Iraq and the War of Sanctions

Iraq and the War of Sanctions

Conventional Threats and Weapons of Mass Destruction

ANTHONY H. CORDESMAN

Westport, Connecticut
London

Library of Congress Cataloging-in-Publication Data

Cordesman, Anthony H.
    Iraq and the war of sanctions : conventional threats and
weapons of mass destruction / Anthony H. Cordesman.
        p.   cm.
    Includes bibliographical references and index.
    ISBN 0-275-96528-7 (alk. paper)
    1. Iraq—Military policy.   2. National security—Iraq.   3. Iraq—
Armed Forces—Weapons systems.   4. Weapons of mass destruction—
Iraq.   5. Iraq—Politics and government—1979-   6. Iraq—Relations—
Foreign countries.   I. Title.
UA853.I75C65   1999
355'.0335567—dc21   98-41447

British Library Cataloguing in Publication Data is available.

Copyright © 1999 by Anthony H. Cordesman

All rights reserved. No portion of this book may be
reproduced, by any process or technique, without the
express written consent of the publisher.

Library of Congress Catalog Card Number: 98-41447
ISBN: 0-275-96528-7

First published in 1999

Praeger Publishers, 88 Post Road West, Westport, CT 06881
An imprint of Greenwood Publishing Group, Inc.

Printed in the United States of America

The paper used in this book complies with the
Permanent Paper Standard issued by the National
Information Standards Organization (Z39.48-1984).

10 9 8 7 6 5 4 3 2 1

*To the men and women who served in UNSCOM and the IAEA,
and the intelligence officers who seek to deny Iraq the ability to proliferate*

Contents

	Preface	xiii
	Acknowledgments	xxv
1.	INTRODUCTION	1
	The UN Resolutions That Shaped the War of Sanctions	2
	Iraq's Struggle Against the UN	4
	Iraqi Threats to the Gulf and the World's Supply of Oil	8
2.	IRAQ'S STRATEGIC CULTURE	10
	The Impact of History	11
3.	THE HIGH COMMAND OF THE IRAQI ARMED FORCES	20
	The Threat to the State from the High Command	21
	The Threat to the Regime from the Armed Forces	22
	The Impact of the Iran-Iraq War	23
	The Gulf War and Its Aftermath	24
	Coup, Counter-Coup, and Rumor from 1991 Onward	25
	The Iraqi National Accord	27
	The Continuing Threat to the Regime from the Iraqi Military	29
	Prospects for a Coup and "One-Bullet Election"	30
4.	TRENDS IN IRAQ'S TOTAL FORCE STRENGTH, MILITARY EXPENDITURES, ARMS IMPORTS, AND MILITARY INDUSTRIES	32
	Militarization and the Cost to the Iraqi People	32
	Iraq's Military Manpower Pool	33

	The Overall Trends in Iraqi Forces Since the Gulf War	34
	Iraqi Military Expenditures	37
	Iraqi Arms Imports	43
	Iraqi Efforts to Smuggle Arms and Parts and Rebuild Its Military Industries Since the Gulf War	59
	Military Expenditures, Arms Transfers, Military Industry, and the Problem of Containment	63
5.	THE THREAT FROM IRAQ'S LAND FORCES	67
	The Impact of the Gulf War on the Iraqi Army	67
	The Iraqi Army Today	71
	The Limited Value of Unit Strength and Order of Battle Data	77
	The Republican Guards	78
	Deployments Against the Kurds and Iran	80
	Deployments Against the Shi'ites and Iran	83
	Land Force Equipment Holdings and Capabilities	86
	Land Force Readiness and War-Fighting Effectiveness	108
	Near-Term Trends and Implications for Containment and Deterrence	113
6.	THE THREAT FROM IRAQI AIR AND AIR DEFENSE FORCES	118
	The Cost of the Gulf War to the Iraqi Air Force	119
	Current Air Force Equipment Holdings	121
	Air Activity Since the Gulf War	128
	Modernization Needs	129
	Readiness, Doctrine, and Training Needs	130
	Overall War-Fighting Capabilities	133
	Land-Based Air Defenses	134
	Land-Based Air Defense Readiness and War-Fighting Capability	137
	Near-Term Trends and Implications for Containment and Deterrence	140
7.	THE THREAT FROM IRAQI NAVAL FORCES	144
	Manning and Overall Strength	144
	Surviving Combat Ships	146
	Naval Readiness and War-Fighting Capability	147
	Near-Term Trends and Implications for Containment and Deterrence	148
8.	UNCONVENTIONAL WARFARE AND TERRORISM	150
	Iraq's Security Structure	151
	Iraqi Terrorist Activity	158

	Attempting to Assassinate President Bush and Attacks on Kuwait	158
	Other Iraqi Acts of Terrorism	161
	Implications for Western and Southern Gulf Strategy	163
9.	CONVENTIONAL FORCES AND THE OUTCOME OF THE WAR OF SANCTIONS	166
	Prospects for Future Conflict	168
	The Value of Military Containment	171
	Additional Measures to Limit Iraqi Conventional Military Capabilities	171
10.	IRAQI WEAPONS OF MASS DESTRUCTION AND THE WAR OF SANCTIONS	175
	Iraq's Long History of Proliferation	175
	Iraq's Capabilities Survive the Gulf War	176
	The UN Cease-Fire Seeks to Eliminate Iraqi Capabilities	178
	UNSCOM and the War of Sanctions	179
	The Biological Weapons Crisis of 1995	212
	The Struggle Continues in 1996 and 1997	215
	The Security Council Splits: The Sanctions Crisis of Fall, 1997	222
	The Sanctions Crisis of 1998	230
	Making "Sanctions Fatigue" and "Oil for Food" a Full-Scale Political Battle	269
	The Strengths and Limits of the War of Sanctions	382
11.	THE SCALE OF IRAQ'S PROGRAMS AND COMPETING IRANIAN AND ISRAELI EFFORTS	394
12.	IRAQ'S STRATEGIC CULTURE AND WEAPONS OF MASS DESTRUCTION	442
	The Beginning of Proliferation	443
	Opportunism and Uncertainty	443
	Persistent Efforts to Acquire Biological, Nuclear, and Chemical Weapons	445
	The Impact of Other Proliferators	449
13.	IRAQ'S ARTILLERY DELIVERY SYSTEMS	450
	Iraqi Artillery	450
	Iraqi Long-Range Unguided Rockets	452
	Iraq's "Super Guns"	454
14.	IRAQ'S AIR DELIVERY SYSTEMS	458

15. IRAQ'S MISSILE CAPABILITIES ... 462

- Iraq's Missile Weapons Before the Gulf War ... 463
- Iraq and the "Scud B" ... 463
- Iraq's Operational Experience During the Iran-Iraq War ... 468
- Iraq's Search for More Advanced Missiles ... 471
- Iraqi Missiles After the Iran-Iraq War ... 475
- Iraq's Missile Capabilities at the Time of the Gulf War ... 478
- The Scud Hunt and Ballistic Missile Defense ... 483
- Iraq's Missile Capabilities Since the Time of the Gulf War and the War of Sanctions ... 488
- Missiles, Weapons of Mass Destruction, and the War of Sanctions ... 505
- The Option of Iraqi Cruise Missiles ... 507

16. IRAQI TERRORISM, UNCONVENTIONAL WARFARE, AND WEAPONS OF MASS DESTRUCTION ... 520

17. IRAQ'S PAST AND FUTURE CHEMICAL WEAPONS CAPABILITIES ... 525

- Iraq's Chemical Weapons Programs Before the Iran-Iraq War ... 525
- Iraq's Use of Chemical Weapons During the Iran-Iraq War ... 527
- Iraq's Expansion of Its Chemical Weapons Production Capability ... 531
- Iraq's Use of Chemical Weapons Against the Kurds ... 534
- Iraq's Chemical Weapons Programs Between the Iran-Iraq War and the Gulf War ... 535
- Iraqi Chemical Weapons Programs at the Time of the Gulf War ... 542
- Iraq's Decision to Not Use Chemical Weapons ... 544
- The Possible Impact of Iraqi Use of Chemical Weapons at the Tactical Level ... 545
- The Possible Impact of Iraqi Use of Chemical Weapons at the Strategic Level ... 547
- Coalition Efforts to Destroy Iraq's Chemical Capabilities During the Gulf War ... 548
- Iraqi Chemical Weapons Programs Since the Gulf War ... 551
- Iraqi Present and Future Chemical Weapons Capabilities and the War of Sanctions ... 552

18. IRAQ'S PAST AND FUTURE BIOLOGICAL WEAPONS CAPABILITIES ... 573

- Iraq's Biological Weapons Efforts Before the Gulf War ... 574
- Coalition Air Strikes Against Biological Weapons Facilities ... 580
- Iraqi Biological Capabilities After the Gulf War ... 581

	UNSCOM versus Iraq and the War of Sanctions	583
	The Continuing Uncertainties Regarding Iraq's Biological Weapons Efforts	590
	The War-Fighting Effectiveness of Iraq's Future Biological Weapons	597
19.	**IRAQ'S PAST AND FUTURE NUCLEAR WEAPONS CAPABILITIES**	**603**
	Iraq's Early Nuclear Efforts	603
	Iraq's Nuclear Facilities at the Time of the Gulf War	609
	Iraqi Progress in Obtaining Fissile Material at the Time of the Gulf War	613
	Iraq's Progress in Nuclear Weapons Design and Assembly	621
	Iraqi Nuclear Programs and the War of Sanctions	627
20.	**THE POLICY IMPLICATIONS OF IRAQ'S WEAPONS OF MASS DESTRUCTION**	**643**
	Living with Iraq's Continuing Capability to Proliferate and the Problem of Iraqi Opportunism	644
	The Limits of Arms Control	645
	Iraq's Future Strategy of Opportunism	646
	Iraqi Proliferation Is Not "Saddam Dependent"	648
	Iraqi Escalation and War-Fighting	649
21.	**IRAQ'S MILITARY FUTURE**	**651**
	Iraq's Near-Term Capabilities	652
	Containment and Deterrence: The Mid-Term and Long-Term Risks of an End to the War of Sanctions	663
	Sources and Methods	667
	Selected Bibliography	669
	Index	679

Preface

The military analysis in this book describes three main themes: Iraq's efforts to rebuild its conventional forces following the Gulf War, the history of its efforts to proliferate, and its long struggle to block UN efforts to deprive it of weapons of mass destruction. It is the history and character of each of these efforts which this book calls the "war of sanctions." The description of Iraq's conventional forces and efforts to proliferate was updated in January, 1999, shortly after Operation Desert Fox. It reflects a remarkable degree of continuity over a nearly ten-year-long period, and suggests that most elements of Iraq's force structure are unlikely to change until there is another major war or Saddam Hussein loses power.

Just as this book was completed, however, the war of sanctions took on a different character. Beginning in July, 1997, Iraq intensified its struggle to end UN sanctions and to block the UN Special Commission (UNSCOM) and International Atomic Energy Agency (IAEA) inspections that sought to halt its efforts to proliferate. As this book describes in detail, these Iraqui actions brought the United States and Britain to the edge of military action in late 1997, in February, 1998, and in the fall of 1998. Nevertheless, in early November, 1998, it still seemed that UNSCOM and the IAEA might be able to continue their operations in Iraq, maintaining many of the elements of an effective inspection and monitoring regime.

As late as November 14, 1998, Iraq's Deputy Prime Minister, Tariq Aziz, sent a letter to UN Secretary-General Kofi Annan stating that the Iraqi leadership had "decided to resume working with the Special Commission and the IAEA and to allow them to perform their normal duties ... not out of fear of the aggressive American campaign and the threat to commit a new aggression against Iraq, but as an expression of our feeling of responsibility and in response to your appeal and those of our friends. The objective of Iraq is to end the suffering of its embargoed people and to see the implementation of paragraph 22 of Security Council Resolution 687 as a first step for lifting the other sanctions.''

The reality, however, was that Aziz's letter was only one more Iraqi political maneuver in the war of sanctions. Iraq did not comply with its promises. It did not provide any meaningful response to a UN request on November 20, 1998, for 12 documents describing Iraq's missile, chemical, biological, and nuclear programs. It began to block "challenge" inspections, and on December 15, Ambassador Richard Butler, the head of UNSCOM, submitted a report on Iraqi compliance with arms inspections to Secretary-General Annan, which effectively stated that the UN could no longer carry out its mission.

The report stated that Iraq had submitted only one of 12 requested documents, and had blocked UNSCOM during four inspection attempts.

Iraq's conduct ensured that no progress was able to be made in either the fields of disarmament or account for its prohibited weapons programs. Iraq did not provide the full cooperation it promised on Nov. 14, 1998. . . . Iraq initiated new forms of restrictions upon the commission's activities. . . . Finally, in the light of this experience, that is, the absence of full cooperation by Iraq, it must regrettably be recorded again that the commission is not able to conduct the substantive disarmament work mandated to it by the Security Council and thus, to give the council the assurances it requires with respect to Iraq's prohibited weapons programs.

The report also said that the one set of documents that Iraq did provide did not contain the information sought by UNSCOM. It said that UNSCOM was prevented from questioning graduate students about biological arms research, although this type of research had been conducted at universities. The most serious standoff came on December 10, when UNSCOM was blocked from entering the ruling Ba'ath Party offices because the inspection team chose not to meet conditions imposed by the Iraqis. Iraqi officials had insisted that only four inspectors would be allowed to enter, and that they would have to declare what it was they were looking for. The report also said that UNSCOM was barred on November 26 from a military base of the People's Mujahideen, an Iranian opposition group.

Additionally, on December 13, a Baghdad-based chemical monitoring team was prevented from inspecting a warehouse on the grounds that it was the Moslem Sabbath. Butler has said that inspectors entered a fourth sensitive site that Iraq said was the former headquarters of its Special Security Organization. The building had been emptied of its contents and Iraq would not disclose their new location. Butler has said that access was granted to a small team to visit a fifth site at the Military Industrialization Corporation, but that "this site too had been prepared to avoid any disclosure of relevant materials."

The report said that Iraq had delayed UNSCOM's work by issuing new restrictions since the inspections resumed in mid-November, and that this made it impossible for inspectors to determine if Baghdad eliminated its weapons of mass destruction, a key requirement for the lifting of sanctions. In contrast, the IAEA has said that Iraq has provided "the necessary level of cooperation" to its inspectors. It has also said that only a few questions relating to Iraq's past atomic program remain.

The Butler report effectively stated that diplomatic efforts had failed, and the ultimate result of his conclusion was a major new series of US and British military strikes on Iraq—Operation Desert Fox. The operation began on December 16, 1998, and was the first major attack on Iraq since the Gulf War. The Pentagon has reported that 415 cruise missiles were fired during the campaign, including 325 Tomahawks fired by US Navy forces and 90 heavier cruise missiles launched from Air Force B-52s. The attacks involved 650 aircraft missions, including 32 sorties by 12 British Tornado fighter-bombers. Iraq claimed its gunners shot down more than 100 Tomahawks, but there was no evidence to prove this.

In addition to the cruise missiles, the first wave of attacks involved bombing raids by attack aircraft including F-14 and F-18 fighter aircraft, and EA-6B aircraft with HARM high-speed anti-radiation missiles from the USS *Enterprise*. Fighters and bombers at bases in Bahrain, Kuwait, and Oman joined in the campaign by the evening of December 17. They included four B-1 bombers from Oman, making it the first time that those advanced aircraft have joined in a combat operation, as well as some dozen F-16 and A-10 fighters from Kuwait. The 60 F-16 and F-15 fighters in Saudi Arabia remained grounded, although Saudi Arabia permitted refueling and AWACS flights. Saudi Arabia has repeatedly refused to allow attacks on Iraq to be launched from its soil since October, 1997. The US Central Command (USCENTCOM) cites "host-nation sensitivities" as a reason not to provide a precise breakdown of where US warplanes in the region are based.

The United States used an undisclosed number of laser-guided bombs and other ordnance. In their first use against a real target, two B-1's bombed a large military complex near Baghdad. No sorties were flown during daytime—a pattern established early in Desert Storm. British forces flew 32–50 sorties with Tornado GR1 fighters from Kuwait. During the fourth night of attacks, for example, 12 Tornadoes flew 24 missions, attacking a large military airfield and a complex near the city of Al Kut in southern Iraq. Not a single US or British casualty was reported after about 70 hours of intensive air strikes involving 650 sorties against nearly 100 targets.

To put these numbers in perspective, the United States fired 23 cruise missiles at Iraqi intelligence headquarters in Baghdad in June, 1993, in retaliation for an alleged plot to assassinate former President George Bush. It fired 27 cruise missiles against military targets in southern Iraq in September, 1996, in retaliation for the movement of Iraqi troops against Kurds in northern Iraq. On the other hand, a total of 2,400 aircraft (1,800 US) were involved in Desert Storm

(January 16–February 28, 1991). They flew a total of 118,000 sorties, 42,000 of which were offensive, against 777 fixed targets. They dropped about 162,000 unguided dumb bombs and used 9,500 smart weapons.

The target mix was carefully chosen to limit the scale of the attacks and the risk of collateral damage. The United States reported on December 20 that Desert Fox was targeting just over 100 total sites between President Saddam Hussein's political and military infrastructure and suspected sites for the production or storage of weapons of mass destruction. The sites targeted during the four-night assault included many targets where the political dimension was far more important that any direct impact on war-fighting. For these sites, the ability to see into a building, to know its contents in real-time, to fully understand dispersal and redundancy, and to know the longer-term political and strategic impact of damage were critical.

Typical sites included:

- Baghdad: Directorate of Military Intelligence, Special Republican Guards barracks, Republican Guards headquarters, TV station, communications center, Air Defense Center, Special Security Organization, Ba'ath Party headquarters, Intelligence Service, Al Karama and Al Kindi missile research and development facilities, Baghdad Museum of Natural History, Ministry of Labor and Social Affairs, Al Mustansiriya University
- Tikrit: Al Sahra Airfield, Republican Guards headquarters, Al Bakr air base
- Mosul: missile research and development facility, air base, two army bases, Republican Guards headquarters
- Taji: military air base, missile design and production facility
- Samarra: air defense sites
- Jabul Makhul: presidential palace that covers 10 square miles and includes 90 structures, suspected nuclear/chemical weapons site, Republican Guards headquarters
- Al Qurnah: communications-related sites
- Ash Shuaybah: radar site
- Ash Rumaylah: communications-related site
- Al Kut: airfield, military complex
- Ibn Al Haytham: missile storage facility in southern Iraq
- Basra: oil refinery

The United States and Britain did hit headquarters and barracks for the intelligence services, Special Republican Guards, and Republican Guards. The first night, they attempted to target and kill personnel in military intelligence, the Special Security Organization, and Special Republican Guards. After that time, it was assumed that most facilities would have limited manning. A point to remember: the largest buildings of the Special Republican Guards have about 400 personnel. The average buildings have 200. Assuming that we hit all of the targeted buildings, that all buildings were fully occupied, and that all the occupants were killed, we would have produced a maximum of 2,600 casualties out of a force of 30,000.

Desert Fox was, however, a limited campaign that was designed to degrade Iraqi capabilities and to show the Iraqi regime that it was vulnerable. It was not an action that was designed to defeat Iraq or to produce major changes in its military capabilities. Iraq did not fight back during Desert Storm. Rather, it chose to ride out the attack. The United States and Britain did not target the major weapons of the Iraqi army, virtually all of its combat aircraft, and most of its actual air defense weapons. As a result, the size and structure of Iraq's conventional forces and order of battle is almost exactly the same as it was before Desert Fox.

Senior US officials warned, even during the first day of the campaign, that the strikes would probably leave the United States with a limited ability to closely monitor Iraq's capability to develop chemical, biological, and nuclear weapons. They warned that the attack would almost certainly mean the end of the seven-year-old UN weapons inspection program in Iraq. They also made it clear that the United States would have to maintain a large military presence in the Gulf region for at least several more years.

The United States and Britain did not target major dual-use facilities that could be used for the production of chemical and biological weapons because of their political sensitivity and the risk of collateral damage. They had no way to target dispersed missiles, and production equipment and weapons for missiles and chemical, biological, and nuclear weapons. They did strike at concealment sites, but did so in order to punish Iraq, and not because they believed that there was equipment and weaponry present. As a result, the only major blow to Iraq's capability to proliferate came as a result of a series of attacks on Iraq's missile production facilities.

Desert Fox ended on the night of December 19. President Clinton declared the attack a success and warned that the United States and Britain would strike again if Iraq took steps to rebuild chemical or biological weapons or to threaten its neighbors: "I am confident we have achieved our mission. We have inflicted significant damage on Saddam's weapons of mass destruction programs, on the command structures that direct and protect that capability and on his military and security infrastructure." Clinton said that the United States would maintain its military forces in the region, keep Iraq under the pressure of comprehensive economic sanctions, continue to enforce the "no-fly" zones in northern and southern Iraq, and work more intensively with the Iraqi opposition to try to change the Iraqi government. Clinton made it clear that the United States had shifted from a strategy of containment and sanctions to a strategy of containment plus replacement. He called for a new government in Iraq. "So long as Saddam remains in power, he will remain a threat to his people, his region and the world. With our allies we must pursue a strategy to contain him and to constrain his weapons of mass destruction program."

Secretary William Cohen repeated his previous assessments of the impact of

Desert Fox in several television interviews. He warned that the Iraqis might try to rebuild their facilities but that the United States would keep a watchful eye.

We are going to be in the region, we are going to maintain our military capability, we are going to continue the sanctions and watch to make sure that he doesn't pose a threat to his neighbors or try to reconstitute these programs. The burden of proof really is on Saddam. He is going to continue to live with the restrictions. He will still have a no-fly zone and a no-drive zone. We will continue the maritime interdiction operations.

In an interview, Secretary of State Madeleine Albright stated that the strikes are a "successfully accomplished mission." She did, however, acknowledge that the threat posed by Iraq's chemical and biological weapons capability cannot be completely erased. "Obviously it is very hard to say that everything that he has in weapons of mass destruction has been destroyed, but his capability of threatening his neighbors and delivering [weapons] has been severely degraded." Albright said that the United States might have to strike at Iraq again if Saddam Hussein rebuilds his country's weapons of mass destruction capability. "We reserve the right to use force again." She also said that US strategy toward Iraq was shifting from one of emphasizing containment to one of containment plus overturning Saddam's regime. "We would like to see a different regime. That is what we are going to be working towards by more active support of the various opposition groups."

The Iraqis also made claims. A statement by Iraq's armed forces general command said that strikes targeted presidential sites, civil establishments, government offices, colleges, students' dormitories, factories, refineries, and some military units. It did not elaborate. Officials said a mass funeral had been held for 68 people killed in and around Baghdad during the bombing raids. Vice President Tariq Ramadan stated that there were 10 times as many civilian casualties as there were military, but he did not cite any figures. Iraq's ambassador to the UN, Nizar Hamdoon, claimed that the British and US attacks had killed or wounded thousands of people. "There has been enormous damage, mainly to the civilian infrastructure and to human life. I am told the casualties are in thousands, in terms of people who were killed or wounded, but we don't have any final figures."

The Iraqis claimed that there were reports of as many as a dozen deaths at a university in a northern Iraqi province, and that there were at least a handful of deaths from the bombing of a major oil field in Basra in the south. US officials confirmed that they had tried to kill large numbers of the Special Republican Guards, which provide crucial support, protection, and muscle for Saddam Hussein. Immediately after the strikes, neither US nor Iraqi officials would give an estimate of Iraqi military losses. In Baghdad, life went on as normal, but reporters did see heavy damage to several buildings where elements of the Iraqi security and military establishments were housed. One missile hit the headquarters of the Iraqi Ministry of Labor and Social Affairs, witnesses said, wounding at least three guards and leaving a crater 20 feet deep just inside the gates. Three other missiles were said to have hit near Al Mustansiriya University in the heart of the Iraqi capital.

Deputy Prime Minister Aziz said on December 21 that four days of US and British air strikes had killed 62 military personnel and wounded 180, and that the air strikes had also ended UN arms inspections in Iraq. Aziz did not give details of civilian casualties but said that they were "much, much more" than those in the military. He also said that while Clinton and Blair had boasted about the damage that the strikes had inflicted on Iraq's elite Republican Guards and Special Republican Guards, only 38 had been killed and 100 wounded from the two guards corps; 24 soldiers from regular army and air defense units were also killed, and 80 were wounded.

Aziz claimed that the United States and Britain had committed "an unjustified crime" in carrying out the raids. He also condemned chief UN arms inspector Richard Butler and said that the inspection process ended when London and Washington began the air strikes. "The moment America and Britain launched missiles against Iraq they killed UNSCOM. I cannot give them another life." He called Butler "a cheap pawn in the hands of the Americans."

Aziz said that the air attacks had taken place in daylight as well as at night because the United States and Britain had wanted to wind up their assault quickly in order to avoid causing greater hostility in the Arab world. He complained of a US–British conspiracy to destabilize the Iraqi government and to finance "terrorist" acts. "The aggression has not stopped, it is continuous." He also complained that Prime Minister Tony Blair had "turned Britain into a tail of the fox which is in Washington." As for Blair's statement about putting Saddam "back in his cage" with the air raids, Aziz said, "This is the old rhetoric of a liar."

The political reaction from Russia was equally unpleasant. Prime Minister Yevgeny Primakov and Defense Minister Igor Sergeyev called for a strategic triangle with India and China, and Sergeyev urged closer military cooperation between the former Soviet republics. Primakov said, "We will never change our position. We are very negative about the use of force bypassing the Security Council." Sergeyev gave a speech in which he stated that, "At this moment, when the United States and their allies are unpredictable, it is essential we reach a common understanding of the military-political problems arising. I hope that strikes on Iraq are not resumed under any circumstances. I hope sense prevails." During televised comments at a meeting in Moscow of defense ministers from the Commonwealth of Independent States, Col.-General Leonid Ivashov, the military's head of international cooperation, stated, "After what has happened we are not going to pretend everything is all right in relations. Though reducing the pace of mutually beneficial cooperation in the military sphere, Russia is not going to sever it totally. Russia will try to encourage the alliance and its separate members to discuss serious and concrete issues of bilateral and European security."

Russia later issued its own damage claims. General Valentin Korabelnikov, the head of Russia's GRU military intelligence agency, estimated that every fifth missile fired on Iraq during December 16–20 had failed to hit its target. "The strikes were not as effective as the Pentagon said. The destruction of several civilian sites, which can have had nothing to do with military installations or possible centers where weapons of mass destruction could be designed or produced, testifies to this."

On December 22, French Foreign Ministry spokeswoman Anne Gazeau-Secret called on the United States and Britain to disclose the results of their attacks against Iraq so as to enable the UN to make new proposals for Baghdad's disarmament. "The United States and Britain should disclose the results of their bombings to the UN Security Council because as things stand, we have no specific tally." She said that such a move would help in drawing up new guidelines to control Iraqi weaponry "because we can in no way allow Iraq to again become a danger to its neighbors," and added that, "once a durable and satisfactory control is established, we can move toward a lifting of sanctions [against Iraq]."

Many of the issues relating to the military effectiveness of Desert Fox are now clear. The first detailed overall damage assessment came at a Pentagon press conference on December 21, several days after the conclusion of the strikes. Secretary Cohen stated that Iraqi development of longer-range missiles was believed to have been pushed back by a year. He indicated that that assessment was based on the amount of time that analysts believe it would take to rebuild the facilities. It could take longer, given the administration's "containment" policy of limiting Iraq's war-making capabilities through sanctions and inspections. Cohen claimed "substantial" success in degrading Iraq's "command and control" systems—systems and networks devoted to communications, intelligence, propaganda, and security. "Saddam may rebuild, and attempt to rebuild, some of this military infrastructure in the future, just as he has replaced many facilities, including lavish palaces, after Desert Storm. But we have diminished his ability to threaten his neighbors with both conventional and nonconventional weapons."

Secretary Cohen warned that that Iraqis might try to rebuild the facilities but stated that the United States would keep a watchful eye. "The policy of containment has been successful. . . . We will keep our forces in place as they've been in place for a number of years now. We will be at the ready should he try to reconstitute those facilities or pose a threat to the region. We'll be prepared to act again in the future." At a similar press conference in London, officials showed images of hits by British forces against Republican Guards installations in southern Iraq. Prime Minister Tony Blair said the Guards were targeted because they guard Saddam Hussein, "keep him in office, have their own system of repression, and of course have been instrumental in putting together the means of concealing the weapons of mass destruction."

On December 21, 1998, the US Department of Defense issued detailed statistics on the impact of Desert Fox. The United States claimed that 85% of all strikes hit their targets, and that 74% were highly effective. Lt. General Anthony Zinni, the Commander of USCENTCOM, summarized Desert Fox during his press conference on December 21 as follows:

The operation involved over 30,000 troops, and 10,000 more outside of our area of responsibility who supported and alerted from bases virtually around the world. We flew over 600 sorties in four days. Over 300 of those were night strike sorties. Over 300 aircraft were involved in strike and support roles. Over 600 pieces of ordnance and 90 cruise missiles were delivered by these aircraft. Over 40 ships performed strike and support roles with ten of them launching over 300 TLAM missiles. Thousands of ground troops deployed to protect Kuwait and to respond to any counteraction. Hundreds of our Special Operations Forces troops also deployed to carry out their assigned missions.

In the days that followed, further data and statements indicated that the United States had been successful in striking at Iraq's missile production facilities. At the same time, it became clear that the fact that US and British forces avoided strikes on major dual-use facilities, and sites with a high probability of storing biological and chemical weapons, meant that many key industrial facilities were left intact.

Serious damage does seem to have been done to some command and control facilities, and probably to large amounts of imported equipment that cannot be fully replaced until Iraq has access to military imports. Nevertheless, General Zinni warned during a press conference on December 23 that Iraq could quickly rebuild the military command and communication systems which were hit during the US and British strikes.

Zinni also said, however, that Saddam Hussein had evidently feared a revolt in his own ranks before the strikes, and had moved Iraqi ground troops into four widely separated sectors where he placed loyal lieutenants in charge. Zinni reported that there were no signs of an imminent overthrow of Saddam, and that Saddam's main aim had been to avert an uprising from within once the British and American strikes began. "That decentralization was done so they ensured they had control" and "to prevent plotting. I think it was done more for internal reasons and internal military problems they thought they might have than for any military preparations they had for us."

To put these remarks in context, Saddam does not seem to have encountered serious problems with the military during 1997 and most of 1998. He was forced to show his concern over the military's loyalty during Desert Fox. In October, 1998, in preparation for possible US and British strikes, Saddam divided Iraq into four major sectors, which he placed under the control of trusted political lieutenants. These lieutenants were given the authority to take command over their sectors if US and British strikes severed the command links with Baghdad, and their authority bypassed the normal chain of command.

The Northern Command, which included the Iraqi 1st and 5th Corps, was given to Staff General Izzat Ibrahim, a long-time supporter of Saddam who had been the target of an assassination attempt a month earlier. The Southern Command, which included the Iraq 3rd and 4th Corps and the Iraqi Navy, was placed under Staff General Hasan al-Majid, one of Saddam's most ruthless lieutenants and a key figure in both Iraq's chemical weapons programs and its persecution of Kurds and Shi'ites. The Central Euphrates Command, which included the Shi'ite areas in the southern-central part of Iraq, was placed under Mohammed Hamzah al-Zubaidi, a Ba'ath Party leader. Zubaidi was not given formal command of any major forces, but was given responsibility for ensuring that no Shi'ite unrest broke out and had the support of two Republican Guards divisions in the area which seemed to be under the control of Qusay Hussein. Finally, the Central Region Command around Baghdad was put directly under the command of Staff General Sultan Hashim Ahmad, who commanded the Iraqi 2nd Corps. This effectively put all of the troops in the Baghdad area directly under the authority of Saddam Hussein since Ahmad reported directly to him, and he already had de facto direct command over the Republican Guards and Special Republican Guards units in the area.

During Desert Fox, Saddam seems to have moved elements of the Republican Guards into positions designed to secure key lines of communication in the north and south, and to have deployed other elements to reinforce the security of Baghdad. After Desert Fox both White House and USCENTCOM officials indicated that Hasan al-Majid had purged elements of the regular forces in the Iraqi 3rd Corps, and that there had been arrests and executions in at least one regular army division in the Corps, as well as of Shi'ite civilians. The commander of the 11th division and several of his officers seem to have been purged or executed.

The strikes on Iraqi air bases were largely symbolic, and Britain and the United States concentrated on striking at attack helicopters and related facilities, which were used in supporting the suppression of the Kurds and Shi'ites. Hitting at the division and corps headquarters of the Republican Guards and regular army probably damaged large amounts of imported equipment that cannot be fully replaced until Iraq has access to military imports. Army units, however, are designed to operate away from their peacetime headquarters, and these facilities were never all that critical during the Iran-Iraq War. Iraq has a very authoritarian government, but it does not need these facilities to execute personal authority down to the major combat unit level. Basic command functions will probably prove relatively easy to replace.

Desert Fox did damage some of the Iraqi air defense command, control, and warning structures in the south. Most air defense weapons remain intact, however, and the Iraqi Integrated Air Defense System has never been a highly effective system. There were 19 Integrated Air Defense System targets planned and only 13 were hit. The Pentagon claimed full success against only 8 targets on December 21, a success rate of 42% against the targets planned. There were

16 SAM targets planned and 9 were hit. The Pentagon claimed full success against 8 targets on December 21, a success rate of 50%.

Before the attacks, the refinery in Basra that the United States and Britain struck was able to handle up to 126,000 barrels of crude oil a day, equal to 36% of Iraq's total refinery capacity of 350,000 barrels per day. It is an important facility, but limited damage is not going to do much to stop Saddam, particularly since most of the real smuggling goes to Turkey through the Kurdish areas in the north.

In short, Desert Fox did not change most of Iraq's military capabilities, and/or the broader problems created by the war of sanctions. US and British efforts to contain and replace Saddam faced the same political problems in dealing with "sanctions fatigue": limited support from Arab allies, hostility on the part of the Arab world, serious questions from many allies and the rest of the developing world, and problems in dealing with Russia, China, and France. It is unclear if any effective inspection and monitoring regime will be found to replace UNSCOM and the IAEA, and Iraq's battle to end economic sanctions and manipulate the UN "oil for food" deal continue, even after Desert Fox. At the same time, the Iraqi regime showed after Desert Fox that it had scarcely changed in character. Saddam Hussein stridently attacked his Arab neighbors in a speech on January 5, 1999, the Iraqi National Assembly threatened to end its recognition of Kuwait and/or its new borders, and Iraq stormed out of an Arab League meeting on January 24, calling the other Arab states puppets of the United States and Britain.

Desert Fox is a clear warning that the war of sanctions remains a highly political war where the battle for perceptions and political influence is far more important than the military damage. It is also a war that has no predictable end, which can turn from a political to a military struggle without warning, and where even an end to sanctions might only be a prelude to decades of containment. On the one hand, Saddam Hussein and those around him are never secure. They are always vulnerable to a "one-bullet election" by the very forces they rely on for security. On the other hand, if Saddam or any similar Iraqi regime survives, the end result will be that any weakening of inspection and sanctions simply makes containment more difficult.

Acknowledgments

The author would like to thank the Smith-Richardson Foundation for a grant that funded part of the research for this book.

Chapter 1

Introduction

Ever since the end of the Gulf War, Iraq has made diplomacy the extension of war by other means. As a result, the Gulf War has been replaced by a new kind of conflict: a "war of sanctions." This conflict is a struggle between Iraq and the United Nations (UN) in which Iraq struggles to break out of the controls and sanctions the UN established as part of the cease-fire in the Gulf War, while the UN attempts to enforce them. It is a struggle between Iraq and the United States and Britain that has already led to several limited UN strikes on Iraq and Operation Desert Fox, and which could escalate to far more serious strikes in the future. In narrow terms, it is a struggle that shapes every aspect of Iraq's conventional military power and efforts to proliferate. In broad terms, it is a strategic struggle in which Iraq attempts to reassert its status as a major Gulf and Arab power, while the UN seeks to limit Iraq's capability to threaten its neighbors and change the character of the Iraqi government.

This is a struggle that Iraq may have begun to win, partly through its grim persistence in attempting to preserve its military capabilities and weapons of mass destruction, and partly by its political efforts to divide the UN, exploit the sympathy of the Arab world, and use its oil wealth as an incentive to win foreign support. Since 1997, the Security Council has become increasingly divided, and Iraq has been able to exploit these divisions. At the same time, Iraq has exploited its Arab identity, the near-breakdown of the Arab-Israeli peace process, and the hardships created by its refusal and delays in accepting the "oil for food" program to win the sympathy of other Arab states and many other nations.

These Iraqi efforts scarcely mean that it has become a reformed or peaceful nation. Iraq remains an aggressive and a revanchist state under the control of an ambitious and dangerous dictator. As a result, Iraq's military capabilities cannot be judged in terms of its current forces and their war-fighting capabilities.

The threat Iraq poses must be judged in terms of its possible strategic intentions and its ability to win the war of sanctions. It must be judged in terms of how Iraq's forces and military capabilities could change if sanctions and export controls were ended, and its current and future capabilities in a range of different scenarios.

Iraq still poses a serious threat in terms of its conventional forces and its ability to retain and rebuild weapons of mass destruction. Its ability to use these forces to intimidate is as important as its ability to use them to attack, and Iraq's future military capabilities are closely tied to its ability to undercut UN military and economic sanctions or bring them to an end.

At the same time, it is far from clear that Iraq can win its "war of sanctions," or its constant struggle to avoid UN controls over its ability to proliferate, without further conflict with the United States, Britain, and their allies. Iraq faces the constant threat that Saddam will push a crisis too far and trigger far more serious military action in the future. Iraq brought the United States and Britain to the edge of major military action in October, 1997 and February, 1998. The United States and Britain began to execute massive strikes against Iraq in November, 1998, and only called them off after last-minute Iraqi concessions. They then struck Iraq a month later in Operation Desert Fox.

While Iraq seems unlikely to face anything like the level of air and missile attacks it faced during the Gulf War, it may suffer military strikes which could serious degrade its conventional forces and ability to proliferate. With or without such strikes, it will face US and British containment, and a major Western military presence in the Gulf, which will almost certainly last as long as either Iraq or Iran pose a threat to a region with two-thirds of all the world's oil reserves and one-third of its gasoline. It also will face continuing efforts to control its oil exports and revenues, prevent conventional arms imports, and prevent the build-up of its capability to proliferate.

THE UN RESOLUTIONS THAT SHAPED THE WAR OF SANCTIONS

The Gulf War liberated Kuwait, but it scarcely ended the struggle against Saddam Hussein. The war of sanctions began almost immediately after the cease-fire. UN Security Council Resolution (UNSCR) 687 was passed on April 3, 1991, and set the terms for the cease-fire in the Gulf War.[1] Resolution 687 calls for the dismantling of Iraq's weapons of mass destruction and long-range missiles and the means to produce them. It does not specifically mention cruise missiles, but the United Nations Special Commission (UNSCOM) has interpreted it to ban long-range cruise missiles.

Resolution 687 gives UNSCOM and the International Atomic Energy Agency (IAEA) the right to conduct challenge inspections and to supervise the destruction of Iraq's assets. At the same time, Article 22 of the Resolution places major restrictions on Iraq's ability to export oil until Iraq fully complies with this part of the cease-fire accords. Resolution 715, which was passed on October 11, 1991, authorizes the UNSCOM plan to carry out its mandate under Resolution 687.

There are similar limits on Iraq's conventional military capabilities and its ability to import "dual use" items which can be used both for civil purposes and to make weapons of mass destruction. Resolution 661, which was passed shortly after Iraq invaded Kuwait, banned the export of all conventional military equipment, spare parts, training and technical support, and technology to Iraq.[2] This ban was continued as part of Resolution 687, although the new resolution did not affect Iraq's ability to manufacture conventional weapons, involve the supervision or dismantling of its conventional weapons manufacturing facilities, or ban the building of ballistic missiles with ranges of less than 150 kilometers.[3]

Other provisions of various UN Security Council Resolutions allow the UN to supervise Iraq's use of its oil revenues to ensure that they are not used to buy arms. At the same time, they limit Iraq's ability to use military force in its northern provinces, which have become a Kurdish enclave, create "no-fly" zones for its military aircraft in northern and southern Iraq, and create "no-drive zones" for its military forces in southern Iraq.

The UN resolutions have no time limit and establish ambiguous conditions for terminating controls and sanctions. Article 22 of Resolution 687 requires UNSCOM and the IAEA to certify that Iraq does not retain any long-range missiles and weapons of mass destruction, or the capability to manufacture them, before Iraq can resume uncontrolled exports. The Resolution requires that Iraq must have fully disclosed all related information, and implies that it must have demonstrated that it has taken no steps to develop a future capability to proliferate. Since 1997, there have been growing debates over whether Article 22 is the only condition for lifting the economic sanctions or whether Iraq must comply with all of the terms of the cease-fire. The history of this debate is described in the chronologies in later chapters.

UNSCOM and the IAEA are responsible for reporting on the status of Iraq's compliance. The Security Council reviews their reports at least every six months, normally in March and October. The provisions of Resolution 687 that affect weapons of mass destruction and Iraq's ability to export oil will remain in force if any permanent member of the Security Council exercises its veto. As a result, virtually any uncertainty regarding Iraq's actions can be interpreted as a reason to not certify compliance, and any permanent member of the Security Council can maintain the sanctions.

The ban on exports to Iraq requires a decision by the Security Council that Iraq has complied with all relevant resolutions, not simply those that apply to weapons of mass destruction. The additional issues include an end of the Iraqi government's repression of its own citizens (UNSCR 688); a halt to all terrorist activity; recognition of Kuwait and Iraq's new border with Kuwait; the payment of reparations for the damage and cost of the Gulf War; and return of Kuwait detainees and property. This is an extremely broad list of issues, and Iraq's level of compliance can be interpreted in many different ways.

The Security Council normally reviews Iraq's compliance with these terms every 60 days, although its members have failed to agree over how to interpret the exact meaning of the terms and Iraq's level of compliance.[4] Since March, 1994. The provisions of Resolution 687 and related resolutions will remain in force, however, if any permanent member of the Security Council exercises its veto.

IRAQ'S STRUGGLE AGAINST THE UN

Almost inevitably, Iraq has struggled to break out of this mix of sanctions, inspections, and controls since the day they were first imposed. Such restraints are an anathema to one of the most nationalistic, aggressive, and militaristic regimes in the world, and it is hardly surprising that the resulting struggle has led to a long series of crises and confrontations that have made diplomacy an extension of war by other means. This struggle seems almost certain to last as long as Saddam Hussein and his coterie are in power, or until Iraq succeeds in mobilizing enough international support to undermine or end UN controls.

No one can predict which outcome will occur, but the war of sanctions now seems more likely to end in Iraq breaking out of the constraints imposed by the UN than it does to end in Saddam's fall from power and replacement by a moderate Iraqi regime. Even if Iraq suffers more military strikes in the process, it is likely to remain a major military threat to its neighbors as long as Saddam Hussein is in power. Iraq retains large conventional forces, and military strikes almost certainly can only degrade, not halt, its capability to proliferate.

Iran may be the rising military power in the Gulf, but Iraq's conventional military forces have been extensively reorganized since the Gulf War, and have regained a substantial part of their pre-war military capabilities. As Table 1.1 shows, Iraq can still deploy massive land forces against Kuwait and the eastern province of Saudi Arabia, and Iraq's conventional forces remain the largest forces in the Gulf in many areas of conventional force strength.

Iraq remains a major proliferator. While it has lost many of the capabilities it possessed at the time of the Gulf War, its half-decade-long struggle to preserve its weapons of mass destruction and missile capabilities continues. It is clear from UN reports that Iraq retains some capability to deliver chemical and biological weapons, and that it has some of the components necessary to rebuild a long-range missile force. It is equally clear that Iraq is conducting a covert effort to rebuild its capabilities and to rapidly expand them the moment UN sanctions weaken.

These Iraqi military capabilities take on special meaning because Saddam Hussein and his coterie have repeatedly demonstrated that they are willing to take extreme political and military risks, and to do so with little warning. Iraq's

Table 1.1
Gulf Military Forces in 1999

	Iran	Iraq	Bahrain	Kuwait	Oman	Qatar	Saudi Arabia**	UAE	Yemen
Manpower									
Total Active	545,600	429,000	11,000	15,300	43,500	11,800	161,500	64,500	66,300
Regular	420,600	429,000	11,000	15,300	37,000	11,800	105,500	64,500	66,300
National Guard & Other	125,000	0	0	0	6,500	0	57,000	0	0
Reserve	350,000	650,000	0	23,700	0	0	20,000	0	40,000
Paramilitary	40,000	55,400	9,850	5,000	4,400	0	15,500	2,700	70,000
Army and Guard									
Manpower	450,000*	375,000	8,500	11,000	31,500	8,500	127,000	59,000	61,000
Regular Army Manpower	350,000	375,000	8,500	11,000	25,000	8,500	70,000	59,000	61,000
Reserve	350,000	450,000	0	0	0	0	20,000	0	40,000
Active Main Battle Tanks	1,390	1,900	106	249	117	34	710	231	1,030
Total Main Battle Tanks***	1,410	2,700	106	341	141	34	1,055	231	1,320
Active AIFV/Recce, Lt. Tanks	555	1,600	71	355	46	84	1,655	558-578	650
Active APCs	550	1,800	340	100	96	172	2,850	570	540
Total APCs	550	2,200	340	140	96	172	3,380	570	540
ATGM Launchers	420+	480+	15	118	68	124+	480+	275	71
Self-Propelled Artillery	290	150	13	41	(59)18	28	200	175	30
Towed Artillery	2,170	1,800	36	0	91	12	260-338	46	452
MRLs	764+	150	9	27	0	4	60	42-66	220
Mortars	6,500	2,000+	18	50+	89	39	510+	135	600
SSM Launchers	46	36?	0	0	0	0	10	6	30
Light SAM Launchers	700	1,100	70+	48?	62	58	650	100	700
AA Guns	1,700	5,500	24	0	16	12	10	72	362
Air Force Manpower	28,000	35,000	1,500	2,500	4,100	1,500	18,000	4,000	3,500
Air Defense Manpower	18,000	17,000	0	0	0	0	4,000	0	0

Table 1.1 (continued)

	Iran	Iraq	Bahrain	Kuwait	Oman	Qatar	Saudi Arabia**	UAE	Yemen
Total Combat Aircraft	307	353	24	76	40	18	432	99	49-89
Bombers	0	6?	0	0	0	0	0	0	0
Fighter/Attack	150	130	12	40	12	18	160	43	27
Fighter/Interceptor	114	180	12	8	0	0	191	22	16
Recce/FGA Recce	8	8	0	0	12	0	10	8	0
AEW C4I/BM	0	0	0	0	0	0	5	0	0
MR/MPA**	5	0	0	0	0	0	0	0	0
OCU/COIN/CCT	0	18	0	28	16	0	21	26	0
Other Combat Trainers	25	155	0	0	0	0	50	0	6
Transport Aircraft****	74	34	3	4	21	6	72	22	16
Tanker Aircraft	5	2	0	0	0	0	15	0	0
Total Helicopters	602	500	33	28	31	24	157	97	25
Armed Helicopters****	100	120	24	16	0	18	12	49	8
Other Helicopters****	502	380	9	12	31	6	145	48	17
Major SAM Launchers	204	340	8	40	0	0	128	36	87
Light SAM Launchers	45	200	0	12	28	9	181	31	200
AA Guns	-	-	-	60	-	-	270-420	-	-
Total Naval Manpower	20,600*	2,000	1,000	1,800	4,200	1,800	13,500	1,500	1,800
Major Surface Combatants									
Missile	3	0	3	0	20	0	8	4	0
Other	2	1-2	0	0	0	0	0	0	0
Patrol Craft									
Missile	21	1	4	6	4	3	9	8	7
(Revolutionary Guards)	5	-	-	-	-	-	-	-	-
Other	42	5	6	5	7	4	21	9	8
Revolutionary Guards (Boats)	40	-	-	-	-	-	-	-	-
Submarines	3	4	0	0	0	0	0	0	0
Mine Vessels	7	4	0	0	0	0	6	0	0

Amphibious Ships	9	0	1	0	2	0	0	3
Landing Craft	17	-	4	2	4	1	8	5	-
Support Ships	25	3	5	4	5	-	7	3	-
Marines	(5,000)	0	0	0	0	0	(3,000)	0	0
Naval Guards	18,000	0	0	0	0	0	0	0	0
Naval Air	2,000	-	-	-	-	-	-	-	-
Naval Aircraft									
Fixed Wing Combat	0	0	0	0	0	0	0	0	0
MR/MPA	8	0	0	0	(7)	0	0	0	0
Armed Helicopters	9	(6)	0	0	0	0	21	(5)	0
SAR Helicopters	0	0	0	0	0	0	4	(6)	0
Mine Warfare Helicopters	2	0	0	0	0	0	0	0	0
Other Helicopters	-	-	2	-	-	-	6	-	-

Note: Equipment in storage shown in the higher figure in parentheses or in range. Air force totals include all helicopters, including army operated weapons, and all heavy surface-to-air missile launchers.

*Iranian total includes roughly 100,000 Revolutionary Guard actives in land forces and 20,000 in naval forces.

**Saudi totals for reserve include National Guard Tribal Levies. The total for land forces includes active National Guard equipment. These additions total 450 AIFVs, 730 (1,540) APCs, and 70 towed artillery weapons.

***Total tanks include tanks in storage or conversion.

****Includes navy, army, national guard, and royal flights, but not paramilitary.

Sources: Adapted by Anthony H. Cordesman from interviews; IISS, *Military Balance*; various data available from *Jane's*; *Military Technology*, *World Defense Almanac*; and Jaffee Center for Strategic Studies, *The Military Balance in the Middle East*.

near-genocidal attacks on its Kurds and its decision to use chemical weapons against Iran are examples of its willingness to take such risks and ignore world opinion. Iraq's attack on Iran, its invasion of Kuwait, and its missile strikes are all the result of sudden, secret shifts in policy by a small decision-making elite, and possibly by one man. In each case, the warning indicators were ambiguous, and many regional leaders and experts argued that Iraq would take a much more moderate course of action.

It is equally dangerous to try to predict the extent to which Iraq will escalate a crisis once it begins. The scope of Iraqi military action expanded sharply during the course of its war with its Kurds, the Iran-Iraq War, and the invasion of Kuwait. Iraq's leaders have not been indifferent to threats to their own survival, but they have often proved willing to escalate in ways that neither their neighbors nor Western experts predicted.

IRAQI THREATS TO THE GULF AND THE WORLD'S SUPPLY OF OIL

Iraq must be regarded as a major military threat to the security of the world's supply of oil exports. There is little prospect that Kuwait can be safe as long as any leader like Saddam Hussein is in power, unless the United States, its Gulf allies, and other Coalition powers maintain a strong deterrent and war-fighting capability to deal with the Iraqi threat. There is a continuing risk of a further conflict between Iraq and Iran, although no one can dismiss the possibility of some alliance of convenience between the two regimes. The Kurds remain a major issue, as does the instability along the Iraqi-Turkish border. Saudi Arabia has a long and vulnerable border with Iraq, and it has done far too little since the Gulf War to improve the defense of its oil-rich eastern province. Iraq remains a potential threat to Israel and Jordan, and to the Arab-Israeli peace process.

Iraq has helped make "creeping proliferation" a key part of the arms race in the Gulf and the Middle East. Its use of chemical weapons and missiles against Iran during the Iran-Iraq War led Iran to become a major proliferator in return. Iraq's missile launches against Israel and Saudi Arabia during the Gulf War broadened the threat of using weapons of mass destruction to include the entire Gulf, and inexorably linked the problem of proliferation in the Arab-Israeli arms race to proliferation in the Gulf.

The threats Iraq can pose have been restricted by Iraq's inability to import arms and the destruction of much of its capacity to produce and deliver weapons of mass destruction. However, there are no guarantees for the future. There is no way to predict how long UN sanctions will endure, or the extent to which they will be weakened or undercut over the next few years. Already there are many states that are openly seeking oil deals with Iraq, and other states that have a strong incentive to sell Iraq arms. "Sanctions fatigue" has already undercut the unity of the UN Security Council, and key nations like China, Egypt,

France, and Russia have shown that their political and economic interests in dealing with Iraq may override their concerns with its military actions.

Iraq cannot compensate quickly for the loss of nearly 40% of its conventional forces during the Gulf War and its inability to import new military technology and dual-use items for nearly a decade. At the same time, it faces only weak military opposition from its southern Gulf neighbors, and it retains the technology to rapidly produce chemical and biological weapons the moment that UNSCOM leaves or loses its effectiveness. Iraq could quickly increase the threat it could pose to key military units and installations in Kuwait and Saudi Arabia, to Western forces in the region, and to ports and air bases. Any third war in the Gulf might involve far more lethal weapons than the Iran-Iraq War and the Gulf War.

As a result, any military analysis of Iraq must examine the history of Iraq's conduct during the long series of crises and confrontations that have shaped the war of sanctions, as well as its present and potential war-fighting capabilities. It must consider how Iraq's forces can evolve while UN sanctions continue, and what Iraq is likely to do once sanctions are lifted. It must consider both Iraq's conventional military capabilities and the threat posed by weapons of mass destruction, and it must consider the near and mid-term impact of any major new transfers of weapons and military technology.

An analysis must also consider the fact that Saddam Hussein, or a similarly ambitious and authoritarian leader, may remain in power in Iraq for many years to come. No one can rule out the possibility of sudden political change in Iraq. Ruthless dictatorships inspire "one-bullet elections," and there are many Iraqis who are far more interested in Iraq's development than in any regional ambitions. At the same time, there is little about Iraq's current power structure that is reassuring, and Saddam and his coterie have done an even better job of building up the instruments of internal control and repression than they have of creating military forces.

NOTES

1. This discussion is based on the full text of UNSCR 687 and the analysis provided in Marjorie Ann Browne, "Iraq-Kuwait: UN Security Council Resolutions, Text and Votes, 1991," Washington, Library of Congress, Congressional Research Service, 91-395F, October 25, 1991.

2. United Nations Security Council Resolution (UNSCR) 661 was passed on August 6, 1990.

3. 93 miles.

4. See Kenneth Katzman, "Iraq: Current Sanctions, Long Term Threat and US Policy Options, CRS 94-465, May 25, 1994; and "Iraqi Compliance with Cease-Fire Agreements," CRS IB92117, October 30, 1997, Washington, Library of Congress, Congressional Research Service.

Chapter 2

Iraq's Strategic Culture

There is a danger in generalizing about Iraq's "strategic culture." It is all too easy to confuse Saddam Hussein's ambitions and the ambitions of those around him with the views and ambitions of the Iraqi people. It is equally easy to forget that Saddam Hussein and his supporters are drawn from a relatively small mix of tribal and clan elites centered around Tikrit, and that they do not even represent the mainstream of Iraqi Sunni history and culture. At least 75–80% of the total population of Iraq is also Shi'ite and/or Kurdish, and Iraq is now a highly urbanized, educated nation.[1] As the fall of other dictatorships has shown, leaders are not peoples, and "strategic cultures" can change rapidly with the regime.

Nevertheless, Saddam Hussein and those around him currently are the Iraqi state, and Saddam's views currently are Iraq's "strategic culture." Saddam has few checks on his power. Although he supposedly was confirmed "president" for seven years by a stage-managed referendum on October 15, 1995, he is a self-appointed authoritarian leader with almost total personal control over the state. He is not only president, but prime minister, minister of defense, minister of finance, commander-in-chief, Secretary General of the Ba'ath Party, and Chairman of the Revolutionary Command Council. He controls the Ba'ath Party Military Bureau, the Defense Council, and the National Security Council.

Saddam and his immediate supporters can exercise direct rule over every aspect of the Iraqi government and the Ba'ath Party. Saddam can rule by decree and exercise his power over every position in the Iraqi civil government, military forces, and security services. He personally approves every promotion in the Iraqi military forces of any field grade rank, and appoints every official down to the level of under-secretary. He can overrule any decision of the National Assembly, and the Revolutionary Command Council of the Ba'ath Party is totally under his control. He can bypass any aspect of Iraq's institutions by formally decreeing martial law or by taking private action in any way he chooses. He secures this rule through a web of overlapping intelligence and internal security services, many of which he controls directly through his youngest son, Qusay, and the Office of the Presidential Palace.

There is little point, therefore, in trying to assess Iraq's military intentions by looking at its public strategic doctrine, or the ideology of the Ba'ath Party. At least for today, Iraq's strategic doctrine is Saddam Hussein, as are its intentions. Iraq is bound only by the limits to Saddam Hussein's personal rule, and to his ability to use Iraq's military forces to further his ambitions.

THE IMPACT OF HISTORY

There is nothing historically inevitable about Iraq's present regime or its militarism. At the same time, much of its current "strategic culture" does not seem to be regime-specific, and the goals and character of its regime may not change radically with the departure of Saddam Hussein. Iraqis are a proud and often warlike people, and Iraq has been highly nationalistic ever since it emerged as a modern state. Iraqi politicians and officers charged that Iraq had been exploited and "cheated" out of just territorial claims long before Saddam came to power. They made claims to the territory of neighboring states, and exhibited desire to be the Arab leader of the Gulf. Several showed a desire for regional hegemony, and fear or resentment of Iran, Turkey, and the West.

Iraq's history has shaped the perceptions of its past leaders, and it is likely to affect the attitudes of its ruling elites long after Saddam is gone. Like other Arab nationalists, Iraq's Arab military and political figures felt that Britain and France betrayed the "Arab nation" following World War I. Iraq, however, had a more troubled genesis than that of many other Arab states. Britain's occupation of Turkish Mesopotamia in 1918 was followed by growing tension between Britain and the native Arab population, the killing of British officers, and a full-scale tribal revolt in June, 1920. This revolt lasted until 1921 and cost Britain 450 dead and over 1,500 wounded.[2]

The creation of Iraq as an independent state did little to ease these tensions. Britain acquired a mandate over Iraq in 1920, and the formal deposal of the Ottoman Sultan in November, 1922 did not create borders that suited the ambitions of either Iraqi nationalists or surrounding states. The resulting border settlements left Arab territories like Kuwait under British control, failed to deal with Iraqi and Arab concerns regarding Iraq's border with Iran and Turkey, limited Iraq's access to the Gulf, and failed to create the desired border with the area that became modern Saudi Arabia and Jordan.

Iraq did not begin to achieve true independence until Britain and Iraq signed a treaty ending the British mandate in 1929, and Iraq was not admitted to the League of Nations until 1932. The Hashemite monarchy that ruled between 1932 and 1958 was seen by some Iraqis as an alien elite of British origin, and came into conflict with the Iraqi military on a number of occasions. This led to five military coups d'etat, beginning in 1936, and a split between nationalists and pro-British Iraqis, which reached the crisis point in 1939. Britain invaded Iraq following a nationalist coup in 1941 and occupied the country until 1945.

Britain effectively dominated Iraqi politics until 1958, often causing the removal of hostile or nationalist Iraqi officials and military officers and exploiting Iraq's oil interests to serve British interests. During this period, Britain made sure that Iraq did not act on any of its major claims and grievances regarding its neighbors, and it pressured Iraq into joining the Baghdad Pact (which included Turkey, Pakistan, and Iran) in 1955. This led to significant clashes and anti-British riots in 1948, 1952, and 1956—all of which had a broader anti-Western character and all of which were suppressed by force.

The coup that overthrew and slaughtered Iraq's Hashemite rulers on July 14, 1958, placed a series of highly nationalist and authoritarian Iraqi leaders in power. The first was a military junta led by Abd al-Karim Qasim, which lasted from 1958 to 1963. The new Iraqi regime almost inevitably turned to Russia and China. It began a series of arms imports from Russia in 1959 that helped institutionalize a continuing arms race between Iraq and Iran. It supported radical political movements that threatened the ruling regimes of virtually all of its neighbors, and made new claims to Kuwait and part of Iran's border area. In fact, Qasim's failure to make good on his attempt to claim Kuwait in 1961 and Britain's successful deterrence of an Iraqi invasion was one of the major reasons for his eventual fall.

The Rise of the Ba'ath and Saddam Hussein

The Ba'ath Party coup that deposed Qasim on February 8, 1963, was an alliance of even more nationalist and pan-Arab officers and politicians. While the leaders of the coup were soon replaced in a new junta under Abd al-Salam Arif, which came to power in November, 1963, the end result was still a regime that was ideologically opposed to the West, a British-dominated Southern Gulf, and a pro-Western Iran, Turkey, and Saudi Arabia. The new regime also sustained the arms race between Iraq and Iran, and Iraq's support of anti-regime movements in neighboring states.

A new Ba'ath coup succeeded on July 17, 1968, that brought General Ahmad Hasan al-Bakr and a small Ba'ath elite to power. This elite ruled through a Revolutionary Command Council (RCC) of which Saddam Hussein became vice chairman. It also adopted policies toward the control of Iraq's oil resources, which led to a steady rise in oil revenues that allowed Iraq to exploit massive rises in oil prices that took place during 1973–1974.

Iraq stepped up its arms imports and military ties to the Soviet Union at precisely the time the United States made Iran the major "pillar" of its policy in the Gulf, and the Shah of Iran began to demonstrate his vaulting ambitions for regional hegemony. Reinforced by the rivalries of the Cold War, this led to a massive acceleration in the Iraqi-Iranian arms race. Further, during the early 1970s, the Shah responded by exploiting an uprising of Iraqi Kurds with the covert support of the CIA. This led to a proxy border war between Iran and Iraq that forced Iraq to concede to Iran partial control of the Shatt al-Arab, its main shipping channel to the Gulf. Iraq also had to make a number of other territorial concessions in its border area with Iran.

Saddam Hussein was the main negotiator of the Algiers Accord that ratified these agreements in 1975. He saw both the extent of the CIA support of the Kurds before the accord, and the way in which the CIA suddenly abandoned them at the Shah's direction within days of its signing. While Saddam's character and ambitions are unique, they must be kept in a broader context. The man who formally shoved General Ahmad Hasan al-Bakr aside on July 16, 1979—and then launched the Iran-Iraq War in September, 1980—came to power as part of an Iraqi ruling elite that has fears and ambitions which are not the product of one man or one party, and which are likely to shape the attitudes of many Iraqi political and military figures long after Saddam and his immediate coterie are gone.

The Iran-Iraq War

Saddam Hussein tacitly supported the Iranian revolution and attempted to reach a modus vivendi with Khomeini, once Khomeini returned to Iran and became the leader of the revolution. Khomeini rejected Saddam's overtures, however, and called for the overthrow of the secular regime in Iraq. He also sent religious "messengers" to the Shi'ites of Iraq, who attempted to provoke an Islamic revolution. During 1980, Iran and Iraq engaged in a steadily escalating series of border clashes and military incidents.

Saddam may have felt threatened by Khomeini and the Iranian revolution, but he also attempted to exploit Iran's apparent military weakness. Iran's military forces underwent a series of purges and upheavals. The new revolutionary government began a series of civil struggles with opposition movements like the People's Mujahideen and hostile ethnic groups like the Kurds. The US embassy hostage crisis cut Iran off from Western arms and military support, and further tensions emerged between the regular Iranian military and new revolutionary militias.

Saddam began by rejecting the Algiers Accord, and then invaded Iran on September 22, 1980. He sent his forces into the oil-rich areas of southwestern Iran, and claimed that this was in support of an Arab uprising. During the time Iraqi forces advanced into Iran, Saddam attempted to claim that much of Iran's richest oil reserves were part of an "Arabastan" that should either be a separate country or part of Iraq.

Saddam's "victory," however, was only the prelude to eight years of war. Iraq could not sustain its advance into Iran, no meaningful popular Iranian support existed for Iraq, and there was no Iranian Arab uprising in what had become a largely ethnic Persian region. Iraq's forces had little capability for urban warfare, failed to seize key strategic objectives like Dezful when they were vulnerable, and then encountered growing popular Iranian resistance. Within a few months, Iraq's slow-moving and road-bound forces were being defeated piecemeal by a steadily growing mass of Iranian Revolutionary Guards, while Iran's regular army deployed and often defeated Iraqi forces.

Between 1981 and 1982, Iran drove Iraq out of virtually all of Iran's territory and began to advance into Iraq. Iraq was forced to use virtually all of its capital reserves to pay for the war and the massive arms imports it needed to compensate for its military incompetence. By 1982, Iranian forces had advanced within 70 kilometers of Basra, and had begun to actively threaten Iraq's control over its Shi'ite south. Iran also had largely defeated its own Kurds, and was supported by key factions of the Iraqi Kurds in their revolt against Saddam. Iran started another front in Iraq's northern border area, and built up its forces in areas that could threaten Baghdad.

Iran retained the military initiative from 1982 to early 1988. However, a war of attrition developed in which Iran relied on revolutionary fervor and human wave attacks, and Iraq relied on a massive superiority in firepower and armored mobility. Iran often scored major initial gains and breakthroughs against Iraqi forces, but lacked the force cohesion and mobility to exploit them. Iraq then concentrated its defenses and inflicted massive casualties on Iran's advancing forces.

Iraq survived near bankruptcy and the loss of most of its oil-export capabilities because of massive aid and loans from Kuwait and Saudi Arabia, and large transfers of modern arms from Europe and the Soviet Union. Iraq made up for its often lackluster military performance with money and weapons, while Iran attempted to improve its methods of attack, exploit surprise, infiltration, night warfare, and attacks through mountain and marsh areas where Iraq could not bring its superiority in arms to bear.

By late 1987, Iran appeared to be winning. It had managed to seize the Faw (Fao) Peninsula in spite of massive Iraqi counter-attacks. It threatened Basra, and Iranian forces had begun to make steady advances in Iraq's northern border areas. Iran was still advancing into Iraq as late as March 15, 1988, when it fought the battle of Halabjah, triggering Iraq's first massive use of poison gas against Iraqi civilians.

Iraq experienced growing difficulties in getting further aid and loans from Kuwait and Saudi Arabia during 1987, and in getting support from other Arab states. The Iran-Contra scandal had cast great uncertainty on the reliability of the support it was getting from the United States, and Iraq had steadily increasing problems in getting French and Russian financing for more arms orders, although deliveries from past orders continued to pour in.

Iran, however, also faced major problems. It had never really succeeded in exploiting its potential advantage in manpower and had begun to experience major recruiting problems. Iranian morale and fervor had faded as Iranian casualties increased. The divisions between Iran's regular and revolutionary forces further undercut Iran's military effectiveness, and Iran had major problems obtaining any resupply for its Western arms and was forced to rely on relatively low-grade Chinese and North Korean weapons.

Several factors decisively tipped the balance during the spring of 1988. Iraq's military capabilities improved more quickly than those of Iran's, partly because Iran's forces were affected by the political divisions within Iran and partly because Saddam Hussein was forced to give his best commanders greater independence and initiative in order to survive. Iraq had built up an advantage in air and long-range missile power that allowed it to strike at Iran's cities and to further undercut morale.

Beginning in 1984, Iraq had slowly developed the capability to conduct massive chemical warfare attacks. By 1987, its growing stockpile of weapons, its wide variety of delivery systems, and improved planning of how to make joint use of its chemical forces and conventional operations resulted in large-scale chemical attacks that were highly effective by regional standards. While these attacks did not produce massive numbers of death, they reached a scale by 1987 where they inflicted many casualties, paralyzed Iranian offensive action, disrupted Iranian rear areas, and steadily undercut Iranian morale. Iraq had decisively "out-proliferated" Iran.

Iraq had slowly developed the capability to effectively attack Iran's oil export facilities in the Gulf and tankers moving to key Iranian loading facilities, such as Kharg Island. Iran had responded by threatening all tanker traffic through the Gulf, especially shipments from Kuwait. It sought both to force other nations to put pressure on Iraq to end its attacks on Iran, and to intimidate Kuwait and Saudi Arabia into reducing their support for Iraq. The end result was the "reflagging" of Kuwaiti tankers with US flags and US escorts of the reflagged tankers. This led to Iranian missile and mine attacks on Kuwaiti and US ships, and a "tanker war" between Iran and the US Navy. The end result was a decisive defeat of the Iranian navy and further reductions in Iran's oil revenues.

Seven years of war had taught the Iraqi army a great deal. It developed a cadre of more competent regular divisions. Iraq's defeats in 1986 led to a rapid expansion of Iraq's elite Republican Guard and forced Saddam to give his corps and divisions commanders far more independence of action. Many of these Iraqi forces regrouped and retrained during late 1987 and early 1988, and Iraq created carefully rehearsed plans to liberate Faw and drive Iran away from Basra.

These Iraqi forces spearheaded a massive Iraqi attack on Iran's positions in southern Iraq in the spring of 1988, and achieved strategic surprise. Iran did not believe Iraq could attack so effectively, and it was unprepared for the scale of chemical warfare that took place. Iran's leaders failed to realize how fragile Iranian morale had become, and they were unprepared for the sudden collapse of their forces.

Iran was decisively defeated during May–July, 1988. Iraq advanced deep into Iran's border area, Iran suffered massive new casualties, and Iran's land forces lost nearly half of their equipment. Khomeini announced the "poison pill" of his acceptance of UN resolutions calling for a cease-fire on July 18, 1988, and a cease-fire came into effect in August. Saddam had won the Iran-Iraq War to the point that he had forced Iran to accept a cease-fire, although he had no real gains to show for eight years of war, had bankrupted Iraq, and had nearly $70–80 billion worth of debt to his neighbors and the West. He had, however, emerged from the Iran-Iraq War with a large and well-equipped military, one which was the most effective and experienced force in the Gulf region.

Iraq's "Strategic Culture" After the Iran-Iraq War

The end of the Iran-Iraq War did not change Iraqi perceptions of its neighbors and the West. While Arab and outside aid was crucial to Iraq's survival and eventual victory during the period between 1982 and 1988, many Iraqis saw this as an opportunistic exploitation of Iraq. Outside arms sales had to be paid for on terms that scarcely encouraged gratitude, and France was the only supplier that backed its sales with useful tactical advice and support.

Saddam and his coterie saw Kuwait's and Saudi Arabia's refusal to forgive its debts and enhance Iraq's oil revenues as ungrateful and as part of a US-led effort to weaken Iraq. The Ba'ath interpreted the growing ties between the United States and the Southern Gulf states that followed the "Tanker War" as part of an effort to encircle Iraq, and the decline of Soviet power as a further threat to its interests. It was this set of conspiracy theories, as well as greed and ambition, that led to Iraq's invasion of Kuwait in August, 1990.

Many Iraqis had come to feel that the United States was deliberately prolonging the Iran-Iraq War to weaken both countries. The Iran-Contra deal reinforced Iraq's distrust of the United States, while occasional Russian tilts towards Iran scarcely led to a solid Iraqi-Russian friendship. Syria's and Libya's hostility to Iraq caused new sources of distrust, and many Iraqis felt that other Arab states should have provided military forces.

Iraq's "Strategic Culture" Since the Gulf War

The aftermath of the Gulf War has scarcely improved this climate. For nearly a half-decade, the "war of sanctions" has kept Iraq under a mix of sanctions, inspection regimes, and export and import controls that have isolated it politically and crippled its economy. During this time, Iraq has been deprived of overt access to arms imports and the technology it needs to proliferate. Iraq's neighbors, including Iran, have been able to continue their efforts to proliferate and to build up their conventional forces, as well as to develop their economies.

Kuwait remains independent, but Iraq has been forced to transfer key territory near its small coastline on the Gulf to Kuwait. Iraq has also been forced to allow UNSCOM and the International Atomic Energy Agency (IAEA) to supervise the destruction of most of its weapons of mass destruction and its ability to produce them, to allow Coalition forces to enforce military restrictions and "no fly zones," and to allow Coalition forces to create an independent Kurdish enclave in Iraq.

During this period, Saddam Hussein has repeatedly shown that he has three major priorities: his own survival; the rebuilding of his conventional military forces; and the preservation of his capability to manufacture and deploy weapons of mass destruction. From the first days of the cease-fire to the present, he has systematically attempted to violate the terms of the cease-fire. He has fought and won a brutal civil war against his Shi'ite opposition in the south, and has kept up constant pressure on the Kurdish enclave in the north. He had mobilized and deployed his army towards Kuwait. He has constantly challenged UNSCOM's efforts to destroy his weapons of mass destruction.

There has never been a three-month period since the cease-fire in early 1991 in which Saddam Hussein has not provoked a new confrontation with the UN, his neighbors, or the West. He has systematically impoverished his people and mortgaged their hopes for future economic development by concentrating Iraq's scarce resources on rebuilding his military forces. He has refused economic aid and relief from limits on Iraq's capability to export oil in an effort to break out of sanctions. He has made constant efforts to divide the Arab world, and he has courted key nations like France and Russia with oil deals and promises of future economic concessions. To all practical purposes, he has turned his defeat and the cease-fire into an extension of war by other means.

The sanctions crisis that Saddam Hussein provoked since the fall of 1997 is simply another series of steps in what has become a near-ritual aspect of Iraqi policy. Every fall since the Gulf War has seen some new challenge to the UN. At the same time, it is clear that Iraq is intensifying its efforts to exploit "sanctions fatigue" and that it has found that it can use UNSCOM as a tool to divide the Security Council. Iraq is increasingly coupling its efforts to rebuild its military forces with propaganda that exploits the hardships of the Iraqi people, the near-collapse of the Arab-Israeli peace process, and the concern Arab nations feel about Iraq's sovereignty and territorial integrity, and the fear that many Southern Gulf states still have of Iran. The individual battles in the "war of sanctions" have often focused on military and security issues, but the strategic goals behind the war are much broader and have clear links to Iraq's "strategic culture."

This mix of history and current strategic priorities helps explain why Saddam Hussein has continued to commit Iraq to new military confrontations with the US-led Coalition. It explains why Iraq has been willing to forgo nearly $120 billion in oil export revenues, and why Iraq's present leaders will continue to use every possible means to break out of UN-sanctioned import restrictions. At least for the foreseeable future, Iraq's official policy towards the rebuilding of its conventional forces and proliferation will continue to be a mix of denial and lies, with occasional bluster and indirect threats. These lies will be told to Iraq's people, media, intellectuals, and military officers, as well as to other nations.

Iraq will make every effort to conceal its true plans and the full nature of its military efforts, and only Saddam Hussein and a few trusted supporters will have any overview of Iraq's military progress and capabilities. Furthermore, Iraq's plans and polices will remain opportunistic and unstable. Iraq's leaders will be unable to predict the exact areas where they will be successful in evading or vitiating UN sanctions and controls. As a result, their strategy, military doctrine, and force development efforts can be expected to evolve on a target-of-opportunity basis. The only thing that seems certain is that Iraq will make a continuing effort to obtain advanced conventional arms and to proliferate in every way that Iraq can conceal.

After Saddam

It is far from certain that Iraq's current "strategic culture" is dependent on whether Saddam and his immediate supporters remain in power. There is little democratic and moderate opposition to Saddam Hussein. The most likely alternative to Saddam, following a "one-bullet election," is another narrowly based authoritarian Sunni elite, and if any "moderates" do seem to rise to power in the immediate aftermath of Saddam's fall, they may end as short-lived figureheads than remain real leaders.

A "quieter Saddam" who patiently waits to acquire significant nuclear or highly lethal biological warfare capabilities and then exploits such capabilities in a more cautious and calculating manner might prove to be just as serious a threat as Saddam the instigator. Few Iraqi regimes of any character are likely to ignore the potential threat of proliferation by Iran, Israel, and Syria. Any civil turmoil or conflict following Saddam's departure might also lead to the use of surviving or covert capabilities against the Iraqi population, and might create new forms of extremism. Regimes may then emerge that are openly revanchist in character, and/or face future financial crises that lead them into new forms of military risk taking.

Nevertheless, any change in Iraq's leadership is likely to be for the better, and such a change might create a very different Iraq. Many, if not most, ordinary Iraqis do not share Saddam's ambitions, near-xenophobia, and paranoia. Figures like Kemal Ataturk and Anwar Sadat have shown that brilliant, moderate leaders can suddenly emerge and change the strategic culture of their nations, and an Iraqi leader with vision might well conclude that focusing on rebuilding Iraq's oil wealth, economic development, and the unification of Iraq's diverse ethnic elements would offer a far greater place in history than continuing with expensive military build-ups and the search for regional hegemony.

Little about the Gulf War or the sanctions that have followed seems likely to reduce Iraqi nationalism or prevent the addition of a strong element of revanchism to Iraq's "strategic culture." Iraqis have little reason to admire the West or Iraq's neighbors. They have obvious reason to resent Britain, Kuwait, Saudi

Arabia, and the United States, and no reason to trust Syria, Iran, Jordan, and Turkey.

Iraqis must be aware that virtually all of Iraq's present "friends" and "supporters" are opportunists seeking future trade and investment opportunities and have no real sympathy for the regime. Further, no Iraqi can ignore the fact that the average Iraqi per capita income was well under one-tenth of its level at the time the Iran-Iraq War began, and that Iraq faces a massive potential reparations and debt repayment bill once sanctions are lifted. There are striking parallels between the cost of peace to Iraq and the cost to Weimar Germany, and the economic consequences of the peace could easily be very similar.

Yet any Iraqi ruling elite must deal with the region in which it lives. Iraq's geography will always present problems in terms of access to the Gulf and dealing with powerful neighbors. Regardless of how friendly a given regime is today, there will always be uncertainties regarding tomorrow. Iraq must deal with other proliferators like Iran and Israel, which remain very real military threats.

Iraq's internal divisions will also present continuing problems. The issue of Kurdish nationalism is unlikely to disappear, and tensions between the Sunni and Shi'ite are unlikely to end—creating inevitable complications in terms of relations with Iran. There will always be tension with fellow exporters, and with importers, over Iraq's need to maximize its oil export revenues. Even a relatively defensive Iraqi regime is likely to feel compelled to go on acquiring weapons of mass destruction to counterbalance the capabilities of Iran and Israel and to limit American power projection options. Any Iraqi regime that survives over time is likely to be highly centralized, relatively ruthless, and to see its neighbors and the West as a potential threat.

NOTES

1. Estimates differ according to source, and other sources are quoted later in this report. This estimate is taken from the International Institute for Strategic Studies (IISS), *Military Balance, 1997–1998*, London, Oxford Press, 1997, p. 127.

2. See David Fromkin, *A Peace to End All Peace*, New York, Henry Holt, 1989, especially pp. 449–462.

Chapter 3

The High Command of the Iraqi Armed Forces

In theory, Iraq has a conventional high command structure. The three military services report to the Ministry of Defense, which reports to the president as the commander-in-chief. The Revolutionary Command of the Ba'ath provides political direction, while the National Defense Council coordinates military activity within the government. In practice, there are a number of highly political bodies that play a major role in virtually every aspect of the command chain. The most important of these bodies is the Ba'ath Party Military Bureau, whose offices are located opposite the Presidential Palace in Baghdad. The Ba'ath Party Military Bureau plays a major role in strategy, making senior appointments, key operational decisions, procurement and resource decisions, and setting policy for each of the services.[1]

Saddam Hussein is the Secretary General of the Ba'ath Party Military Bureau, and his son Qusay is a steadily more important member. The Ba'ath Party Military Bureau is packed with Saddam's closest supporters. Sameer Abdul-Aziz Al-Najim is the Deputy Secretary General, Brigadier Raheem Abed Allu is the Administrative Manager, and the members include senior figures from the Special Security Service (Amn Al-Khass), General Intelligence (Mukhabarat), and Military Intelligence (Estikhabarat). It also includes top officers from each service. Lt. General Mani Abd al Rashid al Takrit, the Director General of the Mukhabarat, serves on the Ba'ath Party Military Bureau. So does Staff Flight General Tahir Saleh Ali al-Tikrit, Saddam's councilor on Ba'ath Party affairs.[2]

The rest of Iraq's command structure is also designed to serve the authoritarian needs of one man. Saddam Hussein, the "president" of the Iraq Republic, is the Supreme Armed Forces Commander. He has direct personal authority over the Presidential Guard and the president's Special Security Committee, which are charged with protecting the president and the regime. He controls the

Defense Council, which is supposedly Iraq's highest ministerial-level body dealing with national security, and the Minister of Defense and Commander of the Armed Forces. The Armed Forces Inspectorate and Military Industry report directly to Saddam, as well as the Defense Council. Saddam coordinates other ministerial-level internal security activities directly through the Ministry of the Interior.[3]

The Chief of the General Staff and Armed Forces headquarters also report directly to Saddam. The Combined Service Staff formally reports to the Chief of the General Staff, as does military intelligence, and the Army headquarters, Naval headquarters, and Air Force and Air Defense headquarters. All of these staffs and headquarters are located in Baghdad. The Republican Guard headquarters and Special Republican Guard headquarters are also located in Baghdad, and seem to report in parallel to Saddam and the Army headquarters. There are also Special Republican Guards units, militias, parallel intelligence organizations, and Ba'ath Party intelligence elements which are designed to protect Saddam and ensure the loyalty of the armed forces.

According to one source, the Iraqi National Security Council provides another coordinating group which focuses on intelligence and internal security issues. Saddam is the formal chairman, but his son Qusay also plays a powerful role. The National Security Council has representatives of the Office of the Presidential Palace, the Special Security Service, the General Intelligence Directorate, Military Intelligence, and the General Security Service, with a representative of the Military Security Service. General Namaq Ismael, a regular army officer from Mosul, also attends meetings. The National Security Council provides Saddam and Qusay with a means of coordinating Iraq's competing intelligence and security services and dealing with key internal security threats and regional intelligence problems.[4]

THE THREAT TO THE STATE FROM THE HIGH COMMAND

In practice, Iraq's high command has military weaknesses that offset many of its strengths in ensuring the security of the regime. Saddam bypasses or alters its formal structure as he pleases. The system emphasizes political loyalty and the security of the regime over military effectiveness, filled with checks and balances to ensure Saddam's safety. Promotion emphasizes loyalty, and positions are regularly rotated to ensure that no officer develops enough personal loyalty to threaten the regime.

Iraqi defectors have made it abundantly clear that major procurement, deployment, and organizational decisions are often made by Saddam and his personnel coterie with little staff work and professional review.[5] Saddam repeatedly bypasses the formal command system down to the small unit level, and major operational decisions are made on the basis of perceived loyalty or personal whim. Major procurement, technical, and industrial decisions are often made by

Saddam on the basis of personal contact, and Saddam has often shown that the most ambitious promise brings more rewards than the real-world prospect of success. Loyalty and the image of success are more important than the reality of success, and many efforts are divided into secret compartments with little coordination of oversight.

This political control of the Iraqi military has been a major part of the problem Iraq had faced in creating effective forces since long before the beginning of the Iran-Iraq War. While Iraq has a formal command structure very similar to that of other regional military forces, with all of the usual C⁴I/BM (command, control, communications, computer/battle management) facilities, the Iraqi armed forces are as much an instrument of state control as they are a means of national defense and military power. They are a key tool in the ruling elite's efforts to secure means of power, to coerce the Kurds, and to suppress systematically any threat from Iraq's Shi'ites.

THE THREAT TO THE REGIME FROM THE ARMED FORCES

At the same time, neither Saddam nor any near-term successor regime will have great reason to trust in the armed forces. The Iraqi army has intervened in politics many times since the emergence of modern Iraq as a state. The politicization of the Iraqi army began with the creation of the state in 1920, when King Faisal placed ex-Ottoman Sunni Arab officers at the head of the political, administrative, and military posts. The first coup d'etat in the Arab world occurred in Iraq in 1936 under the helm of General Bakr Sidki, an Arabized Kurdish officer from Mosul. There were eight successful—among many other unsuccessful—coups d'etat in Iraqi politics between independence and the return of the Ba'athists in 1968. The first Ba'athist regime was overthrown by the military in 1963. In Syria, the Ba'ath came to be dominated by the military—which remains a source of the bitter ideological disputes between a "fraternal" Ba'athist Syria and a Ba'athist Iraq.

Iraq's current military forces have been shaped by this history. Saddam and his coterie fully understand both the risks and advantages of using military force as an instrument of state control. Takriti-dominated Ba'athists took over in 1968 with the help of sympathizers within the armed forces, including fellow Takritis in key armored units. Long before that time, however, they had learned ample and painful lessons in what the armed forces could accomplish through a coup d'etat. Saddam understood all too well that cooperation between the military and the Ba'ath could turn to the advantage of the military, which might seek to govern alone or independently of the Party's principles and directives.[6]

Since 1968, the Ba'athists and especially Saddam Hussein have had considerable success in their constant efforts to improve their political control over the armed forces.[7] The Ba'ath regime began mass purges and the retirement of senior officers immediately after it came to power. By December, 1968, the

Chief of Staff, Faisal al-Ansari, and eight divisional commanders were purged and replaced by trusted Ba'athists. By the end of 1970, 3,000 new commissions had been announced. These new officers led to the genesis of a political commissar system. Furthermore, the regime ensured that loyal officers held key positions. By the early 1970s the Takriti Ba'athists controlled the Ministry of Defense, the air force, Habbaniyah air base outside Baghdad, Baghdad security and the city's garrison, and the Republican Guards brigade.[8]

Saddam Hussein has steadily consolidated his control over the military, making it a key aspect of his control over the state. Not long after coming to full power in 1979, Saddam stated in an interview with the British journalist David Hirst that the stringent measures of political control being adopted by the Ba'ath would prevent any future group of officers from being able to overthrow a revolutionary government, "Without party methods, there is no chance for anyone who disagrees with us to jump on a couple of tanks and overthrow the government. These methods are gone."[9]

Saddam built on formidable methods of exerting control and surveillance over the armed forces. Iraq already had the equivalent of the former Soviet *zampolit* or party commissars who are attached down to the level of the platoon, and who could veto the decisions of professional unit commanders. These commissars, in turn, are controlled by the *Mudiriyat al-tawjih al-siyasi*, the Directorate of Political Guidance, which was formed in 1973. The tasks of this directorate include:

- spreading the ideology of the July 17, 1968, revolution to all military ranks and units;
- supervising the activities of the officers (i.e., political commissars) attached to the Directorate of Political Guidance;
- overseeing the development of military culture on the basis of historic, scientific, and technological data to keep pace with the wind of change;
- seeking to achieve maximum degrees of military discipline; and
- expounding Saddam Hussein's party line and the "aspirations of pan-Arabs."[10]

At the same time, informers and spies from the security and intelligence services permeated the military. Frequent purges, sudden rotations, retirements, and executions were used as a means to keep the officer corps in line and to discourage them from trying to overthrow the government, and Saddam rapidly expanded the Republican Guard during the Iran-Iraq War, both to improve Iraq's military effectiveness and to ensure that a powerful military elite could secure the regime against internal threats.

THE IMPACT OF THE IRAN-IRAQ WAR

Saddam purged the military again in 1979, and rotated or replaced key commanders to ensure their personal loyalty. He also refined his control during the

Iran-Iraq War. From 1981 onward, the Iraqi army had severe morale problems. Many officers resented the excessive political constraints imposed by political officers and felt that the Iraqi leadership's interference in operational matters was a cause of Iraq's defeats.

These developments led Saddam to loosen some of his day-to-day operational controls over the military, but he made sure that the army never forgot who was commander-in-chief. He regularly rotated commanders, downplayed the role of senior commanders in winning victories, gave loyalists in the Republican Guards the credit for victories, and used the media to turn leading officers into virtual nonpersons. For example, Saddam took careful steps to ensure that, militarily, successful generals like Maher Abdul Rashid, who was known as the "Iraqi Rommel" for his outspokenness on political-strategic matters and his military successes, would not pose a political threat in the aftermath of the war. Saddam also used his control over the media and political education process to try to persuade the lower ranks and the Iraqi people that Iraq owed its victories to his "military genius," and that he was responsible for providing the military forces with all of their needs.

After the Iran-Iraq War, Saddam rotated or dismissed many top-ranking officers whose reputation or success made them seem like potential rivals. Some reports of large-scale executions and purges seem to be exaggerated, and many qualified officers were promoted to relatively senior positions. Nevertheless, Saddam altered the military command structure at every level. He reasserted the role of security services and party "commissars" in supervising the military. At the same time, he continued to offer "carrots" to other officers in the form of promotions, housing and land, cash benefits, civil jobs, and a wide range of other benefits.

THE GULF WAR AND ITS AFTERMATH

The Gulf War ended so quickly and disastrously that there was no time for any organized challenge to emerge from within the Iraqi military as a whole, although some of the forces sent to the Kuwaiti theater of operations participated in the uprisings that followed. At the same time, the fighting failed to cripple the Republican Guard and key elements of the regular army because they were either never deployed forward, or they escaped north during the final days of the land battle. As a result, the uprisings right after the war had the effect of spotlighting potentially disloyal forces without depriving Saddam of the power to reassert control. Moreover, the links between the military elements that did participate in the uprisings and various Shi'ite and Kurdish leaders made many in the Iraqi military see such units as traitors.

In the months that followed, Saddam rapidly consolidated Iraq's remaining forces in ways that further emphasized the power of loyalists in the Republican Guards and loyal regular army units. He used the "rebuilding" of the armed forces as a political as well as a military tool. He conducted a series of major shake-ups of his military command structure—four of which were completed before June, 1991. For example, Saddam replaced his Minister of Defense, Lt. General Sa'di Tu'ma 'Abbas al-Juburi—a professional soldier and hero of the Iran-Iraq War—with his paternal cousin and son-in-law, Hussein Kamel al-Majid, on April 6, 1991. He also replaced the Shi'ite Lt. General Husayn Rashid Muhammad al-Tikriti as Chief of Staff with Lt. General Iyad Futayyih Khalifa al-Rawi, the commander of the Republican Guard in June, 1991. Rashid, who had been chief-of-staff since November, 1990, was a respected combat commander and a former commander of the Guard who had overseen its expansion during the Iran-Iraq War.

Some experts feel that Saddam tried to use the fact that al-Juburi was a Shi'ite, and Rashid was Kurd, to signal that part of the blame for Iraq's defeat could be ascribed to these ethnic groups. Yet, al-Juburi was retained as a senior military adviser and Rashid was later made supervisor of the Republican Guard—a position that ranks above the Guard's operational commander. Accordingly, the shifts may have been part of a long series of rotations designed to prevent any center of power from threatening Saddam's authority.

COUP, COUNTER-COUP, AND RUMOR FROM 1991 ONWARD

It is difficult to confirm many of the details of Saddam's other actions in asserting his control over the military. Unconfirmed reports surfaced in late 1991 that Saddam had executed or imprisoned 18 generals for an assassination plot between June and August, 1991. These reports seem uncertain, but it is clear that Saddam continued his policy of shifting and rotating commanders to ensure that no group of military or internal security forces would become loyal to a potential rival. For example, he removed Major General Wafiq Jasim Samarrai as head of military intelligence, purged this command, and put in more loyal officers. General Husayn Rashid was brought back to power as supervisor of the Republican Guards in June, 1992. Lt. General Iyad Futayyih Khalifa al-Rawi—another hero of the Iran-Iraq War, and a key Saddam Hussein loyalist—was made chief-of-staff.

At the same time, Saddam moved more members of his family to senior positions. For example, Kamal Yassin, a member of the Ba'ath ruling council and Saddam's brother-in-law and cousin, was made deputy head of the Ba'ath military bureau. His brother, Arshad Yassin, remained head of Saddam's personal security force—a position he has occupied since 1986.

These actions, however, did not solve Saddam's problems in using the military as an instrument of state control. New reports surfaced in late June, 1992, that Saddam had blocked a coup attempt within the military. Initial reports claimed that a mechanized brigade of the Republican Guard—which was located in Taji, an industrial area northwest of Baghdad—under the command of Brigadier Sabri Mahmoud, was preparing an assault on Saddam Hussein's headquarters in Baghdad, when the coup attempt was detected and halted by Iraqi security forces. Other reports mentioned fighting between the military and security forces. There were reports of clashes between elements of Saddam's personal security force, the Special Republican Guards, and the regular Republican Guards in Baghdad and from June 30 to July 2.

On the other hand, there has been no confirmation of these details, and a few US experts feel that the coup reports were inspired by a series of command upheavals that followed a new large-scale purge of military officers, possibly totaling up to 135 officers. According to these reports, Saddam called a large meeting of his loyal officers together, charged the United States and Jordan with supporting a military coup against him, and used this as a rationale for his purge. While Jordan denied any complicity in a plot against Saddam, Jordan did begin to enforce sanctions on the transshipment of goods and oil to Iraq, although it refused to allow UN inspectors in Aqaba.[11]

There have been reports of similar coup attempts, arrests, and executions from late 1992 to the present—some of which involve the Juburi clan. For example, reports appeared in mid-September, 1992 that Saddam Hussein had executed a total of 26–30 more officers, including General Abed Mutleq Juburi.[12] In October, he was accused of executing 19 more officers, including Brigadier Anwar Ismael Hentoosh and Brigadier Amir Rashid Hasson, two officers blamed for being insufficiently ruthless in putting down the Shi'ite rebellion in the south.[13]

Unconfirmed reports appeared of the execution or arrest of former Interior Minister Samir Abd al-Wahab al-Shaykhali in April, 1993, and another series of arrests and executions of military officers and civilians took place during August through September, 1993. These arrests and executions seem to have begun on August 20, 1993, and to have eventually involved a mixture of military officers and civilians associated with the Juburi clan, Ubayd clan, and Saddam Hussein's home town of Tikrit. Up to 100–150 men were involved, evidently including Jassim Mawlud Mukhlis and Saqr Mukhlis. Saqr was the son of the Mawlud Mukhlis, who was the Tikriti landlord and the original patron who had opened up the officer corps to Tikritis under the monarchy. Another well-known Iraqi executed was Brigadier General Raqhib Tikriti, a military physician who was head of the Iraqi Physician's Association.

While only uncertain reports of fighting and troop movements indicate a major coup attempt took place, there were reports that these arrests followed an effort to obtain Western support for a coup. These reports indicate that the plotters asked for Western air support over Baghdad and assurances that the Kurds would not seize Kirkuk, and that Iran would not intervene in the south.[14] A number of US and British experts feel that these arrests were the result of a serious assassination attempt. Yet Saddam Hussein and the Ba'ath elite may have been reacting to threats that had not yet been transformed into plans. Saddam made little effort to lower his visibility, and he continued to indulge in media events that seemed designed to show his wealth in spite of Iraq's growing economic problems.[15]

A new series of defections occurred in 1995 and 1996, as well as reports of bombings and fighting within military barracks. The most publicized defection was Hussein Kamel al-Majid, Saddam's son-in-law, a Lt. General, and the head of the Military Industrialization Commission and Special Security Service (Amn Al-Khass). Hussein Kamel's flight to Jordan in the summer of 1995, his return to Iraq, and his "execution" created a bizarre sequence of events that exposed both the extent of the internal conflicts within Saddam's family and the true scale of Iraq's chemical and biological warfare programs. Yet another senior officer, General Nizar al-Khazraji, a former chief of staff, fled in late March, 1996 to Jordan, where he announced in early April that he would join the ranks of the opposition to Saddam Hussein by seeking membership in the Iraqi National Accord (*Al Withaq al-Iraqi*), the first Iraqi opposition group to be allowed to open an office in the Jordanian capital of Amman.

THE IRAQI NATIONAL ACCORD

The Iraqi National Accord (INA) was founded by Ayad Alawi, a senior Iraqi intelligence official who had left Iraq in 1971 and Salah Omar Ali Tikriti, a former senior member of the Ba'ath and Minister of Information, who had broken with Saddam over Iraq's invasion of Kuwait. The INA had previously operated in Saudi Arabia with substantial CIA support, and had set up a radio station called the Voice of Free Iraq. The INA also, however, was heavily penetrated by Iraqi security. Iraqi intelligence agents later proved to have provided excellent reporting on the actions of al-Khazraji and other opposition groups in Jordan, and seem to have helped Saddam's security forces round up as many as 100 officers and civilians in the summer of 1996—almost all of whom were executed.[16]

During his stay in Amman, General al-Khazraji gave an extensive interview to *Al-Hayat*, in which he discussed a number of aspects of Saddam Hussein's relationship with the armed forces.[17] Khazraji claimed that he was eased out of his position as Chief of Staff in late 1990 after pointing out the military and strategic dangers to Iraq because of its invasion of Kuwait. His reward was to be "kicked upstairs" as a presidential adviser. Moreover, Khazraji stated that the invasion of Kuwait bypassed the Ministry of Defense and the General Staff, and was undertaken by the Republican Guards on the direct orders of Saddam Hussein. In Khazraji's opinion,

What is left of the Army commanders consists of those who are either grudgingly satisfied or who are weak elements. . . . He orders and they obey because he has gotten rid of the elements who may have had an opinion or were capable of making decisions.[18]

In late June–early July, 1996, reports surfaced that Saddam Hussein had survived yet another coup attempt by the military, which included a plan to assassinate the Iraqi leader. While it is difficult to sort fact from fiction, it seems that elements of the elite Republican Guards were involved, as well as officers from several other army corps. The group took the name of "The Popular Uprising Movement" (*harakat al-intifadhah al-sha'abiyah*), and some reports indicate that it included a number of senior army officers who had decided to rid Iraq of Saddam, and who felt Iraq's external opposition groups were impotent and subservient to foreign powers.[19] Other reports indicate that they had at least some backing from King Hussein of Jordan, the United States, and the Iraqi National Accord—a factor which allowed Iraqi security agents who had penetrated the Iraqi National Accord to warn Saddam.[20]

The Iraqi National Security Council seems to have set up a special committee headed by Qusay and with representatives of the General Intelligence Directorate (Mukhabarat), Military Intelligence Service (Al-Estikhabarat al-Askariyya), General Security Service (Amn al Amm), and Military Security Service (Al Amn al-Askariyya). Saddam seems to have given this group the power to make arrests, regardless of family and tribal connection, and Qusay seems to have taken the lead in directing its operations.[21]

Scores of officers were detained. Some reports indicated that as many as 120–160 officers were arrested and held in the Salamiyeh Prison in Mosul. Other reports indicated that the total included 12 from the Republican Guards and three from the Special Republican or Presidential Guards. Three senior officers who were also provincial governors were arrested as well. They included: Lieutenant General Iyad Khalil Zaki, governor of Al-Muthanna in southwest Iraq, Lieutenant General Mohammed 'Abd al-Qadir 'Abd al-Rahman, governor of Nineveh (Mosul), and Major General Mahmud Shukr Shahin, governor of Al-Wasit in central Iraq. The US State Department reports that some 400 officers were killed in June, including senior Republican Guard officers and Tikritis, and that Saddam's eldest son Uday supervised the implementation of his father's orders. It seems likely, however, that Qusay played at least as important a role.[22]

Most of those executed seem to have been Sunni Arab officers of junior and middle ranks. The executions may, however, have included the following senior officers:

- Staff Brigadier General Ja'afar al-Tayyar, director of training at the Defense Ministry
- Brigadier General Amjad Tariq Aziz, commander of the Administrative Affairs School
- Staff Colonel Khamis Hadi Ni'mah, commander of the 6th Presidential Guards Brigade
- Staff Lieutenant Colonel Ahmad al-Nu'aymi, 6th Brigade staff officer
- Lieutenant Colonel Abdallah Sharif al-Rubay'i, 6th Brigade administrative officer
- Brigadier Suhail al-Admai, an army division commander
- Colonel Adnan Ali al-Ta'i, a brigade commander in the south

Two other senior officers escaped with their lives. Staff Lieutenant General Tali' Ruhayyim al-Duri, a hero of the Iran-Iraq War, fled to northern Iraq and then to Turkey. The alleged participation of this senior officer who held senior commands during the Iran-Iraq War and who is related to Revolutionary Command Council member Izzat Ibrahim al-Duri would seem to indicate serious discontent within the top echelon of the Sunni Arab officer corps, which has constituted the key element of Sunni Arab domination of Iraq.[23] Former Air Force General Hamid Sha'ban, who commanded the Iraqi Air Force for part of the Iran-Iraq War, was initially suspected of involvement in the coup attempt because the dissident officers had planned to make him titular head of state in the event they succeeded in getting rid of Saddam, but he was let go when it transpired that he knew nothing about the affair.[24]

THE CONTINUING THREAT TO THE REGIME FROM THE IRAQI MILITARY

In mid-July, Saddam took the unusual step of making a regular army officer the commander of the Republican Guard, and of appointing a native of Mosul as his office chief of staff. This latter appointee is Awwad al-Bandar, the former head of Iraq's Revolutionary Court, and he seems to have been appointed to counterbalance the internal political impact of Saddam's earlier execution of several officers from Mosul.[25]

At the same time, Saddam seems to have tightened his direct control of the "Special Republican Guard" he uses for his immediate security, increased its readiness and heavy equipment, and possibly strengthened its control over Iraq's surviving covert holdings of biological and chemical weapons and missiles.

The coup and assassination attempts were followed by the Ba'ath regime's customary large-scale purges and dismissals of officers from clans or tribes suspected of dissident behavior. Once again, much of the regime's wrath fell upon officers from the Dulaim and al-Duri tribes of the Al-Anbar Province. Moreover, Saddam Hussein began to admit large numbers of officers from the Al-Sa'dun Sunni Arab tribe from the Al-Basrah Province into the Presidential Guards. Saddam also used his August 31 invasion of the Kurdish security zone to round up and execute Iraqi deserters. This included at least 96 deserters in one town outside of Irbil. Ironically, the Revolutionary Command Council (RCC) issued a decree on August 5 suspending the use of amputation as a punishment for desertion.[26]

Since that time, Saddam has carefully encouraged tribalism within the armed forces from those tribes he feels remain loyal or whose loyalty can be purchased. He seems to have changed and rotated many of the intelligence and security officers responsible for surveillance over the armed forces, and to have strengthened Qusay's role in controlling both the presidential security forces and reviewing security reports on all aspects of the Republican Guard and regular military forces.

PROSPECTS FOR A COUP AND "ONE-BULLET ELECTION"

There is little prospect that Saddam can ever fully secure his control over the military, or can ever eliminate the risk that an assassination or a coup attempt will finally succeed. There have also been growing reports of serious morale problems—including large-scale desertions from within the regular military, breakdowns in morale, and problems in retaining junior officers.

However, Saddam retains a massive apparatus to protect himself from the military, and he continues to demonstrate that he can use the military as an instrument of state control. The Iraqi military continues to deploy nearly 14 of its 23–24 divisions along the border of the area under Kurdish control, and to deploy several divisions that conduct military operations against Shi'ite rebels in the marshes in the south.[27] Saddam has repeatedly demonstrated that he can deploy the Republican Guard for internal security missions, and that he can ruthlessly purge potential power centers within the military.

Moreover, the kind of opposition to Saddam that has surfaced within the military shows little sign of being "democratic." It is the product of clan-oriented struggles for power or a desire to preserve power by getting rid of a man who is perceived as the reason that those sanctions continue. The military may be more "pragmatic" than Saddam, but it will only be as moderate as it has to be. The military will also inevitably use any increase in its political power to favor its own interests.

NOTES

1. Sean Boyne, "Qusay Considers a Reshuffle for Iraq's Command Structure," *Jane's Intelligence Review*, September, 1997, pp. 416–417.

2. Sean Boyne, "Qusay Considers a Reshuffle for Iraq's Command Structure," *Jane's Intelligence Review*, September, 1997, pp. 416–417.

3. Based on interviews and *Jane's Sentinel: The Gulf States*, "Iraq," London, Jane's Publishing, 1997.

4. Sean Boyne, "Inside Iraq's Security Network," *Jane's Intelligence Review*, July, 1997, pp. 312–316, and August, 1997, pp. 365–367.

5. The author has repeatedly visited Iraq since 1973 and has talked to many serving Iraqi officers during the Iran-Iraq War. While such officers never directly criticized Saddam, their discussions of the "high command" often did so in ways that clearly referred to the president. Discussions with defectors in Jordan and Europe since the Gulf War indicate that this situation has grown worse since 1992, and still worse since the defection of Hussein Kamel Majiid in 1995.

6. For extensive details on civil-military relations before the Gulf War, see May Chartouni-Dubarry, "The Development of Internal Politics in Iraq from 1958 to the Present Day," in Derek Hopwood, Habib Ishow, and Thomas Koszinowski, eds., *Iraq: Power and Society*, Reading, Ithaca Press, 1993, pp. 19–36; May Chartouni-Dubarry, "La 'question irakienne' ou l'histoire d'une puissance contrariee," in Bassma Kodmani-

Darwish and May Chartouni-Dubarry, eds., *Perceptions de securite et strategies nationales au Moyen-Orient*, Paris, Masson, 1994, pp. 57–60; Shahram Chubin and Charles Tripp, *Iran and Iraq At War*, Boulder, Westview Press, 1988, pp. 114–120.

7. For more extensive historical background of military politics in Iraqi political life, see Ali Tahir, *Irak: Aux Origines du regime militaire*, Paris, Albin Michel, 1989; Hamid al-Shawi, "L'Intervention des militaires dans la vie politique de la Syrie, de l'Irak et de la Jordanie," *Politique Etrangère*, No. 3, 1974, pp. 343–374.

8. For further details, see *Al Wasat*, June 26, 1995, p. 24.

9. *The Guardian*, November 26, 1971, p. 15.

10. Khalid Al-Ani, *The Encyclopedia of Modern Iraq*, vol. III, Baghdad: *The Arab Encyclopedia House*, n.d., pp. 518–519.

11. *Washington Post*, April 15, 1992, p. A-32, July 3, p. A-1, July 4, 1992, p. A-14, July 10, 1992, p. A-14; *New York Times*, July 4, 1992, p. A-4, July 6, 1992, p. A-6, July 7, 1992, p. A-3, July 10, 1992, p. A-3.

12. *The Sunday Times*, April 18, 1993, p. 19; discussions with Amatzia Baram.

13. *Washington Post*, October 4, 1992, p. A-35.

14. Many of the details in this analysis are based on discussions with Amatzia Baram.

15. *Baltimore Sun*, April 15, 1993, p. 6A; *Washington Times*, April 27, 1993, p. A-2.

16. *Washington Post*, September 15, 1996, p. A-1.

17. *Al-Hayat*, April 16, 1996, p. 5; excerpts of the interview are also in *FBIS-NES*, April 18, 1996, pp. 21–26.

18. Quoted in *FBIS-NES*, April 18, 1996, p. 24. Also see *Jane's Defense Weekly*, March 27, 1996, p. 4.

19. *Philadelphia Inquirer*, August 5, 1996, p. A-3; UPI, July 7, 1996, 1158; Associated Press, July 12, 1996, 0940; *Washington Times*, August 12, 1996, p. A-1, and August 15, 1996, p. A-15; *Wall Street Journal*, February 26, 1996, p. A-8.

20. *Washington Post*, September 1996, p. A-1.

21. Sean Boyne, "Inside Iraq's Security Network," *Jane's Intelligence Review*, July, 1997, pp. 312–316, and August, 1997, pp. 365–367.

22. US State Department Human Rights Report, 1996, Internet version.

23. On Tali' al-Duri, see the exhaustive work on the Iraqi armed forces by Syrian Staff Colonel Ahmad Zaydi, *Al bina'al ma'anawi lil quwat al-musallah al-iraqiyah* (The Development of the Fighting Spirit of the Iraqi Army), Beirut, Dar al-Rawdah, 1990, pp. 336–341.

24. *Al-Hayat*, July 12, 1996, pp. 1, 6.

25. *Washington Times*, July 13, 1995, p. A-5; November 22, 1995, p. A-12; United Press, February 1, 1996, 0932.

26. US State Department Human Rights Report, 1996, Internet version.

27. USCENTCOM map, supplied June, 1996.

Chapter 4

Trends in Iraq's Total Force Strength, Military Expenditures, Arms Imports, and Military Industries

Much of Iraq's propaganda describes a state that has been bankrupted by UN sanctions. There is some truth to these claims, but they ignore the fact that much of Iraq's current poverty is a result of the cost of the Iran-Iraq war and that Iraq could have obtained relief from the economic consequences of sanctions at any time by agreeing to the terms of the cease-fire or to UN resolutions that allowed it to export oil for food under conditions that ensured that the money was spent for the welfare of all of Iraq's people and was not used to illegally import arms or serve Saddam's ambitions. It is also important to note that Iraq's military spending has steadily impoverished Iraq ever since the beginning of the Iran-Iraq War in 1980, and Iraq's efforts to rebuild and sustain its massive military force structure has made its situation far worse since the end of the Gulf War.

Iraq has long treated its economic statistics as a propaganda weapon and manipulates them for domestic and foreign political purposes. It is important to note, however, that Iraq's per capita income peaked just after the Iran-Iraq War began, because Iraq was able to exploit the rise in oil prices following the fall of the Shah. Iraq then had a per capita income in excess of $4,000 in 1997 US dollars, and it was spending about 34% of its national budget and 25% of its GNP on military forces.

MILITARIZATION AND THE COST TO THE IRAQI PEOPLE

By 1982, Iraq was spending over 70% of its budget and 45% of its GNP on military forces, and these spending levels were sustained until the end of the Iran-Iraq War in 1988. By that time, a massive drop in oil exports and the failure to develop the economy had cut Iraq's per capita to around $2,200 dollars, or roughly in half. Iraq had exhausted its national savings and financial reserves and was a major debtor. It had neglected every sector of its economy—especially agriculture—and was importing two-thirds of its food. Iraq did cut its military expenditures following the cease-fire in August, 1988, from levels of around $24 billion in 1988 (in constant 1997 dollars) to levels of around $16 billion in 1989 and the first half of 1990.[1]

Peace, however, led to a major drop in oil prices and revenues, and Iraq's per capita income dropped to levels of around $1,500 in 1989, while military spending remained as high as 60% of the national budget. The build-up of Iraq's military forces in 1990 then raised military spending back to 75% of the national budget, while national mobilization and the oil embargo following Iraq's invasion of Kuwait cut the per capita income to around $750 before any fighting began in the Gulf War.

Since 1991, the "war of sanctions" has almost certainly kept Iraq's per capita income to levels of $500–$900, and increases in prices have impoverished most Iraqis and produced shortages in food and advanced medical care. While reports by the World Health Organization (WHO) and the Food and Agricultural Organization (FAO) often rely so heavily on Iraqi data that they are little more than Iraqi propaganda, they contain enough actual research to indicate that there are problems with malnutrition, infant mortality, and medical services.[2]

At the same time, many of Iraq's statistics contradict some of the more dire reports about the hardship in Iraq. In October, 1997, Iraq imposed a curfew to conduct its first census in 10 years. The census concluded that Iraq had a total of some 22 million people, including an estimated 3.2 million in northern Iraq. The figures also failed to reflect anything approaching the rate of child mortality that some reports had warned about, or the impact of diseases and malnutrition. In fact, outside estimates indicated that Iraq had a population growth rate of 3.69%, one of the highest rates of growth in the world.[3]

The CIA estimated in 1997 that Iraq had a birth rate of 43.07 births/1,000 population, a death rate of 6.57 deaths/1,000 population, and an infant mortality rate of 60 deaths/1,000 live births. Iraq's life expectancy at birth was 66.95 years for the entire population, 65.92 years for males, and 68.03 years for females. In 1989, using exactly the same methodology, the CIA estimated that Iraq had a birth rate of 46 births/1,000 population, a death rate of 7.00 deaths/1,000 population, and an infant mortality rate of 67 deaths/1,000 live births. Iraq's life expectancy at birth was exactly the same for males and females. In short, if the CIA estimates are correct, the death rate in Iraq dropped slightly of more than half a decade of sanctions, and infant mortality and life expectancy were exactly the same. World Bank estimates are very similar.[4]

IRAQ'S MILITARY MANPOWER POOL

One thing is clear. Iraq's economic hardships have not prevented it from mobilizing much of its manpower pool and continuing to make heavy expenditures on military forces. The CIA estimates that Iraq had a military manpower pool of 4,832,001 males between the ages of 15 and 49 in 1996, and had

2,711,312 males fit for military service. An estimated 237,500 males a year reached age 18, the age for military service. The International Institute of Strategic Studies (IISS) estimates that Iraq had a total population of 22.4 million in 1998, and had 1,375,000 males between the ages of 13 and 17, 1,150,000 males between the ages of 81 and 22, and 1,695,000 males between the ages of 23 and 32. It had slightly smaller pools of women, who do not serve in the regular armed forces but can perform support and a number of paramilitary functions.[5]

This is one of the largest pools of manpower in the Arab world, although it is much smaller than Iran's pool of 68.7 million, and is deeply divided along ethnic and religious lines. The ethnic divisions are reflected in the fact that the total population is 75%–80% Arab; 15%–20% Kurdish, Turkoman, and Assyrian, and 5% other. The population is 97% Muslim, but the ruling Sunni elite is only 32% to 37% of the population, 60% to 65% is Shi'ite, and 3% is Christian or other. Most of the population speaks Arabic, but portions speak Kurdish (official in Kurdish regions), Assyrian, and Armenian.[6]

THE OVERALL TRENDS IN IRAQI FORCES SINCE THE GULF WAR

Figure 4.1 shows an estimate of the trends in Iraqi military manpower from 1967 to the present, and Figures 4.2 and 4.3 show how Iraq's manpower, tanks, and air strength compares with that of other Gulf states. Iraq still has an active force structure with over 380,000 men, plus another 650,000 in reserve. It has six corps with 17 regular army divisions, six Republican Guard divisions, 10 special forces and commando brigades, and a Presidential Guard/special security force.

Iraq's equipment holdings after Desert Fox included roughly 2,700 tanks, 4,400 other armored vehicles, 1,980 major artillery weapons, 120 attack helicopters, and over 330 combat aircraft. Iraq has also made a major effort to rebuild its military industries and to compensate for its lack of arms imports with domestic production.

The readiness of Iraq's manpower, major combat formations, and equipment is uncertain. Iraq has slowly improved its training at the company and battalion levels, has created cadres of officers with considerable training and experience, has reorganized its forces, and has repaired and overhauled much of its equipment. Nevertheless, more than half a decade without significant military imports is steadily reducing Iraq's military capabilities. While Iraq was able to rebuild and consolidate its forces after the Gulf War, its rate of recovery declined in late 1993 to early 1994. Iraq made little progress after this time until the fall of 1996, when it again began to increase its readiness and training activity. It also either obtained some imports of spare parts or made more effective use of existing stocks.[7]

While Iraq did step up its smuggling of spare parts after late 1996, and sustained this level of effort during 1997 and 1998, its military consolidation has come almost solely through cannibalizing its pre–Gulf War equipment and

Figure 4.1
Iraq: Military Manning, 1967–1998 (thousands)

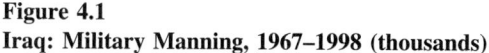

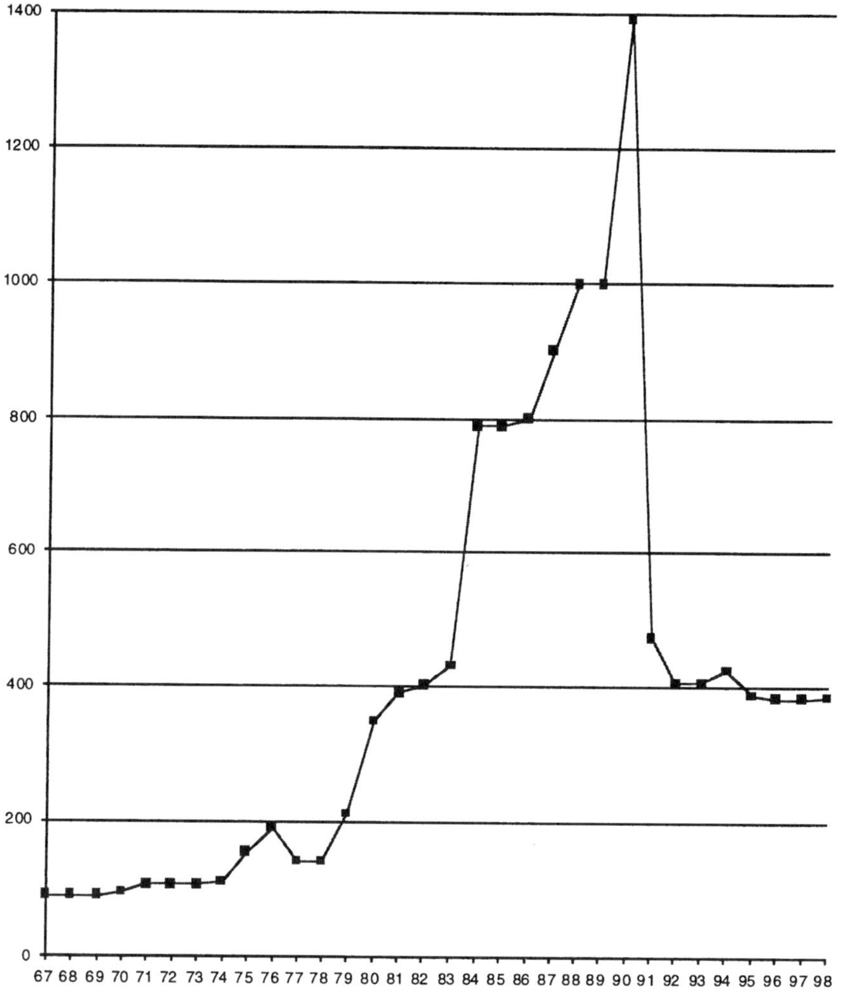

Source: Adapted by Anthony H. Cordesman from ACDA, *World Military Expenditures and Arms Transfers*, Table I1, various editions. Iraqi data after 1991 are author's estimate.

stocks and equipment and spare parts. Iraq has been unable to "recapitalize" its forces by importing major deliveries or new equipment or producing advanced weapons systems in Iraq. Iraq has not been able to import the technology it needs to react effectively to the lessons of the Gulf War and make up key wartime losses, and it has not been able to import or manufacture the massive deliveries of parts, new equipment, and munitions it needs to make up for the inefficiency of its maintenance and logistics capability.[8]

Figure 4.2
Total Active Military Manpower in All Gulf Forces, 1979–1998

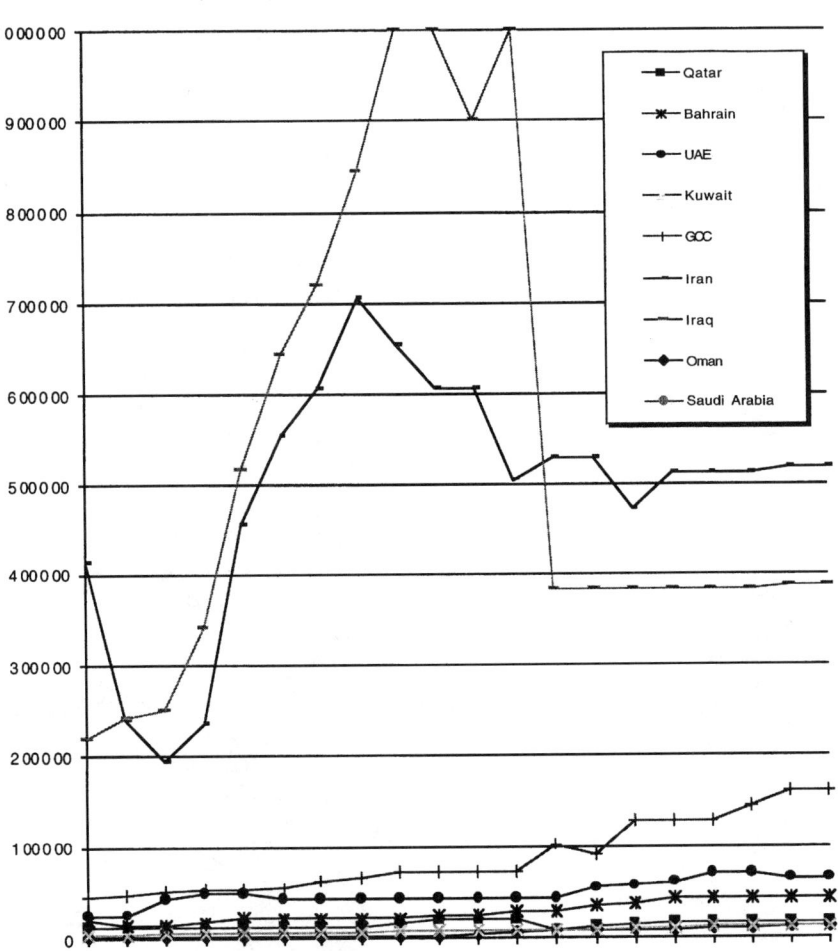

Note: Iran includes active forces in Revolutionary Guards. Saudi Arabia includes active forces in the National Guard.
Sources: Adapted by Anthony H. Cordesman from various sources, and IISS, *Military Balance*.

Iraqi forces have faced other problems. Readiness and morale have declined as a result of Iraq's economic crisis and internal political problems, and desertions have increased. The quality and strength of most units have declined sharply, and even Iraq's elite units have suffered. Iraq has had to cannibalize equipment and take equipment out of some units to maintain the readiness of others.[9]

Iraq is anything but a paper tiger, but it is hardly the military power that won the Iran-Iraq War. Some areas of Iraq's order of battle are becoming a hollow

Figure 4.3
Major Measures of Combat Equipment Strength, 1999

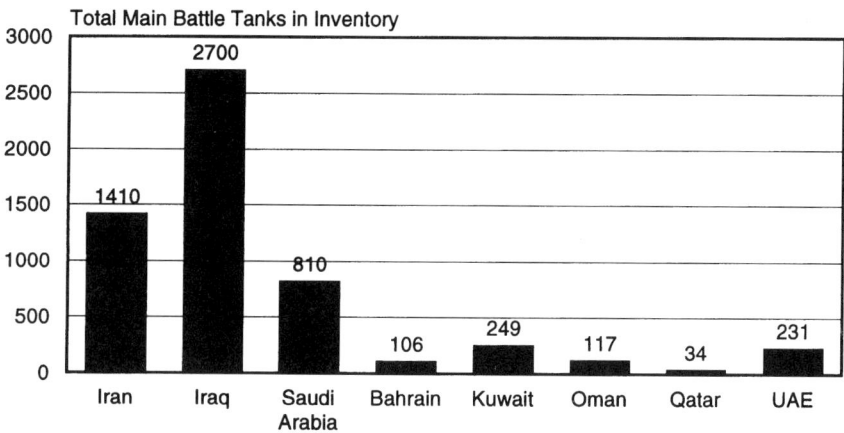

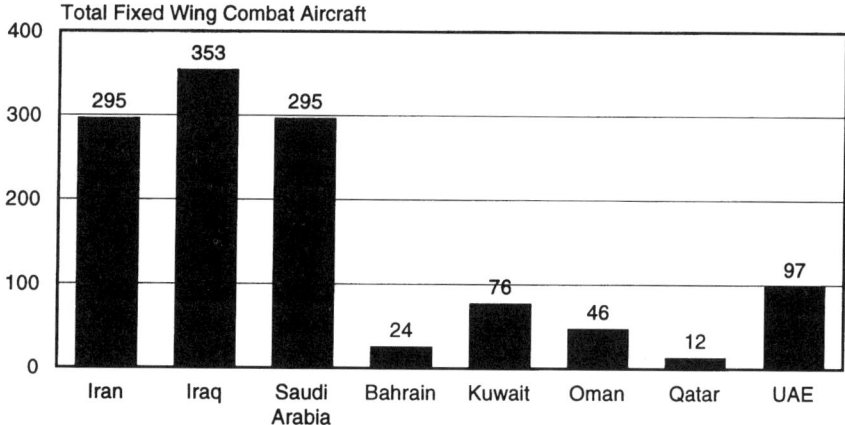

Sources: Adapted by Anthony H. Cordesman from various sources, and IISS, *Military Balance*.

shell. In those areas where Iraq has consolidated its resources effectively, its forces still have to deal with the fact that UN sanctions are denying Iraq the new technology, new equipment, and spare parts it needs. The "war of inspections" is steadily reducing the conventional military threat Iraq can pose to Iran, Kuwait, and other states.

IRAQI MILITARY EXPENDITURES

Iraq has been able to remain a major regional military power largely because of the legacy left by Iraq's immense military expenditures and arms transfers before the Gulf War, and the fact that the regime has given high priority to the military, even at the cost of worsening the plight of Iraq's people.

Iraq imported well over $100 billion worth of conventional arms between 1972 and 1990, and spent over $10 billion on the arms and equipment to assemble, manufacture, and deliver weapons of mass destruction. As Table 4.1 shows, Iraq has been involved in an arms race with Iran since the 1960s. It spent billions fighting the Kurds during the early to mid-1970s, and it then spent nearly $200 billion fighting the Iran-Iraq War. During much of the Iran-Iraq War, Iraq spent 40% to 75% of its GDP on military expenditures. Iraq's losses of weapons and ammunition expenditures alone totaled tens of billions of dollars, and Iraq lost tens of billions more in terms of wartime damage, casualty and death payments, and wasted economic opportunity costs.[10]

Spending During the Iran-Iraq and Gulf Wars

This Iraq effort is also a warning of the level of militarism within the Iraqi state. Iraq's GNP peaked during 1979 and 1980, with totals of $118 billion and $120 billion respectively, measured in constant 1988 dollars. The course of the Iran-Iraq War soon led to cuts in Iraq's oil exports, which reduced its GDP to $70.4 billion in 1981. A combination of wartime damage, the loss of oil export routes through the Gulf and Syria, and lower oil prices then kept Iraq's GNP under $70 billion for the rest of the 1980s. Iraq's GNP was only $65.8 billion in 1988, the year the Iran-Iraq War ended. This was a little over half of Iraq's GNP in 1980.

In spite of these economic problems, Iraq kept its military expenditures at 30% to 40% of its GNP from 1980 to 1984, the first four years of the Iran-Iraq War. When Iran's victories grew more threatening in 1985, Iraqi military spending rose to 52% of the GNP in 1985, and stayed close to 50% for the rest of the 1980s. Iraq could sustain these expenditures only through a combination of massive foreign borrowing and aid from southern Gulf states like Kuwait and Saudi Arabia. Iraq's debt to its Arab neighbors rose to $37 billion.[11]

To put Iraq's military expenditures into perspective, the Arms Control and Disarmament Agency (ACDA) estimates that Iraq spent $10,010 million in current US dollars on military forces in 1978, $11,350 million in 1979, $19,810 million in 1980, $24,610 million in 1981, $25,070 million in 1982, $13,230 million in 1983, $16,680 million in 1984, $12,650 million in 1985, $14,870 million in 1986, $16,450 million in 1987, $18,330 million in 1988, $13,140 million in 1989, $14,110 million in 1990, and $8,776 million in 1991.[12]

The IISS estimates that Iraq spent $13.99 billion in 1987, $12.87 billion in 1988, and $8.61 billion in 1990. It has issued estimates that Iraq spent $2.6 billion in 1992 and 1993 and $1.3 billion in 1995 and 1996, but these estimates seem far too low to include the dollar cost equivalent of the Iraqi effort. The cost of maintaining a well-equipped force of nearly 400,000 men, plus 55,000 men in the paramilitary forces, has to be in excess of $5 billion a year. Further,

Table 4.1
The Iran-Iraq Military Balance, 1967–1997

Country	Manpower (1,000s)**		Tanks	OAVs	Artillery	Combat Aircraft
	Total	Army				
1967 (Time of Arab-Israeli Conflict)						
Iran	221	200	225	278	120	180
Iraq	82	70	400-535	200-250	180-250	215
1973 (Time of October War)						
Iran	212	160	920	1,000	380	159
Iraq	102	90	990	1,330	700	224
1978 (Height of Shah's Military Build-Up)						
Iran	413	280-285	1,620-1,775	1,075-1,300	782-1,225	459-470
Iraq	212	180-200	1,800-2,450	1,500-1,600	956-1,160	450-470
1980 (First Major Year of Iran-Iraq War)						
Iran	240	150	1,735	1,075	1,000	445
Iraq	243	200	2,750	2,500	1,240	332
1987 (Last Year of Iranian Military Superiority and Occupation of Part of Iraq)						
Iran	1,030	605-735	1,000	1,060	1,200	60-100
Iraq	1,000	955	4,500	4,700	3,000	500+
1988 (After August Cease-Fire and Iranian Defeat in Iran-Iraq War)						
Iran	604	550	500-600	700-800	850-900	60-165*
Iraq	1,100	1,000	5,500	4,750	2,800	500-800*
1990 (Before Iraq Invaded Kuwait)						
Iran	605	555	550-650	760-1,200	800-1,100	121-180
Iraq	1,000-1,200	955-1,100	5,500-7,000	6,000-8,800	3,700-5,600	513-770
1991 (In Spring, Operational Forces after Iraq's Defeat by UN Coalition)						
Iran	528-600	400-430	680-750	750-850	1,700-1,500	180-210*
Iraq	500-600	300-400	2,900-3,000	4,000-4,400	1,800-2,000	350-375
1993 (In Spring, Estimated Operational Holdings)						
Iran	500-520	500-520	750-850	950-1,050	2,200-2,400	250-280*
Iraq	430-450	390-410	2,900-3,000	4,000-4,400	1,800-2,000	350-375
1997 (Estimated Operational Holdings)						
Iran	320-540	260-440	1,350	1,000-1,200	2,350-2,700	250-300
Iraq	518	330-350	2,200-2,700	4,000-4,300	1,770-2,000	350-365

*Does not count any of the 131 Iraqi aircraft that flew to Iran during the Gulf War. Their operational status is unknown as of this writing.

**Includes Revolutionary Guards forces and Popular Army forces omitted from some estimates.

Sources: Adapted by the author from interviews and from various annual editions of IISS, *Military Balance*; ACDA, *World Military Expenditures and Arms Transfers*; and the Jaffee Center for Strategic Studies, *Middle East Military Balance*. These sources are extremely uncertain in many areas. The range of estimates has often been adjusted by the author. As is the case with all numbers shown, there is a high degree of uncertainty. Even data like main battle tank counts differ radically.

the IISS estimates do not include substantial expenditures on weapons of mass destruction, and massive civil expenditures on preparing and recovering from the Gulf War.[13]

By 1989, the year between the Iran-Iraq War and Iraq's invasion of Kuwait, Iraq's economy was experiencing a serious economic crisis. Experts disagree over the economic statistics involved, but not over the seriousness of the crisis. According to the CIA, Iraq's GNP was then $35 billion, and its per capita income was only $1,940. This level of per capita income is not unusual by Third World standards, but it was low compared to Iraq's economy in 1979 and to the wealth of a far less developed Saudi Arabia—which had a GNP of $79 billion and a per capita income of $4,800. Iraq also owed $13 billion in annual debt payments to the West, nearly half of its oil revenues in 1989.[14]

While Iraq unquestionably could have funded its economic recovery from the Iran-Iraq War at the cost of further cutbacks in its military expenditures—and done so without risking an attack from Iran or any other neighbor—it chose to try to buy both guns and butter. It was this choice that steadily increased the impact of its debt burden and created the economic crisis which helped lead Iraq to invade Kuwait.[15]

Iraq planned an annual military budget of $12.9 billion in 1990, and it was spending an average of $721 per citizen on military forces before it invaded Kuwait. Although Iraq had cut its rate of new arms orders, it still took delivery on $1.435 billion worth of arms, and ordered $1,125 million more during the first six months of 1990. This level of expenditure raised Iraq's international debt to the West to $40 billion or more. Some experts feel that Iraq's total debt was well in excess of $80 billion by early 1990, if one included all of Iraq's debts to Arab states.[16]

Expenditures Since the Gulf War

There are no reliable estimates of Iraq's military expenditures since the Gulf War, and such estimates are almost impossible to make because Saddam Hussein has used his control over Iraq's economy to shift assets to the military in ways that are not reflected in any Iraqi budget document. However, Figures 4.4–4.9 and Table 4.2 provide reasonable working estimates. Figure 4.4 shows show how Iraq's military expenditures compare with those of other Gulf states. Figure 4.5 compares the trends in Iraq's military spending and arms imports with the overall trends in GNP and total exports to provide a picture of the burden military spending put on the Iraqi economy. Figure 4.6 provides a similar picture of this burden by showing military spending as a percent of GNP and Central Government Expenditures, arms imports as a percent of total imports, and men in uniform per 1,000 in the total population. Figure 4.7 shows the trend in military spending and arms imports in constant dollars. Figure 4.8 shows the trends in military effort as a percent of the 1984 baseline, and Figure 4.9 shows

Figure 4.4
Comparative Military Spending of the Major Gulf Powers (constant $US 1995 millions)

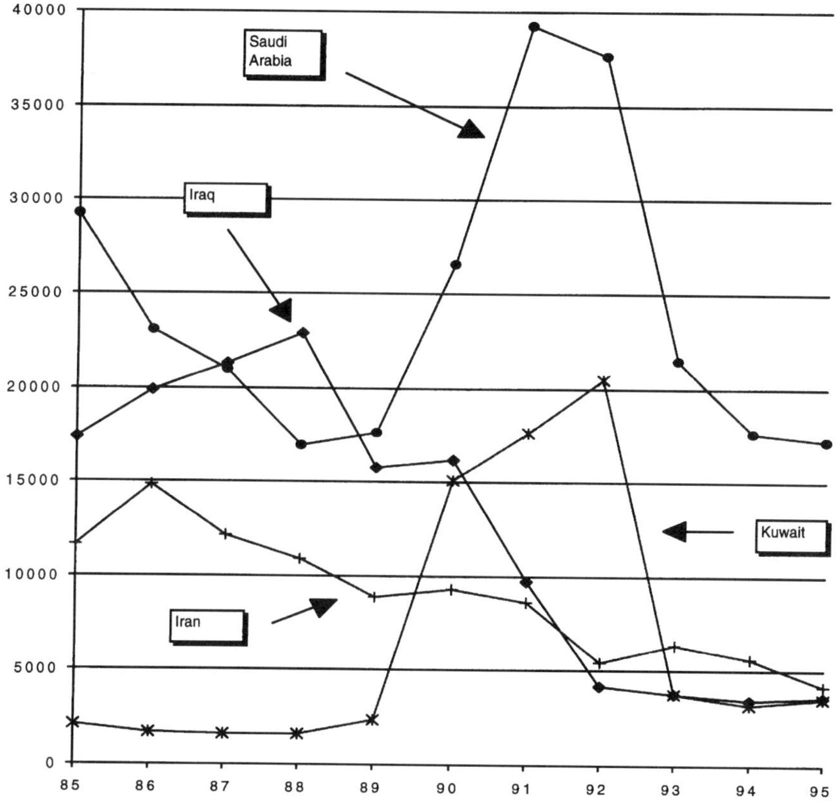

	85	86	87	88	89	90	91	92	93	94	95
Iran	11,680	14,840	12,190	10,860	8,893	9,307	8,654	5,410	6,333	5,586	4,191
Iraq	17,340	19,850	21,290	22,890	15,740	16,210	9,698	4,200	3,800	3,400	3,600
Kuwait	2,057	1,708	1,609	1,565	2,316	15,130	17,620	20,430	3,759	3,146	3,488
Saudi Arabia	29,240	23,080	20,980	16,980	17,600	26,620	39,240	37,650	21,470	17,630	17,210

Source: Adapted by Anthony H. Cordesman from ACDA, *World Military Expenditures and Arms Transfers, 1996*, Table 1.

the relationship between Iraq's military spending per capita and the trend in its per capita income.

Iraq's large force structure is expensive, and it has been active in the field for much of the period since 1991—in dealing with the Shi'ites, surrounding the Kurds, major exercises, and threats like Desert Fox. It has had to be paid a premium to ensure its loyalty. As a result, Iraq's military expenditures had been extremely high for a nation which had only token oil exports for more than half

Table 4.2
Iraqi Military Expenditures and Arms Transfers by Major Supplier (in millions of US dollars)

	Military Expenditures		Arms Imports	
	$ Current	$ 95 Constant	$ Current	$ 95 Constant
1983	13,530	20,440	7,900	11,824
1984	16,880	23,960	9,300	13,270
1985	12,650	17,340	4,900	6,716
1986	14,870	19,850	6,100	8,142
1987	16,450	21,290	5,900	7,637
1988	18,330	22,890	5,600	6,992
1989	13,140	15,740	2,500	2,995
1990	14,110	16,210	2,900	3,333
1991	8,776	9,698	280	300
1992	*4,200*	*4,200*	*195*	*200*
1993	*3,530*	*3,800*	*296*	*300*
1994	*3,330*	*3,400*	*220*	*220*
1995	*3,600*	*3,600*	*206*	*200*
1996	*3,850*	*3,700*	*182*	*170*
1997	*3,930*	*3,800*	*182*	*163*
1998	*3,930*	-	*213*	-

Source: Adapted by Anthony H. Cordesman from ACDA, *World Military Expenditures and Arms Transfers*, Tables I and II, various editions. Data for 1994–1998, and all data in italics, are estimated by Anthony H. Cordesman.

a decade, and which has not been able to import large amounts of arms because of UN sanctions. Iraq has not had to pay market prices for many of these expenditures, or formally include them in its budget, because it has used low-paid conscripts and directly allocated state resources. It has, however, had to pay the economic opportunity cost and divert resources away from its civil economy.

As a result, it is unlikely that Iraqi expenditures have dropped below $5 billion to $7 billion in terms of their dollar value equivalent in purchasing power parity. Many of Iraq's armed forces have been constantly involved in civil wars against the Kurds and Shi'ites, or in expensive field deployments near the Kurdish security zone in the north, and in the urban and marsh areas in the south. Iraq has poured massive resources into rebuilding its military industry and trying to maintain its operational readiness. The government has also offered salary increases and other incentives that have become progressively more expensive with time. While no firm data are available, Iraq has probably spent about 33%

Figure 4.5
Iraqi Gross National Product, Military Expenditures, Total Exports, and Arms Import Deliveries (constant $US 1995 millions)

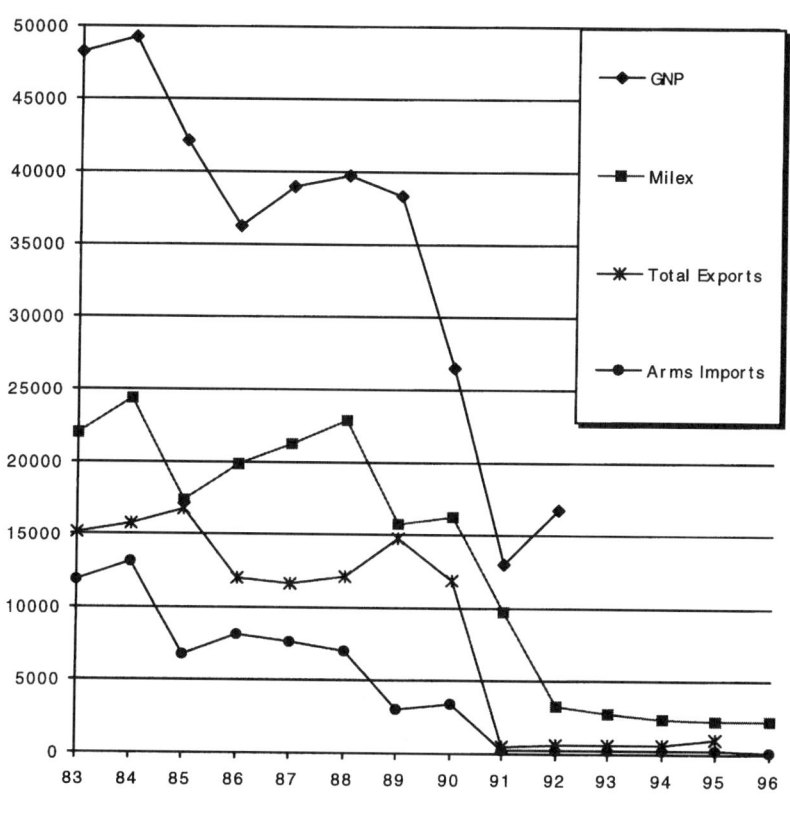

	83	84	85	86	87	88	89	90	91	92	93	94	95	96
GNP	48,270	49,270	42,110	36,190	39,040	39,790	38,320	26,440	12,960	16,740	-	-	-	-
Milex	21,970	24,360	17,340	19,850	21,290	22,890	15,740	16,210	9,698	3,200	2,800	2,400	2,200	2,200
Total Exports	15,140	15,740	16,750	12,020	11,670	12,090	14,720	11,930	517	640	600	627	1000	-
Arms Imports	11,824	13,070	6,716	8,142	7,637	6,992	2,995	3,333	300	200	300	220	200	170

Source: Adapted by Anthony H. Cordesman from ACDA, *World Military Expenditures and Arms Transfers, 1996*, 1997.

to 45% of its post–Gulf War GDP on military expenditures in spite of the economic crisis created by the UN sanctions and Saddam Hussein's refusal to sell oil.

IRAQI ARMS IMPORTS

Until the Gulf War, arms imports served as Iraq's substitute for effective organization and military competence. Table 4.2 and Figures 4.6–4.8 show

Figure 4.6
Iraqi Military Efforts as a Percent of GNP, Government Expenditures, Imports, and Total Population, 1967–1995 (All percentages are measured in absolute manpower and constant 1995 US dollars)

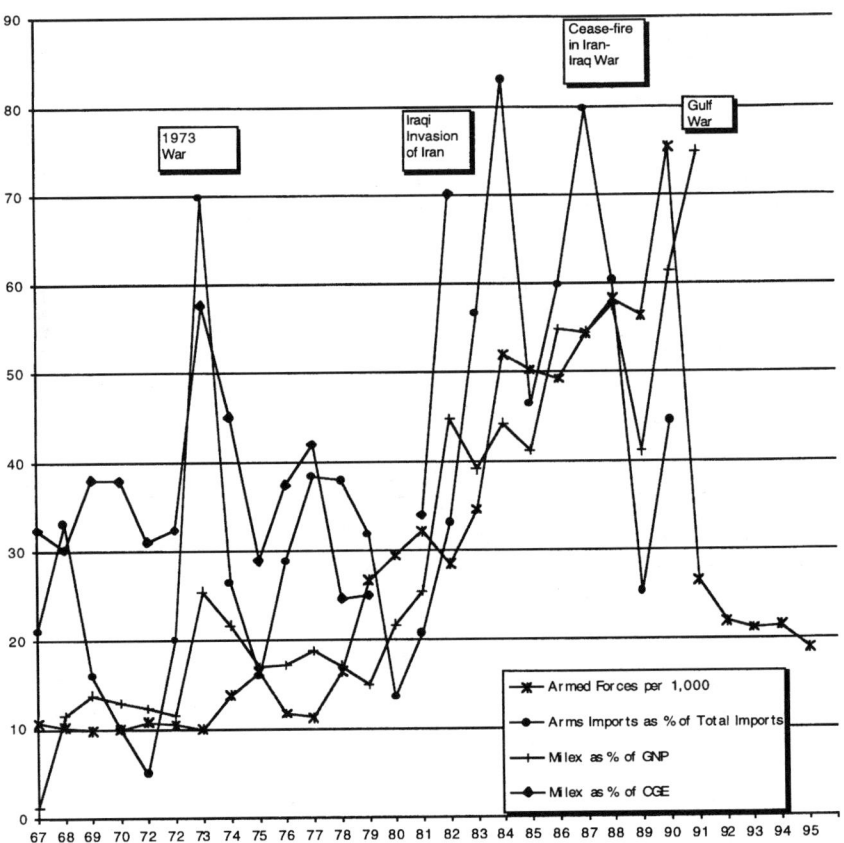

Source: Adapted by Anthony H. Cordesman from ACDA, *World Military Expenditures and Arms Transfers*, various editions.

that Iraq's arms imports placed a major burden on Iraq's economy during the decade before the Gulf War and the beginning of UN sanctions. It was a massive flood of arms imports that kept Iraq alive during the Iran-Iraq War. Similarly, it was Saddam's refusal to accept major reductions in these arms imports that was a major factor in his decision to invade Kuwait.

Ironically, the Gulf War had just the opposite effect. Iraq has now been cut off from major arms deliveries for nearly a decade. It has been unable to modernize, react to many of the lessons in the Gulf War, match the military build-up of its neighbors, and deal with the "revolution in military affairs." It

Figure 4.7
Iraqi Military Expenditures and Arms Transfers (constant $US 1995 millions)

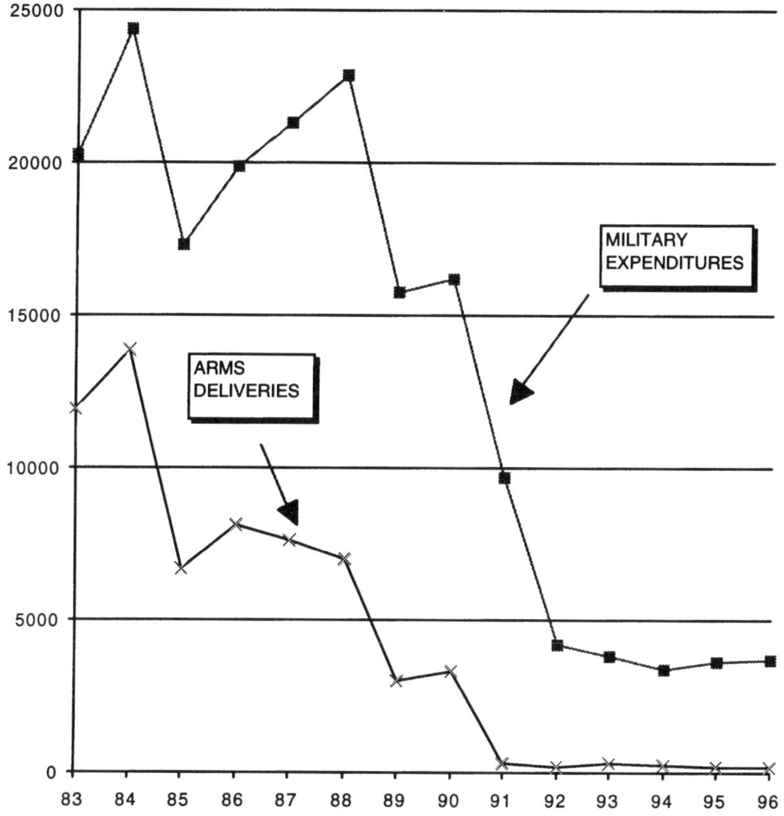

	83	84	85	86	87	88	89	90	91	92	93	94	95	96
Milex	20,240	24,360	17,340	19,850	21,290	22,890	15,740	16,210	9,698	4,200	3,800	3,400	3,600	3,700
Arms Imports	11,924	13,870	6,716	8,142	7,637	6,992	2,995	3,333	300	200	300	220	200	170

Source: Adapted by Anthony H. Cordesman from ACDA, *World Military Expenditures and Arms Transfers, 1996*, 1997.

has also been unable to use arms imports as a substitute for effective maintenance and repair capability, or for an effective logistics system.

In the meantime, Iraq has faced growing problems with obsolescence and wear. While it was able to recover and rebuild substantial amounts of the military equipment it left behind on the battlefield after the Gulf War, it has since had to fight against its Shi'ites, maintain extensive field deployments against its Kurds and Iran, and attempt to rebuild its fighting capabilities through major exercises. The end result has been continuing wear, coupled with the growing obsolescence of Iraq's older equipment and the build-up of a cumulative backlog in the recapitalization of its forces, that now totals at least $20 billion.

Figure 4.8
Iraqi Military Expenditures and Arms Imports as a Percent of 1984 Total, 1984–1994 (measured as percent of constant $US 1994 millions)

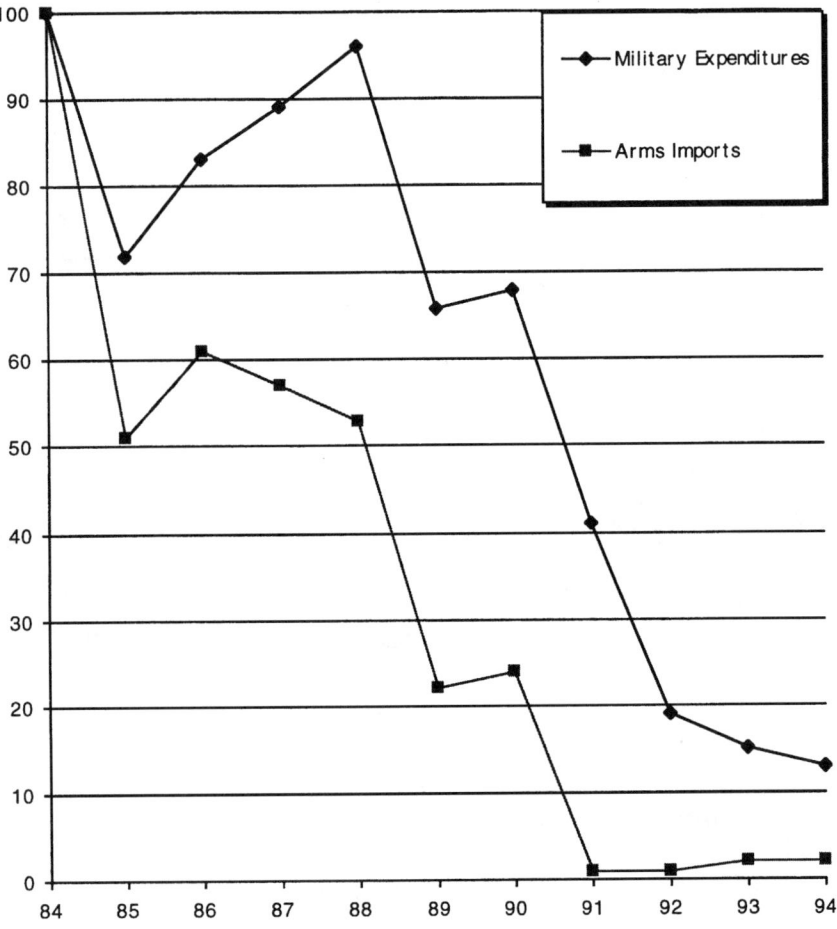

Source: Adapted by Anthony H. Cordesman from ACDA, *World Military Expenditures and Arms Transfers, 1995*, 1996.

The Crisis in Arms Imports Before the Gulf War

Iraq took delivery on $29.7 billion worth of new arms during the latter half of the Iran-Iraq War—the period from 1984 to 1988. These deliveries included $15.4 billion worth of arms from the former Soviet Union, $0.75 billion from Poland, $0.65 billion from Bulgaria, $0.675 billion from Czechoslovakia, and $2.8 billion from the People's Republic of China. Iraq obtained $3.1 billion from France, $0.37 billion from Italy, $0.03 billion from the UK, $0.675 billion

Figure 4.9
Iraqi GNP Per Capita Versus Military Expenditures Per Capita (in constant $US 1995 millions)

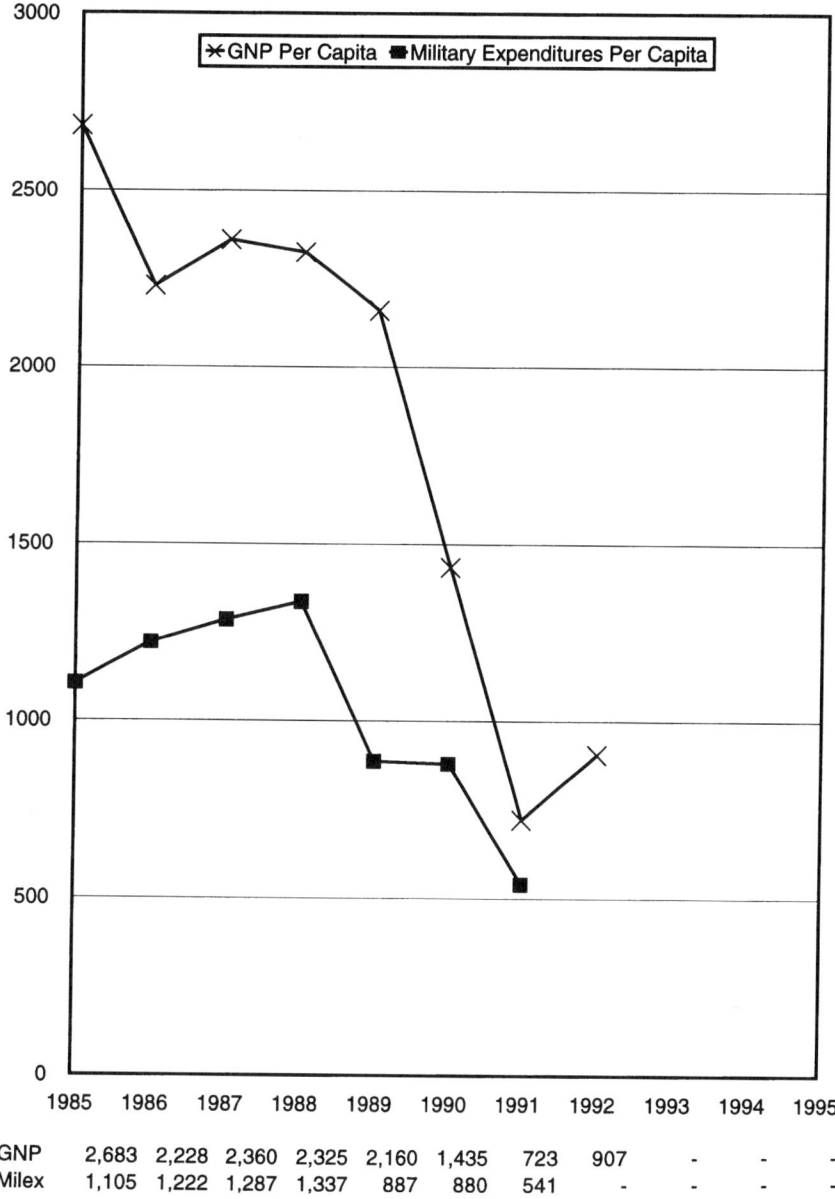

	1985	1986	1987	1988	1989	1990	1991	1992	1993	1994	1995
GNP	2,683	2,228	2,360	2,325	2,160	1,435	723	907	-	-	-
Milex	1,105	1,222	1,287	1,337	887	880	541	-	-	-	-

Source: Adapted by Anthony H. Cordesman from ACDA, *World Military Expenditures and Arms Transfers*, various editions.

from Germany, and $5.2 billion from other countries.[17] These Iraqi arms imports are compared to those of other Gulf countries in Figure 4.10, and it is clear that Iraq's arms imports then vastly exceeded those of Iran and rivaled those of Saudi Arabia in total cost.

Iraq had good reason to reduce its arms imports following the cease-fire in the Iran-Iraq War. It had immense debts and badly needed funds for civil development and reconstruction. Iraq's victories over Iran during the spring and summer of 1988 had cost Iran nearly 50% of its major land force weapons. Iraq had captured thousands of Iranian tanks, other armored vehicles, and artillery weapons that had been abandoned on the field, many with little or no combat damage. Iraq also had an immense backlog of orders it had placed during the peak of the fighting, orders that were scheduled for delivery during 1988–1992.

The size of the backlog of Iraqi arms orders after the Iran-Iraq War is indicated by the fact that Iraq took delivery on $5 billion worth of arms during 1989–1990, including $1.5 billion worth of arms from the former Soviet Union, $400 million from the People's Republic of China, $2.1 billion from major West European states, $600 million from other European states, and $400 million from other countries.

In many ways, therefore, it is not surprising that Iraq only ordered $1.7 billion worth of arms from the end of the Iran-Iraq War in August, 1988, to the beginning of the embargo on arms shipments that followed its invasion of Kuwait in August, 1990. This choice, however, was not voluntary, and it was not the result of some strategic choice that favored civil development or "butter" over military power or "guns." It is quite clear from both intelligence sources and interviews with Iraqi defectors that Iraq's low rate of new arms orders after 1988 was forced upon Saddam Hussein and his coterie by the nation's growing economic crisis.

Iraq's leaders still felt threatened by Iran. The cease-fire was not an agreement, and Iran had a substantial backlog of new arms orders of its own. Iran took delivery on $1.4 billion worth of arms a year during 1989–1990. More important, Iran began to place major new orders of a size that indicated that it was actively attempting to make up for its equipment losses. It placed a total of $6.7 billion in new orders during 1989–1992, and it continued to remain on the "top ten" list. In contrast, Iraq was forced to drop off of the "top ten" list for the first time in a decade.[18]

There were other strategic pressures from an Iraqi perspective. Iraq's leaders saw the United States as a potentially hostile power that did not belong in the Gulf, that had betrayed Iraq in the Iran-Contra arms deal, that had only backed Iraq to checkmate Iran, and that was turning on Iraq now that Iran was no longer the primary threat. They saw Israel as a nuclear threat to Iraq, and Iran's search for weapons of mass destruction as a potentially existential threat.

Iraq's leaders were involved in an incredibly expensive program to develop and mass-produce biological, chemical, and nuclear weapons and long-range missiles. They were committed to maintaining an immense military machine

Figure 4.10
Comparative Arms Import Deliveries of the Gulf Powers, 1983–1995 ($US 1995 constant millions)

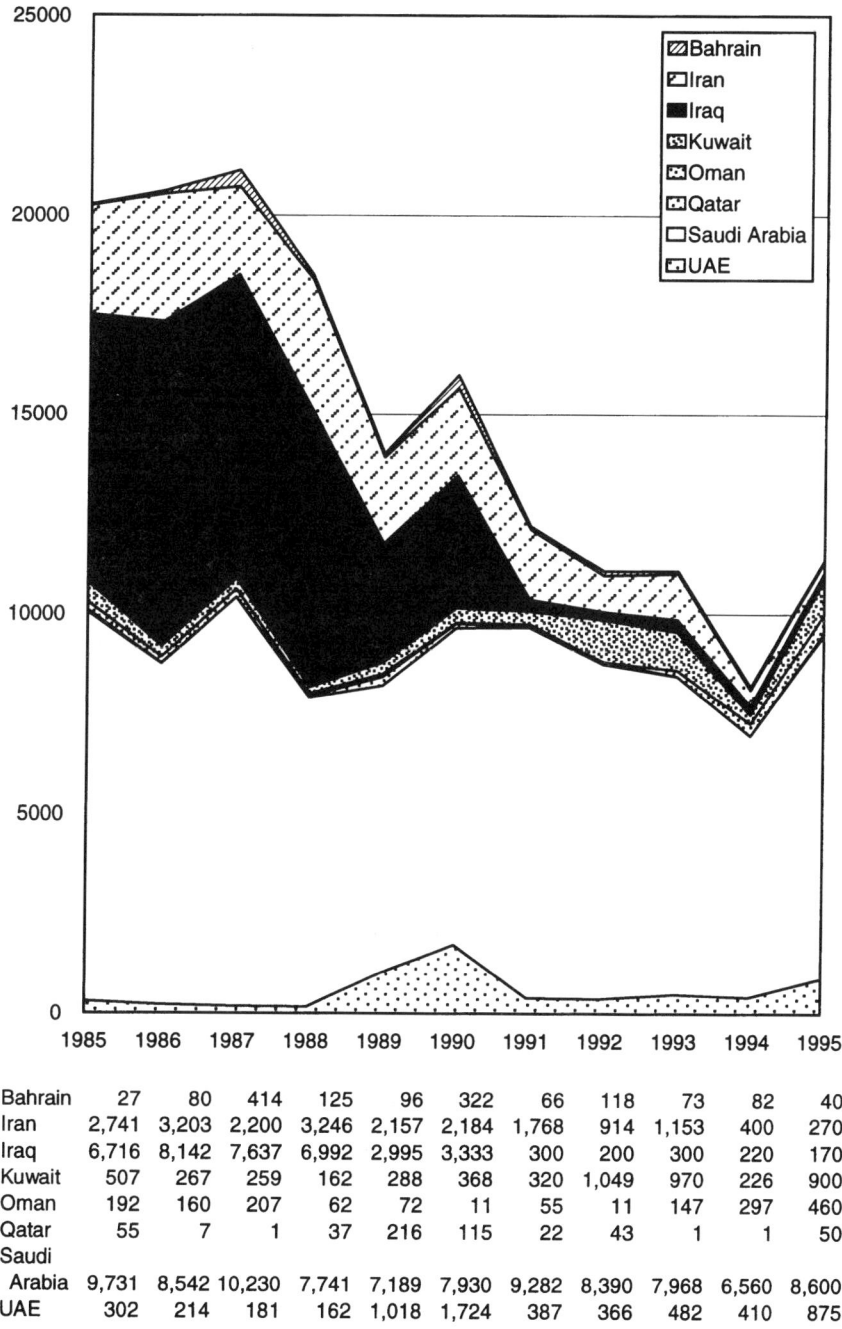

	1985	1986	1987	1988	1989	1990	1991	1992	1993	1994	1995
Bahrain	27	80	414	125	96	322	66	118	73	82	40
Iran	2,741	3,203	2,200	3,246	2,157	2,184	1,768	914	1,153	400	270
Iraq	6,716	8,142	7,637	6,992	2,995	3,333	300	200	300	220	170
Kuwait	507	267	259	162	288	368	320	1,049	970	226	900
Oman	192	160	207	62	72	11	55	11	147	297	460
Qatar	55	7	1	37	216	115	22	43	1	1	50
Saudi Arabia	9,731	8,542	10,230	7,741	7,189	7,930	9,282	8,390	7,968	6,560	8,600
UAE	302	214	181	162	1,018	1,724	387	366	482	410	875

Source: Adapted by Anthony H. Cordesman from ACDA, *World Military Expenditures and Arms Transfers, 1996*, 1997.

that needed roughly $900 million to $1.2 billion a year worth of spares, replacements, and upgrades a year—even given the much lower requirements of peacetime operations. They wanted to complete the conversion of Iraq's military forces to more advanced weapons and technology similar to the kind of first-line equipment used by NATO European forces and Russia. They were particularly concerned with creating an air force using the latest French and Russian aircraft, with upgrading Iraq's obsolescent surface-to-air missile force, and with expanding and modernizing Iraq's Republican Guard and regular heavy divisions with advanced tanks, armored combat vehicles, and self-propelled artillery.

Iraq's leaders realized that new orders averaging less than $1 billion a year were only about one-third to one-half what they needed to meet their goals. The most they could do under the circumstances was to prioritize their new order to focus on modern high technology equipment. This helps explain why $500 million of the $1.7 billion came from major West European states, $100 million from other European states, and $200 million were ordered from the Soviet Union. In contrast, no new orders were placed with the People's Republic of China, although Iraq ordered $900 million worth of new military imports from other countries. Some of the latter orders were designed to resupply and sustain Iraq's existing equipment at the lowest possible cost, some were part of an effort to obtain high-technology systems from third parties, and some were dual-used imports designed to help develop and produce weapons of mass destruction.[19]

At the same time, these pressures steadily increased the tensions between Iraq's leaders and their Southern Gulf neighbors. Saddam and his supporters saw Iraq as the natural military leader of the Gulf and the emerging leader of the Arab world. They felt that continuing aid to Iraq was a legitimate obligation on the part of the wealthy Gulf states like Kuwait, Saudi Arabia, and the United Arab Emirates (UAE) that had stood aside from the fighting in the "Arab cause" against Iran. They felt that Iraq's wartime debts should be treated as aid, and not as a financial burden that helped cripple Iraq's military modernization.

Losing Both Guns and Butter After the Gulf War

Iraq's invasion of Kuwait was partly a result of these perceptions and pressures, and the resulting ironies are obvious. The invasion scarcely met its goals of relieving Iraq's financial problems and consolidating its role as the dominant military power in the Gulf. Instead, Iraq has had no major arms deliveries since it invaded Kuwait, and it has been unable to place any major orders.[20] It has only had limited and erratic deliveries of "black market" parts and munitions, none of which have been significant.

The Gulf War has cost Iraq much of its butter as well as most of its guns, and it has created far greater and longer-term problems in financing a military machine than would ever have been the case if Iraq had focused on recovery and renegotiated its debts. Some estimates indicate that Iraq's GDP would have risen to $35–$40 billion in 1990, if it had not invaded Kuwait. Instead, it dropped to around $25 billion. Any estimate of Iraq's GDP after 1990 is speculative, but it seems to have been about $24 billion in 1991, $20 billion in 1992, and substantially less than $20 billion in 1993. Estimates of Iraq's total foreign debt in 1993, including interest, range from $80 billion to $109 billion.[21]

International institutions like the World Bank and International Monetary Fund (IMF) do not even attempt to make public estimates of the recent trends in Iraq's GDP. It is clear, however, that Iraq remains an economy in crisis and faced steadily growing problems in financing even minimal civil imports after 1994. Further, Iraq's resumption of oil imports in late 1996, under the terms of United Nations Security Council Resolution (UNSCR) 986, required Iraq to use all of the funds it received for civil purposes. The terms of the agreement gave Iraq comparatively limited revenue, and it faced new problems in extending and expanding its imports in the spring of 1997, because of its continuing efforts to conceal weapons of mass destruction from the United Nations Special Commission (UNSCOM). Iraq's actions were so provocative that the Security Council voted on June 4, 1997, to approve UNSCR 111—which warned Iraq that it would face a suspension of the existing "oil for food" deal if it did not change its conduct.[22]

Figures 4.10–4.14 and Table 4.4 put the decline in Iraq's post–Gulf War arms imports into added perspective. Figure 4.10 shows that Iraq suddenly ceased to be one of the largest importers in the Gulf and became one with only token imports—lagging behind even the smallest Southern Gulf states. Figure 4.11 and Table 4.3 show that Iraq was cut off entirely from access to several of its most important pre–Gulf War suppliers after 1990, and that it has only had token access to erratic deliveries of smuggled or black market parts and equipment from the rest. Figure 4.12 shows that this cutoff in access to arms is even more impressive if one looks at Iraq's arms imports during the early part of the Iran-Iraq War. Figure 4.13 describes Iraq's pre–Gulf War suppliers in more detail, and Figure 4.14 highlights the scale of the cut in new arms agreements.

The Iraqi military machine never organized effectively to support and repair its equipment before the Gulf War. It could not deliver the complex mixes of spare parts required by modern military technology in an orderly and efficient fashion, and it solved many of its logistic and resupply problems by flooding the Iraqi military forces with new imports and entire replacements. This same machine has now been virtually cut off from the outside world for five years.

While many of Iraq's internal supply, logistic, and repair capabilities have slowly improved, UN sanctions have had a steadily more crippling impact on a military force structure that required a minimum of $900 million to $1.2 billion in pre–Gulf War military imports in order to sustain its existing readiness, sustainability, and effectiveness. Even when Iraq's more sophisticated military equipment is still operational, it often has limited sustainability and/or partial repair and maintenance. Many subsystems do not work or have no endurance in combat. Iraq's efforts to substitute for imports with domestic modifications

Figure 4.11
Iraqi Arms Agreements and Deliveries by Major Supplier: Before and After the Gulf War (Current $US millions)

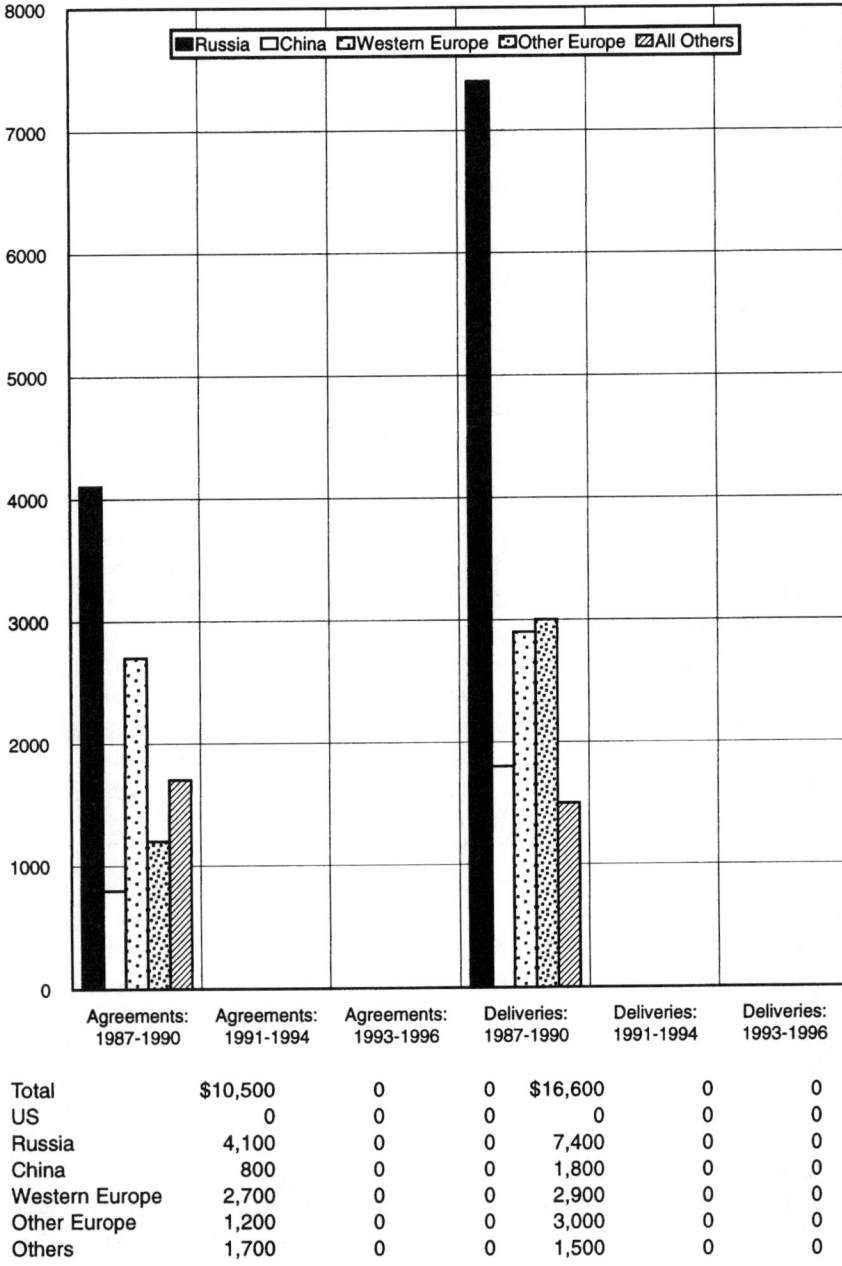

	Agreements: 1987-1990	Agreements: 1991-1994	Agreements: 1993-1996	Deliveries: 1987-1990	Deliveries: 1991-1994	Deliveries: 1993-1996
Total	$10,500	0	0	$16,600	0	0
US	0	0	0	0	0	0
Russia	4,100	0	0	7,400	0	0
China	800	0	0	1,800	0	0
Western Europe	2,700	0	0	2,900	0	0
Other Europe	1,200	0	0	3,000	0	0
Others	1,700	0	0	1,500	0	0

0 = less than $50 million or nil, and all data rounded to the nearest $100 million.
Source: Richard F. Grimmett, *Conventional Arms Transfers to the Developing Nations*, Congressional Research Service, various editions.

Table 4.3
Iraqi Arms Transfers by Major Supplier, 1983–1997 (in millions of current US dollars)

Agreements	1983-1986	1987-1990	1990-1993*	1994-1997
Soviet Union/Russia	11,815	4,090	0	0
China	1,760	615	0	0
United States	0	0	0	0
Major West European	1,005	2,665	0	0
All Other European	3,990	1,020	0	0
All Others	1,920	1,575	0	0
TOTAL	20,490	9,965	200-500	0
Deliveries	**1983-1986**	**1987-1990**	**1990-1993***	**1994-1997**
Soviet Union/Russia	12,179	7,370	400	0
China	3,180	820	200	0
United States	0	0	0	0
Major West European	5,225	1,180	2,100	0
All Other European	3,615	2,765	300	0
All Others	1,920	1,310	0	0
TOTAL	26,119	13,445	3,000	0

*UN sanctions did not prevent arms transfers until August, 1990. Zero transfers are reported after the UN voted for sanctions. 0 = data less than $50 million or nil. All data are rounded to the nearest $100 million. Major West European includes Britain, France, Germany, and Italy.

Source: Adapted by Anthony H. Cordesman from material provided by the US government and Richard F. Grimmett, *Conventional Arms Transfers to the Third World, 1983–1990*, Washington, Congressional Research Service, CRS-9 1–578F, August 2, 1991; *Conventional Arms Transfers to the Third World, 1984–1991*, Washington, Congressional Research Service, CRS-92–577F, July 20, 1991; *Conventional Arms Transfers to the Third World, 1987–1994*, Washington, Congressional Research Service, CRS-95–862F, August 4, 1995; and *Conventional Arms Transfers to the Third World, 1980–1997*, Washington, Congressional Research Service, CRS-97–647F, July 31, 1998.

and production to its major weapons systems have also had only very limited effectiveness.

If Iraq's need for military modernization is included, it would have required about $2–$2.5 billion a year to sustain Iraq's forces, modernize its conventional forces, and support its efforts to deploy large numbers of long-range missiles and weapons of mass destruction. As a result, the impact of the Gulf War and UN sanctions has been devastating. Even if one ignores the cost of replacing Iraq's wartime losses, Iraq's military imports were underfunded by well over $7 billion between 1990 and 1999. Sustaining Iraq's existing force structure, replacing its wartime losses, and modernizing its military forces would have cost

Figure 4.12
Iraqi Arms Agreements and Deliveries by Major Supplier, 1973–1994 (in $US current millions)

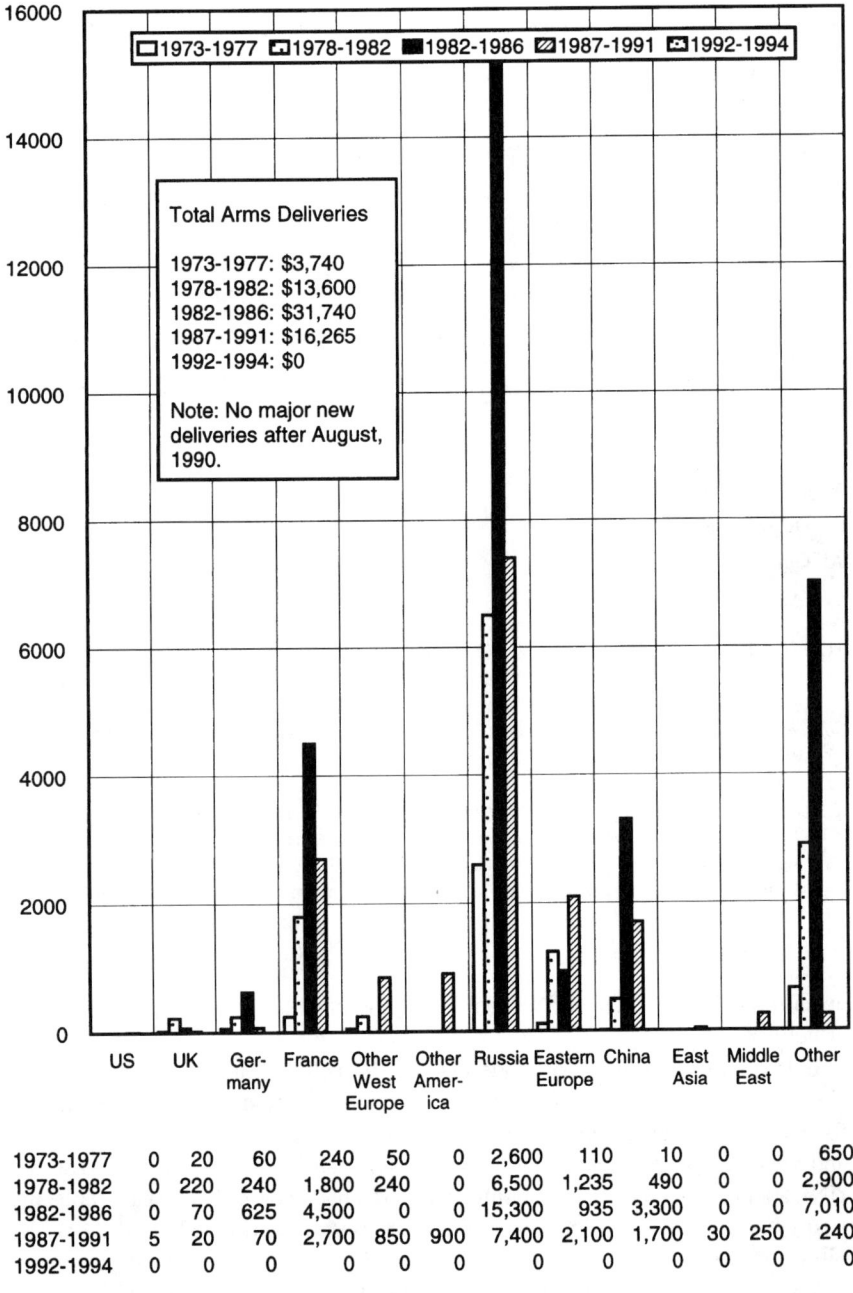

	US	UK	Germany	France	Other West Europe	Other America	Russia	Eastern Europe	China	East Asia	Middle East	Other
1973-1977	0	20	60	240	50	0	2,600	110	10	0	0	650
1978-1982	0	220	240	1,800	240	0	6,500	1,235	490	0	0	2,900
1982-1986	0	70	625	4,500	0	0	15,300	935	3,300	0	0	7,010
1987-1991	5	20	70	2,700	850	900	7,400	2,100	1,700	30	250	240
1992-1994	0	0	0	0	0	0	0	0	0	0	0	0

Total Arms Deliveries

1973-1977: $3,740
1978-1982: $13,600
1982-1986: $31,740
1987-1991: $16,265
1992-1994: $0

Note: No major new deliveries after August, 1990.

Source: Adapted by Anthony H. Cordesman from ACDA, *World Military Expenditures and Arms Transfers*, various editions.

Figure 4.13
Iraqi Arms Agreements and Deliveries by Major Supplier, 1985–1989 (deliveries in current $US millions)

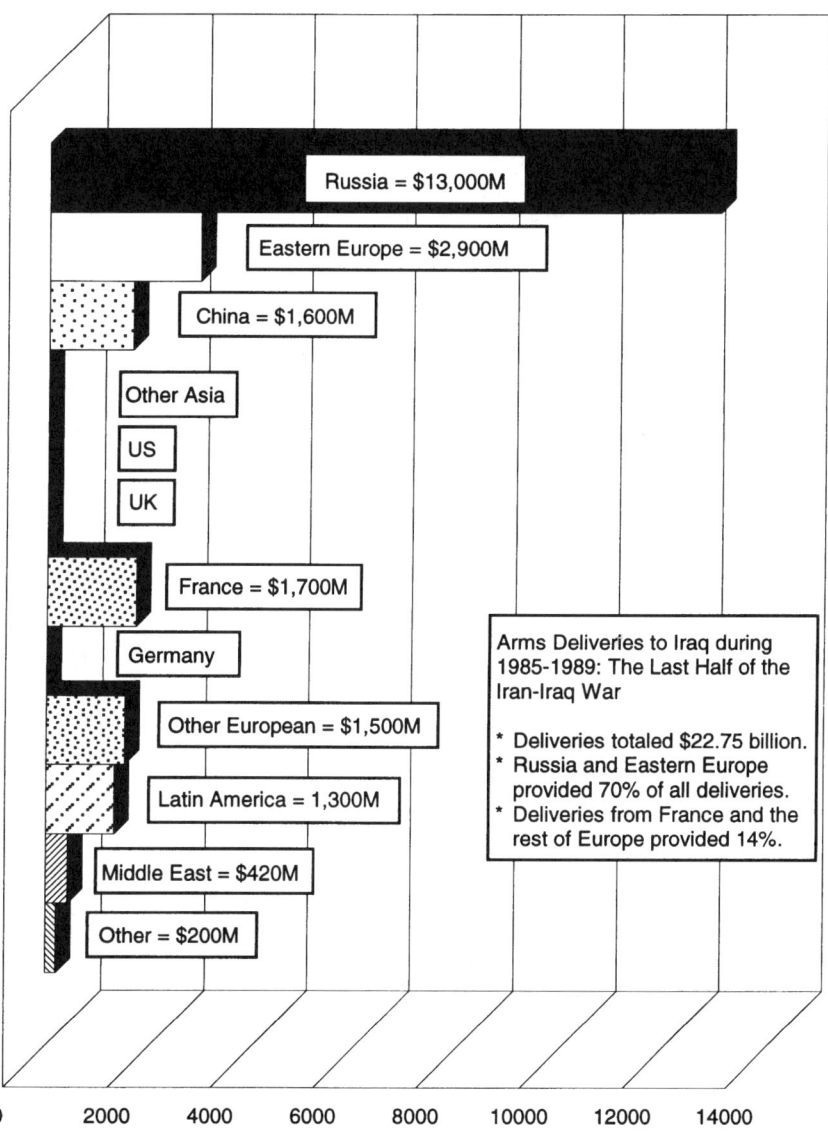

Source: Adapted by Anthony H. Cordesman from ACDA, *World Military Expenditures and Arms Transfers*, various editions.

Figure 4.14
The Impact of UN Sanctions on Iraqi Arms Agreements, 1987–1996 (new agreements in current $US millions)

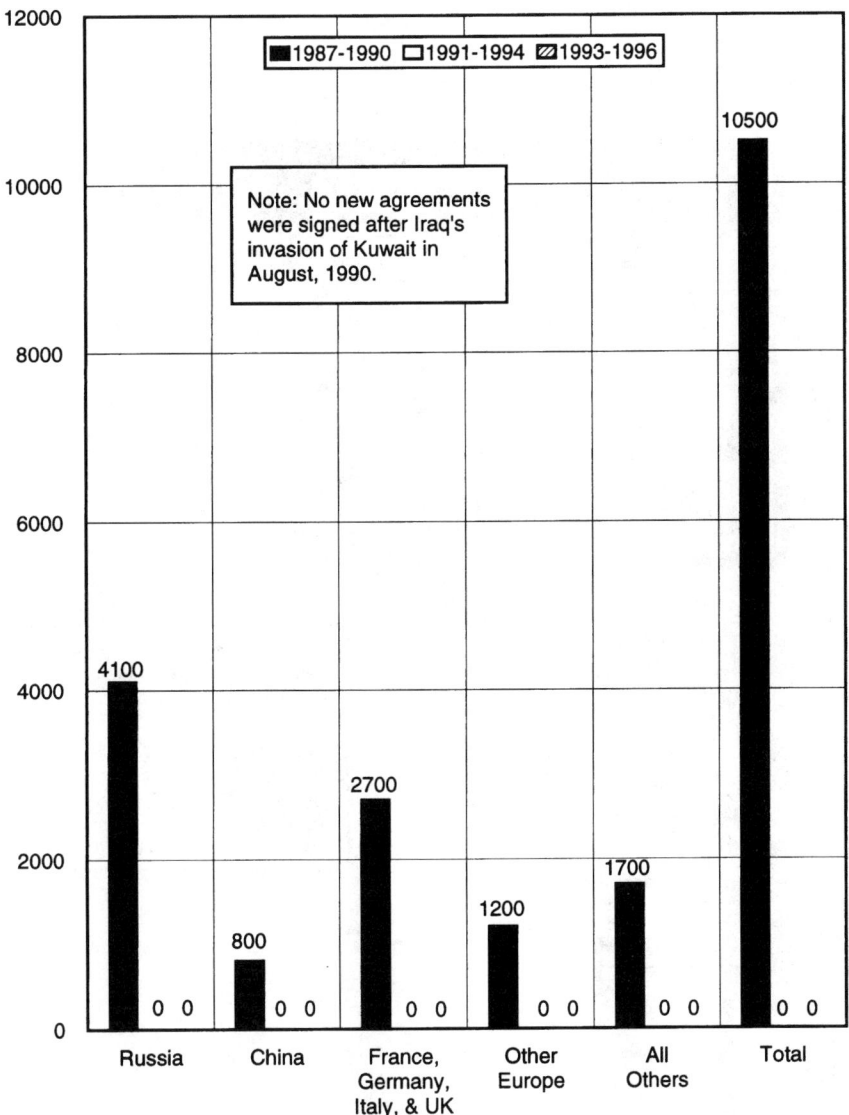

0 = less than $50 million or nil, and all data rounded to the nearest $100 million.
Source: Richard F. Grimmett, *Conventional Arms Transfers to the Developing Nations*, Congressional Research Service, various editions.

Figure 4.15
The Cumulative Iraqi Arms Import Deficit Enforced by UN Sanctions (Measured in $US 1997 constant millions)

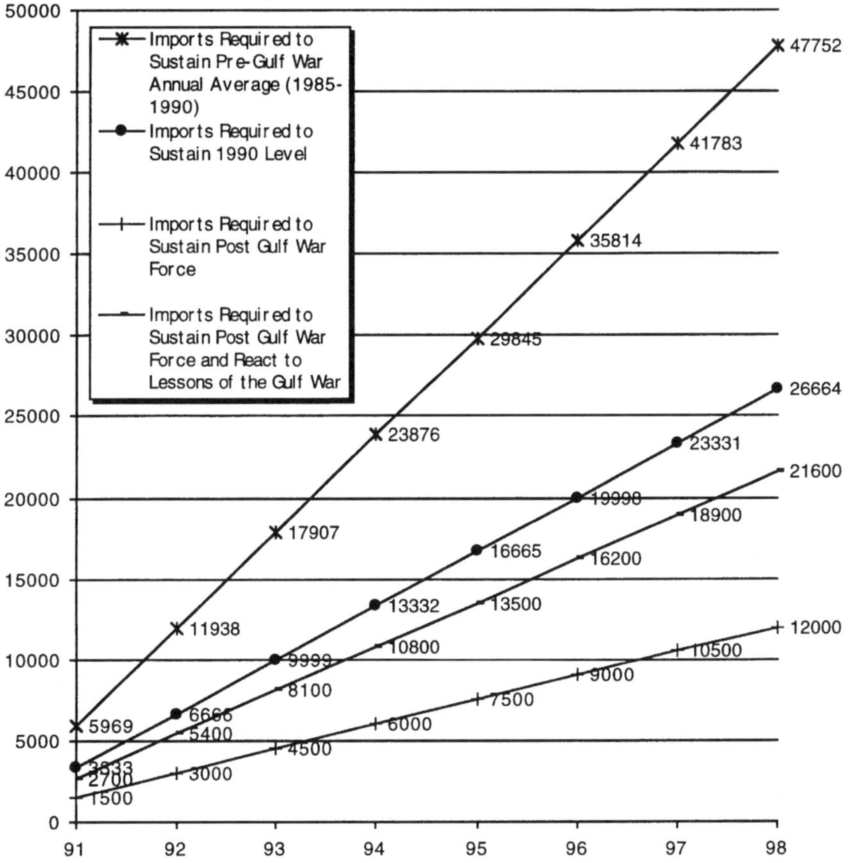

Source: Adapted by Anthony H. Cordesman from ACDA, *World Military Expenditures and Arms Transfers, 1995*, 1996. Data for 1997 and 1998 are estimated by Anthony H. Cordesman.

at least $3 to $4 billion a year after 1991, and the cumulative gap between Iraq's ambitions and its actual military imports between 1991 and 1999 totals at least $21 billion.

The scale of this "recapitalization" problem is indicated by the amount of money Iraq might have spent on arms between 1991 and 1998 if it had not been under UN sanctions. Figure 4.15 shows that if Iraq had imported arms at its average annual rate during the period 1985–1990, it would have had to spend a total of $47.5 billion, nearly half of the oil export earnings it might had received if sanctions had been lifted. A conservative estimate of the cumulative cost of simply modernizing Iraq's existing military forces at the time of the Gulf

War would total $21.6 billion, and it would have cost a minimum of $12 billion simply to keep Iraq's military machine from deteriorating. In contrast, a conservative estimate of the cumulative cost of modernization and moderate force restructuring to react to the lessons of the Gulf War indicates that Iraq would now have to spend at least $26.7 billion on military imports to react to the cumulative impact of sanctions.

Another way of looking at the problem is to consider how much of Iraq's military inventory is now obsolete. If Iraq is judged by US standards, or the best first-line equipment in Southern Gulf forces, this list includes:

- 600–700 M-48s, M-60s, AMX-30, Centurion, and Chieftain main battle tanks;
- 1,000 T-54s, T-55s, T-77s and Chinese T-59 and T-69 main battle tanks;
- 200 T-62 main battle tanks;
- 1,500–2,100 BTR-50, BTR-60, BTR-152, OT-62, and OT-64 armored personnel carriers;
- 1,600 BDRM-2, EE-3, EE-9, AML-60, AML-90 armored fighting vehicles;
- 800–1,200 towed 105 mm, 122 mm, 130 mm, and 155 mm artillery weapons;
- an unknown number of AS-11, AS-1, AT-1, crew-portable, anti-tank-guided missiles;
- more than 1,000 heavy, low-quality, anti-aircraft guns;
- over 1,500 SA-7 and other low-quality, surface-to-air guided missile launchers and fire units;
- 20 PAH-1s (Bo-105s); attack helicopters with AS-11 and AS-12, 30 Mi-24s and Mi-25s with AT-2 missiles, SA-342s with AS-12s, Allouettes with AS-11s and AS-12s;
- 100–180 worn or obsolete transport helicopters;
- 6–7 HD-6s (BD-6s), 1–2 Tu-16s, and 6 Tu-22 bombers;
- 100 J-6s, MiG-23BN, MiG-27, Su-7 and Su-20;
- 140 J-7s, MiG-21, MiG-25 air defense fighters;
- MiG-21 and MiG-25 reconnaissance fighters;
- 15 Hawker Hunter light attack aircraft;
- Il-76 Adnan AEW aircraft;
- AA-6, AA-7 Matra 530 air-to-air missiles;
- AS-11, AS-12, AS-6, AS-14 air-to-surface missiles;
- 25 PC-7, 30 PC-9, 40 L-29 trainers;
- An-2, An-12, and Il-76 transport aircraft;
- 20–30 operational SA-2 batteries with 160 launch units;
- 25–50 SA-3 batteries with 140 launch units;
- 36–55 SA-6 batteries with over 100 fire units;
- 6,500 SA-7s;
- 400 SA-9s;

- 192 SA-13s;
- *Ibn Khaldun* destroyer;
- Osa-class missile boats;
- 13 light combat vessels;
- 5–8 landing craft;
- *Agnadeen* support ship;
- 1 Yugoslav Spasilac-class transport; and
- Polnocny-class LST.

The limitations in each type of equipment are described in the chapters that follow, but it is important to note that this list includes 60–70% of the entire inventory in the Iraqi army, air force, and air defense force, and virtually every combat system in the Iraqi navy, except for some of its anti-ship missile forces. By this standard, sanctions have been anything but a failure. They have seriously weakened Iraq's military forces, and it will take Iraq at least half a decade to compensate for the resulting problems once sanctions are lifted.

IRAQI EFFORTS TO SMUGGLE ARMS AND PARTS AND REBUILD ITS MILITARY INDUSTRIES SINCE THE GULF WAR

Since the cease-fire in the Gulf War, Iraq has attempted to compensate for its loss of access to arms imports by making use of the extensive purchasing and intelligence network it established overseas during the Iran-Iraq War. This network includes a mix of firms in Chile, Europe, the United States, China, Japan, Hong Kong, and other Asian countries. Iraq has refused to provide the UN with a full list of its suppliers, but it is clear that many of its fronts and contacts are still operating. According to one informed UN source, Iraq is known to have at least 15 purchasing organizations and cover groups in Europe alone, with 600–700 full-time staff.

Iraq has used this network to obtain some supplies by using hidden foreign reserves and funds it obtained by smuggling out petrochemical products. It has had some successes. It obtained at least two shipments of tank parts, some additional air-to-air missiles, and one artillery shipment in the early 1990s. It also may have received some significant shipments of spare parts during 1996–1998. These shipments seem to have improved the readiness of some of its surface-to-air units, older fighters and training aircraft, and ground units. Iraq may also have struck deals with some Eastern European states for future deliveries of components like air defense radars. It has not, however, received any major shipments of new weapons that have appeared in any part of its order of battle.[23]

Military Industry After the Gulf War

Iraq has also made a crash effort to restore and improve its domestic military production capabilities. In the process, it has been able to build on an investment in the Iraqi Ministry of Industry and Defense Industry that totaled $14.2 billion between 1985 and 1989. Many of these plants suffered limited damage during the war, and Iraqi officials have claimed that Iraq has repaired and tooled up 200 factory buildings associated with military production since the end of the Gulf War, and that more than 50 establishments of the former Ministry of Industry and Military Industrialization are now operating—many using machine tools and specialized equipment that were originally exported without proper export licenses.[24]

According to a report by the House Foreign Affairs Subcommittee on International Security, International Organizations, and Human Rights, this equipment and related production facilities include the facilities listed in Table 4.4.[25] Iraq has manufactured small arms and artillery ammunition. It has made some artillery weapons like the Ababil multiple launch rocket system, and it has reconditioned and assembled some Soviet tanks, including T-72s. It has manufactured and adapted military electronics and made some small crafts.

Iraq has also continued its efforts to try to produce weapons of mass destruction, often seeking to disguise the true purpose of its plants by changing their names or description. For example, an October, 1995 report by UNSCOM stated that Iraq has resumed "its acquisition efforts in support of its missile facilities," adding that it had "placed a number of orders, both directly and indirectly (through middlemen and front companies), for the purchase of equipment, technologies, supplies and material for both missile and non-missile related activities at these facilities."[26] Iraq replied that it was merely expanding its Ababil-100 program to build surface-to-surface missiles, with ranges between 100km and 150 km, which it is allowed to acquire.

More Claims Than Success

Iraq has, however, faced the problems summarized in Table 4.5. It has had little success in producing and remanufacturing advanced equipment like tanks and aircraft, and only limited success in carrying out many types of major combat repairs. Its efforts have not been able to offset the further attrition of Iraq's surviving equipment, which has been caused by a lack of spares and specialized support equipment. Iraq also seems to have had continuing problems in managing its military industries and making them more efficient—which may explain why Saddam Hussein brought back Abdultawab Mulahwaish, a former minister of industry and minerals, as chairman of the Military Industrial Commission in June, 1997. Mulahwaish replaced Dhaif Abdulmajeed, who seems to have been anything but a success.[27]

Furthermore, Iraq's problems in maintaining its inventory of operational com-

Table 4.4
Major Iraqi Military Production Facilities

- Tank assembly plant operating under Polish and Czech licenses at Al-Amen.
- Major armor refitting center at Base West World (Samawa).
- Manufacture of proximity fuses for 155 mm and cluster munitions at April 7 (Narawan Fuse) Factory.
- Manufacture of 122 mm howitzers, Ababil rockets, tank optics, and mortar sights at Sa'ad 5 (Sa'ad Engineering Complex).
- Manufacture of wheeled APCs under East European license, other armor, and artillery pieces at Al Taji.
- Manufacture and repair of artillery, vehicle parts, and cannon barrels at SEHEE heavy engineering complex (Al Dura).
- Aircraft assembly and manufacturing plant under construction at Sa'ad 38 (Fao).
- Manufacture of aerial bombs, artillery pieces, and tungsten-carbide machine tool bits at Badr (al Yusufiyah).
- Production of explosives, TNT, propellants, and some vehicle production capability at Al Hiteen (Al Iskandariyah).
- Production of cluster bombs and fuel-air explosives at Fao.
- Production of aerial bombs, TNT, and solid rocket propellants at Al Qaqaa.
- Manufacture of small naval boats at Sawary (Basra).
- Production and modification of defense electronics at Mansour (Baghdad).
- Production and modification of defense electronics, radars, and frequency-hopping radios at Sa'ad 13 (Salah al Din-Ad Dawr).
- Digital computer software, assembly of process line controllers for weapons plants, and plastic castings at Diglia (Zaafarniyah).
- Precision machining at Al Rabiyah.
- Manufacture of non-ferrous ammunition cases at Sa'ad 21 (Mosul).
- Liquid nitrogen production at Al Amil.
- Production of ethylene oxide for fuel-air explosives at PCI.
- Production of HMX and RDX explosives at Fallujah chemical plant at Al Muthanna.
- Manufacture of gas masks at Sa'ad 24 (Mosul).

bat equipment are likely to accelerate with time, in spite of its smuggling and manufacturing efforts. Cumulative wear and maintenance defaults will produce steadily more serious—and sometimes unrecoverable—problems, as Iraq's remaining spares are consumed and machines and major subassemblies wear out. Iraq may also exhaust its hidden supplies of hard currency, making it even more difficult to obtain limited supplies of critical spare parts on the world's black market for arms.

Saddam Hussein's cousin, Hussein Kamel al-Majid, was in charge of the

Table 4.5
Iraqi Problems in Military Production

- Iraq developed significant ammunition, small and light arms, and gun barrel production facilities before the Gulf War, and many survive and function, however, focused most resources on weapons of mass destruction.
- Left even high-tech service (e.g., French and Russian aircraft) to foreign technical support teams. Did not attempt to develop major in-house capabilities.
- Pre-1991 production was heavily prototype oriented and largely prestige oriented in nature.
- Did import T-72 kits, in theory as transition to production facilities. However, far from clear that Iraq has industrial base for such manufactures.
- Iraqi modifications sometimes succeeded, but many failed and had an "impress the maximum leader character," for example, T-72 upgrades.
- Historically, assembly of major weapons does not lead to technology transfer or effective reverse engineering capability without extensive foreign support. Net impact is to create over-specialized facilities, waste resources.
- No developing state, including India and China, has yet demonstrated that it can successfully mass manufacture an advanced fighter plane or tank, even on a turn-key basis.
- Few nations have made useful major equipment upgrades for armor and aircraft. Jordan, South Korea, and Turkey are among few successes. Egypt, India, and Pakistan are more typical.
- Iraq has effectively been cut off from all major imports of parts and specialized equipment since the 1990s, although dual-use items, civilian electronics and sensors, and computer gear are not effectively controlled.
- Black market imports, substitution, and local manufactures can only provide an erratic and inefficient substitute for large-scale resources.
- Some indications that Iraq is giving priority to importing equipment for weapons of mass destruction.

Military Industrialization Commission (MIC) and many aspects of this industrialization effort before his defection in 1995. Senior Jordanian officials who talked to Hussein Kamel found that many of his claims regarding the effectiveness of Iraq's military industry had been hollow boasts intended to impress Saddam Hussein. Iraq's claims to produce major weapons systems never went beyond the prototype stage—many of which were unproducable or nonoperational showpiece demonstration systems. They report that Hussein Kamel's successor and former deputy—Lt. General Amir Mohammed Rashid—has found that virtually all of Iraq's efforts to carry out major modifications, to rebuild and recondition sophisticated equipment, and to assemble new advanced weapons from parts have been a failure.[28]

US experts largely agree with this indictment of Iraq's military production. They stress the steady decline of Iraq's equipment readiness and sustainability between late 1993 and mid-1996. They note that Hussein Kamel seemed to deceive Saddam deliberately with showpiece projects, such as putting an SA-2 surface-to-air missile launcher on a truck and claiming he had created a mobile surface-to-air missile system, falsely reporting the indigenous production of transporter-erector-launchers (TELs) for surface-to-surface missiles, and the large-scale production of prototype self-propelled artillery systems like the Majnoon and Al Fao (Al Faw).

At the same time, US experts do believe that Iraq's smuggling efforts have become more efficient, that Iraq has succeeded in importing significant amounts of dual-use equipment in such areas as aircraft parts, and that Iraq has made progress rebuilding some of the plants and facilities necessary to start equipment assembly once sanctions are lifted, and that it will aggressively seek to reduce its past dependence on weapons imports once it can obtain access to foreign production equipment. They also believe that Iraq is steadily improving its ability to produce a wide range of spare parts and to overhaul its land force equipment.[29]

They believe that Iraq can produce indigenous weapons or modifications when given the opportunity, and they believe Iraq will begin by seeking assembly facilities with the goal of moving towards indigenous production and the ability to rebuild and maintain its other equipment for a prolonged period in the face of another cutoff of supplies or embargo. In short, they believe Iraq will seek the capabilities it has been unable to create since the Gulf War.

MILITARY EXPENDITURES, ARMS TRANSFERS, MILITARY INDUSTRY, AND THE PROBLEM OF CONTAINMENT

The trends in Iraqi military expenditures, arms smuggling, and military production argue strongly against any policy that lifts sanctions without retaining controls over how Iraq uses its revenues and without a firm commitment to military containment. They provide overwhelming evidence that Iraq's present regime will divert a large portion of any oil revenues it can to military expenditures, regardless of the cost to the Iraqi people. They also indicate that a major effort will be needed by potential supplier countries to prevent Iraq from importing the equipment it needs to improve its military manufacturing capabilities and restore its military capabilities.

These trends also raise important issues for a ''centrist'' strategy that attempts to replace Saddam with other members of Iraq's present politico-military ruling elite, given the risk that any successor regime may well pursue similar policies towards military expenditures, and strengthening Iraq's military industries.

Finally, the trends in Iraqi military expenditures argue for a strong US and Southern Gulf military deterrent to Iraq. Any state that makes this kind of financial commitment to a military build-up cannot be contained purely through diplomacy or sanctions. Only strong deterrent and defense capabilities can provide security.

NOTES

1. These figures are drawn from the US Arms Control and Disarmament Agency (ACDA) database presented in *World Military Expenditures and Arms Transfers*, Washington, GPO, editions for 1991–1992 and 1996, as converted into constant 1997 dollars using the Office of Management and Budget (OMB) deflators issues for the fiscal year (FY) 1998 federal budget.

2. The text of the recent WHO and FAO reports is available on the Internet, as well as from UN bookstores, and the reader should carefully examine the original reports. They uncritically accept Iraqi figures for the base year of 1990, ignore the previous impact of the Iran-Iraq War, ignore Iraq's civil wars against its Kurds and Shi'ites, do not describe the sampling techniques used in detail, ignore the real-world increase in food output available in Iraqi markets 1994–1997, imply that Iraq's agricultural problems are totally import-driven rather than the result of Iraqi government policy, and even sometimes argue that a shift away from reliance on food imports is damaging the Iraqi environment. Data for recent years are often lacking or are drawn from Iraqi inputs that are directly contradicted by Iraqi reporting in other sources. For example, the WHO reports make claims about lasting damage to Iraqi water purification plants without any analysis of the actual damage done during the Gulf War or mention of Iraqi claims to have repaired the infrastructure involved. The standards of reporting and analysis used by the WHO and FAO are so unbelievably low and politically naive that they could not survive minimal peer group review in any normal research effort, and they cast doubt on the professional integrity of both organizations.

3. CIA, *World Factbook, 1996*, Washington, GPO, 1997, "Iraq"; Reuters, October 16, 1997, 0921.

4. CIA, *World Factbook, 1996*, Washington, GPO, 1997, "Iraq"; CIA, *World Factbook, 1990*, Washington, GPO, 1991, "Iraq."

5. CIA, *World Factbook, 1996*, Washington, GPO, 1997; IISS, *Military Balance, 1997–1998*, p. 127.

6. CIA, *World Factbook, 1996*, Washington, GPO, 1997 "Iraq."

7. USCENTCOM briefing by "senior military official," Pentagon, January 28, 1997, pp. 2, 5–8, 10; *Jane's Defense Weekly*, July 9, 1997, p. 4.

8. USCENTCOM briefing by "senior military official," Pentagon, January 28, 1997, pp. 2, 5–8, 10; *Washington Times*, February 1, 1997, p. A-13.

9. Reuters, September 4, 1996, 0911; *Jane's Pointer*, November 1994, p. 2; Associated Press, September 9, 1996, 0129; *Washington Times*, January 30, 1997, p. A-3; February 1, 1997, p. A-13.

10. US Arms Control and Disarmament Agency (ACDA), *World Military Expenditures and Arms Transfers, 1993–1994*, Washington, GPO, 1995, p. 67.

11. US Arms Control and Disarmament Agency (ACDA), *World Military Expenditures and Arms Transfers, 1989*, Washington, GPO, 1990, p. 51; US Department of Defense, *Conduct of the Persian Gulf War*, Vol. I, Washington, Department of Defense, 1992, p. 4.

12. US Arms Control and Disarmament Agency (ACDA), *World Military Expenditures and Arms Transfers, 1989*, Washington, GPO, 1990, Table I; US Arms Control and Disarmament Agency (ACDA), *World Military Expenditures and Arms Transfers, 1996*, Washington, GPO, 1997, Table I.

13. IISS, *Military Balance*, 1990–1991, 1991–1992, 1997–1998 editions.
14. CIA, *World Factbook, 1991*, pp. 148–149; US Department of Defense, *Conduct of the Persian Gulf War*, Vol. I, Washington, Department of Defense, 1992, p. 4.
15. Richard F. Grimmett, *Conventional Arms Transfers to the Third World, 1983–1990*, Washington, Congressional Research Service, CRS-9 1–578F, August 2, 1991.
16. US Air Force, "Reaching Globally, Reaching Powerfully: The United States Air Force in the Gulf War," Washington, USAF, September, 1991, pp. 3–4.
17. US Arms Control and Disarmament Agency (ACDA), *World Military Expenditures and Arms Transfers, 1989*, Washington, GPO, 1990, p. 117.
18. Richard F. Grimmett, *Conventional Arms Transfers to the Third World, 1985–1992*, Washington, Congressional Research Service, CRS-93–656F, July 19, 1993, pp. CRS-67, 68, 69, 70; Kenneth Katzman, "Iraq's Campaign to Acquire and Develop High Technology," Congressional Research Service, CRS-92–611F, August 3, 1991. US reporting on this subject is inconsistent. US Arms Control and Disarmament Agency (ACDA), *World Military Expenditures and Arms Transfers, 1990*, Washington, GPO, 1992, p. 133, indicates that Iraq imported a total of $22,750 million worth of arms during 1985–1989, including $13,000 million from the Soviet Union, $1,700 million from France, $20 million from the UK, $1,600 million from the PRC, $90 million from West Germany, $2,900 million from other Warsaw Pact countries, $1,500 million from other European countries, $420 million from other Middle Eastern countries, $20 million from other East Asian states, $1,300 million from Latin American countries, and $200 million from other countries in the world.
19. Richard F. Grimmett, *Conventional Arms Transfers to the Third World, 1985–1992*, Washington, Congressional Research Service, CRS-93–656F, July 19, 1993, pp. CRS-56, 57, 58, 59.
20. Richard F. Grimmett, *Conventional Arms Transfers to the Third World, 1989–1996*, Washington, Congressional Research Service, CRS-97–778F, August 13, 1997.
21. Author's estimate based on interviews, EIU reports, the IISS, *Military Balance*, and CIA, *World Factbook*.
22. *Middle East Economic Survey*, June 30, 1997, pp. A-7-A9.
23. USCENTCOM briefing by "senior military official," Pentagon, January 28, 1997, pp. 2, 5–8 10; *Washington Times*, February 1, 1997, p. A-13; Reuters, September 4, 1996, 0911; *Jane's Pointer*, November 1994, p. 2; Associated Press, September 9, 1996, 0129; *Washington Times*, January 30, 1997, p. A-3; February 1, 1997, p. A-13.
24. Germany was Iraq's largest supplier. Iraq imported $4.243 billion worth of equipment during 1985–1989, with $2.4 billion worth of heavy machinery and transportation equipment, $1.3 billion worth of manufactured goods, $425 million worth of chemicals, and $114 million worth of controlling instruments.
25. The analysis of Iraqi procurement networks and industries in this section draws heavily on Kenneth R. Timmerman, "Iraq Rebuilds Its Military Industries," House Foreign Affairs Subcommittee on International Security, International Organizations, and Human Rights, Washington, DC, June 29, 1993; *Jane's Defense Weekly*, July 10, 1993, p. 9; *London Sunday Times*, October 4, 1992, p. 16; *Philadelphia Inquirer*, November 7, 1992, p. A-5; *Washington Times*, March 18, 1992, p. A-2; *New York Times*, July 15, 1993, p. A-3; *Newsweek*, February 1, 1993, pp. 48–50; *Wall Street Journal*, January 19, 1999, p. A-16. June 29, 1993, p. A-6.
26. Quoted in *Jane's Defense Weekly*, October 21, 1995, p. A-6.
27. Reuters, June 16, 1997, 0516.

28. Interviews; Reuters, January 28, 1996, 0438, 1058.

29. Director of Central Intelligence, "The Acquisition of Technology Relating to Weapons of Mass Destruction and Advanced Conventional Munitions, July–December 1996," June, 1997.

Chapter 5

The Threat from Iraq's Land Forces

In spite of a massive UN Coalition victory in the Gulf War, sanctions, and Desert Fox, Iraq maintains an army of 350,000–400,000 full-time actives. This force has an impressive order of battle and a large inventory of combat equipment. It is effective by regional standards, and it can draw on the experience it has gained from both major successes at the end of the Iran-Iraq War and its massive defeat during the Gulf War. The Coalition's success in the Gulf War does not mean that Iraq does not retain impressive military capabilities, and it must be remembered that Iraq emerged from nearly a decade of intense war with Iran as the largest most capable military machine in the region.

At the same time, the Iraqi army has scarcely been able to overcome the effects of the Gulf War. It has been cut off from most arms imports. For nearly the last decade, it has not been able to invest even a tenth of the capital that it invested in modernizing and improving its land forces during the five years before the Gulf War. The devastation of the Gulf War, and the five years of turmoil that have followed, have sharply reduced the composition and capabilities of the Iraqi army.[1]

THE IMPACT OF THE GULF WAR ON THE IRAQI ARMY

The Iraqi army suffered massive losses during the Gulf War, although experts differ sharply on the number of Iraqis who died, on the amount of equipment and munitions destroyed or lost during the air and ground offensive phases of the war, and on the number and identity of the Iraqi combat units that lost cohesion or combat effectiveness at any given time.

Just after the war, USCENTCOM estimated that Coalition forces had virtually shattered more than 15 Iraqi divisions, and only 5–7 of 43 Iraqi divisions in the

Table 5.1
The Impact of Coalition Air and Land Forces on Iraqi Equipment Strength in the Kuwaiti Theater of Operations (KTO) at the Time of the Cease-Fire

	Tanks	APCs	Artillery
Total in KTO on January 16, 1991, at start of Air Campaign (Imagery)	3,475	3,080	2,474
Total left at beginning of the land campaign	2,087	2,151	1,322
Total destroyed or abandoned during the land campaign (USCENTCOM estimate)	2,159	521	1,465
Destroyed by air	(451)	(224)	(353)
Destroyed by land or abandoned	(1,708)	(297)	(1,112)
Total destroyed or abandoned during the land campaign (Imagery Based)	1,245	739	1,044
Total destroyed during air campaign and land offensive (Imagery Based)	2,633	1,668	2,196
Still in Iraqi control on March 1, 1991 (Imagery)	842	1,412	279

Source: Adapted by Anthony H. Cordesman from work by Eliot Cohen, Director, *Gulf War Air Power Survey, Volume II, Section II*, pp. 259–261, and from interviews.

Kuwaiti Theater of Operations (KTO) were still capable of offensive operations. USCENTCOM estimated that the Coalition had captured 86,000 Iraqi prisoners, 64,000 of which were taken by US forces.[2] The Department of Defense estimated after the war that 10 Iraqi infantry divisions, one armored division, and one mechanized division had been reduced to 0–25% of their combat strength. Six more infantry, two mechanized, and four armored divisions had been reduced to 25–50% of their combat strength. Six infantry, two mechanized, and one armored division had been reduced to 50–75% of their combat strength, and five infantry divisions, one special forces division, one mechanized, and two armored divisions retained 75–100% of their combat strength.[3]

There are significant differences between the various US government estimates of Iraqi army equipment losses, and these estimates have been extensively revised based on after-action analysis of intelligence and damage assessment data. This range of estimates is shown in Table 5.1 and Figure 5.1, and is based on imagery data which are probably largely correct.

These estimates indicate that the Iraqi forces deployed in the KTO during the Gulf War lost 76% of their tanks, 54% of their APCs, and 90% of their artillery. Revised US intelligence estimates have also concluded that the Republican Guards units lost roughly 50% of their weapons in these categories as a result of the air campaign and AirLand battle.[4] These estimates of damage to the Guard are much lower than those the United States issued during the Gulf War, and

Figure 5.1
Corrected Intelligence Estimates of the Iraq Military Forces in the Kuwaiti Theater of Operations Before and After the Gulf War

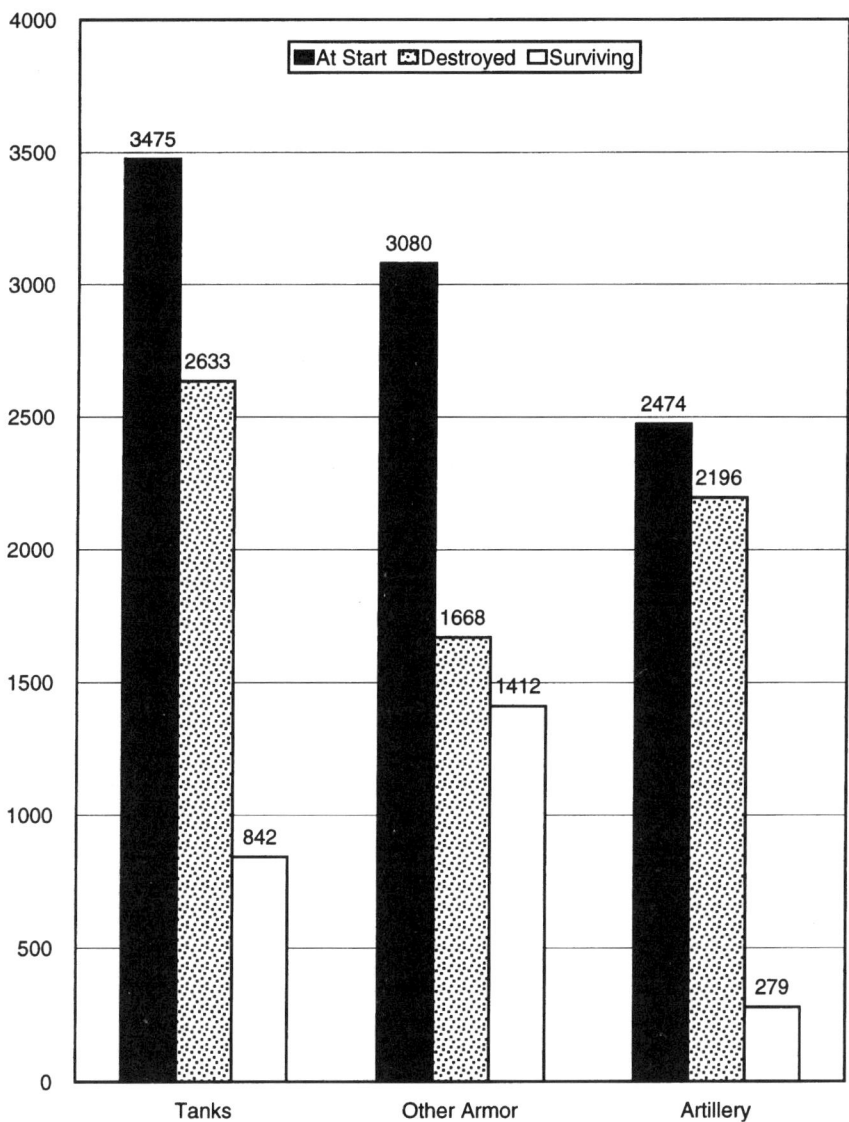

Sources: Adapted by Anthony H. Cordesman from IISS, *Military Balance*, and from material provided by US experts.

again reflect the difference between battlefield estimates based on the claims of combat units and estimates based on satellite imagery. For example, USCENTCOM's estimate of the Republican Guard's tank losses as of February 23 was 388. The CIA estimates based on imagery indicate that the Guard lost 166 tanks.[5]

If one considers the impact of the Gulf War on the entire Iraqi army, rather than just the Iraqi forces in the KTO, US estimates indicate that the army suffered massive losses in operational capability. The Iraqi army emerged from the Gulf War with as little as 25–33% of its pre-war total national division strength fully operational, with only about 20% of its heavy armored and mechanized brigade strength combat effective, and with only 20–25% of its total manpower under full government control.

Some experts feel that Iraq lost about 50% of its total national operational tank strength, 40% of its other armored vehicles, and 50% of its artillery—although such losses count some equipment that was recovered from Kuwait and northern Iraq after the cease-fire. The Iraqi army also lost much of its total stocks and infrastructure as the result of Coalition air attacks.

This situation worsened immediately after the war. Much of the Iraqi army was in a state of disruption and political upheaval. Many Iraqi troops were disaffected. Unrest in the army had triggered the first revolts in the South, and some elements of the armed forces then joined Shi'ite and Kurdish rebels that attempted to seize power. Other commanders and units wavered in their loyalty or hesitated in obeying Saddam Hussein's orders.[6]

However, this near-total disruption of Iraq's forces was relatively short lived. None of the forces that challenged Saddam were strong enough to confront the Republican Guards and the regular military units that remained loyal. It is also clear, in retrospect, that Saddam Hussein began to rush Republican Guards forces out of the theater no later than February 27, 1991, to use them to suppress the uprisings in southern Iraq. It is also likely that the Iraqi commanders negotiating the cease-fire at Safwan manipulated his request to Gen. Norman Schwarzkopf to ensure that Iraq's helicopters could be used to attack both the uprising in the south and the Kurdish uprising in the north.[7]

Iraq then restructured its army command structure. It purged as many as 1,500 senior officers and shot others.[8] The Iraqi army also recovered some of the equipment that it initially abandoned or had fallen into hostile use in Iraq. It conducted a massive scavenger hunt in the Iraqi territory that the Coalition had occupied the moment its forces left. Iraq sent infiltrators into Kuwait in an effort to regain equipment, spare parts, and munitions. In many cases it was able to repair equipment that had been counted as "killed" during the war, because the damage was not sufficient to prevent repair or combining of parts from several damaged systems.[9]

By September, 1992, Iraq's military forces were able to deploy 500,000 to 650,000, including a substantial number of reserves. The Iraqi army retained 300,000–400,000 actives, or about 40% of its pre-war strength. Many of the regular army forces were manned by poorly trained and motivated conscripts, which had been drafted after the Gulf War or who had been defeated in that conflict. These lower-quality forces were stiffened, however, by reorganized and relatively effective Republican Guards forces, a number of moderate to high-quality regular army units, and reorganized internal security forces. By late 1998, Iraqi had built up the total force levels summarized in Figure 5.2. While they scarcely gave it its pre-war force levels, they still made Iraq the largest land power in the Gulf.

THE IRAQI ARMY TODAY

There are a number of different estimates of the current strength of Iraqi land forces. US experts indicate that the Iraqi army had a total of around 375,000 full-time actives (including 100,000 recalled reserves) in 1999, and a total of seven corps, with two Republican Guards corps and five regular army corps. Iraq had a total of 23 divisions. These included six Republican Guard divisions (three armored, one mechanized, and two infantry) and one Presidential Guard/Special Security Force division. There were also 15 independent special forces or commando brigades.

US experts indicate that the land forces had a total of 14 divisions in the north, three divisions in central Iraq, and six divisions south of An Najaf. The Republican Guards had a total of three armored divisions deployed in the vicinity of Baghdad—one near Taji, one near Baghdad, and one near As Suwayrah. These estimates seem to provide the most accurate current picture of Iraqi strength.[10]

Estimates by USCENTCOM are similar, but indicate that the Iraqi land forces had a total strength of 700,000 personnel, including reserves. These estimates indicate that Iraq's major combat formations include 17 regular army divisions (6 heavy and 11 light), and 6 Republican Guards Divisions (3 heavy and 3 light). USCENTCOM also estimated that the total Iraqi army order of battle included six armored divisions, 4 mechanized divisions, 10 infantry divisions, 2 special forces divisions, 1 Special Republican Guards or Presidential Guard Division, 19 reserve brigades, 15 People's Army Brigades, and 25 helicopter squadrons.[11] Both sets of estimates gave Iraq a total force of approximately 23 divisions versus 35–40 divisions in the summer of 1990, and 67–70 divisions in January, 1991—just before the Coalition offensives began in the Gulf War.[12]

USCENTCOM and other US experts estimated that Iraqi divisions had an authorized strength of about 10,000 men, and that about half of the Iraqi 23 divisions had manning levels of around 8,000 men and "a fair state of readiness." Republican Guards divisions had an average strength of around 8,000 to 10,000 men. Brigades averaged around 2,500 men—the size of a large US battalion. USCENTCOM also indicated that Iraqi army company and battalion level training increased significantly after November–December, 1996.[13]

USCENTCOM experts indicated that Iraq's 23 divisions were arrayed north

Figure 5.2
Iraq's Total Military Strength Before the Gulf War and in 1998

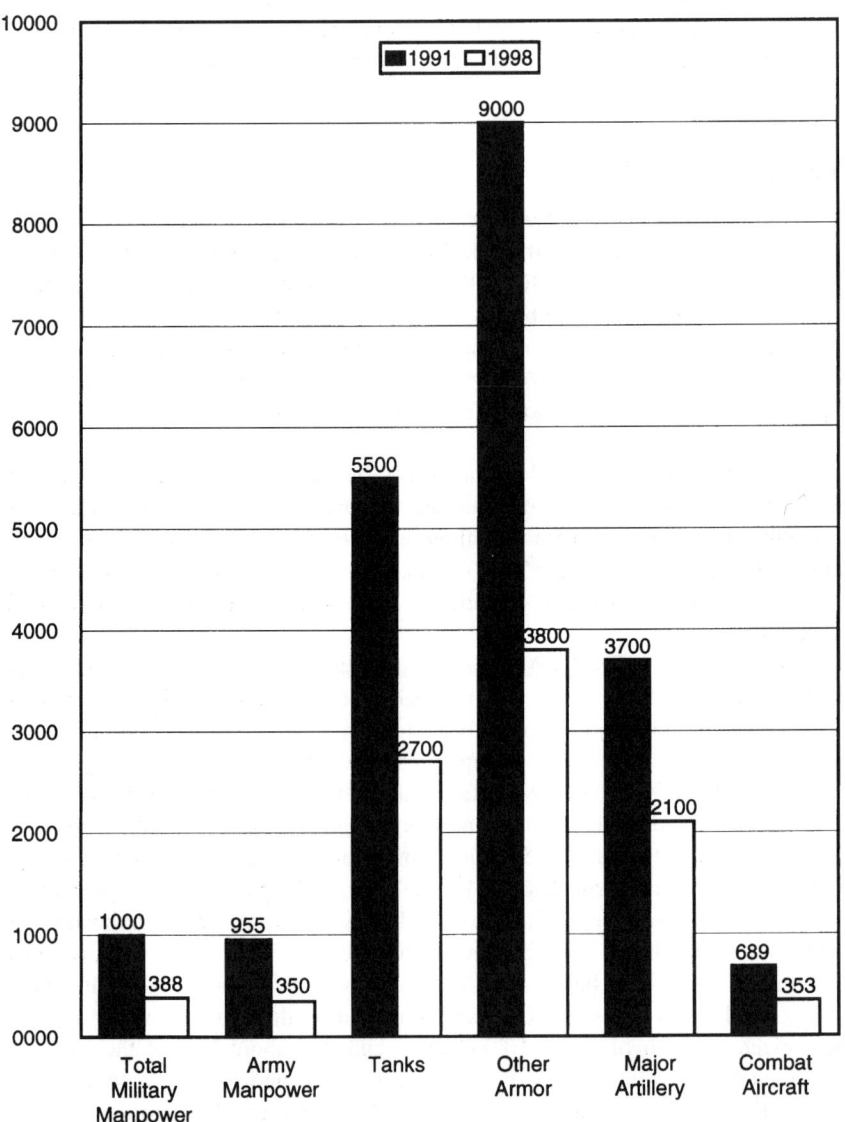

Sources: Adapted by Anthony H. Cordesman from various editions of IISS, *Military Balance*, and from material provided by US experts.

to south in February, 1997, with a mix of regular and Republican Guards divisions. All of the divisions near the Kuwait border were regular, although some Republican Guard divisions could move to the border relatively rapidly. All Republican Guards divisions were located above the 32-degree line. Several additional Republican Guards divisions were located around Baghdad to play a major role in internal security. Several more Republican Guards divisions were located north of Baghdad, closer to the Kurdish area.[14]

In spite of sanctions and Desert Fox, a total of 12 divisions are effective enough to be used in an attack on Kuwait or combat operations against Iran. There were five regular divisions—three relatively combat-ready—in the southern border region, north of Kuwait. There were two Republican Guards divisions that could be rapidly deployed to support the three more capable regular divisions in an attack on Kuwait, which USCENTCOM labeled the "Basrah breakout."[15]

The IISS estimates that the Iraqi army has some 375,000 actives (including 100,000 recalled reserves) in 1999, plus over 600,000 reserves. It estimates that it has seven corps headquarters, six armored and mechanized divisions, 12 infantry divisions, six Republican Guard Force divisions, four special Republican Guard Brigades, 10 commando brigades, and two special forces brigades.[16]

Some other estimates indicate that Iraq's land force had an active strength of up to 400,000 men, five to six corps, and a total of 28–30 divisions with 10 armored and mechanized divisions (four in the Republican Guards and six in the Iraqi regular army), and 18–20 infantry and mountain division equivalents (three in the Republican Guards and 15–17 in the Iraqi regular army), plus a division-sized Special Republican Guards formation.[17]

Work by Sean Boyne provides the most detailed available unclassified estimate of Iraq's order of battle. This work is summarized in Table 5.2, and the total force strength is very similar to the estimates of US experts and the USCENTCOM. Table 5.2 indicates that the regular Iraqi army has five corps and the Republican Guard has two corps. The regular army combat formations shown in Table 5.2 include a total of three armored divisions, three mechanized divisions, and 11 infantry divisions. The Republican Guards units include a total of two armored divisions, two mechanized divisions, and three infantry divisions. It should be noted that US experts do not agree with all of the details in Table 5.2.[18]

Regardless of the precise numbers involved, Iraq's land forces are organized into four major echelons in terms of political and military importance:

- The first echelon is composed of at least one heavy division equivalent of what Iraq called the Special Republican Guards, or "Presidential Guards" force. This force provides Saddam Hussein and Iraq's top leadership with personal protection and reflects the fact that Baghdad is the seat of power and that the Special Republican Guards and the rest of the Republican Guards are critical tools in preserving the regime's security.
- The second echelon includes six other Republican Guards divisions, along with some independent special forces and support units. In practice, the Republican Guards units

Table 5.2
The Iraqi Army Order of Battle

Formation	Command Center	Headquarters Location	Component Brigades
Regular Army			
1st Corps (North)	Al Rashid	Kirkuk, Khaled Camp	-
2nd Infantry Division	Khalid ben Al Walid	Airabee area	-
5th Mechanized Division	Mohammed Alwuasem	Shuwan area	15, 20, 26
8th Infantry Division	Almuthana	Shuwan area	22, 44, 48
38th Infantry Division	Amru Ben Abd Alaziz	Quader Karam area	130, 847, 848
2nd Corps (Baghdad)	Al Yarmouk	Deyala, Mansouria Alijabal Camp	
3rd Armored Division	Salah Aldin	Jalawla	6, 8, 12
15th Infantry Division	Al Farouq	Amerili	76, 104, 436
34th Infantry Division	Alhareth	Khanqin/Alsadia areas	90, 502, 504, 6
3rd Corps (Baghdad)	-		
11th Infantry Division	-	Al Naserria	23, 45, 47, 82
51st Mechanized Division	Sariat Al Jabal	Zubair	41, 31, 25
6th Armored Division	-	Al Nashwa, Shalamcha, Majnon	11, 30, 70
4th Corps (South)	Almajar	Al Amara	-
10th Armored Division	-	Al Teab, Al Amara	17, 24, 42
14th Infantry Division	-	S/SE Al Amara	420, 18, 14
18th Infantry Division	-	Al Musharah & Al Kahla	95, 422, 774

5th Corps (North)		
1st Mechanized Division	Abu Aubaida	Alsalamia Camp, Mosul	1, 27, 34
4th Infantry Division	Al Qaaqaa	Makhmur area	29, 5, 96
7th Infantry Division	Al Mansour	Bashiqa Maoten	38, 39, 116
16th Infantry Division	Thu Al Feqar	Alton Kopri Castle	108, 505, 606
		Saddam Dam, Mosul area	

Republican Guards

Northern Corps	Allah Akbar	Al Rashedia (Baghdad region) & Takrit	-
Adnan Mechanized Division	-	Mosul	11, 12, 21
Baghdad Infantry Division	-	Maqloob Maoten	4, 5, 6
Al Madina Al Munawara Armored Division	-	Al Rasedia & Al Taji Camps	10, 2, 17, 14
Al Abed Infantry Division	-	Kirkuk, Khaleed Camp	38, 39, 40
Southern Corps	Al Fateh Al Mubin		
Nabu Khuth Nussar Infantry Division	-	Al Hafreia, Alsuwera Camp	-
Hamurabi Mechanized Division	-	Alhussainia, Al Khut Governate	19, 22, 23
		Al Wahda area, Alsuwaira	17, 8, 14
Anedaa Armored Division	-	Baaquba, Deyala Governate	27, 28, 29

Source: Adapted from Sean Boyne, "Qusay Considers a Reshuffle for Iraq's Command Structure," *Jane's Intelligence Review*, September, 1997, pp. 416–417.

report directly to the Presidential Palace, and not to the Chief of Staff or Ministry of Defense.
- The third echelon is composed of a number of the best Iraqi regular army units under exceptionally loyal commanders. These units have much of the Iraqi regular army's armor, and have an unusually high level of equipment, total personnel, and combat-experienced personnel.
- Finally, a fourth echelon includes the rest of the Iraqi regular army. The units in this echelon are under loyal commanders, but are often seriously weakened. They lack the manpower and equipment strength of the units in the other echelons, and can only be used in largely defensive or rear area roles.

These forces are supplemented by a number of paramilitary elements, including the Popular or People's Army. The Popular Army began as a Ba'ath Party Militia. It was expanded to a force of several hundred thousand men during the start of the Iran-Iraq War, but generally performed poorly and was reduced to a reserve role. It now seems to be largely an internal security force, although it can provide replacements and reserve elements for the regular army. It is closely tied to the Ba'ath Party and is under the command of Vice President Taha Yassin Ramadan. It is headquartered at Al Hafrethia, near Baghdad.[19] Iraq may be trying to rebuild its Popular Army into a civil defense organization. It seemed to have begun a new recruiting campaign to use the Popular Army for this purpose in 1998, perhaps as a reaction to the threat of new US air and cruise missile strikes in February.[20]

In addition, each of the 15 Iraqi governates that has a largely Sunni or Shi'ite Arab population has a lightly armored Emergency Force unit. These units seem to be about the size of a reinforced battalion or small regiment. Some are reported to have up to 1,500 men, but their actual manning often seems to be under 1,000. These forces seem to be supplemented with tribal militias in some governates. The other three largely Kurdish governates had Kurdish militias before 1991, but it is unclear that any such forces remained after the Kurdish uprising.

There are paramilitary formations or "brigades" in key Iraqi intelligence organizations. These include forces in the Military Intelligence (Estikhabarat), the Special Security Service (Amn Al-Khass), and General Intelligence (Mukhabarat).[21] There are also a number of smaller paramilitary formations, and some may play a role in regional internal security operations.

Finally, Iraq has 20,000 frontier guards. These frontier guards are deployed along every border—except the "border" along the Kurdish security zone, which is covered by regular Iraqi forces. The frontier guards are little more than a light infantry and surveillance force and are armed with light weapons and AA guns. Training has generally been poor, but the force does free the army to perform combat missions elsewhere.

THE LIMITED VALUE OF UNIT STRENGTH AND ORDER OF BATTLE DATA

Iraqi combat formations have never really had standardized tables of organization and equipment (TO&Es) at any point in their recent history. Regardless of their authorized strength and manning, the manning in given divisions, brigades, and regiments has varied sharply with time ever since the first months of the Iran-Iraq War. Iraq's diverse mix of equipment types, wartime losses over more than a decade, and more than half a decade of sanctions have also forced Iraq to make constant changes in the equipment strength and mix of individual combat units.

Most Iraqi formations also have been tailored to a given operational front ever since the beginning of the Iran-Iraq War. This leads to different mixes of combat and service support, and to different tactical, training, and combat engineering concepts. Much has historically depended on the competence of individual commanders, particularly at the region, front, and division levels. Some officers have proved able to do an outstanding personal job of compensating for the overall organizational weaknesses of Iraq's method of organizing its forces, and others have not. Some officers also seem to be better able to obtain equipment and other material resources than others.

As a result, Iraqi units that appeared very similar on paper during the Iran-Iraq War actually had very different mixes of equipment, supply, and manning. Similarly, there were few signs of standardized levels of preparation and equipment along the Iraqi defensive positions in Kuwait and along the Saudi border during the Gulf War. An excellent set of defensives, with good mixes of equipment, could be found next to a poorly equipped "Potemkin position," with little obvious explanation in terms of the relative importance of the position involved.[22] It seems highly unlikely that Iraq has made much progress in solving these problems since the Gulf War, given its internal instability, lack of resupply, equipment shortages, manpower problems, and the regime's focus on loyalty over military effectiveness.

The problems raise a serious challenge to the kind of order of battle analysis that treats all Iraqi units as roughly identical, and efforts to assess the Iraqi army in terms of standardized doctrine, training, and tactics. Iraq simply has no military history to justify such an approach—even if it had ever had historical justification in other countries. As a result, the strength and competence of any given formation, and group of formations, must be based on the best available intelligence on its specific holdings, deployment patterns, organization, command structure, and commanders at the time of the assessment. It must be particularly sensitive to the history of key individual combat units and commanders, and the human factors shaping a unit's competence. A reliance on satellite photos, signals intelligence, and force-wide generalizations can be dangerously misleading in both exaggerating the overall competence of Iraq's forces and in underestimating the competence of particular units and commanders.

THE REPUBLICAN GUARDS

The Iraqi Republican Guards are an important case in point. The Republican Guards are the backbone of the regime's security, and are more privileged in terms of pay, equipment, and status than are the regular army forces. They report to the Presidential Palace, rather than to the Ministry of Defense, although they can be subordinated to a regular army headquarters for specific military operations. They are supervised by Saddam's son, Qusay, and their Chief of Staff is General Ibrahim Abdul Satter Mohammed al-Tikrit, one of Saddam's loyal supporters.[23]

Although their headquarters and some barracks suffered significant damage during Desert Fox, the Republican Guards remain Iraq's most effective land forces and the most effective land forces in the Gulf region. Their combat capability must be kept in perspective. Iraq's regular army heavy divisions scored many of Iraq's defensive victories during the Iran-Iraq War, and many of the breakthroughs and victories in the last months of the Iran-Iraq War. Nevertheless, the Republican Guards did fight well in many battles in the Iran-Iraq War and the Gulf War, and spearheaded Iraq's invasion of Irbil. Like the Soviet Guards and Waffen SS, they may not be more effective than the best regular army units, but they must be taken very seriously.

Iraq has consolidated its Republican Guards forces down from a total of 12 divisions to a total of six divisions since the Gulf War, and it has eliminated a number of smaller formations. In the process, it has given the Republican Guards units priority in terms of equipment, resupply, training, and operational funding. This has increased the gap between the Republican Guards units and regular army units in material terms, although the war-fighting results are untested.

In 1999, the Republican Guards divisions included three heavily armored divisions (the Al Nida, the Hammurabi, and the Al Medina al Munawarrah), and two lighter divisions (the Nebuchadnezzar and the Baghdad). Two special forces brigades seem to have survived from the pre-war special forces division. There are a number of other independent infantry formations.[24]

According to US and Israeli experts, the surviving Republican Guards have a total of between 60,000 and 80,000 men, and 26–30 brigade equivalents (7 armored, 4 mechanized, and the rest infantry). This total manning indicates that Republican Guards have about 65–75% of the total manning needed for their combat units, and about half the total manpower needed to deploy and sustain a force of seven full divisions.[25] This is an indication that Iraq continues to have some manpower problems with even its most prestigious force. Most estimates indicate that the Republican Guards still have six divisions. The order of battle shown in Table 5.2 still counts seven divisions, but the Al Adnan Mechanized Division in the Northern Corps area has been strengthened by consolidating the manpower and equipment of the Al Abed Infantry Division, based at Kirkuk, into the Adnan Division.[26]

US experts note that some of the forces for coup attempts have come from the Guard, that pay and privileges for junior officers and other ranks have declined in real value since late 1993, and that more Shi'ites and non-Takritis are being recruited into the force. Further, Saddam Hussein increasingly seems to be attempting to ensure the security of the Republican Guards by tribalizing the command and manning structure to mix "loyal" tribes in ways that emphasize tribal loyalty to Saddam, while ensuring that units have a wide enough mix of tribes so that no tribal element might serve as a basis of a coup attempt.

There is also a division-sized "Special" or "Presidential" Republican Guards force, under a military command structure reporting directly to Saddam, that acts as a palace guard. This force is deployed in a number of battalions whose mission is to protect Saddam Hussein. It is largely infantry, but has some T-72s, BMPs, D-30s, and 122 mm artillery weapons. Reports of its strength are uncertain, but one report claims a strength of some 13 battalions and 30,000 men before Desert Fox. Iraq lost 600–2,000 men in Desert Fox, many from the Special Republican Guards.

This force is deployed in units which guard Saddam's palaces, guard his movements, and provide emergency response forces. These emergency response forces may include a brigade-sized unit to provide Saddam with personal protection if he is threatened by some element of Iraq's military forces.[27] The "Special Republican Guard" is quite different from the regular Baghdad-based Republican Guard division. The former has three brigades which guard the southern, northern, and western arteries into the city.

Major General Namiq Mohammed is the senior military officer in charge of the Special Republican Guards, but Qusay is the effective commander of the force, just as he is of the regular Republican Guards. If the regular Republican Guards act as the "ring" of forces that defends Baghdad and Saddam Hussein, the Special Republican Guards act as Saddam's last line of defense. According to one report, Qusay has also set up a Joint Operations Room in the Presidential Palace, under the Iraqi National Security Council, to coordinate the operations of the Special Republican Guards with the Republican Guards and the key paramilitary elements of Iraq's security forces. These paramilitary units include the Amn Al-Khass Brigade in the General Security Service, a "brigade" in the General Intelligence Directorate, a paramilitary formation in the Military Security Service, and a "battalion" in military intelligence.[28]

There is also a new formation called the Fedayeen Saddam (Saddam's Men of Sacrifice) that reports directly to the palace, although its strength and status is unclear. Uday formed this force in 1995, and some reports of its strength go as high as 40,000. It seems to consist more of young thugs than a paramilitary force, and its members carry out "patrols" that often amount to little more than extortion and terrorism of any potential opposition. It seems to report to the Presidential Palace and to now be under the control of Qusay, with Lt. General

Mezahem Saab Al Hassan Al-Tikrit as his second in command.[29] It is possible this unit may have a woman's brigade, called the Al Majida Brigade, based in Kirkuk. This seems to be a propaganda effort, however, and it is unclear such a unit exists.

The precise equipment holdings of the surviving Republican Guards units are almost impossible to estimate, but they seem to be about 66–75% of their pre-war size. A very rough estimate of the total equipment holdings of the Republican Guards would be around 650 to 800 tanks (at least 550 T-72s), 800–1,100 other armored vehicles (about half BMP 1/2s and 25% MTLBs), and 350–500 artillery weapons. Unlike other Iraqi army units, these equipment holdings have also been kept largely operational since 1993, largely by consolidating operational equipment out of other combat and support units.

DEPLOYMENTS AGAINST THE KURDS AND IRAN

Iraq's combat-ready land forces are deployed in the area around Baghdad, near the Iranian border, near the Kurdish security zone, and in the Shi'ite south. The army's key formations include a corps headquartered in Mosul and another corps headquartered in Kirkuk. Another Iraqi corps or large-scale formation is concentrated in the Baghdad area, with many of the Republican Guards heavy divisions and the special Republican Guards (or "Presidential guards") formations.[30] Two more corps are deployed in the south, with at least 50,000–75,000 men. These forces seemed to have included 5–10 divisions, with a mix of infantry and heavy divisions, and at least some Republican Guard formations in reserve—although no Republican Guards divisions have been deployed south of the 32nd parallel since October, 1994.

Iraq has kept some 16–18 divisions and 150,000–175,000 troops from its I Corps and V Corps and its Republican Guards deployed in the north-central part of the Iranian border. Many of these forces are stationed along the southern edge of the Kurdish-controlled zone from Dahuk through Al Kuwayr, Irbil, and Kifri to Khanaqin.

In June, 1996, there were three infantry divisions in the north, along the border of Kurdish controlled territory, with one more to the west of Mosul. There were two infantry divisions and two mechanized divisions along the border, southwest of Irbil and north of Kirkuk. Three were three infantry divisions along the border, with Kurdish-controlled territory southeast of Kirkuk, a mechanized division and infantry division east of Tikrit, and an armored division near the Iranian border just south of the Kurdish-controlled area.[31] In contrast, the growing divisions between the two main Kurdish factions—the Kurdish Democratic Party (KDP), led by Masoud Barzani, and the Patriotic Union of Kurdistan (PUK), led by Jalal Talabani—resulted in the collapse of earlier efforts to create a unified Kurdish military force, with a total strength of 16 brigades.

During the years before Iraqi forces invaded the Kurdish enclave in August, 1996, Iraqi forces regularly shelled Kurdish positions near the border of the

Kurdish security zone, and often harassed the UN relief and inspection effort. Iraq used covert operations to bomb and attack UN convoys and sometimes moved combat units closer to the Kurdish enclave in an effort to intimidate the Kurds.

On August 31, 1996, Iraq went much further. In spite of US warnings, it sent the elements of a Corps-sized force into the Kurdish security zone in support of the KDP. Some estimates put this force at three armored divisions, with a total strength of 30,000–40,000 men. This attack occurred after the PUK seized the city of Irbil and came at the invitation of Barzani and the KDP. While the United States fired some 44 cruise missiles at Iraq on September 3 and 4, 1996, it could do little more than extend the southern "no fly zone" from the 32nd to the 33rd parallel. It had little practical ability to protect the Kurds from themselves.

A combination of Iraq military forces and the Iraqi security services then swept through the KDP occupied areas, especially around Irbil. There were some mass executions of Iraqi opposition members, and the Iraqi incursion virtually destroyed any opposition from the Iraqi National Congress (INC). The United States had to evacuate some 2,137 largely Kurdish employees to Guam, while 310 members of the INC and an additional 4,000 local employees of nongovernmental aid organizations and various opposition movements fled north for sanctuary near Turkey.[32]

Substantial Iraqi forces remain near Irbil and around the Kurdish enclave, and the potential size of the forces Iraq might deploy against the Kurds is indicated by the number of divisions Saddam Hussein singled out during a ceremony giving awards to his officers for the operation against the Kurds. Saddam cites the 1st Mechanized Division, 2nd Infantry Division, 5th Mechanized Division, 7th Infantry Division, 8th Infantry Division, and 15th Infantry Division in the Regular Army, and the Adnan Mechanized Division, Baghdad Infantry Division, Al Madina Armored Division, and Al Abed Infantry Division in the Republican Guards.[33]

These forces play a major role in controlling the Kurds and in ensuring that the Iraqi opposition cannot reestablish its bases in the North. Iraq's northern forces also, however, play a major role in defending against Iran and the problems posed by Turkey's military interventions in the area. Turkey has been fighting a civil war against its own Kurds and a violent, hard-line Marxist movement called the Kurdish Workers Party (PKK) since 1984. It entered Iraq to pursue PKK rebels several times during the Iran-Iraq War, and began to cooperate with the Iraqi Kurds in suppressing the PKK in 1992.

When feuding between the KDP and PKK peaked in early 1995, Turkey warned the PUK against its growing alignment with the PKK. On May 20, 1995, some 35,000 Turkish troops entered northern Iraq in pursuit of what Turkey claimed were 2,400–2,800 PKK guerrillas. The operation went on for months, and Turkey established a "security belt" along the Iraqi border that included a 9,000 square kilometer area. Turkey also allied itself with the KDP against the

PKK, adding a new dimension to the military problems in the area and leading the PKK to align itself with Iran.[34] While the Turks eventually withdrew, and aided Saddam's regime by dividing and weakening the Kurds, they also raised the specter of Turkish occupation of part of Iraq and old Iraqi fears that Turkey might sometime seek to regain the rich oil areas around Mosul that it had owned at the time of the Ottoman Empire.

Iraq's system of duplicative and competing intelligence elements makes it difficult to know what additional paramilitary forces are assigned to the Kurdish issue. The Special Security Service plays a major role, and it supported Iraq's military forces when Iraqi forces invaded the Kurdish security zone. It assisted in the arrest and execution of some opposition figures, and probably in at least one mass execution. It still seems to be operating in Irbil, although at a more covert level. Elements of Military Intelligence (Estikhabarat) are present in Kirkuk to deal with Kurdish security issues, and have heavily penetrated the Kurdish security zone. These forces include elements of its "Unit 999." The General Intelligence Directorate, General Security Service, and Military Security Service also have elements dealing with Kurdish opposition movements.[35]

In contrast, the Kurds are not effective, even when they fight each other. When the fighting between the KDP and PUK escalated in August, 1996, it became apparent that both the KDP and PUK were only capable of light, unsustainable, mechanized infantry operations and could not use most of their heavy equipment effectively. Each side fought best in its own territory. The PUK fought very badly against the KDP in KDP territory in August, and the KDP fought very poorly against the PUK in PUK territory in October, 1996. Neither faction seemed likely to have much capability against Iraq, except in guerrilla and mountain warfare.

The Kurds did nothing to improve their unity in 1997 and during most of 1998. In spite of US, Japanese, and other efforts, cease-fire after cease-fire broke down. In the fall of 1997, the fighting between the PUK and KDP produced the worst killing yet. Further, the continuing infiltration of northern Iraq by the PKK, a violent Turkish Kurd movement, triggered another series of major Turkish attacks in northern Iraq.

Turkey launched an offensive in September, 1996 that it called "Dawn 97," and which it claimed killed 860 PKK guerrillas versus 27 Turkish soldiers and 50 Peshmergas from the KDP. The operation ended some 22 days later on October 13, but this time Turkey created a lasting Turkish security zone to block cross raids across the 198-mile Iraqi-Turkish border. After that time, Turkish air forces have bombed PUK and PKK positions as part of the informal alliance between Turkey and the KDP—a development scarcely likely to end the rift between the KDP and PUK, or allay Saddam's concerns regarding Turkish intervention.[36] The KDP and PUK continued to feud, and their forces engaged in minor clashes during the rest of 1996, 1997, and most of 1998.

The United States brokered new attempts to unite the Kurds in September, 1998, and the KDP and PUK began to talk about holding new elections in the spring of 1999. Barzani, however, retained his loose alliance with Turkey and continued to cooperate with Saddam Hussein's government in many aspects of security and smuggling from Iraq to Turkey through the Turkish security zone. Talibani retained his ties to Iran, remained more supportive of the PKK, and had closer ties to the Iraqi opposition groups attempting to drive Saddam from power. Kurdish "unity" seemed to consist largely of a temporary alliance between Barzani and Talibani that seemed likely to last only as long as US aid underpinned the relationship. Furthermore, the Turkish foreign office announced that Turkey opposed the creation of any separate Kurdish entity in Iraq and the use of the Kurdish enclave as a base for opponents of Saddam Hussein.

There is an old Kurdish proverb that "the Kurds have no friends." This seems to be true of the Kurds themselves. Their self-destructive behavior has steadily reduced any threat to Saddam's regime or future control of the Kurdish area. It has led one British observer to state that " 'Kurd' is Iraqi for 'self-inflicted wound.' "

Even if the Kurds were truly united, the Iraqi Kurds would have little capability to defend the Kurdish enclave against Iraqi forces, although the Kurds would have more capability for guerrilla and mountain warfare. In early 1996, the KDP claimed to have 25,000 troops and a militia of 30,000 additional men, but these forces were only armed with light artillery, multiple rocket launchers, mortars, small arms, and SA-7s. Similarly, the PUK claimed to have 12,000 troops plus 6,000 men in support forces, but was armed with some T-54 and T-55 tanks, about 450 mortars, 106 mm recoilless rifles, 200 light anti-aircraft guns, and SA-7s. Their actual strength in late 1998 was only a fraction of these claims.

DEPLOYMENTS AGAINST THE SHI'ITES AND IRAN

Iraq deploys some 7–8 divisions and 75,000 troops from its IV Corps, III Corps and Republican Guards south of Baghdad. These forces are spread out near the Iranian border and in the Shi'ite areas from Karbala and Al Kut in the north to An Nasiriyah and Az Zubayr in the south, although most perform occupation duties and are not involved in any military effort. Iraq has used these forces to destroy the traditional way of life of the marsh Arab Shi'ites. In June, 1996, there was one infantry division in Karbala and one in Al Kut. There were two infantry divisions west of An Nasiriyah, an armored division near Al Amarah, an infantry division near Qalatsalih, an armored division between Qalatsalih and Al Basrah, and a mechanized division near Al Basrah.[37]

The Iraqi regime's burning, draining, and water-diversion projects are part of a process of large-scale environmental destruction in the marshes that continued throughout 1996. The army has constructed canals, causeways, and earthen berms to divert water from the wetlands. Hundreds of square kilometers of marsh areas have been burned, imperiling the marshes' ecosystem.[38]

The Iraqi army has also launched attacks on many villages in the region. On

March 4, 1994, the military began its largest search-and-destroy operation in the marshes in two years. The offensive included the razing of villages and burning operations concentrated in the triangle bounded by Nasiriyah, Al-Qurnah, and Basrah. The magnitude of this operation caused the inhabitants to flee in several directions: deeper into the marshes, to the outskirts of southern Iraqi cities, and to Iran. In late June, 1994, Iraqi military forces attacked several marsh villages in the Nasiriyah province. Sources said that army engineers burned the village of Al-Abra, which contained about 80 homes, to the ground. After the operation, the army transported the village's inhabitants from the scene. In early July, the security forces stormed the villages of Al-Sajiya and Al-Majawid in the Al-Chibaish district, near the main road leading into the marshes. Simultaneously, armor units supported by heavy artillery attacked the village of Al-Kheyout in the district of Al-Madina.[39]

The Iraqi military also conducted large-scale artillery bombardment in the Jindala area of the Al-Amarah marshes. Opposition sources said that the bombardment destroyed several homes and injured several individuals. The military also attacked Al-Hashriya, Al-Wasdiya, and Al-Malha, and arrested some of their inhabitants. In September, 1994, opposition sources reported that military forces used incendiary bombs and launched an armored attack against the area of Al-Seigel in the Al-Amarah marshes. The army later set fire to the entire area.[40]

The UN Special Rapporteur stated in his February, 1994 report that the extent of violations against the marsh inhabitants "places the survival of this indigenous population in jeopardy," and he noted the similarity between the Iraqi regime's "genocide-type operations" against the Kurds and its operations in southern Iraq. In August, he dispatched two of his assistants to the Iran-Iraq border to interview refugees fleeing the marshes. He reported in October, 1994 that the refugees were generally in poor physical and psychological condition, having suffered extreme deprivation of food and medicine. He reiterated his "concern over the survival" of the marsh inhabitants "as a community."

These military operations caused serious civilian casualties, and more than 10,000 refugees from the marshes fled to Iran, where they joined between 50,000 and 60,000 who had fled in previous years. According to the US State Department, large numbers of Shi'ites refugees from southern Iraq fled to Iran, particularly after the escalation in military activity in March, 1994.

In late 1994, the UN High Commissioner for Refugees (UNHCR) estimated that more than 10,000 refugees from the marshes were in camps in Iran. Amar Appeal, a charitable organization operating several of the camps, placed the number at more than 35,000. US government analysts estimated in September, 1994 that more than 200,000 of the 250,000 former inhabitants of the marshes had been driven from the area since 1991, and later reports indicated that further refugees left the area in 1995 and 1996.[41]

Low-level fighting in the marshes persisted into 1999, and the Iraqi armed forces continued to conduct deliberate artillery and infantry attacks against civilians in the southern marshes into the late 1990s. After early 1995, however, there was little real Shi'ite resistance. Many of the government attacks were designed to root out army deserters, dissidents, and displaced civilians, rather than deal with anything approaching effective paramilitary forces. By 1997, there was little meaningful Shi'ite resistance of any kind, although the government continued to have a problem with deserters and bandits.

Once again, Iraq's system of duplicative and competing intelligence elements makes it difficult to know what paramilitary forces are assigned to the Shi'ite issue. The Special Security Service plays a major role, and it supported Iraq's military forces in suppressing the Shi'ite rebellion after the Gulf War. According to one report, it conducted mass executions of Shi'ite prisoners at its prison and security complex near Saddam's farm at Al Ranighwania, near the Baghdad International Airport.[42]

The political branch of the Special Security Service and the Ministry of Interior track Shi'ites through Iraq's identity card system and keep computerized files on known and possible dissidents. This use of personal security files, tied to identity cards, is also applied to Kurds and all other suspect Iraqis. The system seems to be organized to allow tracking by family and tribe, as well as by ethnicity, religion, and region. A modified system tracks all foreign visitors to Iraq by their passports. There are reports that the files on suspect foreign nationals include copies of international telephone calls, transcripts of conversations in hotel rooms and other monitored public areas, and records of movements—including reports by taxi drivers and interviews with Iraqis that foreigners have visited.

The Special Bureau of the General Intelligence Directorate, including Office Five, plays a role in suppressing Shi'ite opposition. Military Intelligence (Estikhabarat) has a base in Basra, and elements of its "Unit 999" have a special section to deal with Shi'ites in the marshes. The General Security Service also plays a major role in dealing with the Shi'ites. Iraq runs a major intelligence effort targeted on Shi'ite opposition groups overseas, and it has heavily penetrated most groups—just as it has virtually all Iraqi opposition movements.[43]

The Shi'ites are, however, only one of the reasons for the deployment of so many forces in the region. The military forces in southern Iraq pose a constant threat to Kuwait, and of new deployments or build-ups that can force the United States to react by moving troops from half the world away. In spite of occasional talks, Iraq and Iran have never fully agreed to a full cease-fire, much less peace. Iran continues to hold well over 100 Iraq combat aircraft that flew to Iran for sanctuary during the Gulf War. Iraq claims that Iran is still holding 18,229 prisoners of war, and Iran claims that Iraq is still holding 5,000–10,000.

Iraq did open its border with Iran in September, 1997 for the first time in 17 years. It claimed it did so to allow Iranians to visit the shrines in Najaf and Karbala in southern Iraq, but it seems to have been attempted to ease relations with Iran in order to obtain support against UN sanctions. Iran rejected the initiative, however, and less than a month later the nations clashed over a raid that the People's Mujahideen e-Khalq (MEK), a violent Iraqi-based Iranian opposition group, launched into Iran. Iran retaliated on September 29, 1997, by bombing the two MEK military bases near the border area, and Iraq responded by sending up sortie after sortie of Iraqi fighters to patrol the area. The end result did more to present problems for the United States in enforcing the southern "no-fly zone" than lead to actual conflict, but it was scarcely a signal that Iraq or Iran was moving toward peace.[44]

There is always a risk of some kind of "devil's bargain" between Iraq and Iran, just as there is of some alignment between Iraq and Syria. So far, however, the tension between Iraq and Iran is one of the few consistent strategic alignments in the Middle East.

LAND FORCE EQUIPMENT HOLDINGS AND CAPABILITIES

While it is difficult to make precise estimates of the strength of Iraq's current land forces, the broad trends are clear. Figure 5.3 shows Iraqi military manning by military service. Figures 5.4 and 5.5 provide estimates of the broad trends in the major weapons strength of Iraqi land forces, showing the trends in Iraqi tank and artillery strength since 1988. These figures clearly reflect Iraq's buildup during the Iran-Iraq War, the impact of its defeat in the Gulf War, and the slow rebuilding of its forces in the years that have followed.

Figures 5.6–5.18 provide a summary net assessment of the trends in the regional military balance. Figure 5.6 compares Iraqi manpower by military service with that of other Gulf states. Figure 5.7 compares land force manpower. Figure 5.8 shows the total armored strength of each Gulf state by major category of armor, and shows that Iraq remains the dominant armored power in the Gulf. Figure 5.9 and 5.10 show the trends in tank strength, Figures 5.11–5.14 compare the strength of various types of other armored vehicles, and Figure 5.16 and 5.17 compare the strength of different major categories of artillery weapons.

It should be noted that the estimates in these figures are those of the author, and that estimates of the equipment holdings of Iraqi forces differ by source. These uncertainties are described in detail in the analysis that follows, and they are of considerable importance. For example, USCENTCOM estimated in mid-1996 that the Iraqi army had 2,200–2,700 tanks, 3,000–3,500 APCs and AFVs, 1,900–2,100 major artillery weapons, and 1,100 other armored vehicles, including recovery, NBC, command, and other vehicles.[45] The IISS estimated that Iraq had 2,700 tanks, 2,900 APCs and AFVs, and 2,100 major artillery weapons.[46] Most of the figures for 1999 that follow are based on interviews as well as the sources shown.

Iraqi Tank Strength

Most estimates of Iraq's tank strength credited it with around 2,700 tanks in 1999, although it is not clear what portion of this total was fully operational. An estimate by other US experts indicates that the Iraqi army's major equipment holdings in late 1998 included about 2,200–2,700 tanks, substantially less than

Figure 5.3
Trends in Total Iraqi Military Manpower, 1978–1997

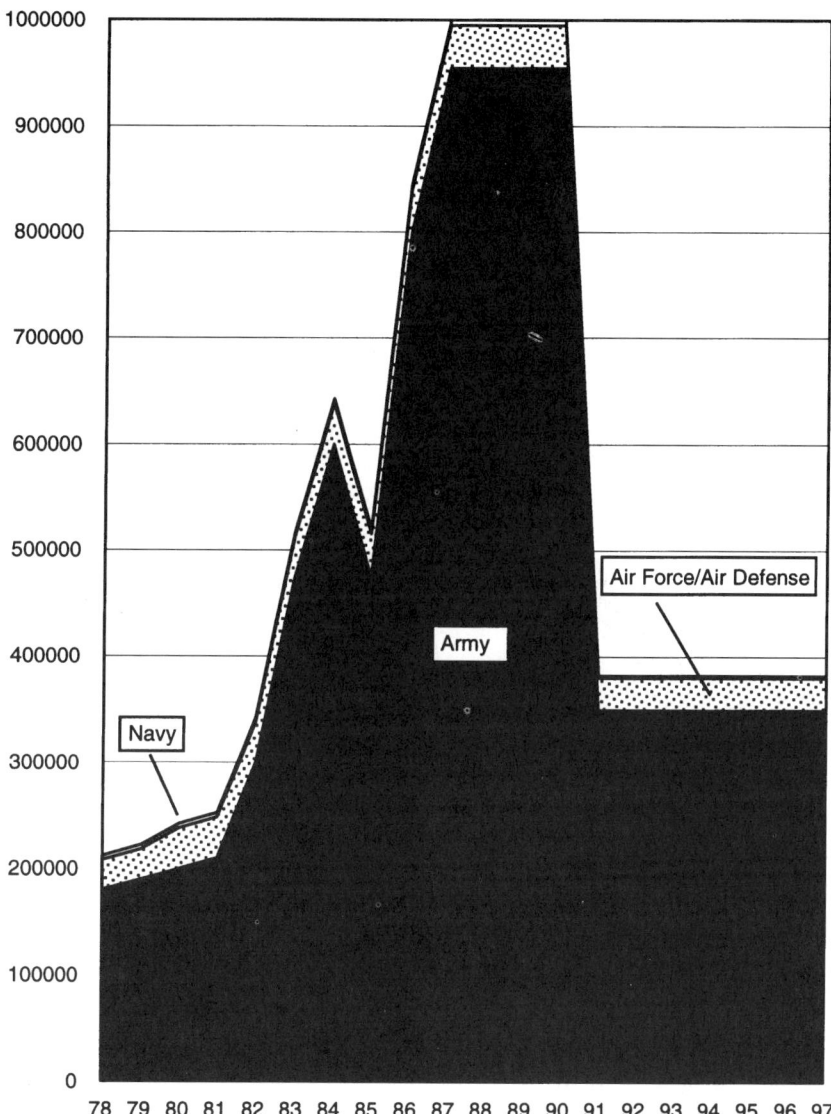

Sources: Adapted by Anthony H. Cordesman from various editions of IISS, *Military Balance*, and interviews with US experts.

Figure 5.4
Iraq: Armored Weapons Strength, 1979–1998

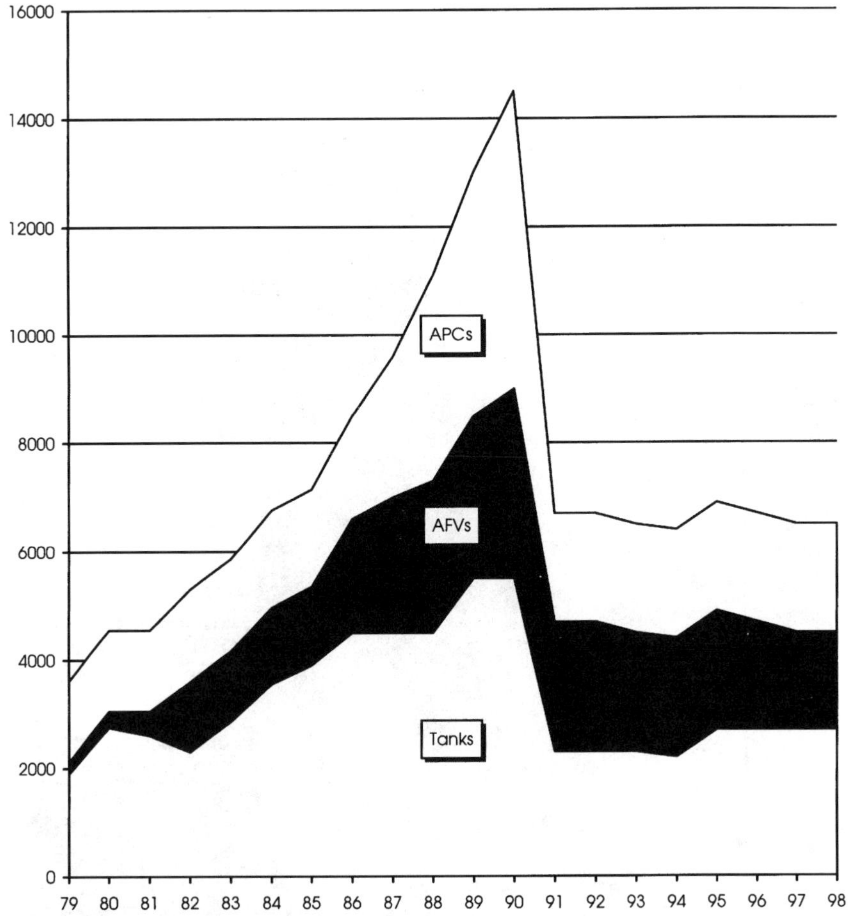

Sources: Adapted by Anthony H. Cordesman from various editions of IISS, *Military Balance*; JCSS, *Military Balance in the Middle East*; and material provided by US experts.

half of the 6,700 tanks it had before the war. About half of these tanks were T-54s, T-55s, T-59s, and T-69s. Iraq also had about 600–700 M-48s, M-60s, AMX-30s, Centurions, and Chieftains captured from Iran, or which it obtained in small numbers from other countries. The IISS estimates that Iraq has roughly 1,000 T-54, T-55, T-77 and Chinese T-59 and T-69 tanks, plus 200 T-62s, and 700 T-72s. It also estimates that Iraq has some Chieftain and M-47 and M-60 tanks it captured from Iran, most of which are inoperable.

One thing is certain. Iraq lost much of its pre-war T-72 strength during the Gulf War. US experts feel that only about 500–600 T-72s and 200–300 T-62s

Figure 5.5
Iraq: Artillery Weapons Strength, 1988–1998

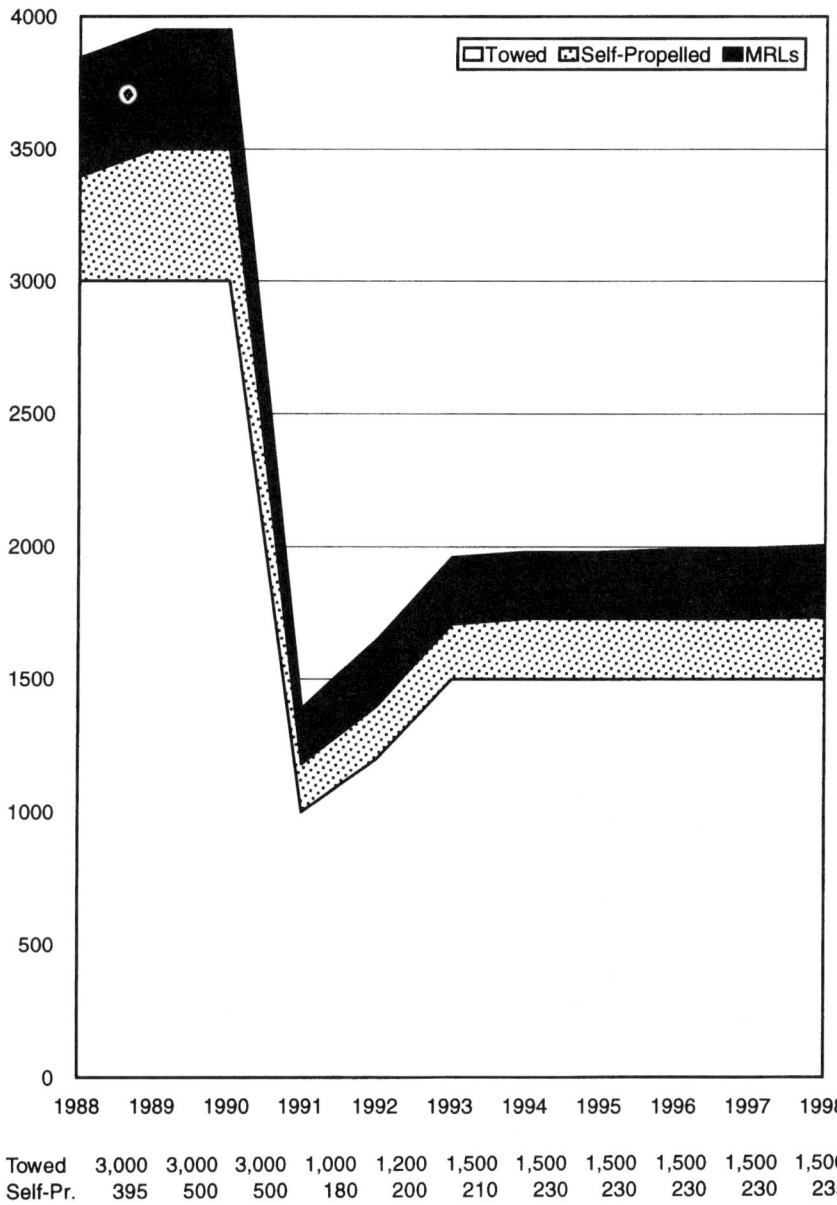

	1988	1989	1990	1991	1992	1993	1994	1995	1996	1997	1998
Towed	3,000	3,000	3,000	1,000	1,200	1,500	1,500	1,500	1,500	1,500	1,500
Self-Pr.	395	500	500	180	200	210	230	230	230	230	235
MRLs	450	450	450	210	250	250	250	250	260	265	270

Sources: Adapted by Anthony H. Cordesman from various editions of IISS, *Military Balance*; JCSS, *Military Balance in the Middle East*; and material provided by US experts.

Figure 5.6
Total Gulf Military Manpower by Service, 1998

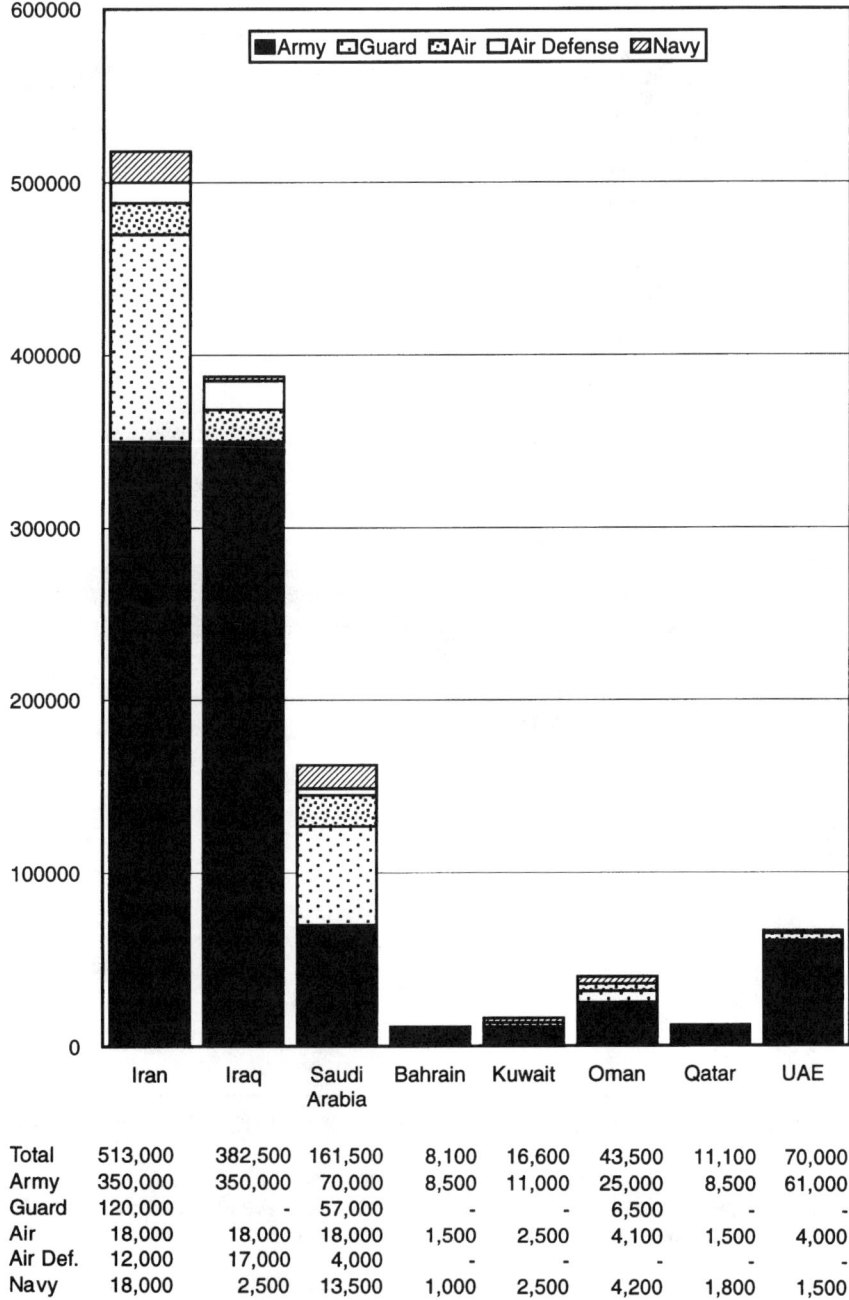

	Iran	Iraq	Saudi Arabia	Bahrain	Kuwait	Oman	Qatar	UAE
Total	513,000	382,500	161,500	8,100	16,600	43,500	11,100	70,000
Army	350,000	350,000	70,000	8,500	11,000	25,000	8,500	61,000
Guard	120,000	-	57,000	-	-	6,500	-	-
Air	18,000	18,000	18,000	1,500	2,500	4,100	1,500	4,000
Air Def.	12,000	17,000	4,000	-	-	-	-	-
Navy	18,000	2,500	13,500	1,000	2,500	4,200	1,800	1,500

Source: Adapted by Anthony H. Cordesman from IISS, *Military Balance*.

Figure 5.7
Total Active Military Manpower in Gulf Armies in 1998

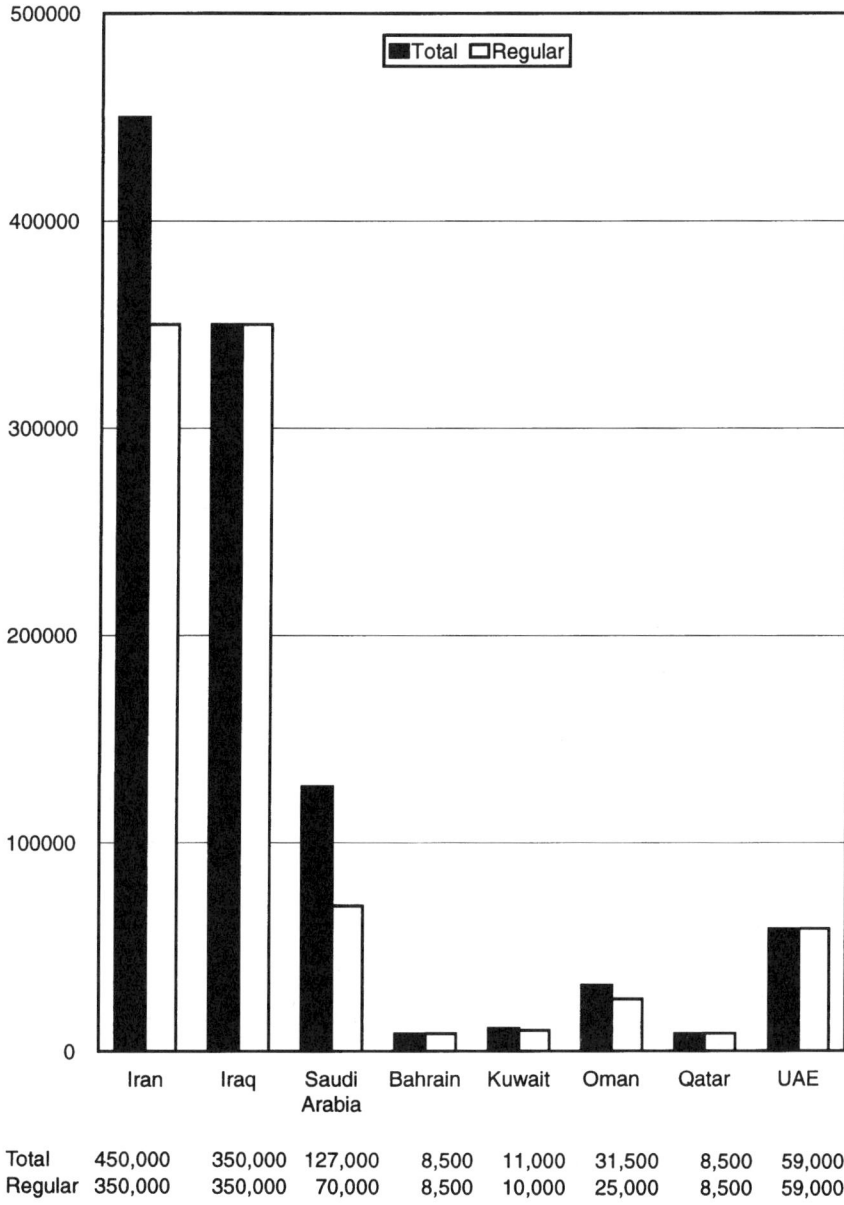

	Iran	Iraq	Saudi Arabia	Bahrain	Kuwait	Oman	Qatar	UAE
Total	450,000	350,000	127,000	8,500	11,000	31,500	8,500	59,000
Regular	350,000	350,000	70,000	8,500	10,000	25,000	8,500	59,000

Sources: Estimated by Anthony H. Cordesman from various sources, and IISS, *Military Balance*. IISS estimates Iran's total land force manpower at 350,000, with over 100,000 men in IRGC forces.

Figure 5.8
Total Gulf Operational Armored Fighting Vehicles, 1998

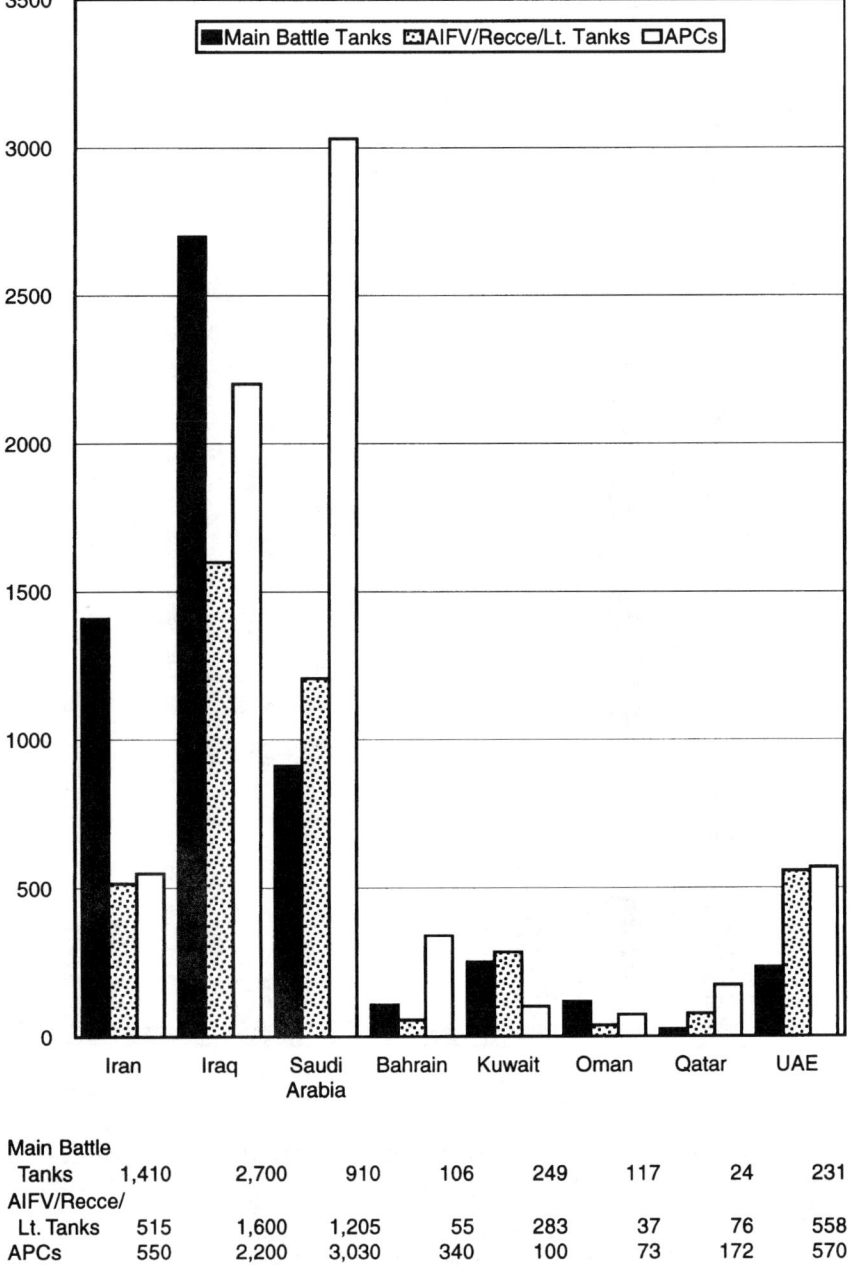

	Iran	Iraq	Saudi Arabia	Bahrain	Kuwait	Oman	Qatar	UAE
Main Battle Tanks	1,410	2,700	910	106	249	117	24	231
AIFV/Recce/Lt. Tanks	515	1,600	1,205	55	283	37	76	558
APCs	550	2,200	3,030	340	100	73	172	570

Sources: Adapted by Anthony H. Cordesman from various sources, and IISS, *Military Balance*.

Figure 5.9
Total Operational Tanks in All Gulf Forces, 1979–1998

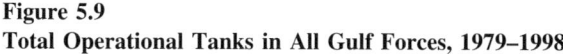

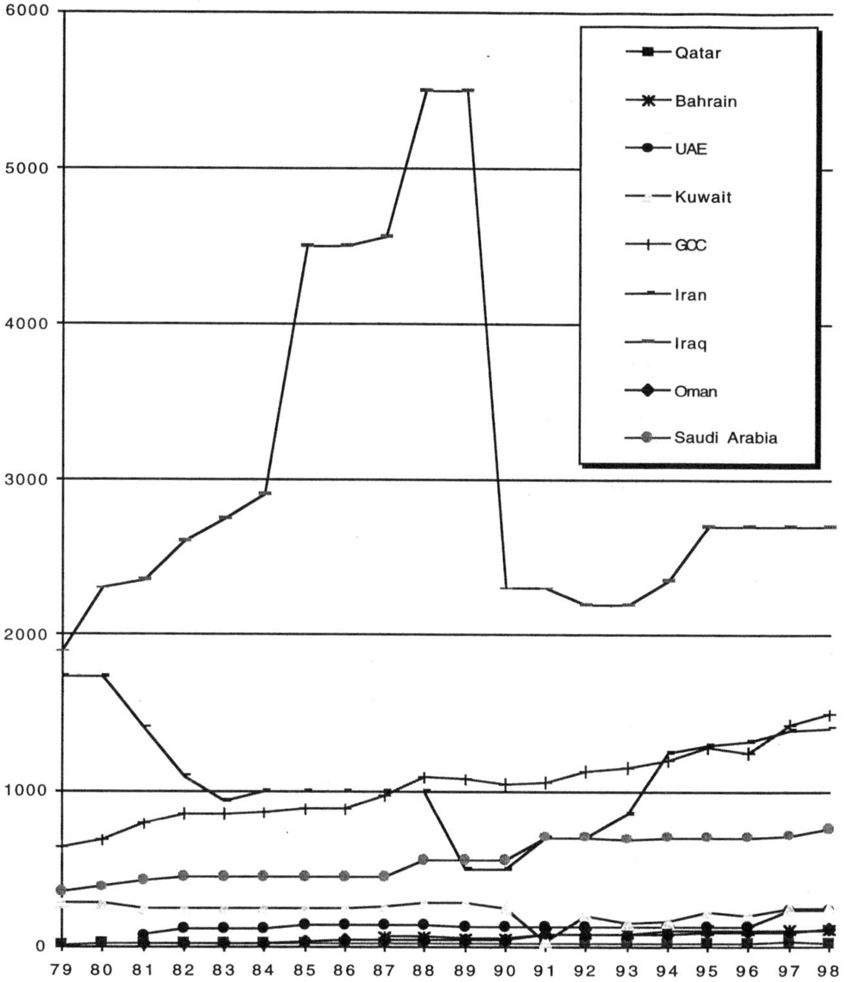

Note: Iran includes active forces in the Revolutionary Guards. Saudi Arabia includes active forces in the National Guard.

Sources: Adapted by Anthony H. Cordesman from various sources, and IISS, *Military Balance*, various editions.

remained after the war, versus nearly 1,500 T-72s and T-62s before the war. According to some estimates, less than 2,200 of Iraq's tanks are fully operational. However, Iraq retained over 1,500 tank transporters and heavy vehicle trailers out of the several thousand it bought during the Iran-Iraq War, and it continued to make effective use of them during exercises in late 1997.[47] Iraq

Figure 5.10
Gulf Modern Tanks in Total Inventory in 1998

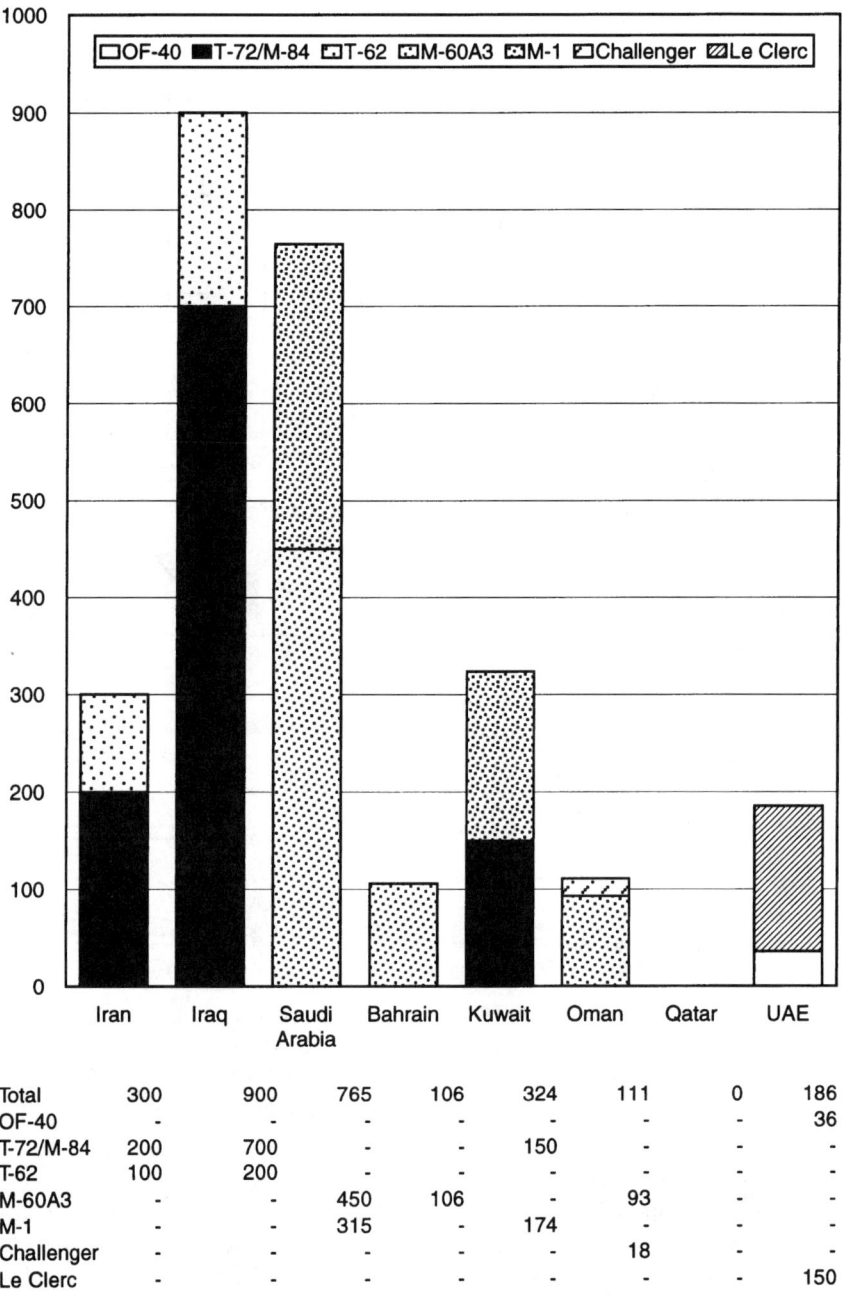

	Iran	Iraq	Saudi Arabia	Bahrain	Kuwait	Oman	Qatar	UAE
Total	300	900	765	106	324	111	0	186
OF-40	-	-	-	-	-	-	-	36
T-72/M-84	200	700	-	-	150	-	-	-
T-62	100	200	-	-	-	-	-	-
M-60A3	-	-	450	106	-	93	-	-
M-1	-	-	315	-	174	-	-	-
Challenger	-	-	-	-	-	18	-	-
Le Clerc	-	-	-	-	-	-	-	150

Sources: Estimated by Anthony H. Cordesman from various sources, and IISS, *Military Balance*.

Figure 5.11
Total Operational Other Armored Vehicles (Lt. Tanks, Scout, AIFVs, APCs, Recce) in Gulf Forces, 1990 and 1998

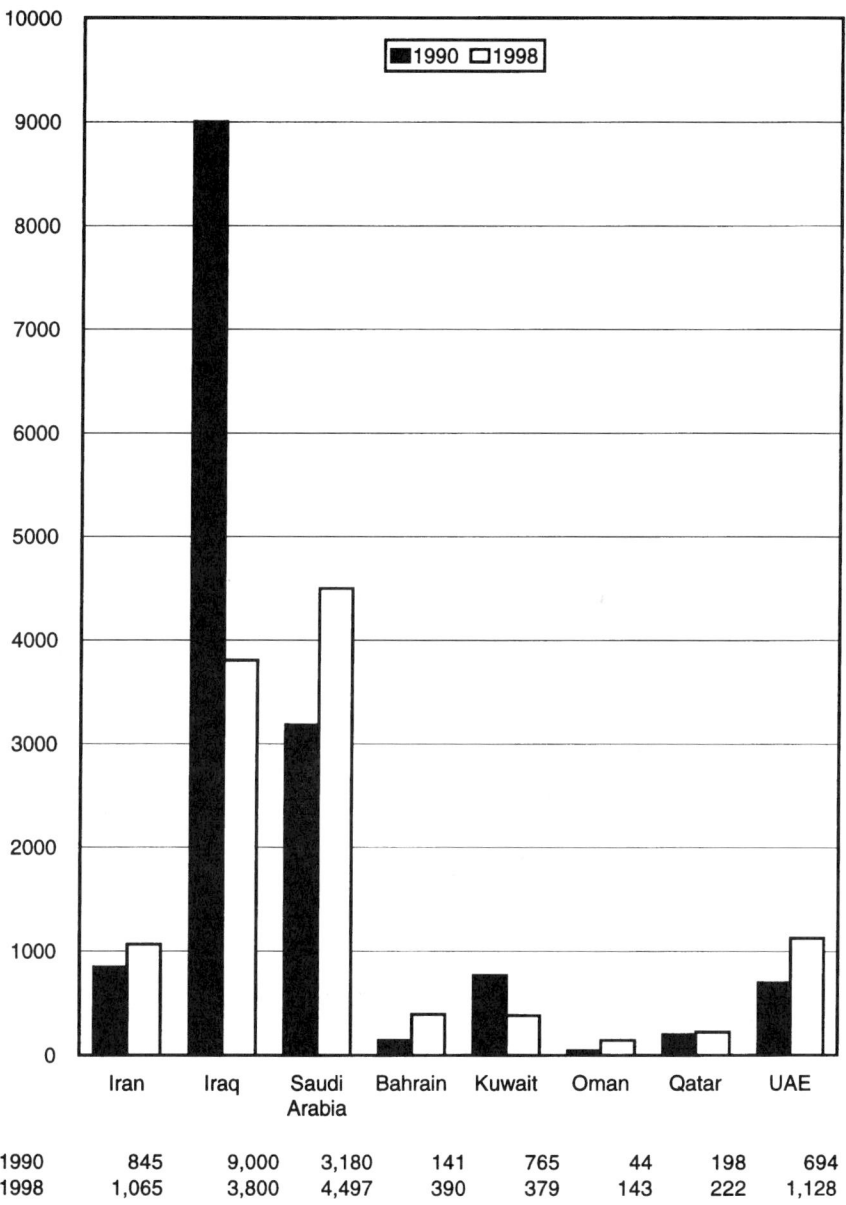

	Iran	Iraq	Saudi Arabia	Bahrain	Kuwait	Oman	Qatar	UAE
1990	845	9,000	3,180	141	765	44	198	694
1998	1,065	3,800	4,497	390	379	143	222	1,128

Note: Iran includes active forces in the Revolutionary Guards. Saudi Arabia includes active forces in the National Guard.
Sources: Adapted by Anthony H. Cordesman from various sources, and IISS, *Military Balance*.

Figure 5.12
Total Gulf Other Armored Fighting Vehicles (OAFVs), 1998

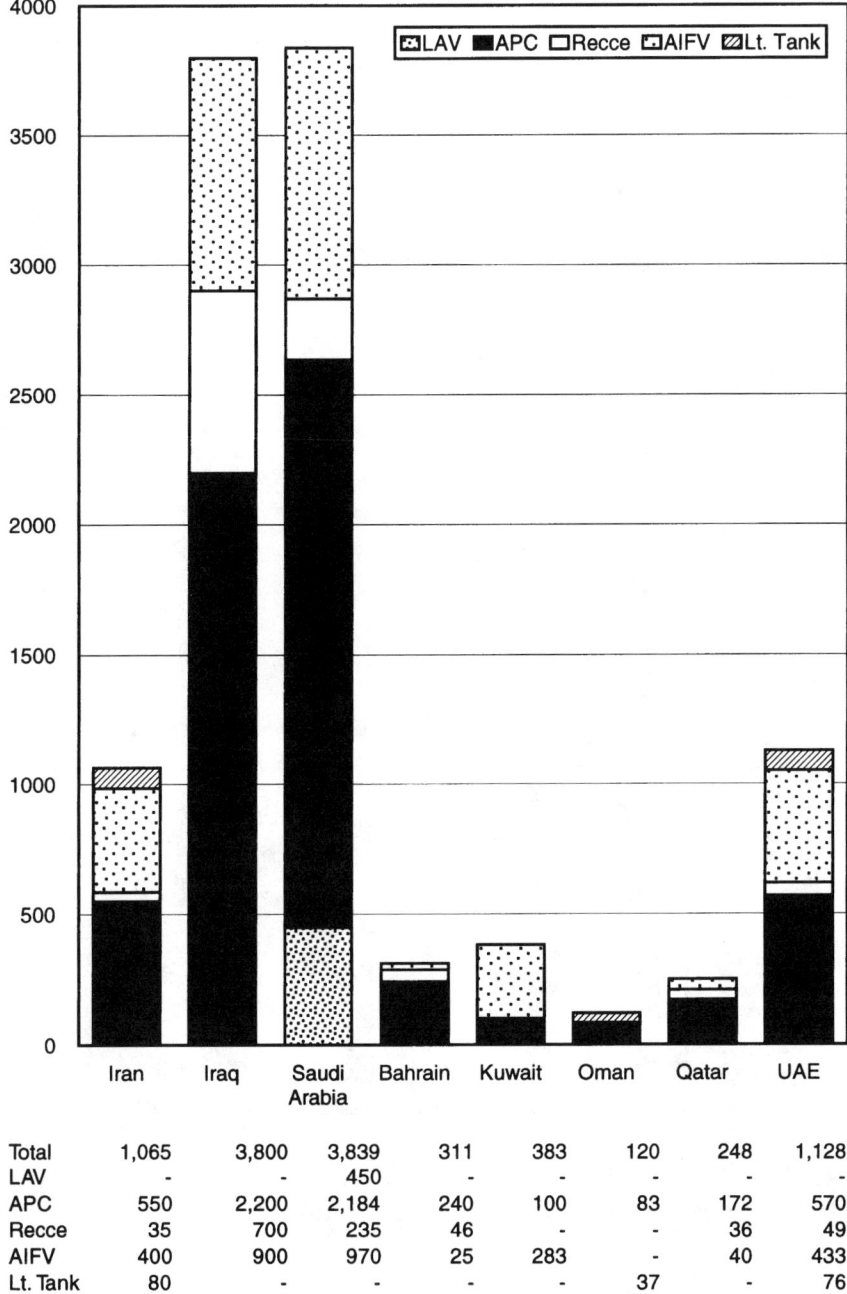

	Iran	Iraq	Saudi Arabia	Bahrain	Kuwait	Oman	Qatar	UAE
Total	1,065	3,800	3,839	311	383	120	248	1,128
LAV	-	-	450	-	-	-	-	-
APC	550	2,200	2,184	240	100	83	172	570
Recce	35	700	235	46	-	-	36	49
AIFV	400	900	970	25	283	-	40	433
Lt. Tank	80	-	-	-	-	37	-	76

Sources: Estimated by Anthony H. Cordesman from various sources, and IISS, *Military Balance*.

Figure 5.13
Advanced Armored Infantry Fighting Vehicles, Reconnaissance Vehicles, Scout Vehicles, and Light Tanks, 1998 (Includes Scorpion, BMP-1, BMP-2, BMP-3, M-2)

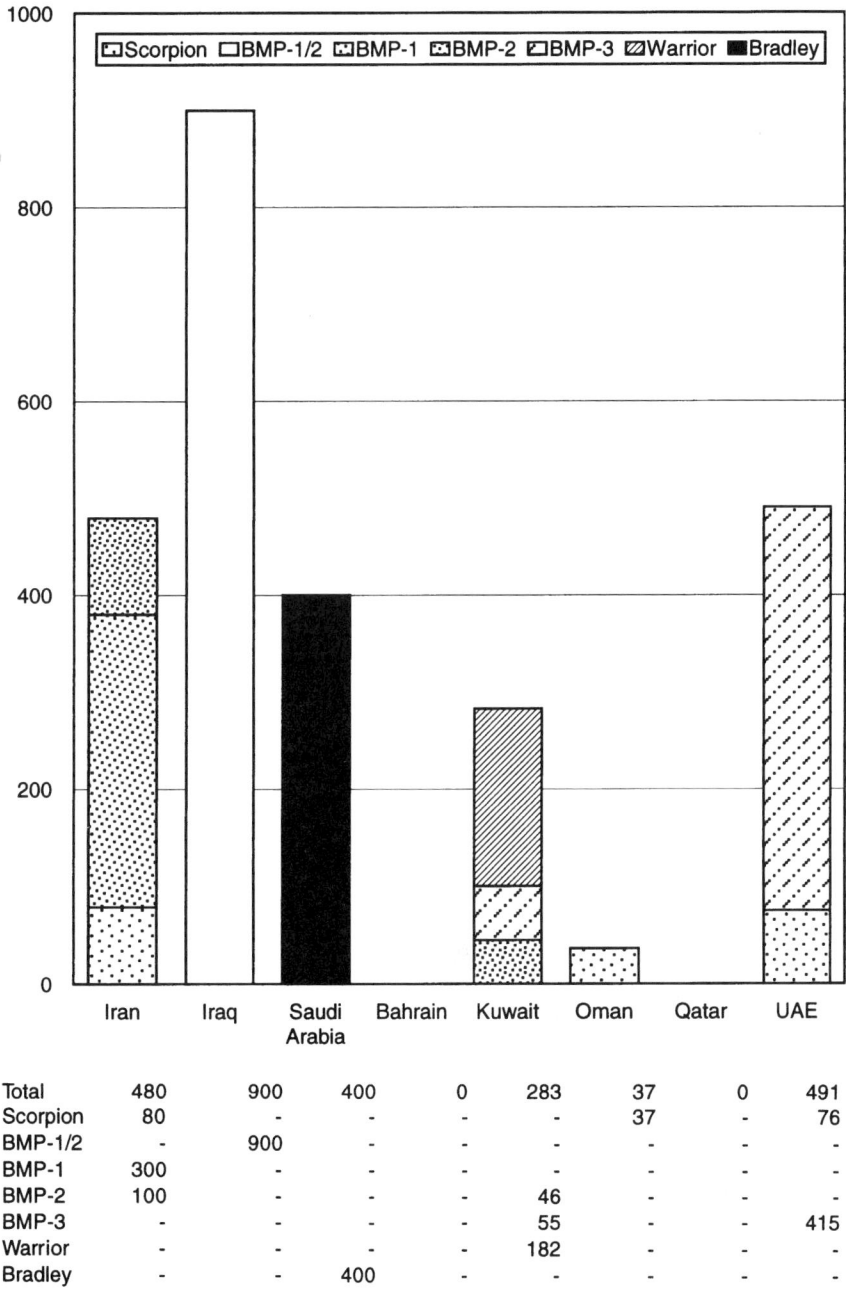

	Iran	Iraq	Saudi Arabia	Bahrain	Kuwait	Oman	Qatar	UAE
Total	480	900	400	0	283	37	0	491
Scorpion	80	-	-	-	-	37	-	76
BMP-1/2	-	900	-	-	-	-	-	-
BMP-1	300	-	-	-	-	-	-	-
BMP-2	100	-	-	-	46	-	-	-
BMP-3	-	-	-	-	55	-	-	415
Warrior	-	-	-	-	182	-	-	-
Bradley	-	-	400	-	-	-	-	-

Sources: Estimated by Anthony H. Cordesman from various sources, and IISS, *Military Balance*.

Figure 5.14
Armored Personnel Carriers (APCs) in Gulf Armies, 1998

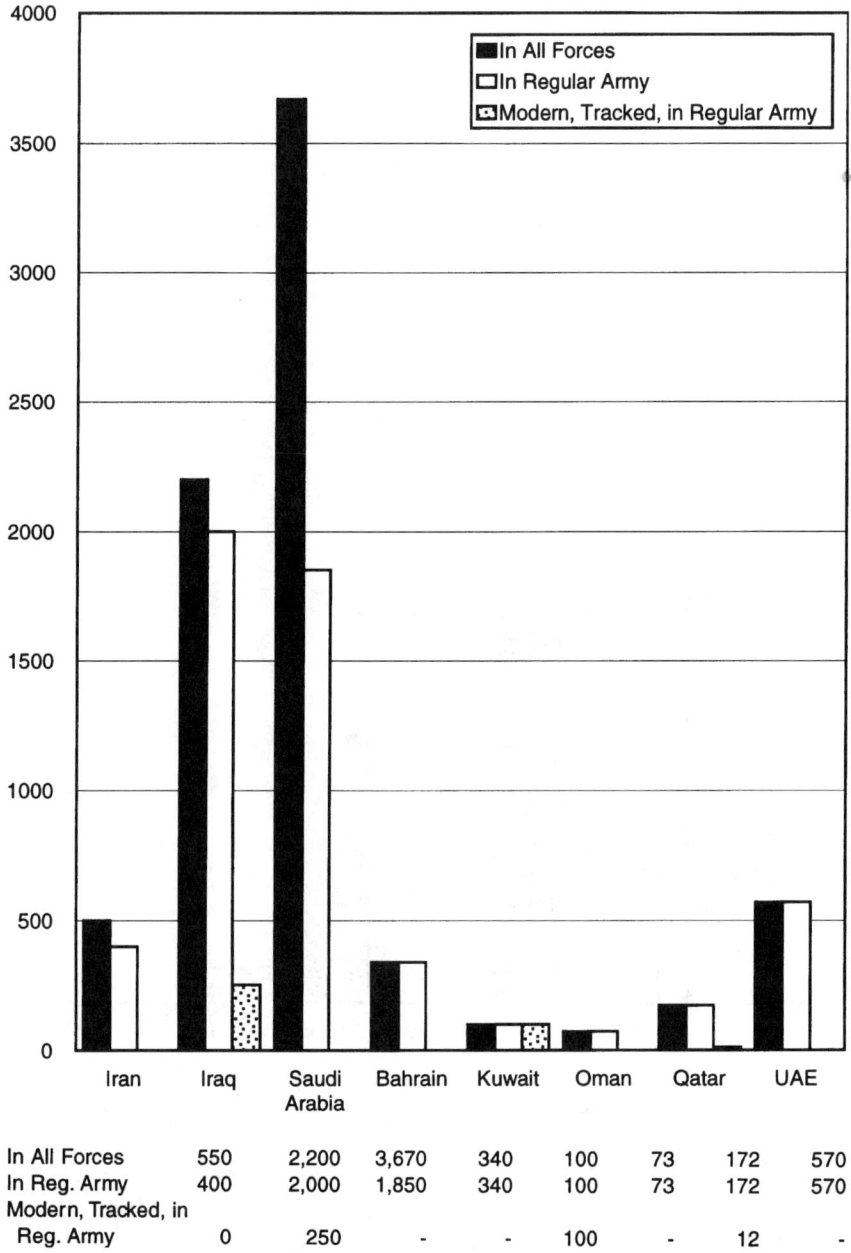

	Iran	Iraq	Saudi Arabia	Bahrain	Kuwait	Oman	Qatar	UAE
In All Forces	550	2,200	3,670	340	100	73	172	570
In Reg. Army	400	2,000	1,850	340	100	73	172	570
Modern, Tracked, in Reg. Army	0	250	-	-	100	-	12	-

Note: Iran includes active land forces in the Revolutionary Guards. Saudi Arabia includes active forces in the National Guard.
Sources: Estimated by Anthony H. Cordesman from various sources, and IISS, *Military Balance*.

Figure 5.15
Total Operational Self-Propelled and Towed Tube Artillery and Multiple Rocket Launchers in Gulf Forces, 1990 and 1998

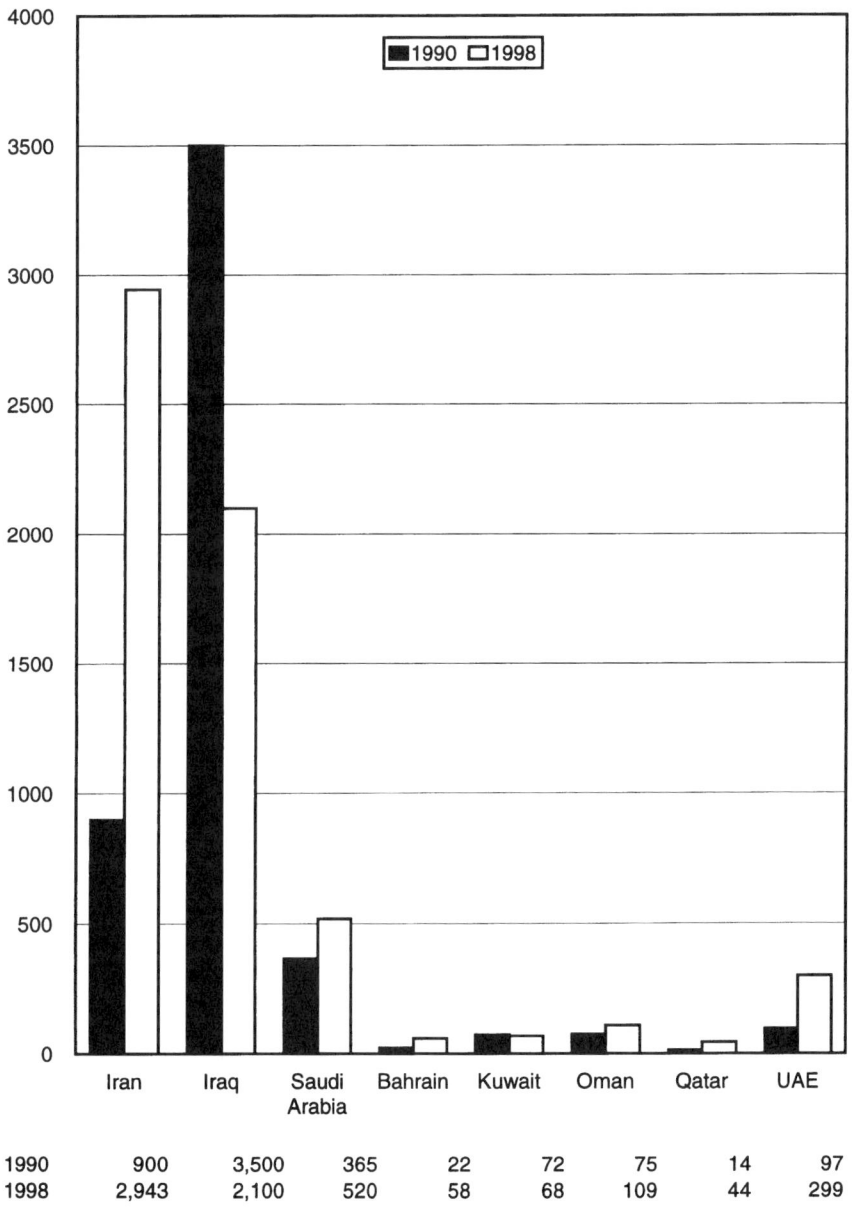

	Iran	Iraq	Saudi Arabia	Bahrain	Kuwait	Oman	Qatar	UAE
1990	900	3,500	365	22	72	75	14	97
1998	2,943	2,100	520	58	68	109	44	299

Note: Iran includes active forces in the Revolutionary Guards. Saudi Arabia includes active forces in the National Guard.

Sources: Adapted by Anthony H. Cordesman from various sources, and IISS, *Military Balance*.

Figure 5.16
Total Operational Gulf Artillery Weapons by Major Category, 1998

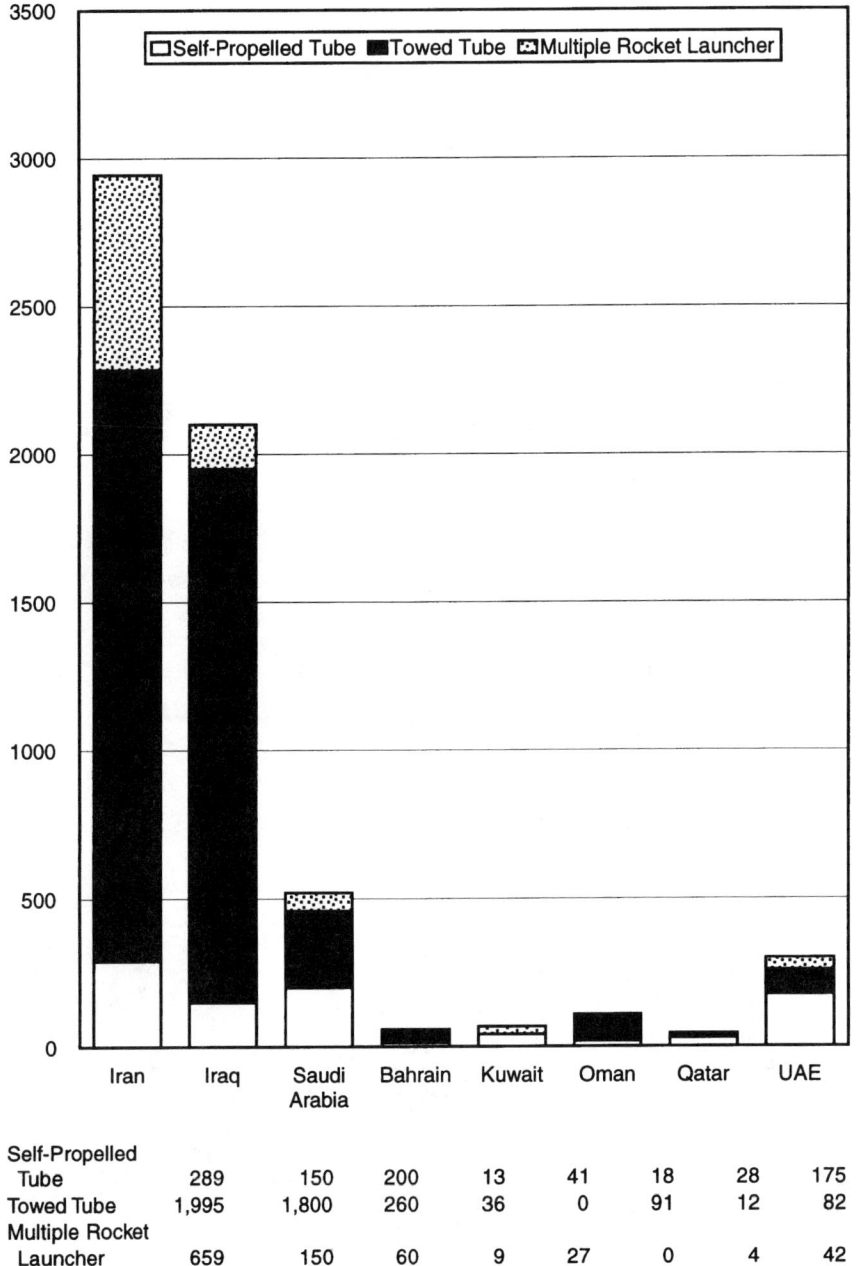

	Iran	Iraq	Saudi Arabia	Bahrain	Kuwait	Oman	Qatar	UAE
Self-Propelled Tube	289	150	200	13	41	18	28	175
Towed Tube	1,995	1,800	260	36	0	91	12	82
Multiple Rocket Launcher	659	150	60	9	27	0	4	42

Sources: Estimated by Anthony H. Cordesman from various sources, and IISS, *Military Balance*.

Figure 5.17
Gulf Tube Artillery Weapons in 1998

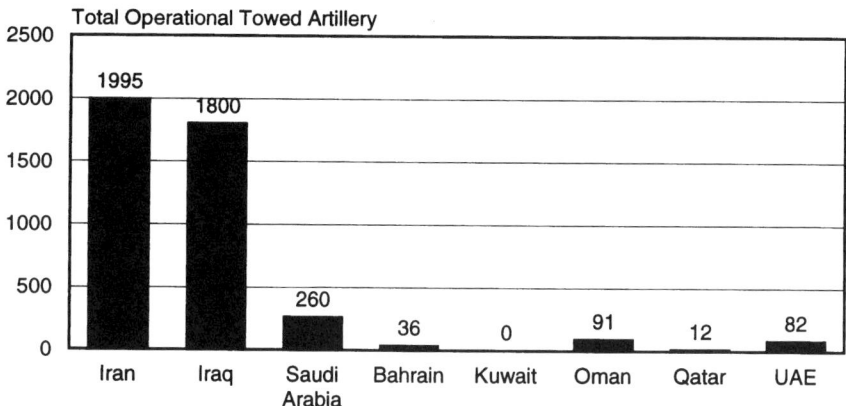

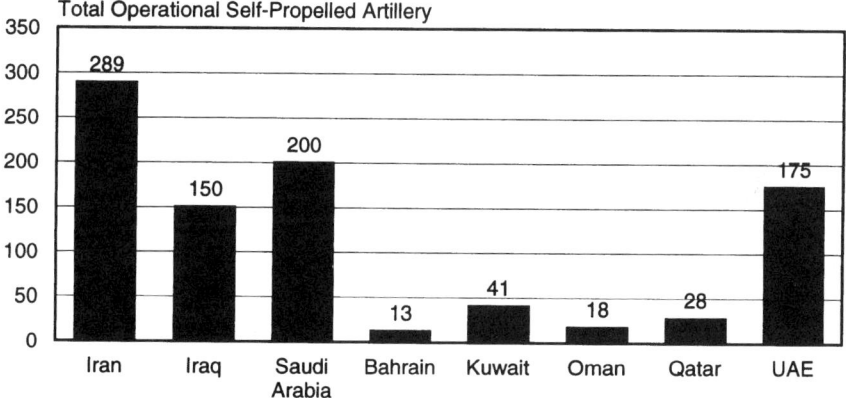

Sources: Estimated by Anthony H. Cordesman from various sources, and IISS, *Military Balance*.

does, however, have a poor history of field repairs for tanks, and of aggressively attempting to recover and repair tanks in battle.

Iraq's current doctrine and tactics for using tanks is unclear. In the past, Iraqi corps and division commanders often set personal standards for training and employing tanks, tailoring them to the specific battlefield conditions they encountered. This worked well during the Iran-Iraq War for selected, battle-experienced unit commanders who were given the time to withdraw from the front, retrain, and exert their own initiative. It also worked well when Iraq had the initiative against slow-moving, infantry-dominated Iranian forces and could attack using pre-planned and well-rehearsed attack plans against a relatively static and slow-reacting enemy. These techniques also compensated for Iraq's poor performance and readiness in combined arms and joint operations.

Figure 5.18
Total Operational Gulf Multiple Rocket Launchers, 1998

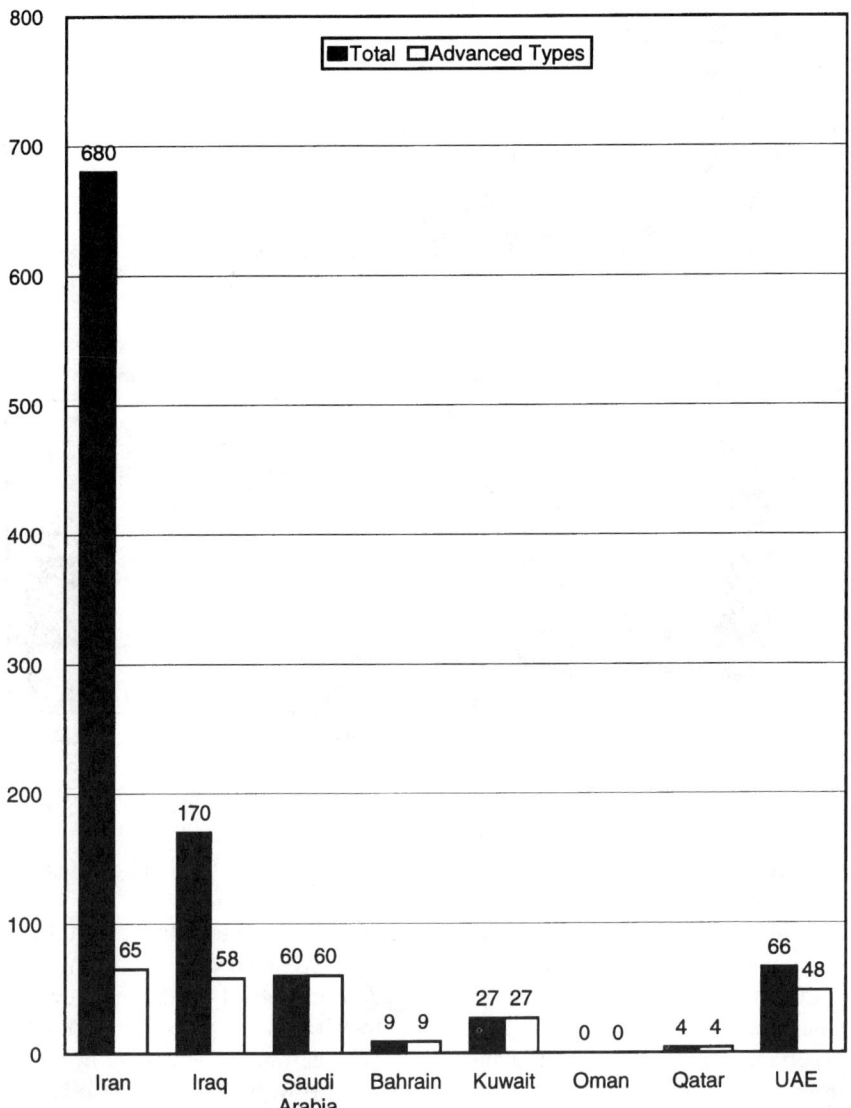

Sources: Estimated by Anthony H. Cordesman from various sources, and IISS, *Military Balance*.

Saddam seems to have felt threatened enough to remove some of his best unit and corps/sector commanders after the Iran-Iraq War, however, and downplayed the role of regular army Iraqi armored units in achieving Iraq's victories. This revealed the depth of the regime's concern with the fact that tanks would be the major weapon in a coup, and Saddam has not had a single year since the Gulf War in which some action by the Iraqi military has not reinforced this concern.

Iraqi armor was almost totally unprepared for the kind of AirLand battle and rapidly moving US Army forces it encountered during the Gulf War. Iraqi tanks showed little ability to deal with anti-tank weapons like the TOW during the battle of Khafji. Iraq was never able to commit most of its best regular army armored and mechanized tank units effectively to the defense of the forward area and then had to rush the surviving elements out of the Kuwait Theater of Operations.

The Republican Guard tank units also either retreated or attempted to fight from ambush without adequate forward scouting and combined arms support. They were almost totally unprepared for the M-1A1's ability to locate Iraqi tanks at long ranges and to fire effectively using nothing more than the "hot spot" on their thermal vision devices, or the threat posed by similar systems on the AH-64. Even when Iraqi tanks did encounter US Army units at shorter ranges, they were not able to engage rapidly enough to avoid massive losses or to inflict significant damage.

Iraq has made a number of claims to have improved the armor, fire control, and night vision capabilities of its tanks since the latter days of the Iran-Iraq War. A tour of the battlefield following the Gulf War revealed that some of these modifications had been deployed, including what seems to be crude reactive armor. There was little indication inside Iraqi tanks, however, that there had been any improvement in the fire control and night vision systems provided with the original tank.[48]

Similarly, there are no confirmed reports of the widespread deployment of such improvements since the Gulf War, even in the tanks held by the Republican Guards. Such improvements might make a difference, but would require a considerable engineering effort to solve the ergonomic problems involved. Older Soviet and Chinese tanks provide little operational work space for such modifications. Further, Iraq would have to radically change its training methods to adopt many of the techniques pioneered by the US Army at Fort Irwin and to give its unit commanders far more initiative. It is unclear that Saddam is able or willing to do this.

Other Fighting Vehicles

Experts estimated that Iraq had some 3,500 other armored vehicles in 1999.[49] Iraq had 1,600 armored reconnaissance and command vehicles (BDRM-2, EE-3, EE-9, AML-60, AML-90, MTLB) versus 2,500 before the war. It had 800–900 armored infantry fighting vehicles (BMP-1, BMP-2, and AMX-10P) versus 2,000 before the war, and 2,300 armored personnel carriers (BTR-50, BTR-60, BTR-152, OT-62, OT-64, MTLB, YW-531, M-113, M-3, EE-11) compared to approximately 7,100 before the war.[50]

The IISS estimates that Iraq retains some 900 BMP-1 and BMP-2 armored fighting infantry vehicles, plus an unknown number of BRDM-2, AML-60, AML-90, EE-9 Cascavel, and EE-3 Jararaca reconnaissance vehicles. It is estimated that Iraq still has about 2,000 armored personnel carriers, including BTR-50s, BTR-60s, BTR-152s, OT-62s, OT-64s, MTLBs, YW-532s, M-113A1s, M-113A2s, Panhard M-3s, and EE-11 Urutus.[51]

Regardless of their number, it is clear that Iraq faces a logistic and maintenance nightmare in supporting so many types of vehicles with such different firepower, mobility, and endurance. Many of these weapons are old or obsolete, and cannot keep up with tanks. Many are also deadlined due to lack of spares or have only limited operational capability. Furthermore, Iraq is forced to equip its heavy divisions with different mixes of armor, with different maneuver capabilities, and often with different training requirements for both the weapons crew and maintenance and support teams. It also has difficulties ensuring that its infantry can keep up with its tanks.

Iraq does, however, retain large numbers of special-purpose armored vehicles like command centers that it had bought during the Iran-Iraq War. Iraqi holdings were also so diverse that they presented major problems in terms of standardization and field repairs, and the different configuration and armament of Iraq's other armored vehicles presented problems in training and tactical operations. Iraq has reduced such problems in the past, however, by attempting to standardize the other armored vehicles in its best Republican Guards and regular army heavy divisions, and by conducting unit training tailored around the equipment holdings of a particular unit.[52]

Iraq's tactical doctrine for using other armored vehicles varies with the major combat unit using a given mix of equipment. Some heavy Republican Guards and regular army units use other armored vehicles much more effectively in supporting tanks than most of the Iraqi army. Iraq has generally overrelied on tanks, however, and has not used its other armored vehicles aggressively in scouting or combat support operations. The Iraqi forces in other armored vehicles often dismount to fight, and lack the training, equipment, and support to fight in their vehicles at night or at the long ranges made necessary by modern Western tanks and anti-tank weapons. Training and doctrine have evidently improved since the Gulf War, but are still best suited to defensive operations against relatively slow-moving mechanized infantry at short to moderate ranges.

Artillery and Multiple Rocket Launchers

Iraq's surviving artillery included about 1,900–2,005 major artillery weapons in 1999. These included 1,500–1,800 towed artillery weapons (105 mm, 122 mm, 130 mm, and 155 mm), and around 150 to 250 self-propelled artillery weapons (2S1 122 mm, 2S3 152 mm, M-109A/1/A2, and GCT AUF-1 155 mm). A significant number of these self-propelled weapons may not have been fully operational. These totals compare with Iraqi holdings of 3,000–5,000 towed weapons, and 500 self-propelled tube weapons before the war. In addition, Iraq had some 4,000–5,000 (60 mm, 81 mm, 120 mm, 160 mm) mortars.

The data on Iraq's holdings of multiple rocket launchers are too contradictory to make any estimate of wartime losses possible, although it is clear that many such weapons were destroyed or abandoned in the Kuwaiti Theater of Operations. However, it is clear that Iraq retains at least 120–140 such weapons (240 mm, 140 mm, Astros I, Astros II, BM-21, 122 mm), and may have over 270. Iraq also seems to retain many of its pre-war holdings of the FROG surface-to-surface rocket launchers, and at least several hundred rockets.[53]

Iraq had over 350 self-propelled mortars mounted on armored vehicles before the Gulf War. These do not seem to have been heavily committed to the Kuwaiti Theater of Operations, and Iraq probably still held several hundred after the conflict. Iraq also retained large numbers of 81 mm and 120 mm Soviet mortars. It has a total of over 2,000 towed and crew-portable mortars.

It is obvious from Iraq's artillery holdings that most units rely heavily on towed weapons, and that Iraq can only equip a few of its heavy combat units with the self-propelled artillery necessary to keep up with Iraqi tanks and Iraq's most modern other armored vehicles. Iraq has tried to solve these problems in the past by mixing tactics and artillery organization borrowed from France, Russia, and China, and tailoring the end result to a given front or campaign.

The end result, however, has rarely been impressive. Only a few Iraqi units have had the radars, training, and organization to allow them to conduct effective counter-battery fire. Targeting and observed fire is heavily dependent on forward observers and is often slow and unresponsive. The ability to use RPVs and other techniques to acquire targets beyond visual range is very limited, and artillery support of mobile Iraqi armored units has been consistently poor—even when the forward armored unit has called in targets and requested support.

Iraq has developed effective techniques for digging in towed weapons and massing tube and multiple rocket fire against slow moving targets like Iranian infantry. It has not, however, demonstrated the ability to quickly shift fires and deal with rapidly moving armored forces. Its towed artillery has been relatively slow-moving and has often been road bound, unless sufficient time existed to support rear areas. During the Iran-Iraq War, Iraqi artillery units usually needed extensive time to deploy large amounts of ammunition into prepared rear areas in order to maintain high rates of fire, and had to pre-survey the battlefield to mass artillery fire effectively. Iraq also relies very heavily on the "feed forward" of large amounts of ammunition, without prior request from the user unit, to make up for its slow-moving and unresponsive logistic and support system.

Iraqi self-propelled artillery units have often had problems extracting themselves from prepared positions and moving rapidly under defensive conditions. Field repair and recovery of artillery systems have been poor.

Anti-Tank Weapons

The Iraqi army lost large numbers of its anti-tank weapons during the fighting, many of which were recovered intact by the UN Coalition forces. Nevertheless, Iraq retained substantial anti-tank warfare capability. In 1999, its guided weapons included an unknown number of HOTs, AS-11s, and AS-12s mounted on PAH-1 and SA-342 helicopters and AT-2s mounted on Mi-8 and Mi-24 helicopters. It had Milan and HOT launchers mounted on VC-TH armored vehicles; Soviet AT-1, AT-3, AT-4 crew-portable anti-tank-guided missiles; and Milan manportable anti-tank guided missiles. It had several thousand 85 mm and 100 mm anti-tank guns and heavy recoilless rifles.

Iraq has rarely employed these weapons well. Even during the Iran-Iraq War, it tended to rely on tanks and massed artillery. During the Gulf War, it showed little understanding of the range at which modern Western armored can engage, the rate of advance and scale of maneuver of modern well-led armor, the impact of night and poor weather warfare in limiting crew-served weapons without night vision aids, the need to rapidly maneuver crew-served weapons rather than rely on static positions, and the need to conduct constant actual training firings of such equipment to develop and maintain proficiency. Iraq also was unprepared for the rapidly moving precision of Coalition artillery and the ability of helicopters and tanks to bypass prepared defenses using such weapons.

Anti-Aircraft Weapons

There are definitional problems in counting Iraq's surviving anti-aircraft guns because some estimates include machine guns, while others only include heavier weapons. Pre-war estimates put the total number of weapons, including machine guns, at around 7,000, and the number of heavier weapons at 4,000.

Iraq lost substantial numbers of self-propelled, anti-aircraft guns during the Gulf War, but it seemed to retain 300–500 heavy weapons, including some AMX-30 SAs, Egyptian-made guns and light missile launchers, and 150–200 radar-guided ZSU-23–4s. Iraq retained 4,000–5,000 other anti-aircraft guns—although many may not be operational or may be deployed as anti-infantry weapons. This gives it a total of approximately 5,500 weapons.

Post-war estimates do not provide many details on Iraqi army surface-to-air missile holdings, although they clearly included thousands of light- and medium-range surface-to-air missiles. These included SA-7, SA-8, SA-9, SA-13, SA-14, and SA-16 vehicle-mounted, crew-served, and manportable weapons, and perhaps 50–100 surviving Roland fire units on self-propelled armored vehicles. According to most estimates, Iraq retained at least 50–66% of its pre-war anti-aircraft weapons strength, or around 3,000 light surface-to-air missile launchers.

Iraq's holdings of such equipment, and its skill in deploying and using it, are of critical importance because of the ability of the US, British, and Saudi air forces to use electronic warfare, precision location systems, stand-off ordnance, stealth, and anti-radiation missiles to suppress Iraq's larger radar-guided, surface-to-air missiles. Iraqi army units did have some success in using systems like the SA-8 and shorter-range air defense missiles and "curtain fire" from anti-aircraft guns to force Coalition aircraft to operate at stand-off ranges during parts of the Gulf War. In general, however, Coalition helicopters took very limited damage and losses, and Iraqi crews rarely made effective use of the radars on their shorter-range air defense missiles because of the fear of being hit by Coalition aircraft.

Iraq would need much larger numbers of the most advanced short-range air defense systems to make a major change in this aspect of its capabilities. It would also need to change its training and acquisition and tracking equipment to emphasize the use of infrared and very short bursts of radar activity restricted to firing under optimal conditions to either break up attacks or hit aircraft after they delivered their munitions. It is unclear that such techniques would be highly effective in any case, but this would require a level of operations research, organization and training, and fire discipline that Iraq has not exhibited in the past.

Attack and Support Helicopters

Estimates of Iraqi helicopter strength are equally uncertain. In 1999, Iraqi army aviation seemed to possess about 120 armed helicopters out of the 159 it had before the war, in spite of some losses during Desert Fox. These included 20 PAH-1s (Bo-105s); attack helicopters with AS-11, AS-12 and HOT missiles, 30 Mi-24s and Mi-25s with AT-2 missiles, 40 SA-342s with AS-12s and HOTs, Allouettes with AS-11s and AS-12s, and 5 SA-321s with Exocet.

No reliable estimate exists of the number of surviving heavy, medium, and light transports and utility helicopters, but it seems likely that Iraq retained 200–300.[54] The IISS estimates that Iraq has roughly 350 transport helicopters, including Mi-6 heavy helicopters, AS-61, Bell 214ST, Mi-4, Mi-8, Mi-17, and SA-330 medium helicopters; and AB-212, BK-117. Hughes 300C, Hughes 500D, and Hughes 530F light helicopters.[55]

Iraq has not demonstrated the ability to use these assets effectively. During the Iran-Iraq War, it used Vietnam-era tactics without anything approaching the effectiveness of US Army operations. Its sortie rates were dismally low, and its reaction times very poor. Large-scale helicopter operations were poorly organized, often failed to exploit the potential tactical opportunity in time to be effective, and rarely pressed the attack home in the face of organized Iranian opposition.

Iraqi helicopter operations were most effective in the north, where they only faced limited air defenses. Even there, they were most effective against poorly armed Kurdish forces, Kurdish civilians, and Iranian infantry forces, and in exploiting terror tactics like the use of poison gas. Iraq never demonstrated the ability to conduct effective air assault operations or coherent long-range helicopter strikes against Iranian armored and mechanized forces.

Iraq acquired no experience in using its helicopters during the Gulf War, and its land forces showed that they were almost totally unprepared for US and French operations using helicopters, particularly the kind of long-range strikes made possible by the AH-64 and long-range air assault operations into Iraqi rear areas. Iraq has conducted some large-scale training exercises involving helicopters since the Gulf War, but it is unclear that it has corrected any of these defects, and it is unclear that it will ever solve them in as rigid and stratified a command system until helicopter operations are put under the command of the Iraqi army, and tactical control is devolved down to the Corps or front level.

Further, Iraq is operating a fleet with some 12 different types of helicopters with very different ages, technologies, and sources of spare parts. The sensor and weapons mix on Iraqi attack helicopters is now nearly 15 years old. Even those helicopters equipped with HOT lack the sensors and fire control systems to effectively use the missile without closing to ranges that make the helicopter vulnerable and then remaining in position for longer than is safe. Much of the potential battlefield limits the effectiveness of the kind of "pop up" tactics and exploitation of terrain masking routinely used by Western, Russian, and Israeli forces, and Iraq has not demonstrated the training and organizational capability to exploit such tactics on a time-sensitive basis or support them through the effective use of scout helicopters and forward observers. This makes advanced helicopter sensors, fire control systems, stand-off missile ranges, and "fire and forget" capabilities even more important.

LAND FORCE READINESS AND WAR-FIGHTING EFFECTIVENESS

Iraq's land forces still retain significant war-fighting capabilities. Iraq has refurbished many of its army weapons, vehicles, and equipment to the extent permitted by its industrial base and spare parts. It has created new tailored logistic organizations to try to improve its sustainment in the absence of military resupply. It has slowly improved the reorganization of its army, and in late 1995, it restored competent military professionals to a number of senior military positions.

Iraq's exercises during 1996–1998 showed that a number of units were improving and that the Iraqi army was still capable of intense exercise activity at the battalion, and sometimes the brigade, level.[56] According to USCENTCOM, many of Iraq's division and corps commanders were purged during 1995 and 1996 and replaced with more capable officers. USCENTCOM also indicates that Iraqi army company and battalion level training began to increase significantly during November–December, 1996.[57]

It can probably defeat any major Iranian attack and should be able to defeat the Iranian army in detail in the border area if given warning about a limited attack. Iraq has already shown that it has the military strength to overrun its Kurds in a matter of weeks if UN forces cease to protect them and Iraq's land forces have effectively defeated all serious Shi'ite resistance. Iraq can pose a threat to Syria, although with some logistical difficulties. Alternatively, it can deploy two to three divisions to Syria and/or Jordan in an Arab-Israeli conflict if it has Syrian or Jordanian host-country support.

Iraq's land forces can still seize Kuwait in a matter of days and/or occupy much of Saudi Arabia's Eastern province, *if* they do not face immediate and coordinated opposition from US, Kuwaiti, and Saudi forces. Kuwait is extremely vulnerable. Iraq has 23 active divisions compared to a total Kuwaiti force of only about four brigades, only two of which are active. The total forward-deployed US strength in the Gulf is 6,500–21,000 men—depending on the season of the year. The United States only has one brigade set of equipment prepositioned in Kuwait, however, and most of its personnel in the Gulf are in the air force, marines, and navy. The United States would have to rush in air power and follow-on ground forces to defend Kuwait, and much would depend on strategic warning and the speed of US reaction to that warning.

Nevertheless, the Iraqi army has severe limitations, and some of its capabilities continue to deteriorate. This deterioration is a product of basic weaknesses in its organization and structure, as well as a result of wartime losses, a postwar loss of imports, political turmoil, and the decline of the Iraqi economy. Iraq's growing readiness, sustainability, and deterioration problems have interacted with these inherent weaknesses to degrade Iraq's ability to conduct effective combined arms and mobile warfare.

As has been touched upon earlier, there are reports that indicate that Iraqi forces may face even more severe resource problems. There are reports that talk of uncertain loyalty and problems in calling up conscripts, desertions, and problems caused by drops in real military pay and fewer benefits in housing and other privileges. Other reports talk about cuts in the size and readiness of the regular army and drops in the activity levels of air units with older aircraft. The most critical of these reports come from opposition sources, however, and other reports indicate that the UN "oil-for-food" program is allowing the Iraqi government to divert other funds to the military and improve its wages and readiness.

Logistics, Sustainability, Interoperability, and Standardization

Like many other Middle Eastern armies, Iraq has armed with little regard to standardization and ease of supply, training, and maintenance. It has emphasized combat arms over service support, sustainability, and maintenance and has never developed an effective cadre of trained noncommissioned officers (NCOs) and technicians. Its officers have shown a striking reluctance to become involved in maintenance activity or the kind of close contact and physical effort necessary to lead troops in such functions, initiative was discouraged, and they were held responsible for losses and damage that resulted from their actions. Iraq has done little to remedy these problems as a result of the Gulf War. If anything, wartime casualties, morale problems, desertions, and pay problems have made the situation worse. Further, Iraq has consolidated much of its manpower and equipment into its combat arms beginning in 1994—steadily increasing the problems inherent in overemphasizing combat arms relative to support and sustainability.

Before the Gulf War, Iraq's logistic system relied on constant resupply and secure rear lines of communication as a substitute for effective maintenance, overhauls, and logistics—particularly at the Corps and division levels. It was dependent on continuing imports of a wide mix of equipment supplied by the former Soviet bloc, France, Italy, other European states, and Third World countries.

This supply of imports ceased in August, 1990, and the UN air offensive did massive damage to the Iraqi army's facilities and stockpiles. As a result, much of Iraq's equipment is now deadlined—or has limited operational effectiveness. Further, Iraq lost many of its logistic vehicles during the Gulf War, including many specialized vehicles and heavy lifters, and it has not been able to replace them. Iraq will find it much harder to sustain operations in the field, particularly in offensive operations, significant distances from its support facilities.

Major Readiness Problems

The human element has deteriorated in many ways. Many of Iraq's best armored and mechanized units were shattered in the fighting, including some of its heavy Republican Guards units. Iraq lost many officers and technicians, and the Iraqi forces have since been subject to recurrent purges and upheavals. It has also been seven years since the end of the Iran-Iraq War, and many combat veterans of the war have now left military service. There has been little large-scale unit training since 1991, and much of Iraq's army has either been kept in static deployments or has been involved in low-grade fighting against the poorly armed Shi'ites in the south.

The Republican Guards and best regular army units are still manned at levels averaging 80% of their authorized strength, and continue to have active field training. The Republican Guards have stayed in garrison more than the regular army units, and this allowed them time to train at the battalion and sometimes the brigade level. Even the Republican Guards, however, still had some manpower problems in early 1997, and had to accept more Shi'ites and promote non-Takritis to more senior positions. They also lost a substantial number of headquarters and barracks facilities in Desert Fox and took some losses in personnel.

Many Iraqi regular army units are now filled in with a mix of inexperienced troops and low-grade conscripts and reservists. Most of Iraq's regular army infantry divisions had only 50–75% of their authorized manning in late 1998. The Iraqi regular army has also been ground down by having to act as an occupation force, carry out low-level counter-insurgency operations, and remain in the field. There were problems with desertions, morale, and call-ups in 1995–1998, and Iraq has been forced to "exempt" its Kurds and some of its Shi'ites from military service for internal security reasons—depriving it of a substantial part of its manpower base. In spite of steady increases in the fee for exemption, a number of Iraqis also buy their way out of conscription.

Saddam Hussein has taken a number of measures designed to improve the loyalty of the armed forces. He has tried to increase salaries to compensate for inflation, and he has set up special stores which provide military personnel with better access to food and consumer goods. He has cut the period for conscription from 36 months to 18 for college graduates, and to four months for the holders of advanced degrees. He has revived special privileges for loyal officers like the car loans, land grants, housing benefits, and low-interest loans used to motivate officers during the Iran-Iraq War. He now allows automatic retirement after 25 years of service.[58] These measures, however, have failed to keep pace with inflation and offset the impact of sanctions. Military salaries and living conditions steadily deteriorated between late 1993 and Saddam's acceptance of the terms of UNSCR 986 in November, 1996—particularly in the regular army forces.

This combination of problems means at least one-third to one-half of the post–Gulf War Iraqi army order of battle consists of hollow forces that will take years to rebuild to the level of capability they had before the Gulf War. Although the "oil for food" deal made under the terms of UNSCR 986 should ease the food and medicine situation, the Iraqi army's equipment problems will continue to worsen until the UN sanctions are lifted.

The most critical mid-term limitation affecting the war-fighting capability of the Iraqi army is now the impact of the UN arms embargo. Iraq can work around some of its equipment problems, but it needs significant imports of spare parts to maintain its army and bring it back to pre–Gulf War readiness. It is also having progressively greater difficulty with "human factors." If the UN embargo continues to be effective, the Iraqi army will continue to lose force strength and war-fighting quality relative to Iran, the Southern Gulf states, and its other neighbors. It is almost impossible to predict the rate at which the Iraqi army will decline, but it is clear that Iraqi forces have already lost a significant amount of their combat effectiveness and sustainability.

Key Force Improvement Priorities

There is no way to predict the future of the Iraqi army, any more than it is possible to make more than near-term predictions about any other aspect of Iraq's military forces. Key variables include the future of UN sanctions, Iraq's access to foreign arms, the nature of Iraq's regime and political leadership, and Iraq's economic and budgetary priorities and the rate at which it can export oil. In addition, much depends on the priority Iraq gives to conventional forces relative to weapons of mass destruction, Iraq's relations with its neighbors, the pace and success in the military build-up in neighboring states, and the relative priority Iraq gives to using its land forces for internal security purposes, to dealing with local external threats, and to developing the kind of military capability necessary to challenge a US-led coalition. Other key uncertainties include the size of the US presence in the region, US and other Western power projection capabilities, the pressures on arms-exporting states to sell to Iraq, and the impact of external factors like the Arab-Israeli conflict.

There are certain basic limitations that must affect Iraq's military future. Once the UN sanctions and embargo are ended, Iraq will require a minimum of several years to modernize its ground forces in order to react to the lessons of the Gulf War. Iraq not only must rebuild its land forces, but it must make major changes in its equipment and technology if it is to compete with the force improvements being made by its neighbors. For example, Iraq needs to upgrade most of its armor, up-gun its older tanks, and use improved tank rounds. Most of its tanks need modern fire control systems, armor, night and thermal vision devices, and need guns and ammunition equal to those in the forces of Saudi Arabia.

If the Iraqi army is to compete directly with Western or Israeli land forces, it must do far more. It must solve its many qualitative defects and convert from the relatively static defensive force that lost the Gulf War to become a force that can match the kind of highly mobile, firepower intensive, maneuver-oriented, 24-hour-a-day force the Coalition deployed during Desert Storm. This is a far more demanding challenge than acquiring spare parts or more modern equipment.

Iraq must greatly improve the long-range sustainability of its forces in maneuver operations and its battlefield recovery and repair capabilities. It must make sweeping improvements in its night and poor weather warfare capabilities, and its ability to rapidly move artillery, mass and shift fires. It must restructure its entire artillery operation to emphasize combined arms and maneuver, precision fire and the ability to shift targets rapidly. Further, it needs to acquire beyond-visual-range and night-targeting systems.

It must restructure its communications, command, control, battle management, and training to support fluid maneuver operations, and a much faster tempo of sustained "24-hour-a-day" operations. This means re-equipping or modifying the fire control, sensors, and communications systems in much of its armor, providing new support and battle management capabilities, retraining the force at the Corps level, and giving officers far more independence of action. Iraq will have to make fundamental changes in tactics and training and acquire advanced training and simulation technology.

The Iraqi army must stress joint operations as well as combined arms. It must greatly improve its helicopter operations, which have been largely ineffective, except in small, independent operations. Maneuver forces must train realistically with helicopters and fixed-wing aircraft. Training must become far more effective above the battalion level, and modern targeting and reconnaissance capabilities must be integrated into its corps, division, and brigade-level operations.

It will need improved mobile short-range air defenses and manportable surface-to-air missiles, tank transporters, secure communications, modern fire control systems, tracked support equipment, and self-propelled artillery.

The Iraqi army must also convert from a politically oriented to a fully professional force. Iraq has many competent officers and force elements by regional standards. However, Saddam Hussein and the Ba'ath still interfere constantly with organizational matters, exercises, training, promotions, and equipment and supply matters. This interference sometimes extends down to the battalion (major and lieutenant colonel) level. Senior commanders still face the constant threat of removal or even execution for the normal failures of war and for petty political reasons. Domestic political considerations and ruthless efforts to ensure the loyalty of all officers to the regime often lead to the promotion of the politically loyal over the professionally competent. In many ways, Saddam Hussein and the Ba'ath elite have been as great a threat to the Iraqi army as Iran and the UN Coalition.

NEAR-TERM TRENDS AND IMPLICATIONS FOR CONTAINMENT AND DETERRENCE

The trends in Iraqi land forces are another clear warning against any policy that lifts sanctions without retaining some sort of controls over how Iraq uses its revenues and without a firm commitment to military containment. These trends also argue for efforts to place strong, long-term limits on Iraq's ability to import modern main battle tanks and the equipment it needs to react to the lessons of the Gulf War. In spite of the deterioration of its land forces, Iraq has no reason to fear a near- or mid-term invasion by Iran. In contrast, Kuwait and Saudi Arabia have good reason to fear that a revitalized Iraqi army will be used to threaten them, or to take new military action against Kuwait.

NOTES

1. A wide range of sources are used in this section and in the following sections on air and naval forces. Most are footnoted by individual source, but major sources also include various editions of the IISS, *Military Balance*, and the Jane's *Sentinel* series; Andrew Rathmell, *The Changing Balance in the Gulf*, London, Royal United Services Institute, Whitehall Papers 38, 1996; Edward B. Atkenson, *The Powder Keg*, Falls Church, NOVA Publications, 1996; Geoffery Kemp and Robert E. Harkavy, *Strategic Geography and the Changing Middle East*, Washington, Carnegie Endowment/Brookings, 1997; and Michael Eisenstadt. *Like a Phoenix from the Ashes? The Future of Iraqi Military Power*, Washington, The Washington Institute, Policy Paper 36, 1993.

2. US Department of Defense, *The Conduct of the Persian Gulf War: Final Report*, Washington, Department of Defense, April, 1992, p. 411.

3. US Department of Defense, *The Conduct of the Persian Gulf War: Final Report*, Washington, Department of Defense, April, 1992, p. 355.

4. US Department of Defense, *The Conduct of the Persian Gulf War: Final Report*,

Washington, Department of Defense, April, 1992, p. 355; Dr. Eliot A. Cohen, draft text of executive summary of *Gulf War Air Power Study*, April 28, 1993, p. 43. Losses include withdrawals and some systems temporarily inoperable. Total losses actually killed or captured are estimated to be 76% of tanks, 55% of APCs, and 90% of artillery. Republican Guards units, however, only lost 50% in these categories.

5. Michael R. Gordon and General Bernard E. Trainor, *The General's War: The Inside Story of the Conflict in the Gulf*, Boston, Little, Brown, 1994, pp. 429–439.

6. *Washington Post*, November 7, 1991, p. A-46, November 14, 1991, p. A-47; *Wall Street Journal*, November 11, 1991, p. A-10; *Jane's Defense Weekly*, November 16, 1991, p. 926, July 13, 1991, p. 61; *The Estimate*, November 22–December 5, 1991, p. 1; *New York Times*, November 7, 1991, p. 3; *Los Angeles Times*, November 14, 1991, p. 4; Michael Eisenstadt, "Recent Changes in Saddam's Inner Circle: Cracks in the Wall?" *Policywatch*, No. 22, November 22, 1991, pp. 1–2; *Baltimore Sun*, June 21, 1991, p. 7.

7. General H. Norman Schwarzkopf, *It Doesn't Take a Hero* (New York: Bantam Books, 1992), pp. 488–489.

8. *Washington Post*, July 16, 1991, p. 14, November 7, 1991, p. A-46, November 14, 1991, p. A-47; *Wall Street Journal*, November 11, 1991, p. A-10; *Jane's Defense Weekly*, November 16, 1991, p. 926, July 13, 1991, p. 61; *The Estimate*, November 22–December 5, 1991, p. 1; *New York Times*, November 7, 1991, p. 3; *Los Angeles Times*, November 14, 1991, p. 4; Michael Eisenstadt, "Recent Changes in Saddam's Inner Circle: Cracks in the Wall?" *Policywatch*, No. 22, November 22, 1991, pp. 1–2; *Baltimore Sun*, June 21, 1991, p. 7; (London) *Daily Telegraph*, July 11, 1991, p. 9; *London Times*, October 4, 1991, p. 12; *Washington Times*, September 4, 1991, p. A7.

9. *New York Times*, August 8, 1991, p. A-12.

10. Based on interviews.

11. Estimate provided by USCENTCOM in June, 1996, plus US Central Command, *Atlas, 1996*, MacDill Air Force Base, USCENTCOM, 1997, pp. 16–18. Also based on interviews.

12. Estimate provided by USCENTCOM in June, 1996, plus US Central Command, *Atlas, 1996*, MacDill Air Force Base, USCENTCOM, 1997, pp. 16–18. Also based on interviews.

13. USCENTCOM briefing by "senior military official," Pentagon, January 28, 1997, pp. 2, 5–8, 10; *Washington Times*, February 1, 1997, p. A-13; Reuters, September 4, 1996, 0911; Jane's *Pointer*, November, 1994, p. 2; Associated Press, September 9, 1996, 0129; *Washington Times*, January 30, 1997, p. A-3; February 1, 1997, p. A-13.

14. USCENTCOM briefing by "senior military official," Pentagon, January 28, 1997, pp. 2, 5–8, 10; *Washington Times*, February 1, 1997, p. A-13; Reuters, September 4, 1996, 0911; Jane's *Pointer*, November, 1994, p. 2; Associated Press, September 9, 1996, 0129; *Washington Times*, January 30, 1997, p. A-3; February 1, 1997, p. A-13.

15. USCENTCOM briefing by "senior military official," Pentagon, January 28, 1997, pp. 2, 5–8, 10; *Washington Times*, February 1, 1997, p. A-13; Reuters, September 4, 1996, 0911; Jane's *Pointer*, November, 1994, p. 2; Associated Press, September 9, 1996, 0129; *Washington Times*, January 30, 1997, p. A-3; February 1, 1997, p. A-13.

16. IISS, *The Military Balance, 1997–1998*, pp. 127–128.

17. In addition to the sources listed at the start of the Iraq section, the author has drawn on interviews with various US and foreign experts in 1993, 1994, 1995, 1996, and 1997. The current estimates also draw on various editions of IISS, *The Military Balance*; USNI Data Base; *Military Technology, World Defense Almanac: The Balance*

of Military Power; Kenneth Katzman, "Iraq: Future Policy Options," Congressional Research Service, CRS 91–596F, December 12, 1991, pp. 23–30; Michael Eisenstadt, "The Iraqi Armed Forces Two Years On," *Jane's Intelligence Review*, March, 1993, pp. 121–127, *Jane's Sentinel: The Gulf States*, "Iraq," London, Jane's Publishing, 1997; RUSI Working Notes; Andrew Rathmell, *The Changing Balance in the Gulf*, London, Royal United Services Institute, Whitehall Papers 38, 1996; Edward B. Atkenson, *The Powder Keg*, Falls Church, NOVA Publications, 1996; Geoffery Kemp and Robert E. Harkavy, *Strategic Geography and the Changing Middle East*, Washington, Carnegie Endowment/Brookings, 1997; and Michael Eisenstadt, *Like a Phoenix from the Ashes? The Future of Iraqi Military Power*, Washington, The Washington Institute, Policy Paper 36, 1993.

18. Sean Boyne, "Qusay Considers a Reshuffle for Iraq's Command Structure," *Jane's Intelligence Review*, September, 1997, pp. 416–417.

19. Sean Boyne, "Qusay Considers a Reshuffle for Iraq's Command Structure," *Jane's Intelligence Review*, September, 1997, pp. 416–417.

20. *Jane's Pointer*, May, 1998, p. 6.

21. Sean Boyne, "Qusay Considers a Reshuffle for Iraq's Command Structure," *Jane's Intelligence Review*, September, 1997, pp. 416–417.

22. The author repeatedly encountered these problems during his visits to Iraqi units during the Iran-Iraq War, and during a tour of the Iraqi positions along the coast of Kuwait, the Kuwait-Saudi border, and the Iraqi-Saudi border after the Gulf War.

23. Sean Boyne, "Qusay Considers a Reshuffle for Iraq's Command Structure," *Jane's Intelligence Review*, September, 1997, pp. 416–417.

24. See the detailed history of the attack on Republican Guards units and the resulting losses by name in the US Department of Defense, *The Conduct of the Persian Gulf War: Final Report*, Washington, Department of Defense, April, 1992, pp. 93–95, 104–113, 355, 401. Also references in the April 15, 1993, draft of the *US Air Force Gulf War Air Power Survey*, pp. 9–10.

25. The author has drawn on interviews with various US and foreign experts; USCENTCOM briefing by "senior military official," Pentagon, January 28, 1997, pp. 2, 5–8, 10; *Washington Times*, February 1, 1997, p. A-13; Reuters, September 4, 1996, 0911; *Jane's Pointer*, November, 1994, p. 2; Associated Press, September 9, 1996, 0129; *Washington Times*, January 30, 1997, p. A-3; February 1, 1997, p. A-13.

26. *Jane's Pointer*, May, 1998, p. 6.

27. Sean Boyne, "Inside Iraq's Security Network," *Jane's Intelligence Review*, July, 1997, pp. 312–316, and August, 1997, pp. 365–367.

28. Sean Boyne, "Qusay Considers a Reshuffle for Iraq's Command Structure," *Jane's Intelligence Review*, September, 1997, pp. 416–417; Sean Boyne, "Inside Iraq's Security Network," *Jane's Intelligence Review*, July, 1997, pp. 312–316, and August, 1997, pp. 365–367.

29. Sean Boyne, "Qusay Considers a Reshuffle for Iraq's Command Structure," *Jane's Intelligence Review*, September, 1997, pp. 416–417; Sean Boyne, "Inside Iraq's Security Network," *Jane's Intelligence Review*, July, 1997, pp. 312–316, and August, 1997, pp. 365–367.

30. Most estimates now indicate a strength of one Special Republican Guards division. Some experts feel that there are two division equivalents.

31. USCENTCOM map, June, 1996; USCENTCOM briefing by "senior military official," Pentagon, January 28, 1997.

32. Alfred Prados and Kenneth Katzman, "Iraq: Attack on Kurdish Enclave and US Response," Congressional Research Service, 96–739, October 17, 1996; Carol Migdalovitz, "Turkey's Military Offensive in Northern Iraq," Library of Congress, 95–487F, April 13, 1995.

33. Sean Boyne, "Qusay Considers a Reshuffle for Iraq's Command Structure," *Jane's Intelligence Review*, September, 1997, pp. 416–417.

34. Carol Migdalovitz, "Turkey's Military Offensive in Northern Iraq," Library of Congress, 95–487F, April 13, 1995; FBIS-WEU-95–061, March 30, 1995, p. 29; *Washington Post*, April 2, 1995, p. A-29; *Financial Times*, March 23, 1995, p. 2; *Christian Science Monitor*, April 3, 1995, p. 18; *Middle East Report*, July–August, 1994, p. 14.

35. Sean Boyne, "Inside Iraq's Security Network," *Jane's Intelligence Review*, July, 1997, pp. 312–316, and August, 1997, pp. 365–367.

36. Associated Press. Ankara, NY, October 22, 1997, 0722 EDT; Reuters, September 27, 1997, 1430; *Khaleej Times*, October 27, 1997; *Baltimore Sun*, October 24, 1997, p. 9A; *Washington Post*, October 25, 1997, p. A-13; *Jane's Defense Weekly*, October 29, 1997, p. 5.

37. USCENTCOM map, June, 1996; USCENTCOM briefing by "senior military official," Pentagon, January 28, 1997, pp. 2, 5–8, 10.

38. Based on US State Department, Country Chapters on Human Rights, Iraq, Internet edition, US State Department on-line database, accessed August 26, 1995, and February 7, 1997, and Amnesty International, Report 1994, and other material.

39. Based on US State Department, Country Chapters on Human Rights, Iraq, Internet edition, US State Department on-line database, accessed August 26, 1995, March 16, 1996, and February 7, 1997; and Amnesty International, Report 1994, and other material.

40. Based on US State Department, Country Chapters on Human Rights, Iraq, Internet edition, US State Department on-line database, accessed August 26, 1995, March 16, 1996, and February 7, 1997; and Amnesty International, Report 1994, and other material.

41. Based on US State Department, Country Chapters on Human Rights, Iraq, Internet edition, US State Department on-line database, accessed August 26, 1995, March 16, 1996, and February 7, 1997; and Amnesty International, Report 1994, and other material.

42. Interviews, Sean Boyne, "Inside Iraq's Security Network," *Jane's Intelligence Review*, July, 1997, pp. 312–316, and August, 1997, pp. 365–367.

43. Interviews, Sean Boyne, "Inside Iraq's Security Network," *Jane's Intelligence Review*, July, 1997, pp. 312–316, and August, 1997, pp. 365–367.

44. *New York Times*, October 8, 1997, p. A-6; *Philadelphia Inquirer*, September 30, 1997, p. A-17; Reuters, September 27, 1997, 0244.

45. USCENTCOM map, June, 1996; USCENTCOM briefing by "senior military official," Pentagon, January 28, 1997, pp. 2, 5–8, 10; USCENTCOM, *Atlas, 1996*, MacDill Air Force Base, USCENTCOM, 1997, pp. 16–17; *Washington Times*, February 1, 1997, p. A-13; Reuters, September 4, 1996, 0911; Jane's *Pointer*, November, 1994, p. 2; Associated Press, September 9, 1996, 0129; *Washington Times*, January 30, 1997, p. A-3; February 1, 1997, p. A-13.

46. IISS, *The Military Balance, 1997–1998*, pp. 127–128.

47. These estimates are based primarily on interviews with various experts, and USCENTCOM briefing by "senior military official," Pentagon, January 28, 1997, pp. 2, 5–8, 10; *Washington Times*, February 1, 1997, p. A-13; Reuters, September 4, 1996, 0911; Jane's *Pointer*, November, 1994, p. 2; Associated Press, September 9, 1996, 0129; *Wash-*

ington Times, January 30, 1997, p. A-3; February 1, 1997, p. A-13. The 1996/1997 IISS data show 2,700 tanks.

48. The author toured the battlefield extensively immediately after the cease-fire in 1991.

49. Discussions with US experts and USCENTCOM, *Atlas, 1996*, MacDill Air Force Base, USCENTCOM, 1997, pp. 16–17.

50. A few experts estimate that Iraq only has about 2,000–2,300 fully operational other armored vehicles. Additional sources include interviews in the United States, London, Switzerland, and Israel.

51. IISS, *The Military Balance, 1997–1988*, pp. 127–128. The IISS estimated 4,200 OAFVs, including 1,500 BTR-50, BTR-60, AML-60, AML-90, EE-9, and EE-3 reconnaissance vehicles; 700 BMP-1 and BMP-2 armored fighting vehicles; and 2,000 BTR-50, BTR-60, BTR-152, OT-62, OT-64, MTLB, YW-531, M-113A1/A2, Panhard M-3, and EE-11 armored personnel carriers in 1993. It later revised this estimate to only provide a partial count in 1996–1997, with 900 BMPs and 2,000 APCs.

52. The author observed these techniques on several occasions during visits to the Iraqi front and rear areas during the Iran-Iraq War.

53. These estimates are based primarily on interviews with various experts, and USCENTCOM briefing by "senior military official," Pentagon, January 28, 1997, pp. 2, 5–8, 10; *Washington Times*, February 1, 1997, p. A-13; Reuters, September 4, 1996, 0911; Jane's *Pointer*, November, 1994, p. 2; Associated Press, September 9, 1996, 0129; *Washington Times*, January 30, 1997, p. A-3; February 1, 1997, p. A-13.

54. Some estimates go as high as 500. It is doubtful that this many are operational and/or armed.

55. IISS, *The Military Balance, 1997–1998*, pp. 127–128.

56. USCENTCOM briefing by "senior military official," Pentagon, January 28, 1997.

57. USCENTCOM briefing by "senior military official, Pentagon, January 28, 1997, pp. 2, 5–8, 10; *Washington Times*, February 1, 1997, p. A-13; Reuters, September 4, 1996, 0911; Jane's *Pointer*, November 1994, p. 2; Associated Press, September 9, 1996, 0129; *Washington Times*, January 30, 1997, p. A-3; February 1, 1997, p. A-13.

58. Many of the details in this analysis are based on discussions with Amatzia Baram.

Chapter 6

The Threat from Iraqi Air and Air Defense Forces

The Iraqi air force has never been able to match the effectiveness of the Iraqi land forces. It developed some effective elements during the Iran-Iraq War, but it was never able to fully exploit its offensive capabilities in spite of the growing weakness of the Iranian air force. It could not approach the effectiveness of the US and Saudi air forces in air-to-air combat during the Gulf War. It played virtually no offensive role, and it suffered major losses from Coalition attacks on Iraqi air bases and facilities and because Iran confiscated the Iraqi aircraft that flew from Iraq to Iran in an effort to find sanctuary from Coalition attacks.

Iraq has slowly rebuilt its air force since the Gulf War, but it has done little to improve the war-fighting effectiveness of its remaining air units, modernize its forces, or improve its training and organization. The air force is still headquartered at Bab-al Mudham in Baghdad. Its headquarters are organized by branch—operations, personnel, training, logistics, and air defense. The air force has regional commands for air defense, which roughly match the command structure of the land-based air defense forces, and garrisons at Baghdad, Mosul, and Talil. It also has regimental and base commands, although little unclassified data are available on the details of this command structure.

In early 1999, the Iraqi Air Force had a total of roughly 35,000–40,000 men, including some 15,000–17,000 air defense personnel.[1] Iraq had been able to rebuild many of the shelters and facilities it lost during the war, and much of the Air Force C^4I/BM system. This C^4I/BM system included an extensive network of optical fiber communications, a TFH 647 radio relay system, a TFH tropospheric communications system, and a large mix of radars supplied by the Soviet Union. Iraq has rebuilt most of the air bases damaged during the Gulf War, and its bases received only very limited damage during Desert Fox. This leaves Iraq with a network of some 25 major operating bases, many with extensive shelters and hardened facilities.[2]

Iraq has not, however, been able to import any new combat aircraft, support and C^{4}I aircraft, advanced air munitions, surface-to-air missiles, major radars and sensors, or advanced C^{4}I/BM equipment since the Gulf War. Its basic technology remains frozen at the level it had achieved in 1990. Iraq's efforts to smuggle in air munitions and C^{4}I/BM equipment had had very limited success. With the exception of some short-range air-to-air missiles, it had not be able to import any of the major new technology it needed in order to react to the lessons of the Gulf War.

US experts believe that the Iraqi air force still had 330 to 370 combat aircraft in inventory, although many of the Iraqi aircraft counted in this total had limited or no operational combat capability. The IISS estimates that Iraq had at least 316 combat aircraft, including six bombers, 130 fighter-ground attack aircraft, and 180 fighters.

The Iraqi air force continues to suffer from the damage inflicted during the Gulf War, and from the impact of nearly a decade of operations without major imports of parts and equipment and foreign technical support. Only about 55% of its fixed wing aircraft are fully serviceable, and helicopter serviceability is poor. While Iraq seemed to have improved its access to smuggled spare parts during some point in 1996–1998, these spares seem to be largely for its Soviet aircraft, and not for its French-made designs.[3]

Although the Iraqi air force occasionally surged to peaks of over 100 sorties per day during 1996–1998, the creation and expansion of the Coalition "no-fly" zones in northern and southern Iraq restricted an already inadequate training program. Iraqi pilots only flew about 60 hours a year versus the 180–250 hours considered normal in advanced air forces. Training sorties generally involved low-grade training aircraft and older Soviet fighters. The Iraqi air force exhibited few signs of being able to react to the lessons learned during the Gulf War. Further, the participation of some air force officers in coup attempts has led Saddam to carefully monitor and control the resources given to the Iraqi air force.[4]

THE COST OF THE GULF WAR TO THE IRAQI AIR FORCE

As is the case with Iraq's land forces, Iraq's losses during the Gulf War have shaped much of the current size and capability of the Iraqi air force. While there are significant differences in unclassified US estimates of Iraqi losses, Table 6.1 shows a USAF and US Marine Corps estimate of Iraqi wartime losses. In addition, the Iranian government seized many of the Iraqi aircraft that flew to Iran. The Iranian government announced in late July, 1992 that it would expropriate the Iraqi combat aircraft that had taken refuge in Iran during the war, which were worth several billion dollars.

Table 6.1
Iraqi Air Strength in Desert Storm and Iraqi Combat Aircraft Losses in Desert Storm

Element of Force Strength	August 1, 1990	January 1, 1991	February 1, 1991	April 1, 1991
Air Force				
Personnel	18,000	18,000	18,000	18,000
Fighters/fighter bombers	718	728	699	362
Bombers	15	15	9	7
Reconnaissance	12	12	12	0
Subtotal	745	755	720	369
Combat capable trainers	370	400	400	252
Total	1,115	1,155	1,120	621
Helicopters	517	511	511	481
Transports	76	70	70	41
Civil transports	59	60	60	42
Air Defense Force				
Personnel	17,000	17,000	17,000	17,000
Surface-to-air missile batteries	120	120	200	85
Anti-aircraft guns	7,500	7,600	7,600	5,850

Iraqi Combat Aircraft Losses in Desert Storm

Aircraft Types	Number on January 12, 1991	Lost in Air Combat	Total Destroyed	Fled to Iran	Remaining on March 1, 1991
Mirage F-1	75	8	10	30	35
Su-24 Fencer	25	0	2	14	9
MiG-29 Fulcrum	41	5	9	7	25
Su-7/17/20/22 Fitter	119	5	14	34	71
MiG-25 Foxbat	33	2	8	0	25
Su-25 Frogfoot	61	2	4	7	50
MiG-23 Flogger	123	8	17	10	96
MiG 21 Fishbed	208	4	16	0	192
TOTAL	685	34	80	102	503

Sources: Adapted by the author from Lt. General Walter E. Boomer, "Desert Storm, MARCENT Operations in the Campaign to Liberate Kuwait," US Marine Corps Headquarters, August 31, 1991; and Eliot Cohen, Director, *Gulf War Air Power Survey, Volume V, Part I*, pp. 17–19 and 653–654.

In 1992, Iraqi Prime Minister Muhammed Hamzah al-Zubayed described this Iranian seizure as part of a plot by Iran that had begun before the Gulf War. He stated,

We realize that all this (Iranian) enthusiasm and readiness to fulfill our demands (before the war)—followed by a chapter of treason and treachery by Iranian elements—was part of a prepared plan. Thus, all that plundering, burning, and destruction within the chapter of treason and treachery took place.[5]

There are different estimates of how many aircraft of a given type went to Iran. Iran's Foreign Minister, Ali Akbar Velayati, said in November, 1995 that Iran would only give back 22 aircraft once sanctions were lifted—all of which seemed to be civilian airliners and transports. The Iraqi government has referred to 115 combat aircraft and 33 airliners, worth some $3 billion.[6] The author's estimate, based on conversations with various experts, is: 24 Mirage F-1s, 20 Su-24s, 40 Su-22s, 4 Su-17/20s, 7 Su-25s, 4 MiG-29s, 7 MiG-23Ls, 4 MiG-23BNs, 1 MiG-23U, and 1 Adnan. This is a total of 112 combat aircraft. Further, some of Iraq's best-trained aircrews flew these aircraft to Iran, and have been held in Iran ever since.

If Iraq's combat losses are combined with its losses to Iran, the resulting estimates indicate that the Iraqi air force retained approximately 330 to 370 combat aircraft in combat units. At the same time, about half of the Iraqi aircraft counted in this total were probably damaged or now lack spare parts. This means that about half of the Iraqi air force's total inventory of combat aircraft has limited or no operational combat capability.

CURRENT AIR FORCE EQUIPMENT HOLDINGS

Iraq retained about 300 aircraft in 1999, organized into two bomber squadrons and 11 fighter and fighter-bomber squadrons.[7] Figure 6.1 shows a rough estimate of the trends in Iraq's air strength, and the impact of the Gulf War. These figures, however, count total aircraft in inventory, and do not reflect the major losses in operational readiness that have resulted from Iraq's loss of import capability and foreign technical support.

Similarly, Figures 6.2–6.5 and Table 6.2 show how the current fixed wing combat aircraft and rotary wing aircraft holdings of the Iraqi air force compare with the air strength of other Gulf states. It is clear from these charts that the Iraqi air force is now quantitatively and qualitatively inferior to the Saudi air force. At the same time, such comparisons exaggerate the strength of both Iraq and Iran. They count all aircraft in inventory and not operational strength—the key measure in terms of war-fighting capability. As a result, all Iraq's surviving aircraft are counted regardless of whether they could engage in sustained combat, and so are those of Iran. While Iran never suffered from the same kind of combat losses during the Iran-Iraq War that Iraq suffered from during the Gulf War, Iran's readiness has suffered sharply from its loss of Western resupply and support. Like Iraq, Iran has far more aircraft in inventory than it can operate, particularly for any sustained number of sorties.

Despite its wartime losses, the Iraqi air force's total surviving inventory of combat aircraft seemed to include 6–7 HD-6 (BD-6), 1–2 Tu-16, and 6 Tu-22 bombers. Roughly 6 of these bombers still seem to be operational.[8] None of the bombers has ever been equipped with advanced air munitions for striking land

Figure 6.1
Iraq: Fixed Wing and Rotary Wing Combat Air Strength, 1979–1998

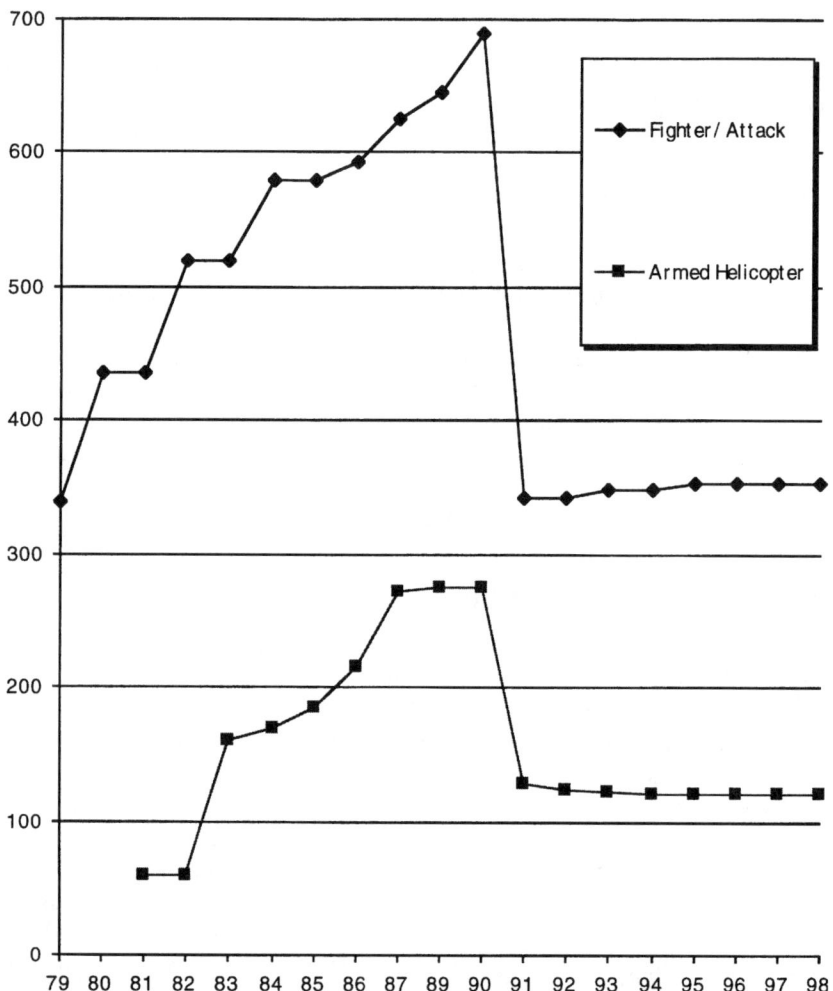

Sources: Adapted by Anthony H. Cordesman from various editions of IISS, *Military Balance*; JCSS, *Military Balance in the Middle East*; and material provided by US experts.

targets, however, or was used effectively against Iranian forces and land targets during the Iran-Iraq War. None of these aircraft flew a single sortie during the Gulf War, and there are no reports of any bomber training or flight activity after the war. The HD-6 bombers do, however, have the technical capability to deliver the CS-601 anti-ship missile, and they played a limited role in attacking shipping to Iran in 1988. At this point, such aircraft are of interest only because a few might be made operational and used in "one-way" sorties in a desperate effort to deliver weapons of mass destruction.

Figure 6.2
Total Operational Combat Aircraft in Gulf Forces in 1990 versus 1998

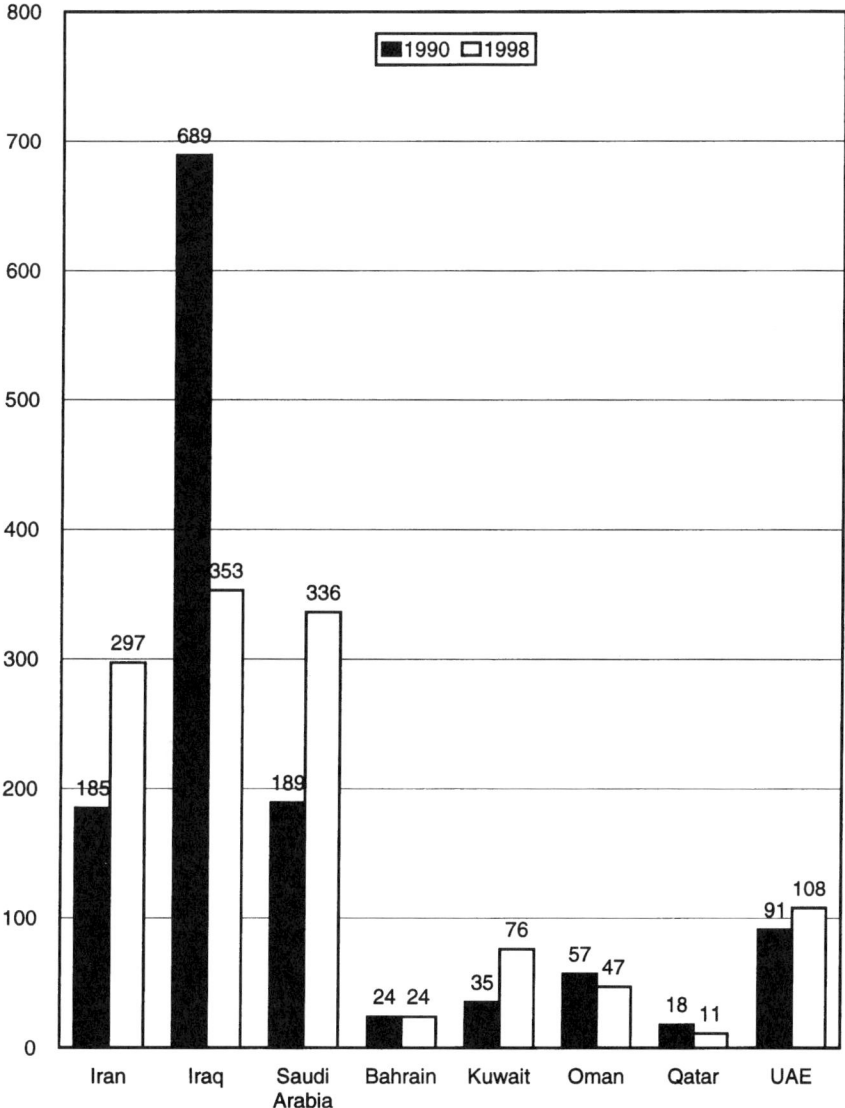

Note: Iran includes active forces in the Revolutionary Guards. Saudi Arabia includes active forces in the National Guard.
Sources: Adapted by Anthony H. Cordesman from various sources, and IISS, *Military Balance*.

Figure 6.3
High-Quality and Advanced Gulf Fixed Wing Fighter Combat Aircraft by Type, 1998 (Includes Mirage F-1, Mirage 2000, F-15, F-16, F-18, Tornado, Su-20/22, Su-24, MiG 25/25R, MiG-29)

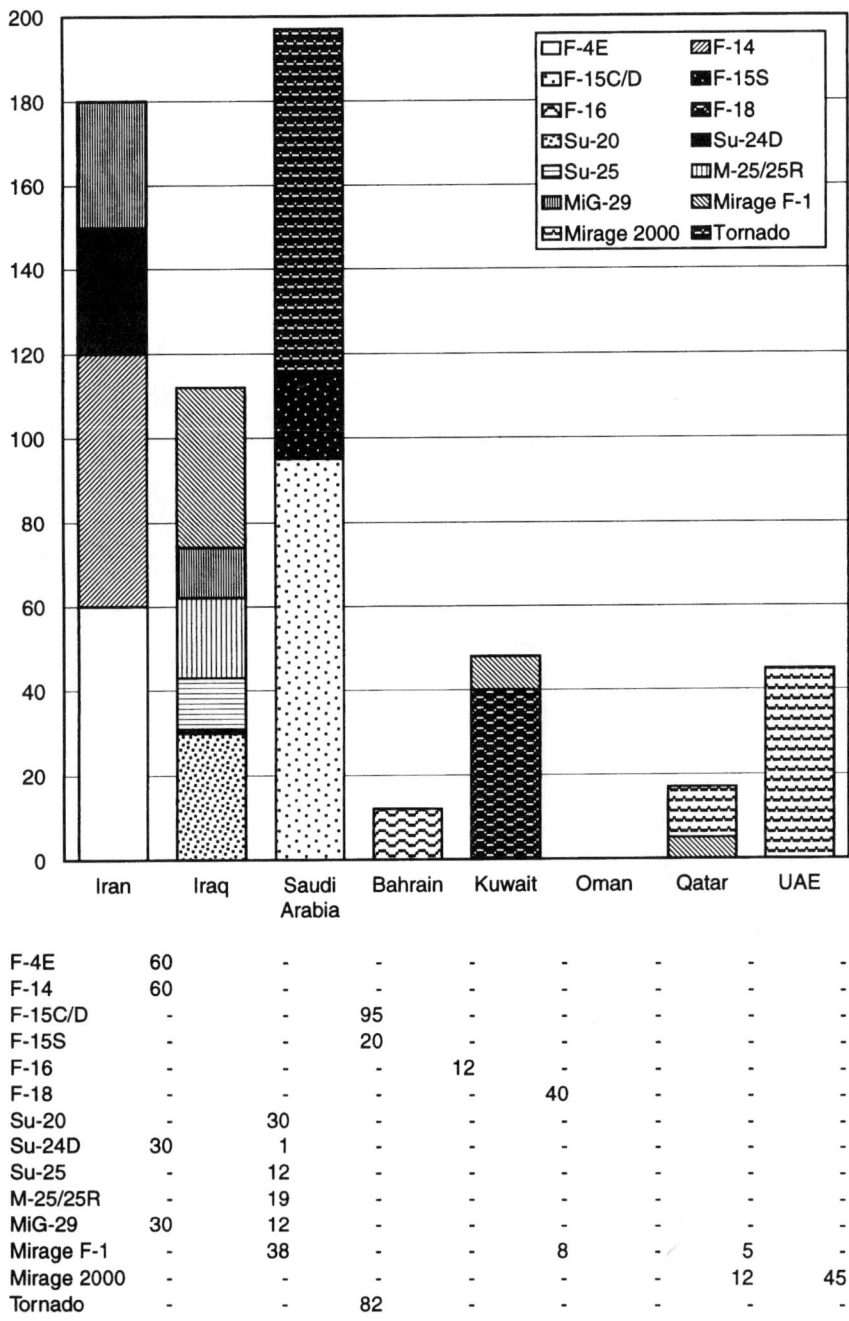

	Iran	Iraq	Saudi Arabia	Bahrain	Kuwait	Oman	Qatar	UAE
F-4E	60	-	-	-	-	-	-	-
F-14	60	-	-	-	-	-	-	-
F-15C/D	-	-	95	-	-	-	-	-
F-15S	-	-	20	-	-	-	-	-
F-16	-	-	-	12	-	-	-	-
F-18	-	-	-	-	40	-	-	-
Su-20	-	30	-	-	-	-	-	-
Su-24D	30	1	-	-	-	-	-	-
Su-25	-	12	-	-	-	-	-	-
M-25/25R	-	19	-	-	-	-	-	-
MiG-29	30	12	-	-	-	-	-	-
Mirage F-1	-	38	-	-	8	-	5	-
Mirage 2000	-	-	-	-	-	-	12	45
Tornado	-	-	82	-	-	-	-	-

Sources: Estimated by Anthony H. Cordesman from various sources, and IISS, *Military Balance*.

Figure 6.4
Iraqi High-Quality Gulf Fixed Wing Fighter Combat Aircraft by Type, 1998 (Includes Mirage F-1, Mirage 2000, F-15, F-16, F-18, Tornado, Su-20/22, Su-24, MiG 25/25R, MiG-29)

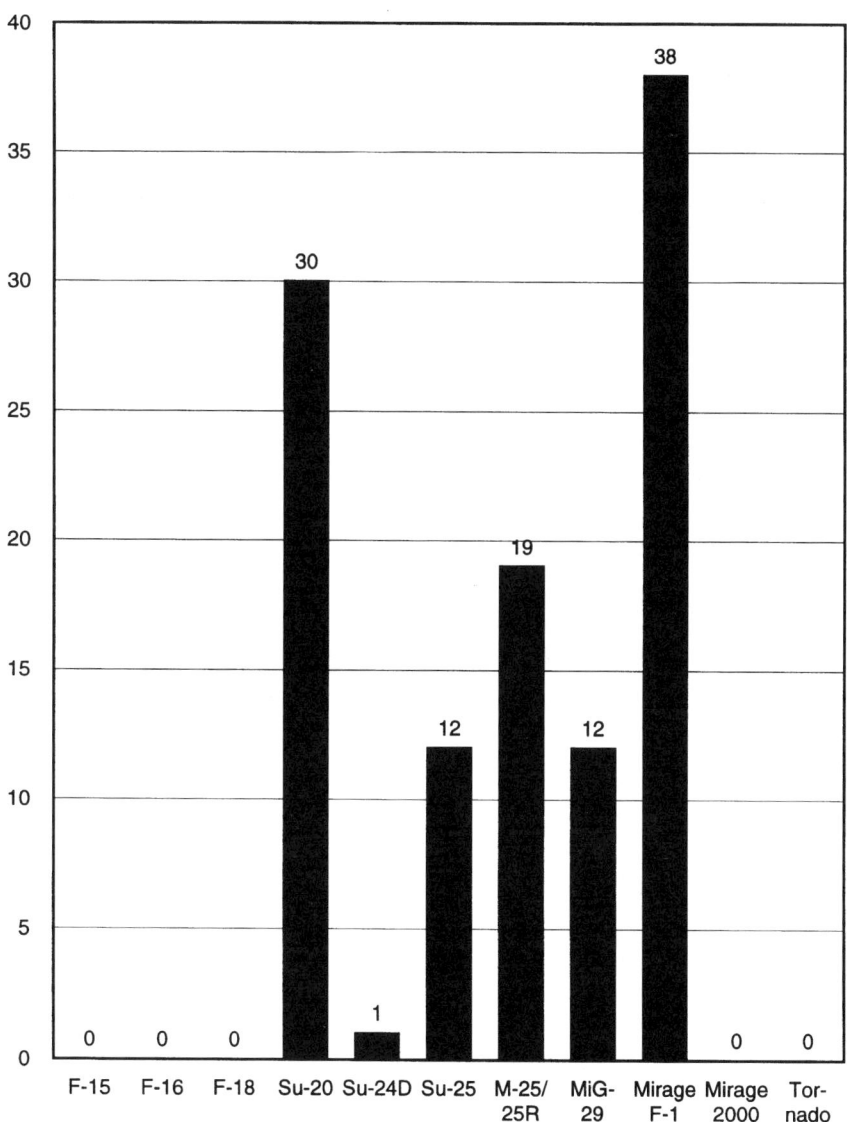

Sources: Estimated by Anthony H. Cordesman from various sources, and IISS, *Military Balance*.

Figure 6.5
Gulf Attack Helicopters in 1998

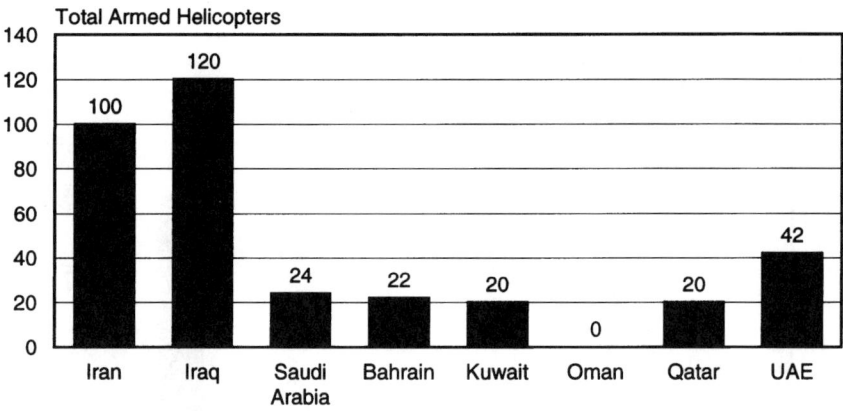

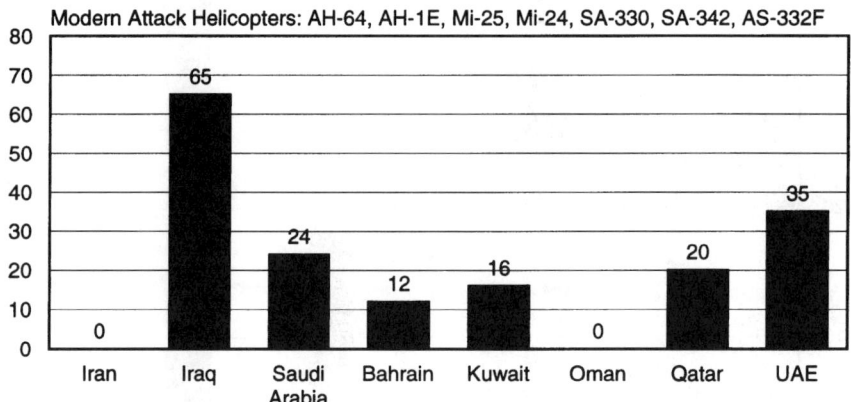

Sources: Estimated by Anthony H. Cordesman from various sources, and IISS, *Military Balance*.

The Iraqi air force's key operational holdings seem to include a total of 255 fighters and fighter bombers, and some 80 trainers—some of which are combat capable.[9] One estimate gives a total of 130 J-6, MiG-23BN, MiG-27, Mirage F-1EQ5, Su-7, Su-20, and Su-25 attack fighters; 180 J-7, MiG-21, MiG-25, Mirage F-1EQ, and MiG-29 air defense fighters; MiG-21 and MiG-25 reconnaissance fighters; 15 old Hawker Hunters; a surviving Il-76 Adnan AEW aircraft; 2 Il-76 tankers; and large numbers of transports and helicopters. Another estimate indicates that Iraq retained about 30 Mirage F-1s, 15 MiG-29s, 50–60 MiG-23s, 15 MiG-25s, 150 MiG-21s, 25–30 Su-25s, and 60 Su-17s, Su-20s, and Su-22s.

An earlier IISS estimate indicates that Iraq had six H-6D and Tu-22 bombers;

Table 6.2
Advanced Combat Aircraft by Type in Gulf Forces in 1998

	Number	Type
Bahrain	24	Total Fixed Wing Combat
	12	F-16C/D
Iran	297	Total Fixed Wing Combat
	60	Modern Combat Aircraft
	30	Su-24D
	30	MiG-29
Iraq	353	Total Fixed Wing Combat
	81	Modern Combat Aircraft
	30	Su-20
	1	Su-24D
	12	Su-25
	38	Mirage F-1EQ5/200
	12	MiG-29
	15	MiG-25
	4	MiG-25R
Kuwait	76	Total Fixed Wing Combat
	40	F/A-18C/D
Oman	46	Total Fixed Wing Combat
	(17)	Jaguar (SO) Mark 1, T-2
Qatar	11	Total Fixed Wing Combat
	5	Mirage F-1EDA/DDA
	(12)	Mirage 2000-5 in delivery
Saudi Arabia	336	Total Fixed Wing Combat
	197	Modern Combat Aircraft
	58	Tornado IDS
	24	Tornado ADV
	95	F-15C/D
	15	F-15S
	5	E-3A
UAE	108	Total Fixed Wing Combat
	45	Modern Combat Aircraft
	9	Mirage 2000E
	22	Mirage 2000EAD
	6	Mirage 2000DAD
	8	Mirage 2000RAD
	(72)	F-16C/D Block 60 on order

Note: Older aircraft with inferior avionics are not included. Supersonic flight performance is not regarded as more than a marginal measure of combat performance.
Source: Adapted by Anthony H. Cordesman from IISS, *Military Balance*.

130 MiG-23BN, Mirage F-1EQ5, Su-7, Su-20, and Su-25 fighter ground-attack aircraft; and 180 F-7, MiG-21, MiG-23, MiG-25, Mirage F-1EQ, and MiG-29 fighters. Iraq was also estimated to have MiG-25 reconnaissance aircraft, two IL-76 tankers, and over 100 trainers, including some Mirage F-1BQs, EMB-312s, and other trainers with combat capability.[10]

Although it is unclear how many air munitions Iraq retained after the Gulf War, some estimates put this figure as low as 50% of the pre-war total. Iraq, however, retains significant numbers of modern air-to-air and air-to-ground munitions. These stocks include AA-6, AA-7, AA-8, AA-10, Matra 530, Matra 550, and Matra Super 530 air-to-air missiles, and AM-39 Exocet, HOT, AS-11, AS-12, AS-6, AS-14, AS-301, AS-37, C-601 Silkworm; air-to-surface missiles; laser-guided bombs, and Cluster bombs.

Iraq has deployed Matra Magic 2 "dogfight" air-to-air missiles on its Mirage F-1s since the war. This is virtually its only major improvement in air force equipment since 1990. It is not clear whether these missiles were delivered before the war, were stolen from Kuwait, or have been smuggled in since. They are an advanced type similar to the more advanced export versions of the US AIM-9, with high energy of maneuver and a maximum range of three nautical miles.[11]

Iraq retained large numbers of combat-capable trainers, transport aircraft and helicopters, and remotely piloted vehicles. The trainers included some Mirage F-1BQs, 25 PC-7s, 30 PC-9s, 50–60 Tucanos (EMB-312s), 40 L-29s and 40 L-39s. Transport assets included a mix of Soviet An-2, An-12, An-24, An-26, and Il-76 jets and propeller aircraft, and some Il-76s modified to act as tankers. The remotely piloted vehicles (RPVs) included some Iraqi-made designs, Italian designs, and Soviet designs. It is unclear how effective Iraq was in using any of these RPV systems, but it did make use of them during the Gulf War.[12]

AIR ACTIVITY SINCE THE GULF WAR

The Iraqi air force has made efforts to improve its air training and has continued to rebuild other aspects of its air defense capabilities. Beginning in April, 1992, Iraq resumed air-to-air and air-to-surface combat training. Its number of training sorties was relatively low during 1992–1995, but began to recover in late 1996, and was significant in 1997 and 1998. The Iraqi air force has also made major efforts to reconstitute its surface-to-air missile net, and it has modified some of its surface-to-air missile systems in an attempt to improve their resistance to US countermeasures. Meanwhile, Iraq has established new missile sites and improved the dispersal of its aircraft.

However, Iraq has had only limited combat experience since the Gulf War. The Iraqi air force flew fighter and attack helicopter sorties against Shi'ites in southern Iraq in June and July, 1992, but the UN then established no fly zones north of the 36th parallel and south of the 32nd parallel. These no-fly zones barred any Iraqi use of fighters and helicopters. The northern zone was established shortly after the cease-fire, and the southern zone was established on August 26, 1992.

Iraqi fighters initially responded by using their radars to track Coalition fighters or by flying into the no-fly zones. At the same time, Iraq moved some of its more expendable land-based air defense systems—like the SA-6—into threatening positions or "surface-to-air missile traps" in or near the no-fly zones. Iraqi fighters also challenged Coalition forces in December, 1992 and January, 1993. These actions—coupled with further efforts to bar UN inspections and a challenge of Kuwait's right to secure its new border—provoked a significant clash between Coalition and Iraqi forces in January, 1993. The Coalition forces shot down at least one Iraqi fighter and attacked the Iraqi surface-to-air missile traps and any Iraqi radars that illuminated Coalition aircraft. They also launched two major attacks on Iraqi command and control facilities.

The Iraqi air force has occasionally challenged Coalition fighters since that time, and its fighters have sporadically "strayed" over the limits of the "no fly" zones ever since 1993. According to some reports, Iraqi personnel also assisted South Yemen during May–July, 1994. Some 40 combat pilots and 50 engineers volunteered, and one report indicates that three pilots were killed before the Iraqi volunteers were repatriated in September, 1994.[13]

Iraqi training has, however, suffered because the Coalition expanded the "no-fly" zone in the south in the fall of 1996, after Iraqi forces had entered the Kurdish security zone in the West. This has furthered reduced the training areas open to the Iraqi air force, particularly for training in combined operations with the Iraqi land forces. Iraq's efforts to challenge US and British aircraft after Desert Fox also show few signs of progress.

MODERNIZATION NEEDS

The Iraqi air force is now operating with considerably less than half of its pre-war ability to generate and sustain combat sorties. It has no major repair facilities for many of its Soviet-made fighters—which had previously been overhauled by Soviet technicians or rebuilt in the former Soviet Union. It still has significant shortages of spare parts—particularly for its French-made and newest Russian fighters—and has no in-country access to the Russian and French technical support which it had relied on before the war. The Mirage F-1 is difficult to maintain, and Iraq is likely to have severe problems in keeping its avionics and weapons subsystems fully operational without access to French technical support and new deliveries of parts and equipment.

Iraq cannot rebuild its air force to anything approaching its pre-war strength without massive arms imports and foreign assistance. At some point, Iraq will also need substantial deliveries of more modern French or Russian combat aircraft, and missiles and electronics for beyond-visual-range (BVR) air-to-air combat and stand-off air-to-ground attacks. It will need the airborne sensor, electronic warfare, and C⁴I/BM assets to end its dependence on ground controlled intercepts, strike deep behind the forward battle zone, and operate as a coordinated force.

The Iraqi air force is still missing critical imports of new aircraft that it had ordered before the Gulf War. These outstanding undelivered orders include 20–30 Mirage F-1EQs, including three two-seat versions. They include up to 70 MiG-29s, 20 Su-25s, 30 Su-20/22s, and 50 MiG-23s. These orders indicate the fact that Iraq had recognized the technical weaknesses in its air order of battle well before the Gulf War, although if Iraq could now obtain delivery of such aircraft, many are sufficiently old designs that they would not be competitive with Western or Southern Gulf fighters. Iraq may also still be missing 12 MiG-21s and 8 MiG-23s that were being repaired in Eastern Europe at the time of the Gulf War.[14]

Iraq would also need much more advanced imports to compete with Western air forces, or the Saudi air force. It would have to acquire some form of "mini-airborne warning and air control system (AWACS)," a large inventory of modern beyond-visual-range air-to-air missiles, modern remotely piloted vehicles (RPVs), and airborne refueling technology. It will require outside support in repairing and reconditioning its fighters. It must find ways of integrating its fighters into an effective air control and warning system that "nets" them with its ground-based air defense system, and which avoids its past overdependence on ground-controlled intercepts.

Iraq needs to acquire modern reconnaissance and intelligence aircraft that are capable of real-time transmission of data to effective command centers and terminals in the field. The air force must work with the army to improve the sensors and weapons on its attack helicopters, and to develop an integrated concept for fixed and rotary wing close air support, and armored operations.

READINESS, DOCTRINE, AND TRAINING NEEDS

Even massive imports of the most advanced aircraft would not be enough to make the Iraqi air force effective. Like most Third World states, Iraq has never organized effectively to fight as an integrated air force—as distinguished from clusters of individual fighting elements. Iraq still seems to confuse having a large order of battle with effectiveness, and it puts far too little emphasis on high sortie rates, the effective massing of air power against given types of targets, planning sustained air campaigns, and testing, exercising, and restructuring its mix of air- and land-based air defense assets to fight as an effective overall force.

Critical Failures in Training and Doctrine

Iraq must reorganize its command structure to provide the same degree of professionalism and freedom from political interference that is needed in its army. Its jury-rigged airborne sensor aircraft is a poor substitute for a true AWACS or integrated airborne sensor and battle management system. Like Iran, Iraq lacks the training and sensors to compete with the West in beyond-visual-range combat, and the advanced training facilities to compete in close or dogfight combat.

Iraqi operations and training have not reflected any significant understanding of modern AirLand battle techniques. It needs to reorganize its training system to stress far more demanding and realistic offensive training that includes training in combined arms exercises and realistic close support and interdiction missions, and strategic bombing missions. This must include constant training with smart munitions and actual ordnance, and far better training in evading air defenses and stand-off attacks. At present, the Iraqi air force has negligible targeting and battle management capabilities for offensive operations, and it tends to deliver munitions into the general area of the target, release them, and leave with little or no effect. Outside experts also indicate that it has probably lost most of its capability to operate its Mirage F-1s with Exocet, due to a lack of maintenance, training, and outside technical support.

In fact, every aspect of Iraqi air defense training needs to be improved. It is a fundamental law of military effectiveness that no force can ever practice what it does not train and exercise to practice, and that training and exercises can never be effective unless they are large enough to develop force-wide competence, involve joint warfare, and ruthlessly test the effectiveness of command at all levels by forcing commanders to learn from defeat and by ending the careers of officers who fail to perform. The failure to respond to this law is a problem that universally cripples the military effectiveness of every force in the Gulf, and Iraqi forces in particular. The Iraqi air force can have no chance of success against Western or Saudi air forces unless it changes these behavior patterns.

Problems in Air-to-Air Combat

The Iraqi air force has generally performed dismally in air-to-air combat, its training levels are still limited and many of its training sorties are unrealistic, and its air combat operations still rely much too heavily on ground-controlled intercept data. The issue is not one of courage; individual Iraqi pilots often pressed home intercepts during the early days of Desert Storm. However, Iraqi air combat tactics were primitive to the point where even the lead pilots of Iraq's MiG-29s often lost their wing man and were forced to seek guidance constantly from ground-based sensors and command facilities. Pilot air combat training rarely rose above the initial levels of Soviet combat training, even before the Gulf War, and there has been no meaningful training since that time.

Iraq performed poorly in reconnaissance, intelligence, airborne warning, and electronic warfare missions during the Iran-Iraq War, and it had no time to gain meaningful experience during the Gulf War. Iraq has tried to improvise some improvements in these mission capabilities since the Gulf War, but its efforts reveal few improvements in the sophistication of Iraq's electronic order of battle and in its ability to use its equipment coherently.

The Iraqi SIGINT/ELINT system suffered considerable damage from air attacks during the Gulf War. It has since been rebuilt and is fully functional, but it lacks the technical sophistication to deal with modern military communications, advanced commercial encryption systems, and air defense operations. Neither Iraqi intelligence nor the Iraqi air force has anything approaching the kind of integrated electronic warfare and intelligence assets available to the US military. It has no meaningful airborne capability, and its integrated air defense C^{4}I/battle management system cannot support its radar system with time-critical SIGINT/ELINT with any efficiency.[15]

Iraq's own analyses of the lessons of the Gulf War show that it recognizes that it must have much more effective air defense capabilities to defend its ground forces in any future war, or be willing to take major ground force losses and risk defeat. At the same time, Iraq has always had severe weaknesses in conducting attack missions as well as in air defense. Its reconnaissance and intelligence aircraft lack the sensors needed to properly characterize ground force attacks on a real-time basis and have limited range and poor night/poor weather performance.

Iraq's air intercept training and tactics are adequate by regional standards—at least as these apply to Iran and the smaller Gulf states. The Iraqi air force is flying higher numbers of training sorties, and it resumed night combat training in 1996—although it remains severely limited in the numbers of sorties it can fly in combat and in the quality of its training.[16] Iraq's air combat capabilities fall far short of the aggressive air battle and aggressor squadron techniques used by the Saudi, US, and British air forces, and ground-controlled intercept tactics are virtually unworkable in modern air warfare and are little more than suicidal. Iraq needs modern airborne warning and air control aircraft, beyond-visual-range combat capabilities, and electronic warfare capabilities. Iraq also needs to reorganize its air defense forces completely if its air defense fighters are to operate effectively in the same environment as its attack aircraft, surface-to-air missiles, and helicopters.

Problems in Strategic, Interdiction, and Close Support Missions

The Iraqi air force did poorly in executing strategic, interdiction, and close-support missions during the Iran-Iraq War. It failed to mass effective numbers of aircraft and rarely pressed its attacks home. It rarely employed guided and unguided attack munitions effectively, often missing its targets. It did not demonstrate an effective stand-off attack capability, except for the Exocets it used in the Gulf, and its evasive tactics and exploitation of countermeasures often left its aircraft far more vulnerable to Iranian short-range air defenses than should have been the case. Its cooperation with ground forces exhibited recurrent command and battle management problems that it had only begun to solve by the time of the cease-fire in 1988. The Iraqi air force constantly exaggerated its success and issued false claims at all levels of command.

The Iraqi air force had even less experience in attack operations during the Gulf War than it did in air defense operations, although it had every opportunity to see what a modern air force could accomplish by watching Coalition operations against Iraq. Its post-war operations have been limited to occasional support of operations against Shi'ites with no air defenses. Its overall attack training has been limited by its inability to operate in the "no fly" zones, and by its lack of access to any of the new major technology it needs to act on the lessons of the Gulf War regarding offensive missions. Its joint training in attack missions has slowly improved, but it remains limited and occurs with land force formations larger than the battalion level.

OVERALL WAR-FIGHTING CAPABILITIES

The Iraqi air force is still relatively effective by regional standards, with the exception of Saudi Arabia. It can probably dominate the skies over the Iran-Iraq border area until Iran fully absorbs its MiG-29s. It can play a major role in defeating the Kurds and can rapidly defeat the Kuwaiti air force if it is not supported by US and Saudi forces. It probably cannot defeat the Saudi and Turkish air forces in the border areas, but these air forces might need US support to win a quick and decisive victory.

The Iraqi air force has little ability to engage US airpower or a US-led Coalition, but it can conduct limited long-range air attacks against its neighbors, retain some refueling capability, and use some precision-guided weapons, chemical weapons, and possibly biological weapons. Iraq could use these capabilities to mass a few air raids against selected targets in Iran or across the Gulf, and it could use its remaining Exocets to attack tankers and other naval targets in the Gulf.

Like Iran, however, Iraq is at least a half decade away from fully rebuilding its air force. Some of its capabilities are frozen in place by its lack of access to new weapons and technology at a time when its Southern Gulf neighbors have relatively free access to the most advanced Western and Russian systems and when Iran has better access than Iraq. Its mission-oriented weaknesses are compounded by a lack of effective central air planning and battle management, a clear concept of how to employ large numbers of aircraft, and a lack of any effective concept for joint operations. The Iraqi air force still fights as individual combat elements, and not as a force.

Iraq needs to greatly improve its sortie rates and sustainability. Like most Arab air forces, Iraq cripples its potential effectiveness by emphasizing aircraft numbers over sustained sortie rates and effective operations. As a result, it could only fly a small fraction of the sortie rates its aircraft strength would have allowed it to fly if the aircraft were operated by a Western air force—roughly one-tenth to one-twentieth of the sortie rate of the Israeli air force. As a result, the operational sortie rate of the Iraqi aircraft would probably decline by 60–75% below its initial surge rate in any combat lasting more than a few days.

The future of the Iraqi air force is impossible to predict for the same reasons that have already been discussed for land forces. It is clear, however, that any major force improvements will take time and require Iraq to make an investment of several billion dollars when the present UN embargo and sanctions are lifted or eased. Much will depend on how far other regional air forces have progressed in the interim, and on the status of US air power in the Gulf. Iraq will find it easier to compete with local air forces, but Saudi Arabia already presents a major challenge, and Iran may modernize substantially before Iraq can begin to catch up. Much will also depend on Iraq's political leadership, the relative priority it gives the air force, and the strategic force planning decisions Iraq makes. In particular, Iraq must decide whether it is going to even attempt to create a professional, modern joint force structure, whether it will be primarily a defensive or full-balanced, multi-role, air force, and whether it intends to try to compete directly with the capabilities of US air power. In general, the more ambitious Iraq's goals become, the less likely it is to succeed.

LAND-BASED AIR DEFENSES

Iraq had a large land-based air defense system before the Gulf War, which had been extensively reorganized after Israel's Osirak raid in 1981. A network of radars, surface-to-air missiles, and anti-aircraft guns surrounded strategic and industrial areas, particularly in the Baghdad area. A French-supplied C^4I/BM system called the KARI (Iraq spelled backwards in French) became operational on a country-wide level in 1986–1987, but it was never really tested during the Iran-Iraq War.

The National Air Defense Operations Center (ADOC) in Baghdad controlled Iraq's air defenses. The ADOC maintained the overall air picture and provided Baghdad with information on the course of the air battle. There were five Sector Operations Centers (SOCs) covering the north, west, center-east, southeast, and far south, which established priorities for air defense engagements. Each was subordinate to the ADOC and controlled air defense operations in a specific geographic area. The SOCs controlled large numbers of ground-based weapons systems and extensive BM/C^4I/SR assets.

There were also a large number of Intercept Operations Centers (IOCs) to provide local air defense control. These had headquarters at Ar-Rutbah, H-1, and H-3 in the west; Mosul and Qayyarah in the north; Al-Taqaddum, Salman Pak, Al-Jarrah, An-Najf, and An-Nukhayb in the center-east; Al-Amrah, As-Salman, and Az-Zubayr in the southeast; and Al-Jahrah in the far south. These systems were linked through an extensive optical fiber communications net and used a TFH 647 radio relay system, a TFH tropospheric communications system, and a large mix of radars supplied by the Soviet Union.

The Strengths and Weaknesses of Iraq's Air Defense System and the Gulf War

The KARI system, however, was a mix of technologies from different nations with uncertain integration. Although part of Iraq's air defense system was French-supplied, Iraq patterned its overall air defense network and operations on Soviet models. It also concentrated its coverage around Baghdad, Basra, and key military and strategic targets. This left many areas uncovered, particularly in southern Iraq, and along air corridors striking north across the Saudi and Kuwait borders.

Iraq's air defenses were fundamentally flawed because the SOCs could not communicate effectively once the ADOC was destroyed or deactivated. This meant that the Coalition could attack and/or overwhelm each sector in isolation from the others. Moreover, the destruction of a given SOC effectively opened up a corridor that could be used to attack the entire country. While it may not be a general lesson of the war, such design defects and vulnerabilities are common in Third World air defense systems, and almost universal in systems dependent on Soviet or PRC (People's Republic of China) surface-to-air missiles, sensors, and electronics.

There were other problems. Iraq had created a strongly inter-netted, redundant, and layered air defense system that included a wide variety of radars, hardened and buried command-and-control sites, interceptors, surface-to-air missiles, and anti-aircraft artillery. In practice, however, much of the communications, data processing, and software were inferior.[17]

Even so, Iraq's air defense forces were formidable in some respects at the start of the Gulf War. According to one US estimate, Iraq had a total of 16,000 radar-guided and heat-seeking surface-to-air missiles, including missiles for the large numbers of lighter army systems described earlier, and smaller numbers of missiles for the heavier SA-2s (S-75 Divina), SA-3s, and SA-6s (2K12). These heavier surface-to-air defense missiles were operated by an air defense force, organized into air defense units that were part of the Iraqi army, but operationally tied to the air force.

Iraq had approximately 137–154 medium surface-to-air missile sites and complexes in Iraq, 20–21 in Kuwait, and 18 major surface-to-air missile support facilities.[18] These included 20–30 operational SA-2 batteries with 160 launch units, 25–50 SA-3 batteries with 140 launch units, and 36–55 SA-6 batteries with well over 100 fire units. Iraq claimed to have modified the SA-2 missile to use an infrared terminal seeker to supplement the SA-2's normal radio command guidance system, but it is unclear that such systems were actually deployed.

All of these systems could still be fired on a target of opportunity basis. Iraq's medium surface-to-air defense sites in Iraq were also a threat to a modern air force. They were widely dispersed, often did not require the use of radar, and could be fired on a target of opportunity basis. The missiles on the sites in Iraq included at least 20 SA-8b (9K33) batteries with 30–40 fire units, 60–100 SA-9 fire units, and some SA-13s (9k25 Strela 10) and 50 to 66 Rolands.[19]

To put this level of air defense strength in perspective, Baghdad had more dense air defenses at the start of the Gulf War than any city in Eastern Europe, and had more than seven times the total surface-to-air missile launcher strength deployed in Hanoi during the height of the Vietnam War. The US Department of Defense released a highly detailed post-war estimate of Iraq's land-based air defense at the outset of the Gulf War that credited Iraq with 3,679 major missiles, not including 6,500 SA-7s, 400 SA-9s, 192 SA-13s, and 288 SA-14s. This report indicated that Iraq had 972 anti-aircraft artillery sites, 2,404 fixed anti-aircraft guns, and 6,100 mobile anti-aircraft guns.

Separate US estimates indicate that Iraq had extensive numbers of crew/vehicle-deployed SA-9s and SA-13s and manportable SA-14s and SA-16s dispersed throughout the KTO. These estimates indicate that Iraq had deployed more than 3,700 anti-aircraft guns in the KTO with barrels larger than 14.5 mm, and that these AA guns were supplemented by more than 10,000 12.7 mm guns in the ground forces in the KTO that could be used in some form of anti-aircraft role. While such weapons lacked accuracy, range, and high lethality, they could be deployed to expose aircraft flying under 12,000–15,000 feet to substantial cumulative risk.[20]

Many of the individual surface-to-air missiles, anti-aircraft guns, and command and control units in the Iraqi system, however, had low operational readiness and proficiency. System-wide and unit-level electronic warfare capability was good by Third World standards, but was scarcely competitive with that of the United States. Iraq's overall sensor/battle management system remained poor. Their training failed to deal with saturation and advanced countermeasure attacks, and was not realistic in dealing with more conventional penetrations by advanced attack aircraft. This was demonstrated all too clearly when Iraqi guns and missiles shot down an Egyptian Alphajet flying to an arms show in Baghdad in April, 1989, even though it flew along a preannounced flight corridor at the scheduled time.[21] Iraq still could not keep its land-based air control and warning and C^4I/BM systems operational 24 hours a day.

Iraq had no real operational understanding of the effectiveness of anti-radiation missiles, electronic warfare, and modern intelligence and targeting assets. It understood Vietnam-era tactics for dealing with US forces, but it did not seem to understand how much these assets had evolved in the 20-odd years since the United States had left Vietnam. It also does not seem to have fully studied the lessons of the Israeli attack on land-based Syrian air defenses in 1982. As a result, its major sensors ceased to operate in an integrated net within the first day of the war. Anti-radiation missiles quickly suppressed both its long- and short-range radar guided missile units. US and similarly equipped Coalition attack aircraft were able to attack ground targets from outside the range of virtually all types of Iraqi short-range air defenses, and cruise missiles and stealth aircraft could penetrate even into the most densely defended Iraqi targets.

Iraq's Air Defense System After the Gulf War

There is no expert consensus on how much of Iraq's land-based air defense assets and air defense system survived the Gulf War, or on Iraq's holdings of surface-to-air missiles in late 1995. Many facilities survived because the Coalition concentrated more on the suppression of air defense activity than on the physical destruction of land-based facilities and trying to hunt down and kill individual air defense weapons.

Table 6.3 shows how Iraq's post-war air defense strength compares with that of other Gulf states. Although Iraq took some losses during Desert Fox, in early 1999 it retained 130–180 SA-2 launchers, 100–125 SA-3 launchers, 100–125 SA-6s, 20–35 SA-8s, 30–45 SA-9s, some SA-13s, and around 30 Roland VI and 5 Crotale surface-to-air missile fire units. Some of these systems were operated by the army. In addition, Iraq had some 2,000 manportable SA-7s and SA-14s, and some SA-16s.[22]

It is unclear whether Iraq learned enough from the Jordanian officers who assisted it during the war, and during the initial period after the war to operate its Hawks. Iraq may also be avoiding any use of the weapons because it fears that the United States would attack any captured Hawks that showed signs of becoming operational.[23]

Most of its other surface-to-air missile units are operational, and there was evidence that Iraq had improved their readiness and training in 1996–1998. Iraq's ground-based defenses remain concentrated around Baghdad, Basra, and Kirkuk, as they were during the pre-war period. Iraqi territory is too large to attempt territorial defense, and Iraq has always concentrated on defending strategic targets and deploying air defense zones to cover critical land force deployments.

However, Iraq redeployed some missiles during 1992 and 1993 to create surface-to-air missile "traps" near the "no-fly zones" that the Coalition established after the war. These traps were designed to attack aircraft with overlapping missile coverage when they attacked launchers deployed near the no-fly zones, and Iraq repeated the tactic after Desert Fox. While the Iraqi efforts failed—and led to the destruction of a number of the missile launchers involved—it is not clear what portion survived or what other detailed redeployments Iraq has made in recent years.[24]

LAND-BASED AIR DEFENSE READINESS AND WAR-FIGHTING CAPABILITY

Iraq has made extensive efforts to improve its use of shelters, revetments, dummies, and other passive defenses. It has used such defenses since the beginning of the Iran-Iraq War, and it has deployed new decoys after the Gulf War in an effort to reduce its vulnerability. According to most experts, it repaired many of the bases and air facilities that were destroyed or damaged during

Table 6.3
Gulf Land-Based Air Defense Systems

Country	Major SAM	Light SAM	AA Guns
Bahrain	None	40+ RBS-70 18 Stinger 7 Crotale	12 Oerlikon 35 mm 12 L/70 40 mm
Iran	12/150 I Hawk 3/? SA-5 45 HQ-2J (SA-2) ? SA-2 15 Tigercat	SA-7 HN-5 30 Rapier FM-80 (Ch Crotale) Type 55	1,700 guns ZU-23, ZSU-23-4, ZSU-57-2, KS-19 ZPU-2/4, M-1939
Iraq	SA-2 SA-3 SA-6	Roland SA-7 SA-8 SA-9 SA-13 SA-14, SA-16	5,500 guns ZSU-23-4 23 mm, M-1939 37 mm, ZSU-57-2 SP, 57 mm 85 mm, 100 mm, 130 mm
Kuwait	4/24 I Hawk 4/16 Patriot	6/12 Aspede	6/2X35 mm Oerlikon
Oman	None	Blowpipe 34 SA-7 28 Javelin 28 Rapier	2 VAB/VD 20 mm 4 ZU-23-2 23 mm 12 L-60 40 mm
Qatar	None	Blowpipe 12 Stinger 9 Roland	?
Saudi Arabia	128 I Hawk ? Patriot	Crotale Stinger 500 Redeye 68 Shahine mobile 40 Crotale 73 Shahine static	92 M-163 Vulcan 20 mm 50 AMX-30SA 30 mm 128 35 mm guns 150 L-70 40 mm (in store)
UAE	5 I Hawk Bty.	20+ Blowpipe 10 SA-16 12 Rapier 9 Crotale 13 RBS-70 100 Mistral	48 M-3VDA 20 mm SP 20 GCF-BM2 30 mm

Source: Estimated by Anthony H. Cordesman.

the Gulf War. It has 16–20 major air bases, with H-3, H-2, and Al Asad in the West; Mosul, Qayarah, and Kirkuk in the north, Al Jarah, Talil, and Shaybah in the South, and 5–7 more bases within a 150 kilometer radius of Baghdad. Many of these bases have surface-to-air missile defenses.

Iraq has been able to restore much of its battle control and management system, reactivate its damaged airfields, and even build one new military airfield in the south.[25] Many of its sheltered air defense and air force command and control centers remained operational. Iraq's French-supplied KARI air defense communications and data-link system is not particularly effective, but it uses fiber optics, and many of the links between its command elements either have survived the bombing or are now repaired.[26]

Many radars and elements of Iraq's air defense C^4I system are also operating, in spite of the Gulf War and Desert Fox, including such pre-war systems as the Soviet Spoon Rest, Squat Eye, Flat Face, Tall King, Bar Lock, Cross Slot, and Thin Skin radars. Iraq also had Soviet, Italian, and French jamming and electronic intelligence equipment. There is no way to know how many of Iraq's underground command and personnel shelters survived the Gulf War, but it seems likely that at least 50–66% survived the Coalition bombing campaign or have been rebuilt since the war.

Nonetheless, Iraq faces major problems in making its land-based air defense forces effective, in modernizing them, and in reacting to the lessons of the Gulf War. Most of Iraq's surface-to-air missile units, radars, automated data processing and transfer system, and central command and communications facilities have only limited to moderate operational capability. Iraq must rehabilitate and improve its radar-guided anti-aircraft guns and most of its short-range air defense systems. It needs to either modernize or replace its Rolands. It should replace its surviving patchwork system of radars and command and control equipment, and in the short term, it must find a reliable source of parts for its SA-3s and SA-6s.

Iraq's most serious challenge will be to find replacements for its French- and Russian-supplied air defense system, and to create a truly modern and effective air defense system. Iraq has recognized this requirement as a lesson of the Gulf War, but it is confronted with the problem that the only way it can create an effective system is to buy the Patriot, sold by the United States, or the S-300, sold by Russia.

The C^4/BM aspects of such a system would have to be tailored to Iraq's needs, that is, to integrate its purchase of the Patriot or S-300 fully into its other air defenses, and provide suitable new sensors and air defense computer technology and software. Such a system could then become operational relatively quickly, but giving full effectiveness by US or Russian standards would require it to be tailored to meet Iraq's specific topographical and operating conditions. This would take a major effort in terms of software, radar deployment and technology, and adaptation of US or Russian tactics and siting concepts to make such a system fully combat effective.[27]

Iraq is reported to be working on its own system and to be attempting to smuggle in radars from Eastern Europe than can detect cruise missiles and stealth aircraft and a "Mother of All Battles" (MOAB) system that could provide the KARI system with much better electronic warfare and low-altitude coverage for the area around Baghdad and key military facilities. Iraq is also reported to be working on defenses against anti-radiation missiles and long-range radar-guided air defense missiles. Like many of Iraq's efforts, however, it is unclear how real such programs are and whether they will ever have any success. If, as some sources suggest, the system has to rely on modifications of the SA-2 and of the Contraves Skyguard system, there is little chance that it can have great effectiveness.[28]

NEAR-TERM TRENDS AND IMPLICATIONS FOR CONTAINMENT AND DETERRENCE

The trends in Iraqi air forces are another warning against any policy that lifts sanctions without retaining any controls over how Iraq uses its revenues and without a firm commitment to military containment. They are a further argument for efforts to create a supplier regime that places strong limits on Iraq's military modernization and provides a particularly strong argument for limits on Iraqi imports of long-range strike aircraft and advanced, heavy, surface-to-air missile defenses.

NOTES

1. US Central Command, *Atlas, 1996*, MacDill Air Force Base, USCENTCOM, 1997, pp. 16–18.

2. Many different lists exist of the names of such bases. Jane's lists A1 Amarah, A1 Asad, A1 Bakr, A1 Basrah-West Maqal, A1 Khalid, A1 Kut, A1 Qayyarah, A1 Rashid, A1 Taqaddum, A1 Walid, Artawi, As Salman, As Samara, As Zubair, Baghdad-Muthenna, Balada, Bashur, Erbil, Jalibah, Karbala, Radif al Khafi, Kirkuk, Mosul, Mudaysis, Nejef, Qal'at Sikar, Qurna, Rumaylah, Safwan, Shibah, Shyaka Mayhar, Sulyamaniya, Tal Afar, Tallil-As Nasiryah, Tammuz, Tikrit, Ubdaydah bin al Jarrah, and Wadi Al Khirr. Many of the bases on this list are of limited size or are largely dispersal facilities. See *Jane's Sentinel: The Gulf States*, "Iraq," London, Jane's Publishing, 1997, p. 22.

3. USCENTCOM briefing by "senior military official," Pentagon, January 28, 1997, pp. 2, 5–8, 10; *Washington Times*, February 1, 1997, p. A-13; Reuters, September 4, 1996, 0911; Jane's *Pointer*, November, 1994, p. 2; Associated Press, September 9, 1996, 0129; *Washington Times*, January 30, 1997, p. A-3; February 1, 1997, p. A-13; *Jane's Sentinel: The Gulf States*, "Iraq," London, Jane's Publishing, 1997.

4. USCENTCOM briefing by "senior military official," Pentagon, January 28, 1997, pp. 2, 5–8, 10; *Washington Times*, February 1, 1997, p. A-13; Reuters, September 4, 1996, 0911; Jane's *Pointer*, November, 1994, p. 2; Associated Press, September 9, 1996,

0129; *Washington Times*, January 30, 1997, p. A-3; February 1, 1997, p. A-13; *Jane's Sentinel: The Gulf States*, "Iraq," London, Jane's Publishing, 1997.

5. FBIS NES 92–054, March 19, 1992, p. 16.

6. *Jane's Defense Weekly*, November 18, 1995, p. 16.

7. *Jane's Defense Weekly*, July 9, 1997, p. 4; US Central Command, *Atlas, 1996*, MacDill Air Force Base, USCENTCOM, 1997, pp. 16–18.

8. US Central Command, *Atlas, 1996*, MacDill Air Force Base, USCENTCOM, 1997, pp. 16–18.

9. US Central Command, *Atlas, 1996*, MacDill Air Force Base, USCENTCOM, 1997, pp. 16–18.

10. IISS, *The Military Balance, 1997–1998*, pp. 127–128.

11. *Washington Times*, September 5, 1996, p. A-1.

12. In addition to the sources listed at the start of the Iraq section, see USCENTCOM briefing by "senior military official," Pentagon, January 28, 1997, pp. 2, 5–8, 10; *Washington Times*, February 1, 1997, p. A-13; Reuters, September 4, 1996, 0911; *Jane's Pointer*, November, 1994, p. 2; Associated Press, September 9, 1996, 0129; *Washington Times*, January 30, 1997, p. A-3; February 1, 1997, p. A-13; The IISS, *Military Balance, 1996/1997*, and *Jane's Sentinel: The Gulf States*, "Iraq," London, Jane's Publishing, 1997; Andrew Rathmell, *The Changing Balance in the Gulf*, London, *Royal United Services Institute*, Whitehall Papers 38, 1996; Edward B. Atkenson, *The Powder Keg*, Falls Church, NOVA Publications, 1996; Geoffery Kemp and Robert E. Harkavy, *Strategic Geography and the Changing Middle East*, Washington, Carnegie Endowment/Brookings, 1997; and Michael Eisenstadt. *Like a Phoenix from the Ashes? The Future of Iraqi Military Power*, Washington, The Washington Institute, Policy Paper 36, 1993.

13. *Jane's Sentinel: The Gulf States*, "Iraq," London, Jane's Publishing, 1997, p. 22.

14. *Jane's Sentinel: The Gulf States*, "Iraq," London, Jane's Publishing, 1997, p. 23; It is unclear that Iraq had ever placed firm orders for more than 26 of the MiG-29s, but may have signed a memorandum of understanding for 70.

15. Interviews.

16. *Jane's Defense Weekly*, July 9, 1997, p. 4.

17. US Department of Defense, *Conduct of the Persian Gulf War: Final Report*, Department of Defense, April, 1992, pp. 13–15; Slides to US Air Force presentation of the April 15, 1993, draft of the Gulf War Air Power study; Brigadier General Robert H. Scales, *Certain Victory: The United States Army in the Gulf War*, Washington, Office of the Chief of Staff, US Army, 1993, pp. 115–116.

18. Some estimates show 129 to 130 sites in Iraq.

19. See Eliot A. Cohen, Director, *Gulf War Air Power Survey, Volume V*, Washington, GPO, 1993, pp. 218–219; US Department of Defense, *Conduct of the Persian Gulf War: Final Report*, Department of Defense, April, 1992, pp. 13–15; Slides to US Air Force presentation of the April 15, 1993, draft of the Gulf War Air Power study; Brigadier General Robert H. Scales, *Certain Victory: The United States Army in the Gulf War*, Washington, Office of the Chief of Staff, US Army, 1993, pp. 115–116. These estimates were projected by different sources, and the launcher or fire unit counts seem to be either rounded or based on standard Soviet battery holdings. According to Dick Palowski, Iraq had the following radar order of battle:

Early Warning and Surveillance

–Spoon Rest D/P-12M	USSR (147–161 MHz)
–Flat Face A/P-15	USSR (800–900 MHz)
–Squat Eye/P-15M	USSR (800–900 MHz)
–Bar Lock/P-35/37	USSR (2,695–3,125 MHz)
–Tall King/P-14	USSR (160–180 MHz)
–TRS-2215 (mobile)	FR (E/F)
–TRS-2230	FR (E/F)
–AN/TPS-32 (3D)	US (2905-3080)
–AWACS (IL-76)	FR

Surface-to-Air Missile Systems

–SA-2	Fansong/Guideline
–SA-3	Low Blow/Goa
–SA-5	Square Pair/Gammon
–SA-6	Straight Flush/Gainful
–SA-7	Grail (IR Hand-Held)
–SA-8	Land Roll/Gecko
–SA-9	Gaskin (IR Vehicle-Mounted)
–SA-13	Gopher (IR Vehicle-Mounted)
–SA-14	Gremlin (IR Hand-Held)
–SA-15	Track with Tube-Launched Missiles (not confirmed)
–SA-16	(not confirmed)
–SA-19	Mounted on 2S6 Gun-Track (not confirmed)
–ROLAND	
–HAWK	
–ASPEDITE	

London Financial Times, April 29, 1989, p. 11, July 26, 1989, p. 20; *Jane's Defense Weekly*, May 13, 1989, p. 837; April 22, 1989, p. 687, August 12, 1989, p. 255, September 30, 1989, p. 674, *Defense News*, May 8, 1989, p. 6; *International Defense Review*, 6/1989, pp. 835–841.

20. Brigadier General Robert H. Scales, *Certain Victory: The United States Army in the Gulf War*, Washington, Office of the Chief of Staff, US Army, 1993, pp. 115–116.

21. The Iraqis were on alert after reports that Israel might attack Iraqi chemical and nuclear facilities. *Washington Post*, April 29, 1989, p. 16.

22. The reader should be aware that these estimates are extremely uncertain and are based largely on expert estimates of the losses during the Gulf War. There is a sharp difference of opinion among some US experts as to the size of Iraq's losses during the conflict. The US Central Command lists 150 SA-2 launchers, 110 SA-3 launchers, 150 SA-6/SA-8 launchers, 30 Roland VII launchers, and five Crotale launchers in *Atlas, 1996*, MacDill Air Force Base, USCENTCOM, 1997, pp. 16–18. Also see USCENTCOM briefing by "senior military official," Pentagon, January 28, 1997, pp. 2, 5–8, 10; *Washington Times*, February 1, 1997, p. A-13; Reuters, September 4, 1996, 0911; *Jane's Pointer*,

November, 1994, p. 2; Associated Press, September 9, 1996, 0129; *Washington Times*, January 30, 1997, p. A-3; February 1, 1997, p. A-13; IISS, *Military Balance, 1996/1997*; and *Jane's Sentinel: The Gulf States*, "Iraq," London, Jane's Publishing, 1997. Other sources include Andrew Rathmell, *The Changing Balance in the Gulf*, London, Royal United Services Institute, Whitehall Papers 38, 1996; Edward B. Atkenson, *The Powder Keg*, Falls Church, NOVA Publications, 1996; Geoffery Kemp and Robert E. Harkavy, *Strategic Geography and the Changing Middle East*, Washington, Carnegie Endowment/ Brookings, 1997; and Michael Eisenstadt, *Like a Phoenix from the Ashes? The Future of Iraqi Military Power*, Washington, The Washington Institute, Policy Paper 36, 1993.

23. The SAM launcher estimates are based on discussions with US and Israeli experts and are highly uncertain.

24. USCENTCOM briefing by "senior military official," Pentagon, January 28, 1997, pp. 2, 5–8, 10; *Washington Times*, February 1, 1997, p. A-13; Reuters, September 4, 1996, 0911; Jane's *Pointer*, November, 1994, p. 2; Associated Press, September 9, 1996, 0129; *Washington Times*, January 30, 1997, p. A-3; February 1, 1997, p. A-13; IISS, *Military Balance, 1996/1997*; and the *Jane's Sentinel* series.

25. *Wall Street Journal*, August 19, 1992, p. A-3; USCENTCOM briefing by "senior military official," Pentagon, January 28, 1997, pp. 2, 5–8, 10; *Washington Times*, February 1, 1997, p. A-13; Reuters, September 4, 1996, 0911; Jane's *Pointer*, November, 1994, p. 2; Associated Press, September 9, 1996, 0129; *Washington Times*, January 30, 1997, p. A-3; February 1, 1997, p. A-13; IISS, *Military Balance, 1996/1997*; and *Jane's Sentinel: The Gulf States*, "Iraq," London, Jane's Publishing, 1997.

26. Michael Eisenstadt, "The Iraqi Armed Forces Two Years On," *Jane's Intelligence Review*, March, 1993, pp. 121–127; *Jane's Sentinel: The Gulf States*, "Iraq," London, Jane's Publishing, 1997.

27. Based on interviews with British, US, Russian, and Israeli experts.

28. See Sean Boyne, "Iraq's MIO: Ministry of Missing Weapons," *Jane's Intelligence Review*, March, 1998, pp. 23–25.

Chapter 7

The Threat from Iraqi Naval Forces

It has been difficult to determine the organization of the Iraqi navy since its near destruction in the Gulf War. Its headquarters remain in Baghdad, and it still seems to have three flotillas, which include its large ships, patrol ships, and mine warfare forces. It also has intelligence, fleet support, land-based anti-ship missiles, and training directorates. The Iraqi navy has naval bases at Basrah, Az Zubayr, and the commercial dock at Umm Qasr. Many of its ships are based at Az Zubayr, although a small channel to Basra along the Shatt al-Arab is used to base some patrol boats. It currently seems to be under the Southern Command that Saddam Hussein created just before Desert Fox.

MANNING AND OVERALL STRENGTH

Figure 7.1 shows the relative strength of Gulf navies. In 1999, the Iraqi navy only had only a core strength of about 1,900–2,500 men, although some estimates indicate a total manning of 5,000. This manpower strength included that used to guard naval bases and man Iraq's land-based anti-ship missiles. It did not, however, include the naval infantry and marine forces, which are subordinate to the army.

The navy's surviving forces included the frigate *Ibn Khaldun*, one Osa-class missile boat, 13 light combat vessels, 5–8 landing craft, the *Agnadeen*, one Yugoslav Spasilac-class transport, a floating dry dock, and possibly one repairable Polnocny-class LST. The IISS and *Jane's* report that Iraq also had three 5,800-ton roll-on, roll-off transport ships with helicopter decks, a capability to carry 250 troops and 18 tanks, and the ability to embark small landing craft. These ships may be under commercial flags and do not have the ability to beach.[1]

Figure 7.1
Gulf Naval Ships by Category in 1998

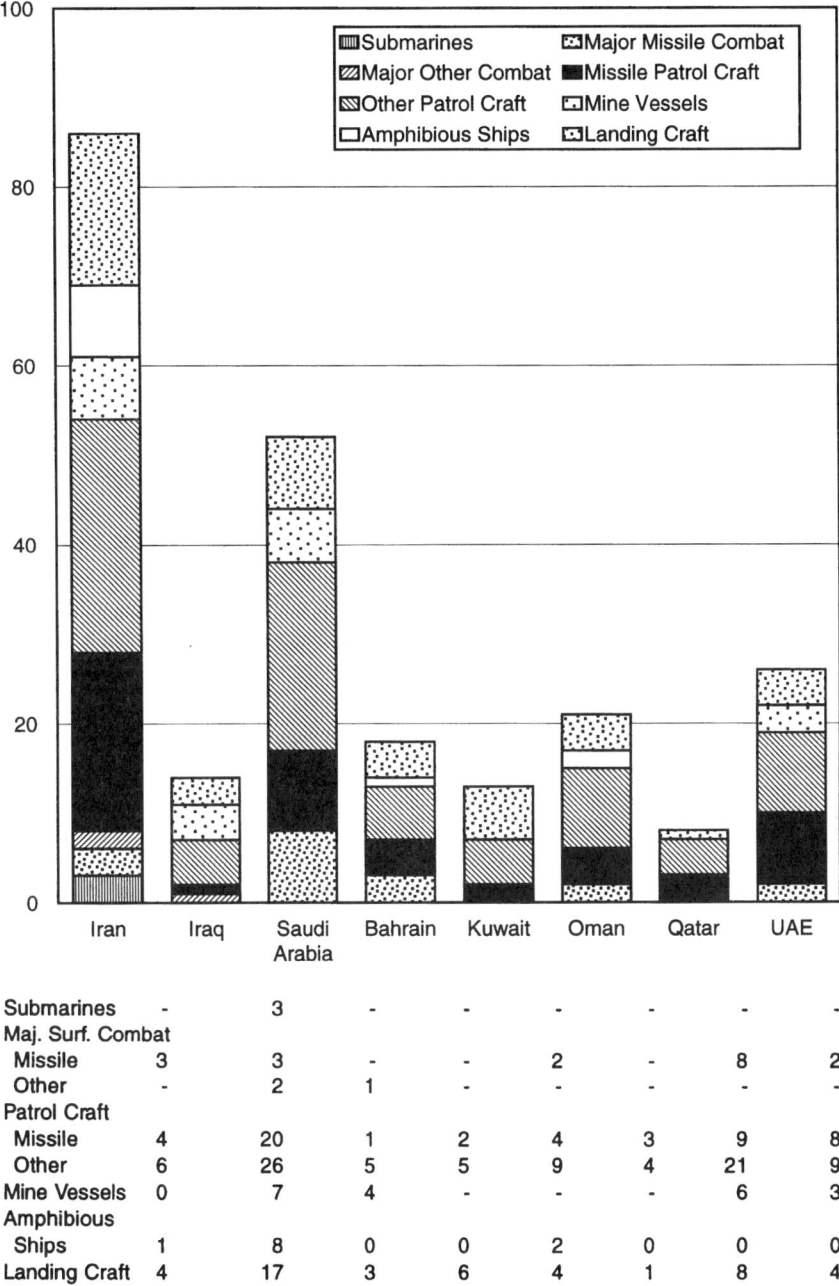

	Iran	Iraq	Saudi Arabia	Bahrain	Kuwait	Oman	Qatar	UAE
Submarines	-	3	-	-	-	-	-	-
Maj. Surf. Combat								
Missile	3	3	-	-	2	-	8	2
Other	-	2	1	-	-	-	-	-
Patrol Craft								
Missile	4	20	1	2	4	3	9	8
Other	6	26	5	5	9	4	21	9
Mine Vessels	0	7	4	-	-	-	6	3
Amphibious								
Ships	1	8	0	0	2	0	0	0
Landing Craft	4	17	3	6	4	1	8	4

Sources: Adapted by Anthony H. Cordesman from IISS, *Military Balance*, and material provided by US experts.

This inventory gives Iraq virtually no naval combat capability. The *Ibn Khaldun* is a comparatively large 1,850-ton ship with a maximum speed of 26 knots, but it is designed for training purposes only. Its armament consists of one 57 mm Bofors gun, one 40 mm Bofors anti-aircraft gun, and a four-barrel 16/20 mm anti-aircraft gun. The *Ibn Khaldun* can carry a quadruple launcher for Exocet missiles, but this launcher has never been fitted. There are reports that the *Ibn Khaldun* may have been rendered largely inoperable during the fighting in 1991, and even if it was not, it probably has only very limited operational capability, because it lacks spares for its Rolls-Royce main engines.

The Iraqi navy does, however, have at least five batteries of HY-2 "Silkworm" anti-ship missiles. In spite of repeated air attacks, there is no evidence that the Coalition destroyed any of Iraq's land-based anti-ship missile launchers, missiles, or fire control equipment during the Gulf War.

SURVIVING COMBAT SHIPS

Iraq's lighter, surviving combat ships include only a maximum of one Osa-class guided missile patrol boat (doubtful), one or two Soviet-supplied Bogomol-class patrol boats, two Zhuk-class patrol boats, six PB-80 coastal patrol craft, some Sawari-class small inshore patrol boats, six SRN-6 Hovercraft, and some small boats. Only one of the hovercraft may be fully operational. Its surviving five mine craft include two Soviet Yevgenya-class and three Yugoslav Nestin-class boats.[2]

The Bogomol-class patrol boats are the only craft large enough to be taken seriously, and they have limited combat capability. Several may also be damaged. These boats are 245-ton vessels and normally carry only a 76 mm gun, a 30 mm Gatling gun, and one SA-N-5 missile.

Iraq does not have access to any of the larger combat ships it ordered from Italy, and little future prospect of obtaining such access. Italy has sold the *Mussa Ben Nussair* and *Tariq Ibn Ziyad* at La Spezia. Italy has turned the four Lupo-class ships that Iraq ordered before the Iran-Iraq War over to its own navy, and it will probably sell the remaining Wadi Mr'agh-class corvettes to some other country.[3]

Iraq has sought to sell some ships to Morocco and two to Malaysia. The *Agnadeen* and Iraq's floating dry dock are held in Alexandria, Egypt. All three of the roll-on, roll-off transports are held in foreign ports. One of the personal yachts that Saddam Hussein ordered before the Iran-Iraq War, the *Al Manuser*, was transferred to King Fahd of Saudi Arabia in 1987, and it has never even entered Iraqi waters. A second yacht, the *Al Qadissiya*, which Saddam Hussein ordered for use on Iraq's rivers, has never been delivered.[4]

Iraq has even less access to the Gulf than it had when it invaded Kuwait. It has been forced to close its naval base at Umm Qasr. Iraq is forced to use small craft and civilian ships for patrols in coastal areas. Virtually all of the larger ships that are still under its control are now laid up in Khor at Zubair, Basra, and Mina al-Bakr.

Iraq has never been able to implement its plans to acquire a large force of naval helicopters with anti-ship missiles and other specialized helicopters. The Iraqi air force does have some Mirage F-1s armed with the Exocet anti-ship missile, but it does not seem to retain any remaining capability to operate Soviet bombers with Soviet air-to-ship missiles. The air force lost some armed helicopters during the Gulf War, but may retain six to seven of the 13 Aerospatiale SA-321s, armed with Exocet air-to-surface missiles obtained during the Iran-Iraq War.

Iraq has a small naval air component, but this seems to be little more than a liaison staff. The Iraqi navy has four Agusta A-109 helicopters for deployment on the corvettes it had ordered from Italy, but these helicopters are in storage. It had also ordered five Agusta Bell AB-212; and 10 Agusta Bell A-103A helicopters from Italy before the Gulf War. It was unable to pay for most of this order, however, and it is unclear that it completed training crews for the few helicopters it did pay for. No armed or special purpose helicopters are currently in service in the Iraqi navy, and the navy still has no meaningful aviation training or capability. Even if the navy can obtain new deliveries, it will be years before it has operational capability.

The helicopters Iraq does use for naval and coastal patrol missions are operated by the air force, as are the Mirage F-1 fighters and Super Frelon helicopters that can be used to launch AM-39 Exocet air-to-ship missiles. However, the Iraqi air force has only a limited ability to conduct anti-ship operations.

It has not taken delivery on any of the major anti-ship helicopter orders it originally negotiated with France in 1989. These orders included six French Aerospatiale AB-332F Super Pumas, with Exocets, and six SA-365N/FF Dauphins, with AS-15TTM air-to-ship missiles. These aircraft might have given Iraq some added anti-ship capability against the Coalition during the Gulf War, although they scarcely would have altered the outcome of the fighting. The AS-332Fs were to be fitted with Varian search and fire control radars, Agrion chin-mounted radars, and four AS-15T air-to-ship missiles each. The AS-15Ts have a range of up to 15 kilometers and are a much cheaper way to attack small ships than the Exocet.[5]

NAVAL READINESS AND WAR-FIGHTING CAPABILITY

Iraq retains some mine warfare capability and most of its land-based Silkworm missile systems. These Silkworms have ranges of up to 100 kilometers, and Iraq has some experience in using them in combat. On February 25, 1991, Iraq fired two Silkworm missiles against Coalition ships in the Gulf. Both missiles missed. One missile failed and crashed into the sea, and the other was destroyed by British Aerospace Sea Darts fired by the *HMS Gloucester*. Iraq can also fire Exocet anti-ship missiles from some of its Mirage F-1 fighters and helicopters. It may also have some Faw 70, Faw 150, and Faw 200 missiles, which it claims are Iraqi-made versions of the Soviet SSC-3 Styx, but these are obsolescent designs at best.[6]

Iraq conducts virtually no naval training, and it rarely has more than one ship on patrol at any given time. Its small bases are vulnerable, and most of its ships, technology, and weapons are at least a decade old. These limitations are so severe that there is no near-term prospect that the Iraqi navy will acquire more than the most marginal war-fighting capability. It can conduct limited raids and fire some anti-ship missiles, but if it attempts to fight Iranian or Western naval and air forces, it is almost certain to be rapidly destroyed.

NEAR-TERM TRENDS AND IMPLICATIONS FOR CONTAINMENT AND DETERRENCE

Iraqi naval forces are so weak that they pose only a limited priority for containment. At the same time, careful attention is needed to two kinds of Iraqi imports: advanced minelaying capabilities and advanced anti-ship missiles. Any supplier regime should focus on such imports as a significant potential risk to the flow of oil and shipping in the Gulf. There are equally good reasons to deny Iraq submarines and modern surface combat ships. Every effort should be made to prevent Iraq from joining Iran as a regional naval threat.

NOTES

1. This analysis draws heavily on interviews and various editions of US Naval Institute, *The Naval Institute Guide to the Combat Fleets of the World, Their Ships, Aircraft, and Armament*, Annapolis, Naval Institute; *Jane's Fighting Ships*; IISS, *Military Balance*; USNI Database.

2. This analysis draws heavily on interviews and USCENTCOM, *Atlas, 1996*, pp. 16–17; various editions of US Naval Institute, *The Naval Institute Guide to the Combat Fleets of the World, Their Ships, Aircraft, and Armament*, Annapolis, Naval Institute; *Jane's Fighting Ships*; IISS, *Military Balance*; USNI Database; Andrew Rathmell, *The Changing Balance in the Gulf*, London, *Royal United Services Institute*, Whitehall Papers 38, 1996; Edward B. Atkenson, *The Powder Keg*, Falls Church, NOVA Publications, 1996; Geoffery Kemp and Robert E. Harkavy, *Strategic Geography and the Changing Middle East*, Washington, Carnegie Endowment/Brookings, 1997; and Michael Eisenstadt, *Like a Phoenix from the Ashes? The Future of Iraqi Military Power*, Washington, The Washington Institute, Policy Paper 36, 1993.

3. *Military Technology*, 2/92, pp. 97–98; *Jane's Defense Weekly*, November 4, 1995, p. 3.

4. *Military Technology*, 2/92, pp. 97–98; *Jane's Defense Weekly*, November 4, 1995, p. 3.

5. *Defense News*, May 8, 1989, p. 6.

6. These estimates are based on interviews and various editions of US Naval Institute,

The Naval Institute Guide to the Combat Fleets of the World, Their Ships, Aircraft, and Armament, Annapolis, Naval Institute; *Jane's Fighting Ships*; IISS, *The Military Balance*, London; USNI Database; *Jane's Sentinel: The Gulf States*, "Iraq," London, Jane's Publishing, 1997.

Chapter 8

Unconventional Warfare and Terrorism

Iraqi security and paramilitary forces are a key tool in Iraq's efforts to use force to put pressure on its Gulf neighbors and the West. Iraq has long manipulated extremist groups and movements to serve its ambitions and ideological goals. Like other radical Middle Eastern states, Iraq has found such exploitation to be a cheap and an effective substitute for overt political and military action. Such activities allow Iraq to partially decouple its actions from public responsibility, and to suddenly shift support from one group to another and disavow a given group at will.

Reporting by the US State Department indicates that Iraq continues to provide haven and training facilities for several terrorist clients. Abu Abbas' Palestine Liberation Front (PLF) maintains its headquarters in Baghdad. The Abu Nidal organization (ANO) also has an office in Baghdad. The Arab Liberation Front (ALF), headquartered in Baghdad, continues to receive funding from Saddam's regime. Iraq provides a home for the former head of the now-defunct 15 May organization, Abu Ibrahim, who masterminded several bombings of US aircraft. It allows the Mojahedin-e Khalq (MEK)—a terrorist group of Iranian exiles opposed to the current Iranian regime—to maintain a base in Iraq and to carry out several violent attacks in Iran from these bases.

Since the beginning of the Iran-Iraq War, Iraqi intelligence has concentrated largely on intelligence operations and on the suppression of dissidents inside and outside of Iraq. It does, however, maintain a large special operations component which operates directly out of Iraqi embassies, and through independent overseas "fronts" like airline and purchasing offices. While Iraqi intelligence is deeply concerned with suppressing opposition to the Ba'ath regime, Iraqi intelligence has also been deeply involved in buying arms, in obtaining the technology for weapons of mass destruction, in providing covert support for ethnic and political movements hostile to the enemies of the Iraqi regime, and in attacks on foreign critics, intelligence agents, and political leaders.

IRAQ'S SECURITY STRUCTURE

Saddam has always relied heavily on Iraq's intelligence services and security structure to maintain his power. The only period in which he made any effort to moderate the public image of these services was after the Gulf War, and this effort virtually ceased by late 1991. On December 23, 1991, the Interior Ministry warned that an amnesty for turning in unlicensed firearms would only last 10 more days. On January 1, 1992, Saddam's son, Uday, called for the public execution of dissidents in his newspaper, *Babil*. From that time onward, the security services ruthlessly suppressed any opposition, with minimal regard for world opinion.

Iraq's security and intelligence forces were the subject of intense strikes during Desert Fox, several key facilities were seriously damaged or destroyed, and some personnel were killed. Nevertheless, most survived, and in early 1999 they included a wide range of formal organizations and militias attached to Saddam Hussein, his sons, the Ba'ath Party, and the military. They remained one of the largest single instruments of government power, and totaled over 100,000 men. They include massive civil police forces, large intelligence and internal security units, and large military and paramilitary forces like the Republican Guards, Special Republican Guards, and Saddam Hussein's bodyguards or special security force. Saddam's elite security forces alone seem to total up to 15,000 men. There are also state political intelligence and security services that help protect Saddam Hussein and his coterie. These organizations are all headed by officers supposedly loyal to Saddam Hussein. Many are related to him, or are members of his Al Bu Nasser tribe and the other two branches of the Tikriti tribe.

As has been mentioned earlier, one source indicates that the Iraqi National Security Council is a coordinating group which ties these organizations together. Saddam is the formal chairman, and his son, Qusay, also plays a powerful role. The National Security Council has representatives of the Office of the Presidential Palace, the Special Security Service, the General Intelligence Directorate, Military Intelligence, and the General Security Service, with a representative of the Military Security Service. General Namaq Ismael, a regular army officer from Mosul, attends meetings, and Saddam's secretary, Abd Hamid Mahmoud, may play some role in its operations. The National Security Council provides Saddam and Qusay with a means of coordinating Iraq's competing intelligence and security services and dealing with key internal security threats and regional intelligence problems.[1]

Iraq's security forces are the subject of constant changes in command, at least some of which involve arrests or executions. The main intelligence and security services include:[2]

- *The Special Security Service (also known as Amn al-Khass, Hijaz Amn al-Khass, Presidential Affairs Department, Special Security Organization, or the SSS).* The Special Security Service is the most powerful of Iraq's security services. Some reports indicate that it controls a Joint Operations Room in the palace that is charged with coordinating the efforts of Iraq's various services to protect Saddam, and which has computer data links to each of the various paramilitary units in the other intelligence services and records section of the General Intelligence Directorate.[3]

It was established in the mid-1980s, after an attempt to assassinate Saddam Hussein highlighted gaps or failures in the already extensive cloak of security around the Iraqi leader. Its top leadership is manned by men personally selected by Saddam Hussein. It was headed by Major General Fanar Zibin Hassan al-Tikriti during the Gulf War, and then by Hussein Kamel, Saddam's ex-son-in-law. It is now headed by Saddam's younger son, Qusay, although other officers perform the day-to-day work and occupy the formal chain of command.

Recruiting is extremely selective. Personnel are generally from Saddam's hometown of Tikrit, or from Hawuija and Samarra—two neighboring cities loyal to Saddam. Many members are recruited from loyal tribes. These tribes included the Dulaim tribe in western Iraq in the past, but it is unclear whether this tribe is still regarded as being loyal. Many recruits are brought in at ages 16–18, are suitably indoctrinated, and then grow up in the service. There are unconfirmed reports of a major new recruiting drive after the coup attempts against Saddam in 1995. It is reported to have grown from around 1,000 personnel before the Gulf War to some 5,000, but such numbers are speculative.

The main function of the Special Security Service is to protect Saddam from assassination attempts emanating from within the army, his family, or the government at large. The tasks of the Special Security Service include:

- guaranteeing the security of the president and providing protection for him during travel and at public meetings;

- ensuring the security of all presidential facilities such as palaces and guest houses, and supervising other security and intelligence services;

- directing and implementing much of Iraq's efforts to conceal its missile, chemical weapons, biological weapons, and nuclear programs;

- surveillance of government ministries and agencies and leadership of the armed forces; and

- supervision of key internal security operations against the Kurds and Shi'ites.

Some experts feel that it manages Saddam Hussein's secret foreign accounts, intelligence operations involving the purchase of foreign arms and technology, and security within Iraq's most critical military industries. It evidently provides some of the liaison staff working with UNSCOM, and closely supervises programs involving missiles and weapons of mass destruction.

The organization has operated within the presidential palace and is headquartered on Palestine Street in Baghdad. It also has a much larger building near the Al Rashid Hotel and small offices in Basra and Mosul. It has a large prison and interrogation complex at Al Ranighwania, near the Baghdad International Airport. Its facilities were severely damaged during Desert Fox.

The Special Security Service has a political branch, which monitors surveillance on all suspect citizens. It has links to the databases maintained by the Ministry of Interior and elements in the Foreign Ministry. It has an operations unit, which can arrest, interrogate, and execute suspects. The Special Branch essentially acts as a watchdog to ensure the loyalty of the members of the Special Security Service and top intelligence and security officials. It also has a paramilitary security force called the Amn Al-Khass Brigade, and it cooperates closely with (and monitors) the Special Republican Guards. The Special Republican Guards would evidently provide the Special Security Service with heavy units in the event of a serious military coup.

- *The General Intelligence Service (also known as the Mukhabaret, Da'irat al Mukhabaret, Mukhabarat al-Amma, or GIS).* The General Intelligence Service is the intelligence and security service of the Ba'ath Party. It grew directly out of the clandestine Ba'ath Party security organization built up by Saddam Hussein in the 1960s, known as the *Jihaz Haneen* (Instrument of Yearning). It was expended when the Ba'ath took power in July, 1968, and it became the General Intelligence Service in the early 1970s. Its first head was Sadoon Shaker, and then Saddam's half-brother, Barzan Al-Tikriti. One director, Fadhil al Barak, was arrested in 1989 for spying for Russia, and he was executed in 1991. Its present head seems to be Lt. General Manee Abd al Rashid, but Qusay plays a major role in its control.

Its tasks include:

- conducting counterespionage and monitoring subversive activities;
- supervising the Ba'ath Party and other political organizations;
- maintaining a watch over internal minorities such as the Kurds and Assyrians;
- suppressing opposition activities emanating from Shi'ites and other minorities;
- maintaining a watch over foreigners in Iraq, including those from Arab countries;
- conducting sabotage, subversion, and terrorist operations against neighboring countries such as Syria and Iran;
- providing financial and military aid, including logistical assistance, to opposition;
- seizure or murder of opposition elements outside of Iraq;
- training key personnel for other intelligence and security agencies;
- technical research into covert operations and procurement of equipment for such operations;
- providing disinformation and attempts to exploit or use Arab and other media; and
- targeting threatening individuals and groups in countries hostile to Iraq.

The GIS is divided into units or bureaus that are spread throughout the country, which are attached to Iraqi embassies and the offices of Iraqi Airways. The GIS has a massive walled headquarters in the Mansour district of Baghdad. It was this headquarters that the United States attacked with cruise missiles on June 27, 1993, after the GIS had been identified as the agency that had sponsored an assassination attempt on President George Bush. Some of its facilities were damaged during Desert Fox.

Like all Iraqi intelligence agencies, personnel are chosen carefully from the groups most loyal to Saddam. The GIS provides excellent career opportunities by Iraqi standards, and its senior personnel are well trained. It runs the National Security College, located in Abughreib on the outskirts of Baghdad. This college trains high school graduates for three years and college graduates for eighteen months. The strength of the GIS is estimated at around 4,000 personnel.

The key elements of the GIS include the Political Bureau, which is organized into a Planning Office for intelligence and covert operations; a Propaganda Office, for psychological warfare and disinformation; a Secret Service, for the collection of foreign intelligence; a training directorate; and a Directorate of Technical Affairs.

There is also a Special Bureau (Office One) which has a number of different subordinate offices that have highly compartmental functions. Office Five ensures the loyalty of other members of the GIS. Office Seven handles special arrests, interrogations, and sometimes executions. It has a special prison and interrogation center in Baghdad, a major prison and interrogation center in Khandair, west of Baghdad, and holds some prisoners in Abugereib. Office Sixteen trains Iraqis and foreigners for covert operations, including terrorism, and may supervise the execution of some operations. Other offices provide foreign counterintelligence with a special focus on Syria, Iran, and Jordan. The GIS also has a paramilitary Mukhabarat Brigade, which is the only part of the GIS that does not normally dress in civilian clothes.

- *Military Intelligence (also known as Estikhabarat, Al-Istikhbarat al-Askariyya).* Military Intelligence traces its origins back to the time of the monarchy. It is still manned largely by army officers, although it was brought under the direct control of the Presidential Palace in the 1980s. It focuses on foreign military threats, but it also is responsible for internal security within the Iraqi military. It has ties to some foreign radical movements and has conducted intelligence operations overseas.

During the Gulf War, Military Intelligence was headed by Major General Sabir Abd al-Aziz Hussein al-Duri—a Sunni Arab from Dur, the hometown of Izzat Ibrahim, the Deputy Chairman of the Revolutionary Command Council. Duri was a traditional, long-serving Ba'athist with ties to the army and senior party leaders. He was replaced after the Gulf War by Major General Wafiq Jassim Sammara'i. Sammara'i was later arrested and fled to Syria, and he was replaced by Major General Khalid Salih al-Juburi. His deputy seems to be Major General Saad al Ghani. Major General Abd al-Khadir Salman Khamis (a Tikriti related to Saddam) also plays a role in the organization.[4]

Military Intelligence has the following tasks:

- ensuring loyalty of the armed forces to the regime;
- supervision of security and counterintelligence in the armed forces;
- collection of intelligence and tactical and strategic research on countries deemed hostile or threatening to Iraq;
- waging of psychological war against military enemies;
- implementation of deception plans during wartime;
- cooperation with foreign intelligence services;
- managing a large network of informants, including foreign personnel, and military human intelligence. This network includes operatives in Jordan, Israel, Gaza and the West Bank, the Gulf states, Egypt, Syria, the Sudan, Turkey, and Yemen;
- managing a large human intelligence network in Iran, with secure covert communications;
- conducting terrorist operations abroad against hostile countries, groups (Kurds), and opponents of Saddam Hussein. During the 1980s, military intelligence operatives in the offices of military attaches in Iraqi embassies in western Europe were involved in such activities. Reportedly, agents of the Istikhbarat were responsible for the assassination of Saddam's opponents in Beirut, London, and Paris. Among the victims

was Abdul Razzaq al-Nayef, a former senior Ba'athist official in the early days, who was murdered in London in 1978; and

- conducting research and studies on technological issues.

Military Intelligence is based in a large complex in the Aladhamia section of Baghdad. This complex has a large base with its own support structure, and it can operate without the support of any other branch of the military. It includes a large prison and an interrogation center. There are other bases at the Al Rashid Camp in Baghdad, and a facility in Baghdad that handles military intelligence on other Arab countries, Iran, opposition movements, and Western threats. Some of its facilities were damaged during Desert Fox.

Work by Sean Boyne indicates that it has regional offices in Kirkuk, Mosul, and Basra. The Kirkuk office deals with intelligence on Iran and the Kurds, the Mosul office handles Turkey, Syria, and Jordan, and the Basra office covers Iran, Kuwait, Saudi Arabia, and the other Gulf states. Military Intelligence is reported to have around 4,000–6,000 personnel. It has three main branches: Political, Special, and Administrative. The Political Branch concentrates on the collection of foreign military intelligence.[5]

The Special Branch includes a security unit to ensure the loyalty of other members of Military Intelligence, and a paramilitary "brigade" with a "battalion" to counter internal security threats in the Baghdad area. It has a covert collection office (possibly known as Unit 999), headquartered at Salman Pak. This organization has "battalions" with special area expertise for infiltrating foreign governments and movements and trains both Iraqi and foreign personnel for such missions. It is reported to have battalions for Iran, Saudi Arabia, Israel, Turkey, maritime operations against Iran or Kuwait, the Kurdish Security Zone, and Shi'ite dissidents.

- *Military Security Service (also known as the Amn Al-Askariya or MSS).* The Military Security Service emerged out of Military Intelligence following the growing signs of unrest within the military forces during 1992. It now has officers in virtually every Iraqi military unit and performs both an internal security and anticorruption function. Like many Iraqi intelligence and security services, it has its own paramilitary unit and a special internal security unit to watch over the operations of the Military Security Service.

  The current head of the Military Security Service seems to be Mu'tamad Ni'mah al-Takriti, who replaced Khalid al-Juburi.[6] Some experts feel that Colonel Abd Hassan al-Majid, Ali Hassan al-Majid's younger brother, was the true power in military intelligence before his defection. The Military Security Service is headquartered in Aladhamia in Baghdad, and it is near the headquarters of the Military Intelligence Service. It reports directly to the Presidential Palace and has grown to a strength as high as 5,000 personnel.

- *General Security Service (also known as the Secret Police, State Internal Security Service, Al-Amn al-Amm, or GSS).* Along with Military Intelligence, this organization traces its routes back to the time Iraq was a monarchy, and it was part of the police forces controlled by the Ministry of the Interior.

  Until the Ba'ath came to power in 1968, it was manned by professional policemen and army officers. It was subsequently purged and "Ba'athized" by Saddam's paternal cousin, Ali Hasan al-Majid, who ran the service from 1980 to 1987. Its headquarters were moved from the Bataween district of Baghdad to the Al Baladiat district in 1990, and the new headquarters area includes yet another special prison.

The General Security Service focuses largely on internal security, but occasionally becomes involved in small foreign operations. It has elements in virtually every major police station in Iraq, and it usually has its own floor or building. It deals with both economic and political crimes.

Major General Abd al-Rahman al-Duri headed the GSS before the Gulf War, but Saddam appointed his half-brother, Siba'awi Ibrahim, as the head after the Gulf War. In July, 1996, Siba'awi Ibrahim was replaced as director of internal security by General Taha Abbas al-Ahbabi. Al-Ahbabi had previously served in the GID and Military Security Service and comes from Tikrit.

Siba'wi Ibrahim's removal reflected a sharp deterioration in Saddam's relations with his half-brothers. The Ibrahims could no longer trust their half-brother. Uday shot Watban in the leg, and the leg had to be removed. This incident was followed by the defection of Hussein Kamel, and then his murder following his return to Baghdad. Barzan responded by publicly attacking Uday. Watban and Sib'awi are reported to have indicated that they wanted to leave Iraq and to have been placed under house arrest in July, 1996.[7]

The GSS seems to have lost some of its influence in spite of the appointment of a new director. This may be the result of the fact that members were involved in the coup attempt against Saddam in 1996, and were arrested and executed. It still, however, is a powerful element of the security structure. Several of its facilities were struck during Desert Fox.

- *Ba'ath Party Security (Amn al Hizb).* This security office develops intelligence on party members and has security cells throughout the Ba'ath Party.
- *The Military Bureau of the Ba'ath Party.* The Military Bureau was also strengthened and reorganized after the Gulf War. It is headed by Saddam, and his deputy is his cousin and brother-in-law, Kamel Rashid Yassin. It acts as a commissar system to indoctrinate the armed forces and check on their political loyalty.
- *The Tribal Chief's Bureau (Maktab al-Shuyukh).* This is a new bureau that was created after the Gulf War. This service pays tribal leaders to control their tribes, spy on possible tribal dissidents, and provide arms to loyal tribesmen to suppress any dissidents. It was headed by Major Saddam Kamel, a cousin and son-in-law of Saddam Hussein and Hussein Kamel's younger brother. Saddam Kamel defected with his brother to Jordan.
- *Saddam's Fedayeen.* Saddam's Fedayeen are led by Saddam's eldest son, Uday. They were formed after the defection of Hussein and Saddam Kamel. They are largely composed of young Takritis and are trained by the Republican Guard. They dress in black and often keep their faces covered. They have limited military capability, but they are equipped with some heavy weapons, including PT-76 light tanks and BTR-70 armored personnel carriers.[8]
- *The Ministry of Information.* Most Middle Eastern governments control their media and the press, and use it as an intelligence and propaganda service. Iraq's Ministry of Information has served as both a particularly strong and ruthless instrument of control. It tolerates some kinds of criticism—many of which seem to be manipulated to give the image that it is safe to make Saddam Hussein aware of the faults of government or to give outsiders the impression of a free press. At the same time, it controls virtually

every word written or spoken in the Iraqi media, uses "journalists" to propagandize internally and abroad, and has a long list of "writers," "academics," and "artists" it can use to influence both domestic and foreign opinion. The Ministry also has close links to other intelligence services, so it can control or spy on foreign visitors and journalists and manipulate crowds and media events in Iraq. For example, it maintains a long list of seemingly private Iraqis who are fluent in foreign languages, and who it ensures appear in front of cameras. Some of these Iraqis are allowed to give private interviews that support Iraqi propaganda—even when the spokesperson appears somewhat critical. The Ministry of Information also attempts to manipulate foreign scholars and international bodies visiting Iraq. It also has a list of quasiacademic institutions it can use to hold and manipulate meetings and conferences and use to develop contacts between foreigners and seeming "moderates" and "opponents" of the regime.

- *The Foreign Ministry.* This ministry mixes legitimate diplomats with members of the intelligence and security services. Like the Soviet diplomatic service during the Cold War, it is so closely linked to intelligence operations that it is impossible to distinguish between diplomats and the Iraqi equivalents of the KGB.

- *The Iraqi telecommunications services and major academic and research institutions.* All of these institutions have intelligence and security cells designed to improve state control. Many have special sections for military and intelligence efforts, for purchasing equipment to be used for military purposes, and for supporting governmental propaganda and outreach efforts in dealing with foreigners.

- *The Iraqi signals and electronic intelligence (SIGINT/ELINT) system.* Iraq received considerable Western and Eastern-bloc technical assistance in developing its SIGINT/ELINT capabilities during the Iran-Iraq War. One source indicates that the intelligence and internal security aspects of Iraqi SIGINT and ELINT operations are unified as part of the Al Hadi Project (Project 858). According to this source, the Iraqi SIGINT/ELINT system has about 800 personnel and is headquartered in Al Rashedia, and it has at least five ground stations in various parts of Iraq. This system collects and translates SIGINT and ELINT and distributes it to both military and intelligence users. It monitors internal communications as well as foreign political and military communications, and it seems to have a highly accurate and rapidly responding direction-finding capability. It uses Japanese and French-supplied computers and communications gear.[9]

Iraq's intelligence and security effort is so large, duplicative, and permeating that it gives Saddam Hussein control over every aspect of Iraqi life. No part of Iraqi society is ever secure from Saddam's surveillance. No element of the military forces or security services is immune to surveillance from its rivals, and no group outside of Iraq is free of penetration by Iraqi intelligence or security officers. At the same time, the power of these organizations and their ties to virtually every element of the Iraqi government and Iraqi society act as a powerful resistance to political change. The intelligence and security structure may not be loyal to Saddam as a man, but it is almost certainly loyal to its own self-interest, and it is likely to prove a lasting barrier to the emergence of any new government or ruling elite which does not make similar use of such instruments of state control.

IRAQI TERRORIST ACTIVITY

Iraq has not been able to act as freely in supporting revolutionary and extremist groups since the end of the Gulf War as it has in the past. Many Iraqi agents were expelled from foreign countries during the Gulf War. The US State Department summarizes this situation as follows, in its annual report on terrorism in April, 1997:

> Iraq's ability to carry out terrorism abroad has been curbed by UN sanctions. As events during 1996 clearly demonstrated, however, Saddam Hussein's regime continues to murder dissidents throughout Iraq and target foreign and local relief personnel in the northern part of the country.[10]

Iraq has still been active in terrorism. The US State Department estimates that Iraqi intelligence conducted 39 terrorist attacks between the end of the Gulf War and April, 1993. Iraqi agents seem to have trained new hit squads to kill enemies in foreign countries, including an Iraqi scientist who was about to defect to Jordan in December, 1992. There have been dozens of attacks on UN relief and aid workers in Iraq, including many bombings. Eight time bombs were found under UN trucks in December, 1992, and explosives damaged 14 UN trucks a week later.

Iraq continues to host a number of terrorist organizations, despite being forbidden to do so by UN Security Council Resolution 687. These groups are described in Table 8.1, and include the People's Mujahideen of Iran (Mojahedin-e Khalq), which is opposed to the government of Iran. As has been discussed, the People's Mujahideen has repeatedly launched raids and conducted terrorist attacks in Iran. Iran has retaliated by sponsoring anti-Iraqi forces in Iran, which operate against Iraq and are led by the Hakim family.[11]

Iraq also continues to supported extremist Palestinian groups like the Abu Nidal Organization (ANO), the Arab Liberation Front (ALF), Abu Abbas's Palestinian Liberation Front (PLF), and Abu Ibrahim. Iraq has also assisted the Turkish Kurdistan Workers Party (PKK). Iraq supports anti-Iranian Kurdish groups in Iran, and it continues to provide safe haven and logistical and military support to several terrorist groups and individuals like the People's Mujahideen and the ANO. It may have given some support to the group that bombed the World Trade Center, although the available evidence is weak.[12] None of the foreign terrorist and extremist groups Iraq supports are particularly strong at the moment, or seem to be attracting major popular support outside of Iraq. They are, however, tools Iraq can use under some conditions. Iraq can also use state terrorism, and it has tried to do so in the past.

ATTEMPTING TO ASSASSINATE PRESIDENT BUSH AND ATTACKS ON KUWAIT

The Iraqi General Intelligence Service sponsored an assassination attempt on President Bush when he visited Kuwait on April 14–16, 1993. Iraqi intelligence

Table 8.1
Major Terrorist Groups with Iraqi Support

- *Abu Nidal organization (ANO) a.k.a.: Fatah Revolutionary Council, Arab Revolutionary Council, Arab Revolutionary Brigades, Black September, and Revolutionary Organization of Socialist Muslims.* The ANO is an international terrorist organization led by Sabri al-Banna. It split from the PLO in 1974. It is made up of various functional committees, including political, military, and financial. It has carried out terrorist attacks in 20 countries, killing or injuring almost 900 persons. Targets include the United States, the United Kingdom, France, Israel, moderate Palestinians, the PLO, and various Arab countries. Major attacks included the Rome and Vienna airports in December, 1985, the Neve Shalom synagogue in Istanbul, the Pan Am Flight 73 hijacking in Karachi in September, 1986, and the *City of Poros* day-excursion ship attack in July, 1988 in Greece; suspected of assassinating PLO Deputy Chief Abu Iyad and PLO Security Chief Abu Hul in Tunis in January, 1991. The ANO assassinated a Jordanian diplomat in Lebanon in January, 1994, and it has been linked to the killing of the PLO representative there. There have been no attacks against Western targets since the late 1980s. Its strength is several hundred men, plus militia in Lebanon and overseas support structure. It is currently headquartered in Libya, with a presence in Lebanon in the Al Biqa' (Bekaa Valley) and also several Palestinian refugee camps in coastal areas of Lebanon. It also has a presence in Sudan, and it has demonstrated an ability to operate over a wide area, including the Middle East, Asia, and Europe. It has received considerable support, including safe haven, training, logistic assistance, and financial aid from Iraq and Syria (until 1987); it continues to receive aid from Libya, in addition to close support for selected operations.

- *Kurdistan Workers' Party (PKK).* The PKK is a Marxist-Leninist insurgent group composed of Turkish Kurds and was established in 1974. In recent years, it has moved beyond rural-based insurgent activities to include urban terrorism. It seeks to set up an independent Marxist state in southeastern Turkey, where there is a predominantly Kurdish population. Its primary targets are Turkish government forces and civilians in eastern Turkey, but it is becoming increasingly active in western Europe against Turkish targets. The PKK conducted attacks on Turkish diplomatic and commercial facilities in dozens of west European cities in 1993 and again in the spring of 1995. In an attempt to damage Turkey's tourist industry, it has bombed tourist sites and hotels and has kidnapped foreign tourists. Its strength is approximately 10,000 to 15,000 full-time guerrillas, 5,000 to 6,000 of whom are in Turkey; 60,000 to 75,000 part-time guerrillas; and hundreds of thousands of sympathizers in Turkey and Europe. It operates in Turkey and western Europe. It receives safe haven and modest aid from Syria, Iraq, and Iran.

- *Mujahedin-e Khalq Organization (MEK or MKO) a.k.a.: The National Liberation Army of Iran (NLA, the militant wing of the MEK), the People's Mujahedin of Iran (PMOI), National Council of Resistance (NCR), Muslim Iranian Student's Society (front organization used to garner financial support).* It was formed in the 1960s by the college-educated children of Iranian merchants. The MEK sought to counter what is perceived as excessive Western influence in the Shah's regime. In the 1970s, the MEK concluded that violence was the only way to bring about change in Iran. Since then, the MEK has followed a philosophy that mixes Marxism and Islam, and it has developed into the largest and most active armed Iranian dissident group. Its history is studded with anti-Western activity and, most recently, attacks on the interests of the clerical regime

Table 8.1 (continued)

- in Iran and abroad. The MEK directs a worldwide campaign against the Iranian government that stresses propaganda and occasionally uses terrorist violence. During the 1970s, the MEK staged terrorist attacks inside of Iran to destabilize and embarrass the Shah's regime. The group killed several US military personnel and civilians working on defense projects in Tehran.

  The MEK also supported the takeover in 1979 of the US embassy in Tehran. In April, 1992, the MEK carried out attacks on Iranian embassies in 13 different countries, demonstrating the group's ability to mount large-scale operations overseas. It has several thousand fighters based in Iraq, with an extensive overseas support structure. Most of the fighters are organized in the MEK's National Liberation Army (NLA). In the 1980s, the MEK's leaders were forced by Iranian security forces to flee to France. Most resettled in Iraq by 1987. Since the mid-1980s, the MEK has not mounted terrorist operations in Iran at a level similar to its activities in the 1970s. Aside from the National Liberation Army's attacks into Iran toward the end of the Iran-Iraq War, and occasional NLA cross-border incursions since, the MEK's attacks on Iran have amounted to little more than harassment. The MEK has had more success in confronting Iranian representatives overseas through propaganda and street demonstrations. Beyond support from Iraq, the MEK uses front organizations to solicit contributions from expatriate Iranian communities.

- *Palestine Liberation Front (PLF)*. The PLF is a terrorist group that broke away from the PFLP-GC in the mid-1970s. The PLP later split again into pro-PLO, pro-Syrian, and pro-Libyan factions. The pro-PLO faction was led by Muhammad Abbas (Abu Abbas), who became a member of the PLO Executive Committee in 1984, but who left it in 1991. The Abu Abbas-led faction has carried out attacks against Israel. Abbas's group was also responsible for the attack in 1985 on the cruise ship *Achille Lauro*, and the murder of US citizen Leon Klinghoffer. A warrant for Abu Abbas's arrest is outstanding in Italy. Its strength is at least 50. It was based in Tunisia until the *Achille Lauro* attack. It is now based in Iraq. It receives logistic and military support mainly from the PLO, but also from Libya and Iraq.

Sources: Adapted from the Internet version of the US State Department report on terrorism, April, 1997 and April, 1998 editions; and Kenneth Katzman, "Terrorism: Middle Eastern Groups and State Sponsors, 1997," Congressional Research Service, CRS 97–692F, July 10, 1997.

agents—including Mohammed Jawad and Abd al-Iman—recruited 11 Iraqis to drive a Toyota Land Cruiser and Chevrolet Suburban across the Kuwait border on April 13. The vehicles contained pistols, hand grenades, timing devices, remote control sensing devices, and 180 pounds of a Semtex plastic explosive. They were also given 12 cases of whiskey to disguise the operation as smuggling. The key device involved in the plot was a car bomb that was intended to be placed along the president's route through Kuwait to kill both him and his entourage. One of the key Iraqis in the plot, Wali Ghazali, was also given a "suicide belt" as a backup if the car bomb failed.

The United States originally suspected that Kuwait might be exaggerating the plot—in part because Iraqi intelligence recruited amateurs and then failed to inform its recruits of changes in President Bush's route. However, later investigations confirmed that Iraqi intelligence was directly involved. While all of the evidence has not been made public, FBI and CIA agents found that a total of 14–17 people were involved in the plot, including 11 Iraqis and three Kuwaitis. Several had clear ties to the Iraqi Intelligence Service, some bomb components were Iraqi, and the bomb design was similar to an Iraqi bomb used in Turkey. Other evidence linked the plot to the highest levels in the Iraqi government.[13]

The United States retaliated on June 26, 1993, by firing 23 Tomahawk cruise missiles against the GIS headquarters in suburban Baghdad. However, the plot on President Bush's life was part of a much broader pattern of challenge and response that Iraq has carried out since the cease-fire in the Gulf War. Iraq continued to challenge UN aircraft in the no-fly zone by tracking them with radar and occasionally subjecting them to anti-aircraft fire. Iraq also continued to attack Shi'ite rebels in the south, to bomb UN aid missions to the Kurds, to keep much of its troop strength on the border of the Kurdish security zone, and to attack Kurdish leaders and villages in the security zone.

The US State Department reports that Iraqi-backed surrogates were probably responsible for two attempts to bomb the Kuwait Airways office in Beirut in 1993, and another attempt to bomb the Kuwaiti embassy in Lebanon. The Iraqi regime has since sent infiltrators into the Kuwaiti border group and conducted sudden arrests of Iraqis living south of Basrah. In April, 1996, it conducted a series of sweeping arrests of Iraqis living near the Kuwaiti border, and it made arrests in the Al-Zubayr and Abu al-Khasib districts.[14]

In June, 1994 the Kuwaiti court found guilty 14 of the individuals accused of participating in the plot to assassinate former President Bush during his April, 1993 visit to Kuwait. The preceding trial had clearly identified Iraq's complicity in the assassination attempt. On March 20, 1995, a Kuwait court confirmed the death sentences against two Iraqis convicted of involvement in the plot in 1993 to assassinate President George Bush, while converting to prison terms the death sentences meted out to four others by a lower court.

OTHER IRAQI ACTS OF TERRORISM

In 1992, the Iraqi government agreed to comply with UN Resolution 687, which requires Iraq to prohibit any terrorist organization from operating within its territory. Nevertheless, Baghdad maintained contacts with the PKK, which has killed hundreds of people in attacks inside Turkey and mounted two separate terrorist campaigns against Turkish interests in Europe in 1993. The PKK has training camps in Iraq.[15] At the same time, Iraq has encouraged fighting between rival factions within the Kurdish movement to encourage divisions like those between the KDP and PUK.

The Iraqi regime has fought a war of attrition against UN and humanitarian targets in northern Iraq aimed at driving the foreign presence out of the area and depriving the Kurdish population of relief supplies. UN and relief workers were shot at, bombs or grenades were tossed at residences and vehicles, and bombs were placed on UN trucks loaded with relief supplies. In March, 1993, a Belgian official of Handicapped International was shot and killed; a local employee of the same organization was killed, and six others were injured when an aid station was bombed in December. The US State Department estimates that the Iraqi regime is responsible for more than 100 attacks on UN and relief agency personnel and aid convoys since 1991.[16]

On September 26, 1993, a UN truck carrying 12 tons of medical supplies was completely destroyed by a bomb attached to the fuel tank, probably by Iraqi agents at an Iraqi checkpoint. The truck driver and 12 civilians were injured by the blast. The incident illustrates Iraqi determination to reduce aid to the Kurds. Later reports indicate that the Iraqi government may have offered a bounty on UN relief workers and other international relief workers working in Iraq. A September 12, 1996, amnesty issued by the Iraqi government specifically excluded anyone accused of espionage—a charge that the Iraqi government has made repeatedly against foreign relief organizations working in the Kurdish enclave.[17]

During 1994–1998, Iraq continued its terrorist attacks against political dissidents, both at home and abroad. It also continued its terrorist war of attrition aimed at driving UN and other foreign aid agencies out of northern Iraq and depriving the Kurdish population of relief supplies. There were at least 17 attacks against UN and international relief personnel. Iraq continued to provide safe haven and training facilities for several terrorist organizations, including Abu Abbas' Palestine Liberation Front (PLF), the ANO, and the Arab Liberation Front (ALF). In April, 1994, a prominent Iraqi member of the opposition residing in Beirut was assassinated. The government of Lebanon stated that it had firm evidence linking the killing to the government of Iraq. Lebanese authorities subsequently arrested two Iraqi diplomats in connection with the incident, and Lebanon broke diplomatic relations with Iraq.[18]

On January 20, 1995, a US district court in California awarded $1.5 million to Dr. Sargon Dadesho, a member of the Iraqi opposition living in the United States, who had brought suit against the Iraqi regime. Early in 1995, a number of members of the Iraqi opposition in northern Iraq were poisoned by thallium. At least one survived and was treated in a British hospital. The British government confirmed that he was a victim of a regime assassination attempt. In October, 1995, the British government expelled an officer of the Iraqi Interests Section in London for engaging in "activities incompatible with his diplomatic status." The London-based Iraqi opposition reported that the official concerned was an employee of the Iraqi Intelligence Services who was responsible for targeting Iraqi exiles for attack. On November 9, 1995, a bomb exploded at the security office in Kurdish-controlled northern Iraq of the opposition Iraqi National Congress (INC), and killed at least 25 persons.

After its invasion of the Kurdish zone in August, 1996, the Iraqi government sent military and civil intelligence agents into Irbil and other KDP areas. The exact details of Iraqi operations are unclear, but Iraq seems to have arrested several thousand persons and executed hundreds of members of the opposition during late August and September. As many as 1,500 people were arrested in Irbil alone, and 150 members of various opposition groups were detained or killed. The government also killed Iraqi "deserters" supporting opposition groups. According to eyewitnesses, these executions included the killing of 96 officers and enlisted men on August 31 in the town of Qushtapa, roughly 20 kilometers south of Irbil.[19]

In spite of KDP denials, Iraqi government military and civil intelligence agents continued to arrange occasional additional disappearances and executions in KDP-controlled areas through early 1997. Iraq also did not halt its attacks on UN personnel. On September 29, 1997, and October 6, 1997, "gunmen" attacked UN convoys in northern Iraq. On October 5, four "gunmen" attacked a UN headquarters in Baghdad. The timing came too close to a crisis Iraq was provoking with the UN Special Commission (UNSCOM) to seem entirely coincidental.[20]

IMPLICATIONS FOR WESTERN AND SOUTHERN GULF STRATEGY

The West, and particularly the United States, often overuse the word "terrorism." Iraq, however, is likely to remain a real "terrorist nation" as long as it is under the control of Saddam Hussein, or any similar "centrist" regime. It also is likely to turn its attention away from dissidents and focus on foreign targets the moment sanctions are eased, or it feels it can do so safely without US or Coalition reprisals. This is not a threat that can be dealt with through sanctions—in fact, Iraq may increase its unconventional warfare and terrorist efforts in reaction to prolonged sanctions. The only answer is strong counterterrorist capabilities and close coordination between the United States and its allies in the Southern Gulf.

NOTES

1. Sean Boyne, "Inside Iraq's Security Network," *Jane's Intelligence Review*, July, 1997, pp. 312–316, and August, 1997, pp. 365–367.

2. The author is deeply indebted to Amatzia Baram for his help in drafting this section. It also draws heavily on the excellent work done by Sean Boyne in "Inside Iraq's Security Network," *Jane's Intelligence Review*, July, 1997, pp. 312–316, and August, 1997, pp. 365–367; and on Michael Eisenstadt, "The Iraqi Armed Forces Two Years On," *Jane's Intelligence Review*, March, 1993, pp. 121–127, and *Like A Phoenix from the Ashes?* pp. 10–13; Judith Miller and Laurie Mylroie, *Saddam Hussein and the Crisis in the Gulf*, New York, Random House, pp. 48–50; Samir al-Khalil, *Republic of Fear*, New York, Pantheon, 1990, pp. 14–16, 30–31, 36–37, 133, 143–145; Adel Darwish and Gregory Alexander, *Unholy Babylon*, London, Victor Gollancz, 1991, pp. 139–140,

219–226, 257–260; *Jane's Sentinel: The Gulf States,* "Iraq," London, Jane's Publishing, 1997.

3. Sean Boyne in "Inside Iraq's Security Network," *Jane's Intelligence Review,* July, 1997, pp. 312–316, and August, 1997, pp. 365–367.

4. *Al-Sharq al-Awsat,* July 4, 1996, p. 4.

5. Sean Boyne, "Inside Iraq's Security Network," *Jane's Intelligence Review,* July, 1997, pp. 312–316, and August, 1997, pp. 365–367.

6. *Al-Sharq al-Awsat,* July 4, 1996, p. 4.

7. *The Times,* July 4, 1996, p. 15.

8. *Jane's Defense Weekly,* October 7, 1995.

9. Interviews, Sean Boyne, "Inside Iraq's Security Network," *Jane's Intelligence Review,* July, 1997, pp. 312–316, and August, 1997, pp. 365–367.

10. On-line edition, access from US State Department, DOSFAN, May 16, 1997. For additional summary reporting, see the annual US State Department reports on terrorism, available through the home page of the US state Department on the Internet; Kenneth Katzman, "Persian Gulf: Radical Islamic Movements," Congressional Research Service, CRS 96–731F, August 30, 1996; and Kenneth Katzman, "Terrorism: Middle Eastern Groups and State Sponsors, 1997," Congressional Research Service, CRS 97–692F, July 10, 1997.

11. *New York Times,* May 26, 1993, p. A-8, June 24, 1992, p. A-3, July 17, 1993, p. A-14; Agence France Presse, April 12, 1993, May 15, 1993, July 19, 1993; BBC ME/1664/A, April 16, 1993, ME/1721/A, June 22, 1993; *Armed Forces Journal,* July, 1992, p. 23; *Financial Times,* May 26, 1993, p. 6; *Washington Times,* April 12, 1993, p. A-2; *Baltimore Sun,* May 24, 1993, p. 5-A.

12. US State Department, 1993, 1994, and 1995 reports on terrorism, *Patterns of Global Terrorism,* Internet on-line editions; US State Department, 1993, 1994, and 1995 reports on human rights, "Iraq," Internet on-line editions; *Wall Street Journal,* June 28, 1993.

13. *New York Times,* June 27, 1993, p. A-1; *Washington Post,* June 27, 1992, p. A-1; November 22, 1993, p. A-14. For an article challenging Iraq's role in the plot, see Seymour M. Hersh, "A Case Not Closed," *New Yorker,* November 1, 1993, p. 80.

14. US State Department, 1993, 1994, 1995, and 1996 reports on terrorism, *Patterns of Global Terrorism,* Internet on-line editions; US State Department, 1993, 1994, 1995, and 1996 reports on human rights, "Iraq," Internet on-line editions; and Kenneth Katzman, "Terrorism: Middle Eastern Groups and State Sponsors, 1997," Congressional Research Service, CRS 97–692F, July 10, 1997.

15. US State Department, 1993, 1994, 1995, and 1996 reports on terrorism, *Patterns of Global Terrorism,* Internet on-line editions; US State Department, 1993, 1994, 1995, and 1996 reports on human rights, "Iraq," Internet on-line editions; and Kenneth Katzman, "Terrorism: Middle Eastern Groups and State Sponsors, 1997," Congressional Research Service, CRS 97–692F, July 10, 1997.

16. US State Department, 1993, 1994, 1995, and 1996 reports on terrorism, *Patterns of Global Terrorism,* Internet on-line editions; US State Department, 1993, 1994, 1995, and 1996 reports on human rights, "Iraq," Internet on-line editions; and Kenneth Katzman, "Terrorism: Middle Eastern Groups and State Sponsors, 1997," Congressional Research Service, CRS 97–692F, July 10, 1997.

17. US State Department, 1993, 1994, 1995, and 1996 reports on terrorism, *Patterns of Global Terrorism,* Internet on-line editions; US State Department, 1993, 1994, 1995,

and 1996 reports on human rights, "Iraq," Internet on-line editions; and Kenneth Katzman, "Terrorism: Middle Eastern Groups and State Sponsors, 1997," Congressional Research Service, CRS 97–692F, July 10, 1997.

18. US State Department, 1993, 1994, 1995, and 1996 reports on terrorism, *Patterns of Global Terrorism*, Internet on-line editions; US State Department, 1993, 1994, 1995, and 1996 reports on human rights, "Iraq," Internet on-line editions; and Kenneth Katzman, "Terrorism: Middle Eastern Groups and State Sponsors, 1997," Congressional Research Service, CRS 97–692F, July 10, 1997.

19. US State Department, 1996 report on human rights, "Iraq," Internet on-line edition.

20. *New York Times*, October 6, 1997, p. A-6; Associated Press, October 7, 1997, 0859.

Chapter 9

Conventional Forces and the Outcome of the War of Sanctions

Iraq's current military weakness does not deprive it of its ability to fight a number of types of war that do not involve committing major forces against the organized opposition of Western and Southern Gulf forces. Iraq can fight irregular or unconventional forms of war. The use of third-party terrorists, extremists, and proxies offers Iraq both a means of revenge and far more security than large-scale military action, as does playing a spoiler role at the political level, and financing political rivals to its enemies in the southern Gulf and the rest of the Arab world. Iraq would also make an exceptionally dangerous partner if it could ever forge any kind of lasting cooperation with Iran or Syria.

A number of types of military conflict remain possible, and typical scenarios could include:[1]

- clashes with Turkey or Iran over Iraqi efforts to attack its Kurds, or support of Kurds hostile to Turkey and Iran;
- mid-intensity conflict with the United States over a major Iraqi attack on the Kurds in the Kurdish security zone;
- war with the Kurds in the Kurdish security zone;
- war with Turkey over Turkish incursions into northern Iraq; cooperation with Turkey in suppressing the Kurds;
- alliance/cooperation with Syria, the Palestinian Authority, and/or Jordan in a future Arab-Israeli conflict or in breaking out of the "US-Israeli encirclement";[2]
- conflict with Iran over Iraqi treatment of the Shi'ites in southern Iraq, and/or Iranian attacks on the Iraqi front group, the People's Mujahideen;
- cooperation with Iran in attempts to pressure some combination of the Southern Gulf

states over oil production, or in pressing the United States to reduce its presence in the Gulf;

- major clashes resulting from refusal to allow UN inspection, over challenges to "no fly zones" and incursions into Kuwait;
- military confrontation growing out of US or UN attacks in response to Iraqi support of terrorism or use of unconventional warfare;
- use of chemical or biological terrorism;
- use of mines or missiles against tanker traffic to Kuwait;
- unconventional attacks on facilities and ships in the Gulf;
- confrontation with Syria over a potential Syrian peace agreement with Israel or some other factor; and,
- conflicts with Syria or Turkey over water.

The most dangerous contingency on this list would be a sudden dash by Iraqi army forces in an attempt to seize Kuwait City. Kuwait has only token air and ground forces by Iraqi standards. The Saudi army has regressed to the point where most of its forces are as static and defensive as they were before the US training effort during Desert Shield. The United States can surge large amounts of air and missile power into the area, but this can still take days. The United States does not normally deploy significant US Army or Marine Corps forces. As a result, Iraqi army forces might be able to thrust into Kuwait City and take the Kuwait people hostage before the United States and Saudi Arabia could react.

Iraq would still suffer serious losses in the process of invading Kuwait, and it would then be virtually defenseless against US strategic bombing. Nevertheless, Iraq has taken serious risks in the past, and the probability of such a scenario could change rapidly if the United States cut its power projection capabilities, Saudi Arabia did not provide full support, and/or Iraq had the opportunity to obtain military resupply and expand its land and air operations in the south.

This list of possible contingencies shows how difficult it is to try to set bounds on the broad range of unpredictable contingencies that could result from the actions of even one of the radical powers in the Gulf. Further, the Southern Gulf states and the West cannot ignore the need to plan for a worst-case scenario: a large-scale Iraqi combined operations attack on Kuwait and/or Eastern Saudi Arabia, launched with limited warning. Once again, the Southern Gulf and the West also cannot simply plan for today. They already must plan forces and capabilities for the year 2000 and well beyond. Someday the UN sanctions will end. Someday Iraq will be able to rebuild its forces with new technology, based on its interpretation of the lessons of the Gulf War.

PROSPECTS FOR FUTURE CONFLICT

Prophecy is a dangerous game at any time, and is virtually impossible in the case of Iraq. There is no way to predict how long Saddam Hussein and the Ba'ath regime will last, or whether any successor government will ultimately prove less authoritarian or aggressive. The future unity and resolve of the UN Coalition is uncertain, and there are limits to how long and how thoroughly the current embargo and sanctions can be applied.

It is clear that Iraq now has less ability to attack its neighbors than it did at the time of the Gulf War. It has lost much of its pre-war offensive capability. It cannot use its present forces in a sustained conflict without major resupply of munitions and spare parts, and its forces will continue to deteriorate with time. Iraq not only is currently limited in military power, the UN embargo on arms and military technology ensures that it will slowly and steadily decline to a limited defensive capability. This decline in Iraq's military forces, however, will not make it vulnerable to Iran, unless Iran receives major additional arms and reorganizes and retrains its forces to the point where they can gain a decisive qualitative edge over Iraq. Such an improvement in Iranian forces now seems highly unlikely.

At the same time, it seems likely that Iraq will be a revanchist state as long as it is under its present Ba'athist regime or under the control of another authoritarian leader or hard-line military officer. Furthermore, the key issue that will shape Iraq's "strategic culture" is not whether Saddam survives, but rather the character of future regimes. As long as any hard-line regime is in power, and Iraq can obtain significant flows of arms and technology, it is likely to be exceedingly dangerous. Iraq is certain to make growing use of the politics of intimidation and may reach the point of risk taking and significant conflict. Further, any successor to Saddam Hussein might find it much easier to develop some form of strategic cooperation with other radical regimes like Iran and Syria.

As a result, the mid- and long-term prospects for future conflict depend heavily on the outcome of the "war of sanctions" and Iraq's access to new supplies of conventional weapons and the technology to make weapons of mass destruction. They depend on the future character of Iraq's regime, and on US and Saudi resolve in maintaining power, conventional deterrent, and defense capabilities. Iran may be able to take care of itself, but Kuwait and the Southern Gulf are only likely to be as safe as US power projection and Saudi military capabilities make them.

What Happens If Sanctions Are Eased or Lifted?

No one can plan on Iraq facing the same limitations on conventional arms imports that it faces today, and the major increases in oil revenues permitted by the oil-for-food program may allow the Iraqi government to divert resources it now spends on food and medical care to paying for military manpower, construction, and some types of dual-use items. In spite of the controls set up under the terms of UNSCR 986, money is still fungible at a national level, and no one should have any illusions about the spending priorities of the Iraqi regime.

If sanctions are lifted or collapse, Iraq can be counted on to try to import carefully targeted weapons and military technologies that react to the lessons of the Gulf War, and which compensate for the critical weaknesses in its conventional forces. It is likely to give priority to its armored forces, air defense systems, and long-range air strike systems, but it is also likely to seek the kind of tactical medium- to long-range guided missiles, mines, and other systems that will allow it to challenge British and US freedom of action in the Gulf, and give it the capability to threaten the oil traffic of its Southern Gulf neighbors.

Iraq will, however, face major short- and mid-term problems even if it does gain relatively free access to conventional arms imports. It has not had any major arms imports for more than a half decade, and it averaged over $3 billion a year worth of arms imports in the decade before the Gulf War. It needs at least $1–$2 billion in annual arms imports to recapitalize and modernize its conventional forces, and it has not had any significant arms imports since August, 1990.

It takes years to order and take delivery on major arms imports. Forces must then be restructured and retrained to use new technology and tactics. Iraq's serious problems with standardization, interoperability, and sustainment will increase—at least for a while—during the conversion process. Iraq can only be fully successful if it adopts new C^4I/battle management systems and concepts, focuses on sustained joint warfare, radically improves the offensive capabilities of its air force, and converts its land forces to allow it to carry out and sustain high-tempo, 24-hour maneuver warfare. It is far easier to make grandiose plans to buy such capabilities than it is to transform actual forces.

Iraq's ruling elite is also the natural enemy of military professionalism. It gives priority to its own security and survival, and this means stifling military initiative. The cult of the leaders means downgrading the status and advice of any military professional who appears to be a potential rival. Saddam Hussein remains a failed law student, and putting him in a field marshal's uniform does not make him a military genius.

What Happens If Sanctions and Export Controls Continue?

If sanctions and export controls continue to have high effectiveness, Iraq seems likely to focus on the survival of the regime in power and on preserving its remaining military capabilities, and to limit itself to internal, low-level, and/or unconventional conflicts.

Internal conflicts are likely to be won by the regime, unless the present Sunni elite divides against itself in some major internal military struggle for power. There is a risk that Kurdish and Shi'ite separatism could provoke some form of

Iraqi civil war, but it is a war that the Ba'ath regime would quickly win unless the UN intervenes. The risk of new fighting between Iraq and its Kurds is particularly high. The Ba'ath elite is almost certain to make every effort to undermine the Kurdish enclave, and to use force the moment it feels it is safe to do so. It will probably have the support of most Iraqi military officers. Turkey's confrontation with its own Kurds and Iran's support of Iraqi Shi'ites are other major wild cards in the equation. Turkey may well reach the point where it fears Kurdish separatism more than Iraq.

Iraq's Shi'ites are now under tight government control, and many are Iraqi nationalists. A new uprising seems unlikely, but it might still occur. If it does, such an uprising seems far more likely to lead to bloody repression than partition of the country or any lasting alignment between Iraqi Shi'ites and Iran. There seems to be only a very limited possibility that a major uprising might create a significant pro-Iranian Shi'ite resistance in Iraq, create a pro-Iranian Shi'ite enclave similar to the Kurdish enclave, or even give Iran part of Iraq's territory.

What seems to be a more likely scenario is that the Ba'ath regime will systematically eliminate the last traces of Shi'ite opposition in the marshes and defeat the Kurds by a mixture of political and economic action, low-level military action, and military intimidation. Such an Iraqi victory over the Kurds, and final elimination of the Shi'ite resistance, could increase tension with Iran and Turkey, and seriously undermine the credibility of Western military capabilities.

Such a victory would also allow Iraq to shift from a focus on internal issues to revenge and efforts at intimidation. Iraq's current regime is almost certain to see reparations, the threat of war crimes trials, and competition for oil quotas and revenues as issues that merit at least the tacit threat of the use of military force. Iraq may be deterred from attacking Kuwait, but it certainly retains the capability to seize Kuwait if Kuwait does not have US support. Iraq could also pose a threat to Saudi Arabia, although it would have to reorganize its logistic and support capabilities to carry out a major invasion of the Eastern province.

Active Iraqi efforts at revenge and intimidation are possible—perhaps likely. At least some border incidents with Iran, Saudi Arabia, and Kuwait are likely, as is the use of terrorism and unconventional warfare against leaders or elites who Saddam Hussein and the Ba'ath see as being responsible for Iraq's defeat, continued sanctions or reparations, or placing limits on the reassertion of Iraqi power in the region.

Even if Iraq does not force another military confrontation with the UN, it will remain a major threat to regional peace. Iraq not only retains a significant capability to build weapons of mass destruction, but its overall mix of conventional forces is still formidable by regional standards. Iraq's forces are still large enough to pose a major threat to Kuwait and Saudi Arabia if the two do not obtain American aid. Iraq has enough conventional forces to enable it to defend against any attack by Iran, and its forces should be fully capable of dealing with any of the various Kurdish or Shi'ite militias that are internal threats to Saddam Hussein's power.

THE VALUE OF MILITARY CONTAINMENT

The trends and risks in Iraq's conventional military power form a strong argument for separating the issue of military containment from other aspects of any strategy for dealing with Iraq. There is every reason to continue to enforce the UN Security Council Resolutions that deny Iraq destabilizing levels of conventional arms imports and imports of dual-use technology it can use for weapons of mass destruction.

Iraq has played the role of an aggressor or a destabilizing state for much of its post-colonial existence. It retains enough military capability, in spite of the Gulf War, to threaten its Southern neighbors if they do not receive outside support and the technical skills and at least some of the equipment to manufacture and deliver weapons of mass destruction. Unless Iran becomes far stronger than it is today, no case can be made for arms transfers unless a more democratic, stable, and ethnically balanced government comes to power in the future. Until a fundamental change takes place in Iraq's government, there is a clear case for military containment, and for taking every possible step to limit Iraq's military build-up and its efforts to rebuild its capacity to deliver weapons of mass destruction.

Every step that strengthens Iraq's military capabilities increases the risk of more military adventures, like its invasion of Iran and Kuwait. A military build-up in Iraq not only threatens the region, it threatens Iraq's people, and it means that an Iraqi regime will allocate resources to military expenditures that do not benefit Iraq's people in any way. It provides an authoritarian regime with the tools necessary to oppress Iraq's Kurds and Shi'ites and maintain control over its Sunnis. It also means the continued diversion of vast resources from recovery and development to useless expenditures on force. To put this in perspective, the United States estimates that Iraq spent over $180 billion (in constant $1995) on military expenditures in the decade before the Gulf War, and over $80 billion on arms imports, plus another $10 billion on weapons of mass destruction.[3]

ADDITIONAL MEASURES TO LIMIT IRAQI CONVENTIONAL MILITARY CAPABILITIES

At the same time, a realistic policy must recognize that the success of military containment will be relative, and that Iraq will eventually succeed in ending or undercutting UN controls. Iraq retains a major military-industrial complex. There are many dual-use technologies that are not practical to ban because they are "civil" in character, but that can aid Iraq in improving its military forces, in strengthening its military industries, and in rebuilding its program to build and deliver weapons of mass destruction.

The backlash from the problems in the Arab-Israeli peace process, the reluctance of Arab states to continue putting pressure on another Arab states, the plight of the Iraqi people, the desire to balance Iraq off against Iran, and the desire to minimize revanchist pressure are all powerful factors that are leading many Arab states to reduce or end their support for sanctions. Nations like China, France, and Russia have powerful commercial interests in Iraq, and the desire to expand their influence in the Middle East and the Gulf. Trading nations like Japan are increasingly reluctant to sacrifice their economic interests, and major regional powers like Turkey have a strong interest in reaching a modus vivendi with Kuwait that will ensure the flow of energy exports and contain the Kurds. Iran has reason to minimize Iraqi hostility and to try to use improved relations with Iraq to improve its own relations with Arab states and counter US strength in the Gulf.

Desert Fox is a warning that UN resolutions and cease-fire accords resulting from the Gulf War cannot provide a lasting basis for preventing all military exports to Iraq, and neither can arms control agreements on supplier regimes. Present international accords allow the sale and transfer of significant amounts of biological, chemical, and nuclear technology to Iraq, once it "complies" with the key sanctions now affecting it. Some nations or individual companies will always be willing to deal with Iraq on a covert or an overt basis. There is no clear difference between "guns" and "butter," and any easing of "civil" economic sanctions will inevitably give Iraq some aid in strengthening its military capabilities.

Given these uncertainties, other Gulf states and those nations which project power into the region must take every possible action to limit Iraq's present and future war-fighting options. This involves four sets of interrelated measures: arms control, supplier regimes and limits on the transfer of technology and equipment, strengthening the deterrent and defensive capabilities of Southern Gulf forces, and building up Western power projection capabilities. It also involves the understanding that action must be taken to restrict both the improvement of Iraqi conventional forces and Iraqi proliferation. Although this analysis has focused on conventional forces, a separate study shows that the threat of Iraqi weapons of mass destruction remains just as high—if not higher.

From a practical viewpoint, it is easier to call for such measures than it is to implement them. Many nations can project token military forces to the Gulf, but only the United States can project major war-fighting capabilities, and only Britain has shown the will and ability to deploy forces as part of a de facto regional alliance with the Southern Gulf states. Other Western nations may sell arms and reach security agreements, but they are unlikely to act as part of a meaningful military deterrent. Iran and Turkey can and will secure their own borders, but they are unlikely to be part of any regional security structure, and Iran still poses a potential threat of its own. Egypt can deploy land forces to the region, but it cannot sustain them or back them with air power. Its performance in the Gulf War was anything but adequate. Syria's token deployments failed to disguise both the inability and lack of willingness to fight.

Bahrain, Kuwait, and Saudi Arabia will determine most of the regional capability to fight in the most probable scenarios for future Iraqi efforts to use force to intimidate or attack. They have made little real individual progress in improving many aspects of their forces since the Gulf War, however, and their cooperation has often been far more rhetorical than real. There is still no joint force or war planning, little effort at sustainability and interoperability, and far too little effort at integrated command, control, and communications. As for the Gulf Cooperation Council, its headquarters building is its most impressive feature.

The slow reemergence of Iraq as a military power may force more effective US, British, and Southern Gulf action. At the same time, the Gulf has little experience in fixing the roof before it rains. Checking Iraq also requires effective action in the full range of possible measures. Focusing on one measure—such as strengthening Southern Gulf military forces—is almost certain to fail.

Every possible step should be taken to pressure Iraq to join international and regional arms control regimes that can bring stability to the Gulf. One point, however, must be kept clearly in mind. Some arms control regimes stress equity to all signatories or tend to penalize moderate states that sign and honor such agreements, while extremist states do not. "Fairness" is not the issue in dealing with Iraq. Security is the issue, and it will best be achieved by understanding that weakening or limiting Southern Gulf and moderate Arab states is scarcely a way of avoiding future conflicts in the Gulf.

Every effort must be taken to develop tight post-sanctions controls on transfers of military and dual-use technology to Iraq, focusing on the risks posed by the transfer of both conventional technologies and those for weapons of mass destruction. Such limits on trade and technology transfers may or may not be part of arms control regimes and formal embargoes.

The worst possible path that outside nations could follow would be to let "sanctions fatigue" result in an end to the "war of sanctions" that treats Iraq as an open market for arms, or to return to the Cold War struggle for influence in the Northern Gulf. The United States and the heirs of the former Soviet Union need to recognize that their past efforts to make either Iran or Iraq into allies or strategic "pillars" have been dismal failures. The United States never benefited from its military support of Iran, and indeed it was forced to intervene against Iran during 1987–1988. The former Soviet Union never obtained any meaningful form of strategic advantage or support from its arms transfers to Iraq.

The ultimate answer to dealing with Iraqi military capabilities must be continued military ties between the United States, Britain, and the Southern Gulf states. Sanctions will end or lose their effectiveness at some point. If this happens without fundamental political changes in Iraq, no one should have any illusions that Saddam Hussein or anyone like him can be "integrated into the family of nations." No set of political agreements with Iraq is likely to last longer than US and British military presence in the Gulf, or be any stronger than a combination of Southern Gulf military forces and US and British power projection capabilities. Diplomacy will at best be an extension of force by other means. As is the case with Iran, the threat from Iraq can ultimately only be contained or countered by war-fighting capability.

NOTES

1. For a wider range of scenarios and contingency considerations, see, Zalmay M. Khalilzad, David A. Shalpak, and Daniel L. Byman, *The Implications of the Possible End of the Arab-Israeli Conflict for Gulf Security*, Santa Monica, RAND, 1997; Shai Feldman, *Nuclear Weapons and Arms Control in the Middle East*, Cambridge, MIT Press, 1997; Andrew Rathmell, *The Changing Military Balance in the Gulf*, London, Royal United Services Institute, Whitehall Papers 38, 1996; and Geoffery Kemp and Robert Harkavy, *Strategic Geography and the Changing Middle East*, Washington, Carnegie/Brookings Endowment, 1997.

2. *Jane's Defense Weekly*, June 25, 1997, p. 15.

3. Author's estimate using $1991 figures from the US Arms Control and Disarmament Agency (ACDA), *World Military Expenditures and Arms Transfers, 1991–1992*, Washington, GPO, 1994, p. 67—converting into 1995 dollars using OMB conversions.

Chapter 10

Iraqi Weapons of Mass Destruction and the War of Sanctions

While Iraq has sought to strengthen its conventional forces, its most bitter struggles in the "war of sanctions" have been over its attempts to preserve its weapons of mass destruction. This war has become a series of battles of attrition which neither side seems likely to fully win. Iraq has suffered major defeats. The UN has maintained an intrusive inspection regime which has been able to verify the destruction of some seven to eight billion dollars of facilities, production equipment, weapon, and related material. It has also maintained controls which have denied Iraq access to dual-use and related imports.

Iraq has, however, resisted the UN's efforts every step of the way. In spite of the best efforts of the UN Special Commission (UNSCOM) and the International Atomic Energy Agency (IAEA), Iraq has succeeded in remaining one of the world's most dangerous proliferators. It has preserved its technology base and many of its capabilities to manufacture and deploy such weapons. It has set up new covert programs, and it has continued to smuggle in equipment and technology. At the same time, it has gradually undermined the UN inspection effort and obtained the support of other nations in its efforts to put an end to sanctions. It is still possible that Iraq may provoke new US and British strikes against its efforts to proliferate it, but many of its capabilities seem likely to survive the best efforts of UNSCOM and the IAEA.

IRAQ'S LONG HISTORY OF PROLIFERATION

Iraq's leadership has given proliferation a high strategic priority for more than three decades. Iraq is the first nation in modern times to make extensive use of weapons of mass destruction. While Egypt used chemical weapons in the Yemeni civil war, and Japan used chemical and biological weapons in World War

II, these uses were limited in scale and produced comparatively few casualties. In contrast, Iraq made extensive use of chemical weapons against Iran during the Iran-Iraq War, and against its own Kurdish population during 1987–1989. Iraq made extensive use of long-range missile attacks against civilian targets during both the Iran-Iraq and Gulf wars.

Iraq made a massive investment in facilities for the production of biological, chemical, and nuclear weapons during the years before the Gulf War that some experts estimate cost Iraq more than $10 billion. Iraq kept much of this effort covert, and it concealed every activity it could. It learned from Israel's raid on Osirak that it needed to take every possible step to reduce the vulnerability of its programs, and had to take steps to conceal its activities from US and other satellites. It adopted new construction techniques to roof its buildings before it added construction features that allowed analysts to determine their function. It used tunnels and underground facilities, and it dispersed facilities in many different areas—often with civilian covers.

Iraq changed its security procedures to disguise both its production efforts and to eliminate special handling procedures in its military forces that provided indicators of where it was storing its chemical and biological weapons. It made use of the global purchasing network it set up to buy arms during the Iran-Iraq War to obtain technology and equipment for weapons of mass destruction, and simultaneously used its civil government and private sector organizations to buy dual-use equipment and technology.

Iraq's efforts were largely successful in concealing the nature and scale of its activities before it invaded Kuwait, and the politics of the Iran-Iraq War reinforced this success. US and other Western decision makers focused on the threat from Iran. They adopted a policy of supporting Iraq to ensure that Iran did not defeat Iraq, and they downplayed the seriousness of Iraq's use of chemical weapons. They gave only limited priority to Iraqi proliferation and underfunded both the intelligence collection effort dealing with Iraq and the military effort to target Iraqi military facilities. While some individual analysts did warn of the potential seriousness of the Iraqi effort, policy makers and intelligence experts failed to allocate the necessary resources to confirm the scale and nature of Iraqi activities.

IRAQ'S CAPABILITIES SURVIVE THE GULF WAR

Iraq took further efforts to conceal its capabilities and intentions after it invaded Kuwait in August, 1990. Before and during the Gulf War, Iraq dispersed its chemical and biological weapons, prepared its missile forces to launch such warheads, and created the capability to attack Coalition forces with large numbers of chemical and biological weapons. There is little doubt that Iraq would have threatened the use of nuclear weapons if it had possessed such weapons at the time. In fact, Iraq attempted to rush its nuclear program forward during the period before the Gulf War, and it was actively working on the design of a nuclear warhead for its missiles.

The end result was that Coalition planners had no way to understand the importance and scale of Iraq's effort and no way to attack it. They could not target most of Iraq's production and military capabilities, attacked only a small part of Iraq's actual effort, and had no way to make meaningful battle damage assessments. The Coalition did make ambitious claims to have destroyed Iraq's weapons of mass destruction during the war, but none of these claims were correct. Coalition air and land forces do not seem to have destroyed a single Iraqi Scud missile. They did little more than token damage to Iraq's well-dispersed stockpile of chemical bombs and munitions, and no damage to its dispersed biological weapons. The Coalition failed to identify more than 80% of Iraq's major facilities for the production of weapons of mass destruction, and only seriously damaged three major facilities.

The US Air Force Gulf War Air Power Survey is almost certainly correct in stating that:

> When all is said and done, too many elements of the Iraqi program were unidentified during Desert Storm, incompletely understood, or were else moved out from under Coalition bombing soon after the air campaign began. . . . In hindsight, this is suggestive of an intelligence failure. Planners cannot target things whose existence is unknown to them, (but) questions about the extent to which active deception and concealment measures by the Iraqis might be able to complicate Coalition targeting, or to substantially reduce the effectiveness of even precision bombing do not seem to have been vigorously pursued. Thus, the intelligence "failure" in this area was . . . accompanied by a conceptual failure to think through the range of feasible countermeasures and responses the Iraqis could take to minimize the effectiveness of bombing against the military programs and capabilities that their leaders valued most.[1]

This experience is a warning that intelligence, arms control, and war planning are not a substitute for the active control of Iraq's, or any other nation's, efforts to develop weapons of mass destruction. No amount of additional intelligence and targeting resources could have guaranteed success. Iraq had learned to conceal the nature of some of its construction activities by building the roof early in the project to conceal the nature of the building, by avoiding highly visible security measures, by converting established civilian facilities, and by the creation of complex cover stories.

Technical means could not have solved some important problems. Key test activities do not require visible signals or electronic emissions. Biological and chemical warfare activities can often be carried out in very compact facilities, and can easily be concealed within state-run civilian plants—particularly in a society where many activities are kept secret on a day-to-day basis. The US community may have failed to make a major effort to obtain human intelligence (HUMINT) on these developments, but interviews with Israeli and Arab intelligence experts indicate that other countries were no more successful. A major HUMINT collection effort is always ultimately dependent on luck, and access, to a few key individuals for success.

THE UN CEASE-FIRE SEEKS TO ELIMINATE IRAQI CAPABILITIES

Fortunately, the Gulf War did not end the Coalition's efforts to destroy Iraq's production facilities, weapons, and delivery capabilities. Although none of the UN negotiators involved in setting the terms of the cease-fire had any idea of the scale and importance of Iraq's surviving capabilities, the terms of the cease-fire required Iraq to destroy or convert all of its weapons of mass destruction, its capabilities to produce them, and its facilities and long-range surface-to-surface missile capabilities.

On April 3, 1991, the UN Security Council passed Resolution 687, which set forth the formal terms for a permanent cease-fire. This resolution required Iraq to renounce and condemn terrorism, repatriate all prisoners, restore all seized and stolen property, establish a fund based on oil revenues as a source for reparations payments to Kuwait, accept a continued arms and economic embargo (except on food, medicine, and essential civilian needs), and accept the eradication of its weapons of mass destruction. Resolution 687 also compelled Iraq to allow the UN to demarcate the Iraqi-Kuwait border, impose a demilitarized zone along that border, and establish an observer force to ensure the continued integrity of such a boundary.

The latter portion of UN Security Council Resolution 687 demanded that Iraq accept the destruction, removal, or dismantling of all biological, chemical, and nuclear weapons; all research, development, and support facilities associated with these weapons; all stocks of chemical and biological agents; all ballistic missiles with ranges exceeding 150 kilometers; and all production and repair facilities associated with the manufacturing of such missiles. It linked Iraqi compliance to Iraq's ability to export oil and other materials by stating that once the UN Security Council agreed that once Iraq had completed the required actions, the UN prohibitions against the export of commodities and products originating in Iraq would have no further force or effect.

To assist in the implementation of Resolution 687, the UN established UNSCOM for the purpose of planning the identification and destruction of Iraq's weapons of mass destruction. UNSCOM in turn created a force of UN inspectors, while also authorizing the IAEA to assist UNSCOM in its objective.

The UN had no idea of what would follow. The negotiators involved felt that the resulting UN effort might last a year or so, two years at the most. They felt that Iraq's assets had largely been destroyed, and that Iraq would do everything possible to speedily comply in order to ensure that the UNSCOM and IAEA inspectors would certify Iraq's compliance and lift sanctions. In practice, however, Iraq still had immense assets it sought to preserve. It became apparent that weapons of mass destruction were the regime's second-highest strategic priority, ranking only after its own survival, and that it was willing to forgo over $100 billion in oil revenues and to impose immense hardships on the Iraqi people in a ceaseless effort to maintain its military capabilities.

UNSCOM AND THE WAR OF SANCTIONS

Saddam accepted Resolution 687 on April 6, 1991—although he called the resolution "unjust"—and the resolution was accepted by the Iraqi National Assembly. The UN Security Council then declared a formal cease-fire to be in effect as of April 11, 1991. Yet this aspect of the war of sanctions began before the UN passed Resolution 687, much less the cease-fire. Iraqi forces were detected salvaging equipment for missiles and weapons of mass destruction, as well as cleaning up suspect sites, as early as April 5, 1991.

On April 18, 1991, the Iraqi government lied to the UN in its first declaration regarding its holdings of weapons of mass destruction. Iraq claimed that its postwar stockpile of such weapons consisted of only 52 regular and modified Scud missiles, 10,000 chemical warheads, 1,500 chemical bombs and shells, and 1,000 tons of mustard and nerve gas. The UN later discovered 46,000 surviving chemical weapons, which proved Iraq's claims that its weapons totaled only 12,500 to be grossly inaccurate. Iraq made similar false claims to the IAEA about its nuclear weapons effort in an April 29, 1991, declaration.

The Iraqi government also seems to have taken almost immediate steps to organize a systematic effort to conceal its surviving weapons, production facilities, and technology. These efforts were directed at the highest levels of the Iraqi government and by the Office of the Presidential Palace (OPP) and personnel in Saddam's private Diwan (office). Saddam's private secretary, Abd Hamid Mahmoud, seems to have long played a major role in coordinating these efforts. So did Lt. General Hussein Kamel Majid, who served as the head of the Military Industrial Organization (MIO) in Iraq before his defection in 1995.

It now seems clear that special organizations were set up in the Special Security Service (SSS) (also known as the Special Security Organization, SSO, and Amn Al Khass) and in the Special Republican Guards to handle the security issues involved, conceal some key equipment, and monitor the activities of UNSCOM and the IAEA. The SSS is reported to have set up a special group called Office 28 to handle the security for Iraq's concealment efforts and ongoing programs at its offices on Palestine Street in Baghdad.[2]

Iraq exploited the complex structure of the MIO, which has over 70 subordinate establishments to conceal its activities or describe them as if they had been used for other activities. The MIO was able to use its ties to a wide range of civil facilities, including research institutions, medical and pharmaceutical facilities, chemical and petrochemical facilities, agricultural and insecticide facilities, other nuclear programs, and food processing plants. This made it extremely difficult to separate Iraq's regular military production activities from its efforts to produce missiles and weapons of mass destruction, and its military activities from its civil programs.

The Iraqi concealment effort seems to have had several major phases. One new phase seems to have begun in 1993, partly as a result of the activities described in Table 10.1. Iraq seems to have created a series of small projects organized as isolated cells which used scientists and engineers that had never previously been associated with Iraq's efforts to build missiles and chemical, biological, and nuclear weapons. These new "black" programs seem to have been designed to ensure that Iraq could go on with its research and development activities even if UNSCOM and the IAEA have traced most of what Iraq did before the cease-fire and defection of Lt. General Majid. There is no way to determine the scale of such efforts, but it does seem fairly clear that the SSS carried out the necessary recruiting effort.

By 1994, Iraq seems to have made extensive use of Saddam Hussein's presidential palaces to conceal documents and key equipment. It is believed that Iraq established a major storage facility at the presidential complex at Jabal Mokhul, on the Tigris north of Tikrit. Iraq also, however, began to shuttle documents and weapons between new hiding sites. This operation is said to have been under the control of the Second and Fourth Brigades of the Special Republican Guards. Some reports indicate that Iraq used mobile freight cars, others that the SSO had two fleets of cars and trucks. One used unmarked green Mercedes trucks from the Segada Transportation Company; another used red and white refrigerator trucks with the name of the Tip Top Ice Cream company. The trucks shuttled between hiding sites that were changed every 90 days until 1997, when UNSCOM efforts led the sites to be changed every 30 days.[3]

Iraqi opposition sources report that another phase began in 1995, after the defection of Hussein Kamel. According to these reports, Qusay took over the broad direction of Iraq's concealment and proliferation efforts, and Abd Hamid Mahmoud began to chair a weekly meeting of representatives from the SSS, Special Republican Guards, and MIO. The members from the MIO are said to include General Amr Mohammed Rashid, the Minister of Oil and a major figure in Iraq's missile programs; Amr Al Saadi, a senior manager in the MIO; and Jaffar Dheilla Jaffar, who has been a key figure in Iraq's nuclear program. Mahmoud is said to chair the committee because Qusay is busy with other activities and has poor relations with Amr Al Saadi.[4] Saddam is also reported to have directed that General Intelligence Directorate (GID) to set up a parallel security office in the MIO in an effort to prevent further defections.

Still other reports indicate that Tariq Aziz is at least an ex officio member of this group and plays a major role in the concealment effort. They also indicate that Abdul Razak, the current head of Iraq's missile program, is a member.

US experts cannot confirm the level of detail provided by Iraqi opposition sources, but have no doubt that the PPO, SSS, and Special Republican Guards

Table 10.1
Iraq's Efforts to Preserve Its Weapons of Mass Destruction

91-1-12:	Congress authorizes the president to use the US armed forces to implement some of the UN resolutions in Public Law 102-1 (H.J. Res. 77), passed by Congress on Jan. 12, 1991, and signed into law by President Bush on Jan. 14, 1991. Congress reaffirms its approval of the use of force against Iraq in the Defense Authorization Act for FY1992 (Section 1095, P.L. 102–190, Dec. 5, 1991).[1]
91–2-1:	The United States and allies drive Iraqi forces from Kuwait. Later in the year, US, British, and French planes start patrolling Iraq's northern skies to shield Iraq's Kurds from attack by Baghdad.
91–3-1:	Kurdish minority launches insurrection but is also crushed. Thousands flee or die of exposure in the mountains. The United States, Britain, and France establish a "safe haven" for the Kurds north of the 36th parallel, an area from which Iraqi planes are banned. Shi'ite Muslims in southern Iraq rebel and are quickly defeated by the elite Iraqi National Guard.
91–3-2:	UN Security Council approves Resolution 686, which sets out the allies' conditions for a cease-fire.
91–3-3:	UN Coalition and Iraq agrees to informal cease-fire. Iraqis accept virtually all allied terms for the cease-fire, which include a ban on Iraq's use of fixed wing military aircraft inside of Iraq. President Bush interprets the resolution as preventing Iraq from using helicopter gunships to quash the Kurdish and Shi'ite rebellions against Saddam that broke out within days of the end of the war. Iraqi helicopter flights were not specifically barred under the informal cease-fire agreement.
	Iraq accepts terms of UN Security Council Resolution 686, establishing a cease-fire.
91–3-6:	Iraqi President Saddam Hussein's cousin, Ali Hassan al-Majid, who was widely blamed for the suppression of the Kurds in 1988, is appointed Interior Minister. The appointment came during the Shi'ite and Kurdish post-war uprisings. Ali was expected to act more forcefully to suppress the rebellions than his predecessor, Samir Abd al-Wahab al-Shaykhali.
91–3-20:	US forces shoot down Iraqi fighters near the northern Kurdish city of Kirkuk, enforcing the March 3 agreement between the UN Coalition and Iraq that Iraq would not use fixed wing aircraft in combat against rebels inside of Iraq.
91–4-1:	In exchange for a formal cease-fire and withdrawal of US forces from southern Iraq, Baghdad promised to get rid of long-range missiles and all weapons of mass destruction. UN monitors, however, have found evidence that Saddam Hussein's regime has falsified reports and hidden stocks of chemical and biological agents, while blocking access to selected sites and excluding Americans from the inspection teams.
91–4-5:	Spokesman for Iraqi dissidents claims that the Iraqi army used chemical weapons against civilians in suppressing the Shi'ite and Kurdish post-war rebellions. No independent confirmation of the charge.

Table 10.1 (continued)

	UN Security Council adopts Resolution 688 in response to reports of the suppression by Iraq of the Kurdish and Shi'ite rebellions, calls for an end to the repression, and demands that Iraq allow humanitarian access to its population.
91–4-6:	Iraq formally accepts the terms of a permanent cease-fire as stipulated in UN 687. Also included in the agreement is UN supervised destruction of Iraq's weapons of mass destruction, ballistic missiles, and Iraq's agreement to contribute to a reparations fund.
91–4-10:	Bush administration warns Iraq not to fly aircraft or undertake military operations in areas where allied relief operations, primarily for the Kurds in the North, were taking place. The administration defines the off-limits area primarily as anywhere north of the 36th parallel, where the allies were trying to create a safe haven for the Kurds and encourage their repatriation.
	American troops report isolated instances of Iraqi forces moving into US-occupied territory in southern Iraq, as US forces thinned out in the region. The Iraqis were reportedly positioning themselves to crush further Shi'ite unrest in the south.
91–4-11:	UN Security Council declares a formal end of the war after reviewing Iraq's message to ensure that Iraq's acceptance of UN terms was unconditional.
91–4-12:	Iraqi forces launch attacks on Kurdish forces around Irbil, north of the 36th parallel, in violation of US warnings. Other Iraqi attacks reportedly occurred in Kurdish areas south of the parallel, including Sulaymaniyah. Bush administration spokesman does not confirm the reports, adding that there had been no attempts by Iraq to impede the refugee relief operations for the Kurds in northern Iraq.
91–4-14:	Iraq tells remaining UN personnel manning the relief center in southern Iraq to leave; the center is then closed down.
91–4-16:	President Bush decides to send US troops into northern Iraq to build refugee camps and guarantee protection for the Kurds, in conjunction with several European allies.
91–4-18:	Iraq and the UN sign Memorandum of Understanding providing for a UN humanitarian presence in Iraq and the stationing of 500 UN security guards in northern Iraq to protect the relief operations. Agreement to remain in force until December 31, 1991, with the possibility for renewal.
91–4-21:	About 200 armed Iraqi policemen enter the Kurdish town of Zakhu as Iraqi soldiers withdraw. The military withdrawal is the result of an agreement between the allies and the Iraqis as the allies were establishing a safe haven for the Kurds. A senior US military officer calls the arrival of the Iraqi police contrary to the spirit of the agreement. Iraq describes establishment of a security zone in northern Iraq as an infringement on its sovereignty.

Table 10.1 (continued)

	Iraq's Revolutionary Command Council, headed and dominated by Saddam Hussein, expands a March, 1991 amnesty for army deserters and grants a pardon for regime opponents. The amnesty does not apply to military officers.
91–4-22:	Iraqi troops, which withdrew from Zakhu under the agreement with the US military, return to the outskirts of Zakhu, deterring many Kurds from returning to their homes. Iraqis in and around Zakhu are reported as being friendly and not seeking confrontation with the allies, but some Iraqi troops overlooking Zakhu fire harassing machine-gun and mortar rounds.
91–4-24:	In response to US warnings, Iraq agrees to move the troops several kilometers away from Zakhu.
	Iraqi Kurdish leaders announce that they have agreed in principle with the Iraqi government on a formula to allow them autonomy in northern Iraq. (However, in later months, Iraq hardened its positions in the talks, and no agreement has been signed.)
91–4-25:	Following US pressure, Iraq begins moving its armed policemen out of Zakhu as well.
91–5-7:	US officials say Iraqi anti-aircraft artillery opened fire on two US reconnaissance jets over northern Iraq, the fifth such incident since the relief operation for the Kurds began.
91–5-8:	US and Iraqi military officials meet to discuss the incident and, on May 9, Iraq assures the United States that such actions will not be repeated.
91–5-13:	British marines exchange fire with Iraqi soldiers guarding Saddam Hussein's summer palace near Dahuk. The allies had allowed the Iraqi forces to retain control of the palace when the security zone for Kurdish refugees was expanded to the outskirts of Dahuk on May 2. The Iraqis, as requested, withdraw from the new areas being occupied by the allies. Dahuk is a Kurdish town in northern Iraq, just outside of the security zone set up by the UN Coalition to facilitate the return of Kurdish refugees to their homes.
91–5-14:	Iraqi troops open fire as a US army helicopter flies past them just outside of the allied security zone in northern Iraq. The helicopter is not hit.
91–5-22:	Iraq agrees to withdraw from Dahuk itself and allow a small contingent of noncombatant military and civilian relief experts into the town to facilitate Kurdish repatriation.
91–5-24:	Iraq, after initial opposition, signs agreement with the UN permitting the presence of UN security guards as a replacement for the allied troops in northern Iraq, when the allies withdraw.
91–6-5:	Clashes between Iraqi troops and Kurdish demonstrators in several towns outside of the allied security zone. US State Department says the Kurds may have provoked the violence in an effort to persuade US troops not to withdraw from northern Iraq.

Table 10.1 (continued)

91-6-6:	The Bush administration charges that massive shipments of flour (over 7 million pounds) intended for Kurdish refugees were diverted into the Iraqi government's food rationing system.
91-6-23 to 91-6-28:	Iraqi soldiers obstructed, and in one case, fired, warning shots at UN inspectors attempting to oversee the destruction of Iraqi nuclear armaments parts.
91-7-15:	Last Coalition troops leave Iraq.
91-7-19:	Clash occurs in Sulaymaniyah, which result in Iraq's loss of control of that city to the Kurds. The Iraqis do not attempt to forcibly recapture Sulaymaniyah after it comes under Kurdish control.
91-7-21:	Iraq's Revolutionary Command Council, headed and dominated by Saddam, expands a March, 1991 amnesty for army deserters and grants a pardon for regime opponents. The amnesty does not apply to military officers.
91-7-30:	UN weapons inspectors report to the UN Security Council that Iraq has attempted to conceal aspects of its nuclear weapons program by destroying or burying essential equipment. The inspectors also reported identifying four times as many chemical weapons as Iraq had reported.
91-8-15:	UN Security Council passes Resolution 76 and tentatively approves a plan under which Iraq could sell up to $1.6 billion worth of oil over six months. Under Security Council Resolution 75, passed the same day, it is determined that 30% of the proceeds would be taken as war reparations. Much of this is to go into an escrow account for the UN to purchase and distribute food and medicine to the Iraqi people. Iraq denounces the plan and refuses to sell oil under these conditions, claiming this was an infringement on its sovereignty.
91-9-3:	Revolutionary Command Council issues law allowing opposition political parties but banning any party but the ruling Ba'ath from organizing in the military or security services. The law also bans parties that advocate the overthrow of the state, possess weapons, or engage in acts of violence. In addition, the formation of parties based on ethnicity or sectarianism is prohibited, preventing the Kurds and Shi'ites from forming their own parties. The law is first approved by the National Assembly on July 4 and amended to include several of the above conditions on August 24.
91-9-8:	Iraq announces its will not allow UN inspectors to use UN aircraft Iraqi military facilities, a violation of the cease-fire agreement.
91-9-10:	Office of Sadruddin Agha Khan, the UN representative for humanitarian affairs in the Persian Gulf, says it has reports of serious clashes between Iraqi and Kurdish forces in northern Iraq. Iraq acknowledged the clashes but says its actions fell within the normal duties of its security forces. The attacks on the Kurds reportedly included air strikes north of the 36th parallel, which were precluded.

Table 10.1 (continued)

91-9-12:	*The Washington Post* reports that in August an Iraqi jet violated the injunction against flights from the southern port of Umm Qasr, which is in the demilitarized zone between Iraq and Kuwait.
91–9-14:	Saddam Hussein ousts Prime Minister Sa'dun Hammadi, appointed at the height of the Shi'ite and Kurdish rebellions in March. Hammadi, a Western-educated Shi'ite Muslim, was an advocate of a more pluralistic, liberal Ba'athist regime, and he supported full compliance with UN and allied cease-fire terms.
91-9-19:	UN Security Council adopts Resolution 712, formally approving the UN oil sale plan set up in Resolution 76. Resolution 712 formally accepts a report by the Secretary-General proposing the means for implementing Resolution 76 and documenting Iraq's humanitarian needs. The report was a requirement laid out in Resolution 76 for the formal approval of the oil sale plan.
91–9-23 to 91-9-24:	Iraqi troops detain UN weapons inspectors in Baghdad on two separate occasions.
91-9-24:	The UN receives a vaguely worded Iraqi statement interpreted as withdrawing Iraq's objections to the use of UN aircraft in monitoring the destruction of Iraq's weapons of mass destruction.
91-9-28:	Iraq ends the multi-day detention of UN inspectors who discovered documents that confirmed Iraq was conducting a clandestine nuclear program. President Bush authorizes US Air Force planes to escort UN aircraft engaged in weapons inspection in Iraq.
91–9-30:	Assistant Secretary of State for Near Eastern Affairs Edward Djerejian meets with Kurdish leader Jalal Talabani in Washington. He reportedly tells Talabani that the United States opposes the fragmentation of Iraq but supports participation for all ethnic groups in Iraq in a pluralistic system of government.
91–10-7:	Kurdish guerrillas shoot and kill about 60 unarmed Iraqi soldiers whom they had captured in clashes outside of Sulaymaniyah. Kurdish citizens in Sulaymaniyah tell journalists that the Iraqi army had launched a surprise, unprovoked attack on the city, which resulted in the capture of the Iraqi soldiers. Kurdish leader Massoud Barzani whose forces had captured the Iraqis, orders an investigation of the killing of the Iraqi military personnel. Rival Kurdish leader Jalal Talabani condemns the murder of the Iraqis but says it may have been perpetrated by Iraqi agents.
91–10-8:	Kurdish guerrillas and the Iraqi government sign a cease-fire after a flare-up of fighting around the cities of Kifri and Sulaymaniyah. Fighting was said to be continuing despite the truce.
91–10-12:	Saddam addresses delegates to an Iraq-sponsored ''conference of Arab popular forces,'' saying that Iraq could withstand the international sanctions for ''20 years.'' Iraq organized the conference to place pressure on

Table 10.1 (continued)

	Arab leaders to violate the international sanctions by resuming commerce with Iraq.
91–10-26:	Kurdish leader Massoud Barzani, leader of the Kurdish Democratic Party (KDP), challenges his rivals, primarily Patriotic Union of Kurdistan (PUK) leader Jalal Talabani, to an election for supreme leadership of the Kurdish movement. Challenge is provoked by an increasing divergence between the two main Kurdish leaders—Talabani advocated abandoning autonomy talks with Baghdad and returning to all-out guerrilla warfare, while Barzani wants to continue to engage Saddam Hussein diplomatically. Barzani generally appeals to more conservative, tribally based Kurds, whereas Talabani draws his strength from urban, better educated, left-leaning Kurds.
91–11-2:	Iraq is reported to be preventing international relief organizations from distributing humanitarian aid directly to the Iraqi people. The Iraqi government is said to be insisting that the food be distributed through Iraq's own distribution and rationing system. As a result, food belonging to international relief organizations is said to be warehoused for several weeks.
91–11-10:	Iraqi troops attack Kurdish guerrilla positions near the city of Irbil. Iraq masses about 18,000 troops on the major roads into Irbil for a possible offensive.
91–11-12:	Iraq agrees to lift a one-month old economic blockade (fuel and food rations) of Kurdish-held territories in northern Iraq if Kurdish guerrilla forces withdrew from the cities they had captured, including Sulaymaniyah and Irbil. The agreement allows Iraqi police and central government employees to resume some of their authority in those cities. (The Kurds later charged that after Kurdish forces complied with that request, Iraq did not lift the blockade and resumed encroaching militarily on the Kurdish cities.)
91–11-25:	After several weeks of stonewalling, Iraq agrees to a UN request to extend for six months the memorandum of understanding which provides for the UN to conduct humanitarian relief operations inside of Iraq. In negotiations on the extension, Iraq continues to refuse to participate in the UN oil sale plan established in UN Security Council Resolutions 76 and 712.
91–11-27:	Senate Foreign Relations Committee releases a report on a visit by a staff member to Iraqi Kurdistan in September, that the Kurds in northern Iraq continue to face major food and shelter shortages as winter approaches. The report notes significant skirting of the international sanctions on the part of Iraq, such as the export of vehicles and machinery to Iran, and notes that divisions exist among the Kurds regarding negotiations with Baghdad for a Kurdish autonomy.

Table 10.1 (continued)

91–12-23:	Iraq's Interior Ministry says it is giving Iraqi citizens a final ten days to turn in unlicensed weapons and ammunition without penalty. The firearm amnesty suggests that the regime is nervous about popular opposition.
	Muhammad Baqr al-Hakim, leader of Iraq's Shi'ite opposition, says he had invited leaders of other Iraqi opposition groups to a gathering in Damascus in an effort to form a common front and to plan strategies for overthrowing Saddam.
92–1-3:	The US State Department issues a document entitled "Humanitarian Issues in Iraq," accusing Iraq of blocking international humanitarian aid to the Iraqi people and condemning its refusal to participate in the UN oil sale plan. The report claims that Iraq refused to concur with a UN proposal to open humanitarian relief centers in the largely Kurdish city of Kirkuk and the Shi'ite city of Nasiriyah in southern Iraq, a misinterpretation of the memorandum of understanding Iraq signed with the UN in April, 1991. The document says there were reports that individuals were sent by the Iraqi government, warning Iraqi citizens individually that they would be arrested if they accepted foreign food assistance. This was a violation, according to the US State Department, of UN Security Council Resolution 688.
92–1-8:	Iraqi troops lay barbed wire and sowing mines around—and occasionally shelling—Kurdish towns in northern Iraq, causing 200,000 Kurds to flee to refugee camps on the border with Iran. However, Kurdish leader Massoud Barzani says an autonomy agreement with the Iraqi government is still possible, and that the main obstacle is Iraq's refusal to cede to the Kurds control of Kirkuk and Khanaqih.
92–1-15:	Iraqi Kurds announce that they will suspend autonomy talks with the Iraqi government and hold elections, by April 3, 1992, for an undisputed Kurdish leader. The elections pit the two main Kurdish leaders, Massoud Barzani and Jalal Talabani, against each other. Barzani favors continued negotiations with Saddam to hammer out a Kurdish autonomy agreement, while Talabani has recently favored renewed military offensives against the government and the declaration of a provisional Kurdish government in Iraqi Kurdistan.
92–1-19:	The Subcommittee on Immigration and Refugee Affairs of the Senate Judiciary Committee releases a report that the security zone in northern Iraq is not providing safety for the approximately 2 million Kurds living outside of the zone. The report states that about 300,000 Kurds have left their homes since October, 1991, fleeing the pressure placed on Kurdistan by the Iraqi military. The report notes considerable smuggling in goods and fuel between Iraq and Turkey, Iran, and Jordan.
92–2-13:	Turkish Prime Minister Demirel imposes restrictions on the importation of Iraqi gasoline by Turkish truckers. The restrictions result in fewer deliveries of supplies to the Kurds, since the Turkish truckers had been

Table 10.1 (continued)

	delivering goods to the Kurds on their way to receive the oil cargo in Iraq. Turkish merchants had complained about the illicit importation, since the low prices for the Iraqi gasoline were depressing the domestic Turkish market.
92–2-14:	Saddam sets up a new security force to protect him and his palace against Shi'ite rebels. The force is said to consist of about 10,000 volunteer troops from Saddam's home town of Tikrit, and neighboring al-Dur. The unit is reportedly led by Saddam's younger son, Qusay.
92–2-22:	Kurdish officials and human rights groups accumulate evidence of Iraqi atrocities against the Kurds in the late 1980s. Kurdish estimates, drawing on captured Iraqi secret police documents, say as many as 180,000 Kurds are killed in the campaign.
92–2-24:	Iraq denounces a report by the UN Human Rights Commission that criticizes Iraq's human rights record. Iraq says it cooperated fully with the UN during its survey of Iraq's human rights behavior.
92–2-26 to 92–2-28:	Iraq refuses to allow UN inspectors to begin dismantling Scud missile production plants and other Scud-related equipment.
92–2-28:	The UN Security Council condemns Iraq for refusing to allow UN inspectors to destroy its weapons of mass destruction and ballistic missiles as agreed in 1991 cease-fire terms.
92–3-1:	Britain and France press the UN Security Council to send a special envoy to Iraq to report on the political situation of the Iraqi Kurds and Shi'ites. The aim of the proposal is to end the Iraqi economic blockade of the Kurdish areas, reduce Baghdad's military pressure on the Shi'ites in the south, and encourage opposition to Saddam among these groups. The proposal was said to be based on UN Security Council Resolution 688 of April 5, 1991.
	Turkey reports that it conducted an air raid against opposition Turkish Kurds operating in northern Iraq. Two days later, Iraq formally protests the cross-border raid on its territory.
92–3-7:	Several members of the House Foreign Affairs Committee, including Chairman Dante Fascell, write a letter to President Bush urging him to consider the use of force to compel Iraq to comply with the cease-fire resolutions. They also urged that humanitarian aid for the Kurds be continued.
	Bomb explodes outside of the headquarters of the Iraqi Kurdistan Front, an umbrella organization for Kurdish rebel groups, just after Kurdish guerrillas ended a meeting there. The rebels blame the Iraqi government for the bombing, which killed four people. Headquarters are located in the Kurdish-controlled town of Sulaymaniyah.
92–3-9:	On the first anniversary of the popular insurrection in Kurdistan, Jalal Talabani, secretary general of the Patriotic Union of Kurdistan (PUK), delivers a speech in Kurdish to the masses of Kurdistan.

Table 10.1 (continued)

92–3-12:	Kurdish leader says Iraqi forces are escalating operations against Kurdish rebels in northern Iraq and that Iraqi troops were massing outside of Sulaymaniyah for a major offensive. The Kurdish leader says the Iraqi military moves were intended to prevent the planned April 3 elections for a unified Kurdish leadership. In a related speech, Saddam told the Kurds that he would not tolerate the elections unless the Kurds distanced themselves from the Western countries protecting them. The Kurds postponed the elections until April 24, because they needed more time to set up an election mechanism.
92–3-13:	Iraq expands military operations against Kurdish rebel positions in the town of Kifri, southeast of Sulaymaniyah.
	UN Security Council formally informs Iraq that it is in violation of the 1991 cease-fire agreement.
92–3-15:	Iraqi troops continue military operations against Shi'ite rebels active in the marshes of southern Iraq. The report estimates that 10,000 guerrillas and 200,000 civilians are living in the marshes.
92–3-19:	Iraq forwards a letter to the UN Security Council, stating that it will cooperate with UN weapons inspection efforts.
92–3-20:	Iraq allows the UN to establish humanitarian aid centers in the largely Shi'ite areas of southern Iraq, including Basra, Nasiriyah, and Hammar. Many observers see the Iraqi move as an effort to appear cooperative with the UN as its delegation, headed by Tareq Aziz, was meeting with the UN Security Council to discuss Iraq's compliance record.
92–3-21:	The "Voice of the Iraqi People" reports that the Iraqi government is mobilizing armor and artillery in northern Iraq and adds that Kurdish sources are 99% certain that an offensive will by ignited within a few days. The radio station adds that Kurds expect two Kurdish-controlled bridges to be the targets of the offensive. A Kurdish source is cited as stating that Iraqi forces in the Aski Kalak have increased by 2,000 soldiers in the last few days.
92–3-31:	Iraq shells Kurdish civilians along the front line between Iraq and Kurdish controlled territories. Shelling forces about 40,000 Kurds to flee their homes.
92–4-5:	Iraqi aircraft fly for the first time since the Gulf War, attempting to intercept Iranian aircraft raiding the bases in Iraq of Iran's opposition, People's Mujahideen, according to the US Department of Defense. Iraqi flights are technically not prohibited under the cease-fire agreement reached with the UN Coalition on March 3, 1991, since the UN Coalition had unilaterally relaxed the ban on Iraqi flights (south of the Kurdish areas in the north) when it discontinued operations in Iraq in 1991.
92–4-14:	The United States, Britain, and France warn Iraq to stop tracking allied reconnaissance aircraft and moving anti-aircraft missiles into the northern no-fly zone. Allied countries say that Iraq had repeatedly illuminated their

Table 10.1 (continued)

	aircraft with tracking radar in recent weeks. Iraq has also moved SA-2 and SA-3 surface-to-air missiles into positions near Mosul, in northern Iraq, and is massing forces close to Kurdish-controlled areas. The Bush administration says that Iraq also conducted a series of combat aircraft training flights recently, though such activity is not prohibited if it is not conducted in the no-fly zones. Iraq fires on an International Committee of the Red Cross jeep in northern Iraq. There are no reports of casualties, but the UN fears that it was part of an Iraqi attempt to intimidate relief workers in northern Iraq.
92–4-22:	The UN says that Iraq imposes new restrictions on the movement of UN vehicles providing humanitarian relief. Iraq requires that use of the UN vehicles have Iraqi Foreign Ministry approval at least 48 hours in advance.
92–5-19:	Iraq's Kurds hold elections for a new assembly and an executive authority in northern Iraq. Each of the two main Kurdish parties, the Kurdish Democratic Party (KDP) and the Patriotic Union of Kurdistan (PUK), ended up with 50 seats, with five additional seats going to smaller parties. No candidate received a clear majority in election for the presidency, and runoff elections for that post were deferred. Iraq had called the elections null and void.
	About 1 million Kurds wait in line for up to eight hours to vote in the first free elections held in the state of Iraq. Thousands of armed guerrillas leave their positions opposite the Iraqi army in order to join the voters. Four candidates for leader of Iraqi Kurdistan, and seven lists for members of a 15-seat National Assembly are put forward by the eight political parties and the few tribal leaders of the Iraqi Kurdistan Front (IKF). The elections were peaceful.
92–5-23:	President Saddam Hussein is preparing to assault the independent Kurdish enclave in northern Iraq in order to retake the territory.
92–6-22:	Iraq's major opposition groups, with the exception of the Shi'ite Islamic groups, meet in Vienna and form a united front, the Iraqi National Congress (INC).
92–6-30:	Memorandum of understanding between Iraq and the UN governing the presence of UN relief workers and guards expires. Iraq refuses to renew the agreement, causing many relief workers to discontinue their operations in Iraq for fear of their security.
92–7-2 to 92–7-8:	Reports circulate in international media regarding a possible failed coup and subsequent army purge in Iraq.
92–7-5 to 92–7-22:	Iraq refuses to allow a UN inspection team to enter a building in Baghdad believed to contain documents related to Iraq's nuclear program. On July 22, inspectors withdrew without gaining access.
92–7-8:	Two UN guards are wounded in a grenade attack in Irbil, in northern Iraq; agents of the Iraqi regime are blamed.

Table 10.1 (continued)

92–7-12:	The "Voice of Rebellious Iraq" says that motorized units surrounded the holy shrines in al-Najaf and Karbala, and prevented ceremonies marking the anniversary of the death of the Imam Hussein (Ashura). Reports from Iraq indicate that Iraqi authorities adopted stringent measures at the beginning of the month of Muharram (beginning July 2). Machine guns were set up on top of mosques. The Ba'athist regime also prevents mourners from assembling in Husseiniyas and mosques around the country, including Kadhemain, near Baghdad, where the 7th and 9th infallible imams of the prophet's household lie in rest.
92–7-16:	A UN guard from Fiji is murdered while asleep, a grenade was thrown at the World Food Program office in Sulaymaniyah, and two UN guards are slightly hurt by a grenade thrown from a speeding car. Another has his car blown up by a 22-pound bomb.
92–7-17:	UN guard is assassinated in Dahuk, in northern Iraq; agents of the Iraqi regime are blamed.
92–7-20:	Bomb explosion destroys a UN vehicle near Sulaymaniyah. Two UN soldiers are injured. Iraqi agents are blamed for the attacks.
92–7-22:	Iraq again refuses to renew the memorandum of understanding governing the UN humanitarian presence in Iraq. The memorandum was eventually renewed on October 22, 1992, but provided for the presence of only 300 UN guards, as opposed to 500 in the original memorandum of understanding.
92–7-25:	Iraq agrees to allow UN monitors into the building to which access was previously refused.
92–8-1:	Iraq launches renewed air attacks on southern Shiite Muslims, prompting the UN to establish a "no-fly" zone along the 32nd parallel. The United States and some allies later begin air patrols, which continue today.
92–8-2 to 92–8-3:	Iraqi media run several articles and carry broadcasts reasserting that Kuwait is a province of Iraq.
92–8-19:	The Bush administration, increasing its confrontation with Saddam Hussein, wins British and French agreement today for a plan to shoot down Iraqi military planes if they move into a wide zone throughout the southern part of the country filled with rebelling Shi'ite Muslims. US-led movement to interdict Iraqi aircraft from flying in southern Iraq is an important shift in Western strategy for taking influence from Saddam Hussein.
	After a long cabinet meeting in London, Prime Minister John Major of Britain states that the allies will develop control over as much as a third of the country. "They will be attacked if they fly in the area that is proscribed."
	US officials says Iraq has refurbished one large air base (Talil in southern Iraq), built a new one, activated other dormant airfields, and revived its

Table 10.1 (continued)

	air defense network. The reconstruction of Iraq's air infrastructure is undertaken to support a revival of military flights in southern Iraq.
92–8-22:	Iraq again refuses to renew the memorandum of understanding governing the UN humanitarian presence in Iraq. The memorandum was eventually renewed on October 22, 1992, but provided for the presence of only 300 UN guards, as opposed to 500 in the original memorandum of understanding.
92–8-26:	UN Security Council votes to accept a UN-sponsored demarcation of the Iraqi-Kuwaiti border and declares this border "inviolable."
	The United States, Britain, and France announce the establishment of a southern "no-fly zone" to protect Iraqi dissidents in southern Iraq from regime air attacks. (A northern "no-fly zone" has been in place since the 1991 cease-fire.)
92–8-27:	Three UN guards in northern Iraq discover a bomb attached to their car, but they defuse it before it can explode. UN officials protest the incident to the Iraqi government, but Iraq denies any connection to it.
92–9-6:	Iraq offers amnesty to army dissenters in the mostly Shi'ite south. Baghdad television says that the ruling Revolutionary Command Council issued a decree offering pardons to dissenters who surrender to authorities in the provinces of Basra, Missan, and Dhiqar.
92–9-8:	The US Department of Defense charges that Iraqi troops were burning Shi'ite villages in southern Iraq in an effort to flush out Shi'ite dissidents hiding in the marshes.
92–9-10:	Two US F-16 fighters patrolling the northern no-fly zone intercept an Iraqi Mirage F-1. The Iraqi aircraft, which displays no hostile intent, quickly turns and leaves the no-fly zone.
92–9-16:	The Kurds' two most important political parties agree to combine their guerrilla forces into a sole unit under the command of the Kurdish government. This is a major step toward further centralizing influence in Kurdish-controlled northern Iraq.
92–9-27:	Opposition leaders lay aside their differences and issue a unified appeal to Iraq's army, the ruling Ba'ath Party, and all citizens to revolt against Saddam Hussein.
92–10-1:	At major meeting in Salahuddin in northern Iraq, Shi'ite groups join the INC, and a three-man leadership council and a 26-member executive council is chosen.
	In an attempt to cool its difficulties with the international community, a high-level Iraqi official signals that Baghdad may be ready to permit more UN humanitarian operations inside of Iraq.
92–10-2 to 92–10-6:	Iraqi Kurds supported by Turkish fighter planes carry out a major military offensive to drive Kurdish separatists from their guerrilla bases in northern Iraq.

Table 10.1 (continued)

92–10-4:	Iraqi Kurdish leaders declare a federalist state.
92–10-12:	Turkish cross-border operations begin.
92–10-19:	A team of aid experts led by the United States warns that there could be a humanitarian emergency on a tremendous scale in the Kurdish-controlled areas of northern Iraq if aid supplies do not reach the area before the start of winter.
92–10-20:	Iraq says it will refuse to allow the stationing of human rights monitors throughout Iraq, as proposed by a special rapporteur of the UN Human Rights Commission, Max Van der Stoel.
92–10-22:	Iraqi officials swear in a memorandum of understanding to cooperate with the UN winter aid program that will transport most of its aid, including fuel, north from the Iraqi capital.
	Turkish troops move across the Iraqi border on three fronts to eradicate the Kurdish separatist movement that has forced southeast Turkey to the brink of civil war.
92–10-26:	Rebel Turkish Kurds were given until this day by the Patriotic Union of Kurdistan leader, Jalal Talabani, to withdraw from Iraqi Kurdistan or receive renewed attack.
92–10-30:	Turkish troops move against Turkish Kurdish rebels who sought refugee in Northern Iraq.
92–10-31:	At Tatvan in Turkey, at least five Turkish soldiers are killed and nine injured when rebel Turkish Kurds invade an outpost on the border with Iran.
	Iraqi opposition groups elect a Kurdish guerrilla chief, a moderate Shi'ite Muslim cleric, and a retired Iraqi general to lead the combat against Saddam Hussein.
92–11-2:	Bomb explodes in a market near the headquarters of the UN guard contingent in Irbil. One person is killed and 16 are injured.
	The UN issues a decision that Iraq cannot remove its weapons from the zone without the permission of UNIKOM, but Iraq claims UNIKOM gave it permission to clear the weaponry from the zone.
92–11-20:	The main opposition group in the South declares that the government in Baghdad has increased repression of Shi'ite Muslim civilians, and that the US-led ban on Iraqi flights in the region is not preventing it.
92–11-23:	The final demarcation of the land border, established by a UN commission pursuant to Resolution 687 (the cease-fire resolution). The new border goes into effect on Jan. 15, 1993; Iraq condemns the findings of the demarcation commission, which allocates additional territory, including a portion of a former Iraqi naval base and several oil wells, to Kuwait. Iraq initially refused to remove its six police posts from what has been designated as Kuwaiti territory. (Later, on January 18, the UN says that Iraq has done so.)

Table 10.1 (continued)

92–12-1:	Iraqi MiG-25 violates no-fly zone; US plane shoots down plane.
92–12-7:	Saddam Hussein declares the opening of the "Saddam River" project, a 350-mile irrigation project flowing from Baghdad to Basra. UN human rights officials criticize the project as an attempt to drain the marshes in southern Iraq, which Iraq's organized Shi'ite opposition uses as a hiding place and base of operations, and to make the vast wetlands accessible to Iraqi armor battling Shi'ite rebels.
92–12-17:	Iraq moves military forces to the northern part of its country within great close proximity to the Kurdish enclave there.
92–12-19:	Following a series of bombings and mining against UN humanitarian relief trucks in northern Iraq, UN relief deliveries are suspended.
92–12-27:	A US F-16 shoots down an Iraqi jet that has violated the allied imposed "no-fly zone" in southern Iraq. Subsequently, Iraq redeploys eight SA-3 and 12 SA-2 anti-aircraft missile launchers in the no-fly zone in a manner threatening to Coalition aircraft patrolling the zone.
93–1-4 to 93–1-5:	Iraq moves anti-aircraft missiles into southern no-fly zone.
93–1-6:	The United States, Britain, France, and Russia give Iraq 48 hours to move the missiles to their original locations or face possible military action. Despite Iraqi statements that it will not comply, and after examining intelligence reports on the movement of the missiles, the United States announces on January 9 that Iraq has complied with the ultimatum. The US House notes that action could be taken without warning if Iraq redeploys the missiles in a threatening manner.
93–1-7:	Iraq tells the UN that it would no longer permit UN weapons inspectors to use their own aircraft to fly into or land in Iraq. It said the inspectors could use chartered Iraqi aircraft (all Iraqi air travel is banned by UN sanctions, however). Iraq does not specifically ban UN U-2 or helicopter surveillance flights, however.
93–1-8 and 93–1-11:	Iraq is described in a Security Council statement as being in material breach of UN Security Council Resolution 687, the principal cease-fire resolution enacted shortly after the Gulf War.
93–1-10:	Iraq bans the flight into Iraq of 70 inspectors who are returning to Iraq after the holidays. The Security Council calls the Iraqi action unacceptable and warns of serious consequences if the decision is not reversed. UN Security Council Resolution 707 states that Iraq must allow the inspectors to use their own transportation in performing their duties. Resolution 715 also provides for the dismantling of Iraqi facilities for developing weapons of mass destruction. These resolutions were passed under Chapter VII of the UN charter (peace and security) and thus can be enforced militarily without further UN authorization.
	500 Iraqis (some armed) cross into the demilitarized zone, seize weapons, including four Silkworm missiles, under guard by UNIKOM, and return to Iraq. (UNIKOM is a monitoring force, and is neither empowered nor

Table 10.1 (continued)

	able to resist militarily a large Iraqi incursion across the border.) The equipment had been left behind by Iraq when it retreated from Kuwait in the Persian Gulf War. Emissaries from the United States, Britain, France, and Russia visit Iraq's ambassador to the UN to protest the seizure.
93–1-11:	US Director of Central Intelligence Robert Gates says that Iraq is continuing to shift anti-aircraft missiles in the exclusion zones in both southern and northern Iraq, but that it is too early to determine whether or not the deployments threatened allied aircraft. The Security Council meets. Several hundred Iraqis again enter the zone and begin dismantling weapons warehouses, and resume this activity on January 12 and early on January 13.
93–1-12:	General John Shalikashvili, Commander-in-Chief of US forces in Europe, says that Iraq has put its anti-aircraft missiles in the northern no-fly zone on operational status. On several subsequent occasions, Iraq again activates its targeting radar in the no-fly zones, precipitating confrontations with Coalition aircraft. US officials cite two legal bases for enforcing the no-fly zones. First, UN Security Council Resolution 688 calls on Iraq to not repress its civilian population, in this case, Shi'ites in southern Iraq and the Kurds in northern Iraq. Second, the March 3, 1992, Safwan Accords concluded between Iraqi and Coalition military commanders prevent Iraq from interfering with allied air operations over Iraq.
	President Bush informs congressional leaders of his intention to launch air strikes against the Iraqi missile sites. In the first hours after the strikes, several members of Congress voice their approval of the use of force. According to reports, the president conferred with selected members of Congress prior to the June 26, 1993, attack on the Iraqi Intelligence headquarters. Most members of Congress support the president's action, although some believe the president should have pursued diplomatic avenues before resorting to military action, and some questioned the wisdom of launching the Tomahawks at night when civilians were more likely to be at home.
93–1-13:	US-led Coalition forces conduct air strikes against eight Iraqi anti-aircraft missile sites and related control facilities in the no-fly zone of southern Iraq (south of the 32nd parallel). Subsequently, administration officials call the raid a success in that it seriously degrades Iraq's air defense network, although several targets were not hit. The raid involves 600 US military 600 US military personnel from the various services and approximately 110 allied aircraft. According to the Defense Department's principal spokesman, only the United States and former Desert Storm partners Britain and France participate in the raid. Iraq says the attack kills 19 and wounds 15, many of them civilians. US officials acknowledge that an apartment building in the southern city of Basra was hit, presumably by mistake. The United States announces that a US-armored battalion, the 1st battalion, 19th regiment, 1st Cavalry Division from Fort

Table 10.1 (continued)

	Hood, Texas—a total of roughly 1,100 soldiers—will go to Kuwait to bolster US forces in the region and underscore the US commitment to Persian Gulf security. Much of their equipment, which includes M1 tanks and Bradley fighting vehicles, is prepositioned in Kuwait under terms of the US-Kuwait Defense Cooperation Agreement, signed in September, 1991. The battalion, scheduled for training exercises in Kuwait, joins the approximately 300 US Special Forces troops already in Kuwait for military exercises. Despite a defiant post-raid speech by Saddam Hussein, Iraq's ambassador to the UN tells the president of the UN Security Council that Iraq would permit flights by UN inspectors in their own aircraft, and that incursions into the demilitarized zone with Kuwait would cease. However, Iraq states that it will continue to resist enforcement of the no fly zones, and Saddam instructed the military to fire on Coalition planes over Iraqi territory.
93–1-14:	The United States, Britain and France deliver an ultimatum to Iraq that it provide such clearance by 4:00 P.M. EST on Jan. 15, 1993. Before the deadline expires, Iraq says the UN aircraft could land, but that Iraq could not guarantee its security, since allied operations were taking place in the southern no-fly zone. UNSCOM rejects that condition and says it would file a new flight request.
93–1-16:	Iraq says it will permit the flights and guarantee their security, but only if they enter Iraqi airspace from Jordan, and not from the south. (The UN flights generally enter from the south, flying from the UNSCOM office in Bahrain.) UNSCOM again rejected this condition, as well as a January 17 Iraqi proposal that the flights could enter from the south if the Coalition suspended its patrols of the no-fly zone during the UN flights.
93–1-17:	Iraq activates its targeting radar in the northern no-fly zone. The Coalition conducts an air strike against an SA-6 ground radar station in northern Iraq and shoots down an Iraqi MiG-23 that crossed into the no-fly zone in the north. Later that day, the United States launches 45 cruise missiles at the Zafaraniya manufacturing complex outside of Baghdad. The Bush administration says the complex, which has been rendered inoperative by UNSCOM in the course of four inspections there, had been used to make components for Iraq's nuclear weapons program. One cruise missile went or was shot off course and hits the A1 Rashid hotel in Baghdad, killing at least three civilians.
93–1-18:	The Coalition launches another raid on the Iraqi air defense installations in the South that it had missed or insufficiently damaged in the January 13 air strike. The Coalition also strikes air defense installations in the northern no-fly zone and shoots at, and probably downs, an Iraqi war plane that tries to resist the Coalition attacks in the north. Iraq's mobile anti-aircraft batteries in the south, however, were moved in advance of the raid. Iraq said 21 were killed in the attacks. There were also reports

Table 10.1 (continued)

	that Iraq fired a Scud missile at the Saudi city of Dhahran, but the Pentagon said it could not confirm that a missile was fired.
93–1-19:	Iraqi planes again challenge the no-fly zone in the north and direct anti-aircraft fire at Coalition aircraft. In response, the Coalition fires cluster bombs and air-to-surface missiles at Iraqi anti-aircraft guns in the northern no-fly zone. Kuwait also announces that an unspecified number of US Patriot missiles have arrived in Kuwait to provide further protection. Four US warships, including the aircraft carrier *Kennedy*, are headed toward the eastern Mediterranean in case they are needed against Iraq. At 1:30 P.M. EST, Iraq's ruling Revolutionary Command Council offers a "cease-fire . . . to enable the new administration to study the no-fly zones." Subsequently, Iraq offers to allow UN aircraft to fly directly from Bahrain to Baghdad without conditions. UN Secretary General Boutros Boutros-Ghali recommends that 3,645 armed UN troops and military support be sent to guard the Iraq-Kuwait border.
93–1-21:	US aircraft fire a missile and drop cluster bombs on an Iraqi ground radar in the northern no-fly zone when the radar beam search was directed at them while they were escorting a French reconnaissance airplane.
93–1-22:	A US F-4G fires two missiles at an air defense battery in the northern no-fly zone after the battery's radar actively tracked US aircraft patrolling the zone. Iraq denies that it had tracked the aircraft and claims there were no air defense batteries at that location. A US A-6 Intruder aircraft fires a laser-guided bomb at an Iraqi anti-aircraft position in the southern no-fly zone after the pilot thought he saw anti-aircraft fire directed at his and other US aircraft patrolling that zone. Iraq denied firing on any US aircraft. US Defense Department officials subsequently say that the US aircraft were not being tracked by Iraqi radar, and that they were trying to establish whether or not Iraq had fired on the US planes.
93–1-23:	More than 100 US, British, and French planes strike missile batteries and radar stations in Iraq. President Bush orders an additional 1,250 troops to Kuwait.
	US A-6 Intruder aircraft fires a laser-guided bomb at an Iraqi anti-aircraft position in the southern no fly zone when the pilot thought he saw anti-aircraft fire directed at his and other US aircraft patrolling the zone. The Defense Department subsequently says that US aircraft were not being tracked by Iraqi radar, and the Department was trying to establish whether or not Iraq had fired on US planes.
93–1-25:	Defense Secretary Les Aspin states that there is some evidence that the Iraqi military is moving surface-to-air missiles into southern Iraq. Movement of those missiles is important because of Iraq deployed the missiles in a threatening pattern in the southern "no-fly zone." US attacks on surface-to-air missile batteries in the last week of the Bush presidency destroyed some of the missiles and forced Iraq to move others.

Table 10.1 (continued)

93–2-2:	A time bomb that was planted on a UN relief truck returning from northern Iraq explodes at a border crossing into Turkey.
93–2-3:	Iraqi anti-aircraft batteries fire on two French Mirages in no-fly zone. French aircraft are not damaged.
93–2-25:	UN officials say an unidentified man ran from a taxi and attached a bomb to an empty UN truck moving through the Iraqi-controlled checkpoint at Fayda in northern Iraq.
93–2-27:	The *London Observer* reports that Iraq had launched a campaign of repression against its Shi'ite population in the south, poisoning and draining its water supplies. On March 1, the United States says it is investigating the report.
93–2-28:	Iraq says that it will welcome visits by foreign reporters to its southern marshes, where a British newspaper said Baghdad launched a campaign of repression against the Shi'ites.
93–3-1:	UN investigator says that it appears as if Iraq has executed hundreds of people from its southern marshes in "death camps."
93–3-2:	UN human rights rapporteur Max Van der Stoel reports to the UN Human Rights Commission that Iraq is guilty of human rights violations on a massive scale, including economic deprivation, torture, and mass executions of ethnic minorities. He renews the appeal he made the previous year for the Human Rights Commission to send human rights monitors to Iraq, a move supported by the UN General Assembly but opposed by Iraq.
93–3-17:	US military officers remind their Iraqi counterparts of the March 3 agreement, but they do not threaten any action against Iraqi helicopters, which Iraq was employing against Kurdish and Shi'ite rebels. The terms of the cease-fire did not call for military efforts to prevent Iraq from using force, including helicopters, to combat the Kurdish and Shi'ite uprisings that began shortly after the end of the war, but several members of Congress, administration officials, and many outside experts argued that the United States should forcibly prohibit Iraq's helicopter use as well.
93–3-19:	Clinton administration releases a US army report on Iraqi war crimes associated with the Persian Gulf crisis. On April 27, 1993, after meeting with visiting INC representatives, Secretary of State Warren Christopher says the United States would propose that the UN Security Council create a commission to investigate alleged Iraqi war crimes and crimes against humanity.
	Increasing reports of unrest in the southern part of the country. Southern Iraq is strictly off limits to Ba'ath Party officials and government employees after dark. In fact, no one wants to travel to the south after sundown, except foreign aid workers and curious journalists.
	Reconstruction in the south of civilian targets of the allied bombing has not been given the same attention as those in the capital. Unlike Baghdad,

Table 10.1 (continued)

	where the rebuilding of bombed bridges in the south is still underway and a primary effort has been given to rebuilding government structures, "Southerners say that the intensive effort by the government to rebuild damaged parts of the holy shrines was a token to the south by the government," said a well-informed resident of al-Basra.
93–3-23:	The UN Security Council, after reviewing Iraq's compliance record and finding several areas of non- or incomplete compliance, decides to maintain economic sanctions against Iraq.
93–4-9:	Iraqi anti-aircraft fires at four US airplanes in the no-fly zone; the planes respond by bombing Iraqi anti-aircraft positions.
93–4-14 to 93–4-16:	Iraq attempts an assassination of President Bush during his visit to Kuwait. The Kuwaitis capture a small van loaded with 180 pounds of explosives and confiscate detonators, timing devices, and other bomb components. Sixteen of the 17 suspects in the plot (11 Iraqi nationals) are in custody in Kuwait and have been charged, and the trial of 14 of them begins in Kuwait on June 5. One of the Iraqi defendants testifies that Iraqi intelligence was behind the plot.
93–4-16 to 93–4-18:	Former US President Bush visits Kuwait.
93–4-16:	Several relief agencies withdraw personnel from northern Iraq after a series of attacks on their personnel, attributed to Iraqi intelligence services.
93–4-18:	According to a US military statement, two US aircraft are targeted by Iraqi anti-aircraft radar while patrolling the northern no-fly zone. Iraqi batteries are located just south of the zone. One of the planes fires a missile in response to the threat. Iraq denies threatening US aircraft.
93–4-26:	US Navy EA-6B patrolling the northern no-fly zone does not respond to an Iraqi surface-to-air missile that was fired on it but fell short.
93–4-27:	After meeting with visiting INC representatives, Secretary of State Christopher says that the United States would propose that the UN Security Council create a commission to investigate alleged Iraqi war crimes and crimes against humanity.
93–4-29:	Kuwait announces the arrest of a group of Iraqis who were charged with planning to assassinate former US President Bush during his visit to Kuwait. The arrests reportedly took place prior to Bush's April visit.
93–4-30:	The State Department releases "Patterns of Global Terrorism: 1992," which states that Iraq is providing a safe haven and support to the radical Turkish-opposition Kurdistan Workers Party (PKK).
93–5-1:	Saddam Hussein orders the cancellation of the Iraqi 25-Dinar notes in an attempt to withhold from the Kurds their main source of commercial exchange. This act has brought anxiety to the 3 million Kurds in northern Iraq.

Iraq and the War of Sanctions

Table 10.1 (continued)

93–5-5:	Iraq abruptly closes its borders and announces that it is taking the pre-war 25-Dinar bank note out of circulation. This wipes out the value of the 25-Dinar note holdings of many Kurds in Iraq.
93–5-19:	US officials state that an FBI investigation had substantiated charges that the Iraqi government plotted the assassination of former President Bush while visiting Kuwait in April, 1993.
93–5-21:	The US Department of Defense announces that US aircraft patrolling the southern no-fly zone encountered anti-aircraft gunfire three times in the past week but did not return fire.
93–5-22:	The UN warns that relief for the Kurds in northern Iraq, as well as for the needy people hurting from the trade embargo in other parts of the country, will be terminated unless Western countries contribute more finances and supplies.
93–5-24:	Secretary of State Christopher warns Iraq not to attack the Kurdish-controlled territories in the north, following reports of an Iraqi military buildup along the front with the Kurds.
93–5-25:	The UN Security Council again decides not to lift economic sanctions against Iraq because Iraq has not complied fully with UN cease-fire resolutions.
93–6-1:	Iran reports that Iraqi troops have surrounded the marsh areas, and the UN inspectors in the area back up that claim. The UN inspectors state that they find Iraqi Shi'ites living in the marshes under appalling conditions with little food or fresh water. Iraqi troops reportedly withdraw when UN humanitarian representative Sadruddin Agha Khan comes to set up the UN relief center, but return a few days later, after Sadruddin had departed.
93–6-3:	US military aircraft detect new efforts by Iraqi anti-aircraft units to track their flights over southern Iraq.
93–6-10 to 93–7-17:	A lengthy stand-off takes place between the Iraqi government and UN inspectors over Iraq's refusal to allow inspectors to monitor two missile test sites south of Baghdad. UN monitors are withdrawn.
93–6-19:	UN Special Commissioner for Iraqi Disarmament Rolf Ekeus and Iraqi government reach agreement on renewing UN inspections of Iraqi weapons programs amid mounting fears that military reprisals will be taken by Coalition forces if a new inspections agreement is not reached.
93–6-24:	Federal Bureau of Investigation (FBI) agents and other US intelligence officers are sent to Kuwait to conduct their own investigation, and report back to the president that their findings confirmed the view that Iraq was behind the plot. Iraq denies that it sponsored the attempt.
93–6-26:	The USS *Peterson*, a Spruance-class destroyer in the Red Sea, and the USS *Chancellorsville*, a Ticonderoga-class cruiser in the Persian Gulf, launch 23 Tomahawk missiles toward the Iraqi intelligence headquarters in western Baghdad. Twenty of the Tomahawks hit the six-winged head-

Table 10.1 (continued)

	quarters building in the center of the intelligence complex. President Clinton states that CIA and FBI reports provide compelling evidence that Iraqi intelligence forces were behind the attempted assassination of former President Bush in April and that the United States was justified in acting against Iraq under the self-defense provisions of Article 51 of the UN Charter. In a briefing following the president's address, Defense Secretary Les Aspin and Chairman of the Joint Chiefs of Staff General Colin Powell say the intelligence headquarters was selected as the target because the Iraqi intelligence services were linked to the attempt on President Bush.
93–6-27:	US Ambassador to the UN Madeleine Albright presents evidence to the Security Council, including pictures of the van with 170 pounds of explosives and the detonator and other bomb components, that link Iraq to the attempt on President Bush. US officials say the attack on the intelligence headquarters was a qualified success based on early damage estimates, but, three of the Tomahawks missed their targets and hit nearby residential areas, destroying several houses and killing eight and wounding 12 civilians. (Iraq claims to have shot down four of the missiles.) The United States moves the aircraft carrier USS *Theodore Roosevelt* and destroyers *Arleigh Burke* and *Spruance* from the Mediterranean to the Red Sea. (The carrier USS *Nimitz* left the Persian Gulf on June 17 at the end of its six-month tour.)
	The British Broadcasting Corporation broadcasts the first extensive report on the mass murder of Iraqi Kurds during 1988–1990.
93–6-28:	President Clinton sends a letter to Congress describing the missile attack on Iraq "consistent with the War Powers Resolution." The president also says the raids crippled Iraq's military intelligence capability, but some observers suggest that this capability was not severely damaged because of redundancies in the system.
93–6-29:	Iraqi anti-aircraft radar "locks on" to US planes flying over the Basra Province in southern Iraq. An F-4G "Wild Weasel" fires one HARM missile at the radar site. President Clinton tells the press that the action follows standard US rules of engagement over the no-fly zones, and that people should not read too much into the incident. Iraqi sources said one Iraqi soldier was wounded in the incident, which it called a "cowardly act of aggression."
93–7-1:	US planes strike at anti-aircraft missile sites in a series of missile attacks in no-fly zones over southern and northern Iraq.
93–7-8:	The approximately 100 foreign relief workers who continue to reside in the autonomous Kurdish northern area of Iraq now solely travel with a backup car filled with armed guards, and they never leave their homes after dark. The relief workers say that they feel as though they are the object of a "low-intensity" campaign by Baghdad to force out the only Western presence in northern Iraq.

Table 10.1 (continued)

93-7-16:	Tehran-based Iraqi Shi'ite political figure Mohammed Baqir Hakim, in a letter to UN Secretary-General Boutros Boutros-Ghali, reports on the recent refugee exodus and asks for UN aid for Iraqi Shi'ites in the South.
93-10-1:	A BBC documentary estimates that the actions of the Iraqi government have reduced the Marsh Arab or Ma'dan population from 700,000 in 1980 (the last census) to less than 200,000.
93-11-12:	The Iraqi government forces step-up military pressure against Shiite villages in southern Iraq, forcing thousands to flee deeper into the marshes or across the border into Iran.
93-11-19:	UN teams enter the marshes of southern Iran to investigate reports that Iraqi forces have used poisoned gas. Iraq is reported to be building a massive earthen barrier along the border with Iran.
93-11-23:	Max van der Stoel, the UN special rapporteur for human rights in Iraq, warns that the survival of the Marsh Arabs (Ma'dan) is threatened in spite of the UN no-fly zone, and that Iraq is continuing to intensify its assaults and use of artillery. He indicates that he did not find signs of use of chemical weapons, but has sent soil samples for analysis, a process that may take some months. He also warns that Iraq is continuing to execute dissidents and occasionally shell Kurdish areas.
94-4-24:	Iraq announces the completion of a 65-mile canal through southern Iraq that would divert river waters away from marshlands inhabited primarily by Shi'ite Iraqis to desert lands. The project has long been the object of concern to human rights groups, who charge that the primary reason for the project is to punish the Shi'ite population in this region for their support of anti-government rebels and to make rebel bases more accessible to government attack.
94-10-3 to 94-10-6:	During a visit to Baghdad by Rolf Ekeus to discuss Iraqi compliance with UN weapons of mass destruction resolutions, Iraq begins to warn of unspecified consequences if the oil export ban is not lifted in conjunction with the October 10, 1994, UNSCOM report to the Security Council. Iraq also warns that it will stop cooperating with UNSCOM.
94-10-6:	A UNSCOM report is formally presented to the Security Council that says that the long-term monitoring program has begun, but, contrary to Iraqi desires, it does not set a timetable for testing the monitoring system.
	During the week, Iraq orders at least two division (Hammurabi, al-Nida) of elite Republican Guard troops to join approximately 40,000 regular troops in southern Iraq, around the city of Basra.
94-10-7:	Secretary of Defense William Perry calls the Iraqi troop movements a cause for concern, and other US defense officials said the troop movements, which include the transport of ammunition and support equipment, are not consistent with routine troop rotations. Iraqi officials say Iraq has a right to deploy its troops anywhere within its own borders. The Kuwaiti Cabinet meets in emergency session, and Kuwait subsequently moves

Table 10.1 (continued)

	most of its 16,000-person force to the border with Iraq, a much larger display of force than it demonstrated in August, 1990. Kuwait's force is still too small and poorly armed and trained to deter Iraq, even though Iraq's total military capability is about 40% of what it was before the 1991 Persian Gulf War.
94–10-8:	President Clinton states, "It would be a grave error for Iraq to repeat the mistakes of the past [the August 1990 invasion of Kuwait] or to misjudge either American will or American power." He states that the United States would honor a commitment to defend Kuwait and to enforce UN resolutions on Iraq. Several US defense officials are quoted by press reports as saying that they do not believe Iraq intends to invade Kuwait again, but that it is wise for the United States to be prepared, given Saddam's record of belligerence. The new US forces join approximately 13,000 US Army, Navy, Air Force, and Marine troops already in the Gulf. The US forces can make use of a brigade's worth of ground equipment (including M1A1 tanks and Bradley Fighting Vehicles) prepositioned in Kuwait. That equipment is there under a September, 1991 US defense pact with Kuwait. The total new forces to be deployed include: two additional Patriot missile batteries; 350 additional combat aircraft, including B-52 bombers, F-117 Stealth fighters, F-15s, F-16s, A-10 attack aircraft, AWACS surveillance aircraft, and U-2 reconnaissance aircraft; the 18,000-member 1st Marine Expeditionary Force; and 16,000 army troops from the 24th Mechanized Infantry Division. The US deployment expands to 36,000 troops. An additional 156,000 troops are placed on alert.
94–10-9:	According to statements by US officials, Iraq had about 80,000 troops in or heading toward southern Iraq, assuming all Iraqi units were eventually filled out. The lead elements of the Iraqi deployment reportedly go as close as 12 miles from the border with Kuwait. UN observers in the Iraq-Kuwait demilitarized zone (six miles into Iraq and three miles into Kuwait) reported that the border area was quiet and they did not see signs of the Iraqi build-up. UNSCOM says that Iraq is not interfering with its operations in Iraq, and a biological inspection team is conducting a mission there. Some Kurdish figures based in Turkey report a movement of Iraqi engineering units toward Kurdish-controlled territory, but US officials said the build-up there was not substantial. Iraq also set up a tent camp along the border with Kuwait, where up to 3,000 stateless Arabs were protesting their expulsions by Kuwait. Iraq's Foreign Minister, Mohammad al-Sahhaf, said that Iraq seeks a diplomatic solution to the crisis.
94–10-10:	Iraq's ambassador to the UN says that Iraq was redeploying its troops from the border area because of "Security Council concerns" about the Iraqi build-up, though he says Iraq reserves the right to place its troops anywhere within Iraq's own territory. President Clinton says the United States has not seen hard evidence that Iraq is pulling back, and the US deployments to the region continue.

Table 10.1 (continued)

94–10-11:	Iraq invites defense attachés from China and Russia to monitor Iraqi troop withdrawals. Chairman of the Joint Chiefs of Staff, John Shalikashvili, says that there were indications that Iraq was undertaking a withdrawal.
94–10-13:	Russian Foreign Minister Kozyrev works out a joint statement with Iraq that implies that Iraq will recognize Kuwait in exchange for the lifting of the oil embargo within six months. The United States rejects the Iraq-Russia statement.
94–10-15:	The United States succeeds in gaining unanimous Security Council approval of Resolution 949, demanding that Iraq not deploy its troops so as to threaten its neighbors. The resolution invokes Chapter VII (peace and security) of the UN Charter but does not specify means of enforcement. US ambassador to the UN, Albright, says the resolution gives the United States authority to strike Iraq if it again moves Republican Guards near Kuwait, but other Security Council members have not yet endorsed that view.
94–10-16:	Secretary of State Christopher indicates that the Iraqi units are withdrawing.
94–10-17:	Iraq pulls back and Secretary of Defense Perry indicates that about 30,000—not the anticipated 36,000—will deploy to Kuwait. The Department of Defense said it was reviewing whether or not to send the 18,000 troops from the 1st Marine Expeditionary Force to Kuwait. In addition, the United States appears to scale back the deployment of combat aircraft to the region. Most of the new US units that arrive in Kuwait have previously conducted exercises with Kuwait, using the US equipment prepositioned there. Many of the combat aircraft are based in Saudi Arabia and Turkey, although Turkey is hesitant to allow an attack on Iraq from its territory. The United States also moves the carrier USS *George Washington* from the Adriatic Sea to the Red Sea, within striking range of Iraq. Britain sends two ships, six Tornado aircraft, and a battalion of troops to the Gulf. France, which had supported the idea of setting a firm timetable for allowing Iraq to resume oil sales, sends a frigate to the Gulf.
94–11-10:	Iraq issues a statement declaring that it "recognizes the sovereignty of the State of Kuwait, its territorial integrity and political independence." (Renunciation of the claim that Kuwait was a "province" of Iraq was one of several UN Security Council conditions to end economic sanctions on Iraq.)
95–1-8:	The United States orders the deployment of 4,000 additional troops to Kuwait.
95–1-10:	Rolf Ekeus, head of the UN special commission monitoring Iraqi disarmament, reports to the Security Council that Iraq had recently turned over information on its chemical weapons programs that it had failed to disclose for four years.

Table 10.1 (continued)

95–1-15:	Saddam Hussein is "re-elected" to another seven-year term as president of Iraq in a referendum in which he was the sole candidate. Saddam reportedly won 99.96% of the vote.
95–2-27:	Max van der Stoel, the former Dutch Foreign Minister who has been charged by the UN with monitoring human rights abuses in Iraq, characterizes Iraq as among "the worst offenders of human rights since the Second World War."
95–4-10:	Rolf Ekeus states that the Iraqi government had withheld information from the UN that suggested that Iraq planned and perhaps began a biological weapons program in the 1980s.
95–4-16:	The Iraqi Cabinet formally turns down a UN Security Council offer to allow Iraq to sell up to $2 billion worth of oil to purchase food and medicines which would have contributed to alleviating supply shortages harming Iraqi citizens. Iraqi troops loyal to Saddam Hussein reportedly put down an uprising led by elite Republican Guard troops. The Iraqi government denied the report.
95–7-11:	The UN votes to renew trade sanctions on Iraq. Observers described the extension as a "foregone conclusion" after UN arms inspector Rolf Ekeus reported that, after four years of denials, Iraq had admitted that it produced biological weapons in 1989 and 1990.
95–8-8:	Jordan grants asylum to two sons-in-law of Saddam Hussein, Lt. Gen. Hussein Kamel Hassan al-Majid, who had supervised Iraq's weapons of mass destruction development programs since 1987, and his brother, Lt. Col. Saddam Kamel Hassan al-Majid, who formerly headed the presidential security forces. The two men were married to the two eldest daughters of Saddam Hussein.
95–8-17:	During a visit to Baghdad, Iraq provides new information to UN arms inspector Rolf Ekeus, admitting inter alia that it began a crash nuclear weapons program in April, 1990 that sought to produce a nuclear weapon by April, 1991. Observers speculated that Iraq's new candor was prompted by the defection of Hussein Kamel, who the Iraqi government believed would cooperate with UN inspectors and Western governments to provide previously undisclosed information on Iraqi weapons programs.
96–2-20:	Hussein and Saddam Kamel, Saddam's two sons-in-law who requested asylum in Jordan in August, 1995, return to Baghdad after receiving Iraqi government "pardons."
96–2-23:	Hussein and Saddam Kamel are killed in Baghdad, allegedly at the hands of family members. Iraq agrees to stop blocking removal of parts of 134 Scud long-range missile motors. This removal has been blocked since November, 1996. UNSCOM stated that "Iraq still possesses a force of operational missiles proscribed by Security Council Resolution 687."

Table 10.1 (continued)

96–3-15:	In response to further Iraqi provocations, the United States dispatches eight F-117A stealth fighters to Kuwait, four B-52 bombers to the British base at Diego Garcia in the Indian Ocean, two Patriot missile batteries to Saudi Arabia, and a second aircraft carrier along with additional aircraft and air defense units to the region. (The second aircraft carrier returns home in October.)
96–5-20:	Iraq and the UN sign an "oil-for-food" deal which would allow Iraq to sell $2 billion worth of oil for food and medical supplies to be supplied to Iraqi civilians under UN supervision.
96–6-22 to 97–6-23:	First Arab Summit since 1990 is held. Iraq is the sole Arab nation not invited to attend.
96–8-1:	Saddam Hussein sends Iraqi forces into northern Iraq, capturing Irbil, a key city inside of the Kurdish safe haven protected by US-led forces.
96–8-2:	Raed Ahmad, an Iraqi weight lifter who carried his country's flag at the 1996 Summer Olympics in Atlanta, requests political asylum in the United States.
96–8-31:	An Iraqi force estimated at three armored divisions comprising 30,000–40,000 personnel invades the Kurdish provisional capital of Irbil, which lies approximately seven miles within the allied-imposed no-fly zone, and had been seized by one of the two leading Kurdish factions, the Patriotic Union of Kurdistan (PUK) in May, 1994. Iraq advances at the invitation of Massud Barzani, leader of a rival Kurdish faction, the Kurdistan Democratic Party (KDP). Over the next few days, and without much additional Iraqi help, the KDP captured major Kurdish cities from the PUK, which is supported by Iran. Numerous PUK members and other Kurds seek refuge in Iran. President Clinton places US forces in the Gulf on alert. The resulting US troop deployments to the Persian Gulf region in the aftermath of the Iraqi incursion bring the total US personnel strength in the region to approximately 30,000 by late September, although some forces are withdrawn by Christmas.
96–9-1:	Responding to Iraqi attacks in northern Iraq and Iraqi efforts to renegotiate the accord, UN Secretary-General Boutros Boutros-Ghali freezes implementation of Iraqi "oil-for-food" accord. US ships and airplanes fire scores of cruise missiles at military targets to punish the Iraqi military and discourage loyalty to Saddam Hussein. President Clinton extends the southern no-fly zone to just south of Baghdad.
96–9-3 to 96–9-4:	US military forces in the Persian Gulf region launch two missile attacks on Iraqi military and command positions in southern Iraq. Iraqi forces withdraw from Erbil. Foreign observers noted that voters were required to sign their ballots. Jordan's King Hussein described the vote as a "farce."

Table 10.1 (continued)

96–9-3:	At 12:15 A.M. Eastern Daylight Time (7:15 A.M. Iraq time), US forces launch 27 cruise missiles at military targets in the southern part of Iraq, 14 from the USS *Laboon* guided missile destroyer and the USS *Shilo* cruiser in the Persian Gulf, and 13 from two B-52 bombers that fly from Guam. The United States says the strikes are a warning to Iraq to comply with Gulf War cease-fire resolutions. A Pentagon spokesman goes on to describe the strikes as a mopping-up operation, designed to destroy Iraqi air defenses that might threaten allied enforcement of an expanded no-fly zone. Subsequently, a US F-16 fighter aircraft fired two anti-radiation missiles at an Iraqi radar. Later on the same day, President Clinton announced that the US mission had been largely accomplished. President Clinton announces that he is widening the no-fly zone over southern Iraq (extending it northward from the 32nd to the 33rd parallel) and would not allow a limited oil sale by Iraq under a recent UN resolution to take place until Iraq abandons its aggressive policies. President Saddam Hussein orders his forces to ignore the no-fly zones and to shoot down intruders.
96–9-4:	The United States launches a second wave of cruise missiles at Iraqi military targets in what America says is an effort to destroy Iraq's ability to attack aircraft enforcing expanded no-fly zones in southern Iraq.
96–9-11:	Iraq fires one surface-to-air missile at two US F-16 jets policing no-fly zones over northern Iraq.
96–9-13:	Iraq announces that it would suspend all attacks against allied war planes patrolling the two no-fly zones. Announcement came as the US military build-up in the Gulf gathered pace, including the dispatch of 5,000 troops. On September 12, the United States moves F-117A stealth bombers and B-52 long-range bombers into position to prepare for possible air strikes. Baghdad announces that it fired three missiles at allied planes in the northern and southern no fly zones.
	Iraq makes a surprise announcement that it will suspend all attacks against allied warplanes patrolling two no-fly zones. The announcement comes as US military build-up in the Gulf gathers pace, including 5,000 troops, and a reinforced squadron of US F-16 fighter aircraft deploys to Bahrain.
96–9-17:	President Clinton orders approximately 3,000 US Army troops from the 1st Cavalry Division at Ft. Hood, Texas, to deploy to Kuwait, joining an additional 1,200 US troops already there. By late September, US troop strength in the region, including personnel embarked on ships, approached 30,000.
96–10-13:	PUK militia regroups and launches a counterattack, recapturing significant portions of territory they had previously lost, and the situation remains fluid. Iran has denied allegations by both KDP and Turkish officials that the PUK counterattack received Iranian military support.

Table 10.1 (continued)

	The United States expresses grave concern, puts forces in the Persian Gulf region on alert, and warns Iraq to withdraw.
96–10-29:	US Secretary of Defense William Perry says the 4,200 troops in Kuwait will depart before Christmas, but adds that 1,800 Marines will remain off shore for rapid deployment and that the F-117A stealth fighters would remain in Kuwait as a warning to Iraq and Iran.
96–11-3:	The United States says that a jet fired a missile at Iraqi radar, but Baghdad denies the incident and accuses the White House of spreading "false news" to help Clinton's re-election chances.
97–1-1:	Russia and France urge Iraq to back down, but both nations say that they are against unilateral action.
97–1-1 to 97–1-6:	The "oil-for-food" program is implemented. The proceeds of this limited oil sale, all of which must be deposited in a UN escrow account, are required to be used to purchase food, medicine, and other material and supplies for essential civilian needs for all Iraqi citizens, and to fund vital UN activities regarding Iraq.
97–2-23:	The government of Iraq agrees to stop blocking removal from Iraq of remnants of some 134 scud long-range missiles motors (with key components stripped by Iraq and still unaccounted for). This removal had been blocked since November 18, 1996, which reinforced UNSCOM concerns that "Iraq still possesses a force of operational missiles proscribed by Security Council Resolution 687." A December 30, 1996, UN Security Council presidential statement had said, "the council deplores the refusal by Iraq" to let UNSCOM remove these remnants for analysis at laboratories of its choice.
97–3-7 to 97–3-20:	A UNSCOM team is delayed for up to three hours at sites labeled "presidential" by Iraqis, who then allow inspectors only limited access. After these delays and limitations, the team finds nothing of concern, but does not claim blockage.
97–4-19:	Iraq agrees to extend the Nov. 5 deadline until after the UN assesses its mission. U-2 flights are suspended.
97–5-20:	Iraq and the UN sign a new "oil-for-food" deal which would allow Iraq to sell $2 billion worth of oil for food and medical supplies to be supplied to Iraqi civilians under UN supervision.
97–6-4 to 97–6-7:	In three separate incidents, Iraqi personnel and aircraft interfere with UNSCOM airborne operations, including Iraqi helicopters spying in front of UNSCOM helicopters to block their mission.
97–6-4:	Iraqis manhandle a UNSCOM photographer while airborne in a UNSCOM helicopter, and grab at the fuel control.

Table 10.1 (continued)

97–6-5:	An Iraqi grabs at a UNSCOM helicopter control stick.
97–6-7:	An Iraqi puts a foot on the UNSCOM helicopter collective control, and Iraqi helicopters fly in front of UNSCOM helicopters to block them, including overlapping of rotors within a few feet.
	UN Security Council Resolution 1111 renews the "oil-for-food" program. Iraqi oil production now averages 605,000 barrels per day. This compares with 2.9 million barrels per day in 1989, before the Gulf War, 2.04 million barrels per day in 1990, 305,000 barrels per day in 1991, 425,000 barrels per day in 1992, 512,000 barrels per day in 1993, 553,000 barrels per day in 1994, 556,000 barrels per day in 1995, and 579,000 barrels per day in 1996. Iraqi production proves to be very erratic in 1997. It ranges from 1–1.3 million barrels per day during January–May, drops to 605,000 barrels per day during June and July, rises to 1.4–1.7 million barrels per day from August to November, and drops to 781,000 barrels per day in December. This is partly the result of a lack of oil field maintenance and repairs and spare parts.
97–6-10:	A UNSCOM team is prohibited entry into a suspected prohibited weapons-procurement facility for seven hours, and finds it to be completely cleared out following wholesale movement of documents in front of the inspectors.
97–6-12:	A UNSCOM team is blocked on a road and simply told it may go no further toward what Iraq claims to be a "presidential" site, even though the chief inspector says his team has no interest in any palaces. Later that day, another team is denied access to a previously inspected Republican Guard site.
97–6-13:	The Security Council adopts a presidential statement that "deplores" the incidents of June 4, 5, and 7, for "endangering the helicopters and their crews," calling on Iraq to "put an end to all such actions."
97–6-18:	Rolf Ekeus, chairman of UNSCOM, briefs the UN Security Council that UNSCOM witnessed Iraqis burning, shredding, and fleeing with stacks of documents while inspectors were blocked.
97–6-21:	Iraq again blocks UNSCOM teams from entering certain sites which have been designated by UNSCOM for inspection.
	The UN Security Council unanimously adopts Resolution 1115: The three key provisions are: (1) condemns Iraq's refusal of access as "clear and flagrant violation" of relevant resolutions; (2) suspends sanctions reviews until after UNSCOM's October six-month report to the council; and (3) expresses the "firm intention to impose additional measures" if Iraq does not comply. The Council also calls for an additional report on Iraq's cooperation with the Commission and suspends the periodic sanctions reviews.

Table 10.1 (continued)

97-7-1: Richard Butler (of Australia) replaces Rolf Ekeus as Executive Chairman of UNSCOM.

[1]Much of this chronology has been adapted from Kenneth Katzman, "Iran and Iraq: US National Security Problems Since the Gulf War—A Chronology," Washington, Congressional Research Service, CRS 93-638F, July 8, 1993.

have played a major role in Iraq's concealment efforts since 1991. They also believe that there are regular meetings between the PPO, SSS, and Republican Guards to direct the concealment effort. Although the United States and Britain struck some of these targets during Desert Fox, virtually all of Iraq's concealment capabilities seem to have survived.

Resolution 707 Fails to Deter Iraq

The initial encounters in the war of sanctions led the UN Security Council to pass Resolution 707 on August 15, 1991. Resolution 707 required Iraq to provide full, final, and complete disclosure of all aspects of its biological, chemical, nuclear, and ballistic missile programs. The resolution also demanded that Iraq allow UN inspectors unconditional and unrestricted access to all areas, facilities, equipment, records, and means which they may wish to inspect.

The resolution further required that Iraq immediately cease any attempt to conceal, move, or destroy any material or equipment relating to these programs. In addition, Resolution 707 called on Iraq to halt all nuclear activities of any kind, except for production of isotopes used for agricultural, industrial, or medical purposes. On October 11, 1991, the UN Security Council also passed Resolution 715, which requires Iraq to meet unconditionally all of its obligations as required in the UN plans for ongoing monitoring of Iraq's compliance with Resolutions 687 and 707.

Passing resolutions, however, did not prevent new challenges from the Iraqi government. As Table 10.1 shows, a long series of confrontations took place between the UN and Iraq, which was particularly intense during the first few years after the Gulf War. UNSCOM and the IAEA completed a total of 53 inspections between June, 1991—the date of the first inspection—and March, 1993. The inspections were comprised of 18 nuclear inspections, 15 chemical inspections, 3 biological inspections, 16 ballistic missile inspections, 5 special missions, and one monitoring team visit.[5] Virtually every inspection encountered significant Iraqi resistance and lies. The Iraqi government engineered confrontation after confrontation and backed down only after it had provoked a crisis, or when the UN Coalition retaliated with force. In March, 1993, these Iraqi actions led Rolf Ekeus—the head of UNSCOM—to declare that he was unable to account for 25% of Iraq's known pre-war Scud force.[6]

Even so, UNSCOM and the IAEA had enough cumulative success to force the Iraqi government to change tactics. On November 26, 1993, Iraq appeared to shift its position and accept the terms of UN Security Council Resolutions 687, 707, and 715. Iraq's Foreign Minister, Mohammed Said Sahaf, sent a letter to the president of the UN Security Council, José Luis Jesus, indicating that Iraq would agree to long-term UN inspection designed to prevent Iraq from resuming its production of weapons of mass destruction so that Iraq could resume its oil exports.

It is important to note, however, that Iraq made this offer only after more than two years of efforts to cheat on the terms of the cease-fire. Furthermore, Iraq's letter came only days after Iraq had again challenged the demarcation of its border with Kuwait, made new claims to Kuwait, had been condemned by the UN for new human rights violations, and had attacked the Shi'ites in its southern marshes. More important, Iraq continued to try to cheat whenever possible.[7]

The detailed history of these developments does not make easy reading, even when it is summarized in chronological form in Table 10.1. It is a history, however, that clearly demonstrates the depth of Iraq's willingness to challenge the UN, even when this led to military action. It is also a history which demonstrates the extent to which Iraq was willing to lie and conceal, and Iraq's growing sophistication in learning how to provoke the United States and Britain without taking serious military risks. While it is possible to understand Iraq's conventional forces, and the structure of its security forces, without understanding the day-by-day history of events following the Gulf War, it is not possible to understand the seriousness of its commitment to preserving and rebuilding its long-range missiles and weapons of mass destruction. This history is also essential to understanding the extent to which the Iraqi government has lied and used "cheat and retreat" tactics.

Challenge and Response in 1994, and Resolution 949

As Table 10.1 has shown, this process of Iraqi "challenge and response" continued throughout 1994 and 1995. During this time, many observers—including a number in the UNSCOM—came to feel that most of Iraq's capabilities had been detected and destroyed. To many, the issue seemed to be the exact point at which UNSCOM and the IAEA would "declare victory and leave." If Iraq had been more cooperative, it might have persuaded a number of UNSCOM experts that their work was complete before the discovery of the full scale of Iraq's biological weapons program and the defection of Hussein Kamel Majid.

Iraq, however, continued to provoke the UN. The most serious crisis during 1994 began on October 6. Iraq issued an ultimatum demanding that the UN set a deadline for lifting sanctions and threatened to halt cooperation with UNSCOM if the UN did not comply by October 10. On October 7, Iraq moved 10,000 troops to within 30 miles of the Kuwaiti border and then moved troops to within 12 miles of the border the next day. Iraq announced on October 12 that its recognition of the new border with Kuwait was dependent on the easing of economic sanctions.

The UN responded on October 8 by expressing "grave concern" over Iraq's lack of cooperation with UNSCOM and stressed the "necessity of full implementation," although it did not use the stronger language "material breach." On October 15, the UN Security Council passed Resolution 949, expressing its determination "to prevent Iraq from resorting to threats and intimidation," although it did not refer to "material breach" or warn of "serious consequences."

THE BIOLOGICAL WEAPONS CRISIS OF 1995

It was biological weapons, however, which led to a major new crisis for UNSCOM. In early 1995, UNSCOM discovered evidence that Iraq had failed to report a far more serious biological weapons program than UNSCOM had previously believed existed. As a result, the UNSCOM called together a conference of international experts on April 6–7, 1995, to examine the new evidence. The result was that the experts concluded that Iraq had failed to declare a full-scale biological weapons program, and UNSCOM reported to the Security Council that Iraq had failed to account for 17–22 tons of biological material. On May 1–3, UNSCOM held a similar conference comprised of of chemical weapons experts which concluded that Iraq had also failed to fully disclose its chemical weapons programs.

New Iraqi Lies

Iraq initially attempted to ignore these developments and to use political threats to bring an end to sanctions. Deputy Prime Minister Tariq Aziz demanded that UNSCOM certify that Iraq had complied with the terms of UN resolutions 687 and 715. UNSCOM rejected this demand and stated in its June, 1995 report that Iraq had not yet "met all these terms" and was still not accounting for its biological weapons material. However, it also declared that "significant progress had been achieved."[8] Iraq claimed to be pleased with its favorable portrayal in the report, and it indicated that it would continue to cooperate with UNSCOM.

Iraq also attempted to persuade UNSCOM that it was fully complying with the terms of cease-fire by admitting that it had a limited biological weapons effort. On July 1, 1995, Iraq officially acknowledged for the first time that it had an offensive biological weapons program. Its declaration admitted to manufacturing a variety of biological agents, but Iraq continued to deny that any weaponization of these agents had occurred.

These disclosures relating to biological weapons did not have the result Iraq had hoped for. They led to further questions from UNSCOM, and to no requests for inspections. As a result, Saddam Hussein declared on July 17, 1995, that Iraqi cooperation with UNSCOM would cease, pending further progress toward certification. Iraqi Foreign Minister Al-Sahaf subsequently proclaimed August 31 as the deadline for compliance by UNSCOM.[9]

As a result, Rolf Ekeus traveled on August 4 to Baghdad, where the Iraqi government presented him with what was called a "full, final, and complete disclosure" of its biological weapons program, which again stated that Iraq had not weaponized its biological agents. During Ekeus's visit, Deputy Prime Minister Aziz reiterated Iraq's warning that a lack of progress on the lifting of economic sanctions through certification would result in cessation of Iraqi cooperation with the UNSCOM, and Aziz urged Ekeus to inform the Security Council of Iraq's intentions.

The Defection of Lieutenant General Husayn Kamel Majid

Ekeus did so on August 7, 1995, but dramatic new events began to unfold in Iraq. That same day, Lieutenant General Husayn Kamel Majid, who had led part of Iraq's weapons of mass destruction program, defected to Jordan.[10] As a result, UNSCOM soon made new major discoveries about the size and nature of Iraq's programs.

The UN discovered new details of Iraq's missile programs that Iraq had concealed from UNSCOM:

- testing activity in 1990 with Scud missile warheads filled with Sarin nerve agent
- research and testing of more energetic liquid propellants
- significant design studies for advanced rocket engines for use with extended range missiles
- research of a missile design intended to deliver a nuclear weapon

UNSCOM discovered that Iraq had hidden four sophisticated chemical warfare capabilities, including a major VX gas program:

- program to develop the nerve agent VX begun in May, 1985 and continued without interruption until December, 1990
- production of large amounts of precursors sufficient to produce 400 tons of VX per year
- development of a binary Sarin-filled artillery round, as well as rockets and aerial bombs in quantities well beyond prototype level
- testing of an Al Hussein variant of the Scud missile with a chemical warhead and a range of 600–650 km.

The UN also discovered that Iraq's biological weapons program had gone far beyond research. The major initial disclosures included

- the existence of major production facilities at Al Hakam, the Daura Foot and Mouth Disease Institute, Taji, and Salman Pak;
- production of 19,000 liters of Botulinum toxin, 8,500 liters of Anthrax, and 2,400 liters of Aflatoxin;
- testing and field trials of Anthrax and Botulinum toxin using aerial bombs;
- testing on animals in March, 1988;
- live firings of 122 mm rockets with biological agents in May, 1990;
- large weaponization of biological agents beginning in December, 1990;
- production of 166 aerial bombs filled with a biological warfare agent;
- production of at least 25 Scud missile warheads filled with biological warfare agent;
- efforts in December, 1990 to modify spray tanks to deliver 2,000 liters of Anthrax. These were planned for use on aircraft or remotely piloted aircraft but were not successful; and
- deployment of biological weapons to operational delivery sites in December, 1990.

Iraq Reacts to Majid's Defection

Baghdad clearly feared that Hussein Kamel Majid's defection would lead to still further disclosures that Iraq was still systematically lying to UNSCOM, and moved quickly to engage in damage control. In an effort to preempt new disclosures and undermine Kamel's credibility, the Iraqi government portrayed him as a rogue officer who had concealed information regarding Iraq's weapons of mass destruction from both UNSCOM and Iraqi officials. They then invited Ekeus to Baghdad to discuss the new information, while simultaneously dropping their August 31 deadline for certification.[11] More substantively, Iraq went on to admit that everything it had told the UN regarding its biological weapons programs during the previous half decade was a lie.

Rolf Ekeus arrived in Iraq on August 17 and met with an Iraqi delegation, which included the Deputy Prime Minister and Foreign Minister. They revealed that Iraq's efforts in regard to acquiring weapons of mass destruction had been seriously understated, and they admitted for the first time that Iraq had produced biological weapons, developed a crash program to manufacture nuclear weapons after its invasion of Kuwait, and made greater progress in producing VX gas and the domestic production of ballistic missiles than it had previously admitted. Iraq then rescinded its deadline of August 31 and pledged to cooperate with the UNSCOM. However, the Iraqis failed to produce any documents to allow UNSCOM to verify Iraq's new disclosures.

When this led to several complaints by Ekeus, the Iraqis reported that they had suddenly "discovered" an immense stock of documents at the farm of General Kamel. These documents—which showed no signs of ever having been stored in the farm—were subsequently turned over to UNSCOM on August 20. A cursory examination revealed that most of the half-million pages were concerned with Iraq's nuclear program, but that a considerable number also discussed chemical, biological, and ballistic missile programs.[12]

In September, 1995, Iraqi officials revealed that other records whose existence they had repeatedly denied, did indeed exist. According to UNSCOM, this acknowledgment and the production of the documents was "... one of the most significant breakthroughs in the four years of its operations in Iraq."[13] Nevertheless, the new information revealed that Iraq's biological and ballistic missile programs were "larger or more advanced in every dimension than previously declared." Further, in regards to chemical weapons, the UNSCOM report revealed that "Iraq acknowledged a much larger and more advanced program than hitherto admitted for the production and storage of the chemical warfare agent VX."[14]

Iraq's Revelations Create New Questions

UNSCOM's October 11, 1995, report to the UN Security Council summarized the situation as follows:

The revelations cast into doubt the veracity of Iraq's previous declaration in the missile area, including the material balance for proscribed weapons and items. . . . In the chemical weapons area . . . (whether) Iraq still keeps precursors in storage . . . has not been fully clarified. . . . The Commission must adjust the direction of some of its monitoring activities, especially to prevent Iraq from using its chemical compounds, equipment, and activities for secret acquisition of chemical weapons. Further destruction of some Iraqi chemical assets has to be contemplated.

. . . a hitherto secret offensive biological weapons program in Iraq, comprising large-scale production of biological warfare agents, the filling and deployment of missile warheads and aerial bombs with these agents, as well as biological weapons research and development activities of considerable width and depth. . . . As late as August of this year, Iraq presented to the Commission a formal, but essentially false, declaration on its biological weapons activities. . . . Much remains to be verified with regard to these weapons, in particular the destruction of munitions and bulk agents. . . . The Commission also detected undeclared efforts by Iraq to establish a covert procurement network for activities under monitoring. . . . Questions can still be raised about the intentions of Iraq as regards possible remnants of its proscribed programs.[15]

THE STRUGGLE CONTINUES IN 1996 AND 1997

It became clear during 1996 that the new disclosures relating to Iraq's missile, biological, and nuclear weapons program had scarcely put an end to Iraq's efforts to proliferate, the "war of sanctions," or Saddam Hussein's struggles with UNSCOM. During 1996 and 1997, Iraq continued to threaten to shoot down UNSCOM helicopters and to use its own aircraft to threaten UNSCOM flights or force them off their desired flight path.

Iraq's National Monitoring Directorate continued to withhold data sent to

UNSCOM by Iraqi facilities, to interrupt UNSCOM interviews, or to ask Iraqis to provide false information. Senior Iraqi military officers and Iraqi intelligence officials continued to interfere with UNSCOM's efforts and/or shelter data and forbidden equipment. UNSCOM also began to encounter growing problems because of the need to inspect sensitive facilities like those of the Special Republican Guard, the Mukhabarat, the General Security Service, and Military Intelligence.[16]

Iraqi Missile Programs

Iraq's missile programs presented growing problems in spite of the improved inspection system that UNSCOM put into place in April, 1994. On November 10, 1995, Jordan intercepted a shipment of Russian-made missile guidance systems and specialized precision machine tools to Iraq. In December, 1995, Jordan also revealed that Iraq had attempted to import 100 sets of advanced missile guidance equipment, including accelerometers and gyroscopes from Russia.[17] This made it clear that Iraq had set up a clandestine import program following the Gulf War to obtain missile guidance systems and furnaces to make missile components for Scud-type missiles. UNSCOM also found that Iraq had attempted to smuggle in Scud missile assemblies from Yemen.

During most of 1996, Iraq refused to allow UNSCOM to inspect several major facilities and to physically examine its remaining records and missiles so that UNSCOM could determine how many missiles Iraq might still be concealing. During June 11–15, 1996, Iraq denied UNSCOM access to several military sites believed to hold materials for the production of weapons of mass destruction. On June 12, the Security Council adopted Resolution 1060, emphasizing the "unacceptability" of Iraq's conduct and calling for "full compliance."

As the chronology in Table 10.1 has shown, these events led to new talks between Rolf Ekeus and Tareq Aziz in June. On June 22, 1996, they reached an agreement that went far beyond the missile issue. Iraq undertook to provide UNSCOM with unrestricted rights of access, while UNSCOM undertook to respect the sovereignty and territorial integrity of Iraq—guarantees already made in the cease-fire. Iraq agreed to a joint program of action, to clarify its concealment policy and to hand over all relevant documents. Iraq's only right to restrict a "sensitive" site was a building where Saddam Hussein was actually present and Iraq agreed to immediately dispatch a high-ranking official to resolve the issue, and that UNSCOM could control all access to and from the site and provide helicopter surveillance. Once the Iraqi official had arrived, it was agreed that a UNSCOM team leader and four other personnel could enter the site with unlimited access, that the team could seal doors or whole buildings, and that it could call in the entire team if it found anything suspicious.

Nevertheless, the war of sanctions continued. UNSCOM inspectors saw the movement of "Scud-like" objects in the vicinity of a site designated for inspection by UNSCOM 155 in July, 1996. They also found evidence that Iraq had covertly been working on space programs using proscribed missiles, and concealing the full scale of the activities of its major programs dealing with missile engines, guidance, and control systems.[18]

On August 23, 1996, Rolf Ekeus went to Baghdad to protest Iraq's latest failure to cooperate with UNSCOM and to comply with the UN resolutions. When this visit had little result, the president of the UN Security Council issued a statement on August 23 stating that Iraq's actions were a ''gross violation'' and called for Iraqi cooperation with UNSCOM, although the statement was the first that failed to describe exactly how Iraq had neglected to comply.

In mid-December, Ekeus reported to the Security Council that Iraq had prevented him from removing 130 Scud engines from Iraq so that international experts could determine whether these were the original engines, or Iraq had destroyed low-quality Iraq-made engines and kept the higher-quality Soviet-made designs. The president of the Security Council responded on December 30, 1996, by again calling for Iraqi cooperation.

In February, 1997, Iraq finally agreed to allow UNSCOM to dig up the missiles that Iraq claimed to have destroyed in 1991, and to send the remains to laboratories in France and the United States. This was necessary because of indications that Iraq might have removed key parts from the missiles and stockpiled them for later use. Iraq also allowed UNSCOM to resume excavations in the ''destruction sites'' in January and February, 1997. The UNSCOM team found additional missile equipment that Iraq had not reported, including four complete engines that Iraq had not previously presented to the Commission. That led UNSCOM to conclude in April, 1997 that Iraq continued to deliberately try to mislead the Commission, and that ''Iraq had not presented sufficient evidence of the destruction of all proscribed missiles.''

More Problems with Iraqi Biological Weapons

Iraq destroyed some of the biological warfare facilities whose existence became public in 1995. The Iraqis had relocated virtually all of their biological agent production equipment to Al Hakam and other facilities before the Coalition air attacks began in 1991, and it had buried all biological agent-filled munitions and agent stockpiles in areas likely to escape bombing. In June, 1996, all bio-production equipment at the Al Hakam facility and some equipment at the Daura facility were destroyed, and the Al Hakam facility was razed.

Iraq claimed that the rest of its biological agents and munitions were unilaterally destroyed after the Gulf War. However, its record of misrepresentation and the lack of documentation to support these claims left the status of Iraqi biological warfare stockpile in doubt. Iraq also retained a number of medical, veterinary, and university facilities where biotechnical research and development could be carried out. Some of these facilities seemed to be staffed by former members of Iraq's biological warfare program, and much of their laboratory equipment was dual use and could be used for biological agent development.

Iraq did allow the UN to inspect some of the sites where it claimed that weapons had been unilaterally destroyed, and UNSCOM found some biological bombs "virtually intact." Nevertheless, Iraq would not allow UN teams to collect soil samples from the locations where Iraq had claimed it had destroyed its biological weapons. Key Iraqi personnel were not made available, and Iraq did not attempt to resolve many of the inconsistencies in its declarations.[19]

By March, 1997, the issue had become serious enough for UNSCOM to call together an international panel of experts to examine Iraq's claims. This panel concluded that:

Iraq had failed to report all imports of equipment and materials, in particular growth material. It had underreported the production of bulk biological warfare agents. The stated production of Aflatoxin could not have happened as declared. The declarations on destruction were not supported by sufficient evidence, and it failed to provide a full accounting of procurement activities for the biological weapons program.[20]

Similarly, UNSCOM reported to the Security Council on April 11 that

what is not accounted for cannot be neglected. . . . Even a limited inventory of long-range missiles would be a source of deep concern if those missiles were filled with the most deadly of chemical nerve agents, VX. . . . If one single missile were filled with the biological agent Anthrax, many millions of lethal doses could be spread in an attack on any city in the region.[21]

Nevertheless, Iraq continued to ask UNSCOM to accept its verbal assurances that it destroyed warheads and weapons that include some 500,000 liters of botulism agent and 50,000 liters of Anthrax. Iraq's Deputy Prime Minister Tareq Aziz reiterated this position on April 23, 1997, in spite of the fact that UNSCOM had declared it could not determine the status of Iraq's biological weapons programs, missile warheads, or bombs.[22]

New Development in Chemical Weapons

UNSCOM reported in April, 1997 that it had found "significant amounts of empty dual-use munitions which Iraq had evaluated for use in its chemical weapons arsenal, but had not declared to the Commission" during a visit in December, 1996. It noted that it was still unable to verify the destruction of chemical warfare equipment and special warheads for biological and chemical weapons that Iraq claimed it had destroyed after April, 1991.

UNSCOM expressed particular concern about Iraq's declarations relating to the production of VX gas, and it found that Iraq had continued to lie about the facilities involved in its chemical weapons program. It found that Iraq's declarations relating to its secret program for biological and chemical weapons were not complete or credible, that Iraq had not declared its entire inventory of chemical bombs, and that "accounting for chemical munitions remains unsolved." It found that Iraq continued to hide key policy documents, contract data, and manuals.[23]

The UN Response

The UN responded to these problems by setting up an import-export monitoring system to deny Iraq the equipment it needs to rebuild its program to deploy weapons of mass destruction. The UN Security Council approved this system in Security Council Resolution 1051 on March 27, 1996. It did so by acting on the basis that it was implementing Security Council Resolution 715, which was passed as part of the cease-fire in 1991. The new regime required exporters to Iraq to notify their governments, the UN, and the IAEA of exports of dual-use items, required Iraq to declare its intentions in using such items, and empowered UN inspectors to inspect all shipments before they arrive in Iraq.

No one, however, had any illusions about the effectiveness of the UNSCOM inspection system. Rolf Ekeus made its limitations clear in his report to the United Nations in April, 1997.

> It is clear that prohibited components . . . still exist. (Iraq) retains a weapons option. The issue is not so much what Baghdad now possesses but what it could produce quickly were the decision made to do so.[24]

Further, Iraq continued to deny the need for any such action by the UN while it impeded UNSCOM's efforts. Tareq Aziz stated in a letter to the president of the Security Council on April 23 that "there are no banned weapons or their components or means to produce them, and there are no banned activities in Iraq."[25] Iraq then demonstrated its commitment to proliferation by harassing UNSCOM inspectors. On four different occasions in early June, Iraqis interfered with the pilots of UNSCOM aircraft. Iraqis attempted to seize the controls of UN helicopters, deliberately flew too close to UNSCOM helicopters, and threatened to shut off the helicopter's fuel pumps in another incident. In addition, Ambassador Ekeus reported that Iraq blocked UN inspectors at three locations, making them wait for five to seven hours while the Iraqi commander cleaned out the facility. Iraq explained these actions publicly by charging that UNSCOM inspectors were committing "flagrant aggression" by attempting to enter Chaldean churches and a "convent for nuns."[26]

Ironically, the Iraqis who were charged with aiding UNSCOM became a serious problem. Iraq's National Monitoring Directorate (NMD) is supposed to be the group that assists the UN. In practice, it is little more than an adjunct to Iraqi intelligence, and UNSCOM reported on April 11 that it "has often discovered that weapons and other facilities have provided accurate information to the NMD but this information has been manipulated so that the monitoring declarations presented to the Commission are misleading and inaccurate." That same UNSCOM report noted that the Iraqi government had implemented a "new policy whereby instructions have been issued to all sites and facilities that access be refused unless representatives of the NMD are present."[27]

On June 21, these new Iraqi actions led the Security Council to pass Resolution 1111, again calling for "full compliance," "stressing the unacceptability" of Iraqi efforts to interfere with the UN inspectors, condemning Iraq's "repeated refusals," and demanding "immediate, unconditional, and unrestricted access." More significantly, the Security Council decided not to conduct any of the reviews called for in paragraphs 21 and 28 of Resolution 687 to consider easing sanctions until UNSCOM's next consolidated progress report on October 11, 1997.[28] The Iraqi Revolutionary Command Council reacted by issuing a press statement that the UN resolution "disregarded all facts and cannot be accepted by fair-minded people throughout the world."[29]

The end result was that Iraq agreed to provide Richard Butler, who replaced Rolf Ekeus as head of UNSCOM on August 1, with yet another full and frank disclosure on its biological weapons program. UNSCOM received the new 800-page document in early September, 1997, and Ambassador Butler visited Baghdad during September 5–9, 1997. He was able to settle several issues relating to Iraq's missile program during this visit, and Iraq undertook to deliver its full, final, and complete disclosure on biological weapons to the UN on September 11.

Iraq's Growing Resistance to UN Inspections

On September 13, however, Iraqis severely manhandled a UNSCOM helicopter crew. Similar problems occurred on September 15. On September 17, UNSCOM inspectors were blocked in visits to a site at the Tikrit military barracks in central Baghdad, and the Sarabdi Republican Guards base, and they were forced to wait while they could do nothing but videotape vehicles carrying away boxes of documents, and ash cans of burned documents being dumped into the river. Iraqis manhandled a UNSCOM photographer attempting to photograph the Tikrit site from a helicopter and threatened the pilot. The UNSCOM team had to wait outside of the Sarabdi site for three hours and watch documents being moved away from the site.[30]

New incidents and detentions occurred on September 27 and 29, and on October 1, 1997. Iraq increasingly responded with claims that "sensitive-sensitive" and "Presidential/residential" sites were out of bounds to UN inspectors. On September 27, UNSCOM inspectors were barred from entering a facility near Baghdad. On September 29, Iraq detained a UNSCOM helicopter at the Rasheed Air Base after UNSCOM inspectors took pictures of movements around a facility near Takrit. Iraqi officials who demanded that UNSCOM inspectors give them the film only relented after a telephone conversation between Tareq Aziz and Ambassador Butler.[31]

On October 1, Iraq barred UNSCOM inspectors from a facility near Baghdad, where it had previously found kits for biological warfare. Further, on September 29, 1997, and on October 6, 1997, "gunmen" attacked UN convoys in northern Iraq. On October 5, four "gunmen" attacked a UN headquarters in Baghdad. The timing of these attacks came too close to the crisis Iraq was provoking with UNSCOM to seem entirely coincidental.[32]

It was also apparent that Iraq had developed a massive intelligence effort designed to defeat the UNSCOM inspection effort. UNSCOM has not commented publicly on this effort in any detail, but reports from US and Iraqi opposition sources indicate that Saddam's intelligence service had concealed microphones in the rooms and offices used by UNSCOM personnel at the Kanat a-Jeish military camp in Baghdad, which serves as UNSCOM's headquarters as well as its living quarters. Bugging equipment was also installed in the inspectors' private and professional gear. The data picked up at UNSCOM headquarters was transmitted to a nearby camp at Al Rashid.[33]

The unit of Iraq's intelligence services that regularly spied on UNSCOM was identified by a member of the Iraqi opposition as "Office 28." It was reported to be one of 32 offices, and to be headed by Col. Abdel Khalifa al Duleimi. It was said to employ 120 persons, most of whom were disguised as drivers or other ordinary-looking people. These Iraqi personnel accompanied UNSCOM staffers from the moment they left their bases until they returned, and could report on virtually every move UNSCOM made.[34]

This same Iraqi source reported that

Each agent is equipped with a small transmitter which enables him or her to report exactly where UNSCOM is going. The people at the prospective inspection site are thus able to get ready for the arms inspectors and hide everything that has to be hidden from them.

He stated that Iraq used its major signals intelligence unit, which is known as the "el Hadi project," or Operation 858. This unit had a headquarters north of Baghdad and six listening posts with a total of up to 1,000 personnel. Operation 858 attempted to monitor all incoming and outgoing UNSCOM communications, locally and internationally. El Hadi was also said to be equipped to listen in on telephone conversations conducted throughout Iraq, although UNSCOM inspectors used scramblers and other secure communications devices.[35]

In addition, Iraq was said to have a facility, situated in Al Rashidiya, 30 kilometers north of Baghdad, which could intercept the satellite telephones used by UNSCOM. Iraq was also said to employ Mi-8 helicopters equipped with special listening devices whenever UNSCOM personnel flew from place to place in Iraq. The airborne conversations were then relayed to al-Rashid camp and to Iraqi intelligence sources operating in the Presidential Palace.[36]

Another technique Saddam used to counter UNSCOM's inspections was to station his Special Republican Guards outside all of his palaces and military facilities. These units normally provide security to the Iraqi military establishment. But in UNSCOM's case, their personnel delayed the entry of arms inspectors until orders were received from within that the site was clear. Simultaneously, the Special Republican Guards notified Iraqi intelligence of UNSCOM's destination, which allowed the Iraqis who were working on unconventional weapons projects to leave, while those who stayed behind concealed or removed all incriminating documents or materials.

THE SECURITY COUNCIL SPLITS: THE SANCTIONS CRISIS OF FALL, 1997

Saddam Hussein had provoked some form of crisis during every fall following the Gulf War, and the fall of 1997 was no exception. At the same time, Iraq created a new kind of confrontation with UNSCOM. Rather than simply provoke a showdown with the United States, Iraq launched an increasingly more sophisticated effort to divide the Security Council and the Arab world, and to break out of the constraints imposed by inspections, import controls, and export. The Iraqi regime proved able to exploit the growing "sanctions fatigue" that many nations felt after six years of confrontations, the growing Arab resentment of the breakdown in the Arab-Israeli peace process, concern with the hardships the sanctions were imposing on the Iraqi people, and the desire of many nations to resume trade and oil deals with Iraq.

Iraq realized during 1997 that these pressures had begun to divide the UN Security Council, and that focusing on the US role in UNSCOM gave it a convenient "foreign threat" and a way to obtain Arab and Third World support on the grounds that the United States and UNSCOM were violating Iraqi sovereignty. Saddam Hussein also seems to have realized that each confrontation he survived became a symbol of his power and a means of further increasing "sanctions fatigue," and that he faced diminishing military risks. In fact, the "pinprick" nature of the US-led attacks that have been described in Table 10.1 seems to have convinced the Iraqi leadership that any damage was more than offset by the regime's image of "strength" in surviving repeated crises with the United States while it made the Iraqi people seem a martyr to US oppression.

The UNSCOM Report of October 6, 1997

The original cause of the crisis was Ambassador Butler's report to the Security Council of October 6, 1997. This report was as critical of Iraq as any report that UNSCOM had made to date. It stated that:[37]

- Analysis had shown that Iraq had destroyed 83 of the 85 missiles it had claimed were destroyed. At the same time, it stated that Iraq had not given an adequate account of its proscribed missile assets, including launchers, warheads, and propellants. It also stated that Tareq Aziz, Iraq's Deputy Prime Minister, "gave an explicit order in the presence of the Executive Chairman, to the Iraqi experts not to discuss such issues with the Chairman."[38]

- Iraq had continued to lie regarding the way in which it has destroyed its pre-war inventory of missile launchers, and major uncertainties remained over its holdings of biological and chemical missile warheads. Iraq initially claimed that it had 45 missile warheads filled with chemical weapons in 1992. It then stated that it had 20 chemical and 25 biological warheads in 1995. UNSCOM established that it had a minimum of 75 operational warheads and that 5 were used for trials. It had evidence of the existence of additional warheads. It can only verify that 16 warheads were filled with Sarin and 34 with chemical warfare binary components, and that 30 were destroyed under its supervision—16 with Sarin and 14 with binary components. Iraq again failed to provide documentation on this issue in September, 1997.[39]

- Iraq had continued to conceal documents describing its missile propellants, and the material evidence relating to its claims to have destroyed its indigenous missile production capabilities indicated it might have destroyed less than a tenth of what it claimed.

- "The Commission identified some other areas of concern related to Iraq's chemical weapons program. The most important among them are the accounting for special missile warheads intended for filling with chemical or biological warfare agent, the material balance of some 550 155-mm mustard gas shells, the extent of VX programs, and the rationale for the acquisition of various types of chemical weapons."[40]

- UNSCOM stated that it had been able to destroy 120 pieces of additional equipment for the production of chemical weapons that Iraq had only disclosed in August, 1997. Major uncertainties still existed regarding some 4,000 tons of declared precursors for chemical weapons, the production of several hundred tons of additional chemical warfare agents, the consumption of chemical precursors, and Iraq's claims to have unilaterally destroyed some 130 tons of chemical warfare agents. Major uncertainties existed regarding 107,500 empty casings for chemical weapons, whether several thousand additional chemical weapons were filled with agents, the unilateral destruction of 15,620 weapons, and the fate of 16,038 additional weapons Iraq claimed it had discarded. 'The margin of error' in the accounting presented by Iraq was in the neighborhood of 200 munitions."[41]

- The uncertainties affecting the destruction of VX gas affected some 750 tons of imported precursor chemicals, and 55 tons of domestically produced precursors. Iraq has made unverifiable claims that 460 tons were destroyed by Coalition air attacks, and that it unilaterally destroyed 212 tons. UNSCOM has only been able to verify the destruction of 155 tons out of this latter total, and to destroy a further 36 tons on its own. Iraq systematically lied about the existence of its production facilities for VX gas until 1995, and it made "significant efforts" to conceal its production capabilities after that date.[42]

- "Iraq has not provided physical evidence (relating to) binary artillery munitions and aerial bombs, chemical warheads for short range missiles, cluster aerial bombs, and spray tanks." Iraq has claimed that these were only prototype programs, but there is no current way to know how many were deployed as weapons.[43]

- "... investigations, along with documents and other evidence available to the Commission, confirmed the assessment that the June, 1996 declaration was deeply deficient.

... The new FFCD, received on 11 September 1997, contains fewer errata and is more coherent. However, with regard to the important issues ... the report contains no significant changes from the June, 1996 FFCD."[44]

- Iraq has never provided a clear picture of the role of its military in its biological warfare program, and it has claimed it only played a token role.

UNSCOM reported that Iraq had never accounted for its disposal of growth media.

Media unaccounted for is sufficient, in quantity, for the production of over three times more of the biological agent—Anthrax—stated by Iraq to have been produced. ... Bulk warfare agent production appears to be vastly understated by Iraq. ... Experts' calculations of possible agent production quantities, either by equipment capacity or growth media amounts, far exceed Iraq's stated results.[45]

There is no way to confirm whether Iraq destroyed 157 bombs of the R400 type, some of which were filled with Botulin or Anthrax spores.[46]

- Iraq's accounting for its Aflatoxin production is not credible. Biological warfare field trials are underreported and inadequately described.
- The account of Iraq's unilateral destruction of bulk biological agents is "incompatible with the facts. ... The Commission is unable to verify that the unilateral destruction of the BW-filled Al Hussein warheads has taken place."[47]
- "The September, 1997 FFCD fails to give a remotely credible account of Iraq's biological program. This opinion has been endorsed by an international panel of experts."[48]

The Security Council Divides

Ambassador Butler's report triggered efforts by the United States and Britain to apply a new kind of sanction against Iraq. The United States and Britain called for sanctions that would only affect Iraq's officials and intelligence officers by denying them the right to travel overseas.[49] These actions led Iraq to threaten to withdraw all cooperation with UNSCOM on October 16, 1997.[50]

More was involved, however, than UNSCOM's report. Iraq had become increasingly concerned that the United States was now targeting Saddam Hussein's regime and would veto any relief from sanctions as long as Saddam was in power. It was conscious that it had steadily growing support from within the Arab world because of the hardship sanctions imposed on Iraq's people. It was aware that many nations did not understand the scale of its violations of the terms of the cease-fire or the threat that its possession of weapons of mass destruction might pose in the future. It had actively courted nations like France and Russia by offering them advantageous oil and trade deals, which were contingent on the end of sanctions, and it had sought support from China, which had a historical policy of opposing any interference in the "sovereignty" of developing nations.

These pressures help explain why Iraq chose to escalate the crisis when it became apparent that the Security Council would not support the original US and British resolution. Key members of the UN Security Council like France and Russia voted against additional sanctions, because they had more interest in regional political influence and their future economic opportunities in Iraq than in the issue of proliferation. Egypt, China, and Kenya joined France and Russia in opposing because they protested additional sanctions on Iraq. The members of the Security Council did agree to condemn Iraq's actions, but effectively refused to support any new initiatives that might force Iraq to cooperate.[51]

A compromise was reached on October 23, 1997, on UN Security Council Resolution 1134. This resolution condemned Iraq's actions and stated the Security Council's "firm intention" that new sanctions would be enforced on foreign travel of Iraqi intelligence officials and Iraqis who interfered with UNSCOM's operations in six months if Iraq failed to comply. The resolution also required UNSCOM to draw up a list of Iraqi officials who had interfered with it, threatened to impose an immediate travel ban on Iraqi officials if Ambassador Butler reported to the Council that his team had been barred from any sites, and continued trade sanctions until April, 1998. At the insistence of France, Russia, China, Egypt, and Kenya, however, the enforcement of any travel ban required a new vote of the Security Council.[52]

Iraq Reacts by Expelling the US Inspectors

These divisions within the Security Council led Iraq's leadership to try divide and conquer tactics. On October 29, Iraq pledged to allow UNSCOM to continue to operate, but declared that the United States was violating Iraqi sovereignty, trying to change Iraq's political system, and spying on Iraq. It demanded that all US members of UNSCOM leave Iraq within one week, and that the United States halt all intelligence overflights by its U-2 reconnaissance aircraft in support of UNSCOM.

Iraq began to implement this ban on October 30. It barred US inspectors from entering the country and gave the US inspectors that were already in Iraq one week to leave the country. It also threatened to shoot down any U-2 flights over Iraq and stated that it was prepared to face the threat of US military action. Deputy Prime Minister Tariq Aziz stated that the US members had to leave until the United States "reconsidered its oppressive policy and its aggressive behavior to the people of Iraq, and its policy of espionage and intervention."[53]

Iraq's demands were clearly aimed at encouraging further splits within the UN Security Council, and called for actions by the UN that would seriously compromise, if not cripple, UNSCOM. UNSCOM had a total of roughly 100 employees in Baghdad, and only 10 of the 40 inspectors in this team were

American. The US personnel in Iraq averaged a total of 10% to 15% of the UNSCOM team, and UNSCOM had staff from 23 different countries. Similarly, UNSCOM's total staff, including its personnel in New York, consisted of 180 people from 35 different countries. Out of this total, 22% came from Chile, 14% from the United States, 11% from Britain, 9% from New Zealand, 6% from Iraq, and 5% from Australia.[54]

US intelligence, however, played a critical role in allowing UNSCOM to make the kind of sudden challenge inspections that prevented Iraq from moving or disguising its efforts. The U-2 flights that the United States carried out for UNSCOM provided the only wide-area surveillance that could track Iraqi activity throughout the country, and provided detailed coverage of all of the physical changes to the hundreds of sites Iraq might use to produce weapons of mass destruction. UNSCOM had permanent observation cameras at only 16 of well over 100 sites of major concern, and these cameras could only cover part of the sites where they were located. The United States was also the only country with the kind of advanced imagery and signals intelligence collection capability to obtain other intelligence information that Iraq might be cheating.

The US intelligence efforts and US inspectors also played an important role in ensuring that UNSCOM's surprise challenge efforts could be successful. Unless intelligence was kept secure among a small cadre in UNSCOM, the Iraqi intelligence effort was able to get enough warning from within UNSCOM to move personnel and more or destroy equipment before UNSCOM could react. Several of the Americans also had unique technical expertise in missile systems and in the production of weapons of mass destruction.

Perhaps even more important, Iraq now had good reason to believe that any weakening of UNSCOM would set a precedent that it could rapidly build upon, and that it might be able to force UNSCOM to abandon its efforts to enter "vital national security facilities" like Presidential and Special Republican Guards facilities. Further, it had reason to believe that exploiting national divisions within UNSCOM would allow it to target the United States as deliberately attempting to keep sanctions in place without proper cause, exploit the growing Arab resentment of the US failure to sustain the Arab-Israeli peace process, and encourage nations like France and Russia to seek an end to sanctions. By early November, Iraq was as concerned with using divide and conquer tactics to bring an eventual end to sanctions as it was with protecting its capability to produce and deploy weapons of mass destruction.[55]

Diplomacy and New Threats of Force

The Security Council reacted on October 30 with a partial show of unity. It strongly condemned Iraq's actions, and France and Russia issued a joint statement on November 1, 1997. The Franco-Russian statement described Iraq's conduct as "unacceptable," called on Iraq to fully comply with the cease-fire in the "strongest terms," and stated that Iraq could not hope for an end to the oil embargo or to rejoin the community of nations unless it did so. This show of unity, however, came too late.

Iraq's leaders had already seen fault lines in the unity of the Security Council, and the effectiveness of the statement was sharply undercut by French and Russian declarations that the UN should not use force to resolve the situation.[56] Iraq reacted by turning back three US inspectors that attempted to enter Iraq on November 2, 1997. On November 3, Iraq warned that it would shoot down any U-2 spy planes flying over its territory in support of UNSCOM if the flights were not halted.

Although US and British diplomats did not rule out the use of force, the UN attempted to resolve the issue diplomatically. On November 4, the Secretary General announced that he was sending a team to Iraq to meet with Iraqi officials and would attempt to solve the situation through negotiation. President Clinton also called for a peaceful solution. These actions led Saddam Hussein to delay the deadline for expelling the US members of UNSCOM, but also led Ambassador Butler to delay a previously scheduled U-2 overflight in support of UNSCOM.[57]

The Secretary General's envoys arrived in Baghdad on November 5, but they did little more than meet with Tareq Aziz and receive a letter for Secretary General from Saddam Hussein. Iraq also continued its efforts to cheat. Ambassador Butler warned on November 5, 1997, that Iraq seemed to be using the interruption in UNSCOM operations to conceal more of its capabilities. He warned that Iraq might be tampering with UNSCOM cameras and monitoring equipment, and that

the Iraqis have moved significant pieces of dual-capable equipment, subject to monitoring by the Commission's remote camera monitoring system, out of view of the cameras ... gyroscope rotor balancing equipment that could be used to balance prohibited gyroscopes ... fermenters to produce seed stocks of biological warfare agent.[58]

Iraq stated that it was merely moving equipment to protect it from US air raids. Nevertheless, the Security Council issued a warning to Iraq against any further tampering with UNSCOM cameras and sensors, a message France deliberately reinforced in a separate message to Iraq. The United States responded with statements that indicated that it would resume U-2 flights the following week, and that they could be protected by flights of up to 50 US combat aircraft equipment with sensors, anti-radiation missiles, and weapons that could attack Iraqi command and control sites.

The United States suspended port calls by the *Nimitz*, and reports surfaced that it had contacted Turkey and Gulf nations about basing additional US aircraft for operations against Iraq. The United States already had about 205 combat aircraft in the Gulf and 50 attack aircraft on the *Nimitz*. The United States had 17 ships in the Gulf, many of which were capable of firing cruise missiles.[59]

On November 6, Iraq responded by stating that it was only moving equipment because of its fear of a US air strike, and that a UN surveillance camera had accidentally been damaged in a missile test. At the same time, it turned back UNSCOM inspectors for the fourth day in a row. Tareq Aziz also accused Ambassador Butler of trying to "mislead the Security Council, and to escalate the situation with the aim of misleading international public opinion." At the same time, Iraqi papers stated that, "We confirm that our opponent is neither the UN nor the Security Council. It is only America."[60]

Further diplomatic exchanges went on until November 10, when Secretary General Kofi Annan met with Tareq Aziz in New York, and failed to convince him to change Iraq's position. Instead, Iraq again threatened to shoot down any U-2 flights, and it stated that it would only end its ban on American inspectors if the UN lifted its trade sanctions and the Security Council sent new representatives from each country to verify its compliance with the UN sanctions.[61]

On November 13, the UN Security Council met and passed a new resolution imposing an international travel ban on Iraqi officials that interfered with UNSCOM's efforts, and which expressed the Security Council's "firm intention" to take unspecified further actions if Iraq did not comply. The Iraqi government responded, however, by stating that it would expel the six remaining US inspectors in Iraq, who were forced to leave by the desert route on November 13. This led Ambassador Butler to remove 68 remaining non-US UNSCOM personnel on November 14, although he left a small cadre to guard UNSCOM's facilities.

These Iraqi actions brought the crisis to the edge of military confrontation. Britain prepared RAF combat aircraft and the carrier *Invincible* for deployment to the Gulf. The United States sent the *George Washington* carrier battle group to join the *Nimitz* carrier battle group in the Gulf, and stepped up its actions to persuade Bahrain, Kuwait, and Saudi Arabia to base additional US aircraft for strikes on Iraq. Britain put a squadron of fighters on alert, and the United States began to prepare two B-1, six B-52, and six F-117 bombers for deployment to Diego Garcia and the Gulf. The United States also deployed an additional 12 F-15s, 18 F-16s, and four tankers, with the entire 347th Expeditionary Wing to Bahrain. These deployments raised the US presence in the Gulf to nearly 250 US planes and 22 warships in the Gulf—including two aircraft carriers, three cruisers, five destroyers, three frigates, two submarines, one amphibious assault ship, one dock-landing ship, one amphibious transport dock, two combat support ships, and two mine counter-measure ships—many of which were capable of firing cruise missiles. The United States also sent four more F-16s and six KC-135 tankers to Turkey, where the United States already had 28 F-15s and F-16s as part of the 40-plane British-Turkish-US force enforcing the northern no fly zone.[62]

Iraq initially responded by accusing UNSCOM of being dominated by US intelligence, and of supporting efforts to topple Saddam Hussein from power. UNSCOM replied by presenting new evidence to the Security Council that showed that a recent U-2 flight had detected a convoy of trucks entering and leaving a site near Baghdad that UNSCOM had indicated it wanted to visit. It reported that it had encountered similar incidents at eight other sites during 1997, and that inspectors had been delayed or denied access to 83% of the facilities that Iraq had declared "sensitive." UNSCOM also warned that Iraq had initially reported making 160 kilograms of VX gas in 1995, but had raised the total to 240 kilograms in 1996, then to 1,250 kilograms, and finally to 3.9 tons. UNSCOM also warned that Iraq had denied making botulism toxins until 1995, when it admitted making 19,000 liters, and had at first admitted making 600 liters of Anthrax and had then had to raise the total to 6,000 liters and then 8,400 liters.[63]

On November 16, Saddam Hussein turned to Russia for help in finding a diplomatic solution, and stated that he hoped a solution could be found that would "lead to the implementation of the Security Council's obligations to Iraq." Tareq Aziz toured the Arab world seeking to build up diplomatic support for Iraq, and the United States hinted that it might increase deliveries under terms of UN Security Council Resolution 986 for Iraqi compliance, although Iraq rejected the offer and the United States sent another U-2 flight over Iraq on November 17.

On November 18, Tariq Aziz met in Moscow with Russian Foreign Minister Yevgeny Primakov, the former head of the Middle East section of the KGB. Primakov then announced that he had found a peaceful solution to the crisis and asked the US, British, Chinese, and French Foreign Ministers to meet with him in Geneva. This meeting took place on November 20, and Iraq appeared to back down and accept the UN terms for the operation of UNSCOM in return for Russian pledges to do everything possible to bring a quick end to inspections and the UN sanctions. After the meeting, Primakov announced that, "We expect that today Iraq will make a decision that absolutely all the inspectors, without any exceptions, will return to Iraq and will begin to work there normally. That is what Russia achieved without a show of force, it was achieved by diplomatic means."[64]

UNSCOM inspection team returned a team of 75 inspectors, including six Americans, to Iraq on November 21. The crisis, however, was scarcely over. The Iraqi press responded by stating that, "Our latest battle with the world oppressors in America has led to a great victory of our pride and glory.... We have proved to everyone that we have a national iron will."[65] Although the Foreign Ministers meeting in Geneva implied that Iraq had not won any new concessions, Russia and Iraq issued a joint statement by President Yeltsin and Saddam Hussein that Russia "will energetically promote the speedy lifting of sanctions against Iraq on the basis of its compliance with the corresponding UN Security Council resolutions and particularly paragraph 22 of Resolution 687 with no additional conditions, and for this and fast steps to increase the work of the Special Commission to be taken."[66]

Russia showed its interest in implementing this agreement on November 24 by unsuccessfully attempting to appoint two new non-US deputies to Butler at the next meeting of UNSCOM. Ambassador Butler's only deputy was an American, Charles Duelfer.[67] France and Russia both cooperated in seeking to obtain a UNSCOM statement that Iraq had made progress in complying with the terms of the cease-fire. They were unsuccessful, but did get agreement that UNSCOM should respect the "legitimate national security, sovereignty, and dignity" of Iraq, and that Ambassador Butler should "initiate early discussions with Iraqi authorities"—which they interpreted to mean discussing access to "sensitive" sites in Iraq.

The Iraqi government issued a statement that,

Upon this Iraq decision, America has made a lot of fuss.... It has resorted as always to reckless threats . . . and hinted it would use its wicked force.... The expulsion of the Americans is a sovereign right as it is the right of every state to expel persona non grata even if they are working in the diplomatic corps. By God, there are not any chemical or biological weapons in Iraq and concerning the nuclear and missile weapons, the non-Iraqis concerned have affirmed that there are no such weapons in Iraq and their files should be closed down.

The joint communiqué (with Russia) "is the beginning towards our central goal, which is a comprehensive end of the embargo on our country."[68]

Several days later, Tariq Aziz stated that,

Actually the crisis is not over because the sanctions on Iraq and the unbalanced position of the Security Council persist.... It has become evident to France and Russia and other Security Council members that dealings with Iraq were arbitrary and unjust.... There will be deliberate delays and insults to Iraq.[69]

UNSCOM resumed its work in Iraq on November 22. The UN inspectors found no evidence that Iraq had attempted to cheat or produce new weapons of mass destruction during their absence. Iraq returned most of the dual-use equipment it had moved during the crisis on November 23, and the United States completed its third U-2 flight over Iraq since the crisis had begun on November 24.

THE SANCTIONS CRISIS OF 1998

During the months that followed, it became all too clear that the crisis was not over, and the situation deteriorated to the point where it seemed that the United States and Britain might launch a major new series of strikes against Iraq. The experiences of October, 1997 and November, 1997 had shown Iraq that it might be able to make fundamental changes in the way it fought the "war of sanctions." The lack of unity within the Security Council, the political divisions within the Gulf and Arab world, and the ability to exploit the hardship of the Iraqi people gave Iraq far more leverage than at any previous point since the cease-fire. The result was a grinding day-by-day battle of attrition in which

Iraq resisted UN efforts, appealed to the outside world, and attacked the US role in both UNSCOM and in every other aspect of sanctions. The United States and Britain responded with threats and demonstrations of force—bringing the situation to the edge of war—but they did so in the face of growing international and Arab resistance. Even Iran began to intervene in partial support of Iraq.

The chronology in Table 10.2 shows that Iraq turned the "war of sanctions" into a struggle to improve its economic position and break out of economic sanctions that it gave as much emphasis as its efforts to preserve its missiles and weapons of mass destruction. In fact, Iraq had laid the ground work for this new campaign long before it had forced a confrontation over inspections in October, 1997. During 1996, it had launched a full-scale propaganda effort to dramatize the hardships imposed by sanctions and blame them on the UN. It publicized visits by a small, fringe group of US doctors that claimed that sanction were causing widespread deaths. It publicized reports by the WHO, FAO, and UNICEF about the hardships suffered by the Iraqi people that were based largely on Iraqi data, and issued claims that 4,000 Iraqi children died every month due to a lack of medicine.[70]

Using Suffering as a Political Weapon

Saddam's regime made every possible effort to exploit this propaganda effort and confuse the sanctions issue with the suffering of the Iraqi people. Table 10.2 shows, for example, that Iraq initially said that it would not renew the food for peace deal and insisted on the lifting of all sanctions. It reversed itself on November 30, but then staged the second funeral in a week for children that it said had died of malnutrition. Hundreds of mourners, wailing and beating their chests, shouted insults against the United States and President Clinton during a funeral for 50 children who Iraqi officials said had died because of UN trade sanctions. The wooden coffins, wrapped in white linen, were mounted on pick-up trucks. Hundreds of people lined Rasheed Street in Baghdad, shouting "God is greatest. America is the enemy of God."[71]

The result of these pressures was that the Security Council voted unanimously on December 4, 1997, to extend the plan that enabled Iraq to sell limited amounts of oil to buy food and medicine for its people suffering under sanctions, although it delayed a decision on whether Iraq could sell more oil until after it received a report from Secretary-General Kofi Annan, due January 30, 1998. The British-drafted resolution allowed Iraq to sell $2 billion worth of oil over six months in order to purchase humanitarian supplies.

The resolution expressed the Security Council's "willingness" to take action on an increase in oil sales, depending on what Annan recommended, but it also reflected all of the previous divisions within the Security Council that had helped trigger a crisis over UNSCOM inspections. France and Russia told the Security Council that the amount should be doubled to $4 billion in oil sales over six months. French Ambassador Alain Dejammet stated that, "Given the scope of

Table 10.2
The Sanctions Crisis of October, 1997 to March, 1998

97–7-1:	Richard Butler (of Australia) replaces Rolf Ekeus as Executive Chairman of UNSCOM.
97–8-4:	Richard Butler, head of the commission investigating Iraqi weapons programs, reports that the Iraqis have declared wide areas off limits and expresses anxiety about the future of the UN program in Iraq. During his visit to Baghdad days earlier, he was lambasted as a US tool by government-controlled media.
97–9-12:	The United States moves F-117A stealth bombers into position to prepare for possible air strikes against Iraq. Baghdad announces it has fired three missiles at Allied planes policing the northern and southern no-fly zones.
97–9-17:	Security Council press statement states that the Council views "in the gravest terms" (1) incidents on September 13 outside of a large military base, including vehicle movements inside of the site while a UNSCOM team was blocked outside, in-flight manhandling of a UNSCOM photographer, and interfering with safety of flight, thus invalidating the inspection; and (2) incidents on September 15 outside of another large Republican Guard base, including vehicle movements while a team was delayed for three hours.
97–9-27, 97–9-29, and 97–10-1:	A UNSCOM team is blocked at three sites termed by Iraq as "presidential." Limited access is gained to sites declared "sensitive" by Iraq, but the team finds clear evidence of recent sanitizing.
97–10-6:	The UNSCOM six-month report to the Security Council notes large gaps in Iraq's declarations for its long-range missile, chemical, and biological weapons programs: (1) In the missile area, specific concern is expressed over "Iraq's actions to retain launchers . . . accounting for special warheads (and) propellants . . . major engine components . . . guidance instruments . . . and proscribed modification, testing, and acquisition activities after the adoption of resolution 687." (2) In the chemical weapons area, large quantities of CW agents, munitions, special warheads, and especially VX nerve agent mass-production capabilities and product denied by Iraq. (3) In the biological weapons area, UNSCOM reports that a panel of experts from 13 member states unanimously found that "the outstanding problems are numerous and grave." (4) As for concealment, "the Commission strongly believes that relevant materials and documents remain in Iraq, and that there have been highly coordinated actions designed to mislead the Commission."
97–10-23:	UNSCR 1134 is adopted (10–0–5, with abstentions by China, Egypt, France, Kenya, Russia). It expresses "grave concern at the report of additional incidents since the adoption of resolution 1115," reaffirms "its determination to ensure full compliance by Iraq with all its obligations under all previous relevant resolutions . . . condemns the repeated refusal of the Iraqi authorities . . . to allow access to sites designated by the spe-

Table 10.2 (continued)

	cial commission ... decides that such refusals to cooperate constitute a flagrant violation of Security Council resolutions ... expresses the firm intention [if Iraq does not comply] to adopt measures which would oblige all states to prevent without delay the entry into or transit through their territories of all Iraqi officials and members of the Iraqi armed forces who are responsible ... [and] decides further, to begin to designate ... individuals whose entry or transit would be prevented ... [as well as] decides not to conduct the day sanctions reviews until after ... 11 April 1998.''
97–10-29:	The government of Iraq informs the president of the Security Council that beginning on October 30, Iraq will not deal with Americans working with the Special Commission, and demands that all UNSCOM Americans leave Iraq within seven days. It demands that the UN set a timetable to lift seven-year-old economic sanctions. The Security Council warns that Iraq faces "serious consequences" for its defiance and the UNSCOM suspends all field operations. A three-week-long crisis ensues, during which the United States assembles force of 30 warships and 250 planes and bombers in the region. In the following days, Iraq refuses to allow UNSCOM inspectors of American nationality to either inspect or arrive in Iraq on UNSCOM aircraft, then delays the expulsion order while a three-member UN delegation sent by the Secretary General visits Baghdad for talks. The Americans are then forced by Iraq, during the night of November 12, to drive overland to Amman, after which UNSCOM and the IAEA immediately draw down to caretaker status.
97–10-30:	Iraq announces that it does not fear the use of force, and officials begin obstructing American involvement in the inspections, turning away two US members of the UNSCOM team. Iraq bars two American inspectors returning from a vacation into the country.
97–10-31:	Rival Kurdish groups in northern Iraq engage in the fiercest fighting since a cease-fire collapsed two weeks earlier. Scores are killed and wounded in the clashes.
97–11-1:	Vice President Taha Yassin Ramadan says that Baghdad will not allow American arms inspectors to take part in weapons inspections resuming on Monday. Russia and France urge Iraq to withdraw its ban, but caution against unilateral anti-Iraqi action.
97–11-2:	UN Secretary-General Kofi Annan announces that he will send a three-man mission to Baghdad to try to resolve the situation. Iraq sends back three American members of a UN team of experts arriving from Bahrain to resume arms inspections. The Arab League says it is against a military solution. US House of Representatives Speaker Newt Gingrich says that Washington should take "whatever steps are necessary" to enforce UN rules against Iraq. Thousands of demonstrators take to the streets of Baghdad, calling for the ouster of the US arms inspectors.

Table 10.2 (continued)

97–11-3:	Iraq issues a less-than-veiled threat that it will shoot down the U-2 spy planes keeping Iraq under surveillance for the UN if the UN does not cancel the flights. Baghdad blocks US members of the UN team from weapons site. The UN halts three inspections. The United States announces that it has moved up the scheduled arrival in the Gulf of the aircraft carrier *Nimitz* to show its concern about enforcing the no fly zones in Iraq.
97–11-4:	Iraq turns back UN weapons inspectors for a second day, saying that it will not grant access to teams that included Americans, Iraq pushes back its deadline to expel American arms inspectors, and the UN, in turn, suspends U-2 spy plane flights while a special UN delegation is in the country. The delay in the expulsion ban and the U-2 flights mean a respite of at least five days, until the special UN delegation returns the following week.
97–11-5:	Annan's three envoys arrive in Baghdad to meet Iraq's Deputy Prime Minister Tariq Aziz. The UN accuses Iraq of obstructing its weapons monitoring system by hiding equipment from surveillance cameras.
97–11-6:	Iraq says that it has removed some weapons equipment from sites to escape possible US military attack. Washington threatens economic sanctions or military action if Iraq does not comply with the UN. Responding to tension over a standoff with Iraq in the Gulf, the United States says it's postponing a scheduled weekend port call for the aircraft carrier *Nimitz* in the United Arab Emirates.
97–11-7:	The head of Annan's delegation, Lakhdar Brahimi, tells reporters that Iraq stood by its ban after their discussions. He says Aziz gave them a letter which they will take back to New York. Aziz says Iraq is ready for "constructive dialogue" with the UN on the dispute, and he wants to go to New York for talks with UNSCOM Chairman Richard Butler. He says Iraq will not expel the American inspectors while talks continue. He condemns what he says is US domination of UNSCOM, and says that Iraq is taking precautions against a US attack.
	US Secretary of State Madeleine Albright says she expects "firm action" to compel Iraqi compliance. Iraq presses its request for UN weapons inspectors to halt U-2 flights and repeat a veiled threat that they could be shot down. Butler says U-2 flights are to resume. UN arms inspectors tell the Security Council that Iraq still refuses to disclose full details of its banned weapons programs and is imposing new restrictions on the inspections. UN envoys hold a press conference and announce that Saddam rejects the UN position on the composition of the UNSCOM inspection team.
97–11-8:	Jan Eliasson, a member of Annan's mission to Baghdad, says that the Iraqi reply insists that US members of the UNSCOM should leave Iraq. President Clinton weighs options towards Iraq in meeting with military and foreign policy advisers.

Table 10.2 (continued)

97–11-9:	Annan characterizes the dispute with Baghdad as being "serious" and worrysome. Saddam declares that his country has to choose between "a life with dignity and honor" or confrontation in its dispute with the UN.
97–11-10:	Annan meets with Aziz, but fails to convince Iraq to rescind its ban on US weapons inspectors. The United States says the Security Council should condemn Iraq, threaten it with "serious consequences," and impose travel sanctions on officials who blocked UN inspections. The UN sends a U-2 spy plane over central Iraq, but there are no incidents, despite Iraqi threats to shoot down such aircraft. Iraqi Foreign Minister Mohammed al-Sahaf issues another veiled threat, saying Baghdad now considered the U-2s alien aircraft and not part of the UN weapons surveillance program. Several hundred Iraqi families head to presidential palaces in Baghdad, vowing to act as human shields in case of a US attack. The UNSCOM provides a list of Iraqi noncompliance with Security Council resolutions.
97–11-11:	Iraqi Foreign Minister Mohammed Saeed al-Sahaf says his government will not call off the ban on American inspectors unless trade sanctions are eased, or the Security Council sends key members to Iraq to verify arms compliance.
97–11-12:	The Security Council unanimously imposes a travel ban on Iraqi officials who interfere with inspections, and condemns Iraq for blocking American UN arms inspectors. The UN Security Council resolution rejects Iraq's proposal to impose conditions on its cooperation with the Special Commission because of the national composition of the inspection teams, and condemns Iraq. UNSCR 1137, "taking note with grave concern of the letter of 29 October 1997, from the deputy prime minister of Iraq, conveying the unacceptable decision of the government of Iraq to seek to impose conditions on its cooperation with the Special Commission . . . condemns the continued violations by Iraq of its obligations. Its denial of entry . . . to sites designated by the Special Commission for inspection to Special Commission inspectors on the grounds of their nationality, its implicit threat to the safety of the reconnaissance aircraft operating on behalf of the Special Commission . . . decides . . . to designate . . . a list of individuals whose entry or transit will be prevented under the provisions of [UNSCR 1134] . . . [and] expresses the firm intention to take further measures as may be required for the implementation of this resolution."
97–11-13:	In a presidential statement of November 13, the Council again condemns the Iraqi decision. Iraq announces that it will expel the American arms monitors immediately, and US weapons inspectors leave Iraq. Iraq ejects six remaining American arms inspectors. UNSCOM Chairman Richard Butler announces that he has decided to withdraw all UNSCOM staff on November 14 and leave a skeleton staff at the Baghdad Center to sustain the UNSCOM facility, pending resolution of the crisis.

Table 10.2 (continued)

97–11-14:	President Clinton orders the USS *George Washington* to the Gulf "as a prudent measure to help assure that we have the forces we need for any contingency." This sends a second US aircraft carrier to the Gulf, and Britain puts a squadron of warplanes on 48-hour alert and dispatches aircraft carrier. UNSCOM head Richard Butler pulls inspection teams out of Iraq, leaves skeleton staff.
97–11-15:	A newspaper owned by the son of Saddam urges Arabs to attack American and British targets in the region to show solidarity with Baghdad.
97–11-16:	The United States says it has received a commitment from Russia to intervene in the crisis and makes a similar appeal to France.
97–11-17:	The United States considers sending more fighter planes to the Gulf region, as well as increasing the amount of oil Iraq can sell to buy food and other humanitarian goods.
97–11-18:	Iraqi Foreign Minister Tariq Aziz meets in Moscow with Foreign Minister Yevgeny Primakov and President Boris Yeltsin. Primakov says Russia has worked out a plan to bring a peaceful end to the crisis.
97–11-19:	Butler and his experts brief the Security Council on Iraq's noncompliance. US Secretary of State Madeleine Albright cuts her trip to India short to attend talks in Geneva on the Iraqi crisis. The UN Security Council has a closed-door meeting on the Iraq situation.
97–11-20:	Iraq announces that UNSCOM may return to resume its ordinary work. P-5 foreign ministers, meeting in Geneva, issue a statement calling for "unconditional and complete fulfillment by Iraq of all relevant resolutions of the UN Security Council," and note that on the following Friday, a meeting of the UN Special Commission will discuss "ways to make UNSCOM's work more effective." An emergency meeting of the commissioners of the UN Special Commission reports "the systematic concealment activities conducted by Iraq." The five permanent members of the UN Security Council underscore the need for action, "aimed at the unconditional and complete fulfillment by Iraq of all of the relevant resolutions of the UN Security Council." Iraq and Russia agree that arms inspectors can return to work. Russia intends to promote lifting of sanctions against Iraq once Baghdad complies with UN resolutions. Iraq says Russia will guarantee measures including "balanced representation" of members in UNSCOM, suspending inspection of presidential sites and flights of US-operated U-2 spy planes. After reviewing a letter from Iraq on resuming weapons inspections, the Security Council gives UNSCOM the go-ahead to return to Baghdad. UN arms inspectors are allowed back into Iraq.
97–11-21:	Emergency meeting of the commissioners of the UN Special Commission. The report of this meeting is given by Executive Chairman Butler

Table 10.2 (continued)

	to the Security Council on November 22, noting among other things "the systematic concealment activities conducted by Iraq." UN arms inspectors, including four Americans, return to Iraq to resume inspections. Upon their return to Iraq, UN arms inspectors find that the Iraqis have dismantled equipment and moved around and destroyed physical evidence and files.
97–11-23:	Iraq announces that it will exclude from inspection sites "palaces and official residences." UN officials have suspected for two years that such sites were being used to conceal illicit items. Some of the excluded areas are several square miles in size.
	The Security Council adopts Resolution 1134, stating its intention to impose travel restrictions on Iraqi officials if Baghdad continues to obstruct weapons inspections.
97–11-26:	The president of the United Arab Emirates, Sheik Zaid bin Sultan al-Nahayan, says a decision on Iraq's return to the Arab fold should be taken by a majority rather than by a consensus, "Let's tell this man that you have erred towards us . . . but we now tell you 'welcome back as a faithful brother.' "
97–11-27:	Iraq's National Assembly recommends that ties with UN inspectors be suspended until a timetable is set to lift Security Council sanctions against Baghdad.
	Kofi Annan announces that he is considering raising the amount of oil Iraq is allowed to sell over the six months for food, medicine, and other goods to $3 billion.
97–11-29:	Iraq drops its all-or-nothing stand on the easing of UN sanctions Saturday, clearing the way for the renewal of limited exemptions that allow it to buy food and medicine. An American U-2 surveillance plane flies another UN mission over Iraq, without interference. Iraq called the flight a violation of its airspace, but it has yet to try to make good on its threat to shoot down the U-2s.
97–11-30:	The UN considers allowing Iraq to sell more oil to buy badly needed food and medicine. The United States says it might consider letting Iraq sell more oil to buy food and medicine, despite the standoff with Iraq.
	Nearly 100 small wooden caskets are paraded through the Iraqi capital Sunday in a government-sponsored funeral procession for children whose deaths Iraq blames on UN sanctions. Iraqi officials said the youngsters, some just babies, died for lack of food or medicine in the past two days. They blamed the deaths on UN sanctions imposed on Iraq after its 1990 invasion of neighboring Kuwait.
	Syria renews its opposition to any military action against Iraq in Baghdad's dispute with UN over weapons inspection.
97–12-1:	Kofi Annan recommends increasing the $2 billion worth of oil Iraq is allowed to sell every six months under a UN "oil-for-food" plan, but stops short of proposing a figure.

Table 10.2 (continued)

	Massive amounts of US military planes and ships remain in the Gulf.
97–12-2:	Saddam Hussein pressures the UN to either lift sanctions against Iraq or change the terms of the oil-for-food program.
97–12-3:	The UN Security Council reiterates its demand "that Iraq fulfill all its obligations as set out in all the relevant resolutions."
	Iraq's deputy prime minister, Tariq Aziz, asks Richard Butler to set timetables for closing arms files when he visits Baghdad the following week, but Butler rejects these proposals.
	The new head of the International Atomic Energy Agency (IAEA), Mohammed El Baradei, says he sees no signs that Iraq had resumed a nuclear weapons program during the temporary absence of Western inspectors. "We can now say that we have managed to remove or destroy or render harmless all nuclear items that came to our knowledge."
	Maj. Gen. Hussam Mohammed Amin, the director of Iraq's National Monitoring Commission says that Iraq has returned all of the monitoring machines removed from suspected weapons-making sites during its standoff with the UN. UN inspectors are told that none of the equipment "was used whatsoever from Oct. 30 to Nov. 22, and that all of the adhesive tape, stamps, monitoring material, and sensors are safe and sound."
97–12-4:	The Security Council unanimously approves a resolution extending its oil-for-food program to help needy Iraqi civilians. The UN Security Council votes to renew and expand the oil-for-food arrangement with Iraq, paving the way for Saddam Hussein to purchase much-needed food and medical supplies for the Iraqi people.
	Britain and the United States warn that they remain prepared to use military force if necessary to force Iraq to allow unrestricted UN searches of the country for chemical and biological arms.
	Iraq releases two Iranians, jailed since 1991.
97–12-5:	Iraq shuts down its oil pipeline to Turkey and says it will not export any more fuel until the UN approves a plan for distributing food bought with oil revenues. Iraqi foreign ministry spokesman expresses deep regret because the Security Council's decision to renew the contract for oil in return for food and medicine does not take into consideration that exports of oil and supply of food, medicine, and other humanitarian needs of the Iraqi people must be simultaneous.
	The UN Committee on Economic, Social, and Cultural Rights urges the Security Council to consider the economic and social rights of a country's poor before imposing sanctions on it. The statement is adopted the same day the Security Council renewed for six months the UN's oil-for-food plan for Iraq as a limited exception to sweeping international economic sanctions imposed since Baghdad's troops invaded Kuwait in August, 1990. The UN Children's Fund published a survey the previous week,

Table 10.2 (continued)

	saying there had been a dramatic deterioration in the nutritional well-being of Iraqi children since sanctions were imposed.
	The United States accuses the Iraqi government of manipulative indifference to suffering in refusing to pump oil until it agrees on a new plan for food distribution with the UN.
	Iraq's foreign minister tells his Iranian counterpart that Baghdad is prepared to resolve disputes hindering better ties between the two former foes.
	Some 20,000 Turkish troops launch an offensive against Turkish Kurds in northern Iraq. Iraq condemns the Turkish raid and calls on its neighbor to withdraw its troops immediately.
97–12-8:	Saddam Hussein, states at a cabinet meeting that the credibility of the United States had been eroded by its repeated showdowns with Baghdad. State television reports that Saddam told his ministers that Washington "is not in the same position as it was two years ago because its credibility has been shaken, while Iraq is more able to break through the veils of deception than two years ago." Saddam reviews the latest plans for construction of a mosque bearing his name and capable of holding 30,000 worshippers.
	Iraqi Deputy President Taha Yassin Ramadan, the highest-ranking Iraqi to visit Iran for years, flies to Tehran for an Islamic summit.
	Iraqi newspapers report that Iraq has formally approved the extension of its oil-for-food deal with the UN for another six months but give no sign that Iraq is backing down on demands for swifter delivery of humanitarian supplies before it resumes oil exports.
97–12-10:	Iraq's oil minister, Lt. Gen. Amer Mohammed Rashid, insists that UN arms inspectors may not enter President Saddam Hussein's palaces, setting the stage for a confrontation two days before a visit by Richard Butler.
97–12-15:	Butler says Iraq's deputy prime minister, Tariq Aziz, told him that Iraq would never allow inspectors to enter presidential sites. Butler says Iraq is prepared to let inspectors into other sensitive sites "in varying degrees." Butler also says his talks with Iraqi officials on Baghdad's chemical and biological weapons programs yielded little new information. "Biology didn't present anything new at all. In fact [Iraq gave] a rather defiant statement that said, 'Nothing, there is nothing . . . chemistry, we are still arguing about the very important nerve gas called VX.''
	The United States condemns Iraq's execution of Jordanian students.
97–12-16 to 97–12-24:	A UNSCOM team inspects various sites declared "sensitive" by Iraq. Limited access is given by Iraq, but with clear evidence of computer materials having been removed during entry delays. Iraq accuses the chief inspector (an American) of being a spy, and blocks a UNSCOM photographer from taking photos at one site.

Table 10.2 (continued)

	A Iraqi newspaper urges rebel Kurds to come to Baghdad for dialogue to resolve their differences with the Baghdad government.
	Butler leaves Iraq.
	The United States welcomes Saudi initiative to enable Libyan and Iraqi pilgrims to meet their Hajj obligations, and announces that it would request appropriate UN approval.
97–12-17:	Iraq rejects a UN offer to work out special arrangements to enable UNSCOM to inspect its numerous presidential sites.
97–12-20:	Tariq Aziz accuses chief UN arms inspector Richard Butler of making "unobjective and inaccurate" statements about banned weapons hidden in Iraq's so-called presidential sites. "Butler is still unobjective and inaccurate, and his statements were aimed at serving an American plot which aims at a fabricated escalation [of a standoff between Iraq and the UN and the United States]."
	Lieutenant-General Amir Muhammad Rasheed, Iraq's oil minister, says his country would resume oil exports as soon as the UN approved plans to distribute food and medicine.
	Iraqi spokesman urges Gulf Arab states to change their attitude toward Baghdad after a Revolutionary Command Council meeting chaired by Saddam Hussein, and praises "statements made by President Sheik Zaid bin Sultan al-Nahayan of the United Arab Emirates and Saudi Crown Prince Abdullah bin Abdul-Aziz. . . . We hope such positive statements will lead to . . . a new Gulf policy among Arabian Gulf states to end the negative state prevailing in the Arab world."
97–12-22:	Following talks in Baghdad, December 12–16, Butler briefs the Council on December 18, and on December 22, a Council presidential statement "stresses that failure by the government of Iraq to provide the Special Commission with immediate, unconditional access to any site or category of sites is unacceptable and a clear violation of the relevant resolutions." The UN Security Council states that Iraq's failure to provide UN weapons inspectors with immediate, unconditional access to any site in Iraq "is unacceptable and a clear violation" of UN resolutions.
	Iraqi Trade Minister Mohammed Mehdi Saleh says that Iraq has successfully concluded talks with the UN over an aid distribution plan under its oil-for-food deal.
97–12-29:	Iraq says that it will ask the UN to allocate some of the revenues of its oil-for-food deal to cover expenses of Iraqis going on pilgrimage to Mecca next March.
	State Department spokesman James Foley criticizes an Iraqi decision to cut food rations for its people on the grounds that food received under its oil deal with the UN has been insufficient. Foley says Iraq ordered the cuts, even though it had acted to defer UN approval of $120 million worth of contracts for food purchases.

Table 10.2 (continued)

	Iraq agrees to supply Jordan with more than 35 million barrels of oil in 1998 at half the world price.
97–12-31:	Iranian President Mohammed Khatami sends a congratulatory message to Iraq's Saddam Hussein to mark the Moslem holy month of Ramadan, the first such gesture in 17 years.
	The US State Department says it has credible reports of mass summary executions of political prisoners in Iraq in recent weeks. "Over the past several weeks we've received a number of, we believe, credible reports that the Iraqi regime may have ordered the summary executions of hundreds if not thousands of political detainees at Abu Graib prison and the Radwaniyah detention camp near Baghdad."
98–1-2:	Iraq condemns a naval exercise Turkey plans to hold with Israel and the United States in the Mediterranean, calling it a provocative act against the Arab world.
98–1-3:	Iraq condemns a rocket attack against UN headquarters in Baghdad, saying it was carried out by "hostile parties."
	Ship loaded with medical supplies donated by the United Arab Emirates arrives in Basra in southern Iraq.
98–1-10:	Pope John Paul II uses his annual state of the world address to condemn the UN economic embargo against Iraq, recalling "our brothers and sisters in Iraq, living under a pitiless embargo."
98–1-11:	A new team of UN weapons inspectors arrives in Baghdad, and an official Iraqi spokesman says its composition is unbalanced in favor of the United States and Britain.
	Mohammed Mehdi Saleh says Iraq will resume oil exports within two days under the third phase of its oil-for-food deal with the UN.
	Dennis Halliday, UN humanitarian coordinator for Iraq, reports that the "economy is a total disaster. Massive unemployment. People on fixed income in dreadful shape and no buying power whatsoever. This is a country that talked up to $20 billion in exports. Now we are down to a minor figure. Halliday says the oil for food program will need to bring much higher revenues to make an impact. "It was seen to be a miracle cure, I think by too many people. Perhaps both sides. But of course $2 billion less the overheads and the compensation is $1.3 billion over six months, very small money for a population of 22 million people. That does not go very far when you realize the huge dependency on imports that this country had. Sadly, it has proven to make a very modest impact here. It has not lifted the level of nutrition probably at all. Roughly 30 percent of adults and children are suffering from malnutrition. We have acute malnutrition that can lead to death. We have chronic malnutrition that leads to stunting of physical and other capabilities which you cannot repair. So it is generational. Twenty-five percent of the kids are not going to school anymore because they are out making money to support the

Table 10.2 (continued)

	family. The whole social structure is crumbling But, it has brought in 2.8 million metric tons of foodstuffs. It is a massive amount of foodstuffs. The last figure I saw is that they would need $15 to $20 billion a year in revenues to begin to get things moving properly.''
98–1-12:	Iraq announces that, following a day of successful inspections, including "sensitive" sites, it will bar further work by a UNSCOM team because of a claimed imbalance of US and UK inspectors on the team. The team is headed by American Scott Ritter, whom Baghdad accuses of spying for the United States.
98–1-13:	Butler reports to the Council that this January 12 team "consisted of 44 persons drawn from 17 nations."
	Babel, the newspaper of President Saddam Hussein's eldest son, Uday, charges that a UN arms inspection team headed by an American is a "hyena which publicly serves the American intelligence.... The arrival of [Scott] Ritter's team with its unbalanced formation has clearly confirmed that the [UN] Special Commission is nothing but an American intelligence apparatus which works to gather security, economic, and scientific information on Iraq."
98–1-14:	Security Council presidential statement "deplores" the Iraqi refusal to let UNSCOM do its work, declaring "that this failure is unacceptable and a clear violation of the relevant resolutions." Butler removes the blocked UNSCOM team from Iraq on January 16.
	Russian Foreign Minister Yevgeny Primakov tells US Secretary of State Madeleine Albright by phone that Moscow strongly opposes any use of force in the latest Iraq–UN standoff.
	Iraq accuses the United States and Britain of prolonging the search for forbidden weapons of mass destruction in Iraq so sanctions would not be lifted.
	Iraq denies allegations Wednesday that it used prisoners as guinea pigs to test biological agents, saying the claim was concocted as a ploy to gain access to sensitive Iraqi sites.
98–1-15:	French foreign ministry says Iraq's decision to block UN arms inspectors from visiting weapons sites was unacceptable. France and Russia offer to take a bigger role in controlling Iraqi weapons, and China says UN inspection teams should be more balanced.
98–1-16:	UN inspection team led by former US Marine Scott Ritter leaves Baghdad after being prevented from carrying out its work for three straight days. Iraq had accused Ritter of being an American spy. In response, UN Security Council issued a statement "deploring" Iraq's failure to comply with the terms of the Gulf War peace agreement by allowing unfettered access to all UN inspectors.
	Russian Defense Minister Igor Sergeyev offers Russian-made spy planes to replace American U-2 reconnaissance aircraft flying UN missions over Iraq after Baghdad repeatedly objects to the flights.

Table 10.2 (continued)

	Britain orders an aircraft carrier with 19 Harrier jets to head for the Gulf, as Defense Secretary George Robertson said he could not rule out the use of force against Iraq.
	Iraq's foreign minister arrives in Iran for talks on normalizing ties between the two countries. Iraqi Foreign Minister Mohammed Saeed al-Sahaf says he wants to resolve all disputes between the two countries peacefully during talks with Iran's Foreign Minister Kamal Kharrazi.
98–1-17:	Saddam threatens to halt UN weapons inspections, warns Washington against military action. Iraq criticizes US Defense Secretary William Cohen for rejecting an offer by Moscow to replace US U-2 surveillance planes hired by the UN arms inspectors to fly over Iraq with comparable Russian aircraft. Saddam calls on Iraqis to volunteer for training to confront continuing threats from the United States.
98–1-18:	Baghdad urges all Iraqis to train against any military threat from the United States.
98–1-20:	Yevgeny Primakov says that the makeup of UN arms inspection teams in Iraq should be better balanced between different countries. China calls for the UN arms inspectors to speed up their work in Iraq and supports a "balanced" composition of inspection teams.
98–1-19 to 98–1-21:	Butler visits Baghdad. Several hundred Iraqis curse the United States at the funeral of 70 children, who Iraq says died due to lack of medicine caused by UN sanctions.
	Iran and Iraq agree to set up committees to discuss ways of resolving outstanding disputes.
98–1-20:	The chief UN weapons inspector admits that he has been unable to persuade Baghdad to open presidential palaces to arms monitors.
98–1-21:	Butler ends two days of crisis talks in Baghdad without reaching agreement on access to suspected weapons sites. The two sides did agree to bring in outside technical experts to assess the situation, but Iraq strengthened its resolve to never allow inspectors into the so-called presidential sites. Washington says the Iraqi proposal to freeze inspection of "presidential sites" is unacceptable.
	Secretary of Defense William S. Cohen announces orders that the aircraft carrier USS *Independence* will relieve the USS *Nimitz* (CVN 68), which departed the Gulf on February 9 and is currently sailing home through the Mediterranean Sea.
	Iraq's foreign minister meets Iranian President Mohammad Khatami to discuss outstanding disputes.
98–1-22:	Russia and China urge the UN Security Council on Thursday to certify that Iraq has halted its nuclear weapons program, despite a UN report indicating that Baghdad may still be withholding information.
	UN officials in Baghdad submit proposals to improve support for sanctions-hit Iraqis and speed up food and medicine under Iraq's oil-for-

Table 10.2 (continued)

	food program. Vice President Taha Yassin Ramadan, who has called for a million men and women to volunteer for armed training, says Iraqis will confront sanctions heroically. "Making excuses for extending the sanctions is one of the series of American aggressions against the Iraqi people.... Iraqis will face the eighth year of sanctions heroically and announce holy jihad [holy war or struggle] to show they will not surrender their principles . . . however great the sacrifice."
98–1-23:	Butler briefs the Council on his January 19–21 Baghdad talks, citing continuing across-the-board lack of Iraqi cooperation in providing either information requested by UNSCOM or access for inspections to seek out the information Iraq refuses to provide. Questioned by a member of the Council, Butler says that, under the current circumstances, UNSCOM cannot fulfill its mandate of disarming Iraq of weapons of mass destruction and preventing Iraqi development of such weapons. UN chief inspector Butler reports to the UN Security Council that Iraq has adopted a dramatically different tone with the weapons inspection teams and is being more secretive than ever before.
	Madeleine Albright warns that a face-off with Iraq is unacceptable, cannot continue. She travels to sound out European and Middle East allies and is followed by Defense Secretary William S. Cohen.
	Butler briefs the UN Security Council on his January 19–21 Baghdad talks, citing Iraqi's lack of cooperation in providing information or access for inspections. Butler said "under the current circumstances, UNSCOM cannot fulfill its mandate of disarming Iraq of weapons of mass destruction and preventing Iraqi development of such weapons." The USS *Independence* gets underway from its forward base homeport of Yokosuka, Japan, for the Arabian Gulf assignment.
98–1-24:	Clinton's advisers discuss Iraq, take no decision. Spokesman Eric Rubin says, "Diplomacy is our preferred course, but we have not ruled out any option."
98–1-25:	Iraq's parliamentary speaker, Saadoun Hammadi, denies that Baghdad violated UN terms for its disarmament in a letter to US legislators, and says the real threat to world order comes from Washington and its "aggressive political aims against Baghdad."
	A report by UNICEF, the UN Children's Fund, compares children's chances of dying from two common diseases, diarrhea and pneumonia, in 1996 with those in 1990, before UN-imposed economic sanctions to punish Iraq for its invasion of Kuwait. Report says that an Iraqi child with diarrhea had a 1-in-600 chance of dying in 1990, rising to 1 in 50 in 1996. For pneumonia, the odds grew from 1 in 60 to 1 in 8 in 1996. "It's the children who are suffering most. The levels of malnutrition that we see are alarming," says Eric Falt, a spokesman for the oil-for-food program.

Table 10.2 (continued)

98–1-26: President Boris Yeltsin sends a special envoy, Deputy Foreign Minister Viktor Posuvalyuk, to Baghdad to seek a diplomatic solution to the crisis. The United States says time is running out for a diplomatic solution. Iraq's UN ambassador says that Iraq could stop all cooperation with UN weapons experts if a military strike is launched over the inspections impasse.

98–1-27: President Clinton intensifies US pressure on Iraq to open its suspect weapons sites, warning Saddam Hussein not to "defy the will of the world." US Republican congressional leaders and united against Baghdad, despite sex scandal dogging Clinton. Pentagon says that Defense Secretary Cohen may visit the Gulf in early February to discuss military action against Iraq.

Russia's Deputy Foreign Minister, Viktor Posuvalyuk, is sent as an envoy to Baghdad and vows every effort to avert military solution.

French President Jacques Chirac proposes to Secretary General Annan that Iraq's maximum oil sale quota under a post-Gulf War oil-for-food pact be doubled.

Iraqi News Agency (INA) says that baby milk rations will be below target for a second month running in February, and accuses the United States of blocking purchases under its UN-approved oil-for-food deal. Infants will get 1.8 kg (four lbs.) of powdered milk next month, just two-thirds of the target ration they had been receiving late last year. "The American administration still insists on its policy of the mass extermination of the Iraqi people, especially the extermination of (Iraq's) children."

Representatives of Russia and China voice their concern that Butler has spoken to the press about matters on which they said he had not yet briefed the Security Council, a Council source said. Council President Alain Dejammet of France alludes to this when he briefs reporters after closed-door consultations. Dejammet says, "several delegations expressed their preoccupation about press articles which were not, in their opinion, consistent with information made available to the Security Council during its informal consultations by the Special Commission."

98–1-28: Deputy Foreign Minister Posuvalyuk meets with Saddam, delivering a letter from Yeltsin.

French Foreign Minister Hubert Vedrine says after meeting with Yevgeny Primakov on Wednesday that using force will not solve the crisis over Iraq's refusal of UN arms inspections. Russia sharply criticizes Butler for making "inappropriate" remarks in which he said Iraq had enough biological material to "blow away Tel Aviv."

Iraqi Foreign Minister Saeed al-Sahaf says he is shocked by a charge by the UN's chief arms inspector Richard Butler that the Baghdad government had enough biological material to "blow away" an Israeli city like Tel Aviv. "We were shocked by the outrageous statements by Mr. Butler. . . . These emphasized that Mr. Butler is not neutral. . . . We are protesting

Table 10.2 (continued)

	against that. I sent a letter to the UN Secretary General. We think this man should be reprimanded for his misbehavior."
98–1-29:	Madeleine Albright leaves for talks with French and Russian foreign ministers and the British foreign secretary. She warned a defiant Saddam that he had "no excuses left." French Foreign Minister Hubert Vedrine says the search for diplomatic solution must be intensified.
	Saddam Hussein declares that Iraqis will fight with "all their capabilities" if the United States launches military strikes against Baghdad. Kofi Annan says he will propose improvements in the oil-for-food deal to the Security Council.
98–1-30:	Madeleine Albright meets with Russian Foreign Minister Primakov, with the two disagreeing on whether force should be used.
	Iraq's Information Minister, Humam Abdel-Khaleq Abdul-Ghafur, says Iraq will not use weapons of mass destruction if struck by the United States because Iraq did not possess any.
98–1-31:	Cohen says any US attack would be "significant," but not intending to destroy Iraq or topple Saddam. Albright meets British Foreign Secretary Cook, says the time is fast approaching for decisions, as diplomacy is unable to resolve the crisis. German Defense Minister Volker Ruehe says that a military strike against Iraq cannot be ruled out if Saddam Hussein refused to allow UN weapons inspectors to continue their work.
98–2-1:	Kuwait tells Albright that it backs the United States if military action is necessary against Iraq. Russian special envoy returns to Baghdad. France and Palestinian President Yasser Arafat agree to send representatives.
	French Interior Minister Jean-Pierre Chevenement reaffirms his opposition to Western military action against Iraq, calling US policy irresponsible.
	Egypt's Foreign Minister, Amr Moussa, calls for diplomacy rather than military action to solve the crisis with Iraq. "We hope there will be de-escalation rather than escalation and that diplomatic and political efforts will be used . . . rather than the military option."
	Saudi officials say, "Saudi Arabia will not allow any strikes against Iraq, under any circumstances, from its soil or bases in Saudi Arabia, due to the sensitivity of the issue in the Arab and Muslim world."
	Iranian President Mohammad Khatami urges the head of the 55-member Organization of the Islamic Conference (OIC) to try to avert a military strike against Iraq.
	Madeleine Albright says the United States supports expanding the Iraqi oil for food program, but would not commit itself to any magnitude. Secretary Albright claims support from Saudi Arabia for a tough stand against Iraq, but request to use Saudi bases is unresolved.

Weapons of Mass Destruction and the War of Sanctions 247

Table 10.2 (continued)

98–2-2:	Kofi Annan proposes that Iraq be allowed to increase its oil sales from $2 billion to $5.2 billion over the next six months to avoid a humanitarian disaster.
	Iraqi parliamentary deputies say that any increase in the oil-for-food deal with the UN will mean nothing to Iraqis unless the United States stopped delaying approval of food and medical purchases.
	Iraq denies Russian report that it agreed to allow inspection of presidential sites.
	Iran's Minister of Defense Rear-Admiral Ali Shamkhani urges, "Islamic states, especially countries of the Persian Gulf region, to resist the new American military moves . . . in order to prevent a new war caused by America."
	International missile and chemical weapons experts meet Iraqi government officials in Baghdad for talks that Iraq hopes can offset UN demands for access to its "presidential sites."
	An official Syrian newspaper reports that US threats of a military strike against Iraq are raising tension in the region and diverting attention from the Arab-Israeli conflict.
	The Secretary-General of the Organization of the Islamic Conference (OIC) calls on the UN to avoid an escalation of the tension and to push for a diplomatic solution to a crisis over weapons inspections in a letter to Secretary General Annan.
	Jordan's Foreign Minister Fayez al-Tarawnah tells deputies that Jordan will never allow its airspace to be used by other states to launch attacks against Iraq.
	Yemen says it opposes any military strike against Iraq and calls for a diplomatic solution.
98–2-3:	British Prime Minister Tony Blair pledges full support to US military action. China reiterates opposition to use of force.
	Russia says that a special envoy progresses in persuading Iraq to comply with UN Russian and French foreign ministers in Baghdad. Kuwait military on high alert.
	Albright says that key Arab leaders agree that Iraq is responsible for "grave consequences" if it continues to defy the UN.
	US Ambassador to UN Bill Richardson says that Washington fully supported a proposal by UN Secretary-General Kofi Annan to double Iraq's exports of oil in exchange for a better supervised food and relief operation, but efforts to find a diplomatic solution to the Iraq crisis over UN arms inspections were "running out of gas."
	Mohammad Khatami says, "Regional states should themselves provide security in this area. . . . The presence of dozens of warships in the Persian Gulf is an affront to the people of the region."

Table 10.2 (continued)

98–2-4: Boris Yeltsin says US President Bill Clinton's actions in crisis could lead to a world war. CNN states that Iraq proposed opening eight presidential sites to inspections for one month. Washington and the UN say the offer is inadequate.

Arab League Secretary General Esmat Abdel-Meguid disbelieves Albright's comments that Arab leaders be prepared to acquiesce to US military action.

France says that it and Russia are aiming for a diplomatic solution. Clinton calls for a "genuine diplomatic solution."

Egyptian President Hosni Mubarak says that Iraq should obey Security Council resolutions to avoid "very dangerous" consequences that could arise from Iraq's standoff with the UN.

Syrian Vice President Abdel-Halim Khaddam warns against any military strike against Iraq, saying, "Any military strike against Iraq will be a serious matter that will create a dangerous situation because such an attack will be totally unjustified. . . . A military strike against Iraq will harm the peoples and countries of the Arab and Islamic worlds."

Talking to reporters after talks in Damascus with Iran's parliament speaker Ali Akbar Nateq-Nouri, Khaddam criticizes what he calls . . . "a double standard at the UN where decisions against Iraq are fully implemented while resolutions against Israel are ignored."

98–2-5: Third US aircraft carrier enters Gulf: USS *Independence* (CV 62), USS *John S. McCain* (DDG 56), USS *Bunker Hill* (CG 52), and USS *Charlotte* (SSN 766) arrive in the Arabian Gulf.

China repeats that it does not favor force.

Indian Prime Minister Inder Kumar Gujral writes to Annan saying the use of military force against Iraq would only complicate the situation and that "any military conflict would aggravate the enormous suffering which the people of Iraq have undergone because of the sanctions."

France announces that it will not take part in any military action, but says that Iraq's position has changed slightly but not enough.

Britain says that Iraqi inspection offer is unacceptable.

Yeltsin says that the worst is over.

Turkey's army takes extra security measures on the Iraqi border in case of any conflict in the crisis over UN weapons inspections.

98–2-6: A further 2,200 US Marines head for the Gulf. The US State Department says a response to any germ attack would be swift. Israel reserves the option to retaliate against any Iraqi attack; the United States urges it not to. Two US F-18 fighters based on the aircraft carrier *George Washington* collide over Gulf, killing one pilot. Clinton concentrates on military build-up, works with the Ambassador to the UN, Bill Richardson, to gather diplomatic support. State Department says there are no plans to

Table 10.2 (continued)

	use nuclear weapons, but response to any germ warfare attack would be "swift, devastating, and overwhelming." Saddam tells Turkish envoy he accepts fate in military standoff. "We are complying with the UN resolutions, but America is distorting this. We are prepared for anything," he said. Israel reserves the option to retaliate against any Iraqi attack; the United States urges it to not fight back.
98–2-7:	Chancellor Helmut Kohl says that Germany will make air bases available in the event of a US-led military strike on Iraq.
	Secretary of Defense Cohen orders the deployment of 43 (initially stated as 50) additional aircraft to Southwest Asia, including six F-117s, six F-16CJs, six B-52s, one B-1, and 23 additional aircraft. About 140 troops and six F-117A Nighthawks from Holloman deploy to Southwest Asia. The six additional B-52s deploy from Barksdale Air Force Base in Louisiana to Diego Garcia, increasing the number of bombers stationed there from eight to 14 by February 15. The one additional B-1 deploys from Ellsworth Air Force Base in South Dakota. The other aircraft include MC-130s, MH-53J helicopters, MH-47E helicopters; HH-60G Black Hawk helicopters, one JSTARS, two AWACS [bringing the total to four], one RIVET JOINT, some KC-10 refuelers, and a couple of HC-130 CSAR aircraft.
98–2-8:	The Pope says that there is still time to resolve the crisis. Albright says any bombardment of Iraq would be substantial. Cohen says Washington has decided to not ask Saudi Arabia for use of bases but that Kuwait and Bahrain are willing to let the United States strike from their territory.
98–2-9:	UN Secretary-General Kofi Annan puts off visit to Middle East because diplomatic efforts reach "critical stage." Saddam discusses crisis with aides. Witnesses say several thousand Turkish troops pour into northern Iraq; security source says troops are setting up tent camps for potential refugees from Iraq. Canada is ready to join military coalition if diplomacy fails.
98–2-10:	Australia pledges military aid for any US-led strike. China says military strikes could trigger more serious conflicts.
98–2-11:	Iraq says it supports Russian proposal to allow UN inspections of all Iraqi sites. The Commander of the US forces in the Middle East says he will be ready to strike Iraq within about a week. Spain will support US-led strike if diplomacy fails. Italy says its air bases would be available. Iraq is ready to open eight presidential sites to inspections conducted under direct authority of UN Security Council for 60 days. Washington dismisses the proposal.
98–2-12:	Cohen visits Moscow; Russia warns him that military strikes against Iraq could do untold damage to US-Russian Minister of Defense ties. Iraq will not accept demand for unfettered UN access to all presidential palaces.

Table 10.2 (continued)

	Saudi Crown Prince Abdullah urges Iraqi President Saddam Hussein on Thursday to listen to the "voice of reason" and to spare Iraqi civilians the punishment of a US military strike.
	UN spokesman says that a military strike on Iraq could disrupt the flow of supplies under the country's oil-for-food program.
98–2-13:	The United States insists that it could not walk away from an obligation to stop Iraq from developing weapons of mass destruction, and Russian objections would not prevent use of force. Russian Foreign Minister Yevgeny Primakov says diplomatic effort should not end before Annan visits Baghdad, and discusses the crisis with the foreign ministers of Iran, Japan, and Sweden.
98–2-14:	The United States plans for military action move forward as calls grow for Annan to go to Baghdad; anti-war protests in London and the Middle East.
98–2-15:	Technical team sent by Annan to survey disputed presidential sites meets senior Iraqi arms negotiators in Baghdad; France and Germany join Russia in pressing Annan to go to Baghdad; the United States threatens to hit Iraq repeatedly if necessary.
	Iraq frees 42 more Egyptians, bringing the total number released to 184 since President Saddam Hussein declared an amnesty for Arab prisoners 10 days earlier.
	Egypt's President, Hosni Mubarak, warns that the situation in the Arab world could deteriorate if the United States attacks Iraq for failing to comply with weapons inspections: "I think things will become much more serious with air strikes.... This is very dangerous—I cannot stand against the whole weight of popular opinion.... You will not find one (Arab) leader who will say publicly we support the air strikes."
	Jordan reaches an accord to supply Baghdad with $255 million worth of exports in return for cheap Iraqi oil supplies in 1998.
98–2-16:	Annan's visit to Iraq is delayed as Security Council members ponder possible peace formula.
	The United States says it will send 5,000 to 6,000 more troops to Kuwait.
	Arab efforts to avert strikes on Iraq intensify. Iraqi foreign minister to deliver message from Saddam to French President Jacques Chirac. The foreign minister of Qatar arrives in Baghdad on Monday to help find a peaceful end to the Iraq crisis. Envoy of Saddam Hussein briefs Libyan leader Muammar Qaddafi.
	The USS *Guam* (LPH 9) Amphibious Ready Group (ARG) arrives on station in the Arabian Gulf. The 12-ship formation in company with the amphibious assault ship includes the other four ships of the ARG: USS *Shreveport* (LPD 12), USS *Ashland* (LSD 48), and USS *Oak Hill* (LSD 51). The USS *John S. McCain* (DDG 56) acted as the group's escort ship. Seven military pre-position ships made up the remainder of the convoy.

Table 10.2 (continued)

	The ships of the Guam ARG carry about 2,000 Marines from the 24th Marine Expeditionary Unit (Special Operations Capable). The USS *Guam*, flagship of the Mediterranean Amphibious Ready Group (MARG) 98–1, cancels a scheduled port visit to Koper, Slovenia, and drops anchor in Augusta Bay, Italy. As three other MARG ships steam toward the Guam, Task Force 61 makes preparations for all four ships to enter the Suez Canal on February 9, 1998.
98–2-17:	An Iraqi newspaper says that UN Secretary-General Kofi Annan must show independence from the United States when he visits Baghdad to try to avert military action against Iraq. Egyptian President Hosni Mubarak said Annan's visit to Baghdad this week was Iraq's last chance to avert a US-led military strike. "A military strike will cause endless problems. I have great hope that this visit will succeed because it will spare Iraq endless problems," Mubarak said after talks with Syrian Vice President Abdel-Halim Khaddam. "We will probably send another letter to [Iraqi president] Saddam Hussein urging him to work hard to make this trip a success because it is the last chance," he added. Russian President Boris Yeltsin sees Annan's planned trip to Baghdad this week as "vitally important." A military strike against Iraq would inflict very substantial damage on Saddam's military might, British Defense Secretary George Robertson said. "We are convinced we can cause massive damage to his military capability," he told BBC radio. French Foreign Minister Hubert Vedrine said Saddam might still cave in under massive international pressure and agree to further UN arms inspections. Iraqi Foreign Minister Mohammed Saeed al-Sahaf arrived in Iran for talks on the crisis.
	Iraq promises to work for the success of any visit by Annan; Annan wins Security Council approval for a peace mission to Baghdad, but the United States reserves the right to disagree with the results; Clinton favors a diplomatic solution, but only if it meets the "immutable" condition of ensuring unfettered access for weapons inspections.
98–2-18:	Kofi Annan says he had a "reasonable chance" of averting military action against Iraq, "I think I have all your support and your prayers. . . . I think I have all I need to be able to undertake this trip."
	The White House says it is not optimistic that Annan would achieve a breakthrough. The United States does say, however, that it could accept a compromise with Iraq in which diplomats from UN Security Council member countries accompany UN arms inspectors on their search for banned weapons. Bill Richardson, the US envoy to UN, says, "In terms of diplomats, observers, that would observe the UN inspection team itself, I think that is something we can deal with."
	Secretary of State Albright, Secretary of Defense Cohen, and the National Security Adviser are drowned out by anti-war demonstrators, yelling from an upper tier of a college gymnasium before 6,000 people in a televised meeting.

Table 10.2 (continued)

98–2-19:	Annan leaves for Paris on his way to Baghdad; 29 UN staff members leave Baghdad for Jordan; about 750 US army troops fly to Kuwait on chartered airliners—the first of an expected 6,000 armored and helicopter unit reinforcements; bomb causes heavy damage at US car dealership building on outskirts of Athens; police believe it was a protest against Washington's plans to attack Iraq.
98–2-20:	Annan arrives in Baghdad, saying he has a "sacred duty" to try to defuse the crisis. He agrees to extend his stay in Baghdad until Feb. 23 to discuss the UN's oil-for-food-deal for Iraq. Annan's spokesman, Fred Eckhard, said that Iraq had given full access to a UN technical team that mapped eight disputed presidential sites earlier this week, accompanied by staff of UNSCOM charged with finding and destroying Iraqi weapons of mass destruction.
	United Arab Emirates President Sheik Zaid bin Sultan al-Nahayan rejects the use of force against Iraq, warning that a US military strike could damage East-West relations and affect the Gulf.
	President Clinton accuses Iraqi President Saddam Hussein of oppressing his people and says the United States would try to avoid harming the innocent in any military strike.
	Israeli Defense Minister Yitzhak Mordechai says he expects Israel to be ready to defend itself against a retaliatory Iraqi strike should the United States attack Baghdad. Asked if the United States would hold back an anti-Iraq strike until Israel had vital Patriot missiles and equipment to detect biological weapons, Mordechai says, "In my estimation, those means will be in our hands in time. We have been working several days so those additional crucial means for the defense of the home front will be in our hands."
	Turkish police clash with hundreds of Islamists demonstrating after Friday prayers against possible US-led military action against Iraq, witnesses said. Hundreds of riot police used batons to break up a protest outside the prominent Beyazit mosque in central Istanbul and rounded up around 80 protesters chanting anti-American slogans.
	Dozens of pro-Iraqi Palestinian demonstrators clashed with Israeli troops in two separate rallies in the West Bank on Friday, witnesses said.
	Around 2,000 Iranian hard-liners march in central Tehran to demonstrate against the US military presence poised against Iraq. The demonstration follows mass prayers at Tehran University, where influential former President Akbar Hashemi Rafsanjani said the West had created the current crisis with Iraq by selling weapons of mass destruction to Baghdad.
98–2-21:	Annan holds three rounds of talks with Deputy Prime Minister Tariq Aziz. In Washington, Clinton and his senior advisers refine plans for air strikes if Baghdad refuses unrestricted access for weapons inspectors.

Table 10.2 (continued)

	Washington urges all of its citizens to leave Iraq. Jordan sends troops and armored vehicles to Maan after fresh clashes erupt between riot police and pro-Iraqi demonstrators.
98–2-22:	Annan holds three-hour meeting with Saddam Hussein, and the UN chief's spokesman later announces a deal on weapons inspections. The United States says it will await Annan's formal report to the Security Council on February 24 before commenting on the deal.
	The USS *John C. Stennis* (CVN 74) departs from Norfolk on a regularly scheduled six-month deployment to proceed directly to the Arabian Gulf, replacing the USS *George Washington* (CVN 73), currently on station there, in mid-March. The USS *George Washington* will return to its home port of Norfolk, Virginia, on time from its six-month deployment.
98–2-23:	Annan announces the details of his agreement with Iraq in a joint news conference with Aziz, and says he hopes the deal will be acceptable to members of the Security Council. He says there are "no time limits or deadlines" in the pact. Aziz says it was diplomacy, not saber-rattling, that helped conclude the agreement. China says it hopes the deal will "disperse the war cloud" over the Gulf. Britain says the agreement looked encouraging but would have to be studied closely. "In my view, the terms of this agreement, which have been concluded in writing, are acceptable and remove a major obstacle to the full implementation of relevant Security Council resolutions. . . . I will so report to the Security Council immediately upon my return to New York on Tuesday. . . . I hope it will be acceptable to all members of the Council." There are "no time limits or deadlines" in the agreement, but adds, "I think it is important that we do our work in a reasonable period. . . . I genuinely believe that if we cooperate and do the kinds of things that we have agreed to do, we will not see that kind of crisis [again]."
	Tariq Aziz states that, "As (Annan) reported to you, we had constructive, intensive, objective discussions about the purpose of his mission. We highly appreciate the nature of the discussions we had, the understandings we reached, and as his excellency said, we happily reached a final agreement on the questions we discussed. We also agreed that we will continue our cooperation with his excellency the Secretary General in order to achieve the common objective. As far as Iraq is concerned, as everybody knows, the priority of the Iraqi people and the Iraqi government is an expeditious implementation of paragraph 22 of (UN) Resolution 687 and a lifting of all sanctions. We are going to work together in good faith and in full cooperation, and we hope that this humanitarian, legal and fair objective, the lifting of sanctions, will be done very soon." He turns away suggestions that the build-up had prompted Iraq to enter into the agreement. "What helped in reaching this agreement . . . is the goodwill that he (Annan) brought with him—not the American or the British build-up in the Gulf and not the policy of saber-rattling. . . . It was diplomacy . . . that enabled us to reach this agreement. . . . This is a great gain. . . .

Table 10.2 (continued)

In fact, there was no crisis between Iraq and the UN ... the crisis was with the United States which is trying to impose its will on the UN."

The US State Department and the White House withhold substantive comment, saying they wish to study the details.

European Union foreign ministers give a cautious welcome to the Accord.

British Foreign Secretary Robin Cook says, "Britain has always wanted a diplomatic solution to the present confrontation with Saddam Hussein. If Kofi Annan achieved that diplomatic solution that will be very welcome and we will be the first to congratulate him on it. ... At the present time we are not aware of the details of that agreement and they will need to be studied closely. ... Our bottom line has always been that we must get an agreement that enables the UN inspectors to get back to work and stops Saddam Hussein developing chemical and biological weapons. ... If we have got that agreement then we have achieved something that will be very valuable and will also justify the strategy that we have been pursuing over recent weeks. If there had been no pressure on Saddam there would have been no deal from Saddam. He has moved under that pressure substantially over the past month. First he said there could be no inspections of its presidential sites, then he said there would be one inspection. If Kofi Annan has got a good deal in Baghdad then he has now agreed to repeat inspections. I welcome what Kofi Annan has said this morning, that you can achieve a lot more from diplomacy when it is backed by firmness and force. If we have got an acceptable deal it will be because of the resolve and the unity that the international community has shown."

Russian President Yeltsin says the latest crisis had been "practically resolved" and indicates he believes Russia played a vital role in averting US military strikes. "From the very beginning we were for a diplomatic solution of the crisis. We were against military action because this would not finish with Iraq. This would involve a much bigger territory, significantly more countries." He warns that US attacks would be "very dangerous especially because the use of chemical weapons [by Iraq] could not be excluded. ... The question has been practically resolved ... [Saddam] Hussein gave his word."

China states that it hopes the deal will "disperse the war cloud" over the Gulf. An Israeli spokesman says the accord leaves Israel no safer from an Iraqi chemical or biological attack. Senior Palestinian negotiator Saeb Erekat welcomes the apparent end of the crisis and calls for world attention to return to Middle East peacemaking.

Egypt's President Mubarak states, "It is a very good agreement. ... I hope that it will be supported by the United States." Foreign Minister Amr Moussa calls for the United States to accept the agreement.

Table 10.2 (continued)

	Turkish Foreign Minister Ismail Cem welcomes the agreement and says he will visit Jordan to propose regional cooperation for a permanent solution.
	Syria welcomes the agreement but expresses skepticism about Washington's intentions towards Baghdad.
	Secretary General Esmet Abdel Meguid of the Arab League welcomes the agreement and states that, "The option for a political solution has averted a very dangerous twist, which would have pushed the entire region into a catastrophe."
	Hassan Rowhani, vice chairman of Iran's Supreme National Security Council, warns that, "The Americans are still looking for pretexts for a military strike against Iraq."
98–2-24:	Annan leaves France to return to New York to brief the Security Council on the deal. The agreement states that, "The Government of Iraq reconfirms its acceptance of all relevant resolutions of the Security Council, including resolutions 687 (1991) and 715 (1991)." The Government of Iraq further reiterates its undertaking to cooperate fully with UN Special Commission (UNSCOM) and the International Atomic Energy Agency (IAEA). The UN reiterates the commitment of all Member States to respect the sovereignty and territorial integrity of Iraq. The Government of Iraq undertakes to accord to UNSCOM and IAEA immediate, unconditional, and unrestricted access in conformity with the resolutions referred to in paragraph 1.... UN and the Government of Iraq agree that the following special procedures shall apply to the initial and subsequent entries for the performance of the tasks mandated at the eight Presidential Sites in Iraq as defined in the annex to the present Memorandum: A Special Group shall be established for this purpose by the Secretary-General in consultation with the Executive Chairman of UNSCOM and the Director-General of IAEA.... United Nations and the Government of Iraq agree to improve cooperation, and efficiency, effectiveness and transparency of work, so as to enable UNSCOM to report to the Council expeditiously under paragraph 22 of resolution 687 (1991). To achieve this goal, the Government of Iraq and UNSCOM will implement the recommendations directed at them as contained in the report of the emergency session of UNSCOM held on 21 November 1997.... The lifting of sanctions is obviously of paramount importance to the people and Government of Iraq and the Secretary-General undertook to bring this matter to the full attention of the members of the Security Council."
	The United States calls for an "enforcement initiative" in the UN Security Council, warning Iraq of "serious consequences" if it reneges on a new deal over weapons inspections. "We want to have an enforcement initiative in the Security Council that says to [Iraqi leader] Saddam [Hussein], if you don't comply, there are going to be very serious consequences," say Bill Richardson, US envoy to UN. "We don't want to be back here in three months. Saddam is not getting away with just signing

Table 10.2 (continued)

a paper . . . I can tell you for sure this is not the last time, Saddam Hussein always pops up, always violates agreements." The wording the United States would like to see would declare Iraq either in "material breach" of Gulf War cease-fire resolutions or open to the "severest consequences." In addition, the United States is determined to keep UN economic sanctions, imposed after Iraq's invasion of Kuwait in 1990, in force for the foreseeable future, even though some US allies want to see them lifted soon. US officials say they see no change in Washington's "broad" interpretation of UN resolutions that Iraq must not only scrap its suspected weapons of mass destruction but compensate Kuwait and account for missing Kuwaitis to win sanctions relief.

Britain calls for UN resolution, making it clear to Iraq that it would face quick retaliation if it breached the deal. "If Saddam is in breach of this agreement . . . the new resolution we intend to go alongside this agreement will make clear that the consequences will be severe," say Prime Minister Tony Blair's chief spokesman. Britain plans to propose a resolution that would nail down the agreement as well as threaten consequences if Iraq departs from it. However, it is questionable whether France, Russia, and China, who are more sympathetic toward Iraq, will approve tough language that, in practice, would give the United States and United Kingdom the right to bomb if the pact is violated.

98–2-26: America's UN Ambassador, Bill Richardson, defends the agreement against criticism from the majority leader of the US Senate, Trent Lott, who called it a sellout to Saddam. "We believe this is a good agreement," Richardson said. "We see the British initiative as a good way to enforce the agreement."

80 UN humanitarian staff pulled out of Baghdad to escape the threat of possible US military strikes return. Around 105 UN humanitarian staff had remained in Baghdad despite the crisis, as well as 164 in the three northern provinces outside of Iraqi government control. About 100 UNSCOM weapons inspectors had also remained in Baghdad and worked throughout the crisis.

Secretary of State Albright reiterates her stated fear that fostering a civil war in Iraq aimed at unseating Saddam could end badly for opposition forces. "This leaves us with a policy that is quite frankly not fully satisfactory to anyone," she told a House of Representatives appropriations subcommittee. "It is a real-world policy, not a feel-good policy. But I am convinced it is the best policy to protect our interests and those of our friends and allies in the Gulf." Albright, repeating comments she made in *Newsweek* magazine this week, said the opposition was divided, "and it would be wrong to create false or unsustainable expectations that could end in bloodshed and defeat."

Iraqi Foreign Ministry Under-Secretary Riyadh al-Qaysi says that although no time limit was specified in the text of the accord, Iraq believes the inspections will be finished "in the shortest possible time." Qaysi

Table 10.2 (continued)

says Iraq is determined to make a success of the agreement, which it considered fair and balanced. "We intend to cooperate to the fullest possible extent," he told Reuters in an interview late on Wednesday. "There was an understanding. And you can see from some provisions in the agreement that the understanding is there," Qaysi said. "The timeframe [is] here. The whole story is reasonably determined to be shorter [rather] than longer. Within the foreseeable future rather than the distant future." Qaysi says the inspectors will not be limited to a single visit to the presidential sites. "But subsequent entry has to be obviously reasonably put within the timeframe envisaged by the Secretary General to come to an end," Qaysi said. He declined to specify how long Iraq considered a reasonable timeframe. Qaysi praises Annan's readiness to listen to Iraq's concerns and for negotiating with trust and good faith. "We faced enormous difficulties since 1991. First of all to have people meet us. Then to have them listen to us. And after they listened to us to interact with what we had to say." Qaysi said Annan's visit to Baghdad has changed the approach of the UNSCOM, "The information seeping back to us is that he has dealt with the individual behavior of some inspectors, using even the word 'cowboy' behavior," Qaysi said. He criticizes the United States and Britain for continuing to build military force and seeking a UN Security Council resolution giving the automatic right to use military force if Iraq hindered any inspection work again. "They claim they speak for the international community, yet when the international community rejoices at the achievement of the agreement, they put themselves outside the fold. . . . Legally you cannot have a blank check for the automatic use of force under the UN charter . . . and politically speaking it means they do not trust the Secretary General."

UN chief weapons inspector Richard Butler says his inspection team had not been weakened by a deal signed by UN Secretary-General Kofi Annan: "I am perfectly satisfied that this document, applied properly with Iraqi cooperation, strengthens my organization. This document is a very important one. . . . It is the first one that Saddam Hussein has personally engaged in since the end of the Gulf War—the fine print in this document is what I call the thumbprint . . . Saddam Hussein has been involved in this and it's got real commitment in it to enable us to get our job done. I just hope they adhere to that." Butler rejects US criticism that the deal, which envisages establishment of a new special group, including diplomats to inspect so-called presidential sites, weakens UNSCOM: "All of it comes through me as executive chairman, and I am looking forward to this development—it expands our staff, it gives us an extra resource. . . . Our inspection group which goes to the presidential sites will be based on our technical expertise."

Jayantha Dhanapala, a former Sri Lankan ambassador to the United States, is formally selected to lead the special team to accompany UN weapons inspectors into the palaces. But Butler says he remains in control

Table 10.2 (continued)

of the weapons inspection operation and would report to the UN Security Council on the campaign to disarm Iraq. "The new special commissioner and I will work together on adding in some diplomatic observers . . . to meet the concerns of Iraq in respect to the dignity of those sites . . . the core function is preserved. The reports will come through me and I will present them to the Security Council. . . ." Butler says the new weapons inspection deal would mean that UNSCOM could possibly complete its mission in Iraq in a very short time, possibly within a year. "If they follow what is in Kofi Annan's document and really cooperate with us, you are not talking years as has been in the past, we are talking a relatively good, short time. . . . I will go to Baghdad in good spirit and determination to work with them to get this job done under these new circumstances, and I expect they will react to me in the same way."

98–2-27:   Kofi Annan sends a letter to UN staff telling them not to be disheartened by criticism of the agreement. He concluded, "It was not unexpected that there would be some criticism of us and misrepresentations of what we have done in Iraq, but you must not be disheartened. The alternative to the agreement would have ended UNSCOM's work. The Memorandum of Understanding has strengthened it. I would want you, therefore, to treat our critics with sympathetic understanding. For my part, I said on Tuesday that I had done my work and that I trust the Security Council will do its duty. We should all await Security Council action on this agreement. It is the Council, not a few critics, which will have the last word."

President Clinton telephones Saudi Arabia's King Fahd and Kuwait's Emir Sheik Jaber al-Ahmad al-Sabah to discuss the agreement. "The president stressed the importance of the Iraqis living up to their commitments and assured the leaders that the military posture would remain the same as a way of backing up our diplomacy with a show of force. . . . He assured both leaders that any interference by the Iraqis would be met with firm and forcible action," he added.

Tariq Aziz says in a French TF1 television interview that, "We believe that this agreement is a victory for Iraq. . . . The threat was there before the arrival of Mr. Annan, and we did not change our positions. We were not scared. . . . The agreement we signed was also our agreement. It was not imposed upon us." He also says he does not trust the special group of arms inspectors and diplomats he agreed to create with Secretary-General Kofi Annan. "I have to be frank. My answer is no, but we will work with them because I trust UN Secretary-General Annan. . . . We have signed a deal, and we are waiting for the Secretary General to send the special group, and we'll begin to work with them when they arrive in Baghdad. . . . UNSCOM must not be left to Anglo-Saxons, not because we have a discriminatory attitude, but because UNSCOM cannot be hijacked by two governments who have a special agenda on Iraq." Aziz says Iraq will "fulfill its commitments correctly and seriously. . . . We

Table 10.2 (continued)

want to finish this very soon.... We also want to help UNSCOM with technical means in order to inform it of some new developments and discoveries regarding missile warheads. [It will] "appear very rapidly that we have done the required work, and we deserve to have the sanctions lifted...."

Richard Butler attempts to refute critics, particularly in the US Congress. "As far as I am concerned, I welcome it. The arrangements are entirely satisfactory to the organization I lead." The new accord is made "at a high political level." Its fine print is less important than the fact it had the "thumbprints of the Secretary-General of UN and the president of Iraq with whom he consulted in this agreement." Butler says he is "delighted" at the appointment of Jayantha Dhanapala—the Sri Lankan UN undersecretary-general for disarmament affairs and a former ambassador to Washington—because Dhanapala is a leading disarmament expert whom he has known for years. Butler says the next step is up to Iraq, and noted that he was still in charge of inspections. "I am very happy with the arrangements. It gives us new resources. It gives us access to sites that Iraq said were absolutely off limits.... What's different? We will have some diplomatic observers with us to see that both sides, not just UNSCOM, behave in an appropriate manner in these rather special sites. I think that is fine." Butler and UN spokesman Fred Eckhard also challenge a report in the *Washington Post* that Lott had quoted. It said Annan referred to UNSCOM inspectors as "cowboys" at a closed-door Security Council meeting earlier in the week. Both said they were at the meeting and that Annan had been quoting Iraqi authorities. Annan has, however, criticized the inspectors by publicly repeating some of Iraq's complaints and saying that UNSCOM staff "have to handle Iraq and the Iraqis with a certain respect and dignity and not push their weight around and cause tensions."

Britain proposes a Security Council resolution to warn Iraq of "the severest consequences" if it violates obligations to give UN arms inspectors unrestricted access to all sites. An early version of the text does not spell out the nature of those "consequences." The draft says Iraq must comply with its obligations to cooperate fully with the UN Special Commission in charge of scrapping its weapons of mass destruction and with the International Atomic Energy Agency, in accordance with Council resolutions "which continue to constitute the governing standard of Iraqi compliance." British Ambassador Sir John Weston says the draft "associates the Council formally with the secretary-general's initiative and the MOU (memorandum of understanding) that he has brought back from Baghdad.... It sends two clear signals: one about 'light at the end of the tunnel' and the other a reminder that this agreement has to be made to work." Britain is expected to be joined by the United States and Japan in sponsoring the resolution. France announces it would back language, warning Iraq that it faced "serious consequences" if it blocked UN in-

Table 10.2 (continued)

spections. But its envoys said Paris wanted to make sure the document did not automatically authorize military action. But China voices objections. Asked whether the language on "most serious consequences" would be satisfactory, its UN ambassador, Qin Huasun, said, "No, I don't think so."

Jordan and Turkey agree that only Iraq's compliance with UN demands would avert a renewed threat of US-led military strikes against Baghdad. A joint communiqué issued at the end of a two-day visit by Turkish Foreign Minister Ismail Cem stresses that Iraq's cooperation with UN demands was the only way Baghdad could hope to bring an end to crippling economic sanctions imposed after its 1990 invasion of Kuwait. Jordanian Deputy Prime Minister and Foreign Minister Jawad Anani states, "The two sides reiterated their view that the only way to prevent the recurrence of such a crisis would be Iraq's full and unconditional compliance with UN Security Council resolutions. . . . Iraq should fully comply . . . but if Iraq complies there should be light at the end of the tunnel."

For the first time in six months, Iraqis will receive in March their full food rations under Baghdad's oil-for-food deal with the UN, a UN official said on Friday. Eric Falt, spokesman for the UN humanitarian coordinator in Iraq, said the basic food basket, which includes flour, rice, sugar, and baby milk, would be topped up by government supplies to reach the agreed target levels. The government will also dig into its own reserves for the first time to help feed the three virtually autonomous Kurdish provinces in the north of the country. Distribution of food will be monitored by UN staff, including 57 personnel who returned to Baghdad on Thursday night. They were evacuated the previous week to escape the threat of US air strikes over a row about weapons inspections in Iraq. Shortages of rice, sugar, tea, pulses, salt, cooking oil, baby food formula, detergent or soap have prevented the full distribution of supplies. For the last two months, babies have been getting just two-thirds of the 2.7 kg (six lbs.) of milk formula they were supposed to receive. "There will be a full ration of infant formula thanks to the utilization of government stocks."

98–2-28: Iraq dismisses a UN draft resolution warning it to comply with a deal to open up its presidential sites to weapons inspectors as "unnecessary." Oil Minister Amir Muhammad Rasheed said the British draft resolution, which sets out severe consequences if Baghdad obstructs inspections, is redundant because the deal clinched by UN Secretary-General Kofi Annan was a cast-iron accord. "We feel [it is] totally unnecessary to have any Security Council resolution to support the memorandum of understanding which we have reached," said Rasheed, a top Iraqi negotiator with UNSCOM weapons inspectors. "It has the power of law. It does not need any endorsement. . . . We have agreed to open them up to international experts so we can prove this was a fallacy like other fallacies

Table 10.2 (continued)

	which the American administration has claimed. . . . The condition is very simple. UNSCOM has to behave according to UN standards. . . . When they yield to pressure from some sources in the American administration . . . we will have problems."
	The United States completes deployment of 3,100 front-line combat troops the 3rd Infantry Division's 1st Brigade to Kuwait City. Their heavy equipment includes 116 M1A2 Abrams tanks and 58 Bradley Fighting Vehicles—waiting on the ground at Camp Doha, nine miles west of the Kuwaiti capital. Since November, the US force level in the Persian Gulf has increased from more than 20,000 to 35,000, almost half on 28 navy vessels, including two aircraft carriers. The number of war planes in the region has risen from about 200 to more than 350.
	British aircraft carrier *Illustrious* enters the Gulf over the weekend to help enforce a no-fly zone over southern Iraq. The *Illustrious* will replace the carrier *Invincible*, which entered the Gulf in January amid rising tension with Iraq over UN weapons inspections. The *Invincible*, with 1,200 men and women on board, is anchored at Bahrain's Mina Sulman. The *Invincible* is due to leave on March 8.
98-3-1:	Russia's special envoy to Iraq, Viktor Posuvalyuk, says he detected a new attitude in the Iraqi leadership, suggesting Baghdad would comply with the provisions of a UN deal on arms inspections in order to get international sanctions lifted. "I have the feeling that their present attitude is completely different, that at present their supreme task—they are literally possessed by it—is to achieve the lifting of sanctions. . . . If we can show that there is light at the end of the tunnel, if we can show that there are guidelines . . . on the basis of Iraq's complete, unconditional, and conscientious fulfilling of the Security Council resolutions, I think that it will be possible to avoid any exacerbation of the situation."
	Kuwait's Foreign Minister, Sheik Sabah al-Ahmad al-Sabah, says Iraqi reconciliation with Kuwait is possible only if Baghdad apologizes for invading the tiny Gulf Arab state. Sheik Sabah says Iraq must also implement all 1990–91 Gulf crisis-related UN resolutions and free some 600 people, mainly Kuwaitis, who Kuwait says have been held by Iraq since the invasion. The "highest authority" in Iraq must admit that the August 2, 1990, invasion of his country was wrong and must also apologize.
98-3-2:	The Security Council votes unanimously for a resolution that "stresses that compliance by the Government of Iraq with its obligations, repeated again in the memorandum of understanding, to accord immediate, unconditional, and unrestricted access to the Special Commission and the IAEA in conformity with the relevant resolutions is necessary for the implementation of resolution 687 (1991), but that any violation would have severest consequences for Iraq," and notes, that "by its failure so far to comply with its relevant obligations Iraq has delayed the moment when the Council can do so." The intensely negotiated resolution council

Table 10.2 (continued)

endorses the agreement that Secretary-General Kofi Annan signed in Baghdad a week earlier that gave the inspectors access to so-called "presidential sites" under special procedures. The resolution contains language to satisfy Council members who insisted on guarantees that the document did not automatically approve any use of force against Iraq if it broke the accord.

Secretary-General Kofi Annan calls on Iraq to fully abide by its obligations, warning that "diplomacy may not have a second chance.... Whether the threat to international peace and security has been averted for all time is now in the hands of the Iraqi leadership. It is now for them to comply in practice with what they have signed on paper.... For its part, the government of Iraq must now fulfill, without obstruction or delay, the continuing obligations that it reaffirmed last week at the very highest level.... Iraq fully understands that if this effort to ensure compliance through negotiation is obstructed, by evasion or deception, as were previous efforts, diplomacy may not have a second chance.... No promise of peace and no policy of patience can be without limits. Certainly UN and the world community lost nothing, gave away nothing, and conceded nothing of substance.... But by halting, at least for now, the renewal of military hostilities in the Gulf, it was a victory for peace, for reason, for the resolution of conflict by diplomacy.... If this agreement is fully implemented and leads over time to a new day in the Gulf, if this exercise in diplomacy, backed by fairness, firmness and force, stands the test of time, it will serve as an enduring and invaluable precedent for UN and the world community."

President Clinton states Iraq faces the "severest consequences" if it again acts to block UN weapons inspectors from carrying out their work. "Tonight's unanimous vote by UN Security Council sends the clearest possible message: Iraq must make good on its commitment to give the international weapons inspectors immediate, unconditional, and unrestricted access to any suspect site, any place, anytime.... [Failure to do so] will result in the severest consequences for Iraq. Iraq now has the responsibility to turn the commitment it has made into full compliance."

British Ambassador Sir John Weston tells the Security Council, "We are not prepared to see a repeat of the Iraqi behavior which led to the present crisis."

China Ambassador Qin Huasun stresses that his delegation "demanded repeatedly and clearly that there must not be any automatic authorization of use of force against Iraq in this draft resolution.... Therefore I wish to stress here that the passing of this resolution in no way means the Security Council automatically authorizes any state to use force against Iraq."

Russia's envoy, Sergei Lavrov, states, "Any hint has been excluded (from the resolution) about automaticity with regard to the application of

Table 10.2 (continued)

force, which would be unacceptable for the majority of the members of the council."

French envoy Alain Dejammet says the resolution confirms "the prerogatives of the Security Council in a way which excludes any idea of automaticity ... this was re-emphasized quite firmly by the representative of Japan on behalf of the co-sponsors of the resolution and I thank them for this."

Tariq Aziz says, "The British wanted ... a resolution to box the Secretary General and add some negative language against Iraq, and also prepare the grounds for a unilateral decision by them and the Americans to attack Iraq when they choose to do so.... We are not going to interrupt their work.... How long do you think it will take to do a correct survey? Not a decade, not a few years. They will need a reasonable period. We will give them the reasonable period for that.... Experts will obviously deal with the technical aspects of the visit. Diplomats will observe and be interested in the political aspect of the visit.... Since November, 1991, UNSCOM has never discovered by its own efforts any prohibited weapons in Iraq.... UNSCOM has never discovered a hidden missile, any hidden chemical or biological stockpile. It was Iraq which either unilaterally destroyed those weapons and informed UNSCOM about their destruction or presented those weapons to UNSCOM for their disposal."

Iraq holds a funeral procession through Baghdad for 43 children it said died as a result of economic sanctions. "At the same time as we shed tears for our children we challenge the United States over its policy against us," said National Assembly member Sultan al-Shawi, who led a protest march in front of the procession. "These children died for the simple fact that they needed food and medicine.... The United States is committing genocide against Iraq. Threatening the use of force against Iraq and prolonging the embargo is not accepted."

98-3-8: Kofi Annan says the United States lacks the authority for automatic use of force against Iraq, even if Baghdad again interfered with UN/ weapons inspectors. "If the United States [felt it] had to strike, I think some sort of consultations with the other members would be required" in the Security Council. Annan's comments are at odds with the Clinton administration's stated view that it does not need further UN permission to strike for any breach of the deal that staved off military action last month.

A UNSCOM inspection team led by Scott Ritter works for 10 hours for a second consecutive day. "They inspected a number of sites on Saturday, three of which again were sensitive," a UN spokesman said. Three such sites also were visited Friday, UN officials said. An Iraqi source said that one was a barracks of the elite Republican Guards. Dacey said that "all sites were inspected to the satisfaction of the inspection team," and that the inspectors "received the full cooperation of the Iraqi authorities."

Table 10.2 (continued)

98-3-9:	French Foreign Minister Hubert Vedrine says all other Security Council members oppose the US and British view that Iraq could be attacked automatically if it hampered UN weapons inspectors again.
	White House spokesman Mike McCurry says the United States expects to consult with the UN before any military strike if Iraq breaks its pledge to grant access to UN weapons inspectors. "If we got to the point where there were serious questions about the government of Iraq's willingness to honor the memorandum of understanding, we would of course be consulting with members of the Security Council. I would expect urgent deliberations to occur if there was any abrogation of the agreement." However, McCurry says later that he understood the question to refer to a need for a Security Council resolution on military action. The United States has repeatedly said it believes it already has the authority to launch a military strike if Iraq violates the agreement it struck with Annan the previous month to allow UN weapons inspectors into sensitive Iraqi sites.
	Iraqi Foreign Minister Sahaf begins talks on a new UN "oil-for-food" program that Iraq says would still not allow enough humanitarian supplies to reach ordinary Iraqis suffering under sanctions. About a third goes to a compensation fund for victims of the 1991 Gulf War and to pay for UN staff for the oil for food program, as well as to cover the costs of UNSCOM. Sahaf, in a letter to the Security Council the previous month, says revenues from oil Iraq sells over the $2 billion mark should no longer include the deductions. He also harshly criticizes UN proposals to update electricity in the northern Kurdish provinces, where the UN rather than Iraq controls the oil-for-food program. The plan includes $1 billion for infrastructure repairs.
	Kuwait's Foreign Minister, Sheik Sabah al-Ahmed al-Sabah, says Kuwait would consider reconciliation with Iraq only if it apologized for invading the oil-rich state, implemented all Gulf crisis-related UN resolutions, and freed some 600 people missing since the crisis.

the humanitarian disaster in Iraq . . . we should have substantially increased the funds available." Britain's deputy UN representative, Stephen Gommersall, said that "The suffering of the Iraqi people would be unnecessary were it not for constant evasions over the last six years in evading its obligations" to destroy its weapons of mass destruction. Similarly, US Ambassador Bill Richardson also accused Iraq of "playing politics" with the oil for food deal. "In short, we call upon the Iraqi leadership to demonstrate as much compassion for the Iraqi people as the council has."

During the rest of 1997 and 1998, Iraq responded with new attempts to exploit the oil for food arrangement, while claiming that it was an unacceptable substitute for the complete lifting of sanctions. It built upon the theme the Iraqi News Agency set forth in December, when it threatened that

Iraq will not embark upon exporting oil under the third phase until the approval of the third (distribution) plan and the acceleration of passage of the accumulated contracts in the 661 committee of the first and second phases.... We asked that the date of the start of the implementation of the decision and beginning of exporting oil (should be) when the UN Secretary-General approves the distribution plan for the third phase, but America and Britain have opposed as usual this legitimate demand.[72]

Divide and Paralyze

The chronology in Table 10.2 shows this growing linkage between Iraq's attacks on UNSCOM and the "hardship" issue. Nizar Hamdoon added a new dimension to the game by claiming that the United States was obstructing the flow of aid and that the money was not helping the Iraqi people. He stated that 80% of the goods Iraq had ordered had not yet reached Iraq, so there was no need to pump oil—although the United States responded with figures that showed that only 60 contracts had been held up since the beginning of the program, and that this was less than 5% of all applications that had been submitted for consideration. It became clear that Iraq was bluffing when it suddenly reversed its position on December 8, 1997, when its actions failed to produce a change in UN policy and threatened to create major cuts in the regime's revenues. Iraq renewed its agreement to the oil for food policy for 180 days without any explanation of why it had reversed its policy.[73]

After November, Iraq's Deputy Prime Minister Tariq Aziz constantly attacked UNSCOM as a tool of the United States:

Butler is still unobjective and inaccurate and his statements were aimed at serving an American plot which aims at a fabricated escalation [of a standoff between Iraq and the UN and United States] . . . Iraq will not remain idle with folded arms while the American game continues to win time and keep the subject [of sanctions on Iraq] suspended from one month to another and from one year to another. . . . We do not have in mind to end the crisis and push the cause of our people once more into dark tunnels of ill-intentioned parties in the Security Council.[74]

Iraq continued to try to force an agreement on a date for ending both UNSCOM's activities and sanctions. Ambassador Butler reported to the Security Council on January 24, 1998, that Iraq appeared determined to withhold any new information and prevent UN inspectors from obtaining it, which meant entering certain forbidden sites. Butler stated in his November report to the Security Council that Deputy Prime Minister Tariq Aziz told him that Iraq was working with UNSCOM to get economic sanctions lifted, and that, "If there was no prospect of this, the government of Iraq had no intention of continuing to work with the Commission. Iraq was ready to face the consequences, including war."[75]

The list of events in Table 10.2 shows that Iraqi diplomacy became steadily more complex and multifaceted in late 1997, and that Iraq became grimly persistent in testing every possible avenue of opportunity. Until this time, Iraq had often been its own worst enemy, forcing the issue to the point which it unified the Security Council and world opinion against it. After the fall of 1997, however, Iraq showed more patience and skill. It still brought events to the brink of US and British military action, but it then compromised at the last moment in ways that steadily improved its position.

Iraq began this new phase of the "war of sanctions" by stating that its agreement to allow US inspectors to return did not mean that UNSCOM could visit sensitive facilities like presidential, intelligence, and Republican Guards compounds. This initially involved about 47 "presidential sites" (although the number was soon reduced to eight), and 63 sites that were said to be "sensitive." Some sites were extremely large, and US sources later referred to a total of 78 sites that Iraq contested.[76]

Once again the Security Council was divided over the proper response. A spokesman for the French Foreign Ministry declared that Ekeus had previously agreed not to inspect sites under the direct supervision of Saddam Hussein. At the same time, Iraqi Foreign Minister Mohammed Said al-Sahaf threatened to throw out any inspectors that entered the sites of the country.[77]

Iraq attempted to split the Security Council from UNSCOM. On November 26, Iraq announced that the Revolutionary Command had decided to invite two representatives and five experts or diplomats from each of the countries on the Security Council to visit Iraq's sites "for a period of a week or more, or for a month, so they could find out the truth." This invitation applied to up to 115 experts and diplomats from 155 countries, who would have had no prior experience in dealing with the problems involved in UNSCOM's inspections.[78]

US officials responded by stating that inspectors from UNSCOM should be allowed to go wherever they choose: "As we have said before, and as the UN Security Council has said unambiguously and unanimously through its resolutions, the UNSCOM inspectors must be permitted to do their jobs and must have unconditional and unfettered access." Lt. General Anthony Zinni, the commander of USCENTCOM, announced to the United States that any future military action would not involve any more "pinpricks," and that there would be a "serious response." He also stated, "I do feel strongly we will get the support we need (from Gulf leaders) when the time comes. . . . They see the threat the way we do, and they've been fully cooperative with what we've needed, to be able to respond and to protect ourselves in this region."[79]

In practice, however, the United States and Britain found that they had little real support for military action. Much of Northern Europe was willing to support military action, and Australia contributed forces for such a contingency. Key members of the Security Council like China, France, and Russia opposed such action, however, as did many other members of the UN.

There was little support for such action in the Arab world, or from Southern Gulf allies, except for Kuwait. Some Southern Gulf states were willing to allow the United States and Britain to base forces. These nations included Bahrain, Kuwait, and Oman. Saudi Arabia, however, made it clear that it did not want the United States to use force unless there was a high probability that Saddam Hussein would be driven from power, and even those Southern Gulf states that reluctantly agreed to support the United States and British position felt that new strikes against Iraq could do as much harm as good. None believed that anything short of all-out war would drive Saddam from power, cripple his conventional military machine, or to target enough of his remaining equipment and facilities for the production of weapons of mass destruction to deny him the capability to proliferate.

These problems are illustrated by the attitudes of key countries in the region, attitudes that did not change significantly when Iraq provoked a nearly identical crisis in October, 1998:

- On February 17, 1998, Bahrain's Crown Prince Sheik Hamad bin Isa al-Khalifa said, "The first priority should be given to the diplomatic effort and a peaceful solution to the crisis, no matter what it takes, because we fear the other alternative in this confrontation will be no less than a catastrophe to this region, the Arab world, and the Middle East."

- Saudi Arabia—America's main partner in the Gulf War—refused access to its bases, and King Fahd, Crown Prince Abdullah, and Defense Minister Prince Sultan opposed the use of force. President Sheik Zaid bin Sultan al-Nahayan of the United Arab Emirates gradually went much further and stated that Iraqi President Saddam Hussein should be forgiven his mistakes and welcomed back into the Arab fold.

- Egypt—another critical partner in the Gulf War coalition—shifted its position towards steadily stronger opposition to the use of force. At the end of November, 1997, Osama el-Baz, the chief adviser to Egypt's President Mubarak, stated that, "As a member of the [United Nations] Security Council, Egypt is concerned with the development of the Iraqi problem.... Our purpose is to move matters in a direction that would guarantee—first—implementation of Security Council resolutions. Second—avoiding any worsening of the lot of the Iraqi people, and this requires avoiding as much as possible any military action.... We believe that the consequences of military action would do more harm than good."[80] By the time US and British strikes became a real possibility in February, 1998, Egypt's President Hosni Mubarak warned that the situation in the Arab world could deteriorate sharply if the United States attacks Iraq for failing to comply with weapons inspections: "I think things will become much more serious with air strikes.... This is very dangerous—I cannot stand against the whole weight of popular opinion.... You will not find one (Arab) leader who will say publicly we support the air strikes."

- Syria—which was a long-standing rival of Iraq and had also fought in the Coalition in 1991—expressed growing concern that so much attention should be paid to Iraq's efforts to proliferate while so little attention was given to Israel. In November, 1997, the leadership of the National Progressive Front (NPF), the ruling coalition led by the Ba'ath Party, issued a statement that

Any military action against Iraq will not solve the problem but will further complicate it, especially that justifications for such an action no longer exist.... The double standard policy adopted by some countries is wrong and will harm principles set for dealing among countries. It will also harm international organizations whose decisions should be compulsory.... Syria is keen to see the removal of all hardships imposed on the Iraqi people as a result of the implementation of sanctions.... Syria believes that Iraq's implementation of all UN Security Council resolutions will create the appropriate climate to remove these sanctions.[81]

By February 18, 1998, intensive Iraqi lobbying and growing Syrian resentment of the breakdown in the Arab-Israeli peace process led Syria's President Hafez al-Assad to take a much harder line. After separate telephone calls with Egyptian and Saudi Arabian leaders, Assad had Syria's official daily newspaper, *Tishreen*, issue a statement that,

It is important for all Arabs to realize that fragments of the military option will hit all without exception. Nothing but solidarity and unity among Arabs would allow them to counter these.... The military strike against Iraq hides evil schemes which in addition to Iraq are directed to harm the Arab and Islamic nations. The strike will serve no one but Israel and enemies of the Arab nation.

Iraq even sought Iranian support in ending sanctions and sent Iraqi Deputy President Taha Yassin Ramadan to Tehran on December 8 to the summit conference of the Organization of Islamic Countries. Iranian Vice President Hassan Habibi was at the airport to greet Ramadan, who was the most senior Iraqi to visit Iran since the beginning of the Iran-Iraq War. Iraq steadily improved its relations with Iran in the months that followed, and Iran too came to oppose any use of force in spite of the fact that Iraq had used chemical weapons in the Iran-Iraq War. Iran's President Mohammad Khatami told Iraq's visiting foreign minister that Baghdad should comply with UN resolutions to avoid possible US-led military strikes. Iranian television reported that, "The president ... asked Baghdad to implement all UN Security Council resolutions in order to deprive America of pretexts for any action."[82]

The Road to the Military Options in Desert Fox

The developments described in Table 10.2 did not deter Britain and the United States from deploying the forces necessary to take unilateral military action, and from making it clear that they were prepared to act if necessary. As Table 10.2 shows, the United States carried out a major military build-up in the Gulf, and would almost certainly have struck Iraq if UN Secretary General Kofi Annan had not brokered yet another last-minute deal.

Iraq only backed down, however, after it succeeded in undermining support for US and British military action to the point where it raised serious doubts about the credibility of any military action in the future. As the day-to-day chronology of developments shows, the political climate of 1998 was very different from that of previous years, and the United States and Britain became increasingly isolated with time.

The United States and Britain did not lack military options, but they did lack a political context in which military action had the necessary international support. "Sanctions fatigue" had reached the point where they needed much greater Iraqi provocation to gain broad Arab and UN support in using them. The chronology of Iraq's actions in Table 10.2 shows, however, that Iraq was far more sensitive to political issues than in previous years. The Iraqi leadership played out the crisis in ways that steadily improved its position and the support it got from key powers like China, France, and Russia.

Furthermore, even US military planners increasingly questioned whether the military benefits of such strikes would outweigh the political costs. It was clear that it would take hundreds of strikes to destroy those missile and dual-capable facilities for the production of weapons of mass destruction that the US could target. Many were near populated areas, and there was certain to be significant collateral damage. Crippling even a single Republican Guards division meant hundreds of more strikes and possibly a new major air battle with Iraq's ground-based air defenses. There was no prospect, however, that the United States could succeed in targeting more than a limited number of the facilities Iraq had been trying to conceal.

There was concern at many levels within the US government that the backlash from the breakdown in the Arab-Israeli peace process and Iraq's skillful political exploitation of the suffering of its own people meant that Saddam Hussein would obtain a political victory from US strikes, and might be able to exploit any popular suffering to further divide the Security Council.

As a result, the Iraqi regime won a significant political victory in terms of support for the easing of sanctions, more than doubled its receipts for the "oil for food" program, and got agreement on diplomatic measures that weakened UNSCOM. In the process, Iraq showed growing confidence that its strategy of attrition was winning the "war of sanctions." It also laid the groundwork for a political war of attrition over the sanctions issue that increasingly focused on ending or bypassing economic sanctions, and which allowed Iraq to create growing doubts that UNSCOM could continue to be effective.

MAKING "SANCTIONS FATIGUE" AND "OIL FOR FOOD" A FULL-SCALE POLITICAL BATTLE

While Iraq backed down to the extent it granted the UN access to its presidential sites, in February, 1998 it effectively "won" the crisis. It increased the divisions within the Security Council, greatly expanded the range of its support from Arab and other countries, and reduced the risk of future military action. Equally important, it levered the UN into agreeing to a $5.256 billion "oil for food" deal.

The new total was an increase of $3.2 billion over the $2 billion previously authorized. The agreement contained in UN Security Council Resolution 1153 more than doubled the cash Iraq would receive every six months. In fact, it potentially allowed Iraq to sell $10.5 billion a year of oil, which compares to average Iraqi annual oil exports of $11.5 billion (in 1998 dollars) during 1981–1989. The net cash flow to Iraq—after deductions for reparations and the cost of UNSCOM—will average about $3.5 billion every six months, or $7 billion a year, plus around $0.5 billion in legal exports to Jordan. This compares with $1.32 billion every six months under the prior agreement, or $2.64 billion a year.

The revised "oil for food" agreement offered Saddam vast new amounts of money to ease internal opposition and conflict. Although the sales and resulting imports were to be under tight UN control, there was no way to avoid Iraqi government control over the flow of many of the imports under the agreement and favoritism in giving "aid" to pro-Saddam groups and regions. Money is also fungible. The Iraqi regime could divert its existing cash flow to arms or proliferation, because the oil for food money provided new ways to meet civil needs. There is no way the UN can monitor every expense.

The expanded agreement involved a much wider range of imports than food and medicine, and it involved more oil exports than Iraq could handle with its current production capability, which can only ship about $4.1 billion worth every six months. Iraq has said it could not handle more than $4 billion worth of oil—equal to almost 2 million barrels per day (bpd) if the oil is sold for $15 a barrel.

Iraq's Oil Minister Amir Muhammad Rasheed stated that Iraq would be unable to export more than $4 billion worth of oil under the third six-month phase of its UN oil for food deal:

Iraq has not rejected the [new] resolution and it has acted positively toward it. . . . However, we have emphasized that we cannot export quantities more than what amounts to $4 billion during six months because of the production limitation . . . and also because of the deterioration of prices and the oil market. Iraq is negotiating with the United Nations for the supply of spare parts for the oil sector. Costs of spare parts and repairs would run to a few hundred million dollars (for) spare parts, chemicals, material required for wells' workover (and) for wet oil extraction treatment and demulsifiers.

Rasheed reported that Iraq was currently exporting 1.2 million bpd of crude oil and had a production capacity of 2.3 million bpd. This production capacity could be increased to 2.65 million bpd in two to three months if the UN agreed to supply Iraq with the spare parts its oil sector needed.

We are now exporting at an average of 1.2 million bpd because of the decline in oil prices to $11.5 a barrel. . . . Our present capacity is 2.65 million barrels a day, which we can achieve in two to three months if the necessary requirements for safe operations of our oil fields have been provided, and we will go up to three million bpd in another three months and to 3.5 million bpd after one year to go back to our production capacity before the aggression [the US-led Gulf War].

Rasheed also made it clear that "oil for food" would be used as a diplomatic weapon.

> We are now coordinating with the United Nations ... to provide the necessary spare parts, materials, and equipment for the oil sector under the memorandum of understanding. Our policy will continue that we give credit to friends who stand with us in our main battle to lift sanctions from the Iraqi people. ... We do this whether in contracting for the purchasing of our oil through the memorandum of understanding or through contracts for the development of our oil fields, which have not developed yet. ... We are continuing discussions with other international oil companies. ... We have reached very advanced stages in some of them.

Dividing the UN and Mobilizing the Arab World and Iran

It is hardly surprising that Iraq followed up on its "victory" by making every possible effort to continue to transform the crisis from a focus on its compliance with the terms of the UN cease-fire into a political crisis between Iraq and the US, Britain, and UNSCOM and sought to make the key issue the ending of all UN sanctions. Iraq worked with Russia, France, and several key Arab states like Egypt and the UAE to oppose any US use of force to ensure that Iraq would open up its "sensitive" sites, and to obtain support in its efforts to end sanctions.

It is clear from Table 10.3 that Saddam Hussein and the Iraqi ruling elite saw the growing divisions within the Security Council as a way of breaking out of sanctions by exploiting the growing level of "sanctions fatigue," even if this meant more hardships for the Iraqi people. Iraq made every possible effort to exploit the near breakdown in the Arab-Israeli peace process, and the resentment of US inaction in the Arab world. It attempted to obtain the support of Gulf states like the UAE, which were more concerned with the Iranian threat than with that from Iraq, and to exploit its vast potential market for imports and oil and gas development to win the support of Europe and major trading states. Throughout this process, the Iraqi leadership turned its own intransigence regarding "oil for food" and compliance with the terms of the cease-fire into charges that the United States, Britain, and the UN were responsible for the suffering of the Iraqi people.

One of the other striking aspects of the chronology in Table 10.3 is Iraq's tireless exploitation of the "big lie." Iraqi leaders like Tariq Aziz endlessly misstated the facts and repeated their denials of activities where UNSCOM had developed incontrovertible evidence. They expanded on their successful "divide and conquer" tactics of October, 1997, and went from attacking the United States to more general attacks on Butler and UNSCOM. They endlessly threatened new crises in an effort to increase "sanctions fatigue," and they issued a series of lies that ignored inconvenient realities like the fact that the Iraq-suggested technical review panels produced conclusions that were even more critical of Iraq than UNSCOM.

Table 10.3
"Oil For Food" and Ending Sanctions Become as Important as Proliferation

98–3-10: Scott Ritter leaves Iraq after inspecting sites without any problem. An official Iraqi newspaper, *al-Iraq*, says Ritter had been sent back to Iraq by the United States to harm a deal over weapons inspections. "Scott Ritter, the owner of a record full of manufactured crises, has returned with an American will to create a new crisis to harm the February agreement."

UN weapons experts announce that they will make their first visits to Iraq's "presidential sites" in about two weeks. Butler will go to Baghdad at about the same time as the experts start work. The visits will be conducted by UNSCOM inspectors and led by diplomat Jayantha Dhanapala. He will remain in Iraq for the first eight inspections and return to New York and appoint a deputy for subsequent visits. His report on inspections will be submitted to Butler. UNSCOM experts will be accompanied by at least two senior diplomats to the presidential compounds, which will be designated by Dhanapala. The diplomats will observe that the terms of the Feb. 23 accord, as well as detailed procedures, are respected and will report on "any matter they deem appropriate" to Dhanapala. The team "shall take into consideration any observations the Iraqi representative may wish to make regarding entry into a particular structure and then decide upon the appropriate course of action." The diplomats have been dubbed a "dignity police." They will almost certainly exclude US and British diplomats as most of the envoys will be drawn from a list of 100 Baghdad-based diplomats that Annan will compile. The first visits to all eight presidential compounds will be "baseline" surveys to set the groundwork for future inspections. The eight compounds are now said to be spread over 12 square miles (31.5 square km). They include 1,058 residences, palaces, warehouses, garages, and other buildings.

India's former UN Ambassador Prakash Shah says he will also be going to Iraq to set up his office by the end of the month. He is to serve as Annan's special representative in Baghdad and as a troubleshooter for all UN programs.

Chairman of the US Joint Chiefs of Staff Army, General Henry Shelton, says that 36,000 troops will remain in the Gulf region until Iraq complies with UN arms inspection demands. "We will make sure that we keep our forces here until such time that we see a trend that Iraq intends to comply fully. Our plans call for remaining deployed until such time when we are convinced that (Iraqi President) Saddam (Hussein) will comply. ... There are no constraints. We are prepared to stay as long as we need," Shelton said of the build-up in the Gulf. Shelton refused to disclose the exact size of the US military force in tiny Kuwait, which various Western military and diplomatic sources put at between 8,000 and 11,000 troops. This is "an operational issue which I prefer not to discuss. ...

Table 10.3 (continued)

	We have a sufficient number of troops on the ground here (from) the Army, Navy, Air Force and Marines to do the job.... We are trained and ready.... We are glad that thus far there has been a diplomatic solution to the current situation."
Air force and navy troops in the Persian Gulf get their first vaccinations against Anthrax. All 1.4 million US military men and women in uniform, as well as the 1 million in the reserves, will get the mandatory vaccinations over the coming months. Civilians working for the Pentagon in the Gulf also will get the inoculations.
98–3-11:	New UN Commissioner Jayantha Dhanapala arrives in Iraq.
President Clinton says the United States would consult Security Council members before any attack on Iraq, but insisted that it did not need UN approval to launch an attack. "We believe that the resolution gives us the authority to take whatever actions are necessary, but of course we would consult."
Ba'ath Party newspaper, *al-Thawra*, rejects conditions set by Kuwait for reconciliation: "Concerning the story of conditions, we advise the Kuwaiti rulers to forget them because it is a story of imagination and mirage." Iraq would accept "frank dialogue (with Iraq), but would not accept conditions.... We are not troubled with it (reconciliation) or desperate for it."
Several hundred Iraqis curse the United States at the funeral procession of 40 children Iraq said died because of shortages of medicine caused by UN sanctions.
The Patriotic Union of Kurdistan (PUK) says that it has obtained a copy of a decree in which the Baghdad government ordered the expulsion of 1,468 Kurdish families within a period of two months starting on March 15. It said the families could choose between migrating to the Arab lands south of Iraq, or move to the mainly Kurdish enclave of northern Iraq, in which case they would have to give up one family member to be held in detention by the government. An Iraqi opposition source says President Saddam Hussein's government has been deporting Kurds from its cities for some time, and many families have arrived in the northern Iraqi cities of Arbil and Sulaymaniyah.
98–3-12:	Iraq's deputy prime minister, Tariq Aziz, meets with Jayantha. Aziz reiterates Iraq's promise to provide access to weapons inspectors visiting the palaces, "taking into consideration the sovereignty and dignity of Iraq and its national security."
98–3-13:	Security Council's Iraqi sanctions committee approves plan to enable up to 22,000 Iraqis to make the pilgrimage to Mecca early next month, though it appeared uncertain whether Baghdad would accept it. Each Iraqi pilgrim should be allocated up to $2,000 from the UN "oil-for-food" program. This would make a total of up to $44 million, if the quota set by Saudi Arabia of 22,000 Iraqi pilgrims is filled. But Baghdad insists

Table 10.3 (continued)

	the money should be funneled through the Iraqi central bank, which would disburse it among the pilgrims, many of whom would fly to Saudi Arabia aboard Royal Jordanian Airline flights. This would be another exception to sanctions, which normally bar flights to and from Iraq.
98–3-14:	President Saddam Hussein urges Iraqi local officials to be more patient in their dealings with Kurds. "If we are weighing our treatment of Iraqis in Baghdad with silver, we should do that in Sulaimaniya and its outskirts and Arbil with gold or diamonds," said Saddam while talking to Iraqi officials near Kirkuk. But any Kurd who was reminded of his wrongdoing and did not correct his ways would be punished. "We shall punish anyone who goes off the road (the rule of the government in Baghdad) after we tell him he should avoid such deviation."
	Britain says it will provide $11 million in humanitarian assistance. Clare Short, Secretary of State for international development, says the aid will be directed through the UN and other international agencies. "The people of Iraq have suffered too much. Saddam manipulates the suffering of his people and uses it for propaganda. But we must do all we can to relieve their suffering. We are channeling our increased aid to organizations that can deliver food and medicine direct to the people in need." Britain had previously provided $4.9 million in aid, largely for removing land mines and assisting vulnerable groups.
	Iraq responds to a US Senate call for war crimes proceedings against President Saddam Hussein by proposing similar trials for President Clinton and other Western leaders. Iraq's National and Arab Front, a coalition of the ruling Ba'ath Party and other pro-government factions, says the Western leaders should be tried for "crimes against Iraq's people (by) causing the deaths of hundreds of thousands of children, elderly and women in Iraq." In addition to Clinton, the Front said leaders who should be prosecuted include former President Bush, former British Prime Minister Margaret Thatcher, Secretary of State Madeleine Albright, and American defense secretaries.
98–3-15:	The United Nations Children's Fund, UNICEF, in cooperation with Iraq's Health Ministry, launches a nationwide campaign to immunize some 3.5 million Iraqi children against polio. Eric Falt, spokesman for the UN humanitarian coordinator in Iraq, says the campaign will cover all children under five years old. "Iraqi children under five represent 15 percent of the overall population or some 3.5 million children." Falt said that a comprehensive survey carried out by UNICEF in 1997 showed that up to 1 million Iraqi children were suffering from malnutrition. This figure represented an increase of 71 percent compared to 1991. UNICEF will carry out a nutritional survey to evaluate the impact of an oil-for-food deal signed with the UN.
	Iraqi officials say that an estimated 1.5 million children have died needlessly in the past seven years, since the imposition of sanctions. Health Ministry sources say hospitals in Iraq are operating at half their normal

Table 10.3 (continued)

capacity because of the shortage of medical supplies. Many are forced to turn away all but emergency cases.

The United States expresses satisfaction with an accord opening Iraq presidential compounds to inspectors, but said Washington wants proof that chemical and biological weapons were destroyed. ''I think as far as the United States is concerned, the procedures are working out in a satisfactory form,'' Defense Secretary William Cohen tells CNN. ''We have gained access to those so-called presidential sites and sensitive sites that have been off limits by virtue of Saddam Hussein's declarations for the past six or seven years. . . . So what we have to do is insist, before there can be any relief in sight for Saddam Hussein or the Iraqi people as far as the sanctions are concerned, that they must produce proof positive. . . . They have failed to do so, and until such time as they do, we cannot say there has been compliance. . . . To the extent that any evidence would continue to document his past activities, that would lend itself to that, then I certainly would support that. . . . But I think the key focus that we have to have is what takes place from this point on. Is he going to fully comply?''

98–3-16: Iraq's Foreign Ministry holds talks with Turkish officials in Ankara to improve ties. The Iraqi delegation, headed by Saad al-Faisel. *Nabdh al-Shabab* (Pulse of Youth), a newspaper owned by President Saddam Hussein's eldest son, Uday, reports that Ankara had expressed a desire to improve ties between the two countries. ''Turkey has stressed that it intended to raise the level of its diplomatic mission in Baghdad from a charge d'affaires to an ambassador.'' Iraq has accused Turkey of being a US lackey in the region because it lets aircraft of the US-led alliance use Turkish bases to protect rebel Kurds from possible attacks by Iraqi armed forces, and for periodically sending Turkish troops across the border into northern Iraq in pursuit of Kurdish rebels. Iraq has also accused Turkey of stealing the region's water by building dams and canals on the Euphrates River.

New Zealand extends deployment of special forces commandos seconded for a possible attack on Iraq. Prime Minister Jenny Shipley says New Zealand ''remained fully convinced of the continuing need for the Multinational Coalition in the Gulf and has agreed to extend the deployment of its contribution to the force.'' The troops will initially remain in Kuwait until the end of April. ''Any extension beyond that [April] date will be considered at the appropriate time.'' Two RNZAF Orion search and reconnaissance aircraft positioned on the island of Diego Garcia will return to New Zealand, but will remain declared as part of the Coalition force to be called on if needed.

The United States welcomes recent efforts by Middle Eastern countries, particularly Iran, to block Iraqi smuggling of petroleum products. The US Energy Information Administration (EIA) says Iraq has been smuggling up to 100,000 barrels a day in crude oil and other petroleum prod-

Table 10.3 (continued)

	ucts, which has provided the country with $700 million a year in revenues. Iraq's major smuggling routes were to Turkey by truck, to India and Pakistan along the Persian Gulf Coast, to Iran across the Fao Peninsula with barges, and to Dubai with small tankers.
	The US State Department says Kurds in Halabja are still suffering much higher rates of serious disease and birth defects. In a statement marking the anniversary of the attack ten years earlier, the spokesman says that even though 5,000 civilians were killed and 10,000 injured, the Iraqi regime has never expressed remorse.
	The UN agrees to make arrangements to monitor the storage and use in Iraq of spare parts for an oil pipeline from Kirkuk, in Iraq, to Yumurtalik, in Turkey. No maintenance work has been carried out on the pipeline for several years, but it is being heavily used to transport oil to the Turkish terminal under the oil-for-food program. The committee had previously approved a year-old Turkish request for the parts to be supplied by Turkey's Tekfen company. But after the United States urged that the parts be stored in Turkey and transported to Iraq as needed, Iraq objected that this was illogical and impractical. The UN secretariat has now made arrangements for the storage and monitoring of the parts to be carried out by a Netherlands-based company called Saybolt, appointed by the UN in 1996 to oversee the export of Iraqi oil under the oil-for-food program. Iraq is required to export the larger share of the oil through the Kirkuk-Yumurtalik pipeline and the rest through its Mina al-Bakr terminal on the Gulf. This is monitored by experts from Saybolt.
98–3-17:	Iraq urges the European Union to ignore British suggestions that aid could be channeled more directly to the Iraqi people, bypassing their government. A Foreign Ministry spokesman says aid should be kept within the framework of Iraq's oil-for-food deal with the UN until Gulf War trade sanctions are lifted. "The world community knows full well that the Iraqi government is cooperating fully, and at the highest level, with the General-Secretariat of the UN to implement the oil-for-food agreement.... The world community also knows very well that during the whole life of the UN deal, the British government has been uniquely helpful to the US administration in impeding the implementation of contracts Iraq has concluded."
	The KDP says Iran has tortured to death one of its members after arresting him and 19 others for allegedly spying against the Islamic state. "Twenty Kurdistan Democratic Party (KDP) officials living in Iran have been arrested.... The detainees are being mistreated and tortured.... as a result, one of the detained was murdered while in custody."
98–3-19:	Richard Butler says he sees a "new spirit" of cooperation from that nation. "Last week we went to some places that Iraq decided to declare sensitive. We had sent a very tough team in to have a look at those places. In the past we'd been blocked. We met with a degree of coop-

Table 10.3 (continued)

eration that I think justifies figuring that maybe there is now a new spirit out there."

Iraq abandons efforts to secure the approval of the UN sanctions committee for up to 22,000 Iraqis to make the pilgrimage to Mecca next month, saying it is too late to make arrangements. Iraqis who want to perform the Moslem pilgrimage in Mecca next month will have to travel to Saudi Arabia via land and by means of 40 buses.

98–3-20: Richard Butler promises Iraq that his team will rapidly complete its work if it is told the whole truth about Baghdad's weapons of mass destruction. "Iraq has the opportunity now, the ball at its feet, to tell us everything that it can about its chemical and biological weapons. . . . I will make a promise in return—if they give us the truth, we will verify in lightning speed and we can be finished with all of this. . . . I would think around about something like a further one year could see us through this job. . . . The basic truth is that Iraq could have been finished with all of this business years ago if it had begun by giving us all of the materials and the truth of the matter. . . . If they give us that full cooperation, they will not find that we are slow. . . . What's different? We will be observed by some diplomats. And that's fine, that's part of the key that unlocked these sites. But make no mistake about it, we'll be doing our job in the normal way."

Iraqi UN representative Nizar Hamdoon says Iraq will not reduce its oil production even if OPEC and non-OPEC nations decide to curtail theirs. "I don't think it's connected because we are a different package." Iraq is expected to produce just under 2 million barrels per day of crude in March, including about 1.37 million barrels per day earmarked for export, according to UN overseers. "Even that figure [$4 billion in sales over six months], unless some money is allocated to repair the damage in the industry, we don't think can be reached . . . [we need] somewhere between $250 million to $300 million to accomplish at least the current figure we are talking about, the $4 billion" in sales over six months.

98–3-21: Iraqi officials say Iraq could raise its oil exports by at least 700,000 barrels per day within six months if the UN approves urgent repairs to crude facilities. Iraq is preparing to increase output from its present capacity of 2.3 million barrels per day to earn the extra sums approved under an enhanced oil-for-food-program that allows Baghdad to sell crude to buy humanitarian supplies. The sales limit has been raised to $5.2 billion in every six months from $2 billion currently, but technical problems and a low oil price severely restrict Baghdad's capacity to increase revenue. Iraqi industry officials told the Monaco Energy Summit they could boost production to 2.6 million barrels per day within three months if they could import oil treatment chemicals, and within another three months could hit 3.0 million barrels per day. With domestic consumption accounting for some 650,000 barrels per day, export levels would be around 2.35 million barrels per day. But experts expect actual

Table 10.3 (continued)

	sales to plateau around 2 million barrels per day until extensive repairs restore to operation the second pipeline from northern Iraq to the Turkish port of Ceyhan, where Iraq's Kirkuk grade currently loads. Abd al-Tikriti, director-general of Iraq's oil ministry, says Baghdad has a three-part, 10-year plan to raise output to 6 million barrels per day. Phase 1 would take output to 3.5 million barrels per day by improving current operations, while Phase 2 would see 10 new fields developed in partnership with foreign oil companies. Phase 3 would lease nine unexplored blocks in the Western Desert to foreign prospectors. Ambitious downstream upgrades, including building a new 150,000 barrels per day refinery, and plans to capitalize on huge gas reserves by building pipelines to Turkey and on into European markets were also on the list, which Iraq estimates has a value of $30 billion. Some 60 foreign companies are reported to be seeking deals in Iraq. Oil Minister Amer Rashid says Iraq is "very near" to signing with Elf, Total, and other European and Asian companies and would close the deals when the political environment was right. Rashid refuses to confirm that it is Iraq's policy to delay deals until after sanctions were lifted to secure better terms, but says such a policy "had merits."
98–3-22:	Prakash Shah, Annan's new envoy to Baghdad, states, "We have been briefed to watch developments in relations between Iraq and the UN and to help avert any escalation of crisis that might develop. . . . It is a question of trying to see the objectives of the UN and its activities here which is trying to bring about peace and peaceful solutions to all questions. . . . I am here to stay for about six months as initiated by the appointment." Sanctions imposed on Iraq for its 1990 invasion of Kuwait would not stay "for ever." The Iraqi paper *Babel*, owned by Saddam's son, Uday, publishes an article stating, "Welcome to Baghdad, Mr. Chairman of the Special Commission once again. . . . Butler is ready to forget a lot of things in order to maintain his special ties with American officials. . . . Before [UN Secretary-General Kofi Annan's] visit [last month] to Iraq the American administration was keen to make sure that Butler maintains his post." Butler is due to meet Iraq's Deputy Prime Minister Tariq Aziz, and other Iraqi officials on Monday and Tuesday and to spend one day with UNSCOM teams before the leaves on Thursday. Richard Butler states, "I am very glad to be here particularly after the agreement was signed between [UN] Secretary-General Mr. Kofi Annan and Iraq. . . . I think the agreement has created a new spirit of cooperation. We are being shown a new degree of cooperation. I welcome it. I hope it continues. If it does we can do our part of this job . . . without the passage of too much time," Butler told a news conference in Baghdad. "I have a sense of a new spirit prevailing in our relationship. . . . The degree of cooperation that Iraq has been showing the commission in all fields . . . is very high and very welcome. . . . I have listened care-

Table 10.3 (continued)

	fully through the noise—what could be called propaganda—and we have adjusted some ways in which we do our work. . . . I will meet the Deputy Prime Minister tomorrow and will offer him my professional commitment to this new spirit and to getting this job done, and I assume he will do the same to me.''
	Water treatment plant inaugurated in Baghdad, which will supply a quarter of a million people after rehabilitation work is carried out with UN support.
98–3-23:	Butler holds first talks in Baghdad since crisis over inspections. Butler meet Iraq's Deputy Prime Minister, Tariq Aziz, for discussions which were expected to cover plans for UN inspectors to visit eight presidential sites at the center of last month's crisis. Iraqi television shows Aziz smiling as he shakes hands with Butler. The two men meet for around two hours. Butler holds an evening session with Iraqi Oil Minister, Lieutenant-General Amir Muhammad Rasheed.
	Oil Minister Amir Muhammad says Iraq's eight ''presidential sites'' would need only two weeks to inspect. ''Work can be achieved in two weeks unless they [UNSCOM] want additional verification of some data which needs some more time,'' Rasheed was quoted in *Nabdh al-Shabab*.
	Iraq's parliament declares that President Clinton and George Bush are war criminals. The National Assembly votes unanimously for the two men to stand trial for the suffering caused by sanctions imposed after its 1990 invasion of Kuwait and on the 1991 Gulf War to evict its forces from the Emirate. The Assembly sets up a committee ''to follow up this matter in order to help send these people to trial.'' The Assembly also demands that ''the crime of imposing oppressive sanctions on the Iraqi people by the United States of America, and a mass extermination of the children, women and elderly of Iraq, be considered a war crime.'' The vote follows a two-day session called in response to a US Senate resolution earlier this month branding Iraqi President Saddam Hussein a war criminal and calling for an international tribunal to be set up to indict him. The tribunal's purpose would be ''indicting, prosecuting, and imprisoning Saddam Hussein and other Iraqi officials who are responsible for crimes against humanity, genocide, and other violations of international law,'' the Senate resolution said.
	Iraq criticizes Doha conference of Islamic states' foreign ministers for urging Baghdad to cooperate with UN weapons inspectors and said Moslems should focus instead on the suffering of ordinary Iraqis.
98–3-24:	*The Sun*, a tabloid newspaper, reports that Britain's air and sea ports are put on alert to the threat of Anthrax being smuggled into the country by Iraq. The all-ports warning follows threat by Iraqi President Saddam Hussein to flood Britain with the toxin disguised inside ''duty free'' bottles of alcohol, cosmetics, cigarette lighters, and perfume sprays. Prime Minister Tony Blair's office confirms the document on which the story is

Table 10.3 (continued)

based, but does not confirm the date of the alert. Blair spokeswoman says government had circulated an all-ports warning, but there was "no evidence that this plot has been implemented, simply that a threat may have been made ... Obviously that has to be taken seriously, but we do not believe there is cause for alarm." Junior Home Office Minister Mike O'Brian tells the BBC, "We do not believe that Anthrax has been brought in Britain, there's no evidence for it, and we're not expecting any imminently. ... There's no imminent or specific threat to Britain." Iraqi officials dismiss charges as "silly and baseless" British government suggestions that Baghdad was planning to smuggle lethal Anthrax into Britain. "The State Department has no comment on whether America was also a target. A spokesman for the Iraqi Ministry of Information and Culture says Iraq has no weapons of mass destruction and was cooperating fully with UN arms inspectors.

Nasser Hindawi, a chemist who helped pioneer Iraq's biological warfare program, is reported to have been arrested in Iraq while preparing to flee the country. Nizar Hamdoon says Hindawi is in jail and Baghdad had informed the UN earlier this month. The UN hoped to interview Hindawi in circumstances in which he could speak freely, but Iraqi secret police agents attend all meetings between UN investigators and local scientists, and Hindawi may not be available. A *New York Times* report quotes Hamdoon as saying Hindawi had been found with military documents which should have been given to the Iraqi government, that he had a forged passport when he was arrested and was about to leave Iraq illegally. UNSCOM says Baghdad had recently handed over documents said to have been taken from Hindawi.

18 diplomats appointed by the UN to accompany inspectors in examining the eight palace compounds arrive in Baghdad, led by Jayantha Dhanapala. Butler ends two days of talks in Iraq saying his talks with Iraqi Deputy Prime Minister Tariq Aziz reflected major changes. "January was tough. That's for sure. Today was a light-year different." Butler said progress was made towards accounting for missile warheads and chemical agents Iraq says it has destroyed. "Today it was just flowers from both sides," said UNSCOM political adviser Gustavo Flauvinen, adding that both sides complimented each other on the trouble-free inspections earlier this month led by UNSCOM inspector Scott Ritter. Butler stated, "I don't think you will have to wait for long" for inspections of presidential palaces. He said in verifying Iraq's claims it had destroyed all stocks and precursors to produce the chemical agent VX, and warheads carrying biological or chemical payloads. "We charted a way forward where in a reasonably short time we might be able to get to the bottom of those issues if Iraq shows this degree of cooperation," Butler said.

98–3-25: Iraq says it will allow UN inspectors to meet Nasser Hindawi. "If the biological team wants to meet him, it can do so. The right of UNSCOM will not be affected by his detention." Butler says his inspectors had

Table 10.3 (continued)

	interviewed Nasser Hindawi a year ago and that he had not yet decided whether to meet him again.
	Security Council agrees unanimously to allow Iraq to sell about $400 million worth of oil in the second half of the current six-month "oil-for-food" period that it failed to sell in the first half that ended on March 4. The shortfall was caused by a five-week delay by Iraq in shipping oil after the official Dec. 5, 1997, start of the current six-month phase.
98–3-26:	UN inspectors visit an Iraqi "presidential site" the first time in seven years. They visit the Radwaniyah presidential complex in west Baghdad. UNSCOM reports that all baseline visits to inspect and survey the eight presidential sites in detail for possible future inspections are expected to be completed by around April 5. UN inspectors will conduct detailed internal and external surveys of the sites while a helicopter surveyed them from the air. Butler says, "We will enter the presidential sites very, very soon and we will do so with our full rights."
	US Ambassador Richardson says, "So far, the inspections of presidential sites, of sensitive sites, have gone well. We are pleased that the secretary-general's agreement is being implemented. . . . The real test will be compliance over an extended period of time. . . . We want to see a consistent pattern of inspections completed."
	Nearly 2,000 Iraqi Moslems leave for Haj in Saudi Arabia in a convoy of 45 buses on the 24-hour journey to Mecca. Endowment Minister Abdul-Muneim Ahmed Saleh says Iraq had to limit its number of pilgrims this year to 3,000 because of financial constraints caused by sanctions. Iraq can send up to 22,000 pilgrims to Mecca under quotas set by the Organization of the Islamic Conference.
98–3-27:	Global fall in petroleum prices drives Iraq to sign 14 new oil contracts to meet its $2 billion limit as part of the oil-for-food deal. The contracts raise to 48 the number of contracts signed under the current six-month stage of the plan. Iraq has been permitted since December, 1996 to sell $2 billion worth of oil every six months. During the first six-month period, Iraq exported a total of 121 million barrels of oil. The volume sold rose to 127 million barrels during the second six-month stage as oil prices fell. Starting in June, Iraq will be permitted to sell $5.2 billion in oil.
	UN weapons experts, accompanied by senior diplomats, end second day of inspections at an Iraqi presidential site.
98–3-28:	Iraq calls on citizens to report information on Iraqis believed missing or detained during the fighting which forced Baghdad's troops out of neighboring Kuwait seven years ago. "The Human Rights Committee at the National Assembly appeals to citizens with information or documents on Iraqis missing in action or detained in Kuwait during the historic showdown, the Mother of all Battles," stated the Iraqi News Agency (INA).
	Iraq's justice minister conveys Saddam Hussein's thanks to United Arab Emirates President Sheik Zaid bin Sultan al-Nahayan for calling for a

Table 10.3 (continued)

	diplomatic solution to the recent crisis between the UN and Iraq. "The Iraqi leadership and the Iraqi people value the honorable and supportive position of the United Arab Emirates with the Iraqi people," During the meeting, Sheik Zaid urged Iraq to "continue complete cooperation with the United Nations to hasten lifting the suffering of the brotherly Iraqi people, who have been led into a tragic situation by the embargo."
98–3-29:	Secretary-General Kofi Annan arrives in Moscow for talks with President Boris Yeltsin on Iraq and other issues.
	Central Bank Governor Isam Hweish predicts Iraq's currency will make strong gains on the back of increased imports under the oil for food deal. "The exchange rate of the Iraqi dinar will tremendously recover during the coming few days.... I recommended people in 1995 in a TV interview to get rid of their hard currency and my advice materialized.... Those who do not exchange their dollar for 1,300 Iraqi dinars will have to exchange them with a lower rate.... Iraq's exchange rate will improve in proportion to the increase in the volume of our imports, which would be realized in the light of the third phase of the memorandum of understanding." The dinar, which slumped to as low as 3,000 to the dollar in 1995, soared to 400 in early 1996 when Iraq agreed to a UN plan allowing it to sell $2 billion worth of oil every six months and to use most of the proceeds to buy food and medicine.
	First Syrian minister to visit Iraq in nearly two decades arrives in Baghdad, saying he was on a humanitarian mission to ease the plight of sanction-hit Iraqis. Health Minister Iyad Shatti arrives with 12 trucks of food and medicine to take part in a Syrian-Iraqi health week. "Our mission today is a humanitarian mission.... Economic relations have started to take their natural course, relations in health have (also) started to take their natural course.... Time will tell. Relations, God willing, will be satisfactory."
98–3-30:	UNSCOM has now entered six of eight palaces. Secretary General Annan says Iraq has so far showed a willingness to fulfill an accord he signed last month on weapons inspections. "I think the record so far regarding Iraqi implementation is good. The inspectors have been able to continue their work unimpeded." Annan says after meeting Russian Foreign Minister Primakov, "I hope that this cooperation will continue into the future and for the longer run." Yeltsin tells Annan, "I am particularly impressed how you and I played out the Iraqi game together."
	Jayanatha Dhanapala, head of the diplomatic corps accompanying UN inspectors, calls Iraq's cooperation "positive." He states that, "Fifty percent of our job is done.... I believe in the next week we should be able to complete the visits to all eight presidential sites."
	UN chief weapons inspector Butler tells the Security Council that Iraq needs to be forthcoming on its chemical weapons projects and he would organize another technical meeting on the deadly nerve agent VX. In a

Table 10.3 (continued)

	report on his talks in Baghdad, Butler emphasizes the new "spirit of cooperation" in carrying out arms inspections since the Feb. 23 agreement signed with Iraqi leaders by Secretary-General Kofi Annan, but says he told Iraq's Deputy Prime Minister Tariq Aziz that his commission was still trying to verify that Baghdad had not produced VX on an industrial scale or prepared it for use in weapons delivery systems. Butler reports that Aziz responded by challenging the methodology used by the commission to reach that assessment. "He (Aziz) could not accept that because Iraq had possessed the necessary equipment and achieved a high level of expertise in the production of other chemical weapons, this necessarily led to the same conclusion in respect of VX." Aziz said Iraq had procured "important quantities" of VX precursors or ingredients, but it had not succeeded in producing them on a scale suitable for military use. The UNSCOM special team reported in February that Iraq had the know-how, equipment, and possibly the ingredients to manufacture as much as 200 metric tons of VX. Butler and Aziz did not discuss biological weapons, where the commission has the largest gaps, because of meetings being held on the subject in Vienna. They also agree on a further technical evaluation meeting on missile warheads, probably at the end of April. UNSCOM maintains that there are discrepancies between the commission's documentation and the warheads probably at the end of April. UNSCOM maintains that there are discrepancies between the commission's documentation and the warheads Iraq said it destroyed unilaterally. Butler also said issues concerning the indigenous production of missile engines and a full accounting of missile propellants needed to be resolved.
98–3-31:	Bahrain's Crown Prince, Sheik Hamad bin Isa al-Khalifa, held talks on Tuesday with visiting Iraqi Justice Minister Shabib al-Maliki. Sheik Hamad welcomed Iraq's "positive cooperation" with the UN to implement the weapons inspection agreement signed last month.
98–4-1:	Iraq tells UN technical team it needs a total of $300 million to repair its sanctions-hit oil industry.
	Iraq asks for all the new money under the expanded oil-for-food program to go for humanitarian goods, with nothing withheld for war reparations. Currently, 30 percent is set aside to pay reparations to Kuwaitis and other for damages incurred during Iraq's seven-month occupation. In addition, 5 percent goes to cover UN expenses in Iraq, including the activities of UN weapons inspectors who must certify that Iraq has eliminated its weapons of mass destruction. After these deductions, Iraq nets about $1.32 billion every six months for food and medicine.
98–4-2:	UN weapons experts and senior diplomats start inspections of the last two of Iraq's presidential sites.
	Iraqi newspaper says Iran will release 6,000 Iraqi prisoners of the 1980–1988 Iraq-Iran War.

Table 10.3 (continued)

UN chief arms inspector Richard Butler says his teams will remain in Iraq for the foreseeable future, even if Baghdad accounts for all its suspected weapons of mass destruction. "If the point of your question is to foresee a day where inspections will end, that day is simply not visible and Iraq knows it. ... When we finish the disarmament process, we will be continuing with the ongoing monitoring process. ... What you should understand is that the process has two parts. One is disarmament and the other is ongoing monitoring. The disarmament part can be brought to an end, [but we must] monitor, to be sure that they are not recreating those weapons. Inspection is an important part of monitoring and we already have some 300 sites in Iraq under ongoing monitoring. ... Inspection is one of the several tools that we use to achieve (our) task. There's been too much focus on inspection as a phenomenon, an end in itself, in the last five-six month period of crisis. ... We must differentiate, as Ritter has been doing, between the initial inspection and the monitoring process. We're not introducing any new element into the discussion this morning. ... That's been there, been agreed to by Iraq for a number of years and is part of the cease-fire agreement. It always was a progression that moved from more intimate inspection to the monitoring process."

$3.5 million worth of spare parts for Iraqi crop spraying helicopters on their way to Baghdad. UN spokesman Eric Falt says, "For the previous season, the spraying campaign was estimated by the Ministry of Agriculture to have covered only 22 percent of the affected." He reports that nearly 5 million tons of food and commodities have arrived in Iraq since the beginning of the deal, but that "there are still deficiencies associated with the nutritional content of the (food) ration as well as the quantity provided."

98-4-3: Britain withdraws the aircraft carrier it sent to the Gulf at the height of the recent Iraqi crisis and sends four extra Tornado aircraft to join the existing force of eight Tornadoes in Kuwait which are better suited to operating in the extreme heat of the coming summer months, it said. British Defense Secretary George Robertson says it is too soon to wind down activity in the area. "Saddam has not yet provided the evidence we need to be sure that he has destroyed all his weapons of mass destruction. Given his track record, it is therefore too soon to relax our vigilance and reduce our military capability in the Gulf."

UN weapons inspectors and diplomats end their first round of inspections of Iraq's highly sensitive presidential sites and leave Baghdad. Iraq's Deputy Prime Minister Tariq Aziz, praises the visits to the presidential sites as a "triumph for the truth over falsehood. ... The group's visit has verified Iraq's credibility and exposed the allegations of America and Britain and their elements in the UN Special Commission [charged with disarming Iraq]. ... If we review the huge fuss made by senior US and British officials over these sites before signing the accord ... and compare that fuss with the current situation ... and after the conclusion of

Table 10.3 (continued)

	the visit, we would notice the great difference between those lies and the truth.''
98-4-5:	Sheik Mohammed bin Rashid al-Maktoum, defense minister of the United Arab Emirates, says in an interview that Iran and Iraq pose no security threat to his country. ''We are under no danger from Iran nor from Iraq . . . Gulf security is the responsibility of Gulf nations in the first degree and the responsibility of friendly Arab states in the second degree.''
	Iraq thanks Syrian President Hafez al-Assad for his stand on its recent crisis with the UN over arms inspections.
	Iranian Foreign Minister Kamal Kharrazi says Iran and Iraq have agreed to exchange all remaining prisoners of war captured during their 1980–1988 war, and that the two countries had reached a deal allowing Iranian pilgrims to visit Shi'ite holy sites in Iraq.
98-4-6:	UN envoy Prakash Shah, the top UN official in Baghdad, says successful completion of the first round of weapons inspections of Iraqi presidential sites has opened a ''new chapter in the relations between the United Nations and Iraq. . . . There was a great deal of a credibility gap in terms of Iraq and the UN before, that's why it ended up in a situation that might have led to use of force. The memorandum of understanding was able to avoid use of military force . . . The visits . . . have gone on well, there has been a remarkable degree of understanding, cooperation, and flexibility shown. . . . If Mr. Butler feels that UNSCOM's work will be finished within one year, I think it is something that all of us must pay a lot of attention to. This is a decision that will have to be taken on the basis of this initial visit, and I think you would need to wait for the report of this initial visit to be presented to the Secretary General and then to the Security Council both by UNSCOM as well as the commissioner that has been appointed Mr. [Jayanatha] Dhanapala as the head of the diplomats' group. . . . What [visits] they will be, when they will be, and where they will be, or how many, will be a decision that will depend upon the report of the initial visit.''
	Russian Foreign Ministry praises Iraq for cooperating with UN weapons experts during inspections of eight presidential sites, and issued a veiled criticism of the United States over the crisis. ''The results of the inspections offer further, clear confirmation of the correctness of the policy of using diplomacy to settle the recent dangerous crisis over Iraq, which made the whole world tense for several weeks. . . . There is a pertinent question—was it necessary to heat up the situation so much? It is obvious the policy of constructive cooperation with Baghdad has had the necessary effect, above all as far as the task of eliminating weapons of mass destruction in Iraq is concerned.'' Foreign Ministry statement says the cooperation over the eight presidential sites set an example which should help speed up the process of completing weapons inspections. The next step should then be to consider lifting the UN oil embargo on Iraq.

Table 10.3 (continued)

98–4-7:	Iraq and Iran finish repatriating more than 5,500 prisoners of war, including an Iranian pilot shot down over Iraq at the outset of the eight-year war in September, 1980. The International Committee of the Red Cross (ICRC) reports it is the biggest repatriation since 1990; and most of the freed prisoners had been in captivity for over 15 years. "Between 2 and 7 April 1998, 5,584 Iraqi prisoners of war held in Iran and three Iranian prisoners of war, as well as 316 other Iranians held in Iraq were repatriated under the auspices of the International Committee of the Red Cross."
	Iraqis claim suffering as the Moslem world celebrated Eid al-Adha feast. UN officials in Baghdad say the country has been hit hard by the sanctions imposed after Iraq invaded Kuwait in 1990, and the harshest hit have been the children. Prakash Shah, the top UN official in Baghdad who took up his post two weeks ago, states, "There are a lot of figures available. More than a million children suffer from malnutrition, and the hospitals are totally devoid of equipment and medicines that are necessary to deal with chronic diseases. . . . Chronic diseases are spreading, and there are new diseases that have been witnessed by the authorities here including WHO [World Health Organization]. Education is another area that has suffered extremely badly."
	Iraqi Parliament Speaker Saadoun Hammadi says Iraq will strictly adhere to the agreement to allow arms inspectors full access to Iraq's presidential sites. Hammadi, addressing an Interparliamentary Union conference in Namibia, also says shortages of foods and medicine as a result of the sanctions have caused more than 1 million deaths, and that Iraq should be allowed to sell oil freely now under the terms of Paragraph 22 of the Security Council Resolution 687 as a stepping-stone to lifting the sanctions.
98–4-8:	Butler's biannual report on Iraq's prohibited weapons programs, due on April 11, is delayed by about a week to include details of the recent inspection by UN teams of so-called Iraqi presidential sites and information about recent technical evaluation meetings in Vienna at which UN, Iraqi, and other experts discussed Iraq's biological warfare program.
98–4-9:	UN report says Iraq is still failing to provide a full account of its biological warfare program and may still be trying to deceive UN weapons inspectors.
	Experts from the International Atomic Energy Agency report that Iraq has met its obligation to the UN to provide information about its secretive nuclear program. In the past six months, IAEA experts found no new evidence of nuclear weapons during 211 inspections, according to a new semiannual report on Iraq's nuclear capabilities. Before that, the report noted, Baghdad had tried to obtain material for nuclear weapons from a foreigner and failed to turn over documents to support its claim that it had abandoned its hidden nuclear program.

Table 10.3 (continued)

98-4-10: Iraq claims that its infant mortality rate has risen nearly fifteen-fold from 450 to 6,500 a month since the embargo began in 1990, despite an improvement in the flow of humanitarian aid since the start of 1998.

Iraqi Parliament Speaker Saadoun Hammadi, heading Iraq's delegation to an Interparliamentary Union conference in Namibia, dismisses as lies Kuwaiti charges that Iraqi is still holding Kuwaiti prisoners, and accuses Kuwait of trying to keep UN sanctions clamped on Baghdad. "Kuwait, by capitalizing on this case and turning it from an issue of missing people to an issue of captives, wants to lengthen the duration of the tyrannical embargo imposed against Iraq."

98-4-11: Iraq's parliament rejects an invitation to attend a London conference to work out ways to speed up the delivery of humanitarian goods under the UN oil-for-food program. Britain had called a meeting of aid organizations and others for April 20–21. Iraqi lawmaker Bahir Jamil says, "The conference is an attempt to dominate (Iraq), including its northern region, so it will naturally worsen the plight of people instead of easing it. The British and US governments have contributed to the deaths of many Iraqi citizens so we cannot depend on them now to help our people."

Iraqi Information Minister Hamam Abdel-Khaliq says there is no need to discuss the oil-for-food program because it was proceeding smoothly with up to 150 UN observers monitoring the distribution of humanitarian supplies throughout the country.

Max van der Stoel said in his report to the annual session of the UN Human Rights Commission in Geneva that, "It is highly probable that more than 1,500 summary, arbitrary, or extrajudicial executions have been carried out throughout the year." Some of those reportedly shot, hanged, or electrocuted had been sentenced to death for plotting against Iraq's government or its officials. A disproportionate number of Iraq's minority Shiites and Kurds were among those killed. Information from several sources, including lists of names, indicates that hundreds of prisoners have been executed at Abu Ghraib and Radwaniyah prisons since last August, the report said. It did not provide the names. The executions apparently increased after President Saddam Hussein's younger son, Qusay, visited Abu Ghraib in November, Van der Stoel said. Qusay is in charge of Iraq's security apparatus.

98-4-12: *Al-Thawra Daily*, organ of the ruling Baath Party, says Baghdad expects UN Chief Kofi Annan to issue a positive report soon on the first round of weapons inspections of Iraq's so-called presidential sites. "The most important result of these visits is that the team did not find in the presidential sites none of what the American and British governments claimed was . . . this was decisive proof of Iraq's credibility and the lying of these two governments which wanted from all their claims to create a pretext to undertake a new military aggression against this struggling country."

98-4-13: Iraqis accuse the United States of genocide against their children and bury 29 infants they said died from shortages of medicine caused by UN

Table 10.3 (continued)

	sanctions. Iraqi officials say the infant mortality rate has risen sharply to 6,500 a month this year from 450 before the stringent economic sanctions were imposed on Iraq after its 1990 invasion of Kuwait. Parliament Speaker Saadoun Hammadi says that 1.5 million Iraqis had died from shortages of food and medicine since 1990. He put the average monthly infant mortality rate at 7,500.
	The IAEA says that Iraq has complied with all requirements to declare and destroy its nuclear weapons capability.
98-4-15:	UN arms experts state that no weapons were found by diplomats and UN inspectors during their initial survey of the 1,058 buildings inside the so-called presidential compounds, from March 26 to April 3, but also says, "It was clearly apparent that all sites had undergone extensive [changes] ... Iraq's explanation for this was that such measures were taken in anticipation of a military strike.... This makes follow-on missions more important." They warn that Baghdad may try to restrict return visits to President Saddam Hussein's palaces. This warning is contained in a report, sent to the Secretary-General, which is not yet released or sent to the Security Council.
	Sources familiar with the report also say it concludes that Iraq has allowed full access to the presidential compounds, in keeping with the Annan agreement. At the same time, that report raises the possibility of future problems for inspectors in gaining access to the sites. An annex written by Charles Duelfer quotes Iraqi officials as saying such surveys were not part of an open-ended process that could go on forever, the envoys said. "They [Oil Minister Amir Muhammed Rasheed] are saying the inspections in the compounds are valid for a limited but undefined period." Iraq made it clear that "the fundamental issue of continuing access is by no means solved and has only been postponed to the future." Duelfer's comments appear in an annex to a Security Council report written by Jayanatha Dhanapala, the UN undersecretary-general for disarmament, who organized the team that included diplomats for the first time.
	Secretary-General Annan says, "The agreement we signed does allow entry and re-entry ... I don't know if General Rasheed can overrule President Saddam Hussein and [Deputy Prime Minister] Tariq Aziz. That agreement was signed by Tariq Aziz and discussed with the president. So if there is any change in the agreement I expect it to come from higher levels."
	Duelfer, an American who is the deputy chairman of UNSCOM, says, "At times it seemed that Iraq was raising spurious issues with the diplomats to put the commission's experts on the defensive.... It is important to recognize that such problems are likely to re-emerge in the future, especially when true no-notice inspections are conducted."
98-4-16:	Secretary-General Annan proposes that Iraq be allowed to import $300 million in equipment to upgrade its dilapidated oil production facilities.

Table 10.3 (continued)

Annan says that even if emergency repairs were carried out, Baghdad could export only $3 billion worth of oil over any six months in 1998, far less than the $5.256 billion authorized by the Security Council under the oil-for-food program. Annan recommends that the Security Council lower its Iraqi oil export allowance to $4 billion, beginning in June and ending in December, and review the sum again later in the year, depending on the arrival of the needed equipment.

Iraq is currently exporting crude at a rate of about 1.57 million barrels per day (bpd), which would generate just under $3 billion in revenues over 180 days at current prices. To reach $5.256 billion, Iraq must increase exports to about 2.8 million bpd at current prices, a level it has not reached since before its war with Iran in 1980.

Iraq demands that the Security Council lift economic sanctions when it meets this month to review the status of Baghdad's weapons program, but UN officials say there is little chance the Council will do so when it meets, possibly the week of April 27. In Baghdad, the ruling Revolution Command Council declares that "the time has come for the discussion of the embargo at the end of April" to consider lifting the sanctions "immediately and with no delay."

A statement by the ruling Ba'ath Party leadership and the Revolutionary Command Council, coming after a joint meeting headed by President Saddam Hussein, says, "The time has come that the discussion of the embargo issue at the end of April lead to ... lifting the embargo completely and comprehensively ... if relations between Iraq and the Security Council are to become balanced and continue on the right basis." The Iraqi statement, carried by the official Iraqi news agency INA, criticizes "evil doers" that accuse Iraq of hiding weapons and says they have responsibility for the "sin of the deaths of our people killed by the embargo and the (previous) military operations ... Only they, if they oppose the lifting of the sanctions, will bear in addition to the burden of previous crises, the burden of new crisis and what harm may hit our people."

Iraqi Trade Minister Mohammed Mehdi Saleh says that Iraq has lost more than $120 billion in trade since the imposition of the economic sanctions.

98–4-17: Butler sends a 36-page UNSCOM report to the UN Security Council saying that UN weapons inspectors made "virtually no progress" over the past six months in verifying that Iraq has destroyed any remaining weapons of mass destruction, a key condition for lifting sanctions. The report states that a series of crises when Iraq repeatedly disrupted the work of the inspectors made it impossible for his experts to do their work. "If this is what Iraq intended by the crisis, then, in large measure, it could be said to have been. ... A major consequence of the four-month crisis authored by Iraq has been that, in contrast with the prior reporting period, virtually no progress in verifying disarmament has been able to

Table 10.3 (continued)

be reported. . . . Iraq's heightened policy of disarmament by declaration, no matter how vigorously pursued or stridently voiced, cannot remove the need for verification as the key means through which the credibility of its claim can be established." The report says that Iraq has focused on process and procedures rather than on "issues related to the destruction, removal, or rendering harmless of Iraq's prohibited weapons systems," and that suggestions by Iraq and other countries for technical evaluation meetings, known as TEMs, on specific weapons programs were time consuming and slowed down the commission's work in the field. "The question of the possible substitution of TEMs for more concrete work in the field, whether by accident or design, is a matter of concern to the commission." The work of these groups of outside experts has "proven to be political in character rather than technical," even when they backed UNSCOM's positions on missing data from Iraq. The report notes that Iraq maintained that it had disclosed or destroyed all its warheads that could carry chemical or biological agents. If any remained, the material in them had degraded. But it also says that a recent UNSCOM visit to Baghdad found that four intact 155 mm shells filled with mustard gas were still of the highest quality, "despite seven years of exposure to extreme climatic conditions." The report says Iraq is still far from fully accounting for its biological warfare program, when it began, and "whether or when it was terminated." It reveals that UNSCOM discovered a 1994 document in March, 1998 that indicated Iraq had a program for the manufacture of nozzles for spray dryers that could be used to help make biological weapons. Iraq has not yet told the commission why it wanted to use the equipment. "Weapons research into other systems . . . is inadequately described [by the Iraqis]. . . . This lack of candor raises the possibility of research or development of undisclosed systems." Consequently, UNSCOM is no closer to certifying that Iraq is in compliance than at the time of the last major report in October, 1997.

Butler gives an interview and says, "They have had an opportunity in the past month since [UN Secretary-General Kofi] Annan's visit to offer a full and complete declaration of past bio-weapons programs and where they stand now. . . . We gave them the opportunity and they blew it." He states that his report raises the same concerns raised in a similar report presented six months ago. "The last time we released a report like this, it triggered the crisis in the Gulf," and he says that the information provided by Iraq is "completely unsatisfactory."

The Security Council considers a previous recommendation from Secretary-General Kofi Annan that Iraq be allowed to spend $300 million on repairs to upgrade its dilapidated oil industry.

The Iraqi News Agency said a statement from the Revolutionary Command Council warned that, "The time has come for the lifting of the embargo completely and comprehensively" when the Security Council

Table 10.3 (continued)

	reviews the sanctions on April 27. The Iraqi statement warns of a new crisis if the sanctions continue.
98–4-18:	Iraqi Foreign Minister Mohammed Saeed al-Sahaf says Iraq has met the requirements of UN resolutions and has the right to an end to sanctions. He tells reporters after meeting Egyptian Foreign Minister Amr Moussa that Iraq "has stuck to security council decisions and has implemented all their essential requirements. . . . It is Iraq's right to ask for an end to the sanctions. . . . According to Iraq's point of view, the weapons inspection committee has been completed and the time has come for the sanctions to be lifted." After meeting the Arab League, Secretary-General Esmat Abdel-Meguid says of the latest UNSCOM report, "It's a monotonous repetition of the past . . . [it] is very easy to answer. It has unfounded deductions. . . . I consider his [Butler's] words unfounded. . . . Answering it [the report] will be easy. I will give the Security Council all the facts. I find no escalation [of the situation] but there is lying to the Security Council and we should clear it up. . . . The accusations proved to be false. . . . So now we are in a new stage, and the task ahead is speedy lifting of the sanctions on the people of Iraq."
	Jumhouriya, an Iraqi government newspaper, calls for a time limit on future inspections of presidential sites and accuses the United States of seeking a "new crisis" between Iraq and UNSCOM weapons inspectors. "It has to be stressed that visits to presidential sites are not an open process without a time ceiling. . . . The repetition of these visits without any limitation is something illogical and unacceptable. . . . It will be considered as a provocative act which aims at prolonging sanctions."
98–4-19:	The Arab League attacks British plan to hold an international conference to speed up implementation of oil for food deal. The Iraqi news agency quotes Deputy Secretary-General Ahmed Benhillias as saying such a meeting should be held only under the auspices of the UN, and that Benhillias "questioned the real motives behind holding this conference in London, outside the context and mechanism of the United Nations in the absence of the essentially concerned party, Iraq."
	Nils Carlstrom, a Swedish major general who heads the Baghdad Monitoring and Verification Center, says UN experts have not accounted for all the warheads filled with biological agents that Iraq says it destroyed and buried in 1991, and that inspectors will return with safety gear to resume the search for the warheads. He reports that a month's work in search of the warheads, involving sophisticated metal detectors, ended March 12. He refuses to say how many warheads have not been accounted for at a site outside Baghdad, but warns that verifying the Iraqi claim that all warheads were destroyed will take a "much longer time than previously thought." Iraqi officials have previously said that 77 warheads were filled with biological agents, and that the United Nations has accounted for 70 of them.

Table 10.3 (continued)

98-4-20:	Deputy Oil Minister Taha Hamoud praises an OPEC deal last month to cut global crude oil output for the first time in a decade, but says, "We consider this deal a bare minimum deal because the cuts should have been bigger.... We hope that everyone will stick to what has been agreed upon.... We blessed all the efforts which aim at the interest of OPEC nations. As for us we can now benefit from the rise in prices because our production capacity at present is limited due to the long years of the [UN] sanctions and the [1991 Gulf War] assaults against our oil.... We think it would have been better if a bigger reduction took place to increase the [oil] price. We have contacted the OPEC oil ministers and informed them of our position that we support all the efforts to boost the standing of OPEC, but unfortunately we ourselves cannot do anything about it."
98-4-21:	The EU, meeting on "oil for food" in London, is told that Saddam Hussein is the biggest block to a smooth flow of humanitarian aid to the Iraqi people. The meeting brings together EU and UN representatives and, for the first time, aid agencies working in Iraq. Iraq has attacked the food program as a conscience salve for the West, and it boycotts the two-day conference, along with most Arab nations and Russia. Britain, the current president of the 15-nation union, is adamant that sanctions should remain in place. Clare Short, Britain's International Development Secretary, says, "If Saddam Hussein would stop producing weapons of mass destruction, sanctions would be lifted." She also says, however, "We have to do better at identifying objectives [for] humanitarian assistance and then make the whole program flow.... One of the most important things to realize is the problem is not just food and medicine. The problems with electricity systems means hospitals can't operate and water and sanitation [systems] are breaking down." Foreign Office Minister Derek Fatchett says, "Sadly, for too long, Iraq has refused to cooperate fully. Indeed, the government has too often been obstructive. This must change if the organizations represented at this conference are going to be successful in... helping the people of Iraq." EU Humanitarian Affairs Commissioner Emma Bonino says it is time to review sanctions, and that they had left Iraq facing "unbearable hardships." She complains that aid bought under the oil-for-food deal was taking too long to reach the people who most needed it. While political circumstances in Iraq had caused some of the problems, "it would be unfair not to bear in mind that the international community has also played a part in the disarray of Iraqi society." The Iraqi News Agency (INA) says, "This conference is an interference in Iraq's internal affairs and a clear attempt to lengthen the duration of the tyrannical embargo imposed against Iraq, although its has lost all its legal justifications." The United States accuses Iraq of failing to cooperate with the UN. State Department spokesman James Rubin says the time is "far away" when

Table 10.3 (continued)

	sanctions on Iraq could be lifted. He says the new UNSCOM report makes "the case that Iraq has not complied with UN Security Council resolutions in any area of substance ... it presents clear and disturbing evidence that Iraq has failed to cooperate in coming forward with the information needed to allow the United Nations to conclude Iraq has indeed destroyed the weapons it says it has destroyed." Rubin says that while Iraq may have complied with its promise to let UN inspectors examine Baghdad's presidential palaces, Iraqis "continue to lie and hide the truth regarding the existence of long-range ballistic missiles, VX, and Sarin chemical weapons, and Anthrax and other biological weapons."
	France says it agrees broadly with the latest UNSCOM report on Iraq's weapons of mass destruction, and that Iraq must give inspectors more information on chemical and biological weapons.
	Iraqi UN envoy Nizar Hamdoon sends a letter to Secretary-General Annan complaining that the deputy executive chairman of UNSCOM, Charles Duelfer, made statements that violated his conditions of employment. The complaint is over an interview published on April 15 in the *New York Times*. Hamdoon says this violated an undertaking by UNSCOM employees not to make statements or give interviews, unless specifically authorized to do so, and represented "contempt for the Security Council on Mr. Duelfer's part and an action ultra vires, inasmuch as information was published in the press of which the Security Council had not been informed."
	Babel prints a front-page editorial claiming that the United States had sent its defense secretary to the Middle East to prepare for a military strike against Iraq. "William Cohen's tour in the Arab homeland aims at consulting with American allies to identify what should be done against Iraq. ... This means that guard dogs start barking again to prepare the ground for an aggression that was impossible to commit because of world condemnation."
98-4-22:	Health Minister Umeed Mubarak says Iraq needs at least $2 billion to re-equip its hospitals after more than seven years of economic sanctions, and claims that severe shortages of medicines and medical equipment have caused the infant mortality rate to soar.
	An Iraqi foreign ministry spokesman says Iraq set free all Kuwaiti prisoners immediately after the 1991 Gulf War and accuses Kuwait of using the issue of Kuwaitis missing in action for political purposes.
	Iraqi Deputy Prime Minister Tariq Aziz, addressing a conference in Baghdad of Arab Labor Unions, accuses Butler of being a US "agent" because of his latest report, and urges Arab states to collectively force an end to the UN trade embargo imposed on Iraq after its 1990 invasion of Kuwait. "Now after seven years of hard work with the UN Special Commission [UNSCOM], after thousands of inspections and hundreds of weapons destruction operations ... America's agent [Richard] Butler

Table 10.3 (continued)

comes and says that Iraq is not cooperating and no horizon is seen for lifting the embargo.... Why does Butler say this? It is not because he is an international weapons expert but because he is executing his masters' orders in Washington, because Washington does not want to lift the embargo imposed on Iraq.... The Special Commission has been working for seven years without its appetite diminishing, and it is not satisfied. It says Iraq must dismantle the long-range missiles. Pertaining to the missiles we have destroyed the engines and the launchers, and they still come and say the missile file is incomplete?... If the Security Council is a just institution ... the embargo would have been lifted at the end of 1991 and the start of 1992. But they did not take any steps to lessen the embargo, on the contrary, they added new tyrannical resolutions to strengthen the embargo.... So long as the Security Council is controlled by America and so long as the Special Commission is formed by America ... then the possibility that the embargo is lifted from Iraq and also Libya and others is weak ... The embargo, if it is rejected by the Arabs and Moslems, will not remain an embargo; even if they wanted in Europe and America to continue the embargo then we don't care.... At the official level the Arab states should meet and tell the Security Council, 'Enough is enough. Lift the sanctions against Iraq. Why do you implement resolutions against Iraq that you don't implement elsewhere?' If this happens then the embargo will not remain."

98-4-23: An Iraqi weekly quotes Iraqi Trade Minister Mohammed Mehdi Saleh as saying that Iraq is poised to sign several deals to import food and medicine from Saudi Arabia under its oil-for-food deal with the UN. "Iraq is preparing to sign deals with Saudi firms to import materials according to the memorandum of understanding.... This year's pilgrimage witnessed a rapprochement in the level of relations between Iraq and Saudi Arabia. Wide-scale contacts with officials there were carried out. ... Official dealings between the two sides were almost normal. Iraq took part in most of the meetings with the delegations there.... An Iraqi trade delegation has concluded a visit to Iran to sign deals to import food according to the oil for food deal." He says Iraq also plans to increase imports from Egypt, Syria, Jordan, the Maghreb states, and other Arab countries.

Deputy Prime Minister Tariq Aziz writes to Security Council President Hisashi Owada of Japan attacking the latest UN weapons report, saying it "represents a flagrant model of lack of objectivity and fairness, denying and distorting the facts and contains numerous flagrant fallacies and lies." Aziz says the report is "almost an American document aimed at justifying the American military concentration in the region, blackmail [of] its population and the aggression it plans against Iraq ... Iraq demands that the Security Council implement paragraph 22 of Resolution 687 immediately without any new restrictions or conditions." He demands the immediate lifting of sanctions imposed on Baghdad in 1990.

Table 10.3 (continued)

	Russia indicates that it may attempt to revive an earlier proposal declaring that Iraq has complied with the order to dismantle all of its nuclear weapons, as indicated in a recent report by the International Atomic Energy Agency. Russian Deputy Ambassador Yuri Fedotov says such a document had a "symbolic and psychological" value for encouraging Iraq rather than any practical effect in lifting sanctions. The United States is expected to oppose this effort.
98–5-3:	Trade Minister Mohammed Mehdi Saleh says that Iraq has lost about $140 billion as a result of UN trade sanctions which include a ban on its oil exports. "Iraq's economy has lost approximately $140 billion. That means the economy lost goods, commodities, equipment, and services which would have been imported by the oil money," Saleh told the Associated Press. Independent experts estimate the loss at about $115 billion from the ban just in oil exports during the years of the embargo. Saleh, a technocrat with a doctorate from Britain's Manchester University, said the sanctions have caused "great material loss" for the economy. But the greatest loss is "the death of 1.5 million Iraqis, most of them children," said Saleh, maintaining that that number of people have died due to lack of food and medicine caused by the embargo.
98–5-4:	Tariq Aziz attacks Arab states for subservience to US hegemony in the Middle East and their support for punitive UN sanctions against Iraq. "The Arab states not only implement resolutions [imposing sanctions on Iraq] but they implement the will of America and the American interpretation of these resolutions rather than the legal.... It is regrettable to say that Arab countries have implemented the embargo on Iraq as if they are the owner of the resolution and most of them are still carrying it out. ... Those [Arab states] who accept American legitimacy should not expect America to stop its evil [policy] against them because they have accepted the American role. America threatens its allies and those who are called its friends with the same manner it threatens its enemies.... Breaking the embargo is an Arab duty by neighboring and other Arab states and only then will the United States lift it." On the Middle East peace process, Aziz says, "This is one of the strangest things in the world ... that the mediator is an ally of one of the parties. The mediator should have at least some neutrality."
	Iraq's Vice President, Taha Yassin Ramadan, says that if the Security Council does not react positively to the open letter addressed to the Council's chairman and members on Friday, Iraq is was ready to fight until the sanctions are lifted. "The age of this letter is not years or months. It has a limited time," Ramadan said in a speech at the closing session of a conference of Arab politicians and dignitaries in Baghdad. The session was open to the press. "Either we accept to die slowly or we fight in order to lift the embargo," Ramadan said. He did not say how Iraq would fight for the lifting of sanctions. "These groups and spies [UNSCOM inspectors] have entered anywhere [in Iraq], even the presidential sites."

Table 10.3 (continued)

	The United States reports that it is compiling files to prove the "criminal conduct" of President Saddam Hussein. David Scheffer, the US ambassador at large for war crimes, tells reporters, "We are working closely with the Kuwaiti government to bring together documentary records of Saddam Hussein's regime with respect to crimes. . . . It is important that the pattern of Saddam Hussein's conduct be extremely well known to the international community," Scheffer said, adding that this conduct "continues to be a threat to international peace and security." The US ambassador is in Kuwait on a three-day visit to discuss the documentation of crimes carried out by Baghdad with Kuwaiti officials.
98–5-5:	The IAEA states that it has obtained a memorandum written by an Iraqi official making reference to an intermediary asking whether Iraq would be interested in contact with a Pakistani scientist. "The implication is clear," says IAEA spokesman David Kyd. "It was only a feeler put out to see if there was interest on the Iraqi side."
98–5-6:	Iraq says, "Oil exports under the memorandum of understanding with the UN have reached more than 130 million barrels, which is more than the amount exported under the second phase, which was 127 million barrels." Saddam Zeban al-Hassan, Director-General of the State Oil Marketing Organization (SOMO), says exports up to April 27 under the third phase totaled 126 million barrels. The third phase will end at the beginning of June. "Because of low world oil prices during the third phase of the memorandum . . . it is necessary to increase oil exports to compensate for losses caused by low prices. . . . If the UN ratifies the required spare parts and they quickly arrive in the country, Iraq will be able to produce up to 2.65 million bpd during two to three months, and this will increase Iraq's export to two million bpd. . . . Oil production could be increased to 3 million bpd in six months, and this would boost Iraq's export capacity to 2.3 million (bpd)."
98–5-7:	Eric Falt, spokesman for Iraq's UN coordinator in Baghdad, says an enlarged oil for food program is needed to address Iraq's humanitarian needs, "The needs of the education sector are enormous, and the impact of the current situation is equally damaging, if not more [so], because it affects the future and spirit of millions of Iraqi schoolchildren and the university students. . . . The great difficulties in agricultural production and the poor state of [the] water sanitation sector throughout Iraq . . . all have direct effect on the physical well-being of 22 million men and women. . . . The situation in the education sector remains very worrisome. . . . So far the efforts of UNESCO . . . have been hampered by the limited funding provided in the context of Security Council resolution 986 (which governs the oil pact)." Baghdad has said that no schools have been built in nearly eight years of UN sanctions and classes were crammed. Tens of thousands of schoolchildren had to sit on the ground for lack of desks, and books had to be recycled. Falt said the $27 million earmarked for the education sector in each of the three phases of the oil-

Table 10.3 (continued)

for-food deal was not enough to address needs. Denis Haliday, UN coordinator for Iraq, says it is "critical that the government be able to rebuild the entire education system as quickly as possible in order to recover from initial damages and now from a severe lack of funding."

The Iraqi Culture and Information spokesman says that Iraq turned down an offer of help to build an atomic bomb with Pakistani expertise and reported the matter to the world's nuclear watchdog organization. He says the offer was made by a Greek intermediary, who asked whether Iraq would be interested in contact with a Pakistani scientist to help build a nuclear bomb. "A Greek national had offered Iraq authorities in mid-1990 that he could supply them with designs to manufacture nuclear weapons, claiming that he could obtain them from Dr. Abdul-Qadir Khan, Chairman of the Pakistani nuclear program.... The Iraqi authorities have neglected the offer as an intelligence trick. They had submitted a document to the International Atomic Energy Agency on the issue... and the subject was over."

Chief UN arms inspector Richard Butler sends letter to Council President Njuguna Mahugu of Kenya, saying Iraq had largely complied since Secretary-General Kofi Annan negotiated an agreement in Baghdad in February assuring UNSCOM of such access. He states that Iraq has met conditions for the lifting of a travel ban on its officials responsible for impeding UN weapons, although the ban never went into force. Security Council members say the ban will terminate automatically, and that the issue would be discussed on Friday in a closed session. They indicate that the Council intends to have Butler give a review of technical weapons issues early in June. The Council imposed the travel ban in November, after Iraq announced it was barring American members of UN teams. The Council, in consultation with UNSCOM in charge of disarming Iraq, was supposed to draw up a list of Iraqi civilian and military officials concerned, but no such list was ever drafted, apparently because of the pressure of events, and the travel ban never took effect. The November resolution provided for the ban to be lifted a day after Butler, the chairman of UNSCOM, reported that Iraq was allowing his inspectors immediate, unconditional, and unrestricted access to all sites, facilities, equipment, and records.

98–5-9: A group of eight foreign ministers tells Iraq that it will face "severest consequences" if it violates its obligations to the UN to permit unfettered weapons inspections. But they also say that full compliance would allow the process of lifting sanctions to begin. At a closing news conference, British Foreign Secretary Robin Cook says the G8 has given Iraq a clear choice. "If Baghdad persists in obstructing the international inspectors, if it continues with its ambitions to develop weapons of mass destruction, then sanctions will remain in place. But if Baghdad adopts the alternative promise and recognizes that it gave a commitment... to abandon its programs of weapons of mass destruction, and if it starts to cooperate in

Table 10.3 (continued)

	demonstrating that it has abandoned that capacity, then we are willing to start lifting the sanctions." The ministers say they look forward to the full implementation of the Annan deal and to Iraqi compliance under UN Security Council Resolution 1154. "We note that any violation by Iraq would have severest consequences. We regret Iraq's failure so far to comply with its relevant obligations, and we note that full compliance with the relevant resolutions would allow the process of lifting sanctions to begin," the communiqué said. The eight countries include Russia and France, the United States, Britain, Germany, Japan, Italy, and Canada.
	Former US Attorney General Ramsey Clark offers $4 million worth of medicine to the Iraqi health authorities on Saturday, saying the aid was in defiance of his government's sanctions policy against Baghdad. Clark says, "Our commitment is to stimulate the flow of medicine from the United States and from other countries . . . in defiance of our government. . . . We are deeply angered by the policies of our government, by the genocide of the sanctions. . . . We are determined that sanctions would be recognized . . . as genocide against humanity. . . . The message we carry is that the American people love the Iraqi people."
98–5-10:	The Security Council votes to renew the sanctions for another six months.
	Tariq Aziz, speaking to CNN-International's "World Report," says that Baghdad sees no chance that sanctions will ever be lifted, and that he hopes other countries will ignore the UN embargo and resume trading with his country. During the same program, UN Secretary-General Kofi Annan says he is pleased with Iraqi cooperation since signing the agreement in Baghdad on Feb. 23 to open all sites, including Saddam's palaces, to UN inspectors. He says Iraq not only has opened the palaces, "but they also have permitted [the inspectors] to go to locations they have not been permitted to go to in more than seven years." Annan says that if cooperation continues and the inspectors can complete their work as soon as possible, "Iraq also ought to be able to see light at the end of the tunnel."
	The Security Council formally terminates a foreign travel ban imposed last November on Iraqi officials, but which was never enforced because of opposition by France, Russia, China, and others.
	Foreign Minister Mohammed Saeed al-Sahaf meets King Hussein of Jordan before starting an African tour aimed at persuading leaders that Baghdad has fulfilled its disarmament obligations under the 1991 Gulf War cease-fire. Sahaf hands the king a letter from President Saddam Hussein, "confirming that Iraq is cooperating with the [UN] commission [of arms inspectors] positively and completely. The letter expresses Iraq's hope "for Jordanian help and support in efforts to lift the sanctions and put an end to the suffering of the Iraqi people under the oppression of these sanctions."
	Tariq Aziz has said that Baghdad was conducting talks with Kurdish rebels in its north, but that Washington was impeding efforts to reach an

Table 10.3 (continued)

	agreement. "Early last week I was receiving a delegation in this building from the Kurdistan Democratic Party [KDP], the group of [Massoud] Barzani. There is another delegation from the [Jalal] Talabani group," KDP rival, the Patriotic Union of Kurdistan [PUK]. Aziz say the two groups had been sending delegations to Baghdad for many years, but blamed Washington for blocking "a national solution" to the Kurdish problem in Iraq. "They [Americans] are preventing the government [in Baghdad] and the Kurds from reaching a political and democratic solution through dialogue. The government's attitude toward the [two] groups is normal."
98-5-11:	Iraq accuses Turkey of threatening the flow of the Euphrates and Tigris rivers by building dams in violation of the rights of countries downstream. "Turkey is violating international law by building several dams on the two rivers without taking into account rights of countries which are sharing these rivers." The Tigris originates in Turkey before flowing into Iraq. The Euphrates starts in Turkey and winds through Syria before entering Iraq. Syria and Iraq say the flow from Turkey is not enough, and both countries depend on the river waters for drinking, irrigation, and electricity generation. In 1996, Turkey announced a plan for its fourth dam on the Euphrates, to produce power and irrigate a large chunk of southeastern Turkey. Syria, Iraq, and Turkey have held several meetings but failed to reach an agreement on water sharing. The Ankara and Damascus governments signed a provisional agreement in 1987 under which Turkey allows the flow of 500 cubic meters per second to Syria. The Syrian government has called for a permanent agreement. Baghdad also opposes Turkey's policy of allowing US and British jet fighters to use a Turkish base to launch surveillance missions in northern Iraq to protect Kurds from possible attacks by Baghdad.
	The *Nabadh al-Shabab* singles out Jordan, France, Russia, and Egypt for failing to provide promised supplies. The newspaper accuses Jordan of snubbing an offer to buy Iraqi sulfur in favor of a deal with Qatar at nearly double the price. The *Nabadh al-Shabab* also criticized French companies for failing to supply Iraq with power generation equipment. "The French fought to strike deals with Iraq . . . to supply stations with power generation units but limited themselves to supply simple stuff that do not live up to Iraq's expectation from the friends in France," the paper said. It also criticizes Iraq's "Russian friends" for acting as "mediators" for Western firms to export materials to Iraq that they are unable to send.
	Iran and Iraq launched their first joint operation to search for the remains of soldiers killed in their 1980–1988 war. Brigadier-General Mirfeisal Baqerzadeh, head of Iran's committee for the war's missing in action, says a 10-man Iranian team entered Iraq to take part in a search in the former battle zones. "The measure marks a turning point in the two

Table 10.3 (continued)

countries' efforts to discover bodies of killed soldiers and those missing in action."

Saddam Hussein removes Labor and Social Affairs Minister Abdul-Hamid Aziz Mohammed Saleh from his position. Saleh, who is also a senior ruling Ba'ath Party member, was dismissed by a presidential decree signed by Saddam on Monday.

Iraq announces that it is replacing most of its foreign ambassadors in a drive to improve its image, which has been severely tarnished since its 1990 invasion of Kuwait. Iraq's most influential newspaper, *Babil*, stated that it is time that Iraqi embassies were "injected with new blood to destroy the wall of isolation the enemies have constructed around Iraq." Iraqi diplomats at several Middle Eastern embassies had said earlier this week that President Saddam Hussein ordered at least 10 ambassadors, including his half-brother, Iraq's representative to the UN offices in Geneva, to return to Baghdad. They included ambassadors to Yemen, Algeria, India, Tunisia, Pakistan, Jordan, and the Cairo-based Arab League.

98–5-12: Secretary General Annan says Iraq is living up to its part of the February 23 memorandum of understanding he has signed with Tariq Aziz.

98–5-14: The International Committee of the Red Cross announces that Iraq and Kuwait have agreed to hold talks on Kuwaitis and Iraqis who have been missing since the Gulf conflict. The talks would involve more than 600 Kuwaitis and 1,037 Iraqis.

Tariq Aziz meets with French President Jacques Chirac as part of a European trip designed to win support for ending sanctions. Aziz also discusses biological and chemical weapons issues with French Foreign Minister Hubert Vendrine.

98–5-15: The Security Council acknowledges Iraq's progress in dismantling its covert nuclear weapons program. The United States and Russia draft a policy statement for the Council stating procedures to reduce or end nuclear inspections if Iraq answers the remaining questions of the IAEA. It calls for the IAEA to present a status report in July, after which the Security Council could endorse the IAEA's position that Iraq has complied with the nuclear arms requirements. It also calls for the IAEA to develop a continuing monitoring program if its questions are answered, and to report on such a program to the Council on October 11, 1998.

98–5-18: Iraq charges that the United States is blocking contracts under the oil for food program as part of its hostility to the Iraqi regime. It claims that 22 contracts have been held up for more than six months because of US requests for more details that are part of a political harassment campaign. The United States replies that some of the proposed contracts involve activities like upgrading Iraqi telecommunications and have nothing to do with food or aid.

Table 10.3 (continued)

	The United States introduces the concept that oil for food should be renewed automatically if the Secretary General indicates it has met given criteria.
98–5-19:	Tariq Aziz visits the Pope in Rome. The Pope expresses support for ending sanctions.
98–5-21:	Iraq rejects the US proposal to automatically renew the oil-for-food agreement every six months as a US plot to prolong sanctions indefinitely.
	The UN reports that a survey of Iraqi children in March shows that 27% are suffering from chronic malnutrition and 24% were underweight, roughly the same percentage as last year. It indicates that Iraq is ignoring UN suggestions to raise the level of food per capita from 2,000 calories to 2,500 under the oil for food program.
98–5-26:	Iraqi Information Minister Humam Abdul-Khaleq says he is optimistic that sanctions will soon be lifted because Iraq has met all of the conditions set forth by UNSCOM.
98–6-2:	UNSCOM announces that it is still looking for the remains of missile warheads, and it is still analyzing samples of 40 warheads. It indicates that Iraq is providing earth-moving equipment to help find the warheads, and that it has conducted surprise visits to 40 sites in an attempt to resolve the uncertainties involved.
	Iraq briefs the Security Council on its position that it has complied with UN inspection requirements at the invitation of Russia.
98–6-3 to 98–6-4:	Butler provides two days of briefings to the Security Council on the evidence that Iraq continues to conceal aspects of its programs, using satellite and U-2 aerial photos, charts, and intelligence data. The briefing raises new questions about Iraq's biological and chemical programs. He provides a road map of unresolved issues to lay out exactly what Iraq must do to fully comply. This effort parallels the similar process already underway for the IAEA and Iraq's nuclear arms program. The principal remaining uncertainties seem to affect biological weapons and VX gas.
98–6-10:	Tariq Aziz denounces protracted UN weapons inspections as an injustice and says UN experts were clutching at straws in their continued search. Speaking on the eve of a visit by chief UN weapons inspector Richard Butler, Aziz say Iraq destroyed all of its prohibited arms in 1991, but the inspectors were determined to find evidence to the contrary. "If they believe they have a one in a million chance to find evidence they will visit . . . a school, a hospital, a factory," he told a conference of Christian leaders in Baghdad. "Until now, they are not satisfied." Aziz says the seven years and two months since the inspectors started their work was time enough to declare the United States, 14 times bigger than Iraq and boasting far greater military force, free of weapons of mass destruction. He once again accuses "Anglo-Saxons"—the United States and Brit-

Table 10.3 (continued)

ain—of deliberately holding up the process to extend sanctions imposed on Iraq for its 1990 invasion of Kuwait. "This is not international work. This is not international law. This is deliberate injustice. . . . The latest discussions which took place in the [UN] Security Council . . . gave an important indication that the game played by the Special Commission is a political game." Citing Iraq's missiles—the area where UNSCOM says it is closest to declaring Iraq in compliance—Aziz said Baghdad had twice proved to the UN that it had destroyed all engines for proscribed long-range missiles. Aziz said that like any other machine, a missile without an engine was useless. "A car without an engine is not a car."

UN spokesman Eric Falt says water quality has benefited from the introduction of disinfectants bought under the oil-for-food agreement, and that none of 280 samples of water in Baghdad had been found to be contaminated, compared to an 8 percent contamination level five months ago. Contamination in the worst-hit governorate of Wasit, southeast of the capital, dropped to 20 percent in April from 28 percent in March. Allocations for water and sanitation programs under the latest expanded stage of the oil-for-food accord have been increased to $210 million from June to December, up from just $40 million in each of the previous six-month phases. UN Secretary-General Annan reports that "the inputs provided under phases one to three have not halted the overall deterioration of the water network." Targets for improvement in water distribution and in sewage disposal were not met because of late arrival of 96 kilometers (60 miles) of pipes and dozens of sewage tankers. "Systematic repairs and plant maintenance have been impossible with the limited volume of supplies delivered to date. . . . In Baghdad losses from these breaks constitute at present 50 percent of production." Power cuts, caused by similar deterioration to the electricity system after the 1991 war and eight years of sanctions, also affect water supply.

Iraqi newspapers say that chief UN weapons inspector Richard Butler was once again overstepping his mandate in his latest visit to Baghdad. *Al-Thawra*, newspaper of the ruling Ba'ath Party, criticizes Butler's reported decision to travel on to Kuwait, and says Butler is following a political agenda and should answer to the UN, not Kuwait. *Babel* calls for the Australian diplomat to be silenced. "Isn't it time we stopped being courteous and cut off the tongue of this dog?"

Crown Prince and Prime Minister Sheik Saad al-Abdullah al-Sabah says Kuwait is not ready for a reconciliation with its Gulf War foe Iraq and is annoyed by calls to mend fences with the country that invaded it in 1990. In an interview with the London-based Arabic daily *as-Sharq al-Awsat*, al-Sabah says he is irked by such calls from some Gulf states, and launched a bitter diatribe against the Iraqi regime. "I am talking with you frankly and I say that if we know (Iraqi President) Saddam Hussein's expansionist intentions, then these remarks (for improved ties) do hurt me indeed. The whole Gulf is targeted, not just Kuwait. We are a member

Table 10.3 (continued)

state of the Gulf Cooperation Council (GCC) and we believe that any aggression in the future against any of the member states is an aggression against all."

Security Council members express concern on Thursday over recent statements by Iraq's vice president, calling into question a 1993 Council resolution on the demarcation of the Kuwait–Iraqi border. Council President Antonio Monteiro of Portugal tells reporters the matter was raised during closed-door consultations on a number of issues. This followed his receipt of a letter earlier this week from Kuwaiti Foreign Minister Sabah al-Ahmad al-Sabah complaining about remarks by Iraqi Vice-President Taha Yassin Ramadan. "The Security Council expresses its strong concern over statements made recently by the vice-president of Iraq calling into question Security Council resolution 833 concerning the demarcation of the boundary between Kuwait and Iraq."

Iraq threatens to halt the UN oil-for-food program if the Security Council adopts a US-backed resolution that adds conditions to Baghdad's bid to buy oil industry equipment. UN ambassador Nizar Hamdoon says, "We will stop the whole thing. Iraq will reject outright this resolution if it is passed. We have conveyed to all that Iraq does not intend to accept that." At issue is a resolution sponsored by Portugal, Britain, and Sweden and backed by the United States that would allow the purchase of $300 million in spare parts to upgrade Iraq's dilapidated oil industry. It also says Iraq's plan on how it purchases and distributes food and other supplies would be ongoing and could be reviewed and amended but not renegotiated every six months, as at present. Iraq objects to this provision, which gives it less control over the program. Until now it has held up oil sales on a regular basis until its plan for distributing the supplies has been approved by the UN. Baghdad has said the language in the draft resolution before the Council implied that the punishing sanctions, imposed when its troops invaded Kuwait in August, 1990, would go on forever. The draft notes that "the distribution plan approved by the Secretary-General on May 29, 1998 will remain in effect as long as the temporary humanitarian arrangements for Iraq are required and that, for this purpose, the plan will be kept under constant review and amended as necessary."

98–6-13: Pope John Paul's envoy, Cardinal Roger Etchegaray, ending a visit to Iraq, calls for an end to the eight-year sanctions imposed on Iraq for its invasion of Kuwait. "The embargo, through its perverse and its uncontrollable effects, is destroying the spirit of the Iraqi people." Last month Iraqi Deputy Prime Minister Aziz, himself a Christian from the northern Iraqi city of Mosul, brought his campaign against the UN embargo to the Vatican where he found a sympathetic ear from the pontiff in a private meeting and from other top Roman Catholic officials.

98–6-15: Iraqi Trade Minister Mohammed Mehdi Saleh says delays in purchases of oil industry spare parts are threatening Baghdad's expanded oil-for-

Table 10.3 (continued)

food deal. Saleh say the United States and Britain were trying to introduce an unnecessary UN resolution covering the purchases, which he says aims at curbing Iraqi oil exports. He says Iraq would reject any decision changing the accord—expanded this month to allow Baghdad to sell $4.5 billion of oil from June to December to finance humanitarian contracts—from a six-month renewable deal into a rolling program. "Expanding the program to many humanitarian sectors would not be achieved unless there will be sufficient amount of revenue from oil . . . which cannot be done unless these spare parts are received."

Chief UN weapons inspector Richard Butler, speaking after talks in Baghdad with Deputy Prime Minister Aziz, says he has agreed to a work schedule with Iraq that could use the road map he presented to the Security Council in early June to could clear up outstanding disarmament issues in as little as two months, and lead to the closure of UNSCOM's files on Iraq's prohibited weapons by October. Butler says the two men will meet again in August to review progress. "Mr. Aziz and I will take stock on the ninth of August and it is my earnest hope that when we do that we will be looking at a slate that's been pretty well ticked off," Butler told a news conference. "He and I will sit down and assess what stage we have reached and what further needs to be done, if anything, hopefully nothing, but what further needs to be done in order to begin to prepare those reports, hopefully for our October report to the Security Council . . . The light at the end of the tunnel is more visible than it has been for a very long time. What this work program does is seek to bring us forward very far and very fast towards the end of this (process)." Butler adds that he believes Iraq will show full cooperation with the fast-track agenda. "My estimation is that that work will be of a high quality with a high degree of cooperation from both sides . . . So it is my hope that we will be entering precisely those kind of (final) reports in October."

The key issues dealt with during the talks are Butler's call for Iraq to provide a wide range of information including its missile "material balance," information on efforts to produce the chemical agent VX, and details of its acquisition of material, agents, and munitions for its biological program. UNSCOM is also seeking information about missile propellant which he says Iraq would be able to supply in 24 hours. Butler presented Iraq with preliminary results of excavations near Baghdad aimed at verifying Iraq had unilaterally destroyed 45 chemical and biological warheads. Other more complex areas could take longer, especially biological weapons, where UNSCOM says it still has a limited understanding of Iraq's capabilities. UNSCOM officials privately acknowledge that certifying Iraq is entirely free of biological weapons, which are relatively simple to produce and store, is a virtually impossible task, but say they are looking at least for a more coherent and consistent declaration by Iraq of its past biological program and what became of it.

Table 10.3 (continued)

	Tariq Aziz confirms the two sides had agreed a schedule of work and gave a positive assessment of their talks. "We had a very fruitful meeting these two days. The exchange of views and discussions were businesslike and professional . . . We will meet again in August and we have made good progress."
Parliament speaker Saadoun Hammadi says, "UNSCOM's comings and goings and the game of excuses it has practiced cannot continue. Our people and the Arab and Moslem masses and free people everywhere will resist it with everything in their power."
98–6-16:	Butler says Iraq's full cooperation with his two-month work plan could earn it an end to the oil embargo imposed on it for invading Kuwait in 1990. But Butler says everything depends on Iraq's full cooperation and compliance with the work program he agreed in Baghdad earlier this week with Tariq Aziz. "We would be able, who knows perhaps in October, to give to the Security Council a report . . . that says Iraq had completed all the actions required of it with respect to disarmament. I'll expect our October report will be different from any the Council had seen before. . . . What we need . . . is full cooperation by Iraq . . . I made a promise to Iraq that we would do this work honestly, competently and quickly. We have no hidden agenda." Butler says that if Iraq met all requirements agreed on this week, the UN's Iraq file for missiles and chemical weapons "could be fairly close to empty. . . . Biological is in a more difficult state and it will be the subject, according to the program of work, of a rather different and special meeting in Baghdad in July because of the unsatisfactory nature of all of Iraq's declarations on the biological area in the past. . . . I believe that everything in the work program could be cleared up by August. . . . We firmly believe that the materials we need exist, are in the possession of the government of Iraq. . . . If they put their shoulder to the wheel, they could step forward and give us what we need in matter of weeks."
Iraq's vice-president, Taha Yassin Ramadan, delivers a letter to Yemeni President Ali Abdullah Saleh on Iraq's "relations with the UN Security Council and what is required from Arab brothers in this stage."
The Clinton administration cautions about lifting UN sanctions against Iraq. Presidential spokesman Mike McCurry says, "We have a lot more to see before we make any judgments about sanctions relief. We evaluate our posture on sanctions based on the performance of the Iraqi government. We will evaluate the performance of the Iraqi government in October when the next review of Iraqi sanctions takes place."
Iraq UN envoy Nizar Hamdoon tells nonaligned members of the Security Council that the UN oil-for-food program would collapse if the Council adopted a resolution to put it on an ongoing basis, instead of being renewable every six months. The resolution, sponsored by Britain, Portugal, and Sweden, would allow for the purchase of $300 million in spare parts to upgrade Iraq's dilapidated oil industry. It would be part of a

Table 10.3 (continued)

                    program letting Baghdad sell $5.25 billion in oil over six months to buy food, medicine, and other necessities to ease the impact of sanctions imposed after its 1990 invasion of Kuwait. But the resolution adds that while Iraq's plan for purchasing and distributing the supplies could be amended as needed, it would no longer be renegotiated every six months. After informing nonaligned members of the Security Council of objections to the resolution, Hamdoon told reporters, "I expressed our concern about that draft and explained to them that Iraq ... cannot deal with any resolution that will give the 'oil-for-food' (program) an ongoing nature." Iraq fears the program is becoming a substitute for the lifting of sanctions, which include a ban on regular oil sales, once UN weapons inspectors have certified that all its chemical, biological, and ballistic weapons have been accounted for and eliminated.

                    Tariq Aziz says his country rejects any attempts to turn its six-monthly oil-for-food accord into a substitute for lifting trade sanctions. Aziz says the accord, an exemption from the trade sanctions designed to allow it to sell oil to pay for humanitarian goods distributed under UN supervision, was never intended to be a long-term solution. "The project is a temporary humanitarian project and on this basis we accepted it," Aziz says. "Any attempt to turn it into an eternal project as a replacement for lifting sanctions cannot be accepted by Iraq and is unacceptable to many countries."

                    Iraqi Ambassador Hamdoon sends the Security Council a letter reaffirming its recognition of the Iraq–Kuwait border, as endorsed by a 1993 Council resolution. The letter is signed by Foreign Minister Mohammed Saeed al-Sahaf, to Council President Antonio Monteiro of Portugal. Monteiro had called in Hamdoon after Council members expressed concern in a statement on Friday over recent statements by Iraqi Vice President Taha Yassin Ramadan apparently calling into question Council resolution 833, adopted five years ago. Kuwaiti Foreign Minister Sabah al-Ahmad al-Sabah had said in a letter to the Council president last week that Ramadan had called the resolution into question and had argued that the Security Council had never previously adopted any resolution on the demarcation of boundaries between two countries. The Kuwaiti minister said such statements represented a "serious threat to the sovereignty, security and integrity" of the emirate. "They reveal both the persistence of Iraq's hostile intentions ... and its real attitude toward the Security Council resolutions concerning its aggression against my country." Sahaf's letter "reaffirmed our recognition of the borders under UN Security Council resolution 833."

98–6-17: Secretary of State Martin Indyk announces that the United States is working with opposition groups outside of Iraq, and plans a new effort funded by Congress to build up a political opposition to Iraqi leader Saddam Hussein. "We will be launching an effort to help them organize and coordinate their case against Saddam Hussein." The effort will go for-

Table 10.3 (continued)

ward "in a visible and effective way" and would focus on Saddam's "brutality and his war crimes" from the 1991 Gulf War and 1990 invasion of Kuwait. There are 73 opposition groups outside of Iraq and "now we're going to get behind them and try to help them.... They represent an alternative vision for Iraq to Saddam Hussein that is democratic in terms of its aspirations. I don't place a high probability on their ability to overthrow Saddam but it's important they demonstrate there is a different way to life for the Iraqi people." Congress approved $5 million to fund Radio Free Iraq to broadcast program in Arabic to Iraq earlier in the year. Republican lawmakers also proposed spending another $33 million to directly help Iraqi opposition movements overthrow Saddam and to provide them with humanitarian assistance.

Iraq's Vice President, Taha Yassin Ramadan, voices his skepticism on Wednesday that a recent agreement with UN weapons inspectors, hailed as a breakthrough by a top Iraqi official, would bring an end to sanctions. "I cannot say the agreement will lead to the lifting of the sanctions," Ramadan told reporters in Sanaa. Ramadan also says Iraq is ready to improve relations with all Arab states, but refused to apologize for its invasion of Kuwait in 1990. "We are ready to turn over a new leaf as brothers with all Arab countries, without exception." Earlier in the year, Kuwaiti Foreign Minister Sheik Sabah al-Ahmad al-Sabah said Iraqi reconciliation with Kuwait was only possible if Baghdad apologized for the invasion, which plunged inter-Arab relations to a low point.

Tariq Aziz says the time has come to take action to lift UN sanctions crippling Iraq. Aziz tells Russian envoy Viktor Posuvalyuk in a meeting in Baghdad that "serious and active work is needed to lift the unjust sanctions on Iraq." The two men met to discuss the UN plan to which Aziz had just agreed to help speed up the final verification of Iraq's disarmament so that the sanctions, imposed after Iraq invaded Kuwait in 1990, could be lifted.

Ewen Buchanan, spokesman for UNSCOM, warns that "there is a big difference from having a work plan and implementing it.... We hope Iraq will actually implement it in good faith and that is what we expect from them."

Iraq and Egypt sign minutes of cooperation on Wednesday to expand trade relations between them.

98–6-18: Iraq calls for the latest six-month phase of the oil-for-food program to be the final one, to be followed by the lifting of sanctions on the normal export of its oil.

A resolution authorizing $300 million in spare parts for Iraq's oil industry is introduced in the Security Council, despite Baghdad's warning that it will cease oil exports if it disapproves of the text.

Table 10.3 (continued)

	Vice President Taha Yassin Ramadan says his country is not ready to apologize for its invasion of Kuwait, even if it would help improve relations with its Gulf neighbors. "Iraq has no intention to apologize for the events that happened in 1990 and will not beg for support from anyone."
98–6-19:	The United States acknowledges that Iraq smuggles about $100 million worth of oil through Turkey annually, and says it is inevitable that some oil will get through. A White House spokesman says, "The amount of oil leakage that we're talking about that gets . . . smuggled across the border into Turkey is something like $100 million a year, obviously much less than 1 percent of the total value of the economic sanctions that the government of (Iraqi President) Saddam Hussein faces. He estimated the total impact of the sanctions at $15 billion annually.
98–6-22:	Iraq attacks Butler's latest report on a recent visit to Baghdad to discuss a so-called "road map" setting out issues to be tackled in the next two months to speed the scrapping of Iraq's weapons of mass destruction. The report has just been made public and says Baghdad refused to include issues relating to VX nerve gas, missile propellants, concealment practices, and other matters in a new work plan. In a letter to the president of the Security Council, Tariq Aziz says the report "reflects the previous attitude of concentrating on controversial points in a manner that fails to give a balanced and objective report of what occurred." Aziz says the report fails to mention that Butler, head of the UN special commission (UNSCOM) in charge of disarming Iraq, had said that samples of water, air, soil, and tree leaves, as well as imprints taken at Iraqi presidential sites in March, "do not indicate the presence of proscribed activities or elements in those sites." He repeats Iraq's contention that it had completed all the disarmament requirements of a 1991 Security Council resolution and that completion of the work schedule "will make it possible to resolve the outstanding issues . . . and will definitely lead to the submission by UNSCOM of its final report to the Security Council," leading to the lifting of Gulf war sanctions. Aziz says the report did not explain Iraq's position that "since the accounting for missile engines, missile launchers and the warheads was completed, the question of missile propellants loses importance and becomes a secondary issue since it is an additional element which was not of interest in itself, in addition to the fact that it did not constitute a very complex substance." He say the only problem concerning the missile propellants was the provision of documents confirming their unilateral destruction. That could be dealt with in the framework of the ongoing monitoring process, referring to the phase of UNSCOM's work due to follow its search-and-destroy operations. He says the report's reference to Iraq's refusal to clarify the extent of its attempts to produce the chemical warfare agent VX was "incorrect," and that Iraq submitted "the relevant clarifications, explanations and docu-

Table 10.3 (continued)

	ments; but the special commission requested additional documents to prove that the production of the aforementioned chemical agent during 1990, which amounted to one and a half tons, even though Iraq had submitted documents proving without any doubt that the chemical agent VX had not been produced in 1990 or 1991 in a sufficiently stable manner to be utilized within the framework of the armament program.'' Regarding Iraq's biological weapons program, Aziz claimed it has ceased to exist since 1991, and that Iraq had already accepted a new approach proposed by Butler that involved ''focusing on the material balances of the weapons, chemical agents, materials and equipment'' at a meeting of experts to be held in Baghdad beginning on July 11. Aziz says that what UNSCOM ''describes as concealment and which does not exist in reality is considered a problem which is unrelated to the disarmament process but which is based on doubts raised by individual occurrences, the circumstances of which have already been fully clarified. Intensive investigations carried out by UNSCOM over the past three years ''have already proved that these doubts were totally unfounded,'' he added. Regarding documents that Iraq acknowledged to be in its possession but refused to provide, Aziz says the ''truth is that [they] are unrelated to the proscribed programs and that they belong to one of the military units.'' He says UNSCOM examined them during an inspection, took notes on them, and ''did not put forward information indicating they were related to disarmament.''
98–6-23:	The Iraqi newspaper *Babel* advises Arab rulers to forsake peace talks with Israel and focus their efforts on holding a summit, involving Iraq, to rally Arab forces. ''If Arab rulers wanted to escape the calamity of being drawn to genocide . . . they should immediately abandon their illusions of peace. They should hold an Arab summit to discuss how to protect the Arab national presence from annihilation.'' The official newspaper *Al-Qadissiya* urges the Arabs to halt normalization of relations with Israel and promote a tight Arab boycott on firms dealing with Tel Aviv. ''We can contain the Zionist entity . . . through stopping all sorts of normalization of relations . . . and tightening the Arab boycott on the companies and persons dealing with this entity in America and around the world.''
	Tariq Aziz says Iraq's oil industry needed urgent renovation after being hit by eight years of economic sanctions. Aziz says Iraq had requested $300 million in spare parts for oil industry repairs to increase the struggling sector's capacity and provide Iraq with the badly needed revenue to pay for food, medicine, and emergency infrastructure projects. ''This is the minimum we need to rehabilitate our oil industry as the whole industry has suffered from sanctions that were extended for eight years. Therefore to implement the UN scheme to sell oil for food, which means production and exportation, we have to maintain the oil industry.''

Table 10.3 (continued)

98–6-24: The *Washington Post* says US army laboratory tests of destroyed Iraqi missiles warheads excavated by UNSCOM in Taji, north of Baghdad, had found "significant amounts" of "VX disulfide... and stabilizer."

Iraq dismisses as "an outrageous lie" a report that UN weapons inspectors found traces of the deadly VX nerve gas in its missile warheads. An Iraqi spokesman says Baghdad never managed to produce VX in a stable state to load into warheads and "flatly rejected" the reported findings of a US military laboratory that the warheads contained traces of the lethal agent. "Once again the Special Commission (UNSCOM) by its incompetence or by design is involved in an outrageous lie that Iraq has concealed weapons of mass destruction.... This lie will be as short-lived as the previous ones." The Iraqi spokesman for Iraq's National Monitoring Department says the *Washington Post* report is "reminiscent of so many allegations made by UNSCOM and US sources which have all been shown to be mere fabrications. The facts are that VX was not [made into a weapon] in any kind of munition because it was not produced in stable form. Finding a trace of a stabilizer in one sample out of seven analyzed is not evidence because if VX was used, a stabilizer would have been found in every sample. Iraq flatly rejects the findings of the US Army laboratory."

A joint meeting of Iraq's Revolutionary Command Council and officials of the ruling Ba'ath Party, chaired by President Saddam Hussein, condemns UN weapons inspectors as US agents and reiterated a warning that prolonging economic sanctions against it will lead to grave consequences. The statements after the meeting make no direct reference to the charge that UNSCOM weapons inspectors had found traces of the deadly nerve agent VX in missile warheads.

UN and US officials have confirmed that tests at the Aberdeen Proving Ground in Maryland indicated the presence of VX in a number of samples of Scud-type warhead fragments recovered from a destruction site at Nibai, north of Baghdad. They were stored at Taji.

Pentagon spokesman Kenneth Bacon says that evidence that Iraq appears to have put the deadly nerve agent VX on a missile warhead will make it "impossible" for the UN to lift sanctions against Saddam Hussein at this time. The information is important because Iraq has denied that it was ever able to produce VX in significant quantities or in a stable state, which would allow it to be stored for potential later use on weapons. "So if this finding is borne out, it will mean that the... UN Special Commission has found evidence that they (Iraqi officials) were not telling the truth and that confirm the long suspicions that the UN Special Commission has had. That's why it's significant. As long as there is new evidence coming out that Iraq has not been honest or truthful about the extent of its weapons of mass destruction program, it's going to be impossible for the UN to lift sanctions."

Table 10.3 (continued)

	President Clinton says, "If this report is true, it will just show that our insistence over these last many years on the UN inspection system is the right thing to do for the safety of America and the safety of the rest of the world."
	France supplies an official, Eric Fournier, for Butler's executive group, to meet Iraqi complaints that the commission had too many Americans and Britons in leading positions. Russia is sending a foreign ministry official, Nikita Zhukov.
	Iraq and Iran agree to seek a speedy resolution to the cases of thousands of prisoners and people missing in action from their 1980–1988 war. In April the two countries repatriated more than 5,500 prisoners of war, including an Iranian pilot shot down over Iraq just days before Iraqi troops poured across the border. Iran has said 5,000 to 10,000 prisoners are still held by Iraq. Baghdad denies holding any Iranians and has said Tehran still holds about 18,000 Iraqi POWs.
98–6-25:	The Security Council meets on sanctions report. Secretary-General Annan says before the Council meeting that he hopes the finding will not damage UN relations with Iraq. "We are dealing with the Iraqis on a large spectrum of issues and I hope this particular development will not destroy the improved relations that has allowed UNSCOM to carry on with its work." Diplomatic sources, speaking on condition of anonymity, say Annan's senior aides have been pressuring Butler to ease up on the Iraqis so the inspection program can be brought to an end.
	Butler tells the Security Council that findings by a US Army laboratory showed "there is no doubt" that Iraq placed deadly VX nerve gas in missile warheads. He says he will send the missile shards to laboratories in France and Switzerland for further analysis, as Iraq has demanded. But he says the tests were conducted by one of the world's premier chemical weapons laboratories. "I explained to the Council that that is very serious because Iraq has always insisted it never weaponized VX. . . . These findings show they did . . . put it in weapons' warheads. I made clear there is no doubt" that "VX was present in some of those weapons warheads . . . These degradation products could be from no other substance. These are unique products. They were of VX, they were found in a munition, namely a missile warhead. That's weaponization."
	Following Butler's briefing, the Council decides to maintain the sanctions against Iraq. No change in the embargoes had been anticipated and members sympathetic to Iraq are not expected to make an attempt to ease sanctions until late this year. Security Council President Antonio Monteiro of Portugal says that "After hearing the views of the members on this matter we concluded there was no still no agreement that necessary conditions existed for a modification" of the sanctions.
	French Ambassador Alain Dejammet, a strong critic of the inspection program within the 15-member Council, says that if the European labo-

Table 10.3 (continued)

	ratories uphold the findings "it would be a matter to be discussed very seriously."
	Iraq's foreign minister, Foreign Minister Mohammed Saeed al-Sahaf, calls on the Security Council to condemn and counter what he says are plans by the United States to build up a political opposition to President Saddam Hussein. In a letter to the Council, he cites a recent Reuters news report about a US State Department seminar for journalists addressed by Assistant Secretary of State Martin Indyk. Sahaf says Indyk, whom he describes as "a known Jew and Zionist," told the seminar that, "with the cooperation of what he called 73 opposition groups outside Iraq, the US is planning a new effort funded by Congress to build up political opposition to President Saddam Hussein." Sahaf said according to the news account, the US Congress had this year approved $5 million to fund what it called "Radio Free Iraq," to broadcast programming in Arabic to Iraq. "Republican members of the US Congress also proposed spending another $33 million to fund US intelligence agents to "overthrow the Iraqi government." Indyk's "explicit statement . . . represents a dangerous development in international relations and is a violation of the Charter of the UN, as well as a flagrant breach of the duties of members of the Security Council." Sahaf calls on the Council "to condemn the hostile and conspiratorial policy of the US towards Iraq and to appeal to the US administration to halt the policy of conspiracy and incitement against a member state and founding member of the UN." Sahaf also urges the Council to take measures that would guarantee respect for Iraq's sovereignty, territorial integrity, and political independence and prevent the "irresponsible US administration from continuing this criminal behavior" against Iraq.
	American UN envoy Bill Richardson protests to the Security Council, and calls for an apology from Iraq's foreign minister over a "dramatically offensive slur" against a senior US official. Richardson is referring to a letter that Foreign Minister Mohammed Saeed al-Sahaf sent to the Council in which he referred to US Assistant Secretary of State Martin Indyk as "a known Jew and Zionist."
98–6-26:	Iraq demands more tests after UN arms inspectors reported finding traces of a lethal nerve gas in destroyed Iraqi missile warheads. Lt. General Amer al-Saadi, a presidential adviser who heads Iraq's talks with UNSCOM weapons inspectors, says more tests are needed. "We demand that other tests be carried out on samples of those warheads which are in Baghdad and on the sites they were taken from. We also demand to hold a scientific conference through which we talk professionally and scientifically. Instead of sending the test results on the warheads to Iraq early as promised, UNSCOM leaked information on these results to the US *Washington Post* newspaper. Any crisis which may take place would rely on the conduct of the said Commission." He emphasizes, however, that Iraq would continue implementing its obligations toward UNSCOM.

Table 10.3 (continued)

	"Iraq will go on meeting commitments vis-à-vis the Special Commission. It will not stop cooperation with it."
98–6-28:	A UN Children's Fund report says that unless a new UN oil-for-food plan for Iraq is properly implemented, it will do little to offset worsening malnutrition suffered by Iraqi women and children. The reports claims the infant mortality rate nearly doubled between 1990 and 1994, while the number of mothers dying while giving birth rose from 117 to 310 per 100,000 between 1990 and 1996. Last year UNICEF conducted a survey which concluded that over 1 million Iraqi children under age 5 are suffering from malnutrition. According to Iraq's Health Ministry figures some, 57,000 Iraqi children under age 5 die every year.
	Iraqi Foreign Minister Mohammed Saeed al-Sahaf tells a National Assembly session that a report by the UN Special Commission in charge of dismantling Baghdad's prohibited weapons has misled the Security Council by failing to highlight Iraq's cooperation. "The past few days have witnessed a shuffling of the cards inside the Security Council by representatives of the US and Britain. They did not reveal the facts and the progress made through Iraq's cooperation with the Special Commission to implement paragraph 22 of resolution 687 (on sanctions). Representatives of Russia, France, and China cast doubt on Butler's report and embarrassed him many times after they realized that the Chairman and members of UNSCOM are tools in the hands of America and Britain."
98–6-30:	A team from IAEA begins talks with Iraqi officials on the dismantling of Iraq's nuclear arms program. The Security Council calls for the IAEA to present a status report in July. After that report the Council could endorse the agency's position that Iraq has compiled with nuclear arms requirements, but officials in New York say they do not expect action until October.
	A US F-16 warplane fires a missile at a radar site in southern Iraq after Iraqi radar locked onto allied jets flying a routine mission over the Iraqi no-fly zone. A spokesman for USCENTCOM says allied planes detected they were being targeted by radar on the ground. "This is considered an action requiring aggressive defensive measures. In response an F-16 pilot assigned to the 4404 wing fired a High Speed Anti-Radiation Missile." The fighter was accompanying the British Tornadoes enforcing the southern no-fly zone. The planes returned safely to base.
	An official at the Iraqi Ministry of Culture and Information denies that its radar locked on to four British patrol planes and called the firing of a US missile "proof of the aggressiveness of Americans. This is an unjustified, aggressive act. No radar was opened." The Iraqi official says the US missile fell 18 kilometers (11 miles) away from the nearest radar.
	Turkey's parliament debates a six-month extension to the mandate for Western force, known as Operation Northern Watch, to operate out of Turkish territory. The motion is passed.

Table 10.3 (continued)

	Jalal Talabani, head of the Patriotic Union of Kurdistan (PUK), urges Turkey to withdraw its troops from northern Iraq, saying the Turkish presence was an obstacle to reconciliation between anti-Baghdad Kurdish forces.
	Russia urges the United States to exercise restraint after an American F-16 fighter jet fired a missile at an Iraqi surface-to-air missile battery in southern Iraq.
	Iraq and Iran open trade talks in Baghdad to boost bilateral economic relations.
	Iraqi Trade Minister Mohammed Mehdi Saleh holds talks in Damascus on ways to increase Syrian imports in line with Baghdad's oil-for-food deal with the UN.
98–7-2:	UN special rapporteur for human rights Max van der Stoel condemns two recent assassinations of Shi'ite Moslem clerics and says they appeared to be the latest killings aimed at silencing dissent in the country. He warns this might be part of an "organized attack by Iraqi officials against the independent leadership of the Sh'ia religious community."
	Jordanian Energy Minister Mohammad al-Hourani arrives in Baghdad to negotiate extra Iraqi energy supplies for a strategic stockpile and discuss a planned pipeline between the two countries. Energy officials say Hourani will negotiate extra crude and petroleum supplies to be stored in new tanks scheduled for completion this year, which add an extra 230,000 ton capacity—or nearly 20 days' consumption.
	UN sources confirm that the US missile attack in southern Iraq left neither human casualties nor structural damage.
	Iraqi Foreign Minister Mohammed Saeed al-Sahaf sends a letter to the Security Council, complaining that it did nothing about Kuwaiti statements that it said threatened the "sovereignty and security" of Iraq. "I should like to inform you and the members of the Council of a number of documented official statements made by senior Kuwaiti officials that have actually threatened the sovereignty and security of Iraq." He cites press reports of a number of "hostile statements and pronouncement concerning Iraq" by Kuwaiti officials, saying they "explicitly acknowledge action taken to replace the political regime in Iraq and the utilization of Kuwaiti funds for this purpose." Sahaf urges the Security Council to "alert Kuwaiti leaders to the consequences" of such statements and to "warn them to desist from the actions in which engage in order to threaten Iraq's security and integrity."
98–7-4:	An IAEA team completes four days of talks with Iraqi officials on the country's nuclear arms program. The team had met with Iraq's Deputy Prime Minister, Tariq Aziz. In its previous report in April, the IAEA had said Iraq had compiled a "full, final and complete" account of its past nuclear weapons programs. At the time, the IAEA also said its monitoring and verification activities since October, 1997 "have not revealed

Table 10.3 (continued)

indications of the existence in Iraq of prohibited equipment or materials or of the conduct of prohibited activity." In response, Russia proposed a plan that would close the so-called nuclear "file" on nuclear weapons in Iraq and shift from an active "search and destroy" disarmament phase to long-term "passive monitoring."

Babel renews its attack on UN Special Commission arms inspectors on Saturday, saying UNSCOM chief Richard Butler and his predecessor should be put on trial.

Iraqi Foreign Minister al-Sahaf says that Iraq has drawn up a new strategy to cope with crippling UN economic sanctions but will continue to press the Security Council to lift the embargoes imposed nearly eight years ago. "We have to prepare ourselves correctly and effectively to implement an alternative strategy drawn up by our leadership, with increased efforts behind the current strategy which is pressing on the Security Council [to end sanctions]. This commission is a tool in the hands of the Americans. Although it was set up by the Security Council, it is dominated by the US administration. The aim of this game is very clear—that is to find excuses to prolong the work of the Special Commission." He says that Iraq is trying to expand its diplomatic ties with Arab and European countries which suffered after the 1991 Gulf War over Kuwait.

US Ambassador Richardson says the United States will oppose any move to certify that Iraq has met its obligation to scrap its nuclear weapons program as premature. "We want Iraq to answer more questions on nuclear design, nuclear exports and uranium technology." Describing Saddam Hussein as a pathological liar, Richardson said the Iraqi leader was constantly trying to divide the UN Security Council by "pulling a fast one." He predicts that UN sanctions imposed on Iraq after its 1990 invasion of Kuwait would stay in place "for a long time" unless Iraq complies with Security Council disarmament demands, deals with restitution to Kuwait and Kuwaiti prisoners of war, and stops "abusing their own people. Iraq is already saying that the nuclear file will be closed and we think that's very premature." He reaffirmed that the United States would oppose lifting sanctions pending verifiable destruction of Iraq's deadliest weapons as well as pending the return of Kuwaiti prisoners and property seized or destroyed in the August 2, 1990, invasion and a general improvement in respecting human rights.

Iraq accuses the United States of blocking UN approval for 40 contracts it signed with international firms to supply spare parts for its oil industry. Oil Minister Lt. General Amer Mohammed Rashid says despite the Council's approval, the UN sanctions committee has not reached agreement yet on how to process the contracts. He blames Washington for the delay. "We have almost no spare parts now," Rashid added. "We are running at a very critical level in terms of production."

Iraq announces it has exported 20 million barrels of oil from its southern Mina-al-Bakr terminal in June under the oil-for-food deal with the UN.

Table 10.3 (continued)

	The head of the Iraqi Southern Oil Company, Mohammed Yassin al-Douboni, says the capacity of the export terminal, which was bombed during the 1991 Gulf War, has been raised to 1.8 million barrels per day.
	Iraq and Lebanon sign a $50 million economic cooperation agreement to export agricultural and other materials to Iraq.
98-7-5:	Iraq accuses the United States and Britain of causing thousands of deaths from cancer as the result of the toxic dust released by depleted uranium rounds. The United States replies that tests have shown no correlation between cancer and any credible contamination from such rounds.
	Talks in Baghdad on the remaining issues blocking the lifting of sanctions on Iraq collapse. The Iraqis return to the belligerent tone which caused an international crisis in October, 1997 and February, 1998, and reject a plan for settling issues proposed by the UN chief arms inspector for Iraq, Richard Butler. Tariq Aziz, the Iraqi delegation leader, accuses Butler, an Australian, of using "old tricks" and following an American policy of continuing sanctions no matter what progress is made. The Iraqis stage a funeral procession for 35 Iraqi children outside the building where Butler and Aziz meet. Their parents tell reporters that the children had died because of sanctions. The Iraqis accuse the United States of "wrecking" the program under which limited oil sales are permitted to pay for food and medicine. UN officials counter that a loosening of the sanctions has increased oil sales sharply and has allowed hundreds of millions of dollars in medical supplies to reach Iraq. They say it was the Iraqi government that recently reduced a UN proposal to raise caloric intake in food distribution.
	The IAEA reports to the UN Security Council that it has found no evidence that Iraq has nuclear weapons. But the agency says that Iraq's failure to account for key nuclear equipment and technical blueprints leaves open the possibility that it has hidden the necessary expertise and material for future use. In their report, the international inspectors criticize Iraq for its lack of full transparency about the secret nuclear program. "Indeed it is prudent to assume that Iraq has retained documentation of its clandestine nuclear program, specimens of important components, and possibly amounts of non-enriched uranium," the agency says in its report. The report also says, "there remains in Iraq a considerable intellectual resource in the form of the cadre of well-educated, highly experienced personnel who were employed in Iraq's clandestine nuclear program." It criticizes Iraq for not providing the agency with drawings of a weapon design, experimental test data, and other documents related to its nuclear program, and in particular its use of centrifuges to produce weapons grade uranium and what is called a vacuum induction furnace. "Iraq did have a program to be able to make these furnaces indigenously," says David Albright, president of the independent Institute for Science and International Security. "This is an essential component in

Table 10.3 (continued)

	making a bomb,'' he added, ''but of equal concern is Iraq's unwillingness to give the inspectors unfettered access to the Iraqi nuclear experts.''
	The report warns the Security Council that if Iraqi inspections can move to long-term monitoring from hands-on disarmament and destruction of material during its next sanctions review in October, a range of intrusive inspection techniques will have to be used. These include unannounced inspections of any site, aerial surveillance photography, and an almost total environmental monitoring of air, water, soil, and vegetation. Providing a list of these measures may be intended to meet concerns of independent arms control experts who charge that the agency has not in the past been rigorous enough in Iraq and cannot be counted on to be as intrusive in the future as the UN Special Commission, which is inspecting and destroying biological and chemical weapons systems and missiles. The report reveals that Iraq is already quibbling over the terms of long-term monitoring. The Iraqis will not allow the agency planes to use the Rashid air base near Baghdad, where the inspectors have their headquarters. The inspectors will have to continue to use the Habanniya base, an isolated wreck of a military installation more than an hour's drive from the capital. Moreover, the Iraqis told agency representatives that if there will be a comprehensive environmental detection program, the intrusive inspections should be reduced. The Iraqis also demanded access to raw data collected in surveillance, ''in particular the data collected through aerial radiation surveys.''
	Saddam Hussein gives an address on the 30th anniversary of the revolution that brought him to power. He states that sanctions will erode, rather than being lifted all at once by the UN. ''This year, and in the time that follows, God willing, will be the virtual erosion of the blockade.'' The speech at least hints at a willingness to compromise.
98–7-21:	Thirty-three Democrats and one house Republican urge President Clinton to lift sanctions on Iraq because of the damage being done to the Iraqi people.
98–7-29:	*Babel* accuses the United States of blocking efforts to wrap up an investigation into Iraq's nuclear program. ''After their visit to Iraq to give a decisive report on closing the Iraqi nuclear file, the International Atomic Energy Agency announced that Iraq had given the required and convincing answers on the program. . . . The US administration, through its UN ambassador, quickly announced it was too early to speak of closing the Iraqi nuclear file next October. The objection of the US . . . means it does not recognize the international agency and rejects the role of the UN.''
	Russia proposes a resolution saying Iraq has complied with demands to destroy its nuclear arms facilities. China and France support the resolution, Britain and the United States oppose it.
98–7-30:	Iraqi Vice President Taha Yassin Ramadan announces that Iraq is losing patience with UNSCOM and the UN and threatens unspecified Iraqi ac-

Table 10.3 (continued)

	tion if the UN does not act to lift sanctions. "We know the influence and the hegemony being practiced on the UN Security Council by America and its ally Britain."
	Iraq's Revolutionary Command Council sends a four-page letter to the Secretary-General demanding that the nuclear inspection effort be downgraded from ongoing inspection to long-term monitoring.
98–7-31:	Richard Butler leaves for Baghdad. He announces that he will try to reconcile the issue of VX nerve gas warheads with Iraqi officials.
98–8-3:	Tariq Aziz meets with Richard Butler and announces that he expects to talks to make no progress and says UNSCOM is "back to its old games and its old tricks." He says Butler is "focusing on minor issues that make no sense from the angle of disarmament. . . . Since this is the wish of the American administration to perpetuate the situation—as long as this is the American wish, you are serving American policy."
	Iraqi security forces announce they have captured two of five men who shot and seriously wounded Uday Hussein on December 12, 1996. A unnamed foreign country is accused of being involved in the attack and as granting sanctuary to the other three attackers.
	Iraq blames UN sanctions for power supply shortages and claims it has only received $29 million out of $180 million worth of contracts to repair the electrical sector.
	The US House of Representatives votes by 407–6 to declare that Iraq has committed a material breech of the terms of the cease-fire.
98–8-4:	Secretary-General Kofi Annan says that the latest confrontation "may be a major hiccup, but a hiccup we can overcome, I hope."
	Butler cuts his visit to Iraq short and describes his meeting with Tariq Aziz in more detail, "I offered him a new accelerated schedule of work for the next five weeks in order to try and resolve most of the outstanding issues, mainly in the chemical and missile areas, before our October report to the Security Council. Iraq must account for all nuclear, biological, chemical and long-range missile systems before sanctions imposed in 1990 can be lifted. Aziz refused to accept the proposal, saying he wasn't ready to continue working with UNSCOM on these issues." He says Aziz had told him that "no more discussion would take place for the present."
	The Clinton administration warns that Iraq's decision to refuse to discuss any further cooperation with UN arms inspectors will only insure that Baghdad remains under sanctions indefinitely. British officials say that recent inspections had uncovered new data on Iraq's efforts to produce VX gas and uncovered evidence showing that 4,000 chemical weapons remain unaccounted for.
	Officials with Butler in Baghdad say that he never got to have a substantive discussion with the Iraqi team, led by Tariq Aziz. Officials say

Table 10.3 (continued)

	that Aziz and his colleagues appeared relaxed, even smug, as they simply stated and restated what apparently had become a high-level policy line that there was nothing left to talk about, that Iraq had ended all its weapons programs and that sanctions should be lifted without further ado.
	Russia and France, which have supported Iraq's demand for an early end to sanctions, react with concern to the breakdown of the talks. The Russians, who served as mediators with Iraq in the past, call for the talks to resume. The French foreign ministry expresses exasperation in a statement that says, "We repeat that good cooperation between UNSCOM and Iraq is necessary and unavoidable if sanctions imposed by the Security Council are to be lifted."
98–8-5:	Iraq issues a statement that it is ending all cooperation with UN arms inspectors in Iraq and effectively demanded the dismissal of Richard Butler through a restructuring of his disarmament commission. The action clearly breaks the agreement made in February with Kofi Annan when Iraq pledged to "cooperate fully with the UN Special Commission and the International Atomic Energy Agency" and to grant them "unconditional and unrestricted access" to sites in Iraq. In their statement, the Iraqis urge that the disarmament panel be moved from New York to Geneva or Vienna, Austria, to free itself of American influence.
	Butler meets with Annan and states later that "the Secretary-General and I certainly agree that there is a syndrome here—going around the same track again and again. We have to find a way to break that. That's up to the Security Council."
	In a statement published in Baghdad, Iraq says that only surveillance cameras set up by UNSCOM will be allowed to operate. Significantly, this would be closer to the level of monitoring Iraq would face if sanctions were to be lifted, as Iraq demands. The statement warns UNSCOM inspectors that they would have to "respect Iraq's sovereignty, security and dignity." Iraq has in the past classified some inspections as intrusions on sovereignty and put areas off limits. More than 100 inspectors, laboratory scientists, and technical experts from a number of countries continue to work at the Baghdad monitoring center or are based there on temporary inspection assignments. Butler says, "I am instructing people to go about their normal work."
	Russia holds Butler at least partly responsible for the latest crisis. Yuri Fedotov, Russia's deputy representative, says, "we are strongly convinced that Iraq is not the only one to blame for this situation, when a decision has been taken to break discussions. . . . This decision we understand was taken by the chairman of UNSCOM without duly consulting the secretary-general and the Security Council."
98–8-6:	Butler briefs members of the Security Council on his trip to Iraq. He discusses the Iraqi leadership's refusal to turn over documents, including one discovered in July that shed light on the amount of "nonconventional

Table 10.3 (continued)

munitions" used during the 1980–1987 war with Iran. The documents could prove that there are larger quantities of chemical—and possibly biological—agents unaccounted for in Iraq than inspectors were told about last year. Iraq says that they had filled 101,080 warheads with chemical weapons in the 1980s, but the new document reveals that fewer than that were actually deployed. The inspectors want to know what happened to the rest. Butler also provides the Security Council with results of a technical evaluation in July of Iraq's "full, final and complete disclosure" on biological weapons, a document the Iraqis say closes the file on that issue. This was the third such technical evaluation demanded by Iraq over the last year, and its findings were no different than earlier ones. "No new material was presented by Iraq at this meeting," Butler wrote in his report of the July technical evaluation. The international experts again concluded that Iraq's latest disclosure "was not adequate to allow for credible verification." The biological experts, whom the Iraqis have accused of being "brainwashed by UNSCOM," found problems with Iraqi accounts of what they had done with bombs, warheads, spraying devices, or quantities of the agents themselves, including Botulinum toxin, Anthrax bacillus and Aflatoxin.

Clinton administration officials say the Iraqis' apparent motive was to provoke a crisis in hope that it would further divide the United States from other members of the UN Security Council, especially Russia and France, who have sought to lift the economic and military sanctions imposed on Baghdad after the 1991 Gulf War. P. J. Crowley, a White House spokesman, says the United States will "keep the pressure on" to persuade Iraq to end its defiance of UN arms inspectors, but that it was too early to contemplate a military response to the latest standoff between Iraq and the UN. "Noncompliance is completely unacceptable.... We will not allow Iraq access to resources necessary to restart their weapons of mass destruction program. We will continue to keep the pressure on until Iraq complies fully with their obligations." James Foley, a State Department spokesman, notes that this was not the first time that Baghdad had refused to cooperate with the arms inspections, only to back down. "We've seen this time and time again. We're not calling it a crisis because, frankly, we don't want to play into Saddam Hussein's hands. Clearly he's in a box. He's trying to squirm his way out. He's trying to provoke a crisis." The Defense Department issues a statement that it has "a very adequate force" in the region of the Persian Gulf—19,000 troops, 167 planes, and the aircraft carrier *Abraham Lincoln*—to deal with Iraq in the case of a military confrontation.

Saddam Hussein issues a statement in Baghdad demanding that UNSCOM headquarters be moved from New York to Vienna to keep UNSCOM away from direct US influence, that the commissions leadership be dissolved and replaced by two members each from each permanent member of the Security Council, that Iraq be made an observer on

Table 10.3 (continued)

	UNSCOM, and that Iraq be recognized as having complied with all Security Council resolutions as a prelude to lifting sanctions. He says that as a goodwill gesture, Iraq will not interfere with monitoring cameras already in place in suspect sites.
98-8-7:	The Security Council unites to condemn Iraq for ending cooperation with UN arms inspectors and calls its conduct "totally unacceptable," but takes no action other than to demand that Baghdad reverse its decision. Secretary-General Annan speaks to the Council about his assessment of Iraq's position after talking Thursday morning with Deputy Foreign Minister Aziz, who leads Iraqi negotiators in dealing with UNSCOM. Annan tells the Council that Iraq is "clearly in violation of the resolutions of the Security Council and the memorandum of understanding I concluded in Baghdad in February. I believe this is well understood by the government of Iraq." Speaking to reporters later, Annan says that he told Aziz that Iraq could not dictate how inspections are conducted and by whom. He says that he had made clear to Aziz "that the Iraqi suggestion that UNSCOM should be restructured and possibly moved from New York is something that was not acceptable. No individual state can tell the UN how to structure itself to carry out tasks or mandates given to it." Annan adds, however, that he feels Iraq's position is "not a closed one," that Baghdad had acted out of frustration and even desperation, and that it might be the right time "to stand back and make a comprehensive reassessment of where we are, where we are going and how to get there. In undertaking this comprehensive review, it might be helpful to engage the Iraqis much more closely than we have hitherto done."
	UNSCOM gives a background briefing that shows that the Iraqis knew that problems in accounting for biological and some chemical compounds were serious and growing and that Iraq had continued to change figures and alter other information earlier presented as "full, final and complete" declarations. The Iraqis had been forced to revise a story when confronted with evidence by inspectors, as in the recent case of the discovery of traces of VX nerve gas on shell casings. At other times they volunteer new information, but that only raises more troubling questions about why an account has changed. In recent examinations of old warhead remnants, for example, weapons experts found more traces of Anthrax than they could explain. When the Iraqis were pressed, they revised earlier "final figures" to say that they had actually filled three times as many warheads with Anthrax (16) as with botulism (five). Until then, Iraq says it had mounted weapons with more than three times more botulism than Anthrax. This admission has revived speculation among inspectors that Iraq had produced not only more Anthrax, but also two kinds of it, one in a dry form that was easier to spray and had a longer shelf life. Officials insist that this is only speculation at this point. Charles Duelfer, deputy chairman of UNSCOM, says that "Every time Iraq changes the figures, it has a ripple effect throughout their entire declaration. That is a very

322   *Iraq and the War of Sanctions*

Table 10.3 (continued)

	complicated procedure because a declaration is built and substantiated to support one set of numbers, and to change that becomes very difficult.''
	Tariq Aziz gives a new explanation of how VX nerve gas could have been found on shells after Iraqis denied they used it. In a letter to the Security Council on Wednesday, he said the traces could have been created from the ''decomposition of other chemical substances or from the use of equipment that has already been used to produce the VX agent.''
	Russian Foreign Ministry spokesman Vladimir Rakhmanin tells a news briefing in Moscow, ''It is now extremely important not to stoke tensions over Iraq.''
	Chinese spokesman Tang Guoqiang says his government would do what it could ''to avoid a worsening of the situation.''
	In a speech on the tenth anniversary of the end of Iraq's war with Iran, President Saddam Hussein says that his country would triumph over the West in its trade sanction standoff. In the war with Iran, from 1980 to 1988, ''will triumphed over might,'' and Hussein added that Iraq would win again in dealing with the outcome of the aftermath of the Gulf War. ''The Americans and their allies underestimated Iraq's ability to resist brute force and that's why they failed. Fooled by their own power, those who attacked Iraq and imposed on it an unjust embargo continue to make the same mistake. Their harvest will be full of thorns, and they will taste bitter defeat.''
98–8-9:	UN Secretary-General Kofi Annan summons his special envoy in Baghdad, Prakash Shah of India, for talks and sends him back with a message asking Saddam Hussein to end Iraq's refusal to cooperate with arms inspectors.
	No active weapons searches have taken place in Iraq since it said that it would no longer cooperate with inspectors. Only the maintenance of long-term surveillance equipment installed at Iraqi sites is being permitted. This type of surveillance was to have been the next stage in the monitoring process, but only after Iraq had been declared free of banned weapons and sanctions had been lifted. Iraq appears to be trying to move itself to that stage by fiat. UN officials and diplomats say it is difficult to see how more intrusive inspections can be resumed unless Saddam Hussein sees some gain in reversing his order.
	The Arab League accuses Richard Butler of overstepping his mandate in continuing to demand a fuller account of weapons programs from Iraq. Arab League spokesman Talaat Hamed says, ''Butler's actions exceed his duties, since Iraq has fulfilled all its commitments concerning weapons of mass destruction.'' Hamed says the league's secretary general, Esmat Abdel-Meguid, was in contact with Annan. ''Abdel-Meguid wants the Iraqi file completely closed.''
	Iraq announces that its oil pipeline between Kirkuk in Iraq and Banias on the Syrian coast will reopen soon.

Table 10.3 (continued)

98–8-10:	Iraqi television and networks show video footage of a tense standoff between Tariq Aziz and Richard Butler in talks that broke down 10 days ago in Baghdad. More than four hours of tapes of two days of meetings are shown in Iraq. Networks have aired mostly one short clip that appears to show Butler getting up from his chair and abruptly ending the meetings August 3. "That never happened," Butler says in an interview, recalling his last, admittedly chilly meeting with Aziz. "The meeting ended in an orderly way. I walked around the table and shook his hand." Aziz discloses that Thyssen of Germany shipped Iraq 35 of the turbo-pumps it used in making its missiles. Health Minister Umeed Madhat Mubarak charges that 1.4 million people have died as a result of UN imposed sanctions. In an interview with the Ba'ath Party paper *al-Thawra*, he claims that more than one million Iraqi children have died, and that an average of 6,452 children under the age of 5 are dying per month versus 539 before the Gulf crisis. He claims the death rate has risen from 24 per 1,000 births in 1989 to 92 in 1998, and that deaths among people over age 5 have risen from 1,600 a month in 1989 to 7,600 in 1998. He says that Iraq used to import $500 million worth of medicine a year in 1989, and that imports have not exceeded $35 million since the beginning of 1998.
98–8-11:	Iraq reopens the Munthiriya complex on the border with Iran with the potential ability to process 3,000 Iranian pilgrims a week. UN Special Envoy Prakash Shah announces he will return to Iraq.
98–8-13:	The UN Security Council is scheduled to debate a draft declaration that acknowledges that its plans to disarm Iraq have suffered a setback. The draft simply instructs the inspectors to press ahead with their work and report any further Iraqi obstruction. The draft the Security Council will consider, and which diplomats say appears to have widespread support, makes no threats of military action against Iraq if it continues to defy the inspectors. Instead, it recalls that the Council has already condemned Iraq's refusal to cooperate as "totally unacceptable," and it acknowledges that "under current circumstances" the inspectors cannot assure the Council that Iraq will not "re-establish its proscribed weapons program." But it also reminds them that they still have a mandate to "carry out a full range of activities including inspections" and says they should report back to the Security Council if they are "hindered in any way from undertaking these activities." Finally, the Council expresses hope that the current visit to Baghdad by UN mediator Prakash Shah of India will result in the "full resumption of cooperation" between Iraq and the inspectors. US and British diplomats acknowledge that the Security Council has no appetite for a repeat of February's confrontation with Baghdad, when only a last-minute agreement between Saddam Hussein and Kofi Annan prevented new military strikes.

Table 10.3 (continued)

	Iraq begins to threaten UNSCOM and IAEA long-term monitoring capability, and blocks inspectors from returning to some sites where cameras and soil-sampling equipment indicates suspicious activities.
98-8-16:	Turkey signs contracts with Iraq as part of the oil-for-food deal which are worth $228 million.
98-8-17:	Prakash Shah fails to persuade Baghdad to resume cooperation with the two agencies trying to find and eliminate its weapons of mass destruction. Iraq's UN representative, Nizar Hamdoon, confirms Baghdad's refusal to change its position and says the inspection agencies had been "unjust and unfair." Hamdoon adds that this was "why we have decided to stop all cooperation" with the two agencies, UNSCOM and the IAEA.
	US Ambassador Bill Richardson says it is up to the Security Council and the Secretary-General to respond adequately. He says the Council would not allow Iraq to goad it into "precipitous action." But, he added, Iraq has "put itself in a box," so that "sanctions are going to stay forever, or until it complies fully."
98-8-18:	Kuwait's Prime Minister and Crown Prince, Sheik Saad al-Abdullah al-Sabah, warns that Iraq is still a threat. "The Iraqi regime is trying to dodge sanctions and will not leave us in peace."
	Babel accuses Israel and the US Jewish lobby of causing the sex scandal President Clinton faces in the United States.
	Syrian Oil Minister Muhammad Mahar Jamal arrives in Iraq on a three-day visit to discuss trade and the July, 1998 agreement to reopen the Kirkuk to Banias pipeline.
98-8-19:	Prakash Shah leaves Baghdad for New York. The Security Council had ordered him to continue his work and invite Baghdad to resume cooperation with his inspectors. But Aziz rejects the UN position, saying Iraq does not trust Butler and will not cooperate with UN inspectors seeking to eliminate its weapons of mass destruction until the Security Council starts lifting the trade embargo. He says Iraq will not change its position "until the Council seriously and sincerely considers, away from American pressure and blackmail, Iraq's legitimate demands," starting with lifting the embargo, according to a Reuters report from Baghdad.
98-8-20:	The UN Security Council maintains trade sanctions on Iraq, and states Iraq's refusal to allow inspections is "totally unacceptable," but defers further action until it hears a report from Prakash Shah.
	Butler appeals again to Iraq to resume its cooperation with UNSCOM.
	Tariq Aziz issues a statement saying, "we no longer trust Butler and those controlling UNSCOM and we think it is futile to resume work with them. Butler is pursuing a policy of maneuvering and procrastination in order not to report to the Security Council that the UNSCOM task of disarming Iraq has been complete. It is no more a secret that Butler and some UNSCOM members . . . are not international personnel; rather they

Table 10.3 (continued)

	are servicing American policy which aims at prolonging the embargo on Iraq.''
98–8-21:	US Ambassador Richardson warns that the sanctions might never be lifted. ''Sanctions may stay on in perpetuity,'' he says, echoing the warning he made after a Council meeting on Monday that ''sanctions are going to stay on forever.''
	Kuwait announces that 1,050 American military personnel have arrived to take part with the Kuwait army in routine maneuvers unrelated to tensions over UN weapons inspection in Iraq.
	Iraqi radio condemns US war games in Kuwait as intended to provoke Iraqi people: ''The coming US maneuvers on Kuwaiti territory near the Iraqi border are part of a campaign of provocation and threats against the Iraqi people. The Sabah ruling family have continued since 1990 to put Kuwait's land, resources and people at the service of aggressive US policies in the Arab Gulf region,'' the statement added.
98–8-25:	The government newspaper *al-Jumhouriya* announces that Iraq will not change its position on UN inspections. It says Iraq will only resume cooperation when Article 22 is implemented and Iraq is free to export oil.
	US officials state that Iraq's ties to the Sudan were a key reason the United States launched cruise missile strikes on the Shifa Pharmaceutical Plant. They say the United States had evidence that Iraqi scientists had aided efforts at a second plant, several miles away, to make precursors for chemical weapons. Emad al-Ani, a senior Iraqi scientist, is reported to have ties to senior Sudanese officials working at the factory, and several Iraqi scientists working for Al-Ani attended the opening of the plant two years earlier
98–8-26:	Scott Ritter, a leading UNSCOM arms inspector, resigns after issuing a scathing criticism of the UN's handling of the inspections. He states that Iraq has succeeded in gutting the inspection program. ''There is an illusion of arms control taking place. Right now, we are not doing meaningful inspections in Iraq.'' Ritter accuses the UN and the United States of refusing to challenge Iraq for fear of creating a confrontation like the one in February. He says Iraq is concealing missiles, biological and chemical weapons, and nuclear efforts, and that the concealment effort is orchestrated by the presidential security forces.
98–8-27:	A spokesman for the Iraqi Ministry of Culture and Information says Ritter is a spy with links to the CIA and Israeli Mossad. ''All plans of UNSCOM and its programs and the behavior of its chairman and competent members are hatched in American and Zionist intelligence rooms.''
	A French foreign ministry official says Ritter's charges are exaggerated and untrue.

Table 10.3 (continued)

	Butler says that UNSCOM still has the support of the Secretary-General and Security Council, but praises Ritter and says there is still work to be done.
	Secretary Albright says that the United States remains a strong supporter of UNSCOM.
98-8-29:	Russian President Yeltsin tells US President Clinton that he will urge Iraq's leader to resume cooperation with UN weapons inspectors. Officials at a US–Russian summit say that Yeltsin had been dismayed by President Saddam Hussein's decision last month to cease cooperation with the inspectors, which broke promises Saddam had made him. Yeltsin told Clinton "that he had been very unpleasantly surprised . . . by Saddam's decision, that it contradicted assurances that Saddam had given him and that he intends to make his own approach to Saddam to stress the need and the urgency of restoring Iraq to compliance."
	Butler tells the Security Council that Iraq had refused three times over the past month to allow inspectors to survey sites they visited previously, thus tightening the curbs it announced on August 5. In written notes to the Council, he says some previously declared sites were now off limits. He lists three incidents when a monitoring team went to look at missile components UNSCOM had tagged previously. Iraq refused to provide access, saying the facility was not a declared site. Two other similar disputes occurred in August when inspectors were refused entry to sites they had monitored in the past. "Iraq has advised the commission, orally, that it may only visit those sites which Iraq alone has declared." Butler tells reporters UNSCOM was "carrying out the monitoring that Iraq is allowing us to carry out. It is less than the whole monitoring program. We are doing no disarmament work."
	Britain and the United States submit a draft resolution to the Security Council on Thursday to suspend periodic reviews of sanctions against Iraq until it resumes full cooperation with UN weapons inspectors. British Deputy UN Representative Stephen Gomersall says the draft to suspend sanctions reviews was submitted during closed-door Council consultations that included the briefing by UNSCOM chief Richard Butler. Gomersall says the proposed draft was "a necessary step to try and get the resumption of Iraq's cooperation with UNSCOM, which is vital if the verification and disarmament task of UNSCOM, which is in itself vital to security in the region, is to be completed." He says discussion of the draft had just begun and predicted a vote in "a matter of days." The draft resolution, invoking the UN Charter's mandatory provisions, would condemn Iraq's non-cooperation with both UNSCOM and the IAEA, which monitors Baghdad's nuclear capacity. It would demand that Baghdad rescind its decision and cooperate fully, in accordance with Council resolutions and an agreement that Secretary-General Kofi Annan negotiated in February that was intended to ensure UN teams unfettered access. The resolution would express the Council's readiness to consider

Table 10.3 (continued)

"in a comprehensive fashion, Iraq's compliance with its obligations under all relevant resolutions," once it had demonstrated it was prepared to honor all its obligations.

UN reports that low oil prices mean that Iraq is expected to produce a little more than half of the $5.2 billion in oil it is allowed to sell over six months. Iraq was authorized by the Security Council to sell $5.2 billion worth of oil during the subsequent six months, but it has only managed to sell $1.06 billion worth of oil because of weak world demand and the damaged state of its oil industry. Because of weak world oil prices, Iraq is currently getting an average price of only $9 to $10 a barrel for its oil, compared with $19 to $20 when it first started selling oil under the program in December, 1996. As a result, oil experts have warned the UN that the country is unlikely to be able to raise more than $2.5 billion to $3 billion during the current six-month period.

While two-thirds of the money raised from oil sales is available for buying food and other humanitarian goods, another 30 percent goes into the Kuwait compensation fund and the remainder is spent on the arms inspectors and administrative expenses. Another important factor is the time it is taking for Iraq to order, receive, and install the $300 million worth of spare parts that the Security Council allowed it to buy last June to repair damage done to its oil industry by the Persian Gulf War and the trade embargo.

Because of the shortfall, UN officials have begun discussions with Baghdad to prioritize its humanitarian purchases. Iraq has complained about delays in contract approvals and deliveries of goods. Iraqi health officials charge that less than 1 percent of the $200 million in medical supplies that Baghdad was permitted to buy during the first six months of 1998 had arrived in the country. UN spokesman Eric Falt acknowledged that medicine deliveries were "slower than expected," but says $17 million, or 9 percent of the medical supplies, arrived during the third phase.

UN officials also say that Iraq will have more money to spend on imported food and humanitarian supplies this year than at any time since sanctions began. Raising between $2.5 billion and $3 billion by the end of November will still give it substantially more than the $2 billion it has been allowed to earn during each of the three previous six-month periods since May, 1996. That was when Iraq finally accepted the Security Council's oil for food offer, 13 months after it was made. According to UN figures, Iraq has imported 6.5 million tons of food and $330 million worth of medical goods since the first shipments under the program in March, 1997. Nevertheless, if the UN is to succeed in its objective of raising the nutritional value of the food ration each Iraqi receives from the government from 2,030 calories a day in 1997—regarded as about the minimum for healthy living—to 2,268 calories this year, it will need to allocate more money to food and less to other humanitarian needs like medicine and health care.

Table 10.3 (continued)

        Iraq's Deputy Oil Minister, Taha Hamoud, says Iraq is ready to export oil under its oil-for-food deal with the UN via the Iraqi-Saudi pipeline, closed since the 1991 Gulf War. "We are ready to pump oil via the pipeline which connect Iraq with the Red Sea with an export capacity of 1,650 million barrels per day."

        Syria opens a trade center in Baghdad, a move seen by officials from the two former foes as a first step toward resuming diplomatic ties severed 18 years ago. Relations have been improving since last year, when both countries agreed to reopen their borders to encourage the flow of Syrian goods under Iraq's oil-for-food deal with the UN. In July, the two countries signed an agreement in Damascus to reopen a pipeline between Iraq's Kirkuk oilfield and the Syrian port of Banias. Iraqi Oil Minister Amir Muhammed Rasheed agreed in Baghdad in August with his Syrian counterpart on a schedule to pump oil via the pipeline, closed since 1982. Officials from the two countries say steps are under way to reopen their embassies, closed for the past two decades. A Syrian trade official says a delegation from the Syrian Foreign Ministry will visit Baghdad on September 15 to check the embassy building, and that trade between the two countries was worth $150 million in 1997 and was expected to reach the same level this year.

        Iraq's Minister of Trade, Mohammed Mehdi Saleh, says Iraq is holding talks with Saudi firms to buy food and medicine under its oil-for-food deal with the UN. "We are conducting trade negotiations with our brothers the Saudis to conclude food and medicine contracts... Representatives of several Saudi companies have visited Baghdad recently and we are currently holding talks with these companies."

98–8-30:   Former UNSCOM inspector Scott Ritter testifies to a joint hearing of the Senate Foreign Relations and Armed Services committees that Iraq would be able to reconstitute its biological and chemical weapons capability and deliver a weapon of mass destruction within six months of the end of UN weapons inspections. "We know in fact that Iraq has a plan to have a breakout scenario for reconstitution of long-range ballistic missiles within six months of the 'go' signal from Iraqi President Saddam Hussein."

        Benon Sevan, UN director of the oil-for-food plan, criticizes the Security Council, especially the United States, for holding up equipment Iraq needs to upgrade its oil industry, one reason the so-called oil-for-food program was falling far below targets. "The program cannot be fully implemented unless the Iraqis can enhance production and enhance capacity to produce oil... This is a crucial issue which needs urgent resolution." Sevan says the delay in obtaining oil industry equipment has led Iraq to tell purchasers it would have to reduce oil supply contracts by some 10 percent over the next three months. All contracts under the program must be approved by the Security Council's sanctions committee. The United States has distinguished between "upstream" equip-

Table 10.3 (continued)

	ment—getting the oil out of the "downstream" operations, which involve getting petroleum products to market. US officials have said that the $300 million approved by the Security Council for spare parts should be used for short-term improvements and not to overhaul Iraq's oil industry for its long-term needs. Ambassador Richardson says, "We are ready to approve spare parts contracts provided that they deal with oil efficiency delivery to the Iraqi people to get humanitarian assistance. But for other frivolous purposes, we will not approve them." Sevan says oil experts from the Dutch Saybolt firm had made it clear to the Security Council that downstream operations were often needed to enable the industry as a whole to operate safely and efficiently. He says he had discussed the issue with US officials, and "I think there is a movement, a little bit on that issue." But he says the entire program is being run in a "suspicious" political atmosphere which made progress difficult. Sevan says 67 equipment contracts were received for approval at a total value of $79.8 million, of which 52 had been circulated to sanctions committee members. A total of 19 were approved and 22 applications had been placed on hold. Sevan says the shortfall in revenues delays a rise in Iraqi food supplies to 2,300 calories a day per person from the current 2,000 calories until at least October, noting that the calorie level was only 1,400 before the program began 18 months ago. Sevan says the quality of foodstuffs was poor and probably could not be improved because of the lower revenues.
	The *Tehran Times* reports that Iran's vice president, Hassan Habibi, is to visit neighboring Iraq, the highest-ranking official to make such a trip in two decades. He is to sign agreements on the exchange of prisoners from the 1980–1988 Iran-Iraq War, war reparations, water sharing, border security, and on ending support for each other's opposition groups.
	Ruling Ba'ath party newspaper *al-Thawra* states in a front-page editorial that the UN Security Council is discussing a "wicked" US-British proposal to suspend regular review of sanctions instead of lifting them. "This is utmost injustice that it has been a month since Iraq submitted its legitimate demands but the Security Council is discussing instead an American-British draft resolution to suspend the periodical review of the embargo. Apart from what would be the stand of the Security Council from the American-British wicked draft resolution . . . Iraq, leadership and people, would stick to their legitimate demands. Any one who thinks that Iraq would bow to the threat of suspending the periodical review of the embargo is mistaken."
98-8-31:	Iraq demands that the UN launch a probe into the UN inspections effort and charges that Ritter's resignation shows UNSCOM is linked to Israeli and US intelligence.
	Iraqi news sources announce that Saddam Hussein has permitted the Iraqi Atomic Energy Organization to conclude deals in the private and public sector to "render services and manufacture materials."

Table 10.3 (continued)

98–9-1:	Vice President Yassin makes a brief visit to the Sudan and inspects the pharmaceutical plant that the United States had attacked with cruise missiles.
98–9-2:	Butler tells the Security Council that Iraq has refused three times in the last month to allow inspectors to visit sites they had inspected previously, and to check the tags on monitored sites.
	The Security Council discusses a possible draft resolution that would give Iraq a comprehensive review of the sanctions process and their status if it allowed inspections.
	Iraq charges that less than 1 percent of the $200 million in medical supplies that Iraq has ordered in the third phase of the oil-for-food deal have been delivered. The UN says that $17 million worth, or 9 percent, have been delivered.
	Massoud Barzani visits Turkey to discuss his alliance with the Turkish government.
98–9-3:	Butler says Iraq is placing new curbs on UN inspection activities, and is interfering with activities in previously declared sites when equipment is tagged. "Iraq has advised the Commission orally that it can only visit the sites that Iraq has declared."
98–9-10:	The Security Council votes unanimously to suspend its regular 60-day review of sanctions against Baghdad but called for a "comprehensive review" of embargoes if Baghdad resumed cooperation with UN arms inspectors.
98–9-13:	*Babel* attacks the UN vote as a "Zionist" conspiracy.
	Saddam Hussein holds a meeting of the Revolutionary Command Council and regional command of the Ba'ath Party on the UN vote.
	Richard Butler of UNSCOM and Mohammed el-Baraedi of the IAEA warn the Security Council that Iraq is blocking follow-up inspections where monitoring devices indicate possible violations and that they can no longer guarantee a high probability that Iraq is not starting new missile and WMD programs.
98–9-16:	An Iraqi official, Hamed Youssef Hummadi, an adviser in Saddam Hussein's office, says in an article in an official newspaper, *al-Qadissiya*, that Annan has failed to honor a promise the Iraqis say he made in February, "which called for ending the embargo imposed on Iraq." Hummadi's comments reflect Iraqi frustration with Annan's insistence that Baghdad must reverse its decision, made on August 5, to stop on-site inspections, a clear violation of the Secretary-General's accord. Annan told diplomats from the Security Council on Monday that he agrees with them that no review of relations with Iraq can be conducted until the decision is reversed.
	Iraqi Foreign Minister Mohammed Saeed al-Sahaf, who is seeking support at a meeting of the Arab League in Cairo, says that Iraq had "no

Table 10.3 (continued)

	confidence in the arms inspection committee and in the policies of the US.''
98–9-17:	President Clinton meets with his top foreign policy advisers and telephones Canadian Prime Minister Jean Chretien to discuss developments in Iraq as tensions escalated once again between Baghdad and Washington. US officials do not rule out the use of force against Iraq to make it comply. Secretary of State Madeleine Albright says all options, including military force against Baghdad, are still on the table.
	Iraq's Revolutionary Command Council endorses a threat to end all cooperation with UN arms inspectors if the Security Council did not restore regular reviews of its sanctions against the country. Iraqi radio announces the Council had endorsed a decision by the Iraqi Parliament on Monday to end cooperation. The legislature is often used to float government policy ideas. The Revolutionary Command Council calls the unanimous Security Council resolution that suspended regular sanctions reviews, effectively keeping Iraq under an indefinite embargo, ''pressure and blackmail.'' The Revolutionary Command Council also criticized Secretary-General Kofi Annan.
	The Iraqis demand a comprehensive review of their relations with the UN. A day earlier, Peter Burleigh, the American representative, said that if such an evaluation took place, the United States would not limit the review to weapons questions but would go back to unmet demands that Iraq turn over or account for missing Kuwaitis, return stolen Kuwaiti property, and show improvement in its human rights record.
98–9-18:	Kofi Annan dismisses charges by Scott Ritter that Iraq could deliver a weapon of mass destruction within six months of the end of UN weapons inspections. During a speech, Annan say he stands by the view of Chief UN Weapons Inspector Richard Butler that Iraq can successfully comply with UN demands.
	Iraqi Foreign Minister Mohammed Saeed al-Sahaf says in Cairo that Iraq wants Kofi Annan to give more details about a Security Council ''comprehensive review'' of its sanctions if Baghdad resumed cooperation with UN weapons inspectors. He rejects US threats to use military force against Iraq to make it comply with UN resolutions, saying Baghdad would not bow to American ''blackmail.'' ''Discussions are being held between Iraq and the Secretary-General in order to know more details about a comprehensive review of the Iraqi file.''
	The UN receives preliminary test results of Iraqi warheads suspected of carrying the deadly VX gas, but UN officials refuse to characterize the findings. The officials say they won't know until the final results if the tests in French and Swiss laboratories back findings by a US army lab, which found that missile fragments had traces of the deadly nerve agent. A French official, speaking on condition of anonymity, say the preliminary results were inconclusive because not all the tests were complete.

Table 10.3 (continued)

	Pentagon spokesman Kenneth Bacon says the United States stands by the Aberdeen results. He says the fragments being tested in Europe came from another part of a large destruction site. The results from the European labs "will not invalidate the US findings of VX." The Swiss and French labs are working off about 40 swipes from fragments of about 43 to 45 missile warheads that were destroyed during the war or shortly after it. Most of the fragments were recovered at al-Nibai, the site where Iraq in 1991 unilaterally destroyed and buried warheads designed to carry chemical weapons. Chief UN weapons inspector Richard Butler had said in June, 1998 that he had no doubts about the findings of a US Army laboratory and tests in Switzerland and France did not invalidate the original findings. "It is utterly unambiguous. These degradation products could be from no other substance. These are unique products. They were VX. They were found in a missile warhead. That is weaponization." Questions have been raised, however, about material used in the rounds of tests. The chunks sent to the United States were dug up from a weapons destruction site near Baghdad. UNSCOM then took swabs from another 80 fragments from a different part of the site and sent half to France and the other half to Switzerland, according to Bacon. He says that the US army tests found traces of decomposed VX on one quarter of 44 fragments salvaged from an Iraqi government al-Hussein missile destruction site.
	Leaders of two Iraqi Kurd groups announce they plan regional elections next summer as part of a US-brokered agreement for the interim sharing of money and power. A brief State Department ceremony is held to announce the agreement reached by Massoud Barzani of the Kurdish Democratic Party and Jalal Talabani of the Patriotic Union of Kurdistan. Barzani says, "What we have accomplished will ensure a prosperous future for our people." Talabani says, "It is a historic day . . . We have closed a sad chapter in the history of the Kurdish people." Secretary of State Madeleine Albright presides and issues an indirect warning to Saddam not to interfere with the reconciliation process. She states there can be "no more campaigns to eradicate a whole population of innocent men, women and children." She also reaffirms her support for UN Security Council resolution 688, which is designed to forbid Saddam from repressing his people, including the Kurds in the north and the Shi'ites in the south.
98–9-19:	Presidential Office Adviser Amir al-Saadi says an Iraqi delegation will travel to New York shortly to discuss the proposals with Annan. "We have heard about those suggestions and we are quite satisfied with them."
	Babel states that "Iraq will not accept anything less than implementation of Section C of [UN Security Council] resolution 687." It accuses Kuwait of plotting against Baghdad at the UN and trying to sabotage efforts to defuse problems over UN sanctions against Iraq. "The Kuwaiti regime is currently inciting the Security Council against Iraq and sabotaging the effort of the Secretary General [Kofi Annan] to defuse what may result

Table 10.3 (continued)

                    from Resolution 1194.'' Babel says Kuwait is ignoring ''the noble Arab efforts to unite rifts and end pan-Arab differences'' and added, ''They returned to their old policy of plotting and they will be fully responsible for their untold future.''

                    Iraqi newspapers quote a spokesman for the Information Ministry as attacking Turkey for proposing a new administration in the north of Iraq and criticized Ankara for military links with Israel. ''Since 1991, Turkey participated in the vacuum of power in northern Iraq because it has been presenting military facilities to US and British forces . . . Turkey's insistence to pursue such delinquent policy besides that of a military pact with the Zionist entity constitutes a serious threat to Arab National Security.''

                    Iraq's top chemical weapons negotiator with the UN, General Amir al-Saadi, repeats Iraq's denial that it had filled missile warheads with the lethal VX agent, as alleged by UN weapons inspectors. He also says Iraq was not able to produce VX in a stable form or use it in weapons. ''Iraq has always maintained that we have neither produced stabilized VX nor weaponized VX agent of any kind in warheads . . . We confirm that once again and therefore there was no VX to be found by the American laboratories and reject the implications of the results.'' Saadi accuses the United States of playing down the results of the French and Swiss laboratory tests. ''We noticed through the press that these laboratories found no VX agent but the Pentagon and some US officials played down and doubted the results of the French and Swiss Laboratories. Iraq is still waiting to be officially notified of the results of the tests at Swiss and French laboratories.''

                    Sami Salih, a former top aide of Saddam Hussein who defected earlier in 1998, gives the *British Sunday Telegraph* details of Iraq's sanction-busting oil smuggling network. He says Iraq smuggled oil across its borders in contravention of UN trade sanctions imposed in 1990 after the Iraqi invasion of Kuwait. The paper says Salih masterminded a network of front companies in Europe and the Middle East to handle the illegal oil trade but was later arrested and imprisoned before escaping. It reports that the smuggling routes have now been closed and the front companies shut down. It adds that Salih had alleged that Iran—seen as a sworn enemy of Iraq—helped ship Iraqi oil cargoes through Iranian territorial waters in return for a large slice of the profits. Salih also says, ''Saddam never had any intention of complying with the inspection teams . . . I have seen missiles hidden all over Iraq. I have seen them stored under swimming pools and on farms. The sanctions should stay in place as long as Saddam is in power.''

98-9-20:   Amir al-Saadi, an adviser at the Presidential Office, announces that Iraq will send a delegation to New York shortly to meet Secretary-General Annan to try to resolve the standoff between Baghdad and UN weapons inspectors. The meeting would discuss a proposal by Annan dealing with

Table 10.3 (continued)

	both the standoff and the review of trade sanctions on Iraq. "We have heard about those suggestions and we are quite satisfied with them."
	Nils Carlstrom, director of UNSCOM's Baghdad Monitoring and Verification Center, says monitoring of declared sites was going on normally. "Monitoring of declared sites is being conducted in a professional way."
	Eric Falt, spokesman for the UN coordinator in Baghdad, says Iraq has received the first medical supplies bought under the fourth phase of its oil-for-food deal with the UN, which began three months ago. He says that Iraq had received $350 million worth of medical items since the beginning of the oil-for-food deal in December, 1998. The fourth phase, which began in June, provided for some $280 million worth of medical supplies to be paid for out of the proceeds from oil sales. "Given the complexity of the process, this shows the significant speed up in deliveries in the health service."
	An Iraqi Foreign Ministry spokesman accused the US and British representatives at the UN sanctions committee of blocking food and medical contracts under the oil-for-food plan. "The American and British representatives in the committee have put on hold 21 contracts of the third phase, 12 out of which are food and medical contracts. The US naval forces illegally embarked on inspecting bitterly and continuously the vessels laden with food and humanitarian needs to Iraqi people... This is a violation to the UN Charter and the related Security Council resolutions, thus causing economic and moral damage to Iraq due to impeding the vessels... and directly pushing insurance and transport taxes up. Such aggression would negatively backfire on status of civilians and their possibility to get food, medicine and humanitarian needs easily and consequently leading to redouble of their suffering."
	Iraq's Minister of Transport and Communications, Ahmed Murtadha Ahmed Khalil, accuses the United States of intercepting an Iraqi vessel inside Iraq's own waters, an act he considered piracy.
	Syrian Economy and Foreign Trade Minister Mohammed Imadi opens an Iraqi trade center in Damascus in a further move toward the restoration of normal ties after 18 years of animosity. Farouq Obeidi, director-general of external relations at the Iraqi Ministry of Trade, says the opening of the center showed that Damascus and Baghdad were determined to boost economic and commercial cooperation, and that the volume of Syrian exports to Iraq was worth more than $150 million in 1997.
98-9-21:	Prakash Shah, UN Secretary-General Kofi Annan's special envoy, leaves Baghdad after spending nearly two weeks trying to avert a new confrontation over Iraq's refusal to let weapons inspectors operate. *Babel* publishes an article stating that "Iraq welcomes proposals from UN Secretary-General Kofi Annan and expressed its readiness for a high-level delegation to discuss them with him."

Table 10.3 (continued)

	An Iraqi oil ministry official says Iraq has not received the first delivery of spare parts for its dilapidated oil industry, nearly four months after UN approval for their purchase. The unnamed source says that only 24 of 80 contracts for oil industry spare parts submitted by Iraq to the UN sanctions committee had been ratified. The Iraqi official accuses the US and British representatives on a UN sanctions committee of delaying or blocking contracts to purchase spare parts for Iraq's oil industry, and says that Iraq had concluded some 270 contracts with oil companies to buy spare parts. "Out of 80 that were submitted to 661 (sanctions) committee, only 24 were approved. Despite the fact that three and a half months have gone since the beginning of the fourth phase, no spare part has arrived in the country."
98–9-22:	French Foreign Minister Hubert Vedrine says Baghdad's behavior makes it impossible even for sympathetic countries such as France to argue in the UN Security Council that Iraq has complied with its obligation to eliminate its weapons of mass destruction. Vedrine says he had written twice to Iraq since Baghdad's decision in August to suspend cooperation with UNSCOM. France's envoy in Baghdad has made representations to President Saddam Hussein, and Vedrine said he planned to meet Iraqi Foreign Minister Mohammed Saeed al-Sahaf in New York. "Iraqis themselves have put the UN Secretary-General in an embarrassing position. This can only work seriously if there is a signal of willingness to co-operate on the Iraqi side. . . . They have accumulated bad behavior that has led to this situation. There has never been a situation where even we could have said that they have met all the conditions."
	Tariq Aziz announces he will go to New York to meet Kofi Annan to try to resolve a dispute over weapons inspections. Vice President Taha Yassin Ramadan tell reporters, "we are waiting for the role of the Secretary-General and what he will do in the next few days."
98–9-23:	The UN sanctions committee has approved two more contracts for spare parts for Iraq's oil industry, bringing the total to 25, with a total value of $54 million. The two latest contracts are with French and Russian companies to supply pipeline equipment and spare parts. Iraq has yet to receive the first delivery of oil spare parts and equipment nearly four months after the UN approved their purchase under an expanded oil-for-food plan.
	Al-Thawra, the newspaper of Iraq's ruling Ba'ath Party, says US allegations that laboratory tests showed traces of deadly VX nerve gas in Iraqi warheads was a lie. "We see that refuting the new lie is taking several months, just like the one concocted about the presidential palaces."
	Turkish Foreign Ministry spokesman Sermet Atacanli objects to parts of a Washington-sponsored peace deal between Iraqi Kurdish factions and says Turkey "will do what is necessary" to prevent any breakup of Iraq. "On Iraq, the most important principle for Turkey is the protection of

Table 10.3 (continued)

its territorial integrity. We will do what is necessary so that this principle is respected and for actions against it not to be undertaken." He said Ankara had expressed its concerns to NATO ally Washington and objected especially to mention in the agreement announced last week of a federal system eventually being set up in Iraq.

The INA says Iraq and Syria began talks on the Tigris and Euphrates river water they share with neighboring Turkey, which declined an invitation to join them. "Coordination meetings of the joint technical committee on water started here with the attendance of the Iraqi and Syrian delegations and in the absence of the Turkish one . . . The Turkish side has not attended the periodical meetings for years despite repeated invitations."

98–9-25: Egyptian Foreign Minister Amr Moussa says eliminating Iraq's weapons of mass destruction must be an integral part of regional disarmament. In a statement to the UN General Assembly, Moussa reiterated Egypt's call for the establishment of a nuclear weapons–free zone in the Middle East. He made no specific mention of Israel, which is widely believed to hold nuclear weapons. Referring to sanctions on Middle East countries such as Iraq, Moussa said such measures shouldn't go indefinitely. This, he said, "will erode their credibility and create sanctions fatigue." He called on Baghdad to comply with Security Council resolutions requiring Iraq to eliminate weapons of mass destruction, so that eight-year-old sanctions against it can be removed. This will require "goodwill, proper conduct and the establishment of stable cooperation" between Iraq and the Council.

Kuwait's Foreign Minister, Sheik Sabah al-Ahmed al-Sabah, calls for continued international pressure on Iraq to comply with UN resolutions, and said Baghdad's defiance was underscored by its refusal to express regret for its 1990 invasion of Kuwait. "The sad certainty, alas, is that all these crises contribute to the perpetuation of the sanctions for which the government of Iraq alone bears full responsibility."

Iraq claims that 4.5 million Iraqi children will return to school next week, but that up to 1 million of them will have to sit on the floor for lack of desks. Many students will read textbooks that have been used for years and sit in classrooms without blackboards or other teaching aids. State-run newspapers, quoting senior education officials, say at least 8,000 schools need urgent rehabilitation and 5,000 more must be built to cope with the rising numbers of students. They also quote senior education officials as saying new school desks are needed immediately.

98–9-26: Turkish Deputy Bulent Ecevit says in a statement that Turkey plans to send an ambassador to Baghdad for the first time since 1992. Turkey, which fears Iraqi Kurdish separatism could encourage its own restive Kurds, will also help to speed up the appointment of an Iraqi ambassador to Ankara. Turkey has complained about being left out of a deal agreed to in Washington between Iraqi Kurdish faction leaders Massoud Barzani

Table 10.3 (continued)

	and Jalal Talabani. The Iraqi Kurdish accord provides for elections next year to re-establish a regional assembly in northern Iraq which collapsed in 1994 amid fighting between the Kurdish groups. Turkey fears the accord will lead to a federation in Iraq that would give the Kurds a greater say in the running of their own affairs. Ecevit says, "In this way, the Ankara peace process has been sidelined. There is no chance of Turkey approving these changes."
98–9-28:	Tariq Aziz meets with Secretary-General Annan in New York, and says that Iraq will continue to block what it calls "provocative" inspections by UNSCOM. Aziz responds positively to Annan's proposal for a comprehensive review of sanctions and Iraq's efforts to disarm, but does not accept the Council's position that no such review take place until Iraq rescinds its August 5 decision to stop cooperating with UN inspectors. "The idea that Iraq should do this or that concession before the comprehensive review takes place is not legal." Aziz says that UNSCOM inspectors are continuing their less-intrusive monitoring activities in Iraq, whereby UNSCOM verifies that Iraq isn't building munitions in locations already declared weapons-free. "The inspectors are already working in Iraq in the monitoring regime. They are very active, and we are providing all the necessary assistance to them," he said. "What we are not allowing them to do is just provocations."
	Major General Nils Carlstrom, director of the Baghdad Monitoring and Verification Center, confirms Aziz's statement and says that "we go out in the morning every day, meet our Iraqi counterparts, do our inspections and send our reports to New York. We continue to monitor as best we can within the restrictions imposed by Iraq." The Iraqis have barred UNSCOM monitors from adding any new sites to the hundreds they already observe. However, Carlstrom says that apart from three incidents since August 5 when Iraq prevented his teams from visiting new sites, work has gone on "at a professional level, with normal cooperation." There are still 40 inspectors divided into six teams for missile sites, chemical, nuclear and biological weapons-related sites, helicopter survey, and export-import control. They are backed by 40 support staff, as well as 40 Chilean air force personnel for the five helicopters at their disposal. Video cameras fixed at many of the sites across Iraq remain linked to screens at UNSCOM headquarters, where data from sensors and air and water sampling stations are also analyzed. The relatively smooth monitoring operation contrasts with the repeated confrontations between Iraq and visiting UNSCOM teams charged with finding evidence of prohibited weapons.
	UNSCOM's commissioners or board of directors from 20 countries begin three days of meetings to discuss proposals for the review and what should be contained in a biannual arms report due in mid-October.
	Kofi Annan names Hans Von Sponeck, a German, as the new field coordinator for the UN's Iraq program, which distributes food and medicine

Table 10.3 (continued)

bought with Iraqi oil revenue. Since the first deliveries in March, 1997, more than seven million tons of food, worth $2.25 billion, have now arrived in Iraq. Denis Halliday, the outgoing UN coordinator of the Iraqi oil-for-food program, made it clear that clashes with his UN superiors were a key reason for his resignation. Halliday had been outspoken about the weaknesses of the plan and was known to have clashed with Benon Sevan, the New York-based executive director of the program.

Shawky Marcus, an Undersecretary at the Iraqi Ministry of Health, claims that at least 1.5 million Iraqis, mostly young children, have died because of UN sanctions. "Mortality has increased day by day. Since the day sanctions were imposed on us until now, we have lost not less than 1.5 million, 70 percent of them in the under-five age group." He gives no detailed breakdown.

98–9-30: In a speech at a General Assembly session, Iraqi Foreign Minister Mohammed Saeed al-Sahaf insists that Iraq no longer has any weapons of mass destruction and that UNSCOM has no proof to back up its claims to the contrary. He urges Secretary-General Annan to personally supervise the review and make sure that it is not "an aimless process with no end in sight." He charges that UNSCOM and its chairman, Richard Butler, are prejudiced against Iraq and operate "under the influence of an arrogant, powerful state."

The *Washington Post* reports that Iraq has three or four "implosion devices" that only lack cores of enriched uranium to make 20-kiloton nuclear weapons. American intelligence assessments concur on the credibility of the reports received from defectors, but cannot fully confirm them. Scott Ritter, the American arms inspector, had made similar charges to a congressional hearing on September 3. He said that UNSCOM had "intelligence information which indicates that components necessary for three nuclear weapons exist (but) lack the fissile material."

The US State Department denies that the United States had been told Iraq possessed the implosion devices, but said it did not doubt Iraq had sought to acquire atomic weapons. Spokesman James Foley says the United States is aware of allegations that Iraq retained "weapons-related components, but that we cannot confirm these allegations.... There's little doubt, however, that Iraq has sought a nuclear capability and has withheld information and weapons-related items from UN inspectors." UN spokesman Fred Eckhard says, "it is not helpful that confidential information continues to spew out but this is a matter for UNSCOM to address and their decision is not to comment." The IAEA indicates that it has not confirmed any of the reports. It had reported to the Security Council on July 28 that the agency had an adequate picture of Iraq's past nuclear programs but that "absolute certainty is simply not possible."

98–10-1: Abdul-Ghani Abdul-Ghafur, a senior member of the ruling Ba'ath Party, tells reporters that Iraq is not moving closer to making a nuclear weapon.

Table 10.3 (continued)

	"The International [Atomic Energy] Agency and the UN know very well that Iraq does not possess nuclear weapons or any other weapons of mass destruction." Abdul-Ghafur charges that the Security Council is applying a double standard and is seeking the destruction of Iraq's weapons of mass destruction while ignoring Israel's nuclear arsenal.
98–10-2:	The Iraqi cabinet decides to review a program to train almost 1 million people in handling arms. The program began in February, when the United States and Britain threatened military action over UNSCOM. The cabinet also orders new efforts to restore border posts and airports. The cabinet also decides to restore the Ar'ar complex on the border with Saudi Arabia so it would be suitable for receiving pilgrims. Funds were allocated for the restoration effort, INA said.
	Abbas al-Janabi, a former personal secretary to Uday Hussein and former editor of *Babel* who defected last spring, says he witnessed the battle in which Saddam's two sons-in-law were gunned down after Lt. General Hussein Kamel al-Majid and Lt. Colonel Saddam Kamel al-Majid returned to Iraq following their defection to Jordan in 1995. Al-Janabi says the two went back to Iraq because of promises of clemency, but that Saddam Hussein summoned them to one of his palaces and demanded they sign documents divorcing his daughters. When they refused, several other relatives threatened to shoot the two brothers, but Saddam said they should have two days to consider. That night, Uday and other members of the family surrounded the house where Hussein Kamel was staying and opened fire. Hussein Kamel was wounded during an ensuing 13-hour gunfight and staggered out of the house. Uday's gunmen shot Kamel, continuing to fire after he was dead. "When he was lying in a lake of blood, they spat on him. He says that Saddam's half-brother, Barzan al-Tikriti, had refused a summons back to Iraq from his post as Iraqi Ambassador to the UN in Switzerland. "Barzan has always had differences with Saddam. Barzan knows his destiny if he goes back to Iraq." He says that Uday had married Barzan's daughter, Saja, but neglected her and that she then fled to Geneva, where she remained with her father. He says Uday has become "more wicked, more cruel" since he was wounded in 1996, that he watched Uday kill four men, and that he was beaten by Uday's bodyguards. He also charges that the Hussein family runs much of the smuggling trade, selling international humanitarian aid sent to Iraq, and illegally exporting millions of dollars of oil.
	Tariq Aziz sends a letter to Kofi Annan calling for "an official investigation into the UN Special Commission's connections and intelligence work that is hostile to Iraq" in order to "guarantee the UN's credibility, neutrality, and reputation." The letter discusses the charges made by Scott Ritter, and says that "these statements show serious facts of which Iraq has warned several times. . . . Namely, that UNSCOM, which works in the name of the UN Security Council and the UN . . . is firmly connected with the intelligence agencies of states that pursue anti-Iraq pol-

Table 10.3 (continued)

icies. These states have declared objectives that have nothing to do with the UN Security Council, particularly the US and Israel . . . UNSCOM acts as an intelligence institution, not as an institution specialized in disarmament and monitoring.'' Aziz says Ritter's comments show that UNSCOM has "studied with the US and Israeli intelligence services ways to carry out its work in Iraq. These facts . . . confirm our complaint and anxiety that the real objective of this body is not to follow up the implementation of the UN Security Council resolutions, but to deliberately act to maintain the embargo against Iraq and to spy against it."

Nearly 10,000 Turkish soldiers cross into northern Iraq to attack Kurdish rebels. Turkey's new incursion into northern Iraq follows two days of air strikes against rebel bases.

98–10-3: The United States announces that Defense Secretary Cohen is due to start a tour of Gulf Arab allies which will bring him to Kuwait in mid-October. The United States has 3,500 troops, mainly ground troops and air force, based in Kuwait. Another 1,500 Marines, part of a 4,000 floating force, were brought ashore late last month. It also has an aircraft carrier group in the region along with other warships, cruise missiles, and additional warplanes. The US presence, including F-117s based in Kuwait, has been reduced since Annan's February accord.

Iraq signs a new agreement with the World Food Program, a UN agency, to expand its special feeding program. Lt. General Saadi Tu'ma, the Iraqi Labor and Social Affairs minister, says the number eligible for the monthly food aid would increase to 943,000 from the current 240,000, starting in November. The special feeding program makes available to the poor 11 pounds of flour, 6.6 pounds of sugar, 4.4 pounds of lentils, and 4.4 pounds of cooking oil. The monthly ration for all Iraqis includes flour, rice, sugar, tea, lentils, salt, cooking oil, soap, and detergent. There's also a special ration of milk for babies.

Iraqi Trade Minister Mohammed Mehdi Saleh and his Iranian counterpart, Mohammed Shariatmadar, agree to expand bilateral trade relations and export Iranian food and medicine to Iraq.

An Iraqi Foreign Ministry spokesman demands that Turkey withdraw its troops from northern Iraq immediately. "The Turkish armed forces have committed a new invasion in northern Iraq, sending more than 10,000 troops on the second of this month. The Iraqi government strongly condemns such military aggression and denounces the Turkish troops' violation of Iraqi sovereignty and territorial integrity."

98–10-4: Iraqi Vice President Taha Yassin Ramadan tells a meeting of Iraqi expatriates in Iraq that Iraq said will not resume its cooperation with UN weapons inspectors unless the UN sets a timetable for scrapping eight years of stringent sanctions. "Iraq's decision to halt cooperation with the UN inspection teams taken on August 5 is irreversible. Iraq is not ready to accept that the situation remains as it is. The situation should be clar-

Table 10.3 (continued)

	ified through setting stages for lifting the embargo.'' Ramadan also demands that UNSCOM be restructured to curb what he said was US and Israeli hostility toward Iraq. ''The Special Commission . . . has to be restructured to make it a neutral body which expresses the will of the Security Council.'' Ramadan says the United States and Britain want ''to overthrow the national government in Iraq and rule the country.'' He says Iraq is ready to resume work with UNSCOM and the IAEA, ''but in a serious, rational and subjective way that would lead to closing the [weapons] files and implementing article 22 of resolution 687.''
98–10-5:	Kofi Annan sends a note to the Security Council outlining elements of a new ''comprehensive review'' of Iraq's compliance with the terms of the cease-fire that could be initiated within weeks if Iraq rescinds its current ban on most arms inspections. He had first suggested the review several weeks earlier. The first phase of the review, which would have its own timetable, would be to determine whether Iraq has accounted for all its weapons of mass destruction, the key requirement for lifting sanctions on oil exports. Annan says UNSCOM and IAEA arms inspectors would be asked to substantiate precisely what ballistic, chemical, biological, and nuclear weapons were still unaccounted for and set a tentative time frame in which they could complete their work, providing Iraq cooperates. Iraq would be asked to submit its account on where it had complied with weapons demands to date and present evidence to substantiate its claims, he added. ''The immediate purpose of the first phase of the comprehensive review would be to define an agreed course of action and a timetable which, if followed would lead to the earlier possible satisfaction of disarmament-related requirements . . . It would be so designed as to make it possible for the Security Council to satisfy itself whether all the necessary conditions for lifting the oil embargo have been fulfilled.'' Once all the information was collected, the Council would draw up a list of remaining requirements to be fulfilled by Iraq as a condition for lifting the oil embargo ''and establish a reasonable time frame for this purpose.'' Annan's proposal does not specify the length of time span, leaving the review of Iraq's performance up to disputes among key members of the Council. Under the terms of the Gulf War cease-fire resolution, the embargo on oil exports can be lifted once Iraq's banned weapons are accounted for and destroyed. The United States alone, however, argues that there are no separate provisions for lifting bans on imports to or exports from Iraq and that all demands for ending sanctions should be considered in one package.
	The Supreme Council for the Islamic Revolution in Iraq and the Iraqi Communist Party report that President Saddam Hussein's forces have attacked villages in southern Iraq and are trying to wipe out the bases of Shi'ite Muslim rebels. They also report anti-government disturbances in Iraqi and other southern Iraqi cities. The Iran-based council states that soldiers backed by tanks and artillery attacked several villages in marshes

Table 10.3 (continued)

near Nasiriya, 225 miles south of Iraqi. The raids are part of a campaign that began last week when troops launched an attack against rebel positions between Nasiriya and Al-Amara, 90 miles to the northeast. The Communist Party reports intensive fighting in the region this week between rebels and army deserters and army units supported by the ruling Ba'ath Party militia. It says dozens of troops were killed or wounded and others were taken prisoner. It did not give figures for opposition casualties. It says offices of the Ba'ath Party in Iraqi, Basra, Amara, Diwanya, and Kerbala were bombed.

Iraq's parliament denounces a decision by the US Congress to permit the American government to spend nearly $100 million on military aid for opponents of President Saddam Hussein. "The Iraqi National Assembly denounces the US Congress' decision to devote money to conspire against Iraq and to overthrow its political regime which was chosen by the people. . . . The American administration in cooperation with international Zionism is conspiring against the revolution in Iraq, using all the means to do so. The National Assembly will take the suitable decision . . . to defend Iraq and its security and sovereignty." The US legislation states the intentions of Congress and gives President Bill Clinton the power to aid the opposition with $97 million in arms and other military equipment, if he chooses. In addition, it permits shipments of US weapons and other military equipment, and also allows $2 million in funding for democratic opposition groups for radio and television broadcasts into Iraq. The House had approved the non-binding legislation, which is called "The Iraq Liberation Act of 1998," by a vote of 360 to 38.

98–10-6: Iraq's ruling Ba'ath party newspaper, *al-Thawra*, urges Arab countries to take a firm stand against Turkey's military threat against Syria. *Al-Thawra* accuses Turkey of following the same hostile policy toward Arab states as the United States in its diplomatic row with Syria. The paper says Turkey represented an anti-Arab alliance which included "the Zionist entity (Israel), America and Britain, who are conspiring and spying against the Arabs."

Richard Butler says in his semi-annual report to the Security Council that Iraq could be near the end of meeting requirements for its ballistic missiles and chemical weapons, but the gap still remains for biological arms. He disputes Iraq's contention that it had accounted for all its weapons of mass destruction. "The disarmament phase of the Security Council's requirements is possibly near its end in the missile and chemical weapons areas but not in the biological weapons area." His report says the Council might have to consider at some stage that UNSCOM could not provide "100 percent verification" that all banned weapons in Iraq had been destroyed. But the report indicates the gap in the data for biological arms is still large and reflects Iraq's failure "to provide the disclosures which are essential to the fulfillment of the disarmament mandate in the biological weapons area." His report accuses Iraq of unilaterally destroying

Table 10.3 (continued)

materials and withholding documents the commission needed. The report indicates Iraq is permitting UNSCOM's monitoring work to be carried out "only at a less than satisfactory level. Full disclosure by Iraq of all necessary materials and information remains the crucial ingredient for both an end to the disarmament process and future monitoring. His report says that full disclosure remains the "crucial ingredient" for completing the disarmament process.

Butler's report raises questions about Secretary-General Annan's concept of a review of Iraq's relations with the UN, if Iraq rescinds its decision suspending cooperation with the arms inspectors. Annan has submitted proposals to the Council suggesting it was up to UNSCOM to prove Iraq had not complied with demands to dismantle its weapons of mass destruction. Butler's report indicates this would reverse "the onus of disclosure clearly placed upon Iraq by the council" and would instead require UNSCOM to disclose fully information that only Iraq had at its disposal. "The question may be asked what sound purpose would be served were the commission to substitute an overall statement of its own for Iraq's statement," the report said. "Would Iraq then be asked to verify the commission's statement?"

Tariq Aziz says in New York that Butler's review did not appear to give Iraq guarantees it would get a fair hearing. Aziz says he has spoken to 14 of the 15 Council members—the United States excluded—he had the sense that they were willing to conduct an honest review. "But that's not yet unanimous." Iraq needs "complete, satisfactory guarantees" to move forward.

John Holum, Acting Under Secretary of State for Arms Control and International Security Affairs and Director of ACDA, says that Iraq can rapidly reconstitute biological and chemical weapon capabilities. "Iraq has the capability within a very short period of time to reconstitute these capabilities and its behavior suggests it also has the intention to do that," Holum said. "So the UN inspectors and the IAEA can't back off, can't back down without completing their work.... That is what the US will insist upon. We hope UNSCOM will be back on track in the very near future."

The IAEA issues its six-month report to the Security Council on Iraqi disarmament which is nearly identical to its previous report. It says it has no indications that Iraq is pursuing nuclear weapons but that its information is still incomplete. "The IAEA has found no indication of Iraq having achieved its program goal of producing nuclear weapons, or of Iraq having retained physical capability for the production of weapons-usable nuclear material or having clandestinely obtained such material." The IAEA also says that the IAEA cannot guarantee that all "readily concealable" items have been found. It indicates that most of its work can now be accomplished through a long-term monitoring program. It also warns that Iraq suspended cooperation with all UN inspectors on August 5 and has prevented UNSCOM and the IAEA from visiting new

Table 10.3 (continued)

	sites. "As a result, the level of assurance the IAEA can give that prohibited activities are not taking place in Iraq is significantly reduced."
98–10-7:	The *New York Times* reports that France has detected traces of nerve gas on Iraqi warheads. Testing on samples taken from the weapons reportedly show evidence of chemicals linked to VX. The *Times* reports that weapons experts told them that the French findings would confirm the American tests. They showed the presence of components found in decomposed VX in missile warheads destroyed by Iraq and dug up by UN inspectors. It reports that diplomats said the French were delaying the release of final tests because they didn't want to undermine Iraq's push at the UN this week to lift the sanctions.
98–10-8:	French Ministry of Defense spokesman Jean-Francois Bureau denies press reports that France had found traces of VX nerve gas on Iraqi warheads and had delayed disclosing the information. It calls for the UN to hold an emergency meeting of chemical experts to stop such reports by making a full assessment of the scientific evidence gathered so far. "Our conclusions right now are that we do not have any definitive conclusions about traces of VX on the samples," he said. Nobody could imagine that France would want to slow down the discussion in UNSCOM. He says that a French military laboratory near Paris had finished examining its Iraqi warhead fragments but had not yet finished its analysis. "We do not have absolute certainty on the conclusions to be drawn."
	US-based arms experts and diplomats say the *New York Times* was correct in reporting that the French defense ministry reported the test results to its partners in Europe but the foreign ministry held them back.
	Tariq Aziz ends a two-week visit to the UN and says he told Secretary-General Annan on his last visit that he needed to consult in Iraqi before any decision on the inspections was made. "We are going to weigh the situation in its entirety in Iraqi. It's premature to say anything. I am still disturbed, disturbed by certain efforts or tactics made by a very few number of members, maybe only one." The United States does not want the review to begin until six to eight weeks after Iraq has cooperated with the arms inspectors and has reservations on the shape it will take. Aziz attacks the latest UNSCOM report and says that Butler never mentioned how many factories and equipment had been destroyed in Iraq in his search for weapons. "It's in the thousands, thousands," he said. "UNSCOM is still playing the same games, the same old business. And they are not telling the truth about each and every matter when they are asked by the secretary-general, by the Security Council and by the press."
	Iraqi Vice-President Taha Yassin Ramadan says that "when Mr. Aziz returns back home, the leadership will assess the situation and if it finds guarantees ... we will cooperate." Ramadan told a closing session of Iraqi expatriates in Iraqi, "If we do not find guarantees we will not cooperate.... They have not yet restructured the Special Commission

Table 10.3 (continued)

	which includes spies and agents of intelligence services," he said, adding "the Security Council should be ashamed of itself to ask us to cooperate with such a commission."
	UN spokesman Fred Eckhard says that that the proposed review of Iraq's relations with the UN will not put the burden of proof on UN arms inspectors, rather than Iraq. "Several press reports have attributed to the Secretary-General a proposal that the UN Special Commission (UNSCOM) and its inspectors should be required to prove that Iraq still has weapons of mass destruction. This is inaccurate." What the Secretary-General has done is to suggest a possible concept for a comprehensive review of Iraq's compliance which the council decided to conduct," he said.
	The US Senate voted to send President Clinton legislation providing up to $97 million in military aid to Iraqi rebels trying to drive Saddam Hussein from power. The bill also gives $2 million to Radio Free Iraq.
	Iraq's Vice-President Taha Yassin Ramadan met Indian Agriculture Minister Son Pal on Thursday for talks aimed at cementing relations between the two countries.
98–10-9:	Iraq rejects Turkish claims that Iraq had links with Turkey's secessionist Kurds and that there contacts between Iraq and the Turkish Kurdistan Workers Party (PKK).
	Secretary of Defense William Cohen indicates that any crisis with Iraq is weeks or months away. Cohen speaks to the press aboard a US aircraft carrier in the Gulf, and says that if President Saddam Hussein fails to obey UN demands, the United States would eventually consider military action He says it is up to the Security Council to support its own resolutions, which require Iraq to resume full cooperation with UNSCOM and the IAEA. "If the UN won't stand behind its resolutions then it doesn't stand for very much. [Saddam Hussein] has a choice to make in the next few weeks and certainly months as to whether he's going to be in compliance, but if he doesn't then we stand ready to exercise military options," he told a questioner.
98–10-11:	Iraq says it will raise the issue of the country's deteriorating environment from UN sanctions when a National Assembly delegation attends an environmental conference in China this week. Delegation leader Mrs. Raja Murad al-Shawi says, "The delegation is to present a paper of action that explains the impact of the unjust embargo on the Iraqi people ... which led to the destruction of the environment in Iraq."
98–10-12:	The IAEA reports that Iraq's nuclear file could be shifted from intrusive inspections to long-term monitoring once Baghdad cooperates again. Its Director, El Baradei, says the IAEA has "no indication that Iraq has nuclear weapons or usable material or capability to produce such items." He says that questions remain but could be resolved under the ongoing monitoring and verification program that was set up in Iraq. The out-

Table 10.3 (continued)

standing issues he reports on include the extent of foreign assistance Iraq had received for the atomic program and how much they were able to weaponize nuclear materials and additional drawings and models of the program, he said. This step would "close" the active nuclear dossier file but the US objects, saying that Iraq still has to answer outstanding questions and needed to pass legislation barring its citizens from reconstructing its weapons of mass destruction. The IAEA recommendation gets immediate approval from Russia, which states that the transfer should occur as soon as Iraq rescinded its August 5 decision banning most inspections.

Security Council President Jeremy Greenstock of Britain reiterates a demand for Iraq to cooperate with UNSCOM. "Members of the Council look to Iraq to take the decision to resume full cooperation." He states the Council has "noted" the comments from the IAEA without specifically endorsing them, and that members "felt there were not many items still to be resolved if cooperation [from Iraq] was forthcoming." In the case of biological weapons, work is needed that depends "crucially on full disclosure by Iraq." Russia's UN ambassador Sergei Lavrov says that as soon as Iraq resumes full cooperation with UNSCOM and the IAEA, there "could be real progress." "In the nuclear file, IAEA reported clearly that, with the cooperation of Iraq fully resumed, there would be no impediment to IAEA's plan for ongoing monitoring and verification to be fully implemented."

Saddam Hussein's half-brother, Barzan al-Takriti, denies reports of a rift with Saddam Hussein. He has not returned from Switzerland, but says, "I am staying here to be with my family and this is being done with the knowledge of the president and due to his understanding of my family situation. I pray to God to help me overcome these circumstances so I can be there [in Baghdad] beside my brother and I hope to be able to offer something that can help him and our people," he was quoted as saying.

The official Iraqi newspaper *al-Qadissiya* attacks Secretary Cohen during his tour of the Arab Gulf states, saying his threats to use force against Iraq were "nonsense." "During his tour to members of the Gulf Cooperation Council the Zionist American Secretary of Defense William Cohen spelled out threats against Iraq which were nonsense and empty. Cohen and the rest of the Zionist crew who are managing the American foreign policy should not spell out such threats against a steadfast people led by an historic leader." Cohen should know that the US military build-up in the Gulf in February "had failed." The Ba'ath party newspaper, *al-Thawra*, says Cohen's threat to use force against Iraq was "silly and unjustifiable."

Turkish State Minister Mehmet Batalli announces that he will go to Iraq to discuss oil and gas joint projects with Iraq's oil minister, Amir Muhammed Rasheed, and several Iraqi ministers during his visit from Oc-

Table 10.3 (continued)

	tober 16–18. Batalli is to discuss several projects, including possible future Iraqi pipeline gas sales to Turkey after an exploration of gas fields in Iraq by Turkish oil company TPAO, Botas, and the Iraqi Oil Ministry. In 1997, Baghdad and Ankara signed a preliminary deal to build a 1,300-kilometer (800-mile) gas pipeline to carry Iraqi exports to Turkey's Mediterranean port of Ceyhan.
98–10-13:	Iraq's Irrigation Minister, Mahamoud Diyab al-Ahmed, accuses Turkey of blocking an agreement on sharing the waters of the two rivers with Iraq and Syria. "The [dam] project . . . which Turkey has built most of, is harmful to Iraq because it will affect the flow of water as well as its quality. The Turkish officials are ignoring demands [by Iraq and Syria] to hold meetings to agree on sharing the waters of the Euphrates." He says a joint committee comprising Iraq, Syria, and Turkey had held 16 meetings since its inception in 1980 but had reached no agreement on sharing the waters because of Turkish objections.
	Iraqi leaders issue a statement that they have discussed Deputy Prime Minister Tariq Aziz's recent visit to New York and accuse the United States of interfering in internal Iraqi affairs. The statement follows a meeting chaired by President Saddam Hussein, and also says that Iraq would hold further discussions on the standoff between Iraq and UNSCOM.
98–10-14:	The Security Council announces that it intends to ask Iraq about the Iraqi air force document requested by UNSCOM inspectors on how many chemical shells and bombs Iraq used in its 1980–1988 war against Iran. The document, discovered by weapons inspectors in July, provides the details of the types of bombs and rockets that Iraq says were used to deliver chemical and biological agents. Butler had requested the document after it was discovered in July during a survey of Iraqi air force headquarters. Security Council diplomats again asked Oil Minister Amir Muhammad Rasheed for the document in October, when he traveled with Tariq Aziz to New York. Rasheed stated that Aziz had the document but that Secretary-General Annan had not requested to see the document during the meeting with Aziz.
98–10-15:	Security Council President Jeremy Greenstock of Britain summons Iraqi Ambassador Nizar Hamdoon for a meeting to remind him that Baghdad has an obligation to turn the document over to UN weapons inspectors. After the meeting, Hamdoon tells reporters that the document has nothing to do with Iraq's disarmament and will only be turned over as part of a "comprehensive review" of sanctions.
98–10-16:	The Iraqi paper *al-Thawra* accuses the United States of plotting against Saddam Hussein, and says the Iraqi leadership is studying how to counter a US "conspiracy" aimed at overthrowing him. "The leadership of the party and revolution continue to study the forms of conspiracy hatched against Iraq by the American government. The American conspiracy

Table 10.3 (continued)

	against Iraq is a declared policy for which a number of [US] State Department officials and CIA agents have been recruited.'' Colonel Alaa Hussein Ali al-Jabour, leader of the so-called Provisional Free Government of Kuwait that was announced following Iraq's invasion, defects from Iraq and is given refugee status in Turkey.
98–10-17:	Tariq Aziz asks Secretary-General Annan to order an investigation into alleged links between weapons inspectors disarming Baghdad and hostile states. ''I demand from your excellency to take necessary measures against those personnel of the commission in addition to an official investigation. Continuation of such serious practices and not taking deterrent measures to put an end to them would compel Iraq to take appropriate measures to protect its security and sovereignty. I remind you that we already drew the attention to the unprofessional conduct of Scott Ritter which was not in compliance with the conduct of an international official working under the banner of the UN.''
98–10-18:	The Iraq-based Mujahideen Khalq Iranian opposition group says that Iranian agents tried to blow up a bus carrying a number of its members on a road north of Baghdad. Iraqi Vice President Taha Yassin Ramadan tells Turkish State Minister Mehmet Batalli that improvements in relations depend on Ankara taking a ''political decision, that should be taken away from foreign pressure.''
98–10-19:	Amir Abdalla Khalil, the Food and Agriculture Organization (FAO) representative in Iraq, says a lack of fertilizers, agricultural machinery, and seeds prevents Iraq from growing the food it needs. ''In spite of the implementation of the memorandum of understanding since 1996, malnutrition has remained a serious problem throughout the whole country.'' He quotes a recent survey by UN agencies working in Iraq, stating that malnutrition and lack of medicines had shown the death toll among children under age 5 was around 5,000 a month. Iraq imported 70 percent of its food needs before 1990. Under sanctions it launched a big drive for self-sufficiency. Khalil says, however, that agriculture is ''deteriorating due to the spread of pests such as sunpest, dubas, humaira and red spider mite as well as the spread of animal diseases.'' He quotes a recent FAO report saying that Iraqi wheat production had decreased to 1.06 million tons in 1997 from 1.24 million tons in 1995, and rice production had declined to 244,000 tons from 315,000 tons in 1995. Iraq suffered a sharp decrease in the number of livestock. The total number of animals fell from 15 million in 1990 to 9 million in 1997, it said. The FAO also said that Baghdad lacked weed killers, and its fleet of 28 helicopters for spraying insecticides was grounded at a vital time by lack of spare parts. The INA reports that ''President Saddam Hussein briefed the ministerial cabinet on the results of a series of joint meetings [of a comprehensive review] which the Revolution Command Council and Iraq's Command of the Arab Ba'ath Socialist Party had held before.'' News of the meeting

Table 10.3 (continued)

	came as a UN official in Baghdad said that the Prakash Shah had met with Tariq Aziz and Foreign Minister Mohammed Saeed al-Sahaf to try to resolve a two-month-long standoff between Iraq and UN weapons inspectors. Sudad Mohammed, of the Iraqi National Monitoring Directorate, accuses a US member of a UN team of spying during an inspection of Iraqi weapons of mass destruction. "During a routine inspection made by UN monitors, an American inspector took photos of a missile warhead despite the fact that his camera does not carry a UN tag. This proves once again that they are collecting information irrelevant to their work. They are wearing UN hats but they are working for parties hostile to Iraq."
98–10-20:	The INA prints a letter from Iraqi Foreign Minister Mohammed Saeed al-Sahaf to Secretary-General Annan stating that "Iraq draws the attention of members of the Security Council to a list of American violations of international law in dealing with Iraq." The list included the two no-fly zones in southern and northern Iraq imposed by the US-led coalition in 1991 and 1993, respectively, as well as three missile and air attacks on Iraq following the 1991 Gulf War, US support for Iraq's opposition groups, and the recent allocation of about $100 million for these organizations to topple the Iraqi government. "These were the grave, illegitimate and illegal acts which should be seriously and responsibly discussed by the Council. Acts like those pose a threat to the international peace and security besides threatening Iraq's security and sovereignty. Hesitating to take firm measures against the government of the US pursuant to the UN Charter and the international law would mean that the Security Council has abandoned its responsibilities. This would subsequently lead to an American continuation in implementing grave hostile policies . . . thus leading to a total loss of confidence in the credibility of the Security Council and the UN."
	The Iraqi press publishes a summary of a thesis by Odai Hussein that concludes that the United States will lose its position as the world's only superpower by the year 2015, and that the Gulf War led to a drop in Washington's power because eight years after UN sanctions were imposed on Iraq, Baghdad still can defy American dictates.
98–10-30:	The UN Security Council completes work on a plan to review Iraq's bid to get eight-year-old sanctions against it lifted, provided Baghdad resumes cooperation with arms inspectors. It divides, however, over two different views of whether trade sanctions would be lifted if Iraq complies with all UN requirements dealing with weapons of mass destruction. France, Russia, and China and chief weapons inspector Richard Butler say they would be. The United States says compliance with arms demands is but one of several criteria for lifting some sanctions, such as the ban on oil exports. The United States says Iraq also has to return stolen Kuwaiti property, account for missing Kuwaiti prisoners, and compensate for its damage to the environment as a result of the invasion of

Table 10.3 (continued)

Kuwait, as well as other demands. The Security Council had adopted resolution 687 after an American-led coalition drove Iraqi troops from Kuwait. Paragraph 22 in this document indicated that the oil embargo could be lifted once Iraq complied with weapons demands. Within months, however, the United States took the stand that paragraph 22 could not be read in isolation. It said complying with weapons demands was not enough to get the oil embargo lifted. Russia, China, and France attempted to put into the Annan letter language on paragraph 22 that would have committed the council to lifting the oil embargo if Iraq complied with all weapons demands. But the United States refused, leaving the Council divided on its own criteria for getting sanctions lifted. Some legal experts say the complicated resolution could support the US position of removing all sanctions at once or leaving them all in place until demands are met, but note that no Council member, including the United States, expressed this interpretation when the document was first adopted.

Iraq states it will suspend all cooperation with UN weapons inspectors, effective immediately, until Chief Weapons Inspector Richard Butler is fired and the eight-year embargo lifted. Iraq had already suspended cooperation with on-site UN weapons inspections on August 5, and made the decision during a joint meeting of the Revolutionary Command Council and the ruling Ba'ath Party, chaired by Saddam Hussein. "Iraq has broken off all cooperation with UNSCOM and its chief and stopped all its activities in Iraq, including the monitoring operations as of today and the Security Council must take radical decisions such as firing UNSCOM chief Richard Butler." The text of Iraq's statement says that "Lifting sanctions is a great national humanitarian mission. Iraq has dealt with the Security Council resolutions since they were issued and complied with all related resolutions, although they were unjust. But this bitter experience, which lasted eight years, has proved that America and its agents are controlling issues connected to this problem, moving it with a clear target that is harming Iraq and the Arab nation. Iraq has been tolerant, patient, dealt diplomatically with all attempts and communications which were supposed to lead to the lifting of sanctions. But the sanctions were not lifted. Events this year have exposed two additional dangerous facts. The first is the American lies about the presidential sites, which almost led to a destructive war. The second is the dirty game that was played by the Special Commission and its head in cooperation with America about the VX claims. When the truth came out through neutral laboratories in France and Switzerland, the head of the commission did not admit the fact but kept requesting of Iraq more explanations with the intention of prolonging and misleading. No act was taken against [UNSCOM chief Richard] Butler, which should have been taken because of his lies and playing with facts . . . The joint meeting decided to halt all kinds of dealings with the Special Commission and its chief and stop all their activities inside Iraq, including the monitoring starting from today.

Table 10.3 (continued)

This does not include the International Atomic Energy Agency. They can continue their monitoring work as per the leadership decision on August 5 as long as these activities are done independently of the Special Commission.''

US-sponsored Radio Free Europe/Radio Liberty (RFE/RL) begins broadcasting two new services into Iraq and Iran.

John Mills, UN spokesman for the Iraqi humanitarian program, reports that Iraq is holding up its contracts for badly needed spare parts for its oil industry. His report shows that 105 spare parts contracts worth $86 million have been approved since July but many of had not been activated. Iraq only sent out letters of credit for 27 of these contracts, worth $46 million. Of this amount, contracts amounting up to $20 million were issued to firms in France, followed by China with $9.8 million and Germany with $8.4 million, according to the documents.

Syrian Industry Minister Ahmed Nezamuldin arrives in Baghdad for talks on expanding economic cooperation between the two countries.

98-10-31: The Security Council calls an emergency session to discuss Iraq's announcement it was halting all dealings with most UN arms inspectors. The UN Security Council unanimously condemns Iraq's decision to cut off all dealings with UN weapons inspectors and demands that Baghdad rescind the decision immediately and unconditionally. ''Members considered this decision a flagrant violation of relevant Council resolutions and of the Memorandum of Understanding signed between the Secretary-General and the Deputy Prime Minister of Iraq. Members demanded that the Iraqi leadership must rescind immediately and unconditionally today's decision, as well as the decision of August 5, to limit cooperation with UNSCOM and the International Atomic Energy Commission [IAEA], as previously demanded by the Council in its [resolution] 1193 and must resume immediate, complete and conditional cooperation with the Special Commission and the IAEA. Once Iraq has rescinded its decisions and has re-established full cooperation with the Special Commission and the IAEA, members remain ready, as clearly reaffirmed in the October 30 letter from the President of the Council to the Secretary-General, to implement a comprehensive review of Iraq's compliance with its obligations under all relevant resolutions. This decision by Iraq has delayed that prospect . . . Today's announcement from Baghdad and also the continuing restrictions on the work of the IAEA are deeply disturbing. In the coming days, the Council will remain actively seized of this matter in order to ensure the full implementation of the relevant resolutions and secure peace and security in the region.''

Ambassador Nizar Hamdoon says that UN inspectors might as well withdraw from Iraq because there was little left for them to do. He also says Iraq wanted Secretary-General Annan ''to get more involved and more active on this issue, because we trust him.'' But Hamdoon says Iraq had been disappointed by the Security Council meeting which decided on

Table 10.3 (continued)

guidelines for a comprehensive review of its relations with Baghdad once it cooperated with inspectors again. "That had a major impact on the Iraqi reaction... the Americans made it clear the review is not about lifting sanctions."

The head of the UN monitoring unit in Baghdad is called in by the Iraqi authorities and told that UNSCOM cannot do any more monitoring, but that Iraq will not expel the inspectors from the country."

98–11-1: Iraq rejects the Security Council statement condemning its decision to halt cooperation with UN weapons inspectors, and says it will not back down.

Iraq allows inspections by the IAEA, but other weapons inspections were stopped after Iraq broke off all cooperation, a UN spokeswoman said.

Iraq and Iran agree to set up committees to develop trade and economic cooperation between the two countries.

Russia states that it is concerned by Iraq's decision to halt cooperation with the UN and urges Iraq to reconsider its move.

Tariq Aziz meets a Russian team headed by ultra-nationalist Vladimir Zhirinovsky.

Tariq Aziz says, "We are not gambling and we are not seeking confrontation.... If the Security Council is serious about lifting the sanctions, if the Security Council is serious about restructuring UNSCOM and about creating a real international, cooperational, honest body to deal with the question of disarmament and to follow up the monitoring mission, OK. In principle we are not against implementing UN resolutions. We are not against working with the international body for the purpose of disarmament. If they change their position and they give Iraq its rights by reducing and lifting the sanctions we will immediately resume cooperation. [UNSCOM] is a subsidiary organ of the Mossad and the CIA. UNSCOM is not an honest impartial professional international agency. It's an instrument in the hands of the CIA and the Mossad."

Butler says Aziz's contentions are "nonsense" and that if Iraq were to fully cooperate, the weapons monitoring would quickly end. "You are quite close to getting towards the end of most of the disarmament issues. Secondly you know exactly what we need: the truth. You own it. You can give it to us. We will be objective. We will get the job of verification done and get to the end of this if you cooperate. That's a true and clear promise. I have to respond I think to the point where the deputy prime minister says that my organization somehow works for the US or Israeli intelligence. This is nonsense. If that's the seriously contended point, leading to restructuring of UNSCOM, then I fear the worst because it rests on contentions that are simply not true."

President Clinton says Iraq's decision to suspend cooperation with UN arms inspectors put it in "clear violation" of its commitments to the UN and of UN Security Council resolutions.

Table 10.3 (continued)

	US Secretary of Defense William Cohen warns Iraq that it could face military attack if Baghdad does not return to compliance with UN arms inspections. "I think everybody is getting weary of dealing with Saddam Hussein." He says the United States prefers that any action against Iraq be taken in concert with the UN and allies, but that unilateral attack by US forces "has always been an option that we could pursue."
	30 countries take part in the Baghdad International Fair, billed as the largest in Iraq since the 1991 Gulf War.
98–11-2:	Iraq allows teams from the IAEA to inspect sites for the second successive day.
	Iraq's parliament supports a decision to stop cooperating with a UN disarmament commission. The 250-member National Assembly votes to end cooperation until the sanctions are lifted and the UN commission is overhauled. The vote comes after Deputy Prime Minister Tariq Aziz says Iraq won't back down from its decision to stop cooperating with the UN disarmament commission, even if threatened with military strikes. "We are not afraid of any reaction or threats. There is no situation worse than the present one."
	Britain and Germany call on Iraq to comply with UN resolutions. New German Chancellor Gerhard Schroeder says, "I must underline that it is not a matter of a conflict between the US and Iraq. Iraq is violating decisions of the international community, decisions of the Security Council." That is the reason why Germany will support the decisions of the Security Council, the current ones and possible future ones."
	Swiss officials prolong a November 5 deadline for Barzan al-Tikriti, Iraqi leader Saddam Hussein's half-brother, to leave the country amid intense speculation on his future.
	Iraq allows UN technicians to change videocassettes on a surveillance camera, although UN officials say it didn't represent a significant change in Baghdad's decision to stop cooperating with weapons inspectors.
	Iraq announces it is considering asking the UN to extend the current oil-for-food plan until it reaches its $5.25 billion target rather than renegotiate the entire program. The program, which expires on November 25, allows Baghdad to sell up to $5.25 billion worth of oil over six months in order to buy food, medicine, and other necessities. Low crude oil prices mean Iraq is only expected to sell about $3 billion worth in the six months ending on November 6.
	Richard Butler calls the new standoff with Iraq the most serious confrontation with the UN to date, and says his teams could no longer carry out any meaningful operations. In a letter to Security Council President Peter Burleigh of the United States, Butler reports Iraq had permitted inspectors from UNSCOM to maintain surveillance cameras by changing tapes. It also permitted maintenance work on the commission's L-100 transport planes. But he says activities are, "by themselves, minor in

Table 10.3 (continued)

	terms of providing credible monitoring. The commission is not in a position to provide the council with any level of assurances regarding Iraq's compliance with its obligations not to re-establish proscribed activities."
98-11-3:	Nizar Hamdoon, Iraq's ambassador to the UN, says he believes there is no support in the Gulf for military action against Baghdad in its latest standoff with the international community over weapons inspections.
	China urges Iraq to drop its opposition to UN weapons inspections and for a review of UN Security Council sanctions against Baghdad.
	The UN Security Council's 661 sanctions committee approves 36 more contracts for spare parts to repair Iraq's sanctions-hit oil industry. Up to this time, 111 contracts worth $88 million for spare parts for the oil industry had been approved. Another 78 contracts worth $39 million were on hold or were sent back to suppliers for more information. Most of the contracts on hold are due to American objections. "This committee now approves 36 new contracts for the supply of spare parts and equipment for Iraq's oil industry," it said. The value of these contracts is $15,468,813, bringing the total approvals for the oil sector to $87.9 million. The contracts are with firms from China, Denmark, France, the Netherlands, United Arab Emirates, Turkey, Switzerland, Italy, and Jordan. They range from pipeline to pump spare parts.
	US Defense Secretary Cohen flies to London to discuss the Iraqi crisis with his counterparts, Britain's George Robertson and France's Alain Richard. Cohen warns that "all options remain open" for ending the Iraqi blockade of arms inspections. A British Defense Ministry spokeswoman says that the defense minister agreed that the decision by Iraq to end cooperation with the UN special commission on disarmament was "unacceptable" and breached his pledge at the beginning of the year to UN Secretary-General Annan, and that Iraq "must comply with the agreement or face the consequences." The spokeswoman says they agreed that they preferred a diplomatic solution, "but we can't rule out a military option. The international community's patience with Saddam isn't infinite." They also said they "can't look at lifting" trade sanctions in place against Iraq since the end of the Gulf War until Saddam complies fully with UN recommendations on disarmament and full cooperation with the inspectors.
	British Foreign Secretary Robin Cook states to Parliament that Iraq "appears to be gambling that the world will grow weary of his constant evasion and his repeated confrontation.... We must remain ready and resolute to prove him wrong. We want to find a diplomatic solution, but we have always made clear that all options remain open.
	A US force of 21 warships and 174 aircraft is now in the Gulf region, and the United States says it is sufficient for any military action against Iraq over UN arms inspections.

Table 10.3 (continued)

	Secretary Cohen heads for the Gulf to discuss the crisis with the leaders of friendly states in the region. US officials warn that the United States has no intention of continuing a costly cycle of building up, then drawing down, forces around Iraq with each new face-off, and that the large number of cruise missiles would suffice along with ability to quickly insert additional forces in a major emergency.
	France recalls its representative in Baghdad for consultations, saying Iraq's decision to end cooperation with UN weapons inspectors would lead to its "total isolation." Foreign Minister Hubert Vedrine writes to Tariq Aziz and says Iraq's decision is "serious," and it aggravates an already tense situation. "France does not understand this attitude which assuredly will not aid Iraq in getting sanctions lifted." He asks Iraq to reverse its position "without delay."
	Saudi Arabia's King Fahd meets with Secretary Cohen in Riyadh. A Saudi official says that "the Saudi leadership conveyed to Cohen its total refusal to have Saudi territory used as a springboard for striking Iraq."
98-11-4:	Secretary Cohen arrives in Kuwait to discuss measures needed to force Iraq to meet UN arms inspection demands. Colonel Ahmed Rahnali, director of national guidance in the Kuwaiti army, says, "Kuwait is not a party to the dispute between the UN and Iraq, but it urges for peace on all international forums." Cohen goes on to Bahrain and Qatar.
	During their meeting in Riyadh, Saudi Arabia's King Fahd told Cohen that he won't let Saudi territory be used "as a springboard" for US attacks on Iraq, Deutsche Press Agentur and the Associated Press reported, citing a Saudi official who spoke on condition of anonymity.
	The Russian Foreign Ministry states it "will do everything it can do" to "prevent military action," and that "any unilateral moves" would only worsen the situation and would have "unpredictable consequences."
	Russian Communist leader Gennady Zyuganov tells the Duma that "I was in Iraq and I spoke to many specialists. They have no weapons of mass destruction. The [UN weapons inspection] commission is continuing only so as to carry out spying activities. They are breaking all norms of ethics and international law." The United States is behaving like a "Big Rambo, that can dictate to the world its norms of behavior. In real life it never turns out as well as it does in films."
	French Foreign Minister Hubert Vedrine says, "We can't see any country that understands what's going on or understands what the Baghdad regime is seeking, especially at a time when the Security Council had adopted a more open position. There is complete agreement in the Security Council—including us, of course, but also the Russians and the Chinese—to tell the Iraqis they're going in completely the wrong direction. [It] is a decision that nobody can support . . . And just when the Security Council was moving a bit towards the French position, in-

Table 10.3 (continued)

	explicably, Iraqi authorities—at the highest level, I think—decide to break off that cooperation."
	European Union defense ministers warned Iraq that its refusal to cooperate is causing a "serious crisis" and may provoke "the most severe consequences." The first informal meeting of all 15 EU defense ministers to discuss defense cooperation outside of the North Atlantic Treaty Organization includes traditionally neutral states such as Austria, Finland, Ireland, and Sweden.
	Kurdistan Democratic Party leader Massoud Barzani says Turkey has little to fear from attempts to create a Kurdish anti-Baghdad front in northern Iraq, and that it does not seek a Kurdish "statelet" that could encourage separatism in Turkey.
	Turkish Deputy Prime Minister Bulent Ecevit states that Iraq's refusal to cooperate with the UN is a cause of concern to Ankara and the Kurds of northern Iraq.
	Egyptian President Mubarak sends a message to Iraqi President Saddam Hussein on the standoff between Iraq and the UN, but no details are reported about the message.
98–11-5:	Iraqi newspapers attack a draft UN resolution demanding that Baghdad stop blocking inspections by UN weapons experts, saying Iraq would not back down, and dismissing Secretary Cohen's visit to the Gulf as a failure.
	The Security Council condemns Iraq's decision to stop cooperating with UN inspections as a "flagrant violation" of its disarmament obligations and calls for an immediate and unconditional reversal. The vote on the British-drafted resolution is a unanimous 15–0, with no abstentions, reinforcing the Council's message to Iraq. The text notes, "with alarm the decision of Iraq on 31 October 1998 to cease cooperation with the UN Special Commission, and its continued restrictions on the work of the International Atomic Energy Agency (IAEA)." It states the Security Council is determined "to ensure immediate and full compliance by Iraq without conditions or restrictions with its obligations under resolution 687 (1991) of 3 April 1991 and the other relevant resolutions." It reaffirms its "readiness to consider, in a comprehensive review, Iraq's compliance with its obligations under all relevant resolutions once Iraq has rescinded its above mentioned decision and its decision of 5 August 1998 and demonstrated that it is prepared to fulfil all its obligations, including in particular on disarmament issues, by resuming full cooperation with the Special Commission and the IAEA consistent with the Memorandum of Understanding signed by the Deputy Prime Minister of Iraq and the Secretary-General on 23 February 1998 (S/1998/166), endorsed by the Council in resolution 1154 (1998)." The resolution condemns the decision by Iraq of 31 October 1998 to cease cooperation with the Special Commission as a flagrant violation of resolution 687 (1991) and other

Table 10.3 (continued)

relevant resolutions; demands that Iraq rescind immediately and unconditionally the decision of 31 October 1998, as well as the decision of 5 August 1998, to suspend cooperation with the Special Commission and to maintain restrictions on the work of the IAEA, and that Iraq provide immediate, complete and unconditional cooperation with the Special Commission and the IAEA.

British UN Ambassador Sir Jeremy Greenstock says, "It is well established that the authorization to use force given by the Security Council in 1990 may be revived if the council decides that there has been a sufficiently serious breach of the conditions laid down by the council for the cease-fire. In the resolution we have just adopted, the council has condemned the Iraqi decision to cease all cooperation as a flagrant violation of its obligations. So Mr. President, this resolution sends a clear message to Iraq: resume cooperation now."

The Ba'ath Party paper *al-Thawra* says, "Whatever the British draft resolution and whatever its final shape, Iraq will not retreat from its decision unless the Security Council responds to Iraq's legitimate rights."

President Clinton calls Iraq's latest defiance of UN resolutions "totally unacceptable" and warns that military force is an option.

Secretary Cohen says he found the Gulf Arab states "united in their condemnation" of Iraq's position after visiting Britain, Saudi Arabia, Kuwait, Bahrain, Qatar, Oman, the United Arab Emirates, Egypt and Jordan.

Jordan's Crown Prince Hassan tells US Defense Secretary William Cohen that military strikes against Iraq could undermine regional stability.

UNSCOM announces it will withdraw 26 people from Iraq out of a permanent staff of about 120 people.

Japan warns Iraq that the international community will not lift sanctions on it unless Baghdad complies with UN inspections of suspected weapons sites.

98–11-6:   Abdul-Ghani Abdul-Ghafur, a senior member of the regional command of the ruling Ba'ath party, says Iraq will not rescind its decision unless the UN Security Council seriously examines the lifting of the trade sanctions in force since Iraq's 1990 invasion of Kuwait. "America and Britain have imposed a new resolution in order to inflict more harm against the Iraqi people and to prolong the unjust embargo. Iraq will not retreat from its decision unless there is a clear response [from the Security Council] to Iraq's legitimate demand to lift the unjust embargo."

Foreign Secretary Robin Cook says that Britain is working on measures to enforce UN economic sanctions more effectively by tackling oil smuggling by Baghdad to sustain Saddam's security forces and buy luxuries for its elite. Industry experts estimate Iraq exports up to 120,000 barrels a day, mainly of diesel oil, through Iran, Turkey, and Jordan. It has also

Table 10.3 (continued)

	been discussing a route through Syria. The proceeds of the smuggling go directly to Saddam Hussein and his family, bypassing UN supervision, unlike the revenue from crude exported officially through an oil-for-food program to buy food and medicines for the civilian population. The scam may be worth up to $250 million a year, about half of the highest Western government estimates. Turkey had imposed a $79 per truck tax in July. Turkish officials estimated the number of vehicles crossing per day has fallen to an average of 500 from a peak of 1,500. Iraq also is smuggling bunker fuel through Iranian territorial waters using barges that carry Iraqi diesel oil down the Shatt al-Arab waterway, along Iranian coastal waters and across the Gulf to Dubai. About half of the illegal Iraqi exports got out via the Iranian route.
	Russia reaffirms its opposition to the use of force against Iraq.
	The United States states that military means remain an option to make Baghdad comply with UN demands on arms inspections. National Security Council spokesman David Leavy says the United States believed it already had "all the necessary authority" under previous UN resolutions to launch military action if President Clinton decided to do so.
	British sources report that Foreign Secretary Robin Cook wants to continue to use diplomacy. "It is his view that there will be a couple of weeks at least of diplomatic activity. We seek a diplomatic solution. But we are not ruling out the use of force, if that is necessary to bring Saddam into compliance with UN Security Council resolutions."
98–11-7:	The United States warns its citizens in the Gulf against possible anti-American attacks as Western powers and regional allies weigh the option of military strikes against Iraq. "US citizens traveling or residing abroad should be aware that tensions have increased."
	Eight Arab foreign ministers from the Southern Gulf states and Egypt warn Iraq that it does not have their support and must comply with the terms of the UN resolutions.
	Trade Minister Mohammed Mehdi Saleh says Iraq is ready for any military confrontation with the United States: "We do not fear any military strike. We are ready to confront any military strike."
	Russian Foreign Minister Igor Ivanov stresses Russia's desire to resolve the Iraqi crisis by diplomatic means in talks with a top Palestinian official and with Arab ambassadors.
	Palestinian leader Yasser Arafat sends a message urging Saddam Hussein not to give the United States an excuse for military strikes against Baghdad.
98–11-8:	President Clinton meets with his top security advisers, but officials say no decision is made on whether to use military force against Iraq.
	Secretary-General Annan appeals to Iraq to rescind its decision to stop cooperating with UN inspectors.

Table 10.3 (continued)

	The UN says 15 arms monitors will leave Iraq on November 9 and 11.
	Saudi Arabian Foreign Minister Prince Saud al-Faisal says his country wanted the crisis between Iraq and the UN settled by diplomacy, not military action. "We prefer a diplomatic solution of the crisis. No one wishes evil on the Iraqi people. But, the responsibility in this issue falls completely on the Iraqi leadership. We think we express the wish of all Arab people which is that the Iraqi leadership bear its responsibilities and go back on its decision."
	About 25,000 Turkish troops, supported by planes and helicopters, move into northern Iraq to fight Kurdish rebels in the PKK.
	British Defense Secretary George Robertson flies into Kuwait and says the military capability is already in place for Western attacks on Iraq, and warns Saddam Hussein that the crisis would not be allowed to drift into 1999. "He [Saddam] would be very foolish to underestimate either our political will or our military capability."
98–11-9:	Baghdad condemns Turkey for launching a new military operation into northern Iraq against Kurdish separatist guerrillas.
	The ruling Ba'ath party newspaper, *al-Thawra*, says that "Iraq will not lose anything if the American administration fulfils its [military] threats but America will be the loser. After this [US] arrogance, oppression and tyranny, Iraq has no option but to re-assess all its relations with the Special Commission and the Security Council."
	The CIA releases a report warning that Iraq could rebuild its chemical and biological arsenals if international arms inspections ceased. It states that Iraq has "the capability to quickly resurrect weapons of mass destruction production absent UN sanctions."
	Five teams of inspectors from the IAEA monitor Iraq's suspected nuclear weapons sites.
	Twenty UNSCOM monitors have left Iraq since Baghdad's decision to halt cooperation, and 10 more are due to leave in the next few days.
98–11-10:	President Clinton discusses military options with senior Defense Department officials. Among those at the meeting are Secretary of Secretary William Cohen, Chairman of the Joint Chiefs of Staff Gen. Henry Shelton, and Secretary of State Madeleine Albright.
	Babel accuses Turkey of pursuing territorial ambitions inside Iraq and following a hostile US policy. "Instead of trying to help restore the central authority in the north of Iraq, they pursue a direction very near to that of American policy [against Iraq]. . . . Turkey would be one of the tools that would be used against the Iraqi people, history and leadership."
98–11-11:	Richard Butler orders the UNSCOM inspection staff out of Iraq. More than 100 inspectors and support personnel head for Bahrain. The IAEA says it is removing its staff immediately as a precautionary measure.

Table 10.3 (continued)

	Several UN humanitarian staff operating Iraq's oil-for-food program leave Baghdad for Jordan.
	Iraq attacks the GCC states for allowing visits by the US and British defense ministers, and *al-Qadissiya* has a front page editorial asking, "How is it that Arab states allow and provide entry visas to a Zionists like Cohen to issue threats against Iraq?"
	Gen. Henry Shelton says, "As of today, no decision has been made.... All options remain on the table ... I would say that Saddam Hussein has been given adequate warning. He has in fact failed to live (up) to his commitments.... We have seen very strong resolve on the part of the UN. They are telling him that he needs to honor these commitments and I think that alone should serve as enough warning for Saddam Hussein ... As we have said in the past, the ball is in Saddam's court. He is the one that made the commitments after he was defeated in the Gulf War in 1991 ... and we expect him to do that to honor his commitments."
	The United States announces it will deploy additional warplanes, including F-117A stealth fighters, to the Gulf. The force will include Air Expeditionary Force of about 50 attack and support jets as well as several radar-avoiding stealth fighters.
	Khalid Shahab al-Douri, head of the Arab and Foreign Relations at the Iraqi parliament, says that Iraq has not expelled the UN. "We have not expelled them and if they have left it is something left to them to decide. We hope that a strike will not take place, but if it happens we will defend ourselves and our country."
98–11-12:	Eight Arab foreign ministers declare that Iraq would be "held responsible for any consequences" from its stopping the work of UN inspectors.
	German Chancellor Gerhard Schroeder urges Iraq to allow UN inspectors to carry out their work in order to achieve a diplomatic solution to the conflict. "I most strongly urge the Iraqi leadership to fulfill comprehensively the resolutions of the UN Security Council. Only on this basis is a political solution of the conflict between Iraq and the international community possible."
	Britain tells its nationals to leave Baghdad as soon as possible and warns that President Saddam Hussein could make biological weapons within weeks. Prime Minister Tony Blair says, "The next step is action if he is not prepared to come back into compliance with his word. He has carried on fabricating evidence, telling lies about his program, attempting to prevent the inspectors doing their work.... We cannot allow such a situation to happen." Defense Secretary George Robertson returns from a tour of Kuwait and Bahrain to seek the support of Gulf Arab states, and says, "Saddam has no option left now but to comply. If he consistently refuses to comply, then military action will have to be the option to be considered. If he continues to defy world opinion, there will be an inevitability, a sad inevitability about force being used."

Table 10.3 (continued)

> Tariq Aziz gives a press conference in which he says, "We don't see any light at the end of the tunnel. . . . There is a tunnel after the tunnel . . . diplomacy did not bring any results. . . . The war has been waged on our people since 1991 and it has not stopped . . . sanctions [are] a war by itself and it is killing Iraqis. . . . We welcome [Annan] if he would like to come here and we would not impose any preconditions on that but the main thing is the lifting of sanctions."
>
> US State Department spokesman James Rubin says, "Clearly Iraq is desperately trying to shift responsibility for the crisis from its doorstep to the US. That effort is failing completely and totally."
>
> Secretary Cohen warns Iraq that it is risking "significant" air strikes in its continuing refusal to allow arms inspections. "They will be significant should they be carried out."
>
> Senator Richard Lugar urges the Clinton administration to follow up any strikes on Iraq with a full-fledged military campaign to remove Saddam Hussein from power.
>
> The UN says that essential humanitarian missions under the oil-for-food program continue despite the withdrawal of most UN staff from Baghdad.
>
> Secretary-General Annan returns and says he has no plans to go to Baghdad because of the Iraq crisis but needed to consult with the Security Council.
>
> Jordan's Prime Minister, Fayez al-Tarawnah, cancels leave for ministers and warns that the government would not tolerate public protests against the threat of US strikes against Iraq.
>
> US officials state that the United States wants Iraqi oil exports to continue under the UN's oil-for-food program and is pushing for a smooth renewal of the scheme in two weeks, even if crisis appears headed toward a military conflict.
>
> The Tunisian government urges restraint from all parties and calls on UN Secretary-General Annan to continue his efforts toward a diplomatic solution.

98–11-13: Secretary-General Annan appeals to Iraq to resume cooperating with UN weapons inspectors but said events on the ground "may be running away from us."

> Saddam Hussein makes his first public statement since the latest dispute began and says that nothing less than a pledge to lift UN sanctions would end the current crisis. Saddam also insists, however, that he is not trying to create a crisis and would accept "positively any initiative" that would lift the sanctions.
>
> President Clinton denounces Iraq's continued defiance of UN weapons inspections. He warns that Saddam Hussein can only avert a devastating attack by ending his ban on the searches. Clinton says, "the Security Council and the world have made it crystal clear now that this is unac-

Table 10.3 (continued)

ceptable. None of us can tolerate an Iraq free to develop weapons of mass destruction with impunity.''

USCENTCOM is given the order to prepare to launch strikes on Iraq on November 13. President Clinton then orders the US military to launch an air strike against Iraq on November 14.

The Iraqi Foreign Ministry announces publicly that it is sending a favorable response to a letter from Secretary-General Annan.

98-11-14: Iraq suddenly agrees to resume unconditional cooperation with UN weapons inspectors and the IAEA. Tariq Aziz's letter to UN Secretary-General Annan states that the Iraqi leadership has "decided to resume working with the Special Commission and the IAEA and to allow them to perform their normal duties ... not out of fear of the aggressive American campaign and the threat to commit a new aggression against Iraq, but as an expression of our feeling of responsibility and in response to your appeal and those of our friends." He refers to a letter from Russian President Yeltsin and Prime Minister Primakov and positions taken by China, France, and Brazil. The letter indicates that Iraq's goal in its decisions on August 5 and October 31 was not to sever relations with UNSCOM and IAEA: "The objective of Iraq is to end the suffering of its embargoed people and to see the implementation of paragraph 22 of Security Council Resolution 687 as a first step for lifting the other sanctions." Aziz refers to an annex to the letter setting out Iraq's views on the proposed comprehensive review and UNSCOM, saying: "If the review were not to be a mere formality ... the adoption of the points we conveyed yesterday, 13/11/1998, to the Ambassadors of Russia, France and China, a copy of which I enclose herewith, will render the review serious, fair and fruitful." Iraq's position on the comprehensive review, as set out in the annex, also asks that "the review to be carried out within a very short time (seven days for example) after the resumption" of UNSCOM work; the Security Council be ready to implement paragraph 22 if the fulfillment of the requirements of section C of Security Council Resolution 687 is established; and if the Council feels more work needs to be done, a short period be set for that and in the meantime the Council takes "measures for lifting or reducing sanctions in proportion to what has been fulfilled of the requirements of paragraph 22." The annex also says, "the question of [UNSCOM chief Richard] Butler and the structure of UNSCOM and its practices are important matters. The Council is to consider them seriously in order to ensure a good relationship in the future. We hope that this will be done as soon as possible."

Prakash Shah, the UN envoy to Baghdad, states that "Iraq accepts to resume cooperation with UNSCOM and the IAEA inspectors in accordance with Security Council resolutions. No conditions have been mentioned in this [Iraqi] letter." In New York, Annan calls the letter "positive" and says he believes it met UN requirements for resolving the latest crisis.

Table 10.3 (continued)

Russia's deputy foreign minister, Viktor Posuvalyuk, praises Iraq's agreement to resume cooperation with UN weapons inspectors and said Russia played a decisive role in Baghdad's change in position. "We have read the message from Iraqi Deputy Prime Minister Tariq Aziz to Secretary-General Annan and we believe that it is clearly written that Iraq agrees to renew the normal work of the special commission. We believe that this opens a real path for political settlement and correspondingly eliminates the possibility of using military force."

Chinese Foreign Ministry spokesman Tang Guoqiang says that "We hope the Iraqi side will honor its pledges and sincerely implement all relevant Security Council resolutions. We also call on all relevant parties to continue political and diplomatic efforts to resolve the weapons inspection crisis as soon as possible."

US National Security Adviser Sandy Berger issues the following statement: "The Iraqi letter . . . is neither unequivocal nor unconditional. It is unacceptable." He makes it clear that the United States is still ready to make armed strikes against Baghdad. "We were poised to take military action and we remain poised to take military action." He warns that the US demands an unequivocal response from Baghdad. "What we have instead is a letter and particularly an annex that's got more holes than Swiss cheese."

President Clinton aborts an air strike at about 8:00 A.M. EST (1300 GMT). The president orders a pause in the strike and requires the US military to carry it out 24 hours later unless otherwise instructed.

Iraq gives the Security Council a two-page letter offering to allow UN inspectors to resume work along with a two-page annex that the United States judged laid down conditions.

US National Security Adviser Sandy Berger publicly rejects the Iraqi offer shortly after 5:00 P.M. EST (2200 GMT).

The White House receives a second letter from Iraq to the Security Council at 7:20 P.M. EST (0020 GMT on Sunday), saying its offer to resume working with UNSCOM was "unequivocal."

The White House receives a third document, a revised version of the Iraqi letter to the Security Council, at 9:06 P.M. EST (0206 GMT on Sunday), saying Baghdad has abandoned its August 5 decision to stop UN field inspections and its October 31 decision to halt all cooperation with UN inspectors.

President Clinton has separate telephone consultations with Vice President Al Gore, Secretary of State Albright, Defense Secretary Cohen, Central Intelligence Agency (CIA) Director George Tenet, and Gen. Henry Shelton, chairman of the Joint Chiefs of Staff. Clinton also speaks to British Prime Minister Tony Blair and French President Jacques Chirac.

Table 10.3 (continued)

	Iraq assures the Security Council that its letter saying UN weapons inspectors could return to Baghdad was "unconditional and unequivocal," and quite separate from an accompanying annex setting out Iraqi wishes. The annex had become a major issue, and the United States and Britain had set unacceptable conditions for the return of the UN weapons teams. Iraqi UN envoy Nizar Hamdoon said he first informed council president Peter Burleigh of the United States orally, and then in a letter, that the annex "contains the views and preferences of the government of Iraq" on a comprehensive review that the council had previously agreed to carry out on how far Baghdad had complied with UN resolutions. The ruling Ba'ath party newspaper, *al-Thawra*, says, "This leadership's decision pulled the rug from under the feet of the American administration, which has become used to distorting the facts relating to Iraq and engineering excuses to commit aggression against it. After this victory we should thank our steadfast people. . . . Victory after victory until we overcome [the sanctions]."
98–11-15:	US National Security Adviser Sandy Berger consults with UN Secretary-General Annan to make sure the White House and the UN have the same understanding of Iraq's promise to comply fully with the UN weapons inspections. Berger ends talks with Annan at 3:00 A.M. EST (0800 GMT). President Clinton decides to abort a second military strike and leaves a meeting in the White House West Wing at about 3:30 A.M. (0830 GMT). Berger calls Shelton to tell him that President Clinton has ordered him to abort a second strike at a time not disclosed by US officials. British Prime Minister Tony Blair says that the crisis over UN weapons inspectors in Iraq is not over and that Britain remains ready, willing, and able to strike if necessary. "This is not over until absolute and unconditional compliance is guaranteed and delivered. Until that we remain on alert." Blair confirms that he and President Clinton had authorized the use of force against Baghdad on November 14, before Iraq sent its letter to the Security Council. Pope John Paul II asks the world to pray for the key figures in the Iraq crisis, asking God to "illuminate their minds and hearts" so that they end the crisis peacefully. President Clinton gives a television address in which he announces that Iraq has agreed unconditionally to allow UN arms inspectors to resume their work in the country, and says the United States remains ready to act militarily pending full compliance. "Last night, Iraq agreed to meet the demands of the international community to cooperate fully with the UN weapons inspectors. Iraq committed to unconditional compliance. Iraq has backed down but that is not enough. Now Iraq must live up to its obligations. . . . Until we see complete compliance we will remain vigilant, keep up the pressure and be ready to act." The president says

Table 10.3 (continued)

Iraq had clarified an earlier letter during the previous night. Clinton makes the US conditions for halting the use of force clear: "As I have said since this crisis began, the return of the inspectors, if they can operate in an unfettered way, is the best outcome, because they have been and they remain the most effective tool to uncover, destroy and prevent Iraq from rebuilding its weapons of mass destruction and the missiles to deliver them. Now let me be clear. Iraq has backed down, but that is not enough. Now Iraq must live up to its obligations. Iraq has committed to unconditionally resume cooperation with the weapons inspectors. What does that mean? First, Iraq must resolve all outstanding issues raised by UNSCOM and the IAEA. Second, it must give inspectors unfettered access to inspect and to monitor all sites they choose, with no restrictions or qualifications, consistent with the memorandum of understanding Iraq itself signed with Secretary-General Annan in February. Third, it must turn over all relevant documents. Fourth, it must accept all weapons of mass destruction–related resolutions. Fifth, it must not interfere with the independence or the professional expertise of the weapons inspectors." Clinton also calls for a new government in Iraq that was "committed to peace" and said the United States would intensify efforts toward that aim.

Iraq welcomes a peaceful resolution to the crisis. Trade Minister Mohammed Mehdi Saleh says, "Any peaceful solution is good." However, Vice President Taha Yassin Ramadan attacks the United States during his address to a celebration in Baghdad to mark the founding of the Iraqi capital. "The leadership of the [ruling Ba'ath] party and the revolution . . . has decided to continue efforts with all means to confront the American threats [and] to lift the siege. We are certain that the complete victory will eventually be on the side of the people of our [Arab] nation."

Tariq Aziz reiterates Iraq's commitment to cooperate with UN inspections. "We will cooperate. We have a commitment and we respect our commitments . . . They can perform their normal work according to the [UN] Security Council resolutions and memorandum of understanding. We will provide them with all the cooperation according to the Security Council resolutions and memorandum of understanding." He also says that "I have to condemn, strongly, the statement of President Clinton regarding the plans of his government to overthrow the government of Iraq . . . This is a flagrant violation of the [UN] Security Council resolutions as well as international law." When he is asked if the crisis is over, he replies that, "I really don't know. I cannot be optimistic and say 'Yes' and I don't want to be pessimistic and say 'No.' The Security Council is still deliberating on the matter and I prefer to wait and see what results they will reach."

The Security Council calls on Iraq to cooperate with UN arms inspectors: "Council members underlined that their confidence in Iraq's intentions needs to be established by unconditional and sustained cooperation." The

Table 10.3 (continued)

	statement also says the Council would undertake a "comprehensive review" of Iraq's compliance with its resolutions once Secretary-General Annan confirms that "Iraq has returned to full cooperation." Baghdad has pushed for the review to begin quickly in hopes it would lead to an easing or lifting of sanctions. Immediately after the meeting ended, Chief Weapons Inspector Richard Butler said his staff of 103, now in Bahrain, would return to Baghdad on November 17. Benon Sevan, head of the UN humanitarian program in Iraq, said 151 international relief workers in Amman, Jordan, would return on November 18.
98-11-16:	Prime Minister Blair speaks by telephone to President Clinton. A statement is issued saying that "The prime minister and the president assessed the situation and agreed on the need to keep up the military presence and make sure agreements are now delivered." Blair then tells parliament, "No warnings, no wrangling, no negotiations, no last minute letters. The next withdrawal of co-operation and he will be hit. If there is a next time, I will have no hesitation in ordering the use of force. President Clinton's position is the same. The US and UK, with far greater international support than ever before, now have Saddam trapped. I hope other countries, more dubious about the use of force, can now see that Saddam is moved by a credible threat of force." Blair says Iraq retains the expertise and equipment to make more weapons of mass destruction and still possessed a large array of conventional weapons, and that there are unanswered questions about the purpose of 610 tons of chemicals that could be used in the production of the nerve gas VX, and of imports of products that could be used in the manufacture of Anthrax bacteria. "Despite UNSCOM, Iraq still has weapons of mass destruction capability. We don't know precisely how much. They still have the skills, the engineers and the equipment to make more." He announces that he had given orders on the morning of November 14 to launch 12 British Royal Air Force Tornado jets stationed in Kuwait before Iraq backed down.

President Clinton warns Saddam Hussein he must comply fully with his promise to allow UN weapons inspectors unfettered access to do their job: "The burden of compliance is where it has always been, with Iraq. Our forces remain strong and ready if he does not."

President Clinton says he'll spend the $97.4 million Congress approved last month to increase the broadcasts of anti-Hussein Radio Free Iraq and to unite the Iraq's splintered opposition forces. State Department spokesman James P. Rubin follows up by saying, "We're not going to lose any sleep if Saddam Hussein suddenly isn't their leader, from whatever reason. No tears will be shed. What we're going to try to do is engage more deeply with opposition groups, work with the Congress on some of the ideas that they've had and try to step up our activity with them." Administration officials say the London-based Iraqi National Congress, an umbrella group for anti-Saddam factions, and two Kurdish groups in northern Iraq were the first organizations the government planned to work |

Table 10.3 (continued)

with. Congress had previously passed the Iraq Liberation Act of 1998 in October. The legislation states as US policy the removal of Saddam's government and authorizes a first installment of up to $97 million in overt military aid to opposition groups. The Administration and Department of Defense say they do not expect quick success. National Security Adviser Sandy Berger states, "This should not be seen as an overnight enterprise or a quick fix, but as a long-term effort to de-legitimize that regime and bring about change. At the State Department, Rubin was asked how the administration planned to bring about a post-Saddam regime. "We're not promising to bring it about. What we're saying is we're going to intensify our work. Right now, we're focused on providing political support for the opposition and Congress has given us the authority and funding to arm the opposition. We don't want any ill-prepared efforts to lead to a tragic or unnecessary loss of life. So what we're going to try to do is engage more deeply with opposition groups, work with the Congress on some of the ideas that they've had and try to step up our activity with them." USCENTCOM commander Marine Gen. Anthony Zinni had warned in October that "We have to be careful what we are doing . . . It should not be a case where the end result is just get rid of Saddam. It has to be done in such a way that the sovereignty and integrity of Iraq remains and that what follows Saddam is a decent government . . . A weakened, fragmented Iraq is more dangerous in the long run than a 'contained' Saddam, as he is now."

Prime Minister Blair tells parliament that the British government will work with the United States "to improve the possibility of removing Saddam Hussein altogether. We want to see Iraq governed by a regime other than that of Saddam Hussein."

State Department spokesman James Rubin gives a briefing on the US estimate of Iraq's holdings of weapons of mass destruction: "There is a large discrepancy between the amount of biological growth media—that's the culture in which you grow biological weapons—procured and the amount of agents that were or could have been produced." He states that Baghdad has not adequately explained where some 8,000 pounds (3,500 kilograms) of the material went out of some 68,000 pounds (31,000 kilograms) of biological growth media it imported. "Iraq's accounting of the amount of the agent it produced and the number of failed batches is seriously flawed and cannot be reconciled on the basis of this full disclosure Iraq has made. Iraq has reported making 8,800 pounds (four tons) of VX nerve gas, 220,000 pounds (100 tons) to 330,000 pounds (150 tons) of nerve agents such as Sarin and 1.1 million pounds (500 tons) to 1.32 million pounds (600 tons) of mustard gas. But Rubin says data from UN weapons inspectors indicates that Iraq may have produced an additional 1.32 million pounds (600 tons) of these agents, divided evenly among the three. "In other words, these are the differences between what they say they have and what we have reason to believe

Table 10.3 (continued)

they have." Rubin provides an itemized list of Iraqi weapons already destroyed under UN supervision, including 48 operational missiles; 14 conventional missile warheads; six operational mobile launchers; 28 operational fixed launch pads; 32 fixed launch pads; 30 missile chemical warheads; other missile support equipment and materials; and a variety of assembled and non-assembled supergun components. They also include 38,537 filled and empty chemical munitions; 90 metric tons of chemical weapons agent; more than 3,000 metric tons of precursor chemicals; 426 pieces of chemical weapons production equipment; 91 pieces of related analytical instruments; the entire al-Hakam biological weapons production facility and a variety of production equipment and materials.

Defense Secretary Cohen says, "I think everyone understands that this is the last go-round as far as Saddam is concerned. I think he has had more than sufficient warning. I don't believe any additional warning is required." A White House spokesman says, "We remain poised to act if there is any evidence that Iraq will not honor the unconditional commitments they made over the weekend. The reconfiguration of forces has enabled us to act quickly and decisively."

Defense Secretary Cohen announces that the United States has halted its forces build-up: "We will keep the forces that are already there for the time being. Those forces that did not yet arrive will in all probability be recycled back in the next several days." Several dozen F-16 and F-15 fighter planes, along with four F-117 Stealth fighters, halt in Europe instead of heading toward the Gulf as originally planned. The United States holds back a total of 91 of the 105 aircraft the Air Force planned to send to the Gulf. It deployed six F-117 Stealth fighters to Kuwait from Holloman Air Force Base, New Mexico, instead of the planned 12. Seven of 12 B-52H model bombers arrived on the island of Diego Garcia in the Indian Ocean. The remaining five are now to stay in the United States. Twenty-four F-16s and 12 F-15C fighters were diverted to England. Four of six B-1B bombers arrive in the Gulf. Two will remain in the United States. Similarly, a Joint Stars surveillance aircraft deployed to the Gulf is returning home. The Army stops deployment of 3,600 troops from Fort Stewart, Georgia, and six to nine batteries of Patriot missiles from Fort Bliss, Texas. Each battery contains about four launchers and 32 missiles. A total of about 4,000 Army troops stand down. Cohen says these forces will "be ready to go at a moment's notice." When a second aircraft carrier (USS *Enterprise*) arrives in the Gulf, the one there—the USS *Dwight D. Eisenhower*—is expected to return home on schedule. The number of aircraft will be about half the 400 US warplanes in the Gulf region the United States had planned. More than 170 US aircraft, one aircraft carrier, and about two dozen other ships—including eight vessels capable of launching Tomahawk cruise missiles—were already in the region, and a total of six F-117 Stealth fighters, six B-52 bombers, four

Table 10.3 (continued)

B-1 bombers, and some support aircraft, including AWACS surveillance planes, were added during the crisis.

The United States announces that its military operations in the Persian Gulf aimed at Iraq have cost almost $6.9 billion since 1991. These costs don't include the latest deployment of additional bombers, fighters, and troops. Costs in fiscal 1998, which ended September 30, are estimated to be $2 billion, primarily because of the massive military buildup that started in January and lasted until May. The United States put two aircraft battle groups on station in January instead of one and increased troops, airmen, and sailors to 40,000 from about 20,000. The figures include costs for continual air patrols over Iraq to stop Iraqi military flights, Tomahawk cruise missile attacks launched twice in 1993 and once in 1996, and major military deployments of troops in October, 1994 and January, 1999. The annual costs include $346 million in fiscal 1991, $106 million in fiscal 1992, $838.5 million in fiscal 1993, $421.8 million in fiscal 1994, $864.3 million in fiscal 1995, $65.2 million in fiscal 1996, $739 million in fiscal 1997, $2 billion in fiscal 1998, and $849 million so far in fiscal 1999.

French Foreign Minister Hubert Vedrine says he will visit Washington for an explanation of reports that Senator John McCain hinted Paris tipped off Iraq about impending American bombing. "The accusation is shameful and completely idiotic. It is especially outrageous coming from a senator and I will ask American authorities for explanations." Vedrine says Iraqi leaders did not need anyone to tip them off that they would be attacked if they failed to allow UN weapons inspectors back into the country. "All they had to do was read any newspaper or watch any television in the world . . . The US knew that France is their friend and their ally though we do not automatically align ourselves on their positions." He adds that France had been in complete agreement with Washington during the last Iraq crisis.

Russian Foreign Minister Igor Ivanov and Chinese Foreign Minister Tang Jiaxuan call for renewed diplomatic efforts to build on progress in resolving the dispute with Iraq over weapons inspections.

UN officials say 84 weapons inspectors, out of more than 100 evacuated last week during the US military build-up, will return to Iraq on November 17, and the rest will follow on November 18.

The UN denies a report that Secretary-General Annan disregarded United States protests when he appealed to Saddam Hussein to rescind his decision not to cooperate with UN weapons inspectors.

The Lloyd's Register oil-for-food monitors return to Iraq. Syria condemns what it calls the US double-standard policy and military build-up against Iraq and calls for solving international problems through dialogue.

Table 10.3 (continued)

Saudi Arabia welcomes the easing of the Iraqi crisis: "The council [of ministers] expressed its satisfaction at the easing of the crisis between Iraq and the UN."

Former UNSCOM Chief Rolf Ekeus states, "One should be skeptical. It is always prudent to be skeptical. We have a history of Saddam Hussein making earlier promises.... which he broke flatly and promptly."

The UN reports Iraq must step up its oil exports to meet its contractual commitments by November 25. Iraq must export an average of 1.8 million barrels per day (bpd) in the last 12 days of the program, well above the 1.49-million-bpd average for the week ending November 13. The four-week average of Iraqi exports is now 1.78 million bpd. The current six-month period of Iraq oil sales expires on November 25, and Baghdad has not indicated whether it will allow the uninterrupted flow of oil when the current six-month phase ends. UN officials said there may be a gap in oil exports of several weeks, but that the oil sale is expected to continue. The UN announces Iraq has shipped 286.8 million barrels in the limited oil sale's fourth six-month phase, and has commitments to ship another 21.655 million barrels in the 12 days from November 14 to November 25. Iraq began the program in December, 1996. More than 7.5 million tons of food, about $400 million of medicine and medical supplies, and more than $200 million of agriculture, electricity, water, sanitation, and education supplies and equipment have arrived in Iraq since oil-for-food shipments first arrived in March, 1997. So far, $2.81 billion of oil has been shipped in the oil sale's fourth phase. By November 25, this sales level is expected to be between $3.0 billion and $3.1 billion. This is far short of the $5.256 billion Iraq is allowed to sell. The shortfall has been caused by Iraq's limited exporting capacity and low oil prices. Another possible problem in the waning days of the oil-for-food program's fourth phase is that more oil has been shipped from Mina al-Bakr, Iraq, than from Ceyhan, Turkey. The Security Council requires the majority of the oil must be shipped from Ceyhan. This is to allow Turkey to gain pipeline fees that it has lost since Iraq invaded Kuwait in August, 1990 and the Kirkuk-to-Yumurtalik pipeline was shut. Through November 13, 153.705 million barrels had been shipped from the Turkish port and 154.750 million barrels had been shipped from Mina al-Bakr. Basrah Light crude is shipped from the Iraqi port and Kirkuk crude is shipped from the Turkish port. The UN's oil-sale overseers—the international oil marketing experts who advise the UN on the oil sale—said that by the time the fourth phase ends on November 25, the volume of Kirkuk sales will be more than Basrah Light sales. "Just barely 50 percent," said a UN official, who wished to remain anonymous. In the past, the UN has allowed shortfalls of sales and other discrepancies to be adjusted in subsequent sales phases.

In June, the UN approved the sale of up to $300 million in oil infrastructure equipment, so-called spare parts, to Iraq. This is funded through Iraqi

Table 10.3 (continued)

	oil sales. In the week ending November 13, seven "spare parts" contracts were approved, with a value of $4.6 million. A passenger boat from Russia ($2.5 million) was the costliest item approved in the week. The UN has now received requests from Iraq for 324 "spare parts" contracts worth $181.1 million. Of these, the UN Security Council's Iraq sanctions committee has approved 139 contracts worth $97.5 million and withheld approval for 96 contracts worth $44.9 million.
98–11-17:	UN arms inspectors leave Bahrain for Baghdad after spending six days outside Iraq. Richard Butler tests Iraq's promises by asking it to turn over two documents, one dealing with chemical and the other with biological weapons. Amer al-Saadi, adviser to President Saddam Hussein, says Iraq is willing to discuss the weapons documents that Butler says he wants Baghdad to hand over. "We took copies of those documents with us to New York and we were ready to show them to fair-minded people." *Babel* says US threats to bomb Iraq over UN weapons inspections was part of a US campaign to overthrow Saddam Hussein's government. "As soon as Iraq foiled this plan, represented in preparations to launch a large scale savage attack on its people . . . the tyrant Clinton announced his full criminal plan to impose his will on the will of the Iraqi people." The Russian Foreign Ministry says US statements calling for Saddam's overthrow "are in direct contradiction to the norms and principles of international law. [UN] Security Council resolutions must be carried out, but it must not be forgotten that they speak of the need to respect Iraq's sovereignty and political independence. The Iraqi people must decide what government Iraq will have." The Ministry softens its statement by referring to "declarations coming out of Washington" and not mentioning Clinton by name. Akram al Watri, a foreign ministry adviser, calls for Richard Butler to be reprimanded for acting without informing the UN Security Council: "Butler withdrew the disarmament experts from Iraq without reference to the [UN] Security Council, thus overstepping his mandate. He only asked the United States' advice, without referring to the Security Council, and his behavior must be sanctioned." The United States made clear that economic sanctions against Iraq will not be lifted at the end of a review of Baghdad's compliance with UN resolutions. Deputy US Ambassador to the UN Peter Burleigh says the US government has always viewed the comprehensive review as just that—a review of Iraqi obligations and the many questions it hasn't answered. "We don't see the sanctions lifting as the end result of the comprehensive review." Burleigh dismisses Baghdad's suggestion that sanctions should be lifted incrementally in proportion to Baghdad's compliance. "It's not allowed under the resolutions. And as far as I know, there's no member of the Council arguing for incremental lifting of sanc-

Table 10.3 (continued)

	tions." Burleigh says that while the Council has focused on resolutions demanding elimination of weapons, the United States demands Iraq's full compliance with resolutions calling for an accounting of missing Kuwaitis and the return of looted Kuwaiti property and government archives. He says the fate of Kuwaiti prisoners is "an extremely important issue."
	Iraq's UN Ambassador, Nizar Hamdoon, states that Baghdad believes it will be able to convince the Security Council that it has met "the bulk of the requirements" in the resolutions. "If the comprehensive review comes up with a conclusion that Iraq has done so, the sanctions obviously and logically should be lifted. The Council may well decide at the end of the comprehensive review to lift the sanctions partially." Hamdoon denies Iraq has any prisoners of war and said Iraq is cooperating on the matter.
98–11-18:	The UNSCOM Baghdad Monitoring and Verification Center resumes its activities and resumes inspections. UN weapons experts resume inspections in Iraq for the first time in three months, testing the Iraq government's promise of full cooperation.
	Foreign Office minister Derek Fatchett announces that he will meet with representatives of 15 Iraqi dissident groups against Saddam Hussein to urge a common line, but a British government official said ministers aren't planning at the moment to match money being put up by the United States, which has pledged $97 million for the opposition parties. A Foreign Office spokesman says Britain will encourage the opposition groups to combine and present proposals for a democratic alternative in Iraq. He said, "it's not a question of providing money or weapons at this stage."
	Oil prices in London drop to their lowest levels in a decade as traders guess that no new Iraqi crisis is imminent. Brent oil for January delivery falls 30 cents, or 2.6 percent, to $11.43 a barrel. In New York, December delivery crude falls 37 cents to $12.45 a barrel.
	Richard Butler says that before the most recent crisis with Iraq, the country had moved close to complying with UN mandates on its chemical weapons and illegal missiles, but the area of biological weapons remained a "black hole." He says UNSCOM had destroyed a substantial portion of Iraq's chemical weapons and made a pretty good account of illegal missiles, but that the same could not be said of biological weapons. He said much more information was needed in the biological area, and he had asked Deputy Prime Minister Tariq Aziz for a fresh start. "I wrote to him today, following last weekend's crisis . . . saying 'Start again. Give us a whole new answer on biology. Break the habit of a lifetime and tell us the truth.' . . . But it's also, I think, been made very clear that if they lie to us again, if they seek to obstruct again, there may well be military action." Butler says a report a concealment committee headed by Aziz, designed to cheat UN inspections, is "substantially true," and

Table 10.3 (continued)

	he had asked Aziz for an explanation on his last trip to Baghdad in a new letter. "Everyone's nightmare about this system is the cheater... and the paradigm case of this is Saddam Hussein's Iraq. The UN asked Iraq to declare the truth to us about its weapons within 15 days; 2,600 days later, we still don't know the truth. Eight and one-half years later, it's still not over. I will probably go to my grave not understanding."
98–11-19:	Iraq protests to the UN against US reconnaissance flights by U-2 aircraft, saying they harm its security and sovereignty.
	Ahmed Chalabi, head of the Iraqi National Congress, an opposition umbrella group, is considered a favorite to receive nearly $100 million in US military assistance. Chalabi met with US Assistant Secretary of State Martin Indyk.
	US and British defense ministers repeat warnings to Baghdad that their forces are ready to strike Iraq if Saddam Hussein breaks an agreement to cooperate with UN arms inspections.
	UN arms experts finish their second day of inspections.
	Iraq's UN ambassador, Nizar Hamdoon, asks the Security Council for a two-month extension in the current round of the humanitarian "oil-for-food" program. Hamdoon says Iraq needs time to reach the oil sales limit of $5.256 billion. Due to low oil prices and poor infrastructure, Iraq is only expected to sell about $3 billion by the deadline of November 25. He also, however, may be seeking to delay a decision on a new round, to which Baghdad has previously objected.
	Butler says it may take four weeks to know if Iraq is now complying and that he is giving priority to data on VX nerve gas, which Iraq first denied having, then admitted. "We demonstrated to them that they made about 4,000 liters, four tons, of this stuff." He says he is also seeking information on liquid propellants used with Scud missiles and a document uncovered at an Iraqi air force base that showed the ordnance was capable of being filled with chemical and biological agents that Iraq had expended in its 1980–1988 war with Iran. Butler says, "This is the last chance and I hope it's the best chance and they see the point. If the only thing preventing Iraq from taking the decision to disclose all of its weapons and to be totally and verifiably disarmed of those weapons of mass destruction was my being removed from this job, then I tell you like any good citizen with a good conscience, I would remove that impediment. But, sadly, that proposition is based on an utterly false premise. So, I'm here to tell you I intend to stay on and get this job done."
98–11-20:	Iraq criticizes Richard Butler for accusing Tariq Aziz of concealing information from his arms teams. Ambassador Hamdoon says, "This kind of behavior and these kinds of remarks do not come from an international employee. He [Butler] talks about Iraq and the president of Iraq in unacceptable language. If he is really a professional international employee ... he should observe a completely different way of working and speak-

Table 10.3 (continued)

ing." *Al-Thawra*, the Ba'ath Party newspaper, says, "It has been proven to the Security Council itself that its Chairman Butler receives his orders from his American overseers and there is concrete evidence that he gives them his reports first to add their hypocritical touches before he presents them to the Security Council."

Richard Butler releases a list of 12 requests for documents sent to Iraq and the replies of Riyadh al-Qaysi, an Under-Secretary in the Iraq's Foreign Ministry. The information was released late on Friday. The requests include:

1. A document UNSCOM inspectors saw briefly on July 18, 1998, at the headquarters of the Iraqi air force that provides the details of the munitions used in the 1980–1988 war with Iran. UNSCOM believes Iraq has given it an inflated figure on the amount of expended ordnance that could be filled with chemical or biological agents, and this raises questions about what happened to the remainder. The Security Council has asked for this document to be surrendered to UNSCOM. Iraq said it was ready to consider disclosing "relevant portions of the paper" in the presence of Secretary-General Annan's special envoy in Iraq, Prakash Shah.

2. A document from the Muthanna State Establishment, dated September, 1988, on future actions concerning the development of chemical weapons. UNSCOM says Iraq had promised to locate the document before and then said it did not exist. Iraq replies that the document had been discussed previously and then not raised by UNSCOM in July high-level meetings on future joint disarmament work.

3. Documents and 1990 records on the status of the production of the deadly nerve agent VX. UNSCOM has said that Iraq had not accounted for thousands of liters of VX. Iraq replies that no such records exist, that it was unsuccessful in its 1990 attempts to produce VX for use in weapons and had given UNSCOM all relevant materials.

4. The full diary of Brigadier Ismail, an officer in the surface-to-surface missile force, which deals with missile-related activities in 1990 and 1991. Several pages of this diary had been provided to UNSCOM earlier dealing with biological weapons warheads. Iraq now says Ismail has destroyed the diary.

5. A January, 1991 report by Lt.-General Hazzem Abdul Razzaq, the commander of the surface-to-surface missile force, mentioned in his recently published memoirs that describes the balance of missiles and warheads that existed at the time. Iraq says the general had taken notes from documents and then destroyed them as ordered. This is noted in the introduction to his memoirs.

6. Governmental and ministerial documents describing the creation of a missile unit in 1990, and its equipment of missile launchers, warheads, ground support equipment, propellants, and other material. UNSCOM said a similar request was contained in a letter to Iraq in November, 1996. Iraq says UNSCOM had not asked for these documents previously but it was ready to relinquish them.

Table 10.3 (continued)

      7. The full diary of "Engineer Muhkdam," which deals with the indigenous production of missile engines in 1990 and 1991. Eleven pages had been provided to UNSCOM earlier. Iraq says the pages from Muhkdam's diary illustrated technological problems with experimental prototypes and showed the missiles were not ready for production, and that Muhkdam had since destroyed his personal diary.

      8. Documentary evidence of unilateral destruction of missile propellants in 1991, including parts of an inventory diary certifying the destruction in 1991. Iraq says: "We made a great effort to search for the diaries but it seems that these documents were amongst those destroyed" in 1991.

      9. Documents dated May, 1991 which provide inventories of available chemical and biological weapons, missiles and their warheads, launchers, and other relevant equipment. Iraq says no such inventory was made and no such documents exist.

      10. Documents detailing decisions made in April, June, and July, 1991 to retain or destroy proscribed weapons and other materials. UNSCOM believes written records were kept. Iraq says Deputy Prime Minister Tariq Aziz had explained to Butler and his predecessor, Swedish diplomat Rolf Ekeus, that he had taken this decision and "communicated it orally to the competent authorities to carry out."

      11. A report on Iraq's investigation of Lt.-General Hussein Kamal and actions he took to conceal weapons capabilities and documents. Iraq says it did not conduct a formal investigation on the defection.

      12. The minutes of meetings of the Iraqi High-Level Committee on the retention of banned weapons and materials that UNSCOM has said Iraq admitted was formed in June, 1991. Iraq says the IAEA, not UNSCOM, had previously requested such minutes. "We pointed out to them on that occasion that there was no such committee in the technical sense of the word."

Iraqi Foreign Ministry Under-Secretary Riyadh al-Qaysi sends two letters to Butler and states the Security Council should proceed first with a promised comprehensive review of Iraq's compliance so far with council resolutions and that the Council would then decide what more needed to be done regarding disarmament. Al-Qaysi says UNSCOM had conducted long searches of many of them but found nothing contrary to Iraq's declarations. "Therefore, the request you made at this time, which is of a general nature, seems to be provocative rather than professional. We hope that UNSCOM will discard this unprofessional approach which would unjustifiably lead to the prolongation of work, and thereby maintaining the inequitable embargo on the people of Iraq." Al-Qaysi says he is replying on behalf of Tariq Aziz, and that Butler's requests fall into two categories. "The first category comprises alleged documents which do not exist, and the second category includes repetition of previous requests in respect of which we had submitted all the available and true clarifications." Al-Qaysi says the "prevailing trend in the deliberations

Table 10.3 (continued)

of the Security Council and the positions resulting therefrom have been to commence with a comprehensive review'' a short time after UNSCOM resumed its activities in Iraq. "The judgment on the remaining issues which should be followed up rests with the Security Council." He appends an annex raising objections or difficulties regarding the handing over of a dozen specific documents.

State Department spokesman James Rubin reacts to these developments by saying the United States is waiting for Butler to determine the significance of the new information.

Secretary-General Annan recommends renewal of the Iraqi oil-for-food program that would permit Baghdad to sell $5.25 billion in oil to purchase food, medicine, and other humanitarian goods for another six months. Annan's report says the program should be continued on the same basis as the current plan that gives priorities for specific categories of food, medicine, and other supplies Iraq needs. Iraq, however, has only been able to export about $3 billion in oil over the last six months because of low crude prices and its dilapidated oil industry equipment. Iraq has argued that a two-month extension would allow Iraq to reach the $5.25 billion target. Diplomats, however, say Iraq's proposal could be a move to delay the next phase of the program, which Baghdad sees as an implicit indication that the sanctions would be in place for at least another six months. The new phase of the program is expected to include a provision that Iraq be allowed to spend a specific amount of the oil revenues to upgrade its pipeline and other equipment. Currently Baghdad is permitted to spend $300 million for this purpose.

Iraqi Trade Minister Mohammed Mehdi Saleh says that there is less pressure to lift the oil embargo because the international community knows Iraqis are being fed, even at a subsistence level: "We accepted this program as a temporary one. Now, it has become a cover to continue sanctions on Iraq. Anyway, people need more than food. We need investment in agriculture and industry, to create job opportunities and to raise income. Oil-for-food can't do this."

98–11-21: President Clinton is taking a more cautious approach to a new barrier Iraq has placed in the path of UN weapons inspectors. "I think it's important we not overreact . . . if they have some independent grounds for objecting to some of this information, that is if they think it's some effort to find out something having nothing to do with matters covered by the UN resolution, they ought to say that and we should immediately resolve it. We will remain vigilant, we will keep up the pressure, we will be ready to act. Iraq must accept once and for all that the only path forward is complete compliance with its obligations to the world."

Sandy Berger, the president's assistant for national security affairs, tells reporters in Seoul that military action is still an option. "We've said all along that the issue here is whether Iraq will meet its obligations under the Security Council resolutions and whether UNSCOM is able to do its

Table 10.3 (continued)

	work. If we reach the conclusion that the answer to those questions is negative we obviously are prepared to act."
	James P. Rubin issues a statement that if Iran tries to undermine Saddam, "We are not going to complain . . . we are not working with [the Iranians] in any shape or form or soliciting their support."
98–11–22:	UN inspection teams in Iraq carry out their work for a fifth consecutive day.
	Al-Jumhuriva says, "We are convinced that UNSCOM is no longer fit to be an international organization carrying out the mandate of the UN. This is why we are not surprised when the American administration makes threats of aggression whenever Iraq takes any legitimate, sovereign position to protest at the deviant behavior of UNSCOM's leaders and members, who are doing things that have nothing to do with their mission and mandate." *Babel* attacks President Clinton's public call for a new government in Iraq and US threats of a military strike. "The aim was not just to keep the sanctions in force but was in line with Clinton's scenario to change the regime in Iraq and replace it with the opposition. Their hands should be paralyzed. They have conspired against Iraq and launched on it the fiercest wars which all ended in defeat and disappointment. It is stupid that Clinton and the corrupt rulers of America . . . do not understand this reality. Our people will not weaken or kneel or submit to threats of destruction. Let the American rulers wake from their sick dreams. . . . Our Iraq is enduring with its dignity and pride and all their schemes will certainly end in failure."

The UN Reaches an Agreement That Seems to Allow UNSCOM to Continue Its Operation

Iraq initially seemed to have conceded a great deal to the UN. Table 10.3 shows that the British and American threat of force led Iraq to reach an agreement with Secretary-General Annan on February 23, 1998, that

The Government of Iraq reconfirms its acceptance of all relevant resolutions of the Security Council, including resolutions 687 (1991) and 715 (1991). The Government of Iraq further reiterates its undertaking to cooperate fully with the UN Special Commission (UNSCOM) and the International Atomic Energy Agency (IAEA). . . . The Government of Iraq undertakes to accord to UNSCOM and IAEA immediate, unconditional, and unrestricted access in conformity with the resolutions referred to in paragraph 1.

The Security Council also showed enough unity so that it voted unanimously on March 2, 1998, for a resolution that "stresses that compliance by the Government of Iraq with its obligations, repeated again in the memorandum of understanding, to accord immediate, unconditional, and unrestricted access to the Special Commission and the IAEA in conformity with the relevant resolutions is necessary for the implementation of resolution 687 (1991), but that any violation would have severest consequences for Iraq,'' and notes, that by its failure so far to comply with its relevant obligations, ''Iraq has delayed the moment when the Council can do so.'' This resolve continued during the following months, and Table 10.3 shows that UNSCOM often won in detailed encounters with Iraq over individual aspects of its efforts to put an end to Iraqi proliferation.

At the same time, the text of agreement the Secretary General reached with Iraq did involve important political compromises that Iraq exploited with great success in the months that followed.

The UN reiterates the commitment of all Member States to respect the sovereignty and territorial integrity of Iraq. The UN and the Government of Iraq agree that the following special procedures shall apply to the initial and subsequent entries for the performance of the tasks mandated at the eight Presidential Sites in Iraq as defined in the annex to the present Memorandum: A Special Group shall be established for this purpose by the Secretary-General in consultation with the Executive Chairman of UNSCOM and the Director-General of IAEA.... UN and the Government of Iraq agree to improve cooperation, and efficiency, effectiveness and transparency of work, so as to enable UNSCOM to report to the Council expeditiously under paragraph 22 of resolution 687 [1991]. To achieve this goal, the Government of Iraq and UNSCOM will implement the recommendations directed at them as contained in the report of the emergency session of UNSCOM held on 21 November 1997.... The lifting of sanctions is obviously of paramount importance to the people and Government of Iraq and the Secretary-General undertook to bring this matter to the full attention of the members of the Security Council.

In the months that followed, Iraq first pursued a campaign to try to pressure the UN into stating that it had fully complied with the terms of the cease-fire and had destroyed its missile and chemical, biological, and nuclear weapons programs. Iraq seems to have seriously hoped that the UN might certify Iraq's compliance as early as the next semi-annual Security Council review of UNSCOM and IAEA activities, which was due in October, 1998. Iraq made relentless use of ''big lie'' techniques. Whenever it was caught lying or failing to meet its obligations to the UN, it issued new statements claiming that it had fully complied and that the United States and Britain were plotting against it.

At the same time, the detailed chronology of events in Table 10.3 shows just how complex and nuanced the Iraqi effort was. Iraq continued to exploit the ''hardship'' issue and the suffering of its own people. It attempted to identify itself with the Arab cause and take advantage of the breakdown in the Arab-Israeli peace process. It charged that UN sanctions had killed some 1.4 million Iraqis, most of them children, and effectively charged the United States with genocide. At the same time, Iraq reached out to old enemies like Iran and Syria, courted Turkey and Egypt, and attempted to rebuild its relations with the rest of the Arab world.

Part of the Iraqi strategy began to unravel in July, 1998. UNSCOM continued to find new problems with Iraq's declarations, particularly those relating to VX gas. The IAEA made it clear that although it had not found new evidence relating to Iraq's nuclear weapons program, it still had serious questions and would demand a continuing monitoring program. At the same time, however, Iraq found that the UN was showing less resolve, and the US threat of force became less credible.

The end result was that Iraq effectively broke all of the major terms of its February agreement with the UN less than six months after it had negotiated the agreement with the Secretary General. On August 3, 1998, Iraq took advantage of Butler's presence in Iraq to accuse him of being a tool of the United States, and announced it would no longer cooperate with UNSCOM and the IAEA. Iraq made this action official on July 5, 1998.

Iraqi officials increasingly went on the political offensive. They made charge after charge condemning Butler, UNSCOM, Britain, and the United States. At the same time, they used every opportunity to try to further divide the Security Council and the Arab world. By October, 1998, the situation was very close to what it had been in October, 1997. Iraq was still subject to sanctions that prevented it from importing conventional arms and equipment to make missiles and weapons of mass destruction. At the same time, UNSCOM and IAEA could not carry out inspections or prevent Iraq from carrying out clandestine programs to research, develop, and build long-range missiles and biological, chemical, and nuclear weapons.

One thing did seem to have changed. The United States stated that it remained ready to use force when Iraq ceased to cooperate with the UN, but it did not threaten to use force as it had in November, 1997 and in February, 1998. Although the United States stated on March 3, 1998, that "military force will be used if Iraq violates this agreement," it seems to have made a decision to avoid the use of force unless Iraq took action provocative enough to unite the Security Council and most of the Arab world. This meant that the United States had shifted from relying on inspections, backed by air and missile strikes, to relying on prolonging sanctions, backed by diplomacy.[83]

The same factors that raised serious questions about the value of using force in November, 1997 seem to have led the United States to try to halt some inspections. For example, when Ambassador Butler attempted to confront Iraq over its refusals to cooperate with UNSCOM in early August, 1998, Secretary of State Madeleine Albright intervened. She delayed the no-notice inspections that Butler had ordered for August 6. When Butler rescheduled these inspections for August 9, the United States intervened again, and Butler brought his team back from Baghdad. According to press reports, the United States had intervened to halt inspections that it feared might trigger a major confrontation on at least six previous occasions between November, 1997 and August, 1998—largely because it did not see any clear benefits from using force unless Iraq took the kind of action that would give the United States broad political support.[84]

More broadly, the events of October, 1997–October, 1998 pose major challenges for future arms control regimes in Iraq and anywhere else in the world.

There is no question that the UNSCOM and IAEA efforts managed to locate and destroy most of Iraq's long-range missiles, chemical and biological weapons, and capabilities to develop and produce weapons of mass destruction. Even so, more than seven years of inspections did not find all of Iraq's assets and, as the following chapters will show, major uncertainties remain regarding its present capabilities to produce and deploy missiles and chemical, biological, and nuclear weapons.

UNSCOM and the IAEA conducted the most intrusive inspection regime in history and supported it with the latest technology for tagging dual-use equipment, automatic soil sampling, and using remote cameras to monitor ongoing activity. They were supported by efforts from more than 40 member countries, including experts, equipment, funds, information, and collection efforts. These efforts included dedicated U-2 flights by the US Air Force and a truly massive national intelligence effort by several member countries of the UN. This effort included large-scale collection efforts by the United States, including extensive satellite photography, and a major British and Israeli analysis effort. It involved extensive European efforts to trace Iraq's pre– and post–Gulf War efforts to import equipment and a considerable effort by the French, German, Italian, and Swiss governments. Japan provided data on Iraqi imports, and even Russia and China provided some intelligence, although they scarcely provided comprehensive data on their export activities.[85]

The previous chronologies show how a dedicated government can block even the most intrusive arms control regime. The coming chapters show just how serious the resulting threat can be. They not only raise serious questions about the future threat from Iraq, but about the potential ability to enforce any arms control regime that depends on inspection and compliance, and the value of concepts like "weapons of mass destruction–free zones." One of the major lessons of the war of sanctions is that arms control may help to halt or roll back proliferation, but it cannot by itself provide a basis for full verification or trust. It may well be that the ultimate lesson of the war of sanctions is that deterrence and the continuing threat of force must underpin every effort to stop a determined proliferator.

The Sanctions Crisis of October–December, 1998: "The More You Remember the Past, the More You Repeat It"

Yet, Iraq did much to snatch defeat from the jaws of victory. In October, 1998, just at the point when Iraq seemed to be gaining support in the Security Council, Saddam Hussein suspended cooperation with UNSCOM and created a virtual repetition of the military confrontation with the United States and Britain that had taken place in October, 1997, and February, 1998. The Iraqi action was so clumsy that, as Table 10.3 shows, the United States and Britain came within hours of a massive missile and air strike on Iraq.

Once again, the details of the crisis provide insight into the nuances in Iraqi diplomacy and the depth of Iraq's commitment to proliferation. They also show the extent to which Iraq had learned to exploit its "cheat and retreat" tactics and could avoid military action even with last-minute diplomacy.

More broadly, however, the detailed history of the course of events from July, 1998 to October, 1998 that is described in Table 10.3 shows how difficult it is to predict the nature and timing of the outcome of the war of sanctions. Only a month later, the United States and Britain were again on the edge of launching strikes against Iraq, and on December 19 they began Operation Desert Fox. As the table shows, the frustrations of October, 1998 led the United States and Britain to declare that they would use force without warning if Iraq did not allow UNSCOM to operate. Furthermore, they declared that they would openly support the Iraqi opposition in seeking the fall of Saddam Hussein.

At the same time, they did not declare whether they intended to enforce the provisions of the resolutions that called for the IAEA and UNSCOM to shift to an open-ended monitoring regime once the inspection phase of their activities ended, exactly what kind of Iraqi delay or interference would trigger the use of force, or what they would do after they used force if Iraq did not agree to comply. Furthermore, a new crisis emerged within days of the resumption of UN inspections when Iraq refused to turn over 12 documents requested by Butler.

Other ambiguities existed over the Security Council's agreement to carry out a "comprehensive review" of the status of Iraq's compliance with the UN, and over whether the sanctions could be lifted under Article 22 if UNSCOM and the IAEA found that Iraq was in compliance. The United States and Britain argued that no comprehensive review could bypass the regular six-month Security Council reviews of UNSCOM and the IAEA, and that Iraq would have to comply with all of the terms of the UN resolutions and cease-fire agreement and not simply with the terms of Article 22. This position, however, had limited support in the Security Council, and China, France, and Russia had major reservations.

Desert Fox did not resolve any of these problems. Iraq's actions during November deprived UNSCOM of its remaining effectiveness, but US and British military action did not bring back UNSCOM or create a climate where the IAEA could carry out challenge inspections. The only light at the end of the tunnel seemed to be the entry to another tunnel. US and British military action did degrade Iraq's conventional capabilities and destroy some key aspects of its missile and dual-use facilities and some targets associated with its efforts to proliferate. Most of Iraq's capabilities survived Desert Fox, however, and US and British support of the Iraqi opposition seemed more symbolic than likely to lead to Saddam's fall. As a result, any new use of force seemed likely to inflict punishment without changing the basic need to contain Iraq and deter and defend against its military threat.

Whether or not more force is used, the war of sanctions seems likely to go on at the political level, with Iraq making slow gains in persuading other nations to lift sanctions but watching its conventional military capabilities degrade from a lack of arms imports. The end result seems likely to make anything like the current Iraqi regime even more committed to retaining and expanding Iraq's missile forces and weapons of mass destruction. The end result is a set of political dynamics that seem almost certain to shape a highly unstable military balance.

THE STRENGTHS AND LIMITS OF THE WAR OF SANCTIONS

There is no way to predict how the struggle will end. It is still possible that Iraq will miscalculate and alienate world opinion or push some future crisis to the point where the United States and Britain feel compelled to take decisive military action and can win world support. At the same time, it is equally possible for the United States or the UN to miscalculate and increase world sympathy for Iraq, or that Iraq may eventually comply with just enough of the terms of the cease-fire to be able to exploit "sanctions fatigue" and either bring an end to sanctions or make them ineffective.

There are also important limits to what UNSCOM and the IAEA can do. It is almost impossible to put technological genies back in the bottle once they emerge. There are too many ways to proliferate, and a modern, authoritarian state can conceal too much. Further, there can be little doubt that Iraq will continue to challenge the UN effort at every possible opportunity, and make every effort to limit and/or end UN inspections.[86]

Rolf Ekeus made these challenges clear in an interview on June 30, 1997—the day he stepped down from UNSCOM:

Our impression after six years is that the present leadership is not interested in giving up these weapons.... People ask how much is left, but we cannot really quantify. We only know that Iraq has not made a list of weapons and production sites available, and that should have been given to us six weeks after the resolution was adopted.[87]

Nothing can change these realities. UNSCOM and the IAEA's efforts are only going to be effective as long as these organizations can continue intrusive inspection efforts. Even under these conditions, UNSCOM and the IAEA cannot prevent Iraq from conducting important covert efforts and from retaining and/or developing some "breakout" capabilities to rapidly recover the ability to deliver weapons of mass destruction the moment that UNSCOM and the IAEA's efforts cease or are undercut to the point where they become ineffective.

UNSCOM has warned of these technical problems in many of its reports, and the events surrounding Desert Fox indicate that they are a grim warning for the future:

For the monitoring system to be effective, it must cast a broad net and cover major facilities such as petrochemical and pesticide plants where chemical and biological warfare agents could be produced. However, such agents can also be clandestinely produced by Iraq in such facilities as breweries, brake fluid factories, and even university microbiology laboratories containing dual use equipment.[88]

Retaining Dual-Use Facilities

Unless Iraq miscalculates and overplays its hand to the point where the United States and Britain carry out further massive air and missile strikes, it will retain large numbers of dual-use facilities. UNSCOM had 90 sites with resident biological weapons teams in late 1997, had tagged some 893 items, and had conducted an average of 240 inspections over a six-month period. UNSCOM identified 79 key sites related to biological warfare by early 1997. Of these, nine were considered Category A, requiring the most intense monitoring, while 15 were Category B, 10 were Category C, and 45 were Category D. Many of the Category A sites were damaged during the Gulf War, but one facility at Al-Hakam was missed entirely by both Coalition intelligence and bombers. These facilities included five sites used to make weapons before the war; five vaccine or pharmaceutical sites; 35 research and university sites; 13 breweries, distilleries, and dairies with dual purpose capabilities; and eight diagnostic laboratories. Virtually all of these facilities survived Desert Fox unscathed. Only the monitoring regime seemed a probable casualty.

Even when there was monitoring it was not enough. In April, 1996, UNSCOM warned that "several pieces of significant undeclared equipment, spare parts, and supplies" were discovered in the inspections of additional facilities, and that, "Iraq has still not declared all sites where dual-use equipment is present. The Commission's resident team continues to identify such sites that should have been declared by Iraq. . . . On a number of occasions, Iraq did not produce the required information on changes that have been uncovered (in key sites).''[89] UNSCOM's declarations in October, 1996, April, 1997, October, 1997, and April, 1998 indicated that this situation had not changed.

The same problems apply to Iraq's future ability to produce chemical weapons. By April, 1997 UNSCOM had conducted some 550 inspections and had 11 full-time inspectors checking on 150 facilities. By October, 1997 it was covering some 160 facilities, had tagged 323 items, was monitoring thousands of others, and was conducting over 170 monitoring inspections in a six-month period. These inspections had discovered some "200 key pieces of undeclared dual-use equipment, such as heat exchangers, glass reactor vessels, and distillation columns capable of use in proscribed chemical weapons activities. About 800 pieces of related equipment have been located. They also discovered after April, 1997 that glass equipment had been imported illegally for the production of chemical weapons. These discoveries point to the fact that Iraq was scarcely meeting in full its requirements with respect to reporting on its holdings of dual-use equipment.''[90]

UNSCOM created a massive effort to monitor Iraq's missile programs. A total of 63 sites have been subjected to regular inspection, 143 items of equipment were tagged, and more than 2,000 missiles were tagged for period verification. UNSCOM averaged 27 inspections a month during 1997. The search for missile technology is also a major part of UNSCOM's export/import monitoring effort, which involve nearly 30 more inspections per month.[91]

Yet, the future of this entire montioring system was at hazard long before Desert Fox because of Iraq's actions since August 5, 1998. Furthermore, Iraq retains a major missile production plant at Ibn Al Haytham. This plant has ongoing activity and two buildings big enough to produce large missiles. It has a major missile research facility at Al Kindi, and UNSCOM found that Iraq continued to conceal the full nature of its key projects for missile development. Iraq lied to UNSCOM about such key activities as Project 1728, the key project for producing missile engines, and Project Karama, the key project for producing guidance and control systems. In addition to the problems listed in its October, 1997 report, UNSCOM found that Iraq used computer simulations and laboratory studies in 1992, 1994, and 1995 to develop forbidden space programs using proscribed missiles. Iraq imported the gyroscopes for long-range missiles in 1995. It attempted to improve its monitoring and inspection of the Iraqi missile programs, such as the Samoud missile, which has a range of under 150 kilometers, and is permitted under the terms of the UN resolutions. UNSCOM was particularly concerned because Iraq has refused to provide computer software and documents on such programs, and missiles such as the Samoud were nearing the production phase.[92]

Iraq's nuclear options are less clear. The IAEA and UNSCOM warned in April, 1997 that it was still unearthing major components from Iraq's nuclear program, and that a previously undeclared and highly expensive cache of unused specialized, corrosion resistant valves had been found since October, 1996.[93] In mid-October, 1997, Hans Blix, then head of the International Atomic Energy Agency (IAEA), stated that he had evidence the Iraq had still not reported all outside assistance for its nuclear weapons program.[94] The IAEA pulled out its inspectors from Baghdad when Iraq banned US inspectors in the weapons inspection program of UNSCOM on October 29, 1997. These inspectors returned with those of UNSCOM's after Iraq allowed UN inspection teams, including Americans, to resume their work.

On December 2, 1997, however, Mohammed El Baradei, Hans Blix's replacement as the head of the IAEA, issued a statement that he saw no signs that Iraq had resumed a nuclear weapons program during the temporary absence of Western inspectors. "We can now say that we have managed to remove or destroy or render harmless all nuclear items that came to our knowledge.... We are now in the middle of investigating changes which took place during our absence, but I think in a couple of weeks we will be able to report to the Security Council [that] so far I don't think we have seen anything that is disturbing."[95] The IAEA went on to issue a statement on April 12, 1998, that indicated that Iraq had complied with all requirements to declare and destroy its nuclear weapons capability. It issued a similar statement in late 1998, just before Desert Fox. Nevertheless, the IAEA warned that this did not mean that Iraq was not retaining significant equipment or did not still have a covert nuclear program. It stated that a monitoring regime would be required for years to come, backed by continuing challenge inspections. UNSCOM and the IAEA continue to investigate the status of the centrifuge and gaseous separation programs conducted by Iraq's Engineering and Design Center before the Gulf War. It is painfully clear that Iraq can begin rebuilding its capabilities to produce and deliver weapons of mass destruction the moment that sanctions end and/or limits on UNSCOM and IAEA activity make this possible.

Clandestine and Covert Programs

No inspection and verification effort can be expected to halt the covert preparation for the rebuilding of an industrial base that will give Iraq the capability to rapidly resume the production of biological and chemical weapons at a limited to moderate scale. Iraq will also continue to have some successes. UNSCOM and the IAEA cannot deny Iraq the technology base, pilot plants, and dual-use facilities necessary to give it a significant breakout capability—at least in chemical and biological weapons. They cannot keep Iraq from conducting research and development at the laboratory level. They cannot prevent Iraq from exploiting any new covert organizations it has created since the Gulf War to carry out test, evaluation, and production planning for biological, chemical, and nuclear weapons, and some missile research.

Iraq has had more than half a decade to covertly develop the capability to produce biological weapons in dry, storable form in the particle sizes necessary to achieve near-nuclear lethality. It has had every incentive to use this time to develop stable forms of dusty mustard gas, and pure and stable "V" and "G" nerve agents. It should be able to make major progress in refining its plans for nuclear enrichment facilities, its basic nuclear weapons designs, and its technology for producing neutron initiators, explosive lenses, and high-speed triggering devices.

Iraq has had time to improve its weaponization programs by developing more effective binary chemical weapons and mechanisms for dispersing chemical and biological agents from rockets, bombs, and missile warheads. It has had time to develop a range of weapons specifically designed for covert or terrorist delivery. Its missile test activities are limited by UNSCOM, but it still may be able to make some advances in the quality of its missile warheads.

Iraq's past efforts have been grandiose enough to leave a considerable trail. Massive imports have provided one kind of warning signal and target for UN operations. The use of extremely large physical facilities has provided another, as has Iraq's insistence on immense documentation and visible paper trails. However, several UNSCOM and IAEA experts believe that Iraq has already created new, parallel, covert proliferation efforts since the Gulf War which do not have links to past efforts, which are small and compartmentalized enough to be extremely difficult to detect, and which allow Iraq to conduct low-level research, development, production facility planning, and preparation in ways that UNSCOM and the IAEA cannot detect.

Iraq does not need to produce the kind of massive amounts of weapons of mass destruction it needed to fight a theater-wide land war with Iran, and developing sufficient amounts of agent to arm missile warheads and a large number of bombs involves far smaller import, facility, and activity requirements. Iraq has had the time to covertly manufacture many of the components it once had to import, many of which can be made to a smaller scale. It has had time to break down its research and development activities into relatively small cells which can be compartmentalized from each other.

Iraq has had time to distribute activity into small, redundant facilities with no links back to its Gulf War programs. Iraq's insistence on large paper trails is obsolete, and UNSCOM and Western intelligence experts report that Iraq is increasingly making use of computer hard drives as a substitute for bulky documentation. The use of commercial scanners, local area networks, CD-ROM, and DVD technology—all of which is readily available without any possibility of export controls—allows Iraq to store even the most massive record-keeping effort on a few CD-ROMs and DVDs, and instantly transfer documentation and research activities to remote sites.[96]

Biological weapons present a special problem, particularly since Iraq's inability to rapidly rebuild a nuclear material production system is likely to make Iraq give biological weapons an even higher priority. Advances in biotechnology, food processing equipment, and related materials are steadily downsizing the area and specialized equipment needed to make far more lethal, dry storable agents than Iraq had at the time of the Gulf War. Iraq has had more than half a decade in which to reverse engineer and manufacture moderate-scale fermenters and spray systems.

As a result, UNSCOM and the IAEA could never have ensured that Iraq would not produce limited amounts of chemical and biological weapons or continue its research and development efforts at a low level, even if they had been allowed to continue to operate. Such programs make some of the suggested compromises in the UN inspection effort, such as a reliance on remote monitoring, little more than an invitation to Iraq to resume and expand its efforts to proliferate.

None of these Iraqi capabilities mean that UNSCOM and the IAEA did not do an excellent job under difficult circumstances, in spite of erratic outside political support and funding. UNSCOM and the IAEA, however, were neither omnipresent nor omnipotent. Virtually every UNSCOM report to the UN showed that Iraqi records were missing, the Iraqi government lied systematically at every stage during UNSCOM's and the IAEA's efforts, and many important aspects of the Iraqi government's declarations were unverifiable.

Further, no one can totally discount the possibility that Iraq could covertly produce significant amounts of highly lethal biological agents, or could assemble a nuclear weapon if Iraq could covertly buy fissile material from some outside source, even if some UN inspection regime is allowed to operate within Iraq. Iraq has several ways of achieving a major "breakout" in weapons of mass destruction that require careful consideration:

- UNSCOM's and the IAEA's success have created new priorities for Iraqi proliferation. The UN's success in destroying the large facilities Iraq needs to produce fissile materials already may well have led Iraq to focus on covert cell-like activities to manufacture highly lethal biological weapons as a substitute for nuclear weapons.
- Most of the biological agents Iraq had at the time of the Gulf War seem to have been "wet" agents with limited storage life and limited operational lethality. Iraq may have clandestinely carried out all of the research necessary to develop a production capability for dry, storage micro-power weapons which would be far easier to clandestinely stockpile and have much more operational lethality.
- Iraq did not have advanced binary chemical weapons, and most of its chemical weapons used unstable ingredients. Iraq has illegally imported specialized glassware since the Gulf War, and it may well have developed advanced binary weapons and tested them in small numbers. It may be able to use a wider range of precursors and it may have developed plans to produce precursors in Iraq. It also may have improved its technology for the production of VX gas.
- Iraq is likely to covertly exploit Western analyses and critiques of its pre-war proliferation efforts to correct many of the problems in the organization of its proliferation efforts, its weapons design, and its organization for their use.
- Iraqi bombs and warheads were relatively crude designs which did not store chemical and biological agents well, and which did a poor job of dispersing them. Fusing and detonation systems did a poor job of ensuring detonation at the right height and Iraq made little use of remote sensors and weather models for long-range targeting and strike planning. Iraq could clandestinely design and test greatly improved shells, bombs, and warheads. The key tests could be conducted using towers, simulated agents, and even be conducted indoors. Improved targeting, weather sensors, and other aids to strike planning are dual-use or civil technologies that are not controlled by UNSCOM. The net impact would be weapons that could be five to 10 times more effective than the relatively crude designs Iraq had rushed into service under the pressure of the Iran-Iraq War.
- UNSCOM's and the IAEA's success gives Iraq an equally high priority to explore ways of obtaining fissile material from the former Soviet Union or other potential supplier country and to prepare for a major purchase effort the moment sanctions and inspections are lifted, and Iraq has the hard currency to buy its way into the nuclear club. Iraq could probably clandestinely assemble all of the components of a large nuclear device except the fissile material, hoping to find some illegal source of such material.
- The components for cruise missiles are becoming steadily more available on the commercial market, and Iraq has every incentive to create a covert program to examine the possibility of manufacturing or assembling cruise missiles in Iraq.

- UN inspections and sanctions may also drive Iraq to adopt new delivery methods, ranging from clandestine delivery and the use of proxies to sheltered launch-on-warning capabilities designed to counter the US advantage in airpower.
- Iraq can legally maintain and test missiles with ranges up to 150 kilometers. This allows for exoatmospheric reentry testing and some testing of improved guidance systems. Computer simulation, wind tunnel models, and production engineering tests can all be carried out clandestinely under the present inspection regime. It is possible that Iraq could develop dummy or operational high explosive warheads with shapes and weight distribution of a kind that would allow it to test concepts for improving its warheads for weapons of mass destruction. The testing of improved bombs using simulated agents would be almost impossible to detect, as would the testing of improved spray systems for biological warfare.
- Iraq has had half a decade in which to improve its decoys, dispersal concepts, dedicated command and control links, targeting methods, and strike plans. This kind of passive warfare planning is impossible to forbid and monitor, but ultimately it is as important and lethal as any improvement in hardware.
- There is no evidence that Iraq made an effort to develop specialized chemical and biological devices for covert operations, proxy warfare, or terrorist use. It would be simple to do so clandestinely, and they would be simple to manufacture.

Dealing with Iraq's Ongoing Efforts

It is impossible to predict what the Security Council will do in the future. No one, however, can afford to deal with Iraqi proliferation by a politically convenient process of denial. Iraq has both the intention and the capability to go with its programs. No major Third World proliferator has ever been open about its intentions and plans, its military strategy and doctrine for using weapons of mass destruction, its production and weaponization plans, or its military capabilities.

Iraq is so committed to deception, lies, and cheating that any attempt towards understanding its future proliferation efforts has to be based on the assumption that the "war of sanctions" will continue indefinitely, and that any attempt to estimate Iraq's current and probable future programs must focus on an analysis of its capabilities, rather than on an analysis of its intentions. This is why a detailed examination of the scale of Iraq's past programs, its strategic culture, and its uses of weapons of mass destruction is so important.

NOTES

1. Eliot A. Cohen, Director, *Gulf War Air Power Survey*, Volume II, Part II, Washington, GPO, 1993, p. 330.
2. See Sean Boyne, "Iraq's MIO: Ministry of Missing Weapons," *Jane's Intelligence Review*, March, 1998, pp. 23–25.
3. *Washington Post*, October 12, 1998, p. A–16.
4. See Sean Boyne, "Iraq's MIO: Ministry of Missing Weapons," *Jane's Intelligence Review*, March, 1998, pp. 23–25.

5. *Arms Control Today*, April, 1993, p. 29.
6. *Jane's Intelligence Review*, March, 1995, p. 115.
7. *Washington Post*, November 27, 1993, p. A-20.
8. United Nations Special Commission, "Report to the Security Council—S/1995/494," 20 June 1995, p. 10.
9. United Nations Special Commission, "Report to the Security Council—S/1995/864," 11 October 1995, p. 7.
10. United Nations Special Commission, "Report to the Security Council—S/1995/864," 11 October 1995, pp. 7–8.
11. United Nations Special Commission, "Report to the Security Council—S/1995/864," 11 October 1995, p. 8.
12. United Nations Special Commission, "Report to the Security Council—S/1995/864," 11 October 1995, pp. 8–10.
13. United Nations Special Commission, "Report to the Security Council—S/1995/864," 11 October 1995, p. 11.
14. United Nations Special Commission, "Report to the Security Council—S/1995/864," 11 October 1995, p. 9.
15. *Jane's Defense Weekly*, January 3, 1996, pp. 17–18; United Nations Special Commission, "Report to the Security Council—S/1995/864," 11 October 1995.
16. United Nations, Note by the Secretary-General, S/1997/301, April 11, 1997, pp. 9–10, 24.
17. *Washington Post*, December 15, 1995, p. A-30; *Jane's Defense Weekly*, January 3, 1996, pp. 17–18.
18. United Nations, Note by the Secretary-General, S/1997/301, April 11, 1997, p. 25.
19. United Nations, Note by the Secretary-General, S/1997/301, April 11, 1997, pp. 16–17.
20. United Nations, Note by the Secretary-General, S/1997/301, April 11, 1997, p. 17.
21. *Jane's Pointer*, June, 1997, p. 6. Rolf Ekeus's successor, Richard Butler, repeated this warning on July 1, 1997. Reuters, July 1, 1997, 1629.
22. Reuters, April 23, 1997, 05:43; United Nations, Note by the Secretary-General, S/1997/301, April 11, 1997, pp. 16–17.
23. United Nations, Note by the Secretary-General, S/1997/301, April 11, 1997, pp. 17–18.
24. *Washington Post*, March 28, 1996, p. A-28; *Jane's Defense Weekly*, April 10, 1996, p. 15; *Philadelphia Inquirer*, April 24, 1997, p. A-3; *Baltimore Sun*, April 25, 1997, p. 22A; Reuters, April 23, 1997, 05:43, April 24, 1997, 09:17; *Washington Times*, April 21, 1997, p. A-13.
25. *Middle East Economic Digest*, May 2, 1997, p. 16; Iraqi News Agency, April 23, 1997.
26. United Nations, Note by the Secretary-General, "Report by the Secretary-General on the Activities of the Special Commission," S/1997/774, October 6, 1997, Annex 1; *New York Times*, June 25, 1997, p. A-1; *Baltimore Sun*, June 19, 1997, p. 15A; *Washington Times*, June 11, 1997, p. A-15.
27. *Jane's Pointer*, June, 1997, p. 6.
28. *Middle East Economic Survey*, June 30, 1997, pp. A-5–A9; *Washington Times*, June 11, 1997, p. A-15, June 22, 1997, p. A-3, June 24, 1997, p. A-15; *New York Times*, June 25, 1997, p. A-1; *Jane's Defense Weekly*, July 2, 1997, p. 15.
29. *Washington Times*, June 24, 1997, p. A-15.

30. Note by the Secretary-General, "Report by the Secretary-General on the Activities of the Special Commission," S/1997/774, October 6, 1997, Annex 1; Reuters, September 17, 1997, 0244.

31. Note by the Secretary-General, "Report by the Secretary-General on the Activities of the Special Commission," S/1997/774, October 6, 1997, Annex 1; Reuters, September 17, 1997, 0244.

32. *New York Times*, October 6, 1997, p. A-6; Associated Press, October 7, 1997, 0859; Reuters, October 2, 1997, 2055.

33. These comments are based on discussions with British members of the UNSCOM team and US experts, and on reports in the *New York Times* on November 25, 1997, but many of the details are drawn from Ahmad Allawi, head of an opposition broadcasting station based in northern Iraq, and reports by exiled Iraqi opponents of the Baghdad regime under the aegis of the Iraqi National Congress.

34. Jay Bushinsky, "Iraqi Opposition: Saddam Bugging Inspectors," *Jerusalem Post*, Friday, November 28, 1997; *New York Times*, November 25, 1997, p. A-1.

35. Jay Bushinsky, "Iraqi Opposition: Saddam Bugging Inspectors," *Jerusalem Post*, Friday, November 28, 1997; *New York Times*, November 25, 1997, p. A-1.

36. Jay Bushinsky, "Iraqi Opposition: Saddam Bugging Inspectors," *Jerusalem Post*, Friday, November 28, 1997; *New York Times*, November 25, 1997, p. A-1.

37. Note by the Secretary General, "Report by the Secretary-General on the Activities of the Special Commission," S/1997/774, October 6, 1997; *Los Angeles Times*, October 2, 1997 p. A-2; *New York Times*, October 2, 1997, p. A-7.

38. Note by the Secretary-General, "Report by the Secretary-General on the Activities of the Special Commission," S/1997/774, October 6, 1997, p. 6.

39. Note by the Secretary-General, "Report by the Secretary-General on the Activities of the Special Commission," S/1997/774, October 6, 1997, paragraphs 58–61.

40. Note by the Secretary-General, "Report by the Secretary-General on the Activities of the Special Commission," S/1997/774, October 6, 1997, paragraph 59.

41. Note by the Secretary-General, "Report by the Secretary-General on the Activities of the Special Commission," S/1997/774, October 6, 1997, paragraph 48.

42. Note by the Secretary-General, "Report by the Secretary-General on the Activities of the Special Commission," S/1997/774, October 6, 1997, paragraphs 62–64.

43. Note by the Secretary-General, "Report by the Secretary-General on the Activities of the Special Commission," S/1997/774, October 6, 1997, paragraph 65.

44. Note by the Secretary-General, "Report by the Secretary-General on the Activities of the Special Commission," S/1997/774, October 6, 1997, paragraphs 69–72, Annex 2.

45. Note by the Secretary-General, "Report by the Secretary-General on the Activities of the Special Commission," S/1997/774, October 6, 1997, paragraphs 74–76, Annex 2.

46. Note by the Secretary-General, "Report by the Secretary-General on the Activities of the Special Commission," S/1997/774, October 6, 1997, paragraphs 81–82.

47. Note by the Secretary-General, "Report by the Secretary-General on the Activities of the Special Commission," S/1997/774, October 6, 1997, paragraphs 79–80, Annex 2.

48. Note by the Secretary-General, "Report by the Secretary-General on the Activities of the Special Commission," S/1997/774, October 6, 1997, paragraph 83.

49. *Washington Times*, October 19, 1997, p. A-7.

50. *New York Times*, October 17, 1997, p. A-5; *Jane's Defense Weekly*, October 22, 1997, p. 4.

51. Associated Press, October 17, 1997, 0503, October 21, 1997, 0459; 1938 EDT.

52. *Washington Times*, October 19, 1997, p. A-7, October 22, 1997, p. A-11; *New York Times*, October 17, 1997, p. A-5, October 22, 1997, p. A-13; *Washington Post*, October 23, 1997, p. A-15; CNN, October 23, 1997, 1216 GMT; Associated Press, NY, October 30, 1997, 0610 EST.

53. Associated Press, NY, October 30, 1997, 0610 EST, 0438 EST, 10–28–97, 1958 EST; *Washington Post*, October 31, 1997, p. A-1; *Washington Times*, October 31, 1997, p. A-1; *New York Times*, October 30, 1997, p. A-1; Reuters, October 29, 1997, 2344 GMT.

54. Associated Press, NY, November 11, 1997, 1211.

55. Associated Press, NY, October 30, 1997, 0610 EST, 0438 EST, 10–28–97, 1958 EST; *Washington Post*, October 31, 1997, p. A-1; *Washington Times*, October 31, 1997, p. A-1; *New York Times*, October 30, 1997, p. A-1; Reuters, October 29, 1997, 2344 GMT.

56. Fax, Embassy of France, November 3, 1997; *Baltimore Sun*, October 30, 1997, p. 16A.

57. Reuters, November 4, 1997;

58. Press release, UN Special Commission, November 5, 1997; *Washington Post*, November 6, 1997, p. A-1; Associated Press, NY, November 5, 1997, 1813 EST, Reuters, November 6, 1997, 1350.

59. Reuters, November 6, 1997, 1510, November 7, 1997, 1511, 1530, 1514 Associated Press, NY, November 5, 1997, 1813, November 6, 1997, 1332 EST, 512 EST, 230 EST; Associated Press, NY, November 25, 1997, 0959.

60. Associated Press, November 6, 1997, 0830.

61. The following chronology is taken from Associated Press and Reuters wire service reports.

62. Based on US Department of Defense and US 5th Fleet Fact Sheets for November 28, 1997, accessed via the Internet on the US Department of Defense web page. Also, *The Estimate*, November 21, 1997, p. 4; ABCNews.com, November 26, 1997, 0412; *New York Times*, November 18, 1997, p. A-9; *Washington Times*, November 25, 1997, p. A-11.

63. *New York Times*, International Internet edition, November 21, 1997.

64. *Washington Post*, November 20, 1997.

65. *al-Thawra*, Baghdad edition, November 21, 1997.

66. Reuters, November 20, 1997, 06:30:09.

67. Reuters, November 22, 1997, 1555.

68. This statement was issued after a meeting by the Revolutionary Command Council and a meeting of the Regional Command of the Ba'ath Party, chaired by Saddam Hussein; Reuters, November 20, 1997, 07:03.

69. Associated Press, November 22, 1997, 2231.

70. Reuters, November 30, 1997, 0829; Associated Press, November 30, 1997, 0742; UNICEF home page on the Internet, "Nearly One Million Children Malnourished in Iraq," December 2, 1997, 1059; FAO, "Special Report, FAO/WFP Food Supply and Nutrition Assessment Mission to Iraq," FAO, Internet home page, October 3, 1997.

71. Reuters, November 30, 1997, 0829; Associated Press, November 30, 1997, 0742.

72. Reuters, December 4, 1997, 2314.

73. The United States responded by accusing the Iraqi government of manipulative indifference to the suffering of the Iraqi people when it refused to pump oil until it agreed on a new plan for food distribution with the United Nations. President Clinton

said that Iraqi President Saddam Hussein was responsible for his people's suffering and was trying to exploit their pain to win support and sympathy abroad. The president was commenting on Iraq's rejection of an extension to the oil for food program under which it sells oil worth $2 billion every six months under UN supervision.

He (Saddam) is in no position to point a finger at anyone else in the world for the suffering of his own people. Today once again he has proved that he is responsible.... This is not about (UN resolution).... This is about some other way that he can manipulate the feelings of people beyond the borders of Iraq, even if he has to let innocent children die to do it, so he can continue to pursue a weapons of mass destruction program.... It's wrong and the world community should not let him get away with it.

Clinton also stated that,

I certainly think he (Saddam) has exposed his motives and his real concerns to the entire world today. It wasn't very long ago that he had this symbolic funeral for children, blaming the world community in general and the United States in particular for the death of Iraqi children.... Let me remind you, when we got the UN resolution passed on [oil for food] ... he delayed full implementation of that for a year and a half.

State Department spokesman James Foley said Iraq's attitude fitted a pattern of Iraqi government attempts to obstruct humanitarian efforts, and that Iraq and the United States also disagreed sharply on the proportion of food contracts that were delayed in the program. Foley stated that,

They fall into three categories—commercial items that are not humanitarian, dual-use items that can also be used for military purposes, and contracts involving problem companies that have a history of sanctions violations. So virtually all the holds are for purposes of obtaining additional information on end-user and uses.... Their (the Iraqis') logic seems to be that they don't have enough money ... to buy sufficient humanitarian goods and so they're going to try to solve the problem by refusing to earn any further income. It's totally illogical.

Reuters, December 4, 1997, 2314, December 5, 1997, 1837; December 8, 1997, 0211; Associated Press, New York, December 7, 1997, 0304.
74. Reuters, December 19, 1997, 1913.
75. Reuters, January 24, 1998, 0624.
76. Associated Press, November 24, 1997, 0823; Reuters, November 24, 1997, 2239. The truly main presidential palace is in Baghdad. Some Iraqis compare its size to Buckingham Palace. It was built by Iraq's former royal family decades before Saddam came to power. The palace—with its ornate ceilings—was shown in television reports filled with Iraqis acting as human shields to protect it from possible US air attacks. The Qadissiya Hawk Palace was built by Saddam near Baghdad Airport during Iraq's 1980–1988 war with Iran, and it contains a large farm with barns and warehouses. Saddam named the palace after the sixth-century Battle of Qadissiya in which the Arabs defeated Persia, today's Iran. There is also a large complex at al-Oja, Saddam's hometown in the Tikrit Province, 120 miles north of Baghdad. Saddam Hussein built residences for his family there after he came to power in 1979. The entire village is sealed off. Among Saddam's newer palaces is a three-story domed building in Baghdad on the banks of the Tigris River, which he built as a sign of defiance to the UN sanctions. Constructed of light brick, with arched windows in the Arab fashion, the palace is called al-Sujod, the Arabic word for the Muslim's touching of his forehead to the ground in prayer. Another large

palace—built before the Gulf War—is 90 miles north of Baghdad and looks over a manmade lake created by diverting the Tigris River. US officials describe this palace as being four times the size of the White House, which has 132 rooms on three floors. Ordinary Iraqis are not allowed near many of the palaces. But some estimate that a few compounds cover hundreds of acres, with date, citrus fruit, or apple orchards and fields so vast that sheep are herded by helicopter.

77. Reuters, November 24, 1997, 1300.
78. Associated Press, November 26, 1997, 1505; Reuters, November 26, 1997, 1359.
79. Associated Press, November 26, 1997, 1135; Reuters, November 26, 1997, 1029, November 27, 1997, 0628, November 28, 1997, 0612.
80. Reuters, November 28, 1997, 1936.
81. Reuters, November 30, 1997, 0525.
82. IRNA, February 18, 1998.
83. *Washington Post*, August 7, 1998, p. A–1.
84. *Washington Post*, August 7, 1998, p. A–1, August 17, 1998, p. A–1, August 27, 1998, p. A–1; *New York Times*, August 7, 1998, p. A–1, August 27, 1998, p. A–1.
85. *Washington Post*, September 29, 1998, p. A–1.
86. Reuters, April 23, 1997, 05:43; *Philadelphia Inquirer*, April 24, 1997, p. A-3.
87. *Washington Times*, June 30, 1997, p. A-9.
88. United Nations, Note by the Secretary-General, S/1997/301, April 11, 1997, p. 8.
89. United Nations, Note by the Secretary-General, S/1997/301, April 11, 1997, p. 17. Note by the Secretary-General, ''Report of the Secretary-General on the Activities of the Special Commission,'' S/1997/774, October 6, 1997, Annex 2.
90. United Nations, Note by the Secretary-General, S/1997/301, April 11, 1997, pp. 17–19.
91. Note by the Secretary-General, ''Report of the Secretary-General on the Activities of the Special Commission,'' S/1997/774, October 6, 1997, paragraph 98.
92. Note by the Secretary-General, ''Report of the Secretary-General on the Activities of the Special Commission,'' S/1997/774, October 6, 1997, paragraph 92; Reuters, April 24, 1997, 09:17; *Washington Times*, April 21, 1997, p. A-13; United Nations, Note by the Secretary-General, S/1997/301, April 11, 1997, pp. 12, 19–23, 24–25.
93. United Nations, Note by the Secretary-General, S/1997/301, April 11, 1997, p. 24.
94. Transcript of Hans Blix interview, Reuters, October 16, 1997, 1928.
95. Reuters, December 2, 1997, 0800.
96. *Los Angeles Times*, November 24, 1997, p. A-1.

Chapter 11

The Scale of Iraq's Programs and Competing Iranian and Israeli Efforts

The past may not always be a model of the future, but Iraq's pre-Gulf War efforts to acquire weapons of mass destruction were so massive that they serve as a powerful demonstration of Iraq's commitment to proliferation. Table 11.1 provides a summary of the details of these Iraqi efforts, based largely on UNSCOM's and IAEA's disclosures. It then compares them with the efforts of Iran and Israel—efforts that any Iraqi regime is likely to see as a strong incentive for future proliferation. It also shows that Egypt, Libya, and Syria are significant proliferators. Iraq may or may not see such states as threats, but it definitely sees them as competitors in terms of prestige and status, and Iraq–Syria relations remain problematic at best.

It is clear from Table 11.1 that Iraq's past efforts involved every type of weapon of mass destruction and involved major parallel efforts of industrial scale. UN experts have estimated that Iraq had 52 missile storage, assembly, and maintenance facilities, 13 facilities associated with biological weapons facilities, 48 facilities associated with chemical weapons, and 21 facilities associated with nuclear weapons at the time of Desert Storm. Even these totals, however, may be an undercount, and they symbolize the fact that the growing risk posed by proliferation is one of the most important lessons of the Gulf War. There is no way to assign a firm cost to this Iraqi effort, but US experts have privately estimated that Iraq may have spent as much as $10 billion during the period 1970–1991, and some experts indicate that it may have cost Iraq an average of nearly 1% of its GNP during these years.

Iraq's efforts have always been founded on exploiting targets of opportunity, lies and deception, compartmentation, and duplication. Iraq has never made hard trade-offs between given paths to proliferation in the past, or adhered to any fixed plan, doctrine, or strategy. Like other authoritarian states, its leadership has shown a fascination with technology per se that may have led it down some very expensive blind alleys, but which has also given it considerable flexibility in terms of future options.

Table 11.1
The Regional Search for Weapons of Mass Destruction

Iraq's Search for Weapons of Mass Destruction

Delivery Systems
- Prior to the Gulf War, Iraq had extensive delivery systems incorporating long-range strike aircraft with refueling capabilities and several hundred regular and improved, longer-range Scud missiles, some with chemical warheads. These systems included:
  - Tu-16 and Tu-22 bombers;
  - MiG-29 fighters;
  - Mirage F-1, MiG-23BM, and Su-22 fighter attack aircraft;
  - A Scud force with a minimum of 819 missiles;
  - Extended range Al Husayn Scud variants (600 kilometer range) extensively deployed throughout Iraq, and at three fixed sites in northern, western, and southern Iraq;
  - Developing Al-Abbas missiles (900 kilometer range), which could reach targets in Iran, the Persian Gulf, Israel, Turkey, and Cyprus; and
  - Long-range super guns with ranges of up to 600 kilometers.
- Iraq also engaged in efforts aimed at developing the Tamuz liquid fueled missile with a range of over 2,000 kilometers, and a solid fueled missile with a similar range. Clear evidence indicates that at least one design was to have a nuclear warhead.
- Iraq attempted to conceal a plant making missile engines from the UN inspectors. It only admitted this plant existed in 1995, raising new questions about how many of its missiles have been destroyed.
- Iraq had design work underway for a nuclear warhead for its long-range missiles.
- The Gulf War deprived Iraq of some of its MiG-29s, Mirage F-1s, MiG-23BMs, and Su-22s.
- Since the end of the war, the UN inspection regime has also destroyed many of Iraq's long-range missiles.
- UNSCOM has directly supervised the destruction of 48 Scud-type missiles, and has verified the Iraqi unilateral destruction of 83 more missiles and 9 mobile launchers.
- A State Department summary issued on November 16, 1998, indicates that UNSCOM has supervised the destruction of.
  - 48 operational missiles;
  - 14 conventional missile warheads;
  - 6 operational mobile launchers;
  - 28 operational fixed launch pads;
  - 32 fixed launch pads;

Table 11.1 (continued)

- 30 missile chemical warheads;
- other missile support equipment and materials, and a variety of assembled and nonassembled supergun components;
- 38,537 filled and empty chemical munitions;
- 90 metric tons of chemical weapons agent;
- more than 3,000 metric tons of precursor chemicals;
- 426 pieces of chemical weapons production equipment;
- 91 pieces of related analytical instruments; and
- The entire al-Hakam biological weapons production facility and a variety of production equipment and materials.

- The UN still estimates, however, that it is able to account for 817 of the 819 long-range missiles that Iraq imported in the period ending in 1988:
  - Pre-1980 expenditures, such as training: 8
  - Expenditures during the Iran-Iraq War (1980–1981), including the war of the cities in February–April, 1988: 516
  - Testing activities for the development of Iraq's modifications of imported missiles and other experimental activities (1985–1990): 69
  - Expenditures during the Gulf War (January–March, 1991): 93
  - Destruction under the supervision of UNSCOM: 48
  - Unilateral destruction by Iraq (mid-July and October, 1991): 83
- UNSCOM's analysis has shown that Iraq had destroyed 83 of the 85 missiles it had claimed were destroyed. At the same time, it stated that Iraq had not given an adequate account of its proscribed missile assets, including launchers, warheads, and propellants.
- UNSCOM also reports that it supervised the destruction of 10 mobile launchers, 30 chemical warheads, and 18 conventional warheads.
- Iraq maintains a significant delivery capability consisting of:
  - HY-2, SS-N-2, and C-601 cruise missiles, which are unaffected by UN cease-fire terms;
  - FROG-7 rockets with 70 kilometer ranges, also allowed under UN resolutions;
  - Multiple rocket launchers and tube artillery; and
  - Experimental conversions such as the SA-2.
- Iraq claims to have manufactured only 80 missile assemblies, 53 of which were unusable. UNSCOM claims that 10 are unaccounted for.
- US experts believe that
  - Iraq may still have components for several dozen extended-range Scud missiles.
  - Iraq is concealing 5–12 missiles, which they have disassembled and scattered in various parts of the country.

Table 11.1 (continued)

- Iraq is also lying about the production of parts for up to 85 missiles, which are also dispersed in many parts of the country. It is unclear how many can be rapidly assembled in to entire missiles.
- Iraq is concealing significant assets of liquid propellants for the missiles.
- In addition, Iraq has admitted to:
  - Hiding its capability to manufacture its own Scuds.
  - Developing an extended-range variant of the FROG-7 called the Laith. The UN claims to have tagged all existing FROG-7s to prevent any extension of their range beyond the UN imposed limit of 150 kilometers for Iraqi missiles.
  - Experimenting with cruise missile technology and ballistic missile designs with ranges of up to 3,000 kilometers.
  - Flight testing Al Husayn missiles with chemical warheads in April, 1990.
  - Developing biological warheads for the Al Husayn missile as part of Project 144 at Taji.
  - Initiating a research and development program for a nuclear warhead missile delivery system.
  - Successfully developing and testing a warhead separation system.
  - Indigenously developing, testing, and manufacturing advanced rocket engines to include liquid-propellant designs.
  - Conducting research into the development of Remotely Piloted Vehicles (RPVs) for the dissemination of biological agents.
  - Attempting to expand its Ababil-100 program designed to build surface-to-surface missiles with ranges beyond the permitted 100–150 kilometers.
  - Importing parts from Britain, Switzerland, and other countries for a 350 mm "super gun," as well as starting an indigenous 600 mm supergun design effort.
- Iraq initially claimed that it had 45 missile warheads filled with chemical weapons in 1992. It then stated that it had 20 chemical and 25 biological warheads in 1995. UNSCOM established that it had a minimum of 75 operational warheads, and five used for trials. It has evidence of the existence of additional warheads. It can only verify that 16 warheads were filled with Sarin, and 34 with chemical warfare binary components, and that 30 were destroyed under its supervision—16 with Sarin and 14 with binary components.
- US and UN officials conclude further that:
  - Iraq is trying to rebuild its ballistic missile program using a clandestine network of front companies to obtain the necessary materials and technology from European and Russian firms.
  - This equipment is then concealed and stockpiled for assembly concomitant with the end of the UN inspection regime.
  - The equipment clandestinely sought by Iraq includes advanced missile guidance components, such as accelerometers and gyroscopes, specialty metals, special machine tools, and a high-tech, French-made, million-dollar furnace designed to fabricate engine parts for missiles.

Table 11.1 (continued)

- Recent major violations and smuggling efforts:
  - In November, 1995, Iraq was found to have concealed an SS-21 missile it had smuggled in from Yemen.
  - Jordan found that Iraq was smuggling missile components through Jordan in early December, 1995. These included 115 gyroscopes in 10 crates, and material for making chemical weapons. The shipment was worth an estimated $25 million. Iraq claimed the gyroscopes were for oil exploration, but they are similar to those used in the Soviet SS-N-18 SLBM. UNSCOM also found some gyroscopes dumped in the Tigris.
- Iraq retains the technology it acquired before the war, and evidence clearly indicates an ongoing research and development effort, in spite of the UN sanctions regime.
- The fact that the agreement allows Iraq to continue producing and testing short-range missiles (less than 150 kilometers range) means it can retain significant missile development effort.
  - The SA-2 is a possible test bed, but UNSCOM has tagged all missiles and monitors all high apogee tests.
  - Iraq's Al-Samoud and Ababil-100 programs are similar test beds. The Al-Samoud is a scaled-down Scud which Iraq seems to have tested.
  - Iraq continues to expand its missile production facility at Ibn Al Haytham, which has two new buildings large enough to make much longer-range missiles.
  - US satellite photographs reveal that Iraq has rebuilt its Al-Kindi missile research facility.
- Ekeus reported on December 18, 1996, that Iraq retained missiles, rocket launchers, fuel, and command system to "make a missile force of significance." UNSCOM reporting, as of October, 1997 is more optimistic, but notes that Iraq "continued to conceal documents describing its missile propellants, and the material evidence relating to its claims to have destroyed its indigenous missile production capabilities indicated it might have destroyed less than a tenth of what it claimed."

Chemical Weapons
- Iraq is the only major recent user of weapons of mass destruction. US intelligence sources report the following Iraqi uses of chemical weapons:

Date	Area	Type of Gas	Approximate Casualties	Target
August, 1983	Haij Umran	Mustard	Less than 100	Iranians/Kurds
October–November, 1983	Panjwin	Mustard	30,000	Iranians/Kurds
February–March, 1984	Majnoon Island	Mustard	2,500	Iranians
March, 1984	Al Basrah	Tabun	50–100	Iranians
March, 1985	Hawizah Marsh	Mustard/Tabun	3,000	Iranians
February, 1986	Al Faw	Mustard/Tabun	8,000–10,000	Iranians

Table 11.1 (continued)

December, 1986	Umm ar Rasas	Mustard	1,000s	Iranians
April, 1987	Al Basrah	Mustard/Tabun	5,000	Iranians
October, 1987	Sumar/Mehran	Mustard/Nerve Agents	3,000	Iranians
March, 1988	Halabjah	Mustard/Nerve Agents	Hundreds	Iranians/Kurds

Note: Iranians also used poison gas at Halabjah and may have caused some of the casualties.

- In revelations to the UN, Iraq admitted that, prior to the Gulf War, it:
  - Procured more than 1,000 key pieces of specialized production and support equipment for its chemical warfare program.
  - Maintained large stockpiles of mustard gas and the nerve agents Sarin and Tabun.
  - Produced binary Sarin-filled artillery shells, 122 mm rockets, and aerial bombs.
  - Manufactured enough precursors to produce 70 tons (70,000 kilograms) of the nerve agent VX. These precursors included 65 tons of choline and 200 tons of phosphorous pentasulfide and di-isopropylamine
  - Tested Ricin, a deadly nerve agent, for use in artillery shells.
  - Had three flight tests of long-range Scuds with chemical warheads.
  - Had a large VX production effort underway at the time of the Gulf War. The destruction of the related weapons and feedstocks has been claimed by Iraq, but not verified by UNSCOM. Iraq seems to have had at least 3,800 kilograms of V-agents by the time of the Gulf War, and 12 to 16 missile warheads.
- The majority of Iraq's chemical agents were manufactured at a supposed pesticide plant at Muthanna. Various other production facilities were also used, including those at Salman Pak, Samara, and Habbiniyah. Though severely damaged during the war, the physical plant for many of these facilities has been rebuilt.
- Iraq possessed the technology to produce a variety of other persistent and nonpersistent agents.
- The Gulf War and the subsequent UN inspection regime may have largely eliminated some stockpiles and reduced production capability.
- During 1991–1994, UNSCOM supervised the destruction of:
  - 38,537 filled and unfilled chemical munitions;
  - 690 tons of chemical warfare agents;
  - More than 3,000 tons of precursor chemicals; and
  - Over 100 pieces of remaining production equipment at the Muthan State Establishment, Iraq's primary CW research, production, filling, and storage site.
- Since that time, the UNSCOM has forced new disclosures from Iraq that have led to:
  - The destruction of 325 newly identified production equipment, 120 of which were only disclosed in August, 1997;
  - The destruction of 275 tons of additional precursors;

Table 11.1 (continued)

- The destruction of 125 analytic instruments; and
- The return of 91 analytic pieces of equipment to Kuwait.
- As of February, 1998, UNSCOM had supervised the destruction of a total of:
  - 40,000 munitions, 28,000 filled and 12,000 empty;
  - 480,000 liters of chemical munitions;
  - 1,800,000 liters of chemical precursors; and
  - Eight types of delivery systems, including missile warheads.
- US and UN experts believe that Iraq has concealed significant stocks of precursors. Iraq also appears to retain significant amounts of production equipment dispersed before or during Desert Storm and not recovered by the UN.
- UNSCOM reports that Iraq has failed to account for:
  - Special missile warheads intended for filling with a chemical or biological warfare agent.
  - The material balance of some 550 155 mm mustard gas shells, the extent of VX programs, and the rationale for the acquisition of various types of chemical weapons.
  - 130 tons of chemical warfare agents.
  - Some 4,000 tons of declared precursors for chemical weapons.
  - The production of several hundred tons of additional chemical warfare agents, and the consumption of chemical precursors.
  - 107,500 empty casings for chemical weapons.
  - Whether several thousand additional chemical weapons were filled with agents.
  - The unilateral destruction of 15,620 weapons, and the fate of 16,038 additional weapons Iraq claimed it had discarded. "The margin of error" in the accounting presented by Iraq is in the neighborhood of 200 munitions.
- Iraq systematically lying about the existence of its production facilities for VX gas until 1995, and making "significant efforts" to conceal its production capabilities after that date. Uncertainties affecting the destruction of its VX gas still affect some 750 tons of imported precursor chemicals, and 55 tons of domestically produced precursors. Iraq has made unverifiable claims that 460 tons were destroyed by Coalition air attacks, and that it unilaterally destroyed 212 tons. UNSCOM has only been able to verify the destruction of 155 tons and to destroy a further 36 tons on its own.
- Iraq has developed basic chemical warhead designs for Scud missiles, rockets, bombs, and shells. It also has spray dispersal systems.
- Iraq maintains extensive stocks of defensive equipment.
- The UN feels that Iraq is not currently producing chemical agents, but Iraq has offered no evidence that it has destroyed its VX production capability and/or stockpile. Further, Iraq retains the technology it acquired before the war and evidence clearly indicates an ongoing research and development effort, in spite of the UN sanctions regime.
- Recent UNSCOM work confirms that Iraq did deploy gas-filled 155 mm artillery and 122 mm multiple rocket rounds into the rear areas of the KTO during the Gulf War.

Table 11.1 (continued)

- Iraq's chemical weapons had no special visible markings, and were often stored in the same area as conventional weapons.
- Iraq has the technology to produce stable, highly lethal VX gas with long storage times.
- Iraq may have developed improved binary and more stable weapons since the Gulf War.
- Since 1992, Iraq attempted to covertly import precursors and production equipment for chemical weapons through Qatar, Saudi Arabia, and Jordan since the Gulf War.
- The current status of the Iraqi program is as follows (according to US intelligence as of February 19, 1998):

Agent	Declared	Potential Unaccounted for	Comments
Chemical Agents	(Metric Tons)	(Metric Tons)	
VX Nerve Gas	3	300	Iraq lied about the program until 1995.
G Agents (Sarin)	100–150	200	Figures include weaponized and bulk agents.
Mustard Gas	500–600	200	Figures include weaponized and bulk agents.
Delivery Systems	(Number)	(Number)	
Missile Warheads	75–100	45–70	UNSCOM supervised destruction of 30.
Rockets	100,000	15,000–25,000	UNSCOM supervised destruction of 40,000, 28,000 of which were filled.
Aerial Bombs	16,000	2,000	
Artillery Shells	30,000	15,000	
Aerial Spray Tanks	?	?	

- A State Department spokesman reported on November 16, 1998, that Iraq had admitted making 8,800 pounds (four tons) of VX nerve gas, 220,000–330,000 pounds (100–150 tons) of nerve agents such as Sarin, and 1.1–1.32 million pounds (500–600 tons) of mustard gas. Data from UN weapons inspectors indicates that Iraq may have produced an additional 1.32 million pounds (600 tons) of these agents, divided evenly among the three. "In other words, these are the differences between what they say they have and what we have reason to believe they have."

Biological Weapons
- Iraq had a highly compartmentalized "black" program with far tighter security regulations than its chemical program.
- Iraq had 18 major sites for some aspect of its biological weapons effort before the Gulf War. Most were nondescript and had no guards or visible indications that they were a military facility.

Table 11.1 (continued)

- The US targeted only one site during the Gulf War. It struck two sites, one for other reasons. It also struck at least two targets with no biological facilities that it misidentified.
- Iraq systematically lied about its biological weapons effort until 1995. It first stated that it had small defensive efforts, but no offensive effort. In July, 1995 it admitted it had a major defensive effort. In October, 1995 it finally admitted a major weaponization effort.
- Iraq has continued to lie about its biological weapons effort since October, 1995. It has claimed that the effort was headed by Dr. Taha, a woman who only headed a subordinate effort. It has not admitted to any help by foreign personnel or contractors. It has claimed to have destroyed its weapons, but the one site UNSCOM inspectors visited showed no signs of such destruction and was later said to be the wrong site. It has claimed only 50 people were employed full time, but the scale of the effort would have required several hundred.
- Since July, 1995 Iraq has presented three versions of FFCDs and four "drafts."
  - The most recent FFCD was presented by Iraq on September 11, 1997. This submission followed the UNSCOM's rejection of the FFCD of June, 1996. In the period since receiving that report, the UNSCOM conducted eight inspections in an attempt to investigate critical areas of Iraq's proscribed activities such as warfare agent production and destruction, biological munitions manufacturing, filling and destruction, and military involvement in and support to the proscribed program. Those investigations confirmed the assessment that the June, 1996 declaration was deeply deficient. The UNSCOM concluded that the new FFCD it received on September 11, 1997, contained no significant changes from the June, 1996 FFCD.
- Iraq has not admitted to the production of 8,500 liters of Anthrax, 19,000 liters of botulinum toxin, and 2,200 liters of Aflatoxin.
- Reports indicate that Iraq tested at least seven principal biological agents for use against humans:
  - Anthrax, Botulinum, and Aflatoxin are known to be weaponized.
  - It looked at viruses, bacteria, and fungi. It examined the possibility of weaponizing gas gangrene and Mycotoxins. Some field trials were held of these agents.
  - It examined foot and mouth disease, hemorrhagic conjunctivitis virus, rotavirus, and camel pox virus.
  - It conducted research on a "wheat pathogen" and a Mycotoxin similar to "yellow rain" defoliant.
  - The "wheat smut" was first produced at Al Salman, and then put into major production during the period 1987–1988 at a plant near Mosul. Iraq claims the program was abandoned.
- The August, 1995 defection of Lieutenant General Husayn Kamel Majid, formerly in charge of Iraq's weapons of mass destruction, revealed the extent of this biological weapons program. Lt. General Kamel's defection prompted Iraq to admit that it:
  - Imported 39 tons of growth media (31,000 kilograms or 68,200 pounds) for biological agents obtained from three European firms. According to the UNSCOM, 3,500 kilo-

Table 11.1 (continued)

    grams or 7,700 pounds remain unaccounted for. Some estimates go as high as 17 tons. Each ton can be used to produce 10 tons of bacteriological weapons.
- Imported type cultures from the United States which can be modified to develop biological weapons.
- Had a laboratory—and industrial-scale capability to manufacture various biological agents, including the bacteria which causes Anthrax and botulism; Aflatoxin, a naturally occurring carcinogen; clostridium perfringens, a gangrene-causing agent; the protein toxin, Ricin; tricothecene Mycotoxins, such as T-2 and DAS; and an anti-wheat fungus known as wheat cover smut. Iraq also conducted research into the rotavirus, the camel pox virus, and the virus which causes hemorrhagic conjunctivitis.
- Created at least seven primary production facilities including the Sepp Institute at Muthanna, the Ghazi Research Institute at Amaria, the Daura Foot and Mouth Disease Institute, and facilities at Al-Hakim, Salman Pak Taji, and Fudaliyah. According to UNSCOM, weaponization occurred primarily at Muthanna through May, 1987 (largely Botulinum), and then moved to Al Salman (Anthrax). In March, 1988 a plant was open at Al Hakim, and in 1989 an Aflatoxin plant was set up at Fudaliyah.
- Had a test site about 200 kilometers west of Baghdad, it used animals in cages and tested artillery and rocket rounds against live targets at ranges up to 16 kilometers.
- Took fermenters and other equipment from Kuwait to improve efforts during the Gulf War.
- Had at least 79 civilian facilities capable of playing some role in biological weapons production still in existence in 1997.
- The Iraqi program involving Aflatoxin leaves many questions unanswered.
  - Iraqi research on Aflatoxin began in May, 1988 at Al Salman, where the toxin was produced by the growth of fungus aspergilus in 5.3 quart flasks.
  - The motives behind Iraq's research on Aflatoxin remain one of the most speculative aspects of its program. Aflatoxin is associated with fungal-contaminated food grains and is considered nonlethal. It normally can produce liver cancer, but only after a period of months to years, and in intense concentrations. There is speculation, however, that a weaponized form might cause death within days, and some speculation that it can be used as an incapacitating agent.
  - Iraq moved its production of Aflatoxin to Fudaliyah in 1989, and it produced 481 gallons of toxin in solution between November, 1988 and May, 1990.
  - Iraq developed 16 R-400 Aflatoxin bombs and two Scud warheads. It conducted trials with Aflatoxin in 122 mm rockets and R-400 bombs in November, 1989 and in May and August, 1990. It produced a total of 572 gallons of toxin and loaded 410.8 gallons into munitions.
  - UNSCOM concluded in October, 1997 that Iraq's accounting for its Aflatoxin production was not credible.
- Total Iraqi production of more orthodox biological weapons reached at least 19,000 liters of concentrated Botulinum (10,000 liters filled into munitions); 8,500 liters of concentrated Anthrax (6,500 liters filled into munitions); and 2,500 liters of concentrated Aflatoxin (1,850 liters filled into munitions).

Table 11.1 (continued)

- Iraq manufactured 6,000 liters of concentrated Botulinum toxin and 8,425 liters of Anthrax at Al-Hakim during 1990; 5400 liters of concentrated Botulinum toxin at the Daura Foot and Mouth Disease Institute from November, 1990 to January 15, 1991; 400 liters of concentrated Botulinum toxin at Taji; and 150 liters of concentrated Anthrax at Salman Pak.
- Iraq is also known to have produced at least
  - 1,850 liters of Aflatoxin in solution at Fudaliyah.
  - 340 liters of concentrated clostridium perfringens, a gangrene-causing biological agent, beginning in August, 1990.
  - 10 liters of concentrated Ricin at Al Salam. It claimed abandoned work after tests failed.
- Iraq weaponized at least three biological agents for use in the Gulf War. The weaponization consisted of at least
  - 100 bombs and 16 missile warheads loaded with Botulinum.
  - 50 R-400 air-delivered bombs and five missile warheads loaded with Anthrax.
  - Four missile warheads and seven R-400 bombs loaded with Aflatoxin, a natural carcinogen. (The warheads were designed for operability with the Al Husayn Scud variant.)
- Iraq had other weaponization activities:
  - Armed 155 mm artillery shells and 122 mm rockets with biological agents.
  - Conducted field trials, weaponization tests, and live firings of 122 mm rockets armed with Anthrax and Botulinum toxin from March, 1988 to May, 1990.
  - Tested Ricin, a deadly protein toxin, for use in artillery shells.
  - produced at least 191 bombs and 25 missile warheads with biological agents.
  - Developed and deployed 250-pound aluminum bombs coverage in fiberglass. Bombs were designed so they could be mounted on both Soviet-and French-made aircraft. They were rigged with parachutes for low altitude drops to allow efficient slow delivery and aircraft to fly under radar coverage. Some debate over whether bombs had cluster munitions or simply dispersed agent like LD-400 chemical bomb.
  - Deployed at least 166 R-400 bombs with 85 liters of biological agents each during the Gulf War. Deployed them at two sites. One was near an abandoned runway where it could fly in aircraft, arm them quickly, and disperse with no prior indication of activity and no reason for the UN to target the runway.
  - Filled at least 25 Scud missile warheads and 157 bombs and aerial dispensers with biological agents during the Gulf War.
- Iraq developed and stored drop tanks ready for use for three aircraft or RPVs with the capability of dispersing 2,000 liters of Anthrax. Development took place in December, 1990. It claimed later that tests showed the systems were ineffective.

Table 11.1 (continued)

- The UN found, however, that Iraq equipped crop spraying helicopters for biological warfare and held exercises and tests simulating the spraying of Anthrax spores.
- Iraqi Mirages were given spray tanks to disperse biological agents.
  - Held trials as late as January 13, 1991.
  - Mirages chosen because they have large 2,200 liter belly tanks and could be refueled by air, giving them a longer endurance and greater strike range.
  - Tanks had electric valves to allow the agent to be released, and the system was tested by releasing simulated agent into desert areas with scattered petri dishes to detect the biological agent. UNSCOM has videotapes of the aircraft.
- Project 144 at Taji produced at least 25 operational Al Husayn warheads. Ten of these were hidden deep in a railway tunnel, and 15 in holes dug in an unmanned hide site along the Tigris.
- Biological weapons were only distinguished from regular weapons by a black stripe.
- The UN claims that Iraq has offered no evidence to corroborate its claims that it destroyed its stockpile of biological agents after the Gulf War. Further, Iraq retains the technology it acquired before the war, and evidence clearly indicates an ongoing research and development effort, in spite of the UN sanctions regime.
- UNSCOM reported in October, 1997 that
  - Iraq has never provided a clear picture of the role of its military in its biological warfare program, and has claimed it only played a token role.
  - It has never accounted for its disposal of growth media. The unaccounted for media is sufficient, in quantity, for the production of over three times more of the biological agent—Anthrax—Iraq claims to have been produced.
  - Bulk warfare agent production appears to be vastly understated by Iraq. Expert calculations of possible agent production quantities, either by equipment capacity or growth media amounts, far exceed Iraq's stated results.
  - Significant periods when Iraq claims its fermenters were not utilized are unexplained.
  - Biological warfare field trials are underreported and inadequately described.
  - Claims regarding field trials of chemical and biological weapons using R400 bombs are contradictory and indicate that "more munitions were destroyed than were produced.
  - The Commission is unable to verify that the unilateral destruction of the BW-filled Al Hussein warheads has taken place."[1]
  - There is no way to confirm whether Iraq destroyed 157 bombs of the R400 type, some of which were filled with Botulin or Anthrax spores.[2]
  - "The September, 1997 FFCD fails to give a remotely credible account of Iraq's biological program. This opinion has been endorsed by an international panel of experts."[3]
- The current status of the Iraqi program is as follows (according to US intelligence as of February 19, 1998):

Table 11.1 (continued)

Agent	Declared Concentrated Amount		Declared Total Amount		Uncertainty
	Liters	Gallons	Liters	Gallons	
Anthrax	8,500	12,245	85,000	22,457	Could be 3–4 times declared amount.
Botulinum toxin	19,400	NA	380,000	NA	Probably twice declared amount. Some extremely concentratred.
Gas Gangrene Clostridium Perfingens Alfatoxin	340 NA	90 NA	3,400 2,200	900 581	Amounts could be higher. Major uncertainties.
Ricin	NA	NA	10	2.7	Major uncertainties.

- UNSCOM cannot confirm the unilateral destruction of 25 warheads. It can confirm the destruction of 23 of at least 157 bombs. Iraq may have more aerosol tanks.
- The UN currently inspects 79 sites—5 used to make weapons before war; 5 vaccine or pharmaceutical sites; 35 research and university sites; thirteen breweries, distilleries, and dairies with dual-purpose capabilities; eight diagnostic laboratories.
- Iraq retains laboratory capability to manufacture various biological agents, including the bacteria which cause Anthrax, botulism, tularemia, and typhoid.
- Many additional civilian facilities are capable of playing some role in biological weapons production.
- A State Department spokesman reported on November 16, 1998, that there was a large discrepancy between the amount of biological growth media-procured and the amount of agents that were or could have been produced. Baghdad has not adequately explained where some 8,000 pounds (3,500 kilograms) of the material went out of some 68,000 pounds (31,000 kilograms) of biological growth media it imported. Iraq's accounting of the amount of the agent it produced and the number of failed batches is seriously flawed and cannot be reconciled on the basis of this full disclosure Iraq has made.

Nuclear Weapons
- Inspections by UN teams have found evidence of two successful weapons designs, a neutron initiator, explosives, and triggering technology needed for production of bombs, plutonium processing technology, centrifuge technology, Calutron enrichment technology, and experiments with chemical separation technology. Iraq had some expert technical support, including at least one German scientist who provided the technical plans for the URENCO TC-11 centrifuge.
- Iraq's main nuclear weapons related facilities were:
  - Al Atheer—center of nuclear weapons program, uranium metallurgy; production of shaped charges for bombs, remote controlled facilities for high explosives manufacture.

Table 11.1 (continued)

- Al Tuwaitha—triggering systems, neutron initiators, uranium metallurgy, and hot cells for plutonium separation, laboratory production of UO_2, UCL_4, UF_6, and fuel fabrication facility.
- Prototype-scale gas centrifuge, prototype EMIS facility, and testing of laser isotope separation technology.
- Al Qa Qa—high explosives storage, testing of detonators for high explosive component of implosion nuclear weapons.
- Al Musaiyib/Al Hatteen—high explosive testing, hydrodynamic studies of bombs.
- Al Hadre—firing range for high explosive devices, including FAE.
- Ash Sharqat—designed for mass production of weapons grade material using EMIS.
- Al Furat—designed for mass production of weapons grade material using centrifuge method.
- Al Jesira (Mosul)—mass production of UCL_4.
- Al Qaim—phosphate plant for production of U308.
- Akashat uranium mine.
- Iraq had three reactor programs:
  - Osiraq/Tammuz I 40 megawatt light-water reactor, destroyed by Israeli air attack in 1981.
  - Isis/Tammuz II 800 kilowatt light water reactor, destroyed by Coalition air attack in 1991.
  - IRT-5000 5 megawatt light water reactor, damaged by Coalition air attack in 1991.
- Iraq used Calutron (EMIS), centrifuges, plutonium processing, chemical defusion, and foreign purchases to create new production capability after Israel destroyed most of Osiraq.
- Iraq established a centrifuge enrichment system in Rashidya and conducted research into the nuclear fuel cycle to facilitate development of a nuclear device.
- After invading Kuwait, Iraq attempted to accelerate its program to develop a nuclear weapon by using radioactive fuel from French and Russian-built reactors. It made a crash effort in September, 1990 to recover enriched fuel from its supposedly safeguarded French and Russian reactors, with the goal of producing a nuclear weapon by April, 1991. The program was halted only after Coalition air raids destroyed key facilities on January 17, 1991.
- Iraq conducted research into the production of a radiological weapon, which disperses lethal radioactive material without initiating a nuclear explosion.
  - Orders were given in 1987 to explore the use of radiological weapons for area denial in the Iran-Iraq War.
  - Three prototype bombs were detonated at test sites—one as a ground level static test, and two others were dropped from aircraft.

Table 11.1 (continued)

- Iraq claims the results were disappointing, and the project was shelved but has no records or evidence to prove this.
- UN teams have found and destroyed, or secured, new stockpiles of illegal enriched material, major production and R&D facilities, and equipment—including Calutron enriching equipment.
- The IAEA believes that Iraq's nuclear program has been largely disabled and remains incapacitated, but warns that Iraq retains substantial technology and established a clandestine purchasing system in 1990 that it has used to import forbidden components since the Gulf War.
- The major remaining uncertainties are:
  - Iraq still retains the technology developed before the Gulf War, and US experts believe an ongoing research and development effort continues, in spite of the UN sanctions regime.
  - Possible concealment and/or dispersal of all the components for two or three implosion-type nuclear devices, except for the fissile material.
  - Possible concealment of an effective, high-speed centrifuge program.
  - Possible elements for radiological weapons.
  - Success in seeking to clandestinely buy components for nuclear weapons and examining the purchase of fissile material from outside Iraq. Iraq is known to be active in this effort.
  - The extent to which Iraq is continuing with the development of a missile warhead suited to the use of a nuclear device.
  - A substantial number of declared nuclear weapons components and research equipment have never been recovered. There is no reason to assume that Iraqi declarations were comprehensive.

Iran's Search for Weapons of Mass Destruction

Delivery Systems

- The Soviet-designed Scud B (17E) guided missile currently forms the core of Iran's ballistic missile forces, largely as a result of the Iran-Iraq War.
- Iran only acquired its Scuds in response to Iraq's invasion. It obtained a limited number from Libya and then obtained larger numbers from North Korea. It deployed these units with a special Khatam ol-Anbya force attached to the air element of the Pasdaran. Iran fired its first Scuds in March, 1985. It fired as many as 14 Scuds in 1985, 8 in 1986, 18 in 1987, and 77 in 1988. Iran fired 77 Scud missiles during a 52-day period in 1988, during what came to be known as the "war of the cites." Sixty-one were fired at Baghdad, nine at Mosul, five at Kirkuk, one at Takrit, and one at Kuwait. Iran fired as many as five missiles on a single day, and once fired three missiles within 30 minutes. This still, however, worked out to an average of only about one missile a day, and Iran was down to only 10–20 Scuds when the war of the cities ended.

Table 11.1 (continued)

- Iran's missile attacks were initially more effective than Iraq's attacks. This was largely a matter of geography. Many of Iraq's major cities were comparatively close to its border with Iran, but Tehran and most of Iran's major cities that had not already been targets in the war were outside the range of Iraqi Scud attacks. Iran's missiles, in contrast, could hit key Iraqi cities like Baghdad. This advantage ended when Iraq deployed extended-range Scuds.

- The Scud B is a relatively old Soviet design which first became operational in 1967, designated as the R-17E or R-300E. The Scud B has a range of 290–300 kilometers with its normal conventional payload. The export version of the missile is about 11 meters long, 85–90 centimeters in diameter, and weighs 6,300 kilograms. It has a nominal CEP of 1,000 meters. The Russian versions can be equipped with conventional high explosive, fuel air explosive, runway penetrator, submunition, chemical, and nuclear warheads.

- The export version of the Scud B comes with a conventional high explosive warhead weighing about 1,000 kilograms, of which 800 kilograms are the high explosive payload and 200 are the warhead structure and fusing system. It has a single-stage storable liquid rocket engine and is usually deployed on the MAZ-543 eight-wheel transporter-erector-launcher (TEL). It has a strap-down inertial guidance, using three gyros to correct its ballistic trajectory, and uses internal graphite jet vane steering. The warhead hits at a velocity above Mach 1.5.

- Most estimates indicate that Iran now has 6–12 Scud launchers and up to 200 Scud B (R-17E) missiles with a range of 230–310 kilometers.

- Some estimates give higher figures. They estimate Iran bought 200–300 Scud Bs from North Korea between 1987 and 1992, and may have continued to buy such missiles after that time. Israeli experts estimate that Iran had at least 250–300 Scud B missiles, and at least 8–15 launchers on hand in 1997.

- US experts also believe that Iran can now manufacture virtually all of the Scud B, with the possible exception of the most sophisticated components of its guidance system and rocket motors. This makes it difficult to estimate how many missiles Iran has in inventory and can acquire over time, as well as to estimate the precise performance characteristics of Iran's missiles, since it can alter the weight of the warhead and adjust the burn time and improve the efficiency of the rocket motors.

- Iran has new long-range North Korean Scuds with ranges near 500 kilometers.

- The North Korean missile system is often referred to as a "Scud C." Typically, Iran formally denied the fact it had such systems long after the transfer of these missiles became a reality. Hassan Taherian, an Iranian foreign ministry official, stated in February, 1995, "There is no missile cooperation between Iran and North Korea whatsoever. We deny this."

- In fact, a senior North Korean delegation traveled to Tehran to close the deal on November 29, 1990, and met with Mohsen Rezaei, the former commander of the IRGC. Iran either bought the missile then, or placed its order shortly thereafter. North Korea then exported the missile through its Lyongaksan Import Corporation. Iran imported

Table 11.1 (continued)

some of these North Korean missile assemblies using its B-747s, and seems to have used ships to import others.

- Iran probably had more than 60 of the longer-range North Korean missiles by 1998, although other sources report 100, and one source reports 170.
- Iran may have 5–10 Scud C launchers, each with several missiles. This total seems likely to include four new North Korean TELs received in 1995.
- Iran seems to want enough missiles and launchers to make its missile force highly dispersible.
- Iran may have begun to test its new North Korean missiles. There are reports it has fired them from mobile launchers at a test site near Qom about 310 miles (500 kilometers) to a target area south of Shahroud. There are also reports that units equipped with such missiles have been deployed as part of Iranian exercises like the Saeqer-3 (Thunderbolt 3) exercise in late October, 1993.
- The missile is more advanced than the Scud B, although many aspects of its performance are unclear. North Korea seems to have completed development of the missile in 1987, after obtaining technical support from the People's Republic of China. While it is often called a "Scud C," it seems to differ substantially in detail from the original Soviet Scud B. It seems to be based more on the Chinese-made DF-61 than on a direct copy of the Soviet weapon.
- Experts estimate that the North Korean missiles have a range of around 310 miles (500 kilometers), a warhead with a high explosive payload of 700 kilograms, and relatively good accuracy and reliability. While this payload is a bit limited for the effective delivery of chemical agents, Iran might modify the warhead to increase payload at the expense of range and restrict the using of chemical munitions to the most lethal agents, such as persistent nerve gas. It might also concentrate its development efforts on arming its Scud C forces with more lethal biological agents. In any case, such missiles are likely to have enough range-payload to give Iran the ability to strike all targets on the southern coast of the Gulf and all of the populated areas in Iraq, although not the West. Iran could also reach targets in parts of eastern Syria, the eastern third of Turkey, and cover targets in the border area of the former Soviet Union, western Afghanistan, and western Pakistan.
- Accuracy and reliability remain major uncertainties, as does operational CEP. Much would also depend on the precise level of technology Iran deployed in the warhead. Neither Russia nor the People's Republic of China seem to have transferred the warhead technology for biological and chemical weapons to Iran or Iraq when they sold them the Scud B missile and CSS-8. However, North Korea may have sold Iran such technology as part of the Scud C sale. If it did so, such a technology transfer would save Iran years of development and testing in obtaining highly lethal biological and chemical warheads. In fact, Iran would probably be able to deploy far more effective biological and chemical warheads than Iraq had at the time of the Gulf War.
- Iran may be working with Syria in such development efforts, although Middle Eastern nations rarely cooperate in such sensitive areas. Iran served as a transshipment point for North Korean missile deliveries during 1992 and 1993. Some of this transshipment

Table 11.1 (continued)

took place using the same Iranian B-747s that brought missile parts to Iran. Others moved by sea. For example, a North Korean vessel called the *Des Hung Ho*, bringing missile parts for Syria, docked at Bandar Abbas in May, 1992. Iran then flew these parts to Syria. An Iranian ship coming from North Korea and a second North Korean ship followed, carrying missiles and machine tools for both Syria and Iran. At least 20 of the North Korean missiles have gone to Syria from Iran, and production equipment seems to have been transferred to Iran and to Syrian plants near Hama and Aleppo.

- Iran has created shelters and tunnels in its coastal areas which it could use to store Scud and other missiles in hardened sites and reduce their vulnerability to air attack.
- Iran can now assemble Scud and Scud C missiles using foreign-made components.
- Iran is developing an indigenous missile production capability with both solid and liquid-fueled missiles, and seems to be seeking the capability to produce MRBMs.
- The present scale of Iran's production and assembly efforts is unclear. Iran seems to have a design center, at least two rocket and missile assembly plants, a missile test range and monitoring complex, and a wide range of smaller design and refit facilities.
- The design center is said to located at the Defense Technology and Science Research Center, which is a branch of Iran's Defense Industry Organization, and located outside Karaj, near Tehran. This center directs a number of other research efforts. Some experts believe it has support from Russian and Chinese scientists.
- Iran's largest missile assembly and production plant is said to be a North Korean–built facility near Isfahan, although this plant may use Chinese equipment and technology. There are no confirmations of these reports, but this region is the center of much of Iran's advanced defense industry, including plants for munitions, tank overhaul, and helicopter and fixed wing aircraft maintenance. Some reports say the local industrial complex can produce liquid fuels and missile parts from a local steel mill.
- A second missile plant is said to be located 175 kilometers east of Tehran, near Semnan. Some sources indicate this plant is Chinese-built and began rocket production as early as 1987. It is supposed to be able to build 600–1,000 Oghab rockets per year, if Iran can import key ingredients for solid fuel motors like ammonium perchlorate. The plant is also supposed to produce the Iran-130.
- Another facility may exist near Bandar Abbas for the assembly of the Seersucker. China is said to have built this facility in 1987, and is believed to be helping the naval branch of the Guards to modify the Seersucker to extend its range to 400 kilometers. It is possible that China is also helping Iran develop solid fuel rocket motors and produce or assemble missiles like the CS-801 and CS-802. There have, however, been reports that Iran is developing extended range Scuds with the support of Russian experts, and of a missile called the Tondar 68, with a range of 700 kilometers.
- Still other reports claim that Iran has split its manufacturing facilities into plants near Pairzan, Seman, Shiraz, Maghdad, and Islaker. These reports indicate that the companies involved in building the Scuds are also involved in Iran's production of poison gas and include Defense Industries, Shahid, Bagheri Industrial Group, and Shahid Hemat Industrial Group.

Table 11.1 (continued)

- Iran's main missile test range is said to be further east, near Shahroud, along the Tehran-Mashhad railway. A telemetry station is supposed to be 350 kilometers to the south at Taba, along the Mashhad-Isfahan road. All of these facilities are reportedly under the control of the Islamic Revolutionary Guards Corps.

- There were many reports during the late 1980s and early 1990s that Iran had ordered the North Korean No-Dong missile, which was planned to have the capability to carry nuclear and biological missile ranges of up to 900 kilometers. This range would allow the missile to reach virtually any target in the Gulf, Turkey, and Israel. The status of the No-Dong program has since become increasingly uncertain, although North Korea deployed some developmental types at test facilities in 1997.

  - The No-Dong underwent flight tests at ranges of 310 miles (500 kilometers) on May 29, 1993. Some sources indicate that Iranians were present at these tests. Extensive further propulsion tests began in August, 1994, and some reports indicate operational training began for test crews in May, 1995. Missile storage facilities began to be built in July, 1995, and four launch sites were completed in October, 1995.

  - The progress of the program has been slow since that time, and may reflect development problems. However, mobile launchers were seen deployed in northeast North Korea on March 24, 1997. According to some reports, a further seven launcher units were seen at a facility about 100 kilometers from Pyongyang.

  - The No-Dong 1 is a single-stage liquid-fueled missile, with a range of 1,000–1,300 kilometers (810 miles), although longer ranges may be possible with a reduce warhead and maximum burn. There are also indications that there may be a No-Dong 2, using the same rocket motor, but with an improved fuel supply system that allows the fuel to burn for a longer period.

  - The missile is about 15.2 meters long—four meters longer than the Scud B—and 1.2 meters in diameter. The warhead is estimated to weigh 770 kilograms (1,200–1,750 pounds) and a warhead manufacturing facility exists near Pyongyang. The No-Dong has an estimated theoretical CEP of 700 meters at maximum range, versus 900 meters for the Scud B, although its practical accuracy could be as wide as 3,000–4,000 meters. It has an estimated terminal velocity of Mach 3.5, versus 2.5 for the Scud B, which presents added problems for tactical missile defense. The missile is be transportable on a modified copy of the MAZ-543P TEL that has been lengthened with a fifth axle and which is roughly 40 meters long. The added support stand for the vertical launch modes brings the overall length to 60 meters, and some experts questioned whether a unit this big is practical.

- Other reports during the later 1980s and early 1990s indicated that Iran was also interested in two developmental North Korean IRBMs, called the Tapeo Dong 1 and Tapeo Dong 2.

  - The Tapeo Dong 1 missile has an estimated maximum range of 2,000 kilometers, and the Tapeo Dong 2 may have a range up to 3,500 kilometers.

Table 11.1 (continued)

- Both Tapeo Dongs are liquid-fueled missiles which seem to have two stages. North Korea tested a two-stage missile body in late August, 1998, with a range of up to 1,200 kilometers.
- Unlike the No-Dong, the Tapeo Dongs must be carried to a site in stages and then assembled at a fixed site. The No-Dong transporter may be able to carry both stages of the Tapeo Dong 1, but some experts believe that a special transporter is needed for the first stage of the Tapeo Dong 1 and for both stages of the Tapeo Dong 2.

- Since the early 1990s, the focus of reports on Iran's missile efforts have shifted, and it has become clear that Iran is developing its own longer-range variants of the No-Dong for indigenous production with substantial Russian and some Chinese aid.
  - As early as 1992, one such missile was reported to have a range of 800–930 miles and a 1,650-pound warhead. Reports differ sharply on its size. Jane's estimates a launch weight up to 16,000 kilograms, provided the system is derived from the No Dong. It could have a launch weight of 15,000 kilograms, a payload of 600 kilograms, and a range of 1,700–1,800 kilometers if it is based on a system similar to the Chinese CSS-5 (DF-21) and CSS-N3 (JL-1). These systems entered service in 1983 and 1987.
  - A longer-range missile was said to have improved guidance components, a range of up to 1,240 miles and a warhead of up to 2,200 pounds.
  - IOC dates were then estimated to be 1999–2001.
  - Russia agreed in 1994 that it would adhere to the terms of the Missile Technology Control Regime and would place suitable limits on the sale or transfer of rocket engines and technology. Nevertheless, the CIA has identified Russia as a leading source of Iranian missile technology, and the State Department has indicated that President Clinton expressed US concerns over this cooperation to President Yeltsin. This transfer is one reason the President appointed former Ambassador Frank Wisner, and then former ambassador Robert Galluci, as his special representatives to try to persuade Russia to put a firm halt to support of Iran.
  - These programs are reported to have continuing support from North Korea, and from Russian and Chinese firms and technicians. One such Chinese firm is Great Wall Industries. The Russian firms include the Russian Central Aerohydrodynamic Institute, which has provided Iran's Shahid Hemmat Industrial Group (SHIG) with wind tunnels for missile design, equipment for manufacturing missile models, and the software for testing launch and reentry performance. They may also include Rosvoorouzhenie, a major Russian arms export agency; NPO Trud, a rocket motor manufacturer; a leading research center called the Bauman Institute; and Polyus (Northstar), a major laser test and manufacturing equipment firm.
  - The CIA reported in June, 1997 that Iran obtained major new transfers of new long-range missile technology from Russian and Chinese firms during 1996. Since that time, there have been many additional reports of technology transfer from Russia.
  - The reports on Chinese technology transfers involve the least detail.
    - There have been past reports that Iran placed orders for PRC-made M-9 (CSS-6/DF-15) missile (280–620) kilometers range, launch weight of 6,000 kilograms.

Table 11.1 (continued)

- - It is more likely, however, that PRC firms are giving assistance in developing indigenous missile R&D and production facilities for the production of an Iranian solid fueled missile.
  - The United States offered to provide China with added missile technology if it would agree to fully implement an end of technology transfer to Iran and Pakistan during meetings in Beijing on March 25–26, 1998.
- Recent reports and tests have provided more detail on these systems.
  - Some US experts believe that Iran tested booster engines in 1997 capable of driving a missile ranges up to 1,500 kilometers. Virtually all US experts believe that Iran is rapidly approaching the point where it will be able to manufacture missiles with much longer ranges than the Scud B. It is less clear when Iran will be able to bring such programs to the final development stage, carry out suitable test firings, develop effective warheads, and deploy actual units. Much still depends on the level of foreign assistance.
  - Eitan Ben Eliyahu, the commander of the Israeli Air Force, reported on April 14, 1997, that Iran had tested a missile capable of reaching Israel. The background briefings to his statement implied that Russia was assisting Iran in developing two missiles, with ranges of 620 and 780 miles. Follow-on intelligence briefings that Israel provided in September, 1997, indicated that Russia was helping Iran developing four missiles. US intelligence reports indicate that China has also been helping Iran with some aspects of these missile efforts.
  - These missiles included the Shihab ("meteor") missiles, with performance similar to those previously identified with Iranian missiles adapted from North Korean designs.
  - The Israeli reports indicated that the Shihab 3 is a liquid-fueled missile with a range of 810 miles (1,200–1,500 kilometers) and a payload of 1,550 pounds (700 kilometers).
  - Israel claimed the Shihab might be ready for deployment as early as 1999.
  - Israel also reported that Iran is developing the Shihab 4, with a range of 1,250 miles (some reports say up to 4,000 kilometers) and a payload in excess of one ton. It indicates that this system could be operational in two to five years. Martin Indyck, the US Assistant Secretary for Near East Affairs testified on July 28, 1998, that the United States estimated that the system still needed added foreign assistance to improve its motors and guidance system.
  - Israeli indicated that Iran might have two other missile programs, including longer-range systems with a maximum range of up to 4,500–5,000 and 10,000 kilometers.
- Iran tested the Shihab 3 on July, 21 1998, claiming that it was a defensive action to deal with potential threats from Israel.
  - The missile flew for a distance of up to 620 miles before its exploded about 100 seconds after launch. US intelligence sources could not confirm whether the explosion was deliberate, but indicated that the final system might have a range of 800–940 miles (a maximum of 1,240 kilometers), depending on its payload. The test confirmed the fact the missile was a liquid-fueled system.

Table 11.1 (continued)

- Gen. Mohammad Bagher Qalibaf, head of the Islamic Revolutionary Guards Corps' air wing, publicly reported on August 2, 1998, that the Shahab-3 is 53-foot-long ballistic missile that can travel at 4,300 miles per hour and carry a one-ton warhead at an altitude of nearly 820,000 feet. He claimed that the weapon was guided by an Iranian-made system that gives it great accuracy: "The final test of every weapon is in a real war situation but, given its warhead and size, the Shahab-3 is a very accurate weapon."
- Other Iranian sources reported that the missile had a range of 800 miles. President Mohammad Khatami said on August 1, 1998, that Iran was determined to continue to strengthen its armed forces, regardless of international concerns: "Iran will not seek permission from anyone for strengthening its defense capability."
- Martin Indyck testified on July 28, that the United States estimated that the system needed further refinement but might be deployed in its initial operational form between September, 1998 and March, 1999.
- There have been other reports that Iran might be using Russian technology to develop very long-range missiles with a range of 3,500–6,250 kilometers.
- It seems clear that Iran has obtained some of the technology and design details of the Russian SS-4. The SS-4 (also known as the R-12 or "sandal") is an aging Russian liquid-fuel designed that first went into service in 1959, and which was supposedly destroyed as part of the IRBM Treaty. It is a very large missile, with technology dating back to the early 1950s, although it was evidently updated at least twice during the period between 1959 and 1980. It has a CEP of two to four kilometers and a maximum range of 2,000 kilometers, which means it can only be lethal with a nuclear warhead or a biological weapon with near-nuclear lethality.
- At the same time, the SS-4's overall technology is relatively simple, and it has a throwweight of nearly 1,400 kilograms (3,000 pounds). It is one of the few missile designs that a nation with a limited technology base could hope to manufacture or adapt, and its throwweight and range would allow Iran to use a relatively unsophisticated nuclear device or biological warhead. As a result, an updated version of the SS-4 might be a suitable design for a developing country.
- Russia has been a key supplier of missile technology.
  - Some sources have indicated that Russian military industries have signed contracts with Iran to help produce liquid-fueled missiles and provide specialized wind tunnels, manufacture model missiles, and develop specialized computer software. For example, these reports indicate that the Russian Central Aerohydrodynamic Institute is cooperating with Iran's Defense Industries Organization (DIO) and the DIO's Shahid Hemmat Industrial Group (SHIG). The Russian State Corporation for Export and Import or Armament and Military Equipment (Rosvoorouzhenie) and Inor are also reported to be involved in deals with the SHIG. These deals are also said to include specialized laser equipment, mirrors, tungsten-coated graphite material, and maraging steel for missile development and production. They could play a major role in helping Iran develop long-range versions of the Scud B and C, and more accurate variations of a missile similar to the No-Dong.

Table 11.1 (continued)

- The Israeli press reported in August, 1997 that Israeli had evidence that Iran was receiving Russian support. In September, 1997, Israel urged the United States to step up its pressure on Iran, and leaked reported indicating that private and state-owned Russian firms had provided gyroscopes, electronic components, wind tunnels, guidance and propulsion systems, and the components needed to build such systems to Iran.
- President Yeltsin and the Russian Foreign Ministry initially categorically denied that such charges were true. Following a meeting with Vice President Gore, President Yeltsin stated on September 26, 1997, that "We are being accused of supplying Iran with nuclear or ballistic missile technologies. There is nothing further from the truth. I again and again categorically deny such rumors."
- Russia agreed, however, that Ambassador Wisner and Yuri Koptyev, the head of the Russian space program, should jointly examine the US intelligence and draft a report on Russian transfers to Iran. This report reached a very different conclusion from President Yeltsin and concluded that Russia had provided such aid to Iran. Further, on October 1, 1997—roughly a week after Yeltsin issued his denial—the Russian security service issued a statement that it had "thwarted" an Iranian attempt to have parts for liquid fuel rocket motors manufactured in Russia, disguised as gas compressors and pumps.
- Russian firms said to be helping Iran included the Russian Central Aerohydrodynamic Institute, which developed a special wind tunnel; Rosvoorouzhenie, a major Russian arms-export agency; Kutznetzov (formerly NPO Trud), a rocket motor manufacturer in Samara; a leading research center called the Bauman National Technical University in Moscow, involved in developing rocket propulsion systems; the Tsagi Research Institute for rocket propulsion development; and the Polyus (Northstar) Research Institute in Moscow, a major laser test and manufacturing equipment firm. Iranians were also found to be studying rocket engineering at the Baltic State University in St. Petersburg and the Bauman State University.
- Russia was also found to have sold Iran high-strength steel and special foil for its long-range missile program. The Russian Scientific and Production Center Inor concluded an agreement as late as September, 1997 to sell Iran a factory to produce four special metal alloys used in long-range missiles. Inor's director, L. P Chromova, worked out a deal with A. Asgharzadeh, the director of an Iranian factory, to sell 620 kilograms of special alloy called 21HKMT, and provide Iran with the capability to thermally treat the alloy for missile bodies. Iran had previously bought 240 kilograms of the alloy. Inor was also selling alloy foils called 49K2F, CUBE2, and 50N in sheets 0.2–0.4 millimeters thick for the outer body of missiles. The alloy 21HKMT was particularly interesting because North Korea also uses it in missile designs. Inor had previously brokered deals with the Shahid Hemat Industrial Group in Iran to supply maraging steel for missile cases, composite graphite-tungsten material, laser equipment, and special mirrors used in missile tests.
- The result was a new and often tense set of conversations between the United States and Russia in January, 1998. The United States again sent Ambassador Frank Wisner to Moscow, Vice President Gore called Prime Minister Viktor Chernomyrdin, and Secretary of State Madeleine Albright made an indirect threat that the Congress might

Table 11.1 (continued)

apply sanctions. Sergi Yastrzhembsky, a Kremlin spokesman, initially responded by denying that any transfer of technology had taken place.
- This Russian denial was too categorical to have much credibility. Russia had previously announced the arrest of an Iranian diplomat on November 14, 1997, that it caught attempting to buy missile technology. The Iranian was seeking to buy blueprints and recruit Russian scientists to go to Iran. Yuri Koptev, the head of the Russian Space Agency, explained this, however, by stating that "There have been several cases where some Russian organizations, desperately struggling to make ends meet and lacking responsibility, have embarked on some ambiguous projects . . . they were stopped long before they got to the point where any technology got out."
- The end result of these talks was an agreement by Gore and Chernomyrdin to strengthen controls over transfer technology, but it was scarcely clear that it put an end to the problem. As Koptev has said, "There have been several cases where some Russian organizations, desperately struggling to make ends meet and lacking responsibility, have embarked on some ambiguous projects." Conditions in Russia are getting worse, not better, and the desperation that drives sales has scarcely diminished.
- Prime Minister Chernomyrdin again promised to strengthen his efforts to restrict technology transfer to Iran in a meeting with Gore on March 12, 1998. The United States informed Russia of 13 cases of possible Russian aid to Iran at the meeting and offered to increase the number of Russian commercial satellite launches it would license for US firms as an incentive.
- New arrests of smugglers took place on April 9, 1998. The smugglers had attempted to ship 22 tons of specialized steel to Iran via Azerbaijan, using several Russia shell corporations as a cover.
- On April 16, 1998, the State Department declared 20 Russian agencies and research facilities ineligible to receive US aid because of their role in transferring missile technology to Iran.
- A US examination of Iran's dispersal, sheltering, and hardening programs for its anti-ship missiles and other missile systems indicate that Iran has developed effective programs to ensure that they would survive a limited number of air strikes, and that Iran had reason to believe that the limited number of preemptive strikes Israel could conduct against targets in the lower Gulf could not be effective in denying Iran the capability to deploy its missiles.
- Iran has shorter-missile range systems.
  - In 1990, Iran bought CSS-8 surface-to-surface missiles (converted SA-2s) from China with ranges of 130–150 kilometers.
  - Iran has Chinese sea and land-based anti-ship cruise missiles. Iran fired 10 such missiles at Kuwait during Iran-Iraq War, hitting one US-flagged tanker.
- Iran has acquired much of the technology necessary build long-range cruise missile systems from China.
  - Such missiles would cost only 10%–25% as much as ballistic missiles of similar range, and both the HY-2 Seersucker and CS-802 could be modified relatively quickly for land attacks against area targets.

Table 11.1 (continued)

- Iran reported in December, 1995 that it had already fired a domestically built anti-ship missile called the Saeqe-4 (Thunderbolt) during exercises in the Straits of Hormuz and Gulf of Oman Other reports indicate that China is helping Iran build copies of the Chinese CS-801/CS-802 and the Chinese FL-2 or F-7 anti-ship cruise missiles. These missiles have relatively limited range. The range of the CS-801 is 8–40 kilometers, the range of the CS-802 is 15–120 kilometers, the maximum range of the F-7 is 30 kilometers, and the maximum range of the FL-10 is 50 kilometers. Even a range of 120 kilometers would barely cover targets in the Southern Gulf from launch points on Iran's Gulf coast. These missiles also have relatively small high explosive warheads. As a result, Iran may well be seeking anti-ship capabilities, rather than platforms for delivering weapons of mass destruction.

- A platform like the CS-802 might, however, provide enough design data to develop a scaled-up, longer-range cruise missile for other purposes, and the Gulf is a relatively small area where most urban areas and critical facilities are near the coast. Aircraft or ships could launch cruise missiles with chemical or biological warheads from outside the normal defense perimeter of the Southern Gulf states, and it is at least possible that Iran might modify anti-ship missiles with chemical weapons to attack tankers—ships which are too large for most regular anti-ship missiles to be highly lethal.

- Building an entire cruise missile would be more difficult. The technology for fusing CBW and cluster warheads would be within Iran's grasp. Navigation systems and jet engines, however, would still be a major potential problem. Current inertial navigation systems (INS) would introduce errors of at least several kilometers at ranges of 1,000 kilometers and would carry a severe risk of total guidance failure, probably exceeding two-thirds of the missiles fired. A differential global positioning system (GPS) integrated with the inertial navigation system (INS) and a radar altimeter, however, might produce an accuracy of 15 meters. Some existing remotely piloted vehicles (RPVs), such as the South African Skua claim such performance. Commercial technology is becoming available for differential global positioning system (GPS) guidance with accuracies of two to five meters.

- There are commercially available reciprocating and gas turbine engines that Iran could adapt for use in a cruise missile, although finding a reliable and efficient turbofan engine for a specific design application might be difficult. An extremely efficient engine would have to be matched to a specific airframe. It is doubtful that Iran could design and build such an engine, but there are over 20 other countries with the necessary design and manufacturing skills.

- While airframe-engine-warhead integration and testing would present a challenge and might be beyond Iran's manufacturing skills, it is inherently easier to integrate and test a cruise missile than a long-range ballistic missile. Further, such developments would be far less detectable than developing a ballistic system if the program used coded or low-altitude directional telemetry.

- Iran could bypass many of the problems inherent in developing its own cruise missile by modifying the HY-2 Seersucker for use as a land attack weapon and extending its range beyond 80 kilometers, or by modifying and improving the CS-801 (Ying

Table 11.1 (continued)

   Jai-1) anti-ship missile. There are reports that the Revolutionary Guards are working on such developments at a facility near Bandar Abbas.
   - Su-24 long-range strike fighters with range-payloads roughly equivalent to US F-111 and superior to older Soviet medium bombers.
   - F-4D/E fighter bombers with the capability to carry extensive payloads to ranges of 450 miles.
   - HY-2 Silkworm missiles and SA-2 surface-to-air missiles can be modified to deliver weapons of mass destruction.
- Iran has made several indigenous-long range rockets:
   - The Iran-130, or Nazeat, since the end of the Iran-Iraq War. The full details of this system remain unclear, but it seems to use commercially available components, a solid-fuel rocket, and a simple inertial guidance system to reach ranges of about 90–120 kilometers. It is 355 mm in diameter, 5.9 meters long, weighs 950 kilograms, and has a 150-kilogram warhead. It seems to have poor reliability and accuracy, and itspayload only seems to be several hundred kilograms.
   - The Shahin 2. It too has a 355 mm diameter, but is only 3.87 meters long, and weights only 580 kilograms. It evidently can be equipped with three types of warheads: A 180 kilogram high explosive warhead, another warhead using high-explosive submunitions, and a warhead that uses chemical weapons.
   - Iranian Oghab (Eagle) rocket with a range of 40+ kilometers.
   - New SSM with a 125-mile range may be in production, but could be modified FROG.
- Large numbers of multiple rocket launchers and tube artillery for short-range delivery of chemical weapons.

Chemical Weapons

- Iran purchased large amounts of chemical defense gear from the mid-1980s onwards. Iran also obtained stocks of non-lethal CS gas, although it quickly found such agents had very limited military impact since they could only be used effectively in closed areas or very small open areas.
- Acquiring poisonous chemical agents was more difficult. Iran did not have any internal capacity to manufacture poisonous chemical agents when Iraq first launched its attacks with such weapons. While Iran seems to have made limited use of chemical mortar and artillery rounds as early as 1985—and possibly as early as 1984—these rounds were almost certainly captured from Iraq.
- Iran had to covertly import the necessary equipment and supplies, and it took several years to get substantial amounts of production equipment and the necessary feedstocks. Iran sought aid from European firms like Lurgi to produce large "pesticide" plants, and began to try to obtain the needed feedstock from a wide range of sources, relying heavily on its Embassy in Bonn to manage the necessary deals. While Lurgi did not provide the pesticide plant Iran sought, Iran did obtain substantial support from other European firms and feedstocks from many other Western sources.
- By 1986–1987, Iran developed the capability to produce enough lethal agents to load its own weapons. The Director of the CIA (and informed observers in the Gulf) made

Table 11.1 (continued)

it clear that Iran could produce blood agents like hydrogen cyanide, phosgene gas, and/or chlorine gas. Iran was also able to weaponize limited quantities of blister (sulfur mustard) and blood (cyanide) agents beginning in 1987, and had some capability to weaponize phosgene gas and/or chlorine gas. These chemical agents were produced in small batches, and evidently under laboratory scale conditions, which enabled Iran to load small numbers of weapons before any of its new major production plants went into full operation.

- These gas agents were loaded into bombs and artillery shells, and were used sporadically against Iraq in 1987 and 1988.
- Reports regarding Iran's production and research facilities are highly uncertain:
  - Iran seems to have completed completion of a major poison gas plant at Qazvin, about 150 kilometers west of Teheran. This plant is reported to have been completed between November, 1987 and January, 1988. While supposedly a pesticide plant, the facility's true purpose seems to have been poison gas production using organophosphorous compounds.
  - It is impossible to trace all the sources of the major components and technology Iran used in its chemical weapons program during this period. Mujahideen sources claim Iran also set up a chemical bomb and warhead plant operated by the Zakaria Al-Razi chemical company near Mahshar in southern Iran, but it is unclear whether these reports are true.
  - Reports that Iran had chemical weapons plants at Damghan and Parchin that began operation as early as March, 1988, and may have begun to test fire Scuds with chemical warheads as early as 1988–1989, are equally uncertain.
  - Iran established at least one large R&D center under the control of the Engineering Research Center of the Construction Crusade (Jahad e-Sazandegi) and had established a significant chemical weapons production capability by mid-1989.
    - Debates took place in the Iranian parliament or Majlis in late 1988 over the safety of Pasdaran gas plants located near Iranian towns, and that Rafsanjani described chemical weapons as follows: "Chemical and biological weapons are poor man's atomic bombs and can easily be produced. We should at least consider them for our defense. Although the use of such weapons is inhuman, the war taught us that international laws are only scraps of paper."
- Post–Iran-Iraq War estimates of Iran chemical weapons production are extremely uncertain:
  - US experts believe Iran was beginning to produce significant mustard gas and nerve gas by the time of the August, 1988 cease-fire in the Iran-Iraq War, although its use of chemical weapons remained limited and had little impact on the fighting
  - Iran's efforts to equip plants to produce V-agent nerve gases seem to have been delayed by US, British, and German efforts to limit technology transfers to Iran, but Iran may have acquired the capability to produce persistent nerve gas during the mid 1990s.
  - Production of nerve gas weapons started no later than 1994.

Table 11.1 (continued)

- Iran began to stockpile cyanide (cyanogen chloride), phosgene, and mustard gas weapons after 1985. Recent CIA testimony indicates that production capacity may approach 1,000 tons annually.
  - Weapons include bombs and artillery. Shells include 155 mm artillery and mortar rounds. Iran also has chemical bombs and mines. It may have developmental chemical warheads for its Scuds, and may have a chemical package for its 22006 RPV (doubtful).
- There are reports that Iran has deployed chemical weapons on some of its ships.
- Iran has increased chemical defensive and offensive warfare training since 1993.
- Iran is seeking to buy more advanced chemical defense equipment, and has sought to buy specialized equipment on world market to develop indigenous capability to produce advanced feedstocks for nerve weapons.
- CIA sources indicated in late 1996 that China might have supplied Iran with up to 400 tons of chemicals for the production of nerve gas.
- One report indicated in 1996 that Iran obtained 400 metric tons of chemical for use in nerve gas weapons from China, including carbon sulfide.
- Another report indicated that China supplied Iran with roughly two tons of calcium hypochlorate in 1996, and loaded another 40,000 barrels in January or February of 1997. Calcium hypochlorate is used for decontamination in chemical warfare.
- Iran placed several significant orders from China that were not delivered. Razak Industries in Tehran and Chemical and Pharmaceutical Industries in Tabriz ordered 49 metric tons of alkyl dimethylamine, a chemical used in making detergents, and 17 tons of sodium sulfide, a chemical used in making mustard gas. The orders were never delivered, but they were brokered by Iran's International Movalled Industries Corporation (Imaco) and China's North Chemical Industries Co. (Nocinco). Both brokers have been linked to other transactions affecting Iran's chemical weapons program since early 1995, and Nocinco has supplied Iran with several hundred tons of carbon disulfide, a chemical uses in nerve gas.
- Another Chinese firm, only publicly identified as Q. Chen, seems to have supplied glass vessels for chemical weapons.
- The United States imposed sanctions on seven Chinese firms in May, 1997 for selling precursors for nerve gas and equipment for making nerve gas, although the United States made it clear that it had "no evidence that the Chinese government was involved." The Chinese firms were the Nanjing Chemical Industries Group and Jiangsu Yongli Chemical Engineering and Import/Export Corporation. Cheong Yee Ltd., a Hong Kong firm, was also involved. The precursors included tionyl chloride, dimethylamine, and ethylene chlorodydril. The equipment included special glass lined vessels, and Nanjing Chemical and Industrial Group completed construction of a production plant to manufacture such vessels in Iran in June, 1997.
- Iran sought to obtain impregnated Alumina, which is used to make phosphorous-oxychloride—a major component of VX and GB—from the United States.

Table 11.1 (continued)

- It has obtained some equipment from the Israelis. Nahum Manbar, an Israeli national living in France, was convicted in an Israeli court in May, 1997 for providing Iran with $16 million worth of production equipment for mustard and nerve gas during the period from 1990 to 1995.
- The CIA reported in June, 1997 that Iran had obtained new chemical weapons equipment technology from China and India in 1996.
- India is assisting in the construction of a major new plant at Qazvim, near Tehran, to manufacture phosphorous pentasulfide, a major precursor for nerve gas. The plant is fronted by Meli Agrochemicals, and the program was negotiated by Dr. Mejid Tehrani Abbaspour, a chief security advisor to Rafsanjani.
- A recent report by German intelligence indicates that Iran has made major efforts to acquire the equipment necessary to produce Sarin and Tabun, using the same cover of purchasing equipment for pesticide plants that Iraq used for its Sa'ad 16 plant in the 1980s. German sources note that three Indian companies—Tata Consulting Engineering, Transpek, and Rallis India—have approached German pharmaceutical and engineering concerns for such equipment and technology under conditions where German intelligence was able to trace the end user to Iran
- Iran ratified the Chemical Weapons Convention in June, 1997.
  - It submitted a statement in Farsi to the CWC secretariat in 1998, but this consisted only of questions in Farsi as to the nature of the required compliance.
  - It has not provided the CWC with any data on its chemical weapons program.

Biological Weapons

- Extensive laboratory and research capability.
- Weapons effort documented as early as 1982. Reports surfaced that Iran had imported suitable type cultures from Europe and was working on the production of Mycotoxins, a relatively simple family of biological agents that require only limited laboratory facilities for small scale production.
- US intelligence sources reported in August, 1989 that Iran was trying to buy two new strains of fungus from Canada and the Netherlands that can be used to produce Mycotoxins. German sources indicated that Iran had successfully purchased such cultures several years earlier.
- The Imam Reza Medical Center at Mashhad Medical Sciences University and the Iranian Research Organization for Science and Technology were identified as the end users for this purchasing effort, but it is likely that the true end user was an Iranian government agency specializing in biological warfare.
- Many experts believe that the Iranian biological weapons effort was placed under the control of the Islamic Revolutionary Guards Corps, which is known to have tried to purchase suitable production equipment for such weapons.
- Since the Iran-Iraq War, Iran has conducted research on more lethal active agents like Anthrax, hoof-and-mouth disease, and biotoxins. In addition, Iranian groups have repeatedly approached various European firms for the equipment and technology necessary to work with these diseases and toxins.

Table 11.1 (continued)

- Unclassified sources of uncertain reliability have identified a facility at Damghan as working on both biological and chemical weapons research and production, and believe that Iran may be producing biological weapons at a pesticide facility near Tehran.
- Some universities and research centers may be linked to biological weapons programs.
- Reports surfaced in the spring of 1993 that Iran had succeeded in obtaining advanced biological weapons technology in Switzerland and containment equipment and technology from Germany. According to these reports, this led to serious damage to computer facilities in a Swiss biological research facility by unidentified agents. Similar reports indicated that agents had destroyed German bio-containment equipment destined for Iran.
- More credible reports by US experts indicate that Iran has begun to stockpile Anthrax and Botulinum in a facility near Tabriz, can now mass manufacture such agents, and has them in an aerosol form. None of these reports, however, can be verified.
- The CIA has reported that Iran has "sought dual-use biotech equipment from Europe and Asia, ostensibly for civilian use." It also reported in 1996 that Iran might be ready to deploy biological weapons. Beyond this point, little unclassified information exists regarding the details of Iran's effort to "weaponize" and produce biological weapons.
  - Iran may have the production technology to make dry storable and aerosol weapons. This would allow it to develop suitable missile warheads and bombs and covert devices.
  - Iran may have begun active weapons production in 1996, but probably only at limited scale suitable for advanced testing and development.
  - CIA testimony indicates that Iran is believed to have weaponized both live agents and toxins for artillery and bombs and may be pursuing biological warheads for its missiles. The CIA reported in 1996 that "We believe that Iran holds some stocks of biological agents and weapons. Teheran probably has investigated both toxins and live organisms as biological warfare agents. Iran has the technical infrastructure to support a significant biological weapons program with little foreign assistance."
- The CIA reported in June, 1997 that Iran had obtained new dual-use technology from China and India during 1996.
- Iran announced in June, 1997 that it would not produce or employ chemical weapons including toxins.

Nuclear Weapons
- The Shah established the Atomic Energy Organization of Iran in 1974, and rapidly began to negotiate for nuclear power plants.
  - He concluded an extendible 10-year nuclear fuel contract with the United States in 1974, with Germany in 1976, and France in 1977.
  - In 1975, he purchased a 10 percent share in a Eurodif uranium enrichment plant being built at Tricastin in France that was part of a French, Belgian, Spanish, and Italian consortium. Under the agreement the Shah signed, Iran was to have full access to the enrichment technology Eurodif developed, and agreed to buy a quota of enriched uranium from the new plant.

Table 11.1 (continued)

- He created an ambitious plan calling for a network of 23 power reactors throughout Iran that was to be operating by the mid-1990s, and sought to buy nuclear power plants from Germany and France.
- By the time the Shah fell in January, 1979, he had six reactors under contract, and was attempting to purchase a total of 12 nuclear power plants from Germany, France, and the United States. Two 1,300-megawatt German nuclear power plants at Bushehr were already 60 percent and 75 percent completed, and site preparation work had begun on the first of two 935-megawatt French plants at Darkhouin that were to be supplied by Framatome.
- The Shah also started a nuclear weapons program in the early to mid-1970s, building upon his major reactor projects, investment in URENCO, and smuggling of nuclear enrichment and weapons related technology from US and Europe.
  - A 5-megawatt light-water research reactor operating in Tehran.
  - A 27-kilowatt neutron-source reactor operating in Isfahan.
  - The started of two massive 1,300-megawatt reactor complexes.
  - An attempted to covertly import controlled technology from the United States.
- US experts believe that the Shah began a low-level nuclear weapons research program, centered at the Amirabad Nuclear Research Center. This research effort included studies of weapons designs and plutonium recovery from spent reactor fuel.
  - It also involved a laser enrichment program which began in 1975, and led to a complex and highly illegal effort to obtain laser separation technology from the United States. This latter effort, which does not seem to have had any success, continued from 1976 until the Shah's fall, and four lasers operating in the critical 16 micron band were shipped to Iran in October, 1978.
  - At the same time, Iran worked on other ways to obtain plutonium, created a secret reprocessing research effort to use enriched uranium, and set up a small nuclear weapons design team.
  - In 1976, Iran signed a secret contract to buy $700 million worth of yellow cake from South Africa, and appears to have reached an agreement to buy up to 1,000 metric tons a year. It is unclear how much of this ore South Africa shipped before it agreed to adopt IAEA export restrictions in 1984, and whether South Africa really honored such export restrictions. Some sources indicate that South Africa still made major deliveries as late as 1988–1989.
  - Iran also tried to purchase 26.2 kilograms of highly enriched uranium; the application to the United States for this purchase was pending when the Shah fell.
  - The Shah did eventually accept full IAEA safeguards but their value is uncertain.
- In 1984, the Ayatollah Khomeini revived nuclear weapons program begun under the Shah. He also:
  - Received significant West German and Argentine corporate support in some aspects of nuclear technology during the Iran-Iraq War.
  - Limited transfers of centrifuge and other weapons related technology from PRC, possibly Pakistan.

Table 11.1 (continued)

- Iran also has a Chinese-supplied heavy-water, zero-power research reactor at Isfahan Nuclear Research Center, and two Chinese-supplied sub-critical assemblies—a light water and graphite design.
- It has stockpiles of uranium and mines in the Yazd area. It may have had a uranium-ore concentration facility at University of Tehran, but the status is unclear.
- Some experts feel that the IRGC moved experts and equipment from the Amirabad Nuclear Research Center to a new nuclear weapons research facility near Isfahan in the mid-1980s, and formed a new nuclear research center at the University of Isfahan in 1984 (with French assistance). Unlike many Iranian facilities, the center at Isfahan was not declared to the IAEA until February, 1992, when the IAEA was allowed to make a cursory inspection of six sites that various reports had claimed were the location of Iran's nuclear weapons efforts.
- Bushehr I and II, on the Gulf Coast just southwest of Isfahan, were partially completed at the time of the Shah's fall. Iran attempted to revive the program and sought German and Argentine support, but the reactors were damaged by Iraqi air strikes in 1987 and 1988.
- Iran may also have opened a new uranium ore processing plant close to its Shagand uranium mine in March, 1990, and it seems to have extended its search for uranium ore into three additional areas. Iran may have also begun to exploit stocks of yellow cake that the Shah had obtained from South Africa in the late 1970s while obtaining uranium dioxide from Argentina by purchasing it through Algeria.
- Iran began to show a renewed interest in laser isotope separation (LIS) in the mid-1980s, and held a conference on LIS in September, 1987.
- Iran opened anew nuclear research center in Isfahan in 1984, located about four kilometers outside the city and between the villages of Shahrida and Fulashans. This facility was built at a scale far beyond the needs of peaceful research, and Iran sought French and Pakistani help for a new research reactor for this center.
- The Khomeini government may also have obtained several thousand pounds of uranium dioxide from Argentina by purchasing it through Algeria. Uranium dioxide is considerably more refined than yellow cake, and is easier to use in irradiating material in a reactor to produce plutonium.
- The status of Iran's nuclear program since the Iran-Iraq War is highly controversial, and Iran has denied the existence of such a program.
  - On February 7, 1990, the speaker of the Majlis publicly toured the Atomic Energy Organization of Iran and opened the new Jabir Ibn al Hayyan laboratory to train Iranian nuclear technicians. Reports then surfaced that Iran had at least 200 scientists and a work force of about 2,000 devoted to nuclear research.
  - Iran's deputy president, Ayatollah Mohajerani, stated in October, 1991 that Iran should work with other Islamic states to create an "Islamic bomb."
  - The Iranian government has repeatedly made proposals to create a nuclear-free zone in the Middle East. For example, President Rafsanjani was asked if Iran had a nuclear weapons program in an interview in the CBS program *60 Minutes* in February, 1997. He replied, "Definitely not. I hate this weapon."

Table 11.1 (continued)

- Other senior Iranian leaders, including President Khatami, have made similar categorical denials. Iran's new foreign minister, Kamal Kharrazi, stated on October 5, 1997, that "We are certainly not developing an atomic bomb, because we do not believe in nuclear weapons. . . . We believe in and promote the idea of the Middle East as a region free of nuclear weapons and other weapons of mass destruction. But why are we interested to develop nuclear technology? We need to diversify our energy sources. In a matter of a few decades, our oil and gas reserves would be finished and therefore, we need access to other sources of energy. . . . Furthermore, nuclear technology has many other utilities in medicine and agriculture. The case of the United States in terms of oil reserve is not different from Iran's. The United States also has large oil resources, but at the same time they have nuclear power plants. So there is nothing wrong with having access to nuclear technology if it is for peaceful purposes."
- The IAEA reports that Iran has fully complied with its present requirements, and that it has found no indications of nuclear weapons effort, but the IAEA only inspects Iran's small research reactors.
  - The IAEA visits to other Iranian sites are not inspections, and do not use instruments, cameras, or seals. They are informal walkthroughs.
  - The IAEA visited five suspect Iranian facilities in 1992 and 1993 in this manner, but did not conduct full inspections.
  - Iran has not had any 93+2 inspections, and its position on improved inspections is that it will not be either the first or the last to have them.
  - Iranian officials have repeatedly complained that the West tolerated Iraqi use of chemical weapons and its nuclear and biological build-up during the Iran-Iraq War, and has a dual standard where it does not demand inspections of Israel or that Israel sign the NPT.
- These are reasons to assume that Iran still has a nuclear program.
  - Iran attempted to buy highly enriched fissile material from Khazakstan. The United States paid between $20 million and $30 million to buy 1,300 pounds of highly enriched uranium from the Ust-Kamenogorsk facility in Khazakstan that Iran may have sought to acquire in 1992. A total of 120 pounds of the material—enough for two bombs—cannot be fully accounted for.
  - Iran has imported maraging steel, sometimes used for centrifuges, by smuggling it in through dummy fronts. Britain intercepted a 110-pounds (50 kilogram) shipment in August, 1996. Iran seems to have a centrifuge research program at Sharif University of Technology in Tehran. A IAEA "visit" did not confirm this.
  - Those aspects of Iran's program that are visible indicate that Iran has had only uncertain success. Argentina agreed to train Iranian technicians at its Jose Balaseiro Nuclear Institute, and sold Iran $5.5 million worth of uranium for its small Amirabad Nuclear Research Center reactor in May, 1987. A CENA team visited Iran in late 1987 and early 1988, and seems to have discussed selling Iran the technology necessary to operate its reactor with 20 percent enriched uranium as a substitute for the highly enriched core provided by the United States, and possibly uranium enrichment

Table 11.1 (continued)

and plutonium reprocessing technology as well. Changes in Argentina's government, however, made it much less willing to support proliferation. The Argentine government announced in February, 1992 that it was canceling an $18 million nuclear technology sale to Iran because it had not signed a nuclear safeguards arrangement. Argentine press sources suggested, however, that Argentina was reacting to US pressure.

- In February, 1990, a Spanish paper reported that Associated Enterprises of Spain was negotiating the completion of the two nuclear power plants at Bushehr. Another Spanish firm called ENUSA (National Uranium Enterprises) was to provide the fuel, and Kraftwerke Union (KWU) would be involved. Later reports indicated that a 10-man delegation from Iran's Ministry of Industry was in Madrid negotiating with the Director of Associated Enterprises, Adolofo Garcia Rodriguez.

- Iran negotiated with KWU and CENA of Germany in the late 1980s and early 1990s. Iran attempted to import reactor parts from Siemens in Germany and Skoda in Czechoslovakia. None of these efforts solved Iran's problems in rebuilding its reactor program, but all demonstrate the depth of its interest.

- Iran took other measures to strengthen its nuclear program during the early 1990s. It installed a cyclotron from Ion Beam Applications in Belgium at a facility in Karzaj in 1991.

- Iran conducted experiments in uranium enrichment and centrifuge technology at its Sharif University of Technology in Tehran. Sharif University was also linked to efforts to import cylinders of fluorine suitable for processing enriched material, and attempts to import specialized magnets that can be used for centrifuges, from Thyssen in Germany in 1991.

- It is clear from Iran's imports that it has sought centrifuge technology ever since. Although many of Iran's efforts have never been made public, British customs officials seized 110 pounds of maraging steel being shipped to Iran in July, 1996.

- Iran seems to have conducted research into plutonium separation, and has published research on uses of tritium that had applications to nuclear weapons boosting. Iran also obtained a wide range of US and other nuclear literature with applications for weapons designs. Italian inspectors seized eight steam condensers bound for Iran that could be used in a covert reactor program in 1993, and high-technology ultrasound equipment suitable for reactor testing at the port of Bari in January, 1994.

- Other aspects of Iran's nuclear research effort had potential weapons applications. Iran continued to operate an Argentine-fueled 5-megawatt, light-water, highly enriched uranium reactor at the University of Tehran. It is operated by a Chinese-supplied neutron source research reactor, and subcritical assemblies with 900 grams of highly enriched uranium, at its Isfahan Nuclear Research Center. This center has experimented with a heavy-water zero-power reactor, a light-water subcritical reactor, and a graphite sub-critical reactor. In addition, it may have experimented with some aspects of nuclear weapons design.

- The German Ministry of Economics has circulated a wide list of such Iranian fronts which are known to have imported or attempted to import controlled items. These fronts include the:

Table 11.1 (continued)

- Bonyad e-Mostazafan;
- Defense Industries Organization (Sazemane Sanaye Defa);
- Pars Garma Company, the Sadadja Industrial Group (Sadadja Sanaye Daryaee);
- Iran Telecommunications Industry (Sanaye Mokhaberet Iran);
- Shahid Hemat Industrial Group, the State Purchasing Organization, Education Research Institute (ERI);
- Iran Aircraft Manufacturing Industries (IAI);
- Iran Fair Deal Company, Iran Group of Surveyors;
- Iran Helicopter Support and Renewal Industries (IHI);
- Iran Navy Technical Supply Center;
- Iran Tehran Kohakd Daftar Nezarat, Industrial Development Group; and
- Ministry of Defense (Vezerate Defa).

- Iran claims it eventually needs to build enough nuclear reactors to provide 20 percent of its electric power. This Iranian nuclear power program presents serious problems in terms of proliferation. Although the reactors are scarcely ideal for irradiating material to produce plutonium or cannibalizing the core, they do provide Iran with the technology base to make its own reactors, have involved other technology transfer helpful to Iran in proliferating, and can be used to produce weapons if Iran rejects IAEA safeguards.
- Russia has agreed to build up to four reactors, beginning with a complex at Bushehr, with two 1,000–1,200-megawatt reactors and two 465-megawatt reactors, and to provide significant nuclear technology.
  - Russia has consistently claimed the light-water reactor designs for Bushehr cannot be used to produce weapons-grade plutonium and are similar to the reactors the United States is providing to North Korea.
  - The United States has claimed, however, that Victor Mikhaliov, the head of Russia's Atomic Energy Ministry, proposed the sale of a centrifuge plant in April, 1995. The United States also indicated that it had persuaded Russia not to sell Iran centrifuge technology as part of the reactor deal during the summit meeting between Presidents Clinton and Yeltsin in May, 1995.
  - It was only after US pressure that Russia publicly stated that it never planned to sell centrifuge and advanced enrichment technology to Iran, and Iran denied that it had ever been interested in such technology. For example, the statement of Mohammed Sadegh Ayatollahi, Iran's representative to the IAEA, stated that "We've had contracts before for the Bushehr plant in which we agreed that the spent fuel would go back to the supplier. For our contract with the Russians and Chinese, it is the same." According to some reports, Russia was to reprocess the fuel at its Mayak plant near Chelyabinsk in the Urals, and could store it at an existing facility, at Krasnoyarsk-26 in southern Siberia.
  - The CIA reported in June, 1997 that Iran had obtained new nuclear technology from Russia during 1996.

Table 11.1 (continued)

- A nuclear accident at plant at Rasht, six miles north of Gilan, exposed about 50 people to radiation in July, 1996.
- Russian Nuclear Energy Minister Yevgeny Adamov and Russian Deputy Prime Minister Vladimir Bulgak visited in March, 1998 and dismissed US complaints about the risk the reactors would be used to proliferate.
  - Russia indicated that it would go ahead with selling two more reactors for construction at Bushehr within the next five years.
  - The first 1,000-megawatt reactor at Bushehr has experienced serious construction delays. In March, 1998, Russia and Iran agreed to turn the construction project into a turnkey plant because the Iranian firms working on infrastructure had fallen well behind schedule. In February, Iran had agreed to fund improved safety systems. The reactor is reported to be on a 30-month completion cycle.
  - The United States persuaded Ukraine not to sell Iran $45 million worth of turbines for its nuclear plant in early March, 1998, and to strengthen its controls on Ukrainian missile technology under the MTCR.
- China is reported to have agreed to provide significant nuclear technology transfer and possible sale of two 300-megawatt pressurized water reactors in the early 1990s, but then to have agreed to halt nuclear assistance to Iran after pressure from the United States.
  - Iran signed an agreement with China's Commission on Science, Technology, and Industry for National Defense on January 21, 1991, to build a small 27-kilowatt research reactor at Iran's nuclear weapons research facility at Isfahan. On November 4, 1991, China stated that it had signed commercial cooperation agreements with Iran in 1989 and 1991, and that it would transfer an electromagnetic isotope separator (Calutron) and a smaller nuclear reactor for "peaceful and commercial" purposes.
  - The Chinese reactor and Calutron were small research-scale systems and had no direct value in producing fissile material. They did, however, give Iran more knowledge of reactor and enrichment technology, and US experts believe that China provided Iran with additional data on chemical separation, other enrichment technology, the design for facilities to convert uranium to uranium hexaflouride to make reactor fuel, and help in processing yellow cake.
  - The United States put intense pressure on China to halt such transfers. President Clinton and Chinese President Jiang Zemin reached an agreement at an October, 1997 summit. China strengthened this pledge in negations with the United States in February, 1998.
  - In March, 1998, the United States found that the China Nuclear Energy Corporation was negotiating to sell Iran several hundred tons of anhydrous hydrogen fluoride (AHF) to Isfahan Nuclear Research Corporation in central Iran, a site where some experts believe Iran is working on the development of nuclear weapons. AHF can be used to separate plutonium, help refine yellow cake into uranium hexaflouride to produce U-235, and as a feedstock for Sarin. It is on two nuclear control lists. China agreed to halt the sale.
  - Iran denied that China had halted nuclear cooperation on March 15, 1998.

Table 11.1 (continued)

- Even so, the US Acting Under Secretary of State for Arms Control and International Security Affairs stated that China was keeping its pledge not to aid Iran on March 26, 1998.
- US estimates of Iran's progress in acquiring nuclear weapons have become more conservative with time.
- In 1992, the CIA estimated that Iran would have the bomb by the year 2000. In 1995, John Holum testified that Iran could have the bomb by 2003.
- In 1997, after two years in which Iran might have made progress, he testified that Iran could have the bomb by 2005–2007.
    - US experts increasingly refer to Iran's efforts as "creeping proliferation," and there is no way to tell when or if Iranian current efforts will produce a weapon, and unclassified lists of potential facilities have little credibility.
    - Timing of weapons acquisition depends heavily on whether Iran can buy fissile material. If so it has the design capability and can produce weapons in one to two years, or must develop the capability to process plutonium or enrich uranium, in which case, it is likely to be 5–10 years.
- The control of fissile material in the FSU remains a major problem:
    - US estimates indicate the FSU left a legacy of some 1,485 tons of nuclear material. This include 770 tons in some 27,000 weapons, including 816 strategic bombs, 5,434 missile warheads, and about 20,000 theater and tactical weapons. In addition, there were 715 tons of fissile or near-fissile material in eight countries of the FSU in over 50 sites, enough to make 35,000–40,000 bombs.
    - There are large numbers of experienced FSU technicians, including those at the Russian weapons design center at Arzamas, and at nuclear production complexes at Chelyabinsk, Krasnoyarsk, and Tomsk.
    - These factors led the United States to conduct Operation Sapphire in 1994, where the United States removed 600 kilograms of highly enriched uranium from the Ulba Metallurgy Plant in Kazakhstan at a time when Iran was negotiating for the material.
    - They also led to Britain and the United States cooperating in Auburn Endeavor, and airlifting fissile material out of a nuclear research facility in Tiblisi, Georgia. There were 10 pounds of material at the institute, and 8.8 pounds were HEU. (It takes about 35 pounds to make a bomb.) This operation was reported in the *New York Times* on April 21, 1998. The British government confirmed it took place, but would not give the date.
- The *Jerusalem Post* reported on April 9, 1998 that Iran had purchased four tactical nuclear weapons from Russian smugglers for $25 million in the early 1990s, that the weapons had been obtained from Kazakhstan in 1991, and that Argentine technicians were helping to activate the weapon.
    - It quoted what it claimed was an Iranian report, dated December 26, 1991, of a meeting between Brigadier General Rahim Safavi, the Deputy Commander of the Revolutionary Guards, and Reza Amrohalli, then head of the Iranian atomic energy organization.

Table 11.1 (continued)

- It also quoted a second document, dated January 2, 1992, saying the Iranians were awaiting the arrival of Russian technicians to show them how to disarm the protection systems that would otherwise inactivate the weapons if anyone attempted to use them.
- The documents implied that the weapons were flawed but did not indicate whether Iran had succeeded in activating them.
- The US intelligence community denied any evidence that such a transfer had taken place.
- The most detailed reports of Iran's nuclear weapons program are the least reliable and come from the People's Mujahideen, a violent, anti-regime terrorist group. Its claims are very doubtful, but the People's Mujahideen has reported that:
  - Iran's facilities include a weapons site called Ma'allem Kelayah, near Qazvin on the Caspian. This is said to be an IRGC-run facility established in 1987, which has involved an Iranian investment of $300 million. Supposedly, the site was to house the 10-megawatt reactor Iran tried to buy from India.
  - Two Soviet reactors were to be installed at a large site at Gorgan on the Caspian, under the direction of Russian physicists.
  - The People's Republic of China provided uranium enrichment equipment and technicians for the site at Darkhouin, where Iran once planned to build a French reactor.
  - A nuclear reactor was being constructed at Karaj, and another nuclear weapons facility exists in the south central part of Iran, near the Iraqi border.
  - The ammonia and urea plant that the British firm M. W. Kellog was building at Borujerd in Khorassan province, near the border with Turkestan, might be adapted to produce heavy water.
  - The Amir Kabar Technical University, the Atomic Energy Organization of Iran (AEOI) (also known as the Organization for Atomic Energy of Iran or AEOI), Dor Argham Ltd., the Education and Research Institute, GAM Iranian Communications, Ghoods Research Center, Iran Argham Co., Iran Electronic Industries, Iranian Research Organization, Ministry of Sepah, Research and Development Group, Sezemane Sanaye Defa, the Sharif University of Technology, Taradis Iran Computer Company, and Zakaria Al-Razi Chemical Company are all participants in the Iranian nuclear weapons effort.
  - Other sources based on opposition data have listed the AEDI, the Laser Research Center and Ibn-e Heysam Research and Laboratory Complex, the Bonab Atomic Energy Research Center (East Azerbaijan), the Imam Hussein University of the Revolutionary Guards, the Jabit bin al-Hayyan Laboratory, the Khoshomi uranium mine (Yazd), a possible site at Moallem Kalayeh, the Nuclear Research Center at Tehran University, the Nuclear Research Center for Agriculture and Medicine (Karaj), the Nuclear Research Center of Technology (Isfahan), the Saghand Uranium mine (Yazd), the Sharif University (Tehran) and its Physics Research Center.

Missile Defenses
- Iran is seeking Russian S-300 surface-to-air missile system with limited anti-tactical ballistic missile capability.

Table 11.1 (continued)

Israel's Search for Weapons of Mass Destruction

Delivery Systems

- A new IRBM/ICBM range high payload booster was developed with South Africa.
- A major missile test took place on September 14, 1989. It was either a missile test or failure of an Ofeq-2 satellite.
- Israel has done technical work on a TERCOM-type smart warhead. It has examined cruise missile guidance developments using GPS navigation systems.
- Up to 50 "Jericho I" missiles are deployed in shelters on mobile launchers with a range of up to 400 miles and a 2,200-pound payload, and with possible nuclear warhead storage nearby.
- Jericho II missiles are now deployed, and some were brought to readiness for firing during the Gulf War.
- These missiles seem to include a single-stage follow-on to the Jericho I and a multistage, longer-range missile.
  - The missile seems to have a range of up to 900 miles with a 2,200 pound payload, and may be a cooperative development with South Africa. (Extensive reporting of such cooperation in press during October 25 and 26, 1989.)
  - Commercial satellite imaging indicates the missile may be 14 meters long and 1.5 meters wide. Its deployment configuration hints that it may have radar area guidance similar to the terminal guidance in the Pershing II.
- A Jericho II missile production facility at Be'er Yakov.
- There are unverified claims that up to 100 missiles are deployed west of Jerusalem.
- A missile base exists at Zachariah, several miles southeast of Tel Aviv.
  - A limestone region with caves, to shelter missiles, TELs, and vehicles.
  - Transport-Erector-Launchers (TELs) have been seen at this base on vehicles 16 meters long, 4 meters wide, and 3 meters high, and may be road mobile for dispersal.
  - They carry missile 14 meters long and 1.5 meters wide.
  - There seem to be 50 missiles deployed at the base.
  - Each TEL has three support vehicles. One is a guidance programmer and power vehicle. Another seems to be a firing control vehicle, and the third seems to be a communications vehicle.
  - The base is not hardened against nuclear attack, and would be vulnerable to chemical and biological attack.
- Israel's current review of its military doctrine seems to include a review of its missile basing options, and the study of possible hardening and dispersal systems. There are also reports that Israel will solve its survivability problems by deploying some form of nuclear-armed missile on its new submarines.
- F-15, F-16, F-4E, and Phantom 2000 fighter-bombers capable of long-range refueling and of carrying nuclear and chemical bombs.

Table 11.1 (continued)

- Tel Nof may be the air base used to arm aircraft with nuclear weapons. Storage facilities may exist at Zachariah.
- Lance missile launchers and 160 Lance missiles with a range of 130 kilometers.
- A variant of the Popeye air-to-surface missile is believed to have nuclear warhead.
- An MAR-290 rocket with a range of 30 kilometers is believed to be deployed.
- An MAR-350 surface-to-surface missile with a range of 56 miles and a 735-pound payload is believed to have completed development or to be in early deployment.
- Israel is seeking super computers for Technion Institute (designing ballistic missile RVs), Hebrew University (may be engaged in hydrogen bomb research), and Israeli Military Industries (maker of "Jericho II" and Shavit booster).

Chemical Weapons

- Reports of a mustard and nerve gas production facility established in 1982 in the restricted area in the Sinai near Dimona seem incorrect. Israel may have additional facilities, and may have the capacity to produce other gases. Probable stocks of bombs, rockets, and artillery, exist.
- Extensive laboratory research into gas warfare and defense.
- An El Al plane crashed in 1992 carrying 50 gallons of dimethyl methylphosphonate that had been purchased from Solkatronic Chemicals Inc. (Air Products and Chemicals) in the United States, and which was being shipping to the Israel Institute for Biological Research. This is enough to produce 594 pounds of Sarin nerve gas.
- Development of defensive systems includes Shalon Chemical Industries protection gear, Elbit Computer gas detectors, and Bezal R&D air crew protection system.
- Extensive field exercises in chemical defense.
- Gas masks were stockpiled and distributed to the population with other civil defense instructions during the Gulf War.
- Warhead delivery capability exists for bombs, rockets, and missiles, but none are now believed to be equipped with chemical agents.

Biological Weapons

- Israel has done extensive research into weapons and defense.
- A large, highly-classified Israel Institute for Biological Research is located in a 14-acre compound in Nes Ziona, south of Tel Aviv. It has high walls and exceptional security, and is believed to have a staff of around 300, including 120 scientists. A former deputy head, Marcu Kingberg, served 16 years in prison for spying for the FSU.
- Israel is ready to quickly produce biological weapons, but there are no reports of active production effort.

Nuclear Weapons

- The director of the CIA indicated in May, 1989 that Israel may be seeking to construct a thermonuclear weapon.

Table 11.1 (continued)

- Israel has two significant reactor projects: the 5-megawatt HEU light-water IRR I reactor at Nahal Soreq and the 40–150-megawatt heavy-water, IRR-2 natural uranium reactor used for the production of fissile material at Dimona. Only the IRR-1 is under IAEA safeguards.
- Dimona has conducted experiments in pilot scale laser and centrifuge enrichment, purifies UO2, converts UF6, and fabricates fuel for weapons purpose.
- Uranium phosphate mining in Negev, near Beersheba, and yellow cake is produced at two plants in the Haifa area and one in southern Israel.
- A pilot-scale heavy water plant is operating at Rehovot.
- Estimates of numbers and types of weapons differ sharply.
- Stockpile of at least 60–80 plutonium weapons.
  - May have well over 100 nuclear weapons assemblies, with some weapons with yields over 100 kilotons.
  - US experts believe Israel has highly advanced implosion weapons. Known to have produced Lithium-6, allowing production of both tritium and lithium deuteride at Dimona. The facility is no longer believed to be operating.
  - Some weapons may be ER variants or have variable yields.
  - A stockpile of up to 200–300 weapons is possible.
- Major weapons facilities include production of weapons-grade plutonium at Dimona, nuclear weapons design facility at Nahal Soreq (south of Tel Aviv), a missile test facility at Palmikim, a nuclear armed missile storage facility at Kefar Zekharya, a nuclear weapons assembly facility at Yodefat, and an tactical nuclear weapons storage facility at Eilabun in eastern Galilee.

Missile Defenses

- Patriot missiles with future PAC-3 upgrade to reflect the lessons of the Gulf War.
- Arrow 2 two-stage ATBM with slant intercept ranges at altitudes of 8–10 and 50 kilometers and speeds of up to Mach 9, plus possible development of the Rafale AB-10 close in defense missile with ranges of 10–20 kilometers and speeds of up to Mach 4.5. Taas rocket motor, Rafael warhead, and Tadiran BM/C4I system and "Music" phased array radar.
- Israel plans to deploy three batteries of the Arrow to cover Israel, each with four launchers, to protect up to 85 percent of its population. It seeks to deploy the system early in the 2000s.
- The program has progressed with considerable success since phase two tests, with successful flights on August 20, 1996 and March 11, 1997. Development costs are estimated at $330 million with Israel paying 28 percent and the United States paying 72 percent. Deployment will be jointly funded under a 1996 accord as a part of a $556 million six-year program. Israel will pay 64 percent and the United States 36 percent. The total program cost is estimated at $1.6 billion.

Table 11.1 (continued)

- The Arrow will be deployed in batteries as a wide-area defense system with intercepts normally at reentry or exoatmospheric altitudes. Capable of multi-target tracking and multiple intercepts.
- Israel is also examining the possibility of boost-phase defenses.

Advanced Intelligence Systems

- The Shavit I launched Israel's satellite payload on September 19, 1989. It used a three-stage booster system capable of launching a 4,000-pound payload over 1,200 miles or a 2,000-pound payload over 1,800 miles. It is doubtful that it had a payload capable of intelligence missions and seems to have been launched, in part, to offset the psychological impact of Iraq's missile launches.
- Ofeq 2 launched in April, 1990—one day after Saddam Hussein threatens to destroy Israel with chemical weapons if it should attack Baghdad.
- Launched first intelligence satellite on April 5, 1995, covering Syria, Iran, and Iraq in orbit every 90 minutes. The Ofeq 3 satellite is a 495-pound system launched using the Shavit launch rocket, and is believed to carry an imagery system. Its orbit passes over or near Damascus, Tehran, and Baghdad.

Syria's Search for Weapons of Mass Destruction

Delivery Systems

- Four SSM brigades: one with FROG, one with Scud Bs, one with Scud Cs, and one with SS-21s.
- New long-range North Korean Scud Cs deployed
- Two brigades of 18 launchers each are said to be deployed in a horseshoe-shaped valley. This estimate of 36 launchers is based on the fact there are 36 tunnels into the hillside. The launchers must be for the Scud C since the older Scud Bs would not be within range of most of Israel. Up to 50 missiles are stored to the north in bunkers as possible reloads. There is a maintenance building and barracks.
- Estimates indicate that Syria has 24–36 Scud launchers for a total of 120 missiles of all types. The normal ratio of launchers to missiles is 10:1, but Syria is focusing on both survivability and the capability to launch a large preemptive strike.
- The Scud Cs have ranges of up to 550–600 kilometers.
- Possible nerve gas warheads with cluster bomblets were reported in September, 1997.
- CEP of 1,000–2,600 meters.
- A training site exists about six kilometers south of Hama, with an underground facility where TELs and missiles are stored.
  - Up to 12 additional Scud B launchers and 200 Scud B missiles with a range of 310 kilometers. Believed to have chemical warheads. Scud B warheads weigh 985 kilograms.
  - 18 SS-21 launchers and at least 36 SS-21 missiles with a range of 80–100 kilometers. May be developing chemical warheads.

Table 11.1 (continued)

- Reports of Chinese deliveries of missiles do not seem correct.
  - Reports of PRC deliveries of missile components by China Precision Machinery Company, maker of the M-11, in July, 1996. The M-11 has a 186-mile range with a warhead of 1,100 pounds.
  - Some sources believe M-9 missile components, or M-9-like components delivered to Syria. Missile is reported to have a CEP as low as 300 meters.
  - Sheltered or underground missile production/assembly facilities at Aleppo and Hamas have been built with aid from Chinese, Iranian, and North Korean technicians. Possibly some Russian technical aid.
  - A missile test site exists 15 kilometers south of Homs, where Syria has tested missile modifications and new chemical warheads. It has heavy perimeter defenses, a storage area and bunkers, heavily sheltered bunkers, and a missile storage area just west of the site.
- Syria has shorter-range systems.
- Short-range M-1B missiles (up to 60 miles in range) seem to be in delivery from China.
- SS-N-3, and SSC-1b cruise missiles.
  - May be converting some long-range surface-to-air and naval cruise missiles to use chemical warheads.
  - 20 Su-24 long-range strike fighters.
  - 30–60 operational MiG-23BM Flogger F fighter ground attack aircraft.
  - 20 Su-20 fighter ground attack aircraft.
  - 60–70 Su-22 fighter ground attack aircraft.
  - 18 FROG-7 launchers and rockets.
  - Negotiations for PRC-made M-9 missile (185–375 mile range).
  - Multiple rocket launchers and tube artillery.

Chemical Weapons
- First acquired small amounts of chemical weapons from Egypt in 1973.
- Began production of non-persistent nerve gas in 1984. May have had chemical warheads for missiles as early as 1985.
- Experts believe 500 to 1,000 metric tons of chemical agents have been stockpiled.
- Syria believed to have begun deploying VX in late 1996 or early 1997.
- The CIA reported in June, 1997 that Syria had acquired new chemical weapons technology from Russia and Eastern Europe in 1996.
- Unconfirmed reports of sheltered Scud missiles with unitary Sarin or Tabun nerve gas warheads deployed in caves and shelters near Damascus.
- Scuds tested in a manner indicating possible chemical warheads in 1996.
- Seems to have cluster warheads and bombs.
- May have VX and Sarin in modified Soviet ZAB-incendiary bombs and PTAB-500 cluster bombs.

Table 11.1 (continued)

- Acquired design for Soviet Scud warhead using VX gas in the 1970s.
- Major nerve gas and possible other chemical agent production facilities north of Damascus. Two to three plants.
- One facility is located near Homs and is located next to a major petrochemical plant. It reportedly produces several hundred tons of nerve gas a year.
- Reports of a new major plant near Aleppo.
- It is reported that a facility co-located with the Center d'Etudes et de Recherche Scientifique (CERS) is developing a warhead with chemical bomblets for the Scud C.
  - Many parts of the program are dispersed and compartmented. Missiles, rockets, bombs, and artillery shells are produced/modified and loaded in other facilities.
- Wide range of delivery systems.
  - Extensive testing of chemical warheads for Scud Bs. May have tested chemical warheads for Scud Cs.
  - Shells, bombs, and nerve gas warheads for multiple rocket launchers.
  - FROG warheads may be under development.
  - Reports of SS-21 capability to deliver chemical weapons are not believed by US or Israeli experts.
  - Israeli sources believe Syria has binary weapons and cluster bomb technology suitable for delivering chemical weapons.

Biological Weapons

- Signed but did not ratify the 1972 Biological and Toxin Weapons Convention. Extensive research effort.
- ACDA report in August, 1996 indicated that "it is highly probably that Syria is developing an offensive biological capability."
- Extensive research effort. Reports of one underground facility and one near the coast.
- Probable production capability for Anthrax and botulism, and possibly other agents.
- Israeli sources claim Syria weaponized Botulin and Ricin toxin in early 1990s, and probably Anthrax.
- Limited indications may be developing or testing biological variations on ZAB-incendiary bombs and PTAB-500 cluster bombs and Scud warheads.

Nuclear Weapons

- Ongoing research effort.
- No evidence of major progress in development effort.
- Announced nuclear reactor purchase plans including 10-megawatt research reactor and six power reactors in 1980s, but never implemented.
- Has miniature 30-kilowatt neutron-source reactor, but unsuitable for weapons production.

Table 11.1 (continued)

Missile Defenses

- Seeking Russian S-300 surface-to-air missile system with limited anti-tactical ballistic missile capability.

Egypt's Search for Weapons of Mass Destruction

Delivery Systems

- Cooperation with Iraq in paying for development and production of "Badar 2000" missile with a 750–1,000 kilometer range. This missile is reported to be a version of the Argentine Condor II or Vector missile. Ranges were reported from 820–980 kilometers, with the possible use of an FAE warhead.
  - Egyptian officers were arrested for trying to smuggle carbon materials for a missile out of the United States in June, 1988.
  - Covert US efforts seem to have blocked this development effort.
- Has Scud B TELs and missiles with approximately 100 missiles with 300 kilometer range.
- Reports that Egypt has developed plant to produce an improved version of the Scud B, and possibly Scud C, with North Korean cooperation.
- North Korean transfers include equipment for building Scud body, special gyroscope measuring equipment, and pulse-code modulation equipment for missile assembly and testing.
- Reports in June, 1996 that Egypt has made major missile purchase from North Korea, and will soon be able to assemble such missiles in Egypt. Seven shipments from North Korea reported in March and April.
- Media reports that US satellites detected shipments of Scud C missile parts to Egypt in February–May, 1996—including rocket motors and guidance devices—do not seem correct. The Scud C has a range of roughly 480 kilometers.
- The CIA reported in June, 1997, however, that Egypt had acquired Scud B parts from Russia and North Korea during 1996.
- The United States suspects that Egypt is developing a liquid-fueled missile called the Vector, with an estimated range of 600–1,200 kilometers.
- Another liquid-fueled missile under development known as "Project T" has an estimated range of 450 kilometers.
- FROG 7 rocket launch units with 40 kilometers range.
- Cooperation with Iraq and North Korea in developing the Saqr 80 missile This rocket is 6.5 meters long and 210 mm in diameter, and weighs 660 kilograms. It has a maximum range of 50 miles (80 kilometers) and a 440 pound (200 kilogram) warhead. Longer range versions may be available.
- AS-15, SS-N-2, and CSS-N-1 cruise missiles.
- F-4E fighter ground attack aircraft.
- Mirage 5E2 fighter ground attack.

Table 11.1 (continued)

- Mirage 2000EM fighters.
- F-16A and 80 F-16C fighters.
- Multiple rocket launcher weapons.
- Tube artillery.

Chemical Weapons

- Produced and used mustard gas in Yemeni civil war in 1960s, but agents may have been stocks the British abandoned in Egypt after World War II. Effort was tightly controlled by Nasser and was unknown to many Egyptian military serving in Yemen.
- Completed research and designs for production of nerve and cyanide gas before 1973.
- Former Egyptian Minister of War, General Abdel Ranny Gamassay, stated in 1975, that, "If Israel should decide to use a nuclear weapon in the battlefield, we shall use the weapons of mass destruction that are at our disposal."[5]
- Seems to have several production facilities for mustard and nerve gas. May have limited stocks of bombs, rockets, and shells.
- Unconfirmed reports of recent efforts to acquire feed stocks for nerve gas. Some efforts to obtain feed stocks from Canada. May now be building feed stock plants in Egypt.
- Industrial infrastructure present for rapid production of cyanide gas.

Biological Weapons

- Research and technical base.
- No evidence of major organized research activity.

Nuclear Weapons

- Low-level research effort. No evidence of more than basic research since the 1960s.

Libya's Search for Weapons of Mass Destruction

Delivery Systems

- Has developed a liquid-fueled missile with a range of 200 kilometers. No evidence of deployment.
- Al-Fatih solid-fueled missile with a range of 300–450 miles is reported to have been under development with the aid of German technical experts but there are no signs of successful development.
- FROG-7 rocket launchers with a range of 40 kilometers.
- Deployed 80 Scud B launchers with a range of 190 miles in 1976, but could not successfully operate system. Many of the launchers and missiles sold to Iran.
- Purchased SS-N-2C and SSC-3 cruise missiles. Little operational capability.
- Pursued other missile development programs with little success.
- Tu-22 bombers with minimal operational capability.
- Su-24 long range strike fighters. These are operational and have limited refueling capability using C-130s.

440   *Iraq and the War of Sanctions*

Table 11.1 (continued)

- Operational Mirage 5D/DE and 10 Mirage 5DD fighter ground attack aircraft.
- Mirage F-1AD fighter ground attack aircraft.
- MiG-23BM Flogger F and 14 MiG-23U fighter ground attack aircraft.
- Su-20 and Su-22 Fitter E, J. F fighter ground attack aircraft.
- Tube artillery and multiple rocket launchers.
- Fired Scud missiles against the Italian island of Lampadusa in 1987.

Chemical Weapons
- Claims will not sign CWC as long as other states have nuclear weapons.
- May have used mustard gas delivered in bombs by AN-26 aircraft in final phases of war against Chad in September, 1987.
- Pilot plant near Tripoli has been producing small amounts of chemical weapons since the early 1980s.
- Are probably two other small research/batch production facilities.
- Main nerve and mustard gas production facilities in an industrial park at chemical weapons plant at Rabta. This plant can produce both the poison gas and the bombs, shells, and warheads to contain it. Are probably two other research facilities.
  - Rabta Plant seems to have started test runs in mid-1988. It is a 30-building facility defended by SAM batteries and special troops. Has sheltered underground areas.
  - Libya has acquired large stocks of feedstocks for mustard gas like thiodiglycol, and precursors for nerve gas, and extensive amounts have been sent to Rabta.
  - At least 100 metric tons of blister and nerve agents have been produced at Rabta since the late 1980s, but production rate has been very low, and the plant is either not successful or is not being utilized because of fear of attack.
  - The plant would have a capacity of 100 metric tons per year if operated at full capacity.
  - Fabricated fire at Rabta in 1990 to try to disguise the function of the plant and the fact that it was operating.
- German courts have convicted a German national in October, 1996 for selling Libya a computer designed for use in chemical weapons programs and helping Libya import equipment to clean the waste emissions from poison gas production from India using an Irish dummy corporation.
- Additional major chemical weapons plant in construction in extensive underground site near Tarhunah, a mountainous area 65 kilometers southeast of Tripoli, but few recent signs of activity.
- Tarhunah has been designed to minimize its vulnerability to air attack and has twin tunnels 200–450 feet long, protected by 100 feet of sandstone above the tunnels and a lining of reinforced concrete. This is far beyond the penetration capabilities of the US GBU-27B and GBU-28 penetration bombs. The GBU-28 can penetrate a maximum of 25–30 meters of earth or 6 meters of concrete.

Table 11.1 (continued)

- Libya rejected the proposal of President Mubarak that it open the Tarhunah facility to third country inspection to prove it was not a chemical weapons facility in April, 1996.
- Reports of construction of another sheltered major facility near Sabha, 460 miles south of Tripoli.
- Reports of Chinese, North Korean, German, Swiss, and other European technical support and advisors.
- Reports of shipments of chemical weapons to Syria and Iran do not seem valid.
- Very low-quality weapons designs with poor fusing and lethality.

Biological Weapons

- Some early research activity.
- No evidence of production capability.

Nuclear Weapons

- Has sought to create a development and production capability, but no evidence of any real progress or success.
- Unsuccessfully attempted to buy nuclear weapons from China in the 1970s.
- Qaddhafi called for Libyan production of nuclear weapons on April 29, 1990.
- Has explored for uranium, but no active mines or uranium mills.
- 10 megawatt, Soviet-supplied nuclear research reactor at Tajura acquired from the USSR in the 1970s. Operates under IAEA safeguards.
- Had plan to build a 440-megawatt, Soviet-supplied reactor near the Gulf of Sidra in the 1970s, but canceled project.
- Ratified NPT is 1975. Declares all facilities under IAEA safeguards.
- Continues to train nuclear scientists and technicians abroad.

1. Note by the Secretary-General, "Report of the Secretary-General on the Activities of the Special Commission," S/1997/774, October 6, 1997, paragraphs 79–80.
2. Note by the Secretary-General, "Report of the Secretary-General on the Activities of the Special Commission," S/1997/774, October 6, 1997, paragraphs 81–82.
3. Note by the Secretary-General, "Report of the Secretary-General on the Activities of the Special Commission," S/1997/774, October 6, 1997, paragraph 83.
4. *Washington Post*, April 6, 1995, p. 1.
5. *Al-Ahram*, July 25, 1975; *Al-Akhbar*, July 25, 1975.

Source: Prepared by Anthony H. Cordesman, Co-Director, Middle East Program, CSIS.

Chapter 12

Iraq's Strategic Culture and Weapons of Mass Destruction

It is far easier to summarize what is known about Iraq's efforts to acquire weapons of mass destruction than it is to draw conclusions about the exact nature of its future strategy, development plans, doctrine, force plans, and war-fighting concepts. The sheer number of the Iraqi efforts listed in Table 11.1 demonstrate, however, that Iraq's "strategic culture" supports massive, if not grandiose, covert efforts and sees arms control agreements largely as a series of constraints that must be dealt with as part of proliferation.

Iraq has never focused on one type of weapon of mass destruction or one type of delivery system. It has always sought a wide range of biological, chemical, and nuclear weapons, and it has investigated a wide range of ways of employing them—ranging from short-range battlefield use to strategic attacks on cities. Iraq has never demonstrated that it links its development efforts to some specific employment doctrine, view of escalation, or some concept of deterrence, retaliation, and conflict termination. Instead, it has simply attempted to proliferate in every possible way, by all available means.

Iraq has also demonstrated that it is willing to take extreme risks with little warning. Iraq's attack on Iran, its near-genocidal attacks on its Kurds, and its invasion of Kuwait were all high-risk steps taken with little warning by a small decision-making elite, and possibly by one man. All of these decisions seem to have been taken relatively quickly, and to have expanded in scope during the months or weeks between the initial decision to act and the actual execution. While Iraq was not indifferent to risk, it often proved willing to escalate in ways that neither its neighbors nor Western experts predicted.

THE BEGINNING OF PROLIFERATION

There is no way to be sure precisely when Iraq began to proliferate, but is likely that it began before the Ba'ath and Saddam came to power. Iraq saw Egypt's use of chemical weapons against tribal forces and civilians during the Yemeni civil war in 1967–1968. It had to have been aware of the fact that Egypt and Syria began programs to acquire chemical and nuclear weapons following the Suez conflict of 1956, and that they were equipped for limited chemical warfare during the 1967 conflict with Israel. Iraq almost certainly knew that Egypt vastly expanded its chemical capabilities during 1967–1973, and definitely knew that Israel captured vast amounts of Egyptian chemical warfare defense gear in October, 1973.

Israel's possible acquisition of nuclear weapons began to be reported as early as 1956, and began to be a major subject of Arab concern in the early 1960s. This concern deepened following Israel's public announcement that it was building a nuclear reactor in Dimona, which was made in the Knesset on December 21, 1960. Iraq also became aware of the Shah's potential nuclear ambitions in the late 1960s, and had every opportunity to track his massive reactor orders and investment in Eurodif during the 1970s.

The detailed analysis which follows suggests that Iraq did not start major chemical and biological warfare programs until the 1980s, but it is clear that both its core programs and nuclear efforts began much earlier. During the 1970s, Iraq created a nuclear program which was clearly designed to give it nuclear weapons, and which might have done so if Israel had not used US-supplied fighters to destroy Iraq's Osirak complex on June 7, 1981. This was the beginning of an effort to acquire nuclear weapons, which has gone on ever since and which has been delayed—not halted—by the events of the Gulf War.

OPPORTUNISM AND UNCERTAINTY

This history helps explain why proliferation is only part of a much broader process of Iraqi "challenge and response" that is a logical result of Iraq's "strategic culture" and view of its neighbors and the West. While Iraq's post-war problems may be largely due to the repeated lies and aggressiveness of its own regime, no Iraqi can ignore the fact that virtually all of its neighbors joined the major Western powers in attacking its forces, driving it out of Kuwait, and in enforcing sanctions.

At least for the foreseeable future, Iraq's official policy towards proliferation will continue to be a mix of denial and lies, and occasional bluster and indirect threats. This declared policy will be internal as well as external, and will be told to its people, media, intellectuals, and military officers as well as to other nations. Iraq's core efforts will be covert, and only Saddam Hussein and a few trusted supporters will have any overview of Iraq's overall efforts and capabilities.

Iraq will almost certainly continue to exploit the line of least resistance in terms of sanctions, controls, and import restrictions. It will make a continuing effort to obtain anything it can by any means it can afford, then make extemporaneous efforts to exploit whatever capabilities it has at the time of a given crisis or confrontation. Since Iraq cannot predict the exact areas where it will be successful in evading or vitiating UN sanctions and controls, Iraqi procurement strategy, doctrine, and employment concepts will evolve on a target of opportunity basis and by responding to given contingencies as they arise.

At the same time, it is unlikely that Iraq's ruling elite has a detailed understanding of the full implications of Iraq's actions in using weapons of mass destruction, its war-fighting capabilities, or the technical and financial details of individual programs. Given Iraq's past experience, it is likely that its decision-making elite will have only an uncertain grasp of the technical details of lethality and other damage effects. It is also unlikely that Iraq's leaders will be able to think beyond what they want to happen, and objectively consider what other states will do or the retaliatory options open to a given enemy.

It is also doubtful that Iraqi proliferation is dependent on a given power elite or set of personalities. As has been touched upon earlier, a "quieter Saddam" who patiently waited to acquire significant nuclear or highly lethal biological warfare capabilities and then exploited such capabilities in a more cautious and calculating manner might prove to be a much more serious threat than Saddam, and even a relatively defensive Iraqi regime is likely to feel compelled to go on acquiring weapons of mass destruction to counterbalance the capabilities of Iran and Israel and to limit American power projection options.

Similarly, Iraq's efforts at proliferation had diverse and changing leadership from the mid-1970s to 1987. Hussein Kamel Hasan al-Majid, Saddam's son-in-law, then became the preeminent official shaping Iraq's military industries and efforts to procure weapons of mass destruction until his defection to Jordan in August, 1995. Hussein Kamel headed the Ministry of Industry and Military Industrialization until 1990, and oversaw Iraq's nuclear weapons research, continued Iraq's development of biological and chemical weapons, and supervised Iraq's successful development of the Al-Husayn missile by modifying the Scud. According to the CIA, Kamel may have directed Iraq's testing of its chemical and biological weapons on Iranian prisoners of war.[1]

Hussein Kamel continued to lead Iraq's efforts after the Gulf War—first as Minister of Defense and then as the director of the Ministry of Industry and Minerals and the Organization of Military Industrialization. His defection in 1995, however, had little impact on the program. CIA sources indicate that Qusay Hussein—Saddam's second son—assumed many of the responsibilities for concealing the proscribed programs.

Iraq has no shortage of technocrats and managers, and many of the leading scientists in Iraq's WMD programs during Hussein Kamel's tenure are still associated with the regime. For example, Lt. General Amir Hamud Sadi—who serves as a presidential advisor and leading official in Iraqi relations with UNSCOM—is one of the principal engineers of Iraq's efforts to proliferate, and served as Hussein Kamel's de facto deputy. Sadi has a doctorate in chemical engineering and has dedicated his entire career to conventional and nonconventional weapons development. Saddam Hussein publicly praised him in 1987 for his role in the development of the Al-Husayn missile.[2]

Somewhat ironically, Iraq's Minister of Culture and Information—Humam Abd al-Khaliq Abd al-Ghafur—is Iraq's leading nuclear official and the former head of its nuclear program. He too was a close associate of Hussein Kamel, and occasionally serves as an interlocutor with the IAEA. He led the Iraqi delegation to the IAEA annual conference in October, 1997.[3]

Other key technocrats include Jafar Dia Jafar, a leading Iraqi nuclear scientist who served as Abd al-Ghafur's deputy in the Iraqi Atomic Energy Organization. Jafar is now officially a presidential advisor, although he may be blamed for some of Iraq's failure to rush the development of a nuclear weapon in 1990–1991, and his position may no longer involve day-to-day control over Iraq's Nuclear program. An Iraqi woman, Dr. Rihab Taha, appears to be the leading official in charge of Iraq's biological weapons program until the cease-fire. While Iraq may be concealing the role of other biologists, she seems to have overseen Iraq's efforts to develop Anthrax and Botulinum toxin and to have directed testing on animal subjects. Like most successful Iraqi technocrats, Taha is highly political. She is married to the Minister of Oil, Amir Rashid Ubaydi, who helps direct Iraqi relations with UNSCOM.[4]

Like other proliferating nations, this does not mean that Iraq cannot be persuaded to sign more arms control agreements, or appear to honor them. Like diplomacy, Iraq is likely to see arms control as an extension of war by other means. It will attempt to use arms control to place limits on its rivals and opponents, while it treats arms control regimes and controls on technology transfer as problems it must solve with lies, concealment, and covert programs. In Iraq's case, and perhaps that of other Middle Eastern proliferators, trust will be impossible, and verification will be extremely difficult.

PERSISTENT EFFORTS TO ACQUIRE BIOLOGICAL, NUCLEAR, AND CHEMICAL WEAPONS

Iraq is likely to continue to seek to develop and deploy all three major types of weapons of mass destruction—biological, chemical, and nuclear—and to acquire advanced air and missile delivery systems. It will probably only prioritize its efforts to acquire such capabilities to the extent that it is forced to do so for resource reasons, because of continuing UNSCOM and IAEA efforts, or because of limitations on its access to foreign technology and materials. Iraq's past efforts have shown that its leaders are well aware of the different strengths and weakness of biological, chemical, and nuclear weapons, summarized in Table 12.1, and of their different lethality, which is illustrated in Table 12.2, and it seems unlikely that any new leaders or leadership elite will think differently.

As a result, it seems unlikely that Iraq's "strategic culture" will ever be satisfied with chemical weapons alone. Similarly, every problem Iraq encounters

Table 12.1
The Strengths and Weaknesses of Weapons of Mass Destruction

Chemical Weapons

Destructive Effects: Poisoning skin, lungs, nervous system, or blood. Contaminating areas, equipment, and protective gear for periods of hours to days. Forcing military units to don highly restrictive protection gear or use incapacitating antidotes. False alarms and panic. Misidentification of the agent, or confusion of chemical with biological agents (which may be mixed) leading to failure of defense measures. Military and popular panic and terror effects. Major medical burdens which may lead to mistreatment. Pressure to deploy high cost air and missile defenses. Paralysis or disruption of civil life and economic activity in threatened or attacked areas.

Typical Military Targets: Infantry concentrations, air bases, ships, ports, staging areas, command centers, munitions depots, cities, key oil and electrical facilities, desalinization plants.

Typical Military Missions: Killing military and civilian populations. Intimidation. Attack of civilian population or targets. Disruption of military operations by requiring protective measures or decontamination. Area or facility denial. Psychological warfare, production of panic, and terror.

Military Limitations: Large amounts of agents are required to achieve high lethality, and military and economic effects are not sufficiently greater than carefully targeted conventional strikes offering major war-fighting advantages. Most agents degrade quickly, and their effect is highly dependent on temperature and weather conditions, height of dissemination, terrain, and the character of built-up areas. Warning devices far more accurate and sensitive than for biological agents. Protective gear and equipment can greatly reduce effects, and sufficiently high numbers of rounds, sorties, and missiles are needed to ease the task of defense. Leave buildings and equipment reusable by the enemy, although persistent agents may require decontamination. Persistent agents may contaminate the ground the attacker wants to cross or occupy and force use of protective measures or decontamination.

Biological Weapons

Destructive Effects: Infectious disease or biochemical poisoning. Contaminating areas, equipment, and protective gear for periods of hours to weeks. Delayed effects and tailoring to produce incapacitation or death, treatable or non-treatable agents, and be infectious on contact only or transmittable. Forcing military units to don highly restrictive protection gear or use incapacitating vaccines antidotes. False alarms and panic. High risk of at least initial misidentification of the agent, or confusion of chemical with biological agents (which may be mixed) leading to failure of defense measures. Military and popular panic and terror effects. Major medical burdens which may lead to mistreatment. Pressure to deploy high cost air and missile defenses. Paralysis or disruption of civil life and economic activity in threatened or attacked areas.

Typical Military Targets: Infantry concentrations, air bases, ships, ports, staging areas, command centers, munitions depots, cities, key oil and electrical facilities, desalinization plants. Potentially fare more effective against military and civil area targets than chemical weapons.

Typical Military Missions: Killing and incapacitation of military and civilian populations. Intimidation. Attack of civilian population or targets. Disruption of military operations by requiring protective measures or decontamination. Area or facility denial. Psychological warfare, production of panic, and terror.

Table 12.1 (continued)

Military Limitations: Most wet agents degrade quickly, although spores, dry encapsulated agents, and some toxins are persistent. Effects usually take some time to develop (although not in the case of some toxins). Effects are unpredictable and are even more dependent than chemical weapons on temperature and weather conditions, height of dissemination, terrain, and the character of built-up areas. Major risk of contaminating the wrong area. Warning devices uncertain and may misidentify the agent. Protective gear and equipment can reduce effects. Leave buildings and equipment reusable by the enemy, although persistent agents may require decontamination. Persistent agents may contaminate the ground the attacker wants to cross or occupy and force use of protective measures or decontamination. More likely than chemical agents to cross the threshold where nuclear retaliation seems justified.

Nuclear Weapons

Destructive Effects: Blast, fire, and radiation. Destruction of large areas and production of fallout and contamination—depending on character of weapon and height of burst. Contaminating areas, equipment, and protective gear for periods of hours to days. Forcing military units to don highly restrictive protection gear and use massive amounts of decontamination gear. Military and popular panic and terror effects. Massive medical burdens. Pressure to deploy high cost air and missile defenses. Paralysis or disruption of civil life and economic activity in threatened or attacked areas. High long term death rates from radiation. Forced dispersal of military forces and evacuation of civilians. Destruction of military and economic centers, and national political leadership and command authority, potentially altering character of attacked nation and creating major recovery problems.

Typical Military Targets: Hardened targets, enemy facilities and weapons of mass destruction, enemy economy, political leadership, and national command authority. Infantry and armored concentrations, air bases, ships, ports, staging areas, command centers, munitions depots, cities, key oil and electrical facilities, desalinization plants.

Typical Military Missions: Forced dispersal of military forces and evacuation of civilians. Destruction of military and economic centers, and national political leadership and command authority, potentially altering character of attacked nation and creating major recovery problems.

Military Limitations: High cost. Difficulty of acquiring more than a few weapons. Risk of accidents or failures that hit friendly territory. Crosses threshold to level where nuclear retaliation is likely. Destruction or contamination of territory and facilities attacker wants to cross or occupy. High risk of massive collateral damage to civilians if this is important to attacker.

Source: Adapted by Anthony H. Cordesman from the Office of Technology Assessment, *Proliferation of Weapons of Mass Destruction: Assessing the Risks*, Washington, US Congress OTA-ISC-559, August, 1993, pp. 56–57.

in nuclear proliferation is likely to lead it to increase its efforts to acquire and deploy biological weapons of similar lethality. Table 12.2 makes the reasons for these motives clear. Chemical weapons are far less lethal than biological and nuclear weapons. Nuclear weapons may confer more status in terms of perceived lethality, but biological weapons can be as—or more—lethal than the kind of nuclear weapon that Iraq is likely to acquire during the next decade.

Accordingly, Iraq has good reason to covertly pursue biological weapons as

Table 12.2
The Comparative Effects of Biological, Chemical, and Nuclear Weapons Delivered Against a Typical Urban Target in the Middle East

<u>Using missile warheads</u>: Assumes one Scud-sized warhead with a maximum payload of 1,000 kilograms. The study assumes that the biological agent would not make maximum use of this payload capability because of design problems. It is uncertain that this assumption is realistic.

	Area Covered in Square Kilometers	Deaths Assuming 3,000–10,000 People per Square Kilometer
<u>Chemical</u>: 300 kilograms of Sarin nerve gas with a density of 70 milligrams per cubic meter	0.22	60–200
<u>Biological</u>: 30 kilograms of Anthrax spores with a density of 0.1 milligram per cubic meter	10.0	30,000–100,000
<u>Nuclear</u>:		
One 12.5 kiloton nuclear device achieving 5 pounds per cubic inch of over-pressure	7.8	23,000–80,000
One 1 megaton hydrogen bomb	190.0	570,000–1,900,000

<u>Using one aircraft delivering 1,000 kilograms of Sarin nerve gas or 100 kilograms of Anthrax spores</u>: Assumes that the aircraft flies in a straight line over the target at optimal altitude and dispenses the agent as an aerosol. The study assumes that the biological agent would not make maximum use of this payload capability because this is inefficient. It is unclear if this is realistic.

	Area Covered in Square Kilometers	Deaths Assuming 3,000–10,000 People per Square Kilometer
<u>Clear, sunny day, light breeze</u>		
Sarin nerve gas	0.74	300–700
Anthrax spores	46.0	130,000–460,000
<u>Overcast day or night, moderate wind</u>		
Sarin nerve gas	0.8	400–800
Anthrax spores	140.0	420,000–1,400,000
<u>Clam, clear night</u>		
Sarin nerve gas	7.8	3,000–8,000
Anthrax spores	300.0	1,000,000–3,000,000

Source: Adapted by Anthony H. Cordesman from the Office of Technology Assessment, *Proliferation of Weapons of Mass Destruction: Assessing the Risks*, Washington, US Congress OTA-ISC-559, August, 1993, pp. 53–54.

a substitute for nuclear weapons, as well as for their intrinsic war-fighting capabilities. Indeed, the more effective outside powers are in denying Iraq nuclear materials, the more Iraq is likely to pursue biological weapons as a substitute—particularly because any Iraqi leadership will know that Iran is making similar efforts, and that no present arms control or export control regime offers any meaningful prospect of denying either Iran or Iraq the ability to conduct a silent arms race in this area.

At the same time, Iraq's leaders must be fully aware that biological and nuclear weapons are not interchangeable. As Tables 12.1 and 12.2 show, such weapons require different employment doctrines and are best delivered using different types of delivery systems. Iraq's leaders also have to be aware that the perceptual balance is of major importance in determining Iraq's ability to use proliferation to achieve political and strategic ends, and that both regional and Western political leaders perceive nuclear weapons as the most "lethal" form of weapon, and that nuclear weapons confer the most status in terms of how the other nations in the region will view Iraq. As a result, it is neither prudent nor cost-effective for Iraq to make hard choices between its final mix of biological and nuclear weapons and key delivery systems, until it knows what it can and cannot acquire and the probable lethality of such weapons.

THE IMPACT OF OTHER PROLIFERATORS

Finally, developments in Iraq will interact with the strengths and weaknesses of other proliferators. This is not a reassuring prospect. With the possible exception of Israel, no Middle Eastern ruling elite is likely to develop a good understanding of the strategic consequences of using weapons of mass destruction, the operational effectiveness and reliability of weapons of mass destruction, and the ability to accurately assess the damage inflicted on an opponent or retaliatory damage.

A combination of the ongoing regional arms race and US counter-proliferation efforts may make some of these uncertainties even worse. The uncertain survivability of weapons, delivery systems, and C^4I/BM capabilities may encourage most regional proliferators to consider preemption, launch on warning, launch under attack, and sudden moves to high levels of escalation. The risks inherent in overt attacks may encourage covert and unconventional attacks and/or the use of terrorist and extremist proxies. Further, all or none or these pressures may affect behavior in a given crisis, and strategic predictability is likely to prove a dangerous fantasy.

NOTES

1. CIA background paper of February 13, 1998.
2. CIA background paper of February 13, 1998.
3. CIA background paper of February 13, 1998.
4. CIA background paper of February 13, 1998.

Chapter 13

Iraq's Artillery Delivery Systems

Some Western analyses of the interaction between Iraq's delivery systems and weapons of mass destruction focus on ballistic missiles. There are good reasons, however, why such a focus may be misleading. As has been noted earlier, Iraq must plan for theater-level war with Iran. Its actions since 1991 show that it is willing to make major deployments in the direction of Kuwait and Saudi Arabia, and it must understand that it cannot win a significant tactical or theater-level conflict with US-supported Southern Gulf forces using conventional arms.

Iraq began chemical warfare by using artillery, rocket launchers, helicopters, and aircraft. It knows it can sustain major forces using such weapons under the terms of the UN cease-fire accords, and that it faces serious near to mid-term difficulties in acquiring and deploying ballistic missiles with ranges in excess of 150 kilometers. Further, Iraq has to understand that covert or proxy attacks offer it significant advantages in terms of cost and deniability.

IRAQI ARTILLERY

Iraq made massive use of artillery weapons and multiple rocket launchers from 1982 onward during the Iran-Iraq War. It initially used such weapons in massed fire with conventional rounds to defend against Iranian mass infantry attacks. As is discussed later, in the section on chemical weapons, it slowly expanded its ability to fire mustard and then nerve gas. It used such fire to halt attacks, attack rear areas, provide area denial, panic Iranian forces, and support Iraqi offensive maneuvers. Iraq never developed the capability to rapidly maneuver artillery, rapidly shift fire, target effectively beyond visual range, and conduct complex combined operations, but its performance gradually became more sophisticated, and artillery and chemical weapons played a critical role in Iraq's defense from 1984 onward, and its defeat of Iran in 1988.

It is not surprising, therefore, that Iraq gave high priority to creating large stockpiles of chemical rounds and developing biological rounds, and organized its artillery forces for possible chemical combat during the Gulf War. While it did not deploy chemical rounds to forward artillery units, it deployed massive numbers of rounds in Iraq and in some support areas in the KTO. Every artillery unit in the KTO had full instruction for the use of chemical weapons, as did higher echelon headquarters. Further, Iraqi forces were generally equipped with chemical defense gear, although Iraq had good reason to know that Coalition forces did not possess such weapons, and that the only risk was fratricide.

UNSCOM has deprived Iraq of most of its inventory of chemical and biological shells and rockets, and of its large-scale production capabilities. Time alone would make many of Iraq's shells and rockets useless because of the poor purity of their chemical agent. As a result, it may be some time before Iraq achieves a significant breakout capability in using such weapons once UN controls are lifted. Iraq also seems likely to give longer-range systems priority as long as its resources are limited, or it must keep them covert, because this has higher political priority.

There is, however, no hard information to confirm Iraq's claims to UNSCOM that it has actually destroyed its inventories of biologically armed shells and rockets. Iraq had so many chemical rounds before UNSCOM began its efforts, that it may retain enough rounds for at least one major engagement. There are also 550 155 mm artillery shells filled with mustard gas that Iraq has claimed were destroyed during the war, but for which it has never provided any supporting evidence.[1]

Further, UNSCOM cannot possibly hope to detect a covert program designed to purify Iraq's agents and make them more storable, improve the lethality of the agent, and improve the fusing and dispersal of its warheads. Iraq also has had more than half a decade in which to improve its artillery organization and training, as well as aspects of its C^4I/SR system that would improve its ability to use chemical and biological rounds.

Iraq also has good reason to retain such chemical and biological capabilities. Wars rarely repeat themselves, but no Iraqi planner or military officer can ignore the possibility that further land/air battles may take place with Iran, other Gulf states, or the United States, and that artillery weapons and rocket launchers offer a way of delivering very large volumes of fire for ranges of 20–40 kilometers. Unless the Iraqi regime changes radically in character and Iran becomes open enough to offer a very high probability that it has ceased to proliferate, no Iraqi leadership elite will be able to ignore the fact that Iran has steadily improved its ability to use artillery and rockets to deliver chemical and potentially biological weapons. Tactics may not have the glamour of strategy, but there may yet be intensive land combat using chemical and possibly biological weapons at the short-range, tactical level. Iraq could use them to strike at rear echelons and advancing offensive forces, achieve tactical area denial, panic or paralyze enemy ground forces, and clear lines of advance.

Iraq retains significant assets of long-range tube artillery. It has about 1,500 towed artillery weapons (105 mm, 122 mm, 130 mm, and 155 mm). It also has around 150 self-propelled artillery weapons (2S1 122 mm, 2S3 152 mm, M-109A/1/A2 and GCT AuF-1) and 4,000–5,000 (60 mm, 81 mm, 120 mm, 160 mm) mortars. These totals compare with 3,000–5,000 towed weapons and 500 self-propelled tube weapons before the Gulf War.

The unclassified data available on Iraq's holdings of multiple rocket launchers are too contradictory to make a precise estimate of wartime losses, but it is clear that many such weapons were destroyed or abandoned in the Kuwaiti Theater of Operations. However, Iraq seems to retain around 120 such weapons (240 mm, 140 mm, Astros I, Astros II, BM-21, 122 mm). It also seems to retain many of its pre-war holdings of the FROG surface-to-surface rocket launchers, and at least several hundred rockets.[2]

Iraq had over 350 self-propelled mortars mounted on armored vehicles before the Gulf War. These do not seem to have been heavily committed to the Kuwaiti Theater of Operations, and Iraq probably retained several hundred of such weapons after the Gulf conflict. Iraq also retained large numbers of towed 81 mm and 120 mm Soviet mortars. It is at least possible that it might equip some weapons with chemical rounds, and Iraq might choose to develop chemical mines.

IRAQI LONG-RANGE UNGUIDED ROCKETS

Iraq also has long-range unguided rockets and has experience in using them. It had FROG rockets when the Iran-Iraq War started, and Iraq began to fire FROG-7s during the first weeks of the conflict. It soon found, however, that these rockets had little military effect. They lacked the lift to carry an effective conventional warhead, and Iraq lacked any means of effective beyond-visual-range (BVR) targeting.

A good example of such ineffectiveness occurred early in the war when Iraq fired four FROG-7 surface-to-surface rockets in an attempt to disorganize some of the staging areas of the Iranian army near Dezful and Ahwaz. The rockets exploded without any military effect, and it is easy to understand the reasons why. The FROG-7, which is also called the R65A or Luna, was designed for nuclear attack, and it has never had more than marginal effectiveness as a conventional weapon.

The FROG has a single stage solid propellant rocket motor. It was first exhibited in 1967. It is 9.0 meters long, 61 centimeters in diameter, and weighs 5,727 kilograms. There is no guidance system other than a spin-stabilized ballistic trajectory. If any trajectory correction is made after launch, it will begin during boost. After boost, the trajectory is ballistic. The FROG's warhead weight is 455 kilograms, and its maximum range is 60 kilometers. The FROG-7 can also carry a nuclear or chemical warhead. It is normally mounted upon and launched from a wheeled erector launcher called the ZIL-135. The main nozzle is surrounded by a ring of much smaller nozzles, and the system is far superior in reliability and accuracy to early FROGs.[3]

The FROG-7's lack of weapons accuracy, lethality, and targeting capability soon forced Iraq to limit its FROG firings to disruptive or "terror" strikes on cities and large economic targets, rather than on military targets or assembly areas. Even then, the resulting fire was so inaccurate when the target was beyond visual range that it often missed the targets or exploded without any meaningful psychological or military effect. For example, the small town of Andimeshk was hit by a FROG rocket early in the war, despite the fact that it had no military or economic value. Later analysis indicated that the rocket was almost certainly meant to strike Dezful and had failed to strike a city-sized target.[4] According to one estimate, Iraq fired 10 FROGs in 1980, 54 in 1981, one in 1982, and two in 1984, for a total of 67 missiles.[5] Even so, Iraq's FROG-7 operators continued to have serious problems finding a meaningful use for the missile, and the FROG never proved to be an effective conventional weapon.

Iraq did, however, improve the training of its FROG crews during the Iran-Iraq War, and improved their ability to site the rocket launcher adequately and provide proper targeting coordinates. It also carried out several development programs. It claimed to have developed its own cluster munitions warhead version of the FROG, called the Laith 90, with a range of 90 kilometers. It also claimed to have developed an Ababil 100 artillery rocket system using a 400 mm diameter rocket mounted in a four launcher canister on a truck. Iraq claimed this rocket has a maximum range of 100 kilometers and a warhead with either 300 anti-tank fragmentation bomblets or 25 anti-tank minelets.[6]

Iraq did not use long-range rockets during the Gulf War, and there do not seem to be any reliable unclassified data on Iraq's current holdings of such systems. It is unclear what Iraq's current holdings of the FROG are, and whether its efforts to produce its own systems have led to significant deployments. Iraq may also choose not to arm the long-range rockets it does have with weapons of mass destruction, as long as UNSCOM can inspect them—as they are obvious areas for UNSCOM concern. Nevertheless, such systems do offer Iraq a number of potential advantages—particularly in delivering biological weapons.

While Iraq may be hiding artillery rounds with biological weapons, and can certainly manufacture them when it can evade UNSCOM inspection, it is not clear whether Iraq found such rounds particularly effective during its pre–Gulf War tests and exercises. With the possible exception of toxins, artillery delivery of biological weapons presents serious safety, control, and fratricide problems. However, unguided artillery rockets offer safer standoff ranges, are much cheaper than guided missiles, and can easily be dispersed and hidden in ways that make them difficult to detect and attack. Further, rockets will remain attractive delivery systems as long as Iraq cannot openly deploy missiles with ranges in excess of 150 kilometers, and faces the near certainty of rapid US air supremacy.

In summary, Iraq's mix of artillery and rockets could easily support substantial chemical war fighting at the Corps level, if Iraq has concealed or can build the necessary rounds. Iraq might also use chemical rounds for terror and tactical purposes in firing at targets in Kuwait, US forces, and ships, and hostile Kurdish enclaves. The main deterrent would be the fear of military retaliation and the political cost of using chemical and biological rounds—factors that may limit their use to conflicts that threaten the security of Iraq's ruling elite.

IRAQ'S "SUPER GUNS"

It seems unlikely that Iraq will revive the advanced "gun" systems it attempted to develop as part of "Project Babylon," or use them to deliver weapons of mass destruction—particularly given the high profile trials of some of Iraq's former Western suppliers.[7] These "super guns" were designed by Dr. Gerald Bull, a Canadian ballistics expert who was murdered outside of his home in Brussels on March 22, 1990. They were an extension of work that Bull had done earlier for the United States and Canada in what was called "Project Harp."[8] Bull's primary interest was in using advanced solid-propellant gun technology to launch satellites, and he headed a firm called the Space Research Corporation (SRC), which was headquartered in Brussels.[9]

UN inspection teams found after the war that Iraq had a 356 mm gun, and confirmed earlier intelligence reports that Iraq was building two 1,000 mm prototype guns. The 356 mm experimental gun had been operational for several years and had been tested seven times. However, the gun had only been tested at relatively short ranges for proof of principle: it had not been used for about a year before the Gulf War, and it had little military value. It was built into the slope of a mountain at Jabal Hamrayn, near Bir Ugla, about 200 kilometers north of Baghdad.[10] It fired a projectile of 75 kilograms (165 pounds), but it could only carry 15 kilograms (30 pounds) of high explosive. While some of its design data claimed a maximum range of 750 kilometers, its real-world range was probably about 150 kilometers (93 miles) to 180 kilometers (120 miles), and it was not particularly accurate even within its fixed trajectory.[11]

Neither of the 1,000 mm guns were assembled, and only one had sufficient components to indicate that it might be operational in the near future.[12] Iraq had ordered large amounts of propellants to be used for the gun from a firm in Belgium, and parts from Britain and Switzerland.[13] Data released by the UN inspection teams also indicate that each gun was to be in 26 sections and about 160 meters long (the length of one and a half football fields). They calculated that it was designed to fire a 1,000 kilogram (2,200 pounds) projective with 408 kilograms (898 pounds) of high explosive or payload.[14] Some experts estimate that it would have been able to fire weapons of mass destruction at ranges range of up to 1,000 miles; others that it was designed to put payloads of 300 to 500 pounds into orbit.[15]

There are indications that Iraq planned to use the guns as weapons and to arm them with biological shells, although it is unclear whether these plans ever moved beyond the conceptual stage. The design of such a shell would have been extremely complicated, and Bull does not seem to have worked on such a design. It is very doubtful that Iraq could have designed such a round. Such a design would challenge the design, manufacturing, test, and evaluation capabilities of even the most sophisticated country.[16]

In short, these "super guns" seem to have been technically impressive "super toys." They were at best rail mobile, and it is very doubtful that the 1,000 mm gun could have been moved without disassembly. Once such a gun fires, its trajectory can be used to target it. As a result, the only feasible way to employ such a weapon would be in the kind of deep-sheltered facility designed to fire against a fixed target that Nazi Germany built in France during World War II to strike London. Although this facility launched what became called the "V-3," it consisted of multiple batteries of pump guns somewhat similar to Bull's designs, which could have fired several rounds an hour.[17]

It is unclear whether they can lift enough payload to launch a satellite for most military purposes, or whether most of the required sensor, processing, and communications technologies could withstand the shock of firing the gun. They are costly and present major problems in terms of designing a reliable shell that can effectively disperse biological agents, and their rate of fire seems to be too slow for high-volume delivery of chemical weapons. They might, however, be more suitable as terror weapons, and Iraq's actions have been so grandiose in the past that it is impossible to totally discount the possibility that it could revive the program.

NOTES

1. Note by the Secretary-General, "Report by the Secretary-General on the Activities of the Special Commission, established by the Secretary-General," UN Security Council, S/1997/774, October 6, 1997, paragraph 61.

2. Sources in addition to those cited at the start of this section include interviews in London, December, 1991, and April, 1993, in Switzerland and Israel, January, 1992, in Switzerland, January, 1993, IISS data, and the views of other experts as of May, June, October, and November, 1993; the IISS estimate is similar to the author's. Also see *Jane's Defense Weekly*, February 22, 1992, p. 284; *Jerusalem Post*, January 25, 1992, p. 9; *New York Times*, March 12, 1992, p. A-10; *Washington Times*, January 20, 1992, p. 10; *Washington Post*, November 7, 1991, p. A-46, November 14, 1991, p. A-47, March 13, 1992, p. A-19; *Wall Street Journal*, November 11, 1991, p. A-19; *Jane's Defense Weekly*, November 16, 1991, p. 926, February 22, 1992, pp. 284; *The Estimate*, November 22–December 5, 1991, p. 1; Michael Eisenstadt, "Recent Changes in Saddam's Inner Circle: Cracks in the Wall?" *Policywatch*, No. 22, November 22, 1991, pp. 1–2; Defense News, February 24, 1992, p. 1.

3. *The World's Missile Systems, Seventh Edition,* General Dynamics, Pomona Division, April, 1982, pp. 65–66.

4. Scott James, "Does Western Technology Offset Larger Soviet Numbers?", *Defense Electronics,* February, 1981.

5. Steven Zaloga, "Ballistic Missiles in the Third World," *International Defense Review,* 11/88, pp. 1423–1437.

6. *London Financial Times,* July 26, 1989, p. 20; *Jane's Defense Weekly,* May 13, 1989, p. 837; April 22, 1989, p. 687, August 12, 1989, p. 255, September 30, 1989, p. 674; *Defense News,* May 8, 1989, p. 6; *International Defense Review,* 6/1989, pp. 835–841.

7. Considerable debate has taken place since the war as to whether British officials knew about the gun much earlier and could have prevented earlier deliveries of equipment to Iraq. *Washington Post,* January 16, 1992, p. 11; *London Financial Times,* January 22, 1992, p. 6.

8. Project Harp had tested a gun based on combining two 16" guns bored out to a caliber of 16.69 inches with a total caliber length of L/86. This project demonstrated that such a device could launch 185 pound payloads up to altitudes of 118 miles (200 kilometers). Bull had claimed that such a device using a solid propellant rocket could deliver a 272 kilogram payload to ranges of 1,150 miles (1,852 kilometers), and 90 kilograms to 2,000 miles (3,200) kilometers. In addition to helping Israel develop 175 mm guns rounds that reached ranges of 40 kilometers, Bull and SRC had previously helped Iraq develop its own Majnoon 155 mm and Al Faw 210 mm artillery weapons. *Jane's Defense Weekly,* April 28, 1990, pp. 770–771, June 2, 1990, p. 1063; *Washington Post,* April 19, 1990, p. A-37; *Economist,* May 5, 1990, p. 99; *Aviation Week,* May 7, 1990, p. 88; *Nature,* April 26, 1990, p. 811.

9. The Space Research Corporation had also done extensive work for Israel. Other firms involved may have included Societa delle Funcine, Firpas SrL and Italian Technology Innovation SrL of Italy; Amalgamated Trading Industries of Belgium; Advanced Technology Institute of Athens; PRB of Belgium, and Astra Defense Systems of the UK. It is uncertain how many of these firms were knowingly involved, or if they were involved at all. *Jane's Defense Weekly,* April 28, 1990, pp. 770–771; *Washington Post,* April 19, 1990, p. A-37; *London Sunday Times,* April 22, 1990, p. 1.

10. William Lowther, *Iraq and the Supergun,* London, Pan, 1992, pp. 226; Reuters, February 1, 1997, 0712.

11. The gun was aimed in the general direction of Israel. *Jane's Defense Weekly,* April 24, 1990, November 24, 1990, September 14, 1991, pp. 458–459; *Defense News,* November 11, 1991, p. 4; *US News and World Report,* November 25, 1991, p. 36; US Department of Defense, *Conduct of the Persian Gulf War: Final Report,* Washington, Department of Defense, April, 1992, pp. 16–18; *New York Times,* September 7, 1989, p. A-9.

12. Some sources estimate a barrel length of 153–160 meters. *Nature,* April 26, 1990, p. 811; *International Defense Review,* 5/1990, p. 481; *Financial Times,* April 18, 1990, p. 22, May 2, 1990, p. 18; *The Middle East,* March, 1990, pp. 17–18.

13. *London Financial Times,* February 20, 1992, p. 8, February 28, 1992, p. 6. The British firm of Matrix Churchill played a significant role in the program, as did the Swiss firm Von Roll. A US firm called Kennametal, Inc. of Pittsburgh has been accused of selling equipment that might have been used in the supergun effort, but the evidence is

ambiguous. *The Philadelphia Inquirer*, February 18, 1992, p. 1; *Wall Street Journal*, January 31, 1992, p. 3; Reuters, February 1, 1997, 0712.

14. *Jane's Defense Weekly*, September 14, 1991, pp. 458–459; *Defense News*, November 11, 1991, p. 4; *Philadelphia Inquirer*, October 9, 1991, p. 12.

15. *Philadelphia Inquirer*, October 9, 1991, p. 12; *US News and World Report*, November 25, 1991, p. 36.

16. The Space Research Corporation had also done extensive work for Israel. Other firms involved may have included Societa delle Funcine, Firpas SrL and Italian Technology Innovation SrL of Italy; Amalgamated Trading Industries of Belgium; Advanced Technology Institute of Athens; PRB of Belgium, and Astra Defense Systems of the UK. It is uncertain how many of these firms were knowingly involved, or if they were involved at all. *Jane's Defense Weekly*, April 28, 1990, pp. 770–771; *Washington Post*, April 19, 1990, p. A-37; *London Sunday Times*, April 22, 1990, p. 1.

17. The underground facility at Mimoyecques in Western France was nearly complete at the time of the Allied invasion of Normandy. It involved a deep underground facility with four sets of five launchers. It is not clear whether the weapon would have worked, but Churchill gave the destruction of this facility top priority to prevent any risk of German recapture.

Chapter 14

Iraq's Air Delivery Systems

The Iraqi air force has always been something of a hollow force. It did not perform well during the Iran-Iraq War in either tactical or strategic missions, and it did not play any significant role in the Gulf War. Iraq has, however, had half a decade to rethink how it might employ its strike aircraft in missions using weapons of mass destruction. Iran has already produced and used chemical bombs, and it has produced biological bombs. Iraq's leadership faces significant near to mid-term problems in deploying large numbers of ballistic missiles and also faces significant constraints on missile warhead testing. It may also feel that many of its older aircraft are expendable if they are dedicated to missions using weapons of mass destruction, and that even its best strike aircraft can be used in one-way missions that greatly extend their range or ability to use very low altitude flight and evasive attack patterns.

Despite its losses, the Iraqi air force's total surviving inventory of combat aircraft seems to include 6 Tu-22s, 1–2 Tu-16s, 30 Mirage F-1s, 15 MiG-29s, 60 MiG-23s, 15 MiG-25s, 150 MiG-21s, 30 Su-25s, and 60 Su-17s, Su-20s, Su-22s.[1] Iraq has recently been able to fly peaks of 100 sorties per day, although many of these aircraft have been low-grade fighters and trainers, and it is not clear whether the bombers are still operational.

Iraq retains large numbers of combat-capable trainers, transport aircraft and helicopters, and remotely piloted vehicles. The trainers include some Mirage F-1BQs, 25 PC-7s, 30 PC-9s, 50–60 Tucanos (EMB-312s), 40 L-29s, and 40 L-39s. Transport assets include a mix of Soviet An-2, An-12, An-24, An-26, and Il-76 jets and propeller aircraft, and some Il-76s modified to act as tankers. The remotely piloted vehicles (RPVs) include some Iraqi-made designs, Italian designs, and Soviet designs. It is unclear how effective Iraq was in using any of these RPV systems, but it did make use of them during the Gulf War.[2]

As Table 14.1 shows, Iraq could dedicate almost any part of its air force to medium-to-long-range missions using weapons of mass destruction against area targets. It may also be able to modify otherwise unusable aircraft for single missions or as unguided drones. While Iraq could not mass large numbers of aircraft and sustain high sortie rates, it could probably mass aircraft to deliver significant numbers of chemical weapons against a force that did not have excellent air cover and ground-based air defense. It could easily use limited numbers of aircraft, drones, or RPVs to deliver chemical or biological weapons against rear area, interdiction, or strategic targets.

Iraq also has the technology to adapt some of its tactical strike fighters as dedicated delivery systems designed to deliver a line-source attack with a biological agent. These attacks would probably not be effective in penetrating a US-controlled fighter screen backed by systems like the Patriot, the AWACS/E-2C, and the Aegis, but Iraq might commit aircraft to long-range, low-altitude strike profiles with a reasonable probability that some could penetrate Iranian and all but the best prepared Southern Gulf air defenses.[3]

It is possible that Iraq might use helicopters to deliver chemical and biological weapons. Iraq used helicopters from the early 1980s onward to deliver chemical weapons against Iranian and Kurdish forces, with growing success in mountain areas. The Iraqi army seems to possess about 120 armed helicopters, including 20 PAH-1 (Bo-105) attack helicopters. No reliable estimate exists of its surviving heavy, medium, and light transports and utility helicopters, but it seems likely that Iraq retains as many as 200–300.[4] The very fact that much of its helicopter force is now incapable of high-intensity combat operations may lead Iraq to consider employing selected aircraft in limited numbers of chemical and biological attacks using the helicopter as a sprayer, or in line-source attacks using dry, storable biological agents. While helicopters are vulnerable and shorter ranged than strike aircraft, they are almost ideal platforms for medium-range biological attacks—particularly if flown in one-way dedicated attacks.

Helicopters provide a high degree of mobility and dispersal, can fly nap of the earth profiles at low speeds that make them difficult to counterattack, and line-source attacks using biological agents, toxins, or persistent nerve gases might be delivered against enemy rear areas sufficiently upwind to be outside of the detection range of SHORAD radars and anti-aircraft weapons.

While there are no unclassified data that provide a clear indication of how Iraq intends to employ its aircraft, its seems almost certain the Iraq has retained some capability to deliver chemical and biological bombs, and that it has exploited the five years since the end of the Gulf War to covertly improve its capability to use fixed and rotary-wing aircraft to deliver biological and chemical weapons. At the same time, any Iraqi efforts to use aircraft in such missions are likely to be subject to the same constraints as Iraq's use of any other delivery system. As long as sanctions and UNSCOM are still in place, planning and preparation will be highly covert and compartmentalized. The actual employment of aircraft in such missions will be highly contingency driven and shaped

Table 14.1
Possible Air Delivery Systems*

Type	Cruise Speed (kilometers/hour) Low**	High	Nominal Range (kilometers)*** Low	High	Maximum Payload (kilograms)
Possible Iraqi Strike Aircraft					
MiG-21	880	800	-	480	1,500
MiG-23	960	950	450	950	3,000
MiG-27	960	890	390	600	4,500
MiG-29	960	890	-	1,150	-
Su-24	930	950	320	1,130	8,000
Mirage F-1	980	980	640	-	4,000
Other Regional Strike Aircraft					
A-4	-	810	-	1,230	4,500
Alphajet	740	710	170	890	2,800
F-4	-	890	-	840	5,900
F-5	-	860	-	310	3,200
F-14	-	980	-	950	4,500
F-15	-	980	-	1,440	10,700
F-16	-	920	550	930	5,400
F/A-18	-	900	-	740	7,700
Hawk	920	780	-	185	2,950
Jaguar	960	880	-	850	4,750
Mirage III	970	950	830	-	1,810
Mirage 5/50	970	950	630	-	4,200
Mirage 2000	-	950	-	690	6,300
Q-5/A-5 Fantan	-	-	400	600	2,000
Su-17/20/22	950	950	430	680	4,000
Tornado IDS	-	820	-	1,390	6,800
Tu-16	-	750	-	2,180	9,000
Tu-22 (Blinder)	-	750	-	1,500	10,000
Tu-22M (Backfire)	-	860	-	4,430	12,000

*Excludes modifications of cruise missiles and RPVs/UAVs, or possible developments of such systems. Egypt, Israel, Iran, Iraq, Libya, and Syria have systems with the capability to be modified for the land attack role and/or some development capability to create such systems.

**Low = Lo-Lo-Lo profile, high = Hi-Lo-Hi profile. Excludes refueling and one-way missions with more than double range. Trade-offs can be made between range and payload in most cases. Some air defense fighters are included, which could be used for such missions because of exceptional flight performance.

***Performance varies sharply with specific variant.

Source: Adapted by Anthony H. Cordesman from the Office of the Secretary of Defense, *Proliferation: Threat and Response*, Washington, Department of Defense, April, 1996 and IISS, *Military Balance, 1996–1997*.

by Saddam or a small political coterie in Iraq's senior leadership, rather than by some cadre of professional military officers. This could lead Iraq to play "wild cards" that are highly unpredictable.

NOTES

1. The IISS estimates are similar.
2. In addition to the source listed at the start of the Iraq section, see Kenneth Katzman, Iraq: Future Policy Options,'' Congressional Research Service, CRS 91–596F, December 12, 1991, pp. 23–30; FBIS, October 13, 1991; *Washington Times*, August 2, 1991, p. B-5; *London Financial Times*, October 4, 1991, p. 4; Associated Press, AM cycle, June 12, 1991; *New York Times*, March 25, 1991, p. A-1.
3. The author participated in one such exercise during the time he was stationed at the US embassy in Tehran.
4. The IISS estimates 500. It is doubtful that this many are operational.

Chapter 15

Iraq's Missile Capabilities

It is as dangerous to discount Iraq's interest in missiles as it is to discount its possible use of other delivery systems. Table 11.1 has shown that Iraq has invested billions of dollars in importing missiles and creating missile production facilities. It has also conducted two major missile wars. The first was during the Iran-Iraq War, where Iran initiated large-scale ballistic missile attacks, but which Iraq dominated by developing extended-range missiles and firing them at far greater rates than Iran could match. Iraq fired a total of 516 Scud and Improved Scud missiles during that conflict. The second missile war took place during the Gulf War, when Iraq fired a total of 93 long-range missiles. The types that have been identified include 84 Al-Husayns, 3 Al Husyan-Shorts, and 1 Al-Hijrarah (with a cement warhead).[1]

There are severe limits on Iraq's current missile capabilities. Its previous missile firings depended on Iraq's ability to import the Scud B before the Gulf War and the massive missile modification and production effort it began during the Iran-Iraq War. UNSCOM has almost certainly been successful in locating and destroying most of these missiles and production capabilities. While Iraq seems to retain some of its long-range Scuds, launchers, and support equipment to reconstitute a small missile force, UNSCOM is still seeking to track down and destroy all of these systems, but it feels it has accounted for 817 of the 819 missiles Iraq imported up to 1988, although Iraq may have produced additional missiles in Iraq. Iraq is unlikely to retain a breakout capability in excess of 10–20 missiles, and it will take some years once sanctions are lifted for Iraq to rebuild its production facilities.[2] Desert Fox damaged Iraq's missile production capabilities enough to delay production by anywhere from six months to two years.

At the same time, Iraq can probably still deploy a limited number of extended range Scud missiles, possibly with chemical or biological warheads. It may well find a source of Scud imports and missile production equipment once sanctions are lifted, or it has the oil revenue to exploit the black market in arms. It has the technology and production skills to modify missiles, and it has had half a decade in which to refine its modifications, production planning, and missile warheads at the technical design level. It has also used missiles with ranges under 150 kilometers—which are permitted under the terms of the UN cease-fire—for some aspects of testing and development.[3]

IRAQ'S MISSILE WEAPONS BEFORE THE GULF WAR

Iraq acquired its first long-range ballistic missiles from the Soviet Bloc in the 1970s, and it had deployed a total of 9–12 Scud transport-erector-launchers (TELs) and an unknown number of Scud B missiles at the time the Iran-Iraq War began. During the course of the war, it conducted a "war of the cites" with Iran in which both nations used missiles to attempt to terrorize the other nation's politicians. This marked the first major use of missiles in combat since World War II. While Egypt and Syria used missiles against Israel in 1967, they fired a total of no more than seven missiles, and none of them had any major effect. The Iran-Iraq War also led Iraq to invest in a massive missile modification and production program. By the time the Iran-Iraq War ended in August, 1988, Iraq had developed two long-range modifications of the Scud and was seeking to design and produce its own long-range missile systems.

IRAQ AND THE "SCUD B"

The Scud is only one member of a large family of ballistic missile systems which potentially affect Iraq's options for proliferation, and which are summarized in Table 15.1. The Scud is, however, the missile which has dominated recent proliferation and missile combat activities in the Middle East.

The design of the Scud is derived from the German V-2 of the 1940s, and the Soviets first deployed it in the 1960s. The Scud is now an aging design with technical limitations. All of the Soviet/Russian designed models of the Scud are single-stage systems using liquid propellants. While the missile has been steadily improved with time, even the later Soviet/Russian-made variants are very large, relative to their range and payload, have limited accuracy, require complex pre-surveying to achieve this accuracy, and normally have a complex and unwieldy set-up and take-down process.[4]

The Scud B first became operational in 1967. It is a Soviet design, and the Soviet Union designates the system as the R-17E or R-300E. The Scud B is a true guided missile. It has a strap-down inertial guidance using three gyros to correct its ballistic trajectory, and it uses internal graphite jet vane steering. It has a nominal CEP of 1,000 meters.[5]

The Scud B has a warhead that detaches from the missile body during the final fall towards target. This provides added stability and allows the warhead to hit at a velocity above Mach 1.5.[6] The Scud B has a range of 290–300

Table 15.1
Comparative Range and Lethality of Surface-to-Surface Systems

Ballistic and Cruise Missiles

Source Country	Type	IOC	Range (km)	Warhead Payload (kg)	Nominal CEP at Range (Meters) Engineering	Nominal CEP at Range (Meters) Operational	Warhead Types
USSR	SS-1b/ Scud A	1957	130	900	900	1,800	HE, N, CB
USSR	SS-1c/ Scud B	1965	290	900	900	1,600	HE, N, CB
	Scud C	?	450	550	900	2,200	HE, N, CB
USSR	SS-21	1978	8-120	1318-1557	300	900	HE, N, CB
USSR	SS-23	1980	500	350	350	900	HE, N, CB
USSR	SS-12	1969	800	300	750	3,000	Nuclear
USSR	SS-22	1979	900	300	300	700	Nuclear
USSR	Sepal SS-C-1b	1962	450	-	-	900	Nuclear
US	BGM-109G GLCM	1983	2,500	-	20	100	Nuclear
US	MGM-31A/B Pershing 1A	1962	160-720	350	400	800	Nuclear
US	Pershing II	1984	160-1,770	-	40	180	Nuclear
US	MGM-52 Lance	1972	110	250	150-400	400-900	HE, N
France	Pluton	1974	10-120	-	150-300	300-500	Nuclear
Argentina	Alacran/ Condor II	?	600-800	600-1000	-	-	?

PRC	CSS-2	1970	2,700	1,800	800	2,000	HE, N
PRC	DF-3						
PRC	CSS-2 DF-3 (Saudi)	1987	2,400-3,000	2,200	800	2,000	HE, N
PRC	CSS-1 DF-2	1970	1,200	1,100	700	1,800	HE, N
PRC	M-9	198?	200-600	2,200	400	700	N, CB
PRC	M-11	1988	650-850	500-1,000	-	-	HE, C, B?
Iran	Scud R-300/ R-17E	1985	320	-	-	-	HE, C?
Iraq	Scud C/D/ R-300/R-17E Variant						
	Al Husayn	1988	650	135-250	900	2,500	HE, C, B?
Iraq	Scud C/D Variant/						
	al Abbas	?	650-850	500-1,000	-	-	HE, C, B?
Israel	Jericho 1	?	200-480	250	-	-	Nuclear
	Jericho II	?	490-750	450-680	-	-	Nuclear
	Jericho III	?	800-1,450	750	-	-	Nuclear

Table 15.1 (continued)

Rockets, Multiple Rocket Launchers, and Artillery

Source Country	Type	IOC	Range (km)	Warhead Payload (kg)	Nominal CEP at Range (Meters) Engineering	Operational	Warhead Types
Iran	Oghab'	1986	40	-	-	-	HE
Iran	Shanin 2	1988	70	180	-	-	HE
Iran	IRAN-130	1987	130-200	-	-	-	HE
USSR	FROG-7	1965	60-70	455	400	900	HE, N, CB
USSR	BM-21 122 mm MRL	1964	20.5	40 X 17	400	900	HE, CW
USSR	M-1972 122 mm MRL	1972	20.5	40 X	400	900	HE, CW
USSR	BM-14/16 140 mm MRL	1952	9.8	40 X	300	800	HE, CW
PRC	T-63 107 mm MRL	-	-	8.1	12 X 15	200	600 HE
PRC	140 mm MRL	-	-	10	19 X 24	300	1,200 HE
US	MLRS 115 mm MRL	1981	30+	12 X 40	50	200	HE
USSR	M-46 130 mm Gun	1954	27.2	74	-	-	HE, CW
USSR	2S5 152 mm Gun		1980	27	96	-	- HE, CW
US	M-107 175 mm Gun	1962	32.7	147	70	150	HE, CW
US	M-109A1 155 mm How	1966	18-30	95	70	120	Nuc, HE, CW
US	M-110 203 mm How	1962	21.3	170	70	120	Nuc, HE, CW

Sources: Adapted from various editions of the *IISS Military Balance, Jane's Weapons Systems,* and working papers by General Dynamics.

kilometers with its normal conventional payload. The export version of the missile is about 11 meters long, 85–90 centimeters in diameter, and weighs 6,300 kilograms. It has a conventional high explosive warhead weighing about 1,000 kilograms, of which 800 kilograms are the high explosive payload and 200 are the warhead structure and fusing system.[7]

It has a single-stage storable liquid rocket engine with about four tons of propellant and a powered flight time of about 70–75 seconds. It does not have a sophisticated guidance system. It follows a calculated ballistic course to target, which is corrected by a simple strap-down inertial guidance system. Course correction is by adjustment of the refractory jet vanes in the motor exhaust. The cruciform long-chord cropped tail fins located at the base of the missile only provide stability. These technical features present significant operational reliability and accuracy problems, and they mean that the operational calibration and instructions for deploying, siting, targeting, and using the regular "Scud B" had to be achieved by extensive practical testing, recalibration, and modification. It also means that the Scud has a large potential "error budget" of things that can go wrong which may degrade its theoretical CEP and accuracy, and that much depends on the skill with which it is employed.

For the missile to be accurate, it must be fired from a presurveyed site against a target whose coordinates are exactly known according to a common grid. This presents major problems—particularly for Third World countries like Iraq, which lacked Global Positioning Systems (GPSs) during the Iran-Iraq War and which does not seem to have used GPSs for missile siting even during the Gulf War. Further, the targeting problem grows progressively more serious as range increases, because the world is not perfectly round, and locating the launch site and target precisely requires both sites to be located using a common system with very high accuracy—a level of mapping that only nations with suitable satellite technology can accomplish. This precision is not as necessary with chemical and nuclear warheads, but it is vital when conventional warheads are aimed at small area targets. It is easy to introduce cumulative targeting errors of several hundred meters or more with normal launch and target location systems.

Cross winds can be a problem at the launch point. The missile accelerates relatively slowly during its initial flight up through the atmosphere, and radiosonde techniques are needed to measure winds, and the guidance must be recalibrated accordingly. It takes about 40 minutes to fully complete the combination of exact siting and wind calibration needed for maximum accuracy with a highly trained crew. The reentry problem is different. The missile travels so quickly that air resistance can affect its accuracy. At the same time, any problem in the shape and weight balance of the warhead or missile can cause tumbling or breakup. This does not affect the performance of Soviet systems, which used well-tested nuclear warheads. It does, however, present another major modification problem for nations like Iraq in modifying either the missile body or warhead. Even minute shifts in weight and size could sharply degrade accuracy and reliability and make them difficult to predict, unless the modification was refined on the basis of extensive range testing.

The Scud can be launched from fixed sites, towed trailers, and a now obsolete tracked IS-3 chassis. The Scud B launchers used in Iraq, however, were normally MAZ-543 vehicles that acted as a transport-erector-launcher (TEL). The MAZ-543 is an eight-wheeled, four-axled vehicle. The missile normally rides flush inside of the vehicle, and it can look like a large fuel truck or tractor trailer from a relatively short distance, a factor that makes it very difficult to target, as Coalition forces learned during the Gulf War. It is normally supported by the ZIL-157 propellant tanker and a mobile command and control van. Both of these vehicles look like commercial vehicles. There is also a special trailer for reloads, which is attached to a ZIL-157 vehicle, and a crane mounted on a Ural-375 truck to move the missile on the launcher. A Scud fire unit is normally supported by an End Tray weather radar, which tracks wind patterns using a radiosonde balloon, but this radar does not have to be collocated with the missile. All of these vehicles can easily be confused with commercial vehicles at a distance.[8]

The warhead is also a critical aspect of the Scud's performance, and Russia had several variations in terms of type and fusing options. These variations included a dummy, conventional high explosive, fuel air explosive, runway penetrator, chemical, biological, nuclear, and developmental cluster or bomblet warhead. The Scuds deployed in Soviet forces, however, were designed almost exclusively to kill area targets using warheads with chemical and nuclear weapons, although some Anthrax warheads seem to have been in inventory. Soviet literature describes a Scud warhead using nerve gas in some detail, but most Soviet exercises seem to have focused on the use of warheads with yields in excess of 100 kilotons, and employed the Scud almost exclusively as a theater nuclear system.

In contrast, the export versions of the Scuds given to countries like Iraq seem to have been designed largely to cater to the desire of Third World nations to have a system with the prestige or glitter factor of a ballistic missile, and the Former Soviet Union (FSU) only exported missiles with conventional warheads. There is no evidence that the FSU or any of the Warsaw Pact countries have ever provided a developing country with the designs for chemical warheads, or even advanced conventional warheads. Further, the FSU never seems to have transferred any technology relating to the biological and nuclear warheads, even to its Warsaw Pact allies.[9] This transfer policy placed important technical limitations on the ability of Iraq and other Third World countries to use the missile, since modern nuclear, chemical, and biological warhead technology is more sophisticated in many ways than the rest of the Scud missile design.

IRAQ'S OPERATIONAL EXPERIENCE DURING THE IRAN-IRAQ WAR

If this technical background seems somewhat esoteric, it is important to understand that it does a great deal to explain Iraq's and Iran's relative success in using the Scud during the Iran-Iraq War. Further, all of the missiles Iraq modified before the Gulf War were based on the Scud B. Given the fact that it has been under UN sanctions and inspection ever since, it seems likely that most of its technology, production, and war-fighting data are still heavily oriented towards the Scud.

Iraq signed its first contract for the Scud in 1973. It took delivery on additional missiles in 1980. As a result, it had limited holdings of Scud missiles when the war began, and a Scud regiment with at least nine operational launchers. It was not until October, 1982, however, that Iraq could make this unit combat effective. It began to fire regular Scud Bs on October 27, 1982, and fired a total of at least 3 missiles in 1982, 33 in 1983, 25 in 1984, 82 in 1985, 25 in 1987, and 193 in 1988.

Iraq used the Scud largely to conduct sporadic "terror attacks" on urban areas or military concentrations, and its strikes seem to have been designed largely to try to put political pressure on Iran to end the war or halt its offensives. Most of the time, Iraq used its Scud missiles against Iranian population centers to the rear of the battlefield.[10] Typical targets were cities relatively near the border like Dezful, Ahwaz, Khorramabad, and Borujerd (190 kilometers from the Iran-Iraq border).[11]

Iraq initially had a monopoly on such systems. Iran acquired its Scuds later in the war—first from Libya and then from North Korea. It deployed these units with a special Khatam ol-Anbya force attached to the air element of the Pasdaran, and fired its first Scuds in March, 1985. It fired as many as 14 Scuds in 1985, 8 in 1986, 18 in 1987, and 77 in 1988. These Iranian missile attacks were more effective than Iraq's attacks, largely because of geography. All of Iraq's major cities were comparatively close to its border with Iran, and Iran could use the Scud B to target key Iraqi cities like Baghdad. Tehran and most of Iran's other major cities outside of the immediate war zone in the border area were outside the range of Iraqi Scud B attacks.

Iran could not really exploit its range advantage, however, because it lacked the number of missiles needed to sustain frequent attacks, Iraq had vastly superior air resources it could use as a substitute for missile attacks, and most Iranian missiles struck outside Baghdad. The optimal theoretical accuracy of the Scud is in excess of a kilometer at long ranges, and its practical accuracy—taking siting and other factors into account—was often in excess of five kilometers. It is scarcely surprising, therefore, that many of the Iranian Scuds that were fired at Baghdad hit the outskirts of the city.

Further, even the missiles that did hit inside of the city often struck in open spaces, and even hits on buildings rarely produced high casualties. Iran never hit any of its proclaimed major targets, which included the Iraqi Ministry of Defense and Iraqi oil facilities. In fact, the net impact of using Scud missiles against urban targets was roughly similar to randomly lobbing a 500-pound bomb into a city every few days or weeks. The Scud strikes usually did little more than produce a loud bang, smash windows, and kill a few innocent civilians. The most lethal attacks on both sides seem to have occurred when missiles hit targets like a school or a large funeral by sheer accident.

Until 1988, the net impact of Iranian and Iraqi missile strikes on the opposite side's public opinion and morale was limited, relatively short lived, and often ambiguous. The side doing the firing was able to propagandize such missile firings as "lethal" retaliation against the enemy. The side receiving the fire, however, experienced only brief periods of panic at worst, and panic often quickly changed into anger and demands for reprisals as the civilians in the target area realized that they could survive the enemy's attacks. There is absolutely no doubt that the leadership elite of both Iran and Iraq came to fully understand that weapons of mass destruction are critical aspects of effective ballistic missile forces, and that the successful proliferation of such missile warheads will be a critical strategic priority as long as they are threatened by other powers or seek to intimidate them.

Since each Scud missile costs around $500,000–$1,000,000, such attacks were extremely expensive as well as relatively ineffective. Nevertheless, both Iran and Iraq attempted to improve their ability to use long-range missiles by acquiring larger numbers of missiles andor building their own. The end result was the beginning of a "missile race" that still continues, which is another powerful incentive for Iraq to both acquire and deploy long-range missiles and arm them with weapons of mass destruction.

Iran responded to the Iraqi missile threat with desperate efforts to obtain large numbers of Scud missiles from Libya, North Korea, and Syria, and to create its own missile manufacturing capabilities. It sought to buy additional Scud Bs, to manufacture them domestically, to develop its own systems, and to obtain alternative systems like the PRC-made M-9. Iran did obtain additional Scud missiles from Libya or Syria in 1986, but it was still only able to fire a total of 18–22 missiles in 1987. Iran then turned to North Korea, and in June, 1987, it obtained agreement to ship 100 more Scuds as part of a $500 million arms package. These missiles were delivered to Iran in early 1988. Iran also seems to have sought Scuds from the PRC, but it was ultimately unable to obtain them.

During the 52 days of the "war of the cites" in 1988, Iran fired at least 77 Scud missiles. Sixty-one were fired at Baghdad, nine at Mosul, five at Kirkuk, one at Takrit, and one at Kuwait. Iran fired as many as five missiles on a single day, and once fired three missiles within 30 minutes. This still, however, worked out to an average of only a little over one missile a day, and Iran was down to only 10–20 Scuds when the war of the cities ended. In contrast, Iraq had now fired a total of 516 missiles against Iran.[12]

This situation might have been very different if Iran had made good on its claims to be able to produce the Scud before the war ended. The minister in charge of the Pasdaran, Mohsen Rafiqdust, started making such claims in November, 1987. Iran also claimed in April, 1988 that it was working on a missile with a 320-kilometer range, and claimed that 80% of the Scuds it fired were produced in Iran. In fact, however, this was pure propaganda. Iran never succeeded in firing an Iranian-made Scud missile.

It was Iraq that eventually was successful in finding the long-range missiles it needed, although it took nearly half a decade to obtain them. Iraq tried actively from 1982 onward to acquire longer range missiles. Various Iraqi statements made in early 1983, for example, suggested that the Soviet Union might be willing to supply newer Soviet missiles with longer ranges like the SS-12 to the Iraqis. No new missile capabilities materialized, however, until February 29, 1988, when Iraq launched five new extended-range missiles that it called the Al Husayn.[13]

The details of Iraq's missile modification efforts will be described shortly, but the resulting pattern of missile strikes during the decisive phase of the war of the cities is summarized in Table 15.2, which is based on Iraqi and Iranian claims. These claims were often exaggerated, but the data in Table 15.2 are valid in indicating the general size of the sudden rise in Iraqi missile attacks and in the total number of air and missile attacks on urban targets.[14]

IRAQ'S SEARCH FOR MORE ADVANCED MISSILES

There is still considerable uncertainty as to exactly how Iraq got all of the technology to modify its Scuds. As has been discussed earlier, modification of the Scud is difficult. The large surface area of the missile cannot be changed without affecting accuracy. Attempting to burn additional propellant affects the ability of the jet vane control system to function, and the sharply pointed warhead is critically shaped and balanced. Any change can cause the missile to wobble, tumble, or break up upon reentry, which also affects accuracy. Like the rest of the missile, the "Scud B's" guidance technology and engineering base may be simple, but they do not permit easy reengineering and modification in ways that fundamentally affect its accuracy and reliability—a factor that may do much to explain the problems Iraq encountered during the Gulf War.

Various sources have claimed that Iraq received Chinese, Egyptian, French, German, andor Soviet help, and technicians and parts from other nations may have been involved. It has also become clear since the Gulf War that Iraq's efforts were dispersed and duplicative, as Iraq's main research effort seems to have occurred at a facility at Taji, its missiles were modified at a facility in the Nasr missile factory, and it began to produce mobile launchers at a facility near Daura. Project 28 focused on reverse engineering the Scud for production in Iraq.[15]

After the Gulf War, UNSCOM found that Iraq was pursuing at least 15 long-range missile projects by the mid-1980s. Another effort, called Project 144, focused on extending the range of the Scud. This project completed a detailed feasibility study of extending the range of its Scuds in late 1986. It then successfully carried out the fourth test of this new variant of the "Scud B"—called the Al Husayn—in August, 1987. One indication of the priority Iraq gave this program is the fact that it then had no radar telemetry. As a result, it had to send out observers at 5 to 10 kilometer intervals for a distance of 600 kilometers, and over a relatively wide angle, to simulate such telemetry.[16]

Table 15.2
Strikes Reported by Iran and Iraq Affecting the "War of the Cities" in 1987 and 1988

		Residential/Economic Attacks[1]			
Date		Iraq		Iran	
		Total Bombing & Missile	Scud[2]	Total Bombing & Missile	Scud[3]
A. 1987					
January	1–15	30	-	3	-
	16–31	18	-	15	3
February	1–15	27	-	5	3
	16–28	8	-	5	5
March	1–15	-	-	-	-
	16–31	4	-	-	-
April	1–15	5	-	-	-
	16–30	2	-	-	-
May	1–15	4	-	1	-
	16–31	1	-	1	-
June	1–15	-	-	-	-
	16–30	1	-	-	-
July	1–15	6	-	-	-
	16–31	-	-	-	-
August	1–15	2	-	-	-
	16–31	13	-	7	-
September	1–15	35	-	8	-
	16–30	19	-	3	-
October	1–15	12	-	6	-
	16–31	4	-	8	4
November	1–15	14	-	9	1
	16–30	10	-	2	2
December	1–15	7	-	2	-
	16–31	1	-	-	-
TOTAL IN 1987		223	-	75	18
B. 1988					
January	1–15	1	-	-	-
	16–31	-	-	-	-
February	1–15	3	-	-	-
	16–28	5	-	3	-
March	1–15	215	101	73	31
	16–31	130	36	143	14
April	1–15	78	40	96	11
	16–30	33	26	63	5
May	1–15	2	-	-	-
	16–31	2	-	-	-
June	1–15	-	-	-	-
	16–30	13	-	1	-

Table 15.2 (continued)

		Residential/Economic Attacks[1]			
Date		Iraq		Iran	
B. 1988 (cont.)		Total Bombing & Missile	Scud[2]	Total Bombing & Missile	Scud[3]
July	1–15	3	-	-	-
	16–31	4	-	-	-
August	1–20[4]	5	-	-	-
TOTAL IN 1988		494	203	379	61

1. Bombing and missile attacks as reported in daily war communiqués and other sources.
2. Includes all long-range missiles, but not Oghabs or any Iran-130s that failed to hit economic or civilian targets.
3. Includes Scud B missiles fired at Baghdad and other Iranian cities.
4. From the beginning of the month to the Iranian acceptance of a cease-fire and UN Resolution 598.

Sources: Adapted from work provided to the author by Gary Sick, and W. Seth Carus and Joseph S. Bermudez, "Iran's Growing Missile Forces," *Jane's Defense Weekly*, July 23, 1988.

This test led Iraq to move forward to production, and Iraq was modifying up to three missiles a month by April, 1988. The precise range-payload capabilities of this missile cannot be determined as a result of the attacks made during either the Iran-Iraq or Gulf wars, because the Iraqis regularly moved the missile launch sites during their attacks. It seems to have about 25% more fuel than the regular "Scud B," or about five tons of propellant.

The US government has released data indicating that the Al Husayn missile has a range of about 650 kilometers (375–400 miles) and a circular effort of probability (CEP) of 1,500–3,000 meters.[17] Other sources provide different data. One Israeli source estimates that the Al Husayn has a maximum range of 600 kilometers, a warhead weight of 300 kilograms, a flight time of 420 seconds, and a CEP of around 1,700–2,300 meters.[18] Other experts indicate that it has a range of 375 miles and a warhead weight of only 250 pounds.[19] Still other sources report that the Al Husayn utilizes a reduced payload package (985 to 190 kg) to effect a 100% growth in range to 600 km (328 nautical miles). Some sources also indicated before the Gulf War that the Al Husayn had re-fire times of 60 minutes versus 160 minutes for the earlier-model Scuds.[20]

In any case, the Al Husayn does not have a high theoretical level of accuracy. Further, the term CEP only describes the distance from the target where 50% of the missiles fired (that function perfectly through launch and are perfectly aimed) will land from the target. The remaining 50% land substantially further away from the target—but the miss distance is difficult to predict. Real world accuracy is also reduced below the CEP, because missile and target locations are rarely known with perfect precision, and many firings involve at least some malfunction within a missile, which further degrades operational accuracy.

Nevertheless, the Al Husayn gave Iraq a missile that could reach Tehran and Qom from positions south of Baghdad. It fired 135–160 missiles at Tehran between February 29 and April 18, 1988, and a total of around 200 Al Husayns at targets in Iran.[21] Other sources indicate that Iraq launched a total of approximately 360 Scud Bs and Al Husayn missiles at Tehran and other Iranian cities during the "War of the Cities."[22]

Iraq fired an average of nearly three Scuds a day—most of which seem to have been Al-Husayns—and the impact of Iraq's missile and air strikes on Iran was far greater in 1988 than its past Scud B strikes. Where the Iranians had previously been able to adapt to the relatively limited and short-lived Iraqi bombing efforts, the constant pounding of missiles interacted with a growing fear that Iraq might use chemical weapons, which had a major impact on Iranian morale. So did the rumors and reports that senior Iranian officials—including Khomeini—had left Tehran. According to some reports, nearly a million Iranians had fled Tehran by mid-March, and several million more had fled by late April.[23]

It is important to stress, however, that the Iraqi missile strikes alone probably would have had relatively little serious impact if they had not interacted with a number of other factors. The Scud strikes were audible over wide areas as they neared their target, made a loud bang, and blew out windows over a wide area. Nevertheless, the Scud strikes did not do serious physical damage to any Iranian target, and they killed substantially less than an average of two dozen people a missile. The variants of the Scuds that Iraq was using only seem to have had 130–250 kilograms of explosive in their warheads, and they were scarcely "city killers."[24]

Some experts suggest that the Al Husayn missiles often broke up during the Iraqi attacks on Iran. One suggests that the missile tended to wobble during its ascent phase, where the impact of the wobble is reduced by the fact that it is still under power and rising, and then experiences growing problems from this wobble as it renters the atmosphere at a high velocity and without power. He also feels that the center of gravity is less forward in the Al Husayn, which can lead to substantial wobble that makes the missile break up at high altitudes during reentry—generally at altitudes of 15–20 kilometers.[25]

What gave the Iraqi missile barrage a radical new strategic impact was that it occurred in combination with (1) the growing fear of chemical weapons, (2) the impact of Iraq's air raids, (3) the effect on morale of Iran's military casualties during the previous year, (4) growing popular and military exhaustion with the conflict, (5) Iran's inability to retaliate, (6) rumors of internal divisions within Iran's leadership, (7) serious economic hardship and growing prices on the black market, and (8) the knowledge that Iran would no longer be threatened if it halted its offensives.[26] This experience is scarcely an incentive for Iraq or any other country to rely on conventional warheads, but it reinforces a lesson from many previous conflicts. The effect of strategic bombardment with conventional weapons is likely to be determined far more by its effect in catalyzing public

IRAQI MISSILES AFTER THE IRAN-IRAQ WAR

Iraq developed still more advanced missiles after the August, 1988 cease-fire in the Iran-Iraq War. It tested a missile on April 25, 1988, which was later renamed the Al-Hijarah or "stones," after the stones used by the Palestinian children and teenagers in the Intifada. The Al-Hijarah missile was a still further modification of the "Scud B," with additional fuel tanks that were relatively crudely welded into the main body. This type of modification may account for the fact that Iraqi missiles proved to be unstable during the Gulf War and often broke up upon reentry. Ironically, this same breakup created the equivalent of a "decoy capability," because the Patriot could not separate the radar signature of the Scud warhead from other missile fragments.[27]

By 1990, the Al-Hijarah matured into a system whose performance was initially estimated as having a maximum range of 700–900 kilometers, a 100 to 300 kilogram payload, a flight time of 540 seconds, and an operational CEP at a maximum range of 2,500 to 3,000 meters.[28] Iraq did not demonstrate this long maximum range during the Gulf War, and some experts now feel that the missile's range may actually be below 800 kilometers, with a payload of around 200 kilograms and an operational CEP of 3,000 meters. Iraq was also working on hydrazine-based propellants to develop missiles with ranges in the thousands of kilometers and new, larger test stands.[29]

Iraq also quietly tested and deployed chemical warheads for its regular and longer-range Scuds.[30] The timing of Iraq's chemical warhead tests is uncertain, but UN inspection efforts later showed that Iraq had binary chemical warheads at the time of the Gulf War.[31] These warhead designs were not particularly reliable or effective. They had crude aluminum welds, some shape and loading stability problems, and relatively crude technology for disseminating the chemical agent as the warhead reached its target. There is also some question about their range and the amount of chemical agent that could be delivered, since even the Soviet-designed VX chemical warhead had 555 kilograms of active agent for a warhead weighing 985 kilograms. The chemical payload of a smaller warhead drops sharply as a proportion of total weight, because the mechanism needed to disperse the agent cannot be reduced in the same proportion. However, the Iraqi chemical warheads could still have been used as terror weapons.

Iraq was seeking even more advanced missile systems at the time it invaded Kuwait, and it spent billions of dollars between 1980 and 1990 on missile development and production facilities, and on facilities to develop and produce weapons of mass destruction to be delivered by missiles. As part of this effort, it funded a massive missile research and development establishment. Iraq established research links with Argentina and Egypt, and joined them in a project called Badar 2000. This project was supposed to turn a large Argentine weather rocket called the Condor—which Argentina had developed in the late 1970s—into a two-stage solid fuel long-range missile, with a payload of 450 kilograms and a maximum range of 950 kilometers.

While Egypt and Argentina eventually canceled their work on the Badar 2000, Iraq tried to continue the project on its own.[32] According to one report, it set up facilities to produce cases and nozzles at the Dhu al-Fiquar Factory at Fallujah, the solid fuel mixing and casting at the Taj al-Ma'arik Factory near Latifyah, and motor assembly and testing at the Al-Yawm al-Azim Factory near Musayib. The project was managed largely by Iraqis, using a wide range of foreign experts and some technical workers hired in Pakistan.[33] Iraq may, however, have had to abandon the Badar 2000 before the war. Argentina's guidance system technology was inadequate, and it had lagged far behind its development schedule. Egypt had not met a single goal for its share of the project, and little serious attention seems to have been paid to warhead design.

Iraq had little success with its efforts to modify the SA-2, SA-3, and SA-6 surface-to-air missiles for use in the surface-to-surface role before the Gulf War. Such modifications have serious inherent accuracy and range-payload problems. Iraq's Sa'ad 16 facility was not able to operate much of the equipment Iraq had imported to build more advanced warheads when the Gulf War began, and Iraq was still seeking carbon fiber warhead technology and manufacturing equipment to improve its warhead capabilities. Iraq's reliance on relatively crude metal warheads helps explain the failure of many of the extended range Scuds that it launched against Israel and Saudi Arabia, as well as some of the problems in the design of its chemical warheads.[34]

Iraq did, however, work on other systems that might have given it improved missile capabilities during the next few years. It hired a separate 23-man missile technology development team from Brazil. This team was led by retired Major General Hugo de Olivera Piva, the ex-director of Brazil's Aerospace Technology Center. Piva headed the effort to convert Brazil's Sonda IV space rocket into a missile large enough to carry a nuclear warhead. This team helped Iraq develop two related systems: the Al-Abid and the Tamuz.

The Al-Abid first attracted world attention on December 5, 1989, when Iraqi TV showed the launching of a long-range booster at the Al-Anbar space research center, which it claimed to have reached a range close to 1,500 nautical miles.[35] According to some reports, this three-stage missile was built with the assistance of the Canadian "Super Gun" designer, Dr. Gerald Bull, as well as with the Brazilian team. The Al-Abid seems to have been a 48-ton missile whose main booster used a cluster of five Scuds. The second stage used two Scuds, and the third stage was of Brazilian design. While the primary reached an altitude of 12,000 meters, the other two stages either failed to separate or may not have been activated during the test. Nevertheless, the test showed that Iraq might eventually be capable of launching a satellite into orbit or of firing much longer-range missiles.[36]

On December 14, 1989, Iraq announced that it had developed another new missile called the Tamuz 1. It claimed that it had tested the missile twice, and that the launches had reached ranges of up to 1,500 kilometers.[37] The Tamuz was also being built with Brazilian assistance, but—in spite of Iraqi claims—it does not seem to have been tested and may still have been in the developmental stage when the war began. The Tamuz appears to have been a three-stage, liquid fueled, 48-ton missile similar to the Al-Abid. It may have used the same booster system—with five al-Abbas boosters in the first stage, two in the second stage, and a one in the third stage, with a 750-kilogram payload.[38]

Some experts feel that the Tamuz could have had a range of roughly 2,000 kilometers once it was fully developed. Others experts believe that a range of 1,250 to 1,500 kilometers was more likely once a military payload and guidance package were added. Such a missile would be very complex, involve a great deal of launch preparation and launch time, and require large, fixed facilities. It would, however, have been the first Iraqi missile with sufficient range payload to deliver a large nuclear weapon, or large chemical or biological weapons payload, against any target in Israel and Iran from launch sites deep in Iraq.[39] UN inspections after the Gulf War confirm that Iraq had been actively working on nuclear warhead designs for such missiles.[40]

Iraq continued to improve its production and test facilities for long-range missiles in the period before it invaded Kuwait. In April, 1990, information surfaced that Iraq might be setting up a new missile test range in Mauritania in West Africa. Such a test range would have given Iraq the ability to test missiles in excess of 1,000 miles—tests that were impossible in Iraq without crossing international borders—but the existence of such a range was never confirmed. In July, 1990, it became apparent that Iraq had quietly sought to buy titanium furnaces from the United States. Such furnaces can be used to manufacture a number of lightweight titanium missile parts, including advanced nose cone designs for warheads.[41]

Iraq made claims to have completed further missile developments after it invaded Kuwait. On October 9, 1990, Saddam Hussein announced that Iraq had developed a new missile that could hit Israel. Some experts now believe that Saddam was talking about modifications to the Adnan 2 drone, but Iraq never used this system against Israel, and no new ballistic missile was ever found.[42] The timing of the Iraqi announcement also indicates that it may have been nothing more than a propaganda ploy. Saddam Hussein made the announcement one day after a major clash between Israelis and Palestinians at the Temple Mount in Jerusalem, at a time when Saddam Hussein was trying to divide and weaken Arab support for the Coalition.[43]

While any estimates of the performance of Iraq's deployed missiles are highly

Table 15.3
Comparative Performance of Iraqi Surface-to-Surface Missile Systems

	"Scud B"	Al Husayn	Al-Hijarah	Tamuz/Al Abid
Date first appeared	March 18, 1968	August 3, 1987	December 7, 1989	-
Number of stages	1	1	2	3
Diameter (meters)	0.884	0.884	0.884	-
Length (meters)	11.7	12.55	13	-
Weight (kilograms)	6,300	7,340	34,500	-
Range (kilometers)	280	600	750	1,200–1,500
Chemical Warhead (kilograms)				
Total weight (kg)	985	190	220	-
Weight of agent (kg)	555	107	-	-
CEP (meters)	900	3,000	3,000–5,000	5,000+
Flight time (minutes)	6.0–6.5	8.0–9.0	10–12	-
Flight mach	4.0	4.0	4.0	-
Fuse	Variable proximity	Variable proximity	Variable proximity	-

Sources: Adapted by the author from material in the US Department of Defense, The *Conduct of the Persian Gulf War: Final Report*, Department of Defense, April, 1992, pp. 16–18, and working paper by Dick Palowski.

controversial, Table 15.3 provides a rough comparison of the characteristics of Iraq's missiles at the time of the Gulf War.[44]

IRAQ'S MISSILE CAPABILITIES AT THE TIME OF THE GULF WAR

By the time of the Gulf War, Iraq had chemical and biological warheads for its missiles, and it was attempting to design a nuclear warhead. It had at least 11 missile programs that were deployed or in development:[45]

- *Standard Scud B*: Russian and Chinese made missile and missile assemblies with a maximum range of 300 kilometers
- *Al Husayn*: an extended-range Scud variants with a 600–650 kilometer range
- *Al Husayn-Short*: an extended-range Scud variant of the Al Husayn with a 600 to 650 kilometer range

- *Al Hijarah*: an extended-range Scud variants with a 600–650 kilometer range
- *Al Fahd*: a conversion of the SA-2 with an intended 300 kilometer range; abandoned in the R&D phase
- *Extended-range Al Fahd*: a 500-kilometer range missile abandoned in the development phase after exhibition at the 1989 arms show in Baghdad
- *Al Abbas*: a longer version of the Al Husayn with a lighter warhead which was intended to have a 900-kilometer range; abandoned during R&D
- *Badar 2000*: a solid-propellant, two-stage missile based on the Condor with a range of 750–1,000 kilometers; was in R&D when Gulf War began; facilities were constructed to begin missile production
- *Tammuz 1*: a missile based on the Scud with an SA-2 sustainer for a second stage. It had an intended range of 2,000 kilometers, but it was not carried through to advanced R&D
- *Al Abid*: a three-stage space vehicle with a first stage of five Al Abbas airframes; test launched in December, 1989
- a solid-fueled missile with a range similar to the Tammuz

When the Gulf War started, Iraq had over 800 Scuds of all types, including several hundred extended-range Al Husayn and Al Abbas missiles. These missiles were deployed in a brigade-sized formation of three to four regiments, based on a Soviet model. This unit seems to have been headquartered near Taji, north of Baghdad, which became the center of Iraqi Scud missile operations during the Iran-Iraq War.

Many US experts initially felt that Iraq's missile forces would be easy to target. They estimated that Iraq had 24–36 Soviet-supplied mobile missile launchers at the time the war began, and that Iraq's surface-to-surface missile brigade had an active strength of three to four regiments of three launchers each, and a deployable strength of only 9–12 launchers.[46] However, Iraq may have had more launchers than the United States estimated. It was deploying new transporter-erector-launchers (TELs), called the Al-Walid or Al-Nida, which it had displayed at the Baghdad International Arms Exhibition in 1989.[47] Some experts feel that at least one unit with Iraqi launchers became operational before the war and supplemented Iraq's standard Soviet-designed MAZ-543 launchers.[48]

In any case, Iraq proved far less predictable in using its forces than many intelligence experts predicted. It had begun to make major changes in the deployment of its Scud forces long before its invasion of Kuwait, and it had expanded its missile deployments to cover its western as well as its eastern borders. In the process, Iraq established a large number of presurveyed sites.

In February, 1990, US intelligence detected Iraqi construction of new fixed missile launcher complexes in Western Iraq. Press reports differ over the size of these complexes. Some indicate that there were five complexes with 28 operational launchers—although such counts seem high. In any case, Iraq could use them to launch the 600-kilometer range Al Husayn to reach the Israeli cities of Tel Aviv and Haifa, Israel's nuclear facility in Dimona, and targets throughout Syria and in much of Turkey.

Some reports also indicate that Iraq deployed from 12 to 18 Al-Abbas missile launchers to three fixed sites in southern, western, and northern Iraq in March, 1990. According to UN reports, the sites included 28 fixed launchers in western Iraq, with other fixed sites near Taji, Baghdad, and Daura.[49] If these reports are accurate, the northern and southern sites would have given Iraq the ability to strike deeper into Iran, and the western and southern sites gave Iraq the ability to strike at other targets and to provide coverage of targets in Israel, Syria, and Turkey.[50]

One source indicates that the site nearest to Israel was close to the H-2 Airfield in Western Iraq, on the road between Iraq and Jordan, and that it had six launchers oriented towards targets in Israel or Syria. Still another report indicates that Iraq had nine prepared launch sites for its regular Scud missiles, with 62 launch positions, although several normally did not have launchers deployed.[51]

The construction of these fixed sites led US intelligence and Coalition air planners to focus on them as major targets, which proved to be a mistake. While Iraq probably felt the fixed sites could be used to launch several volleys of missiles before they could be struck by Coalition or Israeli aircraft, it must have realized that they would be detected by US satellites and could be struck immediately in the event of war. As a result, it seems likely that Iraq, at most, planned to use its fixed launchers to create a first strike or "launch under attack" capability to fire chemical weapons against Israel, and to then shift to mobile launch units and treat the fixed sites as the equivalent of decoys.

In any case, it is unclear whether Iraq made a serious move to deploy significant numbers of missiles to its fixed sites during Desert Shield. It may have felt that such deployments would simply lead to preemptive attacks and result in the loss of trained personnel. Iraq did, however, disperse some of the equipment for its mobile missile units after the beginning of Desert Shield, and it expanded its survey activity to create more presurveyed launch sites in the South. It began to actively redeploy its mobile Scud units into the field at some point in late 1990 or January, 1991, and it deployed fueled Scuds into positions where they could fire "volleys" of Scud missiles at the start of the Coalition attack. (Figure 15.1 shows the range of Iraq's missile developments at the time of the Gulf War.)

The exact range of support equipment Iraq deployed with its mobile missile units is uncertain. Iraq is known to have used the Soviet "End Tray" meteorological radar associated with the FROG-7 and "Scud B" in some of its missile deployments and the UAZ-452T support vehicles. It is not known how effective this equipment was in supporting long-range fire using the Al Husayn and Al-Hijarah. Iraq also deployed at least battalion-sized protection units with its launchers to guard against raids by infiltrators and special forces. [52]

The dispersal of Iraq's mobile missile units near a wide range of potential

Figure 15.1
The Range of Iraq's Missile Developments at the Time of the Gulf War

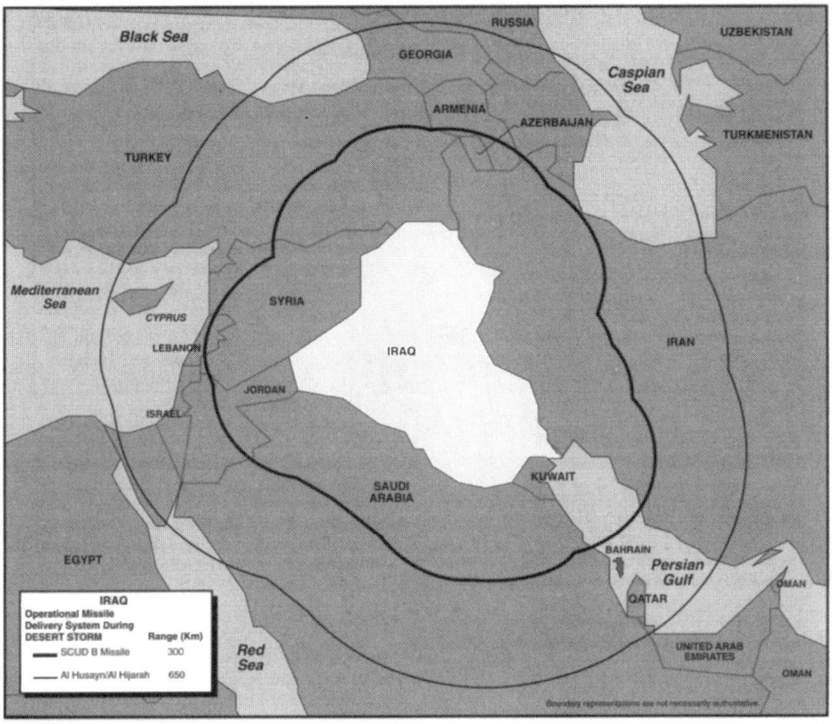

Sources: US Office of the Secretary of Defense, *Proliferation: Threat and Respons*, Washington, Department of Defense, April, 1996, p. 23.

launch sites made them very difficult to target. The large number of presurveyed sites allowed Iraq to create broad launch zones and to disperse its missile units in a large amount of territory. Its TELs and support vehicles were difficult to distinguish from commercial vehicles without extensive reconnaissance. Iraqi forces had also developed the capability to hide their TELs and missiles with camouflage, in civil buildings, underpasses, and in other places of concealment, and they deployed some highly effective decoys.

Once the war began, Iraq used mobile launch units in both the western and southern parts of Iraq to hit targets in Israel and Saudi Arabia.[53] The pattern of these launches is shown in Table 15.4. Iraq launched its first two Scuds against Israel late on the afternoon of January 17, 1991. The first strike on Saudi Arabia took place on January 18, and Iraq eventually launched a total of 93 missiles.[54]

As was the case during the Iran-Iraq War, the Iraqi Scud strikes caused relatively limited direct damage. Detailed statistics on the effects of the Scud strikes

Table 15.4
Iraqi Ballistic Missile Attacks During the Gulf War

Result	Target			Total
	Israel	**Saudi Arabia**	**Bahrain**	
Total fired	40	48	3	91
Missed country	1	3	2	6
Missed target area	15	11	1	27
Intercepted by Patriot	34	11	0	45
Hit target	0	13	0	13
Debris hit	7	7	0	14

Source: OSD Public Affairs, March, 1991. Note that Iraq claims it fired 93 Scuds during the Gulf War, with 43 against Israel and 50 against targets in Saudi Arabia. Israel has reported 39 Scuds as targeted against it. The Iraqi claims were made by Lt. General Hazim Abdulrazaq al-Ayaubi on February 25, 1997 (Reuters, February 2, 1997, 0953; *Washington Post*, February 26, 1997, p. A-15).

on Saudi Arabia are not available, but it is clear that their effect was largely psychological. The threat of Scud strikes cleared the streets of Riyadh, and the fear of chemical attacks had a major impact on morale and forced military units to don chemical gear and take shelter.[55] The one serious effect of Iraq's Scud strikes on Saudi Arabia was an accidental hit on a US barracks near Dhahran on February 25, which produced the only major Coalition losses to any Iraqi long-range strike system.[56]

There are many different estimates of the damage from the Scud attacks on Israel, but Table 15.5 indicates that direct Scud damage killed a maximum of two people in Israel. Only 10 of the 232 people directly hurt by Scuds in Israel suffered more than superficial injuries, and only one was severely hurt, which indicates that the main damage was done by fear, shock, and misuse of civil defense equipment. In contrast, each V-1 falling on London directly killed 2.2 persons, and seriously injured 6.3, and each V-2 falling on London during World War II killed an average of 4.8 persons and seriously injured 11.7.[57]

The physical impact of Iraq's Scud strikes was also limited. While some Israeli newspapers have talked about damage to 2,797 apartments before the deployment of the Patriot, and 9,029 after deployment of the Patriot, this damage generally consisted of broken windows. Only 74 apartments suffered significant damage, 40 before the deployment of the Patriot and 34 afterward.[58] As was the case during the Iran-Iraq War, this experience is almost certainly an important "lesson" to Iraq's leadership that Iraq must have missiles armed with weapons of mass destruction and the option of using warheads lethal enough to pose major or existential threats—which require biological or nuclear warheads.

At the same time, the survivability of Iraq's missile launchers did allow it to achieve its only real military "success" of the war. This success was political

Table 15.5
Casualties from Iraqi Surface-to-Surface Missile Launches During the Gulf War

Direct Casualties Due to Missile Impact

Dead	2
Injured	232
Total	234

Indirect Casualties

Dead due to hear attack	4
Dead due to suffocation from misuse of gas mask	7
Total dead	11
Accidents from running or driving to cover	40
Injuries from misuse of Atropine antidote	230
Hospitalization for acute anxiety	544
Total injured	814
Total dead and injured	825

Source: Adapted from Eliot Cohen, Director, *The Gulf War Air Power Survey, Volume IV, Part I*, Washington, GPO, 1993, pp. 33–332.

and psychological, rather than physical and military, but it was still very real. The continuing Scud attacks gave Saddam Hussein immense prestige in some parts of the Arab world, and helped offset the impression of total defeat that surrounded most aspects of Iraq's performance during the war. The Scuds disrupted some aspects of the Coalition offensive air plan and created the only real risk that the Coalition might be divided by Israel's entrance into the war.[59]

It is certain that Iraq's leaders and military officers see these benefits as being of strategic value, and that they and the leaders and military of other radical states will see Iraq's use of missiles as a valuable lesson of the war. They will view long-range missiles as systems that get immense political attention, even when they were not used, which gave Iraq a symbol of international power, and which could overcome many of the West's advantages in air defense and offensive capabilities. Like Iraq, they are likely to measure the value of such systems in terms of how they influence regional and Western perceptions, rather than simply in terms of war-fighting effects.

THE SCUD HUNT AND BALLISTIC MISSILE DEFENSE

Iraq also is now well aware of two other aspects of the Gulf War that act as an incentive for it to rebuild its missile forces. The Coalition organized a massive, and ultimately futile, effort to find Iraq's Scuds. This effort initially claimed success, but it has since become clear that it wasted hundreds of sorties. While there is some debate over the number of sorties that should be counted, the Coalition flew a total of at least 1,460 strikes against Iraqi ballistic missile forces and capabilities. To put this in perspective, the Coalition flew 260 strikes against leadership targets, 580 strikes against C^4 targets, 970 strikes against military industry, 1,170 strikes against LOCs, 1,370 strikes against SAMs, 1,460 strikes against airfields, and 23,430 strikes against ground forces. A narrow definition of the number of Scud strikes would rank it third after air fields. A broader definition would rank the total strike and reconnaissance sorties flown against both Scuds and NBC targets as second.[60]

The Coalition flew dedicated anti-Scud strikes against mobile missile launchers, fixed-launch sites, and places where mobile launchers might hide (culverts, overpasses, etc.), production facilities, and support facilities. About 50% of the sorties struck at possible hiding places, 30% against production facilities and infrastructure, and 15% (215) against targets believed to be actual mobile launchers. Up to another 1,000 sorties were flown in target collection sensor missions and in "Scud patrols," where the attack aircraft normally diverted to another target.[61]

The reasons these strikes were ineffective are well described in the detailed annexes to the US Air Force Gulf War Air Power Survey:

the Scud hunt unfolded in a way that tended to mask this problem in intelligence from intelligence analysts, strike planners, and commanders alike. The first ten days of the air campaign saw numerous claims of mobile Scud kills by aircrews, backed in some cases, by cockpit video, and the lull in launches during the third and fourth weeks [of Desert Storm] seemed at first to substantiate pilot reports. In retrospect, however, many of the Coalition aircraft had struck decoys, other shorter-range missiles, or traffic such as fuel trucks. Intelligence had not understood the full scope of Baghdad's Scud decoy program, and exploitation of "low signature" firing locations.[62]

In addition, intelligence failed to properly communicate to air planners that most of the missiles were dispersed out of their central bases at locations like Taji in late August, 1990—and that some dispersal actions seemed to have continued until the end of the war. This intelligence failure was partly a collection problem, and partly a result of the fact that the Defense Intelligence Agency (DIA) was so vague and caveated in reporting possible indicators that users did not take note of its reporting. This helped encourage targeteers to focus on fixed-missile sites, although targeting also failed to take proper account of the warnings that it received about uncertainties in the count of mobile missile launchers and Iraq's use of such launchers. As a result, the Coalition wasted sorties on fixed launch sites during the initial air campaign on what the USAF later concluded were little more than decoys.

The failure of the Scud hunt had additional causes. US test and exercise data had shown before the Gulf War that fighters could not find and characterize dispersed mobile missile launchers during the day, and had almost no success at night. These tests indicated that even telling an aircraft with the capability of an F-15E that a Scud launch had occurred within an area of a square mile generally proved inadequate to allow the aircraft to acquire the target. Yet these tests assumed that Scud launches would take the same time to set up, fire, and disperse as Soviet Scud forces. As a result, they made detection much more probable than was the actual case in the Gulf War.

The Iraqis moved very quickly—although at some cost in accuracy. They practiced excellent communications and emitter control to avoid giving setup and launch signatures that patrolling aircraft could find. The Iraqis used land lines and couriers to exercise command and control (which led them to operate near roads in spite of the Scud hunt). While emissions were sometimes detected from their meteorological radars, these were infrequent and could never be correlated with Scud launchers. Further, Iraq conducted some 80% of its launches at night.

Work by UNSCOM revealed after the Gulf War that Iraq also prepared its missile forces to create a retaliatory or launch-under-attack strike capability. It dispersed chemical and biological warheads and bombs in areas where there were few physical indicators of an Iraqi military presence, and where they were almost certain to survive Coalition attacks. Saddam Hussein approved a command system that might have allowed Iraqi missile commanders to launch if the Coalition had destroyed the command and control capabilities of the Iraqi regime.

It is far from clear how real this ''doomsday'' force really was, but biological bombs were left buried in unguarded dispersal strips, and the missile force could almost certainly have launched missiles with chemical and biological warheads *if* it had been given suitable commands. While the creation of such a strike capability may have been more of a grandiose political gesture on Saddam's part than a serious attempt at war fighting, it does illustrate that Iraq was ready to consider retaliatory and launch-under-attack options, and might consider launch on warning or preemptive options in the future. This has serious implications for counter-proliferation planning.

In any case, the Coalition did not properly characterize the Iraqi Scud strike at the time of the Gulf War, and it failed to effectively attack Iraqi Scud forces. It is unclear that the US COMINT and ELINT efforts using TLQ-17 ''Sandcrabs,'' TENCAP, and other detection systems ever reliably detected Scud launches. Even though patrolling aircraft saw 42 actual Scud launches, only eight sightings allowed the patrolling aircraft to go on to actually attempt to attack the target, and no attack produced a confirmed kill. The Iraqis also deployed decoys in their launch areas. Some of these decoys were so realistic that UN inspectors later stated that they could not be distinguished from real launchers on the ground, and they were mixed with low fidelity decoys to make targeting even more difficult.[63]

These data do not mean the Scud hunt was totally ineffective. There are some indications that Iraq came under sufficiently intense attack to reduce the volume of Iraqi missile launches. Thirty-three of Iraq's 88–93 launches occurred during the first week of Desert Storm. As a result, Iraq averaged 4.7 launches per day during the first week of the war versus 1.5 launches per day during the rest of the conflict, and its average launch rate was about 35% lower than during the "war of the cities."

However, such indicators are uncertain. Iraq was seeking to achieve different political-strategic objectives than it had sought during its "war of the cities" with Iran. Iraq only needed a maximum of 10 mobile launchers to achieve its highest launch rate, while 19 launchers are known to have survived the war intact. Iraq suddenly increased its number of launchers when the land offensive seemed likely, and it launched as many missiles in the last eight days of the war as it did during the first seven. Some analysts also feel that Coalition air strikes reduced Iraq's maximum "salvo" size, and the number of Iraqi Scud launches that could occur in a three-minute interval. However, this claim is also uncertain. The problem with this measure of effectiveness is that there is no evidence that Iraq was ever trying to launch as many missiles as possible within a three-minute interval.[64]

It is also interesting to note that the Israeli Air Force (IAF) would have been in a worse position to carry out a Scud hunt—although some Israeli planners feel that the IAF would have been willing to risk much higher losses by flying well below 10,000 feet. Israel did not have either imagery or launch warning satellites. Its best strike aircraft had significantly less targeting characterization capability, and its intelligence effort did not succeed in characterizing the details of the Iraqi missile force any better than US intelligence, although it correctly gave more weight to mobile launches and to the possibility that Iraq would target urban areas in high-risk strikes. Neither the United States nor Israel brought effective operations research efforts into support of their intelligence and targeting efforts, and into creating properly structured models of the search effort required, to achieve the timely location of launchers before striking them.[65]

Similarly, the Scud hunt probably would not have been more effective if it had been supported by the Special Operations teams that Israel considered deploying on the ground. Like the Coalition effort, such teams might have found some launchers and detected the nature of the Iraqi deception effort. They were not, however, trained or prepared to deal with the real world problems of targeting the Iraqi Scud launchers within the time windows involved. They would not have been capable of covering the large search areas required without exceptional risk, and they probably would have produced limited additional disruption of the overall Iraqi launch effort.

The Gulf War Air Power Survey summarizes these problems as follows, and it is almost certain that Iraq has paid at least as much attention to such US studies as most Western military planners:

the evidence suggests that a series of incorrect assumptions were made by intelligence analysts, air planners, and commanders alike. Further, the way the Scud hunt unfolded tended to mask these errors well into the air campaign. The first ten days saw substantial claims of Scud missile launchers by aircrews, backed up by compelling footage from airborne recording systems, and the lull in launches during the third and fourth weeks probably gave the hope that some portion of kill claims were legitimate. Fundamental sensor limitations of Coalition aircraft, coupled with the effectiveness of Iraqi employment tactics, suggest that relatively few mobile Scud launchers were actually destroyed. ... So, beyond the [possible] disruption [of the launch effort] ... Coalition air power does not seem to have been very effective against this launch category.[66]

Iraq is certain to have closely studied such analyses of the Scud hunt, as well as post-war analyses of the success and nonsuccess of the Patriot. It can scarcely be unaware of the fact that the army rushed to judgment on the basis of operator reports, and claimed that the Patriot had intercepted most of the Iraqi Scuds that hit Israel and Saudi Arabia. These statements led President Bush to say that the Patriot was, "proof positive that missile defense systems work."[67] Even in March, 1991—after better data were available—the army issued press releases claiming that "of the 47 Scuds against which it was fired, Patriot successfully intercepted 45 ... throughout its entire period of employment in SWA, the system demonstrated an overall operational readiness rate above 95%."[68]

During the months that followed, outside critics charged that the Patriot was almost totally ineffective. They issued studies indicating that the Patriot had hit no Scud warheads. Some charged that the Patriots might actually have added to the damage the Scuds inflicted on Israel by adding to the missile debris that fell in or near Tel Aviv.

This mix of exaggerated praise and criticism has triggered a debate that has taken on much of the character of the earlier US debate over the Strategic Defense Initiative (SDI)—with each side making extreme claims and treating the issue in ideological, if not quasireligious, terms. The data now available indicate that the truth lies somewhere between the army's position and that of its critics, and that the Patriot had some successes, and its failures often had little to do with the inherent capabilities of the Patriot and follow-on antiballistic missile systems.

This presents interesting, but unanswerable, questions in terms of Iraqi perceptions. There is no way to know if Iraq views US antitactical missile ballistic defense efforts as a major problem, or sees the Gulf War as a lesson in the fact that the United States exaggerates its claims. At the same time, the failures of the Scud hunt raise the issue of whether Iraq sees future missile deployments as highly survivable or feels that new US counterproliferation and intelligence efforts since the war are giving the United States the ability to locate and kill Scud launches in the future.

It is equally impossible to determine how Iraq views these lessons in terms of other regional powers, although it seems likely that it may have concluded that no regional power other than Israel could now be more effective in killing Iraqi missile launchers or defending against incoming missiles than the United States was during the Gulf War. Given the scale and duplicativeness of its past efforts, Iraq may well react by attempting to exploit the survivability of missiles demonstrated during the Gulf War, while taking contingency measures to develop alternative delivery systems.

IRAQ'S MISSILE CAPABILITIES SINCE THE TIME OF THE GULF WAR AND THE WAR OF SANCTIONS

Events since the Gulf War have clarified many aspects of Iraq's wartime missile capabilities, but have left significant uncertainties regarding what it has concealed and its post–Gulf War covert efforts to rebuild its missile capabilities. Iraq has lied about its efforts at virtually every stage of the UN's effort to destroy its capacity to deliver long-range missiles. While it was the UN Coalition which fought Iraqi military forces during the Gulf War, it has been UNSCOM and the IAEA that have had to fight the Iraqi regime ever since.

Iraq declared in its initial report to the UN after the cease-fire that it had 52 surviving ballistic missiles, 38 launchers, 30 chemical-filled warheads, and 23 conventionally armed warheads at five sites.[69] In the years that have followed, the UN has found that the facts are very different, and that Iraq is continuing to conceal both its wartime holdings and production capabilities and to import new components and missile production equipment. UNSCOM soon identified at least 17 facilities where the Iraqi government had conducted research, production, and testing and repair of ballistic missiles, launchers, and rocket fuel.[70] By February, 1992, UNSCOM had destroyed over 80 missiles, 11 missile decoys, dozens of fixed and mobile launchers, eight missile transporters, and 146 missile storage units.[71]

Iraqi efforts to deceive UNSCOM continued after these discoveries. Iraq hid the fact that it was producing its own missile engines, and it concealed the equipment it used in one of its major Scud modification facilities: Project 1728. In July, 1991, it loaded "important tools, dies, and parts of key priority on trucks . . . from all of its major missile establishments. . . . Eleven trucks were turned over to two unidentified officers said to be relatives of Lt. General Husayn Kamel." Iraq also diverted at least three missiles from destruction. While Iraq later claimed it unilaterally destroyed the equipment and missiles later in 1991 and during March, 1992, UNSCOM's inspection efforts proved inconclusive.[72]

Iraq turned inspection after inspection into a confrontation and continued to lie about its efforts. For example, UNSCOM detected the deployment of the special fuel trucks that were used for launching Scud missiles to areas outside of Baghdad in February, 1993, and encountered attempts to deny UN inspectors access to Iraqi missile ranges in June and July, 1993.[73] In 1994, UNSCOM's insistence on the destruction of five pieces of manufacturing equipment designed to produce missile engines evoked new Iraqi challenges and delays before Iraq finally complied. At the same time, satellite photographs showed that Iraq had rebuilt its Al-Kindi missile research facility[74]

The Missile Crisis of 1995

In spite of Iraq's actions, UNSCOM felt that it had managed to account for the history of over 800 Scud missile assemblies by early 1995, including those Iraq fired during the Iran-Iraq and Gulf wars. By the spring of 1995, UNSCOM concluded that it would soon be able to certify that it had destroyed Iraq's missile production and delivery capabilities. UNSCOM was relying on import and usage data that its inspectors had discovered in Iraq and used this data to estimate Iraq's total inventory of Scud variants at 819, and then used this number to set a target for its efforts to dismantle or destroy Iraq's Scuds. UNSCOM also believed that it had managed to identify all of Iraq's major missile production facilities, on the assumption that Iraq had fully destroyed all of the missiles that UNSCOM had counted.

A number of outside experts believed, however, that the UN underestimated the number of Iraqi Scuds. In fact, the director of the CIA had estimated that Iraq might still possess "hundreds" of missiles in testimony before Congress as early as January, 1992.[75]

Iraq's revelations, following Hussein Kamel's defection, showed that the reservations of outside experts were right. The documents Iraq surrendered to UNSCOM in August, 1995 revealed a number of previously undisclosed missile projects. These projects included modification and production of missile systems (Project 144), production of missile guidance and control systems (Project Karama), production of liquid-propellant rocket engines (Project 1728), and development of a two-stage solid-propellant missile (Project Badar-2000).[76] Iraq also admitted that it had manufactured some of its own Scuds before the Gulf War and had a previously undisclosed liquid-fuel engine production capability, and that it was developing new long-range missiles with ranges of 900 kilometers, 3,000 kilometers, and 5,000 kilometers, and a nuclear warhead for its Al Husayn missile. [77]

These developments forced UNSCOM into a major new inspection and verification effort, which illustrates the dangers of relying on the statements of a serious proliferator. As UNSCOM reports,

In 1994, in a spirit of cooperation, the Commission even undertook to write a history of Iraq's proscribed missile program so that Iraq could authenticate it as an official description of relevant Iraqi activities. By mid-1995, this project was close to its completion with many parts certified by Iraq as accurate. However, shortly thereafter, it became obvious that, in many important respects, Iraq had been intentionally misleading the Commission by providing incorrect information as cover for important progress achieved in its proscribed missile programs. This required the Commission to resume verification of those areas.[78]

Further discoveries soon followed. In August, 1995 Iraq admitted that it had carried out an undeclared program ever since 1991 to modify the Volga/SA-2 surface-to-air missile system to a surface-to-surface missile system with a range of over 100 kilometers. This forced UNSCOM to begin tagging the missiles in January, 1996, and to carry out four more tagging of missiles after April, 1996. UNSCOM estimated in October, 1996 that it had tagged nearly 90% of the missiles identified by Iraq and relevant spare parts. However, this tagging only affected declared missiles.[79]

UNSCOM found that Iraq had retained undeclared liquid fuel engine manufacturing facilities for its long-range missiles, and that Iraq had lied about the number of missile warheads it had destroyed before the UNSCOM destruction effort began. It found that Iraq had built or assembled over 80 Scud-type missiles using its own engines, although 53 were unusable. It also found that 10 engines were unaccounted for. In the fall of 1995, UNSCOM also found that Iraq had established a clandestine purchasing network to buy missile components in 1990, and that it had maintained this network following the Gulf War.[80] As a result, UNSCOM reported that the documents Iraq had provided did "not contain the full record of proscribed missile activities," which could have established the extent of Iraqi production.[81]

On November 10, 1995, Jordan intercepted a major shipment of missile guidance components and manufacturing equipment.[82] This shipment made it clear that Iraq set up a clandestine import program to obtain missile guidance systems and furnaces to make missile components for Scud-type missiles following the Gulf War. The shipment was worth nearly $25 million and had been purchased by a front group in Amman headed by a Palestinian named Weamma Gharbiyeh. It included 115 gyroscopes bound for Iraq and a total of 10 crates worth of equipment that were air freighted from Moscow to Amman on November 10, 1995.

The shipment included entire guidance canisters, although these guidance systems would have required massive reengineering to be used with the much slower-reacting missiles that Iraq had developed at the time of the Gulf War. Rolf Ekeus, the chairman of UNSCOM, referred to this effort as "a large shipment of high-grade missile components."[83]

UNSCOM inspectors found additional gyroscopes in a canal of the Tigris on December 9, 1995. The gyroscopes had been smuggled from Russia and were taken from dismantled Russian SS-N-18 or "Stingray" SLBM warheads. The SS-N-18 is an advanced system that entered Russian service in 1977, and which has three variations, with a throwweight of 16,500 kilograms, ranges of 6,500–8,000 kilometers, 1–7 MIRV'd warheads, and CEPs ranging from 900–1,400 meters.

The first detailed report on this Iraqi smuggling effort was issued by the PIR

Center for Policy Studies in Russia on April 12, 1998. It stated that the smuggled gyroscopes had first come to light after UN weapons inspectors received a tip and fished 10 of the gyroscopes out of the Tigris River near the Iraqi capital of Baghdad. According to the PIR, the gyroscopes came from the Research and Testing Institute of Chemical and Building Machines, a defense plant in Sergiyev Posad, a town near Moscow. The plant is involved in the dismantling of long-range strategic missiles, and the gyroscopes were part of the guidance systems for the RSM-50 submarine-launched intercontinental ballistic missiles, which have a range of 5,000 miles. The missiles were dismantled under the START-1 arms reduction treaty between the United States and Russia.

The PIR report indicated that Gharbiyeh initially procured a batch of 10 samples, which were ultimately found in the Tigris River, the report said. He then received the main shipment of 800 missile components, dubbed ''micromotors,'' in official documents that passed through Russian customs at Moscow's Sheremetyevo Airport and on to Jordan. Hussein Kamel al-Majid, the son-in-law of Iraqi President Saddam Hussein and the head of Iraq's weapons program, allegedly ordered the gyroscopes, but defected to neighboring Jordan in the summer of 1995. Gharbiyeh went to Baghdad in a bid to complete the deal, but was arrested and charged with ''working for an enemy state'' because of his connection to al-Majid, who was branded a traitor by Iraq. Al-Majid was killed shortly after he returned to Iraq in 1996, and Gharbiyeh has remained jailed in Iraq ever since.

The report stated that the Russian government investigated the sales but closed the case and never prosecuted anyone at the military plant that allegedly sold the sophisticated devices to a Palestinian. The PIR report indicated that the Russian Criminal Code was not enforced because ''Russian lawmakers and the government failed to notice its serious flaws.'' The report indicated that the most relevant section of Russian criminal law dealing with export controls only barred the sale of weapons of mass destruction. It does not specifically prohibit the transfer, however, of key missile components, such as the gyroscopes, which are used to guide missiles to their targets.

More details were provided in a report by David Hoffman in the *Washington Post* on October 18, 1998. This report was based on joint work by the PIR and the Monterey Institute of International Studies in the United States. It indicated that the gyroscopes were only part of a much larger series of shipments, and were the result of a purchasing effort by a group of top Iraqi missile experts during trip to Russia in late 1994. They signed a letter of intent to buy orders for missile engines, technology, and services in spite of UN sanctions. This report confirms that the Iraqis used Gharbiyeh as a purchasing agent. In addition to the gyroscopes, Iraq signed contract to buy a 5,000-liter fermentation vessel that could be used to produce biological weapons.

According to the PIR Monterey Institute report, Gharbiyeh was given a major order in August, 1994 from the Ibn Al Haythan Missile Center in Iraq. The Center agreed to pay him $3.9 million for key missile components and technology, including precision guidance instruments. Gharbiyeh then brought a delegation of Iraqi missile specialists to Russia in November, 1994. These experts included representatives from the Ibn Al Haythan Center and from Karama, a large Iraqi aerospace and defense firm. They met with senior officials at Russian missile design and production facilities.

The investigation found that the Iraqis and Russians held dozens of protocols and letters of intent for the purchase missile components, technology, and services. "The Russians would supply missile engines, missile design, training, technology, manufacturing and testing for engines, airframes, and guidance and control systems." These included "the most advanced technologies, and eager to work out specific offers as soon as possible, as long as payment was assured."

One of the letters of intent was signed with the Scientific Production Association Energomash, a huge Russian producer of rocket engines based in Moscow. The company agreed to provide "complete technology transfer," including production equipment for two types of liquid-fueled missile engines. "Energomash agreed to provide a complete rocket engine of four-ton thrust as well as design calculations, final design, and five complete samples of a propulsion system for a 'communications satellite' whose size matched the payload specifications for an intermediate-range Scud-derived missile.... The Russians agreed to train the Iraqis in the design, production, and testing of modern rocket engines, and to enter into a project to jointly design a rocket engine," the investigators reported. "Energomash officials assured the Iraqis that they could go ahead with these deals even without the approval of their government by paying bribes to the appropriate people."

Energomash has denied these activities, but the investigation reported that Gharbiyeh remained in Moscow to finish the contracts and returned to Baghdad in early 1995 to negotiate deals with his Iraqi contacts worth more than $65 million.

The PIR and the Monterey Institute also found that Gharbiyeh returned to Russia to purchase the gyroscopes from a missile destruction factory in Sergiyev Posad. He had the gyroscopes tested and certified at a special facility in Moscow, and arranged for the air shipment of 800 sensitive missile gyroscopes and accelerometers from Moscow to Amman.

It was these components that were seized in Amman in November, 1995. They included 240 strategic missile gyroscopes and 240 accelerometers. However, only 120 gyroscopes and 120 accelerometers were seized in Jordan. UNSCOM inspectors found an additional 33 gyroscopes and 26 accelerometers in the Tigris River in Baghdad on December 9, 1995. These seizures, however, leave about 180 gyroscopes and accelerometers—enough for 30 missile guidance systems—still to be accounted for.

The PIR concluded that most of the other equipment and technology was never delivered because of work by the Russian security services and Gharbiyeh's arrest in 1995. The Center also concluded, however, "it is hard to imagine that the Russian authorities at some level were not aware of his [Gharbiyeh's] activities.''

Other sources indicate that the guidance platforms were taken illegally from a Russian facility called the Scientific Testing Institute of Chemical Machine Building, at Sergiyev Pasad. These sources report that they were part of a shipment of 30 gyroscopes that had been air freighted to Jordan as ''electrical measuring equipment'' by a company called TASM, located in Moscow and headed by a former Russian general. The deal had been negotiated during 1993–1994 by a Lebanese middleman. The gyroscopes were roughly the size of a paperback novel, and were easy to smuggle. They evidently ended up in the Karama research center near Baghdad.

It is not yet clear why the guidance platforms were dumped in the river or how the UNSCOM inspectors managed to find them. Some US experts estimate, however, that they were simply too advanced for Iraq and became a potential political embarrassment without offering Iraq any technology it could adapt or weaponize.[84]

Iraq's Smuggling Efforts Continue

These discoveries proved to be part of a much broader pattern of imports from nations like Russia, Germany, and France, and created further uncertainties about how many missiles and warheads Iraq had produced which needed to be destroyed. This series of revelations led Ambassador Rolf Ekeus—the head of UNSCOM—to declare that Iraq's missile and biological weapons programs were ''larger and more advanced in every dimension than previously declared.'' UNSCOM's October, 1995 report stated that there was ''no firm basis for establishing at this time a reliable accounting of Iraq's proscribed missiles.''[85]

Iraq responded by providing yet another supposed full, final, and complete disclosure (FFCD) in November, 1995, but this did not solve the problem. The new document was some 2,500 pages long, but UNSCOM's December, 1995 report to the Security Council stated that, ''Iraq's accounting in the November, 1995 FFCD did not appear to constitute a firm basis for establishing a definite and verifiable material balance for proscribed weapons and activities.''[86]

The new Iraqi FFCD report proved so deficient that UNSCOM was able to pressure Iraq into submitting two more draft FFCDs in February, 1996 and May, 1996. The February, 1996 document did make some progress, but the May document did not. UNSCOM concluded at the end of 1996 that ''Iraq must provide substantial evidence that would allow for the verifiable accounting of all missiles, launchers, propellants, and major components.''[87]

Much of the problem stemmed from the fact that Iraq maintained a global purchasing network of at least some 15 companies, with 600–700 people, as front groups for buying equipment in Europe and Asia. These groups often had significant support from foreign companies and possibly from some elements of foreign governments. UNSCOM recognized the importance of these post-war smuggling efforts in its December 21, 1995, report to the UN Security Council, and Ambassador Ekeus showed the Council a gyroscope that Iraqi engineers had thrown into the Tigris River in an effort to conceal it from the UN inspectors.[88]

While the UN has refused to publicly name the countries and firms found to be involved in this effort, UN and US officials have stated privately that Chinese, French, German, Central European, and Russian firms seem to be most active. One UN official specifically implicated Ukraine, while a senior US official has expressed concern over recent Russian sales of missile-related equipment to Iraq.[89]

New Discoveries in 1996

During 1996, the UNSCOM effort began to focus on the possibility that Iraq had faked some aspects of the destruction of its Scuds in 1991 and had substituted low grade Iraqi-made engines and turbopumps for the much higher grade Soviet made components in the original systems. Where UNSCOM had earlier estimated that it might be dealing with six to 16 concealed missiles, it now faced uncertainties relating to up to 85 missiles and the possibility that Iraq might have as many as 40–48 surviving systems.[90]

Iraq refused to allow UNSCOM to inspect several major facilities and physically examine its remaining records and missiles so that UNSCOM could determine how many missiles Iraq might still be concealing. Nevertheless, UNSCOM inspectors saw the movement of "Scud-like" objects in the vicinity of a site designated for inspection in July, 1996. They also found evidence that Iraq had covertly been working on space programs using proscribed missiles, and concealing the full scale of the activities of its major programs dealing with missile engines, guidance, and control systems.[91]

UNSCOM made repeated efforts to resolve these issues, but the Iraqis refused to cooperate and provide physical evidence from the missile sites where supposedly destroyed Scuds had been buried in 1991. The transfer of this evidence would have allowed UNSCOM to provide missiles to US experts who could have determined whether or not Iraq continued to lie. It seemed likely that Iraq had at least 18–25 operational missile assemblies, and Ekeus reported to the UN on December 18, 1996, that Iraq not only had such missiles, but the TELs, fuel, and command systems to "make a missile force of significance."[92]

Iraq cut its level of cooperation in other areas. It turned meeting after meeting into a confrontation and claimed that UNSCOM should not inspect "presidential areas" because this was a violation of its sovereignty. These problems grew worse after Iraq succeeded in expanding its influence in the Kurdish zone in the fall of 1996, and reached an agreement on "food for oil" under the terms of UNSCR 986. Iraq seemed to have shifted to a strategy of trying to exploit the

Security Council's growing fatigue with the entire sanctions issue—a strategy that UNSCOM officials admitted seemed to be having some success.

UNSCOM was able to keep some 100 experts in a monitoring center in Baghdad, but it had every reason to be concerned about Iraq's claims that there was no new evidence. Iraq disclosed new data about its concealment of missile parts in a letter dated October 3, 1996, but virtually ceased to provide UNSCOM with new documents in January, 1997. Even so, UNSCOM found that Iraq had been concealing a highly sophisticated computer modeling effort to simulate missile tests and development activities ever since 1991—yet another major indication of Iraq's continuing interest in long-range missiles.[93]

Developments in 1997

In February, 1997, Iraq finally agreed to allow UNSCOM to dig up the missiles that Iraq claimed to have destroyed in 1991, and to send the remains to laboratories in France and the United States. This was necessary because of indications that Iraq might have removed key parts from the missiles and stockpiled them for later use. Iraq also allowed UNSCOM to resume excavations in the "destruction sites" in January and February, 1997. The UNSCOM team found additional missile equipment that Iraq had not reported, including four complete engines Iraq had not previously presented to the Commission.

These developments led UNSCOM to conclude in April, 1997 that Iraq had continued to deliberately mislead the Commission, and that "Iraq had not presented sufficient evidence of the destruction of all proscribed missiles." It also concluded that,

With respect to the special warheads for proscribed missiles, both produced for chemical and biological weapons, Iraq has still not provided a credible account on quantities and types of warheads produced, the time frame for their production and filling, and the alleged destruction. The Commission has evidence that Iraq has provided incorrect information in this respect.[94]

UNSCOM found that Iraq continued to conceal missile engines and the full nature of its projects for missile development. Two key Iraqi efforts included Project 1728, the key project for producing missile engines, and Project Karama, the key project for producing guidance and control systems. UNSCOM found that Iraq used computer simulations and laboratory studies in 1992, 1994, and 1995 to develop forbidden space programs using proscribed missiles. As a result, it has attempted to improve its monitoring and inspection of the Iraqi missile programs, like the Samoud missile, which has a range under 150 kilometers and is permitted under the terms of the UN resolutions. UNSCOM is particularly concerned because Iraq has refused to provide computer software and documents on such programs, and missiles like the Samoud are nearing the production phase.[95]

These developments left UNSCOM with considerable uncertainty as to whether Iraq had falsely claimed to have destroyed 130 Scuds, while substituting low-grade, Iraqi-made components for Russian-made motors and parts. Further, there were reports that UN inspectors had uncovered evidence that Iraq was using computer modeling and simulation to develop a new missile with a range of 1,000 miles during an inspection in Iraq from January 5–23, 1997. Other reports indicated that Iraq might have put its surviving missiles on trucks so they could be rapidly moved when inspections occurred, and that 18–25 missiles might still be operational.[96]

The issues relating to the missile engines were largely resolved by the time UNSCOM reported again in October, 1997. Iraq had grudgingly sent rocket motors to the United States and France for testing and had allowed Russian inspection. As a result, UNSCOM confirmed that Iran had destroyed at least 83 out of the 85 missiles it had declared it unilaterally destroyed. This confirmed the fact that UNSCOM had been able to account for 817 of the 819 Scuds Iraq was known to have imported.

UNSCOM reported, however, that questions remained regarding Iraq's indigenous missile production efforts. Iraq had still failed to provide a complete accounting for launchers, warheads, and propellants. There were uncertainties regarding the number and type of warheads and the disposition of key components like turbopumps and guidance platforms.[97] There also were serious problems in accounting for biological and chemical missile warheads. UNSCOM also discovered that Iraq's declarations of August, 1997 regarding Project 1728, and the destruction of missile equipment at Al Alam, near Tikrit, was deeply flawed. UNSCOM could only confirm that "some 10 to 15 percent of the quantities of major engine components that Iraq had declared were destroyed at the site. The Commission was able to remove all of the components excavated from the site in a single 12-ton vehicle, although Iraq claimed that nine truckloads of equipment had been destroyed.[98]

Doubts remained about Iraq's surviving holdings of Soviet-made MAZ-543 transport-erector-launchers (TELs), Iraqi-made al-Nida and al-Walid mobile-erector-launchers (MELs), and the potential readiness state of its Scuds. Iraq had reported that it had destroyed six TELs, four MELs, and 53 missiles after the Gulf War. Some experts felt, however, that Iraq might have up to twice the TELs it had reported, and there was no way to verify the number of MELs it had made.[99]

The potential readiness of Iraq's concealed missile forces presented a problem, because East German military experts had reported that unfueled Scuds could be stored in operational form for up to 20 years in mothballed condition, or could be assembled with the guidance system installed, checked out, and then kept in the field for up to 15 years in static storage facilities or for two years in the field. Scuds fueled with fuel and oxidizers could be stored in operational form for up to a year, be brought to readiness in the field with minimal movement and delectability, and then be deployed to launch sites and fired in 17–30 minutes.

Some experts felt that missiles could be kept in near launch-ready status at a camouflaged launch site for up to a year and fired at a preplanned target in 9–11 minutes, or in a launch-ready state for two hours. Fuel readiness and availability was felt to be an issue, because the oxidizing agent (similar to red-fuming nitric acid) and fuel were said to have a shelf life of 12–18 months, and it was unclear whether Iraq could manufacture such supplies. However, experts felt that some of the training and activity involved could be carried out under the guise of SA-2 fueling exercises.[100]

Developments in 1998

UNSCOM had clearly made great progress by the end of 1997, but Iraq continued to present constant problems. It also pressed UNSCOM and the UN into setting up an independent panel of experts in late 1997. This panel focused on the uncertainties existing regarding Iraq's holdings of warheads, as well as its missile production. It was made up of 13 experts from the United Kingdom, China, France, Germany, Russia, and the United States. It had a parallel panel on chemical weapons, and it met with Iraqi officials in Baghdad from February 1 to 6.

Iraq seems to have had great expectations for the outcome of this technical evaluation meeting. The Iraqi regime clearly saw the missile and chemical weapons panels as a means of closing the UNSCOM files in these areas, and expediting the end of economic sanctions. When the panel reported to the Security Council on February 19, 1998, however, it reached very different conclusions, ones that validated UNSCOM's earlier efforts.

The panel concluded that more work was needed to account for all of Iraq's long-range missile warheads. It also concluded that excavated warhead remnants provided valuable data for overall analysis and evaluation, but that the level of verification was not satisfactory and that more work was required. "Less progress has been achieved in the accounting of Iraq's declared special warheads for chemical and biological weapons. UNSCOM still needs to obtain a full picture of Iraq's warhead production." The experts also stated that "on several occasions, the Iraqi side vehemently objected to the introduction of all relevant facts and information. . . . In many cases, the Iraqi side would withdraw or change its explanations if they were not satisfactory to the team."

US and British intelligence drew similar conclusions in unclassified reports they issued in February, 1998.[101] The details of these reports are summarized in Table 15.6. They agreed with UNSCOM in concluding that Iraq had an active missile force before the Gulf War that included at least 819 operational Scud B missiles (300-km range) purchased from the Soviet Union, an advanced program to extend the Scud's range and modify its warhead (e.g., the Al-Husayn, with

Table 15.6
Iraqi Ballistic Missile Capabilities in 1998

Item	Initial Inventory	Comments
Soviet-supplied Scud missiles (includes the Iraqi modifications of the Al-Husayn, with a range of 650 km, and the Al-Abbas, with a range of 950 km)	819	UNSCOM accepts Iraqi accounting for all but two of the original 819 Scud missiles acquired from the Soviet Union. Iraq hasn't explained the disposition of major components that it may have stripped from operational missiles before their destruction, and some Iraqi claims—such as the use of 14 Scuds in ATBM tests—are not believable. Gaps in Iraqi declarations and Baghdad's failure to fully account for indigenous missile programs strongly suggest that Iraq maintains a small missile force.
Iraqi-produced Scud missiles	Unknown	Iraq denied producing a completed Scud missile, but it produced/procured and tested all major subcomponents.
Iraqi-produced Scud warheads	120	Iraq claims all 120 were used or destroyed. UNSCOM supervised the destruction of 15. Recent UNSCOM inspections found additional CW/BW warheads beyond those currently admitted.
Iraqi-produced Scud airframes	2	Iraq claims testing two indigenous airframes in 1990. It is unlikely that Iraq produced only two Scud airframes.
Iraqi-produced Scud engines	80	Iraq's claim that it melted 63 engines following acceptance tests—53 of which failed quality controls—is unverifiable and not believable. UNSCOM is holding this as an open issue.
Soviet-supplied missile launchers	11	UNSCOM doubts Iraq's claim that it unilaterally destroyed five launchers. The Soviet Union may have sold more than the declared 11 launchers.
Iraqi-produced missile launchers	8	Iraq has the capability to produce additional launchers.

Source: Adapted by Anthony H. Cordesman from material provided by the NSC on February 19, 1998.

a 650-km range and the Al Abbas, with a 950-km range). At the same time, they warned that Iraq had an extensive effort to reverse engineer and indigenously produce complete Scud missiles. It also mentioned that Iraq had programs to indigenously produce long-range missiles (e.g., the Condor) that never entered the production phase.

The US report provided important background on the uncertainties affecting the count of Iraq's remaining missiles and Iraq's indigenous missile production efforts. The US report noted that UNSCOM has only directly supervised the destruction of 48 Scud-type missiles, 10 mobile launchers, 30 chemical and 18 conventional warheads, and related equipment. Similarly, it has only verified Iraq's unilateral destruction of only 83 Scud-type missiles and nine mobile launchers.[102]

The rest of the UNSCOM accounting depends heavily on Iraq's claims that other missiles were destroyed by having fired in the Iran-Iraq and Gulf wars, or were used in static tests or for training. US experts felt that unmonitored claims to unilateral destruction and discrepancies in the Iraqi accounting suggest that Baghdad could still have a small force of Scud-type missiles and an undetermined number of warheads and launchers. Iraq has not adequately explained the disposition of important missile components that it could not produce on its own and may have removed before destruction.[103]

US experts felt that there were still many gaps in the scope of Iraq's indigenous missile programs. Their report noted that Iraq might have pieced together a small inventory of missiles by integrating guidance and control systems it concealed with indigenously produced parts. Iraq had admitted producing Scud engines, airframes, and warheads before the war, but UNSCOM had not been able to verify Iraqi claims that it destroyed all of these components. The US experts also noted that Baghdad probably continues to receive some parts through clandestine procurement networks. They focused on the fact that Jordan interdicted missile-guidance equipment (gyroscopes) bound for Iraq in 1995, and that Baghdad admitted under UNSCOM questioning that it received a similar shipment earlier in 1995. Furthermore, they reported that Iraq turned over a previously undeclared SS-21 short-range ballistic missile launcher in November, 1996 that it acquired from Yemen before the Gulf War, and that this illustrated Iraq's ability to conceal major elements of missile systems from UNSCOM inspectors.[104]

The US experts concluded that Baghdad had not given up its plans to build larger, longer-range missiles. They noted that UNSCOM has uncovered numerous Iraqi design drawings, including multistage systems and clustered engine designs, that theoretically could reach western Europe. UNSCOM inspectors had uncovered evidence that Iraq has continued missile research since the imposition of sanctions. If sanctions were lifted, Iraq could probably acquire enough material to resume full-scale production of Scud-type missiles, perhaps within one year.[105]

The US report stressed that Iraq retained significant research and production capabilities. It had a research facility at Al Kindi, and it continued to expand its missile production facility at Ibn Al Haytham—currently used to support its authorized missile programs. This expansion included the construction of two new fabrication buildings at the facility spacious enough to house the construction of large ballistic missiles. US experts felt that Baghdad's claim that the buildings at Ibn al Haytham were intended to be computer and administrative facilities were inconsistent with the facility's inherent size and capacity.[106]

They also noted that Iraq's Al-Samoud and Ababil-100 missile programs—which are permitted because they fall within the allowed 150-km range limit—serve to maintain production expertise within the constraints of sanctions. They report that Iraq had apparently flight tested the Al-Samoud—which UNSCOM describes as a scaled-down Scud—successfully, and estimated that Iraq would begin converting these programs into long-range missile production programs as soon as sanctions were lifted.[107]

UNSCOM became less concerned with the prospect that Iraq had retained an operational Scud force than US experts as a result of its examination of missile engines. Nevertheless, UNSCOM's April, 1998 report was only marginally more reassuring than its previous reporting, and UNSCOM warned that Iraq's "legal" programs using missiles with ranges under 150 kilometers might well be little more than a means of cloaking a covert long-range missile program:

After the accounting for imported proscribed missiles and their launchers as reported in the Commission's report of October 1997, work continued in the areas of missile warheads and propellants. Warhead issues were the subject of consideration by a technical evaluation meeting that was held in Baghdad from 1 to 6 February 1998. The meeting concluded that the level of verification achieved so far was not satisfactory and stated that further work was required. The meeting made specific recommendations for continuing verification activities by the Commission and actions to be taken by Iraq, including provision of documentation and new declarations. The excavation and analysis of warhead remnants continues with advanced survey equipment. Iraq has not yet provided the information, data and documentation specified by the meeting. The accounting of proscribed missile propellants is still outstanding. As Iraq has not provided the new declarations or documentation requested by the Commission, no substantive progress is able to be recorded in the six months since the Commission's last consolidated report to the Security Council.

The accounting for special (chemical and biological) warheads for the Al Hussein missiles was discussed in depth in the course of the technical evaluation meeting on missile warheads held in Baghdad from 1 to 6 February 1998. The meeting came to the conclusion that the level of verification achieved so far is not satisfactory and that Iraq is required to undertake additional steps to settle this issue.

During the current reporting period, Iraq continued the development of the Al Samoud missile, which, according to its design, is capable of maximum ranges close to 150 kilometers, the limit permitted to Iraq for surface-to-surface missile systems under Security Council resolution 687 (1991). Iraq continued to use non-Iraqi made components, including some from imported Volga surface-to-air missiles, in its Al Samoud missiles. On 26 November 1997, the Commission restated its position that the ongoing monitoring and verification plan did not allow for the use of certain components from surface-to-air missiles in non-proscribed surface-to-surface missiles as they could be used for the conversion of the surface-to-air missiles to surface-to-surface missiles of proscribed ranges. The issue of the use of the components of Volga missiles in the development of Al Samoud missiles was raised by the Executive Chairman during his visit to Iraq in March, 1998. The Iraqi side did not accept the Commission's contentions. Further consideration of these matters will take place. Iraq did not comply with the Commission's requests for technical information on the system.[108]

It was also clear that the sanctions crisis of February, 1998 had not stopped Iraq's efforts to interfere with UNSCOM's efforts to find out the full details of Iraq's missile programs, or any of its other efforts. UNSCOM's April, 1998 report stated:

The Commission's resident monitoring teams continue to experience varying levels of cooperation from the National Monitoring Directorate in the execution of their tasks. While the support at the working level is generally satisfactory, there continue to be incidents of non-compliance. These include late or incorrect declarations; movement of tagged equipment without proper notification; lack of access to sites and rooms through the absence of keys; discrepancies between a site's own declarations and those submitted by the Directorate; interference by personnel of the Directorate in the progress of inspections; false replies by site personnel; site personnel departing sites before inspections could be completed; and sites providing two different directors general for the same site to different teams. In relative terms, such incidents are small in number but nevertheless have a derogatory effect on confidence in the system.[109]

These problems became steadily more severe during June, and helped precipitate the crisis that led Iraq to end cooperation with UNSCOM on July 5, 1998 and eventually to Desert Fox. As Table 10.3 shows, Iraq soon found that it had little reason to be optimistic about UNSCOM's handling of its declarations on missiles, chemical weapons, and biological weapons. On June 4, USCOM experts briefed the Security Council as part of an effort to give Iraq a "road map" that would show it exactly what it needed to do to obtain UNSCOM and IAEA agreement that it had complied with the terms of the cease-fire. During this briefing, UNSCOM released satellite surveillance photographs dating back to 1991 and new U-2 surveillance photos showing that Iraq had lied about the number of missiles it had destroyed and that several of its "destruction pits" had never been used to destroy missiles.[110]

UNSCOM also announced that a team of 27 experts in Iraq had just gathered samples from missile warheads that it dug up from destruction pits in Iraq, and that these samples indicated they might have been loaded with biological and chemical agents. UNSCOM also stated that serious discrepancies still existed regarding missile engines, propellants, warheads, and production facilities. These findings directly contradicted an earlier three-hour-long Iraqi briefing to the Council by a team led by Iraqi Foreign Minister Mohammed Saeed al-Sahaf.

The situation became worse for Iraq on June 22. UNSCOM presented data to the UN showing that the United States had found evidence that Iraq had lied about the deployment of chemical warheads for its missiles and had deployed warheads using stabilized VX nerve gas. The United States based these charges on the basis of work by a military testing laboratory at the Aberdeen Proving Ground in Maryland. The US laboratory found traces of stable VX gas in Scud-type missile warhead fragments recovered from a "destruction site" near Baghdad in early 1998. These results led UNSCOM to suspect that Iraq loaded the VX into warheads before the 1991 Gulf War, and directly contradicted Baghdad's contention that it had never been able to stabilize the volatile nerve agent. Iraq had admitted putting Sarin nerve gas in warheads, but had denied that it had ever succeeded in weaponizing VX.

Butler reported these findings to the Security Council on June 22. Butler also stated publicly on June 24 that he had no doubts about the accuracy of the US tests. The Iraqi reaction was immediate and severe. The same day Butler made his charges, Iraqi Deputy Prime Minister Tariq Aziz denied them, and countercharged that UNSCOM's report was deliberately concealing Iraq's position that, "since the accounting for missile engines, missile launchers, and missile warheads was completed, the question of missile propellants loses importance and becomes a secondary issue since it is an additional element which was not of interest in itself, in addition to the fact that it did not constitute a very complex substance."[111]

Things did not go better when Butler flew to Baghdad to discuss the issue with Iraqi officials. After meeting briefly with Butler on July 3, Tariq Aziz gave a press conference in which he stated that UNSCOM's work since February had not been "honest and quick, but it was a game of maneuvering, protraction and blackmail. I had, before this meeting, the impression that UNSCOM is back to its old games and tricks." Aziz also announced that Iraq would no longer cooperate with UNSCOM, a statement that Iraq's Revolutionary Command Council and National Assembly made official on July 5. That same day, the Iraqi paper *Babel* called Butler a "mad dog." By September 3, it was clear that Iraq was actively interfering with UNSCOM activities even when these only involved efforts to inspect equipment that had been tagged previously, and was refusing UNSCOM inspectors access to sites they had visited previously.

UNSCOM's October, 1998 report to the Security Council did not disclose any new concerns regarding Iraq's missile capabilities, but there is no way to know precisely what aspects of its missile program Iraq is concealing or how far it has gotten in its post–Gulf War efforts to create new missile research, development, and production capabilities. Many Western experts remain convinced that Iraq continues to lie in its accounting of missile engines, missile launchers, and missile warheads. Many also feel that Iraq retains the capability to rapidly deploy long-range missiles, and some estimates go a high as 15–24 combat-capable long-range missiles.

More conservative estimates indicate that Iraq is concealing a number of mobile missile transporter-erector-launchers (TELs), and that it can rapidly build more, perhaps covertly. They indicate that Iraq probably has enough active propellant to fuel several dozen missiles, and possibly far more. Although Iraq has accounted for 817 of the known 819 Scud assemblies it imported before the cease-fire, it has never convincingly accounted for its indigenous production efforts. Accordingly, Iraq may have 5–12 operational al-Husayn missiles that it has disassembled and hidden in various places in Iraq. It could have major components for up to 25 more. Former UNSCOM inspector Scott Ritter has testified that Iraq has lied about its missile production equipment. For example, it has described complex four axis machine tools designed for missile production as much simpler three axis machines.[112]

The following excerpts from UNSCOM's October 6, 1998, report to the Security Council provide a good picture of the degree of Iraq's continuing efforts to disguise its remaining assets and programs:[113]

In the missile area, ... Iraq refused to discuss the issue of proscribed liquid missile propellant and did not respond positively to the Commission's requests for access to specific documents that would facilitate the completion of the verification of outstanding missile disarmament issues.

The following is an account of progress achieved in the missile area and the status of the outstanding issues:

- The Commission was able to account for the destruction of between 43 and 45 of the 45 operational special warheads declared by Iraq as having been unilaterally destroyed in 1991. This constituted a major accomplishment;

- The VX issue needs to be resolved for the Commission to be in a position to assess whether the current accounting of special warheads is sufficient to verify fully both the declared production of proscribed special warheads and their claimed unilateral destruction;

- The Commission arrived at an assessment, based on the discussions with international experts, that Iraq's declarations on the unilateral destruction of the special warheads did not match all the physical evidence collected at the destruction sites. On 3 August, the Commission asked Iraq to discuss this issue;

- The Commission and Iraq have been able to identify jointly steps to clarify some of the problems related to Iraq's actions of 1991 to hide special warheads. The Commission briefed the Security Council on this issue on 3 and 4 June. This effort was terminated by Iraq on 30 July when it refused to provide access to relevant sites and to discuss this issue any further;

- Accounting of proscribed conventional warheads, as a part of resolution of the overall issue of proscribed warheads, has been significantly advanced. Issues related to remnants of some 50 conventional warheads (both imported and indigenously produced by Iraq) that have not been recovered still remain outstanding and clarifications were sought from Iraq. Iraq was also asked to state its opinion on whether the current accounting, regardless of the remaining gaps, should be considered final or further useful work by Iraq and the Commission could be undertaken to close the remaining gaps. No answer has been received;

Considerable progress has been achieved in (indigenous missile production) through the conduct, as agreed in the schedule for work, of expert meetings in Baghdad in July 1998 to review the status of indigenous production, the material balance and the unilateral destruction thereof. In order to obtain sufficient information for verification assessments in this area, it was decided to focus only on complete missiles and on such key missile parts as engines, gyroscopes and warheads;

The issue of seven indigenously produced missiles that were in the possession of Iraq's missile force in 1991 remains unresolved. Iraq maintains that they were training missiles and that they were unilaterally destroyed in 1991. No remnants of indigenous missiles or their engines have been recovered by the Commission at the declared destruction sites;

The team of international experts, invited by the Commission to the July meeting on this issue, came to an assessment that, by the end of 1990, Iraq had the capability to assemble a limited number of engines for its indigenously produced proscribed missiles. The international experts considered that Iraq needed to account for the key components from this program. Progress has been achieved in the development of a rough material balance of components for the production of engines for proscribed missiles. Additional verification work has been recommended;

The team of international experts came to the conclusion that, by the end of 1990, Iraq did not have the capability to manufacture either indigenously, or to assemble from foreign components, gyroscopes for its indigenous missiles. Although the team recommended some additional verification activities to be undertaken by the Commission, it came to the conclusion that, owing to the methods used by Iraq in its unilateral destruction and the incompleteness of destruction inventories provided by Iraq, the establishment of even a rough material balance of proscribed guidance and control components may not be able to be achieved;

Through joint work, Iraq and the Commission were able to account for most of the proscribed missile warheads. However, remnants of some 30 indigenously produced conventional warheads, which Iraq declared as unilaterally destroyed, have not yet been found;

Iraq refuses to address (proscribed liquid missile propellants). The Commission still considers that a solution to the issues related to the unilateral destruction of proscribed liquid missile propellants could be obtained through the provision by Iraq of existing documentation. Were this to be provided, verification could be achieved immediately.

On 3 August 1998, the Executive Chairman outlined specific steps to Iraq directed at bringing remaining issues in the missile area to closure. This schedule included: the provision by Iraq of clarifications on the outstanding issues in the warhead area; a meeting of experts on this issue; and an inspection to verify accountable aspects of the material balance and the unilateral destruction of major components for indigenous missile production. The Executive Chairman also proposed to undertake, during his stay in Iraq, serious consideration of the issue of unilateral destruction of special warheads. These proposals were not accepted by Iraq.

The missile monitoring group at the Baghdad Monitoring and Verification Center currently consists of six resident inspectors from five States. The group currently monitors 63 sites and 159 tagged items of equipment. Over 2,000 operational missiles have been tagged to ensure that they are not modified for proscribed purposes. . . . Iraq has continued its development of the Al-Samoud missile system, which has a declared range of less than 150 kilometers. The issue of reuse by Iraq of Volga surface-to-air missile components in the development of the Al-Samoud missile continues to be unresolved, as detailed in the Commission's report of 16 April 1998.

MISSILES, WEAPONS OF MASS DESTRUCTION, AND THE WAR OF SANCTIONS

Iraq's missile program has been closely tied to its efforts to produce weapons of mass destruction. The UN found that Iraq not only possessed the ability to launch missiles with chemical warheads, but that it had conducted at least three flight tests of Al Husayn Scud variants with chemical warheads. The UN found the 30 chemical warheads for Iraq's Scud missiles stored in the Dujael area, some 18 miles away from the position Iraq had declared. Sixteen of the warheads carried a unitary nerve agent, and 14 carried binary agents.[114]

The warheads were, however, crudely manufactured and had limited carrying capacity. According to some experts, they possessed inadequate welds and might have tumbled or disintegrated in flight. The warheads also lacked the technology to disseminate chemical agents effectively and reliably. There was little internal structure to the warhead, except for three asymmetrically placed metal bars. The chemical agent was placed in a container within the cone that left substantial empty space between the agent and the cone, and the design did not stabilize the liquid agent. As a result, any sudden acceleration or deceleration during the flight could have caused the warhead to tumble or break up. Even so, it is likely that at least some of these warheads would have penetrated their targets and released enough agent to make them successful as a terror weapon.[115]

In addition to chemical warheads, Iraq developed a significant stockpile of biological missile warheads. The August, 1995 defection of Lieutenant General Husayn Kamel Majid, formerly in charge of Iraq's weapons of mass destruction, prompted a number of revelations by the Iraqi government. Chief among these was a detailed accounting of the number of missiles armed with biological agents and the type of agents employed. Iraq admitted to arming 10 missiles with Anthrax-loaded warheads for the Al Husayn missile, and another 15 missiles with Botulinum-loaded warheads in December, 1990 for possible use during the Gulf War. As has been discussed earlier, Iraq also organized part of its Scud force to use these warheads in a possible retaliatory or launch-under-attack strike if the Coalition killed Saddam or most of the Iraqi high command.[116]

The flow of these discoveries is interesting. Iraq declared 30 chemical warheads in 1991, 45 chemical warheads in 1992, and 20 chemical and biological warheads in 1996. UNSCOM found by October, 1997 that Iraq had filled at least 75 warheads with chemical and biological agents, have used five more of these warheads for trials, and that 16 were with filled with Sarin and 34 with a binary chemical agent. It still, however, could only account for the destruction of 44 warheads, and it had no way to make an accurate estimate of the total number of warheads, or of what they were filled with.[117]

These discoveries are a grim warning. It appears almost certain that Iraq will recover some of its Scud launch capabilities relatively soon after the end of the UN inspection effort. According to both UN officials and US experts, Iraq has used its clandestine procurement network and front companies to put major resources into rebuilding its ballistic missile program—a level of effort that may be worth several hundred million dollars a year. The equipment involved includes advanced missile guidance components, such as accelerometers and gyroscopes, specialty metals, special machine tools, and a high-tech, French-made furnace designed to fabricate missile engine parts. According to US and UN officials, these imports are promptly concealed and stored once obtained.

Furthermore, UNSCOM indicates that Iraq is exploiting the fact that the cease-fire agreement allows it to retain short-range missiles (with ranges of 150 kilometers or less) to test and modify missiles and components to produce much longer-range missiles in the future. One such Iraqi effort was the G-1 program, a missile which had several tests prior to 1993, and which had a real-world range well in excess of 150 kilometers. Iraq has also been found to have software for simulating the design and performance of longer-range missiles, although it initially denied this.

The G-1 program has evidently been canceled, but Iraq is known to have six rocket and ballistic missiles with ranges of under 150 kilometers, which are permitted under the terms of UN Security Council Resolution 687:[118]

- *Luna/Frog-7*: a Russian unguided rocket with a 70-kilometer range currently in service and in limited production.
- *Astros II*: a Brazilian unguided rocket with a 60-kilometer range currently in service and in limited production.
- *SA-2*: a Russian surface-to-air missile which China has demonstrated can be converted into a 300-kilometer range surface-to-surface missile. Iraq has designed a surface-to-surface version.
- *SA-3*: a Russian surface-to-air missile which has some potential for conversion to a surface-to-surface missile.
- *Ababil-50*: a Yugoslav-designed, Iraqi-produced 50-kilometer range artillery rocket with very limited growth potential.
- *Ababil-100*: an Iraqi 100–150-kilometer range system with parallel solid-fuel and liquid fuel development programs. It seems to be a "legal" test-bed and foundation for longer range missile programs once sanctions are lifted.
- *"Al Samoud" (Defiance)*: another Iraqi 100–150-kilometer range system with parallel liquid fuel development programs which reverse engineer certain features of the Scud, and which UNSCOM inspectors describe as a scaled-down Scud. It too seems to be a "legal" test bed and foundation for longer range missile programs once sanctions are lifted. Many of the liquid fueled subprograms are compatible with Scud production.

It is relatively easy to increase the range and payload of systems like the Ababil 100 and Al Samoud and use them to test warhead, guidance, and control systems for longer-range systems. Some of this testing is done without telemetry. These efforts are another factor that would have allowed Iraq to rapidly reestablish its missile program once the UN inspections regime was halted if it had not been for Desert Fox.[119]

UNSCOM and US experts also believe that Iraq is still concealing several Scud launchers and several extended-range Scud missile assemblies, as well as some of the manufacturing equipment, test equipment, and parts purchased before the war. Some US experts also assert that Iraq could be hiding these missiles in underground storage sites built before and after the Gulf War.[120]

If Iraq's Scud force is operational—or becomes so—it will face new point defenses based on the improved Patriot missile. The United States might also be able to preclude large-scale Scud assaults by attacking their launch sites with US airpower. Currently, however, the United States has no way to prevent Iraq from confronting the UN, or some future coalition, with the same "Scud hunt" problems encountered by the US-led coalition during the Gulf War. Now, as then, it would be almost impossible for the United States to hunt down and destroy enough of Iraq's missile capabilities to stop all attacks. Further, Iraq's concealment and import efforts provide strong evidence that it continues to attempt to acquire more lethal chemical and biological warheads for its ballistic missiles. Iraq may even be able to deploy chemical and biological warheads rapidly for its missiles that are superior to those it possessed during the Gulf War. Iraq has had five years to carry out research on such warheads, and they could be produced covertly in laboratories and other nonmilitary facilities.[121]

Iraq may also be changing its missile employment doctrine. Some experts believe that Iraq may have concluded that its Scud variants lost much of their "terror effect" if only equipped with conventional warheads. Iraq may also determine that even chemical warheads have a limited terror or deterrent value, prompting it to concentrate on nuclear and biological warheads. While nerve gas warheads might kill several hundred people with a lucky strike and affect some critical targets, Iraq will not be able to launch a large enough volley to achieve critical war-fighting damage until it can access a major source of resupply for its present holdings of missiles and missile parts.

THE OPTION OF IRAQI CRUISE MISSILES

Iraq's potential capability to develop cruise missiles and unmanned aerial vehicles UAVs presents a further uncertainty. Cruise missiles and UAVs are not affected by the terms of the UN cease-fire, and Iraq is not required to destroy them and relevant production facilities, and is not subject to UN inspection relating to cruise missiles. As a result, they offer Iraq important ways of producing delivery systems while avoiding many of the UN constraints on ballistic missiles, and Iraq experimented with weaponizing UAVs and had much of the technology needed to produce cruise missile weapons before the Gulf War. It was working on modifications of the Chinese Silkworm (HY-2) cruise missile, designed to have ranges of 75, 150, and 200 kilometers, at its Nasr missile factory before the war.[122]

Iraq used remotely piloted vehicles (RPVs) during the Gulf War, which led to some initial fears that these RPVs might be equipped with chemical or biological agents. These fears did not prove valid, but Iraq has considerable capability to either modify its RPVs or modify cruise missiles designed for other missions. It is one of some 70 countries that now deploy a total of over 75,000 anti-ship cruise missiles.[123]

Work by Dennis Gormley of Pacific Sierra Research has shown that a number of large Russian, Chinese, Italian, and French RPVs and anti-ship cruise missiles can be modified for land attack missions using commercially available Global Positioning Systems (GPSs) with the possible addition of ring laser gyros, which are available on the commercial market as small packaged electronics for aircraft navigation systems. Such systems cost only about one-tenth the price of ballistic missile guidance systems. While they can be equipped with explosive biological and chemical warheads, or warheads using submunitions, they also can be adapted to slowly release biological and chemical weapons over a pre-selected portion of their line of flight. This "line-source" delivery can achieve up to an order of magnitude more lethality over an area target than using explosive means to distribute such agents over a smaller area.

Iraq has an unknown number of Italian Mirach RPVs, which it calls the Ababil. It has at least explored development of the Mirach 600 into a cruise missile. This RPV normally has a range of about 900 kilometers with a payload of 70 kilograms, but Iraq seems to be working on a version with a 450 kilometer range and a larger payload.

Mirage retains large numbers of French-made Exocets, with ranges of up to 300 kilometers, However, these anti-ship missiles are so highly integrated, and their warhead is so specialized and packed with electronics, that they make a poor platform for conversion. Iraq does, however, have large numbers of Chinese HY-2 and HY-4 Silkworms, and may have some aging Soviet Styx missiles. These weapons can be modified relatively easily and their warheads can be lengthened to carry more biological and chemical weapons.

The liquid-fueled HY-2 could be modified with GPS guidance to achieve accuracies of 100–300 meters, and ranges of over 150 kilometers with a warhead of up to 500 kilograms. Alternatively, commercially available turbojet engines could be used to replace their present engines and extend the range up to 500 kilometers with similar accuracies. Iraq has also been working on air delivered versions of the HY-2 and its own-shorter range Faw air-to-ship cruise missile.

Iraq also may have an unknown number of Chinese C-601 and Russian AS-4 Kitchen and AS-5 Kelt air-launched anti-ship missiles, and may have some large Chinese-made anti-ship cruise missiles similar to the AS-4 and AS-5. The AS-4 and AS-5 are large anti-ship missiles designed for bomber delivery. The AS-4 is a 5,900-kilogram missile with ranges up to 460 kilometers and a 1,000-

kilogram payload. The AS-5 weighs 3,000 kilograms, has a maximum range of 180–230 kilograms, and a 1,000 kilogram warhead. These missiles are surplus now that Iraq has lost its operational bomber force, and it is possible that they could be converted to the land-attack mode.

Cruise missiles offer Iraq a number of major operational advantages over ballistic missiles. They are smaller and easier to conceal. They do not need to be stabilized at their launch points and can be rapidly moved and launched. Most do not produce any detectable heat signature at launch that provides warning. Their technology is simpler than that of advanced fight aircraft and they are easier to service and maintain.

Iraq may also be covertly able to design and build its own cruise missile, RPV, or remotely piloted conversion of an aircraft like the MiG-21 or MiG-23. It is believed that Iraq was developing an RPV that could be armed with biological weapons at the time of Desert Fox. While Iraq has no more capability than Iran to develop and deploy a Tomahawk TLAM-like missile, it may be able to build a missile about half the size of a small fighter aircraft with a payload of about 500 kilograms. Iraq already has the technology needed for fusing and equipping such a system with CBW and cluster warheads. Development of navigation systems and jet engines could be a major problem.

Iraq should be able to solve the problem of acquiring a suitable guidance system over time. Iraq's current inertial navigation systems (INS) would introduce errors of at least several kilometers at ranges of 1,000 kilometers, and the risk of total guidance failure could exceed two-thirds of the missiles fired. Iraq, however, has already made a major effort to acquire better guidance through its clandestine procurement network.

As has been mentioned earlier, Jordan revealed in December, 1995 that Iraq had attempted to smuggle in at least 100 key guidance components from Russia, including gyroscopes and accelerometers. In spite of Iraq's growing economic crisis, the shipment was worth at least $25 million. Further, UNSCOM revealed that Iraq had already received similar components and had thrown missile gyroscopes into a canal of the Tigris River in an effort to conceal its program.[124]

US studies indicate that a commercially available differential global positioning system (GPS), integrated with the inertial navigation system and a radar altimeter, might produce an accuracy of only 15 meters.[125] Some existing remotely piloted vehicles, such as the South African Skua, already claim such performance. Moreover, commercial technology is becoming available for differential global positioning system guidance with accuracies of two to five meters. Iraq would also have to import cruise missile engines. While there are many suitable, commercially available reciprocating and gas turbine engines, finding a reliable and efficient turbofan engine for such an application might be difficult. It is doubtful that Iraq could design and build such an engine, although it has most of the needed design and manufacturing skills.

The ease of building cruise missiles should not be exaggerated. Airframe-engine-warhead integration and testing is challenging and possibly beyond Iraq's manufacturing skills. A cruise missile, however, is inherently easier to integrate than a long-range ballistic missile. It is also less detectable, if using no telemetry or coded telemetry.[126] If Iraq can develop such weapons, these could reach a wide range of targets. A system deployed in border areas with only a 500-kilometer range could cover half of Iran, southeastern Turkey, all of Kuwait, the Persian Gulf coast of Saudi Arabia, Bahrain and most of Qatar, the northern UAE, and northern Oman. A system with a 1,200-kilometer range could reach Israel, the eastern two-thirds of Turkey, most of Saudi Arabia, and all of the other Southern Gulf states, including Oman. Such a system could also be programmed to avoid major air defense concentrations at a sacrifice of about 20% of its range.

NOTES

1. Note by the Secretary-General, "Report by the Secretary-General on the Activities of the Special Commission established by the Secretary-General," UN Security Council, S/1997/774, October 6, 1997, paragraph 23.

2. Note by the Secretary-General, "Report by the Secretary-General on the Activities of the Special Commission established by the Secretary-General," UN Security Council, S/1997/774, October 6, 1997, paragraphs 23–30.

3. Based on interviews with Rolf Ekeus in December, 1996 and January, 1997, *Washington Post*, March 21, 1996, p. A-1; UP, January 13, 1997, 1309; Notes by the Secretary General, UNSCOM S/1996/258, and especially S/1996/848, pp. 24–26, October 11, 1996; *Jane's Defense Weekly*, January 22, 1997, p. 5.

4. Many of the following technical comments are based on interviews, various reporting in *Jane's* and Edward L. Korb, ed. *The World's Missile Systems*, Seventh Edition, General Dynamics, Pomona Division, April, 1988, pp. 244–245; Ray Bonds, *Modern Soviet Weapons*, New York, ARCO, 1986, pp. 88–89.

5. Defense Intelligence Agency, *The Scud Missile: An Unclassified Overview for Policy Makers*, forwarded under U-3,148/SVI-FOIA, October 22, 1997; Edward L. Korb, ed., *The World's Missile Systems*, Seventh Edition, General Dynamics, Pomona Division, April, 1988, pp. 223–226; *Christian Science Monitor*, December 27, 1993, p. 4; *Washington Times*, February 25, 1994, p. A-15, June 16, 1994, p. A-13. The reader should be aware that all such performance data are nominal, and that various sources report significant differences in given performance characteristics. The Soviet Union is also reported to have had two more advanced versions of the missile, which have not been exported. One of these is reported to be a larger missile and has more range. It is 12.2 meters long, is 1 meter in diameter, weighs 10,000 kilograms, and has a range of 450 kilometers. The other is the "Scud D" (SS-le), which is reported to have been designed to deliver submunition busses and is more accurate than previous Scuds. It entered Soviet service in the early 1980s. It has a maximum range of 180 to 190 miles (290 to 310 kilometers) with its normal conventional payload, and a maximum flight time of 325 seconds. US experts do not believe such missiles have been deployed, although a Russia Scud B does exist with a longer, specialized warhead. There are no indications that such missiles have been sent to Iran.

6. Defense Intelligence Agency, *The Scud Missile: An Unclassified Overview for Policy Makers*, forwarded under U-3,148/SVI-FOIA, October 22, 1997; Edward L. Korb,

ed., *The World's Missile Systems*, Seventh Edition, General Dynamics, Pomona Division, April, 1988, pp. 223–226; *Christian Science Monitor*, December 27, 1993, p. 4; *Washington Times*, February 25, 1994, p. A-15, June 16, 1994, p. A-13. The reader should be aware that all such performance data are nominal, and that various sources report significant differences in given performance characteristics. The Soviet Union is also reported to have had two more advanced versions of the missile, which have not been exported. One of these is reported to be a larger missile and has more range. It is 12.2 meters long, is 1 meter in diameter, weighs 10,000 kilograms, and has a range of 450 kilometers. The other is the "Scud D" (SS-le), which is reported to have been designed to deliver submunition busses and is more accurate than previous Scuds. It entered Soviet service in the early 1980s. It has a maximum range of 180–190 miles (290 to 310 kilometers) with its normal conventional payload, and a maximum flight time of 325 seconds. US experts do not believe such missiles have been deployed, although a Russia Scud B does exist with a longer, specialized warhead. There are no indications that such missiles have been sent to Iran.

7. US Office of the Secretary of Defense, *Proliferation: Threat and Response*, Washington, Department of Defense, April, 1996, pp. 12–16; CRS Report for Congress, *Missile Proliferation: Survey of Emerging Missile Forces*, Congressional Research Service, Report 88–642F, February 9, 1989, pp. 52–53.

8. Preparing for launch includes a number of phases. These may be summarized as follows:

State	Warhead	Missile	TEL
6	in storage	in storage	available
5	in storage	sys/comp cks	available
4	attached	fueled	available
3	attached	put on TEL	move to site
2	attached	erected	set up
1	fused	launched	crew dispersed

All of the Scuds are liquid-fueled, and it normally takes a trained team around one hour to fuel and position the missile TEL (transporter-erector-launcher). It normally takes another hour to reload the launcher and an additional hour to prepare it for launching, not counting driving time to and from the reload site. A chemical warhead also has to be filled with the VX agent. These warheads utilize pre-mixed agents that require crews in Military Operational Protection (MOP) gear to fill them.

9. The author has seen Soviet publications with limited technical descriptions of the chemical warhead for the Scud in Arab countries, but no detailed design data.

10. "US Reasserts Aim to Keep Oil Flowing From Persian Gulf," *Washington Times*, February 22, 1984, p. A-1.

11. "Iraqis Fire Missiles on Iranian Cities," *Chicago Tribune*, February 25, 1984, p. 20.

12. One source claims that Iran fired 231 Scuds in 1988. See Steven Zaloga, "Ballistic Missiles in the Third World," *International Defense Review*, 11/88, pp. 1423–1437. Also see Note by the Secretary-General, "Report by the Secretary-General on the Activities of the Special Commission established by the Secretary-General," UN Security Council, S/1997/774, October 6, 1997, paragraph 23.

13. Iraq was only believed to have about 50 Scud missiles before it began this series of attacks. Rafsanjani claimed Iran had evidence that the missiles were standard Scud Bs, which used reduced warhead weight on March 8, 1988. *Washington Times*, March 1, 1988, p. 3; *Washington Post*, March 9, 1988, P. A-19, *Economist*, March 5, 1988, p. 44; *New York Times*, March 2, 1988, p. A-1, March 4, 1988, p. A-8, March 12, 1988, p. A-3, May 1, 1988, p. 18; *Washington Post*, March 2, 1988, p. A-16; *Baltimore Sun*, March 6, 1988, p. 2-A.

14. Steven Zaloga provides the following estimate of missile firings during the course of the war:

| | **Iraqi Firings** | | **Iranian Firings** | |
	FROG-7	Scud	Oghab	Scud
1980	10	-	-	-
1981	54	-	-	-
1982	1	3	-	-
1983	-	33	-	-
1984	2	25	-	-
1985	-	82	14	-
1986	-	-	8	18
1987	-	25	18	61
1988	-	193	231	104
Total	67	361	271	183

Source: Adapted from Steven Zaloga, "Ballistic Missiles in the Third World," *International Defense Review*, 11/88, pp. 1423–1437. Zaloga seems to have inverted the Iranian Scud and Oghab columns in his original article.

15. Michael Eisenstadt, *Like a Phoenix from the Ashes?* Washington, The Washington Institute Policy Paper 36, 1993, p. 36.

16. "Hussein" or "Husayn" is the name of the grandson of Muhammad and the son of Ali. Ali was martyred in An Najaf and Husayn in Karbala, both in Iraq.

17. *New York Times*, May 1, 1988, p. 1; *Los Angeles Times*, May 21, 1988, p. 18; *Washington Post*, May 11, 1988, p. A-1.

18. In spite of the knowledge gained during the Gulf War, sources still differ on other aspects of the performance of this system. According to some reports, the improved Iraqi Scuds have a CEP of 1,300 meters versus 1,000 meters for the Scud B, and carry only 600 kilograms versus 1,000 kilograms for the Scud B. According to other reports, Iraq has obtained Scud Ds from the USSR, although this seems unlikely. The Scud Ds are substantially more accurate than the Scud C, and can use minelet and submunition payloads, but there is no evidence that the USSR has sold such systems to Third World states. Some reports indicate that Iraq has Soviet-made Scud C missiles with strap-on boosters. This seems doubtful, because the missiles Iran recovered did not have such boosters, only a smaller warhead. David C. Isby, *Weapons and Tactics of the Soviet Army*, Fully Revised Edition, London, *Jane's*, 1988, pp. 296–301; For details, see *Jane's Soviet Intelligence Review*, May, 1990, pp. 204–209, and June, 1990, pp. 242–248; *Aviation Week*, January 28, 1991, p. 28; *International Defense Review*, November, 1988, pp. 1423–1427.

19. Working paper issued by the Israeli embassy in Washington, April, 1990. No

author, title, or publisher listed. Also see Duncan Lennox, "Iraq-Ballistic Missiles," *Current News, Supplement*, Department of Defense, October 11, 1990, pp. B-4 to B-6; *Washington Post*, October 10, 1990, p. 19; Dick Palowski, *Changes in Threat Air Combat Doctrine and Force Structure*, 24th Edition, Fort Worth, General Dynamics, DWIC-01, February, 1992, pp. II-330 to II-331; *San Diego Navy Dispatch*, September 8, 1990, p. 26; *DAH-90*, December, 1989, p. 30.

20. Based on interviews.

21. There are substantial differences in the count of missiles launched. The US Department of Defense refers to "almost 200" in US Department of Defense, *Conduct of the Persian Gulf War: Final Report*, Department of Defense, April, 1992, pp. 13–15. Also see the author's detailed tables in *Lessons of Modern War, Volume II: The Iran-Iraq War*, Boulder, 1991, pp. 364, 366, 405, 496–502, 524, 599. The author counts a total of 203 missiles, and over 160 fired at Tehran.

22. Martin Navias, "Ballistic Missile Proliferation in the Middle East," *Survival*, May–June 1989, p. 228; Warren W. Lenhard and Todd Masse, "Persian Gulf War: Iraqi Scud Ballistic Missile Systems," Washington, Congressional Research Service 71-173F, February 14, 1991, p. CRS-3; US Department of Defense, *Conduct of the Persian Gulf War: Final Report*, Department of Defense, April, 1992, pp. 16–19.

23. Based on discussions with Iranians present in the city at the time, Australian intelligence officers, and Robin Wright.

24. The warhead may have been as small as 130 kilograms. Iraq announced in April, 1988, however, that it had an improved missile called the El-Abbas, with a maximum range of 850 kilometers and a payload of 500 to 1,000 kilograms at a range of 650 kilometers. *Jane's Defense Weekly*, October 29, 1988, p. 1045.

25. Theodore A. Postal, "Lessons of the Gulf War Experience with Patriot," *International Security*, Winter, 1991–1992, pp. 128–129.

26. No missiles with chemical warheads were launched during the conflict, although Iraq did make extensive use of bombs, canisters, mortars, and 130 mm and 155 mm artillery shells. (UN working paper.)

27. Rick Atkinson, *Crusade*, Boston, Houghton Mifflin, 1993, pp. 181–183.

28. FBIS, *Middle East*, April 25, 1988, p. 1; Duncan Lennox, "Iraq-Ballistic Missiles," *Current News, Supplement*, US Department of Defense, October 11, 1990, pp. B-4–B-6.

29. US Department of Defense, *Conduct of the Persian Gulf War: Final Report*, Department of Defense, April, 1992, pp. 16–18; *Defense and Foreign Affairs Weekly*, May 8–14, 1989, pp. 3, 6. Iraq's Minister of Industry and Military Industrialization, Husayn Kamil, has denied that Iraq is cooperating in missile development with any foreign country, *Jane's Defense Weekly*, May 13, 1989, p. 843.

30. *New York Times*, November 12, 1991, p. A-3; US Department of Defense, *Conduct of the Persian Gulf War: Final Report*, Department of Defense, April, 1992, pp. 16–18.

31. US Department of Defense, *Conduct of the Persian Gulf War: Final Report*, Department of Defense, April, 1992, pp. 16–18; *New York Times*, September 7, 1989, p. A-9; *New York Times*, March 30, 1990, p. 6, April 3, 1990, p. 1, November 12, 1991, p. A-3; *Christian Science Monitor*, January 23, 1992, p. 1; *The Atlanta Constitution*, January 16, 1992, p. 1.

32. For a good summary report, see *Jane's Defense Weekly*, February 17, 1990,

p. 295; also see *Financial Times*, November 21, 1989, p. 1; *Washington Post*, September 20, 1989.

33. *Flight International*, May 13, 1989, p. 20; *Wall Street Journal*, August 30, 1990.

34. William Lowther, *Iraq and the Supergun*, London, Pan, 1992, especially pages 210–215.

35. US Department of Defense, *Conduct of the Persian Gulf War: Final Report*, Department of Defense, April, 1992, pp. 19. Some sources indicate that the booster is called the al-Abbid or Worshipper.

36. *The Middle East*, November, 1989, p. 19; William Lowther, *Iraq and the Supergun*, London, Pan, 1992, pp. 257–258.

37. US Department of Defense, *Conduct of the Persian Gulf War: Final Report*, Department of Defense, April, 1992, pp. 16–18; *New York Times*, September 7, 1989, p. A-9.

38. The Iraqi Al-Abbas missile was not a success, and some of the five missiles known to have been produced were evidently cannibalized as boosters. Duncan Lennox, "Iraq-Ballistic Missiles," *Current News, Supplement*, US Department of Defense, October 11, 1990, pp. B-4–B-6.

39. *New York Times*, December 5, 1989; *Washington Post*, December 9, 1989; *Aviation Week*, December 11, 1989, p. 31; *Defense Daily*, December 12, 1989, p. 381; *Financial Times*, December 20, 1989; FBIS-WES, December 8, 1989, p. 23; *Jane's Defense Weekly*, December 23, 1989, pp. 1371–1372.

40. Reuters, October 4, 1991, AM Cycle.

41. *New York Times*, April 24, 1990, p. 13; *Washington Times*, May 30, 1990, July 10, 1990.

42. See W. Andrew Terrill, "The Gulf War and Ballistic Missile Proliferation," *Comparative Strategy*, V. 11, 1992, pp. 163–176.

43. *Washington Post*, October 10, 1990, p. 19; *Financial Times (London)*, October 10, 1990, p. 7.

44. For an interesting summary of estimates of Scud capability at the time of the war, see Warren W. Lenhard and Todd Masse, "Persian Gulf War: Iraqi Scud Ballistic Missile Systems," Washington, Congressional Research Service 91–173F, February 14, 1991.

45. US Office of the Secretary of Defense, *Proliferation: Threat and Response*, Washington, Department of Defense, April, 1996, pp. 17–24.

46. The UN has only had formal acknowledgment from Iraq of 10 Soviet MAZ-543, six al-Nida, and three al-Walid launchers, and 11 decoy launchers. Michael Eisenstadt, *Like A Phoenix from the Ashes?* Washington, The Washington Institute Policy Paper 36, 1993, p. 36.

47. There is still considerable uncertainty as to how many mobile launchers Iraq had operational in January, 1991, and estimates generally range from 15 to 30. Most seem to have been MAZ-543s, but some may have been Iraqi-made mobile launchers.

48. Duncan Lennox, "Iraq-Ballistic Missiles," *Current News, Supplement*, US Department of Defense, October 11, 1990, pp. B-4–B-6. Some sources claim that Iraq had up to 100 to 225 homemade launchers by the time of the war, and that the US firm of Terex in Bridgeport, Connecticut, assisted Iraq in making these units; *New York Times*, January 26, 1992, p. A-12. In practice, Iraq seems to have deployed only about six a-Nida TELs, three A1-Walid TELs, and nine decoy launchers. Michael Eisenstadt, *Like a Phoenix from the Ashes?* Washington, The Washington Institute Policy Paper 36, 1993,

p. 36; UN Press Release, IK/79, December 16, 1991; UN Press Release, IK/128, November 5, 1992, pp. 1–2.

49. UN Press Release, IK/79, December 16, 1991; UN Press Release, IK/128, November 5, 1992, pp. 1–2; Michael Eisenstadt, *Like A Phoenix from the Ashes*? Washington, The Washington Institute Policy Paper 36, 1993, p. 36.

50. *Washington Times*, March 29, 1990, pp. A-1, A-8; April 29, 1990; *Washington Post*, April 30, 1990; *Jane's Defense Weekly*, October 29, 1988, p. 1045; *New York Times*, March 30, 1990, p. A-6.

51. US Navy working paper, August, 1990. The sites were Wadi al Jabaryah, Luadl or Ratqa, H-2, Wadi Amil, Ishuayb al Awaj, Qasr Amij East, Qasr Amij West, Wadi Hawran, and Zawr Hawran.

52. Dick Palowski, *Changes in Threat Air Combat Doctrine and Force Structure*, 24th Edition, Fort Worth, General Dynamics, DWIC-01, February, 1992, p. II-332; *UK Recognition Journal*, October, 1988, p. 312.

53. See the deliberate furor Saddam Hussein created over the fixed sites in March, 1990, *New York Times*, March 30, 1990, p. 6.

54. Note by the Secretary-General, "Report by the Secretary-General on the Activities of the Special Commission established by the Secretary-General," UN Security Council, S/1997/774, October 6, 1997, paragraph 23.

55. For typical reporting, see Sir Peter de la Billiere, *Storm Command*, pp. 210–211; Molly Moore, *A Woman at War*, New York, Scribners, 1993, pp. 102–103; General Pagonis, *Moving Mountains*, pp. 148–149.

56. For a detailed description of the effect of the Scud hit on the Dhahran barracks, see United States News and World Report, *Triumph without Victory*, New York, Random House, 1992, pp. 328–330.

57. Widely different figures on the level of physical damage done in Israel have been published in various sources. See Theodore A. Postal, "Lessons of the Gulf War Experience with Patriot," *International Security*, Winter, 1991–1992, pp. 139–151, for high damage estimates and a useful chronology of damage effects in Israel. For a very different examination of the damage effects from the Scud attacks, see Steve Fedtter, George N. Lewis, and Lisbeth Gronlund, "Why Were Scud Casualties So Low?" *Nature*, Vol. 361, January 28, 1993, pp. 293–296.

58. Iran has claimed that each Scud that fell on Tehran killed 10 to 15 and injured at least 30, but these claims are dubious. Steve Fedtter, George N. Lewis, and Lisbeth Gronlund, "Why Were Scud Casualties So Low?" *Nature*, Vol. 361, January 28, 1993, pp. 293–296.

59. For good accounts of these impacts, see General H. Norman Schwarzkopf, *It Doesn't Take a Hero* (New York: Bantam Books, 1992), pp. 409, 415–421, 430, 430, 452, 460–461, 470–472, and 475; also see Rick Atkinson, *Crusade*, pp. 18, 33, 38–50, 66, 81–85, 90–94, 96–103, 124–126, 144–148, 173–175, 181–182, 217–218, 222, 232, 277–278, 417, 496.

60. Figures of up to 2,500 sorties have been estimated. This higher total includes sensors as well as strike sorties, and sorties that were diverted to other targets when Scud targets could not be "found."

61. Eliot A. Cohen, Director, *Gulf War Air Power Survey*, Volume II, Part II, pp. 331–332.

62. See General H. Norman Schwarzkopf, *It Doesn't Take a Hero* (New York: Bantam Books, 1992, pp. 400–402) for an indication that UN commanders still believed they

had hit many Scud launchers after the war. For further technical details, see Thomas A. Keaney and Eliot A. Cohen, *Gulf War Air Power Survey: Summary Report*, Washington, Department of the Air Force, 1993, pp. 124.

63. Eliot A. Cohen, Director, *Gulf War Air Power Survey*, Volume II, Part II, Washington, GPO, 1993, pp. 331, 334–336, 340; Brigadier General Robert H. Scales, *Certain Victory*, Washington, Office of the Chief of Staff, US Army, 1993, pp. 184.

64. Eliot A. Cohen, Director, *Gulf War Air Power Survey*, Volume II, Part II, Washington, GPO, 1993, pp. 335–338.

65. Based on the author's interview with Israeli intelligence analysts and military planners after the war.

66. Eliot A. Cohen, Director, *Gulf War Air Power Survey*, Volume II, Part II, Washington, GPO, 1993, pp. 338–340; Brigadier General Robert H. Scales, *Certain Victory*, Washington, Office of the Chief of Staff, US Army, 1993, pp. 186.

67. A great deal of conflicting material is available on the performance of the Patriot during the Gulf War. The best unclassified source is US Congress, Committee on Appropriations, Subcommittee on the Department of Defense, *Hearings on the FY1993 Defense Budget*, April, 1991; "Performance of the Patriot Missile in the Gulf War," Hearing Before the Legislation and National Security Subcommittee of the Committee on Government Operations, House of Representatives, 102nd Congress, Second Session, April 7, 1992. Also see President George Bush, speech to Raytheon Missile Systems Plant, February 15, 1991. Theodore A. Postal, "Lessons of the Gulf War Experience with Patriot," *International Security*, Winter, 1991–1992, pp. 112–131; Robert M. Stein and Theodore A. Postal, "Correspondence: Patriot Experience in the Gulf War," *International Security*, Summer, 1992, pp. 199–240; Steven A. Hildreth, "Theater Ballistic Missile Defense," CRS 93–585F, June 10, 1993; Steven A. Hildreth and Paul C. Zinsmeister, "The Patriot Air Defense System and the Search for an Anti-Tactical Ballistic Missile System, CRS 91–456F, June 18, 1991; General Accounting Office, "Patriot Missile Defense: Software Problem Led to System Failure at Dhahran," Saudi Arabia, GAO/IMTEC-92-26, February, 1992; Rep. John Conyers, Jr., "The Patriot Myth: Caveat Emptor," *Arms Control Today*, Vol. 22, No. 9, November, 1992; Jorg Bahnemann and Thomas Enders, "Reconsider Ballistic Missile Defense," *Military Technology*, 4/91, pp. 46–52; Statement of Ted A. Postal, "Optical Evidence Indicating Patriot High Miss Rates During the Gulf War," Committee on Government Operations, Subcommittee on Legislation and National Security, April 7, 1992; Eric H. Arnett, "Issue Paper: Ballistic Missile Defense After the Kuwait War," Washington, American Academy for the Advancement of Science, 91–15S, July, 1991; unclassified chronology in Eliot A. Cohen, Director, *The Gulf War Air Power Survey*, Part V, Part II. Washington, GPO, 1993,

68. US Army press release, "Army Weapons System Performance in Southwest Asia, March 13, 1991, p. 3. The press release did note that the Patriot only engaged "threatening" Scuds.

69. *Washington Post*, July 26, 1991, p. A-1; "Ambassador Rolf Ekeus, Unearthing Iraq's Arsenal," *Arms Control Today*, April, 1992, pp. 6–9.

70. The UN refused to name the facilities at the time of this declaration, because it feared Iraq would move some of the equipment and missiles located at those sites.

71. *Washington Post*, February 14, 1992, p. A-33; *Washington Post*, January 15, 1992, p. A-18.

72. UNSCOM, Note by the Secretary-General, S/1996/848, October 11, 1996,

pp. 25–26. Also see the December, 1995 UNSCOM report to the Security Council, S/1995/1308.

73. *New York Times*, February 28, 1992, p. 28; *Washington Times*, February 11, 1992, p. 1, November 6, 1992, p. A-7.

74. Reuters Ltd., July 20, 1995; *Jane's Defense Weekly*, July 29, 1995, p. 13.

75. *Jane's Defense Weekly*, January 3, 1996, pp. 15–18; *Jane's Intelligence Review*, Vol. 7, No. 3, pp. 115–117; *The Atlanta Constitution*, January 6, 1992, p. 1; *New York Times*, February 28, 1992, p. A-28, November 5, 1992, p. A-10; *Washington Times*, February 11, 1992, p. 1, November 6, 1992, p. A-7; *Washington Post*, January 27, 1993, p. A-16, July 7, 1993, p. A-28, March 21, 1996, A-1; *Philadelphia Inquirer*, March 16, 1993, p. E-1; *Arms Control Today*, December, 1992, p. 7.

76. United Nations Special Commission, "Report to the Security Council, S/1995/864," 11 October 1995, pp. 14–15.

77. *New York Times*, August 26, 1995, p. 3.

78. United Nations, Note by the Secretary-General, S/1997/301, April 11, 1997, p. 21.

79. Note by the Secretary-General, S/1996/848, October 11, 1996, pp. 25–26.

80. UN Security Council, Note to the Secretary-General, S/1995/864, 11 October, 1995, p. 15; *Jane's Defense Weekly*, January 3, 1996, pp. 3, 15–19.

81. United Nations Special Commission, "Report to the Security Council, S/1995/864," 11 October 1995, pp. 14–15.

82. *Washington Post*, December 15, 1995, p. A-30; *Jane's Defense Weekly*, January 3, 1996, pp. 17–18.

83. Reuters, December 18, 1995, 0342.

84. *Washington Post*, September 12, 1997, pp. A-1, A-33.

85. United Nations Special Commission, "Report to the Security Council, S/1995/864," 11 October 1995, pp. 14–15.

86. *Jane's Defense Weekly*, January 3, 1996, p. 3; December, 1995 UNSCOM report to the Security Council, S/1995/1308; and UNSCOM, Note by the Secretary General, S/1996/848, October 11, 1996, pp. 25–26.

87. UNSCOM, Note by the Secretary-General, S/1996/848, October 11, 1996, p. 24.

88. *New York Times*, December 22, 1995, p. A-18; *Washington Times*, December 28, 1995, p. A-13; UN Security Council, Note to the Secretary General, S/1995/864, October 11, 1995, p. 15; *Jane's Defense Weekly*, January 3, 1996, pp. 3, 15–19; *Washington Post*, February 5, 1997, p. A-1; UP, January 13, 1997, 1309; Associated Press, October 17, 1996, 2201, December 30, 1997, 2257; *Jane's Defense Weekly*, January 22, 1997, p. 5; *Policywatch*, January 21, 1997 and February 5, 1997.

89. Associated Press, October 14, 1995; *Washington Post*, October 14, 1995, p. A-1.

90. Reuters, December 18, 1996, 0342; Note by the Secretary-General, S/1996/848, October 11, 1996, pp. 25–26; *Washington Times*, July 31, 1996, p. A-15; *Jane's Defense Weekly*, March 5, 1997, p. 16.

91. United Nations, Note by the Secretary-General, S/1997/301, April 11, 1997, p. 25.

92. Reuters, December 18, 1996, 0342; Note by the Secretary-General, S/1996/848, October 11, 1996, pp. 25–26; *Washington Times*, July 31, 1996, p. A-15.

93. Reuters, December 18, 1996, 0342; Note by the Secretary-General, S/1996/848, October 11, 1996, pp. 25–26; *Washington Post*, February 5, 1997, p. A-1; UP, January

13, 1997, 1309; Associated Press, October 17, 1996, 2201, December 30, 1997, 2257; *Jane's Defense Weekly*, January 22, 1997, p. 5; *Policywatch*, January 21, 1997 and February 5, 1997.

94. United Nations, Note by the Secretary-General, S/1997/301, April 11, 1997, pp. 18–20.

95. Reuters, April 24, 1997, 09:17; *Washington Times*, April 21, 1997, p. A-13; United Nations, Note by the Secretary General, S/1997/301, April 11, 1997, p. 12, 19–23, 24–25.

96. *Frankfurter Allgemeine*, February 4, 1997; Associated Press, February 4, 1997, 2003, and April 5, 1997, 1022; *Jane's Defense Weekly*, March 5, 1997, p. 16, March 19, 1997, p. 5; *Jane's Intelligence Review*, Vol. 7, No. 3, pp. 115–117; Reuters, February 23, 1997, 1522.

97. Note by the Secretary-General, "Report by the Secretary-General on the Activities of the Special Commission established by the Secretary-General," UN Security Council, S/1997/774, October 6, 1997, paragraphs 23–41.

98. Note by the Secretary-General, "Report by the Secretary-General on the Activities of the Special Commission established by the Secretary-General," UN Security Council, S/1997/774, October 6, 1997, paragraph 38.

99. David C. Isby, "The Residual Iraqi Scud Force," *Jane's Intelligence Review*, Vol. 7, No. 3, pp. 115–117; Reuters, February 23, 1997, 1522.

100. David C. Isby, "The Residual Iraqi Scud Force," *Jane's Intelligence Review*, Vol. 7, No. 3, pp. 115–117; Reuters, February 23, 1997, 1522.

101. These papers were never formally released with titles and agency identifications. The British white paper and supplementary data sheets are part of an informal Foreign Office report of February 4, 1998. The US paper was prepared by the CIA, and made available in an NSC background briefing of February 13, 1998. Portions appeared in the USIA web page on the Internet as "Iraq Weapons of Mass Destruction Programs: US Government White Paper, February 13, 1998."

102. CIA background paper of February 13, 1998.

103. CIA background paper of February 13, 1998.

104. CIA background paper of February 13, 1998.

105. CIA background paper of February 13, 1998.

106. CIA background paper of February 13, 1998.

107. CIA background paper of February 13, 1998.

108. Report by the Executive Committee of the Special Commission, March 27, 1998, as transmitted by the Secretary-General to the Security Council, April 16, 1998, S/1998/332.

109. Report by the Executive Committee of the Special Commission, March 27, 1998, as transmitted by the Secretary-General to the Security Council, April 16, 1998, S/1998/332.

110. *Washington Times*, June 4, 1998, p. A-1; *New York Times*, June 4, 1998, p. A-6; Reuters, August 10, 1998, 1900; *London Times*, February 12, 1998, p. 15.

111. Reuters, June 22, 1998, 1331.

112. Speech by Scott Ritter, Washington Institute, September 4, 1998.

113. Note by the Secretary-General, S/1998/920(1998), October 6, 1998.

114. *Jane's Defense Weekly*, November 11, 1995, p. 4; UN Security Council, Note by the Secretary-General, S/1995/864, 11 October, 1995.

115. *Christian Science Monitor*, January 23, 1992, p. 1; *Jane's Intelligence Review*, December, 1995, p. 559.

116. *New York Times*, August 26, 1995, p. 3; *Washington Post*, August 26, 1995, p. A-1.

117. Note by the Secretary-General, "Report by the Secretary-General on the Activities of the Special Commission established by the Secretary-General," UN Security Council, S/1997/774, October 6, 1997, paragraphs 58–60.

118. US Office of the Secretary of Defense, *Proliferation: Threat and Response*, Washington, Department of Defense, April, 1996, pp. 17–24.

119. *Washington Post*, October 14, 1995, p. A-1; *Policywatch*, No. 175, November 20, 1995.

120. *Washington Post*, January 15, 1992, p. A-18; *Washington Times*, September 12, 1991, p. A-8, March 5, 1992, p. 1; *US News and World Report* published an article claiming that Iraq might have an underground factory and some 800 missiles on February 10, 1992 (p. 22). General Colin Powell later indicated that he had seen no evidence of any underground facility and that Iraq's maximum holding might be about 250 missiles; *Albany Times Union*, February 5, 1992, p. 7.

121. Michael Eisenstadt, *Like A Phoenix from the Ashes*? Washington, Washington Institute Policy Paper 36, 1993, pp. 36–37.

122. Michael Eisenstadt, *Like A Phoenix from the Ashes*? Washington, Washington Institute Policy Paper 36, 1993, pp. 36–37.

123. Dennis M. Gormley, "Hedging Against the Cruise Missile Threat," *Survival*, vol. 40, no. 1, Spring 1998, pp. 92–111.

124. *Washington Post*, December 8, 1995, p. A-13, December 15, 1995, p. A-30; *Washington Times*, December 8, 1995, p. A-17; Reuters, December 22, 1995, 0240.

125. The United States is considering modifying its own drones to use GPS to achieve such accuracies, *Defense Week*, January 3, 1994, p. 1.

126. *Jane's Defense Weekly*, January 30, 1993, pp. 20–21; *Defense Electronics and Computing*, IDR Press, September, 1992, pp. 115–120; *International Defense Review*, May, 1992, pp. 413–415; *Jane's Remotely Piloted Vehicles 1991–1992*; Keith Munson, *World Unmanned Aircraft*, London, Jane's 1988; *Air Force Magazine*, March, 1992, pp. 94–99, May, 1992, p. 155.

Chapter 16

Iraqi Terrorism, Unconventional Warfare, and Weapons of Mass Destruction

Iraq does not have Iran's history of making extensive use of terrorism, unconventional warfare, and proxies. At the same time, the success of UN sanctions and the efforts of UNSCOM and the IAEA may lead Iraq to change its approach to delivering weapons of mass destruction in the future. Iraq has the option of exploiting a wide range of unconventional delivery methods that are far less expensive, difficult, and detectable than most of the previous delivery systems, and may be able to use other radical nations or groups that either sympathize with Iraq or would strike against Iraq's enemies for their own reasons.[1]

Once again, there is no way to determine what Iraq does or does not plan, and the outcome of the war of sanctions. Iraq's official attitude toward terrorism is the usual one of denial. Further, Iraq's efforts may well be improvised and reactive—and Iraq may suddenly escalate the scale of its use of unconventional warfare/terrorism in reaction to a given contingency or the failure of its military forces. This makes any effort to characterize Iraq's use of such delivery methods purely speculative—whether in terms of warning against such threats or denying their existence.

What is clear is that such attacks are technically feasible and could offer Iraq significant advantages in a wide range of scenarios, and that they apply equally to biological, chemical, and nuclear weapons. Table 16.1 illustrates this point. Many of the attacks postulated in this table may seem to borrow from bad spy novels and science fiction, but all of the scenarios are at least technically possible. These scenarios also illustrate the fact that Iraq does not need sophisticated military delivery systems, does not need highly lethal weapons of mass destruction, can use terrorism to pose existential threats, can use complex mixes of weapons of mass destruction, and can mix terrorism with elements of covert action and deniability.

Table 16.1
Possible Iraqi Unconventional or Terrorist Attack Scenarios Using Weapons of Mass Destruction

- A radiological powder is introduced into the air conditioning systems of Saudi high-rise buildings or tourist hotels. Symptoms are only detected over days or weeks, and public warning is given several weeks later. The authorities detect the presence of such a powder, but cannot estimate its long-term lethality and have no precedents for decontamination. Tourism collapses, and the hotels eventually have to be torn down and rebuilt.
- An Iraqi-backed terrorist group smuggles parts for a crude gun-type nuclear device into Israel or bought in the marketplace. The device is built in a medium-sized commercial truck. A physics student reading the US Department of Defense weapons effects manual maps Tel Aviv to maximize fallout effects in an area filled with buildings with heavy metals and waits for a wind maximizing the fallout impact. The bomb explodes with a yield of only 8 kilotons, but with an extremely high level of radiation. Immediate casualties are limited, but the long-term death rate mounts steadily with time. Peace becomes impossible, and security measures become Draconian. Immigration halts, and emigration reaches crisis proportions. Israel as such ceases to exist.
- Several workers move drums labeled as cleaning agents into a large shopping mall, large public facility, subway, train station, or airport. They dress as cleaners and are wearing what appear to be commercial dust filters, or have taken the antidote for the agent they will use. They mix the feedstocks for a persistent chemical agent at the site during a peak traffic period. Large-scale casualties result, and Draconian security measures become necessary on a national level. A series of small attacks using similar ''binary'' agents virtually paralyze the economy, and detection is impossible, except to identify all canisters of liquid.
- Immunized terrorists visit a US carrier or major Marine assault ship during the first hours of visitors' day during a port call in the Middle East. They are carrying Anthrax powder in bags designed to make them appear slightly overweight. They slowly scatter the powder as they walk through the ship during their visit. The immediate result is 50% casualties among the ship's crew, its Marine complement, and the visitors who follow. The United States finds that it has no experience with decontaminating a large ship where Anthrax has entered the air system and is scattered throughout closed areas. After long debates over methods and safety levels, the ship is abandoned.
- An Iraqi-backed terrorist group seeking to ''cleanse'' a nation of its secular regime and corruption introduces a modified type culture of Ebola or a similar virus into an urban area. It scatters infectious cultures in urban areas for which there is no effective treatment. By the time the attack is detected, it has reached epidemic proportions. Medical authorities rush into the infected area without proper protection, causing the collapse of medical facilities and emergency response capabilities. Other nations and regions have no alternative other than to isolate the nation or center under attack, letting the disease take its course.
- An Iraqi-backed terrorist group modifies the valves on a Japanese remote-controlled, crop-spraying helicopter, which has been imported legally for agricultural purposes. It uses this system at night or near dawn to spray a chemical or biological agent at

Table 16.1 (continued)

altitudes below radar coverage in a line-source configuration. Alternatively, it uses a large, home-built RPV with simple GPS guidance. The device eventually crashes undetected into the sea or desert. Delivery of a chemical agent achieves far higher casualties than any conventional military warhead. A biological agent is equally effective, and the first symptoms appear days after the actual attack—by which time treatment is difficult or impossible.

- A truck filled with what appears to be light gravel is driven through the streets of Riyadh, Kuwait City, Tehran, or Tel Aviv during rush hour or another maximum traffic period. A visible powder does come out through the tarpaulin covering the truck, but the spread of the powder is so light that no attention is paid to it. The driver and his assistant are immunized against the modified form of Anthrax carried in the truck which is being released from behind the gravel or sand in the truck. The truck slowly quarters key areas of the city. Unsuspected passerby and commuters not only are infected but carry dry spores home and into other areas. By the time the first major symptoms of the attack occur some three to five days later, Anthrax pneumonia is epidemic and some septicemic Anthrax has appeared. Some 40% to 65% of the exposed population dies, and medical facilities collapse, causing serious, lingering secondary effects.

- An Iraqi-backed terrorist group scatters high concentrations of a radiological, chemical, or biological agent in various areas in a city and trace elements into the processing intakes to the local water supply. When the symptoms appear, the terrorist group makes its attack known, but claims that it has contaminated the local water supply. The authorities are forced to confirm that water is contaminated, and mass panic ensues.

- Immunized terrorist carry small amounts of Anthrax or a similar biological agent onto a passenger aircraft like a B-747, quietly scatter the powder, and deplane at the regularly scheduled stop. No airport detection system or search detects the agent. Some 70–80% of those on the aircraft die as a result of symptoms that appear only days later.

- Several identical nuclear devices are smuggled out of the FSU through Afghanistan or Central Asia. They do not pass directly through governments. One of the devices is disassembled to determine the precise technology and coding system used in the weapon's PAL. This allows users to activate the remaining weapons. The weapon is then disassembled to minimize detection with the fissile core shipped covered in lead. The weapon is successfully smuggled into the periphery of an urban area outside of any formal security perimeter. A 100 kiloton ground burst destroys a critical area and blankets the region in fallout.

- The same device is shipped to Israel or a Gulf area in a modified standard shipping container equipped with detection and triggering devices that set it off as a result of local security checks, or with a GPS system that sets it off automatically when it reaches the proper coordinates in the port of destination. The direct explosive effect is significant, but "rain out" contaminates a massive local area.

- Iraq equips a freighter or dhow to spread Anthrax along a coastal area in the Gulf. It uses a proxy terrorist group and launches an attack on Kuwait City and Saudi oil facilities and ports. It is several days before the attack is detected, and the attacking

Table 16.1 (continued)

group is never fully identified. The form of Anthrax involved is dry and time encapsulated to lead to both massive prompt casualties and force time consuming decontamination. Iraq not only is revenged, but benefits from the resulting massive surge in oil prices.

- An Iraqi-backed terrorist group scatters small amounts of a biological or radiological agent in a Jewish area during critical stages of the final settlement talks. Near panic ensures, and a massive anti-Palestinian reaction follows. Israeli security then learns that the terrorist group has scattered small amounts of the same agent in cells in every sensitive Palestinian town and area, and the terrorist group announces that it has also stored some in politically sensitive mosques and shrines. Isreali security is forced to shut down all Palestinian movement and to carry out intrusive searches in every politically sensitive area. Palestinian riots and then exchanges of gunfire follow. The peace talks break down permanently.
- Iraq equips dhows to spread Anthrax. The dhows enter the ports of Kuwait as commercial vessels—possibly with local or other Southern Gulf registrations and flags. It is several days before the attack is detected, and the resulting casualties include much of the population of Abu Dhabi and government of the UAE. The UAE breaks up as a result, no effective retaliation is possible, and Iran achieves near hegemony over Gulf oil policy.
- An Iraqi-backed terrorist group attempting to drive Western influence out of Saudi Arabia smuggles a large nuclear device into Al Hufuf on the edge of the Ghawar oil field. It develops a crude fallout model using local weather data, which it confirms by sending out scouts with cellular phones. It waits for the ideal wind, detonates the devices, shuts down the world's largest exporting oil field, and causes the near collapse of Saudi Arabia.
- Alternatively, the same group takes advantage of the security measures the United States has adopted in Saudi Arabia, and the comparative isolation of US military personnel. It waits for the proper wind pattern and allows the wind to carry a biological agent over a Saudi airfield with a large US presence from an area outside of the security perimeter. The United States takes massive casualties and has no ability to predict the next attack. It largely withdraws from Saudi Arabia.
- A freighter carrying fertilizer enters a Middle Eastern port and docks. In fact, the freighter has mixed the fertilizer with a catalyst to create a massive explosion and also carries a large amount of a chemical, radiological, and/or biological agent. The resulting explosion destroys both the immediate target area and scatters the chemical or biological weapon over the area.
- A large terrorist device goes off in a populated, critical economic, or military assembly area—scattering mustard or nerve gas. Emergency teams rush in to deal with the chemical threat, and the residents are evacuated. Only later does it become clear that the device also included a biological agent, and that the response to this ''cocktail'' killed most emergency response personnel and the evacuation rushed the biological agent to a much wider area.

The danger of such scenarios is that they tend to overstate Iraq's willingness to turn to extreme forms of terror, of Iraqis or Iraqi proxies to risk dying, and of Iraq's ability to undetectably execute complex attacks. At the same time, the scenarios in Table 16.1 are not difficult to execute, and only a few require large numbers of people and complex technical activity. The actions of Aum Shinrikyo have already shown that it can be extremely difficult to characterize the level of extremism and capability for sophisticated action within a given group until it has committed at least one act of terror. The cell structure used by the violent elements of most Middle Eastern extremist groups also tends to encourage the creation of compartmentalized groups with different and unpredictable commitments to violence, while the loose and informal chain of contacts between extremist movements, known terrorist groups, and radical governments like Iran creates the possibility of random or unpredictable transfers of technology or weapons. Once again, there are many possibilities and no clear probabilities.

NOTE

1. For further details, see the author's report on "Terrorism and the Threat From Weapons of Mass Destruction in the Middle East: The Problem of Paradigm Shift," Washington, CSIS, October 17, 1996; Brad Roberts, *Terrorism with Chemical and Biological Weapons: Calibrating Risks and Responses*, Alexandria, Chemical and Biological Weapons Control Institute, 1997; and Shai Feldman, *Nuclear Weapons and Arms Control in the Middle East*, Cambridge, MIT Press, 1997.

Chapter 17

Iraq's Past and Future Chemical Weapons Capabilities

The preceding analysis of Iraq's delivery systems helps illustrate the nature of Iraq's strategic culture, the range of uncertainties that both Iraq and its potential enemies must deal with, and many of the reasons Iraq not only has persisted in proliferating since the Gulf War but is likely to do so in the future, even if Saddam is removed from power. Delivery systems, however, are only part of the story. There are additional lessons to be learned from Iraq's chemical, biological, and nuclear warfare programs.

Iraq has produced thousands of tons of chemical weapons since the early 1980s. It used these weapons against the Iranians and the Kurds in the mid and late 1980s. It first used mustard gas against Iranian troops in 1983, using weapons produced in civil laboratories and facilities on a limited scale. It began to use Tabun nerve gas in 1984, and it dropped the first nerve gas bombs in modern warfare. While Iraq initially failed to be able to use chemical weapons in the direct support of ground operations, it developed the skills to do so by 1987, and chemical weapons played a major role in Iraq's victories against Iran in 1987 and 1988. Iraq also used chemical weapons against Kurdish rebels and civilians after the war in late 1988 and in 1989. It has experience using chemical weapons in artillery shells, rockets, mortar rounds, bombs, and spray tanks.[1]

IRAQ'S CHEMICAL WEAPONS PROGRAMS BEFORE THE IRAN-IRAQ WAR

It is not possible to establish a precise date when Iraq acquired chemical weapons, but it seems to have begun to seriously examine acquiring such weapons in the 1960s, and to have decided to create its own production facilities following the October War in 1973. There are some indications that it acquired small numbers of chemical weapons from the USSR at this time, and that it may have had assistance from Egypt in developing suitable production and storage techniques in the period before the Camp David accords.[2] There are also some indications that Iraq may have used poison gas shells or bombs against the Kurds during its campaigns of 1973–1975.[3]

Initial Construction of Production Plants

Iraq seems to have begun the construction of its own chemical weapons plants in the mid-1970s, in response to reports that both Egyptian and Israeli forces were equipped with chemical weapons at the time of the October War, and the threat posed by Iran and its Kurdish rebels.[4] Iraq seems to have weaponized mustard gas for use by mortars and artillery long before the Iran-Iraq War, and to have had shells for at least 120 mm mortars and 130 mm artillery.

One of Iraq's first steps in acquiring a large-scale domestic production capacity was to turn to the Pfaudler Company of Rochester, New York, for assistance in creating a major "pesticide" blending complex.[5] Pfaudler is a large producer of corrosion resistant, glass line steel vessels, the kind suitable for producing large amounts of toxic chemicals. Iraq approached the Pfaudler Company in 1975 and asked about purchasing a relatively small production facility.

Once the company's representatives reached Baghdad, however, it became clear that Iraq sought to immediately create a massive production facility. It rejected the safety concerns of the Pfaudler experts and asked for plans that aimed at rushing ahead without a pilot plant. It also became clear that Iraq wanted to "blend" organophosphate pesticides of a very uncertain value for agricultural purposes, which are commonly recognized as "precursors" for the production of nerve gas.[6]

The Iraqi production goals called for the handling of 600 metric tons per year of Amiton, 300 metric tons of Demiton, 150 tons of Paraoxon, and 150 tons of Parathon. All of these agents are extremely toxic.[7] Amiton and Paraoxon are the most toxic agents, followed by Parathion and then Demeton. Even in 1974, all four were relatively outdated agents for agricultural purposes and had been largely abandoned for safety reasons.[8]

Efforts to Create Large-Scale Production Facilities

During 1975–1976, Pfaudler sought to persuade the Iraqis to proceed on a pilot plant basis. Iraq finally rejected this approached in mid-1976 and insisted on the completion of a massive plant. The Iraqi negotiators also changed from the Ministry of Agriculture to the Ministry of Industry. The resulting impasse gradually led Iraq to break off negotiations.

Iraq then turned to Imperial Chemical Industries, PLC (ICI), with virtually the same proposal. Unlike Pfaudler, ICI was familiar with a British government list of items whose export was controlled because they could be used to produce gas weapons and immediately recognized that Iraq was seeking the precursors for nerve gas. ICI refused to negotiate further.

This refusal did not discourage Iraq, however, who then turned to West German, Swiss, French, Dutch, Belgian, and Italian firms, and seemed to have obtained most of the components it needed.[9] While the precise source of its equipment is unclear, Iraq later seems to have received enough support to build a special "pesticide" plant from Pilot Plant, a unit of Karl Kolb, which is a major West German laboratory equipment supplier, and from three other pilot facilities. The Kolb plant had some of the special equipment necessary to make Sarin, but not special pumps.[10]

Iraq also is believed to have purchased technical assistance from a West German firm called Fritz Werner.[11] It received heavy-duty pumps and chemicals from Water Engineering Trading (WET) GmbH of Hamburg, which sold some $11 million worth of equipment and tons of chemicals, including trichloride, a nerve gas precursor, and equipment from Quast, which provided reactor vessels, centrifuges, and piping line with Hastalloy.[12]

Production Capabilities at the Start of the Iran-Iraq War

It is unclear how far these efforts had gotten when the war began, although at least one major pesticide plant was being operated by the Iraqi "State Ministry of Pesticide Production" in 1980–1981, some mustard gas was probably in production at Samara, and two small pilot plants to produce nerve gas were completing construction at Samara, with a capacity of around 30–50 tons per year.[13] These two plants, however, were only able to produce nerve agents using fairly advanced and specialized feedstock. Finally, Iraq may have obtained additional production equipment for the manufacture of plastics, which could produce massive amounts of hydrogen cyanide as a by-product. This equipment seems to have been modified for the production of cyanide gas.

In summary, Iraq does not seem to have had large stockpiles of chemical weapons when the war began, or to have given gas warfare high priority during, 1980–1982, while it was still on the offensive. It does seem to have had enough CS gas and mustard gas to use some form of gas in the battles around Basra and Mandali in 1982, but evidently it did not have the feedstock and the ability to increase the production capacity it needed for large-scale use of gas in warfare.

IRAQ'S USE OF CHEMICAL WEAPONS DURING THE IRAN-IRAQ WAR

There is some debate over the timing of Iraq's first use of lethal chemical weapons. There is no clear evidence of large-scale use of lethal chemical synthetics and/or biological agents during the initial stages of the Iran-Iraq War, but Iran claimed that Iraq used chemical weapons in the Susangerd area during the first six weeks of the war.[14] There were no casualties to support such claims, and such reports probably reflect Iranian propaganda, although they could be the result of a botched Iraqi attempt to use lethal chemical or biological agents.

Table 17.1 makes it clear, however, that Iraq began to make significant use of chemical warfare against Iran when Iran pushed back the Iraqi forces in Western Iran and put Iraq on the defensive. Beginning in 1982, Iraq began to use tear gas and nonlethal agents, and a broadcast over Baghdad's Voice of the Masses Radio stated in a reference to the Iranians that there was "a certain insecticide for every kind of insect."[15] In December, 1982, Iraq began to use mustard gas to deal with human wave and night attacks.

Large-Scale Use of Chemical Weapons Begins

Iraq again warned Iran that it might make extensive use of poison gas in September, 1983. The Iraqi high command issued a statement that it

was armed with modern weapons that [will] be used for the first time in war . . . not used in previous attacks for humanitarian reasons . . . if you execute the orders of Khomeini's regime . . . your death will be certain because this time we will use a weapon that will destroy any moving creature on the fronts.[16]

The warning was soon followed by further attacks. Iraq made extensive use of lethal chemical weapons in July (Val Fajr 2) and October, 1983 (Panjwin offensive).[17] Chemical warfare seems to have been used extensively on August 9 near Piranshahr, and then around Panjwin in late October and early November, 1983.[18] Two Iranian soldiers wounded by mustard agents during this campaign were sent to Vienna, where they died. Two members of a second group of wounded soldiers were sent to Stockholm for medical treatment, and they also died.

Iran Fails to Mobilize World Opinion

Iran made further charges that Iraq used chemical weapons during the March, 1984 offensive which led to the Iranian seizure of Majnoon Island.[19] These charges stated that Iraq had killed some 1,700 Iranian troops and used GD and GB nerve agents, as well as mustard gas. Many of the Iranian allegations about the Iraqi use of lethal synthetic gases during the following months also related directly to the fighting on the Islands.[20]

Iran attempted to deal with this situation by mobilizing world opinion. After Iran's protests failed to arouse a significant world reaction, it flew chemical warfare casualties to London. A UN team then flew to Iran and found several Iraqi bombs designed for dispersing chemical agents which had Spanish markings. These weapons were later found to have contained mustard gas. Other investigations after the 1984 attacks confirmed a high probability that Iraq was

Table 17.1
Probable Major Uses of Chemical Weapons During the Iran-Iraq War

User/Area	Gas	Delivery Means	Effects/Casualties	Date
Iraq Susangerd	CS	Artillery	Limited	June, 1982
Iraq Mandali and Basra	CS/Mustard	Artillery/Mortars	Unclear	July, 1982
Iraq Southern front	Mustard	Unknown	Used against forces massing for human wave attacks. Effect unknown.	December, 1982
Iraq Haj Omran/ Piranshahr/ Mt. Kordeman	Mustard	Aircraft Helicopters	25–100 casualties	August, 1983
Iraq Panjwin	Mustard	Helicopters/ Artillery	Heavy casualties—3,000 Significant impact on battle	October– November, 1983
Iraq Majnoon Islands	Mustard/CS	Aircraft	Heavy casualties—2,500 Significant impact on battle	February– March, 1984
Iraq Basrah	Nerve (Tabun)/ Mustard	Artillery	Limited—50–100	March, 1984
Iraq Hawizeh Marshes	Nerve (Tabun)/ Mustard	Aircraft/ Artillery	Heavy casualties—3,000 Significant impact on battle	March, 1985
Iraq Al Faw	Nerve/ Mustard	Aircraft Artillery	Heavy casualties—8,000–10,000 Significant impact on battle	February, 1986
Iraq Umm ar Rass	Mustard	Aircraft	Heavy—1,000s Significant impact on battle	December, 1986
Iraq Khorramshahr	Mustard	Bombs	Disrupt build-up against Basra	January– February, 1987
Iraq and Iran* Basra	Nerve/ Mustard	Aircraft Artillery	Heavy casualties—5,000 Significant impact on battle	February– April, 1987
Iraq Khorramshahr	Mustard	Bombs	Disrupt build-up against Basra	April, 1987
Iran Mehran	Mustard/ Cyanogen	Artillery	Limited	July, 1987
Iraq Sardasht	Mustard	Bombs	650–1,000 Kurdish civilians	June– July, 1987
Iraq Somar/Mehran	Mustard/Nerve	Bombs	Disrupt build-up against Basra—3,000 casualties	October, 1987
Iraq and Iran Halabjah	Mustard/Nerve Cyanogen	Aircraft Artillery	Hundred of Kurdish civilians	March, 1988

Table 17.1 (continued)

User/Area	Gas	Delivery Means	Effects/Casualties	Date
Iraq Al Faw, East of Basra	Nerve/ Mustard	Aircraft Artillery	Heavy casualties Significant impact on battle	April, 1988
Iraq Mehran	Nerve/ Mustard	Aircraft Artillery	Heavy casualties Significant impact on battle	May, 1988
Iraq Majnoon, Dehloran, Hawizeh	Nerve/ Mustard	Aircraft Artillery	Heavy casualties Significant impact on battle	June–July, 1988
Iraq Kurdistan	Nerve/Mustard	Aircraft	Terrorize Kurdish rebels and population	August, 1988

Sources: Estimate based on CIA background paper of January 13, 1998, Anthony H. Cordesman and Abraham R. Wagner, *Lessons of Modern War, Volume IV: The Gulf War*, Boulder, Westview, 1996; various editions of the SIPRI Yearbook; Edgar O'Ballance, *The Gulf War*, London, Brassey's, 1988; W. Seth Carus, "Chemical Weapons in the Middle East," *Policy Focus*, Number Nine, Washington Institute for Near East Policy, December, 1988; JCSS, *Military Balance in the Middle East, 1987–1988*, Boulder, Westview, 1988.

*The CIA reports that Iranians also used poison gas at Halabjah and may have caused some of the casualties.

using a nerve gas agent called Tabun.[21] These conclusions were validated by a second UN investigation in 1986, and it later became apparent that Iraq also had Chlorine gas agents, and that Iraq had a major chemical weapons production complex.

Iran's efforts to make a propaganda issue out of Iraq's use of gas may have had some temporary success. Iraq made little use of chemical agents between 1984 and the new Iranian offensive in Faw in 1986. There are, however, alternative explanations. While this pause in Iraqi use of gas may have been because of the hostile reaction in the West and Third World, it may also have been because Iraq lacked the organization and dispensers to use gas safely. There are indications that unfavorable winds caused Iraqi deaths at Haji Omran in August, 1983, at Majnoon in March, 1984, and near Fish Lake in 1987. Iran also seems to have become more cautious after the United States formally condemned Iraqi use of chemical weapons in March, 1984.

Iraq Steadily Improves Its Use of Chemical Weapons

Changes in the training of the Iraqi Chemical Corps also indicate that Iraq was attempting to become more selective in the use of mustard gas, and to attack Iranian rear areas with more care. Further, Iraq was clearly converting its forces to be able to use nonpersistent nerve gases against attacking Iranian troops, or in its own attacks on Iranian positions.

In any case, Iraq resumed extensive use of gas warfare in its defense of Faw in 1986, and made good use of gas in its defense of Basra in 1987. Iraq also found that mustard and nerve gas were effective in defending against attacking Iranian troops in the north during their attacks on Iraq in 1987 and in the early months of 1988. Chemical weapons offered a potential solution to the problem of mountain or rough terrain warfare, and in many cases it allowed Iraq to "secure" a mountainous area with relatively few troops. Iraq was particularly ready to use gas against those Iraqi Kurds fighting on the side of Iran, a group which the government regarded as being nothing but traitors.

Iraq made massive use of chemical weapons during its recapture of Faw in early 1988 and in its assaults to recover its positions outside of Basra. By April, 1988, Iran claimed that the new round of attacks had raised the total number of casualties from chemical weapons since the start of the war to around 25,600, with some 260 dead. These claims may well be legitimate. Although Iran now had extensive defensive equipment, it did not organize or train to use it effectively. Many Iranians died, for example, because they did not shave often enough to allow their gas masks to make a tight seal.[22]

During the final months before the cease-fire, Iraq used chemical weapons in its attacks on Iranian positions in Mehran, the Majnoon Islands, the Hawizeh Marshes, and Dehloran.[23] By the time the war ended in a cease-fire, the Iraqi use of chemical weapons seems to have produced around 45,000 casualties, although there is no way to calculate the seriousness of these casualties or the number of resultant deaths.

The Impact of Chemical Weapons on the Fighting

As for the overall impact of chemical weapons, it is clear that Iraq had substantially greater success in using such weapons after 1987. While 45,000 casualties from gas were a relatively minor part of the well over 1 million military and civilian casualties that resulted from the war, chemical weapons do seem to have had a critical effect on Iranian military and civilian morale in the Iraqi counteroffensives and the "war of the cities" in 1988. Sheer killing power alone is not the issue. Troops that feel they are defenseless may well break and run after limited losses. Populations that fear chemical attacks may well cease to support a conflict. These are lessons that many developing nations have already taken to heart, and further use of chemical, and possibly biological, weapons now seems all too likely.

IRAQ'S EXPANSION OF ITS CHEMICAL WEAPONS PRODUCTION CAPABILITY

Iraq's chemical attacks were made possible by massive efforts to expand its capacity to produce chemical weapons. Many of the details of these efforts are still unclear, but a number of Iraq's efforts are well documented. No later than early 1982, Iraq began to make major new efforts to acquire technology and feedstock from overseas. For example, the Iraqi State Ministry of Pesticide Production turned to a unit of Phillips Petroleum Company in Tessenderloo, Belgium, to obtain 500 metric tons of a chemical called thiodiglycol.[24] Thiodiglycol is not suited for the production of nerve agents, but it can be easily combined with hydrochloric acid to produce mustard gas. About one ton of the chemical is required to produce one ton of mustard gas.[25]

New Production Facilities During the Iran-Iraq War

Phillips Petroleum Company states that it did not react negatively to the order because it was placed by KBS Holland B. V., a Dutch trading firm. It was only after the trading firm began to ship its initial order in July, 1983 that Phillips learned that the actual customer was in Iraq, and then paid little attention because it was said to be a large "agricultural" organization.

In early 1984, when the State Ministry of Pesticide Production placed a second order for 500 tons, Phillips grew suspicious and canceled the order. Phillips then notified the Belgian government, which reacted by canceling Phillips' license to produce the chemical.[26] By this time, Iraq already had enough feedstock for nearly 500 tons of gas, and it began construction of the special refinery and other facilities necessary to make its own thiodiglycol out of more commonly available chemicals. Iraq's industrial complex at Al Fallujah seems to have been able to make thiodiglycol before the cease-fire, as well as the precursors for nerve gas.

Mustard gas offered Iraq significant military advantages. While mustard gas is 10 to 100 times less lethal than the simpler nerve agents in terms of direct exposure, it is easier to produce and handle and to deliver in actual practice. Mustard gas is also more effective when it is actually delivered against infantry or exposed humans in other facilities. It is more persistent, and the casualties consume large amounts of medical services and support. Lethality is not the only issue. Limited exposures to mustard gas can blind or blister for periods of four to six weeks. Mustard gas thus offered Iraq special advantages in dealing with Iranian infantry, which often spent considerable time in static exposed locations and which had relatively poor rear area medical facilities.

Iraq also acquired the equipment and feedstock to make nerve gas. By sheer coincidence, US customs stopped another State Ministry of Pesticide Production order for 74 barrels of potassium fluoride, another precursor of Sarin nerve gas, in February, 1984. The order was placed by Al-Haddad Enterprises Incorporated, owned by Sahib al-Haddad, a naturalized Iraqi citizen. The shipment was not then illegal, because it was not yet controlled, and there is no clear way of determining how many other shipments occurred in the United States or in other countries. However, at least one Dutch firm—Melchemie Holland B. V.—has since been convicted of export violations for selling phosphorous oxychloride, another precursor of nerve gas. Iraqi agents also bought large amounts of equipment from a West German firm in Drereich, which it seems to have claimed would be used to make organophosphate fertilizer but which could help manufacture nerve gas.[27]

These efforts paid off relatively quickly. A major Iraqi research center for chemical weapons was completed at Salman Pak.[28] The facilities necessary to produce mustard gas and Tabun and Sarin nerve agents were established at Iraq's Samara chemical complex, which houses one of the insecticide plants obtained from the West.[29] The Samara facility was heavily sheltered and occupied 26 square kilometers in an area about 100 kilometers north of Baghdad. It was defended by troops and SA-2 missiles. Iraq established another major plant near Karbala, and at least one more gas warfare complex at Fallujah, 65 kilometers west of Baghdad.[30]

Mass Production of Mustard Gas and Nerve Gas

By 1983, Iraqi production of mustard gas was sufficient for Iraq to begin to deliver small amounts with artillery, fighters, and Mi-8 helicopters. It is unclear exactly when Iraq developed bombs using chemical agents, but it seems to have used 250-kilogram bombs it bought from Spain, and to have begun to use Fitter aircraft to deliver such bombs. This mustard gas was exceptionally pure, which indicates that Iraq was still producing batches under laboratory conditions, rather than mass producing mustard gas in tons. This mustard gas seems to have been produced at the Iraqi chemical weapons facility at Samara.[31]

Iraq seems to have begun to produce significant amounts of nonpersistent nerve gas Tabun or GA in 1984, and to have put Sarin or GB into full-scale production in 1986. Its main production facility seems to have been at Samara, although the complex at Al Fallujah may have produced the actual gas as well as the precursors. Iraq also seems to have at least experimented with hydrogen cyanide, cyanogen chloride, and Lewisite.

By late 1985, Iraq could produce about 10 tons a month of all types of gases. This seems to have expanded to a capacity of over 50 tons per month by late 1986.[32] In early 1988, Iraq could produce over 70 tons of mustard gas a month and six tons each of Tabun and Sarin.[33]

By mid-1989, Iraq had at least five major plants for chemical agent research and production.[34] Iraq also seemed to be actively working on the production of biological weapons and on developing a way to deliver gas and biological weapons with surface-to-surface missiles. Some sources feel that Salman Pak is the Iraqi center for the development and production of biological weapons, as well as the development of chemical weapons. There is no reliable way to determine what biological weapons Iraq was developing, and whether actual production was underway. Logical biological weapons include Botulin toxin, Anthrax, tularemia, and equine encephalitis. Iraq also seemed to be producing VX, a persistent nerve gas.[35]

IRAQ'S USE OF CHEMICAL WEAPONS AGAINST THE KURDS

There is no way to document Iraq's first use of chemical weapons against Iraqi Kurds. Pro-Iranian Iraqi Kurdish forces were often intermingled with the Iranian forces deployed in the Northern Front during the Iran-Iraq War, and chemical weapons may have been used against such Kurdish forces as early as 1982. It is clear that Iraq began to make extensive use of lethal chemical weapons in the North during the period 1983–1984, and never made any distinction between Iranian and pro-Iranian Iraqi Kurdish forces between that time and the cease-fire in 1988.

It is even more difficult to establish the extent to which Iraq used chemical weapons against Kurdish civilians. Anti-Iraqi Kurdish factions charged that Iraq began to make extensive use of gas against noncombatant Kurdish villages and areas early in 1987. According to such reports, there were some fifteen such attacks between April 15, 1987, and February 26, 1988. Three of these attacks are claimed to have produced 100 or more casualties: attacks on Arbil, Kanibard, Zeenau, Balookawa, Shaikwassan, the Derasheer Mountains, and the Sawseewaken area on April 16, 1987, the Dahok/Amadia area on May 6, 1987, and the Sulaymania/Sergaloo, Yakhsamar, Haledan, Gweezeela areas on February 25, 1987.[36]

While charges that Iraq made major attacks on noncombatant Kurds during the Iran-Iraq War cannot be independently confirmed, it is clear that poison gas was used against Kurdish civilians during the fighting in the north in early 1988. This use occurred when both Iraq and Iran used gas during an Iranian attack on the Iraqi Kurdish town of Halabjah on February 26, 1988. Up to 5,000 Kurdish civilians were killed in the fighting, although it should be stressed that gas was used in the context of an ongoing military operation during a period when Iran threatened to break through Iraqi lines, and at a time and location when it was difficult to distinguish between Kurds that directly supported Iran and Kurds that were neutral or noncombatant.

Iraq seems to have begun its use of chemical weapons only after its troops were driven from the Halabjah area. It then, however, bombed the town with enough mustard gas to produce burning white clouds. Some of the gas victims seem to have fled toward Iraq, rather than Iran, and this may have confused Iranian forces into thinking that they were Iraqi troops. As a result, Iran seems to have fired hydrogen cyanide gas into the area with artillery shells. The cyanide fired by Iran may have done much of the actual killing, and may have accounted for many of the casualties that Iran blamed on Iraq when it showed the results of the attacks on its state television network.[37]

Iraq did not halt its use of chemical weapons against its Kurds after the cease-fire in the Iran-Iraq War. In spite of the hostile outside reaction to its attacks on Halabjah, Iraq seems to have begun a major new offensive against its own Kurds on August 25, 1988. This offensive was called Operation Anfall, and there is a broad consensus among US and other Western intelligence experts that Iraq made considerable use of gas warfare as part of an effort to depopulate hostile areas. While the exact scale of Iraq's use of gas is uncertain, some 65,000 Kurds fled to Turkey, and many of the refugees gave convincing reports of the use of gas warfare. These attacks only halted after a new wave of world protests, support, and extensive diplomatic pressure from the United States, which tended to isolate Iraq.[38]

IRAQ'S CHEMICAL WEAPONS PROGRAMS BETWEEN THE IRAN-IRAQ WAR AND THE GULF WAR

Iraq did not use chemical weapons in the Gulf War or deploy such weapons forward within the Kuwaiti Theater of Operations (KTO).[39] It did, however, stockpile chemical weapons far enough forward to be rapidly deployed to its front-line troops, and it threatened to use chemical weapons. Iraq armed and dispersed tens of thousands of chemical artillery rounds and bombs and provided its forces with chemical protection equipment. Searches of Iraqi headquarters, artillery, and field units in the KTO after the war found briefing materials and instructions which indicate that Iraq at least considered using mass fire of chemical weapons against the Coalition ground troops attacking its forward defensive barriers.[40]

Although Iraq was a signatory to the Geneva protocols of 1925, which prohibit the use of poison gas, this did not prevent it from producing and using chemical weapons in the Iran-Iraq War. Iraq started to produce mustard gas in small amounts at the laboratory level, and it developed enough mass production capability so it could make extensive use of mustard gas after 1984.[41]

The Advantages of Mustard Gas

While mustard gas is not an advanced gas agent, Iraq found that it offered significant military advantages in fighting Iran which might have applied to the Gulf War, and which may apply to future conflicts.[42] Mustard gas is a blistering agent which is 10 to 100 times less lethal than the simpler nerve agents in terms of direct exposure, and slow to act on those who are exposed.

Lethality, however, is not the only issue in measuring the effectiveness of chemical weapons. Like nerve gas, mustard gas attacks the lungs, eyes, and skin, and gas masks alone are not effective protection. Mustard gas is also easier to produce, handle, and deliver than nerve gas, and it can also be more effective than most nerve gases for several important tactical purposes. It persists for several days to several weeks, and its wounds are slow to heal. Exposed personnel that must work or operate in fixed areas and facilities are difficult to protect over long periods because chemical protection gear has a limited functional life. Exposures to mustard gas can blind or blister for periods of four to six weeks. Casualties consume large amounts of medical services and support.

These properties of mustard gas gave it considerable effectiveness against Iranian infantry, even though nerve gas did not produce high levels of fatalities. Iranian forces often spent considerable time in exposed locations and had relatively poor medical facilities. Their chemical protection gear was often of poor quality, and even the threat of gas often disrupted Iran's operations.

The Use of Nerve Gas

Iraq did not stop at using mustard gas. It began to use small amounts of nerve gas in response to Iran's offensives in 1984. This nerve gas consisted of non-persistent "G-agents," principally Sarin (GB). Such nerve agents are lethal and act almost instantly when the skin, eyes, and wet tissue of their victims are exposed. Nerve gases are difficult to detect, and troops require excellent protection and an antidote in order to prevent high casualties. G-agents also persist for only a few minutes to a few days and normally allow an attacker relatively rapid tactical movement into exposed areas. In contrast, persistent agents like mustard gas and persistent nerve gas may remain lethal for several days to several weeks. Friendly troops can only operate in exposed areas if they have full protection and occupy the area for only a limited amount of time. This is why persistent agents are better suited to fixed targets like air bases and logistic centers, or defensive operations where they can be used against the rear areas of the enemy with only limited risk to friendly troops.[43]

Iraq was able to produce both mustard gas and nerve agents in quantity by 1985 or 1986, although its major plants did not reach full capacity production of either gas until the late 1980s.[44] UN inspectors examining a key Iraqi facility at Muthanna after the war estimated that it eventually reached a peak daily production capacity of 5 tons of mustard gas and 2.5 tons of Sarin. They found that Muthanna still had 225 tons of nerve agent and 280 tons of mustard gas. According to some reports, this plant was the facility that developed nerve gas warheads for Iraq's long-range missiles.[45]

More Plants and Facilities

The UN found a number of other facilities after the war. Iraq completed construction of a special refinery and other gas warfare facilities at Fallujah—about sixty-five kilometers northwest of Baghdad—before the August, 1988 cease-fire in the Iran-Iraq War.[46] These facilities were used to produce precursors like phosphorous trichloride, phosphorous chloride, and thionyl chloride, and to store chemical weapons stocks.[47] Iraq may also have produced some persistent VX nerve gas at this facility.[48]

Iraq had a plant near Basra designed to produce 410,000 tons of ethylene products a year. It began construction of a new Petrochemical Complex No. 2 ethylene plant near Musayyib in 1988, which was scheduled to begin operations in 1991.⁴⁹ The Musayyib facility was designed to produce 420,000 tons of ethylene and 67,000 tons of ethylene oxide.⁵⁰

Iraq expanded its phosphate industry, which is centered at Akashat and Al-Qaim, and it seemed to have adapted powdered detergent and fertilizer plants using phosphate ore to produce feedstocks. Iraq expanded its facility at Rutbah, just south of Ashkhat, to produce acids and other chemical components. It may have established a complex called "Project 9320" in the area, which had three factories to produce secondary chemicals used in manufacturing nerve gas.⁵¹

Some analysts estimate that these developments allowed Iraq to expand its production of all types of poison gas from about 10 tons a month by late 1985 to over 50 tons per month by late 1986.⁵² Iraq may have been able to produce over 60 tons of mustard gas a month and four tons each of Tabun and Sarin by late 1987, and over 70 tons of mustard gas a month and six tons each of Tabun and Sarin by mid-1988.⁵³ These totals do not include the possible production of Soman, a choking agent like phosgene, blood agents like hydrogen cyanide and cyanogen cyanide, vesicants like Lewisite, and agents like Adamsite and Chloropicrin.⁵⁴ The possible range of Iraqi chemical weapons is shown in Table 17.2, although most documented Iraqi uses of chemical weapons involved only the use of mustard gas and nonpersistent nerve gas.

Figure 17.1 shows the location of Iraq's largest chemical, nuclear, and biological facilities at the time of the Gulf War.

Production Capabilities at the Time of the Gulf War

Iraqi production continued to expand until the beginning of the Gulf War. According to some estimates, Iraq had at least 10 major storage bunkers for chemical weapons scattered throughout Iraq by the time Desert Storm began. These estimates indicate that Iraq was able to produce up to 3,500 tons of mustard gas and 2,000 tons of Sarin and Tabun a year by 1989—or more than 20 times the amount it could produce in 1985. They also indicate that Iraq was producing persistent agents VX and VR-55, and that its plant at Fallujah was being expanded to a capacity of 2,000 tons per month.⁵⁵ Such a level of production would have given Iraq enough chemical agents to arm 250,000 to 500,000 tube and rocket artillery rounds a year, as well as smaller numbers of bombs, although such estimates may sharply exaggerate Iraq's capabilities.⁵⁶

Iraq also did not halt its use of poison gas with the end of the Iran-Iraq War. It used poison gas regularly between 1988 and 1989 as part of its military effort to suppress Kurdish military resistance. This use was confirmed by a British defense laboratory that tested soil and bomb damage fragments taken from Kurdish villages the north of Iraq. The chemical and biological defense establishment at Porton Down found low levels of sulfur mustard gas and Sarin (GB). These traces were found in Birjinni, a village of about 200 in northern Iraq. This village had been selected because eyewitnesses had said that Iraqi planes dropped three

Table 17.2
Major Chemical Agents Iraqi Forces Can Use

NERVE AGENTS: Agents that quickly disrupt the nervous system by binding to enzymes critical to nerve functions, causing convulsions and/or paralysis. Must be ingested, inhaled, and absorbed through the skin. Very low doses cause a running nose, contraction of the pupil of the eye, and difficulty in visual coordination. Moderate doses constrict the bronchi and cause a feeling of pressure in the chest, and weaken the skeletal muscles and cause fibrillation. Large doses cause death by respiratory or heart failure. Can be absorbed through inhalation or skin contact. Reaction normally occurs in one to two minutes. Death from lethal doses occurs within minutes, but artificial respiration can help and atropine and oximes act as antidotes. The most toxic nerve agents kill with a dosage of only 10 milligrams per minute per cubic meter, versus 400 for less lethal gases. Recovery is normally quick, if it occurs at all, but permanent brain damage can occur:

Tabun (GA)
Sarin (GB): Nearly as volatile as water and delivered by air. A dose of 5 $mg/min/m^3$ produces casualties, a respiratory dose of 100 $mg/min/m^3$ is lethal. Lethality lasts one to two days.
Soman (GD)
GF
VR-55 (Improved Soman): A thick, oily substance which persists for some time.
VK/VX: A persistent agent roughly as heavy as fuel oil. A dose of 0.5 $mg/min/m^3$ produces casualties, a respiratory dose of 10 $mg/min/m^3$ is lethal. Lethality lasts one to sixteen weeks.

BLISTER AGENTS: Cell poisons that destroy skin and tissue, cause blindness upon contact with the eyes, and which can result in fatal respiratory damage. Can be colorless or black oily droplets. Can be absorbed through inhalation or skin contact. Serious internal damage if inhaled. Penetrates ordinary clothing. Some have delayed and some have immediate action. Actual blistering normally takes hours to days, but effects on the eyes are much more rapid. Mustard gas is a typical blister agent and exposure of concentrations of a few milligrams per meter over several hours generally at least causes blisters and swollen eyes. When the liquid falls onto the skin or eyes it has the effect of second or third degree burns. It can blind and cause damage to the lungs leading to pneumonia. Severe exposure causes general intoxication similar to radiation sickness. HD and HN persist up to 12 hours. L, HL, and CX persist for one to two hours. Short of prevention of exposure, the only treatment is to wash the eyes, decontaminate the skin, and treat the resulting damage like burns:

Sulfur Mustard (H or HD): A dose of 100 $mg/min/m^3$ produces casualties, a dose of 1,500 $mg/min/m^3$ is lethal. Residual lethality lasts up to two to eight weeks.
Distilled Mustard (DM)
Nitrogen Mustard (HN)
Lewisite (L)
Phosgene Oxime (CX)
Mustard Lewisite (HL)

CHOKING AGENTS: Agents that cause the blood vessels in the lungs to hemorrhage and fluid to build up, until the victim chokes or drowns in his or her own fluids (pulmonary edema). Provide quick warning through smell or lung irritation. Can be absorbed through inhalation. Immediate to delayed action. The only treatment is inhalation of oxygen and rest. Symptoms emerge in periods after exposure of seconds up to three hours:

Table 17.2 (continued)

Phosgene (CG)
Diphosgene (DP)
PS Chloropicrin
Chlorine Gas

BLOOD AGENTS: Kill through inhalation. Provide little warning except for headache, nausea, and vertigo. Interfere with use of oxygen at the cellular level. Cyanogen Chloride (CK) also irritates the lungs and eyes. Rapid action and exposure either kills by inhibiting cell respiration or it does not—casualties will either die within seconds to minutes of exposure or recover in fresh air. Most gas masks have severe problems in providing effective protection against blood agents:

Hydrogen Cyanide (AC): A dose of 2,000 mg/min/m^3 produces casualties, a respiratory dose of 5,000 mg/min/m3 is lethal. Lethality lasts one to four hours.

Cyanogen Chloride (CK): A dose of 7,000 mg/min/m^3 produces casualties, a respiratory dose of 11,000 mg/min/m^3 is lethal. Lethality lasts 15 minutes to one hour.

TOXINS: Biological poisons causing neuromuscular paralysis after exposure of hours or days. Formed in food or cultures by the bacterium clostridium botulinum. Produces highly fatal poisoning characterized by general weakness, headache, dizziness, double vision and dilation of the pupils, paralysis of muscles, and problems in speech. Death is usually by respiratory failure. Antitoxin therapy has limited value, but treatment is mainly supportive:

Botulin toxin (A): Six distinct types, of which four are known to be fatal to man. An oral dose of 0.001 mg is lethal. A respiratory dose of 0.02 mg/min/m^3 is also lethal.

DEVELOPMENTAL WEAPONS: A new generation of chemical weapons is under development. The only publicized agent is perfluoroisobutene (PFIB), which is an extremely toxic, odorless, and invisible substance produced when PFIB (Teflon) is subjected to extreme heat under special conditions. It causes pulmonary edema or dry-land drowning when the lungs fill with fluid. Short exposure disables and small concentrations cause delayed death. Activated charcoal and most existing protection equipment offers no defense. Some sources refer to "third" and "fourth" generation nerve gasses, but no technical literature seems to be available.

CONTROL AGENTS: Agents which produce temporary irritating or disabling effects when in contact with the eyes or inhaled. They can cause serious illness or death when used in confined spaces. O-Chlorobenzyl-malononitrile (CS) is the least toxic gas, followed by Chloroacetophenone (CN) and Adamsite (DM). Symptoms can be treated by washing the eyes and/or removal from the area. Exposure to CS, CN, and DM produces immediate symptoms. Staphylococcus produces symptoms in 30 minutes to four hours, and recovery takes 24 to 48 hours. Treatment of Staphylococcus is largely supportive:

Tear: Causes flow of tears and irritation of upper respiratory tract and skin. Can cause nausea and vomiting:

Chlororacetophenone (CN)
O-Chlorobenzyl-malononitrile (CS)

Vomiting: Causes irritation, coughing, severe headache, tightness in chest, nausea, vomiting:
Adamsite (DM)
Staphylococcus

Table 17.2 (continued)

INCAPACITATING AGENTS: Agents which normally cause short-term illness, psychoactive effects (delirium and hallucinations). Can be absorbed through inhalation or skin contact. The psychoactive gases and drugs produce unpredictable effects, particularly in the sick, small children, elderly, and individuals who are already mentally ill. In rare cases they kill. In others, they produce a permanent psychotic condition. Many produce dry skin, irregular heartbeat, urinary retention, constipation, drowsiness, and a rise in body temperature, plus occasional maniacal behavior. A single dose of 0.1 to 0.2 milligrams of LSD-25 will produce profound mental disturbance within a half hour that lasts 10 hours. The lethal dose is 100 to 200 milligrams:

BZ
LSD
LSD-based BZ
Mescaline
Psilocybin
Benzilates

Sources: Adapted from Matthew Meselson and Julian Perry Robinson, "Chemical Warfare and Chemical Disarmament," *Scientific American*, Vol. 242, No. 4, April, 1980, pp. 38–47; "Chemical Warfare: Extending the Range of Destruction," *Jane's Defense Weekly*, August 25, 1990, p. 267; US Marine Corps, *Individual Guide For NBC Defense*, Field Manual OH-11–1A, August, 1990; and unpublished testimony to the Special Investigations Subcommittee of the Government Operations Committee, US Senate, by Mr. David Goldberg, Foreign Science and Technology Center, US Army Intelligence Center on February 9, 1989.

clusters of four chemical bombs on August 25, 1988, and killed at least four people.[57]

Slow Progress in Weapons Technology and Design

Iraq did, however, put more effort into increasing its volume of production than into making its chemical weapons effective. Most of the designs the UN found after the Gulf War had only limited dispersal capability, reliability, and storage problems, and limits to their fusing that affected the ability to reliably set height of burst. Iraq did not have binary nerve gas. Saddam Hussein stated on April 2, 1990, that Iraq had "double-combined chemical" weapons, and had them since the last year of the Iran-Iraq War. Such weapons later proved to be a crude technology for storing alcohol in nerve gas weapons that it acquired in 1984 or 1985, and used during the latter half of the Iran-Iraq War.

There were several other chemical weapons technologies that Iraq does not seem to have been ready to deploy when the Gulf War began.[58] It did not have "dusty" mustard gas that overcomes defenses in a different way. "Dusty" mustard gas is a powdered form of mustard gas which is very persistent, can coat particles so small that they are only several microns in size, and may be able to penetrate protective clothing and filters. Iraq also does not seem to have had "cocktail" chemical weapons which mix several chemical agents together

Figure 17.1
The Location of Iraq's Largest Chemical, Nuclear, and Biological Facilities at the Time of the Gulf War

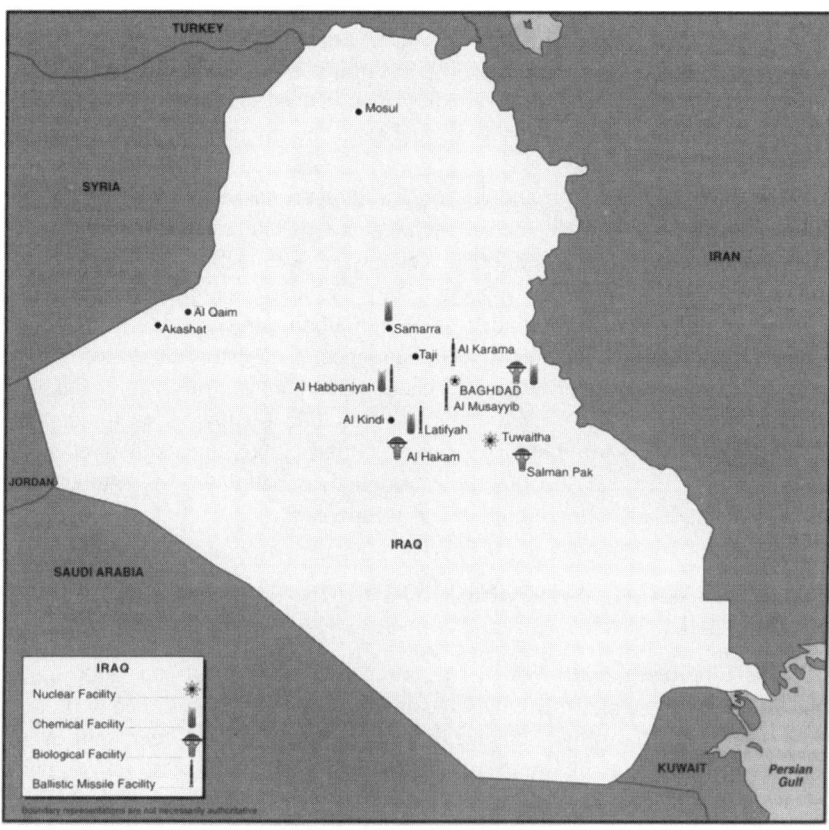

Source: US Office of the Secretary of Defense, *Proliferation: Threat and Response*, Washington, US Department of Defense, April, 1996, p. 19.

to provide different kinds of lethality and/or defeat different forms of protection, including many gas masks. While some sources indicate that Iraq used "cocktails" of cyanogen with mustard gas and Tabun in Kurdistan, this has not been confirmed.[59]

Readiness for Chemical Warfare

Iraqi forces did, however, have considerable readiness for chemical warfare at the time they invaded Kuwait. After 1985, Iraqi doctrine had called for the regular training of all combined arms elements in chemical warfare. Iraqi forces in the KTO were equipped with numerous dual capable delivery systems and sophisticated chemical protection, reconnaissance, and decontamination gear. Delivery systems included rifle grenades, 81 mm mortars, 152 mm, 130 mm, and 122 mm artillery rounds, bombs, bomblets, 90 mm air-to-ground rockets, 216 kilogram Frog and 555 kilogram Scud warheads, and possibly land mines, and cruise missiles. As many as 50% of Iraq's combat aircraft and artillery weapons could deliver chemical rounds.[60] Its units were equipped with chemical protection and decontamination gear, and with the operational instructions for using chemical weapons.[61]

While Iraqi regular army and air force units were tasked with delivering the chemical weapons, Iraq had special chemical troops integrated throughout all of the branches of the Iraqi armed forces which were responsible for the care, build-up, and delivery of chemical weapons. They had a status approaching that of a separate combat arm, and included units and subunits responsible for chemical defense, radiation and chemical reconnaissance, the operation of smoke and flame generators, the identification of chemical targets and meteorological analysis, and decontamination. Each corps had a chemical battalion, each independent brigade or division had a chemical company, regiments had chemical platoons, and chemical sections were assigned to battalions or platoons with weapons capable of delivering chemical weapons.[62]

IRAQI CHEMICAL WEAPONS PROGRAMS AT THE TIME OF THE GULF WAR

At the time of the Gulf War, Iraq had an inventory of around 1,000 metric tons of chemical weapons, and massive amounts of chemicals needed to produce more weapons. Its deployed chemical weapons seem to have been split evenly between blister agents like mustard gas and nerve agents. It was just beginning to weaponize VX, a persistent nerve gas. It was prepared for a massive chemical offensive and had prepared its forces in the Kuwaiti Theater of Operations with chemical defense equipment and extensive written instructions.[63]

Artillery Weapons and Bombs

The primary threat to Coalition ground troops consisted of Iraq's artillery shells. The principal shell was a 155 mm round. Each was filled with 3.5 liters of mustard agent using a tetyl burster charge. In addition to the 155 mm artillery shells, Iraq had 120 mm mortar bombs filled with nonlethal CS gas, some experimental conversions of 130 mm and 152 mm smoke shells, and 122 mm rocket rounds filled with between 6.4 and 9 liters of nerve gas. These rocket rounds were poorly designed and corroded by a combination of the effects of the gas and decomposition of the solid fuel rocket motor.

Iraq had bombs filled with mustard gas and two types of nerve gas. As has been discussed earlier, mustard gas is of only moderate lethality and is most useful in area denial, inflicting panic, and inhibiting operations because of the need to operate in restrictive protective gear or to avoid contaminated areas. It is best suited to attacking static rear areas, suppressing the flanks of an enemy force in a breakthrough, contaminating areas as a defensive barrier, or attacking the rear echelon of an attacking enemy under favorable wind conditions weapons. In the case of the Gulf War, this meant it was not an ideal agent for dealing with any force capable of rapid maneuver, although they would have been effective against rear areas and in delaying operations by forcing Coalition forces to don protective suits, operate armor under sealed conditions, and decontaminate equipment and supplies.

Iraqi nerve gas weapons consisted of GB (Sarin), GF (Tabun), or a mixture of the two. Iraq had not yet begun to produce VX in volume. These nerve agents offered Iraq a much better killing mechanism in dealing with both maneuver forces and area denial. However, Iraq's Tabun and Sarin nerve gas agents were only about 60% pure and had limited shelf lives. Iraq had not yet developed the technology to purify these agents by distilling them, or the capability to add stabilizing chemicals. It did have crude binary weapons which required the chemical components to be stored separately and to be mixed shortly before use.

Iraq's mustard gas munitions tended to leak in storage, although the agent itself has proved stable enough to remain lethal through 1998. Even the nerve agents it kept at a stable 18° C in al-Muthanna had to be used within weeks of production or they started to break down.[64] As a result, Iraq had to produce GB in batches and only loaded its nerve gas weapons a few days before their use. Iraqi did not have not storable binary weapons which kept stable components separate and automatically mixed them in the weapon. Iraq's bombs were pre-filled with suitable alcohols, which then had to be manually added and stirred. Such a procedure is dangerous for the operator and can lead to improper mixture of the agent.

Iraq had four main types of chemical bombs. The smallest was the LD-250, a modification of a Spanish 250-pound smoke bomb. Each LD-250 normally carried 64 liters of mustard gas. It also had bombs filled with CS gas, and a 500-pound bomb called the Aald-500, which contained 150 liters of mustard gas. Iraq had two bombs using nerve gas. One was the DB-2, which contained 400 liters of GB. The other was the R-400, which Iraq used for both chemical and biological weapons, and the chemical version of which contained 102 liters of binary GB.

Drones and Missile Warheads

The United States estimated during the war that Iraq had some MiG-21 derived drones that could be used to deliver chemical weapons. These systems were not found after the war, but the UN found after the war that Iraq had produced warheads for the Al Husayn missile.[65] Some had had unitary GB warheads, and some were of the binary type. The binary warheads were partially filled with alcohol to allow them to be armed by adding a chemical called DF. The UN said later that these warheads were poorly welded, had generally poor construction, and the burster charge was badly placed. It is uncertain whether such warheads could have done any real damage, and some experts feel that they might have tumbled and broken up on reentry.

Post-War UN investigations also showed that Iraq had severe problems with other types of weapons because it had failed to keep its agents pure and to develop corrosion-proof materials. Nearly 25% of the weapons the UN found had leaked, although it was often impossible to distinguish between problems with the chemical agents, problems with the weapons design, and problems because of wartime damage or rapid post-war movement and inadequate storage.[66]

IRAQ'S DECISION TO NOT USE CHEMICAL WEAPONS

There is no way to determine exactly why Iraq did not use its chemical warfare capabilities during the Gulf War without having access to the thoughts and intentions of Iraq's senior leadership.[67] Iraq certainly made threats to use chemical weapons in dealing with the Western and Arab reaction to its invasion of Kuwait and build-up on the Saudi border soon after it invaded Kuwait. For example, Saddam Hussein gave a speech on August 20, 1990, stating that foreign hostages would be dispersed to military and key civil locations throughout Iraq, including Iraq's major chemical weapons production facilities. Iraq also made demonstrative gestures. It conspicuously loaded its aircraft with chemical weapons so that this could be detected by US intelligence before removing the weapons and placing them back in their normal storage sites.

During the fall of 1990, Iraq dispersed chemical weapons in a number of rear area facilities. By November, 1990 Iraq had built up large dispersed and sheltered stocks of chemical weapons in its territory outside of the Kuwaiti Theater of Operations (KTO). It deployed a wide range of chemical-capable delivery systems in its forces supporting its invasion of Kuwait. It also deployed protection and decontamination gear, issued detailed instructions on chemical warfare to its unit commanders, and built decontamination trenches in the forward and rear areas.[68]

Iraq retained large stockpiles of weapons until well after the end of the war. In fact, it was the US destruction of one such supply depot in Iraq after the war that has emerged as the only serious possibility that the forces on either side were exposed to significant amounts of chemical agents. This depot was located at Khamisiyah in Southern Iraq, and US military teams destroyed it in March, 1991. It was later shown to have had from 500 to 2,000 Sarin-filled rockets, and computer models showed that it was at least possible that gas might have reached parts of an area with a 32-mile radius where some 27,000 US troops were then present.[69]

At the same time, Iraq faced many problems in using its chemical weapons. These problems included (1) the purity and storage problems discussed earlier (Iraqi nerve agents were not purified and were not stable in hot weather; they were normally stored in cooled bunkers with instructions that they be used within a week of removal); (2) Iraqi fear of Coalition or Israeli retaliation with nuclear or chemical weapons; (3) the shattering impact of Coalition bombing and the fact that Iraq lost its offensive air capabilities in the first days of the war; (4) the fact that Iraq quickly lost much of its command and control and distribution capability; and (5) poor weather conditions during the ground campaign, whereby winds and rain made effective use of chemical weapons very difficult; and (6) it may not have weaponized large numbers of VX weapons.

All of these factors may have had a significant impact on Iraq's leadership, given Iraq's past willingness to use chemical weapons against Iran and the Kurds. Further, the first few days of the Coalition air campaign showed Iraq that the Coalition could expand its conventional strategic bombing campaign to far more devastating levels by attacking key commercial and government targets. This experience gave Iraq's leadership good cause to fear that such escalation might lead to more intensive Coalition air attacks and to a UN effort to drive them from power.

THE POSSIBLE IMPACT OF IRAQI USE OF CHEMICAL WEAPONS AT THE TACTICAL LEVEL

Iraq faced additional technical and operational problems that deserve serious consideration.[70] None of these problems in employing chemical weapons were "war stoppers," but they were serious, and they may well have had an impact on Iraqi decision making.[71]

The Problem of Tempo of Operations

Iraq's forces in the KTO were unprepared for the tempo and intensity of operations necessary to use chemical weapons effectively against Coalition forces. Its experience during the Iran-Iraq War did little to prepare it for effective operations at the tactical level. Iraq's tactics depended heavily on massed fire against concentrated and relatively static Iranian ground troops with only limited chemical protection gear. It was most successful when it used chemical weapons against massing Iranian attackers that had little maneuverability, or massing Iranian defenders that had little other option except retreat. Iraq's problems in long-range targeting and battle management increased in proportion to the speed, mass, and shock of enemy maneuvers, and the Coalition exploited all of these capabilities. Further, Iraq was unprepared for any form of effective night combat or to deal with the massive weather problems that existed during some of the air and much of the land battle. While weather inhibited Coalition land and air operations, it potentially paralyzed many aspects of Iraqi mobility and greatly increased Iraq's problems in targeting and predicting the weather effects of any use of chemical weapons.

The Cost of Losing Air Superiority

Iraq lost air superiority so early in the war that it had little capability to deliver chemical weapons by air, and it could not have massed enough aircraft over any part of the battlefield at any time to pose a significant threat to Coalition ground troops or rear areas. Iraq suffered serious damage to its forward command and control capabilities during the air campaign, and many Iraqi units lost a substantial amount of their major combat equipment and mobility—creating major problems in making effective use of chemical weapons against a rapidly moving attacker. Iraq also faced serious problems in making effective use of its artillery. Coalition air attacks battered Iraqi forward positions for weeks before Coalition ground troops advanced. By the time the Coalition breached Iraq's forward defenses, Iraqi divisions had taken serious equipment losses, had major supply problems, and suffered from high levels of desertion. Many Iraqi artillery weapons had also been damaged or destroyed.

The Failure of Defensive Barriers

If Iraq had used chemical weapons to augment its forward defenses, this might have delayed the Coalition advance in some areas. Not all Coalition troops had effective chemical protection gear—at least in terms of reliable detection, decontamination, and facility protection equipment. The Coalition troops sent forward did, however, generally have adequate personal protection gear. The Coalition also generally crossed through Iraq's defenses very quickly and did not halt and mass in the forward area. In most cases, their rapid rate of advance would have penetrated and overrun Iraq's artillery before chemical weapons could have had a major tactical effect. Most Iraqi forces in the forward area also lacked the tactical cohesion to use chemical weapons in mass, and to exploit them for either defense or counterattacks.

The Inability to Effectively Target and Strike Maneuver Forces

Iraq would have experienced even greater problems in using chemical weapons to deal with the thrusts of the Coalition armored attack. The US XVIII Corps and VII Corps moved against Iraq from a direction where it had not prepared extensive forward defenses, and had little massed fire capability. The British, French, and US forces in both of these attacking Corps also had extensive chemical protection gear. Slow-moving and disrupted Iraqi forces would, at best, have had limited capability against the most effective forces in the Coalition ground offensive.

Iraq was not organized to use chemical weapons effectively in rear areas or at the theater level once the land battle penetrated its forward defenses and became a fluid war of maneuver. It had no ability to mass chemical artillery fire quickly in most rear areas. Iraq had limited target acquisition capability against maneuvering forces. Coalition armored and heliborne troops had the initiative and overran Iraqi positions before more than limited chemical defense fire could take place. This was particularly true of the Coalition forces attacking from the west, and Coalition forces were sometimes slower in driving north through Kuwait towards Kuwait City.

This does not mean that a major Iraqi attempt to use chemical weapons would not have significantly raised Coalition casualties or would not have had limited tactical successes. It also does not mean that Iraq has any reason to assume that chemical weapons will not be valuable or lethal in the future. Coalition forces like the Egyptian divisions that delayed at Iraq's forward defenses would have made good targets. Units that delayed to regroup or secure their flanks, like a number of the Arab units, exposed themselves to chemical attack. Even limited amounts of fire on British and US armor might have led to some additional delays for decontamination, or to further delays in the double envelopment movement. Use of persistent nerve gas and mustard gas might have affected some Coalition support and supply movements.

THE POSSIBLE IMPACT OF IRAQI USE OF CHEMICAL WEAPONS AT THE STRATEGIC LEVEL

Iraq did not use chemical weapons to attack urban areas, ports, economic targets, or major military concentration and supply areas at the strategic level, but it did make preparations to do so. It dispersed chemical bombs and missile warheads, in some cases to unoccupied dispersal areas, and in ways where the Coalition never detected any Iraqi activity before or during the war to create an option for both aircraft and missile units to launch retaliatory strikes if so directed by the Iraqi leadership, or if the Iraqi leadership came under massive attack.

At the same time, the operational problems that limited Iraq's ability to use aircraft to attack tactical targets with chemical weapons would have been even greater if it had attempted to penetrate more deeply into Coalition air defenses, and Iraq discovered this conclusively within the first two days of Desert Storm. However, Iraq might have launched scattered sorties without warning, and some might have penetrated Coalition air defenses.[72]

Iraq's missile strikes might have had far more impact if it had used chemical warheads—particularly if it had fired in volleys and used VX gas, but again there were operational problems. UNSCOM found after the Gulf War that Iraq's chemical warheads using other agents were still relatively crude and unreliable. Soviet technicians who inspected the Iraqi missiles felt that much of the basic missile modification work was also crude, and that this helped explain the breakup of many Iraqi-modified Scuds during their approach towards targets in Israel. They also felt that the chemical warheads were unbalanced and would have made these problems far worse—potentially making the warheads burn up or depriving them of much of their effectiveness.[73]

Nevertheless, any analysis must consider the fact that a lucky Scud hit near Dhahran with a conventional warhead scored Iraq's only major strike against US forces—killing 28 US soldiers and wounding 97 others. This Scud strike was not only Iraq's only long-range offensive success of the war, it killed more Coalition soldiers than any single land engagement of the war. Iraq has to have been well aware that its Scuds would have done much more damage to the Coalition and Israel if it had used either its chemical or biological warheads, and that even misses would have a powerful political and disruptive effect. The very knowledge that Iraq had actually fired chemically armed warheads or bombs would have led the Coalition, Gulf countries, and Israel to carry out even more intensive chemical defense activities, and might well have forced further dispersal of many elements of Coalition operations.

COALITION EFFORTS TO DESTROY IRAQ'S CHEMICAL CAPABILITIES DURING THE GULF WAR

The Coalition also had important problems and failures in spite of the fact that Iraq did not use chemical weapons. There is no doubt that Coalition war planners made a major effort to destroy Iraq's weapons of mass destruction. At the same time, it is equally clear that they were not properly prepared to carry out such attacks, were poorly supported by US intelligence, and grossly overestimated the effectiveness of their efforts during the war. Many of the chemical weapons activities listed in Table 11.1 were only firmly detected and characterized during 1995, and most of the biological weapons efforts listed in Table 11.1 were not detected until nearly a half decade after the cease-fire in the Gulf War.[74] There is still no reliable inventory of how many of Iraq's weapons were used in the Iran-Iraq war and how many weapons and precursors Iraq still controls.

Iraq's ability to conceal such weapons is a grim warning about the ability of a modern authoritarian state to conceal proliferation while pretending to accede to arms control agreements and systematically lying about its activities. It is a warning that future intelligence and analytic efforts to characterize Iraq's exact intentions, programs, and capabilities may have equal weaknesses, and that the level of military capability the Coalition demonstrated during the Gulf War cannot successfully execute active counterproliferation. Finally, it is a warning of what is likely to happen in the future if UNSCOM and IAEA inspection and destruction efforts are halted.

Many of the weaknesses in the Western intelligence effort were unavoidable. There are tangible limits to what intelligence can do to assess Third World country efforts to develop, build, weaponize, and deploy weapons of mass destruction. While the large-scale use of nuclear reactors can often be observed, characterizing many other aspects of weapons of mass destruction is more difficult. Intelligence coverage of a nation willing to spend billions of dollars a year on a combination of biological, chemical, and nuclear weapons, using many different facilities and methods of production, will always have some inadequacies.

In the case of Iraq, however, these unavoidable intelligence problems were compounded by a failure to dedicate adequate collection and analytic priorities, and to continuously track activity at key facilities. The community failed to properly coordinate all of its reporting and analysis, and it often provided planners and operators with conflicting data—such as its analyses of how Iraq deployed and sorted its weapons, how it marked them, and the shape of its storage bunkers. As a result, US intelligence failed to identify many of Iraq's major facilities, much less characterize their functions and effectiveness. The US Air Force Gulf War Air Power Survey described this intelligence coverage as follows; and its comments came three years before UNSCOM found Iraq had extensive stocks of VX weapons.

The intelligence community could not, of course, have produced a picture as comprehensive as the one that UN Special Commission Inspectors pieced together after recurring and intrusive on-site post-War visits. Nevertheless, certain first order questions do not appear to have been asked.[75]

At the same time, Iraq presented major—if not insuperable—targeting and damage assessment problems. The Coalition conducted some 970 strikes on nuclear-biological-chemical facilities and used some of the most sophisticated strike assets in its inventory. Nearly 80% of the strikes used precision strike aircraft, and 40% of these sorties were carried out by F-117s (the scarcest and most valuable asset for deep penetration strikes in Iraq). The nonprecision strikes were made largely by B-52s, F-16s, F/A-18s, GR-1s, F-111Es, and A-6Es; a few were made by F-111Fs and F-15Es. These strikes were made in cycles, with a heavy peak of strikes during the first week of Desert Storm, a lull during the following few days, and then periods of 10 to 20 strikes per day with occasional peaks. About 54% of the strikes were made during the day, and 46% were made at night.[76]

The Coalition strikes undoubtedly had some effect on Iraq's chemical weapons production capabilities. They struck at the three redundant chemical precursor facilities near Fallujah, at the research centers like Salman Pak (which was also associated with biological toxins), and chemical production plants like Samara. They struck at a number of suspected storage sites throughout Iraq, at the special "S" and cruciform-shaped shelters near Iraqi air bases, and at storage facilities in Kuwait. Suspected delivery systems like the Tu-16 Badger bombers at Al Taquaddum were struck during the second week of the war.[77]

While these attacks damaged Iraqi chemical warfare production capabilities, they did not have the desired or estimated effect. UNSCOM inspections later found that they did far less damage to Iraqi production capability than US Central Command Air Forces (USCENTAF) planners originally estimated, both because the Coalition had failed to identify many of the right targets and because battle damage assessment failed to take into account the fact that physical damage to a building did not mean critical physical damage to key production equipment.

The strikes against Iraq's chemical weapons facilities weakened it's chemical weapons production capabilities, but hardly began to destroy them—a fact not detected by the battle damage assessment effort at the time. The United States concluded after the war that it needed many more lethal weapons to hit hard and underground facilities, and more sophisticated technologies for characterizing the internal layout of large-scale manufacturing facilities. It is now giving high priority to new warhead technologies for destroying underground chemical, biological, and nuclear capabilities, as well as examining ways to improve lethality against the manufacturing equipment inside a plant as distinguished from damaging the building.[78]

Other Coalition air strikes reduced Iraq's ability to move its weapons south, destroyed some of Iraq's artillery forces, and deprived Iraq of almost all of its ability to use offensive airpower. However, the Coalition bombing effect did comparatively little to destroy Iraq's chemical weapons stockpile.[79] Part of the reason the Coalition strikes failed to destroy Iraq's weapons lay in the fact that US intelligence experts assumed that Iraq would be very careful to maintain tight control of the weapons and would have special security arrangements to protect them. In fact, none of the Iraqi chemical weapons had any kind of special markings, and the UN inspectors found chemical and conventional bombs stored together at the Kadzir air base. Other weapons were dispersed outside of plants and storage facilities and covered with loose earth, providing none of the target signatures that intelligence experts expected.

As a result, massive stocks of Iraqi weapons survived. UN inspectors eventually found 12,634 155-mm artillery shells filled with mustard gas.[80] Mustard gas proved to be the only agent Iraq had (other than VX gas) that was stable enough to be stored at length in bulk or munitions. It was about 80% pure, and UNSCOM found that these munitions remained reliable several years after the war.[81] In addition, the UN found 20,000 120-mm mortar bombs filled with nonlethal CS gas (many damaged in the Coalition bombing). It also found 355 tons of mustard gas and nerve agents, 650 tons of intermediate chemicals, 6,920 chemical filled rocket warheads, and 1,376 aerial bombs.[82]

The UN found 915 surviving bombs filled with mustard gas—although Iraq initially declared it only had a total of 110. These included 676 Aald 500-pound bombs, which each contained 150 liters of mustard gas. The UN found 336 R-400s containing 102 liters of binary GB each, and DB-2s containing 400 liters of GB each. It also found some 250 bombs filled with CS gas.

UN inspectors found that Iraq had produced 50 warheads for the Al Husayn missile.[83] Although some significant uncertainties remain, UNSCOM later concluded that nine of Iraq's chemical Scud warheads had been destroyed in static testing, and 11 had been used in training. The UN found that the remaining warheads had been left in an orchard near a road. Sixteen of the 30 remaining warheads had unitary GB warheads, and 14 were of the binary type. The binary warheads were partially filled with alcohol to allow them to be armed by adding DF.

Many of the munitions the UN found were stored at the Al-Muthanna state establishment, mentioned earlier. This is a 25-square kilometer complex about 100 kilometers north of Baghdad, near the air base at Habbaniyah. Large numbers of chemical weapons were also found at four other sites, known as Fallujah 1, Fallujah 2, Fallujah 3, and Muhammediyat Stores. As of February, 1992, the UN had found 45,755 filled chemical munitions, 78,675 unfilled munitions, 355 tons of bulk agent, and 3,173 tons of precursors for chemical weapons versus the 650 tons that Iraq had originally declared. UN and US sources estimated that Iraq might still be concealing up to 50,000 more rounds than it declared.[84]

Finally, the UN found 300 tons of bulk agent stored in containers ranging from barrels to large tanks. Most of this agent was mustard gas, but at least 35 tons was GB. Much of the GB had broken down in storage. The UN found 2,579 tons of precursors out of the 3,173 tons that Iraq had declared. It is possible that much of this total spilled or evaporated, but it is uncertain what happened to the remainder.[85]

In short, the UN investigations found that Iraq had far more problems because it had failed to keep its agents pure, and to develop corrosion-proof materials, than because of the Coalition bombing effort. Nearly 25% of the weapons that the UN found had leaked, although it was often impossible to distinguish between problems with the chemical agents, problems with the weapons design, and problems because of wartime damage or rapid post-war movement and inadequate storage.[86]

IRAQI CHEMICAL WEAPONS PROGRAMS SINCE THE GULF WAR

These UN discoveries are particularly important in light of the fact that US reporting on the effectiveness of the bombing effort during the Gulf War proved to be so grossly exaggerated, as did the estimates made in the US Department of Defense study of the lessons of the war. The US Department of Defense study claimed that

at least 75% of Iraq's CW production capability was destroyed. At Samara, Coalition forces destroyed or severely damaged most known primary CW production, processing, or production support buildings. All three buildings used to fill munitions at Samara were destroyed, although the Iraqis may have moved the equipment from one building before Desert Storm for safekeeping. All three precursor chemical facilities at Habbaniyah were seriously damaged. Although Iraq previously had produced and distributed many CW agents to storage sites throughout the country, the means for delivering these weapons were badly damaged. Coalition air supremacy made Iraqi Air Force delivery of these weapons unlikely; most artillery [Iraq's preferred method of delivering CW] was disabled.[87]

These claims later proved false. In fact, they were made at a time when the United States did not know that Iraq had VX weapons. While the Coalition did damage some key Iraqi facilities and chemical weapons, most of these facilities and virtually all of the weapons survived the bombing. Iraq had time to disperse many of its precursors and key production subsystems before the Gulf War began, and continued to hide and disperse these items after the signing of the cease-fire.[88] It was UNSCOM's Chemical Destruction Group (CDG) that disposed of 398,046 liters (600 tons) of mustard gas, 21,365 liters (30 tons) of Tabun, 64,133 liters (70 tons) of Sarin.

During June, 1992 to April, 1994, the CDG destroyed 481,044 liters at its main facility at al-Muthanna, including 6,773 122-mm rockets, 12,804 155-mm artillery shells, 8,390 bombs, and 29 Al Husayn missile warheads. It destroyed another 11,829 unfilled chemical munitions, 425 122-mm chemical rockets at other sites, and 1,798,593 liters and 1,040,836 kilograms of precursor chemicals. UNSCOM also verified Iraq's claims to have unilaterally destroyed 24,470 additional chemical munitions during the course of 1991, including 45 ballistic missile warheads.[89]

IRAQI PRESENT AND FUTURE CHEMICAL WEAPONS CAPABILITIES AND THE WAR OF SANCTIONS

Impressive as these destruction efforts have been, they have scarcely destroyed all of Iraq's capabilities. Iraq's continuing lies and concealment efforts led Robert Gates, then director of Central Intelligence, to testify to Congress in early 1992 that much of Iraq's "hard to get production equipment" for chemical weapons had been dispersed and "hidden" before the Allied bombing attacks. He also estimated that "if sanctions are relaxed, we believe Iraq could produce modest quantities of chemical agents almost immediately, but it would take a year or more to recover the chemical weapons capability it previously enjoyed."[90]

UNSCOM uncovered lie after lie in the years that followed, and a whole new series of disclosures took place following the defection of Lt. General Hussein Kamel Majid. These disclosures showed that Iraqi declarations of March and May, 1995 were false, and a UNSCOM report stated that, "The new information invalidates the material balances provided in the March, 1995 [declaration] and subsequent amendments."[91]

The Problem of VX Gas

UNSCOM found in the summer of 1995 that Iraq had continued to lie about much of its effort to produce GF and VX nerve gas; it had disguised the fact that it had produced large amounts of VX; and it was hiding the fact that it had been seeking to create an indigenous capability to manufacture cyclohexanol, a precursor of GF, and di-isopropylene, a precursor of VX.

It became clear that Iraq had pursued the development of the deadly nerve agent VX from May, 1985 to December, 1990. As part of this effort, Iraq had engaged in the industrial-scale production of enough chemical precursors to produce 490 tons of VX. These precursors included 65 tons of choline and 200 tons of phosphorous pentasulfide and di-isopropylamine. Iraq also admitted that it had produced binary Sarin-filled artillery shells, 122 mm rockets, and aerial bombs.[92]

While UNSCOM's monitoring failed to reveal any recent chemical production, Ambassador Ekeus also informed the Security Council that it had no documentary evidence verifying Iraqi destruction of its VX precursors and/or any VX stockpiles. Accordingly, UNSCOM reported that it could "not exclude the potential existence of stocks of VX, its direct precursors and undeclared munitions in Iraq."[93]

Since that time, UNSCOM has expressed particular concerns about VX gas, the most lethal chemical weapon that Iraq is still believed to have available. Rolf Ekeus stated in March, 1997 that UNSCOM still had

quite substantial and serious concerns about Iraq's chemical weapons.... They relate to the counting of warheads for chemical warfare. We're talking about the introduction of VX ... a nerve gas more lethal than Sarin.[94]

The Secretary General reported to the UN Security Council in April, 1997 that Iraq was lying about its VX nerve gas, and continued to maintain the capability to manufacture such weapons:

Iraq denied VX activities until 1995, when it was confronted by evidence presented by the Commission. Even following on its admission, Iraq still understates its achievements in the production of VX, asserting that it only carried out such VX activities on the laboratory/pilot plant scale. It claims to have secretly destroyed hundreds of tons of VX precursors in 1991. The Commission has evidence that Iraq obtained this technology and retains equipment for the large-scale production of VX.[95]

The uncertainties affecting the destruction of VX gas affect some 750 tons of imported precursor chemicals and 55 tons of domestically produced precursors. Iraq has made unverifiable claims that 460 tons were destroyed by Coalition air attacks, and that it unilaterally destroyed 212 tons. UNSCOM has only been able to verify the destruction of 155 tons out of this latter total and to destroy a further 36 tons on its own. Iraq systematically lied about the existence of its production facilities for VX gas until 1995, and it made "significant efforts" to conceal its production capabilities after that date.[96]

None of these issues were resolved by the panel of experts which was set up at Iraq's insistence in late 1997. As was the case with the missile panel, discussed earlier, Iraq had great expectation for this panel, which involved experts assembled by UNSCOM and Iraqi officials. The chemical weapons team was headed by UNSCOM staff member Horst Reeps of Germany, and it included 15 chemical weapons experts from the United States, Switzerland, Russia, France, the United Kingdom, China, Sweden, and the Netherlands.

The panel held a technical evaluation meeting on February 2–6, 1998. It examined both Iraq's declarations on the amount of precursor chemicals and VX produced and UNSCOM's independent investigations and data. This material provided a variety of sources to verify Iraq's declarations, including field inspections, interviews with Iraqis involved in VX activities, information from documents Iraq had provided regarding the defection of Hussein Kamal, and data provided by other governments.

The Iraqi regime saw the panel as a means of closing the UN files on its chemical weapons programs and bringing the end of the wide-ranging economic sanctions that much closer. At the same time, Iraq made little serious effort to cooperate. Although Iraq made available personnel involved in VX research and development, UNSCOM said that the head of the Iraqi delegation repeatedly overrode efforts made by Iraqi experts to answer questions so that the experts did not get clear answers. Iraq also failed to provide interpreters for Russian, French, and Chinese experts working for the UN.

When the panel reported it concluded that Iraq was able to produce between 50 and 100 tons of VX before the invasion of Kuwait in 1990, and currently had the know-how, equipment, and possibly the chemicals to manufacture as much as 200 tons of VX.

The team does not feel that the level of verification achieved so far is satisfactory.... There continues to be too much reliance placed by the Iraqi side on unsupported individual statements.... There has been a long history of misrepresentation of the VX program and as of this [technical evaluation meeting], vital information remains to be revealed.... To this end, Iraq has provided only fragmentary evidence in related documentation. No evidence to support Iraq's declarations on its VX activities in 1989 to 1991 has been provided.

... it is clear that the capability to produce VX was regarded as being of the utmost importance to Iraq in 1987 and beyond. Iraq's unilateral destruction of VX essential components and materials, coupled with the denial until 1995 of attempts to produce VX on an industrial scale can only reinforce that view.... There is no credible technical reason why Iraq should fail in the production of VX.... [Iraqi scientists have] demonstrated their understanding of four major synthesis routes, yet have no credible technical justification for not successfully scaling up two of these routes.... Therefore, the retention of a VX capability by Iraq cannot be excluded.

The Limits to UNSCOM Inspections

UNSCOM conducted over 550 inspections affecting Iraq's ability to make chemical weapons between 1991 and April, 1997. It established a monitoring system involving some 150 facilities, including 30 remote-controlled cameras at six Iraqi chemical sites and 19 air samplers at eight sights. In early 1998, the system covered Iraq's research and development institutes, universities, munitions and chemical production sites, chemical storage sites, and pesticide, fertilizer, and petrochemical related facilities with dual use equipment or chemicals.[97] UNSCOM's efforts discovered some "200 key pieces of undeclared dual use equipment, such as heat exchangers, glass reactor vessels and distillation columns capable of use in proscribed chemical weapons activities by April, 1997.[98]

Nevertheless, UNSCOM has made it clear that it has continuing concerns about chemical weapons which go far beyond chemical weapons and was making slow progress, even before Iran suspended inspections on August 5, 1998:

- In October, 1995, UNSCOM stated that, "The Commission believes [Iraq's] FFCD is still incomplete and some of its statements incorrect. Information available to the Commission, including that from Iraq's documents, establishes that not all Iraqi chemical weapons related activities have been disclosed." UNSCOM expressed particular concern about the "production of more stable and storable chemical weapons," and the "design and production of strategic chemical weapons.[99] It also expressed concern over whether Iraq had destroyed all of the chemical weapons production equipment at Muthanna and chemical warheads for the Al Husayn missiles.[100]
- In April, 1997, UNSCOM reported that it had found "significant amounts of empty dual use munitions which Iraq had evaluated for use in its chemical weapons arsenal, but had not declared to the Commission" during a visit in December, 1996. It noted that it was still unable to verify the destruction of chemical warfare equipment and special warheads for biological and chemical weapons that Iraq had claimed it had destroyed after April, 1991. UNSCOM found that Iraq had continued to lie about the size and nature of the facilities involved in its chemical weapons program. It found that Iraq's declarations relating to its secret program for biological and chemical weapons were not complete or credible, that Iraq had not declared its entire inventory of chemical bombs, and that, "accounting for chemical munitions remains unsolved." It also found that Iraq continued to hide key policy documents, contract data, and manuals relating to chemical weapons.[101]
- In October, 1997, UNSCOM reported that "Iraq has not provided physical evidence [relating to] binary artillery munitions and aerial bombs, chemical warheads for short range missiles, cluster aerial bombs, and spray tanks." Iraq has claimed these were only prototype programs, but there is no current way to know how many were deployed as weapons.[102]

Major Remaining Uncertainties

In October, 1997, UNSCOM reported that, "The Commission identified some other areas of concern related to Iraq's chemical weapons program. The most important among them are the accounting for special missile warheads intended for filling with chemical or biological warfare agent, the material balance of some 550 155-mm mustard gas shells, the extent of VX programs, and the rationale for the acquisition of various types of chemical weapons."[103] UNSCOM confirmed that it made no progress in resolving the problem during Ambassador Butler's visit to Baghdad in mid-December 1997.[104]

UNSCOM also stated that "Iraq has not provided physical evidence [relating to] binary artillery munitions and aerial bombs, chemical warheads for short range missiles, cluster aerial bombs, and spray tanks." Iraq has claimed these were only prototype programs, but there is no current way to know how many were deployed as weapons.[105] These uncertainties are summarized in Table 17.3.

UNSCOM and US and European experts believe that Iraq has continued to import some precursors and chemical weapons manufacturing equipment clandestinely since the Gulf War—disguising some imports as pharmaceutical supplies and manufacturing equipment which it imported through Jordan, mixing some gear and chemicals with civilian goods being smuggled in by dhow from Qatar, and moving some components across the Iranian and Turkey borders—sometimes using Kurdish agents.[106]

These beliefs are supported by the developments which took place between April and October, 1997. UNSCOM stated in October that it had been able to destroy 120 pieces of additional equipment for the production of chemical weapons that Iraq had only disclosed in August, 1997. However, serious uncertainties still existed regarding some 4,000 tons of declared precursors for chemical weapons, the production of several hundred tons of additional chemical warfare agents, the consumption of chemical precursors, and Iraq's claims to have unilaterally destroyed some 130 tons of chemical warfare agents. Major uncertainties existed regarding 107,500 empty casings for chemical weapons, whether several thousand additional chemical weapons were filled with agents, the unilateral destruction of 15,620 weapons, and the fate of 16,038 additional weapons Iraq claimed it had discarded. "The margin of error" in the accounting presented by Iraq is in the neighborhood of 200 munitions.[107]

Similarly, UNSCOM's April, 1998 report to the Secretary General stated that,

A significant number of chemical weapons, their components and related equipment were identified and destroyed under UNSCOM supervision in the period from 1991 to 1997. This included over 38,000 filled and unfilled chemical munitions, 690 tons of chemical warfare agents, more than 3,000 tons of precursor chemicals, and over 400 pieces of production equipment. Significant progress was achieved in the investigation of the past CW-related activities with respect to information on types and quantities of chemical weapons developed and produced. This knowledge is essential for effective monitoring activities in Iraq.

Further work is required if the Commission is to be able to report with confidence to the Security Council that Iraq has completed all actions contemplated in relevant chemical weapons-related paragraphs of resolution 687 (1991). In the period under review, the Commission gave priority to the resolution of the four issues outlined in the report of the emergency session of the Special Commission of 21 November 1997 [S/1997/922, annex, para. 13].

Table 17.3
US Estimate of Iraqi Chemical Warfare Capabilities in 1998

CW Agent Stockpiles (in metric tons)

CW Agent	Chemical Agents Declared by Iraq	Potential CW Agents Based on Unaccounted Precursors[1]	Comments
VX	At least 4	200	Iraq denied producing VX until Husayn Kamil's defection in 1995.
G-agents (Sarin)	100–150	200	Figures include both weaponized and bulk agents.
Mustard	500–600	200	Figures include both weaponized and bulk agents.

CW Delivery Systems (in numbers of weapons systems)

Delivery System	Estimated Numbers before the Gulf War	Munitions Unaccounted for[2]	Comments
Missile warheads Al-Husayn (modified Scud B)	75–100	2–25	UNSCOM supervised the destruction of 30 warheads.
Rockets	100,000	15,200–25,000	UNSCOM supervised the destruction of bombs, 28,000 of which were fired.
Aerial bombs	16,000	2,000–8,000	Reflects data disclosed in document in IAF headquarters.
Artillery shells	30,000	15,000	
Aerial spray tanks	Unknown	Unknown	

1. These estimates are very rough. They are derived from reports provided by UNSCOM to the Security Council and to UNSCOM plenary meetings. Gaps in Iraqi disclosures strongly suggest that Baghdad is concealing chemical munitions and precursors. Iraq may also retain a small stockpile of filled munitions. Baghdad has the capability to quickly resume CW production at known dual-use facilities that currently produce legitimate items, such as pharmaceuticals and pesticides. UNSCOM has supervised the destruction of some 45 different types of CW precursors (1,800,000 liters of liquid and 1,000,000 kg of solid).
2. All of these munitions could be used to deliver CW or BW agents. The numbers for missile warheads include 25 that Iraq claims to have unilaterally destroyed after having filled them with biological agents during the Gulf war. UNSCOM has been unable to verify the destruction of these warheads.

Sources: Adapted by Anthony H. Cordesman from material provided by the NSC on February 19, 1998 and by National Intelligence Council on November 17, 1998.

The accounting for special [chemical and biological] warheads for the Al Hussein missiles was discussed in depth in the course of the technical evaluation meeting on missile warheads held in Baghdad from 1 to 6 February 1998. The meeting came to the conclusion that the level of verification achieved so far is not satisfactory and that Iraq is required to undertake additional steps to settle this issue.

In parallel, from 2 to 6 February 1998, the Commission conducted a technical evaluation meeting on the extent of Iraq's efforts to produce and weaponize the chemical warfare agent VX. The meeting confirmed the assessment given in the Commission's October, 1997 report and determined that no full disclosure on the subject of VX had been made by Iraq and that further verification was required. It was also concluded that Iraq was capable of producing VX and that the retention of a VX capability by Iraq could not be excluded. The Commission believes that further progress in the verification of the past VX-related activities could be achieved through finalization of the material balance of special munitions, full verification of the disposition of chemical weapons production equipment, and sampling at VX-related sites.

Recently the Commission sent an international expert team to Baghdad to attempt to clarify the material balance of special munitions procured and produced by Iraq for CW and biological weapons [BW] purposes. For example, there remains concern that significant quantities of 155-mm rounds are unaccounted for. This has acquired additional importance in the light of the recent analysis of four intact 155-mm shells filled with mustard of the highest quality (purity of 94–97%), even after seven years of exposure to extreme climatic conditions. This analysis was undertaken following Iraq's insistence that it was not necessary for the Commission to account for such extant munitions on the grounds that the CW agent with which they were filled would by now have degraded to an inert state. Clearly, these Iraqi munitions could be stored for decades without any loss of quality. Furthermore, the Commission is currently preparing a mission related to the verification of the material balance of production equipment procured by Iraq for CW purposes. This mission will be carried out in the second half of April, 1998. A full accounting on this issue would allow the Commission to have a better overall accounting of Iraq's CW activities.

In addition, the Commission will continue evaluation and verification of other chemical weapons issues mentioned in its report to the Security Council of 6 October 1997 [S/1997/774]. This includes the accounting of all CW-related research and production projects in the area of CW agents and munitions carried out by Iraq in the period from 1988 to 1990; the disposition of "know-how" documentation on the production of various types of CW; and documentation on commercial contracts from Iraq's CW-related procurement activities.

The availability of verifiable substantiation of Iraq's various declarations would immensely speed up the clarification of all outstanding issues in the chemical weapons area. Iraq has been requested on numerous occasions to provide such documentary support. It has not done so. It remains the case that unless such data is provided by Iraq the Commission will be unable to render a full and verified accounting of all Iraq's proscribed CW-related capabilities and for their elimination, as required by the Security Council.[108]

Since this UNSCOM report, there have been further disturbing developments. One is the US discovery that Iraq may have deployed stable VX nerve gas as a weapon and armed Scud missiles with VX. This discovery was particularly important because Iraq had initially denied that it was doing any work on VX gas. Iraq then admitted to have made 3.9 tons of the gas as part of a research project which it claimed it then destroyed in secret, although Tariq Aziz claimed in another letter to the Security Council that Iraq had only produced 1.7 tons of VX and that it was not of weapons grade.

There were more serious contradictions in the statements of Iraqi defectors. When UNSCOM experts met with Iraqi experts in Baghdad in February, 1998, Lt. General Amer Sadi, the head of the Iraqi delegation, stated that, "if there was know-how, it was only on the laboratory scale and without full understanding." This statement directly contradicted statements made four years earlier by Wafiq al Sammurai, then Saddam's chief of military intelligence, who claimed that Iraq had filled at least 10 Scud warheads with VX gas and 10 with Anthrax.[109] Similarly, Hussein Kamel had claimed when he defected that Iraq had begun its VX program in May, 1985, and that it had continued until, December 1990. Such a program would be particularly serious because US experts estimate that Iraq had the capability by 1990 to manufacture some 400 tons a year of precursors for nerve gas.[110]

The history of these discoveries has been discussed earlier, but it is important to note that the work done by the United States at Aberdeen Proving Ground has not been fully confirmed by independent work done in France and Switzerland. This work was reported to UNSCOM in September, 1998, and chemical weapons experts from six countries held two days of talks (September 24–25) to discuss whether Iraq had put the nerve gas VX on warheads.

The meeting included 14 experts from outside the UN, including representatives from US, French, and Swiss laboratories as well as delegates from Russia, Britain, and China. The French and Swiss labs found no VX on swabs on the Iraqi missile warheads they sampled, while the American tests, completed in June, 1998, found traces of decomposed VX on one-quarter of 44 fragments salvaged from an Iraqi government al-Husayn missile destruction site at Taji. The French and Swiss tests, however, had been conducted on 80 fragments from a different part of the site, of which half had been sent to France and the other half to Switzerland. A Pentagon spokesman had stated earlier in September that, "The United States does stand behind its findings. What the French and Swiss find cannot invalidate them, because the fragments came from different places."[111]

These problems illustrate the difficulties in ever firmly verifying Iraq's capabilities, even when inspection is possible. Other issues have emerged, however, since Iraq suspended sanctions on August 5. The United States has cited Iraqi cooperation with the Sudan as a reason it launched cruise missiles to destroy the Shifa Pharmaceutical Industries plant in Khartoum in the Sudan on August 21, 1998. US officials stated that the United States had evidence that Iraqi scientists were helping to produce the chemicals to make nerve gas and that they were involved in helping to produce a precursor chemical called Empta. They also said there is evidence that 40 Iraqi scientists had been working at another heavily guard plant in a military complex several miles away, and that Iraqi scientists had been there since shortly after the end of the Gulf War. As might be expected, Iraq has denied such US claims.[112]

In the months before Desert Fox there were other new discoveries. UNSCOM had the opportunity briefly to examine a document at an Iraqi Air Force headquarters on July 18, 1998, that indicated Iraq might have retained far more chemical weapons than have previously been suspected. The document showed that Iraq had used far fewer chemical weapons during the Iran-Iraq War than it had previously claimed. UNSCOM has good records of how many agents have been manufactured, and the discrepancies between what has been manufactured and what Iraq seems to have used are so great that they could account for as many as 6,300 air-dropped bombs and 730 tons of agents.[113] While US experts feel that the total is more likely to be several thousand bombs and several hundred tons, even the lower estimate is scarcely reassuring.

It is scarcely surprising, therefore, that UNSCOM's October 6, 1998, report to the Security Council left many uncertainties regarding chemical weapons.[114]

The Special Commission has sought to resolve the most important outstanding issues. These include the verification of the material balance of special munitions, including the accounting for 550 artillery shells filled with mustard chemical warfare agent, verification of the unilateral destruction of R-400 chemical and biological aerial bombs, and the provision by Iraq of the document sighted during the inspection at the headquarters of the Iraqi Air Force; accounting for the production of the chemical warfare agent VX; and verification of the completeness of declarations provided by Iraq on the material balance of chemical weapons production equipment.

Iraq declared that 550 shells filled with mustard had been lost shortly after the Gulf War. To date, no evidence of the missing munitions has been found. A dozen mustard-filled shells were recovered at a former chemical weapons storage facility in the period 1997–1998. The chemical sampling of these munitions in April 1998 revealed that the mustard was still of the highest quality. After seven years, the purity of mustard ranged between 94 per cent and 97 per cent. Iraq still has to account for the missing shells and to provide verifiable evidence of their disposition. In July 1998, Iraq promised to provide clarifications on this matter. To date, only preliminary information has been provided by Iraq on its continuing internal investigation;

R-400 aerial bombs. Among 1,550 R-400 bombs produced by Iraq, more than 1,000 bombs were declared as destroyed unilaterally by Iraq, including 157 bombs stated as filled with biological warfare agents. The accounting for about 500 bombs unilaterally destroyed was not possible owing to the state and extent of destruction. In order to bridge the gap, the Commission requested Iraq to provide the documentation on the disposition of the tail parachute sections of R-400 bombs. The accounting for these components would enable the Commission to verify the maximum number of R-400 bombs, which Iraq could have produced. Though this would not resolve the specific issue of the quantity and composition of biological weapons bombs, including allocation of biological weapons agents, it may facilitate the final accounting for the chemical R-400 bombs. Iraq presented the information sought on the disposition of tail sections but field inspection activities are still required;

According to Iraq, 3.9 tons of VX were produced in total: some 2.4 tons in 1988, the remainder in 1990. Iraq provided documents on the 1988 production but did not provide sufficient verifiable evidence on the status of its 1990 production. Iraq has claimed, however, that its VX production program failed owing to the low purity and instability of the agent produced. The Commission's view is that Iraq was certainly able to produce VX, and probably produced it in quantity. However, the achieved level of verification of precisely how much VX was produced by Iraq is not satisfactory. In addition, Iraq denies that it weaponized VX. Sampling by the Commission of special warheads has thrown significant doubt upon this claim;

In April 1998, the Commission decided to remove some remnants of special missile warheads destroyed unilaterally by Iraq and sample them in a laboratory outside Iraq. The purpose was to verify Iraq's declarations on the filling of the special warheads. Forty-four metal fragments of different types of warheads were selected for sampling. Initially Iraq did not permit the removal of samples for analysis. In May 1998, the samples were sent for analysis to a laboratory in the United States of America. This analysis was completed by mid-June. Degradation products of the chemical warfare agent VX were found in some samples. As Iraq had hitherto denied weaponization of VX, it was asked to provide its clarifications. To date no clarifications have been provided;

In July 1998, at Iraq's request, the Commission held an international expert meeting in Baghdad to present and to discuss with Iraq's authorities the results of analysis carried out earlier in the United States laboratory. Iraq did not challenge the analytical results presented, but continues to insist that VX had never been weaponized;

In June and July 1998, the Commission took different wipe samples from other special missile warhead remnants remaining in Iraq in order to collect more data on the types of their chemical fill. Forty-three samples were sent to the same laboratory in the United States, 40 samples sent to a laboratory in France and 40 samples to a laboratory in Switzerland. The analysis of all these samples is not yet complete;

The Commission determined that 197 pieces of glass chemical weapons production equipment had been removed by Iraq from the Muthanna State Establishment, Iraq's prime chemical weapons production site, in 1991, prior to the arrival in Iraq of the first inspection team. This equipment has been repeatedly moved in shipping containers between several facilities in Iraq in the period 1991–1996. One hundred ninety-seven pieces of this equipment were destroyed under UNSCOM supervision in 1997. To ensure that all chemical weapons production equipment removed from Muthanna has been accounted for, the Commission has asked Iraq to provide clarifications on the movement of all such equipment. Iraq presented its clarifications to the Commission in July 1998. However, field verification, which is required, has been blocked since Iraq's 5 August decision.

The chemical monitoring group currently consists of 10 inspectors, three laboratory chemists and one explosive ordnance disposal specialist, from 11 States. The group periodically inspects 120 sites under monitoring and, occasionally, other sites (to date 52) ranging from petrochemical facilities to water treatment plants. There are 518 items of tagged dual-use equipment, as well as thousands of tons of dual-use chemicals now being monitored. The group continues to discover undeclared dual-use items and materials (i.e., equipment subject to monitoring which has not been declared by Iraq). Those items, which should have been declared by Iraq under the Commission's monitoring plan, have subsequently, in the main, been tagged.

British and US intelligence experts warned that Iraq might be concealing significant war-fighting capabilities during the military build-up to the crisis in October, 1998. State Department spokesman James Rubin gave a briefing on the US estimate of Iraq's holdings on November 16, 1998, in which he stated that,

As for chemical weapons, Iraq has reported making 8,800 pounds (four tons) of VX nerve gas, 220,000 pounds (100 tons) to 330,000 pounds (150 tons) of nerve agents such as Sarin and 1.1 million pounds (500 tons) to 1.32 million pounds (600 tons) of mustard gas. Data from UN weapons inspectors indicates that Iraq may have produced an additional 1.32 million pounds (600 tons) of these agents, divided evenly among the three. In other words, these are the differences between what they say they have and what we have reason to believe they have.

One thing *is* clear: Iraq has considerable capability to use any resources it has managed to conceal. US experts estimate that Iraq has rebuilt key portions of its chemical production infrastructure for industrial and commercial use. The facilities are currently subject to UN scrutiny, but they could be converted fairly quickly, allowing Iraq to restart limited agent production. Even though some foreign assistance for equipment and material would be required for all but a minimum effort, Iraq would only need several months to produce a usable stockpile of agents and several years to return to pre-Gulf War stockpile levels.

In spite of these uncertainties, some experts feel that it might take several years and several hundred million dollars worth of imported equipment to develop a major war-fighting capability. They note that Iraq lost much of its feedstock production capacity during the bombing of Samara, which was very heavily damaged during the war. As a result, it will probably take Iraq three to five years to recover a significant capability to employ enough chemical shells, rockets, bombs, and warheads to fight a major land war.[115]

However, Iraq does not need the large amounts of chemical agents needed to support a major land offensive to arm several hundred missile warheads and aircraft bombs, and Table 17.4 shows that even limited numbers of chemical weapons can be highly effective in a number of war-fighting contingencies. It is clear from UNSCOM's reports that Iraq may already have covertly produced enough chemical agents to arm several hundred weapons, including warheads, at small laboratory facilities. It is also clear from UNSCOM statements that it is virtually impossible for any inspection and control regime to prevent this.

Iraq has also had a half decade since the Gulf War in which to develop ways of producing purer chemical agents and more effective bombs and warheads. It, therefore, will almost certainly retain significant capabilities in spite of the "war of sanctions," and it will be able to recover a significant capability to threaten

Table 17.4
Typical War-Fighting Uses of Chemical Weapons

Mission	Quantity
<u>Attack an infantry position</u>: Cover 1.3 square kilometers of territory with a "surprise dosage" attack of Sarin to kill 50% of exposed troops.	216 240-mm rockets (e.g., delivered by 18 12-tube Soviet BM-24 rocket launchers, each carrying 8 kilograms of agent and totaling 1,728 kilograms of agent).
<u>Prevent launch of enemy mobile missiles</u>: Contaminate a 25 square kilometer missile unit operating area with 0.3 tons per square kilometer of a persistent nerve gas like VX.	8 MiG-23 or 4 Su-24 fighters, each delivering 0.9 tons of VX (totaling 7.2 tons).
<u>Immobilize an air base</u>: Contaminate a 2 square kilometer air base with 0.3 tons of VX twice a day for three days.	1 MiG-23 with six sorties or any similar attack aircraft.
<u>Defend a broad front against large-scale attack</u>: Maintain a 300 meter deep strip of VX contamination in front of a position defending a 60 kilometer wide area for three days.	65 metric tons of agent delivered by approximately 13,000 155-mm artillery rounds.
<u>Terrorize population</u>: Kill approximately 125,000 unprotected civilians in a densely populated (10,000 square kilometer) city.	8 MiG-23 or 4 Su-24 fighters, each delivering 0.9 tons of VX (totaling 7.2 tons) under optimum conditions.

Sources: Adapted by Anthony H. Cordesman from Victor A. Utgoff, *The Challenge of Chemical Weapons*, New York, St. Martin's, 1991, pp. 238–242; US Congress, Office of Technology Assessment, *Proliferation of Weapons of Mass Destruction: Assessing the Risks*, US Congress OTA-ISC-559, Washington, August, 1993, pp. 56–57.

enemy population centers and area targets with missile and air strikes shortly after it is freed from UN controls.[116] This potential threat is serious enough to be an important factor behind US efforts to improve its chemical warfare defense capabilities, and US support of the efforts of the United Nations to create an Organization for the Prohibition of Chemical Weapons to enforce the Chemical Weapons Convention if sanctions on Iraq are lifted.[117]

NOTES

1. US Office of the Secretary of Defense, *Proliferation: Threat and Response*, Washington, Department of Defense, April, 1996, pp. 17–24.

2. Based on discussions with Israeli sources in January, 1989.

3. The author visited the area several times during this period. Reports of such use were provided by both Iranian and Israeli officials and confirmed by a British expert.

4. Peter Dunn, "The Chemical War: Journey to Iran," *NBC Defense & Technology International*, pp. 28–37, and "Iran Keeps Chemical Options Open," pp. 12–14.

5. For a good discussion of the early Iraqi effort to acquire chemical weapons, see

David Ignatius, "Iraq's 13-Year Search for Deadly Chemicals," *Washington Post*, Outlook section, September 25, 1988.

6. The building block at the base of the organophosphorus industry is elemental phosphorus. Thus, at a minimum, a supply of phosphorus would be needed to make nerve agents such as the G agents, Tabun (GA), Sarin (GB) and Soman (GD), and the V agents, such as VX and Edemo (VM). There is a very wide range of possible chemical precursors to the production of gas warfare. Ones which may have been sent to Iran and Iraq include Thiodiglycol and chloroethanol (mustard gas); dimethalmine, dimethalmine hydrochloride, and phosphorus oxychloride (Tabun or GA nerve gas); and dimethyl methylphosphonate, difluoro or methylphosphony, and potassium flouride (Sarin or GB nerve gas). For a good description of the technology of proliferation, see Lois R. Ember, "Worldwide Spread of Chemical Arms Receiving Increased Attention," *C&EN*, April 14, 1988, pp. 8–16.

7. All are useful in the production of Tabun nerve gas. The corrosion resistant reactors, pipes, and pumps needed for processing these pesticides can be rapidly converted to nerve gas production. See Ignatius, "Iraq's 13-Year Search for Deadly Chemicals," *Washington Post*, Outlook section, September 25, 1988.

8. Tabun and the more lethal Sarin nerve gases were discovered in Germany in 1936 as part of an effort to develop more advanced pesticides. They could not be used for this purpose because they proved to be as effective in killing people as insects. The Nazis produced some 12,000 tons of nerve gas in World War II, but never used it because they believed that Britain and the United States were also aware of the technology. See John J. Fialka, "Fighting Dirty," *Wall Street Journal*, September 15, 1988, p. 1.

9. Based on work by Leonard Spector of the Carnegie Endowment for International Peace, and other working material.

10. *Christian Science Monitor*, December 12, 1988; and BBC Panorama, 1986.

11. *Christian Science Monitor*, April 13, 1988, p. 32.

12. Some thirteen West German firms are now under investigation by the West German government, W.E.T.

13. This is a small amount. About 15 to 20 tons of a nerve agent like Tabun are need to cover a single square kilometer.

14. Loren Jenkins, "Iraqis Press Major Battle in Gulf War," *Washington Post*, November 17, 1980, p. 1; Taylor and Francis, SIPRI Yearbook, 1985, Philadelphia, 1985, pp. 206–219; W. Andrew Terrill, "Chemical Weapons in the Gulf War," *Strategic Review*, Spring, 1986, pp. 51–58.

15. "Iraq's Scare Tactic," *Newsweek*, August 2, 1982.

16. Chubin and Tripp, *Iran and Iraq at War*, Boulder, Westview, p. 59; BBC, ME, April 14, 1983.

17. Loren Jenkins, "Iraqis Press Major Battle in Gulf War," *Washington Post*, November 17, 1980, p. 1; Taylor and Francis, *SIPRI Yearbook, 1985*, pp. 206–219; W. Andrew Terrill, "Chemical Weapons in the Gulf War," *Strategic Review*, Spring, 1986, pp. 51–58.

18. "In the Pipeline," *The Middle East*, December, 1981, p. 72; "Iraqis Trained for Chemical Warfare," *Washington Post*, November 3, 1980, p. 313. The Iraqis may also have been favorably impressed by the effectiveness of tear gas in instilling panic in Iranian troops. An August, 1982 report in *Newsweek* stated that an entire Iranian division fled in panic when they were exposed to Iraqi tear gas. The Iranians had no idea as to

what type of agent they were being exposed to, and had no defenses against any kind of chemical agent.

19. "In the Pipeline," *The Middle East*, December, 1981; "Iraqis Trained for Chemical Warfare," p. 72; *Washington Post*, November 3, 1980.

20. Beginning in 1982, Iraqi agents bought extensive amounts of equipment from a West German manufacturer of equipment to make organophosphate pesticides. The manufacturer, located in Drereich, claimed it had no way to know whether the Iraqis were buying extensive feedstock for nerve gas in other countries, including the United States. There may now be five major chemical agent production plants in Iraq. See Gustav Anderson, "Analysis of Two Chemical Weapons Samples from the Iran-Iraq War," *NBC Defense and Technology International*, April, 1986, pp. 62–66; Peter Dunn, "The Chemical War; Journey to Iran," Ibid., pp. 28–37; and "Iran Keeps Chemical Options Open," Ibid., pp. 12–14.

21. "Report of the Specialists Appointed to the Secretary-General to Investigate the Allegations of the Islamic Republic of Iran Concerning the Use of Chemical Weapons, United Nations Security Council, Document S 16433, March 26, 1984. Also see the April, 1986 edition of *NBC Defense & Technology International*.

22. W. Seth Carus, "Chemical Weapons in the Middle East," *Policy Focus*, Number Nine, Washington Institute for Near East Policy, December, 1988, p. 7.

23. *Washington Times*, March 23, 1988, p. 1; *Toronto Globe and Mail*, March 24, 1988, p. 1; *Washington Post*, March 24, 24, 1988, p. 1 and April 4, 1988, p. 24.

24. John J. Fialka, "Fighting Dirty," *Wall Street Journal*, September 16, 1988, p. 1.

25. Mustard gas can be made by three easy routes. The first is the reaction of vinyl chloride (readily available or which can be made from ethylene or acetylene) and hydrogen sulfide. The second is the reaction of ethylene and sulfur monochloride. The third is reacting thiodiglycol with hydrogen chloride after making the thiodiglycol from ethylene oxide (from ethylene) and hydrogen sulfide. The sulfur and ethylene feedstocks can be drawn from a typical refinery and hydrogen chloride or chlorine gas are simple to make from a source of chlorine, such as salt, sea water, or produced brines from petroleum operations.

26. Phillips has since claimed that it did not react to the first order for thiodiglycol because such orders were routine. A number of experts disagree, however, and feel that only limited amounts could have credibly been assumed to be used in printing, textiles, and automotive manufacturing. John J. Fialka, "Fighting Dirty," *Wall Street Journal*, September 16, 1988, p. 1.

27. Phillips has since claimed that it did not react to the first order for thiodiglycol because such orders were routine. A number of experts disagree, however, and feel that only limited amounts could have credibly been assumed to be used in printing, textiles, and automotive manufacturing. John J. Fialka, "Fighting Dirty," *Wall Street Journal*, September 16, 1988, p. 1.

28. *Jane's Defense Weekly*, January 9, 1988, p. 3; February 27, 1988, p. 336.

29. Unpublished "Statement of the Honorable William H. Webster, Director, Central Intelligence Agency, Before the Committee on Governmental Affairs, Hearings on Global Spread of Chemical and Biological Weapons," February 9, 1989.

30. Peter Dunn, "The Chemical War: Journey to Iran, *NBC Defense & Technology International*, pp. 28–37, and "Iran Keeps Chemical Options Open," pp. 12–14, *Jane's Defense Weekly*, January 9, 1988, p. 3; February 27, 1988, p. 336.

31. W. Seth Carus, *The Genie Unleashed: Iraq's Chemical and Biological Weapons Production*, Washington, Washington Institute Policy Papers, No. 14., 1989, p. 11.

32. "Iraq's Scare Tactic," *Newsweek*, August 2, 1982; *Washington Post*, April 5, 1988, p. A-1.

33. "Iraq's Scare Tactic," *Newsweek*, August 2, 1982; *Washington Post*, April 5, 1988, p. A-1; W. Seth Carus, *The Genie Unleashed: Iraq's Chemical and Biological Weapons Production*, Washington, Washington Institute Policy Papers, No. 14., 1989, pp. 7–9.

34. Peter Dunn, "The Chemical War: Journey to Iran," *NBC Defense & Technology International*, pp. 28–37, and "Iran Keeps Chemical Options Open," pp. 12–14.

35. W. Seth Carus puts the production of Tabun and Sarin at 50 tons per year, and of mustard gas at 720 tons per year. W. Seth Carus, "Chemical Weapons in the Middle East," *Policy Focus*, Number Nine, Washington Institute for Near East Policy, December, 1988, p. 4. Also see "Iraq's Scare Tactic," *Newsweek*, August 2, 1982; *Washington Post*, April 5, 1988, p. A-1.

36. *Congressional Record*, US Senate, September 9, 1988, p. S12135.

37. *Washington Times*, March 23, 1988, p. 1; *Toronto Globe and Mail*, March 24, 1988, p. 1; *Washington Post*, March 24, 1988, p. 1 and April 4, 1988, p. 24; *Wall Street Journal*, September 16, 1988, p. 1.

38. See Peter W. Galbraith and Christopher Van Hollen Jr., "Chemical Weapons Use in Kurdistan: Iraq's Final Offensive," A Staff Report to the Senate Committee on Foreign Relations, September 21, 1988; and Physicians for Human Rights, *Winds of Death: Iraq's Use of Poison Gas Against Its Kurdish Population*, February, 1989.

39. The author is aware of reports that Czech chemical detection units found two traces of Sarin chemical weapons and one trace of mustard gas, and that a soldier entering an Iraqi bunker may have had exposure to a chemical agent. The evidence supporting any use of chemical weapons and the link to the "Gulf War Syndrome" is so tenuous, however, that the author believes that this statement is largely correct. There is some evidence that one US soldier did have chemical burns. However, the end result of extensive modeling by the CIA and other analysts raises serious doubt as to whether the destruction of chemical weapons by the Coalition allies produced any Coalition casualties.

40. The author was present during several of these searches in headquarters in Iraq and Kuwait. Such materials were widely distributed.

41. For historical background, see Task Force on Terrorism and Unconventional Warfare, *Chemical Weapons in The Third World: 2. Iraq's Expanding Chemical Arsenal*. House Republican Research Committee, US House of Representatives, May 29, 1990, p. 8; Anthony H. Cordesman, *Lessons of Modern Wars—Volume II: The Iran-Iraq War*, Boulder, Westview, 1990, pp. 510–512; W. Seth Carus, *The Genie Unleashed: Iraq's Chemical and Biological Weapons Production*, Washington, Washington Institute Policy Papers, No. 14., 1989, pp. 11–17.

42. W. Seth Carus, *The Genie Unleashed: Iraq's Chemical and Biological Weapons Production*, Washington, Washington Institute Policy Papers, No. 14., 1989, p. 11.

43. The persistence of chemical agents is dependent on wind and temperature, and whether they are dispersed as liquids or aerosols. Gases tend to disperse quickly in very hot weather and to persist far longer in cold weather. It is important to note that gases that may disperse in minutes under some conditions take days to disperse under others,

and that persistent gases that last days or weeks in hot weather can last up to three times longer in cold weather.

44. For general sources for this analysis, see Unpublished "Statement of the Honorable William H. Webster, Director, Central Intelligence Agency, Before the Committee on Governmental Affairs, Hearings on Global Spread of Chemical and Biological Weapons," February 9, 1989; Task Force on Terrorism and Unconventional Warfare, *Chemical Weapons in The Third World: 2. Iraq's Expanding Chemical Arsenal*. House Republican Research Committee, US House of Representatives, May 29, 1990, p. 8; Anthony H. Cordesman, *Lessons of Modern Wars, Volume II: The Iran-Iraq War*, Boulder, Westview, 1991; W. Seth Carus, *The Genie Unleashed: Iraq's Chemical and Biological Weapons Production*, Washington, Washington Institute Policy Papers, No. 14., 1989.

45. *Christian Science Monitor*, January 23, 1992, p. 1; Terry J. Gander, "Iraq—the Chemical Arsenal," *Jane's Intelligence Weekly*, pp. 413–415; Steven R. Bowman, "Iraqi Chemical Weapons Capabilities," Washington, Congressional Research Service 93–292F, February 24, 1993.

46. Nerve gases are more complex to manufacture than mustard gas. There are more ways to manufacture nerve gases than mustard gas, and many types of chemicals that can be used, but sales of most of these chemicals—such as pinacolyl alcohol, potassium fluoride, phosphorous oxychloride, phosphorous trichloride, and trimethyl phosphite—are easy to track, and many have only limited commercial applications. Task Force on Terrorism and Unconventional Warfare, *Chemical Weapons in The Third World: 2. Iraq's Expanding Chemical Arsenal*. House Republican Research Committee, US House of Representatives, May 29, 1990, p. 8; Anthony H. Cordesman, *Lesson of Modern Wars, Volume II: The Iran-Iraq War*, Boulder, Westview, 1991, pp. 510–512; W. Seth Carus, *The Genie Unleashed: Iraq's Chemical and Biological Weapons Production*, Washington, Washington Institute Policy Papers, No. 14, 1989, pp. 11–17.

47. Terry J. Gander, "Iraq—the Chemical Arsenal," *Jane's Intelligence Review*, September, 1992, pp. 413–415; Steven R. Bowman, "Iraqi Chemical Weapons Capabilities," Washington, Congressional Research Service 93–292F, February 24, 1993; Peter Dunn, "The Chemical War: Journey to Iran," *NBC Defense & Technology International*, pp. 28–37; W. Seth Carus, *The Genie Unleashed: Iraq's Chemical and Biological Weapons Production*, Washington, Washington Institute Policy Papers, No. 14., 1989, pp. 22–23; *Foreign Report*, March 31, 1988, p. 12; and Peter Dunn, "Iran Keeps Chemical Options Open," pp. 12–14, *Jane's Defense Weekly*, January 9, 1988, p. 3; February 27, 1988, p. 336. The Austrian firms seems to have included Neuberger Holz und Kunstoffindustrie and Lenhardt Metallbau under Dachdecker. Five West German firms seem to have been involved, including WTB (Walter Thosti Boswau), Infraplan, and Karl Kolb.

48. W. Seth Carus, "Chemical Weapons in the Middle East," *Policy Focus*, Number Nine, Washington Institute for Near East Policy, December, 1988, p. 4; "Iraq's Scare Tactic," *Newsweek*, August 2, 1982; *Washington Post*, April 5, 1988, p. A-1, Task Force on Terrorism and Unconventional Warfare, *Chemical Weapons in The Third World: 2. Iraq's Expanding Chemical Arsenal*. House Republican Research Committee, US House of Representatives, May 29, 1990, p. 8.

49. Task Force on Terrorism and Unconventional Warfare, *Chemical Weapons in The Third World: 2. Iraq's Expanding Chemical Arsenal*. House Republican Research Committee, US House of Representatives, May 29, 1990, p. 8; Anthony H. Cordesman, *Lessons of Modern Wars, Volume II: The Iran-Iraq War*, Boulder, Westview, 1991, pp. 510–512; W. Seth Carus, *The Genie Unleashed: Iraq's Chemical and Biological*

Weapons Production, Washington, Washington Institute Policy Papers, No. 14., 1989, pp. 11–17.

50. It takes 0.45 tons of ethylene oxide to make 1.0 tons of Thiodiglycol, Carus, *The Genie Unleashed*, p. 15.

51. Task Force on Terrorism and Unconventional Warfare, *Chemical Weapons in The Third World: 2. Iraq's Expanding Chemical Arsenal*. House Republican Research Committee, US House of Representatives, May 29, 1990, pp. 9–10.

52. "Iraq's Scare Tactic," *Newsweek*, August 2, 1982; *Washington Post*, April 5, 1988, p. A-1.

53. "Iraq's Scare Tactic," *Newsweek*, August 2, 1982; *Washington Post*, April 5, 1988, p. A-1; W. Seth Carus, *The Genie Unleashed: Iraq's Chemical and Biological Weapons Production*, Washington, Washington Institute Policy Papers, No. 14., 1989, pp. 7–9; Task Force on Terrorism and Unconventional Warfare, *Chemical Weapons in the Third World: 2. Iraq's Expanding Chemical Arsenal*. House Republican Research Committee, US House of Representatives, May 29, 1990, p. 9; US Department of Defense, *Conduct of the Persian Gulf War: Final Report*, Department of Defense, April, 1992, p. 18.

54. Dick Palowski, *Changes in Threat Air Combat Doctrine and Force Structure, 24th Edition*, Fort Worth, General Dynamics, DWIC-01, February, 1992, p. II–325.

55. *The Independent*, July 28, 1991, p. 2, Peter Dunn, "The Chemical War: Journey to Iran," *NBC Defense & Technology International*, pp. 28–37; "Iran Keeps Chemical Options Open," pp. 12–14; W. Seth Carus, *The Genie Unleashed: Iraq's Chemical and Biological Weapons Production*, Washington, Washington Institute Policy Papers, No. 14., 1989, pp. 22; Dick Palowski, *Changes in Threat Air Combat Doctrine and Force Structure, 24th Edition*, Fort Worth, General Dynamics, DWIC-01, February, 1992, pp. II–375.

56. The priority Iraq gave to chemical and biological weapons is illustrated by the fact that Hussein Kamil—Saddam Hussein's son-in-law and cousin—headed the Ministry of Industry and Military Industries during most of this period. The Ministry of Industry and Military Industries is the branch of the Iraqi government which is responsible for the production of chemical and biological weapons. Michael Eisenstadt, "The Sword of the Arabs: Iraq's Strategic Weapons," Washington, Washington Institute for Near East Policy, Policy Paper 21, September, 1990, p. 7; W. Seth Carus, "Chemical Weapons in the Middle East," *Policy Focus*, Number Nine, Washington Institute for Near East Policy, December, 1988, p. 4; "Iraq's Scare Tactic," *Newsweek*, August 2, 1982; *Washington Post*, April 5, 1988, p. A-1; Dick Palowski, *Changes in Threat Air Combat Doctrine and Force Structure, 24th Edition*, Fort Worth, General Dynamics, DWIC-01, February, 1992, pp. II–325 and II–334; *Jane's Soviet Intelligence Review*, June, 1989, p. 256; *Foreign Report*, March 31, 1988, p. 1.

57. *Washington Post*, April 30, 1993, p. A-45; *Christian Science Monitor*, January 25, 1993, p. 18; *Financial Times*, April 2, 1992, p. 3, April 30, 1993, p. 5; *The Economist*, February 6, 1993, pp. 49–50; *New York Times*, June 26, 1993, p. A-19; *Los Angeles Times*, July 20, 1992, p. C2; *Chemical and Engineering News*, May 3, 1993, pp. 8–9.

58. *New York Times*, April 3, 1990, p. 1.

59. The UN did not find signs of the use of chemical weapons during its inspection of the marsh areas in November, 1993, but referred soil samples to experts. *Washington Post*, November 24, 1993, p. A-12; *Jane's Defense Weekly*, January 9, 1988, and January

28, 1989; *Der Spiegel*, January 23, 1989; Task Force on Terrorism and Unconventional Warfare, *Chemical Weapons in The Third World: 2. Iraq's Expanding Chemical Arsenal*. House Republican Research Committee, US House of Representatives, May 29, 1990, p. 10; Baghdad Domestic Service, April 2, 1990.

60. Michael Eisenstadt, "The Sword of the Arabs: Iraq's Strategic Weapons," Washington, Washington Institute for Near East Policy, Policy Paper 21, September, 1990, p. 7; W. Seth Carus, "Chemical Weapons in the Middle East," *Policy Focus*, Number Nine, Washington Institute for Near East Policy, December, 1988, p. 4; "Iraq's Scare Tactic," *Newsweek*, August 2, 1982; *Washington Post*, April 5, 1988, p. A-1; Dick Palowski, *Changes in Threat Air Combat Doctrine and Force Structure, 24th Edition*, Fort Worth, General Dynamics, DWIC-01, February, 1992, pp. II-325 and II-334; *Jane's Soviet Intelligence Review*, June, 1989, p. 256; *Foreign Report*, March 31, 1988, p. 1; *New York Times*, November 12, 1991.

61. The author visited many Iraqi positions the week after the war with senior Saudi officers. At several field headquarters positions, we found orders and instructions for the use of chemical weapons.

62. Dick Palowski, *Changes in Threat Air Combat Doctrine and Force Structure, 24th Edition*, Fort Worth, General Dynamics, DWIC-01, February, 1992, pp. II-326–II-327.

63. There is no evidence of forward deployment of chemical weapons, but the author visited many Iraqi command sites which still had extensive instructions and orders relating to the use of chemical weapons.

64. DF-2 and cyclohexanol and isopropanol were stored separately and had to be hand loaded into the munitions.

65. Rick Atkinson, *Crusade*, pp. 233–224.

66. *Baltimore Sun*, November 3, 1991, p. 16A; *New York Times*, November 12, 1991, p. A-3; *Jane's Defense Weekly*, December 14, 1991, pp. 1144–1145; Associated Press, December 12, 1991, PM cycle; *London Times*, March 4, 1992, p. 10; *Christian Science Monitor*, January 23, 1992, p. 1.

67. For a good overview of the options, see Norman Cigar, "Chemical Weapons and the Gulf War, the Dog That Did Not Bark," *Studies in Conflict and Terrorism*, Vol. 15, 1992, pp. 145–152.

68. There are some indications that a chemical device may have gone off in Iraq. Czech anti-chemical warfare units in the Gulf claim to have detected traces of small amounts of Sarin. This has led to speculation that the Iraqis may have had a warhead or bomb explode accidentally. *Washington Post*, November 11, 1993; Briefing by Secretary of Defense Les Aspin and Undersecretary of Defense for Acquisition and Technology, John M. Deutch, November 10, 1993; *Arms Control Today*, December, 1993, p. 20; *Navy Times*, July 25, 1994, p. 25; *Chemical and Engineering News*, July 11, 1994, p. 26; *Washington Post*, July 24 and July 25, 1994.

69. *Final Report of the Presidential Advisory Committee on Gulf War Veterans*, January 7, 1997; *Economist*, January 11, 1997, pp. 71–74; *Washington Post*, December 15, 1997, p. C-1, December 21, 1996, p. A-3, January 1, 1997, p. A-19, January 2, 1997, p. A-1, January 7, 1997, p. A-11, January 18, 1997, p. A-6, June 27, 1997, p. A-26; *New York Times*, November 26, 1996, p. A-1, December 3, 1996, p. A-1, December 5, 1996, p. A-1, January 9, 1997, p. A-18, January 22, 1997, P. A-17, January 30, 1997, p. A-8, June 15, 1997, 1 NE; *Wall Street Journal*, January 6, 1997, p. A-14; *Washington Times*,

January 8, 1997, p. A-6; *USA Today*, December 12, 1996, p. 6A; *Jane's Defense Weekly*, April 16, 1997, June 25, 1997, p. 8.

70. For a detailed analysis of this issue, see Thomas L. McNaugher, "Ballistic Missiles and Chemical Weapons: The Legacy of the Iran-Iraq War," *International Security*, 15:2, pp. 5–34.

71. See US Department of Defense, *Conduct of the Persian Gulf War: Final Report*, Washington, US Department of Defense, April, 1992, pp. 207; Lt. Colonel Jeffery D. McCausland, "How Iraq's CBW Threat Affected Coalition Operations," *Defense and Foreign Affairs*, September, 1992, pp. 12–16; General Schwarzkopf's Press Conference of February 27, 1991, in *New York Times*, February 28, 1991, p. A-8.

72. *Washington Post*, November 11, 1993.

73. *New York Times*, November 12, 1991, p. A-3; *Christian Science Monitor*, January 23, 1992, p. 1.

74. A number of sources, several Israeli, have claimed after the war that they did provide better estimates of Iraqi capabilities and warned the United States. A close examination of these claims indicates, however, that they either consist of memories that cannot be substantiated with evidence or generic warnings about the seriousness of the threat from Iraq, and the character of Saddam Hussein.

75. Thomas A. Keaney and Eliot A. Cohen, *Gulf War Air Power Survey: Summary Report*, Washington, Department of the Air Force, 1993, p. 123.

76. Eliot Cohen, ed., *Gulf War Air Power Survey*, Volume II, Part II, p. 324.

77. Eliot Cohen, ed., *Gulf War Air Power Survey*, Volume II, Part II, pp. 322–326.

78. *Defense News*, June 27, 1994, p. 10.

79. Eliot Cohen, ed., *Gulf War Air Power Survey*, Washington, GPO, 1993, pp. 242–254, and *Volume II, Part II*, pp. 323–326; US Department of Defense, Volume I, Part II, *Conduct of the Persian Gulf War: Final Report*, US Department of Defense, April, 1992, p. 155.

80. Terry J. Gander, "Iraq—the Chemical Arsenal," *Jane's Intelligence Review*, September, 1992, pp. 413–415; Steven R. Bowman, "Iraqi Chemical Weapons Capabilities," Washington, Congressional Research Service 93–292F, February 24, 1993.

81. *Jane's Intelligence Review*, December, 1995, pp. 556–560.

82. *Washington Post*, July 26, 1991, p. A-1.

83. Rick Atkinson, Crusade, pp. 223–224.

84. *New York Times*, July 31, 1991, p. A-1, November 12, 1991, p. A-3; *Christian Science Monitor*, January 23, 1992, p. 1; Associated Press, December 12, 1991, PM cycle. Terry J. Gander, "Iraq—the Chemical Arsenal," *Jane's Intelligence Review*, pp. 413–415; Steven R. Bowman, "Iraqi Chemical Weapons Capabilities," Washington, Congressional Research Service 93–292F, February 24, 1993.

85. Terry J. Gander, "Iraq—the Chemical Arsenal," *Jane's Intelligence Review*, pp. 413–415.

86. *Baltimore Sun*, November 3, 1991, p. 16A; *New York Times*, November 12, 1991, p. A-3; *Jane's Defense Weekly*, December 14, 1991, pp. 1144–1145; Associated Press, December 12, 1991, PM cycle; *London Times*, March 4, 1992, p. 10; *Christian Science Monitor*, January 23, 1992, p. 1.

87. US Department of Defense, *Conduct of the Persian Gulf War: Final Report*, US Department of Defense, April, 1992, p. 207.

88. *New York Times*, November 12, 1991, p. A-3; *Christian Science Monitor*, January

23, 1992, p. 1; *Jane's Defense Weekly*, December 14, 1991, pp. 1144–1145; Associated Press, December 12, 1991, PM cycle.

89. *Jane's Intelligence Review*, December, 1995, pp. 556–560.

90. US Department of Defense, *Conduct of the Persian Gulf War: Final Report*, US Department of Defense, April, 1992, pp. 16–18; "Ambassador Rolf Ekeus, Unearthing Iraq's Arsenal," *Arms Control Today*, April, 1992, pp. 6–9; *Christian Science Monitor*, January 23, 1992, p. 1; *The Atlanta Constitution*, January 16, 1992, p. 1; *Jane's Defense Weekly*, December 14, 1991, pp. 1144–1145; Associated Press, December 12, 1991, PM cycle. The UN found nearly 100 metal working machines for chemical weapons at the plant during a raid on November 20, 1991.

91. UN Security Council, Note by the Secretary-General, S/1995/864, 11 October 1995, pp. 17–19; *Policywatch*, No. 175, November 20, 1995.

92. *Jane's Defense Weekly*, November 11, 1995, p. 4.

93. United Nations Special Commission, "Report to the Security Council—S/1995/864," 11 October 1995, pp. 18–19.

94. *Jane's Defense Weekly*, March 5, 1997, p. 16.

95. United Nations, Note by the Secretary-General, S/1997/301, April 11, 1997, p. 18.

96. United Nations, Note by the Secretary-General, "Report of the Secretary-General on the Activities of the Special Commission," S/1997/774, October 6, 1997, paragraphs 62–64.

97. United Nations Special Commission, "Report to the Security Council—S/1995/864," 11 October 1995, p. 19.

98. United Nations, Note by the Secretary-General, S/1997/301, April 11, 1997, pp. 17–19.

99. United Nations Special Commission, "Report to the Security Council—S/1995/864," 11 October 1995, p. 19.

100. United Nations Special Commission, "Report to the Security Council—S/1995/864," 11 October 1995, p. 19.

101. United Nations, Note by the Secretary-General, S/1997/301, April 11, 1997, pp. 17–18.

102. Note by the Secretary-General, "Report of the Secretary-General on the Activities of the Special Commission," S/1997/774, October 6, 1997, paragraph 65.

103. Note by the Secretary-General, "Report of the Secretary-General on the Activities of the Special Commission," S/1997/774, October 6, 1997, paragraph 59.

104. Reuters, December 15, 1997, 2003, 1842.

105. Note by the Secretary-General, "Report of the Secretary-General on the Activities of the Special Commission," S/1997/774, October 6, 1997, paragraph 65.

106. *Washington Times*, December 28, 1995, p. A-13.

107. Note by the Secretary-General, "Report of the Secretary-General on the Activities of the Special Commission," S/1997/774, October 6, 1997, paragraph 48.

108. Report by the Executive Committee of the Special Commission, March 27, 1998, as transmitted by the Secretary-General to the Security Council, April 16, 1998, S/1998/332.

109. Washington Post, June 23, 1998, p. A-1; *New York Times*, June 24, 1998, p. A-7.

110. Associated Press, June 24, 1998, 1707; Reuters, June 22, 1998, 13:31 and 0532; *Washington Post*, June 23, 1998, p. A-1; *New York Times*, June 24, 1998, p. A-7

111. *Washington Post*, June 23, 1998, p. A-1; *New York Times*, June 24, 1998, p. A-7, August 25, 1998, p. A-1; Reuters, June 29, 1998, 1314.

112. *New York Times*, August 25, 1998, p. A-1, August 26, 1996, p. A-8.

113. Washington Post, August 17, 1998, p. A-1.

114. Note by the Secretary-General, S/1998/920(1998), October 6, 1988.

115. The technical content of this discussion is adapted in part from the author's discussion of the technical aspects of such weapons in Cordesman, *After the Storm: The Changing Military Balance in the Middle East*, Boulder, Westview, 1993; working material on biological weapons prepared for the United Nations, and from the US Congress, Office of Technology Assessment, *Proliferation of Weapons of Mass Destruction: Assessing the Risks*, United States Congress OTA-ISC-559, Washington, DC, August, 1993; Kenneth R. Timmerman, *Weapons of Mass Destruction: The Cases of Iran, Syria, and Libya*, Los Angeles, Simon Wiesenthal Center, August, 1992; Dr. Robert A. Nagler, *Ballistic Missile Proliferation: An Emerging Threat*, Arlington, Systems Planning Corporation, 1992; and translations of unclassified documents on proliferation by the Russian Foreign Intelligence Bureau provided to the author by the staff of the Government Operations Committee of the US Senate.

116. Cordesman, *After the Storm: The Changing Military Balance in the Middle East*, Boulder, Westview, 1993; working material on biological weapons prepared for the United Nations, and from the US Congress, Office of Technology Assessment, *Proliferation of Weapons of Mass Destruction: Assessing the Risks*, United States Congress OTA-ISC-559, Washington, DC, August, 1993; Kenneth R. Timmerman, *Weapons of Mass Destruction: The Cases of Iran, Syria, and Libya*, Los Angeles, Simon Wiesenthal Center, August, 1992; Dr. Robert A. Nagler, *Ballistic Missile Proliferation: An Emerging Threat*; Arlington, Systems Planning Corporation, 1992; and translations of unclassified documents on proliferation by the Russian Foreign Intelligence Bureau.

117. *Jane's Defense Weekly*, May 14, 1997, p. 4, June 4, 1997, pp. 19–27.

Chapter 18

Iraq's Past and Future Biological Weapons Capabilities

At the time of the cease-fire in the Iran-Iraq War, Iraq was reaching the point where it would have been able to employ biological weapons against Iran if the war had continued. Its capabilities steadily improved between August, 1988 and August, 1990, and Iraq had a major biological weapons program ready to use against the UN Coalition at the time of the Gulf War. It had at least 90,000 liters of Botulinum toxin and 8,300 liters of Anthrax, as well as large stocks of an agent that causes cancer. It had loaded both Botulinum and Anthrax on Scud missile warheads and aerial bombs. Iraq was also experimenting with infectious agents and mycotoxins. These programs were initially centered around Al-Kindi and Salman Pak, but were moved to Al-Hakam and other facilities before the war, and were extensively dispersed before the fighting began.[1]

The activity was completely clandestine, and Iraqi biological weapons initially did not receive the same attention that the world gave to Iraq's other weapons of mass destruction after the end of the Gulf War. In fact, the full scale of Iraq's efforts only became apparent when new evidence surfaced in September, 1995. This comparative lack of attention is evident in the relatively limited number of biological weapons inspections that UNSCOM conducted relative to its chemical and nuclear weapons and ballistic missile inspections during the period between the cease-fire in 1991 and late 1995.[2]

Since that time, UNSCOM has changed its priorities. It has had good reason to do so, since biological weapons can be as effective as small nuclear weapons. One US study of the Gulf War notes that

Experimental data indicate Botulinum toxin is about 3 million times more potent than the nerve agent Sarin. A Scud missile warhead filled with Botulinum could contaminate an area of 3,700 square kilometers (based on ideal weather conditions and an effective dispersal mechanism), or 16 times greater than the same warhead filled with Sarin. By the time symptoms occur, treatment has little chance of success. Rapid field detection methods for biological warfare agents do not exist. Although Botulinum can debilitate in a few hours and kill in as few as 12, and Anthrax takes two to four days to kill, Anthrax is much more persistent and can contaminate a much larger area using the same delivery means.[3]

The UN is still actively engaged in trying to discover and destroy Iraq's biological weapons capabilities. It has included 79 Iraqi facilities in its biological monitoring and verification regime. Of these, nine are considered Category A, requiring the most intense monitoring, while 15 are Category B, 10 are Category C, and 45 are Category D. Many of the Category A sites were damaged during the Gulf War, but one facility at Al-Hakam was missed entirely by both Coalition intelligence and bombers.[4] The Iraqi government has admitted that these plants produced large quantities of Anthrax, Botulinum, clostridium perfringens, and other agents prior to the Gulf War.

IRAQ'S BIOLOGICAL WEAPONS EFFORTS BEFORE THE GULF WAR

Iraq began working on biological weapons in the 1970s, conducted extensive research on mycotoxins beginning in the mid-1980s, and was producing biological weapons in at least four different facilities when the Gulf War began.[5] The origin of the weapons program dates back to at least the period 1972–1973, because major construction activity took place as early as January, 1974. This shows the Iraqi government has to have officially endorsed its development in the early 1970s. The program was initially assigned to the Al Hazen Ibn Al Haytham Institute at Al Salman. Although some reports indicate that the work at this facility was relatively unsophisticated, work by UNSCOM has shown that it had at least two Level 3 biocontainment suites that operated all during the year.

By 1978, poor management and incompetence resulted in the termination of most of the activities at Al Salman, and even to the arrest of some senior members of the problem. Major new construction remained underway, however, and the new facilities at Al Salam were taken over by Dr. Rihab Taha in 1980. Dr. Taha held a doctorate from the University of East Anglia, and she later played a key part in the Iraqi program at Al Hakam.

In spite of this change in leadership, the Iraqi effort remained at a relatively low level until Iraq's defeats in the Iran-Iraq War led Saddam Hussein to reconsider the program. According to some reports, this reconsideration was triggered by a memo that Abdul Nassir Hindawi, one of Iraq's leading microbiologists and a graduate of Mississippi State, wrote for the Revolutionary Command Council and leading officials of the Ba'ath Party.[6] Copies of the paper have never been surrendered to UNSCOM, but it seems to have had a major impact on Iraq's leadership, after Iran's offensives in early 1984.

As a result, the directors of Iraq's poison gas program were instructed to revive the Iraqi biological weapons program in late 1984. The program acquired a presidential priority with almost unlimited funding. Its formal goals were to deter an Israeli nuclear attack, but it is clear that the program was actually directed against Iran. It is also clear that by the mid-1980s, Iraqi was actively conducting research in an effort to weaponize Anthrax, Botulinum, and at least one other weapon whose name UNSCOM still keeps classified.

Iraq Begins Major Research Activity

The Muthanna State Establishment was made Iraq's primary facility for chemical weapons development and production during either 1984 or early 1985. By the end of 1985, the program had a 150-liter fermenter and a staff of 10, who devoted themselves to investigating Anthrax and Botulinum. While many of the details of Iraq's other biological weapons programs remain unknown, it began to import large amounts of biotechnology.

Importing Type Cultures

Iraq imported a reference strain of wheat smut from the American Type Culture Center (ATCC) in Rockville, Maryland, in 1985. Iraq also had detailed one- and five-year development and production plans for biological weapons from 1985 onward.[7] Iraq found that the ATCC placed few controls on the provision of such cultures, other than a check to ensure that the user had suitable scientific experience and only charged a $78 fee for each culture.

Iraq's Ministry of Education imported two Class III fungus samples, and then began to import more lethal cultures. During 1986, Iraq ordered 24 pathogens, including 13 bacteria cultures. The US Department of Commerce cleared the order relatively rapidly, which included the strains of Anthrax, Clostridium Botulinum, and a gangrene-causing culture known as Clostridium Perfringens that Iraq later weaponized. Ironically, the Anthrax culture was derived from a British culture that had originally been developed for biological weapons in World War II. These cultures were sent to the University of Baghdad, but were then transferred to the Iraqi military.[8]

Iraq tried to order other cultures from the British research center at Porton Down and from the Pasteur Center in France. Porton Down rejected the order, but the Pasteur Center shipped many of the same toxins and agents shipped by the ATCC. An Iraqi researcher, Firal al-Saedi, and Iraq seem to have obtained British Anthrax and Botulinum toxins from the University of Birmingham in 1988. Miss Saedi had left England in the early 1980s, but suddenly returned for her former tutor's funeral in 1988. Her tutor, Malcom Jeynes, had kept a selection of lethal cultures in his laboratory refrigerator, including Anthrax, cholera, and bubonic plague. Miss Saedi also attempted to order cultures from the British Public Health Science Laboratory in London, but this order was blocked by a complaint by a British colleague. Miss Saedi then left England.

Iraq carried out extensive testing on mice, guinea pigs, monkeys, sheep, beagles, and donkeys at Muthanna and a facility at Salman Pak. It used both sealed inhalation chambers and animals tethered in fields which were sprayed with aerosols. Although Iraq had attempted to argue that these tests often had only limited success, the results seem to have been impressive enough to persuade the government to authorize the construction of major production facilities.

Imports of Growth Agent and Fermenters

Iraq ordered massive amounts of a biological growth agent from Oxoid in Bedford, England, and Fluka Chemie AG in Bouch, Switzerland. There orders totaled 39 tons, or enough to produce at least four tons of biological weapons agents, and were ordered in 55-, 110-, and 220-pound packages, rather than the normal 10-pound boxes. Neither company expressed any concerns about the orders. Similarly, Iraq began to order the kind of larger fermenters used for making beer and other yeast-based products and spray dryers that could be used to convert liquid slurries that required refrigeration into dried spores that could be stored for indefinite periods at room temperatures.

Iraq installed fermenters at three facilities: a factory located on the outskirts of Baghdad, an agricultural research institute west of Baghdad, and the Al-Hakam Single Cell Protein Production Facility. Al-Hakam was located in the desert and was supposedly a chicken feed factory. The production program was managed by General Amer Saadi, who had a master's degree in chemistry from Oxford and Rihab Taha. Ahmen Murthada, a British-educated engineer, managed the import procurement program. Hussein Kamel Majid had overall control of the program as part of his role as the director of Iraq's Military-Industrial Corporation.[9]

Major Production Facilities

In May, 1987 the core of the Iraqi program, with its fermenters and eight more staff, was transferred to Al Salman (Salman Pak). A second production facility with a 450-liter fermenter was established at Taji to concentrate on the production of Botulinum. The Taji plant produced Botulinum for about six months in 1988, while the Al Salman plant accumulated 1,500 liters of Anthrax. The success of these small trial production runs convinced the Iraqi government to proceed with full-scale production and weapons tests. [10]

Botulinum and Anthrax agents were tested on animals and possibly on human beings, and this testing was followed by the first initial weapons field trials in early 1988. The first known weapons tests occurred in early March, 1988 at al-Muthanna's weapons testing range. Aerial bombs were selected as the weapon of choice for this test and, according to the Iraqis, the results were considered a failure. A second test later the same month, however, proved to be successful. The next weaponization test occurred in November, 1989, when 122-mm rockets were filled with Botulinum, an Anthrax simulate, and Aflatoxin, a naturally occurring carcinogen. These trials were considered successful, as were identical trials held in May, 1990. These trials were followed by tests involving R400 aerial bombs filled with the same three agents.[11]

Construction of a main biological weapons facility started at Al-Hakam in early 1988 and was completed by the end of the year. The complex was constructed to look like ordinary industrial buildings and sheds, and it lacked any obvious signs of being a biological weapons plant—such as sophisticated air filtration equipment. Iraq also avoided actions that might have signaled the true nature of the plant, such as giving most workers vaccinations and masks with air filters.

To expand its production capabilities, the new plant was equipped with two 1,850 liter and seven 1,480 liter fermenters, which were transferred from the Veterinary Research Laboratories in November, 1988. The 450 liter fermenter from Taji was also transferred to Al-Hakam in October, 1988. By April, 1989 production of Botulinum had started, with an Anthrax simulate following in May for the purpose of weapons tests. Iraq claims that production of Anthrax and Botulinum at Al-Hakam during 1990 amounted to 6,000 liters of concentrated Botulinum and 8,425 liters of Anthrax.[12]

Work on Clostridium Perfringens, Aflatoxin, and Ricin

In addition, a parallel research and development activity was started on a number of other biological weapons. In April, 1988 an effort began to weaponize a gangrene-causing agent known as Clostridium Perfringens. Iraq experimented with the infectivity of Clostridium Perfringens, and this program also examined debilitating tricothecene mycotoxins, such as T-2 and DAS. Research into Clostridium Perfringens was transferred to Al-Hakam in 1989, and various reports state that at least 90 gallons or 340 liters of the toxin were produced.

A month later, another program was set up to weaponize Aflatoxin, which is produced by growing the fungus aspergillus. The production of Aflatoxin moved to a plant at Fudaliyah, where 1,850 liters were produced between April and May, 1990 and December, 1990. Still another program examined a grain-destroying fungus known as wheat cover smut. Iraq infected a number of fields in the Mosul area with wheat smut to test its effectiveness as an agent. Work on the wheat cover smut moved to Mosul, but according to the Iraqis, the infected wheat necessary to propagate the fungus was burned at Fudaliyah in 1990.[13]

Iraq also began work on Ricin, a deadly protein toxin, at its Biological Research Center at some point between 1987 and 1988. This work was transferred to Al Salman in 1989, where work was begun on a joint program with scientists at Al Muthanna. Ricin appeared to be a promising weapon, and ten liters of concentrate were prepared for weapons trials using 155-mm artillery shells. According to the Iraqis, these trials were failures, and the project was discontinued.[14] Iraq, however, was later found to have conducted a crash program to harvest castor beans for the production of Ricin in late 1990.

Iraq's production of Ricin has never been fully accounted for, and there are indications that Iraq continued the program well into 1997. Professor Shakir Akidid of Baghdad University is a British-trained biologist who is associated with the Ricin toxin program. UNSCOM attempted to interview him in April, 1997, but he fled the building as they arrived, carrying papers that he claimed belonged to his wife. This program was to be a topic for Iraqi-UNSCOM review during an inspection that was scheduled for November 11, 1997, but which was canceled because of the sanctions crisis.[15]

Mycotoxins, Hemorrhagic Conjunctivitis, Rotavirus, Yellow Fever Virus, and Congo-Crimean Hemorrhagic Virus

There have been charges that Iraq has used mycotoxins against its Kurdish population beginning early in the Iran-Iraq War, but these have never been confirmed, and the timing of many of the claims lacks credibility.[16] Most of the examples and symptoms cited in such charges can be explained more easily by the poor sanitary and health conditions affecting the population in the area.

Iraq is known to have experimented with tricothene mycotoxins in 1990, and its use of mycotoxins or "yellow rain" weapons against the Kurds cannot be ruled out. Nevertheless, reports that the Iraqi secret service used biological agents or toxins to poison the food in Kurdish refugee camps in mid-1989, and produced 700 dead and 4,000 casualties, seem dubious. Iraq does not seem to have produced such agents until 1990, and it is unclear that it produced more than 20 milliliters for animal experimentation.[17]

In July, 1990, while Al-Hakam became the center of toxin production, Al Salman started to conduct research into at least 17 different viruses. It acquired the Foot and Mouth Disease Facility at Daura and subsequently isolated three viruses indigenous to Iraq for possible weapons use. The first was hemorrhagic conjunctivitis, which results in extreme pain and temporary blindness.

This effort was followed by research into a debilitating rotavirus and the virus which causes camel pox. The initiation of this research, however, occurred only months before the eruption of the Gulf War, and the Iraqis have maintained that very little progress was achieved. Yellow Fever Virus and Congo-Crimean hemorrhagic virus were tested, but they were reportedly rejected because they needed human vectors for dispersal.[18]

Shift to Emphasis on Weaponization

Iraq imported two spray dryers from the Niro Atomizer Company in Denmark in 1989, claiming that the dryers were going to be used for civilian nuclear research. The use of the dryers is unclear. One was installed at Al-Hakam as late as 1992 for what Iraq claimed was civilian use. The other was found in a warehouse in Northern Iraq in 1997, but had previously been cleaned and disassembled, and it was not possible to estimate whether it had been used for weapons production purposes.

After Iraq's invasion of Kuwait, it accelerated its biological weapons program and placed a strong emphasis on production and weaponization. The Daura Institute was converted from viral research to Botulinum production and subsequently produced 5,400 liters of concentrate between November, 1990 and January 15, 1991. During the same period, Al Hakam's fermenters were converted from Botulinum production to Anthrax, while its older 150 liter fermenter was used to manufacture 340 liters of Clostridium Perfringens concentrate.[19]

In December, 1990 three of the biological agents—Botulinum, Anthrax, and Aflatoxin—were selected for weaponization. There is no accurate accounting of this effort, and Iraq has told a number of conflicting stories. According to one Iraqi report, 100 R-400 aerial bombs and 13 Al Husayn Scud warheads were filled with Botulinum, 50 bombs and 10 warheads were filled with Anthrax, and 16 bombs and 2 warheads were weaponized with Aflatoxin. UNSCOM experts note, however, that other Iraqi reports indicate that 16 warheads were filly with Botulinum, five with Anthrax, and seven with Aflatoxin.

The R-400 is a parachute-retarded bomb with an exceptionally heavy casing to allow attacks on hard targets, and Iraq has sometimes claimed to have destroyed more R-400s than it has in its inventory. There may well be more bombs than the 157 Iraq now admits to, and up to twice as many missile warheads. As one leading inspector put it, "Everything is filled with errors of fact, errors of commission, and errors of omission."[20]

Iraq claims its biological weapons were subsequently dispersed to four different locations, where they remained throughout the war. The bombs were deployed at two sites—evidently dispersal runways for immediate use by aircraft that could suddenly land on the airstrip, recover a buried bomb, and then fly a strike mission. A total of 25 Scud missile warheads (13 with Botulinum toxin, 10 with Aflatoxin, and two with Anthrax) were deployed to the field. Ten were stored in a deep railway tunnel and 15 in holes dug along the Tigris River.

In addition to warheads and aerial bombs, the Iraqis attempted to develop a drop tank for manned aircraft and RPVs that would dispense up to 2,000 liters of Anthrax. Trials are said to have been conducted in January, 1991, and the Iraqis contend that the tests were a failure. Nevertheless, Iraq maintained three of the drop tanks in a ready-to-use posture until July, 1991, when it says they were destroyed. Iraq has several hundred Italian crop sprayers fitted with nozzles for generating $1\text{-}u$m to $5\text{-}u$m aerosols of the kind that are optimal for biological warfare. There are unconfirmed reports that it also has remote-controlled, Japanese-made crop spraying helicopters.[21]

Some spray systems were installed on aircraft and land vehicles. One MiG-21 was modified for use as a remotely piloted vehicle and equipped with a 2,200 liter belly tank from a Mirage F-1 and one of the sprayer systems. This system was tested with a simulated agent in January, 1991. Iraq also filled an unknown number of 122-mm rocket warheads with Botulinum, Aflatoxin, and a simulant. It claims, however, that these weapons were field tested before the Gulf War and were not deployed in 1990–1991.[22]

To date, Iraq has admitted that it produced a stockpile of some 19,000 liters of concentrated Botulinum, 8,500 liters of Anthrax, 2,220 liters of Aflatoxin, 340 liters of Clostridium Perfringens, and unknown quantities of various other biological agents by the end of the war.[23] Iraq admits that 10,000 liters of Botulinum were weaponized, as were 6,500 liters of Anthrax and 1,580 liters of Aflatoxin.

Iraq also admits, however, that it imported some 39 tons of growth media before the Gulf War. Each ton of growth media can be used to produce 10 tons of biological weapons, and only 17 tons of this growth media are accounted for.[24] UNSCOM inspectors estimate that Iraq's production of Botulinum could be two to three times the amount Iraq claims, that it could have produced far more Anthrax, and that it has no way of accounting for its true production of Ricin.

COALITION AIR STRIKES AGAINST BIOLOGICAL WEAPONS FACILITIES

The disclosure of Iraq's massive biological weapons effort has revealed that the United States could do little more than guess at how to strike Iraqi biological warfare facilities and had no idea that Iraq had successfully weaponized and deployed large numbers of biological weapons. The United States did detect research activity at Salman Pak and Taji, and potential production facilities at al-Latifiyah and abu Ghurayb, and discovered that special refrigerated bunkers had been built throughout Iraq that might hold biological weapons. UN inspection efforts after the war found no evidence that any target that the Coalition struck during the war contained biological weapons. A number of US and foreign intelligence experts feel, however, that this was because intelligence did not detect the removal of most equipment, technology, and possibly weapons from the full range of sites during the war.[25]

The end result was that Coalition targeting information on Iraq's biological weapons was as inadequate as its targeting data on chemical weapons. While the full nature of the problems in the intelligence effort have never been declassified, it is clear that the Coalition could at best broadly identify the nature of a major facility without characterizing what was occurring in a given building, or accurately describing the function of the complex. US intelligence coverage of Iraqi biological warfare capability seems to have focused on a few facilities, but was otherwise largely speculative.

This inability to characterize Iraqi facilities, weapons deployment, and overall capabilities affected the Coalition's war-fighting capabilities. The much publicized attack on an Iraqi infant formula plant is an example of a case where uncertainty alone justified the Coalition attack. It was necessary to attack the baby formula plant as a "suspect" plant because it had many facilities similar to a biological warfare plant, and it adjoined a major military installation.

While UN inspection did not find containment or biological warfare facilities at the plant, Iraq often failed to practice such precautions and may have dispersed much of its biological warfare equipment before Desert Storm began. The plant had been a suspect site since 1983 and had a manned security post and a nine-foot security fence. The Iraqi authorities had applied mottled camouflage to two confirmed biological warfare sites in December, 1990. They applied this same camouflage to the infant formula plant at the same time.[26]

This seems an adequate mix of reasons to attack the plant. Yet, the Gulf War indicates that very hard evidence was needed to deal with the politics of such attack and public opinion. This raises a major challenge for intelligence, since similar "hard" evidence may be needed to justify attacking targets related to weapons of mass destruction if they are located in populated areas, have a sensitive "front," or have dual use or a cover as civilian facilities.

IRAQI BIOLOGICAL CAPABILITIES AFTER THE GULF WAR

There is no way to determine whether Iraq now has significant stocks of dry, storable biological agents. Robert Gates, Director of Central Intelligence for the Bush administration, made this point as early as January, 1992. He responded to questions about Iraq's biological weapons effort by stating that ". . . the biological weapons program was also damaged, but critical equipment for it, too, was hidden during the war." He went on to note that Iraq could produce biological agents within "a matter of weeks," once the UN sanctions and constant intrusive UNSCOM challenge inspections ended.[27]

Total Production of Biological Agents and Toxins

Some things are clear. The Iraqi government has admitted that it had at least five primary production facilities for biological weapons at the time of the Gulf War, including the Sepp Institute at Muthanna, the Ghazi Research Institute at Amaria, the Daura Foot and Mouth Disease Institute, and facilities at Al-Hakam, Salman Pak, and Taji.

Iraq has also admitted that it manufactured 6,000 liters of concentrated Botulinum toxin and 8,425 liters of Anthrax at Al-Hakam alone during 1990 and manufactured 400 liters of concentrated Botulinum toxin at Taji, 150 liters of concentrated Anthrax at Salman Pak, and 1,850 liters of Aflatoxin in solution at Fudaliyah. Additionally, Iraq has admitted that it manufactured a number of agents it claimed it did not weaponize, although some were extensively tested, produced 5,400 liters of concentrated Botulinum toxin at the Daura Foot and Mouth Disease Institute from November, 1990 to January 15, 1991, and there are some indications that it may have attempted to produce a variant of hoof and mouth disease for military purposes.[28]

Total Production of Actual Weapons

The Iraqi government's admissions in the fall of 1995 have provided yet another indication of the massive scale of Iraq's massive weapons production effort. Iraq's known weaponization programs consist of at least 182 bombs and 25 missile warheads. Three of the bombs have been recovered largely intact, and parts have been found for 23 more, but the rest are unaccounted for. At least some of the missile warheads are large components that are three feet wide and 10 feet long, which could hold up to 40 gallons and which could be used by the Al Hussein missile at ranges of up to 400 miles.[29]

As has been indicated earlier, there is no way to estimate Iraq's total weapons production with any precision, but various UNSCOM reports have described holdings of:

- 166 bombs loaded with Botulinum.
- 50 R-400 air-delivered bombs loaded with Anthrax.
- 10 Anthrax-loaded missile warheads for the Al Husayn missile.
- 15 Al Husayn missile warheads loaded with Botulinum.
- 16 missile warheads loaded with Aflatoxin, a natural carcinogen. These warheads were designed for operability with the Al Husayn Scud variant, and were loaded in December, 1990 for possible use during the Gulf War.[30]
- field trials, weaponization tests, and live firings of 122 mm rockets armed with Anthrax and Botulinum toxin (carried out during March, 1988 to May, 1990).[31]
- bombs, 122-mm rockets, and artillery shells filled with 10,000 liters of concentrated Botulinum toxin, and at least 1,580 liters of concentrated Aflatoxin.[32]
- spray tanks prepared for use by helicopters, aircraft, or UAVs. According to one report, Iraq modified a Polish-made Mi-8 helicopter equipped with a crop sprayer to act as an RPV to spray Anthrax.[33]
- development of a 2,000 liter aircraft or RPV drop tank designed to dispense Anthrax. While Iraq claims that its test on the drop tank was a failure, it stored three of them in a ready-to-use posture during the Gulf War.[34]

These reports are based on Iraqi admissions that are often conflicting and are not supported by adequate records, evidence, or testimony. The details of each of Iraq's major production efforts remain uncertain. Furthermore, these same uncertainties apply to the disposition of the weapons and munitions that Iraq could fill with biological agents.

The Iraqi government has claimed that it took its biological bombs to an airfield at some point during May–June, 1991, used a chemical agent to deactivate them, and then explosively destroyed and burned them. The Iraqi government claims that it did the same with its missile warheads at a different site. It has also said, however, that it has no record of the precise dates it carried out such destruction, or even the sites. Iraqi officials took UN inspectors to one site that had no evidence of such destruction, and then changed its story and claimed it could no longer find the site. The Iraqi government also claims to have used such procedures to destroy about 8,000 liters of concentrated Botulinum, over 2,000 liters of concentrated Anthrax, 340 liters of concentrated Perfingens, and an unspecified amount of Aflatoxin that was stored at Al Hakam.[35]

This inability to determine which agents and weapons Iraq did or did not destroy presents the risk that Iraq may have retained lethal agents after the Gulf War, as well as the ability to manufacture them. Aflatoxin may be storable, but it is not particularly lethal, and the fact that it is a carcinogen does not mean that it can produce a significant increase in the rate of cancer in human beings exposed to weaponizable amounts. Botulinum toxin is normally stored in solution and would probably have now lost most of its lethality. Anthrax spores are extremely hardy, however, and can achieve 65% to 80% lethality against untreated patients for years. Iraq may only have deployed wet Anthrax agents, which have a relatively limited life. There are, however, serious uncertainties regarding possible pre–Gulf War Iraqi production of dry, storable Anthrax agents.[36]

UNSCOM VERSUS IRAQ AND THE WAR OF SANCTIONS

Accounting for Iraq's post–Gulf War activities presents problems, because Iraq's effort was only detected a half decade after the Gulf War. Before this time, Iraq had presented six versions of its supposed "full, final, and complete disclosure" (FFCD) regarding biological weapons. The first such declaration was made in 1991 and was a few pages long. It did little more than deny the existence of any biological weapon program and proscribed biological activities. Iraq maintained this position in all of its FFCDs through March, 1995.

The Discovery of the True Scale of Iraq's Program in 1995

It was only after Hussein Kamel defected in 1995 that the UNSCOM became aware of the advanced state of Iraq's biological warfare program. Rolf Ekeus has stated as much in an August, 1995 press interview, "I probably did underestimate the biological program."[37] In an October, 1995 report to the UN Security Council, Mr. Ekeus described the advances achieved in Iraq's biological weapons program as "remarkable."[38]

Iraq did destroy some of the biological warfare facilities whose existence had become public in 1995, and it allowed the UN to inspect some of the sites where weapons had been destroyed—where UNSCOM found some biological bombs "virtually intact." Nevertheless, Iraq would not allow UN teams to collect soil samples from the locations where Iraq had claimed it had destroyed its biological weapons. Key Iraqi personnel were not made available, and Iraq did not attempt to resolve many of the inconsistencies in its declarations.[39]

It also became apparent that Iraq's new disclosures in 1995 told only part of the story. Although the Iraqi government released some 688,000 pages of new documentation after Hussein Kamel defected, it did so under conditions where it claimed the documents had been hidden in a chicken coop and were only found after Hussein Kamel defected. In fact, the documents were spotless and had clearly been moved to the area days before the UNSCOM teams were notified of their existence. These documents are very general, and Iraq seems to have held back most documentation that would reveal the level of sophistication it has achieved, data on any current suppliers, and data that might reveal the development of its program since 1991.[40]

Iraq repeatedly asserted that it destroyed all of its agents after the war, but it still failed to provide any documentation to verify such an action. The inconsistency of these Iraqi assertions regarding the destruction of biological weapons led UNSCOM to state in October, 1995 that, "it does not believe that Iraq has given a full and correct account of its biological weapons program."[41]

Lies in Iraq's FFCDs

This pressure from UNSCOM forced Iraq to issue a completely new FFCD in November, 1995. The new draft was "seriously flawed," however, and resulted in new drafts in March and May, 1996. This helps explain why Rolf Ekeus warned that UNSCOM inspectors believed that Iraq might still have 16 operational Scud variants with biological warheads that Iraq kept moving around Iraq to evade inspection during his testimony to the US Congress on March 20, 1996.[42]

UNSCOM's challenges led Iraq to provide yet another FFCD on June 22, 1996. Although it was 622 pages long, the new FFCD proved to be little more than a copy of the May draft. Further, Iraq actively blocked the efforts of the UN inspection team to verify the contents of the new draft during a visit in July and forced the delay of a visit in August.[43] UNSCOM was able to find a concealed biological laboratory in Tuwaitha and critical undeclared pieces of dual use equipment in spite of Iraq's efforts. However, inventory tags repeatedly disappeared from tagged equipment, and Iraq found many other ways to delay or block the UNSCOM effort.[44]

UNSCOM summarized the situation as follows in late 1996:

The current assessment is that the biological FFCD as written is not credible. Major sections are incomplete, inaccurate, or unsubstantiated. Biological warfare agent production figures are unsupported for the years 1987, 1988, and 1989. Expert estimates of production quantities of biological weapons agents, either by equipment capacity or by consumption of growth media, would far exceed declared amounts. Data on weapons field trials are inaccurate. Weapons agent destruction is undocumented. A lack of documentation to substantiate declarations on the critical areas of biological warfare agent and munitions production, weaponization, and destruction is difficult to accept. Until Iraq is able to provide a full accounting of biological weapons produced and destroyed unilaterally, the Commission cannot report that such weapons and their components do not remain.[45]

By March, 1997 UNSCOM's problems with Iraq remained so serious that UNSCOM called together an international panel of experts to examine Iraq's claims. This panel concluded that,

... Iraq had failed to report all imports of equipment and materials, in particular growth material. It had underreported the production of bulk biological warfare agents. The stated production of Aflatoxin could not have happened as declared. The declaration on destruction was not supported by sufficient evidence, and it failed to provide a full accounting of procurement activities for the biological weapons program.[46]

Nevertheless, Iraq continued to ask UNSCOM to accept its verbal assurances that it destroyed warheads and weapons that include some 500,000 liters of Botulism agent and 50,000 liters of Anthrax. Iraq's Deputy Prime Minister Tariq Aziz reiterated this position on April 23, 1997.[47]

UNSCOM, however, reported that it could not determine the exact status of Iraq's biological weapons programs, missile warheads, or bombs. Although it was monitoring some 86 sites with resident biological weapons teams in April, 1997, the Secretary General of the UN had just reported to the Security Council that "several pieces of significant undeclared equipment, spare parts, and supplies" were discovered in recent inspections of additional facilities, and that "Iraq has still not declared all sites where dual-use equipment is present. The Commission's resident team continues to identify such sites that should have been declared by Iraq. . . . On a number of occasions, Iraq did not produce the required information on changes that have been uncovered [in key sites]."[48]

Issues Unaddressed in Late 1997 and 1998

Iraq's continuing intransigence led the Security Council to threaten further sanctions on June 21, 1997. This threat came at a time when Iraq was already experiencing serious difficulties in selling oil under the terms of UNSCR 986, and it seems to have had some effect. Richard Butler, Rolf Ekeus's replacement, visited Baghdad in late August, 1997, and Deputy Prime Minister Tariq Aziz agreed that Iraq would make yet another full and frank disclosure of its biological weapons effort.

Butler received nearly 800 pages worth of new material from the Iraqis. He reported on these developments to the Security Council in October, 1997 and visited Baghdad again in November.[49] Nevertheless, things did not improve. In October, 1997, UNSCOM reported that,

Until July, 1995 Iraq totally denied it had any offensive biological warfare program. Since then, Iraq has presented three versions of FFCDs and four "drafts." The most recent FFCD was presented by Iraq on 11 September 1997. This latest submission followed the Commission's rejection in April, 1997 of the previous FFCD of June 1996.

... In the period since that report, the Commission conducted eight inspections in an attempt to investigate critical areas of Iraq's proscribed activities, such as warfare agent production and destruction, biological munitions manufacturing, filling and destruction, and military involvement in and support to the proscribed program. Those investigations, along with documents and other evidence available to the Commission, confirmed the assessment that the June, 1996 declaration was deeply deficient.

The new FFCD, received on 11 September 1997, contains fewer errata and is more coherent. However, with regard to the important issues ... the report contains no significant changes from the June, 1996 FFCD. ... The Commission's questions are rephrased in order to avoid having to produce direct answers, or are answered incompletely, or are ignored completely. ... Little of the information the Commission has gathered since June, 1996 has been incorporated into the new document.[50]

UNSCOM also reported that Iraq had never provided a clear picture of the role of its military in its biological warfare program, and had claimed it only played a token role. It had never accounted for its disposal of growth media.

Media unaccounted for is sufficient, in quantity, for the production of over three times more of the biological agent—Anthrax—stated by Iraq to have been produced ... Bulk warfare agent production appears to be vastly understated by Iraq. ... Experts' calculations of possible agent production quantities, either by equipment capacity or growth media amounts, far exceed Iraq's stated results. ... Significant periods when the fermenters were claimed not to be utilized are unexplained.[51]

Iraq's accounting for its Aflatoxin and Ricin production still was not credible. Biological warfare field trials were underreported and inadequately described. Claims regarding field trials of chemical and biological weapons using R-400 bombs were contradictory and indicated that "more munitions were destroyed than were produced." No documentation was provided on munitions filling. The account of Iraq's unilateral destruction of bulk biological agents is "incompatible with the facts. ... The Commission is unable to verify that the unilateral destruction of the BW-filled Al Hussein warheads has taken place."[52] There was no way to confirm whether Iraq destroyed 157 bombs of the R-400 type, some of which were filled with Botulin or anthrax spores.[53] UNSCOM concluded in September, 1997 that, "The FFCD fails to give a remotely credible account of Iraq's biological program. This opinion has been endorsed by an international panel of experts."[54]

The situation did not improve as the "war of sanctions" entered 1998. Iraq refused to provide any additional data when Ambassador Butler visited Baghdad in mid-December, 1997.[55] Iraq then announced in late January, 1998 that it would provide no further data on biological weapons of any kind, and insisted that UNSCOM set a deadline for completing all of its activities within six months.

On January 25, 1998, the Iraqi media challenged remarks by Richard Spertzel, head of UNSCOM's team of biological experts. Spertzel had been asked whether he believed Baghdad had a working plant it was keeping secret from UNSCOM. Spertzel said, "This is very likely." He declined to give any further details, including what agents he believed the plant was making, or whether UN inspectors had sought to visit it. He stated that, "We have good, tantalizing information but no concrete information... that we can take to the Security Council. If we did, I think it would end the debate on ending the sanctions [on Iraq] immediately."[56]

Baghdad responded by saying such statements were "cheap lies," and challenged Spertzel to prove his case to the world. The Iraqi News Agency (INA) quoted senior official Hussam Mohammad Amin as saying, "We are not surprised that such cheap lies should be issued by one of the main American officials.... We challenge Spertzel. We say, 'Visit this site you talk about where you claim the factory is, with representatives of the international media, to end any doubt, to show the truth, and uncover the lie.' " Amin is the head of Iraq's National Monitoring Directorate, the organization which liaisons with UNSCOM's operations in Iraq.

Ironically, however, an Iraqi-sponsored technical evaluation meeting (TEM) reached very different conclusions. Iraq had insisted on the creation of this "neutral body" to correct the "lies" of the UNSCOM. It met in Vienna from March 20 to 27, 1998, and was composed of experts from 15 countries and three members of UNSCOM. When it reported to the UN on April 9, 1998, however, its report concluded that Iraq was still failing to provide a full account of its biological warfare program and might still be trying to deceive UN weapons inspectors.

The report stated that Baghdad's latest so-called "full, final, and complete disclosure" (FFCD) of its germ war program—the fifth to be submitted since 1992—is "judged to be incomplete and inadequate." The report also stated that, "No additional confidence in the veracity and expanse of the FFCD was derived from the TEM... Iraq did not provide any new technical information of substance to support its FFCD." The UN document dismissed Baghdad's description of its production ability for the deadly biological agent Aflatoxin, calling the account "implausible." The report indicated that the experts had "low confidence" in Baghdad's accounting for toxic materials such as Botulinum.

While Iraq claimed to have destroyed all documents related to its biological weapons program, as well as missile warheads capable of carrying the deadly agents, the experts concluded that Baghdad's claims of destroying missiles that can carry biological weapons "cannot be reconciled with physical evidence." The report noted that Iraq had acknowledged concealing its biological warfare program until 1995, but had denied that any deception occurred. "Iraq, however, has presented falsified or altered papers, accounts, and material to conceal its offensive BW.... Since February, 1996, Iraq has not provided further documentation or plausible explanations for many aspects of its BW program. It is not certain whether deception with regard to some elements of the BW program continues."

The report used words and phrases such as "very disturbing," "unacceptable," "not believable," and "absurd." "The attitude of Iraq as evinced by the TEM toward the discussion was disappointing and shows no change since 1995." The report was particularly critical of Iraq's attitude going into the Vienna Technical Evaluation meeting, noting that Baghdad did not send qualified experts. "They did not grasp the opportunity offered. The attitude of Iraq ... toward the discussions was disappointing." The report's only positive finding was that "Iraq ... recognized the need to improve its FFCD and promised to do so.... If this BW TEM [biological warfare technical evaluation meeting] results in a significant improvement of Iraq's declaration, the FFCD, then this is a positive outcome."

Similarly, UNSCOM's April, 1998 report to the Secretary General stated that,

Accordingly, the Commission reported to the Security Council in October, 1997 that Iraq had not disclosed the full scope of its BW program. In meeting Iraq's request that it be allowed to present its view directly to externally appointed experts, an expanded international team of 18 experts from 15 countries was invited to take part in a technical evaluation meeting on all aspects of Iraq's BW program. This took place from 20 to 27 March 1998. The experts used all available information as well as Iraq's explanations and clarifications. Iraq did not provide any new information to the technical evaluation meeting. No additional confidence in the veracity or completeness of the FFCD was derived from the meeting.

Although Iraq contends that it has provided a full and complete account of its BW program, the scope of its program, acknowledged and defined in 1995 and in succeeding FFCDs, still does not cover the entirety of the BW program. Iraq's FFCD is judged to be incomplete and inadequate and to contain major mistakes, inconsistencies, and gaps in information. The FFCD does not provide a clear understanding of the current status of the BW program, nor whether nor when it was terminated. In this overall context, it is important to mention that in March, 1998, the Commission discovered in Iraq a document, dated 1994, which indicated the existence, at a site monitored by the Commission's missile monitoring team, of a program for the manufacture of nozzles for spray dryers to be delivered to Al Hakam, Iraq's principal biological weapons production facility.

Also, in September, 1997 the Commission discovered in Iraq another relevant set of documents relating to discussions held in 1995 by Iraq and a potential supplier for the possible importation of a single-cell protein facility, the potential dual-use character of which is beyond question. Following contact with the potential supplier, the Commission was assured that no contract was concluded, and that no request to supply such materials and equipment had been submitted to the national export control agency of the potential supplier, either in 1995 or in subsequent years.

Specific concerns identified by the technical evaluation meeting of March, 1998 included the following: Iraq has provided a selected and incomplete history of the BW program. It does not include the evolutionary aspects of the BW program, nor an adequate account of the funding and budgetary arrangements. Iraq must provide the Commission with an accurate record of its BW program.

There is a general lack of information concerning relevant organizational arrangements from the highest levels down and their connections to functional organs. All involvement of the Ministries of Defense, Health, Intelligence, or other relevant agencies is denied by Iraq, contrary to the available evidence. The organizations driving or influencing the BW program are not disclosed. This reflects negatively on the credibility of all aspects of the FFCD. Had biological weapons been integrated into Iraq's strategic arsenal, military objectives, concepts of use and mechanisms for releasing the weapons would have been defined. Iraq denies the existence of any such planning.

The FFCD is deficient in reporting the acquisition of supplies, material, seed strains, munitions, and equipment. Substantial quantities of microbial growth media are not reported or included in the material balance. Iraq has not provided complete information on all its acquisition channels.

All research and development is minimized by Iraq. No rationale is presented for selection of agents or inclusion of particular technologies. All planning is denied. Management and development of the research program is not presented in its totality. The quality of all the scientific information in the FFCD is poor, with more emphasis on methods than on results. Iraq's portrayal of the aerobiology development, with no bearing on other components of the research program, is contradicted by information held by the Commission.

Iraq maintains that it is difficult, if not impossible, to provide any verifiable account of production because relevant documents had been unilaterally destroyed. The claimed production quantities of BW agents are inadequately supported. There is low confidence in the stated production figures. The use by Iraq of recollection and back-calculation, based on weapons filling needs and/or the "1990 Al-Hakam report," is flawed and, consequently, the figures are not reliable.

Statements on production and filling of munitions are inadequately supported. Destruction of the BW munitions and weapons cannot be reconciled with the physical evidence. The inability or unwillingness by Iraq to provide a verifiable account of its BW munitions and weapons casts doubts on many aspects of the BW weaponization program. The significance of Iraq's BW aircraft drop-tank project is minimized, and information provided is deficient. The denial of any planning or involvement of relevant agencies in weapons selection, filling, deployment, or destruction is not credible. Weapons research into other systems, including cluster munitions and remotely piloted vehicles, is inadequately described. This lack of candor raises the possibility of research or development of undisclosed systems.

The numerical accounting, based on estimates, of the growth media balance is flawed. Figures of BW agent production are also based on estimated quantities. Figures provided are insufficiently supported to determine a material balance. The construction of a material balance, based primarily on recollection, provides no confidence that weapons, bulk agents, bulk media, and seed stocks have been eliminated.

The Commission will continue its pursuit of the facts of Iraq's proscribed BW program, but given the situation described above, it requires new verifiable information from Iraq before the Commission can assess the full scope of Iraq's BW program. Unless such information is forthcoming, the Commission will not be able to provide a credible report required with respect to Iraq's BW capabilities, as required by the Security Council.[57]

THE CONTINUING UNCERTAINTIES REGARDING IRAQ'S BIOLOGICAL WEAPONS EFFORTS

Biological weapons rival VX gas as the most serious near-term threat Iraq can pose to its neighbors and US power projection forces. Iraq has had ample time to redistribute the equipment, personnel, and technology used to produce biological weapons since the Gulf War, and there is no way to know how many of Iraq's assets survived the war. While some of Iraq's biological weapons production facilities were damaged during the Gulf War, much of their equipment may have been dispersed before or during the war, and Coalition intelligence and bombers missed key facilities like the one at Al-Hakam.[58]

The Inherent Limits to UNSCOM Efforts

It is unclear how much of Iraq's equipment and material can ever be traced. The Iraqi government admits that it had imported extensive amounts of equipment and materials suitable for biological weapons production before the war—largely from Europe. These imports have not yet been accounted for in any detail, and there is no way to know how many have been dispersed or have been used since the Gulf War in undeclared facilities. Iraq's imports also included tons of growth media for biological agents, which were obtained from three European firms. According to UNSCOM, 17 tons of these media still remained unaccounted for.[59] Further, Iraq imported a wide range of type cultures, which can be modified to develop biological weapons, and some came from the United States.[60]

UNSCOM has noted some of the resulting technical problems in its reports:

> ... for the monitoring system to be effective, it must cast a broad net and cover major facilities such as petrochemical and pesticide plants where chemical and biological warfare agents could be produced. However, such agents can also be clandestinely produced by Iraq in such facilities as breweries, brake fluid factories, and even university microbiology laboratories containing dual use equipment.[61]

Similarly, there is no way to be certain exactly what agents Iraq examined before the war, or has examined since. Outside experts add tularemia and typhoid agents to the list Iraq has examined. Iraq's declarations admit to conducting research on a mycotoxin similar to the "yellow rain" defoliant. Iraq examined a wide range of viruses, bacteria, and fungi. It examined the possibility of weaponizing gas gangrene and other mycotoxins, and some field trials were held of these agents. It also examined the use of hemorrhagic conjunctivitis virus, rotavirus, and camel pox virus.[62]

What Iraq May Retain

Once again, the absence of locatable Iraqi facilities and activities provides no reassurance. A senior UNSCOM inspector has described biological weapons as the "black hole" of the UN inspection effort. UNSCOM has been unable to make any progress since its reporting in April, 1998, but virtually all of the independent experts who examined the issue agreed that Iraq continues to pursue its biological warfare programs.[63] There also is no way to determine the level of sophistication Iraq achieved at the time of the cease-fire or has achieved since. It is virtually impossible to locate small, dispersed biological facilities, and suitable research can be carried out under a number of different cover stories. There are also questions about technology transfer. It is possible, for example, that Russia may have given Iraq a strain of Anthrax that has been genetically modified to the point where the US vaccine for Anthrax would no longer be effective.[64] Certainly, Russia seems to have been remarkably careless about controlling its biological equipment exports—such as fermentation vessels—as late as February, 1998.[65]

There are still serious uncertainties about Iraq's exact motives in developing and producing Aflatoxin, and it has still not provided a convincing accounting of how many missile warheads it filled with Anthrax and how many it filled with Botulinum. Iraq has conducted experiments with water processing that indicate it may have examined ways to attack water supplies in ways that are not fully documented. It may have made considerably more progress in developing dry storable agents such as Anthrax, and highly lethal encapsulated micro-powders than it has yet admitted. It may have mobile biological weapons production capabilities, including fermenters, drying equipment, and grinding equipment. UNSCOM also has been unable to determine whether Iraq experimented on live subjects in 1991.

As a result, UNSCOM could never determine the exact types of biological weapons Iraq did or did not develop, how much it modified them before the Gulf War, how well it weaponized them, or what it has done covertly in the five years since the Gulf War ended. Table 11.1 has listed the agents that Iraq is known to have developed, and Table 18.1 provides a more comprehensive list of the range of weapons that Iraq could have examined. It is important to stress that all pre-production research, testing, and weaponization for many of these weapons could be conducted in small covert facilities that have been established since the Gulf War.

At least one Iraqi defector, General Wafic al-Sammaral, a former senior officer in Iraqi military intelligence, has claimed that Iraq "retains 255 containers of biological warfare materials—230 with powder, which has no expiry date, and 25 with liquid, which will deteriorate over time."[66]

Table 18.2 provides an estimate of the major uncertainties that still affected Iraq's biological weapons program in 1998. British, French, German, Swiss, US, and UNSCOM experts are aware of ongoing Iraqi import efforts that seemed to

Table 18.1
Key Biological Weapons That Iraq May Have Examined

Disease	Infectivity	Transmissibility	Incubation Period	Mortality	Therapy
Viral					
Chikungunya fever	high	none	2–6 days	very low (–1%)	none
Dengue fever	high	none	5–2 days	very low (–1%)	none
Eastern equine encephalitis	high	none	5–10 days	high (+60%)	developmental
Tick-borne encephalitis	high	none	1–2 weeks	up to 30%	developmental
Venezuelan equine encephalitis	high	none	2–5 days	low (–1%)	developmental
Hepatitis A	-	-	15–40 days	-	-
Hepatitis B	-	-	40–150 days	-	-
Influenza	high	none	1–3 days	usually low	available
Yellow fever	high	none	3–6 days	up to 40%	available
Smallpox (Variola)	high	high	7–16 days	up to 30%	available
Rickettsial					
Coxiella Burneti (Q-fever)	high	negligible	10–21 days	low (–1%)	antibiotic
Mooseri	-	-	6–14 days	-	-
Prowazeki	-	-	6–15 days	-	-
Psittacosis	high	moderate-high	4–15 days	moderate-high	antibiotic
Rickettsi (Rocky Mountain spotted fever)	high	none	3–10 days	up to 80%	antibiotic
Tsutsugamushi	-	-	-	-	-
Epidemic typhus	high	none	6–15 days	up to 70%	antibiotic/vaccine
Bacterial					
Anthrax (pulmonary)	mod-high	negligible	1–5 days	usually fatal	antibiotic/vaccine

Brucellosis	high	none	1–3 days	up to 25%	antibiotic
Cholera	low	high	1–5 days	up to 80%	antibiotic/vaccine
Glanders	high	none	2–1 days	usually fatal	antibiotic
Meloidosis	high	none	1–5 days	usually fatal	antibiotic
Plague (pneumonic)	high	high	2–5 days	usually fatal	antibiotic/vaccine
Tularemia	high	negligible	1–10 days	low to 60%	antibiotic/vaccine
Typhoid fever	moderate-high	moderate-high	7–21 days	up to 10%	antibiotic/vaccine
Dysentery	high	high	1–4 days	low to high	antibiotic/vaccine
Fungal Coccidioidomycosis	high	none	1–3 days	low	none
Coccidiodes Immitis	high	none	10–21 days	low	none
Histoplasma Capsulatum	-	-	15–18 days	-	-
Norcardia Asteroides	-	-	-	-	-
Toxins[1]					
Botulinum toxin	high	none	12–72 hours	high neuromuscular paralysis	vaccine
Mycotoxin	high	none	hours or days	low to high	?
Staphylococcus	moderate	none	1–2 days	incapacitating	?

1. Many sources classify as chemical weapons, because toxin are chemical poisons.

Sources: Adapted by Anthony H. Cordesman from Report of the Secretary General, Department of Political and Security Affairs, Chemical and Bacteriological (Biological) Weapons and the Effects of Their Possible Use, New York, United Nations, 1969, pp. 26, 29, 37–52, 116–117; *Jane's NBC Protection Equipment*, 1991–1992; James Smith, "Biological Warfare Developments," *Jane's Intelligence Review*, November, 1991, pp. 483–487.

Table 18.2
Iraqi Biological Warfare Capabilities in 1998

BW Agent Production Amounts

BW Agent	Declared Concentrated Amounts	Declared Total Amounts	Comments
Anthrax (Bacillus anthracis)	8,500 liters (2,245 gallons)	85,000 liters (22,557 gallons)	UNSCOM estimates production amounts were actually 3–4 times more than the declared amounts, but is unable to confirm.
Botulinum toxin (Clostridium Botulinum)	19,400 liters (10x and 20x concentrated) (5,125 gallons)	380,000 liters (100,396 gallons)	UNSCOM estimates production amounts were actually 2 times more than the declared amounts, but is unable to confirm.
Gas Gangrene (Clostridium Perfringens)	340 liters (90 gallons)	3,400 liters (900 gallons)	Production amounts could be higher, but UNSCOM is unable to confirm.
Aflatoxin (Aspergillus flavus and Aspergillus parasiticus)	N/A	2,200 liters (581 gallons)	Production amounts and time frame of production claimed by Iraq do not correlate.
Ricin (Castor Bean plant)	N/A	10 liters (2.7 gallons)	Production amounts could be higher, but UNSCOM is unable to confirm.

BW-Filled and Deployed Delivery Systems

Delivery System	Anthrax	Botulinum Toxin	Aflatoxin	Comments
Missile warheads Al-Husayn (modified Scud B)	5	16	4	UNSCOM cannot confirm the unilateral destruction of these 25 warheads due to conflicting accounts provided by Iraq.

R-400 aerial bombs	50	100	7	Iraq claimed unilateral destruction of 157 bombs, but UNSCOM is unable to confirm this number. UNSCOM has found the remains of at least 23.
Aircraft aerosol spray tanks F-1 Mirage modified fuel drop tank	4	NA	NA	Iraq claims to have produced 4, but may have manufactured others.

BW Agent Growth Media

Media	Quantity Imported	Unaccounted-for Amounts
BW Agent Growth Media	31,000 kg (68,200 lbs)	3,500 kg (7,700 lbs)

Total refers to the amount of material obtained from production process, while *concentrated* refers to the amount of concentrated agent obtained after final filtration/purification. The *concentrated* number is the amount used to fill munitions.

Media refers to the substance used to provide nutrients for the growth and multiplication of microorganisms.

Source: Adapted by Anthony H. Cordesman from material provided by the NSC on February 19, 1998.

be designed to produce biological weapons, and most experts believe that Iraq has created the same highly secret and compartmentalized program to carry on with its biological weapons program after the Gulf War that it created for its missile, chemical warfare, and nuclear programs.

Such an Iraqi program is particularly difficult to trace, since all key components are dual use items that can be used for peaceful medical purposes and food processing, and can include everything from biomedical equipment and microencapsulation equipment for cold tablets to brewery fermenters and dry food storage equipment for infant formula. Both Iraq's research and production efforts can be widely dispersed and can be concealed in relatively small buildings—particularly if a government is willing to take moderate risks of contamination of the kind widely taken by the Soviet Union during the Cold War.

These factors led British and US intelligence experts to warn that Iraq might be concealing significant war-fighting capabilities during the military build-up to Desert Fox. More openly, State Department spokesman James Rubin gave a briefing on November 16, 1998, in which he stated that

There is a large discrepancy between the amount of biological growth media—that's the culture in which you grow biological weapons—procured and the amount of agents that were or could have been produced. Baghdad has not adequately explained where some 8,000 pounds (3,500 kg) of the material went out of some 68,000 pounds (31,000 kg) of biological growth media it imported. Iraq's accounting of the amount of the agent it produced and the number of failed batches is seriously flawed and cannot be reconciled on the basis of this full disclosure Iraq has made.

Much depends on whether Iraq did or did not have the capability to make dry, storable weapons at any point before or after the Gulf War. As has been touched upon earlier, some of Iraq's holdings and use of suitable equipment cannot be accounted for. Iraq also initially said that it had tried such production as early as 1989, and then denied this. Similarly, Iraq claims it did not succeed in weaponizing Ricin, and that its trials failed. This, however, is uncertain and is a major potential risk. Iraq still produces tons of castor oil as a commercial lubricant, and 5% of the residual mash is Ricin. UNSCOM experts indicate that the monitoring of this production effort is inadequate to control how the Ricin is disposed of or used.

At this point, only another series of major defections is likely to reveal the full details of Iraq's accomplishments before 1991, or what it has done covertly since that time. At least one of the principal UNSCOM investigators of the Iraqi biological weapons program feels that no effort by UNSCOM can prevent Iraq from retaining a major biological weapons effort and resuming production and deployment within months of the end of UNSCOM's effort.

The Limits of Arms Control and Future Inspection

Most experts agree that even if the UN could account for all growth media, cultures, and Iraq's overt biological weapons production facilities at the time of the Gulf War, Iraq could rapidly establish new covert production at university research centers, medical goods and drug manufacturing plants, or virtually any other facility that can maintain a secure biological research and production activity.

There is no current arms control treaty that could even begin to replace UNSCOM. The Biological Weapons Convention (BWC) has no enforcement provisions to parallel those of the Chemical Weapons Convention (CWC) and Nuclear Non-Proliferation Treaty (NPT). Although 136 countries have adhered to the BWC since it was agreed to in 1972, the United States has not completed drafting a protocol on a possible enforcement regime—in part because it is clear that an enforcement regime would have to be far more complex and intrusive than those now used to enforce the NPT, and that even the most intrusive regime might be unworkable. There simply are too many types of dual use biological research and production facilities that could suddenly be converted to making biological weapons, and there is no way to clearly distinguish between legitimate research and weapons research.[67]

THE WAR-FIGHTING EFFECTIVENESS OF IRAQ'S FUTURE BIOLOGICAL WEAPONS

Iraq has shown that it is prepared to use biological weapons at both the strategic and tactical levels. It dispersed biological weapons to at least four sites in January, 1991 for use during the Gulf War. According to Iraqi sources, the commanders at these main storage sites were given authority in January, 1991 to use these weapons in the case of a devastating attack on Baghdad and the collapse of the Iraqi command and control system. This release authority was granted to ensure that Iraq had a retaliatory capability. It seems to have applied to a massive conventional attack on Baghdad, as well as a nuclear attack, and it may have applied to a successful attack on Iraq's leadership.[68]

Any covert stockpile of highly lethal biological weapons would give Iraq considerable potential to deter and intimidate the Southern Gulf states and the West. Iraq could make use of biological weapons in much the same way as chemical weapons. It could also employ such weapons covertly, since they lend themselves to tailored attacks in terms of delay effects and are well suited to unconventional warfare, or "terrorism." Biological weapons are Iraq's only near-term answer to the effectiveness of the UN's inspection and destruction regime of Iraq's far more visible nuclear, chemical, and missile capabilities. Given Iraq's history, this makes biological weapons an option that Iraq is likely to choose.

Possible Advances in Iraq's Biological Weapons Since 1990

There is no reason to believe that Iraq has not taken advantage of the "war of sanctions," and the years since the Gulf War. Iraq has probably retained some portion of the biological weapons it produced at the time of the Gulf War, and it has had ample opportunity to create small, clandestine production programs or "cells" and/or to develop a program for rapidly reassembling production capabilities using dual use items the moment UNSCOM inspection is halted. As a result, Iraq almost certainly retains some capability to deliver the kind of moderately lethal weapons it had at the time of the Gulf War.

It is doubtful that any of Iraq's biological weapons—particularly any of its missile warheads that date back to the Gulf War era—can take full advantage of the lethality of the biological agents that they carry. While the exact details of Iraq's weapon designs have not been disclosed, Iraq's chemical weapons were relatively unsophisticated, and it seems doubtful that its biological weaponization programs were more advanced. Most of Iraq's pre-war weapons designs were rushed into service, and it seems likely that Iraq's missiles, bombs, and warheads were unreliable and inefficient in disseminating biological agents.

At the same time, Iraq has had well over a half decade to solve the technical challenges in the weaponization and deployment of more lethal munitions and warheads and was known to be working on new RPVs at the time of Desert Fox. It may well have developed advanced dry, storable agents, and has probably solved the problems of microencapsulation, dissemination at critical heights, and predictions of wind and temperature over the target area. Some of UNSCOM's discoveries—like the new glassware production equipment it found between April and October, 1997—indicate that Iraq has developed more biological lethal weapons, improved their storability and resistance to heat and light, and improved the design of its bombs and other dissemination devices. It may already have a genetically engineered strain of Anthrax which Russia developed and which could make the vaccine the US has developed useless.

The "terror" effect of even crude and inefficient biological warheads cannot be dismissed. UAVs and slow-flying civilian aircraft make excellent delivery systems for such weapons, require minimal amounts of advanced technology, do not produce major indications of testing and development, and are inherently difficult to detect and track to a given source and location. Furthermore, the potential consequences of even inefficient dissemination of biological weapons can be disastrous. The amount of Anthrax in the 10 missile warheads that Iraq had filled at the time of the Gulf War had the theoretical ability to kill some 60,000,000 people, while the Botulinum in the remaining 15 missile warheads could have contaminated an area of over 21,000 square kilometers.[69]

Iraq is still likely to have serious problems designing and testing effective missile warheads. There are some experts that question whether Iraq can meet the challenge of developing a suitable combination of biological weapons and compatible warhead technology, and can develop a missile warhead that would achieve extremely high lethalities. Yet, Iraq did have a decade to work on this problem before the Gulf War, and UNSCOM's effort has not been designed to prevent substantial additional further research and development since the war.[70]

A successful weaponization of highly lethal, dry storable, biological weapons with the lethality of theater nuclear weapons could give Iraq major political and strategic advantages in terms of both war fighting and intimidation. It would give Iraq the potential ability to deploy a force rapidly that could be used covertly in "terrorism," or used offensively, under launch-on-warning and launch-under-attack conditions, and/or in a retaliatory mode. Such weaponization could provide Iraq with the ability to launch strikes whose political impact is all out of proportion to their direct military value. The use of toxins or persistent biological agents, like Anthrax, could achieve significant military effects or population damage. Such potential results could prompt Iraq to take the risk of using an agent that was a communicable disease, rather than military agents which require direct exposure to the original payload or which are tailored to control their infectiousness.

NOTES

1. US Office of the Secretary of Defense, *Proliferation: Threat and Response*, Washington, US Department of Defense, April, 1996, pp. 17–24.

2. *Arms Control Today*, April, 1993, p. 29.

3. Eliot Cohen, Director, *Gulf War Air Power Survey*, Vol. II, Part II, Washington, GPO, 1993, p. 327.

4. United Nations Special Commission, "Report to the Security Council—S/1995/864," 11 October 1995, p. 20; *Washington Post*, July 6, 1995, p. A-17.

5. For a range of sources on Iraqi capabilities, see the long series of UNSCOM reports on Iraq's programs, Raymond A. Zilinskas, "Iraq's Biological Weapons," *Journal of the American Medical Association*, Vol. 278, No. 6, August 6, 1997, pp. 418–425; Anthony H. Cordesman, *Weapons of Mass Destruction in the Middle East*, Boulder, Westview, 1992; Anthony H. Cordesman and Ahmed Hashim, *Iraq: Sanctions and Beyond*, Boulder, Westview, 1997; *New York Times*, December 30, 1992; US Department of Defense, *Conduct of the Persian Gulf War: Final Report*, US Department of Defense, April, 1992, pp. 16–19; Andrew Terrill, "Chemical Weapons in the Gulf War," *Strategic Review*, Spring, 1986; *Washington Times*, January 19, 1989, p. A-6; January 27, 189, p. A-2; *Baltimore Sun*, August 19, 1990, p. 5E; Leonard S. Spector, *Proliferation Today*, New York, Vintage Books, 1984; *Arms Control Today*, April, 1992, pp. 7–8.

6. Interviews with UNSCOM personnel; R. Jeffery Smith, "Iraq's Drive for a Biological Arsenal," *Washington Post*, November 21, 1997, p. A-1; *Washington Times*, November 24, 1997, p. A-12.

7. United Nations Special Commission, "Report to the Security Council—S/1995/864," 11 October 1995, p. 22; Interviews with UNSCOM personnel; R. Jeffery Smith, "Iraq's Drive for a Biological Arsenal," *Washington Post*, November 21, 1997, p. A-1; *Washington Times*, November 24, 1997, p. A-12.

8. United Nations Special Commission, "Report to the Security Council—S/1995/864," 11 October 1995, p. 22; Interviews with UNSCOM personnel; R. Jeffery Smith, "Iraq's Drive for a Biological Arsenal," *Washington Post*, November 21, 1997, p. A-1; *Washington Times*, November 24, 1997, p. A-12.

9. United Nations Special Commission, "Report to the Security Council—S/1995/864," 11 October 1995, p. 22; Interviews with UNSCOM personnel; R. Jeffery Smith, "Iraq's Drive for a Biological Arsenal," *Washington Post*, November 21, 1997, p. A-1; *Washington Times*, November 24, 1997, p. A-12.

10. United Nations Special Commission, "Report to the Security Council—S/1995/864," 11 October 1995, p. 23; Interviews with UNSCOM personnel; R. Jeffery Smith, "Iraq's Drive for a Biological Arsenal," Washington Post, November 21, 1997, p. A-1; Washington Times, November 24, 1997, p. A-12.

11. United Nations Special Commission, "Report to the Security Council—S/1995/864," 11 October 1995, pp. 25–26; Interviews with UNSCOM personnel; R. Jeffery Smith, "Iraq's Drive for a Biological Arsenal," Washington Post, November 21, 1997, p. A-1; Washington Times, November 24, 1997, p. A-12.

12. United Nations Special Commission, "Report to the Security Council—S/1995/864," 11 October 1995, pp. 23–24; Interviews with UNSCOM personnel; R. Jeffery Smith, "Iraq's Drive for a Biological Arsenal," Washington Post, November 21, 1997, p. A-1; Washington Times, November 24, 1997, p. A-12.

13. United Nations Special Commission, "Report to the Security Council—S/1995/864," 11 October 1995, pp. 24–25.

14. United Nations Special Commission, "Report to the Security Council—S/1995/864," 11 October 1995, pp. 24–25.

15. *Washington Post*, November 21, 1997, p. A-1.

16. Many sources classify mycotoxins as chemical poisons. Unfortunately, mycotoxins have become one of those weapons that are popular with journalists or propagandists seeking to sensationalize a given conflict, and countries are often accused of using mycotoxins in cases where ambiguous symptoms are present. Iran has also been accused of producing and using mycotoxins.

17. Task Force on Terrorism and Unconventional Warfare, *Chemical Weapons in The Third World: 2. Iraq's Expanding Chemical Arsenal*, House Republican Research Committee, US House of Representatives, May 29, 1990, p. 12; *Wiener Zeitung*, June 25, 1989.

18. United Nations Special Commission, "Report to the Security Council—S/1995/864," 11 October 1995, p. 25.

19. United Nations Special Commission, "Report to the Security Council—S/1995/864," 11 October 1995, p. 26; Raymond A. Zilinskas, "Iraq's Biological Weapons," *Journal of the American Medical Association*, Vol. 278, No. 6, August 6, 1997, pp. 418–425.

20. Interview, January, 22, 1998.

21. United Nations Special Commission, "Report to the Security Council—S/1995/864," 11 October 1995, pp. 26–27; Raymond A. Zilinskas, "Iraq's Biological Weapons," *Journal of the American Medical Association*, Vol. 278, No. 6, August 6, 1997, pp. 418–425.

22. United Nations Special Commission, "Report to the Security Council—S/1995/864," 11 October 1995, pp. 26–27; Raymond A. Zilinskas, "Iraq's Biological Weapons," *Journal of the American Medical Association*, Vol. 278, No. 6, August 6, 1997, pp. 418–425.

23. Some reports indicate 3,117 gallons of Botulinum toxin and 2,265 gallons of Anthrax.

24. *Jane's Defense Weekly*, January 3, 1996, p. 19.

25. Eliot A. Cohen, Director, *Gulf War Air Power Survey*, Volume I, Part II, Washington, GPO, 1993, pp. 242–254, and *Volume II, Part II*, p. 326.

26. Interviews and "Intelligence Success and Failures in Operations Desert Shield and

Desert Storm," Subcommittee on Oversight and Investigations, US House of Representatives, 103rd Congress, 1st Session, August, 1993, pp. 37–39.

27. *The Atlanta Constitution,* January 16, 1992, p. 1.

28. Interviews with UN personnel and UN Security Council; UN Security Council, Note by the Secretary-General, S/1995/864, 11 October 1995.

29. *Washington Post,* November 21, 1997, p. A-1.

30. *New York Times,* August 26, 1995, p. 3; *Washington Post,* August 26, 1995, p. A-1.

31. *Policywatch,* No. 175, November 20, 1995; UN Security Council, Note by the Secretary-General, S/1995/864, 11 October 1995.

32. UN Security Council, Note by the Secretary-General, S/1995/864, 11 October 1995.

33. *Sunday Times,* November 9, 1997; Agence France Press, November 8, 1997, 2325.

34. *Jane's Defense Weekly,* November 11, 1995, p. 4.

35. UN Security Council, Note by the Secretary-General, S/1995/864, 11 October 1995, p. 27.

36. Raymond A. Zilinskas, "Iraq's Biological Weapons," *Journal of the American Medical Association,* Vol. 278, No. 6, August 6, 1997, pp. 418–425.

37. *Washington Times,* August 30, 1995, p. A-10.

38. Reuters Ltd., October 11, 1995.

39. United Nations, Note by the Secretary-General, S/1997/301, April 11, 1997, pp. 16–17.

40. Interviews with UN personnel.

41. United Nations Special Commission, "Report to the Security Council—S/1995/864," 11 October 1995, pp. 27–28.

42. *Jane's Defense Weekly,* April 10, 1996, p. 15.

43. United Nations, Note by the Secretary-General, S/1996/848, 11 October 1996, pp. 22–24.

44. United Nations, Note by the Secretary-General, S/1996/848, 11 October 1996, pp. 22–24.

45. United Nations, Note by the Secretary-General, S/1996/848, 11 October 1996, p. 24.

46. United Nations, Note by the Secretary-General, S/1997/301, April 11, 1997, p. 17.

47. Reuters, April 23, 1997, 05:43; United Nations, Note by the Secretary-General, S/1997/301, April 11, 1997, pp. 16–17.

48. United Nations, Note by the Secretary-General, S/1997/301, April 11, 1997, p. 17.

49. Reuters, August 26, 1997, 0717, September 9, 1997; September 10, 1997, 1954.

50. Note by the Secretary-General, "Report of the Secretary-General on the Activities of the Special Commission," S/1997/774, October 6, 1997, paragraphs 69–72, Annex 2.

51. Note by the Secretary-General, "Report of the Secretary-General on the Activities of the Special Commission," S/1997/774, October 6, 1997, paragraphs 74–76, Annex 2.

52. Note by the Secretary-General, "Report of the Secretary-General on the Activities of the Special Commission," S/1997/774, October 6, 1997, paragraphs 79–80, Annex 2.

53. Note by the Secretary-General, "Report of the Secretary-General on the Activities of the Special Commission," S/1997/774, October 6, 1997, paragraphs 81–82.

54. Note by the Secretary-General, "Report of the Secretary-General on the Activities of the Special Commission," S/1997/774, October 6, 1997, paragraph 83.

55. Reuters, December 15, 1997, 2003, 1842.

56. Reuters, January 25, 1998, 14:18.

57. Report by the Executive Committee of the Special Commission, March 27, 1998, as transmitted by the Secretary-General to the Security Council, April 16, 1998, S/1998/332.

58. *Washington Post*, July 6, 1995, p. A-17.

59. Reuters, December 15, 1997, 2003, 1842.

60. Confirmed by interviews with UN and US State Department personnel. Also see UN Security Council, Note by the Secretary-General, S/1995/284, April, 1995.

61. United Nations, Note by the Secretary-General, S/1997/301, April 11, 1997, p. 8.

62. *Washington Post*, August 26, 1995, p. A-1.

63. Associated Press, April 9, 1998, 2117; *New York Times*, April 10, 1998; Reuters, April 9, 1998, 1639.

64. *Washington Times*, January 14, 1998, p. A-6.

65. *Washington Post*, February 12, 1998, p. A-1.

66. *Jane's Pointer*, September, 1996, p. 6.

67. *Christian Science Monitor*, May 21, 1997, p. 3; *Jane's Defense Weekly*, June 25, 1997, p. 6; Brad Roberts *Terrorism with Chemical and Biological Weapons: Calibrating Risks and Responses*, Alexandria, Chemical and Biological Weapons Control Institute, 1997.

68. UN and US experts commenting on the evidence to date. No clear documentation is available to define the scope of Iraqi release authority.

69. Calculated based on estimates from the Office of Technology Assessment, as cited in *Newsweek*, September 4, 1995, p. 34, and figures provided by the Pentagon as cited in *Time*, September 4, 1995, p. 41.

70. *After the Storm: The Changing Military Balance in the Middle East*, Boulder, Westview, 1993; working material on biological weapons prepared for the United Nations, Office of Technology Assessment, *Proliferation of Weapons of Mass Destruction: Assessing the Risks*, United States Congress OTA-ISC-559, Washington, DC, August, 1993; Kenneth R. Timmerman, *Weapons of Mass Destruction: The Cases of Iran, Syria, and Libya*, Simon Wiesenthal Center, Los Angeles, August, 1992; Dr. Robert A. Nagler, *Ballistic Missile Proliferation: An Emerging Threat*; Systems Planning Corporation, Arlington, 1992; and translations of unclassified documents on proliferation by the Russian Foreign Intelligence Bureau.

Chapter 19

Iraq's Past and Future Nuclear Weapons Capabilities

None of Iraq's weapons development efforts have been subject to more scrutiny than its nuclear weapons program. UN Security Council Resolution 687 forbids Iraq to develop or acquire nuclear weapons or the means to produce them, and to possess or separate both highly enriched uranium (HEU) and plutonium. Iraq agreed to this resolution, and the Security Council approved it on April 3, 1991. As a result, both UNSCOM and the International Atomic Energy Agency (IAEA) have been actively involved in the discovery and destruction of Iraq's massive nuclear weapons program ever since.

IRAQ'S EARLY NUCLEAR EFFORTS

Iraq's nuclear program is so large that it is difficult to summarize, but UNSCOM and IAEA reporting indicates that Iraq spent up to $10 billion on its nuclear program before the Gulf War, and simultaneously pursued several different enrichment methods.[1]

The Iraqi government has stated that it decided to build nuclear weapons in 1988, and that it then set a goal of producing its first weapon in the spring of 1991. In fact, Saddam Hussein took the decision in 1972, when he was still Iraq's Vice President—although he effectively dominated the Iraqi government. Dr. Kiddhir Abdul Abas Hamaza, who defected from Iraq in 1994, has stated that he returned to Iraq in 1970 after studying physics at the Massachusetts Institute of Technology and Florida State University. He then became the chairman of the physics department in Iraq's nuclear research center near Baghdad. He was approached in 1971 by envoys from Saddam Hussein to start a secret nuclear weapons program under the cover of civil research, and he prepared a weapons development plan for Saddam Hussein which he submitted in 1972.[2]

According to Hamza, Saddam immediately adopted the plan, although he rejected a proposal to create a massive "nuclear city" on the grounds that it would be too vulnerable. The project began to gather momentum in 1973, and Saddam began to visit the new facilities. In 1974, Saddam secretly named himself the chairman of the Iraq continues to deny to the IAEA. Saddam also instituted a forced recruiting program, making Iraqi scientists married to foreigners divorce their wives and report every contact with foreigners. In January, 1980, Saddam is reported to have imprisoned and beaten Jafar Dheilla Jafar, a top Iraqi physicist, until he agreed to work on the program.[3]

Iraq was able to establish nuclear cooperation agreements with Brazil, the Former Soviet Union, France, India, and other countries, although no nation could then have doubted Iraq's potential interest in acquiring nuclear weapons. It obtained an IBM mainframe computer from the United States, reactor technology from France, and centrifuge technology from France. It came close to buying a specialized foundry and vacuum furnaces to forge uranium and bomb components from two German firms, Leybold and DeGussa. Saddam only seems to have rejected the offer because he felt the details of the sale would leak and might target Iraq's new weapons development facilities at Al Atheer. Saddam did not hesitate, however, in investing hundreds of millions of dollars in other new Iraqi facilities, and created a cover program for the weapons effort called Peotrochemical-3, or PC-3. The ultimate aim of this program was the production of an implosion-type nuclear device. To accomplish this, PC-3 concentrated on two areas. The first was the production of fissile material through uranium enrichment, and the second was the weaponization of an actual nuclear device.[4]

Iraq denied that it was seeking nuclear weapons from the time such development was first suspected in the 1970s until UN inspectors found direct proof in 1991. Long before this admission, however, there was overwhelming evidence that Iraq was obtaining specialized expertise and technology of a kind that could only be explained by a covert nuclear weapons program.[5] Iraq's major nuclear research efforts began in 1959, when it ordered a small research reactor from the former Soviet Union. This five-megawatt light-water reactor was called the IRT-2000. It used highly enriched uranium and went on line in 1968. It was later used to test the production of plutonium from spent reactor fuel, although no confirmed reports exist regarding such tests until 1988.[6]

Iraq began to seek natural uranium reactors from France and Canada in the 1970s, but it encountered growing problems after most exporters tightened their controls when India exploded a nuclear device in 1974. As a result, Iraq's next major acquisition was the purchase of the "Isis" or "Tammuz II" reactor from France in 1976. This was a small 800-kilowatt light water research reactor using highly enriched uranium, and it went on line in 1980. During this period, Iraq also established a significant nuclear research effort and set up a laboratory scale uranium purification plant at Tuwaitha with Italian support. Iraq is known to have tried unsuccessfully to purchase bulk depleted uranium and reactor fuel pins from the United States and Canada.[7]

The Osirak (Tammuz I) Reactor

The key step Iraq took in developing a nuclear weapon during the late 1970s and early 1980s was the purchase of the Osirak (Tammuz I) light water reactor from France in 1976. This reactor was a 40-megawatt materials test reactor which was originally designed to use 158 pounds (78 kilograms) of highly enriched uranium, and it was the first of two research reactors Iraq planned to buy from France. This amount of enriched material would have been sufficient to manufacture up to three nuclear weapons.[8]

Iraq obtained Italian assistance in developing fuel fabrication capability, and in obtaining a plutonium reprocessing technology with a capacity of up to 8 kilograms per year. This equipment included three radiologically shielded "hot cells" which could extract plutonium from uranium irradiated in a reactor, and related equipment suitable for producing plutonium.[9] The "hot cells" were particularly important to a nuclear weapons effort, because the 40-megawatt Osirak reactor was unusually large for a reactor designed for research purposes.

Experts still disagree over the extent to which the Osirak reactor complex was designed for nuclear weapons purposes, but it seems clear that Iraq was interested in nuclear weapons and not in nuclear power. While Iraq claimed that the reactor was purely for research purposes, the IAEA found that after the Gulf War Iraqi scientists conducted a study in late 1979 that estimated that it had a maximum production capacity of 2 kilograms of plutonium a year.[10] The Iraqi efforts to acquire plutonium "hot cells" and reprocessing capability, which began in 1979, are further evidence. So is Iraq's insistence during this period on trying to obtain 158 pounds of highly enriched uranium from France, after France reacted to international pressure by limiting its supply to Iraq to 55 pounds at any one time.[11]

Iraq bought large amounts of natural uranium from Brazil, Portugal, Niger, and Italy in 1980 and 1981 that it could not process into reactor fuel, but could process into uranium that it could then irradiate into plutonium. Plutonium can be produced by exposing uranium to neutrons within a reactor and then chemically separating out the uranium.[12] Iraq placed an order in early 1980 for 25,000 pounds of depleted uranium fuel pins from a German firm called NUKEM. The pins were sized for irradiation in the Osirak reactor and had no other real purpose than to produce about 10 to 12 kilograms of weapons-grade plutonium. By 1990, Iraq had at least 332,000 kilograms of yellow cake, 116,000 kilograms of UO_2, 2,577 kilograms of UCl_4, 0.465 kilograms of UF_6, 1,850 kilograms of ADU, 2,050 kilograms of UO_3, 310 kilograms of UF_4, and 2,255 kilograms of UO_4.[13]

Iraq could count on being able to use the irradiation approach to proliferation because of the limits on international inspection before the Gulf War. While the Osirak reactor was under IAEA inspection, French technicians were working at the site. Iraq seems to have followed roughly the same approach to disguising its nuclear weapons efforts that Sweden had used in the early 1960s. While the fuel cells at the Osirak reactor were subject to inspection, they were only subject to inspection after Iraq declared that material was present. The IAEA had no right to inspect the cells on an ongoing basis or the fabrication of the material being inspected. According to one Israeli source, the reactor also had a covert chamber for irradiating uranium, which allowed it to produce significant amounts of plutonium—enough to produce one to two bombs over a period of two to three years. This allowed Iraq to "comply" with the IAEA, while developing an ability to handle plutonium technology and stockpiling material for weapons purposes.[14]

This mix of factors led Israel to a series of clandestine efforts to halt construction or destroy the reactor. Israeli agents almost certainly planted a bomb that destroyed the reactor's first set of core structures while they were still awaiting shipment to Iraq in Seine sur Mer, France, in April, 1979. Israeli agents also seem to have assassinated Dr. Yahya el-Meshad, an Egyptian physicist working for Iraq, and to have bombed several of the French and Italian companies working on the project.[15] Finally, on June 7, 1981, Israel launched the highly publicized air raid that destroyed the Osirak reactor before it could become operational.

Iraq's Search for Replacements to Osirak

At the time when Israel attacked and destroyed the reactor, Iraq was negotiating to buy a heavy water power reactor from Italy and a sizable reprocessing facility whose purpose was almost certainly plutonium production. This series of deals seem to have halted after it became clear that Israel would take military action to prevent it from going forward.[16]

While France initially agreed to rebuild the Osirak reactor, it failed to do so because of a mix of US and other international pressure, the new strategic problems created by the Iran-Iraq War, and Iraqi payment problems. Similar pressures blocked Iraq's efforts to obtain help from French, Belgian, Finnish, Italian, and Russian companies in siting and constructing its own reactor facility. Russia evidently examined the idea of building a fortified reactor in Iraq's mountains, but the project proved too costly. Other foreign firms warned Iraq that any such effort would probably be detected by foreign intelligence agencies.[17]

These pressures forced Iraq to find other ways to produce its fissionable material. While Iraq continued to give the search for a replacement for Osirak very high priority, it also started a major separate uranium enrichment effort and an effort to develop a capability to process plutonium.

Like Iran, Iraq continued to use peaceful nuclear power as its "cover" in attempting to obtain new nuclear reactors. In 1984, when Iraq was in the midst of the Iran-Iraq War, unable to export its oil, and nearly bankrupt, it announced that it was seeking to provide 10% of its power needs with nuclear power. It stated that it had contracted with the former Soviet Union to build a 440-megawatt plant at a cost of $2 billion. The plant was supposed to be built by the Soviet Atomnergo group, but there was no sign that Iraq would get the Soviet Union to start construction, or that the former Soviet Union would build a new reactor that Iraq could integrate into a weapons development cycle.

In 1985, Iraq started a new 40-megawatt research reactor project called Project 182, which was based on the design of the Canadian NRX reactor. This design used heavy water as a moderator, natural uranium metal fuel, and water cooling. It was capable of producing 8 to 10 kilograms of weapons-grade plutonium a year. The project called for the reactor to be placed in a bomb and missile-resistant containment vessel, and for the use of the equipment that could be salvaged from the Osirak project.

The same project included an associated plutonium separation plant, using equipment based on designs developed by a small facility that Iraq had created at Tuwaitha. Iraq planned to manufacture some key equipment in Iraq, including fuel loading and unloading machines, the containment vessel, and the primary cooling system. Iraq claims that it halted work on this project in 1988 because it required nearly 30–40 tons of heavy water, and that other projects offered a higher chance of success. There is evidence that it continued work on plans to manufacture heavy water until 1991, but Iraq claims that these were to support a much smaller reactor to provide low enriched uranium (LEU) for Iraq's other enrichment projects.[18]

Iraq's Effort to Find Other Methods of Producing Fissile Material

Iraq was more successful in finding other ways of obtaining fissile materials and in getting nuclear weapons technology. It is now clear that Iraqi scientists completed an evaluation of the possibility of using electromagnetic isotope separation (EMIS) as early as late 1981, and examined gas centrifuge technology.

Iraq initially concluded that centrifuge technology was too complicated, although it later began a major program. In contrast, Iraqi scientists concluded that EMIS had well documented technology, that it could make the necessary prototypes, that it could solve the basic scientific and engineering problems, that the required equipment was not on international export control lists, that the key equipment could be made domestically and clandestinely, that it could make and handle suitable feed material, and that the production effort could be divided into separate stages to reduce vulnerability and deal with the breakdown of subunits.

Iraq also concluded that it was possible to pursue the entire program in ways that would be hard to target and detect, and that it could solve some of the inherent inefficiency problems in EMIS by using other methods to obtain low-enriched uranium to feed its EMIS plants. As a result, Iraq decided to go ahead with the development and construction of EMIS production facilities, each of which could produce 15 kilograms a year of 93% enriched HEU. It selected gaseous diffusion as a way of producing LEU to feed its EMIS plants.[19]

Iraqi progress during the early and mid-1980s reached the point where Iraq was able to complete its first separator and actually separate uranium in 1986. It also developed plans to build EMIS equipment in stages of separators, and it tested separators using both natural uranium and multiple sources of feed. Iraq had at least four separators operating at a test facility at Al Tuwaitha in 1987, and it began enrichment activity in early 1988.

The Iraqi effort was further accelerated when Lt. General Hussein Kamel Majid took over detailed direction of the program in 1987. Hussein Kamel seems to have taken the decision to try to pursue five different paths to producing fissile material in parallel. He also pushed for new imports of technology. According to Hamza, Iraq succeeded in importing triggering components from Poland, although these did not prove adequate and Iraq had to reverse-engineer them and produce its own devices. Hussein Kamel also introduced a policy of torturing scientists who failed to perform or who exaggerated their results. This policy seems to continue to this day. According to Hamza, one key reason that he defected was that the body of Adil Fayadh, a leading nuclear physicist, was found in a ditch in his farm, and Hamza was afraid he might be next.[20]

Iraq contracted with a Yugoslav firm to build an EMIS production facility at Al Tarmiya, north of Baghdad, in late 1987. This plant was supposed to be able to enrich enough natural uranium to produce 15 kilograms of weapons grade material a year, or to use LEU (2.5%) to produce as much as 40–50 kilograms a year. The fear that a single plant might not be successful led Iraq to start work on an Iraqi-constructed second plant at Ash Sharqat, about 200 kilometers northwest of Baghdad. After successful pilot production of uranium tetrachloride feedstock at Al Tuwaitha, Iraq set up a plant to produce this feedstock at Al Jesira, near Mosul, in 1990.

The exact schedule for completion of these plants is unclear, but Iraq seems to have rapidly encountered problems and delays in getting the proper level of production output and enrichment. The completion date for Al Tarmiya soon slipped from 1990 to 1992, and then to 1993, if it were forced to use natural uranium. The plant at Ash Sharqat lagged to the point where civil construction was delayed to late 1990, and the equipment of the plant with EMIS equipment was left to the mid-1990s.[21]

Iraq also had problems with its gaseous diffusion program, and the design team was transferred from the Nuclear Research Center at Al Tuwaitha to the Engineering Design Centre near Rashdiya in 1987. Further problems emerged, and the priority for the program was cut in 1988. These problems led Iraq to attempt to buy LEU on the world market, and Iraq decided to emphasize chemical enrichment. It had plans by 1990 to build a chemical enrichment plant that could produce about five tons a year of LEU (4–8%). The details of these plans, however, remain unclear. These problems and various personality struggles and bureaucratic conflicts among Iraqi scientists also seem to have led to the creation of a centrifuge program at the Engineering Design Centre, with the goal of creating as many as 1,000 centrifuges, producing 10 kilograms of weapons-grade material a year.[22]

Reports of Iraqi cooperation with other proliferating nations during this period are uncertain, but it seems likely that such cooperation took place. Iraq cooperated with Brazil in some aspects of missile research during this period, and Brazil then was actively involved in manufacturing centrifuges, and had used many of the same suppliers for its centrifuge development effort as Iraq. Brazil sold Iraq substantial amounts of uranium and had a research cooperation agreement with Iraq that lasted at least to 1989. Argentina sold Iraq uranium and missile technology, and it may have cooperated with Iraq on some aspects of fissile material manufacture.

While Pakistan had closer ties to Iran than Iraq, Iraq signed a nuclear research cooperation agreement with Pakistan and Egypt in 1985. At least some Pakistani scientists associated with Pakistan's centrifuge plant at Kahuta, near Islamabad, seem to have visited Iraq. Iraq was also the leading member of the Arab Atomic Energy Commission, which was established in December, 1988, and which includes Jordan, Kuwait, Lebanon, Libya, Palestine, Saudi Arabia, Syria, and Tunisia.[23]

IRAQ'S NUCLEAR FACILITIES AT THE TIME OF THE GULF WAR

Iraq had at least 16 major sites with facilities involved in nuclear weapons research and production by the time of the Gulf War. It was heavily involved in massive electromagnetic isotope separation (EMIS) and gas centrifuge enrichment production programs, although each of these efforts had a number of major technical problems. It had developed at least limited amounts of radiological weapons. It had also succeeded in enriching a small quantity of uranium, prior to the Gulf War, in the hot cells of its small reactors at Tuwaitha.[24]

The United States failed to properly characterize this Iraqi nuclear effort before and during the Gulf War. It firmly identified only two out of 21 Iraqi nuclear facilities before the war, and it identified two more facilities as suspect. It never fully identified the actual function of any facility, and it identified the site at Al-Athir so late in the war that this became the last target of the F-117.[25]

By the time the Gulf War took place, the United States had expanded its list to eight targets, but it failed to realistically assess battle damage to these targets. The United States was forced to strike them again in the final days of the war, but it never had the opportunity to examine battle damage and to strike again. UN inspectors found after the war that air strikes did major damage to the Baghdad Nuclear Research Center and to Iraq's two known reactors, but it also found that many of the Coalition air strikes were far less effective than was originally estimated.[26]

Some of these problems in the US targeting and strike effort were a result of the sheer scale of the Iraqi effort. US experts estimate that Iraq spent up to $10 billion during the 1980s to acquire EMIS and centrifuge enrichment facilities, to develop other methods of enrichment, and to acquire the technology and equipment to use fissile material in a nuclear weapon. They also estimate that Iraq had at least 7,000 scientists and technicians working on the program.[27] Key Iraqi leaders of the program—such as Dr. Jafer Dhia Jafar, an Iraqi scientist educated at the University of Manchester and Imperial College—have estimated that Iraqi was spending over $1 billion on this effort when the war began.[28] Iraq's program was so large that the UNSCOM later called it "grandiose and over-designed."[29]

Iraq used a wide range of techniques to conceal its facilities. It sometimes built the shell of a large building that looked like a normal commercial facility and then built a different, special purpose building within it (Tuwaitha). It constructed buildings that looked exactly like other buildings that had previously been built for other purposes (Ash Sharqat and Tarmiya). It deliberately downplayed the importance of facilities by not having visible security activity and special fences (Tarmiya). It took measures to severely reduce off-site emissions and effluents (Tuwaitha and Tarmiya), and it moved critical pieces of equipment from known civil or research facilities after they appeared to be dedicated to peaceful purposes, while building extensive underground basements or annexes after facilities were roofed in.[30] While Iraq normally relied on dispersal and secrecy, it also established surface-to-air missile defenses at major facilities like Tuwaitha.[31] These defenses were combined with hardened shelters at locations like Tuwaitha and Al Atheer, and Iraq had at least one underground facility in a mountain near Irbil.[32]

UN inspectors later found that Iraq had at least 21 nuclear facilities, ones, including 16 major ones. Many of these sites, each of which normally had dozens of major buildings, are listed in Table 19.1. It is important to note, however, that most of these facilities were not declared to the IAEA before the war or subject to its inspection, and most only became known after UN inspections following the Gulf War. US and Coalition forces were not able to identify more than a few of these facilities before the war.

The United States had only firmly identified two out of the eight major Iraqi nuclear facilities at the time Iraq invaded Kuwait, and it identified two more as suspect. Even on January 16, 1991, the targeting list in the ATO only included two Iraqi nuclear facilities, one of which was a mine at al-Qaim, some 300 kilometers northwest of Baghdad.[33] This list was finally increased to eight near the end of the war, when the damage assessment of strikes at secondary targets revealed their true character. By this time, however, it was too late for the Coalition to effectively strike at more than three targets.

The United States did not detect the electromagnetic separation (EMIS) effort at Ash Sharqat or the main Iraqi nuclear weapons design complex at al-Atheer. It did not detect the fact that Iraq removed much of its nuclear technology and production equipment while sheltering other components and dispersing its nu-

Table 19.1
Key Iraqi Nuclear Weapons Facilities

- *Abu Ghraib*: Military base and fuel-rod storage.
- *Abu Sukhayr*: Exploratory mine located about 25 kilometers southwest of Najar. Production from September, 1988 to end of 1990, when it was flooded. Uranium in ore ranged from 80 to 800 ppm.
- *Ahashat*: Phosphate and open faced uranium mine. Uranium extraction.
- *Amil*: Liquid nitrogen for EMIS program.
- *Amir*: EMIS component manufacturing: magnet cores, return irons, ion sources, collector parts.
- *Ameen*: EMIS component manufacturing—prototype components.
- *Atheer*: Some 350,000 square feet of lab space that was largely untouched by the war. Nuclear weapons design and testing of high explosives. Hydrodynamic studies. Large cold isostatic press for shaping explosive charges by Asea Brown Boveri. High temperature vacuum induction furnaces by Arthur Pfeiffer Vacuum Technik GmbH. Planned casting and machining of fissile material, machining of uranium plates, and assembly of explosive structure and core of nuclear weapons. Plasma coating molds and mold fabrication. Design of regular implosion type nuclear weapon.[1]
- *Badar*: Centrifuge component manufacturing. Civil contracting for Al Furat project.
- *Daura (SEHEE)*: EMIS component manufacturing—vacuum chamber parts. Civil contracting for Al Furat project.
- *Dijila*: Electronics plant supporting general fabrication activities for the IAEC. No specialized weapons production equipment.
- *Fao*: Contracting for Al Furat project.
- *Falluja*: Military base and equipment storage.
- *Furat (Farat or Pharat)*: Centrifuge research. Two centrifuge manufacturing sites. Maraging centrifuge facility. Had begun with a Beams type and was capable of making the more advanced Zippe type by mid-1987. Iraq initially claimed they were capable of producing up to 200 centrifuges a year. The manufacturing equipment intended for installation indicates that the true figure was 2,000.
- *IRT-5000*: Po-210 production.
- *Jazirah*: Uranium processing; UCl_4 production. EMIS and centrifuge production.
- *Al Hadre*: High explosives research and hydrodynamic studies.
- *Hatteen*: High explosives research; main explosive structure research.
- *Musayyib*: Materials research and high explosive test site. Test range for shaped charges. Power plant. Nuclear weapons laboratories.
- *Mosel*: UCl_4 production.
- *Nafad*: EMIS component storage.
- *Nasser Works*: Centrifuge component manufacturing and machining.
- *Al Qa Qaa*: Development of nonnuclear components and explosives for nuclear weap-

Table 19.1 (continued)

ons. HMX production and casting for weapon, pressing and machining, main explosive structure of weapon, explosive lens building, and lens assembly. Detonator research. Exploding bridge wire detonators. Research facility for Ministry of Industry and Military Industrialization.

- *Qa'im*: Superphosphate fertilizer plant, Uranium extraction plant and yellow cake production. Heavily damaged during the war.
- *Al Radwan*: Centrifuge component manufacturing: magnet cores, return irons, ion sources, collector parts.
- *Al Rashidiya*: Maraging centrifuge facility.
- *Ar Rabiyah*: Manufacturing workshops for producing metal and ceramic components for the IAEC. Its main function was support of the EMIS program. It had high quality, although not specialized, machine tool capabilities. It was badly damaged by a cruise missile attack in early 1993.
- *Saddam Works*: EMIS component manufacturing and centrifuge machining.
- *Salladine*: EMIS component manufacturing—electrical control panels.
- *Ash Shakyli*: Warehouse storing centrifuge components.
- *Ash Sharqat*: About 250 kilometers north of Baghdad. Worked started in 1988. Three groups of facilities. Uranium enrichment for EMIS. An Iraqi duplicate of Tarmiyah, with 600 mm and 1,200 mm Calutrons, was under construction but not yet operational.
- *Suwayrah*: Nuclear equipment.
- *Tarmiyah*: EMIS research. Main production site for uranium enrichment. Eight working 1,200 mm Calutrons. Seventeen 1,200 mm improved Calutrons being installed. Building for 20 600 mm Calutrons under construction. Capacity of 90 600 mm and 1,200 mm Calutrons. This could have produced 15 kilograms of 93% enriched uranium per year, and more of less enriched uranium. (This complex was built by the Yugoslav Federal Directorate of Supply and Procurement and equipped by the Yugoslav firm of EMO electrical Engineering.)[2] Also, computer facility. Largely destroyed during the war.
- *Technical University of Baghdad*: Streak video cameras and related equipment suitable for weaponization work by Hamamatsu.[3]
- *Tikrit*: Storage of yellow cake.
- *Tuwaitha*: A major research and production center. Site of damaged Tammuz 1 and Tammuz 2 reactors, and IRT-5000 reactor (heavily damaged in war). Nuclear physics labs. Main computer facility with IBM-370 main frame and many IBM PS/2s. Uranium research and development. UCl_4 and UF_6 production. EMIS and centrifuge tests, plutonium separation, and chemical separation. Five working Calutrons. Gaseous diffusion research. Po-210 extraction and neutron initiator research and design. UF_4 production. Metal reduction, casting, and machining. Research on implosion nuclear weapon. Firing system research and design.
- *Zaafarniyah*: Al Dijla and Al-Rabee sites fabricated Calutron components.
- *Walid*: Centrifuge factory.

Table 19.1 (continued)

1. United Nations Security Council, *Report on the Eighth IAEA Inspection in Iraq Under Security Council Resolution 687,* 11–18 November 1991, New York, and United Nations, S/23283 (English), p. 14.
2. *US News and World Report,* November 25, 1991, p. 36.
3. United Nations Security Council, *Report on the Eighth IAEA Inspection in Iraq Under Security Council Resolution 687,* 11–18 November 1991, New York, and United Nations, S/23283 (English), p. 14.

clear material. Had Iraq continued to invade Saudi Arabia in early August, 1990, the United States would have been confronted with a major war in which it had firmly identified only one-tenth of its opponent's peacetime nuclear facilities, and could not detect any wartime activity to relocate or protect nuclear production equipment and material during the war.[34]

US air planners also encountered serious problems in estimating the kind of strikes needed to destroy Iraqi nuclear facilities and assess battle damage effects. Many of the estimates used for targeting had nothing to do with intelligence in the normal sense. They were based on contractor modeling of the potential structure and survivability of Iraqi nuclear facilities, often based on tenuous data, at best, for the Defense Nuclear Agency (DNA). Further, the Defense Intelligence Agency (DIA) found that it could not reliably assess battle damage, and had to request restrikes against five facilities that it had assessed as destroyed a few days earlier. This was a key reason why the Coalition failed to effectively destroy the Iraqi facilities that it identified during the war.[35]

This experience raises serious questions about what the United States would have done if Iraq had waited until it had a nuclear weapon before invading Kuwait. The United States might have entered the Gulf War with no meaningful counter-proliferation capability, or lacked the allied support it needed to challenge the Gulf's only nuclear power. It also raises questions about whether the United States can do a decisively better job of identifying and targeting covert facilities once the UNSCOM and IAEA inspection efforts are ended.

IRAQI PROGRESS IN OBTAINING FISSILE MATERIAL AT THE TIME OF THE GULF WAR

After the Gulf War, UN inspectors found that Iraq was actively involved in trying to produce fissile material from a wide range of different techniques and facilities. The least productive of these activities were gaseous diffusion, laser isotope separation, and chemical separation. Iraq had limited success in gaseous diffusion research during 1982–1987, largely in developing small barrier tubes. Its work on small-sized cascades utilizing small compressors never seems to have been successful. It seems to have canceled the program in 1989 when the design team (Group One) at the Engineering Design Centre near Rashdiya was shifted to centrifuge enrichment, and Iraq claims it dismantled all remaining equipment in 1991.[36]

Iraq showed interest in laser isotope separation (LIS) beginning in 1981, and it had a research and development facility at Al Tuwaitha. It studied molecular LIS and atomic vapor LIS. The program made little progress, however, and its priority was sharply reduced in 1987. Export controls and the refusal of key suppliers to aid Iraq seem to have limited it to low-level research.[37]

Iraq also showed interest in chemical and jet nozzle separation. It approached France and Japan for help in chemical separation technology, which relies on catalysts to speed up the exchanges between U-235 and U-238 and offers a relatively cheap and efficient method of low-level enrichment. Iraq examined both Japanese and French techniques for chemical. It abandoned the Japanese ion-exchange technique developed by ASAHI, but engaged CHEMEX, the major French company involved in such efforts, in a long series of negotiations through which it gradually obtained a full knowledge of the technology involved, and of how France had industrialized it.

Iraq obtained equipment like pulsed columns and pumps, distillation units and mixer-settler barriers from European nations like France, Germany, and Sweden, which it installed at Al Tuwaitha. Iraq did declare to CHEMEX that its technology was too costly and that it was abandoning its efforts. Nevertheless, it began a major clandestine program within Iraq.[38] Iraq kept working to develop the French technique and developed plans for the production scale use of solvent extraction and ion exchange with a capacity to produce 4,000 kilograms of LEU (3%), and studies of a hybrid plant to produce 8% LEU. Even so, Iraq seems to have made only limited progress, and it did not have a pilot plant operating at Al Tuwaitha when the Gulf War began.[39]

Iraq and Plutonium Separation

Iraq's EMIS, centrifuge, and plutonium separation programs were far more serious. Iraq started a small plutonium separation program early in the 1970s, but it made little progress until 1979, when in purchased a research-scale radiochemical laboratory from SNIA-Techint of Italy. This facility was located at Tuwaitha and was steadily expanded with help from SNIA-Techint, and it began "cold tests" during 1983–1987.

In 1988, the facilty began to process spent fuel from its Russian-supplied IRT-5000 reactor, which was exempt from IAEA control. This material was evidently separated between 1982 and 1988, after the IAEA exempted five fuel elements for the Soviet IRT-5000 research reactor from inspection, which contained 10% enriched uranium. Such an IAEA exemption is normal for small amounts of material used for research purposes. Iraq succeeded in using this spent fuel separating 920 grams of uranium and 2.26 grams of plutonium.[40]

Iraq later illegally separated another 2.68 grams of plutonium using natural uranium fuel created in Iraq and irradiated in the IRT-5000. The second batch was also separated at Tuwaitha, and Iraq used natural uranium that it had obtained at a facility at Al Qa'im in Northern Iraq. Iraq inserted about 11 kilograms of this processed uranium into its research reactor. It had sent another 8 kilograms to Tuwaitha by the start of the war, but none of this fuel had been processed by the time the UN inspected the facility. Iraq also conducted experiments to separate plutonium 238 from similarly irradiated neptunium 237. There is no evidence to date, however, that Iraq created a large-scale facility or any form of secret reactor to provide irradiated fuel.[41]

Iraq's plutonium enrichment activity is a further demonstration of its intense interest in nuclear weapons, but Iraq's success must be kept in perspective. Iraq never pursued an intensive effort to develop large amounts of plutonium. In fact, if it had used all of the facilities that existed at the time of the Gulf War for 24 hours a day for a year, it would still only have obtained 100 grams of plutonium. It takes approximately 8–10 kilograms of plutonium to make a nuclear weapon, and there is no evidence that Iraq had a secret reactor or large-scale facility for plutonium production. This is, however, a possibility, and some UN inspectors and outside experts feel that Iraq may still have a facility that the UN has not found.[42]

Iraq's EMIS (Calutron) Programs

Iraq's EMIS or Calutron program reached major proportions by the time of the Gulf War, although the very existence of these Iraqi efforts was only discovered after the war was over.[43] The Iraqi effort was so covert that it led a number of experts to speculate that Iraq had taken advantage of deception techniques to hide its activities from US satellites that it obtained from the Soviets after the Israeli attack on Osirak, and from studying US satellite photos of Iran that the United States had supplied to Iraq during the Iran-Iraq War.[44]

Iraq's major EMIS facilities have been listed earlier. Iraq set up various types of electromagnetic isotope separation (EMIS) facilities at Ad Dijjla, Tarmiya, Ar-Rabiyah, and Al-Hamath and in the Zaafarniya section of Baghdad, and major production facilities at Tarmiya and Ash Sharqat.[45] After the Gulf War, UNSCOM found that Iraq had equipped these plants with at least 30 12-foot disks weighing 60 tons.[46]

EMIS technology has advantages for developing countries. It allows a country to make use of lightly enriched diffusion facilities that cannot produce fissile material, but which are cheaper and easier to build than highly enriched diffusion plants. Even without a feed plant, Calutrons offer the advantage of well-documented designs, relatively simple technology, use of equipment that has not been on export control lists, the ability to covertly manufacture key equipment in country, feed material which is comparatively safe to produce and handle, and final enrichment in separate machines where the failure of one component element does not lead to the failure of the entire system.

If Iraq had been able to exploit all of these advantages, its facilities would eventually have had the capacity to produce between 30 and 100 kilograms a year of weapons-grade uranium, or enough for up to four nuclear weapons a year. UNSCOM experts later estimated, however, that the full output of the plant at Al Tarmiya would have been 12–15 kilograms and would not have exceeded 30 kilograms under real-world conditions.[47]

Iraq poured massive resources into its effort, and it once again exploited every weakness it could find in the IAEA and export control regimes, and the greed of Western firms. For example, it imported mass numbers of specialized pole magnets from an Austrian firm without any questions about their end use, and then trucked them through Turkey or shipped them via Hamburg.[48]

Yet once again Iraq's grandiose plans and rushed efforts resulted in major problems. The UN has not fully disclosed what it has discovered about the effectiveness and technical details of the Iraqi EMIS effort, or the names of its foreign suppliers. Some facts, however, are clear. While several Calutrons were built, their potential efficiency and importance has sometimes been exaggerated in the press. UNSCOM stated in June, 1993 that, "The program was facing serious difficulties in start up and implementation due to a lack of technical depth among Iraqi technicians. It would have been several years before it produced enough uranium for military purposes."[49]

The plants Iraq was building at Al Tarmiya and Ash Sharqat were extremely ambitious in scale. The site at Al Tarmiya covered about 800,000 square meters and was supposed to house 90 alpha (R-120 1,200-mm ion radius) separators and 20 beta (R-60 600-mm ion radius) separators. Iraq's initial plans seem to have called for 70 alpha and 20 beta Calutrons to become operational during August, 1989–December, 1992.[50]

UN officials initially speculated that Iraq's EMIS plants might have produced from 12 to 90 kilograms of uranium a year, with an enrichment level of at least 90%. However, the higher production levels in this estimate require all four beams in each machine at both plants to operate at 145 milliamps, and Iraq was experiencing problems in keeping all of the ion sources operating at once and maintaining stable beams. Its separators at Al Tuwaitha operated only 15–20% of the time, and their design currents averaged only 15% of their design requirement, although Iraqi scientists now feel that they had solved most development problems except the ion source. None of the high-enrichment Calutrons were installed or operating.[51]

These estimates of Iraq's production potential also required all machines to operate an average of 55% of the time. In practice, Iraq had only one plant nearing operation. Its maximum production level seems to have been 12–15 kilograms, and a real-world output of 8–9 kilograms seems more likely. Only eight alpha Calutrons were actually installed by the end of 1989. Iraq was just beginning to install another 17 alpha machines when the Coalition attacked in 1990, but it was still having major reliability and efficiency problems. Installation of separators at the duplicate facility at Ash Sharqat was delayed until the full mix of separators was installed at Al Tarmiya. As a result, the facility at Tarmiya was still the advanced development and test stage when the Gulf War ended.[52]

Although the UN eventually traced about 500 tons of natural uranium that moved into the Iraqi processing system, Iraq claims that the separators at Al Tuwaitha produced only 640 grams of enriched uranium between 1997 and the Gulf War. This output had an average enrichment level of 7.2%, and only 0.06 grams had an enrichment level of over 40%. Other reports indicate that 685 grams were produced at Al Tarmiya by 1991, with an average enrichment level of 4%. These figures give Iraq a maximum of 1.3 kilograms of enriched uranium from EMIS production at the time of the cease-fire in the Gulf War, none of which was weapons grade. The chemical processing of this output also could only be done in small batches at Al Tuwaitha and Al Tarmiya because completion of full-scale production facilities at Tarmiya, had fallen behind schedule.[53]

As a result, some experts feel that it is unlikely that Iraq could have had enough operational EMIS machines to produce one nuclear weapon a year before 1994 at the earliest. Others feel that 12–15 kilograms might have been produced using LEU by mid-1992 or mid-1993 using enriched uranium. These calculations, however, do not examine the possible use of EMIS as a way of preparing enrichment material for further enrichment by centrifuges. UNSCOM has noted, however, that Calutrons could be used for high-capacity, low-enrichment operation and the centrifuges for low capacity, high enrichment.[54]

Iraq's Centrifuge Programs

From at least 1987 onward, Iraq actively sought centrifuge technology from the United States, Europe, and the People's Republic of China. Iraq began with "oil" or "Beams" centrifuges. It had some technical success with this effort. Iraq built a Beams centrifuge at Rashdiya by the end of 1987 and slowly made it operational. In 1988, it considered building 10 to 50 machine cascades, and a major 4,000 Beam centrifuge plant near Al Taji. It also proved that it could use anodized aluminum barrier tubes to separate uranium hexaflouride, and might be able to produce suitable compressors.

Iraq, however, ran into problems with the efficiency of the Beam centrifuge and the manufacture of suitable parts. These problems eventually led to the phaseout of the "oil" centrifuge program during 1989–1991, largely because Iraq obtained access to the technology needed to make much more efficient "magnetic" or "Zippe" centrifuge. In early 1988, Iraq reached an agreement with H&H Metalform GmbH that gave it exceptional access to what the German government regarded as highly classified technology. H&H was already helping Iraq develop long-range ballistic missiles, and it had considerable expertise in centrifuges.

Iraq's access to German technology proved to be a critical breakthrough. The United States had much tighter controls. For example, it blocked an attempt to acquire the specialized pumps needed for cascade facilities in February, 1989, and Iraqi attempts to smuggle centrifuge technology from the United States to Iraq in 1988 and 1989 were blocked by US officials. H&H, however, acted as Iraq's master contractor, and Iraq successfully purchased centrifuge technology and equipment from 13 different German companies.[55]

H&H personnel—including Bruno Stemmler, Walter Busse, and others—visited Iraq in August, 1988. During this visit, they gave Iraq secret technical drawings of sub-and supercritical centrifuges machines developed by MAN Technologies AG, of Munich, Germany, plus at least 70 classified technical reports. As a result, Iraq acquired the "plans" for the URENCO G1 centrifuge design dating back to the 1970s, some of the designs for the URENCO G2 and G3 centrifuges, and possibly data on a 1988 design. The German investigation of the actions of H&H, and technicians associated with MAN, indicated that MAN came to play a major role in setting up a nuclear materials research and centrifuge manufacturing plant at Tuwaitha, and in research and development work on centrifuges taking place at the Sa'ad 16 center near Mosul.[56]

In early 1989, another German expert, Karl Heinz Schabb, who owned a firm called ROSCH in Kaufberen, Germany, began to take an active role in the program. He provided another 90 secret technical reports and key components. According to some reports, Schabb also helped the Iraqis build key parts and assemble machines.[57]

Meanwhile, Bruno Stemmler and Walter Busse continued to visit Iraq under the sponsorship of H&H, and played a major role in coordinating its overall procurement effort. Furthermore, Iraq began to secretly train personnel at a German firm called Interatom, a wholly owned subsidiary of Siemens, and it was able to inspect secret centrifuge facilities and take measurements it could use to reverse engineer them. Interatom only canceled a further training program in 1990 because of reports that German intelligence had become suspicious. According to one German intelligence source, much of this activity was detected by the BND no later than 1989, and it was reported to the German Foreign Office but never received a full investigation.[58]

As early as 1988, Iraq decided to buy enough parts from Europe for the manufacture of key components and for some 50 centrifuge machines to be located at a facility near Al Furat, some 30 kilometers south of Baghdad. Iraqi planners were also confident enough to consider a goal of building facilities with 1,000 operational centrifuges by 1994, and to examine a far more ambitious long-term goal of creating facilities with up to 10,000 operating centrifuges.[59]

Iraq set up a massive procurement effort, much of it coordinated by companies and fronts headed by Iraqi intelligence officers. One such example is the Technology Development Corporation, which was headed by Safa Al-Haboudi. Iraq acquired the specialized drill presses and rolling machines, or lathes, for manufacturing enrichment centrifuges during 1987–1988. It obtained specialized computer numerically controlled machines to make machine casings and aluminum forgings from Nue Magdeburger Werkzeumachinen GmbH in Germany, vacuum induction furnaces from Arthur Pfeiffer Vakuum Tecknik GmbH, preformed scoops from Team GmbH, oxidation furnaces from Degussa SA, and electron-beam welders from Leybold Heraeus. Some components were shipped directly and some through dummy firms as far away as Pakistan. Team GmbH shipped the scoops for centrifuges to Pakistan with customs documents, declaring that they were bodies for ballpoint pens.[60]

In 1989, Iraq acquired at least 100 tons of maraging steel-350 from Europe, a high nickel content steel whose primary use is in uranium centrifuges, although not enough was found to provide for a major centrifuge manufacturing effort, and some experts feel that Iraq's rotors were still of low grade at the time of the UN inspection. Iraq acquired machinery to manufacture end caps and flow-forming machines to make the thin and precisely machined rotors for centrifuges out of maraging-steel tubes from firms like Siemens AG and H&H Metalform in Germany. It acquired 240,000 ferrite magnet spacers from Rhein-Bayern GmbH in Germany, 300 tons of special aluminum alloy for vacuum housings, and 84 tons of special aluminum alloy for molecular pumps.[61]

Iraq obtained five high-frequency inverters suitable for centrifuge cascades from Acomel SA of Neuchatel in Switzerland, and centrifuge balancing machines from Reutlinger und Sohne KG. Ring magnets came from Endshire Export Marketing in Britain, which were ordered by a German firm called Inwako GmbH, a firm directed by an arms dealer named Simon Heiner. Much of the necessary financing for this, and other Iraqi efforts, was handled by the Bank of Credit and Commerce, and then by the Banco Nationale da Lavore, a branch of an Italian bank which was based in Atlanta, Georgia, in the United States.[62]

Iraq obtained the samarium cobalt magnets used to hold the centrifuge in place during high speed rotation. It acquired the specialized vacuum pumps used to circulate uranium hexafluoride gas through gas centrifuges.[63] It obtained 700 bellows valves from Balzer AG and VAT Ag in Switzerland and Nupro in the United States.

Iraq set up a hydrogen fluoride plant at Al-Qa'im, in a facility plant used for phosphate production. Hydrogen fluoride is needed to produce uranium fluoride gas. These orders seem to have attracted remarkably little attention, although Swiss and German customs officers did halt shipments of special numerically controlled machines for the manufacture of baffles and endcaps for the centrifuges.[64]

Iraq eventually made enough progress to set up one centrifuge facility at Al Furat, and another at Al-Rashidiya.[65] By March, 1990, Iraq had enough components for its first prototype centrifuge and was examining both carbon-fibre and maraging steel rotors. By the end of 1990, one machine had reached a test output that would have produced up to 1.9 SWUs a year and which might eventually reach 2.7 SWUs. The UN later found that the capacity of Iraq's plant at Al Furat was being expanded to house 200 centrifuges, and that the facility escaped the Coalition bombing. UN inspectors also found that Iraq had contracted with British and German firms to make two clean-room equipped buildings for the assembly of centrifuges and had given a contract to Interatom in late 1989 to construct a building holding a 100-machine cascade.[66]

At the same time, delays in construction at Al Furat led Iraq to plan a new 120-centrifuge building at Rashdiya called Building 21. This location of a duplicate centrifuge facility at Rashdiya would have improved Iraq's ability to use its technical manpower at Rashdiya more efficiently. The value of centralization also led Iraq to decide to locate its uranium hexaflouride production at Rashdiya, rather than at Al Taji.[67]

Iraq continued to try to import new equipment even after it invaded Kuwait. For example, Iraq tried to buy over $300,000 worth of equipment from the Swiss firm, CETEC, AG, in Sax during September, 1990. The purchase would have included 300 valves for high-speed centrifuges and items for constructing a cascade where several hundred centrifuges operate in tandem. Iraq used a cover firm in Singapore and a delivery address in Jordan.[68]

It is unclear what output Iraq expected at the time Desert Storm began, and what its schedule was for moving towards larger facilities. According to some UNSCOM sources, Iraq planned to have a 100-machine cascade in operation by 1993 and a 500-machine cascade in operation by 1996. If all of these plans had succeeded, Iraq might have had 2,000 machines on line by the late 1990s. Other plans called for the ability to produce up to 1,000 centrifuge machines a year by 1992.

Work by David Albright and others indicates that Iraq might have had 500 operational machines by 1992, 1,000 during 1993–1995, 2,000 by 1996, 3,000 by 1997, and 4,000 after 1998. Depending on efficiency and reliability, this would have produced a separative output of 340–675 SWUs by 1992, 1,000–2,000 SWUs by 1993, and a slow increase to outputs of 4,000–28,000 SWUs in the late 1990s. To put this output in perspective, a nuclear weapon requires about 15 kilograms of weapons-grade uranium. Under the conditions Iraq was likely to face in the mid-1990s, a line or cascade of 2,000 subcritical centrifuges could probably have produced enough SWUs to provide enough fissile material for one bomb a year. A steadily more efficient 4,000 centrifuge production line eventually might have produced 5–11 weapons' worth of material per year.[69]

The centrifuge, however, is a difficult path to enrichment.[70] UNSCOM found serious problems in the quality of Iraq's centrifuge technology and production equipment, and stated that,

> ... Procurement of tons of specialty metals and components, enough to build thousands of machines, was discovered.... Two centrifuge prototypes were tested with some success in test bed experiments.... The Iraqi program was in a very early stage using clandestinely obtained European designs and illicitly obtained materials to build a few research machines.[71]

To put the Iraqi effort in perspective, Pakistan seems to have taken nine years to build a centrifuge enrichment facility, and it still only seems to have about

1,000 out of 14,000 centrifuges running at its plant at any one time. Brazil took 10 years to get a small plant running at Aramar, with only 50–75 centrifuges, although it was well on its way to operating a full-scale 2,000–3,000 centrifuge plant by 1990.[72]

At the same time, there is a wild card in such calculations that indicates that Iraq might actually have been much more successful. Iraq has denied that it made major progress in supercritical centrifuge designs. Unlike other countries, however, Iraq's access to the G-2 design and machines might have allowed it to use such technology. The doors and roof height of the building at Rashdiya seem suited to the larger, 3-meter size supercritical centrifuges, and some of Iraq's orders from France also seem best suited to providing parts for supercritical machines. This issue is important to Iraq's future breakout capability if it can rebuild its nuclear program, because supercritical machines have much more output than subcritical designs: 20–30 SWUs per year versus 2.7 for a smaller, subcritical machine.[73]

IRAQ'S PROGRESS IN NUCLEAR WEAPONS DESIGN AND ASSEMBLY

As these enrichment efforts moved forward, Iraq steadily expanded its nuclear weapons design facility at Al Atheer.[74] Al Atheer was involved in research relating to the production of plutonium, Polonium-210, natural uranium metal, enriched uranium metal, and yellow cerium sulfide.[75] It worked on detonation and neutronic tests, nuclear initiation, and used flash x-rays to see what happened during nuclear weapons detonation tests. It also worked on firing systems, control, and guidance. Projects included explosive lens testing and analysis, natural uranium reflector design, Polonium-210/Beryllium neutron initiators, hardened iron tampers, synchronization and timing systems, pulse power equipment, charging power equipment, junction switches, capacitors, and related measurements.[76]

The UN found some 40,000 pages of documents relating to the Iraqi nuclear weapons design effort, and sophisticated one-and two-dimensional computer codes tailored to nuclear weapons design.[77] Work by the UN inspection teams found that Iraq had concluded that gun-type devices need more material, although they were simpler and had fewer calculation requirements. Iraq concentrated on an intermediary implosion type device, and it was seeking a yield of 20 kilotons—similar to the nominal yield of the weapon dropped on Nagasaki. Iraq had performed 20 detonation experiments relating to such designs by May 31, 1990—the last date referred to in UN-held Iraqi reports.[78] It is important to note that no records have yet been discovered for the period after May, 1990, and that no record exists of design activity using plutonium weapons, although Iraq had plutonium.

At the time the Gulf War began, US experts estimate that Iraq had purchased components for the high melting point explosive (HMX) and rapid detonation explosive (RDX) needed to compress fissile material into a critical mass.[79] The Iraqis had ample supplies of Baratol and HDX high explosives from firms like Carlos Cardoen of Chile, and understood the use of aluminum "flying plates" to increase the pressure wave.

Iraq had obtained x-ray crystal measurement, mass spectrometers, and Beryllium. It bought $96 million worth of computers from the United States between 1984 and 1990, about $26 million of which went to Iraqi military facilities, and large amounts of optical fiber.[80] Further, the IAEA discovered that Iraq was producing, or had obtained, up to 220 pounds of Lithium-6 a year. Lithium-6 can be used both in thermonuclear weapons and to enhance the yield of fission weapons. The UN concluded from Iraqi records that Iraq might have been using Lithium to work on a boosted weapon.[81]

Iraq obtained isostatic presses from Asea Brown Boveri in Switzerland that it could use to shape explosive charges, and high-speed streak cameras from Hamamatsu Photonics in Japan that it could use to photograph the simulated triggering and explosion of a nuclear device. The Iraqis were experimenting with single, high-explosive lenses to test their ability to produce a large enough planar shock wave to set off the critical mass, although there is some question as to whether they could have properly shaped the shock front around such a mass.[82]

Rushing Toward Manufacturing a Weapon

Lt. General Hussein Kamel ordered the development of a program to rush the production of 1–2 weapons after Iraq invaded Kuwait in August, 1990.[83] This program called for the manufacture of the first device by the end of February, 1991, using HEU cannibalized from Iraq's two reactors. The Tammuz-2 had one fresh element of 417 grams, with 93% initial enrichment and 38 elements weighing 11,874 grams, with slight irradiation and 93% enrichment. The IRT-4,000 had 68 fresh elements weighing 13,689 grams, with 68% enrichment, 68 highly irradiated elements weighing 13,490 grams, with 68% enrichment, and 69 highly irradiated elements weighing 13,689 grams, with 10% enrichment.[84]

This inventory of material may seem impressive, but it needs to be kept in perspective. Iraq only had a total of 11.3 kilograms (27.5 pounds) of French-supplied 93% enriched uranium—which was left over from the Tammuz-1 reactor destroyed by Israel—and 22.3 kilograms of Russian-supplied uranium, with levels of enrichment varying from 36% to 80% for its Russian-supplied IRT-5,000 research reactor.[85] Only the French-supplied material could be easily processed for use in a bomb. Using this limited amount of material to build even a single weapon also required the use of very complex implosion technology, since such material cannot be used in the simpler weapons designs made possible by using plutonium or mixes of uranium and plutonium. Iraq would also have had no surplus material to test its weapon design.[86]

Iraq also faced severe problems in processing enough material. It had three projects it could use for such an effort. Project 601 was a solvent extraction unit at Al Tuwiatha using Swedish-made supplier settlers. Conversion of another facility to larger scale production was rushed forward, and the building seems to have been ready on January 17, 1991, when the Coalition bombing campaign began. It was only capable of processing a maximum of one fuel element a day, however, and it would have taken six months to process the freshest elements taken from Iraq's reactors. Project 602 was housed at buildings 64 and 73A at Al Tuwaitha, and it was designed to take the uranyl nitrate solution made by Project 601, convert it into small 250 gram pellets of uranium metal, and then shape the metal into bomb components. It too, however, involved a slow, small-scale process, one that would have lost a considerable amount of fissile material.

Project 521C was a centrifuge project at Rashdiya designed to take Russian-supplied material and enrich it up to 93% fissile material. Iraq had so few operational centrifuges, however, that it could not move forward until April, 1991 at the earliest, and probably until July, 1991. The centrifuge designs to be used in this project also were only achieving 56–80% enrichment in December, 1990, and Iraq only had the carbon rotors for 20 of the 50 centrifuges required. A key European supplied carbon fibre winding machine had also been held up in Jordan. Furthermore, the output from the centrifuge facility required further enrichment by the EMIS facilities at Tuwaitha and Tarmiya. These latter facilities were also experiencing major problems and probably could not have been operational until January, 1992 and possibly a year later.

In short, it is unclear whether Iraq could have developed enough fissile material for even one nuclear device before later 1991, and it might have taken until 1992 or even 1993. Iraq also had very serious problems getting enough fissile material to manufacture additional weapons.

Iraq's Nuclear Weapons Design

The exact status of Iraq's weapons design efforts at the time the Gulf War began is still a matter of some debate.[87] The report of IAEA Director Hans Blix to the UN Security Council on the results of the sixth IAEA inspection of Iraq indicates that Iraq had made substantial progress:[88]

The key result of the sixth inspection is the uncovering of documents that show conclusively that Iraq was very well advanced in a program to develop an implosion-type nuclear weapon and that links existed to a surface-to-surface missile project. Indeed, so advanced has this program been deemed to be that the time needed to reach bomb-making capacity seems to have been determined by the time necessary for the enrichment facilities, rather than the weapons design activities.

... The sixth report also uncovered evidence of broad-based Iraqi international procurement efforts in violation of laws of states from which the export originated. However, much, if not most of the procurement of which evidence will be available, will be found to pertain to equipment and material not subject to export controls elsewhere.[89]

The evidence that the IAEA has found relating to Iraq's nuclear weapons designed still has serious gaps. After the 1995 defection of Lt. Gen. Hussein Kamel, Iraq turned over technical drawings on the use of precision-shaped charges known as "explosive lenses." These consist of spherical-shaped assemblies made of interlocking hexagonal blocks of explosives that are designed to detonate inward and crush enriched uranium to a critically dense mass.[90]

The IAEA could not assess Iraq's final progress in completing such weapons designs, however because, "the chart clearly illustrates several drawings are missing." It also reported major gaps in Iraq's disclosures. Iraq at first denied it had built molds for manufacture of explosive lenses. It then admitted it had such molds, but said that it "can't find" the molds. Iraq initially denied ever casting an explosive lens, and then admitted that Iraqi scientists "had cast one 120mm cylindrical charge and it was tested for 'velocity and pressure.'"[91] This left the IAEA without the data needed to know either the level of sophistication Iraq reached in weapons design or how far it had gotten in manufacturing actual weapons components.

US experts feel that one of these nuclear weapons designs could have produced a weapon weighing about 1,000 kilograms (one metric ton).[92] This mass, and the basic weapons design, was consistent with deployment in the warhead of a Scud missile—although the design of the warhead of the operational Al-Hussein missile was 70–80 centimeters in diameter, and the Iraqi weapon would have required a warhead of 100–120 centimeters in diameter. The developmental Al-Abid could have carried a one-ton warhead with a diameter of 125 centimeters and a distance of up to 1,200 kilometers, and probably would have been operational by 1993.[93]

The basic design was similar in some ways to the US "Trinity" weapon that the United States set off in New Mexico on July 16, 1945. It consisted of a "soccer ball"-shaped set of explosive lenses surrounding a pit of fissile material enclosed in a reflector—made out of depleted uranium or Beryllium. The pit was a solid sphere of uranium, with sufficient highly enriched uranium to approach one critical mass. Using such a large mass of uranium greatly increases the probability that a nuclear device will produce a significant yield, even if the high explosive is relatively unsophisticated and reduces the amount of explosive needed to compress the enriched material to supercriticality.

At the same time, Iraqi experts calculated that minor shifts in design could produce a yield as low as one kiloton, and lacked predetermined values for several critical calculations. As a result, they were using one-dimensional integrated codes for much of their design work. Iraq had not finalized its designs for high explosive lenses or neutron initiators, or its plans for converting HEU into the components that could be compressed into a fissile sphere. Completing these aspects of weapons design and manufacture could have taken Iraq anywhere from mid-1991 to as late as 1993.

The UN did find that Iraq seemed to have carried out enough computation to support weaponization studies, hydrodynamic calculations, exploding wire studies, neutron initiator studies, energy source studies, Neptunium and U-233 experiments, and Lithium-6 experiments. The bulk of this calculation work seems to have been done at Tuwaitha, using an IBM 370 mainframe and smaller IBM PS/2 computers, although the hydrostatic calculations were performed on an NEC mainframe computer.[94]

The UN also found that Iraq planned to use a hardened iron tamper and a Polonium-210 metal/Beryllium neutron initiator. The neutron initiator is the device needed to supply a burst of high-energy neutrons at the correct instant necessary to start the chain reaction and keep it from damping out. Iraq obtained its Polonium-210 from Bismuth, and it completed 20 tests of a Polonium-Beryllium neutron initiator.[95] Iraq had designed and successfully tested its own neutron initiator using explosive lenses and dummy core material just before the Gulf War began. It had also developed and tested high energy pulse junction switches, which can act as a somewhat inferior substitute for krytrons.[96]

The krytrons would have been superior, which helps explain Iraq's effort to smuggle high-speed, high-voltage capacitors from firms like CSI Technologies in the United States in March, 1990.[97] It is not absolutely certain that Iraq wanted the capacitors for nuclear weapons. They have a number of other potential military applications, such as triggering the high-explosive charges in a gas cannon, and the capacitors are co-axial, high-voltage, low-inductance devices that have exceptional resistance to humidity, vibration, and shock. Nevertheless, the krytrons involved were similar to the devices used in US nuclear weapons, and they are perfectly suited to deliver the instant burst of electricity, or triggering charge, necessary to detonate all of the high-explosive hemispheres surrounding nuclear material in order to ensure that it is compressed into critical mass with optimum efficiency.[98]

Without access to such technology, Iraq faced problems in developing effective bridge wire detonators and adequate capacitors. It also faced problems in miniaturizing its nuclear devices, mating them to missile warheads, making effective use of its limited fissile material, and enhancing the yields it could obtain. It risked producing weapons sensitive to shock and accidents. Nuclear weapons are susceptible to accidental triggering and partial detonation from causes ranging from static electricity to misuse of safety interlocks. This might have done devastating damage, and there are some indications that the bomb Iraq designed ''crammed'' so much high explosive into a narrow area that it was highly sensitive to shock and accidental detonation.[99]

Improvising Strategy and Tactics

Iraq faced strategic and tactical problems as well. As long as it was limited to a single weapon, it would not have been able to demonstrate that it had a capability to preserve any significant capability to launch or retaliate. Its nuclear strategy would have had to rely on an unstable mix of deterrent threats and intangibles. Any success in rushing a device forward to completion and actually exploding it might have deterred the United States from launching Desert Storm. On the other hand, possession of a single device might also have confronted Iraq with a "use or lose" option, where anything more than threats that would have triggered a devastating US response.

As has been touched upon earlier, Iraq faced the tactical and technical challenges of mating a nuclear weapon to a delivery system. It had to develop the technology necessary to carry bombs on airplanes in ways that ensured safe and proper release, to develop accurate delivery methods, and to find ways to fuse the bombs to provide reliable control over the height of burst.[100] It needed to develop missiles that were so reliable that there was almost a zero chance of the loss of one of Iraq's limited number of warheads. It needed to improve its warhead design. Iraq's warhead technology was limited and unreliable at the time of the Gulf War, and it presented a risk of missile system failure, reduced accuracy, and catastrophic warhead failure.

Finally, Iraq faced the problem of nuclear weapons security. The seizure of a nuclear weapon could give any political faction a dominant role in a coup attempt or struggle for power. In the case of a revolution, or ideological struggle, it could easily threaten the existence of the regime or lead to the use of a weapon that could trigger a major war. However, creating effective security systems and devices is not easy. Security devices that are internal within the weapon are probably the only way of ensuring a reasonable degree of central government control, but effective designs must be built into every aspect of the weapons design and can interfere with weapons function. Less stringent protection systems can be bypassed in relatively short periods of time, or by disassembling one weapon to learn how to bypass the security systems on the others.

Nevertheless, Iraq might not have found safety or predictability of yield to be critical. Even a partial success, or "fizzle," that only produced a 5 to 6 kiloton yield is still an extremely effective weapon. An outright failure to explode, however, could have cost Iraq roughly $100 to $200 million per weapon until it developed a major fissile material production capability, and any loss would have represented a significant portion of Iraq's total stockpile.

Iraq did attempt to build other types of radioactive weapons. In late 1995, UNSCOM and the IAEA discovered Iraqi efforts aimed at developing a radiological weapon capable of scattering lethal radioactive debris without the necessity of a nuclear explosion, and found that Iraq produced the casings for 80 such weapons. The weapons used irradiated zirconium oxide and were designed to produce an "area denial" weapon for the Iran-Iraq War. Three prototype bombs were detonated at test sites. One was a ground-level static test, and two others were dropped from aircraft.

Iraq claims the irradiated material did not disperse widely enough from the crater, and that these tests proved a failure, but it has no detailed records to prove this or to describe the scale of its program.[101] While UN resolutions do not specifically refer to radiological weapons, Rolf Ekeus, the chief UN weapons inspector, has said that the newly discovered research would be covered by UN Resolution 707, which refers to all Iraqi nuclear programs.

One thing is clear. Iraq would have developed some type of nuclear weapon within several years if had not been for the Coalition bombing and the post-war UNSCOM and IAEA effort. Furthermore, UNSCOM and the IAEA proved more effective in destroying Iraq's nuclear program than Coalition bombers.

IRAQI NUCLEAR PROGRAMS AND THE WAR OF SANCTIONS

Much of Iraq's nuclear equipment was too big to conceal or disperse, and the UN effort has been successful in destroying Iraq's remaining large nuclear facilities and in developing a continuing monitoring effort.[102] By the time the crisis that led to Desert Fox began, UNSCOM and the IAEA were monitoring 150 different sites to prevent a revival of Iraq's chemical and nuclear program. The monitoring effort consisted of 177 remote control cameras and sensors, or "sniffers," linked by microwave signals to a 94 meter tower above the UN base in Baghdad. The UN also used information provided by satellites, U-2Rs of the USAF 9th Reconnaissance Wing, and three helicopters armed with 600-mm cameras, ground penetrating radar, chemical detection systems, and radiation detection systems.[103]

Eliminating Major Facilities for the Production of Fissile Materials

In 1995, Ambassador Ekeus declared that Iraq had "no nuclear program in the sense that there is no centrifuge operating, that there is [not] any production of fissile materials."[104] At the same time, the United States deemed them "inadequate" and urged that UNSCOM's surveillance capability be "upgraded and adjusted."

While admitting the need for minor adjustments, UNSCOM disputed any suggestions of inadequacy relating to its monitoring activities.[105] Nevertheless, UNSCOM and the IAEA continued to investigate the status of Iraq's centrifuge and gaseous separation programs, and UNSCOM stated in April, 1997 that,

patterns of behavior in this area appear to have mirrored Iraq's known concealment activities in other areas. In March, 1997, IAEA excavated three declared equipment burial sites south of Lake Tharthar and unearthed hundreds of items relating to Engineering Design Center operations. Although many of these items are consistent with Iraq's declaration, a previously undeclared and highly expensive cache of unused specialized, corrosion resistant valves was found.[106]

In mid-October, 1997, Hans Blix, then head of the IAEA warhead, said that he had evidence that Iraq had not reported all outside assistance for its nuclear weapons program. Blix said the evidence, indicates there are still a number of questions which we ask ourselves, including the question of possible further external assistance to their nuclear program.... I have also cautioned [the UN Security Council] that beyond questions which arise from our study of the coherent nuclear program in Iraq, from interrogations in Iraq, from talking to suppliers, etc., there are questions that are not prompting answers. There could still be components which we cannot see that they are missing, but which could have been there. There could have been some program or some activity outside of what we have termed the coherent technical pictures.... There will, in the case of Iraq as in the case of any other inspection, always remain an element of uncertainty.[107]

The Nuclear Outcome of the War of Sanctions

There is no way to understand precisely what the IAEA and UNSCOM did or did not accomplish. The IAEA report seemed positive enough, however, for several key members of the Security Council (China, Russia, and France) to begin to put increasing pressure on the IAEA to end sanctions. On January 22, 1998, China and Russia made a strong bid to close the nuclear weapons file on Iraq, and claimed that the IAEA had come up with no new information. France generally supported their position. Ambassador Alain Dejammet said remaining questions on nuclear weapons could be dealt with in the framework of the United Nations' ongoing monitoring system in Iraq rather than through direct inspections.

US Ambassador Bill Richardson replied that an IAEA briefing to the Security Council continued to show "significant gaps, patterns of concealing, and insufficient information." However, Yuri Fedotov, Russia's deputy ambassador to the UN, told reporters that closing the nuclear file did not mean that economic sanctions—which are tied to a scrapping of all weapons of mass destruction—would be eased or lifted. He said that other weapons had to be accounted for first, and that the Security Council should acknowledge that progress had been made and should give a "political and psychological signal to Iraq.... It would show a light at the end of the tunnel—a quite shaky light, but still a light."

China's Ambassador, Qin Huason, said the briefing by the IAEA showed that Iraq had responded to the IAEA's queries raised. "In other words, the IAEA has no evidence to contradict Iraq's response," he said. "Therefore we believe the remaining issues in the nuclear field have been basically solved. It is time to close the nuclear file."

The IAEA report had said that the agency had no information contradicting Iraq's statement that it had never identified nuclear weapon design options beyond preliminary concepts described in a July, 1990 Iraqi document. It also warned, however, that "the IAEA Ongoing Monitoring and Verification plan is predicated on the assumption that Iraq retains the technical capability to exploit, for nuclear weapons purposes, any relevant material to which it might gain access." The IAEA also stated that it was focusing most of its resources on implementing and strengthening its monitoring plan, but would continue to exercise its right to investigate any aspect of Iraq's clandestine nuclear program, particularly through the follow-up of any new information it acquired.[108]

An IAEA panel of experts produced more favorable results in a report to the UN on April 9, 1998. Experts from the IAEA reported that Iraq had met its obligation to the UN to provide information about its secretive nuclear program. In their semi-annual report on Iraq's nuclear weapons capabilities, IAEA experts said they had found no new evidence of nuclear weapons during 211 inspections over the past six months. The report did note, however, that before that time Baghdad had tried to obtain material for nuclear weapons from a foreigner and failed to turn over documents to support its claim that it had abandoned its hidden nuclear program.

On April 12, 1998, the IAEA issued a statement based on these findings that indicated that Iraq had complied with all requirements to declare and destroy its nuclear weapons capability, "The IAEA's ongoing monitoring and verification activities carried out since October, 1997 have not revealed indications of the existence in Iraq of prohibited equipment, material or of the conduct of prohibited activities. . . . Iraq has satisfactorily completed its undertaking to produce a consolidated version of its 'Full, Final, and Complete Declaration' of its clandestine nuclear program."

The agency also said that Iraq had produced a document summarizing its secret nuclear program. "The summary is regarded by the IAEA to be consistent with the technically coherent picture of Iraq's clandestine nuclear program." However, the IAEA also reported that it would continue to monitor and test air samples, focusing particularly on isotopes used for medical purposes.

These IAEA findings led to Russian and French efforts to get the UN to certify that Iraq had complied with the terms of the cease-fire as they applied to nuclear weapons—partly in an effort to persuade Iraq that if it complied with the rest of the terms of the cease-fire, it would see an end to sanctions. The IAEA, however, did not feel the file should be closed. It only regarded its progress to date as a reason to shift its focus to creating a new regime to ensure that Iraq could not restart its efforts or expand any convert programs that the IAEA had not detected. A clear split began to develop between those who felt that the UN effort should end or be sharply reduced in scope, and those who saw a need to concentrate on the threat of new Iraqi activities.

It is important to note that Mohammed El Baradei, the Director General of the IAEA, made the IAEA's qualifications about Iraq quite clear in an editorial in the *Washington Post* on June 1, 1998. El Baradei stated quite clearly that the IAEA was in no position to state that it had found all of Iraq's nuclear weapons efforts and technology:

News stories have been circulating that the IAEA is about to issue Iraq a clean bill of health and to close the nuclear file. Nothing could be further from the truth. . . . Does

Iraq still possess nuclear weapons or weapon-usable material? Does Iraq retain the practical capability—i.e., the scientific and engineering hardware to produce dangerous amounts of weapon-usable fissile material? . . . My agency's answer is that there are "no indications" . . . but it must be understood that "no indications" is not the same as "no existence." . . . no matter how comprehensive the inspection, any country-wide verification process, in Iraq or anywhere else, has a degree of uncertainty.

Because we need continuing reaffirmation that we have in fact neutralized the past program . . . we have introduced . . . a comprehensive and vigorous monitoring regime that . . . has the twin objectives of checking that Iraq's known technical and industrial assets are not used for prohibited purposes, and, perhaps more important, searching country-wide for indications of any prohibited activities. Monitoring inspections are intrusive and involve access to any and all facilities, including industrial sites, scientific establishments and universities, and the use of sensitive environmental sampling and analysis techniques anywhere in Iraq.

The monitoring regime . . . is predicated on the assumption that Iraq has the technical ability to design and construct a nuclear weapon and takes into account the large intellectual resource in Iraq in the corps of scientists and engineers who worked in Iraq's clandestine nuclear program. The agency is cognizant of the technical challenge to the monitoring regime that would result if Iraq were to directly acquire weapon-usable material from abroad. . . . Progress in neutralizing the clandestine program does not mean an end to inspection . . . a future determination by the Security Council that Iraq has satisfied the requirements for lifting the oil embargo would not bring the regime to an end. The monitoring and verification regime would continue unabated.[109]

This statement is unambiguous, and it's clear warning both of the risks Iraq poses and of the limits of any arms control effort and of "nuclear free" and "weapons of mass destruction free" zones. El Baradei's statement also a warning of the possible consequences of Iraq's efforts to limit the IAEA monitoring and inspections since a major IAEA inspection visit in early July, 1998. The IAEA conducted over 211 inspections of some 93 facilities, most in the form of surprise inspections, between October, 1997 and the time Mohammed El Baradei wrote his editorial. If this level of effort cannot provide an assurance that Iraq is not working on a nuclear weapon program, it is all too clear what an ineffective or no inspection program will accomplish.[110]

The IAEA warned in its October, 1998 report to the Security Council that every point El Baradei's statement remained valid if the Security Council decided to shift IAEA activity from the inspection phase to the monitoring phase. Further, UNSCOM provided an additional warning about the difficulties in controlling Iraq's efforts in its October 6, 1998 report to the Security Council on efforts to control Iraq's imports.

The export/import monitoring group consists of five inspectors from five States. The principal aim of such inspections is to verify the arrival of imports of dual-capable items, notifiable under the export/import monitoring mechanism. A separate inspection was conducted of Iraq's customs and general import structure, with the aim of identifying elements of the overall export/import monitoring mechanism which could be refined in the light of the system and procedures currently operating in Iraq. During the reporting period, the joint unit of the Commission and the International Atomic Energy Agency (IAEA) has received notification of some 60 potential or actual transactions involving the import into Iraq of notifiable dual-capable items. The export/import monitoring mechanism is currently being reassessed in order to avoid difficulties in relation to the definition of items which are subject to notification.[111]

There are Western experts who are more pessimistic about Iraq's nuclear programs. Former UNSCOM Inspector Scott Ritter testified to Senate and House committees on September 4 and September 15 that Iraq might retain the components for three nuclear weapons. It later became clear that Ritter based his testimony on information compiled from three Iraqi defectors which came to UNSCOM by way of a "northern European" country.

While US and European policymakers initially indicated that they had no evidence to support Ritter's charges, reports surfaced on September 29, 1998, that UNSCOM inspectors had reported in both 1996 and 1997 that they had credible intelligence evidence that Iraq might have built and retained three to four nuclear "implosion devices" that only needed fissile-grand uranium cores to make kiloton nuclear weapons in the 10–25 kiloton range. US intelligence officials privately indicated that these UNSCOM reports might well be credible.[112]

The defectors involved provided detailed and accurate descriptions of the methods used by Iraq's Special Security Services to hide weapons components which were only known only to a handful of Western inspectors and intelligence experts at the time. These details include the Special Security Services' use of Mercedes trucks to shuttle the weapons between hiding places. These trucks had distinctive markings which included white cabins with red stripes, a red diesel tank and wheel rims, and Ministry of Trade license plates numbered between 30,000 and 87,000. Ritter stated that one defector sketched a map by hand depicting seven depots for those trucks. U-2 surveillance flights later found five of these sites. Ritter also disclosed that one of the defectors identified a secret concealment operations center in the Al Fao Building on Palestine Street in Baghdad. An UNSCOM no-notice inspection found in March, 1996 that Iraq used this center to control several locations for concealing materials, although it seems to have been evacuated in January, 1998.[113]

In spite of the initial denials of policymakers, UNSCOM seems to have first reported on these findings in 1996, and then to have provided an update in a briefing paper for a conference in Washington on May 19 and 20, 1997. The UNSCOM briefing indicated that, "It is assessed that Iraq has retained critical components relating to the most recent weapons design, which has not to date been turned over to the IAEA. These components may comprise several complete weapons minus the HEU [highly enriched uranium] core." The briefing paper also indicated that Iraq might be hiding "undeclared feedstocks of UF6," or uranium hexafluoride, and that UNSCOM suspected Iraq might be maintaining a secret enrichment capacity and machine tools to shape components of a bomb.[114]

There seems to be some tension between UNSCOM and the IAEA over these disclosures. According to press reports, Gary Dillon, the chief of the IAEA Action Team on Iraq, wrote a confidential memo following Ritter's initial disclosures that indicate that they were "unsubstantiated" and had "no credibility." Ritter countered that "I was never authorized by the executive chairman to tell [Dillon] the full extent of the information we had." UNSCOM spokesman Ewen Buchanan said he would not discuss the substance of the case.[115]

Even the experts who feel that Iraq has nuclear weapons assemblies indicate that there is no evidence that Iraq has acquired fissile-grade uranium or plutonium, and obtaining fissile material has long been a more serious technical and supply problem than fabricating the rest of a working nuclear weapon. They also feel that any Iraqi devices are likely to be too large and too heavy to fit inside the 88-centimeter (roughly 34-inch) warhead of one of Iraq's Al Husayn missiles. At the same time, these uncertainties reinforce the warning of the Director General of the IAEA that the IAEA cannot find every aspect of Iraq's nuclear program and that Iraq retains the technology base to make nuclear weapons.

Many Western experts feel that serious uncertainties exist as to how much unenriched uranium Iraq retains and over its progress in developing high-capacity centrifuges. Iraq has not provided the IAEA with drawings of its weapons designs, important experimental test data, and key production and development data on its centrifuge programs and efforts to develop indigenous vacuum induction furnaces to shape fissile materials for use in bombs.[116]

What is clear is that Iraq continues to attempt to buy nuclear technology on the gray and black markets, and authorized its Iraqi Atomic Energy Organization to resume purchases of "peaceful" nuclear technology in 1998. It is also clear that Iraqi scientists are cooperating with other countries.

Khidhir Hamza, a former director of Iraq's program to devise a nuclear weapon who defected in 1994, has said in an interview in the *New York Times* that Iraq planned to produce nuclear components abroad, among them devices to trigger nuclear reactions in warheads, or to import crucial parts to make arms in Iraq. He stated that there was "general planning for removal outside Iraq of some sensitive work or possibly work that requires some imports. The idea is to do it outside and bring the thing back home." Hamza said that at the time he left Iraq in 1995, a friend of his was importing electronic parts for the military from a front company in Jordan that bought the equipment in Malaysia and Singapore. "There are hundreds of these companies in Jordan. They have a whole system of runners in ordinary cars." He said that Iraq repaired its radar after the Gulf War by smuggling in parts. Hamza said there were other front companies in Southeast Asia and overseas bank accounts in areas ranging from the Persian Gulf region to Latin America to draw on to pay for purchases. He said that smugglers carried in parts in their personal luggage, that circuit boards were backed in foam-padded bags and sent through Jordan for a small bribe, and that plastic bags stuffed with goods were stored in the empty tanks of oil trucks returning from Turkey.

Other sources report that Abdulkadir Abdulrahman Ahmed, the director general of Iraq's nuclear research center, is regularly visiting India's leading nuclear research laboratory. This was only discovered when a computer hacker got into the Indian center's files. Hamza stated that Iraq had long worked to build-up a "deep and multilayered cooperation" with India that "seems to be back now."[117]

If the Security Council weakens, and the IAEA effort is ended or loses its effectiveness in the aftermath of Desert Fox, the results seem almost certain. Iraq retains all of the nuclear technology it developed before the Gulf War, and a substantial amount of laboratory and test equipment remains unaccounted for. It can carry out much of its nuclear weapons design effort in small, scattered facilities with limited equipment other than dual use computers and testing equipment. It can aggressively seek enriched or weapons-grade material from the Former Soviet Union or other sources. It can stockpile larger production and test equipment away from areas that are likely to be subject to inspection. For example, the IAEA announced that critical equipment for the manufacture of centrifuges had somehow "gone astray" in Iraq in late January, 1996.[118]

Even if Iraq does allow the UN to resume its monitoring and inspection activities—and UNSCOM can continue intrusive inspection and soil and water sampling at suspect sites—Iraq will retain the technological base that it acquired before the Gulf War. Iraq can still go on with a great deal of research and engineering activity with little fear of a challenge from the UN.[119] Iraq has also developed a long list of secret suppliers, and it is clear that it is reestablishing what is referred to in UNSCOM's September, 1995 report to the UN Security Council as a "very advanced procurement system."[120]

Once again, it is unclear whether there is any real alternative in the form of arms control agreements. The Nuclear Non-Proliferation treaty (NPT) does not currently provide the kind of intrusive inspection regime that would be needed, and it is unclear whether the new rules proposed to strengthen the NPT in May, 1997 would make a critical difference to a closed society as determined as Iraq. Certainly, Iraq would have to fully comply with every aspect of the new NPT inspection regime for there to be any hope that the IAEA could prevent a significant Iraqi effort.[121]

Further, any analysis of Iraq's intentions regarding biological weapons must take into account Iraq's probable reaction if it cannot revive its nuclear program. Biological weapons are sometimes described as the "poor man's nuclear weapons." They are also the "nuclear weapons" of the covert proliferator. As long as Saddam Hussein is in power, Iraq is virtually certain to seek highly lethal biological weapons as a means of compensating for the suppression of its nuclear program. Even when he is gone, successor regimes may feel compelled to follow a similar course because of the risks posed by Iran's nuclear and biological programs, Israel's nuclear forces, and US nuclear capabilities. Ironically, UNSCOM's and the IAEA's success in dealing with the most visible aspects of Iraq's nuclear efforts may ultimately end in stimulating Iraq to develop the kind of biological option that is as close to a nuclear option as time, technology, delivery systems, and Iraq's ability to carry out a covert biological program permit.

NOTES

1. For detailed descriptions of the Iraqi effort, see Anthony H. Cordesman, *Iran and Iraq: The Threat From the Northern Gulf*, Boulder, Westview, 1994; *After the Storm*, Boulder, Westview, 1993; and *Weapons of Mass Destruction in the Middle East*, London, Jane's/RUSI, 1992; and David Albright, Frans Berkhout, and William Walker, *Plutonium and Highly Enriched Uranium, 1996—World Inventories, Capabilities, and Policies*, Oxford, SIPRI-Oxford Press, 1997, pp. 310–350; David Albright and Mark Hibbs, "Iraq's Nuclear Hide and Seek," *Bulletin of the Atomic Scientists*, September, 1991, pp. 14–23; David Albright and Mark Hibbs, "Iraq's Bomb: Blueprints and Artifacts," *Bulletin of the Atomic Scientists*, June, 1992, pp. 8–10; David Albright and Mark Hibbs, "Supplier Spotting," *Bulletin of the Atomic Scientists*, June, 1992, pp. 8–9; David Albright, "Engineer for Hire," *Bulletin of the Atomic Scientists*, December, 1993, pp. 29–36; David Albright and R. Kelley, "Has Iraq Come Clean at Last?" *Bulletin of the Atomic Scientists*, Vol. 51, No. 6, November–December, 1995, pp. 8–9.

2. *New York Times*, August 15, 1998, p. A-1.

3. *New York Times*, August 15, 1998, p. A-1.

4. *Jane's Intelligence Review*, December, 1992, pp. 554–555.

5. Iraq's President Saddam Hussein repeated this denial on July 10, 1990. He stated that, "We do not have nuclear weapons." He also went on to say, however, that ". . . we would see no problem in a Western nation helping us to develop nuclear arms to help compensate for those owned by Israel." French TF1 Television network release, July 9, 1990; *Washington Times*, July 19, 1990, p. 2.

6. Based on work by Leonard Spector and the Atomic Energy Commission of Iraq, *Annual Report for 1988*, Baghdad, Iraq Atomic Energy Commission, 1989, p. 94.

7. Leonard S. Spector, *The Undeclared Bomb*, Ballinger, New York, 1988; Leonard S. Spector and Jacqueline R. Smith, *Nuclear Exports: The Challenge of Control*, Carnegie Endowment for Peace, Washington, April, 1990, pp. 21–26; *New York Times*, March 18, 1980; *Energy Daily*, October 2, 1980; and Dr. Michael Brenner, "Iran as a Nuclear Power in the Middle East," SAI, December 14, 1989, Appendix B.

8. The IAEA estimates that it takes 55 pounds (25 kilograms) of highly enriched uranium to make a nuclear weapon.

9. See Leonard S. Spector, *The Undeclared Bomb*, Ballinger, New York, 1988; Leonard S. Spector and Jacqueline R. Smith, *Nuclear Exports: The Challenge of Control*, Carnegie Endowment for Peace, Washington, April, 1990, pp. 21–26; Jed Snyder, "The Non-Proliferation Regime: Managing the Impending Crisis," *Journal of Strategic Studies*, December, 1985, p. 11; Shyam Bhatia, *Nuclear Rivals in the Middle East*, London, Routledge Paul, 1988, p. 85.

10. David Albright, Frans Berkhout, and William Walker, *Plutonium and Highly*

Enriched Uranium, 1996—World Inventories, Capabilities, and Policies, Oxford, SIPRI-Oxford Press, 1997, pp. 314–315.

11. Half of the 55 pounds would have been in the core of Osirak and unusable for weapons purposes, and the rest would have been irradiated in the nearby Isis reactor, both of which would have been subject to IAEA inspection. Based on work by Leonard Spector.

12. United Nations, *Report on the Eighth IAEA Inspection in Iraq Under Security Council Resolution 687*, 11–18 November 1991, New York, United Nations, S/23283 (English), pp. 21–23 and Annex 2.

13. Leonard Spector, *The New Nuclear Nations*, New York, Vintage, 1985, pp. 165–166; *Energy Daily*, October 2, 1980, p. 1.

14. For an excellent history of Iraq's nuclear weapons effort prior to 1983, see Jed C. Snyder, "The Road to Osirak: Baghdad's Quest for the Bomb," *Middle East Journal*, No. 37, Autumn, 1983, pp. 565–594. Also see Leonard Spector, *The New Nuclear Nations*, New York, Vintage, 1985, pp. 65–67.

15. Leonard Spector, *Proliferation Today*, New York, Vintage Books, 1984, pp. 175–178.

16. Shyam Bhatia, *Nuclear Rivals in the Middle East*, London, Routledge Paul, 1988, p. 85.

17. See Andrew T. Parasiliti, "Iraq, Nuclear Weapons, and the Middle East," The Middle East Institute, December 14, 1989, p. 3; and David Albright, Frans Berkhout, and William Walker, *Plutonium and Highly Enriched Uranium, 1996—World Inventories, Capabilities, and Policies*, Oxford, SIPRI-Oxford Press, 1997, pp. 342–343.

18. See the excellent, detailed description of this effort in David Albright, Frans Berkhout, and William Walker, *Plutonium and Highly Enriched Uranium, 1996–World Inventories, Capabilities, and Policies*, Oxford, SIPRI-Oxford Press, 1997, pp. 343–344.

19. David Albright, Frans Berkhout, and William Walker, *Plutonium and Highly Enriched Uranium, 1996—World Inventories, Capabilities, and Policies*, Oxford, SIPRI-Oxford Press, 1997, pp. 314–315.

20. New York Times, August 15, 1998, p. A-1.

21. David Albright, Frans Berkhout, and William Walker, *Plutonium and Highly Enriched Uranium, 1996—World Inventories, Capabilities, and Policies*, Oxford, SIPRI-Oxford Press, 1997, pp. 314–315, 318–327.

22. David Albright, Frans Berkhout, and William Walker, *Plutonium and Highly Enriched Uranium, 1996—World Inventories, Capabilities, and Policies*, Oxford, SIPRI-Oxford Press, 1997, pp. 314–315, 318–327.

23. Working papers by Leonard Spector, *Journal do Brazil*, May 22, 1988; William H. Webster, Director of Central Intelligence, "Testimony Before the Committee on Governmental Affairs," US Senate, May 18, 1989; *Washington Post*, September 29, 1989; *Mideast Markets*, June 12, 1989, p. 10, September 18, 1989, p. 11; October 16, 1989; *Financial Times Mid-East Market*, December 12, 1989; *Arms Control Today*, April, 1990, p. 27; *The Middle East*, May, 1990, pp. 11–14; *Nucleonics Week*, May 29, 1986, p. 6; *Defense News*, May 8, 1989; *Nuclear Engineering International*, December, 1988, p. 5.

24. US Office of the Secretary of Defense, *Proliferation: Threat and Response*, Washington, US Department of Defense, April, 1996, pp. 17–24.

25. US Department of Defense, *Conduct of the Persian Gulf War: Final Report*, US Department of Defense, April, 1992, pp. 18.

26. US Department of Defense, *Conduct of the Persian Gulf War: Final Report*, US

Department of Defense, April, 1992, pp. 206–207. For some of the reasons and problems in targeting and battle management, see Rick Atkinson, *Crusade*, Boston, Houghton Mifflin, 1993, pp. 295–296.

27. The $10 billion dollar figure is a UN staff estimate. See *New York Times*, October 14, 1991, p. A-6.

28. Al J. Venter, "How Saddam Almost Built His Bomb," *Jane's Intelligence Review*, December, 1997, fax from *Jane's*, December 4, 1997.

29. IAEA comments on CRS-93 323F, fax by IAEA UNSC 687 Action Team, June 23, 1993.

30. Al J. Venter, "How Saddam Almost Built His Bomb," *Jane's Intelligence Review*, December, 1997, fax from *Jane's*, December 4, 1997.

31. James Bruce, "Iraq and Iran: Running the Nuclear Technology Race," *Jane's Defense Weekly*, December 5, 1988, p. 1307; *New York Times*, July 10, 1992.

32. *Washington Times*, August 29, 1990, p. 8; *South*, July, 1987, pp. 99–100; *Stern*, April 6, 1989, pp. 214–217; *Der Spiegel*, December 18–25, 1989, pp. 93–94; Michael Eisenstadt, "The Sword of the Arabs: Iraq's Strategic Weapons," Washington, Washington Institute for Near East Policy, Policy Paper 21, September, 1990, pp. 11–13.

33. Eliot A. Cohen, Director, *Gulf War Air Power Survey*, Volume II, Part II, Washington, GPO, 1993, pp. 317–318.

34. This analysis draws heavily on work in Anthony H. Cordesman in *Weapons of Mass Destruction in the Middle East*, London, Brassey's, 1991; and *After the Storm*, Boulder, Westview, 1993; UN Security Council Report, S/23215, Seventh IAEA on-site inspection, 11–22 October, 1991, November 14, 1991, p. 63; David Kay, "Arms Inspection in Iraq: Lessons for Arms Control," August 12, 1992, p. 3, GWAPS, NA 375; Thomas A. Keaney and Eliot A. Cohen, *Gulf War Air Power Survey: Summary Report*, Washington, Department of the Air Force, 1993, pp. 123; Eliot A. Cohen, Director, *Gulf War Power Survey*, Volume I, Part II Washington, GPO, 1993, pp. 242–254, and *Volume II, Part II*, pp. 317–340.

35. US Department of Defense, *Conduct of the Persian Gulf War: Final Report*, US Department of Defense, April, 1992, p. 239, and Eliot A. Cohen, Director, *Gulf War Air Power Survey*, Volume II, Part II, pp. 328–329.

36. David Albright, Frans Berkhout, and William Walker, *Plutonium and Highly Enriched Uranium, 1996—World Inventories, Capabilities, and Policies*, Oxford, SIPRI-Oxford Press, 1997, pp. 327–328.

37. David Albright, Frans Berkhout, and William Walker, *Plutonium and Highly Enriched Uranium, 1996—World Inventories, Capabilities, and Policies*, Oxford, SIPRI-Oxford Press, 1997, pp. 341.

38. Al J. Venter, "How Saddam Almost Built His Bomb," *Jane's Intelligence Review*, December, 1997, fax from *Jane's*, December 4, 1997.

39. *Washington Post*, October 5, 1991, p. A-1; *Wall Street Journal*, October 29, 1991, p. 24; David Albright, Frans Berkhout, and William Walker, *Plutonium and Highly Enriched Uranium, 1996—World Inventories, Capabilities, and Policies*, Oxford, SIPRI-Oxford Press, 1997, pp. 340–341.

40. Based on interviews with UNSCOM personnel, US experiments, and David Albright, Frans Berkhout, and William Walker, *Plutonium and Highly Enriched Uranium, 1996—World Inventories, Capabilities, and Policies*, Oxford, SIPRI-Oxford Press, 1997, pp. 342–349. See the latter article for more details.

41. See David Albright, Frans Berkhout, and William Walker, *Plutonium and Highly*

Enriched Uranium, 1996—World Inventories, Capabilities, and Policies, Oxford, SIPRI-Oxford Press, 1997, pp. 342–349 for more details.

42. *New York Times*, February 13, 1992, p. A-16; Zachary A. Davis and Warren H. Donnelly, "Iraq and Nuclear Weapons," Congressional Research Service, IB90113, February 13, 1992, p. 3; David Albright and Mark Hibbs, "News That the Front Page Missed," *Bulletin of the Atomic Scientists*, October, 1991, pp. 7–9; Peter D. Zimmerman, "Iraq's Nuclear Achievements: Components, Sources, and Stature," Congressional Research Service, 93-323F, February 18, 1993.

43. David Albright, Frans Berkhout, and William Walker, *Plutonium and Highly Enriched Uranium, 1996—World Inventories, Capabilities, and Policies*, Oxford, SIPRI-Oxford Press, 1997, pp. 314–315, 318–327.

44. *Washington Post*, November 2, 1991, p. C-1.

45. Al J. Venter, "How Saddam Almost Built His Bomb," *Jane's Intelligence Review*, December, 1997, fax from *Jane's*, December 4, 1997; *New York Times*, January 15, 1992, p. A-1; *US News and World Report*, Vol. 112, January 20, 1992, p. 45; *Star Tribune*, November 22, 1991, pp. 22A; *Christian Science Monitor*, October 23, 1991, p. 9.

46. *US News and World Report*, November 25, 1991, p. 36. Vol. 112, January 20, 1992, p. 45; United Nations Security Council, *Report on the Eighth IAEA Inspection in Iraq Under Security Council Resolution 687*, 11–18 November 1991, New York, United Nations, S/23283 (English); David Albright and Mark Hibbs, "Iraq's Shop-Till You Drop Nuclear Program," *Bulletin of the Atomic Scientists*, April, 1992, pp. 27–37.

47. Al J. Venter, "How Saddam Almost Built His Bomb," *Jane's Intelligence Review*, December, 1997, fax from *Jane's*, December 4, 1997.

48. Al J. Venter, "How Saddam Almost Built His Bomb," *Jane's Intelligence Review*, December, 1997, fax from *Jane's*, December 4, 1997.

49. IAEA comments on CRS-93 323F, fax by IAEA UNSC 687 Action Team, June 23, 1993.

50. This summary is taken largely from UNSCOM working reports. For more detail and a slightly different account, see David Albright, Frans Berkhout, and William Walker, *Plutonium and Highly Enriched Uranium, 1996—World Inventories, Capabilities, and Policies*, Oxford, SIPRI-Oxford Press, 1997, pp. 314–315, 318–327.

51. This analysis draws heavily on David Albright and Mark Hibbs, "Iraq and the Bomb: Were They Even Close?" *Bulletin of Atomic Scientists*, March, 1991, pp. 16–25; "US Experts Divided on Whether Iraqi Calutrons Procure U-235," *Nuclear Fuel*, June 24, 1991, pp. 3–4; IAEA comments on CRS-93 323F, fax by IAEA UNSC 687 Action Team, June 23, 1993.

52. This summary is taken largely from UNSCOM working reports. For more detail and a slightly different account, see David Albright, Frans Berkhout, and William Walker, *Plutonium and Highly Enriched Uranium, 1996—World Inventories, Capabilities, and Policies*, Oxford, SIPRI-Oxford Press, 1997, pp. 314–315, 318–327.

53. David Albright, Frans Berkhout, and William Walker, *Plutonium and Highly Enriched Uranium, 1996—World Inventories, Capabilities, and Policies*, Oxford, SIPRI-Oxford Press, 1997, pp. 314–315, 318–327.

54. Zachary A. Davis and Warren H. Donnelly, "Iraq and Nuclear Weapons," Congressional Research Service, IB90113, February 13, 1992, p. 3; David Albright and Mark Hibbs, "Iraq and the Bomb: Were They Even Close?" *Bulletin of Atomic Scientists*, March, 1991, pp. 16–25; David Albright and Mark Hibbs, "It's All Over at Al Atheer,"

Bulletin of Atomic Scientists, June, 1992, pp. 8–10; "US Experts Divided on Whether Iraqi Calutrons Procure U-235," *Nuclear Fuel*, June 24, 1991, pp. 3–4.

55. *US News and World Report*, Vol. 112, January 20, 1992, p. 45; *London Financial Times*, January 15, 1992, p. 1.

56. H&H was headed by Walter Busse, a former employee of MAN Technologies Ltd., which had built the uranium centrifuge assembly plant at Gronau in West Germany for URENCO. It seems to have provided machinery for the production of gas ultracentrifuges. *Washington Post*, June 4, 1991; *Los Angeles Times*, December 12, 1991, A-9; Associated Press, December 11, 1991, AM cycle. Other firms named at this time included Schenk Werzberg and Machinebau, 1989; *Der Spiegel*, December 18, 1989; *FBIS-Western Europe*, December 20, 1989; *Nucleonics Week*, May 4, 1987, p. 1; Gary Milhollin, "Building Saddam Hussein's Bomb," *New York Times*, March 8, 1992, pp. 30–31; Al J. Venter, "How Saddam Almost Built His Bomb," *Jane's Intelligence Review*, December, 1997, fax from *Jane's*, December 4, 1997.

57. For a much more detailed account, see David Albright, Frans Berkhout, and William Walker, *Plutonium and Highly Enriched Uranium, 1996—World Inventories, Capabilities, and Policies*, Oxford, SIPRI-Oxford Press, 1997, pp. 329–338.

58. Interviews; Gary Milhollin, "Building Saddam Hussein's Bomb," *New York Times*, March 8, 1992, pp. 30–31; Al J. Venter, "How Saddam Almost Built His Bomb," *Jane's Intelligence Review*, December, 1997, fax from *Jane's*, December 4, 1997.

59. Maximum ultimate design capability was 2,000 centrifuges per year. *Washington Post*, May 5, 1989; *Rochester Democrat and Chronicle*, March 28, 1989; *New York Times*, January 15, 1992; David Albright and Mark Hibbs, "News That the Front Page Missed," *Bulletin of the Atomic Scientists*, October, 1991, pp. 7–9; *Report on the Seventh IAEA Inspection in Iraq Under Security Council Resolution 687*, 14 November 1991, New York, United Nations, S/232215 (English), p. 19; David Albright and Mark Hibbs, "Iraq's Shop-Till-You-Drop Nuclear Program," *Bulletin of the Atomic Scientists*, April, 1992, pp. 27–37.

60. H&H was headed by Walter Busse, a former employee of MAN Technologies Ltd. which had built the uranium centrifuge assembly plant at Gronau in West Germany for URENCO. *Washington Post*, June 4, 1989; *Der Spiegel*, December 18, 1989; *FBIS-Western Europe*, December 20, 1989; *Nucleonics Week*, May 4, 1987, p. 1; *Wall Street Journal*, October 29, 1991, p. 24; *Nuclear Fuel*, June 20, 1994.

61. *Wall Street Journal*, October 7, 1991, p. A-10; Al J. Venter, "How Saddam Almost Built His Bomb," *Jane's Intelligence Review*, December, 1997, fax from *Jane's*, December 4, 1997.

62. *Wall Street Journal*, October 7, 1991, p. A-10; Al J. Venter, "How Saddam Almost Built His Bomb," *Jane's Intelligence Review*, December, 1997, fax from *Jane's*, December 4, 1997.

63. Michael Eisenstadt, "The Sword of the Arabs: Iraq's Strategic Weapons," Washington, Washington Institute for Near East Policy, Policy Paper 21, September, 1990, pp. 11–13; *Rochester Democrat and Chronicle*, March 28, 1988, pp. 1A and 10A; *Washington Post*, May 5, 1989, p. A-24.

64. *Wall Street Journal*, October 7, 1991, p. A-10; Al J. Venter, "How Saddam Almost Built His Bomb," *Jane's Intelligence Review*, December, 1997, fax from *Jane's*, December 4, 1997.

65. H&H was headed by Walter Busse, a former employee of MAN Technologies Ltd., which had built the uranium centrifuge assembly plant at Gronau in West Germany

Iraq's Past and Future Nuclear Weapons Capabilities 639

for URENCO. It seems to have provided machinery for the production of gas ultracentrifuges. *Washington Post*, June 4, 1991; *Los Angeles Times*, December 12, 1991, A-9; Associated Press, December 11, 1991, AM cycle. Other firms named at this time included Schenk Werzberg and Machinebau, 1989; *Der Spiegel*, December 18, 1989; *FBIS-Western Europe*, December 20, 1989; *Nucleonics Week*, May 4, 1987, p. 1; Gary Milhollin, "Building Saddam Hussein's Bomb," *New York Times*, March 8, 1992, pp. 30–31; Al J. Venter, "How Saddam Almost Built His Bomb," *Jane's Intelligence Review*, December, 1997, fax from *Jane's*, December 4, 1997.

66. *US News and World Report*, Vol. 112, January 20, 1992, p. 45; *London Financial Times*, January 15, 1992, p. 1.

67. David Albright, Frans Berkhout, and William Walker, *Plutonium and Highly Enriched Uranium, 1996—World Inventories, Capabilities, and Policies*, Oxford, SIPRI-Oxford Press, 1997, pp. 314–315, 318–327.

68. *The Middle East*, December, 1996, p. 21.

69. See David Albright, Frans Berkhout, and William Walker, *Plutonium and Highly Enriched Uranium, 1996—World Inventories, Capabilities, and Policies*, Oxford, SIPRI-Oxford Press, 1997, pp. 337–228. The calculations used here are slightly different from those in this reference.

70. *New York Times*, January 15, 1992, p. A-1.

71. IAEA comments on CRS-93 323F, fax by IAEA UNSC 687 Action Team, June 23, 1993.

72. Michael Eisenstadt, "The Sword of the Arabs: Iraq's Strategic Weapons," Washington, Washington Institute for Near East Policy, Policy Paper 21, September, 1990, p. 15.

73. David Albright, Frans Berkhout, and William Walker, *Plutonium and Highly Enriched Uranium, 1996—World Inventories, Capabilities, and Policies*, Oxford, SIPRI-Oxford Press, 1997, pp. 314–315, 318–327.

74. Iraq made this admission to the UN on October 21, 1991. *New York Times*, October 14, 1991, p. A6, October 20, 1991, IV-5; United Nations Security Council, *Report on the Eighth IAEA Inspection in Iraq Under Security Council Resolution 687*, 11–18 November 1991, New York, United Nations, S/23283 (English), p. 9.

75. *Los Angeles Times*, December 12, 1991, p. A-9.

76. A full description of activities is not included because of their value in nuclear weapons design. United Nations Security Council, *Report on the Sixth IAEA Inspection in Iraq Under Security Council Resolution 687*, 8 October 1991, New York, United Nations, S/23122 (English).

77. *Washington Post*, October 5, 1991, p. A-1.

78. Gary Milhollin, "Building Saddam Hussein's Bomb," *New York Times*, March 8, 1992, pp. 30–31.

79. *The Middle East*, May, 1990, pp. 11–14.

80. *US News and World Report*, November 25, 1991, p. 36. This same article named a number of possible US suppliers, including Honeywell (computers), Canberra Industries, Inc. (computer equipment to measure neutrons and for design specifications, Carl Zeiss (computer equipment to process photographic data), Databit, Inc. (computer data transmission and circuit switches), Forney International (computer equipment for power stations), Hewellet-Packard (optical fiber cables, computers, frequency synthesizers, precision electronic and photo equipment), Perkin-Elmer (computers, precision electronic, and photo equipment, Sackman Associates (computers, electronic assemblies, and photo

equipment), and Westinghouse Electric (computer hardware and software for the Iraqi electric system). Many of these supplies almost certainly had little or nothing to do with the Iraqi nuclear effort.

81. Zachary A. Davis and Warren H. Donnelly, "Iraq and Nuclear Weapons," Congressional Research Service, IB90113, February 13, 1992, p. 4; *Washington Post*, October 9, 1991, p. A-17.

82. The core of a nuclear bomb consists of fissile material, a layer of outer explosives, and a firing circuit connected to all parts of the outer high explosive cover to detonate all of it at exactly the same moment and achieve maximum compression at the precise instant high energy neutrons are being injected into the compressed fissile core. *Washington Times*, March 28, 29, 30, 1990; *Washington Post*, March 28, 29, 30, 1990; *New York Times*, March 28, 29, 30, 1990. Also see Peter D. Zimmerman, *Iraq's Nuclear Achievements: Components, Sources, and Stature*," Washington, DC, Congressional Research Service, 93-323F, February 18, 1993; J. Carson Mark, "Some Remarks on Iraq's Possible Nuclear Weapons Capability in Light of Some of the Known Facts Concerning Nuclear Weapons," Washington, Nuclear Control Institute, May 16, 1991; and Al J. Venter, "How Saddam Almost Built His Bomb," *Jane's Intelligence Review*, December, 1997, fax from *Jane's*, December 4, 1997.

83. US Office of the Secretary of Defense, *Proliferation: Threat and Response*, Washington, US Department of Defense, April, 1996, pp. 17–24.

84. See the much more detailed account in David Albright, Frans Berkhout, and William Walker, *Plutonium and Highly Enriched Uranium, 1996—World Inventories, Capabilities, and Policies*, Oxford, SIPRI-Oxford Press, 1997, pp. 347–349.

85. *Nuclear Fuel*, August 5, 1991, Vol. 16, No. 16, p. 14.

86. It takes 15 to 25 kilograms to make one relatively simple nuclear weapon. More advanced weapons take substantially less. The IAEA did, however, certify on May 7, 1990, that all such material was still accounted for. Source: IAEA Office, United Nations, New York, NY.

87. For a good overview, see David Albright and Mark Hibbs, "Iraq's Bomb: Blueprints and Artifacts," *Bulletin of the Atomic Scientists*, June, 1992, pp. 8–10.

88. Report to the UN Security Council on October 8, 1991; *USA Today*, October 10, 1991, p. 6.

89. Gary Milhollin, "Building Saddam Hussein's Bomb," *New York Times*, March 8, 1992, pp. 30–31.

90. *Washington Post*, September 29, 1998, p. A-1.

91. *Washington Post*, September 29, 1988, p. A-1.

92. Many of these details are taken from Peter D. Zimmerman, *Iraq's Nuclear Achievements: Components, Sources, and Stature*, Washington, DC, Congressional Research Service, 93-323F, February 18, 1993. Also see J. Carson Mark, "Some Remarks on Iraq's Possible Nuclear Weapons Capability in Light of Some of the Known Facts Concerning Nuclear Weapons," Washington, Nuclear Control Institute, May 16, 1991.

93. David Albright, Frans Berkhout, and William Walker, *Plutonium and Highly Enriched Uranium, 1996—World Inventories, Capabilities, and Policies*, Oxford, SIPRI-Oxford Press, 1997, p. 311.

94. United Nations, *Report on the Eighth IAEA Inspection in Iraq Under Security Council Resolution 687*, 11–18 November 1991, New York, United Nations, S/23283 (English), pp. 14–15, 29; Gary Milhollin, "Building Saddam Hussein's Bomb," *New*

York Times, March 8, 1992, pp. 30–31; United Nations, S/232215 *Report on the Seventh IAEA Inspection in Iraq Under Security Council Resolution 687*, 14 November 1991, New York, (English), p. 30.

95. *US News and World Report*, November 25, 1991, p. 36; United Nations, *Report on the Eighth IAEA Inspection in Iraq Under Security Council Resolution 687*, 11–18 November 1991, New York, United Nations, S/23283 (English), p. 29.

96. Peter D. Zimmerman, *Iraq's Nuclear Achievements: Components, Sources, and Stature*, Washington, DC, Congressional Research Service, 93–323F, February 18, 1993; J. Carson Mark, "Some Remarks on Iraq's Possible Nuclear Weapons Capability in Light of Some of the Known Facts Concerning Nuclear Weapons," Washington, Nuclear Control Institute, May 16, 1991; and Al J. Venter, "How Saddam Almost Built His Bomb," *Jane's Intelligence Review*, December, 1997, fax from *Jane's*, December 4, 1997.

97. The "sting" operation is a good example of what happens when a company that is concerned with proliferation takes immediate action to contact the officials in the country involved. A US company called CSI Technologies of San Marcos, California, which immediately contacted US customs officials when it was contacted by Euromac, the Iraqi front organization. Euromac was located in Thames Ditton, near London. US officials contacted British officials, and they worked together to set up a series of meetings, some of which were televised, and to make the intercept and arrests at Heathrow Airport. Ironically, Euromac was registered as a "general grocers and provision merchant." It is also unclear whether the Iraqis fully understood what they were ordering. Maxwell Laboratories of San Diego had been delivering other types of capacitors to Iraq, and had delivered 518 slow speed capacitors to Iraq. Iraq then order 185 high speed capacitors. Maxwell Laboratories notified customs and halted the shipment at customs' request. The new type of capacitor, however, was still unsuitable for nuclear weapons. Andrew T. Parasiliti, "Iraq, Nuclear Weapons, and the Middle East," The Middle East Institute, December 14, 1989, pp. 4–5; *Mideast Markets*, Vol. 16, No. 8, April 17, 1989, p. 15, and Vol. 16, No. 9, May 1, 1989, p. 12; *Washington Post*, March 31, 1989, p. A-1; *Los Angeles Times*, March 30, 1990; *Washington Post*, March 31, 1990, p. 2.

98. Peter D. Zimmerman, *Iraq's Nuclear Achievements: Components, Sources, and Stature*, Washington, DC, Congressional Research Service, 93–323F, February 18, 1993; J. Carson Mark, "Some Remarks on Iraq's Possible Nuclear Weapons Capability in Light of Some of the Known Facts Concerning Nuclear Weapons," Washington, Nuclear Control Institute, May 16, 1991; and Al J. Venter, "How Saddam Almost Built His Bomb," *Jane's Intelligence Review*, December, 1997, fax from *Jane's*, December 4, 1997.

99. Gary Milhollin, "Building Saddam Hussein's Bomb," *New York Times*, March 8, 1992, pp. 30–31.

100. The problem of height of burst is critical because it determines the fallout effects of a weapon and the relative importance of blast, radiation, and thermal energy affecting a given target. Fusing is not necessarily different from the fusing needed for ordinary bombs, but the fusing on ordinary bombs often fails to function properly.

101. Reuters, November 7, 1995, December 18, 1995, 0342; *New York Times*, December 22, 1995, p. A–18.

102. For very different views, see Peter D. Zimmerman, *Iraq's Nuclear Achievements: Components, Sources, and Stature*, Washington, Congressional Research Service, 93-323F, February 18, 1993; Gary Milhollin, "The Iraqi Bomb," *New Yorker*, February 1, 1993, pp. 47–55, and Diana Edensword and Gary Milhollin, "Iraq's Bomb—An Update," *New York Times*, April 26, 1993, p. A–17.

103. *Jane's Defense Weekly*, March 11, 1995, pp. 28–29.
104. *Washington Times*, August 30, 1995, p. A–10.
105. *Washington Times*, October 14, 1995, p. A–10.
106. United Nations, Note by the Secretary General, S/1997/301, April 11, 1997, p. 24.
107. Transcript of Hans Blix interview, Reuters, October 16, 1997, 1928.
108. Reuters, January 23, 1998, 02:28.
109. *Washington Post*, June 1, 1998, p. A-17.
110. *New York Times*, July 28, 1998, p. A-3; *Washington Post*, April 14, 1998, p. A-11.
111. Note by the Secretary General, S/1998/920(1998), October 6, 1998.
112. *Washington Post*, September 29, 1998, p. A-1.
113. *Washington Post*, September 29, 1998, p. A-1.
114. *Washington Post*, September 29, 1998, p. A-1.
115. *Washington Post*, September 29, 1998, p. A-1.
116. Speech by Scott Ritter, Washington Institute, September 4, 1998, *New York Times*, April 15, 1998, p. A-12, April 19, 1998, p. A-4, July 28, 1998, p. A-3; Reuters, July 28, 1998, 0218, August 31, 1998, 0927.
117. *New York Times*, November 20, 1998, p. A-1.
118. Reuters, January 30, 1996, 1227; *Jane's Defense Weekly*, January 3, 1996, p. 19.
119. See Kenneth Katzman, "Iraqi Compliance with Cease-Fire Agreements," Congressional Research Service, IB92117, March 25, 1994; and United Nations, Note by the Secretary General, S/26584, November 5, 1993; Note by the Secretary General, S/26825, December 1, 1993; Note by the Secretary General, S/26910, December 21, 1993; Note by the Secretary General, S/1994/31, January 14, 1994; Report on the Twenty-Second IAEA Inspection, 1–15 November 1993; Note by the Secretary General, S/1994/341, March 24, 1994; and Note by the Secretary General, S/1994/355, March 25, 1994.
120. Associated Press, October 14, 1995; A full post–war list has never been published. A US government list published after the Gulf War is contained in the *Federal Register*, Vol. 56, No. 64, April 3, 1991, pp. 13,584–13,589.
121. White House "Fact Sheet," May 14, 1997; *Washington Post*, May 15, 1997, p. A–24. Also see the discussion of monitoring and country activity in US Director of Central Intelligence, "The Acquisition of Technology Relating to Weapons of Mass Destruction and Advanced Conventional Munitions, July–December, 1996," Washington, CIA, June, 1997, and Shai Feldman, *Nuclear Weapons and Arms Control in the Middle East*, Cambridge, MIT Press, 1997.

Chapter 20

The Policy Implications of Iraq's Weapons of Mass Destruction

The most important single conclusion of the preceding analysis is that Iraq's "war of sanctions"—and its continuing efforts to proliferate—create a continuing problem that the UN can limit while sanctions are still in force but cannot hope to end. Iraq will continue to attempt to proliferate as long as Saddam Hussein or any similar leader is in charge. Its efforts will also be far reaching and opportunistic. Iraq's weapons developments, force plans, strategy, doctrine, and war plans are far more likely to be driven by its ability to create new opportunities rather than by any combination of ideology, long-term plans or strategy, or a coherent focus on one path to proliferation in exclusion of another.

The Iraqi leadership can be counted on to block inspections as long as it can and to create new barriers at every opportunity. It can be counted on to continue to exploit "sanctions fatigue" in any way it can. It will exploit the suffering of the Iraqi people to try to make the world ignore the risks of Iraqi rearmament and proliferation. It will exploit divisions within the UN Security Council, and every weakness in the UN inspection and export control effort. It will treat proliferation as Iraq's second-most important strategic priority, ranking only after the survival of the leadership itself. It will seek to undermine and put a final end to the inspection phase of the IAEA and UNSCOM effort, and to either ensure that there is no monitoring phase or that it is rigid and symbolic and is not backed by inspections and the expansion of monitoring to cover new facilities. As the events of October, 1997–October, 1998 show, it may well be willing to lose some equipment to US and British air and missile strikes if it believes this is the price of making the IAEA and UNSCOM ineffective. Similarly, the Iraqi leadership may well be willing to sacrifice substantial amounts of Iraq's conventional military capabilities to such strikes if it feels this preserves its ability to proliferate.

Iraq will continue to lie and deny whenever it can. It will attempt to block every UN effort to limit its efforts to proliferate and to try to find ways to hide its activities from the UN, or stretch the limits of the UN resolutions to carry on research, design, and production activities under the guise of civil or academic programs. It will carry out covert or "black" programs—compartmentalizing duplicate efforts so they cannot be traced back to wartime programs, and the discovery of one program will not halt another.

LIVING WITH IRAQ'S CONTINUING CAPABILITY TO PROLIFERATE AND THE PROBLEM OF IRAQI OPPORTUNISM

The moment Iraq begins to win the "war of sanctions" to the point where it can rebuild its biological, chemical, nuclear, and missile capabilities, it will do so. No matter how successful UNSCOM and the IAEA were while sanctions were in force, Iraq will be able to retain a considerable clandestine "breakout" capability. Its exploitation of this capability will, however, be highly contingency dependent. Much will depend on Iraq's perception of the political and economic costs of overt or large-scale activity. Much will depend on the way in which sanctions are lifted or eased, and the way in which Iraq regains access to arms imports and imports of dedicated or dual use technology.

Iraq will almost certainly give priority to "low-profile" efforts like biological weapons, where it can potentially achieve near-nuclear lethalities with minimum delectability. It is also likely to purse covert delivery programs. This will not prevent it from pursuing nuclear weapons and missiles, but problems in such high-profile efforts will not halt Iraq's process of proliferation. Iraq is also likely to start far more efforts than it is able to finish and to fund major efforts in areas which do not seem cost effective by Western standards. As a result, there are likely to be many confusing and misleading indicators, and even transparent access to the current plans of Iraq's leadership might not be a valid indication of its future efforts.

Nevertheless, there is no way to determine the exact nature of Iraq's ability to recover its capability to produce and deliver weapons of mass destruction. The only thing that is clear is that Iraq is likely to retain significant capability to begin producing biological and chemical weapons the moment that the efforts of UNSCOM and the IAEA are halted or are placed under sharp Iraqi limits, and it is possible that Iraq could achieve a significant "breakout" in developing biological weapons with the lethality of small theater nuclear weapons by conducting a covert parallel program while UNSCOM is still active.

THE LIMITS OF ARMS CONTROL

As has been analyzed earlier, even the full and aggressive implementation of new arms control measures is unlikely to change this situation. The Biological Weapons Convention has been ratified by 140 states. The treaty bans the development, production, and stockpiling of bacteriological and toxin weapons—including such agents as Anthrax, botulism toxin, and bubonic plague—but it currently has no inspection and verification provisions, and years of technical discussions among experts have raised major questions as to whether any inspection and verification regime can stop a closed authoritarian country from developing biological weapons with near-nuclear lethality in sufficient amounts for a strategic attack.

The Clinton administration does hope that negotiations for an inspection protocol to the 1972 Biological Weapons Convention can be completed in 1998, but many Western diplomats feel that the chances of reaching agreement on the verification pact are slipping. The United States sent a delegation to three weeks of closed-door talks at the UN's European headquarters in late January, 1998. Delegates agreed to reconvene from March 9–13, and to conduct longer negotiating sessions in June–July and September–October, but made little real progress.

However, the Clinton administration must present a treaty protocol that is saleable, not only to the US Senate but to the biotechnology industry, which is eager to protect trade secrets. Powers like Germany and Japan will have to decide how many inspections of commercial sites are tolerable, and Russia is reluctant to open up their military and commercial facilities to on-site inspections under the pact. Key officials indicate that, "The Russian position is clear on nonchallenge inspections—they don't want them." There are also uncertainties as to exactly what would constitute a violation. Some disease pathogens have legitimate medicinal purposes for use in vaccines and therapies, and this makes it difficult to allow free challenge inspection and protect valuable biotechnological secrets.[1]

Similarly, even those nations that do accept the terms of the Chemical Weapons Convention may succeed in placing major limitations on the inspectors, and Iraq's experience in attempting to cheat UNSCOM inspectors strongly indicates that even far more intrusive inspection regimes would not offer any assurance that they could prevent a covert program from developing enough chemical weapons to arm a strategic missile and bomb program. Certainly, the resulting duel between the inspection regime and proliferating country would be just as long, grim, and complex as the duel between Iraq and UNSCOM.

The new IAEA inspection regime approved by its board of directors on May 16, 1997, would provide broader coverage and much more intrusive inspection than previous methods, *if* all member nations accepted it. It requires member nations to expand the list of what they report to include "all activities that support the nuclear fuel cycle," and to disclose all holdings of uranium and other radioactive material. It allows inspectors to use more advanced technical equipment and conduct "environmental sampling," such as earth removal, surface swipes, and water testing. It also allows them to inspect any building, not just those declared and authorized by the nation whose facilities are being inspected. Nevertheless, these procedures assume that (1) the government being inspected will not systematically lie and require constant, nation-wide intrusive inspection; (2) there will be no untraceable sales or transfers of weapons grade material; and (3) that intelligence can detect all major facilities and efforts and report them to the IAEA.[2]

One thing is clear: While the UN may not be able to carry out unfettered inspections, a UN monitoring regime with any real capability will be more effective in deterring Iraq from large-scale detectable effort or from resuming open long-range missile, biological, chemical, and nuclear weapons programs and deployments than any Iraqi agreement to an arms control regime. If the UN cannot hope to find all of Iraq's efforts, Iraq can never know what the UN will find. It is unclear that the UN's effort can survive Iraq's relentless "war of sanctions" or that efforts like the "comprehensive review" will ever produce a lasting monitoring regime. Such a regime is, however, a very important goal. Even if the United States and Britain do carry out extensive military strikes against suspect Iraqi facilities, their effect is likely to be temporary and uncertain. The world may have to write off the IAEA and UNSCOM, and Desert Fox is a warning that this could come at any time. However, the fact that the UN inspection efforts have limits, and have reached their point of diminishing returns, is not a reason to give up on either the IAEA and UNSCOM or to treat the monitoring phase of their operations as unimportant.

IRAQ'S FUTURE STRATEGY OF OPPORTUNISM

There is no way to read the mind of the present or future Iraqi regimes, and there are acute limits to the ability to predict how Iraq's politics and strategic culture will affect its acquisition and use of weapons of mass destruction. Both the West and Iraq's neighbors, however, must proceed on the basis of several assumptions about the future course of the "war of sanctions":

- Iraq will seek to end any remaining UN inspection efforts at the earliest possible moment, will continue to lie to the UN, and will do everything possible to make the UN's efforts ineffective.
- Iraq will do everything possible to avoid the conversion of the inspection phase of IAEA and UNSCOM activities to a meaningful and lasting monitoring regime.
- Iraq will continue the covert biological, chemical, nuclear, and missile programs it has instituted since the Gulf War, and it will continue to smuggle in equipment and parts to reinforce its breakout capability in spite of UN inspection efforts.

Policy Implications of Iraq's Weapons of Mass Destruction 647

- Iraq will seek the lifting of UN sanctions in ways that give it maximum access to the capital it needs for weapons of mass destruction and maximum uncontrolled access to dual use technology and production materials like feedstocks and growth cultures.
- Iraq will see arms control as merely an extension of the regional arms race by other means, and it will lie or cheat whenever this suits its interests.
- Iraq will seek the deadliest and most effective weapons of mass destruction it can obtain for the purposes of intimidation, deterrence, and war fighting. Efforts that deny it access to nuclear weapons will end in increasing its interest in biological weapons.
- Iraq will at least seriously consider options for the covert, indirect, or terrorist proxy use of weapons of mass destruction.
- Iraq will, at a minimum, seek to develop a sheltered or highly dispersed capability to launch survivable biological and chemical attacks against Iranian, Kuwaiti, Saudi, and Israeli population centers, and key US power projection facilities in the Gulf the moment UN sanctions are lifted. It will seek to develop launch-on-warning, launch-under-attack, and ride-out retaliatory options.
- Iraq will continue to seek nuclear weapons, although it may shift to covert efforts to acquire fissile materials, actual weapons, and/or centrifuge enrichment and plutonium separation.
- If it can do so, Iraq will seek to rebuild a capability for the massive use of chemical and possibly biological weapons at the tactical war-fighting level, and it will equip its land, air, and naval forces with such weapons.
- Iraqi doctrine and plans for the employment of weapons of mass destruction will in practice reflect the particular personality of Iraq's leader and be highly ideological and theoretical in nature. Iraq will not validate its plans and doctrine through extensive testing and war gaming, and it will react to a crisis on a largely extemporaneous basis. It will not have accurate damage assessment capabilities, and the control of escalation and follow-on strikes will be improvised by a senior leadership with only limited understanding of the effect of its weapons and capabilities.
- Iraq will be deterred primarily by the threat of immediate retaliation with weapons of mass destruction. In practice, this means large-scale Iranian retaliation in kind, or the Israeli or US use of nuclear weapons.

There is no way to be certain how many resources Iraq will allocate to conventional weapons, unconventional warfare and security operations, or weapons of mass destruction in the future. Even if Iraq has formulated detailed plans, which seems doubtful, it must react to outside factors like the duration and intensity of UN sanctions, the level of UN inspections, future oil revenues, its problems in dealing with its Kurds and Shi'ites, its problems with Iran and Kuwait, and the need to balance domestic demand against military ambition. Much will also depend on how long Saddam Hussein remains in power, although it is easy to overemphasize his importance.

The trends in Iraq's efforts to acquire weapons of mass destruction are a strong argument that any strategy for dealing with Iraq must assume that Iraq will pursue its effort to acquire weapons of mass destruction indefinitely into the future, that it will carry out a major clandestine purchasing effort, that it will maintain clandestine facilities, and that it will systematically lie about its efforts. Nothing the present Iraqi government says can be taken seriously without total independent verification. They are also strong arguments for continuing the UN effort as long as possible, for pushing Iraq into arms control agreements and making every effort to enforce them, and for establishing the tightest possible supplier nation controls on this aspect of Iraq's imports.

IRAQI PROLIFERATION IS NOT "SADDAM DEPENDENT"

It is dangerous to assume Iraqi efforts to proliferate are linked to the survival of Saddam Hussein and the Ba'ath elite. Most future Iraqi leaders are likely to have somewhat similar fears and ambitions—at least in the near term. No Iraqi leader will be able to ignore the efforts of Iran or Israel, or the potential challenge posed by the United States and its allies in the Southern Gulf. Such leaders are likely to be products of the same Sunni elite as Saddam, and to rely on a high degree of authoritarianism and use of the instruments of state power. Even "pragmatic" or "moderate" replacements for Saddam will not ignore the potential threat posed by Iran and Iran's weapons of mass destruction programs. They are also likely to seek to use weapons of mass destruction as at least covert counters to US power projection capability and ways of intimidating or influencing their Southern Gulf neighbors.

Barring regional arms control agreements with a degree of intrusiveness that now seems impossible to negotiate or implement, Iraq's leaders are likely to pursue weapons of mass destruction programs at some level, almost regardless of their ideology. For similar reasons, virtually all Iraqi leaders are likely to see arms control agreements as being forced on Iraq from the outside, and see cheating on such agreements while attempting to enforce them on neighboring states as legitimate. Iraqi leaders other than Saddam may use better words, but they are almost certain to continue to lie.

Regardless of which Iraqi leader is in power, it seems likely that Iraq's efforts to develop weapons of mass destruction will be pursued on a target of opportunity basis, and to meet broad political ambitions and the personal goals of Iraq's leaders. Iraq is unlikely to take completely reckless steps or to ignore basic technological realities, but it is also unlikely to articulate and implement highly structured force development plans or develop and implement a detailed military doctrine for employing weapons of mass destruction.

Furthermore, any Iraqi leader is likely to improvise his approach to deploying and using such weapons in reaction to a given crisis, and to alter employment doctrine on the basis of events. It is extremely unlikely that Iraq will seek to create a highly structured pattern of deterrence similar to the one that helped shape the Cold War, and will develop detailed targeting doctrines and escalation ladders.

IRAQI ESCALATION AND WAR-FIGHTING

This does not mean that such leaders, including Saddam, will be suicidal, fanatical, or take what they regard as irrational risks. It may, however, mean that such leaders identify themselves with the state and with Iraq's future. It may mean that they will use weapons of mass destruction against Iraq's neighbors at the tactical level, and/or against Iraq's Shi'ites and Kurds to stay in power or to protect their conventional forces. It may mean that they will strike preemptively against a key enemy like Iran, or create forces designed to deter the United States with a launch-on-warning/launch-under-attack or retaliatory capability. The West and the Southern Gulf states cannot ignore the fact that the Iraqi leadership might well feel that a "ride out" strategy would simply reinforce Iraq's weakness and be fundamentally "irrational" in character.

Iraqi efforts to use weapons of mass destruction for political and war-fighting purposes may follow fundamentally different patterns from those that the United States and Soviet Union institutionalized during the Cold War. Regardless of whether nor not Iraq is led by Saddam, it may

- fail to articulate a strategy of deterrence or employment, or only describe one consisting of rhetoric rather than detailed war-fighting capabilities.
- develop and produce weapons of mass destruction using massive efforts at concealment, denial, and compartmentation—focusing more on the acquisition and development effort than employment. Targeting plans, test and evaluation, and understanding of lethality will be limited. Joint warfare concepts will rarely be articulated, and doctrine will not be practiced.
- keep actual delivery units covert or compartmentalized from other forces, and under the direct control of ruling elites with little real military experience. Actual weapons may often be held separately from delivery systems and by special units chosen more for loyalty than for capability.
- provide separate lines of C^4I/BM reporting, which go directly to the leadership.
- employ weapons in ways which are crisis driven, and utilization and escalation will be more a product of the attitudes and decisions of a narrow, ruling political elite rather than the result of the advice of the military command chain. Risk taking will be leader specific and based on perceptions of a crisis shaped more by internal political attitudes than an objective understanding of the military situation.
- show limited restraint in attacking civilian targets or mass employment against armed forces. Regimes may take existential risks in escalating if they feel they are likely to lose power.
- use proxies and unconventional delivery means where this seems politically desirable, and improvise such employment without warning.
- pay detailed attention to US counter-proliferation and ATBM efforts at the technical level, and the lessons of previous wars. They will seek to steadily improve concealment, denial, and countermeasures.

- see arms control as an extension of conflict and rivalry by other means, not as a valid security option.
- consider using proxy groups or unconventional delivery of weapons of mass destruction to attack outside the context of a war. Such an attack might be launched against a peace process, US commitment to the defense of a given region, a peacekeeping force, an election, a ruling elite, or internal groups hostile to the Iraqi ruling elite.
- find covert or unconventional delivery of weapons of mass destruction preferable to the use of advanced delivery systems. For example, Iraq could use cargo ships, passenger aircraft, commercial vehicles, dhows, or commercial cargo shipments, and route them through multiple destinations. Iraq has a well-established series of covert transport and smuggling networks throughout the region, and it might use proxy or terrorist groups to manufacture biological weapons in situ.
- use biological agents for indirect attacks. Iraq might consider the use of such agents to mirror image local diseases or with long gestation times. Persistent nerve agents could be used in subways, large buildings, shopping malls/bazaars, and so on to create both immediate casualties and long-term risks.
- use mixes of different biological and chemical agents to defeat detection and protection gear or vaccines.
- develop a covert "breakout" capability. The development of a capability to manufacture several hundred biological and chemical weapons suddenly, with little or no warning, is well within Iraq's state of the art, using nothing but commercial supplies and equipment, and much of the effort could be conducted as civil or defensive research.
- see an increasing incentive for the unconventional use of weapons of mass destruction in proportion to Iraq's lack of parity in conventional weapons, and/or the prospect of catastrophic defeat.

The punchline is that any assumptions that Iraq will cease to try proliferating are likely to prove a dangerous exercise in wishful thinking. Iraq will only be constrained as long as UN sanctions provide leverage, and UN inspection efforts can continue to operate with freedom of action and effectiveness. No political or economic argument is going to solve the problem. No export agreement will be "leakproof," and no arms control agreement short of the most Draconian region-wide, intrusive control regime will remove Iraq's incentive to acquire weapons of mass destruction.

NOTES

1. Reuters, January 24, 1998, 0015.
2. IAEA and White House information sheets, May, 1997.

Chapter 21

Iraq's Military Future

The consequences of a status quo are relatively easy to predict. Iraq's military future will only be limited as long as the UN controls Iraq's legal imports and oil revenues, prevents conventional arms imports, and some form of UN monitoring and/or inspection regime is in place. The question is, what will happen if Iraq undercuts UN controls and sanctions, or is able to exploit "sanctions fatigue" to the point where sanctions are lifted?

It is unrealistic to hope for "moderation" in Saddam Hussein's regime or a predictable end to the "war of sanctions." It is equally unrealistic to expect that a new leader will bring a complete end to Iraq's challenge to its neighbors and the West, or its efforts to proliferate. The Gulf War did not change Saddam's fundamental behavior, and neither has the "war of sanctions." Saddam's most probable near-term successors are likely to be products of the Ba'ath, Saddam's coterie, and/or the military than true moderates. They are also more likely to be minority Sunnis from some mix of clans and tribes than a true national government. While no one can rule out the possibility of an Iraqi Ataturk or Sadat, such leadership is more likely to change Iraq's image and moderate the more controversial aspects of its behavior than change its fundamental strategic perspective.

Iraq's mid- to long-term political prospects are more favorable. It is unlikely that any sequence of ruling elites will continue to ignore Iraq's pressing demographic and economic problems to the extent that Saddam has, or that any successors can provide the same mix of political skills and reckless ambition. However, it is unclear when a national leadership will come to power that can bridge Iraq's deep divisions by religion, ethnic group, tribe, and clan. Iraq is likely to have authoritarian minority leaders for some time to come, and Iraq's geography alone makes it likely that Iraq's rulers will believe that they must compete with Iran, Saudi Arabia, and the United States for regional influence and power. Iraq is not proliferating simply because its current regime is radical and extreme; it is proliferating because it has good and enduring strategic reasons to do so.

The West and other Gulf states need to accept this reality. They need to understand the fact that they have a vital interest in maintaining export controls on weapons and dual use items, and the efforts of the UN, just as long as such controls and efforts can be maintained. They need to understand that arms control negotiations with Iraq will be an extension of the "war of sanctions" by other means, and that only strong military forces and counterproliferation efforts can deter and defend against Iraq's breakout capabilities and a post-sanctions expansion of its proliferation effort. The world has to learn to live with the true nature of Iraq's "strategic culture" and its unpredictability and opportunism.

IRAQ'S NEAR-TERM CAPABILITIES

Iraq's near-term contingency capabilities can be predicted with a reasonsable degree of confidence. While it is impossible to dismiss a long list of "wild card" events and changes, it is possible to summarize the most probable trends in Iraq's military future by looking at a range of the most likely contingencies and Iraq's present and future capabilities in each such contingency.

Attacks on Kuwait

Iraq's land forces still retain significant war-fighting capabilities and much of the force structure that made Iraq the dominant military power in the Gulf after its victory over Iran. It seems highly unlikely that Iraq would do more than threaten Kuwait, hoping to gain political status in the process. At the same time, any mix of political factors that forced the United States to withdraw from the Gulf, which separated Kuwait from Saudi Arabia, or which fractured the key elements of the military Coalition that liberated Kuwait in the Gulf War, might change this situation. Saddam Hussein or his successors might also see such an attack as a way of uniting Iraq if they felt their regime was threatened by internal divisions, or might react out of sheer frustration with "sanctions fatigue."

Iraqi forces can still seize Kuwait in a matter of days or occupy part of Saudi Arabia's Eastern province, *if* they do not face immediate opposition from US, Kuwaiti, and Saudi forces. USCENTCOM and US experts indicate that Iraq could assemble and deploy five heavy divisions south into Kuwait in a matter of days. Iraqi divisions now have an authorized strength of about 10,000 men, and about half of the Iraqi army's 23 divisions had manning levels of around 8,000 men and "a fair state of readiness." Republican Guards divisions had an average of around 8,000 to 10,000 men. Brigades averaged around 2,500 men— the size of a large US battalion.

Even today, Iraq has five Republican Guards divisions within 140 kilometers of the Kuwaiti and Saudi border. It can rapidly deploy two to five divisions against Kuwait from the area around Basra. A recent background briefing by USCENTCOM indicates that Kuwait could only rapidly deploy a few combat strength battalions to defend its territory, and Saudi Arabia would take days to deploy even one heavy brigade into areas north of Kuwait City. The tyranny of geography, Kuwait's small size, and Saudi Arabia's widely dispersed army give Iraq a natural advantage in any sudden or surprise attack.

Unless there are weeks of strategic warning, Kuwait, Saudi Arabia, and the United States will lack the land forces to stop Iraq. A force of five Iraqi divisions would compare favorably with total Kuwaiti forces of about four brigades, with only about a brigade equivalent combat ready, and with a total forward-deployed US strength that normally does not include a single forward-deployed land brigade. The Saudi forces at Hafr al Batin are at most the equivalent of two combat-effective brigades, which would probably take two weeks to fully deploy forward to the Kuwait and Saudi borders in sustainable, combat-ready form. The so-called GCC rapid deployment force is largely a political fiction with no meaningful real-world combat capability against Iraqi heavy divisions.

There is little prospect that this situation will improve in the near term. The United States has not been able to pre-position large numbers of equipment sets in or near Kuwait, and pre-positioning brigade sets in Qatar and the UAE means that such forces would take at least a week to 10 days to deploy in combat-ready form in Kuwait. Kuwait is making only limited progress in its military modernization, and the Saudi army has made little progress in improving its capability to move quickly to the defense of Kuwait or to concentrate its forces along the Saudi border with Iraq.

As a result, the ability to deal with a sudden Iraqi attack on Kuwait is likely to depend on the United States' ability to mass offensive air and missile power and to use it immediately against Iraq the moment major troop movements begin. The United States will also require the full support of Saudi Arabia and the other Southern Gulf countries to assist in the deployment and basing of US forces in the region, support from friendly, local forces like the Saudi air force, and a firm and an immediate Kuwaiti willingness to allow the United States and Saudi Arabia to employ force.

Even then, the defense of Kuwait will be an increasingly "close run thing." Even today, Iraqi land forces might penetrate into Kuwait City in spite of US, Saudi, and Kuwaiti airpower—if Iraq was willing to take very high losses in reaching and seizing the city. If Iraq then took the Kuwaiti population hostage, it might succeed. The only way Iraqi forces could then be dislodged would be through a combination of another land build-up in Saudi Arabia by the US and allied forces, and a massive strategic/interdiction air campaign against targets on Iraqi territory.

The essential dilemma in any "second liberation" of Kuwait would be US, Saudi, and Kuwaiti willingness to act in the face of potential massacres of

Kuwaiti civilians, versus the willingness of an Iraqi regime to accept massive damage to Iraq. It seems likely that the United States and Saudi Arabia would show the necessary ruthlessness if the Kuwaiti government supported such action. Oil is too strategically important to cede such a victory to a leader like Saddam Hussein.

The outcome might be different, however, as sanctions ease or end, and Iraq rebuilds more of its military capabilities. There are a number of "wild cards" in such a case:

- Iraq may somehow obtain nuclear weapons, or demonstrate the possession of highly lethal biological weapons.
- The United States may be forced to reduce its forward presence and readiness in the Gulf to the point where it could not rapidly surge air power, and/or had reduced its overall power projection capabilities.
- Iraq may choose a more limited and "acceptable" objective like restoring its pre–Gulf War border or demanding access to Bubiyan, Warbah, the Kwar Abdullah, and the Gulf.
- Saudi Arabia may not immediately and fully support US action and commit its own forces.
- A Kuwait government may refuse to accept the cost of continuing to fight in the face of ruthless Iraqi action against a "hostage" Kuwaiti people.

Civil War in Iraq

Iraq's forces have already shown that they have the military strength to defeat its lightly armed Kurds in a matter of weeks if UN forces cease to protect them. The Iraqi army has effectively defeated all serious Shi'ite resistance. It would take a massive uprising, and possibly a major division within Iraq's military forces, for any civil conflict to challenge the regime.

This does not mean that backing the Iraqi opposition will not eventually shift the military situation, and a coup could come at almost any time. History is a constant warning that dictators can suddenly fall with little or no warning, and at a time when outside experts are confidently talking about their strength and the security of their position.

Saddam's position may erode over time, and US, British, and regional backing of outside opposition groups may eventually create outside opposition movements that are effective. It is dangerous, however, to use nations like Jordan and Kuwait as bases for military resistance movements or to try to treat the Kurdish Security Zone as a base for opposition movements as distinguished from a way to protect the Kurds. The end result may be to create targets the United States and Britain have to try to protect, and which will be vulnerable to penetration by the Iraqi intelligence and security services. Backing the growth of a political opposition is one thing; premature military adventures are quite another.

Power is now so centralized among Sunni tribal elites, who control virtually all senior posts in the military and security forces, that any struggle for power seems more likely to take the form of a coup and counter-coup than civil war. Nevertheless, no one can dismiss the possibility, however, that Saddam Hussein will take another major military risk and end in making another strategic mistake. Saddam may well be able to survive the present situation, but not another major defeat.

At the same time, the military balance is not a reason to be overcautious, nor it is the risk that Iraq may splinter into ethnic and religious faction if there is internal violence. It is possible that the Iraqi military could split over the struggle for power after Saddam, and combine warlordism with regional and ethnic alliances. Any serious north-south split within the army could trigger a significant civil conflict, although it is impossible to predict the resulting balance of power and ethnic and political alignments. Such a struggle might also trigger limited Iranian and Turkish intervention.

Violence is often the key to meaningful political change, and Iraqi nationalism should not be underestimated. Most Shi'ite Arabs in Iraq almost certainly think of themselves as Arabs and not Shi'ites. Both the ordinary Sunni and Shi'ite have suffered under Saddam and have little history of mutual violence, and many Kurds are fully willing to remain Iraqi if they are granted basic human rights, a reasonable share of the nation's oil wealth, and the right to a cultural identify. The status quo is scarcely desirable enough to make it a reason to support Saddam and his kind of rule. Ironically, the authoritarian and militaristic nature of many Iraqi institutions also makes it likely that a new successor elite will come to power with the ability to hold the country together.

Confrontation in the Gulf

Iraq has almost none of the assets necessary to win a naval-air battle against US forces in the Gulf, and it has no prospect of acquiring these assets in the foreseeable future. It would have to rebuild, modernize, and massively expand both its regular navy and air force at levels of strength and capability it simply cannot hope to achieve for the next half decade. Alternatively, Iraq could develop its capabilities to deliver weapons of mass destruction to the point where it could back its conventional military capabilities with a threat that might seriously inhibit US military action and/or the willingness of Southern Gulf states to support the United States and provide air and naval facilities.

Unlike Iran, Iraq cannot conduct meaningful surface ship, naval air force, and amphibious operations. Currently, the Iraqi navy can only conduct limited mine warfare and land-based anti-ship missile attacks and surprise raids on off-shore facilities. Its air force may be able to conduct limited anti-ship missile attacks using its Mirage F-1s, but would have to find a permissive environment to survive. Iraqi Mirage F-1s burdened with the AM-39 Exocet would be unlikely to survive Kuwaiti, Saudi, or Iranian air defenses without a level of air escort capability that Iraq cannot currently provide.

Iraq has little ability to intimidate its neighbors into accepting such operations as long as the United States has the ability to use its air and missile power to inflict enough strategic damage on Iraq to create a massive deterrent to any Iraqi escalation to chemical or biological weapons, and back these capabilities with the ultimate threat of US theater nuclear escalation.

This does not mean that Iraqi air and/or naval forces could not score some gains from a sudden, well-planned raid in the Gulf. Iraq could not sustain any initial success, however, and would probably accomplish nothing more than to provoke a US, a Southern Gulf, or an Iranian reaction that would far offset any advantages Iraq could gain. The only exception might be a proxy unconventional or terrorist attack that allowed Iraq to preserve some degree of plausible deniability.

The "wild cards" in such contingencies are US determination to act, the future size of the US presence in the Gulf, US ability to surge its power projection capabilities at the time of a given crisis, Southern Gulf support for the United States and willingness to provide the United States with suitable facilities, and the political liabilities the United States would face—if any—in terms of the response from nations outside of the region. Far more is involved in a confrontation in the Gulf than Iraq's military capability, and Iraq will be able to acquire far more contingency capability if the United States could not respond for political or budgetary reasons.

Similarly, much will depend over time on Iranian, Southern Gulf, and Western reactions to Iraq's efforts to rebuild the naval strike capability of its air force, and to build up a meaningful blue water navy. A passive response would obviously strengthen Iraq. So would any indifference to Iraqi efforts to improve its access to the Gulf by renewing its pressure on Kuwait to grant Iraq access to Bubiyan and Warbah, or to secure the channels to Umm Qasr. Even then, however, it is difficult to see how Iraq can acquire much contingency capability beyond the upper Gulf, unless Iran and/or Saudi Arabia are indifferent or supportive of Iraqi action.

Confrontation or Conflict with Iran

The cumulative impact of UN sanctions is slowly eroding the capabilities of Iraqi land and air forces relative to those of Iran, and Iraq has only very limited ability to use chemical warfare in another Iran-Iraq conflict. Iraq cannot hope to challenge Iran's naval strength or deny Iran naval and commercial access to the Gulf. Iran is now a much stronger defensive power than it was in 1988, both because of Iran's force improvements and because of Iraq's defeat and the sanctions that have followed.

It is far from clear, however, that Iran will acquire enough of an "edge" over Iraq to win a major conflict and avoid a repetition of the grinding war of attrition that took place during the Iran-Iraq War. In spite of Saddam Hussein, the Iraqi army seems more likely to unite in a defensive conflict than to divide, and it still has nearly twice Iran's tank strength and a superior air force.

The "wild cards" in any contingencies involving a conflict between Iran and Iraq are the possibility of internal unrest and divisions in Iraq that are serious enough to split the Iraqi armed forces, and/or which lead to a new Shi'ite uprising. Similarly, a major Kurdish uprising would greatly complicate Iraq's ability to concentrate its forces to defend against an Iranian attack on Iraq's center and south.

At the same time, any Iranian victory over Iraq might prove to be more apparent than real. It is far from clear that the United States or the Southern Gulf states would tolerate an Iranian victory that did more than depose the present Iraqi regime. Further, the split between Persian, Arab, and Kurd seems likely to remain so great that Iraqi independence would rapidly reassert itself if Iran attempted to occupy or dominate a substantial part of Iraq.

Further, an escalation to the use of weapons of mass destruction against urban, economic, and large military area targets could introduce great uncertainties into such a conflict. Iran now has a major advantage in terms of biological and chemical weapons, and this advantage will grow steadily until UN sanctions on Iraq are lifted. Iraq could then rebuild its strategic delivery capabilities relatively quickly, however, and the end result of any sustained conflict of this kind would be difficult to predict.

The greatest single uncertainty would be the development and use of advanced biological weapons with near nuclear lethality, or the assembly and use of a nuclear device assembled with weapons grade fissile material bought from an outside source. There may be little or no warning of such a strategic development, and the United States is unlikely to extend its deterrent coverage over either Iran or Iraq. Another wild card is that a US or an Israeli counter-proliferation strike on either Iraq or Iran could make the target vulnerable enough for the other country to exploit the resulting window of opportunity.

Adventures in the Southern Gulf

There is little near-term prospect that Iraq will develop enough power projection capability—and supporting power from its navy, air force, and weapons of mass destruction—to win any conflict in the Southern Gulf where it does not attack by land into Kuwait or across the Saudi border. The only exception would seem to be a case where it operated in support of a coup or uprising, or when Iraqi volunteers operated in Southern Yemen in 1994. Any Iraqi attack on a Southern Gulf state is also the contingency most likely to unite the United States and the Southern Gulf states and to ensure European and other support for a strong US-Southern Gulf response.

At the same time, there are three important "wild cards" affecting Iraqi military involvement in the Southern Gulf:

1. Nothing can prevent Iraq from exploiting the fracture lines within and between the Southern Gulf states. Iraq has much less capacity than Iran to exploit the Shi'ite unrest

in Bahrain and Saudi Arabia, but it might be able to exploit future confrontations between Bahrain and Qatar and Saudi Arabia and Yemen.

2. The United States would face serious problems in responding to any change of government in a Southern Gulf state that resulted in a pro-Arab/pro-Iraqi regime and which sought Iraqi military advice or an Iraqi military presence. The United States cannot save a Gulf regime from its own people or (openly) endorse such action by other Southern Gulf countries.
3. Iraq's process of creeping proliferation is making enough progress so that the United States and the Southern Gulf states must reach some degree of agreement on taking suitable counterproliferation measures. A power vacuum in which Iraq proliferates, the Southern Gulf states grow steadily more vulnerable, and US resolve seems progressively more questionable could give Iraq far more capability to directly or indirectly intervene in Southern Gulf affairs.

Wars Against Israel

At least in the near term, Iraq is so weak that it seems unlikely that it would directly provoke Israel by doing anything more than sending limited forces to Jordan or Syria if another major conflict should somehow take place between Israel and its key neighbors. Iraq could move a corps size force into Jordan or Syria within a matter of days, although it would take weeks to give it the substantial capability needed to sustain itself in intensive combat. It could also deploy air units, although it presently does not have the ability to operate within the Jordanian or Syrian C^4I/BM and identification of friend or foe (IFF) system. Improving this situation requires the extensive rebuilding of Iraq's military capabilities, and joint exercises with Jordan and/or Syria.

Until recently, such a prospect seemed very doubtful. Jordan has made peace with Israel, and King Hussein actively supported Iraqi opposition movements during 1994–1996. Syria fought against Iraq in the Gulf War, and its president, Hafaz Asad, has long been a bitter rival of Saddam Hussein. The deterioration of the Arab-Israel peace process in 1996–1997, however, led Syria to take a progressively harder line towards Israel and to reach out for new allies. At the same time, Iraq's search to end sanctions and break out of its containment led it to approach Syria. Iraq and Syria began to hold serious meetings for the first time in a half decade. The border was opened for limited traffic, and key Iraqi papers like *Babel* began to call for Iraqi-Syrian military cooperation as a "useful action to all Arabs," and for Iraq and Syria to "resume diplomatic ties."

It still seems unlikely that such conflicts will take place involving Egypt or Jordan, as long as President Mubarak, King Hussein, or any other moderate leaders remain in power. Asad has shown little interest in taking such risks and remains hostile to Saddam Hussein. Iraq must also realize that it is extremely unlikely that Israel will show restraint in any future missile war, and would probably escalate to the use of nuclear weapons if Iraq made any attributable use of weapons of mass destruction against Israel's civilian population or large formations of Israeli military forces.

Turkey and the Kurds

Iraq is more likely to seek a tacit or an open Turkish alliance against the Kurds, or try to use a Kurdish faction against Turkey, than to seek direct military confrontation. There are, however, possibilities for conflict. One is a future Iraqi-Turkish "alliance" in the form of coordinated operations against the Kurds in the northern border area. Such an "alliance" would offer Turkey the prospect of denying its rebel Kurdish factions sanctuary and bases in the Iraqi border area, and offer Iraq both support in suppressing its Kurds and the prospect that Turkey would cease its raids across the border. Both nations have a strong incentive to secure the area in order to allow them to improve trade and the security of Iraq's pipeline through Turkey.

It is also possible that Turkey's constant incursions into Iraq's border area could trigger some kind of low-level fighting if Iraq's military forces should reoccupy the Kurdish security zone. Iraqi senior officials have increasingly protested Turkey's military actions in Iraq, and its establishment of a "security" zone inside of Iraq to halt Kurdish attacks on Turkey. They cannot ignore the fact that Turkey sent some 20,000 troops and F-16 jets to attack the forces of Kurdistan Workers Party (PKK) in the Khwakurk region of Iraq during the middle of Iraq's sanctions crisis in the fall of 1997.[1] Many senior Iraqi officials also seem to fear that Turkey might still attempt to annex some part of northern Iraq, including some of the oil fields in the area. These fears of Turkish ambitions are almost certainly exaggerated, but they are still very real.

Iraq would also probably react if the Kurdish zone became the basis for a well-organized military opposition to Saddam and the Iraqi regime. If the threat became large enough, it might well accept substantial losses, even if this meant US air and missile strikes. An equally likely result, however, would be divide and conquer tactics in dealing with the KDP and PUK, a massive effort to infiltrate any opposition efforts, and low-intensity combat in the form of assassinations. What is unlikely is that Iraq could be deterred from action by the threat of US military power long enough to allow an opposition movement to emerge as a serious military force when it knew it would have to encounter attacks later under less favorable terms.

Proxy Wars

Unlike Iran, Iraq has never demonstrated much capability to conduct "proxy wars" by training, arming, and funding Arab extremist movements. Iraq does sponsor some extremist and terrorist groups, but the end result has done little for Iraq. Iraq also lacks Iran's bases, training centers, and staging facilities in other countries, and the political support of third nations like the Sudan and

Syria, which are close to the scene of such proxy conflicts. Similarly, Iraq can only hope to win proxy wars fought against vulnerable governments. Attempts to fight such wars will have little impact on a successful Arab-Israeli peace settlement, or in sustaining civil conflict in the face of a government that demonstrates that it has the capacity to govern and deal with its social problems.

At the same time, the failure of the peace process and of secular regimes may make Iraq's use of proxy wars more successful in the future. So would the creation of a radical Arab regime in Jordan, Egypt, or Syria, which might turn to Iraq for support. Iraq also has a strong revanchist motive to use proxy warfare against Israel, Saudi Arabia, and the United States.

Unconventional Offensive Conflicts

Similarly, Iraq may seek to improve its capabilities for unconventional warfare, including the use of chemical and biological weapons. The practical problem Iraq faces will be to find a place and contingency where it can exploit such capabilities that offer more return than using proxies, and which allows Iraq to act at an acceptable level of risk.

In broad terms, there do not seem to be any current contingencies where Iraq can achieve major gains by using unconventional military forces in offensive warfare. The closest case seems to be Turkey's struggle with its Kurds, but Turkey is an extraordinarily dangerous opponent for Iraq to provoke, and any Iraqi aid to Turkey's Kurds would present further problems in Iraq's efforts to control its own Kurds.

The key "wild cards" affecting this set of contingencies are Iraq's willingness to take the risk of using its unconventional forces and alienating other states, the uncertain value of such adventures, and the willingness of other states and movements to accept such Iraqi support and the political price tag that would come with it. This situation might change if:

- Iraq could send volunteers to Lebanon and Syria under circumstances where such conflicts had broad Arab support, and Israel was sufficiently preoccupied with other threats so that it could not retaliate;
- actively supporting some opposition force in Iran appeared to be a safe way of limiting the Iranian threat or ending Iranian support for anti-Iraqi movements;
- supporting an alienated Yemen offered Iraq a low-cost way of using unconventional forces to threaten or put pressure on Saudi Arabia;
- support of some movement in Turkey seemed likely to gain Iraq broader support in Turkey; and
- a civil conflict took place in Kuwait or Saudi Arabia.

None of these contingencies now seem likely. At the same time, the risks of Iraq using its unconventional warfare capabilities should not be discounted. If nothing else, Iraq might act in a "spoiler role," attempting to deny some other nation influence, even if Iraq could not make clear strategic gains on its own.

Weapons of Mass Destruction

Iraq's present holdings of chemical and biological weapons probably are so limited that they do not seriously constrain US freedom of action or do much to intimidate most of Iraq's neighbors. Iran now also has a significant lead over Iraq. Nevertheless, Iraq's possession of such weapons inevitably affects US, British, Israeli, and Southern Gulf perceptions of the risks inherent in attacking Iraq. Much depends on these outside perceptions of the risk in engaging Iraq, refusing its demands, and dealing with Iraqi aggression and/or retaliation.

It seems unlikely that Iraq can reach the point in the near term where its capabilities are great enough to change US, British, Israeli, and/or Southern Gulf perceptions of risk to the point where they would limit or paralyze outside military action. Further, it seems unlikely that Iraq can continue to build up its capabilities without provoking strong US counterproliferation programs, including retaliatory strike capabilities. The same is true of a response by Iran and the Southern Gulf states. As a result, Iraq's acquisition of weapons of mass destruction may end simply in provoking an arms race, even when UN sanctions are lifted.

Arms races do not, however, always bring deterrence and stability. Several "wild cards" deserve special attention:

- One such "wild card" is a successful Iraqi attempt to buy significant amounts of weapons-grade material. This could allow Iraq to achieve a nuclear breakout capability in a matter of months. Both the United States and the region would find it much harder to adjust to such an Iraqi effort than to the slow development of nuclear weapons by creating fissile material in Iraq. It seems likely that the United States could deal with the situation by extending a nuclear umbrella over the Gulf, but even so, the Southern Gulf states might be far more responsive to Iraqi pressure and intimidation. Most, after all, are so small that they are virtually "one-bomb states";

- Another wild card is a change in the US and regional perception of biological weapons. Biological weapons are now perceived largely as unproven systems of uncertain lethality. Regardless of their technical capabilities, they have little of the political impact of nuclear weapons. Iran might, however, conduct live animal tests to demonstrate that its biological weapons have near-nuclear lethality or some power might demonstrate their effectiveness in another conflict. The successful mass testing or use of biological weapons might produce a rapid "paradigm shift" in the perceived importance of such weapons and of Iraq's biological warfare programs;

- Iraq might break out of UN sanctions and reveal a more substantial capability than now seems likely. Paradoxically, such an Iraqi capability would help legitimize Iran's and Israel's programs and the escalation to the use of such weapons;

- Iraq might use such weapons through proxies or in covert attacks with some degree of plausible deniability. Terrorism and unconventional warfare would be far more intimidating if they made use of weapons of mass destruction.

The Defense of Iraq

The previous contingencies assume that Iraq will take offensive action. If it does, it may well be confronted with a US-led attack. If this attack is confined to naval and coastal targets, particularly those Iraqi military capabilities that potentially threaten Gulf shipping, there is little Iraq can do other than to try to ride out the attack by dispersing and hiding its smaller boats, anti-ship missiles, and so on.

If a US-led attack includes strategic conventional missile strikes and bombings, there is equally little Iraq can do in terms of an immediate response, other than to escalate to using weapons of mass destruction in ways that are more likely to end in increasing the risk and damage to Iraq than to deter or damage US forces. Iraq can, however, respond over time with terrorism, unconventional warfare, and proxy wars. It is much easier to use air and missile power to inflict major damage on Iraq than it is to predict or control the political and military aftermath. The resulting casualties and damage will be extremely difficult to translate into an "end game."

Any US use of amphibious and land warfare would be considerably more difficult. Iraq can probably mount a significant defense against amphibious attacks on its coastline and islands. It is impossible to dismiss a popular Shi'ite or Kurdish uprising in support of an outside attack, but the most likely response would seem to be that Iraq's population would unite or remain passive, while US or Coalition forces were forced to advance over water barriers and through built-up areas.

The Iraqi army might collapse in the face of such an assault, but the Republican Guards is more likely to dig in and defend from positions co-located with Iraq's civil population, which would limit the ability to exploit airpower. Attacks on Iraqi territory that went beyond a punitive raid might be costly.

A US-led coalition could probably defeat Iraq's forces, but would have to be at least corps level in size, and occupying Iraq would be impractical without massive land forces of several corps. Further, Iraq's use of terrorism and weapons of mass destruction would be much easier to justify politically in a defensive conflict rather than an offensive one. Such outside attacks would probably end in futility and create an even more revanchist Iraq.

Exploiting "Wars of Intimidation"

The previous contingencies assume that Iraq's strength will be determined largely by the war-fighting capabilities of its military forces. Iraq may, however, be able to achieve some of its objectives through intimidation and/or direct and indirect threats. Iraq's ability to provide such intimidation is now very limited, but will improve steadily once UN sanctions are lifted. In many cases, Iraq's neighbors may be willing to increasingly accommodate Iran to some degree. This is particularly true of those states which see Iran as a more serious threat—such as Bahrain, Oman, Qatar, and the UAE.

Much will depend on regional perceptions of the long-term resolve of the United States, the ability of the Southern Gulf states to avoid major divisions, and the willingness of the Southern Gulf states to show that they will support a firm US response to Iraq, even at some risk. Much will also depend on the ability of Iraq's leadership to set achievable demands and avoid open confrontation. In broad terms, it seems likely that Iraq's ability to intimidate will slowly improve over time, but there is no way to predict how quickly or by how much.

CONTAINMENT AND DETERRENCE: THE MID-TERM AND LONG-TERM RISKS OF AN END TO THE WAR OF SANCTIONS

Like the Cold War, there is no way to predict any end to the war of sanctions. The only thing that is predictable is that the war will end, and Desert Fox is a warning that it may end by slowly lifting the UN's controls on Iraq. This will present major mid- and long-term risks. Until fundamental changes take place in Iraq's regime—changes which are proven by the test of time—the West and Southern Gulf states have every reason to limit Iraq's access to arms and technology and to limit its efforts to acquire weapons of mass destruction to the lowest possible level. The stability of the Gulf is highly dependent on Iraqi perceptions that the United States and Southern Gulf states are not vulnerable to intimidation and attacks, on Iran's ability to preserve rough military parity, and on the continued presence of US forces in the region.

If sanctions are lifted or eased, Iraq still will not be able to rebuild its military power quickly. It averaged nearly $3 billion a year in conventional arms imports during the decade before the Gulf War, and it needed at least $1.5 billion to $2 billion a year to sustain and modernize its conventional forces. While it is impossible to make any precise estimates, it would probably take over $20 billion worth of imports for Iraq to modernize and recapitalize its conventional forces and to react to the technical and force modernization lessons of the Gulf War. It cannot do this quickly, for its economy is too weak. It takes time to place orders and receive delivery, restructure forces, and adopt new training methods and tactics. Iraq's authoritarian leadership also constantly emphasizes its own security over the kind of military reforms that might encourage coups, and sets grandiose and personal goals that limit the influence of Iraq's true military professionals.

It will be far easier for Iraq to acquire and deploy limited numbers of chemical and biological weapons than to rebuild and modernize an effective force to fight any kind of organized war with weapons of mass destruction. It cannot acquire modern ballistic missiles quickly without a major foreign supplier, and it will take at least a half decade to build up a modern air force with advanced strike capabilities. Unless it can obtain fissile material from a foreign source, it will face major problems in rebuilding a nuclear weapons program.

Iraq will also find it easier and cheaper to proliferate than to modernize and rebuild its conventional forces. As a result, the initial stages of any easing of UN sanctions are likely to see Iraq emphasize weapons of mass destruction over conventional weapons, and Iraq may be able to build up a considerable capability to threaten and intimidate its neighbors long before it develops that kind of war-fighting capability that would allow it to directly challenge Iran or a combination of Southern Gulf states and Western military power. The same states that ease UN controls in reaction to "sanctions fatigue" may well find "proliferation fatigue" much worse. Furthermore, the inevitable Iranian, Israeli, and Southern Gulf reaction to Iraqi proliferation is almost certain to add "arms race fatigue" to the problem.

Going on with sanctions is politically difficult and does not offer any predictable time frame or end to the sanctions process. Yet a similar mix of containment and deterrence was critical to creating "peaceful coexistence" during the Cold War, to leading to the meaningful arms control agreements between the East and West, and to ensuring that the collapse of the Soviet empire did not involve military adventures. Further, there may be more consensus in pursing such an approach than some analysts seem to realize. It is easy to forget that the debate over "dual containment" and "critical dialogue" is largely a non-debate in the West and the Southern Gulf when it comes to limiting arms transfers, the sale of dual use technologies, and the need for at least an "over-the-horizon" US military presence in the Gulf. There also is a tendency to ignore the fact that many of these aspects of containment have already proven successful.

Much of the problem with "sanctions fatigue" is not the result of military containment and deterrence. Rather, it is the result of policies which have confused the need to place tight controls on Iraq's regime with a failure to consider the plight and future of the Iraqi people. The UN, the West, and the United States in particular have not been aggressive enough in offering aid and expanding oil sales, and in putting concerted pressure on the Iraqi regime to choose relief and aid over manipulation of the hardships of the Iraqi people. UNSCOM's political masters have been far less effective than UNSCOM in fighting the "war of sanctions."

At the same time, it is important to note that there will be another major loser if UN sanctions and controls are eased to the point where the Iraqi regime can resume major arms imports and a military build-up. Iraq's people have nothing to gain from military adventures, massive Iraqi arms purchases, or any acquisition of weapons of mass destruction that simply intensifies the arms race in the region. Their security is not an issue if Iraq does not launch military adventures and Iran is safely contained. At the same time, the Iraqi people have a great deal to lose from any major war—a reality that the Iran-Iraq War and the Gulf War demonstrated all too well.

NOTE

1. Reuters, December 3, 1997, 0930.

Sources and Methods

This volume has been distributed for comment to a number of experts, intelligence officers, and officials in the United States and other countries to officials in several international agencies and institutions and to various private experts. The author has drawn heavily on the input of such reviewers throughout the text. It was agreed with each reviewer, however, that no individual or agency should be attributed at any point in the text except by specific request, and that all data used be attributed to sources that are openly available to the public. The reader should be aware of this in reviewing the notes section. The data contained in the analysis has often been extensively modified to reflect expert comment.

Data from open sources are deliberately drawn from a wide range of sources. Virtually all of these sources are at least in partial conflict. There is no consensus over demographic data, budget data, military expenditures and arms transfers, force numbers, unit designations, or weapons types.

While the use of computer databases allowed some cross-correlation and checking of such sources, the reporting on factors like force strengths, unit types and identities, and tactics often could not be reconciled. Citing multiple sources for each case is not possible and involves many detailed judgments by the authors in reconciling different reports and data.

The Internet and several on-line services were used extensively. Since such databases are dynamic, and change or are deleted over time, there is no clear way to footnote much of this material. Recent press sources are generally cited, but often are only part of the material consulted.

A broad effort has been made to standardize the analysis of each country, but it became clear early in the project that adopting a standard format did not suit the differences that emerged between countries. The emphasis throughout this phase of the Center for Strategic and International Studies net assessment has been on analyzing the detailed trends within individual states, and this aspect of the analysis has been given priority over country-to-country consistency.

In many cases, the author adjusted the figures and data used in the analysis on a "best guess" basis, drawing on some 30 years of experience in the field. In some other cases, the original data provided by a given source were used without adjustment to ensure comparability, even though this leads to some conflicts in dates, place names, force strengths, and so on within the material presented—particularly between summary tables surveying a number of countries and the best estimates for a specific country in the text. In such cases, it seemed best to provide contradictory estimates to give the reader some idea of the range of uncertainty involved. Some data had to be updated on the basis of interviews with US experts after Desert Fox.

Extensive use is made of graphics to allow the reader to easily interpret complex statistical tables and to see long-term trends. The graphic program used is deliberately standardized and kept relatively simple to allow the material portrayed to be as comparable as possible. Such graphics have a drawback, however, in that they often disguise differences in scale and exaggerate or minimize key trends. The reader should carefully examine the scale used in the left-hand axis of each graph.

Many value judgments regarding military effectiveness were made by the author on the basis of American military experience and standards. Although the author has lived in the Middle East and worked as a US advisor to several Middle Eastern governments, he feels that any attempt to create some Middle Eastern standard of reference is likely to be far more arbitrary than basing such judgments on his own military background.

Mapping and location names presented a major problem. The author used US Army and US Air Force detailed maps, commercial maps, and in some cases, commercial satellite photos. In many cases, however, the place names and terrain descriptions used in different sources presented major contradictions that could not be resolved from available maps. No standardization emerged about the spelling of place names. Sharp differences emerged in the geographic data published by various governments, and in the conflicting methods of transliterating Arabic and Farsi place names into English.

The same problem applied to reconciling the names of organizations and individuals—particularly those being transliterated from Arabic and Farsi. It became painfully obvious that little progress is being made in reconciling the conflicting methods of transliterating such names into English. A limited effort has been made to standardize the spellings used in this text, but many different spellings are tied to the relational database used in preparing the analysis, and the preservation of the original spelling is necessary to identify the source and tie it to the transcript of related interviews.

Selected Bibliography

Al-Ani, Khalid, *The Encyclopedia of Modern Iraq*, vol. III, Baghdad: The Arab Encyclopedia House, n.d., pp. 518–519.
al-Shawi, Hamid, "L'Intervention des militaires dans la vie politique de la Syrie, de l'Irak et de la Jordanie," *Politique Etrangère*, No. 3, 1974, pp. 343–374.
Albright, David, and Mark Hibbs, "Iraq and the Bomb: Were They Even Close?" *Bulletin of Atomic Scientists*, March, 1991, pp. 16–25.
———, "Iraq's Bomb: Blueprints and Artifacts," *Bulletin of the Atomic Scientists*, June, 1992, pp. 8–10.
———, "Iraq's Nuclear Hide and Seek," *Bulletin of the Atomic Scientists*, September, 1991, pp. 14–23.
———, "Iraq's Shop-Till-You-Drop Nuclear Program," *Bulletin of the Atomic Scientists*, April, 1992.
———, "It's All Over at Al Atheer," *Bulletin of the Atomic Scientists*, June, 1992, pp. 8–10.
———, "Supplier Spotting," *Bulletin of the Atomic Scientists*, June, 1992, pp. 8–9.
Albright, David, Frans Berkhout, and William Walker, *Plutonium and Highly Enriched Uranium, 1996—World Inventories, Capabilities, and Policies*, Oxford, SIPRI-Oxford Press, 1997.
Anderson, Gustav, "Analysis of Two Chemical Weapons Samples from the Iran-Iraq War," *NBC Defense and Technology International*, April, 1986, pp. 62–66.
Arnett, Eric H., "Issue Paper: Ballistic Missile Defense After the Kuwait War," Washington, American Academy for the Advancement of Science, 91–15S, July, 1991.
Arnett, Eric H., ed., *Military Capacity and the Risk of War: China, India, Pakistan, and India*, Stockholm, Stockholm Institute of Peace Research Institute, March, 1997.
Atkenson, Edward B., *The Powder Keg*, Falls Church, NOVA Publications, 1996.
Bahnemann, Jorg, and Thomas Enders, "Reconsider Ballistic Missile Defense," *Military Technology*, 4/91, pp. 46–52.

Belyakov, Rostislav, and Nikolai Buntin, "The MiG 29M Light Multirole Fighter," *Military Technology*, 8/94, pp. 41–44.

Bermudez, Joseph S., "Iran's Missile Development," in William C. Potter and Harlan W. Jencks, eds., *The International Missile Bazaar*, Boulder, Westview, 1994, pp. 47–74.

Bhatia, Shyam, *Nuclear Rivals in the Middle East*, London, Routledge, 1988, p. 85.

Blix, Hans, "Verification of Nuclear Nonproliferation: The Lesson of Iraq," *The Washington Quarterly*, Autumn, 1992, pp. 57–65.

Bowman, Steven R., "Iraqi Chemical Weapons Capabilities," Washington, Congressional Research Service, 93–292F, February 24, 1993.

Boyne, Sean, "Inside Iraq's Security Network," *Jane's Intelligence Review*, July, 1997, pp. 312–316, and August, 1997, pp. 365–367.

———, "Qusay Considers a Reshuffle for Iraq's Command Structure," *Jane's Intelligence Review*, September, 1997, pp. 416–417.

Bruce, James, "Iraq and Iran: Running the Nuclear Technology Race," *Jane's Defense Weekly*, December 5, 1988, p. 1307.

Carus, W. Seth, "Chemical Weapons in the Middle East," *Policy Focus*, Number Nine, Washington Institute for Near East Policy, December, 1988, p. 7.

———, *The Genie Unleashed: Iraq's Chemical and Biological Weapons Production*, Washington, Washington Institute Policy Papers, No. 14, 1989, p. 11.

Chartouni-Dubarry, May, "The Development of Internal Politics in Iraq from 1958 to the Present Day," in Derek Hopwood, Habib Ishow, and Thomas Koszinowski, eds., *Iraq: Power and Society*, Reading, Ithaca Press, 1993, pp. 19–36.

———, "La 'question irakienne' ou l'histoire d'une puissance contrariee," in Bassma Kodmani-Darwish and May Chartouni-Dubarry, eds., *Perceptions de securite et strategies nationales au Moyen-Orient*, Paris, Masson, 1994, pp. 57–60.

Chubin, Shahram, and Charles Tripp, *Iran and Iraq at War*, Boulder, Westview, 1988, pp. 114–120.

CIA, *World Factbook, 1996*, Washington, GPO, 1997, "Iraq."

Cigar, Norman, "Chemical Weapons and the Gulf War, the Dog That Did Not Bark," *Studies in Conflict and Terrorism*, Vol. 15, 1992, pp. 145–152.

Cohen, Eliot A., draft text of executive summary of *Gulf War Air Power Study*, April 28, 1993.

Cohen, Eliot A., Director, *Gulf War Air Power Survey, Volumes I-V*, Washington, GPO, 1993.

Conyers, Rep. John Jr., "The Patriot Myth: Caveat Emptor," *Arms Control Today*, Vol. 22, No. 9, November, 1992.

Cordesman, Anthony H., *After the Storm: The Changing Military Balance in the Middle East*, Boulder, Westview, 1993.

———, *The Gulf and the Search for Strategic Stability*, Boulder, Westview, 1984.

———, *Iran and Iraq: The Threat From the Northern Gulf*, Boulder, Westview, 1994.

———, "Terrorism and the Threat From Weapons of Mass Destruction in the Middle East: The Problem of Paradigm Shift," Washington, CSIS, October 17, 1996.

———, *Weapons of Mass Destruction in the Middle East*, London, Jane's/RUSI, 1992.

Cordesman, Anthony H., and Ahmed S. Hashim, *Iran: The Dilemmas of Dual Containment*, Boulder, Westview, 1997.

Cordesman, Anthony H., and Ahmed Hashim, *Iraq: Sanctions and Beyond*, Boulder, Westview, 1997.

Cordesman, Anthony H., and Abraham R. Wagner, *Lessons of Modern War, Volume II: The Iran-Iraq War*, Boulder, Westview, 1991.
Davis, J., and D. Kay, "Iraq's Secret Nuclear Weapons Program," *Physics Today*, July, 1992.
Davis, Zachary A., and Warren H. Donnelly, "Iraq and Nuclear Weapons," Congressional Research Service, IB90113, February 13, 1992.
Defense Intelligence Agency, *The Scud Missile: An Unclassified Overview for Policy Makers*, forwarded under U-3, 148/SVI-FOIA, October 22, 1997.
Defense News, various editions.
Dunn, Peter, "The Chemical War: Journey to Iran," *NBC Defense & Technology International*, pp. 28–37, and "Iran Keeps Chemical Options Open," pp. 12–14.
Eisenstadt, Michael, "The Iraqi Armed Forces Two Years On," *Jane's Intelligence Review*, March, 1993, pp. 121–127.
———, *Like a Phoenix from the Ashes? The Future of Iraqi Military Power*, Washington, Washington Institute, Policy Paper 36, 1993.
———, "The Sword of the Arabs: Iraq's Strategic Weapons," Washington, Washington Institute for Near East Policy, Policy Paper 21, September, 1990.
Ekeus, Ambassador Rolf, "Unearthing Iraq's Arsenal," *Arms Control Today*, April, 1992, pp. 6–9.
Ember, Lois R. "Worldwide Spread of Chemical Arms Receiving Increased Attention," *C&EN*, April 14, 1988, pp. 8–16.
Erlick, Dr. Barry J., Senior Biological Warfare Analyst, US Army, testimony before the Committee on Governmental Affairs, US Senate, February 9, 1989.
The Estimate, various editions.
FBIS-NES, various editions.
Fedtter, Steve, George N. Lewis, and Lisbeth Gronlund, "Why Were Scud Casualties So Low?" *Nature*, Vol. 361, January 28, 1993, pp. 293–296.
Feldman, Shai, *Nuclear Weapons and Arms Control in the Middle East*, Cambridge, MIT Press, 1997.
Fromkin, David, *A Peace to End All Peace*, New York, Henry Holt, 1989.
Galbraith, Peter W., and Christopher Van Hollen Jr., "Chemical Weapons Use in Kurdistan: Iraq's Final Offensive," A Staff Report to the Senate Committee on Foreign Relations, September 21, 1988.
Gander, Terry J., "Iraq—The Chemical Arsenal," *Jane's Intelligence Review*, September, 1992, pp. 413–415.
General Dynamics *The World's Missile Systems, Seventh Edition*, General Dynamics, Pomona Division, April, 1982.
George, Alan, "Iraq: Weapons Sanctions Aren't Working," *The Middle East*, September, 1993, pp. 14–15.
———, "Nuclear Complicity," *The Middle East*, March, 1993, pp. 12–13.
Goldberg, David, Foreign Science and Technology Center, US Army Intelligence Agency, testimony before the Committee on Governmental Affairs, US Senate, February 9, 1989.
Gordon, Michael R., and General Bernard E. Trainor, *The General's War: The Inside Story of the Conflict in the Gulf*, Boston, Little, Brown, 1994, pp. 429–439.
Grimmett, Richard F., *Conventional Arms Transfers to the Developing World*, Washington, Congressional Research Service, various editions.

Harris, Elisa D., "Chemical Weapons Proliferation in the Developing World," *RUSI and Brassey's Defense Yearbook, 1989*, London, 1988, pp. 67–88.

Herdman, Roger C., Director, *Technologies Underlying Weapons of Mass Destruction*, Washington, GPO, Office of Technology Assessment, US Congress, OTA-BP-ISC-115, December, 1993.

Hildreth, Steven A., "Theater Ballistic Missile Defense," CRS 93–585F, June 10, 1993.

Hildreth, Steven A., and Paul C. Zinsmeister, "The Patriot Air Defense System and the Search for an Anti-Tactical Ballistic Missile System, CRS 91–456F, June 18, 1991.

Hopkirk, Peter, *The Great Game*, New York, Kodansha Press, 1991.

Ignatius, David, "Iraq's 13-Year Search for Deadly Chemicals," *Washington Post*, Outlook section, September 25, 1988.

Indyk, Martin, Graham Fuller, Anthony Cordesman, and Phoebe Marr, "US Policy Towards Iran and Iraq," *Middle East Policy*, Vol. III, No. 4, 1994, pp. 1–27.

International Defense Review, various editions.

International Institute for Strategic Studies, *Military Balance*, London, Oxford Press, various editions.

Isby, David C., "The Residual Iraqi Scud Force," *Jane's Intelligence Review*, Vol. 7, No. 3, pp. 115–117; and see Reuters, February 23, 1997, 1522.

Jacobs, Gordon, and Tim McCarthy, "China Missile Sales—Few Changes for the Future," *Jane's Intelligence Review*, December, 1992, pp. 559–563.

James, Scott, "Does Western Technology Offset Larger Soviet Numbers?" *Defense Electronics*, February, 1981. *Jane's Defense Weekly*, various editions.

Jane's Information Group, *Jane's Air-Launched Weapons*, London, Jane's Publishing, various editions.

———, *Jane's Aircraft Upgrades*, London, Jane's Publishing, various editions.

———, *Jane's All the World's Aircraft*, London, Jane's Publishing, various editions.

———, *Jane's All the World's Armies*, London, Jane's Publishing, various editions.

———, *Jane's Armor and Artillery*, London, Jane's Publishing, various editions.

———, *Jane's Avionics*, London, Jane's Publishing, various editions.

———, *Jane's C4I Systems*, London, Jane's Publishing, various editions.

———, *Jane's Fighting Ships*, various editions.

———, *Jane's Helicopter Markets and Systems*, London, Jane's Publishing, various editions.

———, *Jane's Intelligence Review*, Special Report, No. 6, May, 1995.

———, *Jane's Land-Based Air Defense*, London, Jane's Publishing, various editions.

———, *Jane's Military Communications*, London, Jane's Publishing, various editions.

———, *Jane's Military Vehicles and Logistics*, London, Jane's Publishing, various editions.

———, *Jane's Naval Weapons Systems*, various editions.

———, *Jane's Radar and Electronic Warfare Systems*, London, Jane's Publishing, various editions.

———, *Jane's Underwater Technology*, various editions.

———, *Jane's Underwater Warfare Systems*, various editions.

———, *Jane's Unmanned Aerial Vehicles and Targets*, London, Jane's Publishing, various editions.

———, *Jane's World Air Forces*, London, Jane's Publishing, various editions.

Jane's Pointer, various editions.

Jane's Sentinel: The Gulf States, "Iraq," London, Jane's Publishing, 1997.
Kan, Shirley A., "Chinese Proliferation of Weapons of Mass Destruction, Background and Analysis," Library of Congress, CRS-96–767F, September 13, 1996.
Katzman, Kenneth, "Iran and Iraq: US National Security Problems Since the Gulf War— A Chronology," Washington, Congressional Research Service, CRS 93–638F, July 8, 1993.
———, "Iraq: Future Policy Options," Congressional Research Service, CRS 91–596F, December 12, 1991, pp. 23–30.
———, "Iraqi Compliance with Cease-Fire Agreements," Congressional Research Service, CRS IB92117, October 30, 1997.
———, "Persian Gulf: Radical Islamic Movements," Congressional Research Service, CRS 96–731F, August 30, 1996.
———, "Terrorism: Middle Eastern Groups and State Sponsors, 1997," Congressional Research Service, CRS 97–692F, July 10, 1997.
Keaney, Thomas A., and Eliot A. Cohen, *Gulf War Air Power Survey: Summary Report,* Washington, Department of the Air Force, 1993.
Kemp, Geoffery, and Robert E. Harkavy, *Strategic Geography and the Changing Middle East,* Washington, Carnegie Endowment/Brookings, 1997.
Khalizad, Zalmay M., David A. Shalpak, and Daniel L. Byman, *The Implications of the Possible End of the Arab-Israeli Conflict for Gulf Security,* Santa Monica, RAND, 1997.
Korb, Edward L., ed., *The World's Missile Systems, Seventh Edition,* General Dynamics, Pomona Division, April, 1988.
Lenhard, Warren W., and Todd Masse, "Persian Gulf War: Iraqi Scud Ballistic Missile Systems," Washington, Congressional Research Service, 91–173F, February 14, 1991.
Lennox, Duncan, "Iraq-Ballistic Missiles," *Current News, Supplement,* US Department of Defense, October 11; 1990, pp. B-4–B-6.
Lowther, William, *Iraq and the Supergun,* London, Pan, 1992.
Lumpe, Lora, Lisbeth Gronlund, and David C. Wright, "Third World Missiles Fall Short," *The Bulletin of the Atomic Scientists,* March, 1992, pp. 30–36.
Mark, J. Carson, "Some Remarks on Iraq's Possible Nuclear Weapons Capability in Light of Some of the Known Facts Concerning Nuclear Weapons," Washington, Nuclear Control Institute, May 16, 1991.
McCarthy, Tim, "China Missile Sales—Few Changes for the Future," *Jane's Intelligence Review,* December, 1992, pp. 559–563.
McCausland, Lt. Colonel Jeffery D., "How Iraq's CBW Threat Affected Coalition Operations," *Defense and Foreign Affairs,* September, 1992, pp. 12–16.
McNaugher, Thomas L., "Ballistic Missiles and Chemical Weapons: The Legacy of the Iran-Iraq War," *International Security,* 15:2, pp. 5–34.
Middle East Economic Digest, various editions.
Middle East Economic Survey, various editions.
Migdalovitz, Carol, "Turkey's Military Offensive in Northern Iraq," Library of Congress, 95–487F, April 13, 1995.
Milhollin, Gary, "Building Saddam Hussein's Bomb," *New York Times,* March 8, 1992, pp. 30–31.
———, "The Iraqi Bomb," *New Yorker,* February 1, 1993, p. 47–55.

Nagler, Dr. Robert A., *Ballistic Missile Proliferation: An Emerging Threat*, Arlington, Systems Planning Corporation, 1992.
Navias, Martin, "Ballistic Missile Proliferation in the Middle East," *Survival*, May–June, 1989.
Palowski, Dick, *Changes in Threat Air Combat Doctrine and Force Structure*, 24th Edition, Fort Worth, General Dynamics, DWIC-01, February, 1992.
Parasiliti, Andrew T., "Iraq, Nuclear Weapons, and the Middle East," The Middle East Institute, December 14, 1989.
Physicians for Human Rights, *Winds of Death: Iraq's Use of Poison Gas Against Its Kurdish Population*, February, 1989.
Postal, Theodore A., "Lessons of the Gulf War Experience with Patriot," *International Security*, Winter, 1991–1992, pp. 128–129.
Prados, Alfred, and Kenneth Katzman, "Iraq: Attack on Kurdish Enclave and US Response," Congressional Research Service, 96–739, October 17, 1996.
Rathmell, Andrew, *The Changing Military Balance in the Gulf*, London, Royal United Services Institute, Whitehall Papers 38, 1996.
Ripley, Tim, "Iraq's Nuclear Weapons Program," *Jane's Intelligence Review*, December, 1992, pp. 554–558.
Roberts, Brad, *Terrorism with Chemical and Biological Weapons: Calibrating Risks and Responses*, Alexandria, Chemical and Biological Weapons Control Institute, 1997.
Russian Foreign Intelligence Service, *Treaty on the Non-Proliferation of Nuclear Weapons: Problems for Its Prolongation*, Moscow, Russian Foreign Intelligence Service, 1995.
Scales, Brigadier General Robert H., *Certain Victory: The United States Army in the Gulf War*, Washington, Office of the Chief of Staff, US Army, 1993.
Scheinman, Lawrence, "Lessons From Post-War Iraq for the International Full-Scope Safeguard Regime, *Arms Control Today*, April, 1993, pp. 3–6.
Shuey, Robert, and Shirley A. Kan, *Chinese Missile and Nuclear Proliferation*, Congressional Research Service, IB92056, October 4, 1994.
Smith, James, "Biological Weapons Developments," *Jane's Intelligence Review*, November, 1991, pp. 483–487.
Snyder, Jed C., "The Non-Proliferation Regime: Managing the Impending Crisis," *Journal of Strategic Studies*, December, 1985.
Snyder, Jed C., "The Road to Osirak: Baghdad's Quest for the Bomb," *Middle East Journal*, No. 37, Autumn, 1983, pp. 565–594.
Spector, Leonard S., *The New Nuclear Nations*, New York, Vintage Books, 1985.
———, *Proliferation Today*, New York, Vintage Books, 1984; *Arms Control Today*, April, 1992, pp. 7–8.
———, *The Undeclared Bomb*, New York, Ballinger, 1988.
Spector, Leonard S., and Jacqueline R. Smith, *Nuclear Exports: The Challenge of Control*, Carnegie Endowment for Peace, Washington, April, 1990.
Stein, Robert M., and Theodore A. Postal, "Correspondence: Patriot Experience in the Gulf War," *International Security*, Summer, 1992, pp. 199–240.
Tahir, Ali, *Irak: Aux Origines du regime militaire*, Paris, Albin Michel, 1989.
Terrill, W. Andrew, "Chemical Weapons in the Gulf War," *Strategic Review*, Spring, 1986, pp. 51–58.
———, "The Gulf War and Ballistic Missile Proliferation," *Comparative Strategy*, Vol. 11, 1992, pp. 163–176.

Timmerman, Kenneth R., "Iraq Rebuilds Its Military Industries," House Foreign Affairs Subcommittee on International Security, International Organizations, and Human Rights, Washington, DC, June 29, 1993.

———, *Weapons of Mass Destruction: The Cases of Iran, Syria, and Libya*, Los Angeles, Simon Wiesenthal Center, August, 1992.

United Nations, Note by the Secretary-General, S/26910, December 21, 1993.

United Nations, Note by the Secretary-General, S/1994/31, January 14, 1994.

United Nations, Note by the Secretary-General, S/1994/341, March 24, 1994.

United Nations, Note by the Secretary-General, S/1994/355, March 25, 1994.

United Nations, Note by the Secretary-General, S/1995/864, 11 October 1995.

United Nations, Note by the Secretary-General, S/1996/848, October 11, 1996.

United Nations, Note by the Secretary-General, S/1997/301, April 11, 1997.

United Nations, Note by the Secretary-General, S/26584, November 5, 1993.

United Nations, Note by the Secretary-General, S/26825, December 1, 1993.

United Nations, Report on the Twenty-Second IAEA Inspection, 1–15 November 1993.

United Nations, Note by the Secretary-General, "Report by the Secretary-General on the Activities of the Special Commission established by the Secretary-General," UN Security Council, S/1997/774, October 6, 1997.

United Nations, Security Council, *Report on the First and Second IAEA Inspection in Iraq Under Security Council Resolution 687*, 15 July, 1991, New York.

United Nations, Security Council, "Report of the Specialists Appointed to the Secretary-General to Investigate the Allegations of the Islamic Republic of Iran Concerning the Use of Chemical Weapons, Document S 16433, March 26, 1984.

United Nations, Special Commission, "Report to the Security Council—S/1995/494," 20 June 1995.

United Nations, Special Commission, "Report to the Security Council—S/1995/864," 11 October 1995.

United Nations, S/22788 (English), *Report on the Third IAEA Inspection in Iraq Under Security Council Resolution 687*, 25 July 1991, New York.

United Nations, S/23283 (English), *Report on the Eighth IAEA Inspection in Iraq Under Security Council Resolution 687*, 28 August 1991, New York.

United Nations, S/22986 (English), *Report on the Fifth IAEA Inspection in Iraq Under Security Council Resolution 687*, 4 October 1991, New York.

United Nations, S/23112 (English), *Report on the Sixth IAEA Inspection in Iraq Under Security Council Resolution 687*, 8 October 1991, New York.

United Nations, S/23122 (English), *Report on the Seventh IAEA Inspection in Iraq Under Security Council Resolution 687*, 14 November 1991, New York.

United Nations, S/232215 (English), *Report on the Fourth IAEA Inspection in Iraq Under Security Council Resolution 687*, 11–18 November 1991, New York.

United Nations, S/23283 (English), *Report on the Ninth IAEA Inspection in Iraq Under Security Council Resolution 687*, 30 January 1992, New York; S/23505 (English).

United States News and World Report, *Triumph Without Victory*, New York, Random House, 1992.

Unpublished "Statement of the Honorable William H. Webster, Director, Central Intelligence Agency, Before the Committee on Governmental Affairs, Hearings on Global Spread of Chemical and Biological Weapons," February 9, 1989.

US Air Force, "Reaching Globally, Reaching Powerfully: The United States Air Force in the Gulf War," Washington, USAF, September, 1991.
US Arms Control and Disarmament Agency (ACDA), *World Military Expenditures and Arms Transfers*, Washington, GPO, various editions.
US Army press release, "Army Weapons System Performance in Southwest Asia, March 13, 1991.
US Central Command, *Atlas, 1996*, MacDill Air Force Base, USCENTCOM, 1997.
US Congress, Committee on Appropriations, Subcommittee on the Department of Defense, *Hearings on the FY1993 Defense Budget*, April, 1991; "Performance of the Patriot Missile in the Gulf War," Hearing Before the Legislation and National Security Subcommittee of the Committee on Government Operations, House of Representatives, 102nd Congress, Second Session, April 7, 1992.
US Congress, House Committee on Foreign Affairs, Subcommittee on International Security, International Organizations, and Human Rights, "Iraq Rebuilds Its Military Industries," Staff Report, 103rd Congress, 1st Session, June 29, 1993.
US Congress, House Committee on Foreign Affairs, Subcommittees on Europe and the Middle East and on Human Rights and International Organizations, "UN Role in the Persian Gulf and Iraqi Compliance with UN Resolutions," Hearing, 102nd Congress, 1st Session. Reuters, October 21, 1991.
US Congress, Office of Technology Assessment, *Proliferation of Weapons of Mass Destruction: Assessing the Risks*, United States Congress, OTA-ISC-559, Washington, DC, August, 1993.
US Congress, Task Force on Terrorism and Unconventional Warfare, *Chemical Weapons in The Third World: 2. Iraq's Expanding Chemical Arsenal*, House Republican Research Committee, US House of Representatives, May 29, 1990.
US Department of Defense, *Conduct of the Persian Gulf War*, Vol. I, Washington, US Department of Defense, April 1992.
US Director of Central Intelligence, "The Acquisition of Technology Relating to Weapons of Mass Destruction and Advanced Conventional Munitions, July–December, 1996," Washington, CIA, June, 1997.
US General Accounting Office, "Patriot Missile Defense: Software Problem Led to System Failure at Dhahran," Saud Arabia, GAO/IMTEC-92-26, February, 1992.
US Naval Institute, *The Naval Institute Guide to the Combat Fleets of the World, Their Ships, Aircraft, and Armament*, Annapolis, Naval Institute, various editions.
US Office of the Secretary of Defense, *Proliferation: Threat and Response*, Washington, US Department of Defense, April, 1996.
US State Department, *Patterns of Global Terrorism*, Internet on-line editions.
US State Department press release, "Joint US-PRC Statement on Missile Proliferation," Washington, DC, October 4, 1994.
USCENTCOM briefing by "senior military official," Pentagon, January 28, 1997.
Zaloga, Steven, "Ballistic Missiles in the Third World," *International Defense Review*, 11/88, pp. 1423–1437.
Zaydi, Colonel Ahmad, *Al bina' al ma'anawi lil quwat al-musallah al-iraqiyah* (The Development of the Fighting Spirit of the Iraqi Army), Beirut, Dar al-Rawdah, 1990, pp. 336–341.
Ziffereo, Maurizio, "The IAEA: Neutralizing Iraq's Nuclear Weapons Potential," *Arms Control Today*, April, 1993, pp. 7–10.

Zilinskas, Raymond A., "Iraq's Biological Weapons," *Journal of the American Medical Association*, Vol. 278, No. 6, August 6, 1997, pp. 418–425.

Zimmerman, Peter D., "Iraq's Nuclear Achievements: Components, Sources, and Stature," Washington, Congressional Research Service, 93–323F, February 18, 1993.

Index

Aflatoxin, 577
Air and air defense forces, 118–40; equipment holdings, 121–28; fighting capabilities of, 133; after the Gulf War, 137–40; land-based defenses, 134–40; modernization needs, 129–30; readiness, doctrine and training, 130–33; strategic, interdiction and close support missions, 132
Air strikes against biological weapons facilities, 580–81
Air-to-air combat, 131–32
Albright, Madeleine, 201, 204, 379, 416
Algiers Accord, 13
al-Tikriti, Barzan, 339, 346, 353
Anthrax, 273, 279–80
Anti-aircraft weapons, 106–7
Anti-ship missiles, 122
Anti-tank weapons, 106
Arab-Israeli peace process, 1, 269; threats to, 8
Armored vehicles, 86–104
Arms control, limits of, 645–46
Arms imports, 43–59
Arrow missiles, 434–35
Artillery, Iraqi, 104–5, 450–55
Aspin, Les, 197

Assassinations, 154–55; attempt on President Bush, 158, 160–61, 201
Aziz, Tariq, 225, 253, 265, 361, 502

Ba'ath Party, 10–11, 20; intelligence elements of, 21, 153–54, 156; mass purges by, 22–23; return of, 22; rise of, 12–13
Baghdad Pact (1955), 12
Barzani, Massoud, 186, 206, 336–37
Biological weapons, 212–15, 217–18, 387, 539; capabilities after the Gulf War, 581–83; coalition air strikes against, 580–81; effectiveness of Iraq's future, 597–99; growth agent and fermenters, 576; importing cultures, 575–76; of Iran, 422–23; of Iraq, 401–6, 446–47, 573–99; of Israel, 433; production facilities, 576–577; scale of, 401–6; of Syria, 437; uncertainties regarding, 590–97; warheads, 579–80
Biological Weapons Convention, 645
Blair, Tony, 360, 366–67
Blix, Hans, 623–28
Blood agents, 539
Boutros-Ghali, Boutros, 206
Boyne, Sean, 73, 155
Brazil, and missile programs, 476
Britain, 11–12

Bull, Gerald, 454, 476
Burleigh, Peter, 371–72
Bush, George, 158, 160–61, 195, 201
Butler, Richard, 220, 265, 276, 278–80, 284, 352, 371; on concealment, 372–74, 502; report on biological program, 585

Centrifuge programs, 617–21
Chemical weapons: decision not to use, 544–45; efforts to destroy, 548–51; of Egypt, 439; expansion of production of, 531–33; impact of, 531; of Iran, 419–22; before the Iran-Iraq War, 525–27; during the Iran-Iraq War, 527–31; of Iraq, 14–15, 218–19, 367, 385, 387, 446, 525–63; of Israel, 433; of Libya, 440–41; possible impact of, 545–48; scale of, 398–401; of Syria, 436–37; use against the Kurds, 534–35; in warheads, 502
Chemical Weapons Convention, 645
Chernomyrdin, Viktor, 416–17
China: and chemical weapons, 421; missile technology of, 413–14, 418, 436; nuclear technology of, 429–31
Choking agents, 538–39
CIA, 13
Clandestine and covert programs, 385–88
Clark, Ramsey, 298
Clinton, William Jefferson, 203, 207, 366, 376
Clostridium Perfringens, 577
Cohen, William, 275, 368
Cold War, 12–13
Computers, 386
Conspiracy theories, 16
Containment, 113, 140, 148, 171, 663–65
Control agents, 539
Conventional forces, and the war of sanctions, 166–74
Cook, Robin, 354
Coups d'etat, 22, 25–30
Creeping proliferation, 8, 430
Cruise missiles, 387, 418, 436, 507–10

Defectors, 21, 27, 631
Defense Intelligence Agency, 484
Delivery systems: of Egypt, 438–39; of Iran, 408–19; of Iraq, 395–98, 450–55, 458–61; of Israel, 432–33; of Libya, 439–40; of Syria, 435–36
Deserters, 29–30
Deterrence, 113, 140, 148, 380, 663–65
Devil's bargain, 86
Directorate of Political Guidance, 23
"Doomsday" force, 485
Dual-use technologies, 3, 171, 383–85, 555, 596, 598

Eckhard, Fred, 345
Egypt, and weapons of mass destruction, 438–39
Ekeus, Rolf, 205, 209–10, 213–14, 217, 219, 370; on the biological program, 583; on Iraq's missile program, 493; on the limits of sanctions, 382; on missiles, 398; on nerve gas, 553
El Baradei, Mohammed, 629–30
Electromagnetic isotope separation (EMIS), 607, 609–10, 615–17
Exocets, 132, 147, 655

Falt, Eric, 274, 296
Fatchett, Derek, 292
FBI, 200
Fedayeen Saddam, 79
Fedotov, Yuri, 628
Fissile material, 387; eliminating facilities for production of, 627–28; progress in obtaining, 613–21
Foreign Ministry, 157
France, 335
FROG rockets, 452–53
Full, final, and complete disclosure (FFCD), 583–89

Gates, Robert, 195, 552
General Intelligence Service, 153–54
General Security Service, 155–56
Global Positioning Systems, 467, 508
Gommersall, Stephen, 264
Gore, Al, 416
Gulf War: aftermath of, 24–25, 50–59; air activity since, 128–29; chemical weapons at the time of, 542–44, 548–51; and the Iraqi air force, 119–21;

losses during, 68–70; missile capabilities during, 478–83; Scud hunt, 483–88; and strategic culture, 16–18; trends in Iraqi forces since, 34–37; and weapons of mass destruction, 176–78

Halliday, Dennis, 241
Hamza, Kiddhir Abdul Abas, 603, 608, 632–33
Helicopters, 107–8; naval, 147
High command, 20–30; threat to the state from, 21–22
Human wave attacks, 14
HUMINT (human intelligence), 177–78
Hussein, Odai, 349
Hussein, Qusay, 21, 28–29, 79, 444
Hussein, Saddam, 2, 11, 477; alternatives to, 18; and coup attempts, 27–30; "doomsday" force of, 485; and early nuclear efforts, 603–4; and the high command, 21–27; offices of, 10–11, 20–21; priorities of, 17; and proliferation, 443–45; protection of, 79; purges of, 22–27; rise of, 12–13; risks taken by, 4, 8; supporters of, 10
Hussein, Uday, 79, 151, 278, 339; attack on, 318

Incapacitating agents, 540
Indyck, Martin, 415
Inspections, limits to, 554–55
Intelligence, 150–63; Ba'ath Party, 21; and chemical weapons, 549; human, 177–78
International Atomic Energy Agency (IAEA), 3, 16, 178, 296, 300; and the limits of sanctions, 382–84, 387; on nuclear weapons design, 623–24; reviews of, 381; and the War of Sanctions, 627–34
Iran: arms imports of, 48; biological weapons of, 422–23; chemical weapons of, 419–22; delivery systems of, 408–19; deployments against, 83–86; missile defenses of, 431; nuclear program of, 423–31; weapons of mass destruction, 408–31
Iran-Iraq War, 13–16; end of, 16; impact of, 23–24; missile use during, 468–71

Iraq: air and air defense forces, 118–40, 458–61; arms imports of, 43–59; artillery of, 104–5, 450–55; biological weapons of, 401–6, 446–47, 573–99; capability to manufacture Scuds, 397; chemical weapons capabilities of, 525–63; delivery systems of, 395–98, 458–61; domestic military production capabilities of, 60–63; escalation of, 649–50; future strategy of, 646–48; history of, 11–19; land forces of, 67–113; military manpower pool of, 33–34; missile programs of, 216–17, 384, 388, 397, 462–510; naval forces of, 144–48; ongoing efforts of, 388; poverty in, 33; proliferation by, 175–76, 443–49, 644, 648; scale of programs of, 394–408; and the Scud missile, 463–507; security structure of, 151–57; strategic culture of, 10–19, 442–49; struggle with UN, 1, 4, 8; and terrorism, 520–24; threats to the Gulf, 8–9. *See also* Nuclear programs of Iraq
Iraqi armed forces: high command of, 20–30; land forces of, 67–113; readiness for chemical warfare, 541–42; threat to regime from, 22–23; trends since the Gulf War, 34–37
Iraqi National Accord, 27–29
Iraq Liberation Act (1998), 367
Iraq's military future, 651–65; adventures in the Southern Gulf, 657–58; attacks on Kuwait, 652–54; civil war, 654–55; conflict with Iran, 656–57; confrontation in the Gulf, 655–56; defense of Iraq, 662; intimidation, 662–63; proxy wars, 659–60; Turkey and the Kurds, 659; unconventional conflicts, 660–61; wars against Israel, 658; weapons of mass destruction, 661–62
Israel: chemical weapons of, 433; delivery systems of, 432–33; and the Iraqi nuclear program, 606; missile basing options of, 432; missile defenses of, 434–35; nuclear weapons of, 433–34; and weapons of mass destruction, 432–35

Kamel, Hussein, 27, 61–62, 444, 491; assassination of, 339; defection of, 583–84; and the nuclear program, 608
Kharrazi, Kamal, 426
Khatami, Mohammad, 426
Khomeini, Ayatollah, 13, 16, 424
Koptyev, Yuri, 416–17
Kurdistan Democratic Party, 276
Kurdistan Workers' Party, 159
Kurds, 8, 13, 109, 170, 336–37; deployments against, 80–84, 659
Kuwait, 3–4, 336; terrorist attempts on, 161; vulnerability of, 109

Land forces, 67–113; antiaircraft, 106–7, 134–40; armored vehicles, 86–104; artillery, 104–5; improvement priorities, 111–13; readiness problems, 110–11
Libya: nuclear program of, 441; and weapons of mass destruction, 439–41
Logistics, 109–10

Majid, Husayn Kamel, defection of, 213–14
Military expenditures, 32–63
Military Industrial Organization, 179–80
Military intelligence, 154–55
Military risks, 4, 8, 167
Military Security Service, 155
Ministry of Information, 156–57
Missile crisis of 1995, 489–93
Missile defenses: of Iran, 431; of Israel, 434–35; of Syria, 438
Missiles, 216–17, 384, 462–510; anti-radiation, 136; anti-ship, 122; Arrow, 434–35; cruise, 387, 418, 436, 507–10; defense against, 483–88; Exocet, 132, 655; North Korean, 408–13; Patriot, 139, 434, 487; Scud, 397, 408–11, 435, 463–68; Silkworm, 147, 419, 508; testing of, 388; warheads, 301
"Mother of All Battles" (MOAB) system, 140
Moussa, Amr, 336
Mujahedin-e Khalq Organization, 159–60
Multiple rocket launchers, 104–5

Mustard gas, 535–36, 538
Mycotoxins, 578

Naval forces, 144–48
Nerve gas, 536, 538, 552–63
Nidal, Abu, 159
No-Dong missiles, 412
No-fly zones, 128–29
North Korea, missiles of, 408–13
Nuclear Non-Proliferation Treaty (NPT), 633
Nuclear programs: of Iran, 423–31; of Israel, 433–34; of Libya, 441
Nuclear programs of Iraq, 316, 384–87, 406–8, 447–48, 603–34; centrifuge programs, 617–21; early efforts, 603–9; EMIS (Calutron) programs, 607, 609–10, 615–17; fissile material, 387, 613–21; plutonium separation, 614–15; radiological weapons, 626–27; at the time of the Gulf War, 609–13; and the war of sanctions, 627–34; weapons design and assembly, 621–27

Oil: and military spending, 33; price of, 327, 372; threats to supply of, 8–9
"Oil for food" program, 1, 51, 109, 269–377
"One-bullet election," 18, 30
OPEC, 292
Order of battle data, 77–78
Osirak reactor, 605; Israeli attack on, 606

Palestine Liberation Front, 160
Patriotic Union of Kurdistan, 206
Patriot missiles, 139: effectiveness of, 487
Peace process, 1; threats to, 8
People's Mujahideen, 431
Perry, William, 202, 204
Plutonium separation, 614–15
Poison gas, 14
Political commissars, 23
Proliferation: "creeping," 8, 430; Iraq's continuing capability, 644, 648–49; Iraq's history of, 175–76, 443–49

Proxy wars, 659–60
Purges, 22–23, 25–29, 110

Radiological weapons, 626–27
Rafsanjani, Ali Akbar Hashemi, 425
Rasheed, Amir Muhammad, 270
Rashid, Maher Abdul, 24
Reflagging, 15
Republican Guards, 78–80; and coups, 25–26, 28; escape of, 24; and suppression of uprisings, 70; training of, 110
Richardson, Bill, 281, 628
Ricin, 577–78
Ritter, Scott, 263; resignation of, 325–26, 329; testimony of, 328, 631–32
Robertson, George, 360
Rockets, 452–54
Rubin, James, 367, 562, 596
Russia: missile technology of, 413–17, 491–93; nuclear technology of, 428–31

Saddam's Fedayeen, 156
Sanctions, 1–2
"Sanctions fatigue," 8–9, 173, 222, 269–388, 664
Saud al-Faisal, 359
Scud missiles: hunt for, 483–88; impact of, 482–83; of Iran, 397, 408–11; of Iraq, 463–507
Security Council, 1; crisis of 1997, 222–30; and sanctions, 3
Security structure, 151–57
Shalikashvili, John, 195, 204
Shatt al-Arab, 13
Shelton, Henry, 360
Shi'ites, deployments against, 83–86
Short, Clare, 292
Signals and electronic intelligence, 157
Smuggling, 59, 632–33
Soviet Union, 12
Special Republican Guards, 26, 29, 79–80, 221
Special Security Service, 85, 151–53, 179
Spertzel, Richard, 587
Strategic culture, 10–19
"Super guns," 454–55
Surface-to-air missiles, 106–7
Syria, 328; and the Ba'ath Party, 22; biological weapons of, 437; chemical weapons of, 436–37; delivery systems of, 435–36; nuclear program of, 437; and weapons of mass destruction, 435–38

Talabani, Jalal, 186, 193
Tanker war, 15
Tank strength, 86–103, 112
Tapeo Dong missiles, 412–13
Targeting systems, 112
Telecommunications services, 157
TELs (transporter-erector-launchers), 479, 481, 496
Terrorism, 150–63, 520–24, 598–99
Training, failures in, 130–31
Tribal Chief's Bureau, 156
Tribalism, 29
Turkey, 82, 659; and Kurdish separation, 170, 336–37

UN cease-fire, 178–79
Unconventional warfare, 150–63, 520–24, 660–61
UNICEF, 274, 313
United States, and the Iraqi nuclear effort, 610–13
UN resolutions. *See* War of sanctions
UNSCOM, 3, 16–17, 215–72, 280, 282–85, 290, 293; and biological weapons, 212–15, 573–99; chemical monitoring group of, 561; and enforcement, 380; headquarters, of, 320–21, 337; inspections resumed by, 372; limits to inspections, 554–55, 590, 596–97; and the limits of sanctions, 382–87; and missile capabilities, 488–507; on nuclear facilities, 610, 613, 619–20; personnel of, 324–25; and political compromises, 377–79; and propellant, 304; remaining uncertainties, 555–63; requests by, 374–75; reviews of, 381; and VX gas, 552–54; and warheads, 301, 497, 499; and the war of sanctions, 179–212, 583–90, 627–34; and weapons of mass destruction, 175, 643–50
Uranium technology, 315, 338

US Air Force Gulf War Air Power Survey, 177
US inspectors, expelled, 225–26

Van der Stoel, Max, 198, 202, 287
VX nerve gas, 310–11, 332, 344

"War of the cities," 408, 470
Warheads, 387, 543–44; for biological weapons, 579–80; design and testing of, 598
War of sanctions, 1, 16–17, 175–388; chemical weapons and, 552–63; crisis of October, 1998, 380–82; future course of, 646–48; missile capabilities and, 488–510; and nuclear programs, 627–34; outcome of, 166–74, 628–34; strengths and limits of, 382–88; and UN resolutions, 2–4; and UNSCOM, 583–90; weapons of mass destruction and, 175–388, 505–7
Weapons of mass destruction, 2, 661–62; Egypt's search for, 438–39; Iran's search for, 408–31; Iraq's strategic culture and, 442–49; Israel's search for, 432–35; Libya's search for, 439–41; policy implications of, 643–50; terrorism and, 520–24; and the war of sanctions, 175–388, 505–7
Weston, John, 259

Yeltsin, Boris, 416

About the Author

ANTHONY H. CORDESMAN is Senior Fellow and Co-director of the Middle East Program at the Center for Strategic and International Studies, Professor of National Security Studies at Georgetown University, and a special consultant on military affairs for ABC News. The author of numerous books on Middle Eastern security issues, he has served in senior positions for the secretary of defense, NATO, and the United States Senate.